Gender and Law

ASPEN CASEBOOK SERIES

Gender and Law
Theory, Doctrine, Commentary
Seventh Edition

Katharine T. Bartlett
A. Kenneth Pye Professor of Law
Duke University School of Law

Deborah L. Rhode
Ernest W. McFarland Professor of Law
Director, Stanford Center on the Legal Profession
Director, Program in Law and Social Entrepreneurship
Stanford University Law School

Joanna L. Grossman
Ellen K. Solender Endowed Chair in Women
    and the Law and Professor
SMU Dedman School of Law

Wolters Kluwer

Published by Wolters Kluwer in New York.

Wolters Kluwer Legal & Regulatory US serves customers worldwide with CCH, Aspen Publishers, and Kluwer Law International products. (www.WKLegaledu.com)

To contact Customer Service, e-mail customer.service@wolterskluwer.com, call 1-800-234-1660, fax 1-800-901-9075, or mail correspondence to:

Wolters Kluwer
Attn: Order Department
PO Box 990
Frederick, MD 21705

Printed in the United States of America.

1 2 3 4 5 6 7 8 9 0

ISBN 978-1-4548-8086-8

Library of Congress Cataloging-in-Publication Data

Names: Bartlett, Katharine T., author. | Rhode, Deborah L., author. |
    Grossman, Joanna L., author.
Title: Gender and law : theory, doctrine, commentary / Katharine T. Bartlett,
    A. Kenneth Pye Professor of Law, Duke University School of Law, Deborah L.
    Rhode, Ernest W. McFarland Professor of Law, Director, Stanford Center on
    the Legal Profession Director, Program in Law and Social Entrepreneurship
    Stanford University Law School Joanna L. Grossman, Sidney and Walter Siben
    Distinguished Professor of Family Law, Maurice A. Deane School of Law at
    Hofstra University.
Description: Seventh edition. | New York : Wolters Kluwer, [2016] | Series:
    Aspen casebook series | Includes index.
Identifiers: LCCN 2016036170 | ISBN 9781454880868
Subjects: LCSH: Women—Legal status, laws, etc.—United States. | Sex and
    law—United States. | Sex discrimination against women—Law and
    legislation—United States. | Feminist jurisprudence—United States. |
    LCGFT: Casebooks
Classification: LCC KF478 .B37 2016 | DDC 342.7308/78—dc23
LC record available at https://lccn.loc.gov/2016036170

About Wolters Kluwer Legal & Regulatory US

Wolters Kluwer Legal & Regulatory US delivers expert content and solutions in the areas of law, corporate compliance, health compliance, reimbursement, and legal education. Its practical solutions help customers successfully navigate the demands of a changing environment to drive their daily activities, enhance decision quality and inspire confident outcomes.

Serving customers worldwide, its legal and regulatory portfolio includes products under the Aspen Publishers, CCH Incorporated, Kluwer Law International, ftwilliam.com and MediRegs names. They are regarded as exceptional and trusted resources for general legal and practice-specific knowledge, compliance and risk management, dynamic workflow solutions, and expert commentary.

To our students.

Summary of Contents

Contents

4 *Difference*   *513*

6   *Identity*   *807*

Preface

True to its initial vision, this seventh edition organizes the field of gender and law into six theoretical perspectives. These perspectives are not mutually exclusive, nor are they "total" theories intended to answer every doctrinal and policy question that may arise concerning the relationship between gender and law. Rather, they represent alternative diagnostic and normative lenses through which the relationship between law and gender can be understood and improved. We believe that each theoretical framework has significant value *and* limitations. The approach of this book works best if readers attempt to be both open to, and critical of, each perspective.

As the field of gender law has grown, it now touches virtually every area of law and policy. The majority of materials updating this edition continue to focus on work, intimate relationships and family, education, and sexual violence. This applies to most of the new cases added to the book such as United States v. Windsor and Obergefell v. Hodges (same-sex marriage), Videckis v. Pepperdine University (sexual harassment), and Young v. UPS (pregnancy discrimination). As before, however, the materials in this edition demonstrate how gender matters beyond these more obvious contexts—insurance and public benefits law, for example, as well as legal ethics, contract law, and property law. Further, while the majority of materials focus on gender as if it denoted the difference between male and female, this edition has significantly enlarged the attention given to issues that challenge this dichotomy, including transgender and intersex, and interspersed sexual orientation materials throughout the book rather than as a separate section. This edition also reflects the increasing international dimensions of gender law and policy.

This edition retains the integration of theory and practice for which the book is known. We have added dozens more problems, most of them from actual cases or disputes. If anyone believes that the gender problem in this society has been solved, we can report that the easiest part of keeping this book up to date remains finding fresh examples of gender controversy with the potential to challenge ordinary understandings of gender justice and gender progress.

We feel it once more necessary to say that, with respect to edited materials in this book, additions to, deletions from, and other alterations to quoted material are indicated by brackets and ellipses, except for footnotes and citations, which are typically deleted without notice. Where retained, original footnote numbering is used. Paragraph breaks and the order of paragraphs are occasionally modified without notice to make edited excerpts easier to follow.

We appreciate your use of this book and welcome your feedback, including feedback by students, to make it better. The book is committed to helping students think more critically, broadly, and deeply in their analysis of gender and law. But, like gender law more generally, the book is an ongoing work in progress. Thanks for being part of the process of keeping the field responsive to social and legal realities.

Katharine T. Bartlett
Duke University School of Law

Deborah L. Rhode
Stanford Law School

Joanna L. Grossman
SMU Dedman School of Law

August 2016

Acknowledgments

This book has been a truly collaborative effort. While each section had a lead author, it went through numerous drafts as we discussed, refined, expanded, shortened, reorganized and edited the material. In addition, the book benefitted from feedback from an expanding circle of faculty who use the book in their teaching, students enrolled in their courses, and practitioners who have used the book as a source. Since the last edition, Joanna Grossman, who has moved from Hofstra to SMU Dedman School of Law to become the Ellen K. Solender Endowed Chair in Women and the Law, has taken on the responsibilities of lead author from the book's original author, Katharine Bartlett. The book bears the stamp of another round of research assistants, including Grady Jung at Stanford and Brianne Richards at Hofstra, both of whom, like their predecessors, contributed greatly to the research and thought that went into this edition. Thanks also go to Christine Ryan, SJD student from Duke, for her very useful suggestions, and to Eun Sze from Stanford and Frances Avnet from Hofstra for their extraordinarily able administrative assistance.

American Bar Association, Commission on Women in the Profession, Fair Measure: Toward Effective Attorney Evaluations 17-23 (2d ed. 2008). Copyright © 2008 American Bar Association. Reprinted with permission.

Deborah L. Brake, Getting in the Game: Title IX and the Women's Sports Revolution NYU Press 16-17, 112-18, 170, 219-221 (2010). Reprinted with permission of the author and publisher.

Devon W. Carbado and Mitu Gulati, The Fifth Black Woman, 11 J. Contemp. Legal Issues 701, 710-715, 717-720 (2001). Copyright 2001 The
Journal of Contemporary Legal Issues. Reprinted by permission of the
authors and publisher.

L. Camille Hébert, The Economic Implications of Sexual Harassment for
Women, 3 Kan. J.L. & Pub. Pol'y 41, 47-50 (Spring 1994). Reprinted
by permission of the author and publisher.

Catherine A. MacKinnon, Feminism Unmodified: Discourses on Life and Law
16, 31-38, 40-41, 171-172 (1987). Copyright © 1987 by the President
and Fellows of Harvard College. Reprinted by permission from Feminism Unmodified: Discourses on Life and Law by Catharine A. MacKinnon, Cambridge, Mass.: Harvard University Press, Copyright © 1987 by
the President and Fellows of Harvard College.

Catherine A. MacKinnon, Women's Lives, Men's Laws, Harv. Univ. Press 86-
90 (2005). Reprinted by permission from Women's Lives, Men's Laws by
Catharine A. MacKinnon, Cambridge, Mass.: Harvard University Press,
Copyright © 2005 by Catharine A. MacKinnon. Reprinted with permission of author.

Richard A. Posner, Conservative Feminism, 1989 U. Chi. Legal F. 191, 195-
198, 214 (1989). Originally appearing in the University of Chicago Legal Forum, Vol. 1989 Reprinted with permission of the author and from
the University of Chicago Legal Forum and the University of Chicago
Law School.

Gender and Law

1

Formal Equality

Formal equality is the principle of treating like people alike. In determining whether people are alike, and thus deserve the same treatment, formal equality demands that people be judged according to their actual characteristics rather than on the basis of assumptions or stereotypes about who they are or who they ought to be. In the context of sex, formal equality requires the state to provide men and women the same opportunity to exercise civic responsibility, such as by voting and serving on juries. It requires that public benefits such as Social Security and unemployment compensation be available to men and women on the same terms, and that property rules, tax liabilities, and alimony rules be sex-neutral. Formal equality also dictates that employers apply the same hiring and promotion criteria to men and women.

Chapter 1 begins with several cases illustrating traditional legal restrictions against women. It then explores the constitutional and statutory doctrines that evolved to dismantle these restrictions. These doctrines emerged from a series of decisions by the U.S. Supreme Court beginning in the early 1970s, and drew heavily from earlier civil rights cases brought under the Fourteenth Amendment of the United States Constitution and from the formal equality model that undergirded these cases.

One central issue for sex discrimination law involves the appropriate standard of judicial review. Muller v. Oregon and Goesart v. Cleary, set forth in Section A, illustrate the application of the rational basis test. Starting with Reed v. Reed in 1971,[1] the Supreme Court gradually moved to a more stringent "intermediate" standard. Craig v. Boren, decided in 1976, held that a classification based on sex must serve important governmental objectives and

---

1. 404 U.S. 71 (1971).

1

. . . be substantially related to achievement of those objectives."[2] In 1994, the U.S. Supreme Court held in J.E.B. v. Alabama that a sex-based classification be supported by "an exceedingly persuasive justification."[3] Although many sex-based classifications have been invalidated under this standard, a number of sex-based rules have survived as well.

In reviewing the legitimacy of sex-based classifications, a chief concern under both the U.S. Constitution and various civil rights statutes has been the accuracy of the underlying assumptions. Many of the laws and practices challenged in courts were based on stereotypes about women. Some stereotypes make descriptive generalizations that are overbroad or factually unsupported, such as that women do not have the strength or ability to work in certain jobs. Other stereotypes are prescriptive or normative, such as the belief that a woman's place is in the home, not the workplace. Courts have invalidated many laws and practices that were based on stereotypes and those that remain are usually difficult to justify under the formal equality principle.

Some assumptions about women have some factual basis, but nonetheless statutes or practices based on these assumptions are impermissible under the formal equality principle because they are not drawn narrowly enough to support sufficiently important state objectives. Women *on average* may be less strong than men, but not *all women* are less strong than *all men*; thus, ordinarily, formal equality requires that individual women have the opportunity to prove that they have the strength required for a particular job. Not only fairness concerns demand this opportunity, but also the danger that limiting women's opportunities will reinforce and perpetuate the stereotypes on which the limitations were based.

Sometimes job requirements that appear neutral may in fact rest on traditional stereotypes. For example, a workplace may use equipment designed with the heights and weights of men in mind, since the work in question traditionally has been "men's work." Similarly, an employer may require all of its employees—male and female—to work from 8 a.m. to 5 p.m., or attend evening events, even though these hours may be relatively disadvantageous to women because of the greater family obligations they tend to assume. A continuing dilemma within the formal equality framework is what to do about rules and practices that are "formally" equal to men and women, but have a disparate impact on women. Chapter 1 focuses on claims for identical treatment. Chapter 2 focuses on claims for a broader equality that takes into account the practical realities of men's and women's lives.

Formal equality applies to sex-based classifications that discriminate against men, as well as those that discriminate against women. As a result, women's rights advocates have often supported male litigants in their challenges to sex-based rules and practices. As these advocates note, equality for

2. 429 U.S. 190 (1976).
3. 511 U.S. 127 (1994).

Paternity leave

men is justified not only as a matter of fair treatment for men, but also as a means of reducing stereotypes that restrict opportunities for women. For example, a policy that gives parental leaves only to women deprives men of a benefit and also reinforces a domestic division of labor that penalizes women in the world outside of work.

The formal equality framework has facilitated substantial progress for women, but are there problems that it does not adequately address? What additional theoretical tools would be necessary to support an appropriate remedy in those cases?

A. HISTORICAL FOUNDATIONS FOR WOMEN'S CLAIM TO FORMAL EQUALITY

Benevolent Sexism

1. The Historical Legacy: Women as Different and in Need of Protection

a. Economic and Social Legislation to Protect Women

Throughout this nation's history, the conventional view has been that women are unfit for many occupations, and that their biological characteristics and reproductive role make it necessary to limit their employment. This section includes two cases illustrating this conventional view. Muller v. Oregon was decided during a period between 1905 and 1937, referred to as the *Lochner* era,[4] when the U.S. Supreme Court routinely invalidated statutes that interfered with the ability of individuals and businesses to make contracts controlling their own commercial relationships. In upholding economic legislation that limited the terms upon which an employer and employee could contract, the *Muller* case represented a strong message of women's need for protection since it was an exception to the *Lochner*-era cases. The *Lochner* era ended in 1937 with West Coast Hotel Co. v. Parrish,[5] in which the Court upheld a state's Minimum Wage for Women Act, and established the modern principle that courts should defer to legislatures when they enact economic and social legislation unless that the legislation has no rational basis. In Goesart v. Cleary, decided in 1948, the Supreme Court upheld a Michigan law that prevented the licensing of women as bartenders unless the woman was the wife or daughter of a male who owned the bar where she worked, stressing the moral dangers for women who are without the protection of their fathers or husbands. *Goesart* was decided after the *Lochner* period, and

Women cannot own bar, need protection

---

4. The era began with the Supreme Court's decision in Lochner v. New York, 198 U.S. 45 (1905).

5. 300 U.S. 379 (1937).

while its deference to legislatures was typical of that period, the decision is also striking for what it assumed about women's "difference." Note that the laws in both *Muller* and *Goesart* were challenged by employers, not by the women negatively affected by the law.

Muller v. Oregon
208 U.S. 412 (1908)

Mr. Justice BREWER delivered the opinion of the Court.

On February 19, 1903, the legislature of the State of Oregon passed an act, [providing that it would be a misdemeanor to employ any female in any mechanical establishment, or factory, or laundry more than ten hours in any one day. Defendant was charged with violation of the statute for ordering Mrs. E. Gotcher to work more than ten hours per day in defendant's laundry]. . . .

A trial resulted in a verdict against the defendant, who was sentenced to pay a fine of $10. The Supreme Court of the State affirmed the conviction . . . whereupon the case was brought here on writ of error.

The single question is the constitutionality of the statute under which the defendant was convicted so far as it affects the work of a female in a laundry. . . .

It is the law of Oregon that women, whether married or single, have equal contractual and personal rights with men. . . .

[Yet the] legislation and opinions referred to [above, including a brief by Mr. Louis D. Brandeis,] are significant of a widespread belief that woman's physical structure, and the functions she performs in consequence thereof, justify special legislation restricting or qualifying the conditions under which she should be permitted to toil. Constitutional questions, it is true, are not settled by even a consensus of present public opinion, for it is the peculiar value of a written constitution that it places in unchanging form limitations upon legislative action, and thus gives a permanence and stability to popular government which otherwise would be lacking. At the same time, when a question of fact is debated and debatable, and the extent to which a special constitutional limitation goes is affected by the truth in respect to that fact, a widespread and long continued belief concerning it is worthy of consideration. We take judicial cognizance of all matters of general knowledge.

That woman's physical structure and the performance of maternal functions place her at a disadvantage in the struggle for subsistence is obvious. This is especially true when the burdens of motherhood are upon her. Even when they are not, by abundant testimony of the medical fraternity continuance for a long time on her feet at work, repeating this from day to day, tends to injurious effects upon the body, and as healthy mothers are essential to vigorous offspring, the physical well-being of woman becomes an object of public interest and care in order to preserve the strength and vigor of the race.

Still again, history discloses the fact that woman has always been dependent upon man. He established his control at the outset by superior physical strength, and this control in various forms, with diminishing intensity, has continued to the present. As minors, though not to the same extent, she has been looked upon in the courts as needing especial care that her rights may be preserved. Education was long denied her, and while now the doors of the schoolroom are opened and her opportunities for acquiring knowledge are great, yet even with that and the consequent increase of capacity for business affairs it is still true that in the struggle for subsistence she is not an equal competitor with her brother. Though limitations upon personal and contractual rights may be removed by legislation, there is that in her disposition and habits of life which will operate against a full assertion of those rights. She will still be where some legislation to protect her seems necessary to secure a real equality of right. Doubtless there are individual exceptions, and there are many respects in which she has an advantage over him; but looking at it from the viewpoint of the effort to maintain an independent position in life, she is not upon an equality. Differentiated by these matters from the other sex, she is properly placed in a class by herself, and legislation designed for her protection may be sustained, even when like legislation is not necessary for men and could not be sustained. It is impossible to close one's eyes to the fact that she still looks to her brother and depends upon him. Even though all restrictions on political, personal and contractual rights were taken away, and she stood, so far as statutes are concerned, upon an absolutely equal plane with him, it would still be true that she is so constituted that she will rest upon and look to him for protection; that her physical structure and a proper discharge of her maternal functions — having in view not merely her own health, but the well-being of the race — justify legislation to protect her from the greed as well as the passion of man. The limitations which this statute places upon her contractual powers, upon her right to agree with her employer as to the time she shall labor, are not imposed solely for her benefit, but also largely for the benefit of all. Many words cannot make this plainer. The two sexes differ in structure of body, in the functions to be performed by each, in the amount of physical strength, in the capacity for long-continued labor, particularly when done standing, the influence of vigorous health upon the future well-being of the race, the self-reliance which enables one to assert full rights, and in the capacity to maintain the struggle for subsistence. This difference justifies a difference in legislation and upholds that which is designed to compensate for some of the burdens which rest upon her.

We have not referred in this discussion to the denial of the elective franchise in the State of Oregon, for while it may disclose a lack of political equality in all things with her brother, that is not of itself decisive. The reason runs deeper, and rests in the inherent difference between the two sexes, and in the different functions in life which they perform.

For these reasons, and without questioning in any respect the decision in Lochner v. New York, we are of the opinion that it cannot be adjudged that the act in question is in conflict with the Federal Constitution, so far as it respects the work of a female in a laundry, and the judgment of the Supreme Court of Oregon is affirmed.

Goesart v. Cleary
335 U.S. 464 (1948)

Mr. Justice FRANKFURTER delivered the opinion of the Court.

As part of the Michigan system for controlling the sale of liquor, bartenders are required to be licensed in all cities having a population of 50,000 or more, but no female may be so licensed unless she be "the wife or daughter of the male owner" of a licensed liquor establishment. The case is here on direct appeal from an order of the District Court of three judges, . . . denying an injunction to restrain the enforcement of the Michigan law. The claim, denied below, one judge dissenting, and renewed here, is that Michigan cannot forbid females generally from being barmaids and at the same time make an exception in favor of the wives and daughters of the owners of liquor establishments. Beguiling as the subject is, it need not detain us long. To ask whether or not the Equal Protection of the Laws Clause of the Fourteenth Amendment barred Michigan from making the classification the State has made between wives and daughters of owners of liquor places and wives and daughters of non-owners, is one of those rare instances where to state the question is in effect to answer it.

We are, to be sure, dealing with a historic calling. We meet the alewife, sprightly and ribald, in Shakespeare, but centuries before him she played a role in the social life of England. The Fourteenth Amendment did not tear history up by the roots, and the regulation of the liquor traffic is one of the oldest and most untrammeled of legislative powers. Michigan could, beyond question, forbid all women from working behind a bar. This is so despite the vast changes in the social and legal position of women. The fact that women may now have achieved the virtues that men have long claimed as their prerogatives and now indulge in vices that men have long practiced, does not preclude the States from drawing a sharp line between the sexes, certainly in such matters as the regulation of the liquor traffic. The Constitution does not require legislatures to reflect sociological insight, or shifting social standards, any more than it requires them to keep abreast of the latest scientific standards.

While Michigan may deny to all women opportunities for bartending, Michigan cannot play favorites among women without rhyme or reason. The Constitution in enjoining the equal protection of the laws upon States precludes irrational discrimination as between persons or groups of persons in the incidence of a law. But the Constitution does not require situations "which are different in fact or opinion to be treated in law as though they were the same." . . . Since bartending by women may, in the allowable legislative judgment, give rise to moral and social problems against which it may devise preventive measures, the legislature need not go to the full length of prohibition if it believes that as to a defined group of females other factors are operating which either eliminate or reduce the moral and social problems otherwise calling for prohibition. Michigan evidently believes that the oversight assured through ownership of a bar by a barmaid's husband or father minimizes hazards that may confront a barmaid without such protecting oversight. This Court is certainly not in a position to gainsay such belief by the Michigan legislature. If it is entertainable, as we think it is, Michigan has not violated its duty to afford equal protection of its laws. We cannot cross-examine either actually or argumentatively the mind of Michigan legislators nor question their motives. Since the line they have drawn is not without a basis in reason, we cannot give ear to the suggestion that the real impulse behind this legislation was an unchivalrous desire of male bartenders to try to monopolize the calling . . . .

Nor is it unconstitutional for Michigan to withdraw from women the occupation of bartending because it allows women to serve as waitresses where liquor is dispensed. The District Court has sufficiently indicated the reasons that may have influenced the legislature in allowing women to be waitresses in a liquor establishment over which a man's ownership provides control. Nothing need be added to what was said below as to the other grounds on which the Michigan law was assailed.

Judgment affirmed.

Mr. Justice RUTLEDGE, with whom Mr. Justice DOUGLAS and Mr. Justice MURPHY join, dissenting.

While the equal protection clause does not require a legislature to achieve "abstract symmetry" or to classify with "mathematical nicety," that clause does require lawmakers to refrain from invidious distinctions of the sort drawn by the statute challenged in this case.

The statute arbitrarily discriminates between male and female owners of liquor establishments. A male owner, although he himself is always absent from his bar, may employ his wife and daughter as barmaids. A female owner may neither work as a barmaid herself nor employ her daughter in that position, even if a man is always present in the establishment to keep order. This inevitable result of the classification belies the assumption that the statute was motivated by a legislative solicitude for the moral and physical well-being of women who, but for the law, would be employed as barmaids. Since there could be no other conceivable justification for such discrimination against women owners of liquor establishments, the statute should be held invalid as a denial of equal protection.

Putting Theory Into Practice

1-1. An Oregon statute in the mid-1950s makes it a crime for women to "participat[e] in wrestling competition and exhibition." A woman is charged under the statute and offers as a defense that the statute violates her equal protection rights. Defend the statute, and her prosecution, based on the arguments presented in *Muller* and *Goesart*.

1-2. In enacting the statute described in Problem 1-1 above, a court found that

> [the Oregon legislature] intended that there should be at least one island on the sea of life reserved for man that would be impregnable to the assault of woman. It had watched her emerge from long tresses and demure ways to bobbed hair and almost complete sophistication; from a creature needing and depending upon the protection and chivalry of man to one asserting complete independence. She had already invaded practically every activity formerly considered suitable and appropriate for men only. In the field of sports she had taken up, among other games, baseball, basketball, golf, bowling, hockey, long distance swimming, and racing, in all of which she had become more or less proficient, and in some had excelled. In the business and industrial fields as an employe[e] or as an executive, in the professions, in politics, as well as in almost every other line of human endeavor, she had matched her wits and prowess with those of mere man, and . . . in many instances had outdone him.[6]

Does this rationale have any continuing resonance in U.S. society? Assuming the rationale would no longer be constitutionally sufficient, is there another purpose that might justify the statute?

b. Women's Differences and the Practice of Law

For most of this nation's history, the conventional view was that women's "difference" made women unfit for law and law unfit for women. In the colonial era, when labor was scarce and relatively few occupations required formal licenses, a few women did manage to participate in legal transactions either by acting as their husband's representative or by obtaining special authorization to proceed independently. During the late eighteenth century, however, the gradual formalization of bar admission criteria made it increasingly difficult for women to act as lawyers. The inability of married women to make contracts reinforced the barriers to any independent career. And, of course, African-American women under slavery had no capacity to assert even their own legal rights, let alone represent others.

6. State v. Hunter, 300 P.2d 455, 458 (Or. 1956).

After the Civil War, the rise in women's educational and political activism contributed to a growing stream of female applicants to the bar. In 1867, Iowa became the first state to license a woman attorney, Belle Babb Mansfield, and the following decades witnessed a gradual increase in female candidates from largely white middle- and upper-middle-class backgrounds. Women's initial reception as lawyers in most jurisdictions was less than enthusiastic. Many nineteenth-century lawmakers invested the sexes' "separate spheres" with both spiritual and constitutional significance.[7] The following excerpt from Justice Bradley's concurring opinion in Bradwell v. Illinois was typical in rooting women's domesticity in "the divine ordinance." In addition to raising concerns over women's proper role and "peculiar sensibilities," commentators linked female professional careers to infertility, frigidity, and "race suicide." "Theories about the deadly 'brain-womb' conflict warned that women who diverted their scarce energies to cognitive rather than reproductive pursuits risked permanent physical and psychological damage."[8]

Myra Bradwell based her claim for entrance to the bar on the privileges and immunities clause of the Fourteenth Amendment of the U.S. Constitution. This clause provides that "No State shall make or enforce any law which shall abridge the privileges or immunities of citizens of the United States." Her claim arose before other provisions of the Fourteenth Amendment, notably the equal protection clause and the due process clause, became the more important legal foundations for women's rights in the twentieth century.

Bradwell v. Illinois
83 U.S. (16 Wall.) 130 (1872)

Mrs. Myra Bradwell, residing in the State of Illinois, made application to the judges of the Supreme Court of that State for a license to practice law. . . .

[The Supreme Court of Illinois denied the application because she was a married woman. Mrs. Bradwell challenged the denial under the privileges and immunities clause of the Fourteenth Amendment of the U.S. Constitution, but the decision of the Illinois Supreme Court was upheld. The opinion of the Court is omitted here; what follows is the concurring opinion of Justice Bradley.]

Mr. Justice BRADLEY, concurring: . . .

The claim of the plaintiff, who is a married woman, to be admitted to practice as an attorney and counsellor-at-law, is based upon the supposed right of every person, man or woman, to engage in any lawful employment for

7. See Deborah L. Rhode, Justice and Gender 20-24 (1989); Karen Morello, The Invisible Bar: The Woman Lawyer in America (1986); Cynthia Epstein, Women in Law 66-67 (1981).

8. Deborah L. Rhode, Midcourse Corrections: Women in Legal Education, 53 J. Legal Educ. 475, 477 (2003).

a livelihood. The Supreme Court of Illinois denied the application on the ground that, by the common law, which is the basis of the laws of Illinois, only men were admitted to the bar, and the legislature had not made any change in this respect. . . .

The claim that, under the fourteenth amendment of the Constitution, which declares that no State shall make or enforce any law which shall abridge the privileges and immunities of citizens of the United States, the statute law of Illinois, or the common law prevailing in that State, can no longer be set up as a barrier against the right of females to pursue any lawful employment for a livelihood (the practice of law included), assumes that it is one of the privileges and immunities of women as citizens to engage in any and every profession, occupation, or employment in civil life.

It certainly cannot be affirmed, as an historical fact, that this has ever been established as one of the fundamental privileges and immunities of the sex. On the contrary, the civil law, as well as nature herself, has always recognized a wide difference in the respective spheres and destinies of man and woman. Man is, or should be, woman's protector and defender. The natural and proper timidity and delicacy which belongs to the female sex evidently unfits it for many of the occupations of civil life. The constitution of the family organization, which is founded in the divine ordinance, as well as in the nature of things, indicates the domestic sphere as that which properly belongs to the domain and functions of womanhood. The harmony, not to say identity, of interests and views which belong, or should belong, to the family institution is repugnant to the idea of a woman adopting a distinct and independent career from that of her husband. So firmly fixed was this sentiment in the founders of the common law that it became a maxim of that system of jurisprudence that a woman had no legal existence separate from her husband, who was regarded as her head and representative in the social state; and, notwithstanding some recent modifications of this civil status, many of the special rules of law flowing from and dependent upon this cardinal principle still exist in full force in most States. One of these is, that a married woman is incapable, without her husband's consent, of making contracts which shall be binding on her or him. This very incapacity was one circumstance which the Supreme Court of Illinois deemed important in rendering a married woman incompetent fully to perform the duties and trusts that belong to the office of an attorney and counsellor.

It is true that many women are unmarried and not affected by any of the duties, complications, and incapacities arising out of the married state, but these are exceptions to the general rule. The paramount destiny and mission of woman are to fulfil the noble and benign offices of wife and mother. This is the law of the Creator. And the rules of civil society must be adapted to the general constitution of things, and cannot be based upon exceptional cases.

The humane movements of modern society, which have for their object the multiplication of avenues for woman's advancement, and of occupations adapted to her condition and sex, have my heartiest concurrence. But I am not prepared to say that it is one of her fundamental rights and privileges to be admitted into every office and position, including those which require highly special qualifications and demanding special responsibilities. In the nature of things it is not every citizen of every age, sex, and condition that is qualified for every calling and position. It is the prerogative of the legislator to prescribe regulations founded on nature, reason, and experience for the due admission of qualified persons to professions and callings demanding special skill and confidence. This fairly belongs to the police power of the State; and, in my opinion, in view of the peculiar characteristics, destiny, and mission of woman, it is within the province of the legislature to ordain what offices, positions, and callings shall be filled and discharged by men, and shall receive the benefit of those energies and responsibilities, and that decision and firmness which are presumed to predominate in the sterner sex.

For these reasons I think that the laws of Illinois now complained of are not obnoxious to the charge of abridging any of the privileges and immunities of citizens of the United States.

2. The Case for Women's Suffrage

Modern feminism has its roots in the nineteenth century movement for women's suffrage. Although several states briefly allowed women to cast ballots in state and local elections, women did not achieve the vote until the passage of the Nineteenth Amendment in 1920. Efforts to include women in the Civil Rights Amendments that enfranchised former slaves were unsuccessful.

A key document in the history of women's suffrage is the Declaration of Sentiments, adopted at the Seneca Falls Convention in Seneca Falls, New York, in July 1848.[9] As historian Gerda Lerner notes, this Convention was the "first forum in which women gathered together to publicly air their own grievances, not those of the needy, the enslaved, orphans, or widows." The Declaration quite clearly uses the Declaration of Independence as the template. Lerner suggests that naming of "man" as the culprit, which anticipated the subsequent, radical feminist critique of patriarchy detailed in Chapter 3 of this casebook, was probably intended more as part of the Declaration's "rhetorical flourishes" than an "actual analysis of women's situation."[10]

The women's suffrage movement was intertwined with the campaign to abolish slavery. Indeed, the idea for the Seneca Falls Convention was inspired by a London Anti-Slavery Convention a few years earlier at which two

9. The Declaration of Sentiments, as well as all of the other documents excerpted in this section, can be found in a multi-volume collection of women's suffrage documents, History of Woman Suffrage, edited by Elizabeth Cady Stanton, Susan B. Anthony, and Matilda Joslyn Gage (reprint ed. 1985).

10. Gerda Lerner, The Meaning of Seneca Falls, 1848-1998, Dissent 35, 37-39 (Fall 1998).

PETTY

American participants, Lucretia Mott, a Quaker minister, and Elizabeth Cady Stanton, were barred from participation and required to sit behind a curtain.[11] Some suffragettes also had close ties to other social movements, such as campaigns to protect children from abuse, to criminalize sale and consumption of liquor, to combat "vices" such as prostitution and obscenity, and to improve the conditions of the working poor.

The case of United States v. Anthony, excerpted below, involves the conviction of women's suffrage leader Susan B. Anthony, for violation of an 1870 federal civil rights statute intended to prohibit multiple voting by white voters in order to dilute black votes. The excerpt includes Anthony's statements in her defense. After dedicating much of her life to the suffrage struggle, Anthony died in 1906, 14 years before the Nineteenth Amendment was passed.

Another prominent suffragette was Elizabeth Cady Stanton, whose address to the New York State legislature in 1854 forms another basic document in the history of women's suffrage. This reading demonstrates the breadth of the feminist social agenda of the period.

After the turn of the twentieth century, women's rights supporters attracted a mass movement and pursued tactics of escalating pressure, including parades, White House pickets, and hunger strikes. Such strategies, together with women's increasing role in public life and gratitude for their service during World War I, led in 1920 to passage of the Nineteenth Amendment. After that victory, the women's movement dissolved. Although many women remained active in progressive causes, and a few continued to struggle for a constitutional equal rights amendment, an organized feminist campaign did not reemerge until the 1960s.

To what extent do the arguments by leading suffragettes assume that women are the same as men, and to what extent do they assume women are different? Which assumptions about sameness and difference are reflected in contemporary debates? Was it "racist" for women to argue that educated women were even more deserving of the vote than illiterate former slaves?

≡ *Declaration of Sentiments, Seneca Falls Convention, Seneca Falls, New York (July 1848)*

When, in the course of human events, it becomes necessary for one portion of the family of man to assume among the people of the earth a position different from that which they have hitherto occupied, but one to which the laws of nature and of nature's God entitle them, a decent respect to the opinions

11. See Sara M. Evans, Born for Liberty: A History of Women in America 81 (1989).

of mankind requires that they should declare the causes that impel them to such a course.

We hold these truths to be self-evident: that all men and women are created equal; that they are endowed by their Creator with certain inalienable rights; that among these are life, liberty, and the pursuit of happiness; that to secure these rights governments are instituted, deriving their just powers from the consent of the governed. Whenever any form of government becomes destructive of these ends, it is the right of those who suffer from it to refuse allegiance to it, and to insist upon the institution of a new government, laying its foundation on such principles, and organizing its powers in such form, as to them shall seem most likely to effect their safety and happiness. Prudence, indeed, will dictate that governments long established should not be changed for light and transient causes; and accordingly all experience hath shown that mankind are more disposed to suffer, while evils are sufferable, than to right themselves by abolishing the forms to which they were accustomed. But when a long train of abuses and usurpations, pursuing invariably the same object evinces a design to reduce them under absolute despotism, it is their duty to throw off such government, and to provide new guards for their future security. Such has been the patient sufferance of the women under this government, and such is now the necessity which constrains them to demand the equal station to which they are entitled.

The history of mankind is a history of repeated injuries and usurpations on the part of man toward woman, having in direct object the establishment of an absolute tyranny over her. To prove this, let facts be submitted to a candid world.

He has never permitted her to exercise her inalienable right to the elective franchise.

He has compelled her to submit to laws, in the formation of which she had no voice.

He has withheld from her rights which are given to the most ignorant and degraded men—both natives and foreigners.

Having deprived her of this first right of a citizen, the elective franchise, thereby leaving her without representation in the halls of legislation, he has oppressed her on all sides.

He has made her, if married, in the eye of the law, civilly dead.

He has taken from her all right in property, even to the wages she earns.

He has made her, morally, an irresponsible being, as she can commit many crimes with impunity, provided they be done in the presence of her husband. In the covenant of marriage, she is compelled to promise obedience to her husband, he becoming, to all intents and purposes, her master—the law giving him power to deprive her of her liberty, and to administer chastisement.

He has so framed the laws of divorce, as to what shall be the proper causes, and in case of separation, to whom the guardianship of the children shall be given, as to be wholly regardless of the happiness of women — the law, in all cases, going upon a false supposition of the supremacy of man, and giving all power into his hands.

After depriving her of all rights as a married woman, if single, and the owner of property, he has taxed her to support a government which recognizes her only when her property can be made profitable to it.

He has monopolized nearly all the profitable employments, and from those she is permitted to follow, she receives but a scanty remuneration. He closes against her all the avenues to wealth and distinction which he considers most honorable to himself. As a teacher of theology, medicine, or law, she is not known.

He has denied her the facilities for obtaining a thorough education, all colleges being closed against her.

He allows her in Church, as well as State, but a subordinate position, claiming Apostolic authority for her exclusion from the ministry, and with some exceptions, from any public participation in the affairs of the Church.

He has created a false public sentiment by giving to the world a different code of morals for men and women, by which moral delinquencies which exclude women from society, are not only tolerated, but deemed of little account in man.

He has usurped the prerogative of Jehovah himself, claiming it as his right to assign for her a sphere of action, when that belongs to her conscience and to her God.

He has endeavored, in every way that he could, to destroy her confidence in her own powers, to lessen her self-respect, and to make her willing to lead a dependent and abject life.

Now, in view of this entire disfranchisement of one-half the people of this country, their social and religious degradation — in view of the unjust laws above mentioned, and because women do feel themselves aggrieved, oppressed, and fraudulently deprived of their most sacred rights, we insist that they have immediate admission to all the rights and privileges which belong to them as citizens of the United States.

In entering upon the great work before us, we anticipate no small amount of misconception, misrepresentation, and ridicule; but we shall use every instrumentality within our power to effect our object. We shall employ agents, circulate tracts, petition the State and National legislatures, and endeavor to enlist the pulpit and the press in our behalf. We hope this Convention will be followed by a series of Conventions embracing every part of the country.

United States v. Anthony (1873)

Miss ANTHONY: All my prosecutors, from the 8th Ward corner grocery politician, who entered the complaint, to the United States Marshal,

Commissioner, District Attorney, District Judge, your honor on the bench, not one is my peer, but each and all are my political sovereigns; and had your honor submitted my case to the jury, as was clearly your duty, even then I should have had just cause of protest, for not one of those men was my peer; but, native or foreign, white or black, rich or poor, educated or ignorant, awake or asleep, sober or drunk, each and every man of them was my political superior; hence, in no sense, my peer. Even, under such circumstances, a commoner of England, tried before a jury of lords, would have far less cause to complain than should I, a woman, tried before a jury of men. Even my counsel, the Hon. Henry R. Selden, who has argued my cause so ably, so earnestly, so unanswerably before your honor, is my political sovereign. Precisely as no disfranchised person is entitled to sit upon a jury, and no woman is entitled to the franchise, so, none but a regularly admitted lawyer is allowed to practice in the courts, and no woman can gain admission to the bar—hence, jury, judge, counsel, must all be of the superior class.

Judge HUNT: The Court must insist—the prisoner has been tried according to the established forms of law.

Miss ANTHONY: Yes, your honor, but by forms of law all made by men, interpreted by men, administered by men, in favor of men, and against women; and hence, your honor's ordered verdict of guilty, against a United States citizen for the exercise of "that citizen's right to vote," simply because that citizen was a woman and not a man. But, yesterday, the same man-made forms of law declared it a crime punishable with $1,000 fine and six months' imprisonment, for you, or me, or any of us, to give a cup of cold water, a crust of bread, or a night's shelter to a panting fugitive as he was tracking his way to Canada. And every man or woman in whose veins coursed a drop of human sympathy violated that wicked law, reckless of consequences, and was justified in so doing. As then the slaves who got their freedom must take it over, or under, or through the unjust forms of law, precisely so now must women, to get their right to a voice in this Government, take it; and I have taken mine, and mean to take it at every possible opportunity.

Judge HUNT: The Court orders the prisoner to sit down. It will not allow another word.

Miss ANTHONY: When I was brought before your honor for trial, I hoped for a broad and liberal interpretation of the Constitution and its recent amendments, that should declare all United States citizens under its protecting aegis—that should declare equality of rights the national guarantee to all persons born or naturalized in the United States. But failing to get this justice—failing, even, to get a trial by a jury not of my peers—I ask not leniency at your hands—but rather the full rigors of the law.

Judge HUNT: The Court must insist—(Here the prisoner sat down.)

Judge HUNT: The prisoner will stand up. (Here Miss Anthony arose again.) The sentence of the Court is that you pay a fine of one hundred dollars and the costs of the prosecution.

Civil Disobedience

Don't pay taxes don't agree w/

Miss ANTHONY: May it please your honor, I shall never pay a dollar of your unjust penalty. All the stock in trade I possess is a $10,000 debt, incurred by publishing my paper—*The Revolution*—four years ago, the sole object of which was to educate all women to do precisely as I have done, rebel against your man-made, unjust unconstitutional forms of law, that tax, fine, imprison, and hang women, while they deny them the right of representation in the Government; and I shall work on with might and main to pay every dollar of that honest debt, but not a penny shall go to this unjust claim. And I shall earnestly and persistently continue to urge all women to practical recognition of the old revolutionary maxim, that "Resistance to tyranny is obedience to God."

Elizabeth Cady Stanton, Address to the Legislature of the State of New York (February 14, 1854)

The tyrant, Custom, has been summoned before the bar of Common-Sense. His majesty no longer awes his multitude—his sceptre is broken—his crown is trampled in the dust—the sentence of death is pronounced upon him. . . . [A]nd now, that the monster is chained and caged, timid woman, on tiptoe, comes to look him in the face, and to demand of her brave sires and sons, who have struck stout blows for liberty, if, in this change of dynasty, she, too, shall find relief. Yes, gentlemen, in republican America, in the nineteenth century, we, the daughters of the revolutionary heroes of '76, demand at your hands the redress of our grievances—a revision of your State Constitution—a new code of laws. Permit us then, as briefly as possible, to call your attention to the legal disabilities under which we labor.

1st. Look at the position of woman as woman. . . . We are persons; native, free-born citizens; property-holders, tax-payers; yet we are denied the exercise of our right to the elective franchise. We support ourselves, and, in part, your schools, colleges, churches, your poor-houses, jails, prisons, the army, the navy, the whole machinery of government, and yet we have no voice in your councils. . . . We are moral, virtuous, and intelligent, and in all respects quite equal to the proud white man himself and yet by your laws we are classed with idiots, lunatics, and negroes; and though we do not feel honored by the place assigned us in fact, our legal position is lower than that of either; for the negro can be raised to the dignity of a voter if he possess himself of $250; the lunatic can vote in his moments of sanity, and the idiot, too, if he be a made one, and not more than nine-tenths a fool; but we, who have guided great movements of charity, established missions, edited journals, published works on history, economy, and statistics; who have governed nations, led armies, filled the professor's chair, taught philosophy and mathematics to the savants of our age, discovered planets, piloted ships across the sea, are denied the most sacred rights of citizens, because, forsooth, we came not into this republic crowned with the dignity of manhood! . . .

Now, gentlemen, who would fain know by what authority you have disfranchised one-half the people of this State? You who have so boldly taken possession of the bulwarks of this republic, show us your credentials, and thus prove your exclusive right to govern, not only yourselves, but us. . . . Can it be that here, where we acknowledge no royal blood, no apostolic descent, that you, who have declared that all men were created equal—that governments derive their just powers from the consent of the governed, would willingly build up an aristocracy that places the ignorant and vulgar above the educated and refined—the alien and the ditch-digger above the authors and poets of the day—an aristocracy that would raise the sons above the mothers that bore them? Would that the men who can sanction a Constitution so opposed to the genius of this government, who can enact and execute laws so degrading to womankind, had sprung, Minerva-like, from the brains of their fathers, that the matrons of this republic need not blush to own their sons!

. . . [Y]ou place the negro, so unjustly degraded by you, in a superior position to your own wives and mothers; for colored males, if possessed of a certain amount of property and certain other qualifications, can vote, but if they do not have these qualifications they are not subject to direct taxation; wherein they have the advantage of woman, she being subject to taxation for whatever amount she may possess. . . .

[W]e demand in criminal cases that most sacred of all rights, trial by a jury of our own peers. . . .

Shall an erring woman be dragged before a bar of grim-visaged judges, lawyers, and jurors, there to be grossly questioned in public on subjects which women scarce breathe in secret to one another? Shall the most sacred relations of life be called up and rudely scanned by men who, by their own admission, are so coarse that woman could not meet them even at the polls without contamination? [A]nd yet shall she find there no woman's face or voice to pity and defend? Shall the frenzied mother, who, to save herself and child from exposure and disgrace, ended the life that had but just begun, be dragged before such a tribunal to answer for her crime? How can man enter into the feelings of that mother? How can he judge of the agonies of soul that impelled her to such an outrage of maternal instincts? How can he weigh the mountain of sorrow that crushed that mother's heart when she wildly tossed her helpless babe into the cold waters of the midnight sea? Where is he who by false vows thus blasted this trusting woman? Had that helpless child no claims on his protection? Ah, he is freely abroad in the dignity of manhood, in the pulpit, on the bench, in the professor's chair. The imprisonment of his victim and the death of his child, detract not a tithe from his standing and complacency. His peers made the law, and shall law-makers lay nets for those of their own rank? Shall laws which come from the logical brain of man take cognizance of violence done to the moral and affectional nature which predominates, as is said, in woman?

Statesmen of New York, whose daughters guarded by your affection, and lapped amidst luxuries which your indulgence spreads, care more for their nodding plumes and velvet trains than for the statute laws by which their persons and properties are held—who, blinded by custom and prejudice to the degraded position which they and their sisters occupy in the civil scale, haughtily claim that they already have all the rights they want, how, think ye, you would feel to see a daughter summoned for such a crime—and remember these daughters are but human—before such a tribunal? Would it not, in that hour, be some consolation to see that she was surrounded by the wise and virtuous of her own sex; by those who had known the depth of a mother's love and the misery of a lover's falsehood; to know that to these she could make her confession, and from them receive her sentence? . . .

2d. Look at the position of woman as wife. Your laws relating to marriage—founded as they are on the old common law of England, a compound of barbarous usages, but partially modified by progressive civilization—are in open violation of our enlightened ideas of justice, and of the holiest feelings of our nature. If you take the highest view of marriage, as a Divine relation, which love alone can constitute and sanctify, then of course human legislation can only recognize it. Men can neither bind nor loose its ties, for that prerogative belongs to God alone, who makes man and woman, and the laws of attraction by which they are united. But if you regard marriage as a civil contract, then let it be subject to the same laws which control all other contracts. Do not make it a kind of half-human, half-divine institution, which you may build up, but can not regulate. Do not, by your special legislation for this one kind of contract, involve yourselves in the grossest absurdities and contradictions.

. . . The wife who inherits no property holds about the same legal position that does the slave on the Southern plantation. She can own nothing, sell nothing. She has no right even to the wages she earns; her person, her time, her services are the property of another. She can not testify, in many cases, against her husband. She can get no redress for wrongs in her own name in any court of justice. She can neither sue nor be sued. She is not held morally responsible for any crime committed in the presence of her husband so completely is her very existence supposed by the law to be merged in that of another. Think of it; your wives may be thieves, libelers, burglars, incendiaries, and for crimes like these they are not held amenable to the laws of the land, if they but commit them in your dread presence. For them, alas! there is no higher law than the will of man. . . .

4th. Look at the position of woman as mother. There is no human love so strong and steadfast as that of the mother for her child; yet behold how ruthless are your laws touching this most sacred relation. Nature has clearly made the mother the guardian of the child; but man, in his inordinate love of power, does continually set nature and nature's laws at open defiance. The father may apprentice his child, bind him out to a trade, without the mother's consent—yea, in direct opposition to her most earnest entreaties, prayers and tears.

He may apprentice his son to a gamester or rum-seller, and thus cancel his debts of honor. By the abuse of this absolute power, he may bind his daughter to the owner of a brothel, and, by the degradation of his child, supply his daily wants; and such things, gentlemen, have been done in our very midst. Moreover, the father, about to die, may bond out all his children wherever and to whomsoever he may see fit, and thus, in fact, will away the guardianship of all his children from the mother. . . . [B]y your laws, the child is the absolute property of the father, wholly at his disposal in life or at death.

In case of separation, the law gives the children to the father; no matter what his character or condition. At this very time we can point you to noble, virtuous, well-educated mothers in this State, who have abandoned their husbands for their profligacy and confirmed drunkenness. All these have been robbed of their children, who are in the custody of the husband, under the care of his relatives, whilst the mothers are permitted to see them but at stated intervals. . . .

Many times and oft it has been asked us, with unaffected seriousness, "What do you women want? What are you aiming at?" Many have manifested a laudable curiosity to know what the wives and daughters could complain of in republican America, where their sires and sons have so bravely fought for freedom and gloriously secured their independence, trampling all tyranny, bigotry, and caste in the dust, and declaring to a waiting world the divine truth that all men are created equal. What can woman want under such a government? Admit a radical difference in sex, and you demand different spheres—water for fish, and air for birds.

. . . When we plead our cause before the law-makers and savants of the republic, they can not take in the idea that men and women are alike; and so long as the mass rest in this delusion, the public mind will not be so much startled by the revelations made of the injustice and degradation of woman's position as by the fact that she should at length wake up to a sense of it.

If you, too, are thus deluded, what avails it that we show by your statute books that your laws are unjust—that woman is the victim of avarice and power? . . .

Would to God you could know the burning indignation that fills woman's soul when she turns over the pages of your statute books, and sees there how like feudal barons you freemen hold your women. Would that you could know the humiliation she feels for sex, when she thinks of all the beardless boys in your law offices, learning these ideas of one-sided justice—taking their first lessons in contempt for all womankind—being indoctrinated into the incapacities of their mothers, and the lordly, absolute rights of man over all women, children, and property, and to know that these are to be our future presidents, judges, husbands, and fathers; in sorrow we exclaim, alas! for that nation whose sons bow not in loyalty to woman. . . .

But if, gentlemen, you take the ground that the sexes are alike, and, therefore, you are our faithful representatives—then why all these special laws for woman? Would not one code answer for all of like needs and wants? Christ's golden rule is better than all the special legislation that the ingenuity of man can devise: "Do unto others as you would have others do unto you." This, men and brethren, is all we ask at your hands. We ask no better laws than those you have made for yourselves. We need no other protection than that which your present laws secure to you.

In conclusion, then, let us say, in behalf of the women of this State, we ask for all that you have asked for yourselves in the progress of your development, since the Mayflower cast anchor beside Plymouth rock; and simply on the ground that the rights of every human being are the same and identical. You may say that the mass of the women of this State do not make the demand; it comes from a few sour, disappointed old maids and childless women.

You are mistaken; the mass speak through us. A very large majority of the women of this State support themselves and their children, and many their husbands too. . . .

Now, do you candidly think these wives do not wish to control the wages they earn—to own the land they buy—the houses they build? To have at their disposal their own children, without being subject to the constant interference and tyranny of an idle, worthless profligate? Do you suppose that any woman is such a pattern of devotion and submission that she willingly stitches all day for the small sum of fifty cents, that she may enjoy the unspeakable privilege, in obedience to your laws, of paying for her husband's tobacco and rum? Think you the wife of the confirmed, beastly drunkard would consent to share with him her home and bed, if law and public sentiment would release her from such gross companionship? Verily, no! Think you the wife with whom endurance has ceased to be a virtue, who, through much suffering, has lost all faith in the justice of both heaven and earth, takes the law in her own hand, severs the unholy bond, and turns her back forever upon him whom she once called husband, consents to the law that in such an hour tears her child from her—all that she has left on earth to love and cherish? The drunkards' wives speak through us, and they number 50,000. Think you that the woman who has worked hard all her days in helping her husband to accumulate a large property, consents to the law that places this wholly at his disposal? Would not the mother whose only child is bound out for a term of years against her expressed wish, deprive the father of this absolute power if she could?

For all these, then, we speak. If to this long list you add the laboring women who are loudly demanding remuneration for their unending toil; those women who teach in our seminaries, academies, and public schools for a miserable pittance; the widows who are taxed without mercy; the unfortunate ones in our work-houses, poor-houses, and prisons; who are they that we do not now represent? But a small class of the fashionable butterflies, who, through the short summer days, seek the sunshine and the flowers; but the cool breezes of autumn and the hoary frosts of winter will soon chase all these away; then they, too, will need and seek protection, and through other lips demand in their turn justice and equity at your hands.

NOTE ON THE BIRTH AND REBIRTH OF MODERN FEMINISM

The women's movement resurfaced in the 1960s in response to a variety of social, economic, and political trends. One was demographic; the increase in women's life expectancy and control over reproduction, and the rise in divorce rates meant that domesticity was a less stable basis for an entire life. At the turn of the twentieth century, women's average life expectancy was 48, and she could contemplate living only 10 to 15 years after her last child left home. By the 1960s, the average woman could contemplate living two-thirds of her adult life with no children under 18.[12] So, too, women's increasing education and employment experience, particularly during World War II, made them less content with full-time domesticity. Rising economic expectations also propelled more women into the paid labor force, and led to frustration with the discrimination they encountered there. Women's discontent was captured in Betty Friedan's widely read publication, The Feminine Mystique (1963). The book, which became an instant best-seller, reported the results of Friedan's interviews with affluent fellow graduates of Smith College, then suburban housewives like Friedan herself. Despite their material privilege, these women were deeply unhappy: "desperately in search of stimulation and challenge, some had sexual affairs, others spent their time shopping and accumulating consumer goods, and still others gulped tranquilizers, cooked gourmet meals, or scrutinized their children as though they were rare insects." Friedan labeled their disaffection "the problem that has no name."

So, too, as was true of the first wave of feminism, the contemporary women's rights movement drew inspiration and supporters from the civil rights struggle and other progressive social movements. Female activists who encountered gender discrimination in those movements began increasingly to turn their energy to the emerging struggle for "women's liberation," based on a fundamental equality between the sexes. Materials in this chapter represent many of the key legal outcomes of these efforts, while subsequent chapters reflect theories that developed once the basic civil rights framework for gender equality was in place.

---

12. Rhode, Justice and Gender, supra note 7, at 54.

B. FORMAL EQUALITY AND THE CONSTITUTIONAL RIGHT TO EQUAL PROTECTION

1. The Right to Equal, Individualized Treatment

Equality claims often arise in the context in which a person asks to be treated as an individual, and without regard to membership in a particular category. The state cannot avoid categories when it makes laws. For example, the state sets age limits concerning rights to vote, drink alcoholic beverages, and marry, even though maturity levels vary, because it would be too difficult to make an individual determination of maturity in every case. So, too, employers' hiring decisions may depend on applicants' educational levels, years of experience, or test scores, even though these are not perfect measures of job fitness.

The state is not allowed to rely on some categories, however, regardless of administrative convenience. Classifications based on race and national origin are subject to strict scrutiny, meaning they must be based on a compelling state interest that cannot be achieved through other, more tailored means. The Supreme Court has never held that strict scrutiny is required for sex-based classifications. Instead the Court has opted for the "intermediate standard of review" developed in the cases that follow.

Reed v. Reed
404 U.S. 71 (1971)

Mr. Chief Justice Burger delivered the opinion of the Court.

[This case challenges an Idaho statute that designates an order of priority for courts to designate the administrator of an estate of a person who dies intestate (without a will). Parents are one priority group, and for all priority groups, Idaho law provides that males are preferred to females. The case is brought by the mother of a child who died intestate, after the probate court issued an order naming the child's father as the administrator of the child's estate.]

In issuing its order, the probate court implicitly recognized the equality of entitlement of the two [parent] applicants; . . . the court ruled, however, that appellee, being a male, was to be preferred to the female appellant [under Idaho law]. In stating this conclusion, the probate judge gave no indication that he had attempted to determine the relative capabilities of the competing applicants to perform the functions incident to the administration of an estate. It seems clear the probate judge considered himself bound by statute to give preference to the male candidate over the female, each being otherwise "equally entitled." . . .

[handwritten margin notes: "Mother came forward when estate given to father"]

[handwritten note: "Judge bound by male prefer."]

[W]e have concluded that the arbitrary preference established in favor of males . . . cannot stand in the face of the Fourteenth Amendment's command that no State deny the equal protection of the laws to any person within its jurisdiction.

In applying that clause, this Court has consistently recognized that the Fourteenth Amendment does not deny to States the power to treat different classes of persons in different ways. . . . The Equal Protection Clause of that amendment does, however, deny to States the power to legislate that different treatment be accorded to persons placed by a statute into different classes on the basis of criteria wholly unrelated to the objective of that statute. A classification "must be reasonable, not arbitrary, and must rest upon some ground of difference having a fair and substantial relation to the object of the legislation, so that all persons similarly circumstanced shall be treated alike. . . ." . . .

In upholding the [Idaho statute], the Idaho Supreme Court concluded that its objective was to eliminate one area of controversy when two or more persons, equally entitled under [Idaho law], seek letters of administration and thereby present the probate court "with the issue of which one should be named." The court also concluded that where such persons are not of the same sex, the elimination of females from consideration "is neither an illogical nor arbitrary method devised by the legislature to resolve an issue that would otherwise require a hearing as to the relative merits . . . of the two or more petitioning relatives. . . ." . . .

Clearly the objective of reducing the workload on probate courts by eliminating one class of contests is not without some legitimacy. The crucial question, however, is whether [Idaho law] advances that objective in a manner consistent with the command of the Equal Protection Clause. We hold that it does not. To give a mandatory preference to members of either sex over members of the other, merely to accomplish the elimination of hearings on the merits, is to make the very kind of arbitrary legislative choice forbidden by the Equal Protection Clause of the Fourteenth Amendment; and whatever may be said as to the positive values of avoiding intrafamily controversy, the choice in this context may not lawfully be mandated solely on the basis of sex. . . .

Reversed and remanded.

Frontiero v. Richardson

411 U.S. 677 (1973)

Mr. Justice BRENNAN announced the judgment of the Court in an opinion in which Mr. Justice DOUGLAS, Mr. Justice WHITE, and Mr. Justice MARSHALL join.

The question before us concerns the right of a female member of the uniformed services to claim her spouse as a "dependent" for the purposes of obtaining increased quarters allowances and medical and dental benefits under [federal law] on an equal footing with male members. Under the [federal statutes at issue], a serviceman may claim his wife as a "dependent" without regard to whether she is in fact dependent upon him for any part of her support. . . . A servicewoman, on the other hand, may not claim her husband as a "dependent" under these programs unless he is in fact dependent upon her for over one-half of his support. . . . [T]he question for decision is whether this difference in treatment constitutes an unconstitutional discrimination against servicewomen in violation of the Due Process Clause of the Fifth Amendment.

In an effort to attract career personnel through reenlistment, Congress established . . . a scheme for the provision of fringe benefits to members of the uniformed services on a competitive basis with business and industry. [Under this scheme] a member of the uniformed services with dependents is entitled to an increased "basic allowance for quarters" and . . . a member's dependents are provided comprehensive medical and dental care.

Appellant Sharron Frontiero, a lieutenant in the United States Air Force, sought increased quarters allowances, and housing and medical benefits for her husband, appellant Joseph Frontiero, on the ground that he was her "dependent." Although such benefits would automatically have been granted with respect to the wife of a male member of the uniformed services, appellant's application was denied because she failed to demonstrate that her husband was dependent on her for more than one-half of his support. [Joseph Frontiero, a student who received veterans' benefits, was not dependent upon Sharron Frontiero.] Appellants then commenced this suit, contending that, by making this distinction, the statutes unreasonably discriminate on the basis of sex in violation of the Due Process Clause of the Fifth Amendment. In essence, appellants asserted that the discriminatory impact of the statutes is twofold: first, as a procedural matter, a female member is required to demonstrate her spouse's dependency, while no such burden is imposed upon male members; and, second, as a substantive matter, a male member who does not provide more than one-half of his wife's support receives benefits, while a similarly situated female member is denied such benefits. Appellants therefore sought a permanent injunction against the continued enforcement of these statutes and an order directing the appellees to provide Lieutenant Frontiero with the same housing and medical benefits that a similarly situated male member would receive.

Although the legislative history of these statutes sheds virtually no light on the purposes underlying the differential treatment accorded male and female members, a majority of the three-judge District Court [which voted to uphold the statutes] surmised that Congress might reasonably have concluded that, since the husband in our society is generally the "breadwinner" in the family — and the wife typically the "dependent" partner — "it would be more economical to require married female members claiming husbands to prove actual dependency than to extend the presumption of dependency to such members." Indeed, given the fact that approximately 99% of all members of the uniformed services are male, the District Court speculated that such differential treatment might conceivably lead to a "considerable saving of administrative expense and manpower."

At the outset, appellants contend that classifications based upon sex, like classifications based upon race, alienage, and national origin, are inherently suspect and must therefore be subjected to close judicial scrutiny. We agree and, indeed, find at least implicit support for such an approach in our unanimous decision only last Term in Reed v. Reed. . . .

[The Court reviews the attitude of "romantic paternalism" discussed in *Reed*.] As a result of notions such as these, our statute books gradually became laden with gross, stereotyped distinctions between the sexes and, indeed, throughout much of the 19th century the position of women in our society was, in many respects, comparable to that of blacks under the pre-Civil War slaves codes. Neither slaves nor women could hold office, serve on juries, or bring suit in their own names, and married women traditionally were denied the legal capacity to hold or convey property or to serve as legal guardians of their own children. . . . And although blacks were guaranteed the right to vote in 1870, women were denied even that right . . . until adoption of the Nineteenth Amendment half a century later.

It is true, of course, that the position of women in America has improved markedly in recent decades. Nevertheless, it can hardly be doubted that, in part because of the high visibility of the sex characteristic, women still face pervasive, although at times more subtle, discrimination in our educational institutions, in the job market and, perhaps most conspicuously, in the political arena. . . .

Moreover, since sex, like race and national origin, is an immutable characteristic determined solely by the accident of birth, the imposition of special disabilities upon the members of a particular sex because of their sex would seem to violate "the basic concept of our system that legal burdens should bear some relationship to individual responsibility." . . . And what differentiates sex from such non-suspect statuses as intelligence or physical disability, and aligns it with the recognized suspect criteria, is that the sex characteristic frequently bears no relation to ability to perform or contribute to society. As a result, statutory distinctions between the sexes often have the effect of invidiously relegating the entire class of females to inferior legal status without regard to the actual capabilities of its individual members.

We might also note that, over the past decade, Congress has itself manifested an increasing sensitivity to sex-based classifications. In [Title VII] of the Civil Rights Act of 1964, for example, Congress expressly declared that no employer, labor union, or other organization subject to the provisions of the Act shall discriminate against any individual on the basis of "race, color, religion, sex, or national origin." Similarly, the Equal Pay Act of 1963 provides that no employer covered by the Act "shall discriminate . . . between employees on the basis of sex." And §1 of the Equal Rights Amendment, passed by Congress on March 22, 1972, and submitted to the legislatures of the States for ratification, declares that "(e)quality of rights under the law shall not be denied or abridged by the United States or by any State on account of sex." Thus, Congress itself has concluded that classifications based upon sex are inherently invidious, and this conclusion of a coequal branch of Government is not without significance to the question presently under consideration. . . .

With these considerations in mind, we can only conclude that classifications based upon sex, like classifications based upon race, alienage, or national origin, are inherently suspect, and must therefore be subjected to strict judicial scrutiny. Applying the analysis mandated by that stricter standard of review, it is clear that the statutory scheme now before us is constitutionally invalid.

The sole basis of the classification established in the challenged statutes is the sex of the individuals involved. . . .

[T]he Government concedes that the differential treatment accorded men and women under these statutes serves no purpose other than mere "administrative convenience." In essence, the Government maintains that, as an empirical matter, wives in our society frequently are dependent upon their husbands, while husbands rarely are dependent upon their wives. Thus, the Government argues that Congress might reasonably have concluded that it would be both cheaper and easier simply conclusively to presume that wives of male members are financially dependent upon their husbands, while burdening female members with the task of establishing dependency in fact.[22]

The Government offers no concrete evidence, however, tending to support its view that such differential treatment in fact saves the Government any money. In order to satisfy the demands of strict judicial scrutiny, the Government must demonstrate, for example, that it is actually cheaper to grant increased benefits with respect to all male members, than it is to determine which male members are in fact entitled to such benefits and to grant increased benefits only to those members whose wives actually meet the dependency requirement. Here, however, there is substantial evidence that, if put to the test, many of the wives of male members would fail to qualify for benefits. And in light of the fact that the dependency determination with respect to the husbands of female members is presently made solely on the basis of affidavits rather than through the more costly hearing process, the Government's explanation of the statutory scheme is, to say the least, questionable.

In any case, our prior decisions make clear that, although efficacious administration of governmental programs is not without some importance,

---

22. It should be noted that these statutes are not in any sense designed to rectify the effects of past discrimination against women. . . . On the contrary, these statutes seize upon a group—women—who have historically suffered discrimination in employment, and rely on the effects of this past discrimination as a justification for heaping on additional economic disadvantages.

"the Constitution recognizes higher values than speed and efficiency. . . ." And when we enter the realm of "strict judicial scrutiny," there can be no doubt that "administrative convenience" is not a shibboleth, the mere recitation of which dictates constitutionality. . . . We therefore conclude that, by according differential treatment to male and female members of the uniformed services for the sole purpose of achieving administrative convenience, the challenged statutes violate the Due Process Clause of the Fifth Amendment insofar as they require a female member to prove the dependency of her husband. Reversed.

Mr. Justice POWELL, with whom THE CHIEF JUSTICE and Mr. Justice BLACKMUN join, concurring in the judgment. . . .

It is unnecessary for the Court in this case to characterize sex as a suspect classification, with all of the far-reaching implications of such a holding. Reed v. Reed, [1971], which abundantly supports our decision today, did not add sex to the narrowly limited group of classifications which are inherently suspect. . . . In my view, we can and should decide this case on the authority of *Reed* and reserve for the future any expansion of its rationale.

There is another, and I find compelling, reason for deferring a general categorizing of sex classifications as invoking the strictest test of judicial scrutiny. The Equal Rights Amendment, which if adopted will resolve the substance of this precise question, has been approved by the Congress and submitted for ratification by the States. If this Amendment is duly adopted, it will represent the will of the people accomplished in the manner prescribed by the Constitution. . . . It seems to me that this reaching out to pre-empt by judicial action a major political decision which is currently in process of resolution does not reflect appropriate respect for duly prescribed legislative processes. . . .

≡≡≡ *Orr v. Orr*
440 U.S. 268 (1979)

Mr. Justice BRENNAN delivered the opinion of the Court.

The question presented is the constitutionality of Alabama alimony statutes which provide that husbands, but not wives, may be required to pay alimony upon divorce.

The fact that the classification expressly discriminates against men rather than women does not protect it from scrutiny. . . . "To withstand scrutiny" under the Equal Protection Clause, "classifications by gender must serve important governmental objectives and must be substantially related to achievement of those objectives." . . .

Appellant [husband, who was ordered to pay alimony and challenges the Alabama alimony statutes as a violation of the equal protection clause in a contempt action brought against him for being in arrears on his alimony obligations] views the Alabama alimony statutes as effectively announcing the

State's preference for an allocation of family responsibilities under which the wife plays a dependent role, and as seeking for their objective the reinforcement of that model among the State's citizens. . . .

The opinion of the Alabama Court of Civil Appeals suggests other purposes that the statute may serve. Its opinion states that the Alabama statutes were "designed" for "the wife of a broken marriage who needs financial assistance." This may be read as asserting either of two legislative objectives. One is a legislative purpose to provide help for needy spouses, using sex as a proxy for need. The other is a goal of compensating women for past discrimination during marriage, which assertedly has left them unprepared to fend for themselves in the working world following divorce. We concede, of course, that assisting needy spouses is a legitimate and important governmental objective. We have also recognized "[r]eduction of the disparity in economic condition between men and women caused by the long history of discrimination against women . . . as . . . an important governmental objective." It only remains, therefore, to determine whether the classification at issue here is "substantially related to achievement of those objectives."

Ordinarily, we would begin the analysis of the "needy spouse" objective by considering whether sex is a sufficiently "accurate proxy" . . . for dependency to establish that the gender classification rests "upon some ground of difference having a fair and substantial relation to the object of the legislation." [Reed v. Reed (1971).] . . . Similarly, we would initially approach the "compensation" rationale by asking whether women had in fact been significantly discriminated against in the sphere to which the statute applied a sex-based classification, leaving the sexes "not similarly situated with respect to opportunities" in that sphere. . . .

But in this case, even if sex were a reliable proxy for need, and even if the institution of marriage did discriminate against women, these factors still would "not adequately justify the salient features of" Alabama's statutory scheme. . . . Under the statute, individualized hearings at which the parties' relative financial circumstances are considered already occur. . . . There is no reason, therefore, to use sex as a proxy for need. Needy males could be helped along with needy females with little if any additional burden on the State. In such circumstances, not even an administrative-convenience rationale exists to justify operating by generalization or proxy. Similarly, since individualized hearings can determine which women were in fact discriminated against vis-à-vis their husbands, as well as which family units defied the stereotype and left the husband dependent on the wife, Alabama's alleged compensatory purpose may be effectuated without placing burdens solely on husbands. Progress toward fulfilling such a purpose would not be hampered, and it would cost the State nothing more, if it were to treat men and women equally by making alimony burdens independent of sex. "Thus, the gender-based distinction is gratuitous; without it, the statutory scheme would only provide benefits to those men who are in fact similarly situated to the women the statute aids," . . . and the effort to help those women would not in any way be compromised.

Moreover, use of a gender classification actually produces perverse results in this case. As compared to a gender-neutral law placing alimony obligations on the spouse able to pay, the present Alabama statutes give an advantage only to the financially secure wife whose husband is in need. Although such a wife might have to pay alimony under a gender-neutral statute, the present statutes exempt her from that obligation. Thus, "[t]he [wives] who benefit from the disparate treatment are those who were . . . nondependent on their husbands" . . . . They are precisely those who are not "needy spouses" and who are "least likely to have been victims of . . . discrimination," . . . by the institution of marriage. A additional benefits only for those it has no reason to prefer cannot survive equal protection scrutiny.

Legislative classifications which distribute benefits and burdens on the basis of gender carry the inherent risk of reinforcing the stereotypes about the "proper place" of women and their need for special protection. . . . Thus, even statutes purportedly designed to compensate for and ameliorate the effects of past discrimination must be carefully tailored. Where, as here, the State's compensatory and ameliorative purposes are as well served by a gender-neutral classification as one that gender classifies and therefore carries with it the baggage of sexual stereotypes, the State cannot be permitted to classify on the basis of sex. And this is doubly so where the choice made by the State appears to redound—if only indirectly—to the benefit of those without need for special solicitude. Reversed and remanded.

Putting Theory Into Practice

1-3. The following exchange is reported as part of a voir dire examination conducted by a judge in a criminal case in a municipal court in California:

The Court: Miss Bobb, what is your occupation?
Miss Bobb: I'm an attorney.
The Court: And in your practice do you practice criminal law as well as civil law?
Miss Bobb: No, I practice entirely bankruptcy law.
The Court: All right. Is there a Mr. Bobb?
Miss Bobb: I have some difficulty with that question because I've noticed only the women have been asked to answer that.
The Court: Yes, I know. Do you have a Mr. Bobb—is there a Mr. Bobb?
Miss Bobb: Are you going to [poll] the men to see if they care to disclose—
The Court: No, I'm just going to ask you if you have a husband or not. Do you have a husband?
Miss Bobb: I don't care to answer it then. What's relative to women is relative to men.

The Court: Yes, I know. What is your husband's occupation?

Miss Bobb: I don't care to answer that.

The Court: I instruct you to answer.

Miss Bobb: I don't think I should.

The Court: I've got—you understand that you'll be in contempt of Court—jury—you're an attorney, you understand these rules, don't you?

Miss Bobb: No, I do not understand why only the women are asked certain questions and the men aren't asked the same questions.

The Court: The question to you, Mrs. Bobb—you're an attorney at law, you understand the rules and regulations of—of—of being an attorney. And the question to you now simply is: What is your husband's occupation?

Miss Bobb: I refuse to answer.

The Court: You're held in contempt of Court, Mrs. Bobb.[13]

Is Mrs. Bobb's resistance reasonable? To what extent will formal equality principles provide relief to Mrs. Bobb?

Upon appeal, the Court of Appeals of California decided that Carolyn Bobb was improperly held in contempt of court. The reviewing court found no compelling state interest for posing some questions to female jurors, but not to male jurors, and thereby held that requiring Mrs. Bobb to answer the question denied her equal protection of the law. Is this ruling good for women? Does it prevent the court from learning the information, or is there another way to get an answer that is consistent with formal equality principles?

2. The Right to Equal Group Treatment

In *Reed* and *Orr*, the state had in place a system of individualized fact-finding; the only question was whether part of that fact-finding could be abbreviated by using sex as a proxy—in *Reed*, a proxy for ability and interest in administering an estate, and in *Orr*, a proxy for financial dependency. In both of these contexts, eliminating sex as a proxy (as the Supreme Court did) does not impose a great administrative burden and is likely to produce more accurate results in terms of the goals of the statutes.

In many contexts, however, the state needs to draw lines to decide questions that do not lend themselves to individualized fact-finding. Common examples include the right to vote, marry, drive, serve in the military, and attend public schools. This section examines two other examples.

13. Bobb v. Municipal Court, 192 Cal. Rptr. 270, 270-71 (Cal. App. 1983).

Stanton v. Stanton
421 U.S. 7 (1975)

[handwritten: → Diff. age of majority for men + women]

Mr. Justice BLACKMUN delivered the opinion of the Court.

This case presents the issue whether a state statute specifying for males a greater age of majority than it specifies for females denies, in the context of a parent's obligation for support payments for his children, the equal protection of the laws . . . .

[The case is an appeal arising from divorce proceedings, following a judgment requiring the father to pay child support to the mother for a daughter and a son. The father discontinued support payments for the daughter when she turned 18, pursuant to Utah law, which set the age of majority for girls at 18 and the age of majority for boys at 21. The trial court denied the mother's motion for further support, which the Supreme Court of Utah affirmed.]

We find it unnecessary in this case to decide whether a classification based on sex is inherently suspect. . . . [Reed v. Reed (1971)] we feel, is controlling here. . . . "A classification 'must be reasonable, not arbitrary, and must rest upon some ground of difference having a fair and substantial relation to the object of the legislation, so that all persons similarly circumstanced shall be treated alike.'" . . . The test here, then, is whether the difference in sex between children warrants the distinction in the appellee's obligation to support that is drawn by the Utah statute. We conclude that it does not. It may be true, as the Utah court observed and as is argued here, that it is the man's primary responsibility to provide a home and that it is salutary for him to have education and training before he assumes that responsibility; that girls tend to mature earlier than boys; and that females tend to marry earlier than males. The last mentioned factor, however, under the Utah statute loses whatever weight it otherwise might have, for the statute states that "all minors obtain their majority by marriage"; thus minority, and all that goes with it, is abruptly lost by marriage of a person of either sex at whatever tender age the marriage occurs.

[handwritten margin: Diff. in sex does not constitute diff. compensation (child support)]

Notwithstanding the "old notions" to which the Utah court referred, we perceive nothing rational in the distinction drawn by [the statute] which, when related to the divorce decree, results in the appellee's liability for support for Sherri only to age 18 but for Rick to age 21. This imposes "criteria wholly unrelated to the objective of that statute." A child, male or female, is still a child. No longer is the female destined solely for the home and the rearing of the family, and only the male for the marketplace and the world of ideas. . . . Women's activities and responsibilities are increasing and expanding. Coeducation is a fact, not a rarity. The presence of women in business, in the professions, in government and, indeed, in all walks of life where education is a desirable, if not always a necessary, antecedent is apparent and a proper subject of judicial notice. If a specified age of minority is required for the boy in

[handwritten margin: Society is changing]

order to assure him parental support while he attains his education and training, so, too, is it for the girl. To distinguish between the two on educational grounds is to be self-serving: if the female is not to be supported so long as the male, she hardly can be expected to attend school as long as he does, and bringing her education to an end earlier coincides with the role-typing society has long imposed. And if any weight remains in this day to the claim of earlier maturity of the female, with a concomitant inference of absence of need for support beyond 18, we fail to perceive its unquestioned truth or its significance, particularly when marriage, as the statute provides, terminates minority for a person of either sex. . . .

[Whether the common law age of 21 applies to both children or the remedy for the unconstitutional inequality is to treat males as adults at age 18] is an issue of state law to be resolved by the Utah courts on remand. . . .

≡≡≡ *Craig v. Boren*
429 U.S. 190 (1976)

Mr. Justice BRENNAN delivered the opinion of the Court, with whom Mr. Justice POWELL, Mr. Justice STEVENS, Mr. Justice BLACKMUN (in part), and Mr. Justice STEWART concurred.

The interaction of two sections of an Oklahoma statute . . . prohibits the sale of "nonintoxicating" 3.2% beer to males under the age of 21 and to females under the age of 18. The question to be decided is whether such a gender-based differential constitutes a denial to males 18-20 years of age of the equal protection of the laws in violation of the Fourteenth Amendment.

This action was brought in the District Court for the Western District of Oklahoma on December 20, 1972, by appellant Craig, a male then between 18 and 21 years of age, and by appellant Whitener, a licensed vendor of 3.2% beer. The complaint [alleged] that [the law] constituted invidious discrimination against males 18-20 years of age. A three-judge court . . . sustained the constitutionality of the statutory differential and dismissed the action. . . . We reverse. . . .

To withstand constitutional challenge . . . classifications by gender must serve important governmental objectives and must be substantially related to achievement of those objectives. . . . We accept for purposes of discussion the District Court's identification of the objective underlying [the statutes in question] as the enhancement of traffic safety. Clearly, the protection of public health and safety represents an important function of state and local governments. However, appellees' statistics in our view cannot support the conclusion that the gender-based distinction closely serves to achieve that objective and therefore the distinction cannot under [Reed v. Reed (1971)] withstand equal protection challenge.

The appellees introduced a variety of statistical surveys. First, an analysis of arrest statistics for 1973 demonstrated that 18-20-year-old male arrests for "driving under the influence" and "drunkenness" substantially exceeded female arrests for that same age period. Similarly, youths aged 17-21 were found to be overrepresented among those killed or injured in traffic accidents, with males again numerically exceeding females in this regard. Third, a random roadside survey in Oklahoma City revealed that young males were more inclined to drive and drink beer than were their female counterparts. Fourth, Federal Bureau of Investigation nationwide statistics exhibited a notable increase in arrests for "driving under the influence." Finally, statistical evidence gathered in other jurisdictions, particularly Minnesota and Michigan, was offered to corroborate Oklahoma's experience by indicating the pervasiveness of youthful participation in motor vehicle accidents following the imbibing of alcohol. Conceding that "the case is not free from doubt" . . . , the District Court nonetheless concluded that this statistical showing substantiated "a rational basis for the legislative judgment underlying the challenged classification." . . .

Even were this statistical evidence accepted as accurate, it nevertheless offers only a weak answer to the equal protection question presented here. The most focused and relevant of the statistical surveys, arrests of 18-20-year-olds for alcohol-related driving offenses, exemplifies the ultimate unpersuasiveness of this evidentiary record. Viewed in terms of the correlation between sex and the actual activity that Oklahoma seeks to regulate—driving while under the influence of alcohol—the statistics broadly establish that .18% of females and 2% of males in that age group were arrested for that offense. While such a disparity is not trivial in a statistical sense, it hardly can form the basis for employment of a gender line as a classifying device. Certainly if maleness is to serve as a proxy for drinking and driving, a correlation of 2% must be considered an unduly tenuous "fit." Indeed, prior cases have consistently rejected the use of sex as a decisionmaking factor even though the statutes in question certainly rested on far more predictive empirical relationships than this.

Moreover, the statistics exhibit a variety of other shortcomings that seriously impugn their value to equal protection analysis. Setting aside the obvious methodological problems,[14] the surveys do not adequately justify the salient features of Oklahoma's gender-based traffic-safety law. None purports

---

14. The very social stereotypes that find reflection in age-differential laws, see *Stanton*, are likely substantially to distort the accuracy of these comparative statistics. Hence, "reckless" young men who drink and drive are transformed into arrest statistics, whereas their female counterparts are chivalrously escorted home. . . . Moreover, the Oklahoma surveys, gathered under a regime where the age-differential law in question has been in effect, are lacking in controls necessary for appraisal of the actual effectiveness of the male 3.2% beer prohibition. In this regard, the disproportionately high arrest statistics for young males—and, indeed, the growing alcohol-related arrest figures for all ages and sexes—simply may be taken to document the relative futility of controlling driving behavior by the 3.2% beer statute and like legislation, although we obviously have no means of estimating how many individuals, if any, actually were prevented from drinking by these laws.

ABV

Low ABV

to measure the use and dangerousness of 3.2% beer as opposed to alcohol generally, a detail that is of particular importance since, in light of its low alcohol level, Oklahoma apparently considers the 3.2% beverage to be "nonintoxicating." . . . Moreover, many of the studies, while graphically documenting the unfortunate increase in driving while under the influence of alcohol, make no effort to relate their findings to age-sex differentials as involved here. Indeed, the only survey that explicitly centered its attention upon young drivers and their use of beer — albeit apparently not of the diluted 3.2% variety — reached results that hardly can be viewed as impressive in justifying either a gender or age classification.[16]

. . . [T]he showing offered by the appellees does not satisfy us that sex represents a legitimate, accurate proxy for the regulation of drinking and driving. In fact, when it is further recognized that Oklahoma's statute prohibits only the selling of 3.2% beer to young males and not their drinking the beverage once acquired (even after purchase by their 18-20-year-old female companions), the relationship between gender and traffic safety becomes far too tenuous to satisfy *Reed*'s requirement that the gender-based difference be substantially related to achievement of the statutory objective.

We hold, therefore, that under *Reed*, Oklahoma's 3.2% beer statute invidiously discriminates against males 18-20 years of age. . . .

Mr. Justice STEVENS, concurring.

There is only one Equal Protection Clause. It requires every State to govern impartially. It does not direct the courts to apply one standard of review in some cases and a different standard in other cases. Whatever criticism may be leveled at a judicial opinion implying that there are at least three such standards applies with the same force to a double standard. . . .

In this case, the classification is not as obnoxious as some the Court has condemned, nor as inoffensive as some the Court has accepted. It is objectionable because it is based on an accident of birth, because it is a mere remnant of

---

16. The random roadside survey of drivers conducted in Oklahoma City during August 1972 found that 78% of drivers under 20 were male. Turning to an evaluation of their drinking habits and factoring out nondrinkers, 84% of the males versus 77% of the females expressed a preference for beer. Further 16.5% of the men and 11.4% of the women had consumed some alcoholic beverage within two hours of the interview. Finally, a blood alcohol concentration greater than .01% was discovered in 14.6% of the males compared to 11.5% of the females. "The 1973 figures, although they contain some variations, reflect essentially the same pattern." . . . Plainly these statistical disparities between the sexes are not substantial. Moreover, when the 18-20 age boundaries are lifted and all drivers analyzed, the 1972 roadside survey indicates that male drinking rose slightly whereas female exposure to alcohol remained relatively constant. Again, in 1973, the survey established that "compared to all drivers interviewed, . . . the under-20 age group generally showed a lower involvement with alcohol in terms of having drunk within the past two hours or having a significant BAC (blood alcohol content)." [Id.] In sum, this survey provides little support for a gender line among teenagers and actually runs counter to the imposition of drinking restrictions based upon age.

the now almost universally rejected tradition of discriminating against males in this age bracket, and because, to the extent it reflects any physical difference between males and females, it is actually perverse [because males are on average heavier than females and thus have a greater capacity to consume alcohol without impairing their ability to drive]. The question then is whether the traffic safety justification put forward by the State is sufficient to make an otherwise offensive classification acceptable.

The classification is not totally irrational. For the evidence does indicate that there are more males than females in this age bracket who drive and also more who drink. Nevertheless, there are several reasons why I regard the justification as unacceptable. It is difficult to believe that the statute was actually intended to cope with the problem of traffic safety, since it has only a minimal effect on access to a not very intoxicating beverage and does not prohibit its consumption. Moreover, the empirical data submitted by the State accentuate the unfairness of treating all 18-20-year-old males as inferior to their female counterparts. The legislation imposes a restraint on 100% of the males in the class allegedly because about 2% of them have probably violated one or more laws relating to the consumption of alcoholic beverages. It is unlikely that this law will have a significant deterrent effect either on that 2% or on the law-abiding 98%. But even assuming some such slight benefit, it does not seem to me that an insult to all of the young men of the State can be justified by visiting the sins of the 2% on the 98%. . . .

Mr. Justice REHNQUIST, dissenting. . . .

I think the Oklahoma statute challenged here need pass only the "rational basis" equal protection analysis . . . and I believe that it is constitutional under that analysis.

Most obviously unavailable to support any kind of special scrutiny in this case, is a history or pattern of past discrimination, such as was relied on by the plurality in [Frontiero v. Richardson (1973)] to support its invocation of strict scrutiny. There is no suggestion in the Court's opinion that males in this age group are in any way peculiarly disadvantaged, subject to systematic discriminatory treatment, or otherwise in need of special solicitude from the courts.

The Court does not discuss the nature of the right involved, and there is no reason to believe that it sees the purchase of 3.2% beer as implicating any important interest, let alone one that is "fundamental" in the constitutional sense of invoking strict scrutiny. . . .

It is true that a number of our opinions contain broadly phrased dicta implying that the same test should be applied to all classifications based on sex, whether affecting females or males. . . . However, before today, no decision of this Court has applied an elevated level of scrutiny to invalidate a statutory discrimination harmful to males, except where the statute impaired an important personal interest protected by the Constitution. There being no such interest here, and there being no plausible argument that this is a discrimination against females,[2] the Court's reliance on our previous sex-discrimination cases is ill-founded. It treats gender classification as a talisman which—without regard to the rights involved or the persons affected—calls into effect a heavier burden of judicial review.

The Court's conclusion that a law which treats males less favorably than females "must serve important governmental objectives and must be substantially related to achievement of those objectives" apparently comes out of thin air. The Equal Protection Clause contains no such language, and none of our previous cases adopt that standard. I would think we have had enough difficulty with the two standards of review which our cases have recognized—the norm of "rational basis," and the "compelling state interest" required where a "suspect classification" is involved—so as to counsel weightily against the insertion of still another "standard" between those two. How is this Court to divine what objectives are important? How is it to determine whether a particular law is "substantially" related to the achievement of such objective, rather than related in some other way to its achievement? Both of the phrases used are so diaphanous and elastic as to invite subjective judicial preferences or prejudices relating to particular types of legislation, masquerading as judgments whether such legislation is directed at "important" objectives or, whether the relationship to those objectives is "substantial" enough. I would have thought that if this Court were to leave anything to decision by the popularly elected branches of the Government, where no constitutional claim other than that of equal protection is invoked, it would be the decision as to what governmental objectives to be achieved by law are "important," and which are not. As for the second part of the Court's new test, the Judicial Branch is probably in no worse position than the Legislative or Executive Branches to determine if there is any rational relationship between a classification and the purpose which it might be thought to serve. But the introduction of the adverb "substantially" requires courts to make subjective judgments as to operational effects, for which neither their expertise nor their access to data fits them. And even if we manage to avoid both confusion and the mirroring of our own preferences in the development of this new doctrine, the thousands of judges in other courts who must interpret the Equal Protection Clause may not be so fortunate. . . .

2. I am not unaware of the argument from time to time advanced, that all discriminations between the sexes ultimately redound to the detriment of females, because they tend to reinforce "old notions" restricting the roles and opportunities of women. As a general proposition applying equally to all sex categorizations, I believe that this argument was implicitly found to carry little weight in our decisions upholding gender-based differences. . . . Seeing no assertion that it has special applicability to the situation at hand, I believe it can be dismissed as an insubstantial consideration.

Notes

1. "Simple Little Case"?   At a distance of three decades, the cases in this section do not seem difficult, but at the time they were decided, most members of the all-male Court did not perceive them as straightforward. Justice Blackmun's papers offer a window into how one of those who voted ultimately to overturn the gender preference in *Reed* viewed the case and the arguments underlying it. The brief in *Reed*, on which now-Justice Ruth Bader Ginsburg had collaborated as an advocate, argued that the probate code compounded the "subordination of women." It claimed that "American women have been stigmatized historically as an inferior class and are today subject to pervasive discrimination. . . . A person born female continues to be branded inferior for this congenital and unalterable condition of birth." Justice Blackmun found the brief "mildly offensive and arrogant" and out of proportion in what he considered "a very simple little case." It was "much ado about nothing" since the estate in dispute amounted to less than $1,000 — clothes, a clarinet, and fewer than $500 in savings of an adolescent who had committed suicide. However, Justice Blackmun also recognized that it was meant as a "test case," and he was prepared to join the majority because "there can be no question that women have been held down in the past in almost every area." He advised the Court to write a "brief and simple opinion" and hoped that "we do not get into a long and emotional discussion about women's rights."[14]

Was the Court's decision to write a "brief and simple" opinion in *Reed* the right choice? How much guidance does it provide about which kinds of classifications do not pass constitutional scrutiny? Does Justice Blackmun's reference to "emotional" arguments about women's rights reflect the very same stereotypes that underpinned the classifications in *Reed*, *Orr*, and the cases that followed?

As in *Reed*, an irony of Craig v. Boren is that one of the nation's most important sex discrimination cases arose in one of the least important factual contexts. Ruth Bader Ginsburg, then director of the Women's Rights Project of the American Civil Liberties Union, filed an amicus curiae brief in the case and noted later: "It was a petty law, mercifully terminated. One might wish the Court had chosen a less frothy case" for announcing a crucial principle.[15]

2. The Role of Stereotyping in Formal Equality Analysis.   The articulated standard in these cases, at least from Craig v. Boren forward, is that the challenged classification must bear a substantial relationship to important governmental objectives. Note the frequency with which the Supreme

---

14. For the full story, see Linda Greenhouse, Becoming Justice Blackmun: Harry Blackmun's Supreme Court Journey 209-11 (2005).

15. Ruth Bader Ginsburg, Remarks for the Celebration of 75 Years of Women's Enrollment at Columbia Law School, 102 Colum. L. Rev. 1441, 1445 (2002).

Court's analysis focuses on the fact of stereotyping by the legislature. What is the problem with stereotyping? Is it that stereotypes are "archaic" and "overbroad," and therefore too often inaccurate? Or is the problem that individuals are harmed by stereotypical assumptions even when they are at least partially true about women, or men, as a group? Or is the concern that stereotypes, even when they are accurate, perpetuate the inequalities that they reflect? What stereotypes underlie the classification in *Craig*?

3. Sexual Orientation Discrimination as a Form of Gender Discrimination. Gay rights advocates have frequently attempted to establish that homosexuals as a class have the characteristics required for special constitutional protection under the equal protection clause. The Supreme Court has never recognized such protection despite several federal court rulings strongly protecting gay and lesbian individuals from various forms of discrimination.[16]

Do gays and lesbians, as a group, meet the following criteria that are often used to identify a protected class: (1) a history of discrimination; (2) exhibition of obvious, immutable, or distinguishing characteristics that define them as members of a discrete group; and (3) political powerlessness, or the burdening of a fundamental right?

Although the Court has never formally deemed sexual orientation a suspect or quasi-suspect class, it has used the equal protection clause to invalidate laws disadvantaging gays and lesbians. In Romer v. Evans, the Court invalidated a Colorado constitutional amendment (Proposition 2) repealing and prohibiting all state and local anti-discrimination policies with respect to homosexuals.[17] In the majority's view, this amendment failed to meet the rational relationship standard under the equal protection clause because it arbitrarily prevented a group from protecting its interests through the normal political process. This discrimination, the Court stated, could not be justified by a "bare desire to harm a politically unpopular group."[18] The Court then drew on *Romer* when invalidating the federal Defense of Marriage Act (explored in Chapter 2, Section D(1)), which prohibited a valid same-sex marriage from being given effect for any federal-law purpose. Congress' departure from a longstanding history of deference to state marriage rules was a "discrimination of unusual character" under *Romer* and thus invalid under the Equal Protection Clause. But in neither of these cases did the Court expressly consider or hold that sexual orientation classifications merit heightened scrutiny.

---

16. See Note 7, below (discrimination in the military); Section C of this chapter (employment); Section D of this chapter (public accommodations); Chapter 2, Section D(1) (same-sex marriage); Chapter 2, Section D(3) (child custody); Chapter 2, Section C(2) (Title IX); Chapter 3, Section B (sexual harassment).

17. 517 U.S. 620 (1996).

18. Dep't of Agric. v. Moreno, 413 U.S. 528, 534 (1973).

3rd tenet questionable

Gay and lesbian advocates have argued in many cases and in many contexts that heightened scrutiny is appropriate. But it is not clear which way the history of discrimination against gays and lesbians cuts, nor whether gays and lesbians are politically powerless. The issue of "immutability" also poses a dilemma for gays and lesbians. On the one hand, part of the harm of discrimination is the pressure it creates to suppress, and thereby alter, same-sex orientation. On the other hand, if sexual orientation is alterable, gays and lesbians have the ability to avoid discrimination. The costs of such alteration might be clearer to heterosexuals if they imagined the tables turned:

> Would heterosexuals living in a city that passed an ordinance banning those who engaged in or desired to engage in sex with persons of the *opposite* sex find it easy not only to abstain from heterosexual activity but also to shift the object of their sexual desires to persons of the same sex?[19]

Should the immutability requirement be redefined? Judge Norris argued that "the Court has never meant strict immutability in the sense that members of the class must be physically unable to change or mask the trait defining their class. People can have operations to change their sex. . . . Reading the case law in a more capacious manner, 'immutability' may describe those traits that are so central to a person's identity that it would be abhorrent for government to penalize a person for refusing to change them, regardless of how easy that change might be physically."[20] Janet Halley has argued that a focus on immutability is inappropriate because it misrepresents the complex and changing way that sexual orientation evolves and misperceives the harm of discrimination. Rather, she explains, "[such] discrimination encourages people to manipulate the identity they attach to themselves, both in the secrecy of their own minds and on the public stage, in . . . their subjective and their public identities. It ensures that personal desires, sexual behavior, subjective identity and public identity will frequently get out of sync with each other."[21]

Is there a plausible constitutional theory there? Or should full protection for gays, lesbians, bisexuals, and transgender persons depend upon the legislative process?

---

19. Watkins v. United States Army, 847 F.2d 1329, 1347-48 (9th Cir. 1988), after reh'g, 875 F.2d 699 (9th Cir. 1990) (en banc).

20. *Watkins*, 875 F.2d at 726 (Norris, J., concurring).

21. Janet E. Halley, The Politics of the Closet: Towards Equal Protection for Gay, Lesbian, and Bisexual Identity, 36 UCLA L. Rev. 915, 933 (1989); see also Janet E. Halley, Sexual Orientation and the Politics of Biology: A Critique of the Argument from Immutability, 46 Stan. L. Rev. 503 (1994); Gary Mucciaroni & Mary Lou Killian, Immutability, Science, and Legislative Debate over Gay, Lesbian, and Bisexual Rights, 47 J. Homosexuality 53 (2004); Qazi Rahman & Glenn D. Wilson, Born Gay? The Psychobiology of Human Sexual Orientation, 34 Personality & Individual Differences 1337 (2003).

4. Remedying Inequality in Formal Treatment.   Problems of formal equality often can be eliminated in more than one way. Formal gender neutrality could be achieved in *Orr* either by eliminating alimony for both husbands and wives or by leaving the state's system of individualized alimony determinations in place and extending eligibility to husbands who can prove their dependency. The latter alternative, which is the option Alabama chose, presents the classic "won the battle but lost the war" scenario for Mr. Orr: He prevails on the constitutional point, but remains liable for alimony under a different, gender-neutral regime. The formal equality principle applied in *Craig* and *Stanton* also did not compel any particular resolution: The state could use the higher age or the lower age or some other age altogether, just so long as it used the same age for both males and females.

Frontiero v. Richardson also presents the rule-maker with options — either require all employees to demonstrate dependency, or extend dependency benefits to all spouses. The first option would have the same effect as the ultimate result in *Orr*: all spouses would have to show dependency in order to receive the benefits. Instead, the court extended the presumption of dependency to all spouses, putting the burden on Congress to eliminate the presumption if it so chose. Thus, in *Orr*, a benefit previously available only to women was extended to men, but only if they proved dependency (which Mr. Orr could not). By contrast, in *Frontiero* the effect of extending the benefit was to give a windfall to some employees — female as well as male. It seems clear enough why Mr. Orr should not have relief — escape from alimony obligations — simply because other husbands (dependent ones) were victims of unconstitutional discrimination: Mr. Orr was not like those other, dependent husbands. But should Sharron Frontiero and her husband have received dependency benefits when her husband was not a dependent, simply because some other potential claimants, who also were not dependent, were receiving them? Another way of looking at this issue is that while in *Reed, Orr, Craig*, and *Stanton* the Court forces the state to abandon gender-based stereotypes and adopt an approach that is *more* accurate, in *Frontiero*, extension of the presumption actually renders the fringe-benefit scheme *less* accurate. Should this be a problem, constitutionally speaking? Alternatively, does it reflect legitimate differences in the administrative burdens associated with individualized determinations of eligibility?

5. Who Is the Protected Victim?   One question in some of these cases is who the victim of discrimination is. In *Frontiero*, for example, is it the female wage-earner whose benefits are lower because her husband is not presumed to be a dependent, or the male dependent himself?

What are the consequences of the answer to this question? None, if you think that discrimination against men should be analyzed in the same way as discrimination against women. But Justice Rehnquist's view in his dissenting opinion in *Craig* (and other early cases) was that when the "victim" of the discrimination is male, the constitutional standard of review appropriate to other forms of "social welfare legislation" —i.e., the rational basis test—is all that is required (and that administrative convenience satisfies this standard). Consider this position, in light of the Court's view, shared by Chief Justice Rehnquist and explored in Chapter 2 of this book, that affirmative action plans designed to eliminate the effects of past discrimination against racial minorities be subject to the same strict standard as rules and practices that exclude or disadvantage those minorities.

One approach to the "victim" problem is reflected in such cases as *Orr* and *Craig*, but found frivolous by Justice Rehnquist in Footnote 2 to his dissent in *Craig*. That approach assumes that women are harmed not only by discrimination against them, but also by discrimination that favors them, when this "benign" discrimination reflects, and thus perpetuates, traditional stereotypes. How would you evaluate this claim? Are women harmed by preventing men from buying 3.2 percent beer? How? Does it matter what the legislative history of the statute suggests about the role of stereotypes? In *Craig*, the sparse information available on the state legislature's 1972 retention of different ages for alcohol purchases suggests the influence of religious fundamentalist concerns. The principal testimony opposing equalization of ages came from a minister who wanted to protect young men from the "pool, beer, and girls syndrome."[22]

Finally, Footnote 22 of Justice Brennan's opinion in *Frontiero* notes that the statutes at issue in that case were not designed to rectify the effects of past discrimination against women. If they had been so designed, should the result in the case be different? This issue is explored in Chapter 2.

6. Women in the Military. Throughout the nation's history, cultural expectations and legal restrictions expressly limited female involvement in the armed forces. Until the early 1970s, women constituted less than 2 percent of the American military and discrimination in placement and promotion was widespread, particularly for women of color. Enrollment was limited through quotas on female applicants; exclusion from combat positions, military academies, and training programs; and disqualification of women who became pregnant or had minor children. The prevailing view was apparent in one 1968 federal district court opinion: "In providing for involuntary service for men and voluntary service for women, Congress followed the teachings of history that if a nation is to survive, men must provide the first line of defense while women keep the home fires burning."[23] Accordingly, in 1981 the Supreme Court upheld the male-only draft in Rostker v. Goldberg, concluding that the "decision to exempt women from registration was not the 'accidental

22. Brief of Appellants at 11, Craig v. Boren, No. 75-628 (1976).
23. United States v. St. Clair, 291 F. Supp. 122, 125 (S.D.N.Y. 1968).

[handwritten in left margin: Allow women more active role in military in the 70s]

by-product of a traditional way of thinking about females,'" but rather a rational decision to prepare a draft of combat troops.[24]

In the mid-1970s, many of these restrictions were modified or withdrawn, without judicial intervention. As a result, female participation in the armed forces substantially increased, reaching 10 percent by the late 1980s, 13 percent by the turn of the twentieth century, and 15 percent by 2009.[25] Despite this gradual integration, the combat exclusion would last several more decades before being lifted, piecemeal, by the Department of Defense. The Defense Advisory Committee on Women in the Services (DACOWITS), a civilian advisory group within the Defense Department, played a particularly important role. In December 1991, Congress repealed the statutory prohibitions, dating from 1948, on assigning women in the Air Force, Navy, and Marines to combat aircraft. In addition, the statute created a "Commission on the Assignment of Women in the Armed Forces" to "assess the laws and policies restricting the assignment of female service members."[26] Finally, in December 2015, Secretary of Defense Ash Carter announced that all remaining barriers to women's service in combat would be lifted. This means, he explained, "They'll be allowed to drive tanks, fire mortars and lead infantry soldiers into combat. They'll be able to serve as Army Rangers and Green Berets, Navy SEALs, Marine Corps infantry, Air Force parajumpers, and everything else that was previously open only to men."[27]

What changes and challenges might you expect from more gender integration in the military, especially in combat roles? According to a Pew Research survey, the female force is more racially diverse than the male force, just as likely to experience the "struggles and benefits of service upon discharge," and more likely than their male counterparts to be critical of the wars in Iraq and Afghanistan.[28] But opponents of women in combat also raise a host of concerns about pregnancy, promiscuity, and "gender-norming"—the practice of adjusting strength and fitness standards to reflect sex-based differences. According to these commentators, the military's effort to accommodate women is fostering resentment, diluting performance requirements, creating double standards, inspiring inappropriate chivalry, compromising morale, impairing recruitment, and diverting attention from more central goals of combat preparedness. Underlying these concerns has been a host of symbolic

---

24. 453 U.S. 57, 70-72, 74, 76-77 (1981).

25. Currently women serve in 95 percent of all Army occupations and make up approximately 16 percent of the active Army. For current data, see Women in the U.S. Army, http://www.army.mil/women/today.html.

26. Jill Elaine Hasday, Fighting Women: The Military, Sex, and Extrajudicial Change, 93 Minn. L. Rev. 96, 132-51 (2008).

27. DOD, Press Release, Carter Opens All Military Occupations, Positions to Women (Dec. 3, 2015), http://www.defense.gov/News-Article-View/Article/632536/carter-opens-all-military-occupations-positions-to-women.

28. Id.

issues about masculinity, manhood, and dominance. General William West-moreland expressed a common attitude with uncommon candor. "No man with any gumption wants a woman to fight his nation's battles."[29] Proponents of equal treatment point out that the most comprehensive studies conclude that with appropriate training, the vast majority of women can meet the physical demands of combat, and that their presence does not cause declines in unit cohesiveness.[30] As in civilian contexts, military positions requiring particular levels of strength, endurance, or agility can be allocated under gender-neutral guidelines that match individual capabilities with job requirements. Moreover, as many experts have noted, technological changes in warfare have reduced the relevance of physical strength in combat and eroded the distinctions between combat and combat-related positions. Judge Richard Posner puts it this way: "We live in an age of push-button warfare. Women can push buttons as well as men."[31]

If service in the military is a responsibility of citizenship, should women feel obligated to serve? Some feminists argue that women should seek to challenge military culture, not to assimilate within it. In opposing proposals for gender-neutral draft registration, a New Haven women's group issued the following response: "Women have traditionally fought for peace, and there is no reason for us to abandon that position now."[32]

7. Gays and Lesbians in the Military. For most of American military history, gays and lesbians were excluded from service. Former President Bill Clinton attempted to ease the exclusion in 1993 with the Don't Ask Don't Tell (DADT) policy, which allowed gay and lesbian individuals to serve as long as they did not admit their sexual orientation or engage in homosexual conduct.[33] However, this supposed compromise resulted in the firing of 14,500 service members across all branches, and a disproportionate number

29. William Westmoreland, quoted in Judith Wagner Decrew, The Combat Exclusion and the Role of Women in the Military, Hypatia 62 (Winter 1995).

30. See, e.g., J. Michael Brower, Undermining Old Taboos: U.S. Studies Say Women Can Meet Physical Demands of Combat, Armed Forces J. Int'l, May 1996, at 13 (reporting on studies sponsored by the Army Research Institute and the British Ministry of Defense); Martha McSally, Women in Combat: Is the Current Policy Obsolete?, 14 Duke J. Gender L. & Pol'y 1011, 1029-40 (2007); Blythe Leszkay, Feminism on the Front Lines, 14 Hastings Women's L.J. 133, 161 (2003).

31. Richard Posner, Overcoming Law 55 (1995). Maia Goodell argues that the physical-strength rationale for excluding women from combat is clearly traceable to ideology rather than biology. See Maia Goodell, Physical-Strength Rationales for De Jure Exclusion of Women from Military Combat Positions, 34 Seattle U. L. Rev. 17 (2010).

32. Feminist Opposition to the Draft, quoted in Catharine MacKinnon, Sex Equality 270-71 (2001).

33. National Defense Authorization Act of 1994, Pub. L. No. 103-160, 107 Stat. 1547 §571, codified as amended at 10 U.S.C. §654 (2006); About "Don't Ask, Don't Tell," Servicemembers Legal Def. Network, http://www.sldn.org/pages/about-dadt.

But can w/ trans?

of the discharges were women. For example, in 2009 women made up 14 percent of the Army, but 48 percent of discharges. Women were 20 percent of the Air Force in the same year, but 51 percent of Air Force discharges under the policy.[34] During his campaign for the Presidency, President Obama stated his intention to abolish the DADT policy. Repeal efforts were stalled at first, but catalyzed by a federal district court's ruling that DADT violated the Fifth Amendment's guarantee of due process and the First Amendment's guarantee of freedom of speech.[35] While the case was pending on appeal, Congress repealed DADT during a lame-duck session in December 2010.[36] The repeal became effective in September 2011, replacing DADT with a policy of nondiscrimination under which the military may not take administrative action against any personnel, or persons seeking to become personnel, on the basis of sexual orientation.

8. The Equal Rights Amendment. The Equal Rights Amendment (ERA), discussed in both Justice Brennan's and Justice Powell's opinions in *Frontiero,* failed by three states to gain the support of two-thirds (38) of the states by the 1982 congressional deadline (a date extended three years beyond the original 1979 deadline). The proposed amendment read: "Equality of rights under the law shall not be denied or abridged by the United States or by any state on account of sex." The text of the Amendment did not resolve when differences between the sexes justify different treatment. However, debate over the Amendment generally assumed that it would require "strict scrutiny" of sex-based classifications, along the lines favored by four Justices in *Frontiero.*

The Amendment, initially proposed in 1923, has been reintroduced in every congressional session since 1982, but it has never emerged from committee. The United States is one of a small number of nations that does not have an explicit guarantee of women's rights in its Constitution. Opinion polls find support for such a guarantee; according to a survey taken by Opinion Research Corporation in 2001, 88 percent of Americans favored the Equal Rights Amendment and 72 percent believed that it had already been adopted.[37]

Given such support, what has prevented passage? Opponents such as Concerned Women for America claim that women already have equal opportunity, and that the ERA will strip women of laws and institutions that protect

---

34. See Andrea Stone, "Don't Ask, Don't Tell" Discharges Hit Lesbians Hardest (Aug. 16, 2010), http://www.aolnews.com/2010/08/ask-don't-tell-discharges-hit-lesbians-hardest/.

35. Log Cabin Republicans v. United States, 716 F. Supp. 2d 884 (C.D. Cal. 2010).

36. Don't Ask, Don't Tell Repeal Act of 2010, Pub. L. No. 111-321, §2(a)(2)(C), 124 Stat. 3515 (2010).

37. The Equal Rights Amendment Campaign Network, A Nationwide Survey Shows that Americans Want a Constitutional Guarantee of Equal Rights for Women, http://2passera.org/survey.shtml.

them. One writer states that the ERA would eliminate the Violence Against Women Act, the Women's Bureau, the Office of Women's Health, National Women's History Month, and Mother's Day.[38] Commentator Christina Hoff Sommers believes the Amendment would "hand radical feminist groups . . . a 'powerful weapon' to achieve other 'terrible' outcomes: 'Boy Scouts would be forced to "integrate," sororities and fraternities would be eliminated or required to merge. . . . Single sex schools and summer camps for boys would be phased out.'"[39] The ERA website responds that the Amendment would not make all single-sex institutions unconstitutional, only those that "perpetuate the historical dominance of one sex over another."[40]

As efforts to pass a federal Equal Rights Amendment continue, 23 states have enacted versions of an equal rights amendment in their own constitutions.[41] While a few states have incorporated the same review standards as the federal equal protection clause, and while numerous decisions interpreting state ERAs have not had the effect proponents may have desired,[42] one comprehensive review of state ERAs concluded that they have been "an extremely important tool in advancing sex equality for women,"[43] especially with respect to women's reproductive autonomy, disparate impact cases, and discrimination based on sexual orientation.[44] Another commentator, however, argues that state ERAs have often been deployed to protect men's rights instead of women's and to this extent are ineffective for women "except as symbols."[45] Formal equality, of course, does not distinguish between men's rights and women's rights. Is this a strength, or a weakness, of the formal equality principle?

Putting Theory Into Practice

1-4. In response to acts of violence in and around school by rival gangs, a school board instituted a ban on students wearing or displaying any gang symbol. This ban is interpreted in one school to bar males, but not females, from wearing earrings, because some males who wear earrings do so as a sign of

---

38. Sarah Rode, Equal Rights Amendment Strips Women of Their Rights (May 27, 2007), http://www.freerepublic.com/focus/news/1840583/posts.

39. Christina Hoff Sommers, "Equal Rights" Time Warp, Wall St. J., Apr. 3, 2007, at A15.

40. See http://www.equalrightsamendment.org/faq.htm#q13.

41. See http://www.equalrightsamendment.org/faq.htm#q7.

42. Linda J. Wharton, State Equal Rights Amendments Revisted: Evaluating Their Effectiveness in Advancing Protection Against Sex Discrimination, 36 Rutgers L.J. 1201, 1243-47 (2005) (discussing Rhode Island and Florida).

43. Id. at 1204.

44. Id. at 1248-68.

45. See Paul Benjamin Linton, State Equal Rights Amendments: Making a Difference or Making a Statement?, 70 Temp. L. Rev. 907, 941 (1997) (arguing that the "ultimate irony" of state ERAs is that "in many respects women have given up 'privileges' they always enjoyed in exchange for 'rights' that never were in jeopardy").

gang allegiance while earrings on females do not have any gang significance. Should the rule be allowed to stand? Does it offend formal equality principles? Would a dress code by a state employer that prevented males but not females from wearing earrings be permissible? Would it depend on the nature of the job (teacher versus police officer)?

1-5. Although women are now allowed in all positions in the military, they are not required to register with the Selective Service at age 18, which men are required to do.[46] This policy, which was upheld by the U.S. Supreme Court when women could not serve in combat roles,[47] is now being reconsidered, and a few cases have challenged the differential treatment.[48] Is the policy constitutional? In one poll, 61 percent of men said women should be required to register, while only 39 percent of women said so.[49] Is this disparity surprising?

1-6. At the public high school graduation in East Haddam, Connecticut, boys wear blue robes; girls wear white robes and carry flowers. Also, boys and girls file into the graduation venue in separate lines. Does this practice violate the Equal Protection Clause? If so, is the violation remedied by allowing boys and girls to choose which color they wish to wear?[50]

3. Indirect Discrimination

The cases examined so far are examples of "facial" or "direct discrimination," which means that the classifications are explicitly based on sex. When

---

46. Kristy Kamarch, Women and the Selective Service, CRS Insight (Dec. 15, 2015), https://www.rt.com/usa/310058-women-draft-usa-lawsuit.

47. Rostker v. Goldberg, 453 U.S. 57 (1981). The case is discussed in the note following the next section.

48. See Bill Chappell, 'Things Have Changed,' U.S. Judge Says of Case Over Men-Only Military Draft, NPR (Dec. 12, 2015), http://www.npr.org/sections/thetwo-way/2015/12/12/459473353/things-have-changed-says-judge-in-case-over-men-only-military-draft (describing challenge now before the Ninth Circuit Court of Appeals brought by the National Coalition for Men); Girls Just Want to Get Drafted: Lawsuit Challenges Male-Only Selective Service, RT News (July 16, 2015), https://www.rt.com/usa/310058-women-draft-usa-lawsuit/ (describing class action).

49. Stephanie Akin, Women and the Draft, Roll Call (June 28, 2016), rollcall.com/news/politics/women-draft-poll-shows-don't-favor-registration.

50. See Joanna L. Grossman & Katharine T. Bartlett, Blue for Boys, White with Flowers for Girls: When Commencement Is an Exercise in Discrimination, in Justia's Verdict (May 3, 2016), at https://verdict.justia.com/2016/05/03/blue-for-boys-white-with-flowers-for-girls; Elizabeth T. Ryan & Jordan E. D'Addeo, Issuing Graduation Gowns By Sex is Wrong, Hartford Courant, May 4, 2016, http://www.courant.com/opinion/op-ed/hc-op-fresh-talk-ryan-east-haddam-graduation-robes-0504-20160503-story.html. This problem should be reconsidered after you read the Title IX materials in Chapter 2, Section C(2).

an employer fires or fails to promote someone because of her sex, this is also a case of direct discrimination. Examples of direct discrimination under employment discrimination law are explored later in this chapter.

Discrimination can also be indirect, such as when a state acts on a basis other than sex, but the impact of its laws or practices disproportionately affects members of one sex. Personnel Administrator of Massachusetts v. Feeney, excerpted below, concerns the disproportionate effect of a veterans' preference system on women's opportunities for state civil service positions.

Personnel Administrator of Massachusetts v. Feeney
442 U.S. 256 (1979)

Mr. Justice STEWART delivered the opinion of the Court.

This case presents a challenge to the constitutionality of the Massachusetts veterans' preference statute . . . on the ground that it discriminates against women in violation of the Equal Protection Clause of the Fourteenth Amendment. Under [this statute], all veterans who qualify for state civil service positions must be considered for appointment ahead of any qualifying nonveterans. The preference operates overwhelmingly to the advantage of males.

The appellee Helen B. Feeney is not a veteran. She brought this action pursuant to 42 U.S.C. §1983, alleging that the absolute preference formula established in [the Massachusetts statute] inevitably operates to exclude women from consideration for the best Massachusetts civil service jobs and thus unconstitutionally denies them the equal protection of the laws. The three-judge District Court agreed, one judge dissenting. . . .

The Federal Government and virtually all of the States grant some sort of hiring preference to veterans. The Massachusetts preference, which is loosely termed an "absolute lifetime" preference, is among the most generous. It applies to all positions in the State's classified civil service, which constitute approximately 60% of the public jobs in the State. It is available to "any person, male or female, including a nurse," who was honorably discharged from the United States Armed Forces after at least 90 days of active service, at least one day of which was during "wartime." Persons who are deemed veterans and who are otherwise qualified for a particular civil service job may exercise the preference at any time and as many times as they wish. . . .

[The record shows that Ms. Feeney, who entered the state civil service system in 1963, did quite well in the competitive civil service examinations she took in order to obtain a promotion, but was "consistently eclipsed by veterans."]

The sole question for decision on this appeal is whether Massachusetts, in granting an absolute lifetime preference to veterans, has discriminated against women in violation of the Equal Protection Clause of the Fourteenth Amendment. . . .

The cases of Washington v. Davis, [1976], and Arlington Heights v. Metropolitan Housing Dev. Corp., [1977], recognize that when a neutral law has a disparate impact upon a group that has historically been the victim of discrimination, an unconstitutional purpose may still be at work. But those cases signaled no departure from the settled rule that the Fourteenth Amendment guarantees equal laws, not equal results. *Davis* upheld a job-related employment test that white people passed in proportionately greater numbers than Negroes, for there had been no showing that racial discrimination entered into the establishment or formulation of the test. *Arlington Heights* upheld a zoning board decision that tended to perpetuate racially segregated housing patterns, since, apart from its effect, the board's decision was shown to be nothing more than an application of a constitutionally neutral zoning policy. Those principles apply with equal force to a case involving alleged gender discrimination.

When a statute, gender-neutral on its face, is challenged on the ground that its effects upon women are disproportionably adverse, a twofold inquiry is thus appropriate. The first question is whether the statutory classification is indeed neutral in the sense that it is not gender-based. If the classification itself, covert or overt, is not based upon gender, the second question is whether the adverse effect reflects invidious gender-based discrimination. . . . In this second inquiry, impact provides an "important starting point," but purposeful discrimination is "the condition that offends the Constitution." . . .

Veteran status is not uniquely male. Although few women benefit from the preference the nonveteran class is not substantially all female. To the contrary, significant numbers of nonveterans are men, and all nonveterans—male as well as female—are placed at a disadvantage. Too many men are affected by [the statute] to permit the inference that the statute is but a pretext for preferring men over women. . . .

Discriminatory intent is . . . either . . . a factor that has influenced the legislative choice or it is not. The District Court's conclusion that the absolute veterans' preference was not originally enacted or subsequently reaffirmed for the purpose of giving an advantage to males as such necessarily compels the conclusion that the State . . . intended nothing more than to prefer "veterans." Given this finding, simple logic suggests that an intent to exclude women from significant public jobs was not at work in this law. To reason that it was, by describing the preference as "inherently nonneutral" or "gender-biased," is merely to restate the fact of impact, not to answer the question of intent. . . .

The basic distinction between veterans and nonveterans, having been found not gender-based, and the goals of the preference having been found worthy, [the statute] must be analyzed as is any other neutral law that casts a greater burden upon women as a group than upon men as a group. The enlistment policies of the Armed Services may well have discriminated on the basis of sex. . . . But the history of discrimination against women in the military is not on trial in this case. . . .

"Discriminatory purpose" . . . implies more than intent as volition or intent as awareness of consequences. . . . It implies that the decisionmaker, in this case a state legislature, selected or reaffirmed a particular course of action at least in part "because of," not merely "in spite of," its adverse effects upon an identifiable group. Yet, nothing in the record demonstrates that this preference for veterans was originally devised or subsequently re-enacted because it would accomplish the collateral goal of keeping women in a stereotypic and predefined place in the Massachusetts Civil Service. . . .

Veterans' hiring preferences represent an awkward—and, many argue, unfair—exception to the widely shared view that merit and merit alone should prevail in the employment policies of government. After a war, such laws have been enacted virtually without opposition. During peacetime, they inevitably have come to be viewed in many quarters as undemocratic and unwise. Absolute and permanent preferences, as the troubled history of this law demonstrates, have always been subject to the objection that they give the veteran more than a square deal. But the Fourteenth Amendment "cannot be made a refuge from ill-advised . . . laws." . . . The substantial edge granted to veterans by [the Massachusetts statute] may reflect unwise policy. The appellee, however, has simply failed to demonstrate that the law in any way reflects a purpose to discriminate on the basis of sex.

The judgment is reversed, and the case is remanded for further proceedings consistent with this opinion. . . .

Mr. Justice MARSHALL, with whom Mr. Justice BRENNAN joins, dissenting. . . .

In the instant case, the impact of the Massachusetts statute on women is undisputed. Any veteran with a passing grade on the civil service exam must be placed ahead of a nonveteran, regardless of their respective scores. The District Court found that, as a practical matter, this preference supplants test results as the determinant of upper level civil service appointments. . . . Because less than 2% of the women in Massachusetts are veterans, the absolute-preference formula has rendered desirable state civil service employment an almost exclusively male prerogative. . . .

As the District Court recognized, this consequence follows foreseeably, indeed inexorably, from the long history of policies severely limiting women's participation in the military. . . .

The legislative history of the statute reflects the Commonwealth's patent appreciation of the impact the preference system would have on women, and an equally evident desire to mitigate that impact only with respect to certain traditionally female occupations. Until 1971, the statute and implementing civil service regulations exempted from operation of the preference any job requisitions "especially calling for women." . . . In practice, this exemption, coupled with the absolute preference for veterans, has created a gender-based civil service hierarchy, with women occupying low-grade clerical and secretarial jobs and men holding more responsible and remunerative positions. . . .

Thus, for over 70 years, the Commonwealth has maintained, as an integral part of its veterans' preference system, an exemption relegating female civil service applicants to occupations traditionally filled by women. Such a statutory scheme both reflects and perpetuates precisely the kind of archaic assumptions about women's roles which we have previously held invalid. . . . The Court's conclusion to the contrary—that "nothing in the record" evinces a "collateral goal of keeping women in a stereotypic and predefined place in the Massachusetts Civil Service" —displays a singularly myopic view of the facts established below.

To survive challenge under the Equal Protection Clause, statutes reflecting gender-based discrimination must be substantially related to the achievement of important governmental objectives. . . . Appellants here advance three interests in support of the absolute-preference system: (1) assisting veterans in their readjustment to civilian life; (2) encouraging military enlistment; and (3) rewarding those who have served their country. . . . Although each of those goals is unquestionably legitimate, the "mere recitation of a benign, compensatory purpose" cannot of itself insulate legislative classifications from constitutional scrutiny. . . . And in this case, the Commonwealth has failed to establish a sufficient relationship between its objectives and the means chosen to effectuate them. . . .

I would affirm the judgment of the court below.

NOTE ON NONDISCRIMINATORY AND DISCRIMINATORY INTENT

Did the Idaho and Alabama legislatures in *Reed* and *Orr* "intend" to disadvantage people because of their sex? Probably not, but the point of these cases is that laws based on stereotyped thinking about women are unacceptable, even if—perhaps *especially* if—they are unintentional.

Why, then, in *Feeney*, does the Court allow to stand a system that has a substantially disproportionate impact against women—a much greater practical impact, indeed, than the statutes in *Reed* and *Orr*? One explanation is that an explicit sex-based distinction is, by definition, discriminatory (whether or not it is justified), while it is less clear that a rule or practice with a disproportionate impact on women has discriminated based on sex.

Does it follow that intent should be required when the challenged statute is neutral on its face? On the one hand, as noted above, the requirement reflects the fact that it is harder to know if a facially neutral classification was the result of discrimination or some more benign explanation. On the other hand, rules and practices that are not explicitly sex-based but that have a disproportionate, negative impact against women may be even more dangerous than cases of explicit sex-based discrimination; the stereotypes that guide decisionmaking in such cases may be more hidden and thus easier to perpetuate. In fact, Title VII of the Civil Rights Act of 1964, explored later in this chapter, requires that rules and practices in the employment context that have a disparate impact on women and minorities be job-related, regardless of the "intent" of the employer.

Ironically, some direct or explicit sex-based classifications are actually "saved" by the intention to discriminate. For example, in the 1981 case of Rostker v. Goldberg (discussed in Note 6 in Section 2, above), the Supreme Court upheld a male-only draft registration system on the theory that, since females could not serve in combat, they were not likely to be subjected to future drafts.[51] Because reasons for the exclusion of women were well reviewed in the legislative history, the statute was not an "accidental by-product" of narrow, outmoded stereotypes about women, but a deliberate, reasoned choice. Similarly, in Mississippi University for Women (MUW) v. Hogan, discussed in Chapter 2, the Court's conclusion that an all-female, state-supported nursing school was a violation of the equal protection clause turned in part on the origins of the school and stereotyped notions about what it was appropriate to train women to do.[52] Justice O'Connor suggests in her opinion for the Court that if the intent had been to compensate women for the disadvantage they experienced in their educational or employment opportunities, another result might have followed. An example in the affirmative action context is Contractors Ass'n of Eastern Pennsylvania v. City of Philadelphia, which held that an affirmative action plan favoring women will pass intermediate scrutiny if it is shown to be "a product of analysis rather than a stereotyped reaction based on habit."[53]

To the extent that a showing of discriminatory intent seems desirable, how should it be demonstrated? In *Feeney*, the fact that a few women qualified as veterans is taken as a neutral fact that disproves discriminatory intent. Is this analysis sound?

Putting Theory Into Practice

1-7. A Veterans Administration rule requires that all chaplains at VA hospitals be "ordained" clergy members. The requirement is shown to have a disparate impact on women because the Roman Catholic Church, among others, will not ordain women as priests. Does the rule offend formal equality

51. 453 U.S. 57 (1981).
52. 458 U.S. 718 (1982).
53. 6 F.3d 990, 1010 (3d Cir. 1993).

principles? Is this an example of direct discrimination, or indirect discrimination, or neither?

1-8. Although women make up about 50 percent of medical school graduates, only about 15 percent of surgeons are women and in some sub-specialties, like neurosurgery and orthopedic surgery, women comprise less than 5 percent.[54] A significant part of the gender gap is thought to be attributable to the high stress and irregular hours involved in the surgical profession.[55] Is this a problem that needs fixing? If so, who has responsibility for it, and what should be done?

1-9. Customer evaluations of marketers show that female marketers are undervalued by customers, as against objective criteria, by about 20 percent.[56] Student evaluations of teachers also show a systematic bias against women.[57] Are companies that use customer evaluations to help evaluate their employees, or schools that use students' evaluations to help evaluate their teachers, engaged in sex discrimination? If so, what should be done?

1-10. Good Eats is a restaurant that, in order to develop new markets to boost sagging sales, decides to offer a 20 percent discount to all groups of eight who are meeting during the lunch service for the purpose of a bridal shower, baby shower, birthday party, book club meeting, bridge club meeting, or sewing circle. As it turns out, groups that meet for these purposes during the lunch period are almost exclusively female. Public accommodation laws in the state prohibit discrimination on the basis of sex. Is the Good Eats discount unlawful?

54. See Liz Kowalczyk, Female Surgeons Say Explicit Bias Is Rare, but Subtler Obstacles Still Exist in Boston, boston.com (Feb. 25, 2013), http://www.boston.com/lifestyle/health/2013/02/25/female-surgeons-say-explicit-bias-rare-but-subtler-obstacles-still-exist-boston/CqDZ25e2R1g8IL4ky4LzKJ/story.html.

55. See Suvarna Bhatt, Is There a Glass Ceiling for Female Surgeons?, Health Careers Network (Nov. 2, 2010), http://www.healthecareers.com/article/is-there-a-glass-ceiling-for-female-surgeons/158279.

56. See Bryce Covert, Female Client Service Reps Get Lower Scores Despite Better Performance and Experience (May 22, 2014), http://thinkprogress.org/economy/2014/05/22/3440725/wordstream.

57. Adam Driscoll et al., What's in a Name: Exposing Gender Bias in Student Ratings of Teachers, 40 J. Innovative Higher Ed. 291 (2015); William Arthur Wines & Terence J. Lau, Observations on the Folly of Using Student Evaluations of College Teaching for Faculty Evaluations, Pay, and Retention Decisions and Its Implications for Academic Freedom, 13 Wm. & Mary J. Women & L. 167 (2006); Sylvia R. Lazos, Are Student Evaluations Holding Back Women and Minorities?: The Perils of "Doing" Gender and Race in the Classroom, in Presumed Innocent: The Intersections of Race and Class for Women in Academic (Gabriella Gutierrez y Muhs et al., eds., 2012).

C. FORMAL EQUALITY IN EMPLOYMENT

The preceding cases involve constitutional challenges to classifications by Congress or state legislatures. The U.S. Constitution, of course, is but one legal tool to address sex-based discrimination. State and federal anti-discrimination laws also play a critically important role. Important federal statutes include the Equal Pay Act of 1963,[58] which requires employers to give women and men equal pay for equal work, and Title VII of the Civil Rights Act of 1964 (Title VII),[59] which prohibits employers from discriminating with respect to the compensation, terms, conditions, or privileges of employment based on the individual's race, color, religion, sex, or national origin. Both of these statutes track formal equality principles in ways that are illustrated in the discussion that follows.

1. The Equal Pay Act: Formal Equality Paradigm

The Equal Pay Act requires that men and women receive "equal pay" for "equal work." Equal work is defined as "jobs the performance of which requires equal skills, effort, and responsibility, and which are performed under similar working conditions." The Act also includes some exceptions for factors not related to sex, such as a seniority or merit system.

≡≡≡≡ *EEOC v. Madison Community Unit School*
≡≡≡≡ *District No. 12*
≡≡≡≡ **818 F.2d 577 (7th Cir. 1987)**

Female Coaches paid less than male coaches

Posner, Circuit Judge.

The Equal Employment Opportunity Commission brought this suit against the school district of Madison, Illinois, charging that the district was paying female athletic coaches in its high school and junior high school less than male coaches, in violation of the Equal Pay Act of 1963. . . .

The trial brought out the following facts:

[Luvenia] Long was paid substantially less for coaching girls' track than Steptoe, a man, was paid for coaching boys' track. Although the boys' track program included more students and had more meets than the girls', Steptoe had two assistant coaches compared to Long's one, and as a result Long and Steptoe devoted approximately equal time to their coaching jobs. Long also coached the girls' tennis team, and Jakich, a man, the boys' tennis team;

58. 29 U.S.C. §206 (2012).
59. 42 U.S.C. §2000 et seq. (2012).

and Jakich was paid more than Long even though there were no significant differences between the teams in number of students, length of season, or number of practice sessions; however, the boys' team played almost twice as many matches as the girls' team. Long was also assistant coach of the girls' basketball team one year and received lower pay than Tyus, the male assistant coach of the boys' track team. The district judge found that the work of the two assistant coaches was substantially equal and required the same skill, effort, and responsibility—except that Long worked longer hours than Tyus. [Carol] Cole, who coached the girls' volleyball, girls' basketball, and girls' softball teams, was paid less for coaching volleyball than the male coach of the boys' soccer team, less for coaching basketball than the male coach of the boys' soccer team, and less for coaching softball than the male coach of the boys' baseball team. Also, as assistant coach of the girls' track team she was paid less than the assistant coach of the boys' track team. In all of these cases the judge found that the work of the female coach and her male counterpart was the same in skill, effort (including time), and responsibility. Any potential differences in effort and responsibility stemming from the fact that the boys' teams were sometimes larger and played longer seasons were, he found, offset by the fact that the head coaches of the boys' teams had more assistants than their female counterparts. . . .

The first question we must decide is whether the pairs of jobs that the district judge compared in finding unequal pay are sufficiently similar to be "equal work" within the meaning of the Equal Pay Act. The Act is not a general mandate of sex-neutral compensation. It does not enact "comparable worth" —the principle that wages should be based on "objective" factors, rather than on market conditions of demand and supply which may depress wages in jobs held mainly by women relative to wages in jobs held mainly by men. . . . A female secretary paid less than a male janitor cannot complain under the Equal Pay Act that the disparity in their wages is not justified by "objective" factors such as differences in skill, responsibility, and effort. . . . The Act requires equal pay only when men and women are performing "equal work on jobs the performance of which requires equal skill, effort, and responsibility, and which are performed under similar working conditions." The working conditions of a janitor are different from those of a secretary, and so are the skills and responsibilities of the two jobs. The Act does not prohibit paying different wages even if the result is to pay a woman less than a man and by doing so "underpay" her because the difference in the wage rate is greater than necessary to compensate the male for any greater skill, effort, or responsibility required by, or any inferior working conditions encountered in, his job.

Thus the jobs that are compared must be in some sense the same to count as "equal work" under the Equal Pay Act; and here we come to the main difficulty in applying the Act: whether two jobs are the same depends on how fine a system of job classifications the courts will accept. If coaching an athletic team in the Madison, Illinois school system is considered a single job rather than a congeries of jobs, the school district violated the Equal Pay Act prima facie by paying female holders of this job less than male holders, and the only question is whether the district carried its burden of proving that the lower wages which the four female coaches received were lower than the wages of their male counterparts because of a factor other than sex. If on the other hand coaching the girls' tennis team is considered a different job from coaching the boys' tennis team, and a fortiori if coaching the girls' volleyball or basketball team is considered a different job (or jobs) from coaching the boys' soccer team, there is no prima facie violation. So the question is how narrow a definition of job the courts should be using in deciding whether the Equal Pay Act is applicable.

. . . The Act requires that the jobs compared have "similar working conditions," not the same working conditions. This implies that some comparison of different jobs is possible. It is true that similarity of working conditions between the jobs being compared is not enough to bring the Act into play — the work must be "equal" and the jobs must require "equal" skill, effort, and responsibility, as well as similar working conditions. But since the working conditions need not be "equal," the jobs need not be completely identical.

Estimating and comparing the skill, effort, responsibility, and working conditions in two jobs are factual determinations. . . . We can overturn them, therefore, only if they are clearly erroneous. . . . The district judge found (among other things) that coaching a girls' tennis team is sufficiently like coaching a boys' tennis team, coaching a girls' softball team is sufficiently like coaching a boys' hardball team, and, indeed, coaching a girls' volleyball or basketball team is sufficiently like coaching a boys' soccer team, to allow each pair of jobs to be described as involving equal work, as requiring equal skill, effort, and responsibility, and as being performed under similar working conditions. . . .

There are pitfalls in allowing any comparisons between different jobs, and they are illustrated by this case. One is a tendency to focus entirely on the measurable differences and ignore the equally or more important but less readily measurable ones. The witnesses in this case concentrated on the amount of skill and time required for coaching girls' and boys' teams and paid little attention to responsibility. It may be true that because the boys' teams tend to have more assistant coaches than the girls' teams, the head coaches of the boys' teams put in no more time than the head coaches of the girls' teams even when the boys' teams are larger and play more matches. But normally there is greater responsibility (one of the dimensions in which the statute requires equality between the jobs compared) if you have a staff than if you don't. That is one reason why the president of a company is paid more than a junior executive who, lacking staff assistance, may work longer hours. . . .

Effort is inconclusive

Another difference tends to be ignored when effort, which is hard to measure, is equated to time, which is easy to measure. Boys and girls differ on average in strength, speed, and perhaps other dimensions of athletic ability; there may also be important differences in their attitudes toward athletic competition. The differences between boys and girls in athletic aptitude and interest may make coaching a boys' team harder—or easier—than coaching a girls' team; there can be no confidence that the two jobs require equal effort. The district judge set aside this consideration by ruling that a difference in the sex of students, customers, etc., can't be used to justify a pay difference under the Equal Pay Act. But this is wrong. The reference to "factor other than sex" refers to the sex of the employee, not the sex of the employer's customers, clients, or suppliers. . . . Suppose that the school district happened to have just male, or just female, coaches and paid coaches more for coaching boys' teams than girls' teams. Men paid less than other men for coaching, or women paid less than other women, could not complain of a violation of the Equal Pay Act. . . . The Act did not seek to eliminate whatever differences between the sexes might make it harder to coach a boys' team than a girls' team. If it is harder (we are not saying it is harder—we are just discussing possibilities), the statutory requirement of equal effort is not met and the differential in pay is outside the scope of the Act.

Nevertheless, we are unwilling to hold that coaches of girls' and boys' teams can never be found to be doing equal work requiring equal skill, effort, and responsibility and performed under similar working conditions. Above the lowest rank of employee, every employee has a somewhat different job from every other one, even if the two employees being compared are in the same department. So if "equal work" and "equal skill, effort, and responsibility" were taken literally, the Act would have a minute domain. . . .

But the words "very much alike," "closely related," or, as the cases sometimes say, "substantially equal"—even the words "virtually identical"—are not synonymous with "identical." . . . There is a gray area, which we must be vigilant to police, between "very much alike," which is within the scope of the Act, and "comparable," which is outside; for it is plain that Congress did not want to enact comparable worth as part of the Equal Pay Act of 1964. . . .

Whatever answer we might give, if we were the finders of fact, to the question whether coaching a girls' tennis team and coaching a boys' tennis team are sufficiently alike to be equal work within the meaning of the Act, we cannot, on the record compiled in this case (a potentially important qualification), deem the district court's determination clearly erroneous. . . .

Although we conclude that there is no objection in principle to comparing different coaching jobs, the record of the present case does require us to distinguish between coaching boys' and girls' teams of the same sport and coaching boys' and girls' teams of different sports. [The court sets aside as arbitrary the judge's equation of girls' basketball and girls' volleyball with boys' track.] . . .

With this exception we conclude that the plaintiffs did establish a prima facie case of violation of the Equal Pay Act, and we move on to consider defenses, of which only one ("factor other than sex") is relevant. Madison argues that the sex of the teams is a factor other than sex. . . . If Madison, having decided for reasons unrelated to the sex of the coaches that coaches of male teams should be paid more than coaches of female teams, neither prohibited nor even discouraged women from coaching male teams, the difference in pay between male coaches of boys' teams and female coaches of girls' teams would be due to a decision unrelated to the sex of the coaches. But Madison discouraged women, including Cole and Long, from applying to coach boys' teams, which not only adds a reason related to the sex of the coaches for a difference in pay between men and women to a reason related solely to the sex of the team members, but also casts doubt on the bona fides of the school district's claim to have based the difference in the pay of coaches of male and of female teams solely on the sex of the team members. . . .

The reason for discouraging women from coaching boys' teams was that the school authorities were concerned about the "locker room problem." This may or may not be a good reason . . . but it does suggest that women receive less pay than men for doing what the district court found was equal work within the meaning of the Equal Pay Act because they are women; their sex makes them ineligible to receive the higher wage that men receive for equal work. Even if the school district is entitled to insist that coaches and coached be of the same sex, if the work of each coach is the same and the reason for the difference in pay is the difference in the sex of the coach, the Equal Pay Act is violated. An employer cannot divide equal work into two job classifications that carry unequal pay, forbid women to compete for one of the classifications, and defend the resulting inequality in pay between men and women by reference to a "factor other than [the] sex" of the employees. . . . It would not be the sexual segregation that had caused the inequality in pay, but a decision to pay men more for doing the same work as women (albeit with a "clientele" of a different sex from the women's "clientele").

═══ ***Sandor v. Safe Horizon, Inc.***
2011 WL 115295 (E.D.N.Y.)

GOLD, United States Magistrate Judge.

Plaintiff Stephanie Sandor brings this action against her former employer, Safe Horizon, Inc., alleging that defendant unlawfully discriminated against her on the basis of her gender and race. [Among other causes of action, Sandor claimed that Safe Horizon] discriminated against her on the basis of her gender in violation of the Equal Pay Act. . . .

Facts . . .

1. Background

Safe Horizon is a nonprofit organization that provides "support and advocacy for victims of crime and abuse." In July of 2009, Safe Horizon employed about 720 staff members. Plaintiff Sandor, a Hispanic female, worked in Safe Horizon's Human Resources Department. The essence of plaintiff's claim is that another employee, a black male, was hired after plaintiff at a higher salary than plaintiff was earning. . . .

2. Plaintiff's Employment at Safe Horizon

Plaintiff was hired by Safe Horizon as a Recruitment Coordinator in the Human Resources Department in December 2001. She was promoted to Human Resources Manager in January 2005. In January 2007, plaintiff applied for a promotion to Senior Director. George Johnson, Vice President of Human Resources, declined to promote plaintiff. Plaintiff resigned from her employment with Safe Horizon and accepted a higher-paying position with the National Resources Defense Council in August of 2007.

As Human Resources Manager, plaintiff provided advice and support to various Safe Horizon departments run by approximately 40–45 managers and directors. Plaintiff also worked on defendant's Domestic Shelter Programs Task Force, an initiative undertaken to reorganize the way the Safe Horizon shelters were run. Plaintiff's responsibility on the Task Force was to help with recruitment and prevent high staff turnover. As part of the Task Force, plaintiff attended bi-weekly meetings with managers of the shelters to instruct them on human resources policies and procedures. . . .

Plaintiff's written performance evaluations from October 2004, August 2005, February 2006, and April 2007, all indicated that plaintiff was almost without exception meeting or exceeding expectations in all relevant categories. Johnson prepared plaintiff's final performance evaluation in April 2007. Johnson's summary of plaintiff's performance states, in pertinent part, that Sandor "is knowledgeable of the work that must be accomplished and adept at the administrative implementation. She has a wealth of education to compliment [sic] her human resource foundation." In addition, Johnson identified "building/developing customer relationship[s]" and "build[ing] customer confidence in her advice and counsel" as two areas where plaintiff required "continued growth and development." . . .

Excellent employee

3. Brown's Employment at Safe Horizon

Safe Horizon hired Richard Brown, a black male, in June 2006. At the time, Brown was unemployed and Johnson, who knew Brown, was aware that Brown was looking for employment. Abigail Saunders, an Employee Relations Manager, was going out on maternity leave and Safe Horizon was looking to hire a temporary replacement. . . . Robinson hired Brown for the temporary position on or about June 14, 2006.

Brown, like Sandor and Saunders, was responsible for supporting various Safe Horizon departments and programs. Johnson ultimately decided to keep Brown on as a permanent employee at Safe Horizon. Brown was promoted to Senior Director in either January 2007 or May 2007.

Brown reported to Robinson and Johnson. Robinson testified that Brown was "not as skilled in understanding and in the application of [Safe Horizon's] employee re[tention] policy and . . . [human resources] law as he needed to be in order to do the work that he was doing." Posner, who interacted with Brown in the Human Resources Department, stated that Brown "didn't know the main things of HR," that it took from several months to a year for Brown to learn how to work the human resources database, and that Brown did not enforce basic human resources guidelines. Collins, who also worked with Brown, stated that Brown "never had a grasp on our compensation system." . . .

4. Plaintiff's Education and Prior Work Experience

Plaintiff holds a Bachelor of Arts from St. Lawrence University in Political Science and Spanish, and completed a Master's of Science in Human Resources Management in 2004 while working at Safe Horizon. In addition, plaintiff is a certified mediator and has taken a variety of human resources certification courses. Beginning in 1998 and continuing until her employment with Safe Horizon in 2001, plaintiff worked primarily as a recruiter for employment and advertising agencies.

5. Brown's Education and Work Experience

Brown graduated from high school and completed certificate programs from Columbia University's Institute for Not-for-Profit Management and the Zenger Miller Frontline Leadership. According to Brown's resume, he worked as a manager and assistant director of human resources for two hotels from 1996–2000 and as the director of quality assurance at a third hotel from 2000 to 2002. Brown served as Director of Human Resources/Chief Business Officer of the Cathedral of St. John the Divine, a nonprofit organization, from 2002 to 2006. Brown stated that his responsibilities at The Valley included "oversight [of the] HR department that was being developed," handling leases, negotiating agreements with vendors, and supervising the information technology and facilities departments. Brown was laid off from The Valley when it ceased operating in 2006.

6. Salaries

Brown, Saunders and plaintiff were all Human Resources Managers in June 2006. At the time, plaintiff was receiving an annual salary of $47,577.98 as a 100% full time employee. Before she went out on maternity leave, Saunders was receiving $44,752.25 as a 100% full time employee. Brown was hired in June 2006 as an 80% full time employee, meaning he worked from Monday to Thursday, at a salary of $44,752.00. The 100% full time equivalent of Brown's salary would have been $55,940.00.

Johnson determined Brown's starting salary. Johnson decided to pay Brown a higher salary than plaintiff and Saunders based upon Brown's experience "working with large populations in a hotel management situation and managing human resources . . . at The Valley." He testified that he felt that Brown's salary was "equal" given the work experience he brought to the position. Johnson also acknowledged, however, that he did not discuss in detail the experience Brown had managing people at his previous job and how it might compare to the experience of the managers already employed at Safe Horizon. . . .

Discussion. . . .

Plaintiff Sandor next claims that she was unlawfully denied her right to equal pay pursuant to the Equal Pay Act. The EPA prohibits employers from discriminating among employees on the basis of sex by paying unequal wages for equal work. "The purpose behind the enactment of the EPA was to legislate out of existence a long-held, but outmoded societal view that a man should be paid more than a woman for the same work." Both parties assert that they are entitled to summary judgment on plaintiff's EPA claim.

To prove a violation of the EPA, Sandor must demonstrate that: "(i) the employer pays different wages to employees of the opposite sex; (ii) the employees perform equal work on jobs requiring equal skill, effort, and responsibility; and (iii) the jobs are performed under similar working conditions." Unlike Title VII, the EPA is essentially a strict liability statute; a plaintiff need not demonstrate discriminatory intent to prevail.

It is undisputed that plaintiff has established a *prima facie* case. Brown was hired to replace Saunders at a salary of $44,752.00 as an 80% full time employee; the full time equivalent would have been $55,940. At the time, plaintiff was paid $47,577.98 as a 100% full time employee and, prior to her maternity leave, Saunders was paid $44,752.00 as a 100% full time employee. It is also undisputed that Brown, plaintiff and Saunders all served as Human Resource Managers and performed equal work under similar working conditions.

Now that Sandor has established her *prima facie* case, the burden of persuasion shifts to Safe Horizon to justify the wage disparity based upon one of the EPA's affirmative defenses: "(i) a seniority system; (ii) a merit system; (iii) a system which measures earnings by quantity or quality of production; or (iv) a differential based on any other factor other than sex." The Second Circuit has noted that, "[t]he burden of establishing one of the four affirmative defenses is a heavy one, . . . because the statutory exemptions are narrowly construed." Therefore, Safe Horizon "'cannot attain summary judgment unless the evidence . . . on that issue is conclusive.'"

Defendant contends that it should not be held liable under the EPA because its decision to pay plaintiff less than Brown was based on "factor[s]

#4 → other than sex

other than sex." "[T]o successfully establish the 'factor other than sex' defense, an employer must . . . demonstrate that it had a legitimate business reason for implementing the gender-neutral factor that brought about the wage differential."

Defendant Safe Horizon maintains that it had two legitimate business reasons for paying Brown a higher salary than it paid to plaintiff and Saunders. First, defendant argues that Brown was hired to fill an immediate need in the Human Resources Department that arose when Saunders went out on maternity leave. Second, defendant contends that Brown possessed "superior relevant human resources experience" that justified the higher salary. . . .

This evidence is insufficient to meet Safe Horizon's burden. . . . Moreover, defendant has not presented any evidence indicating that it conducted a search for other qualified candidates willing to accept the same rate of pay earned by Saunders and plaintiff but failed to find anyone.

Second, Brown was unemployed at the time he was hired, and defendant has not explained why, even if its need to fill Saunders' position was "immediate," it was necessary to pay Brown a higher salary than plaintiff was earning to persuade him to accept the position. For example, there is no evidence indicating that Brown was offered the same salary being paid to Saunders and plaintiff but declined. Nor has defendant proffered evidence of Brown's salary at his previous job as some indication that Brown could reasonably have demanded the salary he received from Safe Horizon. Moreover, because Brown was unemployed, defendant did not need to offer Brown higher compensation in order to "lure him away from his prior employer," a practice that has been recognized as a legitimate business reason for a wage differential.

Finally, it might arguably have been reasonable for defendant to have initially paid Brown a higher salary because he was a temporary employee and may not have been receiving other non-wage benefits. However, Brown's salary was not adjusted after he became a permanent employee and presumably began receiving the same benefits as plaintiff and other permanent staff. In fact, Johnson testified that Safe Horizon provides benefits even to temporary employees after they have worked for more than two months. Thus, it appears that Brown would have been receiving benefits even before he secured a permanent position with defendant. Accordingly, defendant has failed to establish that it needed to pay Brown a higher salary than plaintiff and Saunders in order to fill an immediate need.

Defendant next argues that the wage differential was justified by Brown's background and experience. More specifically, defendant emphasizes that Brown had experience working with shelter programs, and Saunders was the employee relations person responsible for Safe Horizon's shelter program.

When an employer claims that a wage differential is based upon experience, it bears the burden to demonstrate both that the "experience is a job-related qualification for the position in question" and that the employer "based [the] higher salary on this factor." According to the job posting for

Brown's position, Safe Horizon was seeking a candidate with the following qualifications: "[An u]ndergraduate degree and at least three to five years delivering HR generalist services or three to five years of solid experience in at least two HR disciplines that require ongoing client interface. Masters in HR or OD a plus." Brown's education includes a high school diploma and certificate programs from Columbia University's Institute for Not-for-Profit Management and the Zenger Miller Frontline Leadership. Prior to joining Safe Horizon, Brown had approximately six years of experience working in human resources for various hotels and four years as the chief business operator and director of human resources of a nonprofit organization.

It is clear that, at least with respect to his education, Brown did not possess even the minimum qualifications required for the position. According to his resume, Brown did have more work experience than the position required. Even if Brown's work experience were relevant to the vacant position that Safe Horizon needed to fill, defendant could not obtain summary judgment without conclusively establishing that Brown's experience was the reason he was paid a higher salary than plaintiff or Saunders. Johnson testified that he paid Brown a higher salary based upon Brown's "background and experience," which included "hotel management, human resources, training and some program management." Johnson further testified that he hired Brown because he had worked with "large populations in a hotel management situation and managing human resources before at the Valley," but also acknowledged that Brown managed only three to five staffers in the human resources department at The Valley. This is particularly significant because, according to Johnson's testimony, the responsibilities of the Safe Horizon position were much more substantial; Brown was hired to provide support for approximately 700 Safe Horizon employees and was expected to interact with approximately 60 managers. There is no indication that Brown had experience working with an organization of Safe Horizon's size. Moreover, although Brown's title at The Valley was "Director of Human Resources," Brown testified that this role involved "oversight [of the] HR department that was being developed."

Defendant also asserts in its memorandum that Johnson believed that the wage differential was justified because of Brown's "experience with shelters, and he was filling in for Ms. Saunders, who was the employee relations person for the domestic violence shelters." The evidence in support of this argument consists of Collins' statement that Johnson told her that Brown "had experience with shelters and . . . could step into [Saunders'] role pretty easily." However, Johnson never testified that this was the reason for offering Brown a higher salary. More importantly, there is nothing in Brown's resume or his deposition transcript to support defendant's assertion that Brown had significant experience working with shelters.

Having considered all of the evidence, I conclude that defendant has failed to establish that it based Brown's higher salary on his background and experience. Although Safe Horizon's decision to pay Brown a higher salary may not have been the result of gender bias, defendant bears the burden of demonstrating that it had a legitimate business reason for the wage differential. Because Safe Horizon has failed to meet this "heavy burden," plaintiff's motion for summary judgment on her EPA claim is granted.

Notes

1. The Formal Equality Paradigm. The Equal Pay Act of 1963 is a paradigmatic application of formal equality principles. The main interpretative task is defining what work is equal. It obviously would be unfair to allow employers to circumvent the Act by minor variations in job titles or job descriptions. Thus, the Act has been applied to require the same wages for different job classifications entailing substantially equal duties and involving comparable skill, responsibility, and effort, such as female "cleaners" and male "janitors," "beauticians" and "barbers," and "seamstresses" and "tailors."[60]

Successful Equal Pay Act cases, however, are relatively rare, particularly in cases involving upper-level employees. The main problem with administrative and executive positions is the difficulty of finding a close enough comparison. Courts generally require the plaintiff in an Equal Pay Act suit to identify a particular employee, working for the same employer, who is earning more for the same work, and it is more difficult to compare the substance of white-collar jobs than lower-level positions.[61] A representative example is Georgen-Saad v. Texas Mutual Insurance Co.[62] There, the plaintiff, a Senior Vice President of Finance, alleged underpayment in comparison with other senior vice presidents in the company. The court dismissed that claim on the ground that "the assertion that any one of these jobs requires 'equal skill, effort, and responsibility' . . . cannot be taken seriously. . . . These are Senior Vice Presidents in charge of different aspects of Defendant's operation; these are not assembly-line workers or customer-service representatives." In the court's view, the Equal Pay Act could deal with "commodity-like" work, not the functions of high-level executives.[63]

60. See, e.g., Aldrich v. Randolph Central Sch. Dist., 963 F.2d 520 (2d Cir. 1992).

61. See, e.g., Juliene James, The Equal Pay Act in the Courts: A De Facto White-Collar Exemption, 79 N.Y.U. L. Rev. (2004); Mary E. Graham & Julie L. Hotchkiss, A Systematic Assessment of Employer Equal Employment Opportunity Efforts as a Means of Reducing the Gender Earnings Gap, 12 Cornell J.L. & Pub. Pol'y 169 (2002).

62. 195 F. Supp. 2d 853 (W.D. Tex. 2002).

63. See also Stopka v. Alliance of American Insurers, 141 F.3d 681 (7th Cir. 1998) (jobs of five male vice presidents required insurance skills that were substantially different from responsibilities of only female vice president whose job required administrative skills, even though all division vice presidents were ranked equally under Alliance's Salary Administration Program). But see Lawin-McEleney v. Marist College, 239 F.3d 476 (2d Cir. 2001) (female professor's use of statistical averages from pool of entire college faculty could establish liability when there were only three other professors in her department).

The Equal Pay Act addresses unjustified wage differentials based on sex but does not deal with gender biases that underlie the disparities. For example, the Act would not encompass discriminatory behavior that may have prevented women from becoming coaches of male sports teams at Madison Community Unit School. Such claims would need to proceed under Title VII, discussed below.

2. Lilly Ledbetter and Pay Discrimination Claims Under Title VII. Plaintiffs can bring wage discrimination claims under Title VII as well as the Equal Pay Act. The Equal Pay Act has some advantages, including a longer statute of limitations and the lack of an intent requirement, but under Title VII, a plaintiff can prove wage discrimination without necessarily proving that a particular man was being paid more than the plaintiff for doing the same job.

In 2006, the Supreme Court considered a Title VII wage discrimination claim in Ledbetter v. Goodyear Tire & Rubber Co., a case that captured the public attention and led to Congressional action.[64] The lawsuit was brought by Lilly Ledbetter, the only female production supervisor at a Goodyear plant in Gadsen, Alabama. She proved to a jury that she suffered illegal pay discrimination on the basis of sex—her salary was as much as 40 percent lower than that of the lowest-paid male supervisor—and was awarded the maximum available damages under Title VII. On appeal, Goodyear successfully argued before the Eleventh Circuit that her claim was time-barred because every discriminatory pay decision occurred more than 180 days prior to when she first filed a charge with the EEOC.[65] Title VII provides that an EEOC charge must be brought within 180 or 300 days (depending on the jurisdiction) "after the alleged unlawful employment practice occurred." There are three possible dates from which the 180-/300-day clock could run: (1) from the date of the pay decision that sets a discriminatory wage, (2) from the date an employee learns her pay is discriminatory (a "discovery" rule), or (3) from the date any paycheck that contains an amount affected by a prior discriminatory pay decision is issued (the "paycheck accrual" rule). The Supreme Court opted for the first approach, holding that a plaintiff has 180/300 days after the pay decision that sets the discriminatory wage to file her charge with the EEOC in compliance with Title VII's statute of limitations. The majority flatly rejected the paycheck accrual rule, reasoning that a paycheck containing a discriminatory amount of money is not a present violation, but, instead, is merely the present effect of a prior act of discrimination. "[C]urrent effects alone cannot breathe life into prior, charged discrimination," the Court wrote; "such effects have no present legal consequences."[66]

64. 550 U.S. 618 (2007).
65. 421 F.3d 1169 (11th Cir. 2005).
66. 550 U.S. at 628.

Although *Ledbetter* dealt with a rather technical rule, it promised significantly adverse effects for victims of pay discrimination who were not able to quickly learn of, and promptly complain about, pay disparities. The ruling provoked public outcry and became a hot-button issue in the 2008 presidential campaign. After President Barack Obama was elected, a new version of the bill, the Lilly Ledbetter Fair Pay Act of 2009, was passed and it became the first bill signed into law during his presidency.[67] The new law provides that an

> unlawful employment practice occurs, with respect to discrimination in compensation in violation of this title, when a discriminatory compensation decision or other practice is adopted, when an individual becomes subject to a discriminatory compensation decision or other practice, or when an individual is affected by application of a discriminatory compensation decision or other practice, including each time wages, benefits, or other compensation is paid, resulting in whole or in part from such a decision or other practice.[68]

In effect, the Act takes a broad view of the employment practices that trigger the limitations period under Title VII, adopting the "paycheck accrual" rule that the Supreme Court rejected in *Ledbetter.* Lilly Ledbetter, who campaigned for the Act and testified before Congress, received no benefit from the law in her name, since her jury verdict was vacated and subject to no further appeals. But she became a civil rights folk hero who does extensive public speaking and published a memoir in 2012, entitled Grace and Grit: My Fight for Equal Pay at Goodyear and Beyond.

Litigation over the meaning of the Act has continued. Regardless of how broadly the Ledbetter Act is construed, however, it deals only with the narrow issue of the statute of limitations and does nothing to deal with other obstacles to successful proof of pay discrimination.[69] One of these obstacles is the well-documented phenomenon of pay secrecy, which some employers enforce by penalizing employees who discuss their pay with other employees.[70] The Paycheck Fairness Act (PFA), which has been introduced in several sessions of Congress to make it easier to prove wage discrimination,[71] would

---

67. See Lilly Ledbetter Fair Pay Act of 2009, Pub. L. No. 111-2, 123 Stat. 5 (codified as amended at 42 U.S.C. §2000e-5(e)(3)(A) (2012)).

68. Id.

69. On the "glass ceiling" of the EPA, see Deborah Thompson Eisenberg, Shattering the Equal Pay Act's Glass Ceiling, 63 SMU L. Rev. 17 (2010).

70. Leonard Bierman & Rafael Gely, "Love, Sex and Politics? Sure. Salary? No Way": Workplace Social Norms and the Law, 25 Berkeley J. Emp. & Labor L. 167, 168, 171 (2004) (explaining that social norms discourage discussion of salaries in the workplace and observing that one-third of U.S. private sector employers have policies that, although illegal, bar employees from discussing their salaries, while many other employers informally communicate an expectation of salary confidentiality).

71. See Paycheck Fairness Act, S. 84, https://www.govtrack.us/congress/bills/113/s84.

make it illegal for employers to penalize employees who discuss their salaries. The PFA would also expand damages under the EPA and narrow the fourth affirmative defense, which allows employers to justify pay disparities by "any factor other than sex." One of the changes would be to require employers to show that a "factor other than sex" explains the entirety of a pay disparity and that the factor is justified by business necessity. Some courts, including in *Sandor*, above, have begun to require the latter showing, but a new statute would clearly impose that and other requirements.[72] The legislation, however, has been repeatedly defeated in Congress.[73]

Perhaps because of the lack of success on the federal level, states have begun to enact more aggressive equal pay laws. California led the way in 2015, with a law predicated on a legislative finding that "the state's equal pay provisions and law regarding wage disclosures must be improved" in order to "eliminate the gender wage gap in California," which "extends across all occupations" and is "far worse for women of color." The new law increases protection in the following ways: (1) it changes the "equal work" standard to "substantially similar work"; (2) it eliminates the requirement that the plaintiff and comparator work for the same "establishment," and allows comparisons as long as they work for the same employer; (3) it narrows the affirmative defenses to equal pay claims, most importantly by requiring that employers prove that a "factor other than sex" explains the entirety of the wage differential and is justified by business necessity; (4) it expands the available remedies for equal pay claims; and (5) it attacks pay secrecy by providing that an employer "shall not prohibit an employee from disclosing the employee's own wages, discussing the wages of others, inquiring about another employee's wages, or aiding or encouraging any other employee to exercise his or her rights [to equal pay]."[74] A few months later, New York adopted a similar law, as part of Governor Andrew Cuomo's Women's Equality Act, which increased protections for women in a whole range of areas.[75]

3. The Wage Gap. Although the wage gap between women's and men's earnings has been slowly eroding, it remains significant. Adjusting for hours worked (but not for differences in education, experience, or time in the work force), women's median weekly earnings are about 82.5 percent those of men, as compared to 62.3 percent in 1979. The gap is narrower among

---

72. See also Riser v. QEP Energy, 776 F.3d 1191 (10th Cir. 2015); Belfi v. Prendergast, 191 F.3d 129 (2d Cir. 1999); Dreves v. Hudson Group Retail, LLC, 2013 U.S. Dist. LEXIS 82636 (D. Vt. June 12, 2013). For an analysis of this and other Equal Pay Act trends, see Deborah L. Brake, The Shifting Sands of Employment Discrimination: From Unjustified Impact to Disparate Treatment in Pregnancy and Pay, Geo. L. J. (forthcoming 2017).

73. David S. Joachim, Senate Republicans Block Bill on Equal Pay, N.Y. Times (Apr. 9, 2014).

74. Cal. Labor Code §1197.5 (2016).

75. N.Y. Labor Law §194 (2016).

African-Americans (90 percent) and Hispanics (89 percent).[76] The disparity for older women is greater than for younger women; full-time working women in the 16–24 age bracket earn on average 95 percent of what men earn, while women in the 55–64 age range earn only 75 percent.

Part of the explanation for the overall gender gap in wages is the occupational distribution of male and female workers. As compared to men, women are much less likely to work in construction (9 percent women) or in repair and maintenance services (12 percent women), which are relatively well paid, and they are more likely to work in lower-paid job categories such as human resources (71 percent women) and personal care and service occupations (72.5 percent women).[77] Even within their industry groups, women are over-represented in the lower-paying job categories. In the legal profession, for example, women are over 87 percent of paralegals and legal assistants, but only 33 percent of lawyers.[78] And women make less than men within the same job category. Female financial managers, for example, earn only 67 percent of what male financial managers make,[79] female physicians make only 62 percent,[80] and females in sales positions only 68 percent.[81] Over a lifetime, this adds up. One estimate places the disparity between men's and women's wages in a 40-year legal career to average almost $1.5 million.[82]

4. Factors Justifying Differences in Pay. What explains wage disparities? One factor, mentioned above in Note 2, is that women often don't know whether or not they are being paid less than their male colleagues. Another factor is that women do not negotiate as effectively as men for their own salaries. An illustrative study found that male Carnegie Mellon graduates were eight times more likely to negotiate a starting salary than their female classmates.[83] This is especially crucial with respect to starting salaries, where the difference between a $25,000 and a $30,000 starting job salary, assuming 3 percent wage increases, would amount to over $350,000 over the next 28 years.[84]

76. U.S. Bureau of Labor Statistics, Women in the Labor Force: A Databook at 2-3, 61, tbl. 16 (Dec. 2015).

77. *Id.* at 51, 55, 58, 69, 70, 71, 75, tbl. 14, 18.

78. Id. at 37, tbl. 11.

79. Id. at 64, tbl. 18.

80. Id. at 67, tbl. 18.

81. Id. at 69, tbl. 18.

82. Jessica Arons, Center for American Progress, Lifetime Losses: The Career Wage Gap (Jan. 6, 2009), http://www.american-progress.org/issues/2009/01/wage_gap_numbers.html, at 1.

83. See Linda Babcock & Sara Laschever, Women Don't Ask: Negotiations and the Gender Divide (2003).

84. See Shankar Bedantam, Salary, Gender and the Social Cost of Haggling, Wash. Post, July 30, 2007.

Another set of factors is the well-documented "wage premium" for married men that married women generally do not receive; the wage penalty experienced by mothers that is not experienced by fathers; and the disproportionate penalty placed on women who take leaves.[85] What do you think explains these various penalties? Are these stereotypes, or facts?

A still further factor is the common practice of employers matching a recruited employee's former salary, which serves to perpetuate market discrepancies between men's and women's wages. This common practice is, on the one hand, a practical response to competitive market conditions; on the other hand, it serves to immunize pay disparities that begin elsewhere and to perpetuate the social conditions that the Equal Pay Act was designed to eliminate. Courts have not been uniform in their approach to wage disparities based on matching offers and similar market forces.[86] Only where there is evidence of past discrimination in a particular work force are market forces typically insufficient to prove that the discrimination was for a reason other than sex. In Corning Glass Works v. Brennan, for example, the Supreme Court rejected an employer's claim that market forces justified paying more to night workers than day workers given that women had previously been excluded from such positions.[87] Was Massachusetts right to pass a law in 2016 banning employers from asking a candidate about prior salary until after an offer with compensation is made?[88]

A case study in the difficulties of applying equal pay principles involves athletic coaches, addressed in the *Madison* case. In intercollegiate sports, women hold fewer than 3.5 percent of the coaching jobs in men's sports in all divisions and the coaches for men's teams are paid more than twice the amount paid to coaches for women's teams. The percentage of women who are head coaches of women's teams has declined from 90 percent to 42 percent since enactment of Title IX, largely due to the increase in resources and status of women's sports.[89]

85. See AAUW, The Simple Truth About the Gender Pay Gap 10 (2012); Shelley J. Correll & Stephen Benard, Getting a Job: Is There a Motherhood Penalty?, 112 Amer. J. Sociol. 1297 (2007).

86. Compare, e.g., Wernsing v. Illinois Dep't of Human Servs., 427 F.3d 466 (7th Cir. 2005) (court "not even slightly tempted" to change its longstanding position that prior salary may be taken into account when setting an employee's starting pay) with Glenn v. General Motors Corp., 841 F.2d 1567 (11th Cir. 1988) (rejecting employer justification for wage disparity based on male clerks' transfer from higher-paying positions than female clerks).

87. 417 U.S. 188, 205-07 (1974).

88. Mass. Bill S. 2119 (enacted Aug. 1, 2016).

89. Linda Jean Carpenter & R. Vivian Acosta, Women in Intercollegiate Sport: A Longitudinal, National Study—Thirty-Five Year Update 1977-2012, at 17-18 (2012), http:// acostacarpenter .org/AcostaCarpenter2012.pdf; see also NCAA, Gender-Equity Report 2004-2010. Some evidence suggests that if football, basketball, and ice hockey were excluded, the salaries for male and female head coaches would be nearly equal. Robert Drago et al., Final Report for Cage: The Coaching and Gender Equity Report 11 (2005), http://lser.la.psu.edu/ workfam/CAGEfinalreport.doc.

What might justify the substantial pay differential between male and female coaches? Judge Posner in *Madison* reasoned that revenue-based differentials might be justified as long as women have equal access to the higher-paid coaching jobs. Is he right? Does the challenge of coaching a team that produces revenues, and thus additional stress and media demands, justify the large gap in coaching salaries between men's teams and women's teams? Where does the difference in revenue capacity come from? If it is from a greater interest by paying fans to attend games, is there a problem to be solved and, if so, what is the solution?[90]

In an effort to clarify the treatment of sex-based pay disparities in coaching under the Equal Pay Act and Title VII discussed below, the federal Equal Employment Opportunity Commission has promulgated guidelines providing that relevant factors justifying pay differences include experience, duties, and working conditions. Where job responsibilities are equivalent and the primary justification for a salary disparity is the profitability of the sport or prevailing wage rates, however, sex-based disparities can constitute an equal pay violation. To justify differential salaries based on differential revenues, the institution must demonstrate that the revenue discrepancy in no way relates to (1) institutional discrimination in opportunity, or (2) societal discrimination. In effect, the school must show that the female coach received the same opportunities as the male coach to be a revenue producer, and that the differences in revenue did not relate to lower interest in female sports or fewer resources for female athletic programs. The guidelines also make clear that that "[s]ex discrimination in the marketplace which results in lower pay for jobs done by women will not support the marketplace value defense."[91]

5. "Comparable Worth" or "Pay Equity." Should teachers and secretaries be paid less than sanitation workers, maintenance staff, and mechanics? Should child care workers be paid less than gas station attendants and pet sitters? What do you suppose explains the differences? Can they be successfully challenged through the principle of formal equality?

The Equal Pay Act requires that women and men be paid the same for the same work, but it does not require pay equity between job categories. In other words, it demands that male and female nurses be paid the same, but not that the wage structures for traditionally female occupations like nurses, teachers,

---

90. See Katharine T. Bartlett & Mitu Gulati, Discrimination by Customers, 102 Iowa L. Rev. __ (forthcoming 2016) (arguing that colleges and universities could use tools, like ticket-bundling, to help build demand for women's sports and thus even out current inequities attributable to differences in fan preference for men's over women's sports).

91. Enforcement Guidance on Sex Discrimination in the Compensation of Sports Coaches in Educational Institutions (1997), http://www.eeoc.gov/policy/docs/coaches.html. For discussion, see Deborah L. Rhode & Christopher J. Walker, Gender Equity in College Athletics, 4 Stan. J. C.R. & C.L. 101, 117-19 (2008).

and secretaries be fair in relation to wage structures for traditionally male occupations like sanitation workers, mechanics, and appliance repair workers.

A principle that goes beyond the Equal Pay Act and Title VII to address these kinds of arguable inequities *between* job categories is referred to as comparable worth or pay equity. Pay equity seeks not only to ensure equal pay for equal work, but also to achieve salary comparability for workers in different, sex-segregated job classifications requiring equivalent degrees of training, experience, and effort. In the *Madison* case, Justice Posner makes clear that the Equal Pay Act does not encompass comparable worth. Should it? Does the principle of pay equity satisfy formal equality?

Arguments for and against pay equity turn on assumptions about the causes of occupational segregation, and on the form of equality to which one is committed. If occupational segregation follows from the different priorities and lifestyle choices of men and women, there is arguably no problem to solve. Human capital theorists posit that women anticipate working fewer years than men with more interruptions, and so "self-select" into occupations requiring lower levels of skill and less educational investment. They may also choose jobs that offer lower pay in exchange for more pleasant and less hazardous working conditions, and more flexible schedules.[92] Some argue that these choices are, at least in part, hard-wired into women's biology.[93] Opponents of pay equity argue also that free markets will operate to eliminate pay structures that are unequal: If men are overpaid, women will move into those fields, creating surpluses in those occupations and shortages in traditionally female occupations. The result will be to eliminate pay discrepancies that are not justified by the nature and demands of the work. Under this market view, women not satisfied to be teachers at existing salary levels should seek higher pay as sanitation workers or mechanics. Are you persuaded by these points?

Even if sex-segregated job categories help to explain why women's earnings are only 83 percent of men's,[94] they do not explain why, within the same occupational category, significant salary disparities exist.[95] Does this phenomenon demonstrate the fundamental failure of the Equal Pay Act to eliminate discrimination in wages? Or does it show that women are making trade-offs not only between occupational categories, but within them? One expert, Claudia Goldin, suggests that occupations that most value long hours, face time at the office, and being on call—like business, law and surgery—tend to have the widest pay gaps, whereas professions like pharmacy, where employees

92. See Warren Farrell, Why Men Earn More: The Startling Truth About the Pay Gap—and What Women Can Do About It (2005).

93. See Kingsley Browne, Sex and Temperament in Modern Society: A Darwinian View of the Glass Ceiling and the Gender Gap, 37 Ariz. L. Rev. 971 (1995) (excerpted in Chapter 4, Section A).

94. U.S. Bureau of Labor Statistics, Women in the Labor Force: A Databook, supra note 76, at 2 & tbl. 21.

95. See Note 3, above.

can easily substitute for one another and are paid in proportion to the hours they work, have the narrowest pay gaps.[96] What implications do you draw from this?

To what extent do women's "choices" in the paid labor market simply reflect the same broader patterns of societal discrimination that affirmative action in the hiring context are designed to overcome—i.e., gendered definitions of work and past discrimination? Or workplace policies that steer employees in gendered directions?[97] Will supply and demand take care of job segregation and low pay in traditionally female occupations? Some say no, especially given the social reason why men tend to invest more heavily in their human capital and do not participate as much in the family responsibilities that constrain the job choices of many women.

If affirmative action is justified to overcome these factors on the hiring side, should wage structures be proactively examined with the goal of recalibrating the wage scales for job categories that have been historically dominated by women? A number of states have done so, undertaking pay equity studies and making adjustments in various pay categories in state employment where bias was identified. In addition, Minnesota and Iowa have passed legislation requiring pay equity in state employment, and Maine requires it for private sector jobs as well. Other countries, including Sweden, England, Australia, and Canada (specifically, Ontario), also have pay equity requirements. European Council Directive 75.117, Article I, provides that the principle of equal pay under Article 119 of the EEC Treaty requires equal pay for "work to which equal value is attributed."

6. Women and Contingent Work. A significant sector of the U.S. work force is made up of "contingent workers"—i.e., those employed other than on a full-time, permanent basis. This group includes part-time workers, on-call workers, temporary workers, independent contractors, day laborers, and home-based workers. Part-time workers have lower wages, fewer benefits, and less job stability than full-time workers.[98] According to data from the Bureau of Labor Statistics, almost 20 percent of the American work force work part time, with women making up 67 percent of the part-time work force.[99] In 2013, 26 percent of employed women worked part time, compared

96. See Claire Cain Miller, Pay Gap Is Because of Gender, Not Jobs, N.Y. Times, Apr. 23, 2014.

97. For examples and analysis, see Vicki Schultz, Telling Stories About Women and Work: Judicial Interpretations of Sex Segregation in the Workplace in Title VII Cases Raising the Lack of Interest Argument, 103 Harv. L. Rev. 1749, 1808 (1990).

98. For a full inventory of the differences in consequences between full-time and contingent work, see U.S. Government Accountability Office, Contingent Workforce: Size, Characteristics, Earnings, and Benefits (Apr. 20, 2015), http://gao.gov/assets/670/669766.pdf.

99. Barry T. Hirsch, Why Do Part-Time Workers Earn Less? The Role of Worker and Job Skills, 58 Ind. & Lab. Rel. Rev. 525, 525-26 (2005).

with about 13 percent of employed men.[100] Contingent work has been growing, and some researchers argue that it is increasingly necessary to provide flexibility in a global environment characterized by cheap overseas labor and "just in time" production methods. Does women's role in the contingent work force raise gender equity concerns? If so, how should they be addressed?

Putting Theory Into Practice

1-11. Jennifer Lawrence, an Oscar-winning actress, wrote an open letter in 2015 entitled "Why Do I Make Less Than My Male Co-Stars?" She wrote:

> When the Sony hack happened [revealing salaries] and I found out how much less I was being paid than the lucky people with dicks, I didn't get mad at Sony. I got mad at myself. I failed as a negotiator because I gave up early. I didn't want to keep fighting over millions of dollars that, frankly, due to two franchises, I don't need. (I told you it wasn't relatable, don't hate me.)
>
> But if I'm honest with myself . . . I didn't want to seem "difficult" or "spoiled." At the time, that seemed like a fine idea until I saw the payroll on the Internet and realized every man I was working with definitely didn't worry about being "difficult" or "spoiled." . . . We've only been able to vote for what, 90 years? . . . Could there still be a lingering habit of trying to express our opinions in a certain way that doesn't "offend" or "scare" men?[101]

Is Lawrence right about the reason she got paid less? What other reasons might explain the gap she discovered? What feminist strategies could be deployed by women in Hollywood to remedy the problem of pay inequity? How would you respond to actress Kate Winslet, who told a reporter that she doesn't like talking about money because "it's a bit vulgar isn't it?"[102]

1-12. Since 2007, all of the Grand Slam tennis events have paid men and women winners the same prize money. In 2012, the 13th-seeded male tennis player at Wimbledon, Gilles Simon, made news when he complained that men should be paid more than women because "men spend twice as long

---

100. U.S. Bureau of Labor Statistics, Women in the Labor Force: A Databook, supra note 76, at 2 & tbl. 21.

101. Jennifer Lawrence, Why Do I Make Less Than My Male Co-Stars?, http://us11. campaign-archive1.com/?u=a5b04a26aae05a24bc4efb63e&id=64e6f35176&e=1ba99d671 e#wage; see also Madeline Berg, Everything You Need to Know About the Hollywood Pay Gap, Forbes, Nov. 12, 2015.

102. Alicia Adamczyk, Why You Should Care About the Hollywood Wage Gap, Time. com (Feb. 26, 2016), http://time.com/money/4207416/hollywood-wage-gap/ (noting, also, that earnings for female actresses peak around age 34, while those for male actors do not peak until age 51).

on court as women do."[103] Men play best-of-five set matches, while women play best-of-three, which means men's matches are longer and more demanding. Men's tennis is also arguably more competitive than women's in the top ranks and, for this reason, some fans and sports commentators believe, more entertaining. If the standard of the Equal Pay Act was applied to Grand Slam tennis tournaments, would it require that men and women be paid the same? What should the law be? Assuming it is not required by law, is it good policy to equalize tennis tournament winnings? Give your reasons.

1-13. In 2011, two employees at the University of Tennessee sued, claiming that they were paid less to serve to serve as the Director and Associate Director for Women's Strength and Conditioning than were the employees who worked for Men's Strength and Conditioning. The University's "Office of Equity and Diversity" denied their claims, with this reasoning:

> Football overwhelmingly is the top revenue-generating sport in Athletics and the sport that generates the most fan interest. If the University's football team is successful, then the entire Athletics program reaps the monetary benefits. If the University's football team is unsuccessful even partly because football injuries are not being prevented, diagnosed, treated and rehabilitated successfully, then the entire Athletics program suffers. With no disrespect being intended to [the claimants], the Director of Men's Strength and Conditioning is more important to athletics because of its football-related responsibilities.[104]

In bringing a claim in court, how would you respond to the internal ruling? Would it matter whether the two complainants are both female?

1-14. The all-female nursing faculty at a major university sues the university for violation of the Equal Pay Act, arguing that the skill, effort, and responsibility of their jobs are functionally equivalent to the salaries of the majority-male, higher-paid faculties at the university's architecture, urban planning, and environmental health schools. Should they prevail?[105]

1-15. A member of Congress proposes a bill that goes even further than the proposed Paycheck Fairness Act—mandating that all salaries be posted in a database available to all current employees. Would this be an effective

103. CBS Sports, Wimbledon Should Pay Men More Than Women: Gilles Simon (June 27, 2012), at http://www.cbc.ca/sports/tennis/story/2012/06/27/sp-atp-wta-tennis-wimbledon-gilles-simon.html.

104. Erin Buzuvis, Title IX Blog (Nov. 17, 2011) (describing case and ruling); see also Steve Megargee, Settlement Reached in Tennessee Discrimination Lawsuit, Wash. Post., Jan. 4, 2016 (reporting on settlement for more than $1 million for pay and retaliation claims arising out of this complaint).

105. Spaulding v. Univ. of Wash., 749 F.2d 686 (9th Cir. 1994).

mechanism for reducing pay inequity? By what mechanism? Would it impose any adverse consequences on women?

2. Title VII: Finding the Limits of Formal Equality

The linchpin of employment discrimination law is Title VII of the Civil Rights Act of 1964. Two theories of employment discrimination have emerged under Title VII. The *disparate treatment* theory addresses employment rules or decisions that intentionally treat an employee less favorably than others because of the employee's race, sex, religion, or national origin. When plaintiffs challenge a formal policy that discriminates on the basis of sex, the employer's only statutory defense is to prove that a sex-based requirement or restriction is a bona fide occupational qualification (BFOQ). While a number of different tests for the BFOQ defense exist, the standard basically requires the employer to show that "the essence of the business operation would be undermined" by hiring employees without the qualification in question and that either virtually all members of the excluded sex lack the qualification or it is impossible to test for it individually. When plaintiffs challenge adverse employment actions that are not rooted in a formal policy, they must prove that the decisions were made "because of sex." In systemic cases, they do so through a combination of statistical evidence and individual anecdotes that reveal the underlying discriminatory motive;[106] in individual cases, they utilize the proof structures laid out below.

The second theory under Title VII is *disparate impact* discrimination. Under this theory, the plaintiff must show that a facially neutral job requirement or policy disproportionately affects women. Unlike discrimination cases brought under the U.S. Constitution, like Massachusetts v. Feeney (excerpted earlier), the plaintiff in a Title VII disparate impact case need not show discriminatory intent. Once the plaintiff introduces facts showing disparate impact, the employer must either refute those facts, or demonstrate that the facially neutral job requirement is both job-related and consistent with business necessity. Even then, the plaintiff has the opportunity to show that the employer's goals could be met in a less restrictive manner. To the extent that the discriminatory impact approach focuses on the *effects* of a rule rather than its *form*, it more closely fits the model of substantive, rather than formal, equality—a model examined more closely in Chapter 2.

---

106. Most systemic disparate treatment claims are litigated as class actions. The likelihood of obtaining class certification in an employment discrimination case is less likely after the Supreme Court's ruling in Wal-Mart Stores, Inc. v. Dukes, 564 U.S. 338, 131 S. Ct. 2541 (2011), in which it rejected certification of a class of more than 1.5 million plaintiffs who alleged pay and promotion discrimination on the basis of sex. The impact of this case is discussed in detail below.

Title VII has been a significant tool in helping women gain access to areas of employment previously closed to them. The statute has had greater difficulty, however, with rules that are based on women's actual differences from men. Such questions tend to divide into two separate phases of Title VII analysis: (1) whether the claimed discrimination constitutes "discrimination on the basis of sex"; and (2) whether, if a classification constitutes sex discrimination, it is nonetheless justified because of its relationship to legitimate business concerns.

a. What Is Discrimination "Because of Sex"?

When an employer clearly discriminates "because of sex," the only remaining question is whether or not the sex-based discrimination is justified (see next section). But the meaning of that phrase took many years to take shape. In Phillips v. Martin Marietta Corp., the Supreme Court first considered this question when asked to determine whether a policy against hiring women with preschool-age children constituted sex discrimination.[107] Although the Court ruled that it did—adopting the so-called sex-plus doctrine that treats discrimination against a subclass of one gender as unlawful—questions during oral argument showed the lack of consensus on the meaning of the phrase. As Gillian Thomas writes, the Justices displayed a "skeptical, even bemused tenor to several of their questions about the scope of Title VII's sex provision."[108] Justice Hugo Black asked the plaintiff's lawyer whether Title VII required an employer to "give the woman a job of digging ditches and things of that kind," while Justice Blackmun asked whether a hospital that hired only female nurses for a long time and "like[d] them and got along well" would now have to hire male nurses?[109] Justice Burger, meanwhile, asked whether "if a federal judge as a matter of policy would decline to hire a law clerk who had an infant child, a lady law clerk, but was willing to hire a man whose wife had infant children, they would be in violation of the statute, if the statute applied to them?"[110] After this plodding start, the Supreme Court would gradually hammer out a robust definition of sex discrimination, but it is still not always easy to determine whether an action was taken "because of sex."

Courts have recognized two proof structures for individual disparate treatment claims: pretext and mixed-motive. In pretext claims, the plaintiff bears the burden of proof that the discrimination complained of was based on sex. The first step (the "prima facie case") requires the plaintiff to establish

107. 400 U.S. 542 (1971).
108. Gillian Thomas, Because of Sex: One Law, Ten Cases, and Fifty Years That Changed American Women's Lives at Work 24 (2016).
109. Id.
110. Id.

several factors that eliminate some of the obvious nondiscriminatory explanations for the adverse decision (e.g., that the applicant was not qualified for the position). The defendant then has the burden to articulate a legitimate, nondiscriminatory reason for the decision. The plaintiff then has the ultimate burden of proving that the reason given is a pretext for sex discrimination. Ezold v. Wolf, Block, Schorr & Solis-Cohen, excerpted below, is an example.

In mixed-motive cases, both discriminatory and nondiscriminatory reasons are present. Price Waterhouse v. Hopkins, excerpted below, is an example.

Ezold v. Wolf, Block, Schorr & Solis-Cohen
983 F.2d 509 (3d Cir. 1992)

HUTCHINSON, Circuit Judge.

Wolf, Block, Schorr and Solis-Cohen (Wolf) appeals from a judgment of the United States District Court for the Eastern District of Pennsylvania granting relief in favor of Nancy O'Mara Ezold (Ezold) on her claim that Wolf intentionally discriminated against her on the basis of her sex in violation of Title VII . . . when it decided not to admit her to the firm's partnership effective February 1, 1989. . . .

The district court held that the nondiscriminatory reason articulated by Wolf for its rejection of Ezold's candidacy—that her legal analytical ability failed to meet the firm's partnership standard—was a pretext. . . .

Ezold was hired by Wolf as an associate on a partnership track in July 1983. She had graduated in the top third of her class from the Villanova University School of Law in 1980 and then worked at two small law firms in Philadelphia. . . . Ezold was hired at Wolf by Seymour Kurland, then chairman of the litigation department. The district court found that Kurland told Ezold during an interview that it would not be easy for her at Wolf because "she was a woman, had not attended an Ivy League law school, and had not been on law review." . . . [She] was assigned to the firm's litigation department. From 1983-87, Kurland was responsible for the assignment of work to associates in the department. He often delegated this responsibility to partner Steven Arbittier. . . . The district court found that Arbittier assigned Ezold to actions that were "small" by Wolf standards. . . .

Senior associates within two years of partnership consideration are evaluated annually; non-senior associates are evaluated semi-annually. The firm's partners are asked to submit written evaluations on standardized forms. . . . Ten criteria of legal performance are listed on the forms in the following order: legal analysis, legal writing and drafting, research skills, formal speech, informal speech, judgment, creativity, negotiating and advocacy, promptness and efficiency. Ten personal characteristics are also listed: reliability, taking and managing responsibility, flexibility, growth potential, attitude, client relationship, client servicing and development, ability under pressure, ability to work independently, and dedication. As stated by Ian Strogatz, Chairman of the Associates Committee: "The normal standards for partnership include as factors for consideration all of the ones . . . that are contained [on] our evaluation forms." . . .

The firm's partners evaluated Ezold twice a year as an associate and once a year as a senior associate from October 1983 until the Associates Committee determined that it would not recommend her for partnership in September 1988. The district court found that "in the period up to and including 1988, Ms. Ezold received strongly positive evaluations from almost all of the partners for whom she had done any substantial work." . . . Ezold's overall score in legal skills in the 1988 bottom line memorandum before the Associates Committee was a "G" for good [the second highest rating on a 5-part scale ranging from exceptional to unacceptable]. . . .

Evaluations in Ezold's file not mentioned by the district court show that concerns over Ezold's legal analytical ability arose early during her tenure at the firm. In an evaluation covering the period from November 1984 through April 1985, Arbittier wrote:

> I have discussed legal issues with Nancy in connection with [two cases]. I found her analysis to be rather superficial and unfocused. I am beginning to doubt that she has sufficient legal analytical ability to make it with the firm. . . . She makes a good impression with people, has common sense, and can handle routine matters well. However these traits will take you just so far in our firm. I think that due to the nature of our practice Nancy's future here is limited. . . .

That same year Schwartz wrote:

> I have worked a great deal with Nancy since my last evaluation. . . . Both cases are complex, multifaceted matters that have presented novel issues to us. While her enthusiasm never wanes and she keeps plugging away—I'm often left with a product that demonstrates uncertainty in the analysis of a problem. After extensive discussions with me, the analysis becomes a little more focused, although sometimes I get the sense that Nancy feels adrift and is just marching as best she can to my analytical tune. . . . In my view her energy, enthusiasm and fearlessness make her a valuable asset to us. While she may not be as bright as some of our best associates, her talents will continue to serve us well.

. . . Also in 1985, partner Donald Joseph rated Ezold's legal analytical ability as marginal and wrote "its [sic] too early to tell but I have been disappointed on her grasp of the problem, let alone performance." . . .

During her next evaluation period from April through November 1985, Ezold received similar negative evaluations. Arbittier, Robert Fiebach and Joseph rated her legal analytical abilities as marginal. Arbittier wrote:

> She took a long time getting [a summary judgment brief] done and I found it to be stilted and unimaginative. One of the main issues—dealing with the issue of notice—she missed completely and did not grasp our position. . . . Also,

in considering whether to file a defensive motion . . . she failed to cite me to a clause in the agreement that was highly relevant leaving me with the impression that the motion could not succeed. I think Nancy tries hard and can handle relatively straight-forward matters with a degree of maturity and judgment, but when she gets into more complicated areas she lacks real analytical skill and just does what she is told in a mechanical way. She is not up to our minimal Wolf, Block standards. . . .

Boote made the following report on his performance review with Ezold after this evaluation period:

Nancy appeared to accept the judgment, albeit a little grudgingly, that her analytical, research and writing ability was not up to our standards and that she should focus on the types of matters that she can handle effectively. . . . We made it very clear to Nancy that if she pursues general civil litigation work she is not on track toward partnership and that her only realistic chance for partnership in our opinion is to develop a good reputation for herself in one of the specialized areas of practice. . . .

In the evaluation period covering November 1985 to April 1986, Boote wrote the following to the Associates Committee:

Nancy continues to get mixed reviews. Her pluses are that she is mature, courageous, pretty good on her feet and has the capacity to inspire confidence in clients. Her minuses are that there is doubt about her analytic and writing ability. . . . In considering Nancy's prospects for the long range, I think we should bear in mind that we have made mistakes in the past in letting people go to other firms who really could have filled a valuable niche here. Whether Nancy is such a person, of course, remains to be seen. . . .

A summary of Ezold's performance review from October 1986 prepared by Schwartz stated:

Nancy was advised that several of the lawyers feel she has made very positive progress as a lawyer, Sy [Kurland] being one of them. However, he told her that other lawyers had strong negative sentiments about her capabilities and they feel she has a number of shortcomings in the way of complicated analysis of legal problems and in being able to handle the big complicated corporate litigation, and therefore, does not meet the standard for partnership at Wolf, Block. . . . Both Sy and I urged Nancy to seriously consider looking for employment elsewhere as she may not be able to turn the tide. . . .

Although several partners saw improvement in Ezold's work, negative comments about her analytical ability continued up until, and through, her 1988 senior associate evaluation, the year she was considered for partnership. . . . [In the 1988 review,] the Associates Committee voted 9-1 not to recommend Ezold for . . . partnership. . . .

Out of a total of eight candidates in Ezold's class, five male associates and one female associate were recommended for regular partnership. One male associate, Associate X, was not recommended for either regular or special partnership. . . . Ezold resigned from the firm on June 7, 1989. . . .

Ezold claims Wolf intentionally discriminated against her because of her sex. Intentional discrimination in employment cases falls within one of two categories: "pretext" cases and "mixed-motives" cases. See Price Waterhouse v. Hopkins, 490 U.S. 228, 247 n.12 (1989) (plurality). . . . [She] litigated this case as a pretext case. . . . The plaintiff must first establish by a preponderance of the evidence a prima facie case of discrimination. . . . The plaintiff can establish a prima facie case by showing that she is a member of a protected class; that she was qualified for and rejected for the position; and that non-members of the protected class were treated more favorably. . . . The parties do not dispute the district court's conclusion of law that Ezold demonstrated a prima facie case. . . .

The defendant may rebut the presumption of discrimination arising out of the plaintiff's prima facie case by producing evidence that there was a "legitimate, nondiscriminatory reason" why the plaintiff was rejected. . . . The burden then shifts to the plaintiff to show that the defendant's articulated reasons are pretextual. This burden merges into the plaintiff's ultimate burden of persuading the court that she has been the victim of intentional discrimination. The plaintiff must demonstrate "by competent evidence that the presumptively valid reason[ ] for [the alleged unlawful employment action was] in fact a coverup for a . . . discriminatory decision." . . . Explicit evidence of discrimination—i.e., the "smoking gun"—is not required. . . . A plaintiff can establish pretext in one of two ways: "either directly by persuading the court that a discriminatory reason more likely motivated the employer or indirectly by showing that the employer's proffered reason is unworthy of credence." . . .

In proving that the employer's motive was more likely than not the product of a discriminatory reason instead of the articulated legitimate reason, sufficiently strong evidence of an employer's past treatment of the plaintiff may suffice. . . . The employer's "general policy and practice with respect to minority employment" may also be relevant. . . . Alternately, if a plaintiff produces credible evidence that it is more likely than not that "the employer did not act for its proffered reason, then the employer's decision remains unexplained and the inferences from the evidence produced by the plaintiff may be sufficient to prove the ultimate fact of discriminatory intent." . . .

Wolf's articulated nondiscriminatory reason for denying Ezold's admission to the partnership was that she did not possess sufficient legal analytical skills to handle the responsibilities of partner in the firm's complex litigation practice. Ezold attempted to prove that Wolf's proffered explanation was "unworthy of credence" by showing she was at least equal to, if not more qualified than, similarly situated males promoted to partnership. She also contended that her past treatment at the firm showed Wolf's decision was based on a discriminatory motive rather than the legitimate reason of deficiency in legal analytical ability that the firm had articulated.

The district court compared Ezold to eight successful male partnership candidates. . . . It found:

> The test that was put to the plaintiff by the Associates Committee that she have outstanding academic credentials and that before she could be admitted to the most junior of partnerships, she must demonstrate that she had the analytical ability to handle the most complex litigation was not the test required of male associates. . . .

The district court then concluded:

> Ms. Ezold has established that the defendant's purported reasons for its conduct are pretextual. The defendant promoted to partnership men having evaluations substantially the same or inferior to the plaintiff's, and indeed promoted male associates who the defendant claimed had precisely the lack of analytical or writing ability upon which Wolf, Block purportedly based its decision concerning the plaintiff. The defendant is not entitled to apply its standards in a more "severe" fashion to female associates. . . . Such differential treatment establishes that the defendant's reasons were a pretext for discrimination. . . .

[The district court was wrong.]

The record does not show that anyone was taken into the partnership without serious consideration of their strength in the category of legal analytic ability. . . . Wolf reserves for itself the power to decide, by consensus, whether an associate possesses sufficient analytical ability to handle complex matters independently after becoming a partner. It is Wolf's prerogative to utilize such a standard. . . . The partnership evaluation process at Wolf, though formalized, is based on judgment, like most decisions in human institutions. A consensus as to that judgment is the end result of Wolf's formal process. In that process, the Associates Committee has the role of collecting and weighing hundreds of evaluations by partners with diverse views before reaching its consensus as to a particular associate's abilities. . . . The differing evaluations the partners first submit to the Associates Committee are often based on hearsay or reputation. No precise theorem or specific objective criterion is employed. . . .

Were the factors Wolf considered in deciding which associates should be admitted to the partnership objective, as opposed to subjective, the conflicts in various partners' views about Ezold's legal analytical ability that this record shows might amount to no more than a conflict in the evidence that the district court as factfinder had full power to resolve. . . . [The difficulty in this case] is the lack of an objective qualification or factor that a plaintiff can use as a yardstick to compare herself with similarly situated employees. . . .

When an employer relies on its subjective evaluation of the plaintiff's qualifications as the reason for denying promotion, the plaintiff can prove the articulated reason is unworthy of credence by presenting persuasive comparative evidence that non-members of the protected class were evaluated more favorably, i.e., their deficiencies in the same qualification category as the plaintiff's were overlooked for no apparent reason when they were promoted to partner.

A plaintiff does not establish pretext, however, by pointing to criticisms of members of the non-protected class, or commendation of the plaintiff, in categories the defendant says it did not rely upon in denying promotion to a member of the protected class. . . .

The district court's failure to consider the negative evaluations of Ezold's legal analytic ability because the partners making them had little contact with Ezold cannot be excused in the face of the credence the district court gave to positive comments about Ezold's ability from those who likewise had little or no contact with her. While a factfinder can accept some evidence and reject other evidence on the basis of credibility, it should not base its credibility determination on a conflicting double standard.

Moreover, . . . [t]here is no evidence that Wolf's practice of giving weight to negative votes and comments of partners who had little contact and perhaps knew nothing about an associate beyond the associate's general reputation was not applied equally to female and male associates. . . .

This Court has recognized that when an employer discriminatorily denies training and support, the employer may not then disfavor the plaintiff because her performance is affected by the lack of opportunity. . . . Even if we assume that Ezold received "small" cases at the beginning of her tenure at Wolf, however, there is no evidence this was the result of sex discrimination. Her evaluations indicate, rather, that it may have been her academic credentials that contributed to her receipt of less complex assignments. For example, Davis stated that "the Home Unity case was the first really fair test for Nancy. I believe that her background relegated her to . . . matters (where she got virtually no testing by Wolf, Block standards) and small matters." . . . It is undisputed that Arbittier opposed hiring Ezold because of her academic history and lack of law review experience. In one of Ezold's early evaluations, Kurland wrote: "She has not, in my view, been getting sufficiently difficult matters to handle because she is not the Harvard Law Review type. . . . We must make an effort to give her more difficult matters to handle." . . . He also stated: "I envisioned . . . her when I hired her as a 'good, stand-up, effective courtroom lawyer.'" . . . In urging the Executive Committee to reconsider Ezold's candidacy Magarity wrote:

> [The] perception [that she is not able to handle complex cases] appears to be a product of how Sy Kurland viewed Nancy's role when she was initially hired. For the first few years Sy would only assign Nancy to non-complex matters, yet,

at evaluation time, Sy, and some other partners, would qualify their evaluations by saying that Nancy does not work on complex matters. . . .

Nancy was literally trapped in a Catch-22. The Chairman of the Litigation Department would not assign her to complex cases, yet she received negative evaluations for not working on complex matters. . . . While it would be unfortunate if these academic and intellectual biases were perpetuated after the decision was made to hire Ezold, academic or intellectual bias is not evidence of sex discrimination. The district court made no finding that Ezold was given small assignments because of her sex. . . .

The district court found that when Ezold suggested to Schwartz in her early years at Wolf that an unfairness in case assignments may have occurred because she was a woman, Schwartz replied: "Nancy, don't say that around here. They don't want to hear it. Just do your job and do well." . . . This statement, made years before the 1988 decision to deny Ezold partnership, does not show that Wolf's evaluation of her legal ability was pretextual. . . .

Finally, the district court found that by allowing partners to bypass the formal assignment system, Kurland and Arbittier "prevented the plaintiff from securing improved assignments . . . [and] impaired her opportunity to be fairly evaluated for partnership." . . . The fact that Wolf's formal assignment process was often bypassed does not support the district court's finding of pretext. Title VII requires employers to avoid certain prohibited types of invidious discrimination, including sex discrimination. It does not require employers to treat all employees fairly, closely monitor their progress and insure them every opportunity for advancement. "Our task is not to assess the overall fairness of [Wolf's] actions." . . . It is a sad fact of life in the working world that employees of ability are sometimes overlooked for promotion. Large law firms are not immune from unfairness in this imperfect world. The law limits its protection against that unfairness to cases of invidious illegal discrimination. This record contains no evidence that Wolf's assignment process was tainted by a discriminatory motive. . . .

The district court found that Ezold was "evaluated negatively for being 'very demanding,' while several male associates who were made partners were evaluated negatively for lacking sufficient assertiveness in their demeanors." . . . The criticisms of Ezold's assertiveness related to the way in which she handled administrative matters such as office and secretarial space, and not legal matters. . . . In particular, David Hofstein's evaluation of Ezold in 1984 stated:

> My one negative experience did not involve legal work. When my group moved to the south end of the 21st floor, Nancy had a fit because she had to move. As I. Strogatz and our [Office Manager] know, Nancy's behavior was inappropriate and I think affected everyone's perception of her. Dealing with administrative matters professionally is almost as important as dealing with legal matters competently, and at least in that instance, Nancy blew it. . . .

The district court refers to criticisms of male associates for lacking assertiveness, but in connection with their handling of legal matters. The district court was comparing apples and oranges. The record shows that male associates were also criticized for their improper handling of administrative problems. . . . The district court also quotes an evaluation of Ezold as a "prima donna" on administrative matters, but leaves out the full context of the statement which compares her to a male associate: "Reminds me of [a male associate]—very demanding, prima donna-ish, not a team player." . . .

The district court's finding that this evidence supports its conclusion that Ezold was treated differently because of her gender is clearly erroneous. An "unfortunate and destructive conflict of personalities does not establish sexual discrimination." . . . Further, by the time of Ezold's final evaluation in 1988, there was no mention of her attitude on administrative matters. Rosoff testified that in independently reviewing the Associate Committee's decision not to recommend Ezold for partnership, he disregarded the criticisms of her handling of administrative matters from earlier years as "ancient history." . . .

We have reviewed the evidence carefully and hold that it is insufficient to show pretext. Despite Ezold's disagreement with the firm's evaluations of her abilities, and her perception that she was treated unfairly, there is no evidence of sex discrimination here. . . .

Accordingly, we will reverse the judgment of the district court in favor of Ezold and remand for entry of judgment in favor of Wolf.

≡ ### *Price Waterhouse v. Hopkins*
≡ **490 U.S. 228 (1989)**

Justice BRENNAN announced the judgment of the Court and delivered an opinion, in which Justice MARSHALL, Justice BLACKMUN, and Justice STEVENS join.

Ann Hopkins was a senior manager in an office of Price Waterhouse when she was proposed for partnership in 1982. . . . When the partners in her office later refused to repropose her for partnership, she sued Price Waterhouse under Title VII . . . charging that the firm had discriminated against her on the basis of sex in its decisions regarding partnership. Judge Gesell in the Federal District Court for the District of Columbia ruled in her favor on the question of liability . . . and the Court of Appeals for the District of Columbia Circuit affirmed. . . . We granted certiorari to resolve a conflict among the Courts of Appeals concerning the respective burdens of proof of a defendant and plaintiff in a suit under Title VII when it has been shown that an employment decision resulted from a mixture of legitimate and illegitimate motives. . . .

Ann Hopkins had worked at Price Waterhouse's Office of Government Services in Washington, D.C., for five years when the partners in that office proposed her as a candidate for partnership. Of the 662 partners at the firm at that time, 7 were women. Of the 88 persons proposed for partnership that year, only 1—Hopkins—was a woman. Forty-seven of these candidates were admitted to the partnership, 21 were rejected, and 20—including Hopkins—were "held" for reconsideration the following year. Thirteen of the 32 partners who had submitted comments on Hopkins supported her bid for partnership. Three partners recommended that her candidacy be placed on hold, eight stated that they did not have an informed opinion about her, and eight recommended that she be denied partnership.

In a jointly prepared statement supporting her candidacy, the partners in Hopkins' office showcased her successful 2-year effort to secure a $25 million contract with the Department of State, labeling it "an outstanding performance" and one that Hopkins carried out "virtually at the partner level." Despite Price Waterhouse's attempt at trial to minimize her contribution to this project, Judge Gesell specifically found that Hopkins had "played a key role in Price Waterhouse's successful effort to win a multi-million dollar contract with the Department of State." Indeed, he went on, "[n]one of the other partnership candidates at Price Waterhouse that year had a comparable record in terms of successfully securing major contracts for the partnership."

The partners in Hopkins' office praised her character as well as her accomplishments, describing her in their joint statement as "an outstanding professional" who had a "deft touch," a "strong character, independence and integrity." Clients appear to have agreed with these assessments. At trial, one official from the State Department described her as "extremely competent, intelligent," "strong and forthright, very productive, energetic and creative." Another high-ranking official praised Hopkins' decisiveness, broadmindedness, and "intellectual clarity"; she was, in his words, "a stimulating conversationalist." Evaluations such as these led Judge Gesell to conclude that Hopkins "had no difficulty dealing with clients and her clients appear to have been very pleased with her work" and that she "was generally viewed as a highly competent project leader who worked long hours, pushed vigorously to meet deadlines and demanded much from the multidisciplinary staffs with which she worked."

On too many occasions, however, Hopkins' aggressiveness apparently spilled over into abrasiveness. Staff members seem to have borne the brunt of Hopkins' brusqueness. Long before her bid for partnership, partners evaluating her work had counseled her to improve her relations with staff members. Although later evaluations indicate an improvement, Hopkins' perceived shortcomings in this important area eventually doomed her bid for partnership. Virtually all of the partners' negative remarks about Hopkins—even those of partners supporting her—had to do with her "interpersonal skills." Both "[s]upporters and opponents of her candidacy," stressed Judge Gesell, "indicated that she was sometimes overly aggressive, unduly harsh, difficult to work with and impatient with staff."

There were clear signs, though, that some of the partners reacted negatively to Hopkins' personality because she was a woman. One partner described her as "macho"; another suggested that she "overcompensated for being a woman"; a third advised her to take "a course at charm school." Several partners criticized her use of profanity; in response, one partner suggested that those partners objected to her swearing only "because it's a lady using foul language." Another supporter explained that Hopkins "ha[d] matured from a tough-talking somewhat masculine hard-nosed mgr to an authoritative, formidable, but much more appealing lady ptr candidate." But it was the man who, as Judge Gesell found, bore responsibility for explaining to Hopkins the reasons for the Policy Board's decision to place her candidacy on hold who delivered the coup de grace: in order to improve her chances for partnership, Thomas Beyer advised, Hopkins should "walk more femininely, talk more femininely, dress more femininely, wear make-up, have her hair styled, and wear jewelry."

Dr. Susan Fiske, a social psychologist and Associate Professor of Psychology at Carnegie-Mellon University, testified at trial that the partnership selection process at Price Waterhouse was likely influenced by sex stereotyping. Her testimony focused not only on the overtly sex-based comments of partners but also on gender-neutral remarks, made by partners who knew Hopkins only slightly, that were intensely critical of her. One partner, for example, baldly stated that Hopkins was "universally disliked" by staff, and another described her as "consistently annoying and irritating"; yet these were people who had had very little contact with Hopkins. According to Fiske, Hopkins' uniqueness (as the only woman in the pool of candidates) and the subjectivity of the evaluations made it likely that sharply critical remarks such as these were the product of sex stereotyping—although Fiske admitted that she could not say with certainty whether any particular comment was the result of stereotyping. Fiske based her opinion on a review of the submitted comments, explaining that it was commonly accepted practice for social psychologists to reach this kind of conclusion without having met any of the people involved in the decisionmaking process.

In previous years, other female candidates for partnership also had been evaluated in sex-based terms. As a general matter, Judge Gesell concluded, "[c]andidates were viewed favorably if partners believed they maintained their femin[in]ity while becoming effective professional managers"; in this environment, "[t]o be identified as a women's lib[b]er" was regarded as [a] negative comment. In fact, the judge found that in previous years "[o]ne partner repeatedly commented that he could not consider any woman seriously as a partnership candidate and believed that women were not even capable of functioning as senior managers—yet the firm took no action to discourage his comments and recorded his vote in the overall summary of the evaluations."

Judge Gesell found that Price Waterhouse legitimately emphasized interpersonal skills in its partnership decisions, and also found that the firm had not fabricated its complaints about Hopkins' interpersonal skills as a pretext for discrimination. Moreover, he concluded, the firm did not give decisive emphasis to such traits only because Hopkins was a woman; although there were male candidates who lacked these skills but who were admitted to partnership, the judge found that these candidates possessed other, positive traits that Hopkins lacked.

The judge went on to decide, however, that some of the partners' remarks about Hopkins stemmed from an impermissibly cabined view of the proper behavior of women, and that Price Waterhouse had done nothing to disavow reliance on such comments. He held that Price Waterhouse had unlawfully discriminated against Hopkins on the basis of sex by consciously giving credence and effect to partners' comments that resulted from sex stereotyping. Noting that Price Waterhouse could avoid equitable relief by proving by clear and convincing evidence that it would have placed Hopkins' candidacy on hold even absent this discrimination, the judge decided that the firm had not carried this heavy burden.

The Court of Appeals affirmed the District Court's ultimate conclusion, but departed from its analysis in one particular: it held that even if a plaintiff proves that discrimination played a role in an employment decision, the defendant will not be found liable if it proves, by clear and convincing evidence, that it would have made the same decision in the absence of discrimination. Under this approach, an employer is not deemed to have violated Title VII if it proves that it would have made the same decision in the absence of an impermissible motive, whereas under the District Court's approach, the employer's proof in that respect only avoids equitable relief. We decide today that the Court of Appeals had the better approach, but that both courts erred in requiring the employer to make its proof by clear and convincing evidence. . . .

Justice KENNEDY, with whom THE CHIEF JUSTICE and Justice SCALIA join, dissenting. . . .

The ultimate question in every individual disparate-treatment case is whether discrimination caused the particular decision at issue. Some of the plurality's comments with respect to the District Court's findings in this case, however, are potentially misleading. As the plurality notes, the District Court based its liability determination on expert evidence that some evaluations of respondent Hopkins were based on unconscious sex stereotypes,[5] and on the

---

5. The plaintiff who engages the services of Dr. Susan Fiske should have no trouble showing that sex discrimination played a part in any decision. Price Waterhouse chose not to object to Fiske's testimony, and at this late stage we are constrained to accept it, but I think the plurality's enthusiasm for Fiske's conclusions unwarranted. Fiske purported to discern stereotyping in comments that were gender neutral—e.g., "overbearing and abrasive"—without any knowledge of the comments' basis in reality and without having met the speaker or subject. "To an expert of Dr. Fiske's qualifications, it seems plain that no woman could be overbearing, arrogant, or abrasive: any observations to that effect would necessarily be discounted as the product of stereotyping. If analysis like this is to prevail in federal courts, no employer can base any adverse action as to a woman on such attributes." . . . Today's opinions cannot be read as requiring factfinders to credit testimony based on this type of analysis. . . .

fact that Price Waterhouse failed to disclaim reliance on these comments when it conducted the partnership review. The District Court also based liability on Price Waterhouse's failure to "make partners sensitive to the dangers [of stereotyping], to discourage comments tainted by sexism, or to investigate comments to determine whether they were influenced by stereotypes."

Although the District Court's version of Title VII liability is improper under any of today's opinions, I think it important to stress that Title VII creates no independent cause of action for sex stereotyping. Evidence of use by decisionmakers of sex stereotypes is, of course, quite relevant to the question of discriminatory intent. The ultimate question, however, is whether discrimination caused the plaintiff's harm. Our cases do not support the suggestion that failure to "disclaim reliance" on stereotypical comments itself violates Title VII. Neither do they support creation of a "duty to sensitize." As the dissenting judge in the Court of Appeals observed, acceptance of such theories would turn Title VII "from a prohibition of discriminatory conduct into an engine for rooting out sexist thoughts."

Notes

1. Assessing the Facts in *Ezold*. The evidence showed that only one of 55 litigation partners in the law firm in *Ezold* was a woman, that most of the law firm partners had gone to a more prestigious law school than the plaintiff, that some male associates with less favorable evaluations than the plaintiff had made partner, and that the plaintiff was involved with women's issues at the firm, especially concerning the firm's treatment of paralegals. Although the trial court ruled in the plaintiff's favor, the appellate court reversed because it was persuaded that two-thirds of the partners voted against the plaintiff primarily because she lacked the analytic ability to handle complex litigation. The only woman litigation partner voted against her, no women testified in her favor, and several gave evidence concerning the firm's fairness toward women. How would you assess such evidence? Which factors seem the most important?[111]

2. The Significance of Stray Remarks. In evaluating claims of sex discrimination, what significance should be given to "stray remarks" concerning the plaintiff? The district court found that Nancy Ezold "was evaluated negatively for being too involved with women's issues . . . specifically her concern about the [firm's] treatment of paralegals." How significant is this finding? Although a partner had written in one evaluation that Ezold's

---

111. For a case history of the litigation, see Deborah L. Rhode, What's Sex Got to Do with It: The Challenge of Diversity in the Legal Profession, in Legal Ethics: Law Stories 233 (Deborah L. Rhode & David Luban eds., 2005); see also Thomas, supra note 108, at 127-47.

"[j]udgment is better, although it still can be clouded by over-sensitivity to what she misperceives as 'womens' [sic] issues," the appellate court concluded that the criticism was for her misperception that the firm's treatment of paralegals was a women's issue. What is your view? The Supreme Court in *Price Waterhouse* found that certain remarks by partners about Ann Hopkins were based on sex-role stereotypes, and thus discriminatory. Is there a difference in the way the courts treat "stray remarks" in the two cases?

In other cases involving such comments, courts have reached inconsistent results. In one 2005 case, the Tenth Circuit Court of Appeals held that evidence that male supervisors referred to a woman physician as "Jane" instead of "Dr." and called her a "femi-Nazi" were relevant and precluded summary judgment, even though they were not directly related to the termination decision.[112] But in another case, decided in 1999, the Fifth Circuit Court of Appeals upheld a judgment against a terminated surgical resident, finding irrelevant various remarks about her based on her sex and national origin. These remarks included a statement that "her difficulties in the program were 'cultural'"; a concern by one superior about why women would put themselves through surgical residency particularly if they plan on having children because, "they're constantly tired, and they don't have time to put on their makeup and put on clothes and do a lot of things girls need to do . . . "; and the observation of one superior that the plaintiff was "not accepted well by the 'good old boys.'"[113]

A federal district court dismissed a systemic disparate treatment case brought by the EEOC against Bloomberg, L.P. on grounds that the plaintiff's anecdotal evidence of pregnancy discrimination was insufficient, given the lack of statistical data to support the claim of pattern and practice of discrimination. In the words of the court, "'J'accuse!' is not enough in court." While the EEOC presented evidence of comments that the court viewed as stereotyped or biased—such as the CEO's asking "is every fucking woman in the company having a baby or going to have a baby?"—it concluded that they were not sufficient to support an inference of systemic discrimination. "Isolated remarks by a handful of executives . . . do not show that Bloomberg's standard operating procedure was to discriminate against pregnant women and mothers."[114] And remarks such as a threat by a manager to "'kill your

112. Plotke v. White, 405 F.3d 1092 (10th Cir. 2005).

113. Sreeram v. La. State Univ. Med. Ctr., 188 F.3d 314 (5th Cir. 1999); see also Heim v. State of Utah, 8 F.3d 1541, 1546 (10th Cir. 1993) (holding that a supervisor's comment, "Fucking women, I hate having fucking women in the office," was insufficient to show discrimination because it appeared directed at "women in general," rather than at plaintiff).

114. EEOC v. Bloomberg, L.P., 778 F. Supp. 2d 458, 461, 478-81 (S.D.N.Y. 2011).

children and burn down your house' if a deadline was missed ha[ve] nothing to do with the type of discrimination the EEOC allege[d] . . . ."[115]

In a highly publicized sex discrimination case in Silicon Valley, Ellen Pao presented several pieces of evidence suggesting that the venture capital firm where she had worked, Kleiner Perkins, bore animosity toward women, yet the jury voted against her claim. The facts included that Ellen's boss and most prominent partner, John Doerr, told "an investigator that Ms. Pao had a 'female chip on her shoulder.' Chi-Hua Chien, a partner, said women should not be invited to a dinner with former Vice President Al Gore because they 'kill the buzz.' A senior partner at the time, Ray Lane, joked to a junior partner that she should be 'flattered' that a colleague showed up at her hotel room door wearing only a bathrobe. Another senior partner, Ted Schlein, seemed never to have heard of the exhortation of Sheryl Sandberg, a senior Facebook executive, that women should 'sit at the table,' testifying, 'I really don't think it was a very big deal to us who sits at a table or who does not.' "[116] Does this environment give women an equal opportunity to succeed?

3. "Mixed-Motive" Discrimination. The plaintiff in *Price Waterhouse*, Ann Hopkins, presented evidence of the partners' discriminatory motivation. The firm presented evidence of nondiscriminatory reasons for denying her partnership. The Supreme Court decided that if a plaintiff could show that sex was a substantial motivating factor for the employment action at issue, the burden would shift to the employer, who must then prove by clear and convincing evidence that it would have made the same decision even in the absence of a discriminatory motive. After the decision, Congress enacted the Civil Rights Act of 1991, which codified a modified version of the *Price Waterhouse* rule. Title VII now provides that if sex or any other protected characteristic is "a motivating factor for any employment practice, even though other factors also motivated the practice," the employer is liable for committing an unlawful employment practice. The employer can avoid monetary damages and certain other remedies, however, by proving it "would have taken the same action in the absence of the impermissible motivating factor."[117] In such cases, remedies are limited to declaratory relief, injunctive relief, and attorney fees. Financial damages, reinstatement, hiring, and promotion are not available.

115. Id. at 479; see also David M. Litman, What Is the Stray Remarks Doctrine? An Explanation and a Defense, 65 Case W. Res. L. Rev. 823 (2015); Kerri Lynn Stone, Taking in Strays: A Critique of the Stray Comment Doctrine in Employment Discrimination Law, 77 Mo. L. Rev. 149 (2012).
116. David Streitfeld, Ellen Pao Loses Silicon Valley Bias Case Against Kleiner Perkins, N.Y. Times, Mar. 27, 2015, at A1.
117. Id. at §§2000e-2(m) & 2000e-5(g)(2)(B) (2012).

4. Determining and Proving Intent in Disparate Treatment Cases. In *Price Waterhouse*, the trial court found that the firm had discriminated against Hopkins on the basis of sex "by consciously giving credence and effect to partners' comments that resulted from sex stereotyping." The statements provided "circumstantial" evidence of intent. Was it appropriate for the court to infer discriminatory intent from this evidence? Can the low percentage of women among the employer's partners itself be probative of discrimination? One commentator notes:

> Glass ceiling cases are rarely stronger than this. At the time when Price Waterhouse withheld her promotion, all but 7 of the firm's 662 partners were male. Hopkins billed more hours and brought in more business than any other person nominated for partnership in the year of her reject, and clients generally had given her high ratings. . . . Several men who obtained partnerships [in the year that Hopkins did not] were characterized as "abrasive," "overbearing," or "cocky." No one mentioned charm school for them.[118]

Is this analysis convincing, even without expert evidence about unconscious discrimination?

What constitutes unconscious gender bias? Consider the following analysis by the American Bar Association's Commission on Women in the Profession:

> [T]he characteristics traditionally associated with women are at odds with many characteristics traditionally associated with professional success such as assertiveness, competitiveness, and business judgment. Some lawyers and clients still assume that women lack sufficient aptitude for complex financial transactions or sufficient combativeness for major litigation. Particularly in high stakes matters, risk averse managers are often reluctant to gamble on female practitioners.
>
> Yet professional women also tend to be rated lower when they depart from traditional stereotypes and adopt "masculine," authoritative styles. Negative evaluations are particularly likely when the evaluators are men, or the role is one typically occupied by men.
>
> As a consequence, female lawyers often face a double standard and a double bind. They risk appearing too "soft" or too "strident," too "aggressive" or "not aggressive enough." And what appears assertive in a man often appears abrasive in a woman. . . .
>
> The force of traditional stereotypes is compounded by the subjectivity of performance evaluations and by other biases in decisionmaking processes. People are more likely to notice and recall information that confirms prior assumptions than information that contradicts them. Attorneys who assume that working mothers are less committed tend to remember the times they left early, not the nights they stayed late.

118. Deborah Rhode, Speaking of Sex: The Denial of Gender Equality 161 (1997).

A related problem is that people share what psychologists label a "just world" bias. They want to believe that, in the absence of special treatment, individuals generally get what they deserve and deserve what they get. Perceptions of performance are frequently adjusted to match observed outcomes. Individuals are also motivated to interpret information in ways that maintain their own status and self-esteem.[119]

A substantial body of research indicates that the likelihood of bias in performance evaluations is greater in settings where women constitute a minority of the work force, the applicant pool, and the senior management.[120] The expert testimony of Professor Susan Fiske in the *Price Waterhouse* case, introduced to explain the influence of gender stereotypes, drew on the influential work of Rosabeth Moss Kanter. Kanter's research on tokenism established that groups constituting 15 percent or less of an organization are particularly vulnerable to stereotyping.

Fiske stated that when there is dramatic underrepresentation of a group, the token individuals are much more likely to be thought about in terms of their social category. People expect token individuals to fit preconceived views about the traits of the group. . . . When a token person behaves in a way that is counterstereotypical—for example, when a woman acts in an aggressive, competitive, ambitious, independent, or active way—she is more likely to be regarded as uncaring or lacking in understanding. This does not mean that women can play safe by conforming to conventional stereotypes. The Catch-22 or double bind of the powerless group is that stereotypes associated with nondominant groups are also traits that are not highly valued in the organization. A woman who acts womanly acts in a way that may cast doubt on her competence and effectiveness; a woman who is thought to be too masculine may be regarded as deviant.

In describing how persons respond to an individual whose behavior is incongruent with prevailing stereotypes, Fiske referred to Kanter's four "role traps." Under this scheme, the dominant male group perceives token women as mothers, seductresses, iron maidens, or pets. . . . The role trap most applicable to Hopkins was that of the "iron maiden." . . . Under Fiske's theory, the explicitly sex-based comments describing Hopkins were a predictable response to her status as a token woman who did not fit the conventional feminine mold. . . .

An additional cue Fiske found which indicated that stereotyping was influencing decisionmaking was the intensity of the negative reaction toward Hopkins. . . . Claims were made, for example, that Hopkins was universally disliked, potentially dangerous, and likely to abuse authority. Fiske contrasted

---

119. ABA Comm'n on Women in the Profession, The Unfinished Agenda: A Report on the Status of Women in the Legal Profession 15-16 (2001); see also Deborah L. Rhode & Barbara Kellerman, Gender Differences and Gender Stereotypes—Crossing the Bridge: Reflections on Women and Leadership, in Women and Leadership: The State of Play and Strategies for Change 1, 6-11 (Barbara Kellerman & Deborah L. Rhode eds., 2007).

120. Virginia Valian, Why So Slow?: The Advancement of Women 139-41 (1998).

these extremely negative comments with positive comments by others in the organization who seemed to describe the same behavior. Supporters found Hopkins as "outspoken, sells her own ability, independent, [has] the courage of her convictions." Detractors found her "overbearing, arrogant, abrasive, runs over people, implies she knows more than anyone in the world about anything and is not afraid to let anybody know it." Fiske's testimony on this phenomenon of "selective perception" suggested that the differing reactions to Hopkins were not simply a function of the slice of Hopkins' behavior that each individual evaluator had witnessed. Instead, when all the evidence was in, the "real" Ann Hopkins might still not clearly emerge from putting all the pieces together. Fiske's use of Kanter's role traps also demonstrated how other people can contribute to the social construction of the personality of an individual. This made it more difficult to separate Hopkins' "real" personality from the environment in which she worked.[121]

Is this testimony persuasive? Of what? Would it have helped Nancy Ezold? If Fiske's theory is accepted, would employers safely be able to make suggestions to female employees for improving deficiencies that could be related to gender roles? What if a woman *is* ineffective because she is too assertive? Or not assertive enough? Or does not maintain a professional appearance? Does it matter that the "walk more femininely" comment came from her strongest mentor at the firm, who testified he thought he was providing helpful advice?[122]

5. Upper-Level Employees. Cases such as *Ezold* and *Price Waterhouse* demonstrate the difficulties for plaintiffs in proving discrimination in professional and upper-level employment positions. Such cases are costly to litigate and "smoking guns" like the charm school comment are rare. Human resources personnel advise managers to ensure that written performance reviews include concrete examples of employee weaknesses and avoid stereotypical characterizations. Many researchers believe that unconscious bias in evaluations, mentoring, and assignments, along with inflexible workplace structures, have largely replaced deliberate sex discrimination in employment, particularly for managerial and professional positions.[123]

A threshold question in *Price Waterhouse* and *Ezold* is the extent to which Title VII regulates employment practices by partnerships. The United States Supreme Court, in Hishon v. King & Spalding, held that the decision by a

---

121. Martha Chamallas, Listening to Dr. Fiske: The Easy Case of *Price Waterhouse v. Hopkins*, 15 Vt. L. Rev. 89, 96-99 (1990).

122. Thomas, supra note 108, at 130.

123. See Susan Sturm, Second Generation Employment Discrimination: A Structural Approach, 101 Colum. L. Rev. 458, 460 (2001). For more on unconscious bias, see Jerry Kang, Trojan Horses of Race, 118 Harv. L. Rev. 1489 (2005); Linda Hamilton Krieger, The Content of Our Categories: A Cognitive Bias Approach to Discrimination and Equal Employment Opportunity, 47 Stan. L. Rev. 1161 (1995).

private law firm whether to offer partnership to a law associate falls under Title VII because opportunities for partnership constituted a term or privilege "linked directly with an [associate's] status as an employee."[124] It is not clear, however, whether Title VII covers an employment package which, from the outset, decouples partnership consideration from performance as an associate. Justice Powell, in a concurring opinion in *Hishon*, stated his view that absent a claim based on the law firm's promise of partnership consideration, Title VII would not apply to such decisions.

> The relationship among law partners differs markedly from that between employer and employee—including that between the partnership and its associates. The judgmental and sensitive decisions that must be made among the partners embrace a wide range of subjects [including participation in profits, work assignments, approval of commitments in bar association, civil and political activities, questions of billing, and acceptance of new clients]. The essence of the law partnership is the common conduct of a shared enterprise.[125]

Subsequent cases have confirmed that even if Title VII covers the partnership decision, it does not necessarily cover treatment of partners by the partnership, at least when the partner has equity in the partnership, has a significant degree of management over the partnership, and is subject to liability.[126] Similarly, the EEOC issued guidelines in 2000 that would bring Title VII into play when "the individual is subject to the organization's control," although they would not apply when "the individual acts independently and participates in managing the organization."[127]

6. Sexual Orientation Discrimination. As noted earlier in the chapter, courts have interpreted the U.S. Constitution not to protect gays, lesbians, bisexuals, or transgender individuals who experience employment discrimination by public employers.[128] Likewise, there is currently no federal law that expressly prohibits discrimination on the basis of sexual orientation by private employers.

Some advocates have attempted to secure protection for these groups under Title VII, but these have been largely unsuccessful efforts, except in a few sexual harassment cases examined in Chapter 3, Section B. In 2015, the EEOC issued an adjudication in an individual case in which it held that

124. 467 U.S. 69, 76 (1984).

125. Id. at 79-80 & n.3 (Powell, J., concurring).

126. See, e.g., EEOC v. Sidley Austin Brown & Wood, 315 F.3d 696, 703-07 (7th Cir. 2002) (partners may still be employees when they lack equity in the partnership, receive regular salary, and lack meaningful management over the partnership).

127. See EEOC Compliance Manual, ¶7110, §2-III-A.1.d (2000).

128. See, e.g., Shahar v. Bowers, 114 F.3d 1097 (11th Cir. 1997) (en banc); Padula v. Webster, 822 F.2d 97 (D.C. Cir. 1987).

"sexual orientation is inherently a 'sex-based' consideration" and therefore[129] actionable under Title VII. It remains to be seen how influential this position will be.[130] Continuing efforts have been made to secure statutory protection against sexual orientation discrimination. The first bill to try to do so was introduced by Congresswoman Bella Abzug in 1974. The bill proposed broad protection for gays and lesbians against discrimination in employment, housing, and public accommodations. Similar bills were introduced at regular intervals through the 1970s and 1980s, but none was passed into law. In 1994, the first version of the Employment Non-Discrimination Act (ENDA) was introduced in the Senate, which held hearings on the bill. ENDA was narrower than the unsuccessful bills of earlier decades, focusing only on employment. It has been proposed in different forms on multiple occasions since then. In its most common version, ENDA would prohibit employers from taking any employment action on the basis of sexual orientation or from retaliating against any individual who sought to enforce these protections.

In addition to opposition from conservatives, ENDA provoked heated controversy among gay rights advocates over whether to include protection for transgender persons. A version of ENDA that included protection against gender identity discrimination was introduced into the House of Representatives in 2007, but a sexual orientation-only version was the one that passed in the House. In 2013, by a vote of 64 to 32, the U.S. Senate passed another version of ENDA, which included gender-identity protection, but the Republican-controlled House never brought it to a vote.[131] Advocates abandoned ENDA in 2014 and began pushing a broader anti-discrimination agenda. The Equality Act, introduced in the federal House of Representatives on July 23, 2015, bans sexual orientation and gender identity discrimination in employment, housing, public accommodations, and any other context in which federal law bans discrimination.[132]

Gay rights advocates have met with greater success at the state level. As of 2016, 21 states and the District of Columbia had enacted laws prohibiting sexual orientation discrimination in various contexts, including employment, housing, and public accommodations; nineteen of these expressly cover gender identity discrimination.[133] Increasing numbers of Fortune 500 companies also prohibit discrimination based on sexual orientation and gender

129. Baldwin v. Foxx, 2015 WL 4397641 (EEOC July 15, 2015).

130. See, e.g., Hively v. Ivy Tech Comm. Coll., 2016 WL 4039703 (7th Cir. July 28, 2016).

131. Employment Non-Discrimination Act of 2013, S. 815, 113th Cong. (2013), https://www.govtrack.us/congress/bills/113/s815/text/is.

132. H.R. 3186, Equality Act, 114th Cong., 1st Sess. (2015-16); see also Lisa Bornstein & Megan Bench, Married on Sunday, Fired on Monday: Approaches to Federal LGBT Civil Rights Protections, 22 Wm. & Mary J. Women & L. 31 (2015).

133. Movement Advancement Project, Non-Discrimination Laws (2016), http://www.lgbtmap.org/equality-maps/non_discrimination_laws.

identity.[134] Despite such protections, surveys find that between one-quarter and two-thirds of LGBT employees report experiencing discrimination at work.[135] For further discussion of legal issues with respect to transgender discrimination, see Chapter 6, Section C.

Backlash against protections based on sexual orientation and gender identity is evident in laws enacted in a number of Southern states, all of which are being challenged in court. One comprehensive effort to roll back such protection is HB 2, in North Carolina, discussed in detail in Chapter 6, Section C. In April 2016, Mississippi passed a law effectively allowing people with religious objections to discriminate against LGBT people, single mothers, and anyone who has a sexual relationship outside a heterosexual marriage.[136] Similar laws are under consideration around the country.

7. Systemic Bias. Many commentators have argued that employment discrimination today is more a problem of the "structure" of the workplace, rather than individual acts of bias.[137] Employee search processes, for example, may not access the best sources of female or minority candidates, or they may use selection criteria that are incomplete in a way that disfavors candidates who are not already well represented in the work force. Workplaces may lack strong mentoring for workers who may feel isolated by reason of their sex or minority status. Work groups may be organized to reinforce rather than reduce status differentials and other factors that facilitate stereotyping. "Diversity" programs are often poorly designed and mere window dressing that obscures institutional bias.

The law recognizes that employers may engage in systemic discriminatory practices that affect multiple employees. The theory of the systemic disparate treatment claim is that, left unexplained, a significant gap between members of the plaintiff-class in the at-issue jobs and in the qualified labor pool raises an inference of discrimination.[138] Title VII allows the EEOC to sue employers for such a "pattern and practice" of discrimination. In addition, class actions may

134. See Human Rights Campaign, Corporate Equality Index 2016: Rating American Workplaces on Lesbian, Gay, Bisexual and Transgender Equality.

135. Catalyst, Making Change: LGBT Inclusion—Understanding the Challenges 18 (2007); Brad Sears & Christy Mallory, The Williams Institute, Evidence of Employment Discrimination on the Basis of Sexual Orientation in State and Local Government (2011); Brad Sears & Christy Mallory, The Williams Institute, Documented Evidence of Employment Discrimination and its Effects on LGBT People (2011).

136 See Mike McPhate, Mississippi Law on Serving Gays Proves Divisive, N.Y. Times, Apr. 14, 2016.

137. See, e.g., Sturm, supra note 123; Tristin K. Green, Insular Individualism: Employment Discrimination Law After Ledbetter v. Goodyear, 43 Harv. C.R.-C.L. L. Rev. 353 (2008); Tristin K. Green, A Structural Approach as Antidiscrimination Mandate: Locating Employer Wrong, 60 Vand. L. Rev. 849 (2007); see also discussion of unconscious bias in Notes 2 & 4, above, and 8, below.

138. Teamsters v. United States, 431 U.S. 324 (1977).

be brought on behalf of groups of individuals under Federal Rule of Civil Procedure Rule 23 if there are sufficiently common questions of fact or law and if the rule's other requirements (e.g., numerosity, representativeness) are met.

In fact, however, even though Title VII contemplates collective claims, the theories it provides, as interpreted by courts, are not particularly conducive to the recognition of systemic claims of discrimination. Disparate treatment law addresses treating a woman worse than a man, but it is inconsistent in addressing discrimination where evidence of discriminatory intent is absent, and it does not hold employers responsible for failing to use "best practices" in gender equity. In theory, disparate impact analysis should apply where women fare badly in a particular workplace in a systematic way, but a disparate impact claim requires that plaintiffs identify a specific practice that disproportionately disadvantages women; an employer's failure to adopt any particular practice that might curtail the exercise of unconscious bias or otherwise eliminate disparities in the workplace generally is not sufficient. The law imposes a duty on employers not to discriminate, but it does not require them to address disparities that cannot be traced to an employer policy, or that arise from broader, society-wide dynamics.

The difficulties of framing a case of systemic discrimination are apparent in, and made more difficult by, the Supreme Court's 2011 ruling in Wal-Mart Stores, Inc. v. Dukes.[139] Plaintiffs in *Wal-Mart* alleged in 2001 that Wal-Mart's personnel system was plagued by several factors that set the stage for biased and stereotyped decisionmaking, including a highly subjective and discretionary system that allowed mostly male supervisors to make biased pay and promotion decisions. Their evidence included statistical studies showing disparities in women's pay, which was on average $1,100 less annually for women who were in hourly positions and $14,500 less for women in salaried management positions. Plaintiffs also presented evidence that the women, despite being paid less, had greater seniority and higher performance ratings on average. With respect to promotion, while women comprised 67 percent of hourly workers and 78 percent of hourly department managers, only 35.7 percent of assistant managers, 14.3 percent of store managers, and 9.8 percent of district managers were women. Plaintiffs showed that women were significantly less likely to be promoted than men in the same position and had to wait longer for promotions. They also showed that competitor big-box stores had significantly higher percentages of women in higher management positions than Wal-Mart. Plaintiffs sought certification of a class of approximately 1.5 million women who were employed at any Wal-Mart domestic retail store at any time since December 26, 1998 and who had been or may have been

---

139. 564 U.S. 338 (2011). See generally Roger W. Reinsch & Sonia Goltz, You Can't Get There from Here: Implications of the *Walmart v. Dukes* Decision for Addressing Second-Generation Discrimination, 9 N.W. J.L. & Soc. Pol'y 264 (2014).

subjected to Wal-Mart's challenged pay and management track promotions policies and practices.

After years of litigation, in 2010 the Ninth Circuit Court of Appeals meeting en banc affirmed the district court's certification of a class.[140] The Supreme Court reversed on two different grounds. In a unanimous part of the decision, the Supreme Court held that the class certification was improvidently granted under Rule 23(b)(2) because the monetary relief sought was not simply incidental to the injunctive and declaratory relief sought under that section. This ruling will complicate all (b)(2) class actions in which both injunctive relief and monetary relief are sought, not just those involving discrimination. More troubling for sex discrimination law, though, was the 5-4 ruling that class certification was also inappropriate under Rule 23(a), which requires that the claims of class members present common questions of law and fact. The five Justices reasoned that the commonality requirement was not met because plaintiffs did not adequately establish a company-wide policy of discrimination against women, or a common source of discrimination. According to the Court's majority, individuals are free to make their own discrimination claims, subject to individual defenses Wal-Mart might assert, but they cannot sue as a class for Wal-Mart's allegedly discriminatory personnel practices.

Under prior case law, beginning with Teamsters v. United States, systemic (or "pattern and practice") discrimination claims may be proven through statistical evidence of gaps between, for example, the percentage of women in particular jobs in an employer's work force and the percentage of women in the qualified labor pool. Left unexplained, such a gap raises an inference of discrimination, especially when supported by anecdotal evidence of discriminatory motives.[141] Many recent cases also rely on so-called "social framework" evidence, which draws on social science research about the types of structures and conditions that give rise to biased or stereotyped decision-making, as a way of bolstering the inference that the disparity reflects discriminatory decision-making. The testimony in *Price Waterhouse* by Susan Fiske, drawing on the work of Rosabeth Moss Kanter, discussed above, is an example of such evidence. Although the *Wal-Mart* ruling was technically interpreting Rule 23, the Court's reasoning throws the substantive theory of systemic discrimination into question. Can plaintiffs in a future case prove unlawful discrimination based on statistical evidence and bolstered by anecdotal evidence? The Court's opinion reveals skepticism about systemic, institutional bias, and narrowly defines discrimination as the product of an individual actor with a conscious bad intent. The Court also heavily criticizes the social framework

---

140. 603 F.3d 571 (9th Cir. 2010) (en banc).
141. 431 U.S. 324 (1977).

evidence offered by the plaintiffs.[142] With this precedent, absent a company-wide policy of discrimination, plaintiffs can only win by showing that individual decisions were the product of discriminatory motive. Yet individual plaintiffs are unlikely to be able to prove discrimination on their own facts alone; the discrimination becomes apparent only when the evidence is viewed collectively.

Why wasn't the broad discretion Wal-Mart gave to its supervisors itself a "policy" of discrimination? Probably because the company's stated, official policy was one of nondiscrimination. Can an employer have a policy of discrimination without knowing it? Should employers be held responsible even for "innocent" discrimination? Arguably, the disparate impact theory is intended to cover discrimination not motivated by discriminatory intent. Yet there is an understandable reluctance to treat employers who do not mean to discriminate the same as those who do. Some commentators have suggested reformulations of the disparate treatment and disparate impact theories to more fully recognize discrimination when employers do not intend discriminate but fail to take steps to restructure a workplace that they should realize does not promote gender equity and inclusiveness.[143] Is it reasonable to expect employers affirmatively to identify potential sources of discrimination in the workplace and take steps to eliminate them? Or to structure decision-making in a way that reduces the chance that bias will infect it? Why or why not?

8. Strategies for Countering Bias in the Workplace.   Some scholars such as Richard Epstein have argued that employer self-interest is a sufficient check against gender bias. Their assumption is that a free market rewards efficiency, and that it is inefficient for employers to discriminate against qualified women. If they are not advancing at the same rate as men, the reason must be sex-based differences in female employees' choices and capabilities.[144] Other experts respond that the economic market is not always efficient and that unconscious biases and preferences for individuals who are like them restrict

---

142. For opposing views on the admissibility and usefulness of social framework evidence, compare Melissa Hart & Paul M. Secunda, A Matter of Context: Social Framework Evidence in Employment Discrimination Class Actions, 78 Fordham L. Rev. 37 (2009) (arguing that social framework evidence should be admissible in many employment class actions) with John Monahan et al., Contextual Evidence of Gender Discrimination: The Ascendance of "Social Frameworks," 94 Va. L. Rev. 1715 (2008).

143. See, e.g., David Benjamin Oppenheimer, Negligent Discrimination, 141 U. Pa. L. Rev. 899 (1993) (suggesting a theory of "negligent discrimination"); Deborah M. Weiss, A Grudging Defense of *Wal-Mart v. Dukes*, 24 Yale J. Law & Feminism 119 (2012) (developing a "notice theory" of discrimination): Tristin K. Green, The Future of Systemic Disparate Treatment Law, Berkeley J. Emp. & Labor Law (forthcoming) (suggesting a "context" model of systemic discrimination).

144. Richard A. Epstein, Forbidden Grounds: The Case Against Employment Discrimination Laws (1992).

opportunities and cause subordinate groups to choose workplaces with less discrimination.[145]

Approaches to dealing with employment bias involve both individual and managerial initiatives. Commonly recommended strategies for employees are to be clear about their values and goals, seek mentors, negotiate for what they need, and adopt a style that they and others are comfortable with. Members of groups who perceive themselves as subject to negative stereotypes often feel the need to do what Devon Carbado and Mitu Gulati label "identity work to counter those stereotypes." Examples include acting harried and tired to overcome the impression that they are not busy, or sending emails late at night to indicate that they have worked late. Some strategies may compromise individuals' identities or have other psychic costs: heterosexual "performances" to counter suspicions of homosexuality; avoidance of social events that might suggest racial "cliquishness"; and laughing at racist or sexist jokes to demonstrate a sense of humor, prevent discomfort, and indicate a lack of obsession with "outsider status."[146]

Evidence suggests that when members of subordinate groups do succeed at climbing the employment ladder, incentives exist for them to differentiate themselves from less successful members of these groups and to conform with existing workplace landscapes instead of trying to change them.[147] What are these incentives? If the only women and minorities who succeed in the workplace are those who are most like the individuals already there, what kind of equality (or diversity, for that matter) is achieved? Is it enough to level the playing field, or do the rules of the game also need to change?

Some commentators believe that the most promising approach to reducing gender inequality in the work force is to shift emphasis away from after-the-fact enforcement of anti-discrimination prohibitions and to rely more on improving an employer's capacities to identify, prevent, and redress unconscious bias and exclusionary practices. Consider Susan Sturm's analysis:

> [Current inequalities] frequently involve patterns of interaction among groups within the workplace that, over time, exclude nondominant groups. This exclusion is difficult to trace directly to intentional, discrete actions of particular actors. . . .
>
> [Take the example of a large law firm that] aggressively recruits women at the entry level and [yet] fails to track patterns in work assignment and promotion so [that] the firm's management [was] largely unaware of any problem

---

145. See, e.g., Scott A. Moss, Women Choosing Diverse Workplaces; A Rational Preference with Disturbing Implications for Both Occupational Segregation and Economic Analysis of Law, 27 Harv. Women's L.J. 1 (2004).

146. Devon W. Carbado & Mitu Gulati, Working Identity, 85 Cornell L. Rev. 1259, 1262 (2000) (excerpted in Chapter 6, Section A).

147. See Devon W. Carbado & Mitu Gulati, Race to the Top of the Corporate Ladder: What Minorities Do When They Get There, 61 Wash. & Lee L. Rev. 1645 (2004).

until [the following] complaints arose: . . . differences in patterns of work assignment and training opportunities among men and women; tolerance of a sexualized work environment by partners who are otherwise significant "rainmakers"; routine comments by male lawyers, particularly in the predominantly male departments, on the appearance, sexuality, and competence of women; harsh assessments of women's capacities and work styles based on gender stereotypes; avoidance of work-related contact with women by members of particular departments; and hyper-scrutiny of women's performance by some, and the invisibility of women's contributions to others. These complaints coincide with a concern about low morale and productivity among diverse work teams. Upon examination, the firm discovers dramatic differences in the retention and promotion rates of men and women in the firm.

The problems of bias described in this scenario result from ongoing patterns of interaction shaped by organizational culture. These interactions influence workplace conditions, access, and opportunities for advancement over time, and thus constitute the structure for inclusion or exclusion. They cannot be traced solely to the sexism of a single "bad actor." Nor can they be addressed by disaggregating the problem into discrete legal claims. The overall gender impact of this conduct may be discernible only if examined in context and in relation to broader patterns of conduct and access. The absence of systematic institutional reflection about these patterns and their impact on workplace conditions, access, and opportunity for advancement contributes to their cumulative effect. The overall organizational culture affects the extent to which particular acts produce bias in a given workplace. Comments or behavior occurring in conjunction with sex segregation and marginalization may be discriminatory, while the same statements may produce little gender exclusion in a more integrated context. . . .

[These] second generation problems cannot be reduced to a fixed code of specific rules or commands that establishes clear boundaries governing conduct. Instead, their resolution requires a different process, namely problem solving. That process identifies the legal and organizational dimensions of the problem, encourages organizations to gather and share relevant information, builds individual and institutional capacity to respond, and helps design and evaluate solutions that involve employees who participate in the day-to-day patterns that produce bias and exclusion. An effective system of external accountability, including judicial involvement as a catalyst, would encourage organizations to identify and correct these problems without creating increased exposure to liability, and to learn from other organizations that have engaged in similar efforts.

A rule-enforcement approach . . . discourages this type of proactive problem solving. That approach treats regulation as punishing violations of predefined legal rules and compliance as the absence of identifiable conduct violating those rules. . . .

In a rule-enforcement process, problems tend to be redefined as discrete legal violations with sanctions attached. Fear of liability for violation of ambiguous legal norms induces firms to adopt strategies that reduce the short-term risk of legal exposure rather than strategies that address the underlying problem. They accomplish this in significant part by discouraging the production of information that will reveal problems, except in the context of preparation for litigation. Under the current system, employers producing information that reveals problems or patterns of exclusion increase the likelihood that they will be sued. Thus, lawyers counsel clients not to collect data that could reveal racial or gender problems or to engage in self-evaluation, because that information could be used to establish a plaintiff's case. . . .

Fundamentally, the rule-enforcement model encourages lawyers to see issues as potential legal claims, rather than as problems in need of systemic resolution. This narrow focus on avoiding liability diverts attention from the structural dimensions underlying the legal violations, as well as the organizational patterns revealed through aggregating claims. . . .[148]

Professor Sturm, like other experts, proposes that employers should be obligated to establish systems to collect information on recruitment, hiring, promotion, retention, and quality of life issues; monitor evaluation, assignment, and mentoring practices; provide adequate diversity training, family leave, and alternative schedule policies; and hold managers accountable for their performance in achieving diversity-related goals.[149]

Many commentators urge more expansive liability for implicit bias or "unconscious" discrimination.[150] Will stronger legal standards coerce more egalitarian behavior by employers? Katharine Bartlett draws on social science research to suggest that measures that affirm people's intentions to act in nondiscriminatory ways may be more effective in reducing discrimination than legal coercion that assumes the worst in people. She argues that

[t]hreat and confrontation about race and gender bias, which people do not want to possess or exhibit, may inadvertently provoke shame, guilt, and resentment, which lead to avoidance and resistance, and ultimately to more stereotyping. In other words, pressure and threat will often deepen bias rather than correct it. Positive strategies that affirm people's good intentions, in contrast, engage people constructively in defining their better, nondiscriminatory selves

148. Sturm, supra note 123, at 468, 470-71, 475-76; see also Tristin K. Green, Insular Individualism: Employment Discrimination Law after *Ledbetter v. Goodyear*, 43 Harv. C.R.-C.L. L. Rev. 353, 354 (2008) (noting a "potentially devastating conceptual shift" in employment discrimination law based on "the belief that discrimination can be reduced to the action of an individual decisionmaker (or group of decisionmakers) isolated from the work environment and the employer").

149. Sturm, supra note 123; Rhode & Kellerman, supra note 119, at 29-31; Tristin K. Green, Work Culture and Discrimination, 93 Cal. L. Rev. 623, 684 (2005).

150. See, e.g., Russell K. Robinson, Perceptual Segregation, 108 Colum. L. Rev. 1093 (2008); Tristin K. Green & Alexandra Kalev, Discrimination-Reducing Measures at the Relational Level, 59 Hastings L.J. 1435, 1457 (2008); Ivan Bodensteiner, The Implications of Psychological Research Related to Unconscious Discrimination and Implicit Bias in Proving Intentional Discrimination, 73 Mo. L. Rev. 83, 108, 120-27 (2008); Ann C. McGinley, ¡Viva La Evolucion!: Recognizing Unconscious Motive in Title VII, 9 Cornell J.L. & Pub. Pol'y 415, 482 (2000).

and aligning their conduct accordingly. While coercion and threat make people defensive, opportunity and engagement leverage people's good intentions into a deeper commitment to a more inclusive, nondiscriminatory workplace. It is this type of commitment—not legal coercion—that will best address the implicit bias that is most characteristic of today's workplace . . . . [A]ttention needs to be given to the means by which internal commitment to those standards, or what I refer to as good intentions, is generated . . . . [P]eople who have an internal commitment to nondiscrimination norms will combat implicit discrimination more effectively than those motivated by traditional legal sanctions.[151]

Is she right? What are the implications for law?

Putting Theory Into Practice

1-16. Plaintiff, who was the only female among her employer's four top-level executives, brought a lawsuit for sex discrimination after she was terminated. The employer claims that the dismissal was because of unsatisfactory performance. The plaintiff presents evidence of remarks by one vice president who questioned the ability of women to have children and still remain committed to work. She also presents evidence of a company hiring goal (or "profile") in favor of unmarried, childless women, which another vice president said was justified by the fact that such women are more committed to their work and available for long hours and travel. Should this evidence be sufficient to prove pretext in plaintiff's termination?[152]

1-17. At one point during the *Ezold* litigation, the plaintiff would have accepted an offer of $75,000 (one year's pay) to settle the matter. That was less than the cost of just one of the lawyers who worked on the firm's appeal, and the costs in reputation, acrimony, and time, as well as fees, were considerable. Ezold later noted, "it was ironic that the partners criticized me for lack of analytic ability when any lawyers in their right mind would have advised settlement." In a press interview after the trial, however, the co-chair of the firm's executive committee indicated that he felt there was "no choice" but to challenge the "impression that maybe there was sex discrimination," which would have hurt recruiting efforts and tarnished the firm's reputation as a champion of civil rights. By contrast, even after the firm won its appeal, Robert Segal, another firm leader expressed doubts about whether he would make the same judgment again. "The litigation was very expensive and very painful. This may have been a case that wasn't worth winning."[153]

---

151. Katharine T. Bartlett, Making Good on Good Intentions: The Critical Role of Motivation in Reducing Implicit Workplace Discrimination, 95 Va. L. Rev. 1893, 1901-02 (2009).
152. Santiago-Ramos v. Centennial P.R. Wireless Corp., 217 F.3d 46 (1st Cir. 2000).
153. Rhode, What's Sex Got to Do with It, supra note 111, at 245.

If you had been a member of the firm's executive committee, would you have advised settlement? If you had been a female associate at the firm who had experienced sexist comments, would you have been willing to disclose them to Ezold's lawyer?

1-18. Ellen Pao's lawsuit brought attention to the treatment of women in Silicon Valley, but there have been many other lawsuits as well. A survey called *Elephant in the Valley* focused on women with at least ten years of experience and who had reached positions of power and influence. Eighty-four percent of them had been told they were too aggressive, and 47 percent were asked to do low-level tasks not asked of their male counterparts. Eighty-eight percent reported that clients or colleagues had addressed questions to their male peers that should have been addressed to them; and 87 percent had been on the receiving end of demeaning comments from male colleagues. Seventy-five percent were asked during job interviews whether they had spouses and children; some were asked for their views on abortion and religion.[154] Are the best methods for improving the treatment of women likely to be industry specific? If you were at the helm of a tech start-up, what measures might you take to prevent this type of culture from developing?

1-19. After retiring from the federal bench, Judge Nancy Gertner began to write about her views of law and justice. She has this to say about the challenges facing employment discrimination plaintiffs:

> Just as the social-psychological literature is exploding with studies about implicit race and gender bias—in organizational settings, in apparently neutral evaluative processes, and among decisionmakers of different races or genders—federal discrimination law lurches in the opposite direction, often ignoring or trivializing evidence of explicit bias. And just as empirical studies highlight the stubborn persistence of discrimination at all levels of jobs and in salaries, federal discrimination law assumes the opposite. In summary judgment decisions, judges search for explicitly discriminatory policies and rogue actors; failing to find them, they dismiss the cases. It is as if the bench is saying: "Discrimination is over. The market is bias-free. The law's task is to find the aberrant individual who just did not get the memo." The complex phenomenon that is discrimination can be reduced to a simple paradigm of the errant discriminator or the explicitly biased policy, a paradigm that rarely matches the reality of twenty-first-century life. . . .
>
> When the defendant successfully moves for summary judgment in a discrimination case, the case is over. Under Rule 56 of the Federal Rules of Civil Procedure, the judge must "state on the record the reasons for granting or denying the motion," which means writing a decision. But when the plaintiff wins, the judge typically writes a single word of endorsement—"denied"—and the case moves on to trial. Plaintiffs rarely move for summary judgment. They bear the burden of proving all elements of the claim, particularly intent, and

154. Women in Tech, Elephant in the Valley (2015).

must do so based on undisputed facts. Defendants need only show contested facts in their favor on one element of a plaintiff's claim. The result of this practice—written decisions only when plaintiffs lose—is the evolution of a one-sided body of law.[155]

If you were given the opportunity to speak to judges about the substance and procedure of discrimination law, what might you say? Would the perspectives in this book help frame your remarks?

b. What Is Discrimination? The Special Case of Appearance Regulation

Many workplaces require their employers to meet certain appearance standards, which are often sex-based—for example, only women may be required to wear skirts, while only men may be required to have short hair. These cases often present difficult issues about what constitutes sex discrimination. On the one hand, a rule that allows (or requires) only women to wear skirts explicitly discriminates on the basis of sex. On the other hand, it may seem reasonable to give employers some latitude in regulating appearance and courts do not want to spend scarce resources micromanaging workplace dress codes.

Courts have avoided finding that sex-specific grooming codes constitute unlawful sex discrimination through various approaches. The first federal appellate case on the subject upheld a hair length requirement imposed only on male employees on the grounds that the "discrimination" was based not on the "immutable characteristics" of sex, but rather characteristics over which the individual had control.[156] Other courts have determined that appearance regulations discriminate not on the basis of sex but rather on "neutral" generally accepted community grooming standards (that happen to be sex-specific).[157] Such reasoning is explored more fully in the notes below. The following case, Jespersen v. Harrah's Operating Company, took a still different approach.

≡≡≡ **Jespersen v. Harrah's Operating Company, Inc.**
444 F.3d 1104 (9th Cir. 2006) (en banc)

SCHROEDER, Chief Judge:
We took this sex discrimination case en banc in order to reaffirm our circuit law concerning appearance and grooming standards, and to clarify our evolving law of sex stereotyping claims.

155. Nancy Gertner, Losers' Rules, 122 Yale L.J. Online 109, 110-15 (2012).
156. See Baker v. Cal. Land Title Co., 507 F.2d 895 (9th Cir. 1974).
157. See, e.g., Willingham v. Macon Tel. Publ'g Co., 507 F.2d 1084 (5th Cir. 1975).

The plaintiff, Darlene Jespersen, was terminated from her position as a bartender at the sports bar in Harrah's Reno casino not long after Harrah's began to enforce its comprehensive uniform, appearance and grooming standards for all bartenders. The standards required all bartenders, men and women, to wear the same uniform of black pants and white shirts, a bow tie, and comfortable black shoes. The standards also included grooming requirements that differed to some extent for men and women, requiring women to wear some facial makeup and not permitting men to wear any. Jespersen refused to comply with the makeup requirement and was effectively terminated for that reason.

The district court granted summary judgment to Harrah's on the ground that the appearance and grooming policies imposed equal burdens on both men and women bartenders because, while women were required to use makeup and men were forbidden to wear makeup, women were allowed to have long hair and men were required to have their hair cut to a length above the collar. The district court also held that the policy could not run afoul of Title VII because it did not discriminate against Jespersen on the basis of the "immutable characteristics" of her sex. The district court further observed that the Supreme Court's decision in *Price Waterhouse v. Hopkins*, prohibiting discrimination on the basis of sex stereotyping, did not apply to this case because in the district court's view, the Ninth Circuit had excluded grooming standards from the reach of *Price Waterhouse*. The district court granted summary judgment to Harrah's on all claims. [The en banc court affirmed.]

I. Background

Plaintiff Darlene Jespersen worked successfully as a bartender at Harrah's for twenty years and compiled what by all accounts was an exemplary record. During Jespersen's entire tenure with Harrah's, the company maintained a policy encouraging female beverage servers to wear makeup. The parties agree, however, that the policy was not enforced until 2000. In February 2000, Harrah's implemented a "Beverage Department Image Transformation" program at twenty Harrah's locations, including its casino in Reno. Part of the program consisted of new grooming and appearance standards, called the "Personal Best" program. The program contained certain appearance standards that applied equally to both sexes, including a standard uniform of black pants, white shirt, black vest, and black bow tie. Jespersen has never objected to any of these policies. The program also contained some sex-differentiated appearance requirements as to hair, nails, and makeup.

In April 2000, Harrah's amended that policy to require that women wear makeup. Jespersen's only objection here is to the makeup requirement. The amended policy provided in relevant part (emphasis added):

All Beverage Service Personnel, in addition to being friendly, polite, courteous and responsive to our customer's needs, must possess the ability to physically perform the essential factors of the job as set forth in the standard job descriptions. They must be well groomed, appealing to the eye, be firm and body toned, and be comfortable with maintaining this look while wearing the specified uniform. Additional factors to be considered include, but are not limited to, hair styles, overall body contour, and degree of comfort the employee projects while wearing the uniform. . . .

Beverage Bartenders and Barbacks will adhere to these additional guidelines:

Overall Guidelines (applied equally to male/female):

> Appearance: Must maintain Personal Best image portrayed at time of hire.
>
> Jewelry, if issued, must be worn. Otherwise, tasteful and simple jewelry is permitted; no large chokers, chains or bracelets.
>
> No faddish hairstyles or unnatural colors are permitted.

Males:

> Hair must not extend below top of shirt collar. Ponytails are prohibited.
>
> Hands and fingernails must be clean and nails neatly trimmed at all times. No colored polish is permitted.
>
> Eye and facial makeup is not permitted. . . .
>
> Shoes will be solid black leather or leather type with rubber (non skid) soles.

Females:

> Hair must be teased, curled, or styled every day you work. Hair must be worn down at all times, no exceptions.
>
> Stockings are to be of nude or natural color consistent with employee's skin tone. No runs.
>
> Nail polish can be clear, white, pink or red color only. No exotic nail art or length. . . .
>
> Shoes will be solid black leather or leather type with rubber (non skid) soles.
>
> *Make up (face powder, blush and mascara) must be worn and applied neatly in complimentary colors. Lip color must be worn at all times.*

Jespersen did not wear makeup on or off the job, and in her deposition stated that wearing it would conflict with her self-image. It is not disputed that she found the makeup requirement offensive, and felt so uncomfortable wearing makeup that she found it interfered with her ability to perform as a bartender. Unwilling to wear the makeup, and not qualifying for any open positions at the casino with a similar compensation scale, Jespersen left her employment with Harrah's.

. . . In her complaint, Jespersen sought damages as well as declaratory and injunctive relief for discrimination and retaliation for opposition to discrimination, alleging that the "Personal Best" policy discriminated against women by "(1) subjecting them to terms and conditions of employment to which men are not similarly subjected, and (2) requiring that women conform to sex-based stereotypes as a term and condition of employment."

Harrah's moved for summary judgment, supporting its motion with documents giving the history and purpose of the appearance and grooming policies. Harrah's argued that the policy created similar standards for both men and women, and that where the standards differentiated on the basis of sex, as with the face and hair standards, any burdens imposed fell equally on both male and female bartenders.

In her deposition testimony, attached as a response to the motion for summary judgment, Jespersen described the personal indignity she felt as a result of attempting to comply with the makeup policy. Jespersen testified that when she wore the makeup she "felt very degraded and very demeaned." In addition, Jespersen testified that "it prohibited [her] from doing [her] job" because "it affected [her] self-dignity . . . [and] took away [her] credibility as an individual and as a person." . . .

The record therefore does not contain any affidavit or other evidence to establish that complying with the "Personal Best" standards caused burdens to fall unequally on men or women, and there is no evidence to suggest Harrah's motivation was to stereotype the women bartenders. Jespersen relied solely on evidence that she had been a good bartender, and that she had personal objections to complying with the policy, in order to support her argument that Harrah's " 'sells' and exploits its women employees." Jespersen contended that as a matter of law she had made a prima facie showing of gender discrimination, sufficient to survive summary judgment on both of her claims.

II. Unequal Burdens

. . . [T]his case involves an appearance policy that applied to both male and female bartenders, and was aimed at creating a professional and very similar look for all of them. All bartenders wore the same uniform. The policy only differentiated as to grooming standards.

In Frank v. United Airlines, Inc. [2000], we dealt with a weight policy that applied different standards to men and women in a facially unequal way. The women were forced to meet the requirements of a medium body frame standard while men were required to meet only the more generous requirements of a large body frame standard. In that case, we recognized that "an appearance standard that imposes different but essentially equal burdens on men and women is not disparate treatment." The United weight policy, however, did not impose equal burdens. On its face, the policy embodied a requirement that categorically " 'applied less favorably to one gender[,]' " and the burdens imposed upon that gender were obvious from the policy itself.

This case stands in marked contrast, for here we deal with requirements that, on their face, are not more onerous for one gender than the other. Rather, Harrah's "Personal Best" policy contains sex-differentiated requirements regarding each employee's hair, hands, and face. While those individual requirements differ according to gender, none on its face places a greater burden on one gender than the other. Grooming standards that appropriately differentiate between the genders are not facially discriminatory. . . .

Not every differentiation between the sexes in a grooming and appearance policy creates a "significantly greater burden of compliance." For example, . . . this court upheld Safeway's enforcement of its sex-differentiated appearance standard, including its requirement that male employees wear ties, because the company's actions in enforcing the regulations were not "overly burdensome to its employees." Similarly, as the Eighth Circuit has recognized, "where, as here, such [grooming and appearance] policies are reasonable and are imposed in an evenhanded manner on all employees, slight differences in the appearance requirements for males and females have only a negligible effect on employment opportunities." . . .

Jespersen asks us to take judicial notice of the fact that it costs more money and takes more time for a woman to comply with the makeup requirement than it takes for a man to comply with the requirement that he keep his hair short, but these are not matters appropriate for judicial notice. . . .

. . . Jespersen did not submit any documentation or any evidence of the relative cost and time required to comply with the grooming requirements by men and women. As a result, we would have to speculate about those issues in order to then guess whether the policy creates unequal burdens for women. This would not be appropriate.

III. Sex Stereotyping

In *Price Waterhouse*, the Supreme Court considered a mixed-motive discrimination case. There, the plaintiff, Ann Hopkins, was denied partnership in the national accounting firm of Price Waterhouse because some of the partners found her to be too aggressive. While some partners praised Hopkins's " 'strong character, independence and integrity,' " others commented that she needed to take "a course at charm school" . . . .

The stereotyping in *Price Waterhouse* interfered with Hopkins' ability to perform her work; the advice that she should take "a course at charm school" was intended to discourage her use of the forceful and aggressive techniques that made her successful in the first place. Impermissible sex stereotyping was clear because the very traits that she was asked to hide were the same traits considered praiseworthy in men.

Harrah's "Personal Best" policy is very different. The policy does not single out Jespersen. It applies to all of the bartenders, male and female. It requires all of the bartenders to wear exactly the same uniforms while interacting with the public in the context of the entertainment industry. It is for the most part unisex, from the black tie to the non-skid shoes. There is no evidence in this record to indicate that the policy was adopted to make women bartenders conform to a commonly accepted stereotypical image of what women should wear. The record contains nothing to suggest the grooming standards would objectively inhibit a woman's ability to do the job. The only evidence in the record to support the stereotyping claim is Jespersen's own subjective reaction to the makeup requirement.

Judge Pregerson's dissent improperly divides the grooming policy into separate categories of hair, hands, and face, and then focuses exclusively on the makeup requirement to conclude that the policy constitutes sex stereotyping. This parsing, however, conflicts with established grooming standards analysis. . . . The requirements must be viewed in the context of the overall policy. The dissent's conclusion that the unequal burdens analysis allows impermissible sex stereotyping to persist if imposed equally on both sexes . . . is wrong because it ignores the protections of *Price Waterhouse* our decision preserves. If a grooming standard imposed on either sex amounts to impermissible stereotyping, something this record does not establish, a plaintiff of either sex may challenge that requirement under *Price Waterhouse*.

We respect Jespersen's resolve to be true to herself and to the image that she wishes to project to the world. We cannot agree, however, that her objection to the makeup requirement, without more, can give rise to a claim of sex stereotyping under Title VII. If we were to do so, we would come perilously close to holding that every grooming, apparel, or appearance requirement that an individual finds personally offensive, or in conflict with his or her own self-image, can create a triable issue of sex discrimination.

This is not a case where the dress or appearance requirement is intended to be sexually provocative, and tending to stereotype women as sex objects. The "Personal Best" policy does not, on its face, indicate any discriminatory or sexually stereotypical intent on the part of Harrah's. . . . Jespersen's claim here materially differs from Hopkins' claim in *Price Waterhouse* because Harrah's grooming standards do not require Jespersen to conform to a stereotypical image that would objectively impede her ability to perform her job requirements as a bartender.

We emphasize that we do not preclude, as a matter of law, a claim of sex stereotyping on the basis of dress or appearance codes. Others may well be filed, and any bases for such claims refined as law in this area evolves. This record, however, is devoid of any basis for permitting this particular claim to go forward, as it is limited to the subjective reaction of a single employee, and

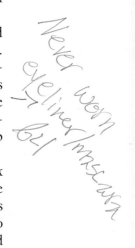

Never worn eyeliner/mascara
by/

there is no evidence of a stereotypical motivation on the part of the employer. This case is essentially a challenge to one small part of what is an overall apparel, appearance, and grooming policy that applies largely the same requirements to both men and women. . . . [T]he touchstone is reasonableness. A makeup requirement must be seen in the context of the overall standards imposed on employees in a given workplace.

Pregerson, Circuit Judge, with whom Judges Kozinski, Graber, and W. Fletcher join, dissenting:

. . . I believe that the "Personal Best" program was part of a policy motivated by sex stereotyping and that Jespersen's termination for failing to comply with the program's requirements was "because of" her sex. Accordingly, I dissent from Part III of the majority opinion and from the judgment of the court.

The majority contends that it is bound to reject Jespersen's sex stereotyping claim because she presented too little evidence—only her "own subjective reaction to the makeup requirement." I disagree. Jespersen's evidence showed that Harrah's fired her because she did not comply with a grooming policy that imposed a facial uniform (full makeup) on only female bartenders. Harrah's stringent "Personal Best" policy required female beverage servers to wear foundation, blush, mascara, and lip color, and to ensure that lip color was on at all times. Jespersen and her female colleagues were required to meet with professional image consultants who in turn created a facial template for each woman. Jespersen was required not simply to wear makeup; in addition, the consultants dictated where and how the makeup had to be applied. . . .

This policy did not, as the majority suggests, impose a "grooming, apparel, or appearance requirement that an individual finds personally offensive," but rather one that treated Jespersen differently from male bartenders "because of" her sex. I believe that the fact that Harrah's designed and promoted a policy that required women to conform to a sex stereotype by wearing full makeup is sufficient "direct evidence" of discrimination.

The majority contends that Harrah's "Personal Best" appearance policy is very different from the policy at issue in *Price Waterhouse* in that it applies to both men and women. . . . The fact that a policy contains sex-differentiated requirements that affect people of both genders cannot excuse a particular requirement from scrutiny. By refusing to consider the makeup requirement separately, and instead stressing that the policy contained some gender-neutral requirements, such as color of clothing, as well as a variety of gender-differentiated requirements for "hair, hands, and face," the majority's approach would permit otherwise impermissible gender stereotypes to be neutralized by the presence of a stereotype or burden that affects people of the opposite gender, or by some separate non-discriminatory requirement that applies to both men and women. . . . But the fact that employees of both genders are subjected to gender-specific requirements does not necessarily mean that particular requirements are not motivated by gender stereotyping.

Because I believe that we should be careful not to insulate appearance requirements by viewing them in broad categories, such as "hair, hands, and face," I would consider the makeup requirement on its own terms. Viewed in isolation—or, at the very least, as part of a narrower category of requirements affecting employees' faces—the makeup or facial uniform requirement becomes closely analogous to the uniform policy held to constitute impermissible sex stereotyping in Carroll v. Talman Federal Savings & Loan Ass'n of Chicago, [1979]. In *Carroll*, the defendant bank required women to wear employer-issued uniforms, but permitted men to wear business attire of their own choosing. The Seventh Circuit found this rule discriminatory because it suggested to the public that the uniformed women held a "lesser professional status" and that women could not be trusted to choose appropriate business attire.

Just as the bank in *Carroll* deemed female employees incapable of achieving a professional appearance without assigned uniforms, Harrah's regarded women as unable to achieve a neat, attractive, and professional appearance without the facial uniform designed by a consultant and required by Harrah's. The inescapable message is that women's undoctored faces compare unfavorably to men's, not because of a physical difference between men's and women's faces, but because of a cultural assumption—and gender-based stereotype—that women's faces are incomplete, unattractive, or unprofessional without full makeup. We need not denounce all makeup as inherently offensive, just as there was no need to denounce all uniforms as inherently offensive in *Carroll*, to conclude that *requiring* female bartenders to wear full makeup is an impermissible sex stereotype and is evidence of discrimination because of sex. Therefore, I strongly disagree with the majority's conclusion that there "is no evidence in this record to indicate that the policy was adopted to make women bartenders conform to a commonly-accepted stereotypical image of what women should wear."

I believe that Jespersen articulated a classic case of *Price Waterhouse* discrimination and presented undisputed, material facts sufficient to avoid summary judgment. Accordingly, Jespersen should be allowed to present her case to a jury.

KOZINSKI, Circuit Judge, with whom Judges GRABER and W. FLETCHER join, dissenting:

I agree with Judge Pregerson and join his dissent—subject to one caveat: I believe that Jespersen also presented a triable issue of fact on the question of disparate burden.

The majority is right that "the [makeup] requirements must be viewed in the context of the overall policy." But I find it perfectly clear that Harrah's overall grooming policy is substantially more burdensome for women than for men. Every requirement that forces men to spend time or money on their appearance has a corresponding requirement that is as, or more, burdensome for women: short hair v. "teased, curled, or styled" hair; clean trimmed nails v. nail length and color requirements; black leather shoes v. black leather shoes. The requirement that women spend time and money applying full facial makeup has no corresponding requirement for men, making the "overall policy" more burdensome for the former than for the latter. The only question is how much.

It is true that Jespersen failed to present evidence about what it costs to buy makeup and how long it takes to apply it. But is there any doubt that putting on makeup costs money and takes time? Harrah's policy requires women to apply face powder, blush, mascara and lipstick. You don't need an expert witness to figure out that such items don't grow on trees.

Nor is there any rational doubt that application of makeup is an intricate and painstaking process that requires considerable time and care. Even those of us who don't wear makeup know how long it can take from the hundreds of hours we've spent over the years frantically tapping our toes and pointing to our wrists. It's hard to imagine that a woman could "put on her face," as they say, in the time it would take a man to shave — certainly not if she were to do the careful and thorough job Harrah's expects. Makeup, moreover, must be applied and removed every day; the policy burdens men with no such daily ritual. While a man could jog to the casino, slip into his uniform, and get right to work, a woman must travel to work so as to avoid smearing her makeup, or arrive early to put on her makeup there.

It might have been tidier if Jespersen had introduced evidence as to the time and cost associated with complying with the makeup requirement, but I can understand her failure to do so, as these hardly seem like questions reasonably subject to dispute. We could — and should — take judicial notice of these incontrovertible facts.

Alternatively, Jespersen did introduce evidence that she finds it burdensome to *wear* makeup because doing so is inconsistent with her self-image and interferes with her job performance. My colleagues dismiss this evidence, apparently on the ground that wearing makeup does not, as a matter of law, constitute a substantial burden. This presupposes that Jespersen is unreasonable or idiosyncratic in her discomfort. Why so? Whether to wear cosmetics — literally, the face one presents to the world — is an intensely personal choice. Makeup, moreover, touches delicate parts of the anatomy — the lips, the eyes, the cheeks — and can cause serious discomfort, sometimes even allergic reactions, for someone unaccustomed to wearing it. If you are used to wearing makeup — as most American women are — this may seem like no big deal. But those of us not used to wearing makeup would find a requirement that we do so highly intrusive. Imagine, for example, a rule that all judges wear face powder, blush, mascara and lipstick while on the bench. Like Jespersen, I would find such a regime burdensome and demeaning; it would interfere with my job performance. I suspect many of my colleagues would feel the same way.

Everyone accepts this as a reasonable reaction from a man, but why should it be different for a woman? It is not because of anatomical differences, such as a requirement that women wear bathing suits that cover their breasts. Women's faces, just like those of men, can be perfectly presentable without makeup; it is a cultural artifact that most women raised in the United States learn to put on—and presumably enjoy wearing—cosmetics. But cultural norms change; . . . a large (and perhaps growing) number of women choose to present themselves to the world without makeup. I see no justification for forcing them to conform to Harrah's quaint notion of what a "real woman" looks like.

Nor do I think it appropriate for a court to dismiss a woman's testimony that she finds wearing makeup degrading and intrusive, as Jespersen clearly does. Not only do we have her sworn statement to that effect, but there can be no doubt about her sincerity or the intensity of her feelings: She quit her job—a job she performed well for two decades—rather than put on the makeup. That is a choice her male colleagues were not forced to make. To me, this states a case of disparate burden, and I would let a jury decide whether an employer can force a woman to make this choice.

Finally, I note with dismay the employer's decision to let go a valued, experienced employee who had gained accolades from her customers, over what, in the end, is a trivial matter. Quality employees are difficult to find in any industry and I would think an employer would long hesitate before forcing a loyal, long-time employee to quit over an honest and heart-felt difference of opinion about a matter of personal significance to her. Having won the legal battle, I hope that Harrah's will now do the generous and decent thing by offering Jespersen her job back, and letting her give it her personal best—without the makeup.

Notes

1. Dress, Appearance, and Judicial Ideology. The lineup of votes in *Jespersen* is somewhat surprising. Judge Mary Schroeder, who wrote the majority decision, is widely viewed as liberal, while Judge Alex Kozinski, one of the nation's most prominent conservative judges, dissented. Some have speculated that Schroeder was aware that Jespersen would lose and voted with the majority in order to assign herself the opinion and to minimize its negative impact on discrimination law. Others have suggested that she decided that the burdens involved were relatively trivial and wanted to discourage comparable litigation. If either of those reasons is true, how would you evaluate it? Is your view affected by research finding that although Harrah's changed its policy, the decision has not significantly influenced practices in the casino industry and has not triggered further lawsuits? Part of the reason is that female work-ers generally see makeup as a way to ensure good tips, and lawyers do not believe these cases are sufficiently remunerative to file.[158]

2. The Importance of Appearance. Beauty may be only "skin deep," but that is deep enough to confer significant advantages.[159] Attractive indi-viduals are more likely to be hired and promoted, and it is estimated that they make 14 percent more per hour than their less attractive counterparts.[160] Even in fields like law, where appearance bears no obvious relation to job perfor-mance, one study found that attractive attorneys, regardless of qualification and experience, earned significantly more than their less attractive counter-parts, and that the disparity increases over time.[161] In a national poll, about 16 percent of individuals believed that they had been subject to appearance-related discrimination, a higher percentage than those in other polls reporting gender or racial discrimination (12 percent).[162]

What are the costs of appearance-related bias to employees, employers, and society generally? Are they justified or inevitable? Is a person's appearance something like intelligence, which produces different opportunities that we must simply accept? Or is it an unfair basis for discrimination that we should attempt to eliminate, as a matter of law? Does it matter that research shows that some appearance preferences such as facial symmetry and unblemished skin appear to be innate?[163] If so, should it matter that the "in-group" pref-erences underlying racial and ethnic discrimination also appear to be hard-wired? Should we expect employers to avoid using attractiveness as a proxy for effective job performance?

158. Tracey E. George et al., The New Old Legal Realism, 105 Nw. L. Rev. 689, 715-16, 723, 727 (2011) (noting lack of change in practice); Deborah L. Rhode, The Beauty Bias 14 (2010) (noting change in Harrah's policy).

159. See Rhode, Beauty Bias, supra note 158, at 23-44; Daniel S. Hamermesh, Beauty Pays (2011).

160. See the studies reviewed in Deborah L. Rhode, The Injustice of Appearance, 61 Stan. L. Rev. 1033, 1038-39 (2009); Megumi Hosoda et al., The Effects of Physical Attrac-tiveness on Job Related Outcomes: A Meta-Analysis of Experimental Studies, 56 Personnel Psychol. 431 (2003); Kristie M. Engemann & Michael T. Owyang, So Much for That Merit Raise: The Link Between Wages and Appearance, Q. Rev. Bus. & Econ. Conditions 10 (Apr. 2005) (14 percent estimate).

161. See Jeff E. Biddle & Daniel S. Hamermesh, Beauty, Productivity and Discrimina-tion: Lawyers' Looks and Lucre, 16 J. Lab. Econ. 172, 185-90 (1998). For a general account of the importance of appearance for women lawyers, see Peggy Li, Physical Attractiveness and Femininity: Helpful or Hurtful for Female Attorneys, 47 Akron L. Rev. 997 (2015).

162. See polls cited in Rhode, The Injustice of Appearance, supra note 160, at 1068-69.

163. See Nancy Etcoff, Survival of the Prettiest: The Science of Beauty 31-32 (1999) (describing study of babies).

3. Legal Standards. The unequal burden test endorsed in the *Jespersen* test marks an advance over prior law, which saw grooming codes as neutral and acceptable as long as they merely reflected "community standards." Commentators often had pointed out that reliance on community standards, discussed further below, only served to reinforce the very stereotypes that Title VII was intended to eliminate.[164] Does the unequal burden test do much better? What would Jespersen have needed to show to demonstrate that the makeup requirement imposed an unequal burden on women? Couldn't a court take judicial notice of the fact that cosmetics don't grow on trees and that it takes time to style hair? Does the equal burden test capture all that is objectionable in Harrah's policy? Consider Rhode's claim:

> The problem with this prevailing approach to appearance regulation is not only that judges often seem clueless about the disproportionate demands that many codes impose on women. The difficulty is also that a framework comparing male and female burdens fails to capture all of what makes these regulations objectionable. Darlene Jespersen resisted Harrah's makeup requirement not because it took more time and money for her to be presentable than her male counterparts, but because she felt that being "dolled up" was degrading and undermined her credibility with unruly customers. Dress codes that require women to wear skirts and high heels are problematic for similar reasons, regardless of what the codes demand of men.[165]

In Rhode's view,

> [j]ustifications for banning appearance discrimination rest on three basic claims. The first is that such discrimination offends principles of equal opportunity; individuals should be judged on merit and performance, not irrelevant physical characteristics. A second rationale is that appearance-related bias reinforces group subordination; it exacerbates disadvantages based on gender, race, ethnicity, class, age, and sexual orientation. A third justification is that some decisions based on appearance unduly restrict self-expression and cultural identity. Although opponents of prohibiting appearance discrimination raise some legitimate concerns, these can be met through well-designed statutory schemes. The excessive liability and business backlash that critics have predicted have not in fact materialized in the few jurisdictions that have prohibited appearance-related bias.[166]

What is your view? Should judges take a less permissive view toward appearance discrimination? In general, courts have upheld sex-specific requirements even when the standards are stricter or more burdensome for one sex

---

164. See, e.g., Katharine T. Bartlett, Only Girls Wear Barrettes: Dress and Appearance Standards, Community Norms, and Workplace Equality, 92 Mich. L. Rev. 2541 (1994).

165. Rhode, Beauty Bias, supra note 158, at 121.

166. Id. at 93.

(although not when they also discriminate by race).[167] Are these rulings defensible? What would happen in most workplaces if courts held that sex-specific grooming codes constituted unlawful discrimination? Would it have a major effect on dress and grooming practices? Would there be any significant negative consequences?

Plaintiffs' claims that they were discriminated against for being too attractive and dressing too sexily have also been largely unsuccessful.[168] However, a few courts have been willing to see standards of attractiveness as a form of sex stereotyping. In Lewis v. Heartland Inns of America, the Eighth Circuit Court of Appeals found that the plaintiff had established a prima facie case of sex discrimination based on allegations that she had lost her position as a front desk hotel clerk because she was not "pretty," and lacked the "Midwestern girl look."[169]

Why do organizations want to control the appearance of their employees? Ordinarily, a business cannot discriminate on the basis of race, sex, or other prohibited factors just because customers may prefer it. The reasons are obvious, and explored more fully in Wilson v. Southwest Airlines, discussed below. Often these preferences reflect precisely the biases that antidiscrimination laws seek to address. Are dress and appearance standards just a version of this? A highly publicized example is the 1983 case of Craft v. Metromedia, Inc.[170] There, a local television station anchorwoman, Christine Craft, filed suit against her employer after she was moved to an off-camera position because producers found her hair and makeup to be inappropriate. Craft claimed that she was judged by harsher standards than male anchors. The station responded with audience research including focus groups and a telephone survey, which showed that the plaintiff's appearance had an adverse impact on her acceptance among viewers. The court determined that she was properly reassigned due to the demonstrated negative viewer response.[171] By that logic, could television stations require that female but not male anchors look young and attractive because viewers will accept a Bill O'Reilly but not his female equivalent?

---

167. See, e.g., Schiavo v. Marina Dist. Dev. Co., 123 A.3d 272 (N.J. Super. Ct. 2015); Jordan D. Bello, Attractiveness as a Hiring Criteria: Savvy Business Practice or Racial Discrimination, 8 J. Gender, Race & Just. 483, 483 (2004). Abercrombie & Fitch ultimately settled a case charging discrimination based on its policy of hiring attractive "All American" white sales personnel. Steven Greenhouse, Abercrombie & Fitch Bias Case Is Settled, N.Y. Times, Nov. 17, 2004, at A16.

168. See Goodwin v. Harvard Coll., JVR No. 806230, 2005 WL 4256570 (D. Mass. May 17, 2005).

169. 591 F.3d 1033, 1036 (2010).

170. 572 F. Supp. 868 (W.D. Mo. 1983), rev'd in part, 766 F.2d 1205 (8th Cir. 1985).

171. For Craft's own account of her experience, see Christine Craft, Too Old, Too Ugly, and Not Deferential to Men (1988).

One problem with such double standards is that they can become self-perpetuating. Viewers may expect youth and beauty in female newscasters partly because they lack exposure to an alternative—women who gained their position through merit-related qualifications. Reconsider how to approach this question after reading Wilson v. Southwest Airlines.

In December 2015, the New York City Commission on Human Rights announced new guidelines for the municipal human rights law that expressly prohibits "enforcing dress codes, uniforms, and grooming standards that impose different requirements based on sex and gender."[172] Is this blanket prohibition the right approach?

4. Weight. One of the most common forms of appearance discrimination concerns weight. A wide array of research finds that women are judged more harshly than men for being overweight, that a majority of overweight women report experiencing discrimination, and that those who are obese or significantly overweight earn less than average-sized women.[173] Because being overweight is most common in African-American and low-income women, weight requirements have a disproportionate impact based on race and class.

Weight limits have been a common appearance requirement in some occupations. Flight attendants have been the most widely noted examples. Courts initially upheld strict restrictions even when the standards for men took into account large frame sizes while the standards for women presupposed small or medium builds. One court relied on the "fact" that the weight restrictions for women did not concern an "immutable characteristic": Weight, unlike height, is subject to the "reasonable control" of most individuals.[174] Frank v. United Airlines, Inc., cited in *Jespersen*, reversed such rulings. There, the Ninth Circuit Court of Appeals found that a policy permitting men's weight to vary within a broader range of frame sizes than women constituted unlawful sex discrimination.

Despite the commonly held view that weight is a matter of personal choice and self-discipline, a wide array of research indicates that body size is influenced by genetic and environmental factors and that over 90 percent of individuals are unable to achieve long-term weight loss through dieting.[175]

172 Vanessa Friedman, The End of the Office Dress Code, N.Y. Times, May 25, 2016.

173. Rhode, The Injustice of Appearance, supra note 160, at 1039; Dalton Conley & Rebecca Glauber, Gender, Body Mass, and Socioeconomic Status: New Evidence from the PSID, 17 Advances in Health Econ. & Health Servs. 253 (2007) (finding that women earn 0.6% less family income for each 1 percent increase in body mass); John Cawley, The Impact of Obesity on Wages, 39 J. Hum. Res. 451, 468 (2004) (finding that obese women average 9 percent less per hour than average-sized women).

174. Jarrell v. Eastern Airlines, Inc., 430 F. Supp. 884, 892 (E.D. Va. 1977), aff'd mem., 577 F.2d 869 (4th Cir. 1978).

175. Sunaina Assanand et al., Personal Theories of Hunger and Eating, 28 J. Applied Soc. Psych. 998 (1998) (discussing popular assumptions). For the role of genetic and environmental factors, see Gina Kolata, Rethinking Thin (2007); John C. Peters et al., From Instinct

Should this matter, from a legal standpoint? Discrimination based on weight contributes to eating disorders, which disproportionately affect women and girls.[176] Over 90 percent of those suffering from anorexia or bulimia are female, although some recent research suggests that the problems are growing among men.[177] Should this matter, from a legal standpoint?

Some plaintiffs have successfully sued for weight discrimination under the federal Americans with Disabilities Act (ADA) and analogous state provisions. However, governing regulations under the ADA interpret the Act to cover only extremely severe obesity (100 percent over average weight) caused by a physiological disorder.[178] Although a few state and local ordinances offer broader coverage, the vast majority of individuals remain unprotected.[179]

In a widely publicized lawsuit against an Atlantic City casino, a number of "Borgata Babes" claimed, inter alia, that the defendant's Personal Appearance Standards were based on gender stereotypes and were not enforced as rigorously against men as against women.[180] The standards required that the plaintiff beverage servers not gain or lose more than 7 percent of their baseline weight—the weight at which they were hired. Undisputed evidence showed that over 20 women and no men were suspended for noncompliance with the weight policy, and that weight checks were much more common for women than men. The appellate court rejected the plaintiff's claim on the ground that "simple statistical disparities are insufficient to show that the weight standard was facially discriminatory."[181] Does this make sense? Although the court criticized the plaintiffs for relying on "sheer numbers," how else could they prove a disparate impact claim? Is it relevant that many women appear eager for jobs involving a sexualized appearance that generates high tips? Four thousand women applied for the first 200 Borgata Babes jobs.[182]

5. Laws Against Discrimination Based on Appearance. A few jurisdictions have specific prohibitions against appearance discrimination. Michigan and San Francisco ban discrimination based on height and weight. Local

to Intellect: The Challenge of Maintaining Healthy Weight in the Modern World, 3 Obesity Revs. 69, 70 (2002). On the ineffectiveness of diets, see Rhode, Injustice of Appearance, supra note 152, at 1042, 1063.

176. See Kathleen Zelman, More Men Facing Eating Disorders, WebMd (Oct. 25, 2005), http://www.cbsnews.com/stories/2005/10/25/health/webmd/main972825.shtml.

177. Id. (research shows that up to 25 percent of men are on diets at any given time).

178. 29 C.F.R. §1630 (2016).

179. Rhode, The Injustice of Appearance, supra note 152, at 1078-79; Elizabeth E. Theran, Legal Theory of Weight Discrimination, in Weight Bias: Nature, Consequences and Remedies 195, 206 (Kelly D. Brownell et al. eds., 2005).

180. Schiavo v. Marina Dist. Dev. Co., 123 A.3d 272 (N.J. Super. Ct. 2015), review denied, 123 A.3d 272 (N.J. 2016).

181. Id.

182. Joanna L. Grossman, Hit the Gym, BorgataBabes, Justia's Verdict (Sept. 29, 2015), http://verdict.justia.com/2015/09/29/hit-the-gym-borgatababes.

ordinances in Madison, Wisconsin; Urbana, Illinois; Santa Cruz, California; and Howard County, Maryland ban appearance discrimination more generally, although with certain exceptions such as for grooming requirements or for characteristics within an individual's control.[183]

Should more jurisdictions enact such prohibitions? In one opinion poll, 33 percent of Americans thought that laws should protect unattractive people from hiring discrimination, while 39 percent believed that employers should be allowed to discriminate based on appearance.[184] Scholars are also divided. Some worry that extending civil rights acts to such claims will erode support for such legislation and trivialize more serious forms of bias. Stanford law professor Richard Ford frames a common objection:

> [T]here are practical limits of human attention and sympathy. The good-natured humanitarian who listens attentively to the first claim of social injustice will become an impatient curmudgeon after multiple similar admonishments. . . . And a business community united in frustration at a bloated civil rights regime could become a powerful political force for reform or even repeal. . . . The growing number of social groups making claims to civil rights protection threatens the political and practical viability of civil rights for those who need them most.
>
> The law can identify a small set of social prejudices—race, sex, religion, national origin, age and disability—that are so unjustified and so socially destructive that we're confident that the benefits of prohibiting them outweigh the costs. . . . But there are limits. . . . It's a mistake to turn civil rights against truly invidious discrimination into an omnibus requirement that we reward intrinsic merit. . . . The fantastic aspiration to somehow make society perfectly "fair" through force of law reflects a dangerous combination of gauzy idealism, narcissistic entitlement and reckless hubris.[185]

Is this a fair point? One survey of appearance discrimination laws found no evidence of such backlash, but also highly limited enforcement activity, partly due to the costs and difficulties of proof and the limited remedies available. Such regulation did, however, remedy some of the worst abuses, increase complainants' bargaining leverage, and attract public attention to the problems.[186] The same appears true for the one other jurisdiction abroad,

---

183. For the impact of these laws, see Rhode, The Injustice of Appearance, supra note 160, at 1081-90. For further discussion of the problem of obesity discrimination, see Lucy Wang, Weight Discrimination: One Size Fits All Remedy?, 117 Yale L.J. 1900 (2008); Kari Horner, A Growing Problem: Why the Federal Government Needs to Shoulder the Burden in Protecting Workers from Weight Discrimination, 54 Cath. U. L. Rev. 589 (2005).

184. Press Release, Employment Law Alliance, National Poll Shows Public Opinion Sharply Divided on Regulating Appearance—From Weight to Tattoos—in the Workplace (Mar. 22, 2005), http://www.prnewswire.com/news-releases/national-poll-shows-public-opinion-sharply-divided-on-regulating-appearance-in-the-workplace-54313802.html.

185. Richard Ford, The Race Card 176-77 (2007).

186. Rhode, The Injustice of Appearance, supra note 160, at 1095-96.

Victoria, Australia, that explicitly prohibits appearance discrimination.[187] Is this an adequate justification for the laws? What other policy strategies might be useful? Would modifying employment-at-will doctrine to require just cause for dismissals or demotion be a partial solution?[188]

6. Sex and Age.   Sex and age can be a devastating combination particularly for women. Even in jobs where appearance is considered less important, older women earn lower salaries than men and younger women, and they may lack opportunities to obtain higher-paying and more prestigious jobs.[189] Older women's concerns about the economic and social consequences of "letting themselves go" is part of what has fueled the dramatic increase in cosmetic procedures. In 2014, Americans spent over 12 billion dollars on cosmetic treatments, and doctors performed twice as many procedures as in 2000.[190]

A few high-profile cases have produced successful verdicts for women claiming age and appearance discrimination.[191] In the Borgata Babes lawsuit, discussed above, cocktail servers, including women ages 54, 57, and 66, claimed that they had been dismissed after having to audition in "skimpy flapper" costumes. Gloria Allred, who represented the women, maintained that maybe owners believed that "they can profit by using young women as bait to hook in young men to buy drinks, but it's wrong. Women are not just sex objects."[192] One commentator responded, "The whole point of being a cocktail waitress in a casino is to be a sex object. . . . And eventually, grandma needs to take off the cocktail underwear."[193] Who is right?

7. Feminism and Appearance.   Issues of appearance have long been divisive issues for feminists. While some leaders of the women's movement have denounced makeup, high heels, and cosmetic surgery as forms of objectification and subordination, other feminists see them as a source of pleasure and agency. Where do you fall in this debate? Is there a way to find common

---

187. Rhode, The Beauty Bias, supra note 158, at 134-36.

188. William R. Corbett, Hotness Discrimination: Appearance Discrimination as a Mirror for Reflecting on the Body of Employment Discrimination Law, 60 Cath. U. L. Rev. 615, 657 (2011).

189. See Nicole Buonocore Porter, Sex Plus Age Discrimination: Protecting Older Women Workers, 81 Denv. U. L. Rev. 79, 94-99 (2003).

190. Joel Stein, Nip. Tuck. Or Else: Why You'll Be Getting Cosmetic Procedures Even if You Don't Really Want to, Time, June 29, 2015, 45. According to one researcher, cosmetic surgery has become the "new makeup." Id. (quoting Abigail Brooks).

191. See, e.g., Eduardo Porter, UBS Ordered to Pay $29 Million in Sex Bias Lawsuit, N.Y. Times, Apr. 15, 2005, at C4 (reporting on case against bank where plaintiff was called "old and ugly").

192. Elie Mystal, Women Are Not Sex Objects; Cocktail Waitresses, on the Other Hand . . . , Above the Law (May, 31, 2011), http://abovethelaw.com/2011/05/women-are-not-sex-objects-cocktail-waitresses-on-the-other-hand/ (quoting Allred).

193. Id.

ground by focusing not on individual practices but on social forces that shame and stigmatize women, and that fail to provide sufficient safeguards against unsafe or fraudulent cosmetic practices?[194] Consider Rhode's view:

> The overemphasis of attractiveness diminishes women's credibility and diverts attention from their capabilities and accomplishments. In the long run, these are more stable sources of self-esteem and social power than appearance. Prevailing beauty standards also place women in a double bind. They are expected to conform, yet condemned as vain and narcissistic for attempts to do so. Neither should they "let themselves go," nor look as if they were trying too hard not to. Beauty must seem natural, even, or especially, when it can only be accomplished through considerable unnatural effort . . . . Feminists are in a particularly problematic situation. Those who defy conventional standards are ridiculed as homely harpies; those who comply are dismissed as hypocrites.
>
> Whatever their other disagreements on these issues, most individuals appear to share certain core values. Appearance should be a source of pleasure, not of shame. Individuals should be able to make decisions about whether to enhance their attractiveness without being judged politically incorrect or professionally unacceptable. Our ideals of appearance should reflect diversity across race, ethnicity, age, and body size. In this ideal world, the importance of appearance would not be overstated. Nor would it spill over to employment and educational contexts in which judgments should be based on competence, not cosmetics. Women would not be held to higher standards than men. Neither would they be subject to sexualized grooming requirements unless sex is the commodity being sold. Women's self-esteem would be tied to accomplishment, not appearance. In order for appearance to be a source of enjoyment rather than anxiety, it cannot dictate women's self-worth.[195]

Do you agree? Is a unifying agenda for feminists possible on this issue? How important is it? Is fighting appearance discrimination a fruitless diversion from more important battles? Comedian Joan Rivers advised women "It's the way things are, accept it, or go live under a rock."[196] How would you respond?

Putting Theory Into Practice

1-20. Can a retail cosmetics saleswoman be fired for "not being hot enough"? What about a cocktail server?[197]

194. Rhode, The Beauty Bias, supra note 158, at 69-89.
195. Id. at 76, 87.
196. Emily Nussbaum, Last Girl in Larchmont, The New Yorker, Feb. 23 & Mar. 2, 2015, at 171 (quoting Rivers).
197. Yanowitz v. L'Oreal U.S.A., 131 Cal. Rptr. 2d 575, 588 (Cal. App. 2003); Gersh Kuntzman, Casino Gal's Fat Chance—Hotel's Waitress Rule: Gain Pounds, Lose a Job, N.Y. Post, Feb. 18, 2005, at 3.

1-21. A temp worker, Nicola Thorp, was sent home from at her receptionist job at PricewaterhouseCoopers in east London for wearing flat shoes,
rather than the two-inch to four-inch high heels required by her agency, Portico. "If you can give me a reason as to why wearing flats would impair me
to do my job today, then fair enough," she is reported as saying, "but they
couldn't. I was expected to do a nine-hour shift on my feet escorting clients
to meeting rooms. I said I just won't be able to do that in heels." Portico
responded, "In line with industry standard practice, we have personal appearance guidelines across many of our corporate locations. These policies ensure
staff are dressed consistently and include recommendations for appropriate
style of footwear for the role."[198]

Who prevails under U.S. law? Is it relevant to the law that 90 percent of
all forefoot surgery is performed on women, and that "seventy-five percent of
the problems eventuating in [the foot] corrections performed annually in the
United States either result from or are greatly aggravated by the use of high-
fashion footwear."[199] Or that, in addition to the adverse health consequences,
high heels have long been used as a symbol of idleness or, in Thorstein Veblen's
words, of "the wearer's abstinence from productive employment"?[200]

1-22. At the Seventh Circuit Annual Judicial Conference, some judges
complained of distracting attire—"blouses so short there's no way the judges
wouldn't look" and a velour outfit that looked as if the lawyer was "on her
way home from the gym."[201] Is it appropriate for firms to monitor what lawyers wear to court on the grounds that some judges have complained about
overly sexy or informal attire? Is it appropriate for judges to comment publicly
on women's attire?

1-23. Jazzercise refused a franchise to Jennifer Portnick, a 245-pound
aerobics instructor, on the ground that the company sold "fitness." According
to its lawyer, "One of the keys to success is extending franchises to instructors
with a fit, toned body. Being able to portray this image inspires students. The
fit and toned body image is a necessary part of what students seek to achieve."
Portnick was in fact fit. She worked out six days a week, taught back-to-back

---

198. Nadia Khomami, Receptionist "Sent Home from PwC for Not Wearing High Heels,"
The Guardian, May 11, 2016, http://www.theguardian.com/uk-news/2016/may/11/
receptionist-sent-home-pwc-not-wearing-high-heels-pwc-nicola-thorp. After Ms. Thorp started
a petition drive for a parliamentary hearing on the subject, Portico changed its policy. Id.

199. See Marc Linder, Smart Women, Stupid Shoes, and Cynical Employers: The Un-
lawfulness and Adverse Health Consequences of Sexually Discriminatory Workplace Footwear
Requirements for Female Employees, J. Corp. L. 295, 296 (Winter 1997).

200. Thorstein Veblen, The Theory of the Leisure Class: An Economic Study of Institutions 121 (1899).

201. John Schwartz, At a Symposium of Judges, a Debate on the Laws of Fashion, N.Y.
Times, May 23, 2009, at A10.

exercise classes, and had no history of performance problems or lack of students. Can she win a lawsuit against Jazzercise under San Francisco's ordinance banning discrimination based on height or weight, or does the company have a legitimate reason for refusing to be associated with an overweight instructor?[202]

1-24. In 2013, at a public event with California's Attorney General Kamala Harris, President Barack Obama stated, "You have to be careful to, first of all, say she is brilliant and she is dedicated and she is tough, and she is exactly what you'd want in anybody who is administering the law, and making sure that everybody is getting a fair shake. She also happens to be by far the best-looking attorney general in the country." When the crowd began laughing, Obama added, "It's true! C'mon."[203] Public outcry was immediate. Within hours, according to White House spokesperson Jay Carney, the President called Harris to apologize: "They are old friends and good friends and he did not want in any way to diminish the attorney general's professional accomplishments and her capabilities."[204]

Media commentary was mixed. In an article headlined, "Obama in Need of Gender Sensitivity Training," Jonathan Chait of *New York Magazine* claimed that Obama's comment "was not a compliment," and that the example he set was "disgraceful."[205] By contrast, Jonathan Capehart of the *Washington Post* commented, "Lighten up, people. You'd swear the President was guilty of luridly cat-calling a woman he doesn't know."[206] Similarly, Liza Minnelli didn't see anything wrong with Obama's compliment. After all, she pointed out, Harris was applying makeup and styling her hair in order to "be thought of as attractive. She's not doing that for no reason."[207]

If you were commenting on the incident, what would you say?

1-25. Middle and high school dress codes have become an increasing concern. A survey by the Gay, Lesbian and Straight Education Network found that almost one in five students reported being prevented from wearing clothing deemed inappropriate based on their gender.[208] In 2016, Fresno,

---

202. Letter from C. Robert Sturm, Law Firm of Littler Mendelson, to the San Francisco Commission on Human Rights, Oct. 26, 2001, at 6. The case was mediated to a successful resolution and the complaint dismissed.

203. Eun Kyungh Kim, Obama Apologizes to Kamala Harris for "Best Looking Attorney General" Comment, Today (Apr. 5, 2013) (quoting Obama).

204. Id. (quoting Carney).

205. Jonathan Chait, Obama in Need of Gender-Sensitivity Training, New York Magazine, Apr. 4, 2013.

206. Kim, supra note 203 (quoting Capehart).

207. Id. (quoting Minnelli).

208. Gay, Lesbian and Straight Education Network, the 2013 National School Climate Survey: The Experiences of Lesbian, Gay, Bisexual and Transgender Youth in Our Nation's Schools (2014).

California high school students came to school staged a protest after trustees retained a policy refusing to allow boys to have long hair and earrings, and restricting dresses and skirts to girls. Boys showed up at school wearing dresses.[209] Administrators claim that such codes are useful by focusing student attention on academic rather than appearance-related issues and that unconventional attire is distracting. How would you assess that argument? Should courts intervene? What if any dress code restrictions would you impose on middle and high school students?

1-26. Sarah Robles, who is 23 years old and weighs 275 pounds, is the highest-ranked weightlifter of either gender in the United States. Robles has had trouble gaining a corporate sponsor, requiring her to live on a subsistence allowance from the U.S. Weightlifting Federation while she trains for the 2016 Olympics. Critics claim that the lack of corporate support for Robles is due to her masculine appearance, pointing out that only female athletes who are feminine and attractive receive lucrative sponsorships (including two slimmer, though less accomplished, female weightlifters). Former professional basketball player Lisa Leslie appears in one Nike ad, stating "I'm a fashion model who can dunk."

Is it sex discrimination for corporations to support attractive female athletes and not unattractive ones? Should there be a law prohibiting corporations from engaging in this practice?

c. When Is Sex a "Bona Fide Occupational Qualification"?

Once plaintiffs demonstrate that they have been treated differently on the basis of sex, employers are liable under Title VII unless they can meet the high burden of showing that sex is a "bona fide occupational qualification," or BFOQ. For cases brought under the disparate impact theory of Title VII, the employer must meet the somewhat lower burden of "business necessity." Can you think of particular jobs where sex should be either a BFOQ or a business necessity?

≣
≣ *Dothard v. Rawlinson*
≣ **433 U.S. 321 (1977)**

Mr. Justice STEWART delivered the opinion of the Court.

Appellee Dianne Rawlinson sought employment with the Alabama Board of Corrections as a prison guard, called in Alabama a "correctional counselor."

---

209. Gabrielle Sorto, Student Protests Growing over Gender-Equal Dress Codes, CNN (Feb. 25, 2016), htt:www.cnn.com/2016/02/25/living/dress-code-protests-irpt/index.

Issue: Not hired @ Correctional facility

After her application was rejected, she brought this class suit under Title VII of the Civil Rights Act of 1964 . . . .

At the time she applied for a position as correctional counselor trainee, Rawlinson was a 22-year-old college graduate whose major course of study had been correctional psychology. She was refused employment because she failed to meet the minimum 120-pound weight requirement established by an Alabama statute. The statute also establishes a height minimum of 5 feet 2 inches. [Rawlinson subsequently amended her complaint to challenge Alabama Administrative Regulation 204 that established a "gender criteria" for assigning correctional counselors to "contact positions" requiring close physical proximity to inmates.] . . .

Gendered req.

Like most correctional facilities in the United States, Alabama's prisons are segregated on the basis of sex. . . . A correctional counselor's primary duty within these institutions is to maintain security and control of the inmates by continually supervising and observing their activities. . . .

At the time this litigation was in the District Court, the Board of Corrections employed a total of 435 people in various correctional counselor positions, 56 of whom were women. Of those 56 women, 21 were employed at the Julia Tutwiler Prison for Women, 13 were employed in noncontact positions at the four male maximum-security institutions, and the remaining 22 were employed at the other institutions operated by the Alabama Board of Corrections. Because most of Alabama's prisoners are held at the four maximum-security male penitentiaries, 336 of the 435 correctional counselor jobs were in those institutions, a majority of them concededly in the "contact" classification. Thus, even though meeting the statutory height and weight requirements, women applicants could under Regulation 204 compete equally with men for only about 25% of the correctional counselor jobs available in the Alabama prison system. . . .

It is asserted . . . that these facially neutral qualifications standards work . . . disproportionately to exclude women from eligibility for employment by the Alabama Board of Corrections. We dealt in Griggs v. Duke Power Co. [1971] [and other cases] with similar allegations that facially neutral employment standards disproportionately excluded Negroes from employment, and those cases guide our approach here.

Those cases make clear that to establish a prima facie case of discrimination, a plaintiff need only show that the facially neutral standards in question select applicants for hire in a significantly discriminatory pattern. Once it is thus shown that the employment standards are discriminatory in effect, the employer must meet "the burden of showing that any given requirement (has) . . . a manifest relationship to the employment in question [*Griggs*]." If the employer proves that the challenged requirements are job related, the plaintiff may then show that other selection devices without a similar discriminatory effect would also "serve the employer's legitimate interest in 'efficient and trustworthy workmanship.'" . . .

. . . In considering the effect of the minimum height and weight standards on this disparity in rate of hiring between the sexes, the District Court found that . . . [w]hen the height and weight restrictions are combined, Alabama's statutory standards would exclude 41.13% of the female population while excluding less than 1% of the male population. Accordingly, the District Court found that Rawlinson had made out a prima facie case of unlawful sex discrimination.

The appellants argue that a showing of disproportionate impact on women based on generalized national statistics should not suffice to establish a prima facie case. They point in particular to Rawlinson's failure to adduce comparative statistics concerning actual applicants for correctional counselor positions in Alabama. There is no requirement, however, that a statistical showing of disproportionate impact must always be based on analysis of the characteristics of actual applicants. . . . The application process might itself not adequately reflect the actual potential applicant pool, since otherwise qualified people might be discouraged from applying because of a self-recognized inability to meet the very standards challenged as being discriminatory. . . . A potential applicant could easily determine her height and weight and conclude that to make an application would be futile. Moreover, reliance on general population demographic data was not misplaced where there was no reason to suppose that physical height and weight characteristics of Alabama men and women differ markedly from those of the national population.

For these reasons, we cannot say that the District Court was wrong in holding that the statutory height and weight standards had a discriminatory impact on women applicants. . . .

We turn, therefore, to the appellants' argument that they have rebutted the prima facie case of discrimination by showing that the height and weight requirements are job related. These requirements, they say, have a relationship to strength, a sufficient but unspecified amount of which is essential to effective job performance as a correctional counselor. In the District Court, however, the appellants produced no evidence correlating the height and weight requirements with the requisite amount of strength thought essential to good job performance. Indeed, they failed to offer evidence of any kind in specific justification of the statutory standards. . . .

[T]he District Court was not in error in holding that Title VII . . . prohibits application of the statutory height and weight requirements to Rawlinson and the class she represents.

III

Unlike the statutory height and weight requirements, Regulation 204 [excluding women from maximum security "contact positions"] explicitly discriminates against women on the basis of their sex. In defense of this overt discrimination, the appellants rely on [Title VII's BFOQ defense], which permits sex-based discrimination "in those certain instances where . . . sex . . . is a bona fide occupational qualification reasonably necessary to the normal operation of that particular business or enterprise." . . .

We are persuaded by the restrictive language of [Title VII], the relevant legislative history, and the consistent interpretation of the Equal Employment Opportunity Commission that the BFOQ exception was in fact meant to be an extremely narrow exception to the general prohibition of discrimination on the basis of sex. In the particular factual circumstances of this case, however, we conclude that the District Court erred in rejecting the State's contention that Regulation 204 falls within the narrow ambit of the BFOQ exception.

The environment in Alabama's penitentiaries is a peculiarly inhospitable one for human beings of whatever sex. Indeed, a Federal District Court has held that the conditions of confinement in the prisons of the State, characterized by "rampant violence" and a "jungle atmosphere," are constitutionally intolerable. . . . The record in the present case shows that because of inadequate staff and facilities, no attempt is made in the four maximum-security male penitentiaries to classify or segregate inmates according to their offense or level of dangerousness—a procedure that, according to expert testimony, is essential to effective penological administration. Consequently, the estimated 20% of the male prisoners who are sex offenders are scattered throughout the penitentiaries' dormitory facilities.

In this environment of violence and disorganization, it would be an oversimplification to characterize Regulation 204 as an exercise in "romantic paternalism." [Frontiero v. Richardson.] In the usual case, the argument that a particular job is too dangerous for women may appropriately be met by the rejoinder that it is the purpose of Title VII to allow the individual woman to make that choice for herself. More is at stake in this case, however, than an individual woman's decision to weigh and accept the risks of employment in a "contact" position in a maximum-security male prison.

The essence of a correctional counselor's job is to maintain prison security. A woman's relative ability to maintain order in a male, maximum-security, unclassified penitentiary of the type Alabama now runs could be directly reduced by her womanhood. There is a basis in fact for expecting that sex offenders who have criminally assaulted women in the past would be moved to do so again if access to women were established within the prison. There would also be a real risk that other inmates, deprived of a normal heterosexual environment, would assault women guards because they were women.[22] In a prison system where violence is the order of the day, where inmate access to guards is facilitated by dormitory living arrangements, where every institution

22. The record contains evidence of an attack on a female clerical worker in an Alabama prison, and of an incident involving a woman student who was taken hostage during a visit to one of the maximum-security institutions.

is understaffed, and where a substantial portion of the inmate population is composed of sex offenders mixed at random with other prisoners, there are few visible deterrents to inmate assaults on women custodians.

Appellee Rawlinson's own expert testified that dormitory housing for aggressive inmates poses a greater security problem than single-cell lockups, and further testified that it would be unwise to use women as guards in a prison where even 10% of the inmates had been convicted of sex crimes and were not segregated from the other prisoners. The likelihood that inmates would assault a woman because she was a woman would pose a real threat not only to the victim of the assault but also to the basic control of the penitentiary and protection of its inmates and the other security personnel. The employee's very womanhood would thus directly undermine her capacity to provide the security that is the essence of a correctional counselor's responsibility. . . .

The judgment is accordingly affirmed in part and reversed in part, and the case is remanded to the District Court for further proceedings consistent with this opinion. . . .

Mr. Justice MARSHALL, with whom Mr. Justice BRENNAN joins, concurring in part and dissenting in part. . . .

The Court properly rejects two proffered justifications for denying women jobs as prison guards. It is simply irrelevant here that a guard's occupation is dangerous and that some women might be unable to protect themselves adequately. Those themes permeate the testimony of the state officials below, but as the Court holds, "the argument that a particular job is too dangerous for women" is refuted by the "purpose of Title VII to allow the individual woman to make that choice for herself." . . . Some women, like some men, undoubtedly are not qualified and do not wish to serve as prison guards, but that does not justify the exclusion of all women from this employment opportunity. . . .

What would otherwise be considered unlawful discrimination against women is justified by the Court, however, on the basis of the "barbaric and inhumane" conditions in Alabama prisons, conditions so bad that state officials have conceded that they violate the Constitution. . . . To me, this analysis sounds distressingly like saying two wrongs make a right. It is refuted by the plain words of [Title VII, which] requires that a BFOQ be "reasonably necessary to the normal operation of that particular business or enterprise." But no governmental "business" may operate "normally" in violation of the Constitution. . . .

The Court's error in statutory construction is less objectionable, however, than the attitude it displays toward women. Though the Court recognizes that possible harm to women guards is an unacceptable reason for disqualifying women, it relies instead on an equally speculative threat to prison discipline supposedly generated by the sexuality of female guards. There is simply no evidence in the record to show that women guards would create any danger to security in Alabama prisons significantly greater than that which already exists. All of the dangers with one exception discussed below are inherent in a prison setting, whatever the gender of the guards.

The Court first sees women guards as a threat to security because "there are few visible deterrents to inmate assaults on women custodians." . . . In fact, any prison guard is constantly subject to the threat of attack by inmates, and "invisible" deterrents are the guard's only real protection. No prison guard relies primarily on his or her ability to ward off an inmate attack to maintain order. Guards are typically unarmed and sheer numbers of inmates could overcome the normal complement. Rather, like all other law enforcement officers, prison guards must rely primarily on the moral authority of their office and the threat of future punishment for miscreants. As one expert testified below, common sense, fairness, and mental and emotional stability are the qualities a guard needs to cope with the dangers of the job. . . . Well qualified and properly trained women, no less than men, have these psychological weapons at their disposal.

The particular severity of discipline problems in the Alabama maximum-security prisons is also no justification for the discrimination sanctioned by the Court. . . . If male guards face an impossible situation, it is difficult to see how women could make the problem worse, unless one relies on precisely the type of generalized bias against women that the Court agrees Title VII was intended to outlaw. For example, much of the testimony of appellants' witnesses ignores individual differences among members of each sex and reads like "ancient canards about the proper role of women." . . . The witnesses claimed that women guards are not strict disciplinarians; that they are physically less capable of protecting themselves and subduing unruly inmates; that inmates take advantage of them as they did their mothers, while male guards are strong father figures who easily maintain discipline, and so on. Yet the record shows that the presence of women guards has not led to a single incident amounting to a serious breach of security in any Alabama institution.[3] And, in any event, "[g]uards rarely enter the cell blocks and dormitories" . . . where the danger of inmate attacks is the greatest.

It appears that the real disqualifying factor in the Court's view is "[t]he employee's very womanhood." . . . The Court refers to the large number of sex offenders in Alabama prisons, and to "[t]he likelihood that inmates would assault a woman because she was a woman." . . . In short, the fundamental justification for the decision is that women as guards will generate sexual assaults. With all respect, this rationale regrettably perpetuates one of

3. The Court refers to two incidents involving potentially dangerous attacks on women in prisons. . . . But these did not involve trained corrections officers; one victim was a clerical worker and the other a student visiting on a tour.

the most insidious of the old myths about women that women, wittingly or not, are seductive sexual objects. The effect of the decision, made I am sure with the best of intentions, is to punish women because their very presence might provoke sexual assaults. It is women who are made to pay the price in lost job opportunities for the threat of depraved conduct by prison inmates. Once again, "[t]he pedestal upon which women have been placed has . . . , upon closer inspection, been revealed as a cage." . . . It is particularly ironic that the cage is erected here in response to feared misbehavior by imprisoned criminals.

The proper response to inevitable attacks on both female and male guards is not to limit the employment opportunities of law-abiding women who wish to contribute to their community, but to take swift and sure punitive action against the inmate offenders. Presumably, one of the goals of the Alabama prison system is the eradication of inmates' antisocial behavior patterns so that prisoners will be able to live one day in free society. Sex offenders can begin this process by learning to relate to women guards in a socially acceptable manner. To deprive women of job opportunities because of the threatened behavior of convicted criminals is to turn our social priorities upside down.[5] . . .

≡≡≡ ## Wilson v. Southwest Airlines Co.
517 F. Supp. 292 (N.D. Tex. 1981)

HIGGINBOTHAM, District Judge.

This case presents the important question whether femininity, or more accurately female sex appeal, is a bona fide occupational qualification ("BFOQ") for the jobs of flight attendant and ticket agent with Southwest Airlines. Plaintiff Gregory Wilson and the class of over 100 male job applicants he represents have challenged Southwest's open refusal to hire males as a violation of Title VII. . . .

---

5. The appellants argue that restrictions on employment of women are also justified by consideration of inmates' privacy. It is strange indeed to hear state officials who have for years been violating the most basic principles of human decency in the operation of their prisons suddenly become concerned about inmate privacy. It is stranger still that these same officials allow women guards in contact positions in a number of non-maximum-security institutions, but strive to protect inmates' privacy in the prisons where personal freedom is most severely restricted. I have no doubt on this record that appellants' professed concern is nothing but a feeble excuse for discrimination. As the District Court suggested, it may well be possible, once a constitutionally adequate staff is available, to rearrange work assignments so that legitimate inmate privacy concerns are respected without denying jobs to women. Finally, if women guards behave in a professional manner at all times, they will engender reciprocal respect from inmates, who will recognize that their privacy is being invaded no more than if a woman doctor examines them. The suggestion implicit in the privacy argument that such behavior is unlikely on either side is an insult to the professionalism of guards and the dignity of inmates.

At the phase one trial on liability, Southwest conceded that its refusal to hire males was intentional. . . . Southwest contends, however, that the BFOQ exception to Title VII's ban on sex discrimination justifies its hiring only females for the public contact positions of flight attendant and ticket agent. The BFOQ window through which Southwest attempts to fly permits sex discrimination in situations where the employer can prove that sex is a "bona fide occupational qualification reasonably necessary to the normal operation of that particular business or enterprise." Southwest reasons it may discriminate against males because its attractive female flight attendants and ticket agents personify the airline's sexy image and fulfill its public promise to take passengers skyward with "love." Defendant claims maintenance of its females-only hiring policy is crucial to the airline's continued financial success. . . .

Factual Background . . .

Southwest was incorporated in March of 1967 and . . . as a result of the defensive tactics of Southwest's competitors . . . [i]n December of 1970, Southwest had $143 in the bank and was over $100,000 in debt, though no aircraft had ever left the ground.

Barely intact, Southwest, in early 1971, called upon a Dallas advertising agency, the Bloom Agency, to develop a winning marketing strategy. Planning to initiate service quickly, Southwest needed instant recognition and a "catchy" image to distinguish it from its competitors.

The Bloom Agency evaluated both the images of the incumbent competitor airlines as well as the characteristics of passengers to be served by a commuter airline. Bloom determined that the other carriers serving the Texas market tended to project an image of conservatism. The agency also determined that the relatively short haul commuter market which Southwest hoped to serve was comprised of predominantly male businessmen. Based on these factors, Bloom suggested that Southwest break away from the conservative image of other airlines and project to the traveling public an airline personification of feminine youth and vitality. A specific female personality description was recommended and adopted by Southwest for its corporate image: This lady is young and vital . . . she is charming and goes through life with great flair and exuberance . . . you notice first her exciting smile, friendly air, her wit . . . yet she is quite efficient and approaches all her tasks with care and attention. . . .

From the personality description suggested by The Bloom Agency, Southwest developed its now famous "Love" personality. Southwest projects an image of feminine spirit, fun, and sex appeal. Its ads promise to provide "tender loving care" to its predominantly male, business passengers. The first advertisements run by the airline featured the slogan, "AT LAST THERE IS SOMEBODY ELSE UP THERE WHO LOVES YOU." Variations on this theme have continued through newspaper, billboard, magazine and television advertisements during the past ten years.[4] . . .

Over the years, Southwest gained national and international attention as the "love airline." Southwest Airlines' stock is traded on the New York Stock Exchange under the ticker symbol "LUV." During 1977 when Southwest opened five additional markets in Texas, the love theme was expanded to "WE'RE SPREADING LOVE ALL OVER TEXAS."

As an integral part of its youthful, feminine image, Southwest has employed only females in the high customer contact positions of ticket agent and flight attendant. From the start, Southwest's attractive personnel, dressed in high boots and hot-pants, generated public interest and "free ink." Their sex appeal has been used to attract male customers to the airline. . . . The airline also encourages its attendants to entertain the passengers and maintain an atmosphere of informality and "fun" during flights. According to Southwest, its female flight attendants have come to "personify" Southwest's public image.

Southwest has enjoyed enormous success in recent years.[6] This is in no small part due to its marketing image. . . . The evidence was undisputed that Southwest's unique, feminized image played and continues to play an important role in the airline's success.

Less certain, however, is Southwest's assertion that its females-only hiring policy is necessary for the continued success of its image and its business. Based on two on-board surveys, one conducted in October, 1979, before this suit was filed, and another in August, 1980, when the suit was pending, Southwest contends its attractive flight attendants are the "largest single component" of its success. In the 1979 survey, however, of the attributes considered most important by passengers, the category "courteous and attentive hostesses" ranked fifth in importance behind (1) on time departures, (2) frequently scheduled departures, (3) friendly and helpful reservations and ground personnel, and (4) convenient departure times. . . . Apparently, one of the remaining eight alternative categories, "attractive hostesses," was not selected with sufficient frequency to warrant being included in the reported survey results. . . .

[R]ather than Southwest's female personnel being the "sole factor" distinguishing the airline from its competitors, as Defendant contends, the 1980

---

4. Unabashed allusions to love and sex pervade all aspects of Southwest's public image. Its T.V. commercials feature attractive attendants in fitted outfits, catering to male passengers while an alluring feminine voice promises in-flight love. On board, attendants in hot-pants (skirts are now optional) serve "love bites" (toasted almonds) and "love potions" (cocktails). Even Southwest's ticketing system features a "quickie machine" to provide "instant gratification."

6. From 1979 to 1980, the company's earnings rose from $17 million to $28 million when most other airlines suffered heavy losses. As a percentage of revenues, Southwest's return is considered to be one of the highest in the industry.

survey lists Southwest's "personnel" as only one among five characteristics contributing to Southwest's public image. . . . Accordingly, there is no persuasive proof that Southwest's passengers prefer female over male flight attendants and ticket agents, or, of greater importance, that they would be less likely to fly Southwest if males were hired.

In evaluating Southwest's BFOQ defense, therefore, the Court proceeds on the basis that "love," while important, is not everything in the relationship between Defendant and its passengers. Still, it is proper to infer from the airline's competitive successes that Southwest's overall "love image" has enhanced its ability to attract passengers. To the extent the airline has successfully feminized its image and made attractive females an integral part of its public face, it also follows that femininity and sex appeal are qualities related to successful job performance by Southwest's flight attendants and ticket agents. The strength of this relationship has not been proved. It is with this factual orientation that the Court turns to examine Southwest's BFOQ defense.

Interpretations of the Bona Fide Occupational Qualification . . .

Southwest concedes with respect to the *Weeks* test that males are able to perform safely and efficiently all the basic, mechanical functions required of flight attendants and ticket agents. . . . Southwest's position, however, is that females are required to fulfill certain non-mechanical aspects of these jobs: to attract those male customers who prefer female attendants and ticket agents, and to preserve the authenticity and genuineness of Southwest's unique, female corporate personality.

A similar, though not identical, argument that females could better perform certain non-mechanical functions required of flight attendants was rejected in Diaz v. Pan American World Airways, Inc., [1971]. There, the airline argued and the trial court found that being female was a BFOQ because women were superior in "providing reassurance to anxious passengers, giving courteous personalized service and, in general, making flights as pleasurable as possible within the limitations imposed by aircraft operations." . . . Although it accepted the trial court findings, the Court of Appeals reversed, holding that femininity was not a BFOQ, because catering to passengers' psychological needs was only "tangential" to what was "reasonably *necessary*" for the business involved (original emphasis). . . . Characterizing the "essence" or "primary function" of Pan American's business as the safe transportation of passengers from one point to another, the court explained:

> While a pleasant environment, enhanced by the obvious cosmetic effect that female stewardesses provide as well as, according to the findings of the trial court, their apparent ability to perform the non-mechanical functions of the job in a more effective manner than most men, may all be important, they are tangential to the essence of the business involved. No one has suggested that

having male stewards will so seriously affect the operation of the airline as to jeopardize or even minimize its ability to provide safe transportation from one place to another. . . .

Similar reasoning underlay the appellate court's rejection of Pan American's claim that its customers' preference for female attendants justified its refusal to hire males. Because the non-mechanical functions that passengers preferred females to perform were tangential to the airline's business, the court held, "the fact that customers prefer (females) cannot justify sex discrimination." . . . The Fifth Circuit in *Diaz* did not hold that customer preference could never give rise to a sex BFOQ. Rather, consistent with the EEOC's exception for authenticity and genuineness, the Court allowed that customer preference could "be taken into account only when it is based on the company's inability to perform the primary function or service it offers," that is, where sex or sex appeal is itself the dominant service provided.

Diaz and its progeny establish that to recognize a BFOQ for jobs requiring multiple abilities, some sex-linked and some sex-neutral, the sex-linked aspects of the job must predominate. Only then will an employer have satisfied [the] requirement that sex be so essential to successful job performance that a member of the opposite sex could not perform the job. An illustration of such dominance in sex cases is the exception recognized by the EEOC (Equal Employment Opportunity Commission) for authenticity and genuineness. In the example given in [EEOC Regulations], that of an actor or actress, the primary function of the position, its essence, is to fulfill the audience's expectation and desire for a particular role, characterized by particular physical or emotional traits. Generally, a male could not supply the authenticity required to perform a female role. Similarly, in jobs where sex or vicarious sexual recreation is the primary service provided, e.g. a social escort or topless dancer, the job automatically calls for one sex exclusively; the employee's sex and the service provided are inseparable. Thus, being female has been deemed a BFOQ for the position of a Playboy Bunny, female sexuality being reasonably necessary to perform the dominant purpose of the job which is forthrightly to titillate and entice male customers. . . . One court has also suggested, without holding, that the authenticity exception would give rise to a BFOQ for Chinese nationality where necessary to maintain the authentic atmosphere of an ethnic Chinese restaurant. . . .

Application of the Bona Fide Occupational Qualification to Southwest Airlines

Applying the first level test for a BFOQ, with its legal gloss, to Southwest's particular operations results in the conclusion that being female is not a qualification required to perform successfully the jobs of flight attendant and ticket agent with Southwest. Like any other airline, Southwest's primary function is to transport passengers safely and quickly from one point to another.[24]

To do this, Southwest employs ticket agents whose primary job duties are to ticket passengers and check baggage, and flight attendants, whose primary duties are to assist passengers during boarding and deboarding, to instruct passengers in the location and use of aircraft safety equipment, and to serve passengers cocktails and snacks during the airline's short commuter flights. Mechanical, non-sex-linked duties dominate both these occupations. Indeed, on Southwest's short-haul commuter flights there is time for little else. That Southwest's female personnel may perform their mechanical duties "with love" does not change the result. "Love" is the manner of job performance, not the job performed.

While possession of female allure and sex appeal have been made qualifications for Southwest's contact personnel by virtue of the "love" campaign, the functions served by employee sexuality in Southwest's operations are not dominant ones. According to Southwest, female sex appeal serves two purposes: (1) attracting and entertaining male passengers and (2) fulfilling customer expectations for female service engendered by Southwest's advertising which features female personnel. As in *Diaz*, these non-mechanical, sex-linked job functions are only "tangential" to the essence of the occupations and business involved. Southwest is not a business where vicarious sex entertainment is the primary service provided. Accordingly, the ability of the airline to perform its primary business function, the transportation of passengers, would not be jeopardized by hiring males.

Southwest does not face the situation . . . where an established customer preference for one sex is so strong that the business would be undermined if employees of the opposite sex were hired. Southwest's claim that its customers prefer females rests primarily upon inferences drawn from the airline's success after adopting its female personality. But according to Southwest's own surveys, that success is attributable to many factors. There is no competent proof that Southwest's popularity derives directly from its females-only policy to the exclusion of other factors like dissatisfaction with rival airlines and Southwest's use of convenient Love and Hobby Fields. Nor is there competent proof that the customer preference for females is so strong that Defendant's male passengers would cease doing business with Southwest as was the case in [Fernandez v. Wynn Oil Co.]. In short, Southwest has failed in its proof to satisfy Diaz's business necessity requirement, without which customer preference may not give rise to a BFOQ for sex. . . .

24. Southwest's argument that its primary function is "to make a profit," not to transport passengers, must be rejected. Without doubt the goal of every business is to make a profit. For purposes of BFOQ analysis, however, the business "essence" inquiry focuses on the particular service provided and the job tasks and functions involved, not the business goal. If an employer could justify employment discrimination merely on the grounds that it is necessary to make a profit, Title VII would be nullified in short order.

It is also relevant that Southwest's female image was adopted at its discretion, to promote a business unrelated to sex. Contrary to the unyielding South American preference for males encountered by the Defendant company in *Fernandez*, Southwest exploited, indeed nurtured, the very customer preference for females it now cites to justify discriminating against males. . . . Moreover, the fact that a vibrant marketing campaign was necessary to distinguish Southwest in its early years does not lead to the conclusion that sex discrimination was then, or is now, a business necessity. Southwest's claim that its female image will be tarnished by hiring males is, in any case, speculative at best. . . .

[S]ex does not become a BFOQ merely because an employer chooses to exploit female sexuality as a marketing tool, or to better insure profitability. . . .

Conclusion . . .

Rejecting a wider BFOQ for sex does not eliminate the commercial exploitation of sex appeal. It only requires, consistent with the purposes of Title VII, that employers exploit the attractiveness and allure of a sexually integrated workforce. Neither Southwest, nor the traveling public, will suffer from such a rule. More to the point, it is my judgment that this is what Congress intended.

Notes

1. The Business Necessity Defense. The Supreme Court reasoned in *Dothard* that the height and weight requirements were proxies for strength, which could have been measured more directly and without sex discrimination. (The state did not present any evidence to support the height and weight minimums it had imposed.)[210] How likely do you think it is that substantially more women could qualify under a strength test? Of course, if a disproportionate impact remained, that rule, too, would need to be justifiable under the business necessity test. What if the defendant had shown that the height and weight restrictions were necessary to create the *appearance* of strength, as vital to prison security as strength itself? (Justice Rehnquist, concurring in the opinion, raises this possibility.)

2. BFOQ and Sexual Authenticity. As facially discriminatory exclusions based on sex, the prison regulation excluding women as prison guards in maximum-security areas in *Dothard* and the exclusion of men as flight attendants in *Wilson* are examples of disparate treatment discrimination, which are justified under Title VII only if the sex of the employee in each case is shown to be a bona fide occupational qualification, or BFOQ. Sex is a BFOQ in the

---

210. Thomas, supra note 108, at 44-45.

entertainment industry if an actor's or actress's plausibility depends on sexual identity with the character portrayed. It may sometimes also be a BFOQ, according to *Wilson*, when the "essence" of a business requires a certain kind of sex appeal.[211] Thus, while a family restaurant cannot discriminate between men and women for waiter positions, it generally is assumed that a topless bar may hire only women dancers, and may discharge an employee for failure to meet the employer's criteria relating to sexual image. Ironically, then, the more explicitly the employer's business exploits sex for money, the more easily sex will be viewed as a BFOQ. Is this perverse? Does it fail to protect women when they most need it? This issue is explored in Chapter 3.

Some expensive New York French restaurants hire only male waiters, in line with the tradition of the "classiest" Continental establishments. Are they violating Title VII? What if they hire only French waiters, and thereby virtually exclude waiters of color? What is the "essence" of such a job?

3. BFOQ and Customer Preferences. Under what circumstances might customer preference justify discriminatory conduct? In the lower court decision in *Diaz*, the airline introduced evidence of a survey indicating that 79 percent of all passengers, male and female, preferred being served by female flight attendants. Expert psychological evidence was also introduced to explain the general preference of airline passengers for female attendants. It posited that: The unique experience of being levitated off the ground and transported through the air at high speeds creates feelings of apprehension, boredom, and excitement; females were psychologically better equipped to cope with these conflicting states and especially adept at relieving passenger apprehension; and passengers of both sexes responded better to the presence of females. This and other evidence persuaded the district court that sex was a BFOQ for flight attendants. The Fifth Circuit Court of Appeals, held, however, that although the airline could take the interpersonal skills of flight attendant applicants into account, it could not do so by categorically excluding all men.

As noted in the previous section, the court in Craft v. Metromedia came to a different conclusion. There, the court determined that a television anchorwoman could be properly reassigned due to the demonstrated negative viewer response. Is the rejection of the survey evidence in *Diaz* and *Wilson* reconcilable with its use in *Craft*? Fernandez v. Wynn Oil Co., cited in *Wilson*, held that an oil company could not refuse to hire female executives because its South American clients would refuse to deal with them.[212] Is this the correct decision? Is it reconcilable with *Craft*? When do you think positive viewer or customer response becomes a "business necessity"?

---

211. On when sex constitutes the essence of the business, see Kimberly Yuracko, Private Nurses and Playboy Bunnies: Explaining Permissible Sex Discrimination, 92 Calif. L. Rev. 147 (2004).

212. 653 F.2d 1273 (9th Cir. 1981).

4. BFOQ and Privacy Considerations. Courts have also found the BFOQ test to be satisfied in some cases in which sex-specific hiring accommodates privacy or other related interests. In Fesel v. Masonic Home of Delaware, Inc., for example, nine of the nursing home's female residents signed an affidavit objecting "most strenuously" to male nurses or male nurses' aides, though apparently not to male physicians.[213] The court accepted the employer's defense that female sex was a BFOQ for the nursing positions. Quite a number of cases in the context of hospitals and nursing homes have reached the same conclusion. Does it seem reasonable to hire only men, or only women, when the employment at issue implicates sex-specific privacy or therapeutic interests?[214] UAW v. Johnson Controls, excerpted in Chapter 2, includes suggestions that the Court was prepared to endorse a privacy application of the BFOQ defense.

Yet allowing the BFOQ exception in this context would seem to perpetuate age-old stereotypes that Title VII was meant to condemn—i.e., that women's role is washing and cleaning up after people, and men's role is that of the skilled professional.[215] A more recent case suggests that the BFOQ privacy defense is narrow, and only comes into play when hiring members of one sex would undermine the institution's safety and effectiveness. In Slivka v. Camden-Clark Memorial Hospital, the West Virginia state supreme court struck down a hospital policy to hire only female obstetrics nurses, despite evidence that 80 percent of patients demanded female nurses and female nurses were needed as chaperones for male physicians.[216] The *Slivka* court noted the importance of not deferring to personal preferences based on dated world views.

When the privacy claim is by a prisoner, it is unlikely to prevail.[217] Courts that do recognize a right to privacy for inmates tend to give more respect to women's privacy than to men's.[218] Is this fair?

5. BFOQs and Formal Equality Analysis. Justice Stewart's opinion upholding the female ban on maximum security positions in *Dothard* articulates the most common defense to a formal equality claim: Women are different

213. 447 F. Supp. 1346 (D. Del. 1978), aff'd mem., 591 F.2d 1334 (3d Cir. 1979).

214. See Emily Gold Waldman, The Case of the Male OB-GYN: A Proposal for the Expansion of the Privacy BFOQ in the Healthcare Context, 6 U. Pa. J. Lab. & Emp. L. 357, 366-92 (2004) (proposing that employers should be able to hire, for example, only female obstetricians and gynecologists).

215. See Amy Kapczynski, Same-Sex Privacy and the Limits of Antidiscrimination Law, 112 Yale L.J. 1257 (2003).

216. 594 S.E.2d 616 (W. Va. 2004).

217. See, e.g., Gunther v. Iowa State Men's Reformatory, 612 F.2d 1079 (8th Cir.).

218. Compare, e.g., Oliver v. Scott, 276 F.3d 736 (5th Cir. 2002) (holding that privacy rights did not bar cross-sex surveillance of male prisoners or require shower partitions and that such conditions did not violate equal protection rights) with Everson v. Michigan Department of Corrections, 391 F.3d 737 (6th Cir. 2004) (upholding sex as a BFOQ in Michigan's women's prisons, because the duties required officers to patrol sleeping, shower, and bathroom areas, and Michigan sought to address a deplorable record in caring for its female inmates).

from men in ways that justify different treatment. The reasoning of the opinion leaves no room for a woman to become qualified for the position. Safety at the prison—safety of the woman and of the prison population more generally—would be compromised by "womanhood," referring to both women's relative weakness, and their vulnerability to sexual assault. Viewed this way, women's unsuitability for the position reflects inherent sex differences, not ones that the state has produced or perpetuated by excluding them from the position.

Justice Marshall's dissent challenges the majority's assumptions about women's differences on multiple grounds. It (1) disputes the factual premises of the rule—for example, that female guards would create a danger to the prison's basic security; (2) identifies the stereotypes about women as "seductive sexual objects" that are reinforced through the exclusion; (3) insists that some women will be able to protect themselves and should be given the chance to prove their individual ability despite the average characteristics of their sex; and (4) claims that improvements in staffing (as a prior case had already required) was essentially a less restrictive alternative to excluding women from the positions.

If you think *Dothard* is wrongly decided, is it because the Court failed to apply standard formal equality principles correctly? Or because formal equality does not provide the tools necessary to analyze an exclusion based on factors "unique" to women?

Is excluding women where they might present temptation for the prisoners comparable to giving in to "consumer preference"? Is the concern for prison safety and security sufficiently distinguishable from the kinds of business justifications rejected in other cases? Isn't it just a question of economics? Why should Southwest Airlines be required to forgo the income attributable to being the "LUV" airline, while the state of Alabama may defend its exclusion of women based on inadequate protection of their safety under present staffing arrangements? Should courts be more sympathetic when taxpayers are footing the bill and underfunding causes chronic security problems?

Is *Dothard* less troubling if courts require a detailed "basis in fact" for assumptions about how men or women are likely to behave on the job? A number of courts in recent years have denied employer motions for summary judgment in BFOQ cases because the factual predicate was insufficient.[219] One

---

219. See, for example, White v. Dep't of Correctional Servs., 814 F. Supp. 2d 374 (S.D.N.Y. 2011) (denying summary judgment because a reasonable jury could find that the prison could find less restrictive ways to ensure that strip frisks and urine tests were performed by an officer of the same gender as the prisoner); Reese v. Mich. Dep't of Corrections, 105 Fair Empl. Prac. Cas. (BNA) 1584 (E.D. Mich. 2009) (denying summary judgment because factual record was not clear on how frequently male officers would have to perform pat-downs on female prisoners); Inscore v. Doty, 2009 WL 2753049 (E.D. Ark. Aug. 27, 2009) (denying summary judgment to employer who refused to hire women for undercover positions in narcotics unit because there was a genuine issue of material fact "as to whether being a young black male was an essential qualification to the investigation unit's business of infiltrating the culture of crack cocaine dealers").

court observed that "the BFOQ defense generally requires a 'case-by-case' analysis."[220] Are juries any less likely than judges to be convinced that a gender-based BFOQ is justified?

6. His Very Manhood?   The majority in *Dothard* allowed the prison's BFOQ defense in part because a female correctional officer's "very womanhood" would "directly undermine her capacity to provide the security that is the essence of a correctional counselor's responsibility."[221] Can the "very manhood" of male correctional counselors undermine their ability to carry out the essence of a prison's business? In several cases over the last decade, prisons have been sued over policies that exclude men from certain positions in women's prisons as a means of curbing the sexual abuse of female prisoners.[222]

In Everson v. Michigan Dep't of Corrections, the Sixth Circuit upheld such a policy of the Michigan Department of Corrections (MDOC) on the theory that being female was a BFOQ for 250 designated positions in housing units at female prisons.[223] This policy was enacted as part of the response to a problem of sexual abuse of female inmates that had "long plagued the MDOC." In addition to the prevalence of sexual abuse (189 allegations of sexual abuse by male officers over a 6-year period), the problem was exacerbated by a fear of reporting incidents of abuse and tolerance of sexual misconduct by higher-ups. The court relied heavily on *Dothard* for the proposition that excluding officers of one gender can be an appropriate response to an "inhospitable" environment in which security cannot be otherwise maintained.[224] The court concluded that "a basis in fact exists that privacy screens preclude proper surveillance of inmates and that allegations of sexual abuse engender hesitancy in male officers and mistrust between inmates and guards, and thus the 'very manhood' of male [officers] undermines their capacity to provide security."[225] And even though most male officers will "conduct themselves professionally," the MDOC "cannot predict which officers will engage in sexual abuse." Based on the data provided by MDOC, the court was persuaded that "some male officers possess a trait precluding safe and efficient job performance—a proclivity for sexually abusive conduct—that cannot be ascertained by means other than the knowledge of the officer's gender."[226]

220. *Reese*, 105 Fair Empl. Prac. Cas (BNA) at *4.
221. *Dothard*, 433 U.S. at 336.
222. In addition to the cases discussed below, see Henry v. Milwaukee County, 539 F.3d 573 (7th Cir. 2008) (invalidating gender-based staffing policy in juvenile detention center because insufficient evidence of sexual abuse problem and same-gender mentoring/rehabilitation plan did not require same-gender staffing at night).
223. 391 F.3d 737 (6th Cir. 2004).
224. Id. at 754.
225. Id. at 755.
226. Id.

Thus gender was a "legitimate proxy for a safety-related job qualification" given "the endemic problem of sexual abuse in Michigan's female facilities."[227]

In Breiner v. Nevada Dep't of Corrections (NDOC), the Ninth Circuit considered a similar policy, in which men could not be hired as "correctional lieutenants," but reached the opposite conclusion.[228] NDOC argued that the exclusion of male officers would reduce sexual misconduct because male officers are more likely to "condone sexual abuse by their male subordinates"; are "themselves likely to sexually abuse female inmates"; and lack the "instinct" that female officers possess that makes them less susceptible to manipulation by inmates.[229] The court rejected all three justifications for the exclusion of men and held that NDOC had not established a gender BFOQ. For the policy to stand, NDOC had to show a "high correlation between sex and the ability to perform job functions" that are "reasonably necessary" to the business of running prisons. NDOC did not meet its burden of showing "a basis in fact" (required by *Dothard*) for concluding that "all male correctional lieutenants would tolerate sexual abuse by their subordinates; that all men in the correctional lieutenant role would themselves sexually abuse inmates; or that women, by virtue of their gender, can better understand the behavior of female inmates." Nor did NDOC refute "the viability of alternatives that would achieve [the goal of reducing abuse] without impeding male employees' promotional opportunities."[230] Moreover, NDOC's explanation for its policy "relies on the kind of unproven and invidious stereotype that Congress sought to eliminate from employment decisions when it enacted Title VII."[231] The court was particularly disturbed by NDOC's suggestion that "all men are inherently apt to sexually abuse, or condone sexual abuse of, female inmates."[232]

Which of these courts has the better of the argument? Is reliance on a guard's "very manhood" to predict his likelihood to commit or tolerate sexual abuse equally reliant on stereotypes as reliance on a female officer's "very womanhood" to predict her likelihood of being victimized? Does the protection of female inmates offset any harm from the possible perpetuation of gender stereotypes?

7. The Ministerial Exception. Besides the BFOQ exception, there is an exception to Title VII for employment decisions made by religious organizations. In the unanimous 2012 decision of Hosanna-Tabor Evangelical

---

227. Id. at 755, 762; see also Teamsters Local Union No. 117 v. Washington Dep't of Corrections, 789 F.3d 979 (9th Cir. 2015) (upholding designation of 11 positions as female-only in response to sexual misconduct by male correctional officers in women's prisons).

228. 601 F.3d 1202 (9th Cir. 2010).

229. Id. at 1211.

230. Id. at 1216.

231. Id. at 1211.

232. Id. at 1215.

Lutheran Church and School v. EEOC,[233] the United States Supreme Court held that both the establishment clause and the free exercise clause bar employment discrimination lawsuits based on the termination of employees by a religious institution when that employee is a "minister" within the "ministerial exception" to nondiscrimination statutes. The Court determined that the plaintiff in *Hosanna-Tabor*, allegedly fired because of a disability in violation of the Americans with Disabilities Act, was a minister on the basis of her title ("Minister of Religion, Commissioned") and the fact that she taught religious as well as secular subjects.

There is some question whether the ministerial exception should apply even when the religious institution's discrimination has nothing to do with a religious belief or practice. A decision of the Ninth Circuit Court of Appeals prior to *Hosanna-Tabor* had held that the ministerial exception did not extend to cases of sexual harassment, where the employer did not claim a religious purpose for the harassment.[234] But in *Hosanna-Tabor*, the Supreme Court stated that the claimed discriminatory behavior need not be connected to a particular tenet of the religion: "The purpose of the exception is not to safeguard a church's decision to fire a minister only when it is made for a religious reason. The exception instead ensures that the authority to select and control who will minister to the faithful . . . is the church's alone."[235] At the same time, the Court limited the case to the church's decision to fire an employee, and holds that the ministerial exception operates as an "affirmative defense to an otherwise cognizable claim, not a jurisdictional bar."[236]

Other potential conflicts between women's equality interests and religion are explored in Section D of this chapter (public accommodations) and Chapter 6, Section B (gender, culture, and religion in the international context).

Putting Theory Into Practice

1-27. A mid-sized law firm handles, among other things, insurance and employment discrimination defense. A number of the firm's oldest and best clients prefer to work with male attorneys, because they have more confidence in their abilities. Most recently, an insurance client threatened to take his business elsewhere if a Jewish female lawyer, who was assigned to handle a personal injury trial for his company, was not replaced by one of the firm's

---

233. 132 S. Ct. 694 (2012).

234. Bollard v. California Province of the Soc'y of Jesus, 196 F.3d 940, 944 (9th Cir. 1999). Bollard was applied and reaffirmed in Elvig v. Calvin Presbyterian Church, 375 F.3d 941 (9th Cir. 2004) (holding that a supervising pastor's sexual harassment of a female minister was not related to the church's "constitutionally protected prerogative to choose its ministers" nor "a constitutionally protected religious practice," and therefore Title VII was applicable).

235. *Hosanna-Tabor*, 132 S. Ct. 694, 709 (2012).

236. Id. at 709 n. 4 (citing *Bollard* with approval).

"bright, new" (male) attorneys. The client claims that the man will be more effective in the "redneck" Southern town where the case is scheduled for trial. The law firm makes the reassignment to please the client. Is this discrimination based on sex? Is use of sex valid as a BFOQ?[237]

1-28. The firm in Problem 1-27 above also has a practice of assigning women attorneys to employment discrimination cases brought by women claiming sex discrimination, and assigning minority attorneys to employment discrimination cases in which race is an issue. A white male attorney with the firm believes that this policy in assigning cases reduces his opportunities to excel at the firm. Is this discrimination based on sex? Is it justified? Would the issue be different if a black woman is assigned as defense counsel in a rape trial before a largely black jury on the theory that she would have the most credibility in cross-examining the black woman complainant?

1-29. A trucking company has a policy that new drivers must be accompanied by an experienced driver for six months. In response to a sexual harassment lawsuit, the company implemented a "same-sex trainer policy," under which female drivers could only be accompanied by other female drivers, to alleviate safety and privacy concerns. However, new female drivers were often placed on a "female waiting list" because there were no female drivers available to train. Is this policy legal?[238]

1-30. Transition House, New England's first battered women's shelter, caused controversy by hiring a man as its interim executive director. About Women, a collective of psychologists and social workers who were influential in creating shelters, including Transition House, wrote a public letter of protest. In their view, the decision constituted a "flagrant violation" of the organization's founding principle to establish a space where women could feel safe from male intrusion and could openly unburden themselves of the experiences of male violence they had undergone without fear of censure, criticism, or inhibition by male presence. The male interim director responded by noting that he spent his time in administrative offices in a separate location from the shelter and had limited contact with residents.[239] Who is right? If the male director is fired based on the rationale of About Women, would he have a sex discrimination claim under Title VII?

1-31. Professor V. works for a state university and conducts many research projects under grants obtained through the university. One of these projects

---

237. This case is modeled on Karen Horowitz, a video vignette from Stephen Gillers's Series, Adventures in Legal Ethics (1992).

238. See EEOC v. New Prime, Inc., 42 F. Supp. 3d 1201 (W.D. Mo. 2014).

239. Courtney E. Martin, Violence Shelter Considers Hiring Male Director (Aug. 22, 2005), www.womensenews.org.

is a study of women who have rejected settlement offers by a trust fund set up to satisfy the claims of women injured by the Dalkon Shield intrauterine birth-control device and who must pursue their claims through non-judicial adjudicatory hearings. The purpose of the project is to study the effectiveness of those hearings and the surrounding process. The research requires lengthy interviews of women claimants both before and after the hearings, with questions that probe, among other things, the intimate details of their sex lives, their sex partners, their contraception histories, and other matters relating to their experiences with the Dalkon Shield. Most of these women have suffered substantial distress and harm as a result of these experiences and many find it understandably difficult to discuss these experiences with strangers.

Professor V. wants to hire only white women, ages 35 to 45, to conduct these interviews. His reason is that the validity of his research requires the interviewer to create a neutral, nonjudgmental atmosphere in which the interviewees feel comfortable talking about one of the most private aspects of their lives. Research has shown that people of virtually every race, sex, and background, including blacks, Hispanics, men, and women, feel most comfortable talking about the intimate details of their lives with middle-aged, white women between the ages of 35 and 45.

He asks your advice. May he hire only white women ages 35 to 45 as interviewers without violating any law?

1-32. Hooters is an Atlanta-based restaurant chain that hires only female food servers, bartenders, and hosts. These women wear tight short-shorts and tank tops or half-tees with a large-eyed owl on the front. Some shirt backs read "More than a Mouthful." Hooters sells food, drink, posters, T-shirts, calendars, and other products. It also offers an atmosphere of what a spokeswoman described as "good-humored, wholesome sex appeal" that the Hooters girls embody. Although it "welcomes" children, the sexy cheerleader image of the Hooters' girls is designed to attract its target audience of adult males.

Does Hooters have a BFOQ defense to a sex discrimination suit brought by male applicants who were rejected for jobs because of their sex?

1-33. Defendant operates Pin-Ups, a live adult entertainment venue. The business has "numerous image-related requirements for its entertainers in order to make sure the entertainers present the image and service that the defendant sells." Plaintiff worked as a dancer at Pin-Ups, but was terminated when she became pregnant. Defendant argued that the discharge was lawful because "sex appeal" is a job requirement that is an integral part of its business. Who should prevail?[240]

240. See Berry v. Great American Dream, Inc., 88 F. Supp. 3d 1378 (N.D. Ga. 2015).

1-34. A teacher at a Catholic girls' school was dismissed after she lent her name to an advertisement supporting abortion rights on the thirtieth anniversary of Roe v. Wade. Title VII prohibits discrimination based on religion.[241] Does the teacher have a claim against the school?

D. STATE PUBLIC ACCOMMODATIONS LAWS AND ASSOCIATIONAL FREEDOMS

In addition to federal and state laws prohibiting sex discrimination in employment, many states have passed civil rights acts prohibiting sex discrimination in public accommodations and in private clubs and organizations. Challenges to the application of these statutes have claimed infringement of rights of expression, association, and privacy protected by the federal and state constitutions. Such rights have long served to protect the activities and privacy of politically unpopular groups, including those involved in the civil rights movement. The question is how far this protection extends, and to whom.

In 1984, the United States Supreme Court faced this issue with respect to sex discrimination in the case of Roberts v. United States Jaycees. There, the Court rejected First Amendment challenges to a Minnesota anti-discrimination statute under which the Jaycees had been required to admit women as full voting members.[242] Three years later, the Court considered a challenge to California's Unruh Act, a broad public accommodations law that had been used to require Rotary Clubs in the state to admit women.

≡≡≡ ***Board of Directors of Rotary International v. Rotary Club of Duarte***
481 U.S. 537 (1987)

Mr. Justice POWELL delivered the opinion of the Court.

We must decide whether a California statute that requires California Rotary Clubs to admit women members violates the First Amendment.

Issue → Must admit women?

---

241. See Curay-Cramer v. Ursuline Academy of Wilmington Del., Inc., 344 F. Supp. 2d 923 (D. Del. 2004) (no, because it would require the court to become entangled in church doctrine, which would violate the First Amendment); see also Fassl v. Our Lady of Perpetual Help Roman Catholic Church, 2005 U.S. Dist. LEXIS 22546 (E.D. Pa. Oct. 5, 2005) (refusing to hear employee Family and Medical Leave Act complaint against a Catholic Church, on First Amendment grounds).

242. 468 U.S. 609 (1984).

I

Rotary International (International) is a nonprofit corporation founded in 1905, with headquarters in Evanston, Illinois. It is "an organization of business and professional men united worldwide who provide humanitarian service, encourage high ethical standards in all vocations, and help build goodwill and peace in the world." . . . Individual members belong to a local Rotary Club rather than to International. In turn, each local Rotary Club is a member of International. . . . In August 1982, shortly before the trial in this case, International comprised 19,788 Rotary Clubs in 157 countries, with a total membership of about 907,750. . . .

Individuals are admitted to membership in a Rotary Club according to a "classification system." The purpose of this system is to ensure "that each Rotary Club includes a representative of every worthy and recognized business, professional, or institutional activity in the community." . . . Each active member must work in a leadership capacity in his business or profession. The general rule is that "one active member is admitted for each classification, but he, in turn, may propose an additional active member, who must be in the same business or professional classification." Thus, each classification may be represented by two active members. In addition, "senior active" and "past service" members may represent the same classifications as active members. . . . There is no limit to the number of clergymen, journalists, or diplomats who may be admitted to membership. . . . Subject to these requirements, each local Rotary Club is free to adopt its own rules and procedures for admitting new members. . . .

Membership in Rotary Clubs is open only to men. . . . Herbert A. Pigman, the General Secretary of Rotary International, testified that the exclusion of women results in an "aspect of fellowship . . . that is enjoyed by the present male membership," . . . and also allows Rotary to operate effectively in foreign countries with varied cultures and social mores. Although women are not admitted to membership, they are permitted to attend meetings, give speeches, and receive awards. Women relatives of Rotary members may form their own associations and are authorized to wear the Rotary lapel pin. Young women between 14 and 28 years of age may joint Interact or Rotaract, organizations sponsored by Rotary International . . . .

In 1977 the Rotary Club of Duarte, California, admitted Donna Bogart, Mary Lou Elliott, and Rosemary Freitag to active membership. International notified the Duarte Club that admitting women members is contrary to the Rotary constitution. After an internal hearing, International's board of directors revoked the charter of the Duarte Club and terminated its membership in Rotary International. The Duarte Club's appeal to the International Convention was unsuccessful.

The Duarte Club and two of its women members filed a complaint in the California Superior Court for the County of Los Angeles. The complaint alleged, inter alia, that appellants' actions violated the Unruh Civil Rights Act.[2] . . . [fn. 2: The Unruh Civil Rights Act provides, in part: "All persons within the jurisdiction of this state are free and equal, and no matter what their sex, race, color, religion, ancestry, or national origin are entitled to the full and equal accommodations, advantages, facilities, privileges, or services in all business establishments of every kind whatsoever." Cal. Civ. Code Ann. §51 (West 1982).

II

In Roberts v. United States Jaycees, [468 U.S. 609 (1984),] we upheld against First Amendment challenge a Minnesota statute that required the Jaycees to admit women as full voting members. *Roberts* provides the framework for analyzing appellants' constitutional claims. As we observed in *Roberts*, our cases have afforded constitutional protection to freedom of association in two distinct senses. First, the Court has held that the Constitution protects against unjustified government interference with an individual's choice to enter into and maintain certain intimate or private relationships. Second, the Court has upheld the freedom of individuals to associate for the purpose of engaging in protected speech or religious activities. In many cases, government interference with one form of protected association will also burden the other form of association. In *Roberts* we determined the nature and degree of constitutional protection by considering separately the effect of the challenged state action on individuals' freedom of private association and their freedom of expressive association. We follow the same course in this case . . . .

A

The Court has recognized that the freedom to enter into and carry on certain intimate or private relationships is a fundamental element of liberty protected by the Bill of Rights. Such relationships may take various forms, including the most intimate . . . . We have not attempted to mark the precise boundaries of this type of constitutional protection. The intimate relationships to which we have accorded constitutional protection include marriage . . . the begetting and bearing of children . . . child rearing and education . . . and cohabitation with relatives . . . . In determining whether a particular association is sufficiently personal or private to warrant constitutional protection, we consider factors such as size, purpose, selectivity, and whether others are excluded from critical aspects of the relationship. [468 U.S. at 620.]

The evidence in this case indicates that the relationship among Rotary Club members is not the kind of intimate or private relation that warrants constitutional protection. The size of the local Rotary Clubs ranges from fewer than 20 to more than 900. . . . There is no upper limit on the membership of any local Rotary Club. About 10 percent of the membership of a typical club moves away or drops out during a typical year. . . . The clubs therefore are instructed to "keep a flow of prospects coming" to make up for the attrition and gradually to enlarge the membership . . . . The purpose of Rotary "is to produce an inclusive, not exclusive, membership, making possible the recognition of all useful local occupations, and enabling the club to be a true cross section of the business and professional life of the community." . . . The membership undertakes a variety of service projects designed to aid the community, to raise the standards of the members' businesses and professions, and to improve international relations. Such an inclusive "fellowship for service based on diversity of interest," . . . however beneficial to the members and to those they serve, does not suggest the kind of private or personal relationship to which we have accorded protection under the First Amendment. To be sure, membership in Rotary Clubs is not open to the general public. But each club is instructed to include in its membership "all fully qualified prospective members located within its territory," to avoid "arbitrary limits on the number of members in the club," and to "establish and maintain a membership growth pattern."

Many of the Rotary Clubs' central activities are carried on in the presence of strangers. Rotary Clubs are required to admit any member of any other Rotary Club to their meetings. Members are encouraged to invite business associates and competitors to meetings. At some Rotary Clubs, the visitors number "in the tens and twenties each week." . . . Joint meetings with the members of other organizations, and other joint activities, are permitted. The clubs are encouraged to seek coverage of their meetings and activities in local newspapers. In sum, Rotary Clubs, rather than carrying on their activities in an atmosphere of privacy, seek to keep their "windows and doors open to the whole world." . . . We therefore conclude that application of the Unruh Act to local Rotary Clubs does not interfere unduly with the members' freedom of private association.

B

The Court also has recognized that the right to engage in activities protected by the First Amendment implies "a corresponding right to associate with others in pursuit of a wide variety of political, social, economic, educational, religious, and cultural ends." Roberts v. United States Jaycees, [468 U.S. at 622] . . . . For this reason, "[i]mpediments to the exercise of one's right to choose one's associates can violate the right of association protected by the First Amendment . . . ." Hishon v. King & Spalding, [467 U.S. 69, 80 n.4 (1984)] (Powell, J., concurring) (citing NAACP v. Button, [371 U.S. 415 (1963)]; NAACP v. Alabama ex rel. Patterson, [357 U.S. 449 (1958)]). In this case, however, the evidence fails to demonstrate that admitting women to Rotary Clubs will affect in any significant way the existing members' ability to carry out their various purposes.

As a matter of policy, Rotary Clubs do not take positions on "public questions," including political or international issues . . . . To be sure, Rotary Clubs engage in a variety of commendable service activities that are protected by the First Amendment. But the Unruh Act does not require the clubs to abandon or alter any of these activities. It does not require them to abandon their basic goals of humanitarian service, high ethical standards in all vocations, good will, and peace. Nor does it require them to abandon their classification system or admit members who do not reflect a cross section of the community. Indeed, by opening membership to leading business and professional women in the community, Rotary Clubs are likely to obtain a more representative cross section of community leaders with a broadened capacity for service.

Even if the Unruh Act does work some slight infringement on Rotary members' right of expressive association, that infringement is justified because it serves the State's compelling interest in eliminating discrimination against women. See Buckley v. Valeo, [424 U.S. 1, 25 (1976)] (per curiam) (right of association may be limited by state regulations necessary to serve a compelling interest unrelated to the suppression of ideas). On its face the Unruh Act, like the Minnesota public accommodations law we considered in *Roberts*, makes no distinctions on the basis of the organization's viewpoint. Moreover, public accommodations laws "plainly serv[e] compelling state interests of the highest order." [468 U.S. at 624.] In *Roberts* we recognized that the State's compelling interest in assuring equal access to women extends to the acquisition of leadership skills and business contacts as well as tangible goods and services. [Id. at 626.] The Unruh Act plainly serves this interest. We therefore hold that application of the Unruh Act to California Rotary Clubs does not violate the right of expressive association afforded by the First Amendment . . . .

[handwritten margin note: Holding]

Justice SCALIA concurs in the judgment.

Justice BLACKMUN and Justice O'CONNOR took no part in the consideration or decision of this case.

≡ ***Foster v. Back Bay Spas***
1997 Mass. Super. LEXIS 194
(Sept. 29, 1997)

[handwritten margin note: Issue: Men join health club]

BURNS, Judge . . .

This motion for summary judgment arises out of plaintiff James Foster's action to require the defendant . . . to allow him to join the health club. The club does not admit men. Foster argues that this policy violates [the Massachusetts public accommodations statute that prohibits discrimination based on sex].

Background

Plaintiff James Foster [lives] in Boston. Defendant Back Bay Spas, Inc. d/b/a Healthworks Fitness Center ("Healthworks") owns and operates a health club facility in the Back Bay area of Boston which accepts only women. Foster is a member of the Marriott Health Club at Copley Place, directly across the street from a Healthworks facility. There exist a large number of other, co-ed exercise facilities in the Boston area with similar resources as Healthworks. Nevertheless, Foster seeks membership at Healthworks Fitness Center, the one facility which caters only to women.

Healthworks was developed and designed for use by women, and thus its programs and facilities—including locker rooms and restrooms—cater to women. Healthworks, in addition to providing a full range of exercise equipment and facilities, offers various fitness and health classes, including classes tailored towards female concerns such as pre-natal programs and special nutrition counseling for women. Healthworks has also contracted with the YWCA Boston so that its members may use its facility. Healthworks promotes itself as an all women's facility, by its advertising and facility window displays.

Healthworks opened its Back Bay facility in February 1996 and its membership is now over 3,500. Foster inquired about membership at Healthworks in February 1996 and was turned away because he is a man.

Affidavits submitted by Healthworks reveal that many of the club's members based their decision to join and to remain members of the facility because it is only open to women. Moreover, Healthworks submitted an affidavit of a Robert Tanenbaum, Ph.D., an expert on areas that impact exercise behavior and fitness including knowledge of gender differences, human sexuality, and reduction of performance anxiety . . . . In his affidavit, Dr. Tanenbaum concludes that over 80% of the members he interviewed stated that the all female aspect of the club was the most important reason for joining Healthworks; that many of the members are of "post-childbearing age and have experienced bodily changes resulting from pregnancy and childbirth which alter their appearance . . . older members who have recently gone through menopause . . . feel intimidated exercising in a coed environment;" that many of the women expressed concern about being watched by members of the opposite sex while exercising; and, that several were recovering from past physical or sexual abuse, or had specific religious concerns about exercising in a coed facility. Most significantly, Dr. Tanenbaum concluded that "approximately 87% of the women . . . said that they would stop exercising at Healthworks if men were permitted to join. . . . Healthworks meets an existing need among the women described and minimizes the hurdles typically found in a coed setting, particularly for women who do not have a consistent fitness history."

Discussion

No material facts are in dispute. The Court, therefore, is charged with determining whether Foster has proved, as a matter of law, that Healthworks' refusal to allow men membership in its facility is in violation of the Massachusetts Public Accommodation Law, . . . and, if so, whether there is any exception to the anti-discrimination provisions in that law.

[Massachusetts law] provides [that]:

> No . . . place of public accommodation, resort or amusement shall, directly or indirectly . . . distribute or display . . . any . . . notice or sign, . . . intended to discriminate against or actually discriminating against persons of any . . . sex . . . in the full enjoyment of the accommodations, advantages, facilities or privileges offered to the general public by such places of public accommodation. . . .

The statute further defines a "place of public accommodation" [to include]:

> any place, . . . which is open to and accepts or solicits the patronage of the general public and . . . (8) a place of public amusement, recreation, sport, exercise or entertainment. . . .

[The law provides]:

> Whoever makes any distinction, discrimination or restriction on account of . . . sex . . . relative to the admission of any person to, or his treatment in any place of public accommodation, resort or amusement, as defined in Section ninety-two A, . . . shall be punished. . . . All persons shall have the right to the full and equal accommodations, advantages, facilities and privileges of any place of public accommodation, resort or amusement subject only to the conditions and limitations established by law and applicable to all persons.

Healthworks has stipulated that it is "a place of public accommodation." . . . On its face, therefore, there is no dispute that the exclusion of males from this place of public accommodation is in violation of the public accommodation law. Healthworks claims, however, that women have a privacy right to exercise in an all female environment.

The privacy statute grants a right to privacy. [The statute provides that] "a person shall have a right against unreasonable, substantial or serious interference with his privacy." The central issue in this case, therefore, is whether a privacy right exists, or can be read into the public accommodations statute, which would permit the exclusion of all men from an all women's exercise facility.

Healthworks claims that its customers' privacy rights are protected by [the law]; that there exists within the public accommodations statute an implied right of privacy for all women to exercise in an all women environment; and that the public accommodation statute was amended to protect women, not men. Specifically, Healthworks argues that a privacy right exists, based on the customer gender preferences of Healthworks's membership. [In a Pennsylvania case identical to this one,] the Commonwealth Court of Pennsylvania held that based on a "customer gender privacy" defense, an all women's health club would be permitted to exclude all men from its facility, stating that "this defense recognizes a pervasive public policy that certain conduct that relates to and between genders is inappropriate." . . . In determining that the membership had a privacy interest in exercising in a single sex club the court concluded that "they [the members] expose parts of the body about which they are most sensitive, assume awkward and compromising positions, and move themselves in a way which would embarrass them if men were present."

This Court recognizes the difficulty in defining what constitutes "privacy rights." Nevertheless, it is clear that the cases relied upon [in the Pennsylvania case] all involve the exposure or the touching of intimate body parts. This case, on the other hand, involves exercising—an activity—performed before numerous other people, in full exercise attire. Moreover, as Foster points out, at the Healthworks facility in Boston's Back Bay area, the exercisers can be seen from the street as there are two large windows at the front of the facility. Healthworks argues that although there is little nudity involved, and recognizes that any such nudity is voluntary, the compromising positions and contours the customers must invariably assume while exercising raises this clothed activity to a level of exposure akin to nudity or physical contact and thus requires the protection of a privacy right. Again, this Court disagrees. No exercise position, performed while dressed, would result in the sort of exposure of intimate body parts which has been protected by the privacy right.

. . . Here, the putative privacy right is only the right to exercise in a same-sex facility. No private information is being disclosed, and no highly personal or intimate facts are being revealed. The only basis for the claimed right is the exposure of one's clothed anatomy while exercising. Massachusetts case law supports no such right.

Healthworks' affidavits and personal statements describe the sense of intimidation certain women, including post-menopausal women, and women who have undergone mastectomies or who have suffered abuse, will feel in a coed exercise atmosphere, such that they would cease their exercise program. While the Court recognizes the impact that the admission of men into the club may have on these women, intimidation and the assumption that all male Healthworks members will harass and leer at their exercise compatriots is still an insufficient ground on which to create a privacy exception. Absent the unclothed exposure of intimate body parts, or the touching of body parts by members of the opposite sex, this Court can find no basis for overriding the public accommodations statute's mandate.

Further, an affidavit from a member of the Islamic faith stated that Islamic women, who are forbidden from revealing any part of their body (except for their face and hands) while in the presence of men, would no longer be able to use the Healthworks facility at all if men were allowed to join. Healthworks, however, is not a religious facility providing exercise facilities only to Islamic women. It is a public health club. And while this Court recognizes the disparate impact the inclusion of men will have on women of the Islamic faith, this Court cannot allow Healthworks to discriminate against men by allowing women of all faiths access to a single-sex exercise space on the basis of the religious beliefs of a portion of its members.

Because this Court concludes that there is no legitimate privacy interest to be recognized or protected which would excuse the discriminatory exclusion of males in violation of the public accommodations statute, the inquiry need not go further. Since the customers of Healthworks have no privacy right to be protected, the Court is not required, indeed cannot, consider whether Healthworks' policy is reasonable.

For the reasons set forth above, [Foster's motion for summary judgment is granted].

Notes

1. First Amendment Challenges. Under *Roberts* and *Rotary Club*, the more personal and intimate the association in terms of its size, purpose, selectivity, and agenda, and the more engaged in a specific political, social, or religious agenda, the greater the protection the First Amendment affords. Is it appropriate that the more exclusive the association, the greater autonomy it will enjoy? Is it perverse that a neo-Nazi group but not a Little League may be able to exclude Jews?

Anti-discrimination statutes similar to the one applied in the Healthworks case also have faced First Amendment challenges. An important early case involved a successful challenge to the exclusion of girls by the Boys' Club of Santa Cruz. The Club's mission was to combat delinquency in boys, who were four times more likely than girls to get into trouble with the law. Club owners, and the principal donor, had determined that male juvenile delinquency could be most effectively addressed in an all-male setting.[243] After the Club lost its First Amendment challenge, the donor attempted to cancel the $15 million trust fund that brought in 75 percent of the club's annual budget. She was unable to do so because her original gift had not required the exclusion of girls. A few years after the litigation, 30 percent of the members of the Boys' Club in Santa Cruz were girls, involved in all aspects of the club,

---

243. Isbister v. Boys Club of Santa Cruz, 707 P.2d 212 (Cal. 1985).

including football and baseball. According to one report, there were "no signs of tension" as a result of the change in admission policy.[244]

In California, similar litigation was unsuccessful in forcing the Boy Scouts to admit girls.[245] The Boy Scouts still exclude girls, although the Explorers allow female adolescents between 14 and 20 to join. Moreover, since 1988, adult women have been allowed to become Boy Scout troop leaders. The Boy Scouts have taken no steps to include transgender boys; after some initial resistance, the Girl Scouts of Colorado admitted a transgender boy to a troop. The organization said it would welcome a child who "lives life as a girl" and would not require any proof of anatomical gender from parents' requesting membership for a daughter.[246]

A divided U.S. Supreme Court in Boy Scouts of America v. Dale upheld the right of the Boy Scouts to exclude members based on sexual orientation.[247] The case involved James Dale, who joined the Scouts at age eight and for the next 12 years was an exemplary member. He earned 25 merit badges and the honored status of Eagle Scout. Shortly after being appointed an assistant troop leader, Dale enrolled at Rutgers University, where he became co-president of the Lesbian and Gay Alliance. His membership in the Scouts was revoked after a Newark newspaper identified him as president and quoted comments that he made in connection with a seminar on health needs of gay and lesbian teens.

Dale then filed a complaint under New Jersey public accommodation law, which bars discrimination based on characteristics such as race, ethnicity, and sexual orientation. The New Jersey Supreme Court upheld his claim, and in a 5-4 decision, the U.S. Supreme Court reversed. Writing for the majority, Chief Justice Rehnquist concluded that the New Jersey law violated the Boy Scouts' rights of speech and association. Under the Court's analysis, "the presence of a gay rights activist would force the organization to send a message that the Boy Scouts accepts homosexual conduct." According to Scout leadership, such a message would be inconsistent with its oath and laws requiring Scouts to be "morally straight" and "clean" in body and mind.

In upholding the Scouts' policy, the majority relied heavily on its prior decision in Hurley v. Irish-American Gay, Lesbian and Bisexual Group of Boston, Inc.[248] In *Hurley*, the Court ruled that organizers of a St. Patrick's Day parade could not be compelled by Massachusetts public accommodation law to let gays and lesbians march behind a GLBT banner. Just as those parade organizers had the right "not to propound a particular point of view," the

---

244. Jill Zuckman, Boys' Club Finds Sugar and Spice, San Jose Mercury News, Aug. 14, 1987, at 1B.

245. See Yeaw v. Boy Scouts of America, 64 Cal. Rptr. 2d 85 (Ct. App. 1997).

246. See Phil Gast, Parents Urged to Support, Safeguard Children as They Explore Gender, CNN.com (Oct. 28, 2011).

247. 530 U.S. 640 (2000).

248. 515 U.S. 557 (1995).

Boy Scouts had a right not to convey the message of legitimacy that Dale's membership would imply.[249]

Justice Stevens, writing for himself and three other Justices, took issue with the majority's analysis of both the facts and the law.

> [N]either one of [the Scouts' guiding] principles — "morally straight" and "clean" — says the slightest thing about homosexuality. Indeed, neither term in the Boy Scouts' Law and Oath expresses any position whatsoever on sexual matters.
>
> BSA's published guidance on that topic underscores this point. Scouts, for example, are directed to receive their sex education at home or in school, but not from the organization. . . .
>
> Several principles are made perfectly clear by [the Court's past cases in this area]. First, to prevail on a claim of expressive association in the face of a State's antidiscrimination law, it is not enough simply to engage in *some kind* of expressive activity. . . . Second, it is not enough to adopt an openly avowed exclusionary membership policy. . . . Third, it is not sufficient merely to articulate *some* connection between the group's expressive activities and its exclusionary policy. . . .
>
> Rather, [the question is whether an anti-discrimination law] "impose[s] any *serious burdens*" on the group's "collective effort on behalf of [its] shared *goals.* . . ."

The evidence before this Court makes it exceptionally clear that BSA has, at most, simply adopted an exclusionary membership policy and has no shared goal of disapproving of homosexuality.[250]

The *Dale* holding has been controversial among constitutional scholars, policymakers, and the general public. Some commentators have viewed the decision as inconsistent with prior cases involving discrimination by private associations (discussed in Chapter 1). They are also troubled by granting First Amendment protection to an organization that discriminates on the basis of status, not conduct: heterosexual troop leaders who support gay rights were not dismissed.

Should the Jaycees and Rotary Club be required to admit women, while the Boy Scouts are entitled to exclude gays?

In piecemeal fashion, Boy Scouts lifted their bans on participation by gay scouts, leaders, and employees, but allowed local chapters to continue excluding gay volunteer leaders at their discretion.[251] Should its discriminatory legacy continue to influence the decision whether to join?

---

249. Boy Scouts of America v. Dale, 530 U.S. 640, 651, 653, 655-56 (2000).

250. Id. at 668-69, 682-84.

251. See Michelle Boorstein, Boy Scouts of America Votes to End Controversial Ban on Openly-Gay Scout Leaders, Wash. Post, July 27, 2015.

2. Separate but Equal. At the time the *Jaycees* and *Rotary Club* cases were decided, there were no comparable organizations for women that provided the same networking advantages. Should it have made a difference if there were? In contrast, girls who could not join the Boy Scouts were able to join the Girl Scouts. Should this make a difference?

If the Boy Scouts should be required to admit girls, should the Girl Scouts be required to admit boys? Could the Girl Scouts claim that their case for sex segregation is stronger, as a strategy to remedy past discrimination against girls?[252]

3. The Scope of State and Local Public Accommodations Laws. Federal law prohibits discrimination in public accommodations on the basis of race, color, religion, national origin or disability, but not sex.[253] Federal constitutional guarantees of equal protection apply only to public entities. Thus, challenges to sex-based exclusions from private associations, as in *Rotary Club*, from private businesses, or from retail establishments have been brought under state civil rights acts. The public accommodations laws in some states do not apply to sex-based exclusions at all.[254] Among the many that do, however, the scope varies. Some prohibit discrimination only as to places of public accommodation, construed to mean entities that exist at a particular place, such as hotels or restaurants, and thereby excluding organizations that may meet in different locations, such as the Jaycees, Rotary Clubs, and some scouting organizations. Others apply to private clubs only in areas or at functions where nonmembers are present. Some apply only to businesses, although business may be quite broadly construed. Some statutes specifically exempt "private" or "distinctly private" clubs.[255]

Although the plaintiff won his case against Healthworks, the Massachusetts legislature then passed legislation exempting fitness facilities from its general public accommodations law. A handful of other states have also carved out narrow exemptions for health clubs, changing rooms, bath houses and other places where privacy concerns might be relevant.[256] Are targeted

---

252. These questions should be considered again in the context of the materials in Chapter 2, Section C.

253. 42 U.S.C. §2000a (2012); 42 U.S.C. §12182 (2012). The Equality Act, discussed above, would add "sex" to the list of prohibited characteristics.

254. For a comprehensive listing of public accommodations laws, see Joseph William Singer, No Right to Exclude: Public Accommodations and Private Property, 90 Nw. U. L. Rev. 1283, 1478-95 (1996).

255. Examples of each of these types of statutes are discussed in Sally Frank, The Key to Unlocking the Clubhouse Door: The Application of Antidiscrimination Laws to Quasi-Private Clubs, 2 Mich. J. Gender & L. 27 (1994).

256. See Mass. Gen. Laws ch. 272 §92A (2016); 775 Ill. Comp. Stat. 5/5-103 (West 2012); Tenn. Code Ann. §4-21-503 (2016); see also Michael R. Evans, The Case for All-Female Health Clubs: Creating a Compensatory Purpose Exception to State Public Accommodation Laws, 11 Yale J.L. & Feminism 307 (1999).

exemptions a reasonable compromise? If Massachusetts wants to allow all-women's health clubs, is it also required to allow all-men's health clubs?

All-male golf and country clubs have been another site of controversy. Public pressure led the Augusta National Golf Club to integrate racially in the 1970s, and caused the withdrawal of corporate sponsorships from the prestigious Masters tournament in 2003 and 2004. When major companies again began supporting the event, the National Council of Women's Organizations organized shareholder resolutions charging that the corporate sponsorship violated company anti-discrimination policy.[257] As late as 2012, the club reaffirmed its all-male policy, with chairman Billy Payne calling it a "private matter," but later that year, the club admitted its first two female members—former Secretary of State Condoleeza Rice and business executive Darla Moore.[258] An advisory opinion from the Arizona state attorney general's office stated that the exclusion of women from the Phoenix Country Club violated state anti-discrimination laws.[259] The Club now offers a Women's Golf Association.[260] Why do you suppose that it has been harder to get clubs and corporate sponsors to take sex discrimination as seriously as race discrimination?

4. Gender-Based Pricing. In states with broad public accommodations laws, men and women have challenged pricing differentials that benefit the other sex.[261] Early cases upheld the differentials.[262] However, the law has begun to shift the other way. The California Supreme Court ruled in *Koire v. Metro Car Wash* that several car washes and a bar violated the public accommodations law by providing "ladies' day" discounts to women.[263] The legislature later adopted a law making clear that price differentials cannot be based

257. On the controversy, see Frank J. Ferraro, Prerogative or Prejudice?: The Exclusion of Women from Augusta National, 1 DePaul J. Sports L. Contemp. Probs. 39 (2003); Elizabeth Dwoskin, Burk Swings at Exxon (Apr. 17, 2006), www.womensenews.org; Martha Burk, Cult of Power: Sex Discrimination in Corporate America and What Can Be Done About It (2005).

258. Karen Crouse, Touchy Day at Augusta National Men's Club, N.Y. Times, Apr. 4, 2012, at B11; Elisabeth Bumiller, Avid Golfer Rice Jumps a Barrier Again, N.Y. Times, Aug. 20, 2012, at B9.

259. See Jennifer Steinhauer, A Cozy Spot to Eat After Golf, but Out of Bounds to Women, N.Y. Times, June 28, 2008, at A1.

260 . See http://www.phoenixcc.org/club/scripts/library/view_document.asp?GRP=1 4417&NS=PG&APP=80&DN=WGA.

261. See Mark Allan Herzberg, "Girls Get in Free": A Legal Analysis of the Gender-Based Door Entry Policies, 19 S. Cal. Rev. L. & Soc. Just. 479 (2010).

262. See, e.g., Tucich v. Dearborn Indoor Racquet Club, 309 N.W.2d 615, 619 (Mich. Ct. App. 1981); The Dock Club, Inc. v. Illinois Liquor Control Comm'n, 428 N.E.2d 735 (Ill. App. Ct. 1981); MacLean v. First Northwest Indus., 635 P.2d 683 (Wash. 1981).

263. 707 P.2d 195 (Cal. 1985); see also Ladd v. Iowa W. Racing Ass'n, 438 N.W.2d 600 (Iowa 1989) (racetrack's policy of giving free admission and discounted concessions to women constituted unlawful discrimination).

on sex and requiring certain businesses, including dry cleaners and hair salons, to post a notice informing customers that state law prohibits discrimination "with respect to the price charged for services of similar or like kind, against a person because of the person's gender."[264] In 2004, the New Jersey Director of Civil Rights issued a ruling that a restaurant's "ladies' night"—a night each week when it admitted women free of charge and charged them less for drinks—violated the state's anti-discrimination law.[265] The restaurant argued that it had a legitimate purpose for the promotion—to increase patronage and revenue by bringing more women to the restaurant because of the reduced prices and more men because of the greater number of women. It also argued that this type of discrimination was too trivial to matter and, in any event, was canceled out by similar promotions, on different nights, for men. The director rejected all these arguments and held that the New Jersey law contained no exceptions.

Are gender-based price differentials ever justified? Are some forms of discrimination too trivial to bother with? Is equality served more by strict interpretation of anti-discrimination laws or by focusing only on the most severe types of discrimination? Are women helped or harmed by a policy that charges them less for alcoholic drinks?

5. Public Breastfeeding. As these materials make clear, private businesses have the right to exclude unless doing so violates a public accommodations law. Likewise, they have the right to set rules for customer behavior—"no shirt, no shoes, no service"—unless that power is circumscribed. Women who breastfeed in stores or restaurants, or on airplanes, have sometimes encountered hostility and, in some cases, been thrown out. These incidents are sometimes met with public protests, such as "nurse-ins," in which large numbers of women show up to the location of a controversy and simultaneously breastfeed.[266] Almost every state now has a public breastfeeding law that overrides the state's criminal indecent exposure laws (if they even apply to women's breasts; many do not) and amends the public accommodation laws specifically to protect breastfeeding. Most of these laws give a woman the right to breastfeed anywhere she otherwise has the right to be.[267] Yet, despite

264. Cal. Civ. Code §51.6 (2016).

265. Gillespie v. Coastline Restaurant, CRT 2579-03, Order, N.J. Dep't of Law & Public Safety (June 1, 2004), http://www.state.nj.us/lps/Gillespie.Order.06.01.04.html.

266. See Cavan Sieczkowski, Moms Stage "Nurse-In" to Protest Anthropologie Breastfeeding Incident, Huffpost Parents (Aug. 21, 2014), http://www.huffingtonpost.com/2014/08/21/nurse-in-anthropologie-breastfeeding_n_5697858.html.

267. For a current list of laws, see State Breastfeeding Laws, Nat'l Conf. of State Legis., http://www.ncsl.org/research/health/breastfeeding-state-laws.aspx#State. Although the federal accommodations law does not cover sex-based exclusion, a 1999 amendment to a postal appropriations bill provides that women can breastfeed in any federal building or on federal property. See Treasury and General Government Appropriations Act, Pub. L. No. 106-58, §647, 113 Stat. 478 (1999).

these protections, women are sometimes still ordered to leave public and private places when they breastfeed.[268] Emily Gilette was forced off a Delta Airlines plane in 2006 for refusing to cover her baby's head with a blanket, even though she and her family occupied an entire row and were seated in the rear of the plane; she was in Vermont, which had (and has) broad protections for breastfeeding.[269] She was awarded damages. Why do people object to public breastfeeding?

6. Sexual Orientation and Public Accommodations. Public accommodations laws are also being used to challenge exclusions based on sexual orientation. A growing number of states ban discrimination by public accommodations on grounds of sexual orientation and, in a smaller number of states, gender identity.[270] The Supreme Court of California held that California's Unruh Act, invoked in *Koire* and *Isbister*, was violated by a medical group's refusal to provide infertility treatment to lesbian women. The statute at the time did not prohibit sexual orientation discrimination, although it was amended in 2005 to provide protection for sexual orientation and gender identity and expression.[271] But even before that amendment, the list of protected characteristics in the statute was treated as illustrative rather than exhaustive, and courts had repeatedly applied it to exclusions on the basis of sexual orientation. The court in North Coast Women's Care Med. Grp., Inc. v. San Diego Cnty. (Cal. 2008) rejected the argument that the doctors' religious objections to inseminating a lesbian, unmarried woman were sufficient to excuse the clear violation of the public accommodations law. Medical practices, like other business establishments, must provide "full and equal" access to all patients. A 2009 report by the American Society for Reproductive Medicine concluded that there is no ethical basis for physicians to deny access to fertility services on the basis of marital status or sexual orientation.[272] The American College of Obstetricians and Gynecologists gives doctors more room to exercise conscientious objection by refusing to provide particular services or to treat particular patients.[273] Regardless of the ethics,

268. See, e.g., Martha Neil, Public Breastfeeding May Be Legal in Mich., But It's Not OK in My Court, Judge Told Mom, ABA J. (Nov. 11, 2011); Pastor Calls Breastfeeding Mom a Stripper, SFGate (Oct. 18, 2012), http://blog.sfgate.com/sfmoms/2012/02/28/pastor-calls-breastfeeding-mom-a-stripper.

269. 9 Vt. Stat. Ann. §4502j (2016).

270. A map of current state laws on this subject is available at http://www.aclu.org/maps/non-discrimination-laws-state-state-information-map.

271. Cal. Civ. Code §51 (2016).

272. ASRM-Ethics Committee, Access to Fertility Treatment by Gays, Lesbians, and Unmarried Persons, 92 Fertility & Sterility 1190 (2009).

273. ACOG-Committee on Ethics, The Limits of Conscientious Refusal in Reproductive Medicine, 110 Obstetrics & Gynecology 1203 (2007, aff'd 2010).

however, surveys suggest that many fertility specialists do indeed discriminate on the basis of sexual orientation and marital status.[274]

The Supreme Court's ruling in Obergefell v. Hodges,[275] which held bans on same-sex marriage unconstitutional, has provoked a number of new lawsuits about the denial of public accommodations to gay and lesbian individuals by bakers, photographers, and wedding venues. The individuals and businesses in these cases have argued that providing goods or services in connection with gay or lesbian weddings violates their religious freedom. These challenges have not made it far in court. The Supreme Court of New Mexico upheld a trial court's ruling that a photographer who refused to provide services for a lesbian wedding had violated state law prohibiting sexual orientation discrimination. The nondiscrimination law was generally applicable and did not infringe the photographer's free exercise rights.[276] Likewise, an appellate court in Colorado upheld an order requiring a bakery to fill a gay couple's order for a wedding cake.[277]

Despite these losses in court, social conservatives have rallied behind the bakers, florists, and photographers who object to playing a role in a wedding, when, they say, the marriage violates their deeply held religious beliefs. Are courts reaching the correct results in these cases? Do women have a stake in the outcome? Consider Mary Anne Case's observations about the "live-and-let-live" solution that some have urged in the era of marriage equality:

> Although the claim of the proponents of living-and-letting-live is that "we can and should protect the liberty of both sides in the culture wars," every proposal I have seen provides far more protection to the religious objectors than to the proponents of sexual liberty and equality, among which latter group I unequivocally count myself. In particular, while it is clearly correct to say, as [Douglas] Laycock does, that, "[i]f we are to preserve liberty for both sides in the culture wars, then we have to preserve some space where each side can live its own values and where its rules control," no proposal I yet have seen offers my side in the culture wars anything like the "space . . . [to] live its own values and where its rules control" such proposals insist our conservative religious opponents are entitled to. As a strong supporter of rights to sexual liberty and equality, I instead observe that many religiously motivated opponents of such rights seem to want to have their cake, eat it too, and shove it down my throat; and that most, if not all, religious liberty scholars who claim their goal is a live-and-let-live solution seem to support my religious opponents in their ongoing efforts to realize these desires at my expense.

274. See Liza Mundy, Everything Conceivable: How the Science of Assisted Reproduction is Changing Men, Women, and the World 202 (2008) (citing 2005 study of doctors finding that half would refuse infertility services to a lesbian woman).

275. 135 S. Ct. 2584 (2015). This case is excerpted in Chapter 3, Section D of this book.

276. Elane Photography, LLC v. Willock, 309 P.3d 53 (N.M. 2013).

277. Craig v. Masterpiece Cakeshop, Inc., 370 P.3d 272 (Colo. Ct. App. 2015).

Nor am I reassured by the insistence of proponents of live-and-let-live that while religious liberty may be in great peril, women's rights are secure, that there is of course no danger of retrogression on aspects of our current law crucial to women's legal and social equality. . . .[278]

7. Social Stigma Harms. Victims of sex discrimination will sometimes be ostracized by the members of the clubs and associations they must sue in order to gain admittance, which seriously undermines the value of the protection public accommodations statutes are able to offer. One revealing New York Times account of a lawsuit to end discriminatory practices at a Massachusetts country club described the ostracism and frustration of plaintiffs, which contributed to divorce, and the loss of clients and business, among other things.[279] These difficulties also occur in the employment context when a plaintiff sues to protect her rights, but there, employers have an obligation to protect an employee from retaliation as a result of pursuing her employment rights; they also tend to have greater control over the other employees than private clubs may have over their members. Is this problem a necessary price of litigation? Can the law realistically address it?

Putting Theory Into Practice

1-35. A law firm advertises on billboards with the tagline: "Divorce: Men Only" and describes its mission as "fighting for men's rights." The firm accepts only male clients and also provides fee discounts for all law enforcement officers and "firemen." Is this lawful in a state with a public accommodations law that protects against sex discrimination? Do any potential justifications for the focus on men's rights offset any harms to women?[280] What about a competitor to Uber called Chariot for Women, which operates under the tagline "Driving Women Towards Empowerment and Safety" and accepts only female drivers and riders.[281] Is this lawful? Might it be even if the men-only divorce firm is not? Why or why not?

---

278. Mary Anne Case, Why "Live-and-Let-Live" Is Not a Viable Solution to the Difficult Problems of Religious Accommodation in the Age of Sexual Civil Rights, 88 S. Cal. L. Rev. 463, 471, 489 (2015).

279. Marcia Chambers, The High Price of Victory, N.Y. Times, Apr. 2, 2001, at D1.

280. This problem is modeled on one described in Michele N. Struffolino, For Men Only: A Gap in the Rules Allows Sex Discrimination to Avoid Ethical Challenge, 23 Am. U. J. Gender Soc. Pol'y & L. 487 (2014). In Nathanson v. Commonwealth, 16 Mass. L. Rep. 761 (Super. Ct. 2003), the court affirmed a ruling of the Massachusetts Commission Against Discrimination that fined a female matrimonial lawyer $5000 for refusing to accept male clients. For discussion, see the symposium in 20 W. New Eng. L. Rev. 5 (1998).

281 Justin Wm. Moyer, A 'Female-Only Uber' Called Chariot is Coming to Boston Next Week. But Is It Legal?, Wash. Post, Apr. 11, 2016.

1-36. Under the Massachusetts law cited in *Foster*, could a public golf course run all-male tournaments if it also holds all-female tournaments?[282]

1-37. Harvard has a long tradition of all-male social clubs. In 1984, the university required these clubs to admit women. At that point, the clubs broke official ties with Harvard and were no longer recognized by the university. Under informal pressure to admit women in 2016, a spokesman for the 215-year-old all-male Porcellian Club justified the group's policy on the ground that admitting women could increase the chances of sexual misconduct.[283] A couple of weeks later, the University announced a new policy prohibiting members of single-sex clubs from holding leadership positions on campus, including captains of athletic teams, and barring them from receiving official recommendations required for prestigious fellowships such as the Rhodes and Marshall Scholarships. An estimated 30 percent of Harvard undergraduates belong to the six male "final clubs," five women's "final clubs," and nine sororities and fraternities. At least one club has already begun a lawsuit challenging the new policy on First Amendment grounds.[284] Is the challenge likely to prevail? Should it? Is the new policy a good way to promote gender equality on campus?

1-38. The Las Vegas Athletic Club offers cheaper sign-up rates for women than for men, because it has more trouble attracting women as members and seeks to increase its female clientele. Nevada has a law prohibiting discrimination based on sex in public accommodations.[285] Does the Athletic Club policy violate that statute? Should its practice be illegal? What about offering a women-only workout room? What about the sex-segregated topless swimming pools also available in some Las Vegas fitness centers?[286] Is it legal for the Nevada Hard Rock Hotel and Casino to promise that "ladies dressed in schoolgirl outfits drink free Champagne all night"?[287]

282. See Joyce v. Town of Dennis, 705 F. Supp. 2d 74 (D. Mass. 2010).

283. Jess Bidgood, Social Club at Harvard Rejects Calls to Admit Women, Citing Risk of Sexual Misconduct, N.Y. Times, Apr. 13, 2016, at A17.

284. Stephanie Saul, Harvard Restrictions Could Reshape Exclusive Student Clubs, N.Y. Times, May 6, 2016, at A9.

285. See Steve Friess, A Las Vegas Gym Faces a "Ladies' Night" Bias Case, N.Y. Times, Dec. 12, 2007, at A27.

286. See Phillips v. Las Vegas Athletic Club, Nev. Dep't Empl., Training and Rehab., Charge No. 0828-07-0563L (2008).

287. Friess, supra note 285 (describing Nevada litigation); Lauren Collins, Hey LA-A-A-Dies!, New Yorker, Aug. 6, 2007, at 22-23 (describing litigation against several nightclubs in New York that offer ladies' nights).

1-39. The Black Women's Health Imperative is a membership organization dedicated to "health education, research, advocacy and leadership development" for black women and girls. Its website describes itself as follows:

> Founded in 1983 by health activist Byllye Y. Avery, it has been a pioneer in promoting the empowerment of African American women as educated health care consumers and a strong voice for the improved health status of African American women. The organization is gaining the well-earned reputation as the leading force for health for African American women. Black Women's Health Imperative possesses national stature as the only national organization devoted solely to the health of the nation's 19 million Black women and girls.[288]

The organization's services and programs are all geared toward Black women and girls. Should this organization be subject to state legislation banning race and sex discrimination? How would you respond to the view propounded in relation to the organization's predecessor organization, the National Black Women's Health Project?

> If African-American women do not exclude white women from their association, their sharing will be chilled by the presence of white women. African-American women will spend valuable time listening to white women defend their actions. In essence, African-American women will spend time concentrating on white women, instead of focusing on themselves. Their communications will become stilted until they are effectively silenced in their own associations.[289]

1-40. Nineteenth-century hotels used to have separate floors for women. These were abandoned by the 1980s, but they are returning, as customer research has indicated that many women prefer the privacy and special amenities of floors that cater particularly to women. Is this a positive development, or a throwback to a discriminatory era?

1-41. Ansel O'Keefe is a well-known and highly successful photographer in New Mexico, who is well known for a very distinct style that integrates people and nature, most often in desert settings. Last fall, he turned down the request of two women to photograph their wedding on the explicit ground that he does not photograph people or subject matters of which he disapproves. He often does weddings, and accepts work from gays and lesbians in non-wedding matters, but he does not approve of same-sex weddings and thus will not accept an assignment of this nature. The applicable public accommodations law protects against sexual orientation discrimination, but O'Keefe argues that, as an artist, his work is "expressive." Just as "I would be

---

288. http://www.blackwomenshealth.org/site.
289. Pamela J. Smith, We Are Not Sisters: African-American Women and the Freedom to Associate and Disassociate, 66 Tul. L. Rev. 1467, 1511 (1992).

perfectly within my rights to refuse to photograph other subject matters that offend me—such as a uniformed Nazi or a bigamist surrounded by his 35 children," O'Keefe has stated, "the law cannot force me to express the state's misguided and morally repugnant views of marriage." Who should prevail if the couple sues?

1-42. How do the identity-based student organizations on your campus handle membership and leadership? Do you see any problem with their approaches?

2 Substantive Equality

When men and women are similarly situated, requiring that they be treated equally often opens up opportunities for women that were previously unavailable to them. To the extent that men and women are differently situated, however, applying the same rules to them may produce different, unequal outcomes. Theories of substantive equality seek to avoid these unequal outcomes by taking differences into account and eliminating their negative effects on women. Deciding which differences matter and what alternative approach will best accommodate them can involve complex, contested judgments.

One source of unequal outcomes for women is past discrimination. Women historically have been excluded, either by law or by gender roles and customs, from obtaining jobs equal to men in status and compensation. Examples of remedial measures intended to reverse the effects of past discrimination include "affirmative action" plans designed to increase female representation in traditionally male occupations and "pay equity" schemes designed to restructure wage scales that historically have developed job categories held disproportionately by women.

Biological differences are another potential target of substantive equality strategies. Only women become pregnant, for example, and pregnancy can disadvantage workers with respect to hiring, promotion, and job security. Measures to make those environments more compatible with pregnancy and related conditions aim to neutralize this disadvantage.

Many differences between men and women are matters of averages, rather than definitional or categorical differences. Formal equality rules level the playing field for the exceptional or "non-average" woman who can compete successfully for an opportunity on the same basis as the average man. Other more result-oriented approaches may be necessary, however, if the goal is to ensure that women and men have functionally equivalent opportunities. In the educational context, for example, some argue that all-female classrooms or sports teams are necessary to ensure that competition with boys does not deprive girls of equally valuable opportunities. In the family law, similarly, some rules are better than others at recognizing women's economic vulnerability and the greater investment they make in their children.

In considering the examples of substantive equality in this chapter, it is important to note (1) which differences in circumstances or characteristics between men and women are, or should be, significant, (2) what outcomes are just, and (3) what strategies are most likely to lead to those outcomes. To what extent does a substantive equality approach differ from formal equality?

A. REMEDYING THE EFFECTS OF PAST DISCRIMINATION

1. Sex-Specific Public Benefits to Remedy Past Societal Discrimination

One of the circumstances that might justify different treatment for otherwise similarly situated people is past discrimination that has disadvantaged members of one group. This rationale has been at the heart of affirmative action programs for racial and ethnic minorities and is also used to justify some measures to remedy past discrimination against women. Kahn v. Shevin, excerpted below, would likely be decided differently today, but the opinion is an important historical marker for use of affirmative remedies to address gender inequalities.

Kahn v. Shevin
416 U.S. 351 (1974)

Mr. Justice DOUGLAS delivered the opinion of the Court.

Since at least 1885, Florida has provided for some form of property tax exemption for widows. The current law granting all widows an annual $500 exemption . . . has been essentially unchanged since 1941. Appellant Kahn is a widower who lives in Florida and applied for the exemption to the Dade County Tax Assessor's Office. It was denied because the statute offers no analogous benefit for widowers. [T]he Circuit Court for Dade County, Florida, held the statute violative of the Equal Protection Clause of the Fourteenth Amendment. . . . The Florida Supreme Court reversed. . . .

There can be no dispute that the financial difficulties confronting the lone woman in Florida or in any other State exceed those facing the man.

Whether from overt discrimination or from the socialization process of a male-dominated culture, the job market is inhospitable to the woman seeking any but the lowest paid jobs. There are, of course, efforts under way to remedy this situation. . . . But firmly entrenched practices are resistant to such pressures, and, indeed, data compiled by the Women's Bureau of the United States Department of Labor show that in 1972 a woman working full time had a median income which was only 57.9% of the median for males—a figure actually six points lower than had been achieved in 1955. . . . The disparity is likely to be exacerbated for the widow. While the widower can usually continue in the occupation which preceded his spouse's death, in many cases the widow will find herself suddenly forced into a job market with which she is unfamiliar, and in which, because of her former economic dependency, she will have fewer skills to offer.

There can be no doubt, therefore, that Florida's differing treatment of widows and widowers "rest[s] upon some ground of difference having a fair and substantial relation to the object of the legislation." [Reed v. Reed (1971).] . . .

This is not a case like Frontiero v. Richardson . . . where the Government denied its female employees both substantive and procedural benefits granted males "solely . . . for administrative convenience." We deal here with a state tax law reasonably designed to further the state policy of cushioning the financial impact of spousal loss upon the sex for which that loss imposes a disproportionately heavy burden. . . .

Affirmed.

Mr. Justice BRENNAN, with whom Mr. Justice MARSHALL joins, dissenting. . . .

In my view . . . a legislative classification that distinguishes potential beneficiaries solely by reference to their gender-based status as widows or widowers, like classifications based upon race, alienage, and national origin, must be subjected to close judicial scrutiny, because it focuses upon generally immutable characteristics over which individuals have little or no control, and also because gender-based classifications too often have been inexcusably utilized to stereotype and stigmatize politically powerless segments of society. See Frontiero v. Richardson [1973]. . . .

I agree that, in providing special benefits for a needy segment of society long the victim of purposeful discrimination and neglect, the statute serves the compelling state interest of achieving equality for such groups. No one familiar with this country's history of pervasive sex discrimination against women can doubt the need for remedial measures to correct the resulting economic imbalances. . . . [T]he purpose and effect of the suspect classification are ameliorative; the statute neither stigmatizes nor denigrates widowers not also benefited by the legislation. Moreover, inclusion of needy widowers within the class of beneficiaries would not further the State's overriding interest in remedying the economic effects of past sex discrimination for needy victims of that discrimination. While doubtless some widowers are in financial need, no one suggests that such need results from sex discrimination as in the case of widows.

The statute nevertheless fails to satisfy the requirements of equal protection, since the State has not borne its burden of proving that its compelling interest could not be achieved by a more precisely tailored statute or by use of feasible, less drastic means. [The statute] is plainly overinclusive, for the $500 property tax exemption may be obtained by a financially independent heiress as well as by an unemployed widow with dependent children. The State has offered nothing to explain why inclusion of widows of substantial economic means was necessary to advance the State's interest in ameliorating the effects of past economic discrimination against women. . . .

By merely redrafting that form to exclude widows who earn annual incomes, or possess assets, in excess of specified amounts, the State could readily narrow the class of beneficiaries to those widows for whom the effects of past economic discrimination against women have been a practical reality.

Mr. Justice WHITE, dissenting.

The Florida tax exemption at issue here is available to all widows but not to widowers. The presumption is that all widows are financially more needy and less trained or less ready for the job market than men. It may be that most widows have been occupied as housewife, mother, and homemaker and are not immediately prepared for employment. But there are many rich widows who need no largess from the State; many others are highly trained and have held lucrative positions long before the death of their husbands. At the same time, there are many widowers who are needy and who are in more desperate financial straits and have less access to the job market than many widows. Yet none of them qualifies for the exemption. . . .

I find the discrimination invidious and violative of the Equal Protection Clause. There is merit in giving poor widows a tax break, but gender-based classifications are suspect and require more justification than the State has offered. . . .

It may be suggested that the State is entitled to prefer widows over widowers because their assumed need is rooted in past and present economic discrimination against women. But this is not a credible explanation of Florida's tax exemption; for if the State's purpose was to compensate for past discrimination against females, surely it would not have limited the exemption to women who are widows. Moreover, even if past discrimination is considered to be the criterion for current tax exemption, the State nevertheless ignores all those widowers who have felt the effects of economic discrimination, whether as a member of a racial group or as one of the many who cannot escape the cycle of poverty. It seems to me that the State in this case is merely conferring an economic benefit in the form of a tax exemption and has not adequately explained why women should be treated differently from men.

I dissent.

NOTE ON "BENIGN" CLASSIFICATIONS FAVORING WOMEN

As a result of the statute upheld in Kahn v. Shevin, a wealthy widow could receive a $500 property tax exemption while an impoverished widower could not. Can this result be justified under equal treatment principles?

Justice Douglas, one of the Court's most liberal members and strongest supporters of gender equality, was convinced that Florida's preference for women was justifiable. Some commentators have attributed this view to Douglas' own experience. At age six, his mother was left destitute by the death of his father, a rural preacher. Douglas and his older sister washed store windows and picked fruit to earn the nickels and dimes that, as he later recalled, "often meant the difference between dinner and no dinner." At oral argument, the lawyer for the widower, Ruth Bader Ginsburg, attempted to convince the Court that the preference was an inadequate way of responding to widows' plight: "if need is the concern, then sex should not substitute for an income test. And if widowed state is the concern, then it is irrational to distinguish between taxpayers based on their sex."[1] Does Justice Douglas' opinion respond to this argument?

Kahn v. Shevin is one of a few public benefits decisions that have allowed group-based treatment more favorable to women than to men. The other principal case along this line is Califano v. Webster (1977), a case that upheld a Social Security provision applicable to retirements before 1972 and computed old-age benefits under a formula more favorable to women than to men. The benefits for both sexes were determined according to an average monthly wage earned during certain years, but women were given the opportunity of excluding three additional lower earning years than men. In a per curiam opinion, the Court concluded:

> The more favorable treatment of the female wage earner enacted here was not a result of "archaic and overbroad generalizations" about women . . . or of "the role typing society has long imposed" upon women . . . such as casual assumptions that women are "the weaker sex" or are more likely to be child-rearers or dependents. . . . Rather, "the only discernible purpose of [the statute's more favorable treatment is] the permissible one of redressing our society's longstanding disparate treatment of women."

The challenged statute operated directly to compensate women for past economic discrimination. Retirement benefits under the Act are based on past

1. Fred Strebeigh, Equal: Women Reshape American Law 63 (2009).

earnings. But as we have recognized: "Whether from overt discrimination or from the socialization process of a male-dominated culture, the job market is inhospitable to the woman seeking any but the lowest paid jobs." [Kahn v. Shevin.] Thus, allowing women, who as such have been unfairly hindered from earning as much as men, to eliminate additional low-earning years from the calculation of their retirement benefits works directly to remedy some part of the effect of past discrimination.[2]

How "benign" is the classification that *Kahn* upheld? In an illuminating international study by Peter Glick and Susan Fiske, some 15,000 men and women were rated on attitudes of hostile sexism and benevolent sexism (an example of the latter would be "women should be cherished and protected by men"). They found that the two forms of sexism were related and together were better predictors of gender inequality than either alone.[3] What are the policy implications of this research?

A premise of many of the cases considered in Chapter 1, such as Orr v. Orr, is that sex-based classifications that appear to benefit women, in fact, may foster the kind of stereotypes that do more harm than good. Is there any other problem with "benign" classifications? Consider Catharine MacKinnon's observation about Kahn v. Shevin:

> The special benefits side of the difference approach has not compensated for the differential of being second class. . . . Under its double standard, women who stand to inherit something when their husbands die have gotten the exclusion of a small percentage of the inheritance tax to the tune of Justice Douglas waxing eloquent about the difficulties of all women's economic situation. If we're going to be stigmatized as different, it would be nice if the compensation would fit the disparity.[4]

Is MacKinnon's criticism fair to Justice Douglas? Aren't legislatures entitled to partially address an inequality? Or is the complaint that Kahn v. Shevin is mere tokenism?

Putting Theory Into Practice

2-1. The U.S. Navy at one time had a policy in which male officers were terminated after they were passed over for promotion a second time after nine years, while female officers were discharged for non-promotion only after 13 years. The rationale was that women could only be assigned to hospital ships

2. Califano v. Webster, 430 U.S. 313, 317-18 (1977).
3. Peter T. Glick et al., Beyond Gender Prejudice as Simple Antipathy: Hostile and Benevolent Sexism Across Cultures, 79 J. Personality & Soc. Psychol. 763 (2000).
4. Catharine A. MacKinnon, Feminism Unmodified: Discourses on Life and Law 38 (1987).

and transports and not to vessels involved in combat, so they did not have the same opportunities as men to compile records warranting promotion.[5] Was this a reasonable policy? Is it still justified? Chapter 1 addresses further issues relating to women in the military.

2. "Affirmative Action" in Employment

Under certain circumstances, Title VII permits affirmative action to redress a significant gender imbalance in the workplace. An affirmative action plan might give preference to qualified women for a job they previously would not have obtained because of past discrimination, or because of historical patterns that channeled male and female workers into separate and unequal positions.

Litigation may force employers to implement an affirmative action plan to remedy past discrimination, but employers might also wish to voluntarily integrate their work force even in the absence of legal liability. The latter situation was at issue in Johnson v. Transportation Agency. There, the Supreme Court held that the agency could appropriately take into account the sex of the female employee in its promotion decisions, even though past discrimination by the Agency could not be proved.

What limits on affirmative action does the Court place on employers that want to address a gender imbalance in their work force? What differences among the Justices exist on this question? Should sex-based affirmative action plans be evaluated under the same standard as race-based affirmative action plans?

≡ *Johnson v. Transportation Agency*
≡ 480 U.S. 616 (1987)

Justice BRENNAN delivered the opinion of the Court.

Respondent, Transportation Agency of Santa Clara County, California, unilaterally promulgated an Affirmative Action Plan . . . pursuant to which the Agency passed over petitioner Paul Johnson, a male employee [for promotion to road dispatcher], and promoted a female employee applicant, Diane Joyce. The question for decision is whether in making the promotion the Agency impermissibly took into account the sex of the applicants in violation of Title VII of the Civil Rights Act of 1964. [No constitutional issue was raised.] The District Court for the Northern District of California . . . held

Issue [handwritten annotation]

---

5. See Schlesinger v. Ballard, 410 U.S. 498 (1975).

Allowing ♀ over ♂ for promotion ≠ violation

Affirmative Action

that respondent had violated Title VII. The Court of Appeals for the Ninth Circuit reversed. . . . We affirm.[2]

I

In December 1978, the Santa Clara County Transit District Board of Supervisors adopted an Affirmative Action Plan (Plan) for the County Transportation Agency. The Plan implemented a County Affirmative Action Plan, which had been adopted, declared the County, because "mere prohibition of discriminatory practices is not enough to remedy the effects of past practices and to permit attainment of an equitable representation of minorities, women and handicapped persons." . . . Relevant to this case, the Agency Plan provides that, in making promotions to positions within a traditionally segregated job classification in which women have been significantly underrepresented, the Agency is authorized to consider as one factor the sex of a qualified applicant.

In reviewing the composition of its work force, the Agency noted in its Plan that women were represented in numbers far less than their proportion of the County labor force in both the Agency as a whole and in five of seven job categories. Specifically, while women constituted 36.4% of the area labor market, they composed only 22.4% of Agency employees. Furthermore, women working at the Agency were concentrated largely in EEOC job categories traditionally held by women: women made up 76% of Office and Clerical Workers, but only 7.1% of Agency Officials and Administrators. . . . As for the job classification relevant to this case, none of the 238 Skilled Craft Worker positions was held by a woman. . . . The Plan noted that this underrepresentation of women in part reflected the fact that women had not traditionally been employed in these positions, and that they had not been strongly motivated to seek training or employment in them "because of the limited opportunities that have existed in the past for them to work in such classifications." . . . The Plan also observed that, while the proportion of ethnic minorities in the Agency as a whole exceeded the proportion of such minorities in the County work force, a smaller percentage of minority employees held management, professional, and technical positions.

The Agency stated that its Plan was intended to achieve "a statistically measurable yearly improvement in hiring, training, and promotion of minorities and women throughout the Agency in all major job classifications where they are underrepresented." . . . As a benchmark by which to evaluate progress, the Agency stated that its long-term goal was to attain a work force whose composition reflected the proportion of minorities and women in the area labor force. . . . Thus, for the Skilled Craft category in which the road dispatcher position at issue here was classified, the Agency's aspiration was that eventually about 36% of the jobs would be occupied by women. . . .

2. No Constitutional issue was either raised or addressed in the litigation below. . . . We therefore decide in this case only the issue of the prohibitory scope of Title VII. . . .

The Agency's Plan . . . set aside no specific number of positions for minorities or women, but authorized the consideration of ethnicity or sex as a factor when evaluating qualified candidates for jobs in which members of such groups were poorly represented. . . .

On December 12, 1979, the Agency announced a vacancy for the promotional position of road dispatcher in the Agency's Roads Division. Dispatchers assign road crews, equipment, and materials, and maintain records pertaining to road maintenance jobs. . . .

Twelve County employees applied for the promotion, including Joyce and Johnson. Joyce had worked for the County since 1970, serving as an account clerk until 1975. She had applied for a road dispatcher position in 1974, but was deemed ineligible because she had not served as a road maintenance worker. In 1975, Joyce transferred from a senior account clerk position to a road maintenance worker position, becoming the first woman to fill such a job. . . . During her four years in that position, she occasionally worked out of class as a road dispatcher.

Petitioner Johnson began with the County in 1967 as a road yard clerk, after private employment that included working as a supervisor and dispatcher. He had also unsuccessfully applied for the road dispatcher opening in 1974. In 1977, his clerical position was downgraded, and he sought and received a transfer to the position of road maintenance worker. . . . He also occasionally worked out of class as a dispatcher while performing that job.

Nine of the applicants, including Joyce and Johnson, were deemed qualified for the job, and were interviewed by a two-person board. Seven of the applicants scored above 70 on this interview, which meant that they were certified as eligible for selection by the appointing authority. The scores awarded ranged from 70 to 80. Johnson was tied for second with a score of 75, while Joyce ranked next with a score of 73. A second interview was conducted by three Agency supervisors, who ultimately recommended that Johnson be promoted. Prior to the second interview, Joyce had contacted the County's Affirmative Action Office because she feared that her application might not receive disinterested review.[5] The Office in turn contacted the Agency's

[handwritten margin note: Proactive]

[handwritten note: Bias]

---

5. Joyce testified that she had had disagreements with two of the three members of the second interview panel. One had been her first supervisor when she began work as a road maintenance worker. In performing arduous work in this job, she had not been issued coveralls, although her male co-workers had received them. After ruining her pants, she complained to her supervisor, to no avail. After three other similar incidents, ruining clothes on each occasion, she filed a grievance, and was issued four pairs of overalls the next day. . . . Joyce had dealt with a second member of the panel for a year and a half in her capacity as chair of the Roads Operation Safety Committee, where she and he had several differences of opinion on how safety should be implemented. ". . . In addition, Joyce testified that she had informed the person responsible for arranging her second interview that she had a disaster preparedness class on a certain day the following week. By this time about 10 days had passed since she had notified the person of her availability, and no date had yet been set for the interview. Within a day or two after this conversation, however, she received a notice setting her interview at a time directly in the middle of her disaster preparedness class. . . . This same panel member had earlier described Joyce as a "rebel-rousing, skirt-wearing person." . . .

Affirmative Action Coordinator, whom the Agency's Plan makes responsible for, *inter alia*, keeping the Director informed of opportunities for the Agency to accomplish its objectives under the Plan. At the time, the Agency employed no women in any Skilled Craft position, and had never employed a woman as a road dispatcher. The Coordinator recommended to the Director of the Agency, James Graebner, that Joyce be promoted.

Graebner, authorized to choose any of the seven persons deemed eligible, thus had the benefit of suggestions by the second interview panel and by the Agency Coordinator in arriving at his decision. After deliberation, Graebner concluded that the promotion should be given to Joyce. As he testified: "I tried to look at the whole picture, the combination of her qualifications and Mr. Johnson's qualifications, their test scores, their expertise, their background, affirmative action matters, things like that. . . . I believe it was a combination of all those." . . .

The certification form naming Joyce as the person promoted to the dispatcher position stated that both she and Johnson were rated as well qualified for the job. . . . Graebner testified that he did not regard as significant the fact that Johnson scored 75 and Joyce 73 when interviewed by the two-person board. . . .

Petitioner Johnson filed a complaint with the EEOC alleging that he had been denied promotion on the basis of sex in violation of Title VII. . . .

II

As a preliminary matter, we note that petitioner bears the burden of establishing the invalidity of the Agency's Plan. . . .

The assessment of the legality of the Agency Plan must be guided by our decision in Steelworkers v. Weber, [1979]. In that case, the Court [held that] a voluntary affirmative action plan designed to "eliminate manifest racial imbalances in traditionally segregated job categories" [did not violate Title VII]. As we stated:

> It would be ironic indeed if a law triggered by a Nation's concern over centuries of racial injustice and intended to improve the lot of those who had "been excluded from the American dream for so long" constituted the first legislative prohibition of all voluntary, private, race-conscious efforts to abolish traditional patterns of racial segregation and hierarchy. . . .

We noted that the plan did not "unnecessarily trammel the interests of the white employees," since it did not require "the discharge of white workers and their replacement with new black hirees." Nor did the plan create "an absolute bar to the advancement of white employees," since half of those trained in the new program were to be white. . . . Finally, we observed that the plan was a temporary measure, not designed to maintain racial balance, but to "eliminate a manifest racial imbalance." . . . As Justice Blackmun's concurrence made clear, *Weber* held that an employer seeking to justify the adoption of a plan need not point to its own prior discriminatory practices, nor even to evidence of an "arguable violation" on its part. Rather, it need point only to a "conspicuous . . . imbalance in traditionally segregated job categories." Our decision was grounded in the recognition that voluntary employer action can play a crucial role in furthering Title VII's purpose of eliminating the effects of discrimination in the workplace, and that Title VII should not be read to thwart such efforts.

The first issue [in this case] is therefore whether consideration of the sex of applicants for Skilled Craft jobs was justified by the existence of a "manifest imbalance" that reflected underrepresentation of women in "traditionally segregated job categories." In determining whether an imbalance exists that would justify taking sex or race into account, a comparison of the percentage of minorities or women in the employer's work force with the percentage in the area labor market or general population is appropriate in analyzing jobs that require no special expertise. . . . Where a job requires special training, however, the comparison should be with those in the labor force who possess the relevant qualifications. . . .

A manifest imbalance need not be such that it would support a prima facie case against the employer . . . since we do not regard as identical the constraints of Title VII and the Federal Constitution on voluntarily adopted affirmative action plans. Application of the "prima facie" standard in Title VII cases would be inconsistent with *Weber*'s focus on statistical imbalance, and could inappropriately create a significant disincentive for employers to adopt an affirmative action plan. . . .

As the Agency Plan recognized, women were most egregiously underrepresented in the Skilled Craft job category, since none of the 238 positions was occupied by a woman. . . .

[H]ad the Plan simply calculated imbalances in all categories according to the proportion of women in the area labor pool, and then directed that hiring be governed solely by those figures, its validity fairly could be called into question. This is because analysis of a more specialized labor pool normally is necessary in determining underrepresentation in some positions. If a plan failed to take distinctions in qualifications into account in providing guidance for actual employment decisions, it would dictate mere blind hiring by the numbers. . . .

The Agency's plan emphatically did not authorize such blind hiring. It expressly directed that numerous factors be taken into account. . . .

We next consider whether the Agency Plan unnecessarily trammeled the rights of male employees or created an absolute bar to their advancement. In contrast to the plan in *Weber*, which provided that 50% of the positions in the craft training program were exclusively for blacks, . . . the Plan sets aside no positions for women. The Plan expressly states that "[t]he 'goals' established for each Division should not be construed as 'quotas' that must be met." . . . Rather, the Plan merely authorizes that consideration be given to affirmative action concerns when evaluating qualified applicants. As the Agency Director testified, the sex of Joyce was but one of numerous factors he took into account in arriving at his decision. . . . The Plan thus resembles the "Harvard Plan" approvingly noted by Justice Powell in Regents of University of California v. Bakke, [1978,] which considers race along with other criteria in determining admission to the college. As Justice Powell observed [in *Bakke*]: "In such an admissions program, race or ethnic background may be deemed a 'plus' in a particular applicant's file, yet it does not insulate the individual from comparison with all other candidates for the available seats." Similarly, the Agency Plan requires women to compete with all other qualified applicants. No persons are automatically excluded from consideration; all are able to have their qualifications weighed against those of other applicants.

In addition, petitioner had no absolute entitlement to the road dispatcher position. Seven of the applicants were classified as qualified and eligible, and the Agency Director was authorized to promote any of the seven. Thus, denial of the promotion unsettled no legitimate, firmly rooted expectation on the part of petitioner. . . .

Finally, the Agency's Plan was intended to attain a balanced work force, not to maintain one. The Plan contains 10 references to the Agency's desire to "attain" such a balance, but no reference whatsoever to a goal of maintaining it. . . .

Express assurance that a program is only temporary may be necessary if the program actually sets aside positions according to specific numbers. . . . In this case, however, substantial evidence shows that the Agency has sought to take a moderate, gradual approach to eliminating the imbalance in its work force, one which establishes realistic guidance for employment decisions, and which visits minimal intrusion on the legitimate expectations of other employees. . . .

Justice STEVENS, concurring.

While I join the Court's opinion, I write separately to explain my view of this case's position in our evolving antidiscrimination law and to emphasize that the opinion does not establish the permissible outer limits of voluntary programs undertaken by employers to benefit disadvantaged groups.

I

Antidiscrimination measures may benefit protected groups in two distinct ways. As a sword, such measures may confer benefits by specifying that a person's membership in a disadvantaged group must be a neutral, irrelevant factor in governmental or private decisionmaking or, alternatively, by compelling decisionmakers to give favorable consideration to disadvantaged group status. As a shield, an antidiscrimination statute can also help a member of a protected class by assuring decisionmakers in some instances that, when they elect for good reasons of their own to grant a preference of some sort to a minority citizen, they will not violate the law. The Court properly holds that the statutory shield allowed respondent to take Diane Joyce's sex into account in promoting her to the road dispatcher position. . . .

It remains clear that the [Civil Rights] Act does not require any employer to grant preferential treatment on the basis of race or gender, but since 1978 the Court has unambiguously interpreted the statute to permit the voluntary adoption of special programs to benefit members of the minority groups for whose protection the statute was enacted. . . .

II . . .

Given the interpretation of the statute the Court adopted in *Weber*, I see no reason why the employer has any duty, prior to granting a preference to a qualified minority employee, to determine whether his past conduct might constitute an arguable violation of Title VII. Indeed, in some instances the employer may find it more helpful to focus on the future. Instead of retroactively scrutinizing his own or society's possible exclusions of minorities in the past to determine the outer limits of a valid affirmative-action program—or indeed, any particular affirmative-action decision—in many cases the employer will find it more appropriate to consider other legitimate [diversity-related] reasons to give preferences to members of under-represented groups. Statutes enacted for the benefit of minority groups should not block these forward-looking considerations. . . . The Court today does not foreclose other voluntary decisions based in part on a qualified employee's membership in a disadvantaged group. Accordingly, I concur.

Justice O'CONNOR, concurring in the judgment. . . .
In my view, the proper initial inquiry in evaluating the legality of an affirmative action plan by a public employer under Title VII is no different from that required by the Equal Protection Clause. In either case, consistent with the congressional intent to provide some measure of protection to the interests of the employer's nonminority employees, the employer must have had a firm basis for believing that remedial action was required. An employer would have such a firm basis if it can point to a statistical disparity sufficient to support a prima facie claim under Title VII by the employee beneficiaries of the affirmative action plan of a pattern or practice claim of discrimination. . . .

As I read *Weber* . . . the Court . . . determined that Congress had balanced [its intent to root out invidious discrimination against any person on the basis of race or gender, and its goal of eliminating the lasting effects of discrimination against minorities] by permitting affirmative action only as a remedial device to eliminate actual or apparent discrimination or the lingering effects of this discrimination.

[handwritten margin note: Prove discr. in past. What if want to avoid in future?]

Contrary to the intimations in Justice Stevens' concurrence, this Court did not approve preferences for minorities "for any reason that might seem sensible from a business or a social point of view." . . . I concur in the judgment of the Court.

Justice SCALIA, with whom THE CHIEF JUSTICE joins, and with whom Justice WHITE joins in Parts I and II, dissenting. . . .

The Court today completes the process of converting [Title VII] from a guarantee that race or sex will *not* be the basis for employment determinations, to a guarantee that it often *will*. Ever so subtly, without even alluding to the last obstacles preserved by earlier opinions that we now push out of our path, we effectively replace the goal of a discrimination-free society with the quite incompatible goal of proportionate representation by race and by sex in the workplace. . . .

I . . .

Several salient features of the plan [at issue in this case] should be noted. Most importantly, the plan's purpose was assuredly not to remedy prior sex discrimination by the Agency. It could not have been, because there was no prior sex discrimination to remedy. The majority, in cataloging the Agency's alleged misdeeds . . . neglects to mention the District Court's finding that the Agency "has not discriminated in the past, and does not discriminate in the present against women in regard to employment opportunities in general and promotions in particular." . . . This finding was not disturbed by the Ninth Circuit.

Not only was the plan not directed at the results of past sex discrimination by the Agency, but its objective was not to achieve the state of affairs that this Court has dubiously assumed would result from an absence of discrimination—an overall work force "more or less representative of the racial and ethnic composition of the population in the community." . . . Teamsters v. United States, [1977]. Rather, the oft-stated goal was to mirror the racial and sexual composition of the entire county labor force, not merely in the Agency work force as a whole, but in each and every individual job category at the Agency. In a discrimination-free world, it would obviously be a statistical oddity for every job category to match the racial and sexual composition of even that portion of the county work force *qualified* for that job; it would be utterly miraculous for each of them to match, as the plan expected, the composition of the entire work force. Quite obviously, the plan did not seek to replicate what a lack of discrimination would produce, but rather imposed racial and sexual tailoring that would, in defiance of normal expectations and laws of probability, give each protected racial and sexual group a governmentally determined "proper" proportion of each job category. . . .

II

The most significant proposition of law established by today's decision is that racial or sexual discrimination is permitted under Title VII when it is intended to overcome the effect, not of the employer's own discrimination, but of societal attitudes that have limited the entry of certain races, or of a particular sex, into certain jobs. . . .

In fact, . . . today's decision goes well beyond merely allowing racial or sexual discrimination in order to eliminate the effects of prior societal discrimination. The majority opinion often uses the phrase "traditionally segregated job category" to describe the evil against which the plan is legitimately (according to the majority) directed. As originally used in *Weber*, that phrase described skilled jobs from which employers and unions had systematically and intentionally excluded black workers—traditionally segregated jobs, that is, in the sense of conscious, exclusionary discrimination. But that is assuredly not the sense in which the phrase is used here. It is absurd to think that the nationwide failure of road maintenance crews, for example, to achieve the Agency's ambition of 36.4% female representation is attributable primarily, if even substantially, to systematic exclusion of women eager to shoulder pick and shovel. It is a "traditionally segregated job category" not in the *Weber* sense, but in the sense that, because of longstanding social attitudes, it has not been regarded by women themselves as desirable work. . . . There are, of course, those who believe that the social attitudes which cause women themselves to avoid certain jobs and to favor others are as nefarious as conscious, exclusionary discrimination. Whether or not that is so (and there is assuredly no consensus on the point equivalent to our national consensus against intentional discrimination), the two phenomena are certainly distinct. And it is the alteration of social attitudes, rather than the elimination of discrimination, which today's decision approves as justification for state-enforced discrimination. This is an enormous expansion, undertaken without the slightest justification or analysis.

III . . .

It is impossible not to be aware that the practical effect of our holding is . . . effectively [to require] employers, public as well as private, to engage in intentional discrimination on the basis of race or sex. This Court's prior interpretations of Title VII, especially the decision in Griggs v. Duke Power Co., [1971,] subject employers to a potential Title VII suit whenever there is a noticeable imbalance in the representation of minorities or women in the employer's work force. Even the employer who is confident of ultimately prevailing in such a suit must contemplate the expense and adverse publicity of a trial. . . . If, however, employers are free to discriminate through affirmative action, without fear of "reverse discrimination" suits by their nonminority or male victims, they are offered a threshold defense against Title VII liability premised on numerical disparities. Thus, after today's decision the failure to engage in reverse discrimination is economic folly, and arguably a breach of duty to shareholders or taxpayers, wherever the cost of anticipated Title VII litigation exceeds the cost of hiring less capable (though still minimally capable) workers. (This situation is more likely to obtain, of course, with respect to the least skilled jobs—perversely creating an incentive to discriminate against precisely those members of the nonfavored groups least likely to have profited from societal discrimination in the past.) . . . A statute designed to establish a color-blind and gender-blind workplace has thus been converted into a powerful engine of racism and sexism, not merely permitting intentional race- and sex-based discrimination, but often making it, through operation of the legal system, practically compelled.

It is unlikely that today's result will be displeasing to politically elected officials, to whom it provides the means of quickly accommodating the demands of organized groups to achieve concrete, numerical improvement in the economic status of particular constituencies. Nor will it displease the world of corporate and governmental employers (many of whom have filed briefs as amici in the present case, all on the side of Santa Clara) for whom the cost of hiring less qualified workers is often substantially less—and infinitely more predictable—than the cost of litigating Title VII cases and of seeking to convince federal agencies by nonnumerical means that no discrimination exists. In fact, the only losers in the process are the Johnsons of the country, for whom Title VII has been not merely repealed but actually inverted. The irony is that these individuals—predominantly unknown, unaffluent, unorganized—suffer this injustice at the hands of a Court fond of thinking itself the champion of the politically impotent. I dissent.

Notes

1. Affirmative Action: Definitions and Background. Affirmative action plans vary across multiple dimensions: which employees are covered; whether the plans are voluntarily adopted or imposed under law or court order; and what measures they require. Some plans seek to expand the group of qualified applicants through recruitment and training, but do not show any preference in terms of hiring or promotion to members of the underrepresented group. At the other end of the spectrum are "quotas" that go so far as to compel the hiring or promotion of a certain number or percentage of group members. In between are various forms of goals, timetables, and tie-breaking preferences that favor members of the underrepresented group without changing the applicable qualification standards.

Affirmative action became part of U.S. law in 1965, when President Lyndon Johnson approved Executive Order 11246, which was subsequently strengthened under President Nixon and further modified under President

Clinton. The Order requires firms over a certain size doing a certain level of business with the federal government to employ qualified individuals from targeted groups in percentages roughly proportional to their representation in the available applicant pool. If those groups are underrepresented, the employer must develop a corrective plan and make good-faith efforts to implement it. Another form of affirmative action involves "set-asides"—preferences for targeted groups in the government contracting process. The concept originated in the 1950s as a way to help small businesses. Set-asides were expanded in the 1970s to encompass minority-owned businesses, and further extended in the 1980s to include women-owned businesses. However, the Supreme Court has cut back on minority set-aside plans that are not narrowly tailored to meet a compelling governmental interest—the same standard used to evaluate practices that discriminate *against* minorities.[6] For a set-aside plan to be valid, it is not sufficient that a particular minority group is underrepresented in an industry; instead, there must have been a previous pattern of pervasive and systematic discrimination in which the government itself participated.[7]

The federal government has between 150 and 200 other laws and regulations supporting some form of affirmative action. Most are aspirational: they express a desire for proactive strategies and goals but not methods of implementation or sanctions for noncompliance. One goal, which was reached in 2016, is that 5 percent of the federal government's contracting dollars go to businesses owned by women.[8] About one-fifth of American employees work for the U.S. government or for contractors and subcontractors who are subject to federal affirmative action requirements. Many more workers are covered by state or local mandates or voluntary private sector plans.[9]

With respect to affirmative action and women, *Johnson* still appears to be good law, meaning that courts do not apply the same strict standard requiring a showing of past discrimination. But note that the different opinions in *Johnson* represent a wide range of judicial perspectives. Justice Scalia believes that, as in the race cases, voluntary affirmative action should be permitted only by employers who previously engaged in discrimination against the group in question. Justice O'Connor believes that the disparity that the state is attempting to correct should be substantial and provide a "firm basis for believing that remedial action is required." Justice Brennan, writing for a plurality of the Court, maintains that a voluntary affirmative action plan is justified to address a "manifest imbalance" (or substantial underrepresentation

6. Adarand Constructors, Inc. v. Pena, 515 U.S. 200 (1995).

7. See, e.g., Associated General Contractors of Ohio, Inc. v. Drabnik, 214 F.3d 730 (6th Cir. 2000).

8. See Stacy Cowley, Government Meet Goal Set in 1994 for Women's Business Contracts, N.Y. Times, Mar. 2, 2016.

9. For specific facts and figures, public opinion data, and related issues, see Faye J. Crosby, Affirmative Action Is Dead: Long Live Affirmative Action (2004).

of women in "traditionally segregated job categories"). Justice Stevens thinks that the employer should be given even more leeway, in order to achieve a "forward-looking" diversity.

Given that the objective of affirmative action is to reverse the effects of past discrimination and/or to enhance diversity, is there any reason why gender-based affirmative action should be treated more leniently than race-based plans? Indeed, if race is the more suspect category, isn't it perverse to impose greater barriers to ending past race discrimination than to eliminating past sex discrimination? Courts have not been entirely consistent in dealing with affirmative action in the gender context, and there is conflicting authority on the question. The Sixth Circuit Court of Appeals has applied strict scrutiny to both race-based and sex-based affirmative action plans.[10] Other circuits, including the Third, Fifth, Ninth, Tenth, and Eleventh, have required intermediate scrutiny, with a lesser evidentiary burden.[11] Cases allowing gender-based affirmative action plans have generally required some showing of past discrimination, but not necessarily discrimination by the governmental entity whose affirmative action plan is in dispute.[12] Moreover, to an extent not apparent in judicial analysis of race-based affirmative action plans, courts emphasize that the purpose for reviewing gender-based discrimination is less to "smoke out" hidden, invidious discrimination than to make sure that sex-based rules are not based unintentionally on archaic stereotypes.[13] Does this difference justify a different legal standard?[14]

10. See, e.g., Builders Ass'n v. City of Chicago, 298 F. Supp. 2d 725 (N.D. Ill. 2005) (applying Brunet v. City of Columbus, 1 F.3d 390 (6th Cir. 1993)). The issue is not yet settled in the Seventh Circuit. In Northern Contracting, Inc. v. Illinois, 473 F.3d 715 (7th Cir. 2007), the court applied strict scrutiny, but the county had failed to argue for a different standard. The district courts in the circuit have gone both ways. Compare Builders Ass'n of Greater Chicago v. City of Chicago, 298 F. Supp. 2d 725 (N.D. Ill. 2005) (applying strict scrutiny to invalidate sex-based affirmative action program), with Builders Ass'n of Greater Chicago v. County of Cook, 123 F. Supp. 2d 1087 (N.D. Ill. 2000) (finding sex-based affirmative action plan invalid under "exceedingly persuasive" standard).

11. See, e.g., Dallas Fire Fighters Ass'n v. City of Dallas, 150 F.3d 438 (5th Cir. 1998) (intermediate scrutiny applied to sex-based preferences); Contractors Ass'n of Eastern Pennsylvania v. City of Philadelphia, 6 F.3d 990 (3d Cir. 1993); Western States Paving Co. v. Wash. Dep't of Transp., 407 F.3d 983 (9th Cir. 2005); Concrete Works of Colo., Inc. v. City and County of Denver, 321 F.3d 950 (10th Cir. 2003); Engineering Contractors Ass'n of South Florida., Inc. v. Metro. Dade County, 122 F.3d 895 (11th Cir. 1997).

12. See, e.g., Ensley Branch, N.A.A.C.P. v. Siebels, 31 F.3d 1548, 1580 (11th Cir. 1994).

13. See Contractors Assoc. of Eastern Pennsylvania v. City of Philadelphia, 6 F.3d 990, 1010 (3d Cir. 1993) (affirmative action plan favoring women will pass intermediate scrutiny if it is shown to be "a product of analysis rather than a stereotyped reaction based on habit.").

14. See Rosalie Berger Levinson, Gender-Based Affirmative Action and Reverse Gender Bias: Beyond *Gratz, Parents Involved,* and *Ricci,* 34 Harv. J. Law & Gender 1, 36 (2011) (arguing that although the race/gender anomaly is not justified, the incongruity should not be resolved by subjecting gender-based affirmative action to strict scrutiny).

Most surveys reflect between 10 and 20 percent greater popular support for affirmative action programs on behalf of women than for programs on behalf of African Americans. In both cases, whether people say they support affirmative action depends upon the way the plan is described, and how the question is asked. In general, support is much lower for quotas or for "preferential treatment" than for other strategies that seek to equalize opportunities or that take qualifications into account. Support for affirmative action is greater when specific practices are described, when policies are characterized in terms of promoting diversity rather than giving preferences, and when socially usefully functions are presented.[15]

Reversals of government-sponsored affirmative action plans, especially in the context of higher education, have occurred in response to popular opposition to such plans. For example, in 1996, California voters passed the California Civil Rights Initiative (Proposition 209), which prohibits "discrimination against, or . . . preferential treatment to, any individual on the basis of race, sex, color, ethnicity, or national origin in the operation of public employment, public education, or public contracting." Proposition 209 was upheld in both federal and state courts. It has had significantly greater impact on racial diversity than on gender diversity,[16] and most of the continuing controversy concerns race-based plans.[17] In 2016, the Supreme Court upheld the University of Texas' affirmative action plan, which, in addition to admitting all students who graduate in the top 10% of their class from a Texas high school (mandated by state law), allows consideration of race as one factor in each applicant's "Personal Achievement Index."[18] The University successfully defended its plan under strict scrutiny with a "reasoned, principled explanation" for its pursuit of a diverse educational body and extensive evidence that race-neutral alternatives would not produce the same results.

One reason sex-based affirmative action in the educational setting is less of a hot-button issue than race-based affirmative action is that women earn about 57 percent of all bachelor's degrees[19] and represent 59 percent of

15. For studies, see Loan Le & Jack Citrin, Affirmative Action, in Public Opinion and Constitutional Controversy 162, 171-76 (Nathaniel Persily et al. eds., 2008); see also Corey A. Ciocchetti & John Holcomb, The Frontier of Affirmative Action: Employment Preferences & Diversity in the Private Workplace, 12 U. Pa. J. Bus. L. 283, 285, 308-09 (2010).

16. Susan W. Kaufmann, The History and Impact of State Initiatives to Eliminate Affirmative Action, 111 New Directions for Teaching and Learning 3, 5 (Fall 2007).

17. Id. at 7.

18. Fisher v. Univ. of Tex., 579 U.S. __ (2016).

19. See Liz Dwyer, Rejected from College: If You're a Woman, A Less-Qualified Man Probably Took Your Spot, Good Education (Apr. 15, 2011), http://www.good.is/post/rejected-from-college-if-you-re-a-woman-a-less-qualified-man-probably-took-your-spot. The female-male ratio of college and university students is larger for private colleges and universities (59.3 percent vs. 40.7 percent) than for state schools (56.4 percent vs. 43.6 percent). See Daniel Borzelleca, The Male-Female Ratio in College, Forbes, Feb. 16, 2012, http://www.forbes.com/sites/ccap/2012/02/16/the-male-female-ratio-in-college/#470773131525.

enrollment in graduate programs.[20] Except in programs like science and engineering, where women are still underrepresented, some schools favor men in the application process in order to avoid having more than 60 percent women.[21] For consideration of whether this data warrants affirmative intervention on behalf of males, see Section C(2)(a) of this chapter.

2. Women's "Choices": Explanation or Symptom of Gender Inequality? In his dissent in *Johnson*, Justice Scalia attributes women's underrepresentation in traditionally male job categories to women's choices. In his view, it is "absurd" to think that women could be "eager to shoulder pick and shovel." Could he be right? If so, should a "lack of interest" by women generally in certain jobs be a defense to the absence, or severe underrepresentation, of women in those jobs?

This defense was the focus of an important lawsuit by the Equal Employment Opportunity Commission (EEOC) against Sears, Roebuck & Co. in the late 1980s. The suit alleged a nationwide pattern and practice of discriminating against women for commission sales positions. To support its claim, the EEOC offered extensive statistical evidence that women who applied for sales positions were less likely than men with similar qualifications to receive high-paying commission jobs involving "big ticket" items, such as major appliances, furnaces, roofing, and tires. Rather, women disproportionately ended up in non-commission lower-paying jobs selling apparel, linen, toys, paint, and cosmetics. In defending its employment practices, Sears introduced testimony by a female historian, Rosalind Rosenberg, that such patterns were consistent with women's traditional preferences, including their reluctance to work irregular hours, their desire for "social contact and friendship," and their discomfort with the stress of competitive pay structures. The trial court found such evidence more credible than testimony by other historians called by the EEOC, who asserted that women are influenced by the opportunities presented to them, and have been eager to take higher-paying nontraditional jobs when such options have been available.

Other evidence in the case showed that Sears relied on tests measuring applicants' "vigor" by reference to their views on boxing, wrestling, and swearing. One witness explained that female employees weren't in higher-paid retail sales positions because they "didn't like going outside when it's snowing, raining, or whatever." In addition, Sears had taken no steps that might

---

20. Shirley M. Clark & Patricia S. Reed, Are We Losing the Best and the Brightest? Highly Achieved Women Leaving the Traditional Workforce, Final Report, at 9 (Nov. 2007), http://www.doleta.gov/reports/pdf/AreWeLosingThebest.pdf; see also Nat'l Center for Education Statistics, The Condition of Education 32 (May 2015), http://nces.ed.gov/pubs2015/2015144.pdf (in 2014, 37 percent of females attained a bachelor's degree, as compared to 31 percent of men; 9 percent of females had completed a master's degree or higher, as compared with 6 percent of males).

21. Dwyer, supra note 19.

have made the higher-paid positions more attractive to women, such as flexible schedules or outreach and support programs.[22] Should this evidence have concerned the court? The judgment for Sears was affirmed on appeal, over the dissent of Judge Cudahy who challenged the stereotypes implicit in the court's analysis and its failure to recognize the employer's role in shaping the interests of applicants.

Is the *Sears* case about the failure of courts to recognize stereotypes at work? Or does it simply recognize reality and decline to impose responsibility on employers to alter employee preferences? According to one commentator:

> The liberal prohibition against stereotyping assumes that the problem is that the employer has inaccurately identified the job interests of (at least some exceptional) women who have already formed preferences for nontraditional work. By stopping at this level of analysis, however, liberal courts fail to inquire into or discover the deeper process through which employers actively shape women's work aspirations along gendered lines. . . . [For example, through] their recruiting strategies, employers do more than simply publicize job vacancies to those who are already interested: They actually stimulate interest among those they hope to attract to the jobs.[23]

To what extent does the affirmative action plan at issue in *Johnson* address this concern?

Women do disproportionately "choose" lower-paying jobs, resulting in sex segregation in many occupation categories. For example, women constitute 87 percent of paralegals and legal assistants, but only 33 percent of lawyers.[24] They also constitute 97 percent of preschool and kindergarten teachers and 91 percent of nurse practitioners, but less than 3 percent of electricians and carpenters.[25] Should these disparities be a concern? If so, what should be done about it? For further discussion of these differentials in the pay area, see Chapter 1, Section C.

3. Affirmative Action and the "Merit" Principle. One of the differences between Kahn v. Shevin and Johnson v. Transportation Agency is that Florida's tax exemption, designed to address general societal discrimination against women, had no single, specific victim, where in *Johnson*, the district court found that the plaintiff would have gotten the job at issue were it not

22. EEOC v. Sears, Roebuck & Co., 628 F. Supp. 1264, 1307 (N.D. Ill. 1986), aff'd, 839 F.2d 302 (7th Cir. 1988).

23. Vicki Schultz, Telling Stories About Women and Work: Judicial Interpretations of Sex Segregation in the Workplace in Title VII Cases Raising the Lack of Interest Argument, 103 Harv. L. Rev. 1749, 1808 (1990).

24. See U.S. Bureau of Labor Statistics, Women in the Labor Force: A Databook, Rep. 1059, tbl. 11, at 37 (Dec. 2015), http://www.bls.gov/opub/reports/cps/women-in-the-labor-force-a-databook-2015.pdf.

25 Id. at 38-39, 42.

for Santa Clara's "affirmative action" plan. This finding allowed Justice Scalia to conclude that affirmative action employers violate the merit principle.

> [Acceptance of the brief's contention] effectively constitutes appellate reversal of a finding of fact by the District Court in the present case ("[P]laintiff was more qualified for the position of Road Dispatcher than Diane Joyce. . . ."). More importantly, it has staggering implications for future Title VII litigation, since the most common reason advanced for failing to hire a member of a protected group is the superior qualification of the hired individual.[26]

Responding to this point, Justice Brennan, citing an amicus curiae brief from the American Society for Personnel Administration, disputes that underlying assumption:

> It is a standard tenet of personnel administration that there is rarely a single, "best qualified" person for a job. An effective personnel system will bring before the selecting official several fully-qualified candidates who each may possess different attributes which recommend them for selection. Especially where the job is an unexceptional, middle-level craft position, without the need for unique work experience or educational attainment and for which several well-qualified candidates are available, final determinations as to which candidate is "best qualified" are at best subjective.[27]

Who is right? Are you persuaded that Joyce was less "qualified" than Johnson? Note that her quantitative score included subjective interview evaluations. Is there an argument that a woman who compiled her record in a workplace with so much gender bias is at least as qualified as a man who ranked marginally higher? What do you make of Footnote 5 in the opinion?

The debate about the meaning of merit was at the heart of a highly contested case, Ricci v. DeStefano, which concerned the constitutionality of the City of New Haven's failure to certify the results of a promotion exam that relied 60 percent on scores from written tests.[28] The results of the exam would have excluded all African Americans and all but one Hispanic from promotion. In holding that an employer cannot abandon a test that produced disparate results based on a good faith fear of liability for that disparate impact, the Supreme Court assumed that the test was a valid predictor of performance. In her dissenting opinion, Justice Ginsburg concluded that the heavy reliance on written tests to select fire officers was "flawed," "dubious," and "a questionable practice, to say the least."

> Successful fire officers, the City's description of the position makes clear, must have the "[a]bility to lead personnel effectively, maintain discipline, promote harmony,

26. 480 U.S. at 675 n.5 (Scalia, J., dissenting).
27. 480 U.S. at 641 n.17.
28. 557 U.S. 557 (2009).

exercise sound judgment, and cooperate with other officials." These qualities are not well measured by written tests. [As testified by one expert,] [l]eadership skills, command presence, and the like "could have been identified and evaluated in a much more appropriate way.[29]

Justice Ginsburg's skepticism about the value of written tests to judge leadership skills is supported by the research of Susan Sturm and Lani Guinier, who argue that standardized paper-and-pencil tests leave out criteria indicative of potential future success, such as discipline, emotional intelligence, commitment, drive to succeed, reliability, creativity, judgment, honesty, courage, the ability to manage anger, and leadership. The criteria that are overvalued in relation to their correlation with preparation for higher education or employment are the willingness to guess, conformity, and docility.[30] Along these lines, Professor Marjorie Shultz at the University of California at Berkeley School of Law and others have questioned the overreliance of law school admissions on the LSAT, and argued for criteria that better measure potential as an effective lawyer.[31] What criteria do you think might be more relevant?

4. The Problem of Stigma. One primary objection to affirmative action is that singling out women for special assistance risks reinforcing the very assumptions of inferiority that society should be trying to eliminate. Even when women perform effectively, their success may be devalued and their advancement may be assumed to reflect preferential treatment rather than individual merit. One commentator responds:

> Assumptions of inferiority predate preferential treatment and would persist without it. Affirmative action is not responsible for adverse stereotypes. Racism and sexism are. White males who long benefited from preferences in schools, jobs, and clubs have suffered no discernible loss of self-esteem. What, moreover, is the likely alternative to affirmative action programs? A return to the "neutral" policies that have perpetuated gender and racial hierarchies is scarcely preferable. Women who benefit from preferential treatment may experience some stigma, but the absence of women is stigmatizing as well. Many members of underrepresented groups find it demeaning to lose affirmative action on the ground that they will find it demeaning.[32]

Do you agree? Why or why not?

29. Id. at 633 (Ginsburg, J., dissenting).
30. Susan Sturm & Lani Guinier, The Future of Affirmative Action: Reclaiming the Innovative Ideal, 84 Cal. L. Rev. 953, 957, 976-77 (1996); see also Lani Guinier & Susan Sturm, Trial by Firefighters, N.Y. Times, July 11, 2009, at A17 (*Ricci* case fails to question relevance of written tests for leadership skills).
31. See Jonathan D. Glater, Study Offers a New Test of Potential Lawyers, N.Y. Times, Mar. 10, 2009, at A22.
32. Deborah L. Rhode, Speaking of Sex: The Denial of Gender Equality 169 (1997).

5. "Positive Action" in European Law. The European Union (as well as Canada) has explicit constitutional commitments to "positive action," or affirmative action programs for women. Tax breaks are available to firms that hire women in traditionally male-dominated fields, and advancement plans for women are sometimes mandatory. Still, these commitments are mixed with legal rules that reflect the same tensions apparent in U.S. debates on affirmative action, particularly when a man objects that he would have gotten a job but for gender preferences. In one case, the European Court of Justice struck down an affirmative action plan under facts strikingly similar to *Johnson*.[33] Yet European Union countries are considerably more generous in providing social and economic support for women when they are pregnant or raising small children (explored later in this chapter). Are the two approaches to "special treatment" consistent? What do you make of the fact that sex segregation remains high even in Scandinavian countries with the most progressive work/family policies?

A number of European countries have passed legislation requiring companies to have a certain minimum percentage of women on their corporate boards. Norway, Spain, France, and Iceland have quotas that set the minimum at 40 percent. Italy has a quota of one-third, and Belgium and Germany require 30 percent. The Netherlands has a voluntary target of 30 percent, and Great Britain has launched a voluntary effort known as the 30% Club. The European Union considered measures to require up to 40 percent representation but these were not passed. Are these a good idea? From a formal equality perspective, what is the downside?[34] What information would you need to answer that question? According to Viviane Reding, the EU's former Justice Commissioner, without intervention it would take more than 40 years for women to hold 40 percent of board positions in Europe's publicly traded companies.[35] Is that sufficient reason?

33. Anderson v. Fogelqvist, Case C-407/98, 2000 E.C.R. I-5539. For recent cases, see Thomas Trelogan et al., Can't We Enlarge the Blanket and the Bed? A Comparative Analysis of Positive/Affirmative Action in the European Court of Justice and the United States Supreme Court, 28 Hastings Int'l & Comp. L. Rev. 39, 40-41 (2004); Christopher D. Totten, Constitutional Precommitments to Gender Affirmative Action in the European Union, Germany, Canada and the United States: A Comparative Approach, 21 Berkeley J. Int'l L. 27 (2003).

34. See Louisa Peacock, EU Quotas Would "Patronise Women," The Telegraph (Mar. 5, 2012), http:www.telegraph.co.uk/finance/jobs/9123991/EU-quotas-would-patronise-women.html; James Kanter, Europe to Study Quotas for Women on Boards, N.Y. Times, Mar. 15, 2012, at B3.

35. Kanter, supra note 34, at B3.

Putting Theory Into Practice

2-2. Reconsider the issue of pay equity discussed in Chapter 1, Section C(1). Is it a problem that teachers and secretaries, who are disproportionately women, are paid less than sanitation workers and mechanics, who are disproportionately men? If so, what additional tools does substantive equality add to address the problem?

2-3. A state university typically provides financial incentives to encourage departments to make hires that are consistent with university priorities. The physics department faculty is all men. This year the university is offering $10,000 in extra research funds to the physics department for every female it hires and additional hiring lines subsidized by the central administration for departments that hire underrepresented minorities. Is this plan appropriate? Is it constitutional?

2-4. In 2014, only 2.7 percent of venture capital-funded companies had a female CEO. To address the absence of women in start-up companies, the law firm Perkins Coie offered to discount its services by 15 percent for all startups that are founded or led by a woman.[36] Is this a good idea? To what extent, if any, does it violate the principle of equality?

2-5. The Federal Communications Commission seeks to give preferences to women in the granting of operation licenses for radio and television stations, on the theory that they have faced discrimination as a general population and thus have "separate needs and interests with respect to which the inclusion of women in broadcast ownership and operation can be of value."[37] Should such preferences be allowed?[38] Does women's ownership affect programming? What is women's programming?

---

36. Nell Gluckman, Perkins Coie Offers Discount to Female-Run Startups, Amer. Lawyer, Mar. 23, 2016.

37. In re Application of Mid-Florida Tel. Corp., 70 F.C.C.2d 281, 326 (Rev. Bd. 1978), set aside on other grounds, 87 F.C.C.2d 203 (1981).

38. See Lamprecht v. FCC, 958 F.2d 382 (D.C. Cir. 1992) (striking down broadcast preferences).

B. ELIMINATING THE DISADVANTAGES OF WOMEN'S DIFFERENCES

1. Pregnancy

Different treatment of women might also be justified on the basis of genuine differences (i.e., not stereotypes) between men and women. The most obvious difference between women and men is their reproductive capacity. Although this difference has a "real" biological basis, it has also given rise to gender stereotypes. Women's childbearing role was one of the nineteenth- and early twentieth-century justifications for excluding them from positions ranging from serving on juries to working as lawyers or bartenders. The question for contemporary sex discrimination law is whether different treatment based on pregnancy can reduce the disadvantages that childbearing produces, without also reinforcing other practices and attitudes that disadvantage women.

The first modern Supreme Court case concerning pregnancy discrimination, Cleveland Board of Education v. LaFleur, addressed the constitutionality of a rule requiring public school classroom teachers to take unpaid maternity leave once they reached the fourth month of pregnancy and to stay out of the classroom until their child was at least three months old. The Court invalidated the policy on due process grounds. Although the state could prevent an individual woman from working if she was not fit for the job as a result of pregnancy, the Court held that it could not compromise her procreative rights by conclusively presuming an inability to work.[39]

In the same year, however, the Court upheld a California law that excluded pregnancy from an otherwise comprehensive list of disabilities covered by the state disability insurance plan. In Geduldig v. Aiello, the Court distinguished prior precedents involving the exclusion of women, by characterizing the exclusion as one based on pregnancy, not sex:

> [T]his case is . . . a far cry from cases like [*Reed*] and [*Frontiero*], involving discrimination based upon gender as such. The California insurance program does not exclude anyone from benefit eligibility because of gender but merely removed one physical condition—pregnancy—from the list of compensable disabilities. While it is true that only women can become pregnant, it does not follow that every legislative classification concerning pregnancy is a sex-based classification. . . . Normal pregnancy is an objectively identifiable physical condition with unique characteristics. Absent a showing that distinctions involving pregnancy are mere pretexts designed to effect an invidious discrimination against the members of one sex or the other, lawmakers are constitutionally free

---

39. 414 U.S. 632 (1974). For a comprehensive history of pregnancy discrimination law, see Deborah Dinner, The Costs of Reproduction: History and the Legal Construction of Sex Equality, 46 Harv. C.R.-C.L. L. Rev. 415 (2011).

to include or exclude pregnancy from the coverage of legislation such as this on any reasonable basis, just as with respect to any other physical condition.

The lack of identity between the excluded disability and gender as such under this insurance program becomes clear upon the most cursory analysis. The program divides potential recipients into two groups—pregnant women and nonpregnant persons. While the first group is exclusively female, the second includes members of both sexes. The fiscal and actuarial benefits of the program thus accrue to members of both sexes.[40]

Is the distinction between women and non-pregnant persons persuasive?

The Court in General Electric Co. v. Gilbert (1976) applied the reasoning in *Geduldig* in the Title VII context, holding that pregnancy discrimination is not a form of actionable sex discrimination.[41] That decision was overruled by Congress by an amendment to Title VII known as the Pregnancy Discrimination Act of 1978 (PDA). The PDA explicitly declares that discrimination based on pregnancy was discrimination based on sex, for purposes of Title VII:

> The terms "because of sex" or "on the basis of sex" include, but are not limited to, because of or on the basis of pregnancy, childbirth, or related medical conditions; and women affected by pregnancy, childbirth, or related medical conditions shall be treated the same for all employment-related purposes, including receipt of benefits under fringe benefit programs, as other persons not so affected but similar in their ability or inability to work, and nothing in section 703(h) of this title shall be interpreted to permit otherwise.[42]

The PDA amended Title VII but not the U.S. Constitution. Pregnancy discrimination can still be lawful where Title VII or other statutes are inapplicable. Under the PDA, employers cannot treat pregnant workers worse than other workers who are temporarily disabled. Can they treat them better?

California Federal Savings & Loan Association v. Guerra
479 U.S. 272 (1987)

Justice MARSHALL delivered the opinion of the Court.

The question presented is whether Title VII of the Civil Rights Act of 1964, as amended by the Pregnancy Discrimination Act of 1978 (PDA), preempts a state statute that requires employers to provide leave and reinstatement to employees disabled by pregnancy.

---

40. 417 U.S. 484 , 496-97 n.20 (1974).
41. 429 U.S. 125, 133-40 (1976).
42. 42 U.S.C. §2000e(k) (2012).

I

California's Fair Employment and Housing Act (FEHA) . . . is a comprehensive statute that prohibits discrimination in employment and housing. In September 1978, California amended the FEHA to proscribe certain forms of employment discrimination on the basis of pregnancy. [At issue in this case is a provision that] requires these employers to provide female employees an unpaid pregnancy disability leave of up to four months. [It has been construed] to require California employers to reinstate an employee returning from such pregnancy leave to the job she previously held, unless it is no longer available due to business necessity. In the latter case, the employer must make a reasonable, good-faith effort to place the employee in a substantially similar job. The statute does not compel employers to provide paid leave to pregnant employees. Accordingly, the only benefit pregnant workers actually derive . . . is a qualified right to reinstatement. . . .

[margin note: Issue]

II

Petitioner California Federal Savings & Loan Association (Cal Fed) is a federally chartered savings and loan association based in Los Angeles; it is an employer covered by both Title VII and [the relevant state FEHA law]. Cal Fed has a facially neutral leave policy that permits employees who have completed three months of service to take unpaid leaves of absence for a variety of reasons, including disability and pregnancy. Although it is Cal Fed's policy to try to provide an employee taking unpaid leave with a similar position upon returning, Cal Fed expressly reserves the right to terminate an employee who has taken a leave of absence if a similar position is not available.

Lillian Garland was employed by Cal Fed as a receptionist for several years. In January 1982, she took a pregnancy disability leave. When she was able to return to work in April of that year, Garland notified Cal Fed, but was informed that her job had been filled and that there were no receptionist or similar positions available. Garland filed a complaint with respondent Department of Fair Employment and Housing, which issued an administrative accusation against Cal Fed. . . . Prior to the scheduled hearing . . . , Fair Employment and Housing Commission, Cal Fed, joined by petitioners Merchants and Manufacturers Association and the California Chamber of Commerce, brought this action in the United States District Court for the Central District of California. They sought a declaration that [the California unpaid pregnancy disability leave requirement] is inconsistent with and pre-empted by Title VII and an injunction against enforcement of the section. The District Court granted petitioners' motion for summary judgment. . . .

The United States Court of Appeals for the Ninth Circuit reversed. . . .
We granted certiorari . . . and we now [uphold the statute.] . . .

[margin note: Facts]

[margin note: Woman replaced while on mat. leave]

III

Petitioners argue that the language of the federal statute itself unambiguously rejects California's "special treatment" approach to pregnancy discrimination. . . . They contend that the PDA forbids an employer to treat pregnant employees any differently from other disabled employees. . . .[6]

[S]ubject to certain limitations, we agree with the Court of Appeals' conclusion that Congress intended the PDA to be "a floor beneath which pregnancy disability benefits may not drop, not a ceiling above which they may not rise." . . .

The context in which Congress considered the issue of pregnancy discrimination supports this view of the PDA. Congress had before it extensive evidence of discrimination against pregnancy, particularly in disability and health insurance programs like those challenged in *Gilbert*. . . . Opposition to the PDA came from those concerned with the cost of including pregnancy in health and disability-benefit plans and the application of the bill to abortion, not from those who favored special accommodation of pregnancy. . . .

We . . . find it significant that Congress was aware of state laws similar to California's but apparently did not consider them inconsistent with the PDA. In the debates and Reports on the bill, Congress repeatedly acknowledged the existence of state antidiscrimination laws that prohibit sex discrimination on the basis of pregnancy. Two of the States mentioned [Connecticut and Montana] then required employers to provide reasonable leave to pregnant workers. . . . [B]oth the House and Senate Reports suggest that these laws would continue to have effect under the PDA.

Title VII, as amended by the PDA, and California's pregnancy disability leave statute share a common goal. The purpose of Title VII is "to achieve equality of employment opportunities and remove barriers that have operated in the past to favor an identifiable group of . . . employees over other employees." . . . Rather than limiting existing Title VII principles and objectives, the PDA extends them to cover pregnancy. As Senator Williams, a sponsor of the Act, stated: "The entire thrust . . . behind this legislation is to guarantee women the basic right to participate fully and equally in the workforce, without denying them the fundamental right to full participation in family life." . . .

[The California law at issue in the case] also promotes equal employment opportunity. By requiring employers to reinstate women after a reasonable

---

6. [The PDA provides that] [t]he terms "because of sex" or "on the basis of sex" include, but are not limited to, because of or on the basis of pregnancy, childbirth, or related medical conditions; and women affected by pregnancy, childbirth, or related medical conditions shall be treated the same for all employment-related purposes, including receipt of benefits under fringe benefit programs, as other persons not so affected but similar in their ability or inability to work, and nothing in [this law] shall be interpreted to permit otherwise.

pregnancy disability leave, [this law] ensures that they will not lose their jobs on account of pregnancy disability. California's approach is consistent with the dissenting opinion of Justice Brennan in General Electric Co. v. Gilbert . . . :

> [D]iscrimination is a social phenomenon encased in a social context and, therefore, unavoidably takes its meaning from the desired end products of the relevant legislative enactment, end products that may demand due consideration of the uniqueness of the "disadvantaged" individuals. A realistic understanding of conditions found in today's labor environment warrants taking pregnancy into account in fashioning disability policies. . . .

By "taking pregnancy into account," California's pregnancy disability-leave statute allows women, as well as men, to have families without losing their jobs.

We emphasize the limited nature of the benefits [this law] provides. The statute is narrowly drawn to cover only the period of *actual physical disability* on account of pregnancy, childbirth, or related medical conditions. Accordingly, unlike the protective labor legislation prevalent earlier in this century, [this law] does not reflect archaic or stereotypical notions about pregnancy and the abilities of pregnant workers. A statute based on such stereotypical assumptions would, of course, be inconsistent with Title VII's goal of equal employment opportunity. . . .

Moreover, even if we agreed with petitioners' construction of the PDA, we would nonetheless reject their argument that the California statute requires employers to violate Title VII. [The challenged statute] does not prevent employers from complying with both the federal law (as petitioners construe it) and the state law. This is not a case where "compliance with both federal and state regulations is a physical impossibility," . . . or where there is an "inevitable collision between the two schemes of regulation." . . . [The California law] does not compel California employers to treat pregnant workers better than other disabled employees; it merely establishes benefits that employers must, at a minimum, provide to pregnant workers. Employers are free to give comparable benefits to other disabled employees, thereby treating "women affected by pregnancy" no better than "other persons not so affected but similar in their ability or inability to work." Indeed, at oral argument, petitioners conceded that compliance with both statutes "is theoretically possible." . . .

Herma Hill Kay, Equality and Difference: The Case of Pregnancy
1 Berkeley Women's L.J. 1, 26-31 (1985)

Philosophers recognize that, just as the concept of equality requires that equals be treated equally, so it requires that unequals be treated differently. To treat persons who are different alike is to treat them unequally. The concept of formal equality, however, contains no independent justification for making unequals equal. A different concept, that of equality of opportunity, offers a theoretical basis for making unequals equal in the limited sense of removing barriers that prevent individuals from performing according to their abilities. The notion is that the perceived inequality does not stem from an innate difference in ability, but rather from a condition or circumstance that prevents certain uses or developments of that ability. As applied to reproductive behavior, the suggestion would be that women in general are not different from men in innate ability. During the temporary episode of a woman's pregnancy, however, she may become unable to utilize her abilities in the same way she had done prior to her reproductive conduct. Since a man's abilities are not similarly impaired as a result of his reproductive behavior, equality of opportunity implies that the woman should not be disadvantaged as a result of that sex-specific variation.

As applied to the employment context, the concept of equality of opportunity takes on the following form. Let us postulate two workers, one female, the other male, who respectively engage in reproductive conduct. Assume as well that prior to this activity, both were roughly equal in their ability to perform their similar jobs. The consequence of their having engaged in reproductive behavior will be vastly different. The man's ability to perform on the job will be largely unaffected. The woman's ability to work, measured against her prior performance, may vary with the physical and emotional changes she experiences during pregnancy. At times, her ability to work may be unaffected by the pregnancy; at other times, she may be temporarily incapacitated by it. Ultimately, she may require medical care to recover from miscarriage, or to complete her pregnancy by delivery, or to terminate it earlier by induced abortion. In order to maintain the woman's equality of opportunity during her pregnancy, we should modify as far as reasonably possible those aspects of her work where her job performance is adversely affected by the pregnancy. Unless we do so, she will experience employment disadvantages arising from her reproductive activity that are not encountered by her male co-worker . . . .

[P]regnancy differs from sex . . . in that pregnancy is an episodic occurrence, rather than an immutable trait. The category of pregnant persons is a sub-class within the larger category of women . . . .

This interpretation of Title VII based on an episodic analysis of biological reproductive differences will permit pregnancy to be recognized as the normal consequence of reproductive behavior that can and should be accommodated in the workplace. . . . If she is temporarily impaired from performing at work up to her normal level of ability, the concept of equal employment opportunity embodied in Title VII requires not only that she remain free of resulting job reprisals, but also that she secure compensatory benefits to offset any potential work-related disadvantage. Under this analysis, women will be equal to men in their ability to work and to make reproductive choices . . . .

Richard A. Posner, Conservative Feminism
1989 U. Chi. Legal F. 191, 195-98

Where the libertarian is apt to part company with the liberal or radical feminist in the field of employment is over the question whether employers should be forced to subsidize female employees, as by being compelled to offer maternity leave or pregnancy benefits, or to disregard women's greater longevity when fixing pension benefits. To the extent that women workers incur higher medical expenses than men (mainly but not entirely due to pregnancy), or live longer in retirement on a company pension, they cost the employer more than male workers do. So the employer should not be required to pay the same wage *and* provide the same package of fringe benefits. (Of course, to the extent that women impose lower costs—for example, women appear to be more careful about safety than men, and therefore less likely to be injured on the job—they are entitled to a correspondingly higher wage or more extensive fringe benefits.) This is not to suggest—which would be absurd—that women are blameworthy for getting pregnant or for living longer than men. It is to suggest merely that they may be more costly workers and that, if so, the disparity in cost should be reflected in their net compensation. If this disparity is not reflected, then male workers are being discriminated against in the same sense in which women would be discriminated against if they received a lower wage than equally productive (and no less costly) male workers. What is sauce for the goose should be sauce for the gander. More than symmetry is involved; we shall see in a moment that laws designed to improve the welfare of women may boomerang, partly though not wholly because of the economic interdependence of men and women.

I anticipate three objections to my analysis. The first is that in speaking of employers' subsidizing women I am taking as an arbitrary benchmark the costs and performance of male workers. I am not. Consider an employer who is female in a hypothetical female-dominated society and whose entire labor force is also female, so that for her the benchmark in setting terms of employment is female. A man applies for a job. He asks for a higher wage on the ground that experience shows that the average male employee's medical costs are lower than the average female employee's medical costs. If the employer refuses to pay him the higher wage, then, assuming that this worker is just as good as the employer's average female worker, the employer is discriminating against him. This should answer the second objection—that nature should not be allowed to determine social outcomes. I agree that natural law does not compel the conclusion that women should be penalized in the marketplace or anywhere else for living longer or for incurring greater medical costs on average than men. But neither is there any reason why men should be penalized for not living as long as women by being forced to pay for women's longer years of retirement. The matter should be left to the market.

The third objection to my analysis is that, in suggesting that the employer be allowed to make cost-justified differentiations based on sex, I am necessarily implying that he should be permitted to treat employees as members of groups whose average characteristics the particular employee may not share, rather than as individuals. That is true. Some women die before some men, just as some women are taller than some men. The difference is that while it is obvious on inspection whether a given woman is taller than a given man—and therefore it would be absurd for an employer to implement a (let us assume valid) minimum-height requirement of 5 feet 8 inches by refusing to accept job applications from women, it is not obvious which women employees will not live as long as which men employees or will not take as much leave or incur as high medical expenses. Any cost-based differentiation in these areas must be based on probabilistic considerations, of which sex may be the most powerful in the sense of having the greatest predictive power. The average differences between men and women are not invidious, and many cut in favor of women—they are safer drivers, and they live longer, and in a free insurance market would therefore be able to buy liability insurance and life insurance at lower rates than men. Women would not be stigmatized if the market were allowed to register these differences.

It is not even clear, moreover, that women benefit, on balance, from laws that forbid employers to take into account the extra costs that female employees can impose. Such laws discourage employers from hiring, promoting, and retaining women, and there are many ways in which they can discriminate in these respects without committing detectable violations of the employment-discrimination laws. Sometimes there is no question of violation, as when an employer accelerates the substitution of computers for secretaries in response to an increase in the costs of his female employees.

There is an additional point. Most women are married—and many who are not currently married are divorced or widowed and continue to derive a benefit from their husband's earnings. The consumption of a married woman is, as I have noted, a function of her husband's income as well as of her own (in the divorce and widowhood cases as well, for the reason just noted). Therefore a reduction in men's incomes as a result of laws that interfere with profit-maximizing and cost-minimizing decisions by employers will reduce women's welfare as well as men's. Moreover, women who are not married are less likely to have children than women who are married; and where employer benefits are child-related—such as pregnancy benefits and maternity leave—their effect is not merely to transfer wealth from men to women but from women to women. The effect could be dramatic. Compare the situation of a married woman with many children and an unmarried woman with no children. Generous pregnancy benefits and a generous policy on maternity leave will raise the economic welfare of the married woman. Her and her husband's wages will be lower, because all wages will fall in order to finance the benefit, but the reduction will probably be smaller than the benefits to her—in part because the unmarried female worker will experience the same reduction in wages but with no offsetting benefit. Feminists who support rules requiring employers to grant pregnancy benefits and maternity leave may therefore, and I assume unknowingly, be discouraging women from remaining single or childless. Feminists of all persuasions would think it outrageous if the government required fertile women to have children, yet many feminists support an oblique form of such a policy—a subsidy to motherhood. They do this, I suspect, because they have not considered the economic consequences of proposals that *appear* to help women.

≡≡≡ ### *Troupe v. May Department Stores Co.*
20 F.3d 734 (7th Cir. 1994)

POSNER, Chief Judge.

The plaintiff, Kimberly Hern Troupe, was employed by the Lord & Taylor department store in Chicago as a saleswoman in the women's accessories department. . . . Until the end of 1990 her work was entirely satisfactory. In December of that year, in the first trimester of a pregnancy, she began experiencing morning sickness of unusual severity. The following month she requested and was granted a return to part-time status, working from noon to 5:00 p.m. Partly it seems because she slept later under the new schedule, so that noon was "morning" for her, she continued to experience severe morning sickness at work, causing what her lawyer describes with understatement as "slight" or "occasional" tardiness. In the month that ended with a warning from her immediate supervisor, Jennifer Rauch, on February 18, she reported late to work, or left early, on nine out of the 21 working days. The day after the warning she was late again and this time received a written warning. After she was tardy three days in a row late in March, the company on March 29 placed her on probation for 60 days. During the probationary period Troupe was late eleven more days; and she was fired on June 7, shortly after the end of the probationary period. She testified at her deposition that on the way to the meeting with the defendant's human resources manager at which she was fired, Rauch told her that "I [Troupe] was going to be terminated because she [Rauch] didn't think I was coming back to work after I had my baby." Troupe was due to begin her maternity leave the next day. . . . [A]t argument Lord & Taylor's counsel said that employees of Lord & Taylor are entitled to maternity leave with half pay. . . .

The great, the undeniable fact is the plaintiff's tardiness. Her lawyer argues with great vigor that she should not be blamed—that she was genuinely ill, had a doctor's excuse, etc. That would be pertinent if Troupe were arguing that the Pregnancy Discrimination Act requires an employer to treat an employee afflicted by morning sickness better than the employer would treat an employee who was equally tardy for some other health reason. This is rightly not argued. If an employee who (like Troupe) does not have an employment contract cannot work because of illness, nothing in Title VII requires the employer to keep the employee on the payroll. . . .

Against the inference that Troupe was fired because she was chronically late to arrive at work and chronically early to leave, she has only two facts to offer. The first is the timing of her discharge: she was fired the day before her maternity leave was to begin. . . . Thus, her employer fired her one day before the problem that the employer says caused her to be fired was certain to end. If the discharge of an unsatisfactory worker were a purely remedial measure rather than also, or instead, a deterrent one, the inference that Troupe wasn't really fired because of her tardiness would therefore be a powerful one. But that is a big "if." We must remember that after two warnings Troupe had been placed on probation for sixty days and that she had violated the implicit terms of probation by being as tardy during the probationary period as she had been before. If the company did not fire her, its warnings and threats would seem empty. Employees would be encouraged to flout work rules knowing that the only sanction would be a toothless warning or a meaningless period of probation.

[I]t might appear to be an issue for trial whether it is superior to Troupe's interpretation. But what is Troupe's interpretation? Not (as we understand it) that Lord & Taylor wanted to get back at her for becoming pregnant or having morning sickness. The only significance she asks us to attach to the timing of her discharge is as reinforcement for the inference that she asks us to draw from Rauch's statement about the reason for her termination: that she was terminated because her employer did not expect her to return to work after her maternity leave was up. We must decide whether a termination so motivated is discrimination within the meaning of the pregnancy amendment to Title VII.

Standing alone, it is not. (It could be a breach of contract, but that is not alleged.) . . . We must imagine a hypothetical Mr. Troupe, who is as tardy as Ms. Troupe was, also because of health problems, and who is about to take a protracted sick leave growing out of those problems at an expense to Lord & Taylor equal to that of Ms. Troupe's maternity leave. If Lord & Taylor would have fired our hypothetical Mr. Troupe, this implies that it fired Ms. Troupe not because she was pregnant but because she cost the company more than she was worth to it.

The Pregnancy Discrimination Act does not, despite the urgings of feminist scholars . . . require employers to offer maternity leave or take other steps to make it easier for pregnant women to work . . . to make it as easy, say as it is for their spouses to continue working during pregnancy. Employers can treat pregnant women as badly as they treat similarly affected but nonpregnant employees. . . .

The plaintiff has made no effort to show that if all the pertinent facts were as they are except for the fact of her pregnancy, she would not have been fired. So in the end she has no evidence from which a rational trier of fact could infer that she was a victim of pregnancy discrimination. . . . The Pregnancy Discrimination Act requires the employer to ignore an employee's pregnancy, but . . . not her absence from work, unless the employer overlooks the comparable absences of nonpregnant employees. . . . Of course there may be no comparable absences . . . ; but we do not understand Troupe to be arguing that the reason she did not present evidence that nonpregnant employees were treated more favorably than she is that . . . there is no comparison group of Lord & Taylor employees. . . . We doubt that finding a comparison group would be that difficult. Troupe would be halfway home if she could find one nonpregnant employee of Lord & Taylor who had not been fired when about to begin a leave similar in length to hers. She either did not look, or did not find. Given the absence of other evidence, her failure to present any comparison evidence doomed her case.

═══ ## *Young v. United Parcel Service, Inc.*
135 S. Ct. 1338 (2015)

Justice BREYER delivered the opinion of the Court.

The Pregnancy Discrimination Act makes clear that Title VII's prohibition against sex discrimination applies to discrimination based on pregnancy. It also says that employers must treat "women affected by pregnancy . . . the same for all employment-related purposes . . . as other persons not so affected but similar in their ability or inability to work." 42 U.S.C. §2000e(k). We must decide how this latter provision applies in the context of an employer's policy that accommodates many, but not all, workers with nonpregnancy-related disabilities.

In our view, the Act requires courts to consider the extent to which an employer's policy treats pregnant workers less favorably than it treats nonpregnant workers similar in their ability or inability to work. And here—as in all cases in which an individual plaintiff seeks to show disparate treatment through indirect evidence—it requires courts to consider any legitimate, nondiscriminatory, nonpretextual justification for these differences in treatment. See McDonnell Douglas Corp. v. Green, 411 U.S. 792, 802 (1973). Ultimately the court must determine whether the nature of the employer's policy and the way in which it burdens pregnant women shows that the employer has engaged in intentional discrimination. The Court of Appeals here affirmed a grant of summary judgment in favor of the employer. Given our view of the law, we must vacate that court's judgment.

I

A

Facts

We begin with a summary of the facts. The petitioner, Peggy Young worked as a part-time driver for the respondent, United Parcel Service (UPS). Her responsibilities included pickup and delivery of packages that had arrived by air carrier the previous night. In 2006, after suffering several miscarriages, she became pregnant. Her doctor told her that she should not lift more than 20 pounds during the first 20 weeks of her pregnancy or more than 10 pounds thereafter. UPS required drivers like Young to be able to lift parcels weighing up to 70 pounds (and up to 150 pounds with assistance). UPS told Young she could not work while under a lifting restriction. Young consequently stayed home without pay during most of the time she was pregnant and eventually lost her employee medical coverage.

Young subsequently brought this federal lawsuit. We focus here on her claim that UPS acted unlawfully in refusing to accommodate her pregnancy-related lifting restriction. Young said that her co-workers were willing to help her with heavy packages. She also said that UPS accommodated other drivers who were "similar in their . . . inability to work." She accordingly concluded that UPS must accommodate her as well. Comparison

UPS responded that the "other persons" whom it had accommodated were (1) drivers who had become disabled on the job, (2) those who had lost their Department of Transportation (DOT) certifications, and (3) those who suffered from a disability covered by the Americans with Disabilities Act of 1990 (ADA). UPS said that, since Young did not fall within any of those categories, it had not discriminated against on the basis of pregnancy but had treated her just as it treated all "other" relevant "persons."

B . . .

This case requires us to consider the application of the second clause [of the PDA] to a "disparate-treatment" claim—a claim that an employer intentionally treated a complainant less favorably than employees with the "complainant's qualifications" but outside the complainant's protected class. . . .

In *McDonnell Douglas*, we considered a claim of discriminatory hiring. We said that, to prove disparate treatment, an individual plaintiff must "carry the initial burden" of "establishing a prima facie case" of discrimination by showing

> "(i) that he belongs to a . . . minority; (ii) that he applied and was qualified for a job for which the employer was seeking applicants; (iii) that, despite his qualifications, he was rejected; and (iv) that, after his rejection, the position remained open and the employer continued to seek applicants from persons of complainant's qualifications." 411 U.S., at 802.

If a plaintiff makes this showing, then the employer must have an opportunity "to articulate some legitimate, nondiscriminatory reason for" treating employees outside the protected class better than employees within the protected class. If the employer articulates such a reason, the plaintiff then has "an opportunity to prove by a preponderance of the evidence that the legitimate reasons offered by the defendant [i.e., the employer] were not its true reasons, but were a pretext for discrimination." Texas Dept. of Community Affairs v. Burdine, 450 U.S. 248, 253 (1981). . . .

C . . .

Young introduced further evidence indicating that UPS had accommodated several individuals when they suffered disabilities that created work restrictions similar to hers. UPS contests the correctness of some of these facts and the relevance of others. . . . [The District Court granted summary judgment to UPS; the Fourth Circuit affirmed, writing that] "UPS has crafted a pregnancy-blind policy" that is "at least facially a 'neutral and legitimate business practice,'" and not evidence of UPS's discriminatory animus toward pregnant workers."

II

The parties disagree about the interpretation of the Pregnancy Discrimination Act's second clause. . . . [T]he Act's first clause specifies that discrimination "'because of sex'" includes discrimination "because of . . . pregnancy." But the meaning of the second clause is less clear; it adds: "[W]omen affected by pregnancy, childbirth, or related medical conditions shall be treated the same for all employment-related purposes . . . as *other persons* not so affected but *similar in their ability or inability to work*." 42 U.S.C. §2000e(k) (emphasis added). Does this clause mean that courts must compare workers *only* in respect to the work limitations that they suffer? Does it mean that courts must ignore all other similarities or differences between pregnant and nonpregnant workers? Or does it mean that courts, when deciding who the relevant "other persons" are, may consider other similarities and differences as well? If so, which ones? . . .

The parties propose very different answers to this question. Young and the United States believe that the second clause of the Pregnancy Discrimination Act "requires an employer to provide the same accommodations to workplace disabilities caused by pregnancy that it provides to workplace disabilities that have other causes but have a similar effect on the ability to work." In other words, Young contends that the second clause means that whenever "an employer accommodates only a subset of workers with disabling conditions," a court should find a Title VII violation if "pregnant workers who are similar in the ability to work" do not "receive the same [accommodation] even if still other non-pregnant workers do not receive accommodations."

UPS takes an almost polar opposite view. It contends that the second clause does no more than define sex discrimination to include pregnancy discrimination. Under this view, courts would compare the accommodations an employer provides to pregnant women with the accommodations it provides to others *within* a facially neutral category (such as those with off-the-job injuries) to determine whether the employer has violated Title VII.

A

We cannot accept either of these interpretations. . . .

The problem with Young's approach is that it proves too much. It seems to say that the statute grants pregnant workers a "most-favored-nation" status. As long as an employer provides one or two workers with an accommodation—say, those with particularly hazardous jobs, or those whose workplace presence is particularly needed, or those who have worked at the company for many years, or those who are over the age of 55—then it must provide similar accommodations to *all* pregnant workers (with comparable physical limitations), irrespective of the nature of their jobs, the employer's need to keep them working, their ages, or any other criteria. . . .

We agree with UPS to this extent: We doubt that Congress intended to grant pregnant workers an unconditional most-favored-nation status. The language of the statute does not require that unqualified reading. The second clause, when referring to nonpregnant persons with similar disabilities, uses the open-ended term "other persons." It does not say that the employer must treat pregnant employees the "same" as "*any* other persons" (who are similar in their ability or inability to work), nor does it otherwise specify *which* other persons Congress had in mind.

Moreover, disparate-treatment law normally permits an employer to implement policies that are not intended to harm members of a protected class, even if their implementation sometimes harms those members, as long as the employer has a legitimate, nondiscriminatory, nonpretextual reason for doing so. There is no reason to believe Congress intended its language in the Pregnancy Discrimination Act to embody a significant deviation from this approach. . . .

C

We find it similarly difficult to accept the opposite interpretation of the Act's second clause. UPS says that the second clause simply defines sex discrimination to include pregnancy discrimination. But that cannot be so.

The first clause accomplishes that objective when it expressly amends Title VII's definitional provision to make clear that Title VII's words "because of sex" and "on the basis of sex" "include, but are not limited to, because of or on the basis of pregnancy, childbirth, or related medical conditions." 42 U.S.C. §2000e(k). We have long held that " 'a statute ought, upon the whole, to be so construed that, if it can be prevented, no clause'" is rendered "'superfluous, void, or insignificant.'" But that is what UPS' interpretation of the second clause would do. . . .

Moreover, the interpretation espoused by UPS and the dissent would fail to carry out an important congressional objective. As we have noted, Congress' "unambiguou[s]" intent in passing the Act was to overturn "both the holding and the reasoning of the Court in the *Gilbert* decision." Newport News Shipbuilding & Dry Dock Co. v. EEOC, 462 U.S. 669, 678 (1983). In *Gilbert*, the Court considered a company plan that provided "nonoccupational sickness and accident benefits to all employees" without providing "disability-benefit payments for any absence due to pregnancy." 429 U.S., at 128, 129. The Court held that the plan did not violate Title VII; it did not discriminate on the basis of sex because there was "no risk from which men are protected and women are not." *Id.*, at 138. Although pregnancy is "confined to women," the majority believed it was not "comparable in all other respects to [the] diseases or disabilities" that the plan covered. *Id.*, at 136. Specifically, the majority explained that pregnancy "is not a 'disease' at all," nor is it necessarily a result of accident. Neither did the majority see the distinction the plan drew as "a subterfuge" or a "pretext" for engaging in gender-based discrimination. *Ibid.* In short, the *Gilbert* majority reasoned in part just as the dissent reasons here. The employer did "not distinguish between pregnant women and others of similar ability or inability *because of pregnancy.*" It distinguished between them on a neutral ground—*i.e.*, it accommodated only sicknesses and accidents, and pregnancy was neither of those. See 429 U.S., at 136.

Simply including pregnancy among Title VII's protected traits (*i.e.*, accepting UPS' interpretation) would not overturn *Gilbert* in full—in particular, it would not respond to *Gilbert*'s determination that an employer can treat pregnancy less favorably than diseases or disabilities resulting in a similar inability to work. As we explained in California Fed. Sav. & Loan Assn. v. Guerra, 479 U.S. 272 (1987), "the first clause of the [Act] reflects Congress' disapproval of the reasoning in *Gilbert*" by "adding pregnancy to the definition of sex discrimination prohibited by Title VII." *Id.*, at 284. But the second clause was intended to do more than that—it "was intended to overrule the holding in *Gilbert* and to illustrate how discrimination against pregnancy is to be remedied." *Id.*, at 285. The dissent's view, like that of UPS', ignores this precedent.

III

The statute lends itself to an interpretation other than those that the parties advocate and that the dissent sets forth. Our interpretation minimizes the problems we have discussed, responds directly to *Gilbert*, and is consistent with longstanding interpretations of Title VII.

In our view, an individual pregnant worker who seeks to show disparate treatment through indirect evidence may do so through application of the

McDonnell Douglas framework. That framework requires a plaintiff to make out a prima facie case of discrimination. But it is "not intended to be an inflexible rule." Rather, an individual plaintiff may establish a prima facie case by "showing actions taken by the employer from which one can infer, if such actions remain unexplained, that it is more likely than not that such actions were based on a discriminatory criterion illegal under" Title VII. The burden of making this showing is "not onerous." *Burdine*, 450 U.S., at 253. In particular, making this showing is not as burdensome as succeeding on "an ultimate finding of fact as to" a discriminatory employment action. Neither does it require the plaintiff to show that those whom the employer favored and those whom the employer disfavored were similar in all but the protected ways.

Thus, a plaintiff alleging that the denial of an accommodation constituted disparate treatment under the Pregnancy Discrimination Act's second clause may make out a prima facie case by showing, as in *McDonnell Douglas*, that she belongs to the protected class, that she sought accommodation, that the employer did not accommodate her, and that the employer did accommodate others "similar in their ability or inability to work."

The employer may then seek to justify its refusal to accommodate the plaintiff by relying on "legitimate, nondiscriminatory" reasons for denying her accommodation. But, consistent with the Act's basic objective, that reason normally cannot consist simply of a claim that it is more expensive or less convenient to add pregnant women to the category of those ("similar in their ability or inability to work") whom the employer accommodates. After all, the employer in *Gilbert* could in all likelihood have made just such a claim.

If the employer offers an apparently "legitimate, non-discriminatory" reason for its actions, the plaintiff may in turn show that the employer's proffered reasons are in fact pretextual. We believe that the plaintiff may reach a jury on this issue by providing sufficient evidence that the employer's policies impose a significant burden on pregnant workers, and that the employer's "legitimate, nondiscriminatory" reasons are not sufficiently strong to justify the burden, but rather—when considered along with the burden imposed—give rise to an inference of intentional discrimination.

The plaintiff can create a genuine issue of material fact as to whether a significant burden exists by providing evidence that the employer accommodates a large percentage of nonpregnant workers while failing to accommodate a large percentage of pregnant workers. Here, for example, if the facts are as Young says they are, she can show that UPS accommodates most nonpregnant employees with lifting limitations while categorically failing to accommodate pregnant employees with lifting limitations. Young might also add that the fact that UPS has multiple policies that accommodate nonpregnant employees with lifting restrictions suggests that its reasons for failing to accommodate pregnant employees with lifting restrictions are not sufficiently strong—to the point that a jury could find that its reasons for failing to accommodate pregnant employees give rise to an inference of intentional discrimination.

This approach, though limited to the Pregnancy Discrimination Act context, is consistent with our longstanding rule that a plaintiff can use circumstantial proof to rebut an employer's apparently legitimate, nondiscriminatory reasons for treating individuals within a protected class differently than those outside the protected class. . . .

Our interpretation of the Act is also, unlike the dissent's, consistent with Congress' intent to overrule *Gilbert*'s reasoning and result. The dissent says that "[i]f a pregnant woman is denied an accommodation under a policy that does not discriminate against pregnancy, she *has* been 'treated the same' as everyone else." This logic would have found no problem with the employer plan in *Gilbert*, which "denied an accommodation" to pregnant women on the same basis as it denied accommodations to other employees—*i.e.*, it accommodated only sicknesses and accidents, and pregnancy was neither of those. . . .

IV

Under this interpretation of the Act, the judgment of the Fourth Circuit must be vacated. . . . Viewing the record in the light most favorable to Young, there is a genuine dispute as to whether UPS provided more favorable treatment to at least some employees whose situation cannot reasonably be distinguished from Young's. . . .

Young also introduced evidence that UPS had three separate accommodation policies (on-the-job, ADA, DOT). Taken together, Young argued, these policies significantly burdened pregnant women. See App. 504 (shop steward's testimony that "the only light duty requested [due to physical] restrictions that became an issue" at UPS "were with women who were pregnant"). The Fourth Circuit did not consider the combined effects of these policies, nor did it consider the strength of UPS' justifications for each when combined. That is, why, when the employer accommodated so many, could it not accommodate pregnant women as well?

We do not determine whether Young created a genuine issue of material fact as to whether UPS' reasons for having treated Young less favorably than it treated these other nonpregnant employees were pretextual. We leave a final determination of that question for the Fourth Circuit to make on remand. . . .

≡≡≡ ### UAW v. Johnson Controls, Inc.
≡≡≡ **499 U.S. 187 (1991)**

Mr. Justice BLACKMUN delivered the opinion of the Court.

In this case we are concerned with an employer's gender-based fetal-protection policy. May an employer exclude a fertile female employee from certain jobs because of its concern for the health of the fetus the woman might conceive?

I

Respondent Johnson Controls, Inc., manufactures batteries. In the manufacturing process, the element lead is a primary ingredient. Occupational exposure to lead entails health risks, including the risk of harm to any fetus carried by a female employee.

Before [Title VII] became law, Johnson Controls did not employ any woman in a battery-manufacturing job. In June 1977, however, it announced its first official policy concerning its employment of women in lead-exposure work:

> [P]rotection of the health of the unborn child is the immediate and direct responsibility of the prospective parents. While the medical profession and the company can support them in the exercise of this responsibility, it cannot assume it for them without simultaneously infringing their rights as persons. . . .
>
> Since not all women who can become mothers wish to become mothers (or will become mothers), it would appear to be illegal discrimination to treat all who are capable of pregnancy as though they will become pregnant. . . .

Consistent with that view, Johnson Controls "stopped short of excluding women capable of bearing children from lead exposure," . . . but emphasized that a woman who expected to have a child should not choose a job in which she would have such exposure. The company also required a woman who wished to be considered for employment to sign a statement that she had been advised of the risk of having a child while she was exposed to lead. The statement informed the woman that although there was evidence "that women exposed to lead have a higher rate of [miscarriage]," this evidence was "not as clear . . . as the relationship between cigarette smoking and cancer," but that it was, "medically speaking, just good sense not to run that risk if you want children and do not want to expose the unborn child to risk, however small. . . ."

Five years later, in 1982, Johnson Controls shifted from a policy of warning to a policy of exclusion. Between 1979 and 1983, eight employees became pregnant while maintaining blood lead levels in excess of 30 micrograms per deciliter. . . . This appeared to be the critical level noted by the Occupational Health and Safety Administration (OSHA) for a worker who was planning to have a family. . . . The company responded by announcing a broad exclusion of women from jobs that exposed them to lead:

> [I]t is [Johnson Controls'] policy that women who are pregnant or who are capable of bearing children will not be placed into jobs involving lead exposure or which could expose them to lead through the exercise of job bidding, bumping, transfer or promotion rights. . . .

The policy defined "women . . . capable of bearing children" as "[a]ll women except those whose inability to bear children is medically documented."

Or provide proof of infertility

. . . It further stated that an unacceptable work station was one where, "over the past year," an employee had recorded a blood lead level of more than 30 micrograms per deciliter or the work site had yielded an air sample containing a lead level in excess of 30 micrograms per cubic meter. . . .

II

In April 1984, petitioners filed in the United States District Court for the Eastern District of Wisconsin a class action challenging Johnson Controls' fetal-protection policy as sex discrimination that violated Title VII. . . . Among the individual plaintiffs were petitioners Mary Craig, who had chosen to be sterilized in order to avoid losing her job, Elsie Nason, a 50-year-old divorcee, who had suffered a loss in compensation when she was transferred out of a job where she was exposed to lead, and Donald Penney, who had been denied a request for a leave of absence for the purpose of lowering his lead level because he intended to become a father. . . .

[The District Court granted summary judgment for defendant and the court of appeals affirmed.] . . .

III

The bias in Johnson Controls' policy is obvious. Fertile men, but not fertile women, are given a choice as to whether they wish to risk their reproductive health for a particular job. [Title VII] prohibits sex-based classifications in terms and conditions of employment, in hiring and discharging decisions, and in other employment decisions that adversely affect an employee's status. Respondent's fetal-protection policy explicitly discriminates against women on the basis of their sex. The policy excludes women with childbearing capacity from lead-exposed jobs and so creates a facial classification based on gender. . . .

[The assumption by the appellate courts that sex-specific fetal-protection policies do not involve facial discrimination was incorrect.]

First, Johnson Controls' policy classifies on the basis of gender and childbearing capacity, rather than fertility alone. Respondent does not seek to protect the unconceived children of all its employees. Despite evidence in the record about the debilitating effect of lead exposure on the male reproductive system, Johnson Controls is concerned only with the harms that may befall the unborn offspring of its female employees. . . . Johnson Controls' policy is facially discriminatory because it requires only a female employee to produce proof that she is not capable of reproducing.

Our conclusion is bolstered by the Pregnancy Discrimination Act of 1978 (PDA), in which Congress explicitly provided that, for purposes of Title VII, discrimination "on the basis of sex" includes discrimination "because of or on the basis of pregnancy, childbirth, or related medical conditions." . . .

In its use of the words "capable of bearing children" in the 1982 policy statement as the criterion for exclusion, Johnson Controls explicitly classifies on the basis of potential for pregnancy. Under the PDA, such a classification must be regarded, for Title VII purposes, in the same light as explicit sex discrimination. Respondent has chosen to treat all its female employees as potentially pregnant; that choice evinces discrimination on the basis of sex.

[T]he absence of a malevolent motive does not convert a facially discriminatory policy into a neutral policy with a discriminatory effect. Whether an employment practice involves disparate treatment through explicit facial discrimination does not depend on why the employer discriminates but rather on the explicit terms of the discrimination. . . .

We hold that Johnson Controls' fetal-protection policy is sex discrimination forbidden under Title VII unless respondent can establish that sex is a "bona fide occupational qualification."

IV . . .

The wording of the BFOQ defense contains several terms of restriction that indicate that the exception reaches only special situations. The statute thus limits the situations in which discrimination is permissible to "certain instances" where sex discrimination is "reasonably necessary" to the "normal operation" of the "particular" business. . . .

Johnson Controls argues that its fetal-protection policy falls within the so-called safety exception to the BFOQ. Our cases have stressed that discrimination on the basis of sex because of safety concerns is allowed only in narrow circumstances. In Dothard v. Rawlinson, . . . this Court indicated that danger to a woman herself does not justify discrimination. We there allowed the employer to hire only male guards in contact areas of maximum-security male penitentiaries only because more was at stake than the "individual woman's decision to weigh and accept the risks of employment." . . . Similarly, some courts have approved airlines' layoffs of pregnant flight attendants at different points during the first five months of pregnancy on the ground that the employer's policy was necessary to ensure the safety of passengers. . . . In two of these cases, the courts pointedly indicated that fetal, as opposed to passenger, safety was best left to the mother. . . .

We considered safety to third parties in Western Airlines, Inc. v. Criswell . . . in the context of the [Age Discrimination in Employment Act]. We focused upon "the nature of the flight engineer's tasks," and the "actual capabilities of persons over age 60" in relation to those tasks. Our safety concerns were not independent of the individual's ability to perform the assigned tasks, but rather involved the possibility that, because of age-connected debility, a flight engineer might not properly assist the pilot, and might thereby cause a safety emergency. . . .

Third-party safety considerations properly entered into the BFOQ analysis in *Dothard* and *Criswell* because they went to the core of the employee's job performance. Moreover, that performance involved the central purpose of the enterprise. . . . The concurrence attempts to transform this case into one of customer safety. The unconceived fetuses of Johnson Controls' female employees, however, are neither customers nor third parties whose safety is essential to the business of battery manufacturing. No one can disregard the possibility of injury to future children; the BFOQ, however, is not so broad that it transforms this deep social concern into an essential aspect of batterymaking. . . .

The PDA's amendment to Title VII contains a BFOQ standard of its own: unless pregnant employees differ from others "in their ability or inability to work," they must be "treated the same" as other employees "for all employment-related purposes." This language clearly sets forth Congress' remedy for discrimination on the basis of pregnancy and potential pregnancy. Women who are either pregnant or potentially pregnant must be treated like others "similar in their ability . . . to work." [Id.] In other words, women as capable of doing their jobs as their male counterparts may not be forced to choose between having a child and having a job. . . .

We conclude that the language of both the BFOQ provision and the PDA which amended it, as well as the legislative history and the case law, prohibit an employer from discriminating against a woman because of her capacity to become pregnant unless her reproductive potential prevents her from performing the duties of her job. We reiterate our holdings in *Criswell* and *Dothard* that an employer must direct its concerns about a woman's ability to perform her job safely and efficiently to those aspects of the woman's job-related activities that fall within the "essence" of the particular business.[4]

V

We have no difficulty concluding that Johnson Controls cannot establish a BFOQ. Fertile women, as far as appears in the record, participate in the manufacture of batteries as efficiently as anyone else. . . .

---

4. The concurrence predicts that our reaffirmation of the narrowness of the BFOQ defense will preclude considerations of privacy as a basis for sex-based discrimination. . . . We have never addressed privacy-based sex discrimination and shall not do so here because the sex-based discrimination at issue today does not involve the privacy interests of Johnson Control's customers. Nothing in our discussion of the "essence of the business test," however, suggests that sex could not constitute a BFOQ when privacy interests are implicated. See, e.g., Backus v. Baptist Medical Center [(E.D. Ark. 1981)] (essence of obstetrics nurse's business is to provide sensitive care for patient's intimate and private concerns).

VI

A word about tort liability and the increased cost of fertile women in the workplace is perhaps necessary.

[The Court concedes the possibility that it may cost the employer more to protect pregnant women, at the risk of tort liability if it does not.] . . .

[T]he extra cost of employing members of one sex . . . does not provide an affirmative Title VII defense for a discriminatory refusal to hire members of that gender. . . . Indeed, in passing the PDA, Congress considered at length the considerable cost of providing equal treatment of pregnancy and related conditions, but made the "decision to forbid special treatment of pregnancy despite the social costs associated therewith." . . .

We, of course, are not presented with, nor do we decide, a case in which costs would be so prohibitive as to threaten the survival of the employer's business. We merely reiterate our prior holdings that the incremental cost of hiring women cannot justify discriminating against them.

VII

Our holding today that Title VII . . . forbids sex-specific fetal-protection policies is neither remarkable nor unprecedented. Concern for a woman's existing or potential offspring historically has been the excuse for denying women equal employment opportunities. See, e.g., Muller v. Oregon. . . . Congress in the PDA prohibited discrimination on the basis of a woman's ability to become pregnant. We do no more than hold that the Pregnancy Discrimination Act means what it says. . . .

The judgment of the Court of Appeals is reversed and the case is remanded for further proceedings consistent with this opinion.

Justice WHITE, with whom THE CHIEF JUSTICE and Justice KENNEDY join, concurring in part and concurring in the judgment. . . .

I . . .

Common sense tells us that it is part of the normal operation of business concerns to avoid causing injury to third parties, as well as to employees, if for no other reason than to avoid tort liability and its substantial costs. This possibility of tort liability is not hypothetical; every State currently allows children born alive to recover in tort for prenatal injuries caused by third parties . . . and an increasing number of courts have recognized a right to recover even for prenatal injuries caused by torts committed prior to conception. . . .

The Court's narrow interpretation of the BFOQ defense in this case . . . means that an employer cannot exclude even pregnant women from an environment highly toxic to their fetuses. It is foolish to think that Congress intended such a result, and neither the language of the BFOQ exception nor our cases require it.[8]

II

Despite my disagreement with the Court concerning the scope of the BFOQ defense, I concur in reversing the Court of Appeals because that court erred in affirming the District Court's grant of summary judgment in favor of Johnson Controls. First, the Court of Appeals erred in failing to consider the level of risk-avoidance that was part of Johnson Controls' "normal operation." . . . If the fetal protection policy insists on a risk-avoidance level substantially higher than other risk levels tolerated by Johnson Controls such as risks to employees and consumers, the policy should not constitute a BFOQ.

Second, even without more information about the normal level of risk at Johnson Controls, the fetal protection policy at issue here reaches too far. This is evident both in its presumption that, absent medical documentation to the contrary, all women are fertile regardless of their age . . . and in its exclusion of presumptively fertile women from positions that might result in a promotion to a position involving high lead exposure. . . .

Third, it should be recalled that until 1982 Johnson Controls operated without an exclusionary policy, and it has not identified any grounds for believing that its current policy is reasonably necessary to its normal operations. . . .

Finally, the Court of Appeals failed to consider properly petitioners' evidence of harm to offspring caused by lead exposure in males. . . . It seems clear that if the Court of Appeals had properly analyzed that evidence, it would have concluded that summary judgment against petitioners was not appropriate because there was a dispute over a material issue of fact.

Mr. Justice SCALIA, concurring in the judgment.

I generally agree with the Court's analysis, but have some reservations, several of which bear mention. . . . [T]he Court goes far afield, it seems to me, in suggesting that increased cost alone — short of "costs . . . so prohibitive as to threaten survival of the employer's business" . . . — cannot support a

---

8. The Court's cramped reading of the BFOQ defense is also belied by the legislative history of Title VII, in which three examples of permissible sex discrimination were mentioned — a female nurse hired to care for an elderly woman, an all-male professional baseball team, and a masseur. . . . In none of those situations would gender "actually interfer[e] with the employee's ability to perform the job," as required today by the Court. . . . the Court's interpretation of the BFOQ standard also would seem to preclude considerations of privacy as a basis for sex-based discrimination, since those considerations do not relate directly to an employee's physical ability to perform the duties of the job. The lower federal courts, however, have consistently recognized that privacy interests may justify sex-based requirements for certain jobs. . . .

BFOQ defense . . . I think, for example, that a shipping company may refuse to hire pregnant women as crew members on long voyages because the on-board facilities for foreseeable emergencies, though quite feasible, would be inordinately expensive. In the present case, however, Johnson has not asserted a cost-based BFOQ.

Notes

1. The Feminist Debate over "Equal" vs. "Special" Treatment. A broad coalition of feminist groups advocated the passage of the PDA, but after its passage they split over its meaning. Dispute centered on the legality and desirability of rules that attempt to eliminate some of the special disadvantages associated with pregnancy and childbirth.

Supporters of "special" treatment, like Professor Kay, argued that neutral rules cannot ensure equality between men and women when their circumstances are different, as in the case of pregnancy. By contrast, opponents like Wendy Williams claimed:

> Pregnancy [is] the centerpiece, the linchpin, the essential feature of women's separate sphere. The stereotypes, the generalizations, the role expectations [are] at their zenith when a woman [becomes] pregnant. . . .
>
> [F]eminists who seek special recognition for pregnancy are starting from the same basic assumption, namely, that women have a special place in the scheme of human existence when it comes to maternity. . . .
>
> The special treatment model has great costs. . . . [T]he reality [is] that conceptualizing pregnancy as a special case permits unfavorable as well as favorable treatment of pregnancy. Our history provides too many illustrations of the former. . . .[43]

Judge Posner's analysis offers a market-based rationale against "special treatment." Does his analysis have the same consequences as Williams' rationale? To what extent is Judge Posner correct that maternity leave policies "subsidize" women? Are there ordinary employment policies that subsidize men?

Is *Cal Fed* consistent with *Johnson Controls*? *Cal Fed* permits special legislation or employer policies that give pregnant employees unique protection while *Johnson Controls* prohibits special protection. Is the rule that protections favoring pregnant women are permissible, but that protections that compromise their work opportunities are not? Is this distinction satisfactory?

43. Wendy W. Williams, The Equality Crisis: Some Reflections on Culture, Courts, and Feminism, 7 Women's Rts. L. Rep. 175, 191, 195-196 (1982).

2. Stereotypes v. Facts. *Troupe* represents the prevailing interpretation of the PDA as a mandate to treat pregnant women like other similarly situated non-pregnant employees — no worse, but not necessarily any better. But *LaFleur* and the first clause of the PDA make clear that employers must base decisions on a pregnant woman's actual work capacity, rather than on stereotypes about how pregnant women or mothers behave. Proving the basis for an employer's decision can be a challenge. Is it realistic to expect Ms. Troupe to show that she was treated worse because of her actual condition and performance, even if she was? Consider the view of Ruth Colker: "[w]hat was she supposed to find — a nonpregnant employee with a sudden record of tardiness after a nearly spotless work record who also had scheduled a lengthy leave?"[44] Kimberly Troupe argued unsuccessfully that the problem was not her lateness, but the fact that the employer had impermissibly assumed that she would not return to work after her pregnancy leave. If she had proved this fact, should she have won?

In a case also from the Seventh Circuit Court of Appeals, Maldonado v. U.S. Bank, a new part-time bank employee was terminated, after notifying her supervisor that she was pregnant and due in July, because the bank needed a teller who could fill in for full-time tellers during summer vacations.[45] The court held that the bank could not take advance adverse action against Maldonado, noting that Maldonado had not asked for leave and had even hinted to her supervisor that she might not carry the pregnancy to term. The court qualified its holding, however, by suggesting that

> under narrow circumstances that we are not convinced are present here, [an employer may] project the normal inconveniences of pregnancy and their secondary effects into the future and take actions in accordance with and in proportion to those predictions. . . . But an employer cannot take anticipatory action unless it has a good faith basis, supported by sufficiently strong evidence, that the normal inconveniences of an employee's pregnancy will require special treatment.[46]

A growing number of mothers also have had success in court where they were harmed by stereotypical assumptions about their work commitments. These cases are discussed in the next section on caregiver discrimination. Chapter 4, Section B considers further the issue of work/family balance.

3. Pregnancy Bias? With many types of discrimination, the nature of the bias workers experience is clearly rooted in animus toward employees with a particular characteristic or trait. Is that the likely nature of bias with pregnancy? Is pregnancy something people find generally distasteful? If not, then what accounts for evidence of widespread pregnancy discrimination in the

---

44. Ruth Colker, Pregnancy, Parenting, and Capitalism, 58 Ohio St. L.J. 61, 80 (1997).
45. 186 F.3d 759 (7th Cir. 1999).
46. 186 F.3d, at 767.

workplace? A plaintiff in a recent case offered evidence that her supervisor said she couldn't do her job and "be pregnant."[47] Is this evidence of pregnancy bias?

Early studies found pregnancy to be a source of bias in almost every aspect of work—from hiring to performance appraisals to pay.[48] One study noted the contrasting reaction of store workers to pregnant customers (soft and nurturing responses combined with overly friendly touches and terms) and to pregnant job applicants (hostility).[49] Another noted especially hostile reactions to pregnant women applying for traditionally male-dominated jobs.[50] Do these studies support the conclusion that pregnancy bias reflects ambivalence to combining work and motherhood rather than animus against pregnant women per se? If so, does that support any particular approach to eradicating pregnancy discrimination?

4. Pregnancy as a Disability. Note that California's pregnancy leave requirement that was challenged in the *Cal Fed* case was a "disability leave." Should pregnancy be considered a disability under the Americans with Disabilities Act of 1990 (ADA)?[51] The ADA provides employees with a covered disability the right to reasonable accommodations that do not impose undue hardship.[52] The ADA does not expressly mention pregnancy, but most courts have interpreted it to exclude coverage for women who suffer temporary disability from the complications of normal pregnancy.[53] In 2008, Congress passed the Americans with Disabilities Act Amendments Act (ADAAA), which restores protections for the disabled that had been gutted

---

47. Martin v. Winn-Dixie Louisiana, Inc., 132 F. Supp. 3d 794 (M.D. La. 2015).

48. Jane A. Halpert et al., Pregnancy as a Source of Bias in Performance Appraisals, 14 J. Org. Behav. 649 (1993) (finding negative stereotyping against pregnant workers with significantly more negative performance appraisals, especially when reviews were done by men); Sara J. Corse, Pregnant Managers and Their Subordinates: The Effects of Gender Expectations on Hierarchical Relationships, 26 J. Applied Behav. Sci. 25 (1990) (finding that pregnant managers are penalized for acting firmly in the face of a conflict, rather than conforming to expectations that pregnant women should be soft and nurturing).

49. See Michelle R. Hebl et al., Hostile and Benevolent Reactions Toward Pregnant Women: Complementary Interpersonal Punishments and Rewards that Maintain Traditional Roles, 92 J. Applied Psychol. 1499 (2007); Shelley J. Correll et al., Getting a Job: Is There a Motherhood Penalty?, 112 Am. J. Soc. 1297, 1306 (2007); Amy J.C. Cuddy et al., When Professionals Become Mothers, Warmth Doesn't Cut the Ice, 60 J. Soc. Issues 701, 703 (2004).

50. Id. at 1508-09.

51. 42 U.S.C. §§12101-12213 (2012).

52. 42 U.S.C. §12102(1)(A) (2012).

53. See, e.g., Gorman v. Wells Mfg. Corp., 209 F. Supp. 2d 970, 976 (S.D. Iowa 2002) (noting that "the majority of federal courts hold that pregnancy-related complications do not constitute a disability under the ADA"); Gudenkauf v. Stauffer Communications, Inc., 922 F. Supp. 465, 474 (D. Kan. 1996) (rejecting plaintiff's ADA claim because her "pregnancy was not unusual or abnormal" and the "conditions she experienced with the pregnancy were not outside the normal range").

by federal court rulings over two decades. Among other changes, the ADAAA expands the definition of disabled to include conditions that interfere with mundane, work-related tasks like standing, lifting, or bending.[54] It also directs courts to construe the statute broadly in favor of the disabled. In response, the EEOC issued an interpretive guidance stating that temporary disabilities can be covered if "substantially limiting," which is "not meant to be a demanding standard," and should be understood to encompass an employee with a "20-pound lifting restriction that lasts or is expected to last for several months." Yet, the EEOC guidance expressly excludes pregnancy from coverage under the ADAAA based on the theory that because "pregnancy is not the result of a physiological disorder," it is "not an impairment."[55] Given that the amended statute is designed to cover potentially short-term disabilities, including those whose only manifestation is a lifting restriction, can the continuing exclusion of pregnancy be justified? Is there any benefit to women to refusing to treat pregnancy as a disability? On the one hand, the purpose of the ADA is to eliminate stereotyped thinking about disability. On the other hand, this exclusion avoids associating pregnancy with the dependence implied in the notion of disability, upon which traditional legal restrictions against women were often based. Given the stereotypes associated with pregnancy, why exclude it from the Act, which requires reasonable accommodation?

5. Accommodation Under the Second Clause of the PDA. Unlike the ADA, the PDA provides only a comparative right of accommodation—employers need only accommodate the pregnant workers' needs if they accommodate the needs of those similar in their ability or inability to work, but unaffected by pregnancy. As interpreted in *Young*, this does not necessarily mean a pregnant woman is entitled to accommodations provided to *any* other person—the accommodation must be available to enough people to raise an inference of discrimination against the pregnant worker who is denied the accommodation. But the accommodation must be provided to at least one person in order for the comparative right of accommodation to be activated. In one incident, Wal-Mart fired a pregnant woman who worked the fitting room for carrying a water bottle throughout the day because her doctor had advised that she drink water regularly to prevent recurring bladder infections.[56] Could the plaintiff have sought relief under the PDA? If Wal-Mart allows other employees to eat or drink on the job (say a diabetic in need of frequent snacks), then it would have to make a similar accommodation for a pregnant employee with a comparable medical need. But if the company

---

54. 42 U.S.C. §12102(2)(A) (2012).

55. See EEOC Compliance Manual §902.2(c)(3) (2016); see also 29 C.F.R. §1630.2(j)(1)(ii) (2016). For detailed discussion of the law before and after the ADAAA, see Jeannette Cox, Pregnancy as 'Disability' and the Amended Americans with Disabilities Act, 53 B.C. L. Rev. 443, 460-66 (2012).

56. Wiseman v. Wal-Mart Stores, Inc., No. 08-1244-EFM, 2009 U.S. Dist. LEXIS 62079 (D. Kan. July 21, 2009).

makes no exceptions to its policy, can it deny her this medically indicated and costless accommodation?

In a post-*Young* case, Sanchez-Estrada v. Mapfre Praico Insurance Co., the trial court found no violation of the second clause when an employer refused to provide a pregnant employee with a maternity fit uniform.[57] The employer allowed her to work in regular clothing instead because its uniform budget for the year had been exhausted, and the company had suffered significant financial losses. Although, under *Young*, cost cannot be used to justify the failure to extend otherwise available accommodations to pregnant workers, the plaintiff could not point to any other employee whose need for a new uniform was accommodated differently.

What if the employer *does* provide accommodations to some temporarily disabled workers, but not to pregnant women? In *Young*, the employer provided light-duty assignments to three broad classes of workers temporarily unable to perform certain requirements of their jobs. Pregnant women were not the only ones excluded by the formal policy, but they were part of a small group. Although several federal appellate courts had ruled that similar policies did not violate the PDA,[58] the Supreme Court held that this one might. It remanded the case for a determination whether UPS had a legitimate nondiscriminatory reason for its differential treatment of some temporarily disabled workers—a reason that cannot "consist simply of a claim that it is more expensive or less convenient to add pregnant women to the category of those . . . whom the employer accommodates"—and the weighing by a factfinder whether the employer's reason is sufficient to outweigh the burden on pregnant workers. If the benefit does not outweigh the burden, the factfinder is entitled to draw an inference of intentional discrimination and invalidate the policy under the PDA. How might employers justify such policies without reference to cost savings? What benefits to the employer are likely to be deemed sufficiently important in this context to avoid a finding of discrimination? What burdens are too great to justify the benefits? How might you expect employers to draft light-duty policies in the wake of this ruling?[59] Early cases in the wake of *Young* suggest that courts are doing as the Supreme Court instructed—taking a more careful look at the facts surrounding the denial of accommodation. A federal court in Louisiana, in the wake of *Young*, held that summary judgment for an employer in an accommodation

57. 126 F. Supp. 3d 220 (D. Puerto Rico 2015).

58. See, e.g., Urbano v. Cont'l Airlines, 138 F.3d 204 (5th Cir. 1998); Spivey v. Beverly Enterprises, Inc., 196 F.3d 1309 (11th Cir. 1999); Reeves v. Swift Transportation Co., Inc., 446 F.3d 637 (6th Cir. 2006).

59. On the potential implications of this ruling, see Joanna L. Grossman & Deborah L. Brake, Forceps Delivery: The Supreme Court Narrowly Saves the Pregnancy Discrimination Act in *Young v. UPS*, Justia's Verdict (Mar. 31, 2015), https://verdict.justia.com/2015/03/31/forceps-delivery-the-supreme-court-narrowly-saves-the-pregnancy-discrimination-act-in-young-v-ups.

case was inappropriate because there were disputed facts about whether the employer's explanation for the denial of accommodation was pretextual and whether it had offered accommodations to comparably restricted workers.[60] The Supreme Court of Iowa, interpreting a state law co-extensive with the PDA, held that the treatment of pregnant workers could not be compared only to those also injured off the job, but had to be compared to all workers with temporary disabilities.[61]

Even after *Young*, is the PDA deficient insofar as it prevents explicit discrimination against pregnant women but stops short of requiring accommodations necessary to meet their needs? A bill entitled The Pregnant Women's Fairness Act was introduced in Congress in 2012, and again in 2013 and 2015.[62] It proposes a right of reasonable accommodation for pregnancy-related disability, modeled after the Americans with Disabilities Act.[63] Is this a better approach? What objections might you expect from employers? Are there any downsides to women of having a right of reasonable accommodation?

6. Disparate Impact Theory. Another theory potentially available under existing law is that the failure to accommodate pregnancy has a disparate impact against women.[64] In *Cal Fed*, the Court specifically declined to address the issue, and few plaintiffs have succeeded under this theory.[65] Consider the following analysis of disparate impact claims under the PDA:

> In theory, disparate impact law should compensate for some of the shortcomings of the PDA's comparative right of accommodation by invalidating some of the harsh employment policies that make it difficult for women to work through pregnancy. . . . The reality is that plaintiffs almost never prevail on such claims in the pregnancy context.
>
> There are a number of reasons why disparate impact theory has not turned out to be more useful for pregnant workers. Although most courts acknowledge the theoretical existence of disparate impact theory under the PDA, some refuse to apply it in its true form. These courts treat the second clause of the PDA . . . as a ceiling on what accommodations employers can be forced to provide.

---

60. Martin v. Winn-Dixie Louisiana, Inc., 132 F. Supp. 3d 794 (M.D. La. 2015).

61. McQuistion v. City of Clinton, 872 N.W.2d 817, 830 (Iowa 2015).

62. H.R. 5647 (introduced May 8, 2012); H.R. 1975 (introduced May 14, 2013); H.R. 2654 (introduced June 4, 2015). On the development of pregnancy discrimination law and the need for greater protection, see Joanna L. Grossman, Nine to Five: How Gender, Sex, and Sexuality Continue to Define the American Workplace (2016).

63. On the bill, see Joanna L. Grossman, The Pregnant Workers' Fairness Act: Accommodating the Needs of Pregnant Working Women, Justia's Verdict (May 11, 2012), https://verdict.justia.com/2012/05/11/the-pregnant-workers-fairness-act.

64. See Christine Jolls, Antidiscrimination and Accommodation, 115 Harv. L. Rev. 643 (2001).

65. Several of the relevant cases are collected in Joan C. Williams & Nancy Segal, Beyond the Maternal Wall: Relief for Family Caregivers Who Are Discriminated Against on the Job, 26 Harv. Women's L.J. 77, 134-36 (2003).

Judge Posner, for example, in *Troupe*, described disparate impact as a "permissible theory" under the PDA but cautioned that "properly understood," it was not a "warrant for favoritism" and could not be used to prevent employers from treating pregnant workers "as badly as they treat similarly affected but nonpregnant employees." Other courts have taken a similar tack—claiming to recognize disparate impact law but refusing to allow it to provide anything more than a comparative right to accommodation or leave. The Fifth Circuit . . . refused to apply disparate impact to claims "in which the plaintiff's only challenge is that the amount of sick leave granted to employees is insufficient to accommodate the time off required in a typical pregnancy. To hold otherwise would be to transform the PDA into a guarantee of medical leave for pregnant employees, something we have specifically held that the PDA does not do." . . .

Even when courts are not openly dismissive of disparate impact claims, plaintiffs have not met with much success. One potential obstacle is the inability to identify, as required under the statute, a particular "employment practice" that produces the disparate impact. Courts have held, for example, that any discretionary decision—such as the decision to deny a particular woman's request for pregnancy-related leave—cannot be challenged as a practice. . . .

A second obstacle arises when courts prejudge the merits of the claim by refusing to apply disparate impact analysis to "legitimate" job requirements like attendance. . . .

A final, but important, obstacle is that courts tend to require statistical proof of a disparate impact. Courts have been largely unwilling to accept nonstatistical showings of impact, or to rely on broader societal data to support a claim of disparate impact. And plaintiffs have been mostly unsuccessful in making the requisite statistical showing. . . .[66]

Should courts be more accepting of disparate impact claims in the pregnancy context?[67] Is it consistent with the aims of the PDA? With its structure?

7. Before the PDA: AT&T v. Hulteen (2009). This case involves a group of female employees who took pregnancy-related disability leaves between 1968 and 1974, before the PDA became law. Under company policy at the time, an employee who took disability leave was entitled to full service credit during the leave, while those who took pregnancy leaves could receive no more than 30 days credit. AT&T amended this policy in 1979 to comply with the PDA, but many of the women currently reaching retirement age are penalized by the pre-1979 policy because they have amassed fewer service credits. As a result, they now collect lower pensions than retirees who took other kinds of disability leave during that period. The Supreme Court

---

66. Joanna L. Grossman, Pregnancy, Work, and the Promise of Full Citizenship, 98 Georgetown L.J. 567, 615-17 (2010).

67. For analysis of disparate impact analysis and pregnancy accommodation claims, see L. Camille Hebert, Disparate Impact and Pregnancy: Title VII's Other Accommodation Requirement, 24 Am. U. J. Gender Soc. Pol'y & L. 107 (2015).

ruled 7-2 for AT&T, reasoning that the company's pension system was based on a bona fide seniority system (one defense to pay discrimination claims under either Title VII or the Equal Pay Act) that was itself not the product of intent to discriminate.[68] AT&T did intend to discriminate on the basis of pregnancy prior to 1979, but the Court ruled that its retirement system was not tainted by that prior intent. Justice Ginsburg, in dissent, noted that "[c]ertain attitudes about pregnancy and childbirth, throughout human history, have sustained pervasive, often law-sanctioned, restrictions on a woman's place among paid workers and active citizens." And while the PDA "does not require redress for past discrimination," it does "protect women, from and after April 1979 . . . against repetition or continuation of pregnancy-based disadvantageous treatment."[69] What accounts for the two different readings of the statute's scope? With which one do you agree?

8. European Community Law. European Community law has developed in a direction far more favorable to the claims of pregnant women than American law. One representative case found a violation of the nondiscrimination provisions of a Council Directive of the European Community Union when an employer discharged a pregnant woman who had been hired without knowledge of her pregnancy, even though the only reason she got the job was to replace another employee on maternity leave. The European cases go well beyond *Troupe* and the PDA by protecting pregnancy regardless of whether other disabilities are protected. As one commentator explains, the European "no comparison necessary" approach places a "badge of protection" on pregnant women, which shields them from adverse employment-related consequences whether or not other disabling conditions would receive similar treatment.

Which is the better approach? Would the European approach violate the PDA? As Chapter 4, Section B indicates, European Union law also provides greater accommodation than the American law for caretaking responsibilities.

9. Johnson Controls as a Reprieve of the Protective Legislation Debate. In Muller v. Oregon, excerpted in Chapter 1, the famous Brandeis brief cited the protective legislation of 19 states and 7 foreign countries, and then brought to the Court's attention

> . . . over ninety reports of committees, bureaus of statistics, commissioners of hygiene, inspectors of factories, both in this country and in Europe, to the effect that long hours of labor are dangerous for women, primarily because of their special physical organization. . . . Perhaps the general scope and character of all these reports may be summed up in what an inspector for Hanover says: "The

68. 556 U.S. 701 (2009).
69. Id. at 719 (Stevens, J., concurring).

reasons for the reduction of the working day to ten hours—(a) the physical organization of women, (b) her maternal functions, (c) the rearing and education of the children, (d) the maintenance of the home—are all so important and so far reaching that the need for such reduction need hardly be discussed."[70]

In *Muller*, the issue was whether the danger to women of a long work day was sufficient to overcome the Fourteenth Amendment freedom of contract rights of the employer. In *Johnson Controls*, the question was whether the danger to women and their fetuses justified their exclusion from certain job categories under Title VII (as a "bona fide occupational qualification" under Title VII). Freedom of contract no longer has the recognition it once had and women's equality is now a protected value, both constitutionally and statutorily. Nonetheless, Justice Blackmun, and many legal commentators, have drawn parallels between fetal protection policies and protective legislation of the nineteenth century, which was also backed by "scientific" data.

For contemporary law outside the employment context that reflects the "protective" approach toward pregnant women, see Chapter 5, Section B(4). What are the costs and benefits of contemporary protective legislation? What, if anything, should be inferred from the fact that these policies are more common in certain industries—typically those with higher pay and benefits that have been traditionally dominated by men?[71]

10. Women Workers and "Choice." The issue of women's choice with respect to fetal protection policies can be posed in different ways. Fetal protection policies do give women one kind of choice—between sterilization and losing their jobs. One woman at Johnson Controls, Betty Riggs, submitted to sterilization although she wanted more children because her marriage was breaking up and she needed the money. Not long after Betty Riggs and four other women were sterilized, the company shut down its pigments department and their jobs were eliminated.[72] The Court in *Johnson Controls*, in invalidating fetal protection policies, concludes that women workers should make their own decisions about whether to assume the risks of the workplace for themselves and their potential offspring. In fact, this has been the general response to the Court's decision in *Johnson Control*.

Is this the best approach for women? Or should Johnson Controls have been required to make the workplace safer for pregnant women? The law in the United Kingdom requires employers to assess risks to expectant mothers and their fetuses and then to control the risk if possible. If the risk cannot be controlled, then suitable alternative work or paid leave must be given until the

70. 208 U.S. 412, 419 n.1 (1908).
71. Mary E. Becker, From *Muller v. Oregon* to Fetal Vulnerability Policies, 53 U. Chi. L. Rev. 1219, 1238-39 (1986).
72. David Kirp, Fetal Hazards, Gender Justice and the Justices: The Limits of Equality, 34 Wm. & Mary L. Rev. 101, 104-06 (1992).

woman is no longer pregnant.[73] Could this approach be justified under formal equality, or does the possibility of paid leave treat women better than men?

11. Equality Analysis in Johnson Controls. The *Johnson Controls* case reveals a number of different ways to identify the groups to compare for purposes of equality analysis. The Seventh Circuit Court of Appeals, in effect, compared employees who could bear children against employees who could not. On that basis, the appellate court concluded that the policy was facially sex-neutral and justifiable as a way to protect women's unconceived offspring. This approach is similar to the one used by the U.S. Supreme Court when it concluded in Geduldig v. Aiello that discrimination on the basis of pregnancy (even though only women were thereby affected) was not discrimination between women and men but rather discrimination between pregnant and non-pregnant persons.[74]

For his part, Justice Blackmun in *Johnson Controls* compared fertile women to fertile men, concluding that the fetal protection policy violates Title VII because it treats these two groups differently. Justice Blackmun referred in his opinion to evidence that lead exposure may damage sperm as well as ova to strengthen his analysis that men and women are similarly situated and thus the relevant groups for comparison. Justice Scalia did not specify the groups to be compared. In his view, whether or not the Court thought the policy in question was a form of sex discrimination, Congress unequivocally had determined with the Pregnancy Discrimination Act that it was. For the same reason, Justice Scalia's analysis is not affected by whether or not there are any comparable fetal risks to be passed through male employees.

If the *Johnson Controls* case satisfies formal equality requirements, does it also satisfy substantive equality—i.e., does it ensure that women and men enjoy the same opportunities? Arguably so, except that women may face damage to their reproductive capacities that men do not face.

Is it unfair to employers to prevent them from excluding women but holding them potentially liable for miscarriages or birth defects attributable to lead exposure? Or is this simply a cost to the employer of being engaged in a risky business, which is best dealt with by ordinary business means, such as insurance, or passing the risks of business along to the consumer?

Putting Theory Into Practice

2-6. Barbara works the 8-to-5 shift as a department store cashier. She is entitled to an hour break for lunch and two ten-minute breaks during the day.

---

73. See Michael Thomson, Reproductivity, the Workplace and the Gendering of the Body (Politic), 14 Cardozo Stud. L. & Lit. 565, 571 (2004).
74. 417 U.S. 484 (1974).

Ordinarily, the supervisor manages lunch hours and breaks for all employees by staggering the lunch hours on a rotating basis and trying to fit in the shorter breaks around lulls in store business. An employee may have her lunch hour at 11 a.m. one day, and 3 p.m. the next.

Barbara is returning to work after a maternity leave. She wants to have her breaks timed so that she can use her lunch break to breastfeed her baby (at an adjacent day-care center) and her short breaks to pump her breast milk. For this to work well, she needs a regular daily lunch hour and evenly spaced breaks. Should she be entitled to these accommodations? What if another mother returning to work wants a similar arrangement? Alternatively, what if such accommodations would prevent the supervisor from attending a management-training seminar given over the lunch break? How should fairness to other workers be juggled?

2-7. A local police department has a limited number of temporary desk-duty positions for its officers. Those officers injured on the job or in the course of military service are given priority; officers temporarily disabled for any other reason can hold a light-duty position only if no higher-priority officer needs it. When Cynthia applied for a light-duty position during the last trimester of her pregnancy, when her doctor had told her to avoid long prolonged standing or physical exertion, she was told that none was available. Two of the three positions were held by men injured during a weekend training session with the military reserves, and the third was held by a man who broke his ankle at work (he didn't realize his foot had fallen asleep while doing paperwork at his desk and fell over when he tried to stand up). Without a temporary desk assignment, Cynthia was forced to go on unpaid leave until after she delivered her baby. Has she suffered actionable pregnancy discrimination under *Young*?

2-8. An inner-city community center runs after-school programs for teenage girls, many of whom lack positive adult role models. The center has a policy against hiring unmarried pregnant woman, on the theory that these individuals present negative role models. Does the policy wrongfully discriminate on the basis of sex?[75]

2. Caregiver Discrimination

Discrimination against women because of their unique role in the reproductive process does not end with childbirth. Discrimination against mothers, especially those with young children, is well documented and can take a wide variety of forms. One problem for all new parents is the lack of adequate

75. See Chambers v. Omaha Girls Club, Inc., 834 F.2d 697 (8th Cir. 1987).

caretaking leave. In 1993, Congress passed the federal Family and Medical Leave Act (FMLA). The FMLA requires that employers of more than 50 workers allow up to a three-month, unpaid leave for the care of a new infant or ill family member, with the right to return to the same or an equivalent position without loss of pre-leave benefits. The Act covers employees who have worked for the employer for at least 12 months and for 1250 hours during the year preceding the start of the leave. (In February 2015, new regulations were enacted to extend the FMLA to same-sex married couples.)[76] Only half of the work force is covered by the Act and the U.S. Department of Labor found that 88 percent of eligible employees who need time off do not take it, largely because they cannot afford to go without a paycheck. Even many who can afford to take leave sometimes do not do so because of resistance by supervisors and colleagues. One study of highly educated individuals found that about one-third of women and almost half of men reported that their workplace culture penalized employees for taking advantage of family-friendly policies.[77] Other research has indicated that many employees did not assert their rights because of well-founded concerns of informal retaliation and blacklisting; they feared being branded as a "troublemaker" or "slacker" and not getting favorable assignments, shifts, or recommendations if they changed jobs.[78] Fewer men take family leave than women, and fewer employers offer paid leave to men. What accounts for this difference? Is it a problem that employers or public policy should address?[79]

Should the government require *paid* family leave? If so, who should subsidize it? In 2002, California became the first state to amend a state disability program to include up to six weeks of compensation for leave to care for an ill family member, or the birth, adoption, or foster care placement of a new child. New Jersey, Rhode Island, Washington and the District of Columbia followed suit, and a handful of other states have expanded their unemployment insurance programs to provide wage replacement for parental leave.[80] Should such legislation be a top priority? Paid leave did receive some attention

76. Press Release, U.S. Dep't of Labor, Federal Job-Protected Family & Medical Leave Rights Extended to Eligible Workers in Same-Sex Marriage (Feb. 23, 2015).

77. Sylvia Ann Hewlett & Carolyn Buck Luce, Off-Ramps and On-Ramps: Keeping Talented Women on the Road to Success, Harv. Bus. Rev. 43 (Mar. 2005).

78. Catherine R. Albiston, Bargaining in the Shadow of Social Institutions: Competing Discourses and Social Change in the Workplace Mobilization of Civil Rights, 39 Law & Soc'y Rev. 11, 23-27, 31-38 (2005); see also Catherine Albiston & Lindsey Trimble O'Connor, Just Leave, 39 Harv. J.L. & Gender 1 (2016) (reporting results of an original survey on the barriers to using family leave).

79. See Joanna L. Grossman, Job Security Without Equality: The Family and Medical Leave Act of 1993, 15 Wash. U. J.L. & Pol'y 17 (2004) (noting negligible impact of FMLA on caretaking leaves by men).

80. Sarah Fass, Paid Leave in the States: A Critical Support for Low-Wage Workers and Their Families (2009); see also Gillian Lester, A Defense of State Paid Family Leave, 28 Harv. J.L. & Gender 1, 3 (2005).

during the 2016 presidential campaign, but, so far, has not gained any traction in Congress.[81] The United States is now the only high-income country without paid family leave.[82]

An important legal precedent is the U.S. Supreme Court's decision in Nevada Dep't of Human Res. v. Hibbs, upholding the constitutionality of the FMLA as applied to state employees.[83] The primary legal issue in the case concerned sovereign immunity. The Eleventh Amendment to the U.S. Constitution prohibits money damages against a state except to the extent Congress has validly limited that immunity through specific legislation. *Hibbs* raised the question whether the FMLA constituted such a limitation, and whether it was valid under Section Five of the Fourteenth Amendment as a congruent and proportional response to a state-sponsored history of discrimination. The plaintiff was a man and the expansive language of then-Chief Justice Rehnquist is noteworthy in its recognition of the power of gender stereotyping with respect to family care issues and the intent of the gender-neutral provisions of the FMLA to address the resulting disadvantages.

> The FMLA aims to protect the right to be free from gender-based discrimination in the workplace. . . . The history of the many state laws limit[ing] women's employment opportunities is chronicled in—and, until relatively recently, was sanctioned by—this Court's own opinions. . . . Congress responded to this history of discrimination by abrogating States' sovereign immunity in Title VII of the Civil Rights Act of 1964. . . . According to the evidence that was before Congress when it enacted the FMLA, states continue to rely on invalid gender stereotypes in the employment context, specifically in the administration of leave benefits. . . . Congress . . . heard testimony that . . . "Even . . . [w]here child-care leave policies do exist, men, *both in the public and private sectors*, receive notoriously discriminatory treatment in their requests for such leave." . . . Many States offered women extended 'maternity' leave that far exceeded the typical 4- to 8-week period of physical disability due to pregnancy and childbirth, but very few States granted men a parallel benefit: Fifteen States provided women up to one year of extended maternity leave, while only four provided men with the same. . . . This and other differential leave policies were not attributable to any differential physical needs of men and women, but rather to the pervasive sex-role stereotype that caring for family members is women's work.[84]

Note that the Act was inspired by a problem that disproportionately affects women, but by insisting that men receive the same parental leave

---

81. See, e.g., Anna Louie Sussman & Laura Meckler, Clinton Offers New Details About Paid Family Leave Plans, Wall St. J., Jan. 7, 2016.

82. See Katy Hall & Chris Spurlock, Paid Parental Leave: U.S. v. The World, Huff. Post (Feb. 4, 2013); Paul Cleary, Norway Is Proof That You Can Have it All, The Australian (July 15, 2013).

83. 538 U.S. 721 (2003).

84. Id. at 728-31.

benefits as similarly situated women, the FMLA reflects formal equality principles. If women disproportionately use parenting leave, is this benefit a "subsidy" for women?

In an interesting twist, nine years after *Hibbs*, the Supreme Court distinguished the FMLA's family leave provisions from the FMLA's provision entitling a covered employee to leave when that employee's own "serious health condition . . . interferes with the employee's ability to perform at work." According to the Court in Coleman v. Maryland Court of Appeals,[85] the FMLA's "self-care" provision was not a response to any identified pattern of gender-based discrimination, and thus does not constitute a valid Congressional abrogation state sovereign immunity. Thus, while individuals under *Hibbs* can obtain money damages against a state for violations of the FMLA family-care provisions, sovereign immunity protects states against such suits under the FMLA's self-care provision. Is the Court's distinction between the FMLA's family-care and self-care persuasive? In a dissenting opinion, Justice Ginsburg emphasized the importance of job security for pregnant women with maternity-related disabilities before and after childbirth to the achievement of gender equality—an importance underlined in the legislative history of the Act. To Justice Ginsburg, an essential aspect of the FMLA is the way the family-care and the self-care provisions work together to protect women from discrimination on account of their pregnancies. "It would make scant sense to provide job-protected leave for a woman to care for a newborn, but not for her recovery from delivery, a miscarriage, or the birth of a stillborn baby."[86]

Does it matter that the plaintiff in *Coleman* was a man? According to Justice Ginsburg, the availability of FMLA rights to men was intended, among other things, to blunt the force of stereotypes of women as primary caregivers—in other words, to recognize the historic pattern of discrimination against pregnant women and female caregivers in a gender-neutral way. Does this intention supply the necessary connection between the self-care provision and an identified pattern of gender discrimination?

At its best, the FMLA only protects parents who need (and can afford) unpaid leave in the first months of caregiving. But both mothers and fathers often continue to face conflicts between work and the obligations of parenting for many more years. In the cases that follow, consider whether the mother in *Back* and the father in *Ayanna* faced the same type of discrimination. How well does the law protect them from caregiving discrimination? (The problem of work/family balance is revisited in Chapter 4 through the perspective of difference.)

85. 132 S. Ct. 1327 (2012).
86. Id. at 1345 (Ginsburg, J., dissenting).

Back v. Hastings on Hudson Union Free School District
365 F.3d 107 (2d Cir. 2004)

CALABRESI, Circuit Judge.

In 1998, Plaintiff-Appellant Elana Back was hired as a school psychologist at the Hillside Elementary School on a three-year tenure track. At the end of that period, when Back came up for review, she was denied tenure and her probationary period was terminated. She alleged that the termination violated her constitutional right to equal protection of the laws. Defendants-Appellees contend that Back was fired because she lacked organizational and interpersonal skills. Back asserts that the real reason she was let go was that the defendants presumed that she, as a young mother, would not continue to demonstrate the necessary devotion to her job, and indeed that she could not maintain such devotion while at the same time being a good mother.

This appeal thus poses an important question, one that strikes at the persistent "fault line between work and family—precisely where sex-based overgeneralization has been and remains strongest." Nev. Dep't of Human Res. v. Hibbs, 538 U.S. 721 (2003). It asks whether stereotyping about the qualities of mothers is a form of gender discrimination, and whether this can be determined in the absence of evidence about how the employer in question treated fathers. We answer both questions in the affirmative. . . .

A. Background

i. *Back's Qualifications*

As the school psychologist at Hillside Elementary School, Elana Back counseled and conducted psychological evaluations of students, prepared reports for the Committee on Special Education, assisted teachers in dealing with students who acted out in class, worked with parents on issues related to their children, and chaired the "Learning Team," a group made up of specialists and teachers which conducted intensive discussions about individual students. Defendant-Appellee Marilyn Wishnie, the Principal of Hillside, and defendant-appellee Ann Brennan, the Director of Pupil Personnel Services for the District, were Back's supervisors. They were responsible for establishing performance goals for her position, and evaluating Back's work against these standards.

In the plaintiff's first two years at Hillside, Brennan and Wishnie consistently gave her excellent evaluations. . . . In her first annual evaluation, on a scale where the highest score was "outstanding," and the second highest score was "superior," Back was deemed "outstanding" and "superior" in almost all categories, and "average" in only one.

In her second year at Hillside, Back took approximately three months of maternity leave. After she returned, she garnered another "outstanding" evaluation from Brennan, who noted that she was "very pleased with Mrs. Back's performance during her second year at Hillside." Other contemporaneous observations also resulted in strongly positive feedback, for example, that Back "demonstrate[d] her strong social/emotional skills in her work with parents and teachers, and most especially with students," and that she was "a positive influence in many areas, and continues to extend a great deal of effort and commitment to our work." In her annual evaluation, Back received higher marks than the previous year, with more "outstandings" and no "averages." The narrative comments noted that she "continues to serve in an outstanding manner and provides excellent support for our students," and that her "commitment to her work and to her own learning is outstanding." At the beginning of Back's third year at Hillside, she again received "outstanding" and "superior" evaluations from both Brennan and Wishnie.

Defendant-Appellant John Russell, the Superintendent of the School District, also conducted ongoing evaluations of Back's performance. In January 1999, he . . . rated her performance "superior." In February 2000, he again sat in on a Learning Team meeting, and again indicated that Back's performance was "superior." He also noted that she was effective without being overly directive, and worked well with the other members of the team. In addition, according to Back, all three individual defendants repeatedly assured her throughout this time that she would receive tenure.

ii. Alleged Stereotyping

Back asserts that things changed dramatically as her tenure review approached. The first allegedly discriminatory comments came in spring 2000, when Back's written evaluations still indicated that she was a very strong candidate for tenure. At that time, shortly after Back had returned from maternity leave, the plaintiff claims that Brennan, (a) inquired about how she was "planning on spacing [her] offspring," (b) said " '[p]lease do not get pregnant until I retire,' " and (c) suggested that Back "wait until [her son] was in kindergarten to have another child."

Then, a few months into Back's third year at Hillside, on December 14, 2000, Brennan allegedly told Back that she was expected to work until 4:30 p.m. every day, and asked " 'What's the big deal. You have a nanny. This is what you [have] to do to get tenure." 'Back replied that she did work these hours. And Brennan, after reportedly reassuring Back that there was no concern about her job performance, told her that Wishnie expected her to work such hours. But, always according to Back, Brennan also indicated that Back should "maybe . . . reconsider whether [Back] could be a mother and do this job which [Brennan] characterized as administrative in nature," and that Brennan and Wishnie were "concerned that, if [Back] received tenure, [she] would work only until 3:15 p.m. and did not know how [she] could possibly do this job with children."

A few days later, on January 8, 2001, Brennan allegedly told Back for the first time that she might not support Back's tenure because of what Back characterizes as minor errors that she made in a report. According to Back, shortly thereafter Principal Wishnie accused her of working only from 8:15 a.m. to 3:15 p.m. and never working during lunch. When Back disputed this, Wishnie supposedly replied that "this was not [Wishnie's] impression and . . . that she did not know how she could perform my job with little ones. She told me that she worked from 7 a.m. to 7 p.m. and that she expected the same from me. If my family was my priority, she stated, maybe this was not the job for me." A week later, both Brennan and Wishnie reportedly told Back that this was perhaps not the job or the school district for her if she had "little ones," and that it was "not possible for [her] to be a good mother and have this job." The two also allegedly remarked that it would be harder to fire Back if she had tenure, and wondered "whether my apparent commitment to my job was an act. They stated that once I obtained tenure, I would not show the same level of commitment I had shown because I had little ones at home. They expressed concerns about my child care arrangements, though these had never caused me conflict with school assignments." They did not—as Back told the story—discuss with her any concerns with her performance at that time. . . .

On April 30, 2001, Brennan and Wishnie purportedly repeated the same concerns about her ability to balance work and family, and told Back that they would recommend that she not be granted tenure and that Superintendent Russell would follow their recommendation. They reportedly also "stated they wanted another year to assess the child care situation."

iii. Denial of Tenure

Back retained counsel in response to Brennan and Wishnie's alleged statements, and in a letter dated May 14, 2001, informed [Superintendent] Russell of these comments, and of her fear that they reflected attitudes that would improperly affect her tenure review. On May 29, 2001, Brennan and Wishnie sent a formal memo to Russell informing him that they could not recommend Back for tenure. . . .

On or around June 13, 2001, Wishnie and Brennan filed the first negative evaluation of Back, which gave her several "below average" marks and charged her with being inconsistent, defensive, difficult to supervise, the source of parental complaints, and inaccurate in her reports. Their evaluation, which was submitted to Russell, concluded that Back should not be granted tenure. Around the same time, several parents who had apparently complained about Back were encouraged by Russell to put their concerns in writing. Several parents submitted letters, reporting a range of complaints about Back's work, including that she was defensive, immature, unprofessional, and had misdiagnosed children.

In September 2001, the Board notified Back that her probationary appointment would be terminated. . . .

Plaintiff presses three arguments on appeal. First, she contends that an adverse employment consequence imposed because of stereotypes about motherhood is a form of gender discrimination which contravenes the Equal Protection Clause. . . .

A. Theory of Discrimination

Individuals have a clear right, protected by the Fourteenth Amendment, to be free from discrimination on the basis of sex in public employment. . . .

To make out such a claim, the plaintiff must prove that she suffered purposeful or intentional discrimination on the basis of gender. Discrimination based on gender, once proven, can only be tolerated if the state provides an "exceedingly persuasive justification" for the rule or practice. The defendants in this case have made no claim of justification; thus our inquiry revolves solely around the allegation of discrimination. . . .

To show sex discrimination, Back relies upon a *Price Waterhouse* "stereotyping" theory. Accordingly, she argues that comments made about a woman's inability to combine work and motherhood are direct evidence of such discrimination. . . .

It is the law, then, that "stereotyped remarks can certainly be evidence that gender played a part" in an adverse employment decision. The principle of *Price Waterhouse*, furthermore, applies as much to the supposition that a woman *will* conform to a gender stereotype (and therefore will not, for example, be dedicated to her job), as to the supposition that a woman is unqualified for a position because she does *not* conform to a gender stereotype.

The instant case, however, foregrounds a crucial question: What constitutes a "gender-based stereotype"? *Price Waterhouse* suggested that this question must be answered in the particular context in which it arises, and without undue formalization. We have adopted the same approach, as have other circuits. Just as "[i]t takes no special training to discern sex stereotyping in a description of an aggressive female employee as requiring 'a course at charm school,'" *Price Waterhouse*, 490 U.S. at 256, so it takes no special training to discern stereotyping in the view that a woman cannot "be a good mother" and have a job that requires long hours, or in the statement that a mother who received tenure "would not show the same level of commitment [she] had shown because [she] had little ones at home." These are not the kind of "innocuous words" that we have previously held to be insufficient, as a matter of law, to provide evidence of discriminatory intent.

Not surprisingly, other circuit courts have agreed that similar comments constitute evidence that a jury could use to find the presence of discrimination . . . .

The defendants argue that stereotypes about pregnant women or mothers are not based upon gender, but rather, "gender plus parenthood," thereby implying that such stereotypes cannot, without comparative evidence of what was said about fathers, be presumed to be "on the basis of sex." *Hibbs* makes pellucidly clear, however, that, at least where stereotypes are considered, the notions that mothers are insufficiently devoted to work, and that work and motherhood are incompatible, are properly considered to be, themselves, gender-based. *Hibbs* explicitly called the stereotype that "women's family duties trump those of the workplace" a "*gender* stereotype," and cited a number of state pregnancy and family leave acts—including laws that provided *only* pregnancy leave—as evidence of "pervasive sex-role stereotype that caring for family members is women's work."

Defendants are thus wrong in their contention that Back cannot make out a claim that survives summary judgment unless she demonstrates that the defendants treated similarly situated men differently. Back has admittedly proffered no evidence about the treatment of male administrators with young children. Although her case would be stronger had she provided or alleged the existence of such evidence, there is no requirement that such evidence be adduced. Indeed we have held that,

> In determining whether an employee has been discriminated against "because of *such individual's* . . . sex," the courts have consistently emphasized that the ultimate issue is the reasons for *the individual plaintiff's* treatment, not the relative treatment of different *groups* within the workplace. As a result, discrimination against one employee cannot be cured, or disproven, solely by favorable, or equitable, treatment of other employees of the same race or sex.

Brown v. Henderson, 257 F.3d 246, 252 (2d Cir. 2001) (citations omitted). . . .

Because we hold that stereotypical remarks about the incompatibility of motherhood and employment "can certainly be *evidence* that gender played a part" in an employment decision, we find that *Brown* applies to this case. As a result, stereotyping of women as caregivers can by itself and without more be evidence of an impermissible, sex-based motive.

* * *

We hold that Back has clearly produced sufficient evidence to defeat summary judgment as to Brennan and Wishnie. . . . We conclude that a jury could find, on the evidence proffered, that Brennan and Wishnie's cited justifications for their adverse recommendation and evaluation were pretextual, and that discrimination was one of the "motivating" reasons for the recommendations against Back's tenure.

═══ *Ayanna v. Dechert, LLP*
914 F. Supp. 2d 51 (D. Mass. 2012)

GORTON, District Judge.

Plaintiff Ariel Ayanna sues defendant law firm Dechert, LLP for retaliation under the Family Medical Leave Act and sex discrimination in violation of M.G.L. c. 151B, §4(1). Currently before the Court is defendant's motion for summary judgment and plaintiff's opposition thereto.

Ayanna, a male attorney, was an associate at Dechert from September, 2006 until his termination in December, 2008. He is married and has two children. His wife suffers from chronic mental illness. During Ayanna's first year of employment at Dechert he met his assigned objective for billable hours, received positive performance reviews and was awarded a bonus.

During his second year, Ayanna requested to work from the Munich office of Dechert for nine months while his wife completed a Fulbright scholarship in Germany. Dechert did not transfer Ayanna to the Munich office, but, instead, agreed that he could work from Munich while remaining assigned to the Boston office. Ayanna contends that because attorneys in Munich worked fewer hours, he was told by his supervisors in Boston that he did not need to meet the billable hours requirement for United States based attorneys while working from Germany. Despite that reassurance, once in Germany, Ayanna expressed concern to the Boston office about his reduced hours. He requested additional work but was not assigned any. Although Ayanna's billable hours were lower than stateside attorneys, he billed more hours than the other associate in the Munich office.

During their time in Munich, Ayanna's wife became pregnant with their second child and experienced a deterioration of her mental health. After she attempted to commit suicide, Ayanna took emergency FMLA leave to care for his wife. Following the birth of their second child, he took four weeks of paid paternity leave. His wife's condition improved and he was able to return to the Boston office of Dechert in August 2008, despite being scheduled to remain on FMLA leave until September. As a result of his early return, Ayanna remained eligible for an additional four weeks of FMLA leave that year. He continued to care for his wife and children after returning to work.

When he returned to the Boston office Ayanna was assigned to be the "right hand man" to Partner Christopher Christian. Ayanna contends that Christian was immediately hostile to him due to his recent leave and monitored his work and presence in the office more closely than other associates. After Ayanna's wife was briefly hospitalized at the end of September 2008, the assignment of work from Christian to Ayanna dropped off and Christian began assigning work to other associates.

In his annual performance evaluation Ayanna was given an overall "fair" rating. Dechert claims that rating took into account both billable hours and supervisor evaluations but placed a far greater emphasis on the former. Of the ten performance evaluators, one rated Ayanna as "fair", the others gave him ratings of "good" or "very good." Between January 2008 and October 2008 Ayanna billed 850 hours and 41 pro bono hours. He also completed 554 non-billable hours on internal firm projects while in Germany. Ayanna's "annualized" billable hours were adjusted to 1,460 to account for his FMLA and paternity leave. His total billable hours fell far short of the 1,950 target for associates in the Boston office and Ayanna ranked 62nd out of 65 associates in his practice group.

On December 17, 2008 Ayanna was terminated. All of the associates who received a rating of fair (except one who had only recently joined the firm) were also terminated. . . .

1. Retaliation for Exercising Rights Afforded Under the Family Medical Leave Act (Count I)

Ayanna claims that Dechert retaliated against him for taking FMLA leave by withholding work assignments, thus decreasing his billable hours for the year and, ultimately, terminating him on the ground that his billable hours were too low.

Although the text of 29 U.S.C. §2615(a) makes no reference to retaliation, the First Circuit has recognized such a cause of action in the statute and the interpretative regulation. When there is no direct evidence of retaliation for taking FMLA leave, the Court applies the *McDonnell Douglas* three step burden-shifting framework. . . .

To make out a prima facie case of retaliation under the FMLA, an employee must prove that 1) he engaged in the protected conduct of taking FMLA leave, 2) he was fired, and 3) the protected conduct and the termination were causally connected. Only the third prong is in dispute in this case.

Although courts are hesitant to find a causal connection between an employee's FMLA leave and firing if the intervening time was several months, "[t]emporal proximity can create an inference of causation in the proper case." Pomales v. Celulares Telefonica, Inc., 447 F.3d 79, 85 (1st Cir. 2006). As discussed below, when viewed in the light most favorable to Ayanna, there is sufficient evidence to support a finding that his FMLA leave and his termination were related, whether or not there was "temporal proximity."

Dechert avers that Ayanna was fired for the nondiscriminatory reason that his billable hours during 2008 were too low. While the Court finds plaintiff's claims somewhat dubious at this stage, viewing the facts in the light most favorable to Ayanna and drawing all reasonable inferences in his favor, it acknowledges that Ayanna has presented sufficient evidence to raise a genuine issue of material fact as to whether that proffered reason was actually a pretext for retaliation.

First, at the time he was fired, Ayanna was told by Dechert Partner Joseph Fleming that he was terminated due to his "fair" rating and his "personal issues." A reasonable jury could find that the comment was directed at Ayanna's recent need to take FMLA leave.

Furthermore, there remains a factual dispute as to whether Ayanna's billable hours were low because the firm purposefully withheld work from him in retaliation for taking FMLA leave. Viewing the facts in the light most favorable to Ayanna, Christian monitored Ayanna very closely following his return from FMLA leave. When Christian became aware that the condition of Ayanna's wife had worsened to the point that she needed further hospitalization, Christian shared his concern with other Dechert employees regarding Ayanna's ability to handle his workload. At the same time, Ayanna's work for Christian was curtailed. Christian informed Ayanna he no longer considered him "reliable" and was spreading work that previously would have gone to Ayanna to other associates thus decreasing his billable hours.

As proof that Ayanna was not denied work assignments in retaliation for taking FMLA leave, Dechert asserts that he billed more hours in September and October after returning from leave than he did prior to taking FMLA leave. However, Ayanna was working from Germany immediately prior to taking FMLA leave. Because it remains disputed whether the firm approved of his reduced billing while in Germany, his number of billable hours is not dispositive of his claim that he was denied work assignments.

When considering his annual billable hours, Dechert did not take into account Ayanna's time in Germany but, nevertheless, directly compared those billable hours to other Boston based associates when deciding whether to terminate him. The Court acknowledges that not adjusting the hours of associates temporarily working in foreign offices may have been standard practice at Dechert. Without evidence in the record of such a policy, however, and without knowing how many other retained associates failed to reach Dechert's billable hours target that year, a direct comparison of Ayanna's pre- and post-FMLA leave hours is not enough to disprove the inference that he was denied work in retaliation for taking leave. A reasonable jury could find that had Ayanna not taken FMLA leave, Dechert would have treated his reduced billable hours simply as an expected byproduct of his temporary assignment to Germany.

Finally, unlike most of the attorneys who were terminated contemporaneously, Ayanna met his billable hours requirement the previous year. While several other associates who were terminated were warned during 2008 that their billable hours were disappointingly low, Ayanna apparently was not given any such warning prior to his termination. That calls into question Dechert's claim that Ayanna was terminated solely because of his low billable hours.

Drawing all inferences in Ayanna's favor, there remains a genuine issue of material fact as to whether Dechert's termination of Ayanna on the ground of his low billable hours was actually a pretext for retaliation. . . . Dechert is not entitled to summary judgment.

2. Violation of M.G.L c. 151B §4(1) (Count II)

Ayanna alleges disparate treatment sex discrimination in violation of Chapter 151B on the grounds that he was fired because he was a male caregiver. Ayanna contends that his decision to take FLMA and paternity leave and to prioritize family obligations did not comport with Dechert's firm culture, which he asserts is dominated by a traditional male "macho" stereotype that promotes relegating family responsibilities to women.

Disparate treatment sex discrimination claims under Chapter 151B are also subject to the three step *McDonnell Douglas* burden-shifting test. . . . While Dechert asserts that Ayanna was fired for failing to meet performance expectations, as discussed above, there remains a dispute as to whether his low billable hours were actually caused by Dechert's alleged discriminatory treatment.

Even presuming that Ayanna can make out a prima facie case of disparate treatment sex discrimination, however, he has offered no evidence that his termination for low billable hours was actually a pretext for terminating him because he was a male who was also a caregiver. His broad claims about the "macho" culture at Dechert, without any facts specifically showing instances of discrimination against him, are inadequate to support a finding that he was fired due to his gender.

In fact, the record reflects that female attorneys who took on caregiving roles also experienced negative outcomes at Dechert. For example, a female attorney who was fired at the same time as Ayanna indicated that she was unable to obtain adequate work assignments when she returned from maternity leave. Further, the evidence does not support a finding that Christian was antagonistic to Ayanna because he is a male caregiver. At most the record suggests that Christian may have disfavored him because Ayanna prioritized his family over his employment responsibilities. While those facts suggest Ayanna may have been terminated because of the time he allotted to his caregiving duties, Chapter 151B does not provide protection for employees based on their caregiver status alone. Because Ayanna has proffered no evidence that his termination was based on his gender, Dechert is entitled to summary judgment on this count.

Notes

1. Caregiver Discrimination Lawsuits.   Lawsuits alleging discrimination against caregivers are on the rise. One study noted a 590 percent increase between 1998 and 2012 (a time when employment discrimination lawsuits decreased overall), and a plaintiff success rate of 52 percent—far better than plaintiffs bringing other employment discrimination claims.[87] *Ayanna* is one of the few alleging discrimination against a male caregiver.[88] Were you convinced that the plaintiff's family responsibilities in *Ayanna* were the reason

---

87. Cynthia Thomas Calvert, Caregivers in the Workplace Family Responsibilities Discrimination Litigation Update 2016, http://www.worklifelaw.org/pubs/FRDupdate2016.pdf.

88. See Keith Cunningham-Parmeter, Men at Work, Fathers at Home: Uncovering the Masculine Face of Caregiver Discrimination, 24 Colum. J. Gender & L. 253 (2013).

for his adverse treatment at work? What is the difference in the stereotypes that were applied to the male plaintiff in *Ayanna* and the female plaintiff in *Back*? Does it matter whether their supervisors ever treated them favorably? One author has argued that although social psychology research has "thoroughly refused the validity of the same-actor inference"—a "presumption of non-discrimination that arises when the same actor who engaged in an adverse action against the employee previously engaged in a positive action toward that employee"—courts continue to rely on it in caregiver discrimination cases.[89]

In addition to problems of proof, caregiver discrimination suits are difficult because caregiving is not one of the protected characteristics under Title VII or any other federal anti-discrimination law. In 2007, however, the EEOC issued an enforcement guidance to explain the circumstances under which caregiver discrimination might nonetheless be actionable.[90] For example, it is unlawful, as a form of illegal sex stereotyping, for an employer to assume that female employees will have caregiving responsibilities that interfere with job performance or labor force commitment. Employers cannot assume that women with young children will not work long hours or be available for travel or that they will be more likely to leave the work force. The EEOC also issued four press releases in 2012, indicating a renewed commitment to focus on caregiver discrimination.[91] If you were the school psychologist in the *Back* case, how would you have reacted to the supervisors' running commentary and skepticism?

In another case, Lust v. Sealy, the plaintiff was a sales representative who lost a promotion to a man. Evidence of discrimination included her supervisor's admission that he didn't consider recommending her for promotion because she had children. He didn't think she would want to relocate her family, even though she had not told him that and, in fact, had indicated frequently how much she wanted the promotion. When the plaintiff asked about that promotion, the supervisor also asked why her husband wasn't going to take care of her.[92] The plaintiff won at trial and the verdict was upheld on appeal in a decision written by Richard Posner, the same judge who wrote the

89. Andrea L. Miller, The Use (and Misuse) of the Same-Actor Inference in Family Responsibilities Discrimination Litigation: Lessons From Social Psychology on Flexibility Stigma, 41 Wm. Mitchell L. Rev. 1032 (2015); see also Victor D. Quintanilla & Cheryl R. Kaiser, The Same-Actor Inference of Nondiscrimination: Moral Credentialing and the Psychological and Legal Licensing of Bias, 104 Cal. L. Rev. 1 (2016) (arguing that the same-actor inference is "one of the most egregious examples of the tension between federal employment discrimination law and psychological science" and should be curtailed).

90. EEOC, Enforcement Guidance: Unlawful Disparate Treatment of Workers with Caregiving Responsibilities, 915.002 (May 23, 2007), http://www.eeoc.gov/policy/docs/caregiving.html.

91. See, e.g., EEOC, Press Release, Unlawful Discrimination Based on Pregnancy and Caregiving Responsibilities Widespread Problems, Panelists Tell EEOC (Feb. 15, 2012).

92. Lust v. Sealy, 383 F.3d 580, 583 (7th Cir. 2004).

opinion in *Troupe*. The court reduced the damages award to $150,000—half the maximum statutorily allowed—because the employer had taken steps to remedy the discrimination.

A wide body of research and reported cases document adverse stereotypes that working mothers face, such as a presumed lack of dependability, productivity, and commitment.[93] Should such research be admissible in sex discrimination cases where women claim that they were subject to the "motherhood penalty" but lack explicit statements like those present in *Back* and *Sealy*? How else might this body of work be helpful in preventing workplace bias?

The EEOC guidance also makes clear that it is unlawful to treat male employees with caregiving responsibilities less favorably than female employees in the same situation (or vice versa), especially if motivated by the belief that men should not assume such responsibilities. For example, an employer who told a male employee that he was not eligible for leave to take care of a newborn unless his wife was "in a coma or dead" committed actionable discrimination of this nature.[94] Two years later, in 2009, the EEOC issued a "best practices" document that encourages employers to provide accommodations for caregiving beyond those required by law in order to promote a better work/life balance for all employees.[95] The EEOC recommends that employers adopt a "caregiver" policy that describes common stereotypes or biases about caregivers and provides examples of prohibited discriminatory conduct. It also encourages employers to take proactive efforts to purge the hiring process of unfair stereotypes about caregivers and to ensure that applicants are not evaluated or steered into particular jobs on the basis of caregiving responsibilities. Finally, the EEOC recommends a number of policies to alleviate common conflicts faced by caregiving employees. Flexible work arrangements are at the top of the list, along with voluntary overtime, reasonable leave time for caregiving obligations, and other "family-friendly" modifications of conventional workplace rules. Should such policies be mandated? What objections do you see to them?

2. Accommodation vs. Discrimination. Should policies concerning childrearing, like childbearing, be seen as *accommodations* to employees with special needs, or as necessary components of a *nondiscriminatory* workplace? Some scholars, drawing on frameworks applicable to religious beliefs or disabilities, argue that employers have an obligation to undertake some expense and inconvenience if necessary to enable caretakers to participate fully in the

---

93. Stephen Benard et al., Cognitive Bias and the Motherhood Penalty, 59 Hastings L.J. 1359 (2008).

94. Knussman v. Maryland, 272 F.3d 625, 629-30 (4th Cir. 2001).

95. EEOC, Employer Best Practices for Workers with Caregiving Responsibilities (2009), http://www.eeoc.gov/policy/docs/caregiver-best-practices.html.

work force. Viewed this way, as measures to overcome disadvantages women experience from engaging in gendered activities, such workplace accommodations reflect values of substantive, rather than formal, equality.

Other scholars have resisted the equal treatment/special treatment dichotomy. They argue that the workplace is not a neutral structure that needs restructuring to accommodate women, but rather a set of arrangements already favoring an ideal worker, typically male, who lacks substantial caretaking responsibilities. On this view, reforming the workplace to acknowledge employees' caretaking responsibilities is not "special treatment" for women, but rather a recognition of the fundamental reality of women's lives and the importance of caretaking to society. Joan Williams' call for a "reconstructive feminism" is in this vein.[96] Williams argues that the focus of discussion should be not on theories of equality, but on how household work should be allocated within the household, how the cost of childrearing should be shifted from the private to the public arena, and what workplace restructuring should occur.[97] Does this formulation escape the choice between nondiscrimination and accommodation?

How might this agenda be achieved? An important rationale for work/family reforms is that they can be effective for employers as well as society.

> [E]mployers who provide family-friendly workplaces often save money because of decreased attrition and absenteeism, as well as enhancing recruitment and productivity. Practices that employees deem to reflect business necessity may in fact reflect business-irrational practices driven by gender stereotypes.[98]

Are employers who do not provide family-friendly workplaces overemphasizing short-term costs at the expense of long-term savings? If so, will the market eventually provide correctives or do we need policy interventions?

3. Parenting Leave: An International Perspective.   Three years after the passage of the FMLA, the European Council adopted the European Union Directive on Parental Leave, which provides minimum standards with which the member states must comply. These standards include a right to

---

96. Joan C. Williams, Reconstructive Feminism: Changing the Way We Talk About Gender and Work Thirty Years After the PDA, 21 Yale J.L. & Feminism 79 (2009).

97. Id.; Joan C. Williams, Reshaping the Work-Family Debate: Why Men and Class Matter (2010); Joan C. Williams, Do Women Need Special Treatment? Do Feminists Need Equality?, 9 J. Contemp. Legal Issues 279, 285-96 (1998).

98. Williams & Segal, Beyond the Maternal Wall, supra note 65, at 79; see also Barbara Kellerman & Deborah L. Rhode eds., Women and Leadership: The State of Play and Strategies for Change 16 (2007) (documenting the "business case for work/family policies"); James T. Bond et al., The 2002 National Study of the Changing Workforce 34-35 (Families and Work Institute, 2002) (finding that employees with greater access to flexible work arrangements are more committed and have lower attrition and higher satisfaction rates than employees who lack such opportunities).

parental leave for at least three months, protection against dismissal, and the right to return to the same or similar position. Most of the Member States of the European Union apply standards that exceed European Union standards for parental leave. For example, Finland allows "47.5 weeks of leave per childbirth: 17.5 weeks of maternity leave, four weeks of paternity leave, and 26 weeks of parental leave." Similarly, Sweden offers parents comparable amounts of leave — 14 weeks of maternity leave, two weeks of paternity leave and an additional 13 months of parental leave. In many Scandinavian countries, leaves may be split between parents or extended over a number of years. For example, Norway allows parents to spread 29 weeks of childcare over a two-year period following the birth of a child, and Sweden allows a parent to take a 25 percent reduction in working hours until the child is 8 years old.[99]

The comparative generosity of other countries' family leave policies, however, obscures complex issues about implementation and equity. In some countries, liberal leave policies foster employer resistance against women workers. In Mexico, for example, where women are guaranteed 12 weeks' paid maternity leave, many employers believe they have the right to deny employment to women if they state an intention to take a leave; others administer illegal pregnancy tests. These infractions are only weakly sanctioned. Similarly, Japan's Equal Employment Opportunity Law, effective in 1986, provides for equal opportunity and treatment in the job market for men and women. However, as one commentator notes, "the provisions of the law were not mandatory and no enforcement provisions were provided, resulting in minimal effectiveness."[100]

Some countries have achieved much higher rates of male involvement by a "use it or lose it approach." Sweden, for example, requires that 60 days of paid leave be taken by fathers; it is not transferable to mothers. That requirement, coupled with an extensive public education campaign, has resulted in 70 percent of fathers taking parental leave.[101] Sweden also pays a "gender-equality" bonus if parenting leave is shared. Studies of Scandinavian approaches find that when fathers take more leave, it results in shorter leave by mothers and a smaller loss in their earning potential. One study found that a mother's income increased 7 percent for every month of paternity leave her husband

---

99. See Rebecca Ray, A Detailed Look at Parental Leave Policies in 21 OECD Countries, Center for Economic Policy and Research, at 10, 22-23, 27-28 (Sept. 2008), http://www.lis-datacenter.org/wp-content/uploads/parent-leave-details1.pdf; Jan Tormod Dege & Erik Aas, Norway, in Employment Law in Europe 710, 714 (Susan Mayne & Susan Maylon eds., 2001).

100. Id. at 713; see also Ray, supra note 99, at 19 (noting that in Japan although "maternity leave is nearly universally guaranteed, maternity pay is not").

101. Steven Erfors, Sweden, in Employment Law in Europe, supra note 99, at 710, 830; see also Ray, supra note 99, at 27-28; Elina Pylkkhanen & Nina Smith, OECD Study, Career Interruptions Due to Parental Leave: A Comparative Study of Denmark and Sweden 11 (2003); Katrin Bennhold, In Sweden, Men Can Have It All, N.Y. Times, June 9, 2010, at A6.

takes.[102] However, Swedish fathers account for only about 12 percent of total benefit days claimed. One reason is employer resistance. Another is mothers' preferences: About half of those surveyed wanted all the days for themselves. Gender differences persist after the parental leave period. Sixty percent of mothers of young children work part time compared with only 5 percent of fathers.[103]

Drawing on such evidence, several American commentators argue that the FLMA should be amended to reward employers for encouraging men to take more parental leave.[104] Are these proposals worth considering?

Putting Theory Into Practice

2-9. In 2015, the Pentagon standardized maternity leaves for all branches of the service, offering women who give birth twelve weeks of paid leave. For the Army, this represents a doubling of the available leave, but for the Navy and Marine Corps, this is a reduction from eighteen weeks. Secretary of Defense Ash Carter noted that women at "peak ages" for childbearing leave the military at higher rates than other servicemembers and predicted that the new policy will "strengthen [the Pentagon's] position in the battle for top-tier talent."[105] The same policy, however, only grants men four days of paid leave. Is it possible that the reduction of leave for some servicewomen could actually promote equality? How? Does the new policy overall enhance equality? Does it matter from what perspective you evaluate it?

2-10. If one problem with parental leaves is that men don't choose to take them, would it be a good idea to make paternity leave mandatory?[106] If not, why not?

2-11. You are the head of the litigation department at a mid-sized firm. A senior associate who has just had a second child asks not to be assigned to

---

102. Elly-Ann Johansson, The Effect of Own and Spousal Parental Leave on Earnings 28 (2010).

103. See surveys discussed in Ira Mark Ellman, Marital Roles and Declining Marriage Rates, 41 Fam. L.Q. 455, 482 (2007).

104. See, e.g., Keith Cunningham-Parmeter, (Un)Equal Protection: Why Gender Equality Depends on Discrimination, 109 Nw. U. L. Rev. 1 (2014) (proposing bonuses for men who take paternity leave); Lester, supra note 80, at 80-81 (listing various proposals made by others, including required parental leave for fathers, linking federal contract eligibility of family leave uptake rates by male employees, and public awareness campaigns); Bryce Covert, Women Won't Have Equality Until Dads Stay Home: Here's How It Works, The Nation, Apr. 20, 2016.

105. Max J. Rosenthal, Most Military Moms Just Got Expanded Benefits, But Here's How Dads Got Screwed, Mother Jones, Jan. 28, 2016.

106. See Michael Selmi, Family Leave and the Gender Wage Gap, 78 N.C. L. Rev. 707, 774-75 (2000).

any cases requiring overnight travel. She also tends to avoid late or weekend hours at the firm, although she is accessible at home for conference calls and last-minute assignments. She is a hard-working and competent litigator but not a superstar. Other attorneys with families are annoyed that they are bearing a disproportionate share of document review work in other cities, and tasks that require office face time. You believe that the woman's choices may signal a lack of commitment that will hurt her at partnership. When you raise this concern, she claims that it reflects gender bias. How do you respond? How should the firm?

C. RECOGNIZING SEX-LINKED AVERAGE DIFFERENCES

Some sex-based differences affect matters where group-based judgments remain highly relevant. For example, on average, women live longer than men, have fewer driving-related accidents, have higher health care costs, and stay out of the work force for longer periods. Does our commitment to sex equality require that we ignore such average differences—for example, in the setting of insurance rates? Similarly, researchers document some differences in the way girls and boys learn (again, on average). Does that justify "separate but equal" classroom treatment? Can athletic programs take account of average sex-based differences in strength, size, and speed?

1. Fringe Benefit Plans, Insurance, and Other Actuarially-Based Systems

City of Los Angeles, Department of Water & Power v. Manhart
435 U.S. 702 (1978)

Mr. Justice STEVENS delivered the opinion of the Court.

As a class, women live longer than men. For this reason, the Los Angeles Department of Water and Power required its female employees to make larger contributions to its pension fund than its male employees. We granted certiorari to decide whether this practice discriminated against individual female employees because of their sex in violation of [Title VII].

For many years the Department has administered retirement, disability, and death-benefit programs for its employees. Upon retirement each employee is eligible for a monthly retirement benefit computed as a fraction of his or her salary multiplied by years of service. The monthly benefits for men and women of the same age, seniority, and salary are equal. Benefits are funded entirely by contributions from the employees and the Department, augmented by the income earned on those contributions. No private insurance company is involved in the administration or payment of benefits.

Based on a study of mortality tables and its own experience, the Department determined that its 2,000 female employees, on the average, will live a few years longer than its 10,000 male employees. The cost of a pension for the average retired female is greater than for the average male retiree because more monthly payments must be made to the average woman. The Department therefore required female employees to make monthly contributions to the fund which were 14.84% higher than the contributions required of comparable male employees. Because employee contributions were withheld from paychecks a female employee took home less pay than a male employee earning the same salary.[5] . . .

[The plan was subsequently amended based on state law. This action concerns the old plan, which the District Court found to violate Title VII. The United States Court of Appeals for the Ninth Circuit affirmed.] . . .

I

There are both real and fictional differences between women and men. It is true that the average man is taller than the average woman; it is not true that the average woman driver is more accident prone than the average man. Before [Title VII] was enacted, an employer could fashion his personnel policies on the basis of assumptions about the differences between men and women, whether or not the assumptions were valid.

It is now well recognized that employment decisions cannot be predicated on mere "stereotyped" impressions about the characteristics of males or females. Myths and purely habitual assumptions about a woman's inability to perform certain kinds of work are no longer acceptable reasons for refusing to employ qualified individuals, or for paying them less. This case does not, however, involve a fictional difference between men and women. It involves a generalization that the parties accept as unquestionably true: Women, as a class, do live longer than men. The Department treated its women employees differently from its men employees because the two classes are in fact different. It is equally true, however, that all individuals in the respective classes do not share the characteristic that differentiates the average class representatives. Many women do not live as long as the average man and many men

---

5. The significance of the disparity is illustrated by the record of one woman whose contributions to the fund (including interest on the amount withheld each month) amounted to $18,171.40; a similarly situated male would have contributed only $12,843.53.

outlive the average woman. The question, therefore, is whether the existence or nonexistence of "discrimination" is to be determined by comparison of class characteristics or individual characteristics. A "stereotyped" answer to that question may not be the same as the answer that the language and purpose of the statute command.

[Title VII] makes it unlawful "to discriminate against any individual with respect to his compensation, terms, conditions, or privileges of employment, because of such individual's race, color, religion, sex, or national origin." . . . The statute's focus on the individual is unambiguous. It precludes treatment of individuals as simply components of a racial, religious, sexual, or national class. If height is required for a job, a tall woman may not be refused employment merely because, on the average, women are too short. Even a true generalization about the class is an insufficient reason for disqualifying an individual to whom the generalization does not apply.

That proposition is of critical importance in this case because there is no assurance that any individual woman working for the Department will actually fit the generalization on which the Department's policy is based. Many of those individuals will not live as long as the average man. While they were working, those individuals received smaller paychecks because of their sex, but they will receive no compensating advantage when they retire.

It is true, of course, that while contributions are being collected from the employees, the Department cannot know which individuals will predecease the average woman. Therefore, unless women as a class are assessed an extra charge, they will be subsidized, to some extent, by the class of male employees. It follows, according to the Department, that fairness to its class of male employees justifies the extra assessment against all of its female employees.

But the question of fairness to various classes affected by the statute is essentially a matter of policy for the legislature to address. Congress has decided that classifications based on sex, like those based on national origin or race, are unlawful. Actuarial studies could unquestionably identify differences in life expectancy based on race or national origin, as well as sex. But a statute that was designed to make race irrelevant in the employment market . . . could not reasonably be construed to permit a take-home-pay differential based on a racial classification.

Even if the statutory language were less clear, the basic policy of the statute requires that we focus on fairness to individuals rather than fairness to classes. Practices that classify employees in terms of religion, race, or sex tend to preserve traditional assumptions about groups rather than thoughtful scrutiny of individuals. The generalization involved in this case illustrates the point. Separate mortality tables are easily interpreted as reflecting innate differences between the sexes; but a significant part of the longevity differential may be explained by the social fact that men are heavier smokers than women.

Finally, there is no reason to believe that Congress intended a special definition of discrimination in the context of employee group insurance coverage.

It is true that insurance is concerned with events that are individually unpredictable, but that is characteristic of many employment decisions. Individual risks, like individual performance, may not be predicted by resort to classifications proscribed by Title VII. Indeed, the fact that this case involves a group insurance program highlights a basic flaw in the Department's fairness argument. For when insurance risks are grouped, the better risks always subsidize the poorer risks. Healthy persons subsidize medical benefits for the less healthy; unmarried workers subsidize the pensions of married workers; persons who eat, drink, or smoke to excess may subsidize pension benefits for persons whose habits are more temperate. Treating different classes of risks as though they were the same for purposes of group insurance is a common practice that has never been considered inherently unfair. . . .

An employment practice that requires 2,000 individuals to contribute more money into a fund than 10,000 other employees simply because each of them is a woman, rather than a man, is in direct conflict with both the language and the policy of the Act. Such a practice does not pass the simple test of whether the evidence shows "treatment of a person in a manner which but for that person's sex would be different." It constitutes discrimination and is unlawful unless exempted by the Equal Pay Act of 1963 or some other affirmative justification. . . .

III

[T]he Department argues that the absence of a discriminatory effect on women as a class justifies an employment practice which, on its face, discriminated against individual employees because of their sex. But even if the Department's actuarial evidence is sufficient to prevent plaintiffs from establishing a prima facie case on the theory that the effect of the practice on women as a class was discriminatory, that evidence does not defeat the claim that the practice, on its face, discriminated against every individual woman employed by the Department.

In essence, the Department is arguing that the prima facie showing of discrimination based on evidence of different contributions for the respective sexes is rebutted by its demonstration that there is a like difference in the cost of providing benefits for the respective classes. That argument might prevail if Title VII contained a cost justification defense comparable to the affirmative defense. . . . But neither Congress nor the courts have recognized such a defense under Title VII.

Although we conclude that the Department's practice violated Title VII, we do not suggest that the statute was intended to revolutionize the insurance and pension industries. All that is at issue today is a requirement that men and women make unequal contributions to an employer-operated pension fund. Nothing in our holding implies that it would be unlawful for an employer to set aside equal retirement contributions for each employee and let each retiree purchase the largest benefit which his or her accumulated contributions could command in the open market. Nor does it call into question the insurance industry practice of considering the composition of an employer's work force in determining the probable cost of a retirement or death benefit plan. . . .

Mr. Justice BRENNAN took no part in the consideration or decision of this case.

[The opinion of Mr. Justice BLACKMUN, concurring in part and concurring in the judgment, is omitted.]

Mr. CHIEF JUSTICE BURGER, with whom Mr. Justice REHNQUIST joins, concurring in part and dissenting in part. . . .

Gender-based actuarial tables have been in use since at least 1843, and their statistical validity has been repeatedly verified. The vast life insurance, annuity, and pension plan industry is based on these tables. As the Court recognizes . . . it is a fact that "women, as a class, do live longer than men." It is equally true that employers cannot know in advance when individual members of the classes will die. . . . Yet, if they are to operate economically workable group pension programs, it is only rational to permit them to rely on statistically sound and proved disparities in longevity between men and women. Indeed, it seems to me irrational to assume Congress intended to outlaw use of the fact that, for whatever reasons or combination of reasons, women as a class outlive men. . . .

Here, of course, petitioners are discriminating in take-home pay between men and women. . . . The practice of petitioners, however, falls squarely under the exemption provided by the Equal Pay Act of 1963 . . . [for] a differential based on any "other factor other than sex. . . ." The "other factor other than sex" is longevity; sex is the umbrella-constant under which all of the elements leading to differences in longevity are grouped and assimilated, and the only objective feature upon which an employer—or anyone else, including insurance companies—may reliably base a cost differential for the "risk" being insured.

This is in no sense a failure to treat women as "individuals" in violation of the statute, as the Court holds. It is to treat them as individually as it is possible to do in the face of the unknowable length of each individual life. Individually, every woman has the same statistical possibility of outliving men. This is the essence of basing decisions on reliable statistics when individual determinations are infeasible or, as here, impossible.

Of course, women cannot be disqualified from, for example, heavy labor just because the generality of women are thought not as strong as men—a proposition which perhaps may sometime be statistically demonstrable, but will remain individually refutable. When, however, it is impossible to tailor a program such as a pension plan to the individual, nothing should prevent application of reliable statistical facts to the individual, for whom the facts cannot be disproved until long after planning, funding, and operating the program have been undertaken. . . .

Mr. Justice MARSHALL's opinion, concurring in part and dissenting [to the Court's holding that the opinion should not be retroactive, is omitted].

Notes

1. Group-Based vs. Individual-Based Equality. In an important sense, *Manhart* chooses formal equality over a form of "reverse" substantive equality: women and men must be treated alike at the pay-in side, even though as a (substantive) result women, on average, will live longer and obtain greater pay-out benefits than men. Put another way, the employer may not take account of men's and women's differences and make adjustments so that the outcomes (again, on average) are the same. Formal equality in these circumstances means that each employee will be treated as an individual rather than as a member of a group, but it also means that women will tend to obtain more benefits over their lifetimes than men, unless the employer shifts to a different system. Is that "fair"?

Despite the concern expressed by the defendant in *Manhart* that women as a group receive disproportionately more pension benefits than they earn, women as a group are less likely to be covered by a pension plan (39 percent, as compared to 46 percent for men), and the average pay-out for female retirees is less than half the pension benefits paid out to male retirees.[107] Are these facts relevant to the legal issues in *Manhart*?

Justice Stevens concedes that an employer could simply give a fixed benefit to employees from which they could purchase their own retirement plan on the open insurance market. A functionally equivalent alternative would be for employers to make fixed contributions to a private insurance carrier, which would then pay out different monthly amounts on retirement according to the employee's sex in recognition of the longer life expectancy of women. This alternative, too, however, has been found to be a violation of Title VII.[108]

2. Efficiency vs. Nondiscrimination in Fringe Benefit and Insurance Plans. The correlation between sex and longevity is largely explained by the fact that men engage in more self-destructive behaviors than women. Critics of *Manhart* have argued that sex is the most efficient proxy for these

---

107. See Dana M. Muir, From Yuppies to Guppies: Unfunded Mandates and Benefit Plan Regulation, 34 Ga. L. Rev. 195, 1220-21 (1999). On the story behind the *Manhart* case, see Gillian Thomas, Because of Sex: One Law, Ten Cases, and Fifty Years That Changed American Women's Lives at Work 60 (2016).

108. See Arizona Governing Committee for Tax Deferred Annuity and Deferred Compensation Plans v. Norris, 463 U.S. 1073 (1983) (giving employees a choice of carriers when all carriers used sex-segregated mortality tables violates Title VII); see also Probe v. State Teachers' Retirement Sys., 780 F.2d 776 (9th Cir. 1986) (joint life-survivor option that gives lower monthly payments to male employee who designates a female beneficiary violates Title VII).

behaviors and that monitoring these behaviors directly would be too expensive and inefficient.[109] Those who favor the result in *Manhart* argue that critics have confused correlation with causation: Sex is not the cause of the actuarial differences but only the most efficient correlate. Where efficiency is the only value to be served, pro-*Manhart* advocates argue that the nondiscrimination principles of Title VII should prevail.[110] Is the result unfair to men? Consider the following:

> It is hard to understand why the use of merged-gender mortality tables is unfair to men. It has a disparate impact on men as a group because it disadvantages self-destructors, and more men than women are self-destructors. The total annuity payout to [men] is less than the total amount paid to [women] because the total number of years the men [live] would be less. But are men, especially non-self-destructors, entitled to cash in on the fact that many of their sex self-destruct, and is this "entitlement" one that rises to the level of a right protected by Title VII?[111]

As long as sex is not the "cause" but only a correlate, isn't using sex as a predictor in setting rates and benefits similar to using race or ethnicity as a selection criterion for credit, college admissions, or hiring?[112]

Among the reasons offered for allowing risk classifications based on gender and other protected characteristics are that these classifications more accurately distribute the costs of insurance to those who are at higher risk.[113] Opponents respond that it is unfair to treat individuals as members of groups whose characteristics they may not share, which often "trades on preexisting social inequities and stereotypes."[114]

Until the mid-1990s, nearly half of insurers refused to insure domestic abuse victims because actuarial statistics showed that they are more likely to be victimized and thus draw disproportionately on health, life, and disability insurance plans. State laws vary widely on the subject. Some states have no legislation on the subject, or have only weak protections, such as a prohibition only against "irrational" discrimination against victims of domestic

---

109. See, e.g., George J. Benston, The Economics of Gender Discrimination in Employee Fringe Benefits: *Manhart* Revisited, 49 U. Chi. L. Rev. 489, 517-19, 530-31 (1982).

110. See, e.g., Lea Brilmayer et al., The Efficient Use of Group Averages as Nondiscrimination: A Rejoinder to Professor Benston, 50 U. Chi. L. Rev. 222, 223-25 (1983).

111. Id. at 226-27.

112. For a fuller statement of these arguments, see Brilmayer et al., supra note 110. For Benston's response to these arguments, see George J. Benston, Discrimination and Economic Efficiency in Employee Fringe Benefits: A Clarification of Issues and a Response to Professors Brilmayer, Laycock, and Sullivan, 50 U. Chi. L. Rev. 250 (1983).

113. Ronen Avraham et al., Understanding Insurance Antidiscrimination Rules, 87 So. Cal. L. Rev. 195, 204-14 (2014) (examining the problems of adverse selection, moral hazard, and inefficiency).

114. Id. at 214-20.

violence, or against denial or limitation of coverage "solely" because a person is a victims of domestic violence while still allowing insurers to limit coverage because abuse victims are at a higher risk of injury or death.[115] Should insurers be able to charge women higher rates because of what some men do to them? Is charging victims of domestic violence (a predominantly female group) more for insurance any different than charging victims of high blood pressure more?

3. Life Insurance. At one time, life insurance rates were the same for men and women, although the amount of life insurance coverage available to a married woman sometimes depended upon the amount sold to her husband. Gender-distinct mortality tables emerged after the Civil War, especially for annuities, as these financial instruments substituted for the dower rights and other benefits of coverture that were in decline during this period.[116] Today, all but one U.S. jurisdiction allows insurers to take gender into account in setting life insurance rates.[117] Only Montana bans sex-based rates and benefits for all types of insurance.[118]

If women, on average, live longer than men, why shouldn't they pay less for life insurance? One scholar has argued that gender-distinct rates reflected, in part, the growing emphasis on men's and women's separate spheres after coverture rules were dismantled, and the tendency thereafter to emphasize gender differences in order to support this ideology.[119] Does this affect your thinking?

4. Health Insurance. A survey by the National Women's Law Center found that, depending upon their age, women had to pay between 6 and 45 percent more for health coverage because they use more medical services.[120] Not only have women been paying more, they have also had less access to

---

115. Emily C. Wilson, Stop Re-Victimizing the Victims: A Call for Stronger State Laws Prohibiting Insurance Discrimination Against Victims of Domestic Violence, 23 Amer. U. J. Gender, Soc. Pol'y & Law 413, 424-25 (2015). For a fuller discussion of discrimination by the insurance industry against victims of domestic violence, see Deborah S. Hellman, Is Actuarially Fair Insurance Pricing Actually Fair?: A Case Study in Insuring Battered Women, 32 Harv. C.R.-C.L. L. Rev. 355 (1997). For a state-by-state survey of the law on this subject as of 2010, see National Women's Law Center, Health Care: Making the Grade on Women's Health: A National and State by State Report Card, http://hrc.nwlc.org/policy-indicators/domestic-violence-insurance; see also Chapter 3, Section C for discussion of violence against women in general.

116. See Mary L. Heen, From Coverture to Contract: Engendering Insurance on Lives, 23 Yale J. Law & Feminism 335, 373-83 (2011); Mary L. Heen, Nondiscrimination in Insurance: The Next Chapter, 49 Go. L. Rev. 1, 12-13 (2014).

117. Avraham et al., supra note 113, at 250.

118. Mont. Code Ann. §49-2-309 (2016).

119. See Heen, From Coverture to Contract, supra note 116, at 373-83.

120. Lisa Codispoti et al., National Women's Law Center, Nowhere to Turn: How the Individual Health Insurance Market Fails Women 8 (2008).

employer-provided plans, due to their disproportionate concentration in low-paying jobs and part-time work that lack full benefits.[121]

One of the provisions of the federal Patient Protection and Affordable Care Act is a prohibition of sex discrimination in health insurance.[122] Based on this law, a number of complaints were filed in 2014 claiming that the nation's largest insurance companies continued to charge women more than men for the same coverage.[123] No other federal law specifically prohibits gender discrimination in setting insurance rates.

5. Auto Insurance.   Only nine states ban the use of gender in auto insurance.[124] Sex has typically been a significant factor in car insurance premiums, reflecting the fact that male drivers under the age of 21 are twice as likely to have accidents as female drivers under the age of 21.[125] If you think that it is not fair for women to be charged more for health insurance, do you think that men should be charged more for car insurance?

6. Europe.   In March 2011, the European Court of Justice held in a case referred by the Constitutional Court of Belgium, that insurance companies could not use sex as a risk factor in determining insurance rates.[126] Since 2012 new commercial insurance policies sold in Europe require unisex rates and benefits.[127] Some qualifications temper this approach; for example, safe-driver premiums, as long as sex itself was not used as a risk factor,[128] and family history or health status may be used as factors.[129] Is Europe's prohibition route the best approach?

121. Walter L. Steihm, Poverty Law: Access to Healthcare and Barriers to the Poor, 4 Quinnipiac Health L.J. 279, 287-88 (2001).

122. See 42 U.S.C. §18116 (2012); Nat'l Fed'n of Indep. Bus. v. Sebelius, 132 S. Ct. 2566 (2012).

123. Jessica Mason Pieklo, Four Insurance Companies Accused of Widespread Sex Discrimination, in RH Reality Check (Jan. 17, 2014), http://rhrealitycheck.org/article/2014/01/17/four-insurance-companies-accused-widespread-sex-discrimination.

124. Avraham et al., supra note 113, at 201.

125. See Jill Insley & Rupert Jones, ECJ Gender Ruling Hits Insurance Costs, The Guardian (Mar. 1, 2011), http://www.guardian.co.uk/money/2011/mar/01/ecj-gender-ruling-insurance-costs.

126. Case C-236/09, Test-Achats v. Conseil des Ministres (Mar. 1, 2011), http://curia.europa.eu.

127. Heen, Nondiscrimination in Insurance, supra note 116, at 6.

128. See Press Release, European Commission (Dec. 22, 2011), http://europa. eu/rapid/pressReleasesAction.do?reference=IP/11/1581&format=HTML&aged=0&language=EN&guiLanguage=en.

129. Heen, Nondiscrimination in Insurance, supra note 116, at 75.

Putting Theory Into Practice

2-12. After the European Court of Justice decision forbidding use of sex as a determining risk factor in insurance premiums, the Association of British Insurers estimated that women under 25 could as a result pay 25 percent more for car insurance, while men's rates would likely fall by an average of 10 percent. Similarly, women could see a rise in cost of up to 20 percent for life insurance, and while men approaching retirement could see an 8 percent reduction in annuity rates, women's annuity rates could rise by 6 percent.[130] If true, from women's standpoint, is this "equality" worth it? In addition to the actuarial arguments made by the insurance industry, is there an equality argument justifying use of sex in setting insurance rates?

2. Education

a. Sex-Segregated Schools

During much of early American history, it was often assumed that women needed no formal education; informal training in the household arts was thought sufficient. In the nineteenth century, as elementary and secondary education opportunities increased, prominent medical experts warned that women faced a deadly "brain-womb conflict." Rigorous study assertedly would divert needed physical resources from reproductive to cognitive capacities. Even those who favored expanded female education, such as Catherine Beecher, generally believed that its primary objective should be "the preparation of woman for her distinctive profession as housekeeper, mother, nurse, and chief educator of infancy and childhood." Defenders of academic rigor emphasized that the point of women's instruction in traditional disciplines was not only to "enlarge their sphere of thought" and to render them "more interesting companions to men." Chemistry might be significant in its own right, but its principles were also applicable in the kitchen. Smith College's first president and early administrators denied that the college would produce competitors with men or diminish the "innate capacities which have been the glory and charm of true womanhood."[131]

These views are long out of date, of course, but disputes still arise about whether girls and boys have different abilities, learning styles, or interests that should shape their educations. One issue concerns single-sex schools. In 1982, the U.S. Supreme Court held in Mississippi University for Women

---

130. Insley & Jones, supra note 125.

131. Sheila M. Rothman, Woman's Proper Place 40 (1978); see also Deborah L. Rhode, Association and Assimilation, 81 Nw. U. L. Rev. 106, 131-32 (1986); Deborah L. Rhode, Justice and Gender 291-92 (1989).

(MUW) v. Hogan that a traditionally all-female state nursing school could not exclude men. Underlying the Court's decision was evidence that the school's sex segregation reflected not legitimate educational or compensatory justifications, but rather stereotypical views of nursing as an exclusively female occupation.[132] The Court did not, however, declare all single-sex schools unconstitutional. Justice O'Connor reserved the possibility that under "limited circumstances," a gender-based classification favoring one sex might be justified "if it intentionally and directly assists members of the sex that is disproportionately burdened." Justice Powell, joined by Justice Rehnquist, wrote a strong dissent emphasizing the "honored" tradition of single-sex education, its benefits especially to women, and its contributions to educational diversity. Quoting from the Brief for the MUW Alumnae Association, Justice Powell noted the value of sex-segregated schools in freeing women from the distraction of romantic relationships:

> [I]n the aspect of life known as courtship or mate-pairing, the American female remains in the role of the pursued sex, expected to adorn and groom herself to attract the male. . . .
>
> An institution of collegiate higher learning maintained exclusively for women is uniquely able to provide the education atmosphere in which some, but not all, women can best attain maximum learning potential. It can serve to overcome the historic repression of the past and can orient a woman to function and achieve in the still male-dominated economy. It can free its students of the burden of playing the mating game while attending classes, thus giving academic rather than sexual emphasis.[133]

Fourteen years after *Hogan,* the Supreme Court was faced with another challenge—this time, to an all-male state military college, the Virginia Military Institute (VMI).

═══ ### *United States v. Virginia*
518 U.S. 515 (1996)

GINSBURG, J., delivered the opinion of the Court, in which STEVENS, O'CONNOR, KENNEDY, SOUTER, and BREYER, JJ., joined.

Virginia's public institutions of higher learning include an incomparable military college, Virginia Military Institute (VMI). The United States maintains that the Constitution's equal protection guarantee precludes Virginia from reserving exclusively to men the unique educational opportunities VMI affords. We agree. . . .

132. 458 U.S. 718 (1982).
133. 458 U.S. at 739 n.5 (Powell, J., dissenting).

II

From its establishment in 1839 as one of the Nation's first state military colleges, VMI has remained financially supported by Virginia and "subject to the control of the [Virginia] General Assembly." . . .

VMI today enrolls about 1,300 men as cadets. Its academic offerings in the liberal arts, sciences, and engineering are also available at other public colleges and universities in Virginia. But VMI's mission is special. It is the mission of the school to produce educated and honorable men, prepared for the varied work of civil life, imbued with love of learning, confident in the functions and attitudes of leadership, possessing a high sense of public service, advocates of the American democracy and free enterprise system, and ready as citizen-soldiers to defend their country in time of national peril. . . .

In contrast to the federal service academies, institutions maintained "to prepare cadets for career service in the armed forces," VMI's program "is directed at preparation for both military and civilian life;" "[o]nly about 15% of VMI cadets enter career military service."

VMI produces its "citizen-soldiers" through "an adversative, or doubting, model of education" which features "[p]hysical rigor, mental stress, absolute equality of treatment, absence of privacy, minute regulation of behavior, and indoctrination in desirable values." . . .

VMI cadets live in spartan barracks where surveillance is constant and privacy nonexistent; they wear uniforms, eat together in the mess hall, and regularly participate in drills. Entering students are incessantly exposed to the rat line, "an extreme form of the adversative model," comparable in intensity to Marine Corps boot camp. Tormenting and punishing, the rat line bonds new cadets to their fellow sufferers and, when they have completed the 7-month experience, to their former tormentors.

VMI's "adversative model" is further characterized by a hierarchical "class system" of privileges and responsibilities, a "dyke system" for assigning a senior class mentor to each entering class "rat," and a stringently enforced "honor code," which prescribes that a cadet "'does not lie, cheat, steal nor tolerate those who do.'"

VMI attracts some applicants because of its reputation as an extraordinarily challenging military school, and "because its alumni are exceptionally close to the school." "[W]omen have no opportunity anywhere to gain the benefits of [the system of education at VMI]." . . .

In 1990, prompted by a complaint filed with the Attorney General by a female high-school student seeking admission to VMI, the United States sued the Commonwealth of Virginia and VMI, alleging that VMI's exclusively male admission policy violated the Equal Protection Clause of the Fourteenth Amendment. . . .

In the two years preceding the lawsuit, the District Court noted, VMI had received inquiries from 347 women, but had responded to none of them.

"[S]ome women, at least," the court said, "would want to attend the school if they had the opportunity." The court further recognized that, with recruitment, VMI could "achieve at least 10% female enrollment"—"a sufficient 'critical mass' to provide the female cadets with a positive educational experience." And it was also established that "some women are capable of all of the individual activities required of VMI cadets." In addition, experts agreed that if VMI admitted women, "the VMI ROTC experience would become a better training program from the perspective of the armed forces, because it would provide training in dealing with a mixed-gender army."

[The District Court ruled in favor of VMI, because admission of women would require alterations of some of the distinctive and beneficial aspects of VMI; the Fourth Circuit Court of Appeals reversed and remanded, holding that the state could not achieve its purposes by favoring one gender and that VMI had to either admit women, establish a parallel institution or program, or abandon state support. In response to the Fourth Circuit's ruling, Virginia proposed a parallel program at Mary Baldwin College, a private liberal arts school for women: Virginia Women's Institute for Leadership (VWIL). The program was to be open, initially, to 25 to 30 students. The District Court decided that the program plan met the requirements of the equal protection clause, and a divided Court of Appeals affirmed.]

III

The cross-petitions in this case present two ultimate issues. First, does Virginia's exclusion of women from the educational opportunities provided by VMI—extraordinary opportunities for military training and civilian leadership development—deny to women "capable of all of the individual activities required of VMI cadets," the equal protection of the laws guaranteed by the Fourteenth Amendment? Second, if VMI's "unique" situation,—as Virginia's sole single-sex public institution of higher education—offends the Constitution's equal protection principle, what is the remedial requirement?

IV . . .

To summarize the Court's current directions for cases of official classification based on gender: Focusing on the differential treatment or denial of opportunity for which relief is sought, the reviewing court must determine whether the proffered justification is "exceedingly persuasive." The burden of justification is demanding and it rests entirely on the State. [See Mississippi Univ. for Women v. Hogan (1982).] The State must show "at least that the [challenged] classification serves 'important governmental objectives and that the discriminatory means employed' are 'substantially related to the achievement of those objectives.'" The justification must be genuine, not hypothesized or invented post hoc in response to litigation. And it must not rely on overbroad generalizations about the different talents, capacities, or preferences of males and females. . . .

The heightened review standard our precedent establishes does not make sex a proscribed classification. Supposed "inherent differences" are no longer accepted as a ground for race or national origin classifications. Physical differences between men and women, however, are enduring: "[T]he two sexes are not fungible; a community made up exclusively of one [sex] is different from a community composed of both." . . .

"Inherent differences" between men and women, we have come to appreciate, remain cause for celebration, but not for denigration of the members of either sex or for artificial constraints on an individual's opportunity. Sex classifications may be used to compensate women "for particular economic disabilities [they have] suffered," . . . to "promot[e] equal employment opportunity," . . . to advance full development of the talent and capacities of our Nation's people. But such classifications may not be used, as they once were, . . . to create or perpetuate the legal, social, and economic inferiority of women.

Measuring the record in this case against the review standard just described, we conclude that Virginia has shown no "exceedingly persuasive justification" for excluding all women from the citizen-soldier training afforded by VMI. We therefore affirm the Fourth Circuit's initial judgment, which held that Virginia had violated the Fourteenth Amendment's Equal Protection Clause. Because the remedy proffered by Virginia—the Mary Baldwin VWIL program—does not cure the constitutional violation, i.e., it does not provide equal opportunity, we reverse the Fourth Circuit's final judgment in this case.

V . . .

Single-sex education affords pedagogical benefits to at least some students, Virginia emphasizes, and that reality is uncontested in this litigation.[8] Similarly, it is not disputed that diversity among public educational institutions can serve the public good. But Virginia has not shown that VMI was established, or has been maintained, with a view to diversifying, by its categorical

---

8. On this point, the dissent sees fire where there is no flame. "Both men and women can benefit from a single-sex education," the District Court recognized, although "the beneficial effects" of such education, the court added, apparently "are stronger among women than among men." The United States does not challenge that recognition. Cf. C. Jencks & D. Riesman, The Academic Revolution 297-98 (1968): "The pluralistic argument for preserving all-male colleges is uncomfortably similar to the pluralistic argument for preserving all-white colleges. . . . The all-male college would be relatively easy to defend if it emerged from a world in which women were established as fully equal to men. But it does not. It is therefore likely to be a witting or unwitting device for preserving tacit assumptions of male superiority—assumptions for which women must eventually pay."

exclusion of women, educational opportunities within the State. In cases of this genre, our precedent instructs that "benign" justifications proffered in defense of categorical exclusions will not be accepted automatically; a tenable justification must describe actual state purposes, not rationalizations for actions in fact differently grounded. . . .

Neither recent nor distant history bears out Virginia's alleged pursuit of diversity through single-sex educational options. In 1839, when the State established VMI, a range of educational opportunities for men and women was scarcely contemplated. Higher education at the time was considered dangerous for women; reflecting widely held views about women's proper place, the Nation's first universities and colleges — for example, Harvard in Massachusetts, William and Mary in Virginia — admitted only men. . . . VMI was not at all novel in this respect: In admitting no women, VMI followed the lead of the State's flagship school, the University of Virginia, founded in 1819. . . .

Debate concerning women's admission as undergraduates at the main university continued well past the century's midpoint. . . . If women were admitted, it was feared, they "would encroach on the rights of men; there would be new problems of government, perhaps scandals; the old honor system would have to be changed; standards would be lowered to those of other coeducational schools; and the glorious reputation of the university, as a school for men, would be trailed in the dust." . . .

Ultimately, in 1970, "the most prestigious institution of higher education in Virginia," the University of Virginia, introduced coeducation and, in 1972 [by court order], began to admit women on an equal basis with men. . . .

Virginia describes the current absence of public single-sex higher education for women as "an historical anomaly." But the historical record indicates action more deliberate than anomalous: First, protection of women against higher education; next, schools for women far from equal in resources and stature to schools for men; finally, conversion of the separate schools to coeducation. . . .

[I]t is uncontested that women's admission would require accommodations, primarily in arranging housing assignments and physical training programs for female cadets. It is also undisputed, however, that "the VMI methodology could be used to educate women." The District Court even allowed that some women may prefer it to the methodology a women's college might pursue. "[S]ome women, at least, would want to attend [VMI] if they had the opportunity," the District Court recognized, and "some women," the expert testimony established, "are capable of all of the individual activities required of VMI cadets." The parties, furthermore, agree that "some women can meet the physical standards [VMI] now impose[s] on men." In sum, as the Court of Appeals stated, "neither the goal of producing citizen soldiers," VMI's *raison d'etre*, "nor VMI's implementing methodology is inherently unsuitable to women."

In support of its initial judgment for Virginia, a judgment rejecting all equal protection objections presented by the United States, the District Court made "findings" on "gender-based developmental differences." These "findings" restate the opinions of Virginia's expert witnesses, opinions about typically male or typically female tendencies." For example, "[m]ales tend to need an atmosphere of adversativeness," while "[f]emales tend to thrive in a cooperative atmosphere." "I'm not saying that some women don't do well under [the] adversative model," VMI's expert on educational institutions testified, "undoubtedly there are some [women] who do"; but educational experiences must be designed "around the rule," this expert maintained, and not "around the exception."

The United States does not challenge any expert witness estimation on average capacities or preferences of men and women. Instead, the United States emphasizes that time and again since this Court's turning point decision in Reed v. Reed, [1971], we have cautioned reviewing courts to take a "hard look" at generalizations or "tendencies" of the kind pressed by Virginia, and relied upon by the District Court. . . .

It may be assumed, for purposes of this decision, that most women would not choose VMI's adversative method. As Fourth Circuit Judge Motz observed, however, in her dissent from the Court of Appeals' denial of rehearing en banc, it is also probable that "many men would not want to be educated in such an environment." . . . (On that point, even our dissenting colleague might agree.) Education, to be sure, is not a "one size fits all" business. The issue, however, is not whether "women—or men—should be forced to attend VMI"; rather, the question is whether the State can constitutionally deny to women who have the will and capacity, the training and attendant opportunities that VMI uniquely affords.

The notion that admission of women would downgrade VMI's stature, destroy the adversative system and, with it, even the school, is a judgment hardly proved, a prediction hardly different from other "self-fulfilling prophec[ies]," . . . once routinely used to deny rights or opportunities. When women first sought admission to the bar and access to legal education, concerns of the same order were expressed. . . .

[Such] fear, according to a 1925 report, accounted for Columbia Law School's resistance to women's admission, although

> [t]he faculty . . . never maintained that women could not master legal learning. . . . No, its argument has been . . . more practical. If women were admitted to the Columbia Law School, [the faculty] said, then the choicer, more manly and red-blooded graduates of our great universities would go to the Harvard Law School! . . .

More recently, women seeking careers in policing encountered resistance based on fears that their presence would "undermine male solidarity," . . . deprive male partners of adequate assistance, and lead to sexual misconduct. . . .

History of oppression

Women's successful entry into the federal military academies, and their participation in the Nation's military forces, indicate that Virginia's fears for the future of VMI may not be solidly grounded. . . .

The State's misunderstanding and, in turn, the District Court's, is apparent from VMI's mission: to produce "citizen-soldiers," individuals "imbued with love of learning, confident in the functions and attitudes of leadership, possessing a high sense of public service, advocates of the American democracy and free enterprise system, and ready . . . to defend their country in time of national peril." . . .

Surely that goal is great enough to accommodate women, who today count as citizens in our American democracy equal in stature to men. Just as surely, the State's great goal is not substantially advanced by women's categorical exclusion, in total disregard of their individual merit, from the State's premier "citizen-soldier" corps. Virginia, in sum, "has fallen far short of establishing the 'exceedingly persuasive justification'" . . . that must be the solid base for any gender-defined classification.

VI

In the second phase of the litigation, Virginia presented its remedial plan—maintain VMI as a male-only college and create VWIL as a separate program for women. . . .

The constitutional violation in this case is the categorical exclusion of women from an extraordinary educational opportunity afforded men. A proper remedy for an unconstitutional exclusion, we have explained, aims to "eliminate [so far as possible] the discriminatory effects of the past" and to "bar like discrimination in the future." . . .

Virginia chose not to eliminate, but to leave untouched, VMI's exclusionary policy. For women only, however, Virginia proposed a separate program, different in kind from VMI and unequal in tangible and intangible facilities. . . .

VWIL affords women no opportunity to experience the rigorous military training for which VMI is famed. . . . Instead, the VWIL program "deemphasize[s]" military education, and uses a "cooperative method" of education "which reinforces self-esteem."

VWIL students participate in ROTC and a "largely ceremonial" Virginia Corps of Cadets, but Virginia deliberately did not make VWIL a military institute. The VWIL House is not a military-style residence and VWIL students need not live together throughout the four year program, eat meals together, or wear uniforms during the school day. VWIL students thus do not experience the "barracks" life "crucial to the VMI experience," the spartan living arrangements designed to foster an "egalitarian ethic." "[T]he most important aspects of the VMI educational experience occur in the barracks," the District Court found, yet Virginia deemed that core experience nonessential, indeed inappropriate, for training its female citizen-soldiers.

VWIL students receive their "leadership training" in seminars, externships, and speaker series, episodes and encounters lacking the "[p]hysical rigor, mental stress, . . . minute regulation of behavior, and indoctrination in desirable values" made hallmarks of VMI's citizen-soldier training. Kept away from the pressures, hazards, and psychological bonding characteristic of VMI's adversative training, VWIL students will not know the "feeling of tremendous accomplishment" commonly experienced by VMI's successful cadets.

Virginia maintains that these methodological differences are "justified pedagogically," based on "important differences between men and women in learning and developmental needs," "psychological and sociological differences" Virginia describes as "real" and "not stereotypes." The Task Force charged with developing the leadership program for women, drawn from the staff and faculty at Mary Baldwin College, "determined that a military model and, especially VMI's adversative method, would be wholly inappropriate for educating and training *most women*" . . . [and noted that while "some women would be suited to and interested" in a VMI-style experience, VMI's adversative method "would not be effective for *women as a group*."] . . .

As earlier stated, generalizations about "the way women are," estimates of what is appropriate for *most women*, no longer justify denying opportunity to women whose talent and capacity place them outside the average description. Notably, Virginia never asserted that VMI's method of education suits *most men*. It is also revealing that Virginia accounted for its failure to make the VWIL experience "the entirely militaristic experience of VMI" on the ground that VWIL "is planned for women who do not necessarily expect to pursue military careers." By that reasoning, VMI's "entirely militaristic" program would be inappropriate for men in general or *as a group*, for "[o]nly about 15% of VMI cadets enter career military service."

In contrast to the generalizations about women on which Virginia rests, we note again these dispositive realities: VMI's "implementing methodology" is not "inherently unsuitable to women," "some women . . . do well under [the] adversative model," "some women, at least, would want to attend [VMI] if they had the opportunity," "some women are capable of all of the individual activities required of VMI cadets," and "can meet the physical standards [VMI] now impose[s] on men." . . .

In myriad respects other than military training, VWIL does not qualify as VMI's equal. VWIL's student body, faculty, course offerings, and facilities hardly match VMI's. Nor can the VWIL graduate anticipate the benefits associated with VMI's 157-year history, the school's prestige, and its influential alumni network.

Mary Baldwin College, whose degree VWIL students will gain, enrolls first-year women with an average combined SAT score about 100 points lower than the average score for VMI freshmen. The Mary Baldwin faculty holds "significantly fewer Ph.D.'s," and receives substantially lower salaries than the faculty at VMI.

Mary Baldwin does not offer a VWIL student the range of curricular choices available to a VMI cadet. VMI awards baccalaureate degrees in liberal arts, biology, chemistry, civil engineering, electrical and computer engineering, and mechanical engineering. . . . VWIL students attend a school that "does not have a math and science focus," they cannot take at Mary Baldwin any courses in engineering or the advanced math and physics courses VMI offers. . . .

For physical training, Mary Baldwin has "two multi-purpose fields" and "[o]ne gymnasium." VMI has "an NCAA competition level indoor track and field facility; a number of multi-purpose fields; baseball, soccer and lacrosse fields; an obstacle course; large boxing, wrestling and martial arts facilities; an 11-laps-to-the-mile indoor running course; an indoor pool; indoor and outdoor rifle ranges; and a football stadium that also contains a practice field and outdoor track."

Diff. facilities

Although Virginia has represented that it will provide equal financial support for in-state VWIL students and VMI cadets, and the VMI Foundation has agreed to endow VWIL with $5.4625 million, the difference between the two schools' financial reserves is pronounced. Mary Baldwin's endowment, currently about $19 million, will gain an additional $35 million based on future commitments; VMI's current endowment, $131 million—the largest per-student endowment in the Nation—will gain $220 million.

The VWIL student does not graduate with the advantage of a VMI degree. Her diploma does not unite her with the legions of VMI "graduates [who] have distinguished themselves" in military and civilian life. . . . A VWIL graduate cannot assume that the "network of business owners, corporations, VMI graduates and non-graduate employers . . . interested in hiring VMI graduates," will be equally responsive to her search for employment. . . .

No network w/ new school

Virginia, in sum, while maintaining VMI for men only, has failed to provide any "comparable single-gender women's institution." Instead, the Commonwealth has created a VWIL program fairly appraised as a "pale shadow" of VMI in terms of the range of curricular choices and faculty stature, funding, prestige, alumni support, and influence.

HBC

Virginia's VWIL solution is reminiscent of the remedy Texas proposed 50 years ago, in response to a state trial court's 1946 ruling that, given the equal protection guarantee, African Americans could not be denied a legal education at a state facility. . . . Reluctant to admit African Americans to its flagship University of Texas Law School, the State set up a separate school for Herman Sweatt and other black law students. [In holding that the all-black school was not equivalent to the University of Texas facility, the Court emphasized not only the size of the full-time faculty, library, and extracurricular offerings, but also the alumni network.]

More important than the tangible features, the Court [in *Sweatt*] emphasized, are "those qualities which are incapable of objective measurement but which make for greatness" in a school, including "reputation of the faculty, experience of the administration, position and influence of the alumni, standing in the community, traditions and prestige." Facing the marked differences reported in the *Sweatt* opinion, the Court unanimously ruled that Texas had not shown "substantial equality in the [separate] educational opportunities" the State offered. Accordingly, the Court held, the Equal Protection Clause required Texas to admit African Americans to the University of Texas Law School. In line with *Sweatt*, we rule here that Virginia has not shown substantial equality in the separate educational opportunities the State supports at VWIL and VMI.

[Reversed and remanded.]

Justice SCALIA, dissenting.

Today the Court shuts down an institution that has served the people of the Commonwealth of Virginia with pride and distinction for over a century and a half. To achieve that desired result, it rejects (contrary to our established practice) the factual findings of two courts below, sweeps aside the precedents of this Court, and ignores the history of our people. As to facts: it explicitly rejects the finding that there exist "gender-based developmental differences" supporting Virginia's restriction of the "adversative" method to only a men's institution, and the finding that the all-male composition of the Virginia Military Institute (VMI) is essential to that institution's character. As to precedent: it drastically revises our established standards for reviewing sex-based classifications. And as to history: it counts for nothing the long tradition, enduring down to the present, of men's military colleges supported by both States and the Federal Government.

Much of the Court's opinion is devoted to deprecating the closed-mindedness of our forebears with regard to women's education, and even with regard to the treatment of women in areas that have nothing to do with education. Closed-minded they were—as every age is, including our own, with regard to matters it cannot guess, because it simply does not consider them debatable. The virtue of a democratic system with a First Amendment is that it readily enables the people, over time, to be persuaded that what they took for granted is not so, and to change their laws accordingly. That system is destroyed if the smug assurances of each age are removed from the democratic process and written into the Constitution. So to counterbalance the Court's criticism of our ancestors, let me say a word in their praise: they left us free to change. The same cannot be said of this most illiberal Court, which has embarked on a course of inscribing one after another of the current preferences of the society (and in some cases only the counter-majoritarian preferences of the society's law-trained elite) into our Basic Law. Today it enshrines the notion that no substantial educational value is to be served by an all-men's military academy—so that the decision by the people of Virginia to maintain such an institution denies equal protection to women who cannot attend that institution but can attend others. Since it is entirely clear that the Constitution of the United States—the old one—takes no sides in this educational debate, I dissent.

I . . .

[I]n my view the ~~function of this Court is to *preserve* our society's val-~~ ~~ues regarding (among other things) equal protection,~~ not to *revise* them; to prevent backsliding from the degree of restriction the Constitution imposed upon democratic government, not to prescribe, on our own authority, progressively higher degrees. For that reason it is my view that, whatever abstract tests we may choose to devise, they cannot supersede—and indeed ought to be crafted *so as to reflect*—those constant and unbroken national traditions that embody the people's understanding of ambiguous constitutional texts. More specifically, it is my view that "when a practice not expressly prohibited by the text of the Bill of Rights bears the endorsement of a long tradition of open, widespread, and unchallenged use that dates back to the beginning of the Republic, we have no proper basis for striking it down." . . .

The all-male constitution of VMI comes squarely within such a governing tradition. Founded by the Commonwealth of Virginia in 1839 and continuously maintained by it since, VMI has always admitted only men. And in that regard it has not been unusual. For almost all of VMI's more than a century and a half of existence, its single-sex status reflected the uniform practice for government-supported military colleges. Another famous Southern institution, The Citadel, has existed as a state-funded school of South Carolina since 1842. And all the federal military colleges—West Point, the Naval Academy at Annapolis, and even the Air Force Academy, which was not established until 1954—admitted only males for most of their history. Their admission of women in 1976 (upon which the Court today relies), came not by court decree, but because the people, through their elected representatives, decreed a change. . . . In other words, the tradition of having government-funded military schools for men is as well rooted in the traditions of this country as the tradition of sending only men into military combat. The people may decide to change the one tradition, like the other, through democratic processes; but the assertion that either tradition has been unconstitutional through the centuries is not law, but politics-smuggled-into-law.

And the same applies, more broadly, to single-sex education in general, which, as I shall discuss, is threatened by today's decision with the cut-off of all state and federal support. Government-run *non*military educational institutions for the two sexes have until very recently also been part of our national tradition. "[It is] [c]oeducation, historically, [that] is a novel educational theory. From grade school through high school, college, and graduate and professional training, much of the Nation's population during much of our history has been educated in sexually segregated classrooms." Mississippi Univ. for Women v. Hogan, [1982] (Powell, J., dissenting). These traditions may of course be changed by the democratic decisions of the people, as they largely have been.

Today, however, change is forced upon Virginia, and reversion to single-sex education is prohibited nationwide, not by democratic processes but by order of this Court. Even while bemoaning the sorry, bygone days of "fixed notions" concerning women's education, the Court favors current notions so fixedly that it is willing to write them into the Constitution of the United States by application of custom-built "tests." This is not the interpretation of a Constitution, but the creation of one.

II.

To reject the Court's disposition today, however, it is not necessary to accept my view that the Court's made-up tests cannot displace longstanding national traditions as the primary determinant of what the Constitution means. It is only necessary to apply honestly the test the Court has been applying to sex-based classifications for the past two decades. . . . We have denominated this standard "intermediate scrutiny" and under it have inquired whether the statutory classification is "substantially related to an important governmental objective." . . .

Only the amorphous "exceedingly persuasive justification" phrase, and not the standard elaboration of intermediate scrutiny, can be made to yield this conclusion that VMI's single-sex composition is unconstitutional because there exist several women (or, one would have to conclude under the Court's reasoning, a single woman) willing and able to undertake VMI's program. Intermediate scrutiny has never required a least-restrictive-means analysis, but only a "substantial relation" between the classification and the state interests that it serves. . . .

Not content to execute a *de facto* abandonment of the intermediate scrutiny that has been our standard for sex-based classifications for some two decades, the Court purports to reserve the question whether, even in principle, a higher standard (i.e., strict scrutiny) should apply. . . . [The Court's] statements are misleading, insofar as they suggest that we have not already categorically *held* strict scrutiny to be inapplicable to sex-based classifications. . . . And the statements are irresponsible, insofar as they are calculated to destabilize current law. Our task is to clarify the law—not to muddy the waters, and not to exact over-compliance by intimidation. The States and the Federal Government are entitled to know *before they act* the standard to which they will be held, rather than be compelled to guess about the outcome of Supreme Court peek-a-boo.

The Court's intimations are particularly out of place because it is perfectly clear that, if the question of the applicable standard of review for sex-based classifications were to be regarded as an appropriate subject for reconsideration, the stronger argument would be not for elevating the standard to strict scrutiny, but for reducing it to rational-basis review. The latter certainly has a firmer foundation in our past jurisprudence: Whereas no majority of the Court has ever applied strict scrutiny in a case involving sex-based classifications, we routinely applied rational-basis review until the 1970's. . . .

It is hard to consider women a "discrete and insular minorit[y]" unable to employ the "political processes ordinarily to be relied upon," when they constitute a majority of the electorate. And the suggestion that they are incapable of exerting that political power smacks of the same paternalism that the Court so roundly condemns. Moreover, a long list of legislation proves the proposition false. . . .

III . . .

There can be no serious dispute that, as the District Court found, single-sex education and a distinctive educational method "represent legitimate contributions to diversity in the Virginia higher education system." As a theoretical matter, Virginia's educational interest would have been best served (insofar as the two factors we have mentioned are concerned) by six different types of public colleges—an all-men's, an all-women's, and a coeducational college run in the "adversative method," and an all-men's, an all-women's, and a coeducational college run in the "traditional method." But as a practical matter, of course, Virginia's financial resources, like any State's, are not limitless, and the Commonwealth must select among the available options. Virginia thus has decided to fund, in addition to some 14 coeducational 4-year colleges, one college that is run as an all-male school on the adversative model: the Virginia Military Institute.

Virginia did not make this determination regarding the make-up of its public college system on the unrealistic assumption that no other colleges exist. Substantial evidence in the District Court demonstrated that the Commonwealth has long proceeded on the principle that " '[h]igher education resources should be viewed as a whole—public and private' "—because such an approach enhances diversity and because " 'it is academic and economic waste to permit unwarranted duplication.' " It is thus significant that, whereas there are "four all-female private [colleges] in Virginia," there is only "one private all-male college," which "indicates that the private sector is providing for th[e] [former] form of education to a much greater extent that it provides for all-male education." In these circumstances, Virginia's election to fund one public all-male institution and one on the adversative model—and to concentrate its resources in a single entity that serves both these interests in diversity—is substantially related to the State's important educational interests. . . .

[handwritten margin note: More private female schools than priv. male schools]

IV . . .

In an odd sort of way, it is precisely VMI's attachment to such old-fashioned concepts as manly "honor" that has made it, and the system it represents, the target of those who today succeed in abolishing public single-sex education. The record contains a booklet that all first-year VMI students (the so-called "rats") were required to keep in their possession at all times. Near the end there appears the following period-piece, entitled "The Code of a Gentleman":

Without a strict observance of the fundamental Code of Honor, no man, no matter how "polished," can be considered a gentleman. The honor of a gentleman demands the inviolability of his word, and the incorruptibility of his principles. He is the descendant of the knight, the crusader; he is the defender of the defenseless and the champion of justice . . . or he is not a Gentleman.

A Gentleman . . .

Does not discuss his family affairs in public or with acquaintances.

Does not speak more than casually about his girl friend.

Does not go to a lady's house if he is affected by alcohol. He is temperate in the use of alcohol.

Does not lose his temper; nor exhibit anger, fear, hate, embarrassment, ardor or hilarity in public.

Does not hail a lady from a club window.

A gentleman never discusses the merits or demerits of a lady. Does not mention names exactly as he avoids the mention of what things cost.

Does not borrow money from a friend, except in dire need. Money borrowed is a debt of honor, and must be repaid as promptly as possible. Debts incurred by a deceased parent, brother, sister or grown child are assumed by honorable men as a debt of honor.

Does not display his wealth, money or possessions.

Does not put his manners on and off, whether in the club or in a ballroom. He treats people with courtesy, no matter what their social position may be.

Does not slap strangers on the back nor so much as lay a finger on a lady.

Does not "lick the boots of those above" nor "kick the face of those below him on the social ladder."

Does not take advantage of another's helplessness or ignorance and assumes that no gentleman will take advantage of him.

A Gentleman respects the reserves of others, but demands that others respect those which are his.

A Gentleman can become what he wills to be. . . .

I do not know whether the men of VMI lived by this Code; perhaps not. But it is powerfully impressive that a public institution of higher education still in existence sought to have them do so. I do not think any of us, women included, will be better off for its destruction.

Joanna L. Grossman & Grant Hayden, The Thin Pink Line: Policing Gender at Every Corner

Verdict: Legal Analysis and Commentary from Justia (May 24, 2016)

[handwritten: 2♀, King & Queen of prom]

A recent editorial in the *Tallahassee Democrat* reported on, and praised, the students at Leon High School, who elected two women to serve as prom king and queen. The two women had dated for three years and were viewed by their peers perhaps as the most popular couple. The surprising part of this story was that after the story reached over 200,000 people on Facebook, many of the comments were supportive and celebratory, or expressed the simple idea that this was no big deal.

But this story is the exception, as we see uproars across the country to people, rules, and events that challenge conventional gender norms. When students at a California high school tried to elect a lesbian couple as prom king and queen, school officials issued a royal edict that for all-important prom purposes, qualification for "king" or "queen" is defined by sex at birth. Meanwhile, across the country in Harrisburg, Pennsylvania, a girl who showed up in a tuxedo was turned away at the prom door for violating the established dress code that says "girls must wear formal dresses." And in nearby East Haddam, Connecticut, boys and girls walk in different lines at commencement, with boys dressed in blue, and girls in virginal white carrying flowers.

And if all this seems trivial—rules that affect people on only one night in high school—recall the sweeping (and unconstitutional) law passed by North Carolina recently, requiring that transgender individuals only use public bathrooms that align with their birth sex and wiping out the state's protections against employment discrimination simply to ensure that no LBGT person ever benefited from them. Or remember that the state refused to comply with a federal order stating that the bathroom portion of the bill violates Title IX and must be repealed. Or take notice of the efforts of Oklahoma legislators—at the same time they were passing an unconstitutional bill to ban *all* abortions (vetoed by their governor)—to pass a law that would grant students a right to avoid sharing a bathroom with a transgender student in the name of religious freedom.

Why all the hubbub? People simply cannot care this much about what people wear to a high school dance, whether the prom king is a boy (particularly when the students themselves don't care), or whether girls are both differentiated and robed in pristine white at a high school graduation.

Now people might care about sharing bathrooms with transgender people, but only because they are misinformed, acting out of a misplaced fear of predation, or bigoted. The transgender bathroom problem has been framed in some circles as one as one of safety—protecting girls and women from bathroom predators. But there is no empirical support for this fear. The number of transgender people is very low—the best estimate, by the Williams

Institute, is that a mere 0.3 percent of the population is transgender. But, more importantly, as Mark Joseph Stern recently pointed out on Slate, there is "overwhelming evidence and professional consensus" that this fear is entirely baseless. (Not to mention that, with or without laws protecting transgender access to bathrooms, predatory men could dress up as women and enter women's rooms. Or, of course, they could just prey on little boys like Jerry Sandusky and Dennis Hastert, both of whom used all-male locker-rooms as their hunting grounds. But nobody is banning men from using communal restrooms).

There must, then, be some reason underlying all these scandals and stories. The real reason, we suggest, is that transgender people present a direct challenge to the existence of a simple division between the sexes. People who were born with one set of sexual organs but identify and present as members of the opposite sex blur the lines between sexes, and make clear there that the relationship between sex and gender is complicated. It's hard to maintain sexual inequality when you can't tell, exactly, what makes someone a boy or a girl, a man or a woman.

And when people are not transgender, but simply refuse to be segregated by sex or to conform to conventional sex norms, society has the same reaction: "make sure we can tell the difference between girls and boys." When the girls in East Haddam wrote an opinion piece in the local paper, it met with scores of angry comments (now deleted) about how their efforts to change the school's discrimination graduation robe policy were frivolous or stupid. But that argument cuts both ways. If it doesn't mean anything, then why don't the boys and girls wear the same graduation robes? Why wouldn't the default be that everyone earning the same degree wears the same genderless attire in the ceremony to honor their achievements?

What [bans on same-sex marriage, dress codes in the workplace, and gender restrictions in schools] have in common is that they are attempts to police the gender line. Maintaining the distinction between men and women wouldn't be important if, for most everything, they weren't treated differently. That is, when equality is the rule, then drawing a distinction really doesn't matter—whether you're on one side of the gender line or the other (or somewhere in between), you're treated the same. At home. At school. At work. At church. At the country club. The distinction matters precisely because equality isn't the rule in many of those places—the gender division reflects a longstanding hierarchy, with men on top. And if we can't tell who's who because people challenge gender conventions—by wearing the wrong color, or marrying someone of the wrong gender, or, even worse, trying to become someone of the other gender, chaos ensues.

This kind of behavior is not unique to sex discrimination. Systemic racial oppression depends, too, on a policing of boundaries. The "one drop" rule is the most notorious example. But a key facet of any system of oppression is the ability to clearly distinguish between classes of people. Any impediments to those distinctions, or suggestions that, even if they do exist, they don't really support the kind of radical distinctions that get drawn in the law or, more generally, society, are dismissed.

This isn't to say that people who are gay, transgender, or graduating from high school aren't being independently targeted for discrimination. They are, and their suffering is real. But they are also pawns in a larger game of gender oppression, one that depends on having clearly drawn battle lines.

Notes

1. What's at Stake Here? The *VMI* case started with an anonymous complaint by a northern Virginia female high school student to the U.S. Department of Justice that the school did not accept applications from women. One of the issues in the case was whether women would really attend VMI, although the case record revealed that 347 women had made inquiries about VMI in the two years preceding the lawsuit.[134] Another subject of debate was whether the presence of women would significantly change the school and eliminate its benefits for men. The government argued that women could thrive at VMI, without changing it. Was this a realistic claim? VMI contended, and the District Court agreed, that women would change the fundamental dynamic of the school and ruin what was unique and valuable about it. Was this plausible? Or was it beside the point? Should women be excluded from a public institution simply because their presence might change that institution?

Despite a claim that VMI would not have to change after the Supreme Court decided the case, the government pressured VMI to make changes to accommodate women, such as more privacy in bedrooms and bathrooms, and less severe haircuts. Was this appropriate?[135] With which theory of equality was this measure most consistent?

Given VMI's highly gendered approach to education, was VMI's exclusion of women the only constitutional defect? Or should it also be unconstitutional for a state-supported institution to implement such a pedagogy, no matter who has access to that institution?[136]

---

134. See United States v. Virginia, 518 U.S. 515, 523 (1996).

135. A parallel case was filed against South Carolina's The Citadel, the only other state-supported, all-male military college. While the case was still on appeal, the Fourth Circuit ordered immediate admission of the named plaintiff, Shannon Faulkner, who dropped out less than a week later, "overcome by stress and terror as the only woman alone in the barracks with 1800 male cadets, most of whom hated her guts." Faulkner v. Jones, 10 F.3d 226 (4th Cir. 1993); Citadel's First Female Case Tells of the Stress of Her Court Fight, N.Y. Times, Sept. 10, 1995, §1, at 36. After the ruling in *VMI*, The Citadel decided to admit women.

136. Katharine T. Bartlett, Unconstitutionally Male?: The Story of United States v. Virginia, in Women and the Law Stories 133, 167 (Elizabeth Schneider & Stephanie Wildman eds., 2011).

While the exclusion of women from VMI was the central legal issue, another concern, not directly addressed in the parties' briefs or in the Supreme Court decision, was the propriety of the adversative method itself. The adversative method, which defined the essence of the institution, was deliberately and pervasively gendered. Its purpose was to create leaders by giving them near-impossible challenges, and then equating success in meeting those challenges with masculinity. Given this purpose, the problem with admitting women to VMI was as much that they might succeed, as that they would fail. As one researcher put it, "if women could perform well on [the rat line], how could it continue to function as evidence of manhood?" To reinforce the machismo ethos, gendered obscenities and hostility toward women . . . served as official motivational techniques in the rat line. . . . Other familiar phrases [included] "raping your virgin ducks" (peeling apart the stiffly starched legs of a new pair of white trousers), [and] "rolling your hay tight as a tampon" (rolling up thin mattress in the morning).[137]

The VWIL program at Mary Baldwin College has consistently enrolled more students than the number of women enrolled at VMI — sometimes more than double. More VWIL graduates receive military commissions, and these women have been serving with distinction.[138] Does this surprise you? Does it indicate the VWIL is actually the superior program for women?

Mary Anne Case visited both VMI and VWIL after the *VMI* decision. She found the "rats" at VMI "a sorry lot — terrified, sweating, shaking, and exhausted . . . they were unable to tell their left feet from their right." By contrast, the VWIL's equivalent to rats (nULLS) were working together, learning the same values of accountability and discipline in a more supporting, encouraging, and non-intimidating environment. She noted, however, that VMI was still the more prestigious, sought-after alternative, even by many women.

The paradoxes here are many: First, the dominant class, men, have selected what appears to be the less attractive standard for themselves. Second, in part because they have selected it, this standard is assumed unquestionably to be desirable; inquiry into it is generally limited only to how far it will be extended to women. Much less attention is paid to whether the separate standard sought to be applied to women might in fact make some sense for women and men alike.[139]

What do you make of this analysis?

What does VMI look like now — twenty years after first admitting female students? Reporting results of a survey of current VMI students, Abigail Perdue drew the following conclusions:

---

137. Id. at 174; see also Valorie K. Vojdik, Gender Outlaws: Challenging Masculinity in Traditionally Male Institutions, 17 Berkeley Women's L.J. 68, 98-99 (2002) (describing the culture of hyper-masculinity at The Citadel).

138. Bartlett, supra note 136.

139. See Mary Anne Case, Two Cheers for Cheerleading: The Noisy Integration of VMI and the Quiet Success of Virginia Women in Leadership, 1999 U. Chi. Legal F. 347, 349, 378.

On May 15, 1999, Chih-Yuan Ho and Melissa Graham became the first women to graduate from VMI. Nearly two decades later, tensions between the sexes and institutional myths regarding coeducation remain alive and well. . . . Only twenty-three respondents, or 6.52%, stated that coeducation at VMI had been "very successful."[287] As one cadet explained, "[b]eing a woman here is one of the hardest things I have ever done." Yet most women felt that coeducation had been somewhat successful, and a majority — 63.26% — believed it had positively impacted their lives. By comparison, a sizeable minority — 48.36% — of men described coeducation as unsuccessful, and 65.69% of men asserted that coeducation had affected them negatively, with a quarter opining that it had affected them very negatively. Significantly, these results come nearly twenty years after assimilation at a time when the expected initial "kinks" of assimilation should have subsided.

[G]iven the tradition of single-sex education, especially within VMI's androcentric environment, the continued presence of gender polarization at VMI is unsurprising. The data paints a picture of some men fiercely defending their traditionally masculine domain and the power and privilege that they derive from it. Their animosity toward female cadets whom they perceive as intruders and their frustration with coeducation are reflected in their perception of female cadets as being more masculine than women in general. Moreover, displeasure with female cadets is further manifested in the pressure for hyper-masculinity among male cadets in conjunction with a surprisingly high level of pressure for female cadets to be gender neutral. Gender strategies, such as gender neutrality and emphatic sameness, allow "otherized" female cadets to avoid having to accept the lower status domain of femininity within androcentric, gender polarized environments like VMI while simultaneously being denied access to the advantages associated with masculinity. Hence, at VMI, the behaviors of male and female cadets not only confirm their gendered place and status level at VMI but their gendered identities as well. For men, preserving their male domain maintains male privilege and a firm grip on each man's masculine identity. The pressure toward hyper-masculinity suggests that coeducation may cause male cadets to feel as if their control and gendered identity are under assault.

For women, the relationship between status and gender identity is more problematic. Assuming that a female cadet has lived as a female-gendered being prior to entering VMI, she likely has a vested interest in seeing herself as feminine after matriculation and throughout her transformation into a cadet. After all, her femininity is likely an important part of her personal identity. On the other hand, she is attempting, whether intentionally and consciously or not, to assimilate into a stronghold of masculinity. By opting for gender neutrality or emphatic sameness, she hopes to avoid the lower status of being a feminine "shedet." Yet, in so doing, she may unintentionally forfeit a vital part of her gender identity as Woman. Thus, perhaps VMI women "have access only to so much of privilege or influence as [their peers] are willing to accede . . . and only for so long as [the female cadets] will pay the price for male approval."[290] What

---

290. Adrienne Rich, Of Woman Born 58 (1976).

remains unclear, however, is whether the price of assimilation comes at too high a cost.

In conclusion, United States v. Virginia is not a case about a simple change to an admissions policy. Instead, it is about a fundamental alteration of VMI cultural landscape that has had far-reaching implications on the Institution as well as its student body. . . . Thus, one unintentional and unforeseen consequence of coeducation is the exacerbation of existing gender polarization at VMI. This may help to explain the stigmatized status often associated with female cadets who, for the most part, simply wish to receive the same excellent training that has been historically available to men.[140]

2. Single-Sex Schools at the Elementary and Secondary Level. While the number of women's colleges has declined from 300 in 1960 to about 50 today, single-sex education at the secondary level has increased significantly since the Supreme Court decided United States v. Virginia. In 1995, the nation had only two single-sex public high schools; by 2009 there were 95, and the number of single-sex classrooms is estimated to have grown from about a dozen in 2002 to more than 500 in 40 states in 2011.[141] Newer data is not readily available because the single-sex-education advocacy group that had been tallying it—to show that the idea was gaining interest—removed their list from the website to avoid triggering interest of the ACLU, which, as discussed below, has been challenging programs it alleges are unlawfully discriminatory.[142]

Changes in federal regulations reflected and reinforced the interest in single-sex approaches. In 2001, Congress passed the No Child Left Behind Act, which included a clause stating that "funds made available to local educational agencies . . . shall be used for innovative assistance programs, which may include . . . programs to provide same-gender schools and classrooms (consistent with applicable law)."[143] In 2006, the U.S. Department of Education amended its regulations under Title IX to allow elementary and secondary non-vocational schools that receive federal funding to be single-sex as long as there is a "substantially equal" single-sex or co-educational school for students of the excluded sex. They may also offer single-sex classes or extracurricular activities when they are voluntary and substantially related to improving stu-

140. Abigail Perdue, Transforming "Shedets" into "Keydets": An Empirical Study Examining Coeducation Through the Lens of Polarization, 28 Colum. J. Gender & L. 371, 431-32 (2015).

141. Elizabeth Weil, Teaching to the Testosterone, N.Y. Times Mag., Mar. 3, 2008, at 39, 40; Jennifer Medina, Schools Try Separating Boys from Girls, N.Y. Times, Mar. 10, 2009; Tamar Lewin, Single-Sex Education is Assailed in Report, N.Y. Times, Sept. 22, 2011, at A19.

142. See Nat'l Ass'n for Single Sex Public Education, http://www.singlesexschools.org/schools-schools.htm.

143. Pub. L. No. 107-110, 115 Stat. 1425 (2002).

dents' educational achievement, as long as a "substantially equal" opportunity is available to the excluded sex. Funding recipients must conduct at least biennial evaluations to ensure that single-sex opportunities are "based on genuine justifications and do not rely on overly broad generalizations about the different talents, capacities, or preferences of either sex to ensure they remain constitutional."[144]

Some of the impetus for the revival of girls-only educational opportunities in the 1990s came from research by the American Association of University Women (AAUW) identifying significant differences between boys and girls as they progress through educational institutions, with girls experiencing a much steeper decline than boys in self-image and in career aspirations, especially those related to math and science:

> Girls, aged eight and nine, are confident, assertive, and feel authoritative about themselves. They emerge from adolescence with a poor self-image, constrained views of their future and their place in society, and much less confidence about themselves and their abilities. Sixty percent of elementary school girls say they are "happy the way I am," a core measure of personal self-esteem. More boys, 67 percent of those surveyed, also strongly agreed with the statement. Over the next eight years, girls' self-esteem falls 31 percentage points, with only 29 percent of high school girls saying they are happy with themselves. Almost half of the high school boys (46 percent) retain their high self-esteem. By high school, this gender gap increases from 7 points to 17 points.[145]

The AAUW findings have been challenged by other experts who claim that the conclusion that schools shortchange girls is based on "soft and slippery issues, like the 'silencing' of girls in the classroom," rather than on educational achievement tests, college entrance and graduation rates, and earnings. Self-esteem measures may in part reflect boys' self-deception, bravado, and immaturity.[146] Moreover, on many measures, female students do better. They receive higher grades and receive more honors in every field but science and sports. On standardized tests, although boys do better in mathematics, science, and geopolitics, the margins are small; girls do better in reading achievement, and surpass boys in writing skills by a significant amount. Boys are also more likely to be at the bottom of their class, to be assigned to special

---

144. 34 C.F.R. §106.34(b)(4) (2016); see also Doe v. Wood County Bd. of Educ., 888 F. Supp. 2d 771 (S.D. W. Va 2012) (holding a single-class classroom is only "voluntary" under the regulations if parents give affirmative consent prior to enrollment; an opt-out provision is not sufficient).

145. Am. Ass'n of Univ. Women, Survey, Shortchanging Girls, Shortchanging America 4 (1991).

146. Judith Kleinfeld, The Myth That Schools Shortchange Girls: Social Science in the Service of Deception (Women's Freedom Network 1998); see Kingsley R. Browne, Sex and Temperament in Modern Society: A Darwinian View of the Glass Ceiling and the Gender Gap, 37 Ariz. L. Rev. 971, 1032 (1995).

education programs, to repeat a grade, to have a learning disability, and to create a discipline problem. So too, they participate less in extracurricular activities and attend college at lower rates than their female counterparts, suggesting a "new gender gap."[147] What can be done about it is less clear.

Also open to dispute is whether single-sex education is likely to address the disadvantages confronting either sex. Advocates argue that male and female students learn differently, and that they benefit from classrooms geared toward their special needs and without the distractions related to sex.[148] Evidence on this point is mixed. Not all studies find fewer distractions or greater academic achievements in single-sex environments, and some school districts have discontinued such initiatives. However, other evidence, including studies of Catholic schools, indicates that single-sex settings significantly benefit some students, particularly those from poor and minority communities.[149] The most comprehensive meta-analysis of existing studies, by the Department of Education and American Institute for Research, found that 41 percent documented advantages, 45 percent found no influence; 8 percent favored co-ed schools, and 6 percent found mixed effects (positive results for one sex but not the other).[150] Authors of another meta-analysis criticized the "pseudoscience" of single-sex education, arguing that it "is deeply misguided, and often justified by weak, cherry-picked, or misconstrued scientific claims rather than by valid scientific evidence." According to their analysis of existing studies, "[t]here is no well-designed research showing that single-sex education improves students' academic performance, but there is evidence that sex segregation increases stereotyping and legitimizes institutional sexism."[151]

Women's rights groups, including the Women's Rights Project of the American Civil Liberties Union and the National Organization for Women,

147. See, e.g., Mark Hugo Lopez & Ana Gonzalez-Barrera, Women's College Enrollment Gains Leave Men Behind, Pew Research Center (Mar. 6, 2014), http://www.pewresearch.org/fact-tank/2014/03/06/womens-college-enrollment-gains-leave-men-behind/; Michelle Conlin, The New Gender Gap: From Kindergarten to Grad School, Boys Are Becoming the Second Sex, Bus. Wk. Online (May 26, 2003), http://www.businessweek.com/magazine/content/03_21/b3834001_mz001.htm; Christina Hoff Sommers, The War Against Boys: How Misguided Feminism Is Harming Our Young Men (2000).

148. For reviews of the evidence, see Rebecca A. Kiselewich, In Defense of the 2006 Title IX Regulations for Single-Sex Public Education: How Separate Can Be Equal, 49 B.C. L. Rev. 217, 229-30 (2008); Sara Mead, The Evidence Suggests Otherwise: The Truth About Boys and Girls (2006), www.educationsector.org.

149. See William Raspberry, Same-Sex Schools Work—Sometimes, Wash. Post, Mar. 16, 1998, at A21.

150. Elizabeth Weil, Teaching Boys and Girls Separately, N.Y. Times Mag., Mar. 2, 2008, at 8; see also U.S. Dep't of Educ., Early Implementation of Public Single-Sex Schools: Perceptions and Characteristics (2008).

151. Diane F. Halpern et al., The Pseudoscience of Single-Sex Schooling, 333 Science 1706 (2011); see also Rosalind C. Barnett & Caryl Rivers, The Truth About Girls and Boys (2011) (analyzing international research on single-sex education and reaching conclusions similar to Halpern's).

have opposed sex-segregated schools and classrooms, and have challenged the Department of Education regulations that allow them. These groups argue that the single-sex model reinforces gender stereotypes. They also draw on evidence that the positive outcomes from same-sex schooling are due less to gender segregation than to other factors, such as student background, small class size, favorable faculty-student ratio, or special mentoring programs—features that could be replicated in co-ed schools.[152] The AAUW believes "single-sex education without proper attention to civil rights protections can reinforce problematic gender stereotypes, increase discrimination, and restrict the educational opportunities open to both girls and boys. Where separate programs are established for boys and girls, such programs have tended to be distinctly unequal, with fewer resources allocated for girls programs."[153]

In 2012, the ACLU launched a campaign styled "Teach Kids, Not Stereotypes"; the group claims that many single-sex programs violate Title IX and the Equal Protection Clause and has filed complaints against several public school districts. A preliminary report documents widespread instances of reliance on stereotyped attitudes and discredited science, including the idea that "boys are better than girls in math because boys' brains receive several daily 'surges' of testosterone, whereas girls can perform well on tests only a few days per month when they experience 'increased estrogen during the menstrual cycle.'"[154] Is the ACLU right that the 2006 regulations green-lighting the establishment of more single-sex public schools and classes should be repealed?

In 2014, OCR issued a new guidance, presented in a user-friendly Q&A format, designed to ensure single-sex opportunities in public schools comply with federal law. It directly addresses some of the concerns identified in the ACLU report, particularly with respect to generalized claims about teaching methods that work for "all boys" or "all girls."[155] The guidance explains, for example, that even if there were reliable evidence to show that girls learn better

152. For a summary of the debate on these issues, see Rosemary Salomone, Feminist Voices in the Debate over Single-Sex Schooling: Finding Common Ground, 11 Mich. J. Gender & L. 63 (2004); see also Gary J. Simson, Separate but Equal and Single-Sex Schools, 90 Cornell L. Rev. 443, 452-53 (2005).

153. AAUW, Position on Single-Sex Education, http://www.aauw.org/act/issue_advocacy/actionpages/singlesex.cfm.

154. ACLU, Preliminary Findings of ACLU "Teach Kids, Not Stereotypes" Campaign, at 3 (Aug. 20, 2012), https://www.aclu.org/files/assets/doe_ocr_report2_0.pdf. (quoting Michael Gurian & Arlette Ballew, The Boys and Girls Learn Differently Action Guide for Teachers 100 (2003)); see also Feminist Majority Foundation, The State of Public School Sex Segregation in the United States (June 26, 2012), http://www.feminist.org/research/fmf.asp (finding, in study of single-sex education in public schools from 2007-10, widespread noncompliance with Title IX and the Equal Protection Clause).

155. OCR, Questions and Answers on Title IX and Single-Sex Elementary and Secondary Classes and Extracurricular Activities (Dec. 1, 2014), http://www2.ed.gov/about/offices/list/ocr/docs/faqs-title-ix-single-sex-201412.pdf.

in warmer classrooms and boys in colder ones, that evidence would be insufficient to support single-sex classrooms with different temperatures. A school could establish a co-educational "warm" classroom and a co-educational "cold" classroom and allow students to choose. But to mandate sex-segregated classes because of temperature, the school would have to prove not only that boys learn better in a cold environment, but also that they "would learn better in a cold environment *with no girls.*"

David Cohen and Nancy Levit reviewed developments after the 2006 regulation change. They concluded that "seven years into an unconstitutional experiment that is promising a false bill of goods to parents and children and delivering significant damage in the form of stereotypes and sexism," the "arguments against sex segregation in public schools are even stronger than they were before. . . ."[156] Rosemary Salomone reviews the same history, but argues that the debate has become too ideological and strident, trampling on the evidence that single-sex education can be beneficial to some students in some circumstances.[157] What role, if any, do you believe sex segregation should play in public education?

3. Race and Single-Sex Schooling. Although female students routinely graduate from high school and college at a higher rate than their male classmates, the most significant disparities in educational achievement are not based on gender but on race, ethnicity, and income levels.[158] In the 1980s and 1990s, the rise in single-sex secondary schools reflected a desire to assist racial and ethnic minorities. During this period, schools for boys in inner-city neighborhoods were founded, and a Young Women's Leadership School in East Harlem was launched. Other urban centers later followed suit. These single-sex schools have aimed to increase positive role models, raise self-esteem, and nurture academic values. All-female academies have been especially successful in achieving high levels of college enrollments and low dropout rates.[159] Opinion within the African-American community is mixed, with groups like the NAACP opposing sex-segregated schools, and others welcoming the extra help they might bring to at-risk children who suffer from disproportionate homicide and school dropout rates, as well as poor grades and test performance.

156. David S. Cohen & Nancy Levit, 44 Seton Hall L. Rev. 339, 392 (2014).

157. Rosemary Salomone, Rights and Wrongs in the Debate Over Single-Sex Schools, 93 B.U. L. Rev. 971 (2013).

158. Tamar Lewin, Girls' Gains Have Not Cost Boys, Report Says, N.Y. Times, May 20, 2008, at A17.

159. Leonard Sax, Why Gender Matters: What Parents and Teachers Need to Know About the Emerging Science of Sex Differences (2006); National Association for Single Sex Public Education, Advantages for Girls and Advantages for Boys (2006); Rosemary Salomone, Same, Different, Equal: Rethinking Single Sex Education (2003).

In *Garrett v. Board of Education of School District of Detroit*, plaintiffs (represented by the ACLU and the NOW Legal Defense and Education Fund) successfully challenged the exclusion of girls from the Detroit all-male, black academies.[160] A federal district court held that excluding girls served no substantial interest and violated both the federal and the state constitutions, as well as Title IX. Critics of the academies argued that

> [t]he all-male black school is paternalistic. It stigmatizes boys, ignores girls, and brazenly discounts women as capable teachers of boys. In the minds of all-male black school advocates, only males can teach boys to become men.[161]

Is this a fair critique? Data at the time showed that the homicide rate for black males between the ages of 18 and 24 in Wayne County, Michigan, was 14 times the national rate, that the dropout rate for males was twice that of females, that boys were suspended three times as often as girls, and that scores on standardized tests were consistently lower.[162] Does this data change the picture?

Explicitly all-black academies would be difficult to sustain under existing race discrimination law, which requires the almost impossible task of showing that these schools are a narrowly tailored means to address specific prior intentional discrimination or to achieve a compelling state purpose.[163] General societal discrimination will not do. As a practical matter, however, given the small number of white residents in most inner-city school districts, de facto racial segregation is common.

Putting Theory Into Practice

2-13. In a footnote to her *VMI* opinion, Justice Ginsburg cites a claim by educational experts that: "The all-male college would be relatively easy to defend if it emerged from a world in which women were established as fully equal to men." What underlies this claim?

2-14. A female Women's Studies professor at a co-educational college does not let men enroll in her feminist ethics course, arguing that, in her experience, male students inhibit the participation of women. As an alternative for male students, she offers one-on-one tutorials, which about two dozen men have taken since she began teaching in 1966. She is sued by a male student

---

160. 775 F. Supp. 1004 (E.D. Mich. 1991).

161. Michael Meyers, The Non-Viability of Single-Race, Single-Sex Schools, 21 N.Y.U. Rev. L. & Soc. Change 663, 665-66 (1994-1995).

162. Note, Inner-City Single-Sex Schools: Educational Reform or Invidious Discrimination?; 105 Harv. L. Rev. 1741, 1743-44 (1992).

163. City of Richmond v. J.A. Croson Co., 488 U.S. 469 (1989).

under Title IX, and under the Fourteenth Amendment's equal protection clause. Who should win?

2-15. In 1983, the first public high school in the United States was established geared specifically to gay and lesbian adolescents and their problems.[164] In 2016, Atlanta established Pride School Atlanta, a K-12 school designed for LGBT students. Is a separate school for LGBT students still a good model? What reasons might justify this model? What questions might you ask before advising a student to attend the Atlanta school? Of what relevance is a 2013 study showing that the overall climate for LGBT students across the country has improved, but that 55 percent report feeling unsafe because of their sexual orientation?[165]

2-16. King Abdalaziz University paid Virginia Tech $246,000 to design and operate a faculty development program for teachers from Saudi Arabia. In keeping with the preferences of the University, Virginia Tech created one class for about 30 male faculty members and a separate class for the 30 female faculty members. Eloise Coupey, an associate professor of marketing, filed a sex discrimination complaint.[166] Should she win?

2-17. In the early 1970s, college enrollments in the United States were roughly 43 percent female and 57 percent male. Today, these figures are reversed; about 56 percent of students are women. The widening gender gap is especially acute in lower-income categories.[167]

Should it be permissible for the university to enact an affirmative plan to boost male enrollment? Could private schools do the same under Title IX? One admissions officer explained the pressures: "gender balance matters in ways both large and small on a residential college campus. Once you become decidedly female in enrollment, fewer males, and, as it turns out, fewer females find your campus attractive."[168] Does this justify preferential treatment for male applicants? According to another admissions officer, such treatment is "not an issue of equity; it's an issue of institutional prerogative [to create] a

164. Michael Bronski, Rethinking the Harvey Milk School: Not-So-Fast Times at Queermont High, The Boston Phoenix, News & Features (Aug. 8-14, 2003), http://www.boston phoenix.com/boston/news_features/other_stories/documents/03073221.asp. For further information about the school, see www.hmi.org.

165. Gay, Lesbian & Straight Education Network, 2013 National School Climate Survey, http://www.glsen.org/article/2013-national-school-climate-survey.

166. See Virginia: Separate-Sex Classes, N.Y. Times, Aug. 11, 2005, at A19.

167. Nat'l Center for Education Statistics, The Condition of Education (May 2015), http://nces.ed.gov/programs/coe/indicator_cha.asp.

168. Jennifer Delahunty Britz, To All the Girls I've Rejected, N.Y. Times, Mar. 23, 2006, at A25.

community that will best serve both the men and the women who elect to be members of that community."[169] Do you agree?

2-18. Reconsider the practice of a school district requiring boys and girls to wear different color gowns at graduation.[170] Are complaints about such a practice too trivial to take seriously, or are they, as Grossman and Hayden suggest, part of a "larger game of gender oppression" that are important to stop? Do you feel the same way about a school district rule requiring that a prom king and queen need to be, respectively, a boy and a girl?

b. School Athletics

Some of the issues raised by single-sex education arise in the context of school athletics. Differences in boys' and girls' experiences with sports begin early and have lasting consequences. Is this justified by biological sex differences? Or is it a matter of stereotyping? What does the equality principle require?

One issue concerns whether school sports teams should be sex-segregated. Separate teams explicitly discriminate on the basis of sex, but they are generally thought to be justified because if female athletes had to compete with male athletes, their opportunities would be more limited. Given the physical differences between the sexes, it seems fair to let girls compete against girls, and boys against boys, as long as they each have equal opportunities to participate in sports. Separate girls' and boys' basketball teams would seem to benefit both. Opportunities may be separate, in other words, as long as they are equal. Is this reasoning consistent with the *VMI* case?

What happens, then, if because of student demand, a school only offers a particular sport either to girls or boys rather than separate teams for each? Should a boy, then, be able to compete for the girls' field hockey team, or a girl for the football team? Title IX of the Education Amendments of 1972 denies the right to try out for a team offered only to the other sex when the sport involved is a contact sport. However, courts have uniformly ruled that federal or state equal protection clauses prohibit the exclusion of girls from both contact and non-contact sports teams, if no girls' team is offered in the sport.[171] Thus, schools have been ordered to allow girls to try out for boys' teams in sports like wrestling, football, tennis, cross-country skiing, soccer,

---

169. Alex Kingsbury, Many Colleges Reject Women at Higher Rates Than for Men, U.S. News & World Report, June 17, 2007 (quoting Henry Broaddus, director of admissions at William and Mary).

170. See Problem 1-6 in Chapter 1.

171. See, e.g., Adams v. Baker, 919 F. Supp. 1496 (D. Kan. 1996); see also cases reviewed in Eileen McDonagh & Laura Pappano, Playing with the Boys: Why Separate Is Not Equal in Sports 137-44 (2008).

and golf. In sports like wrestling, some 6500 women compete on high school teams, largely against male competitors on predominately male teams. These female athletes are not always welcome participants, and some boys have forfeited matches rather than compete against girls.[172] What accounts for this resistance, and how do you think it should be handled?

One cluster of cases has involved boys who sued to be on all-girls' teams when there are no teams for boys in the same sport (e.g., volleyball or field hockey). These cases have been generally unsuccessful.[173] Under Title IX, only persons whose athletic opportunities have been limited historically by sex have the right to try out for a team offered to members of the other sex. This restriction has left male athletes with little hope of using Title IX to gain access to sports typically offered only to women, such as field hockey and volleyball. They have generally fared no better with constitutional equal protection rights (federal or state), on the grounds that their exclusion is substantially related to the important purpose of remedying athletic discrimination against girls and protecting their still-limited opportunities. Is this fair?

In an outlier case, the Massachusetts Supreme Judicial Court applied the state's equal rights amendment to permit boys to try out for female-only teams in sports not otherwise available to them such as field hockey.[174] The few boys who did so were often considerably larger, faster, and stronger than their female competitors, and parents, players, and coaches expressed safety as well as fairness concerns. And some team members complained that when "you win, people think it's only because of the boys on your team. It's so defeating."[175] Critics of allowing boys to play on girls' teams question whether such integration rights are fair to girls. For example, average height differences between boys and girls might create an unfair advantage in volleyball, where there is a nearly seven-inch difference in the height of the net used in girls' and boys' games. Skeptics also question whether letting boys onto a girls' team will change the experience of the game for girls, making it less fun and empowering for girls. How would you address these concerns?

Another group of cases involve girls who are especially talented and who want to compete on boys' teams instead of girls' teams, even though the

172. Robin Wilson, Oklahoma Hold 'Em, Chronicle of Higher Education, Apr. 4, 2008, at A8; see also Deborah L. Brake, Wrestling with Gender, 13 Nev. L.J. 486 (2013) (analyzing the phenomenon of match forfeitures as a form of gender backlash in response to the assertion of equality from the presence of girls in the sport).

173. See Petrie v. Illinois High Sch. Ass'n, 394 N.E.2d 855 (Ill. App. Ct. 1979); Williams v. Sch. Dist of Bethlehem., 998 F.2d 168 (3d Cir. 1993).

174. Williams v. Sch. Dist. of Bethlehem, 998 F.2d 168 (3d Cir. 1993). Atty. Gen. v. Mass. Interscholastic Athletic Ass'n, Inc., 393 N.E.2d 284 (Mass. 1979). For a discussion of this case, see Deborah L. Brake, Getting in the Game: Title IX and the Women's Sports Revolution 58 (2010).

175. Rick Reilly, Not Your Average Skirt Chaser, CNN/SI (Nov. 21, 2001), http://www.si.com/vault/2001/11/26/314458/not-your-average-skirt-chaser; see also Mike Wise, High School Sports in Field Hockey, a Twist on Title IX, N.Y. Times, Oct. 18, 2001, at S1.

school offers both (e.g., basketball). Plaintiffs in these cases have not fared well.[176] Title IX limits integration rights to sports that are offered only to one sex; constitutional claims also typically fail where there is already a girls' team in that sport. Should they succeed? Is the existence of a team for each sex a sufficient guarantee of equality for all players? Why might a girl prefer to play on a boys' team?

These two sets of cases are quite different. In the first, boys claim that, *as a group,* they are denied an opportunity that girls have. They lose because if boys were allowed on girls' teams, they could take over the team and substantially reduce opportunities for girls. In the second, girls seek to be treated *as individuals,* rather than as members of a group. Few will qualify for boys' teams, so their presence will have only a slight impact on opportunities for boys. Are the two cases comparable? If the boys lose their claims to participate on girls' teams, should girls also lose their claims to participate on boys' teams?

Some scholars have argued that separate teams are not justified, even on biological terms.[177] Katherine M. Franke, for example, questions the rationality of athletic sex segregation, given studies showing that as a result of women's increased access to coaching, nutrition, fitness, and sports medicine, the gap between men's and women's performance has narrowed. As she notes, between 1964 and 1985, female marathon runners "knocked more than an hour-and-a-half off their running times, while men's times during the same period have decreased by only a few minutes." She predicts that if "the gap between highly trained male and female athletes were to continue to close at the current rate, in thirty to forty years men and women would compete in these sports on an equal basis."[178] Is this plausible? Eileen McDonagh and Laura Pappano argue against "coercive sex segregation in sports," which is embodied in law, custom and tradition. The key problem they see with this system is

> that these policies are not based on the athletic ability of any particular girl or woman who seeks to 'play with the boys,' but are based solely on the sex categorization of girls and women as 'female.' Thus, coercive sex-segregated sports policies prescribe such segregation, regardless of the athletic talent or demonstrated qualifications of any particular girl or woman.[179]

McDonagh and Pappano argue that gender segregation turns primarily on stereotypes rather than physical differences and that separation perpetuates the

---

176. See, e.g., O'Connor v. Bd. of Educ., 545 F. Supp. 376 (N.D. Ill. 1982); cf. Thomka v. Mass. Interscholastic Ath. Ass'n, 22 Mass. L. Rptr. 263 (2007).

177. See evidence reviewed in McDonagh & Pappano, supra note 171, at 53-68.

178. Katherine M. Franke, The Central Mistake of Sex Discrimination Law: The Disaggregation of Sex from Gender, 144 U. Pa. L. Rev. 1, 37-38 (1995).

179. McDonagh & Pappano, supra note 171, at 8.

notion that women's sports are not "real," but rather a watered-down version of men's sports. The norm of separation codifies "historic myths about female physical inferiority and fosters a system which, while offering women more opportunities than ever before, still keeps them from being perceived as equal athletes to men."[180] Deborah Brake counters that neither sex separation nor integrated teams can solve the dilemma of difference as it plays out in this context:

> Neither model is costless. Shifting to a framework that offers coed opportunities for all athletes with no attention to gender could potentially wipe out the biggest gains Title IX has produced: the burgeoning numbers of girls and women who participate in competitive school sports. With gender-blind team selection and competition, the majority of female athletes could well be relegated to second-tier teams or club and intramural games with only token representation at the varsity level. . . . Although some individual female athletes might be better off with coed teams because of their ability to excel in competition with male athletes, women as a group would likely face diminished opportunities to play sports at the most elite levels.
>
> On the other hand, accommodating gender difference has its costs, too. It reinforces an ideology that has historically been used to justify the outright denial of sports opportunities to women and, more recently, to place a lower value on women's sports. Having separate men's and women's teams risks sending the message that women are inherently lesser athletes. . . . As the feminist sport historian Jennifer Hargreaves explains the dilemma, separation can increase women's control over sport, mobilize women to fight for equal resources, and enable them to participate in sports free from male domination, but it also re-creates social gender divisions and can exaggerate sexism, with the message that biological sex, rather than culture, defines athleticism.[1]
>
> This is the classic dilemma of difference, leaving advocates for gender equality damned if they ignore gender and damned if they don't. Title IX negotiates this terrain with a flexible and pragmatic approach. . . .[181]

How would you resolve this "dilemma of difference?" Does segregation or integration best serve equality?

≣ ### *Cohen v. Brown University*
101 F.3d 155 (1st Cir. 1996)

Bownes, Senior Circuit Judge.

This is a class action lawsuit charging Brown University, its president, and its athletics director (collectively "Brown") with discrimination against

---

180. Id. at 7.

1. Jennifer Hargreaves, Sporting Females: Critical Issues in the History and Sociology of Women's Sports (New York: Routledge Press, 1994), 25-34, 207, 208.

181. Brake, Getting in the Game, supra note 174, at 16-17.

women in the operation of its intercollegiate athletics program, in violation of Title IX of the Education Amendments of 1972, and its implementing regulations. . . . The plaintiff class comprises all present, future, and potential Brown University women students who participate, seek to participate, and/or are deterred from participating in intercollegiate athletics funded by Brown.

This suit was initiated in response to the demotion in May 1991 of Brown's women's gymnastics and volleyball teams from university-funded varsity status to donor-funded varsity status. Contemporaneously, Brown demoted two men's teams, water polo and golf, from university-funded to donor-funded varsity status. As a consequence of these demotions, all four teams lost, not only their university funding, but most of the support and privileges that accompany university-funded varsity status at Brown.

[Following a bench trial, the district court found Brown to be in violation of Title IX, and ordered a comprehensive plan for compliance be submitted. The court found the plan submitted was not comprehensive and did not comply with the opinion. The court rejected the plan and ordered Brown to elevate and maintain the women's teams at university-funded varsity status.]

. . . Brown challenges on constitutional and statutory grounds the test employed by the district court in determining whether Brown's intercollegiate athletics program complies with Title IX. . . .

I . . .

As a Division I institution within the National Collegiate Athletic Association ("NCAA") with respect to all sports but football, Brown participates at the highest level of NCAA competition. Brown operates a two-tiered intercollegiate athletics program with respect to funding: although Brown provides the financial resources required to maintain its university-funded varsity teams, donor-funded varsity athletes must themselves raise the funds necessary to support their teams through private donations. The district court found . . . that it is difficult for donor-funded varsity athletes to maintain a level of competitiveness commensurate with their abilities and that these athletes operate at a competitive disadvantage in comparison to university-funded varsity athletes. . . .

Brown's decision to demote the women's volleyball and gymnastics teams and the men's water polo and golf teams from university-funded varsity status was apparently made in response to a university-wide cost-cutting directive. The district court found that Brown saved $62,028 by demoting the women's teams and $15,795 by demoting the men's teams, but that the demotions "did not appreciably affect the athletic participation gender ratio." . . .

Plaintiffs alleged that, at the time of the demotions, the men students at Brown already enjoyed the benefits of a disproportionately large share of both the university resources allocated to athletics and the intercollegiate participation opportunities afforded to student athletes. Thus, plaintiffs contended, what appeared to be the even-handed demotions of two men's and two women's teams, in fact, perpetuated Brown's discriminatory treatment of women in the administration of its intercollegiate athletics program.

The district court . . . summarized the history of athletics at Brown. . . . It found that, in 1993-94, there were 897 students participating in intercollegiate varsity athletics, of which 61.87% (555) were men and 38.13% (342) were women. During the same period, Brown's undergraduate enrollment comprised 5,722 students, of which 48.86% (2,796) were men and 51.14% (2,926) were women. . . . [I]n 1993-94, Brown's intercollegiate athletics program consisted of 32 teams, 16 men's teams and 16 women's teams. Of the university-funded teams, 12 were men's teams and 13 were women's teams; of the donor-funded teams, three were women's teams and four were men's teams. At the time of trial, Brown offered 479 university-funded varsity positions for men, as compared to 312 for women; and 76 donor-funded varsity positions for men, as compared to 30 for women. In 1993-94, then, Brown's varsity program—including both university- and donor-funded sports—afforded over 200 more positions for men than for women. Accordingly, the district court found that Brown maintained a 13.01% disparity between female participation in intercollegiate athletics and female student enrollment, and that "[a]lthough the number of varsity sports offered to men and women are equal, the selection of sports offered to each gender generates far more individual positions for male athletes than for female athletes." . . .

The district court found from extensive testimony that the donor-funded women's gymnastics, women's fencing and women's ski teams, as well as at least one women's club team, the water polo team, had demonstrated the interest and ability to compete at the top varsity level and would benefit from university funding. . . .

The district court did not find that full and effective accommodation of the athletics interests and abilities of Brown's female students would disadvantage Brown's male students.

II

Title IX provides that "[n]o person in the United States shall, on the basis of sex, be excluded from participation in, be denied the benefits of, or be subjected to discrimination under any education program or activity receiving Federal financial assistance." . . . As a private institution that receives federal financial assistance, Brown is required to comply with Title IX.

The agency responsible for administering Title IX is the United States Department of Education, through its Office for Civil Rights. Congress expressly delegated to Department of Education the authority to promulgate regulations for determining whether an athletics program complies with Title IX. The regulation at issue in this case . . . provides:

(a) *General.* No person shall, on the basis of sex, be excluded from participation in, be denied the benefits of, be treated differently from another person or otherwise be discriminated against in any interscholastic, intercollegiate, club or intramural athletics offered by a recipient, and no recipient shall provide any such athletics separately on such basis.

(b) *Separate teams.* Notwithstanding the requirements of paragraph (a) of this section, a recipient may operate or sponsor separate teams for members of each sex where selection of such teams is based upon competitive skill or the activity involved is a contact sport. However, where a recipient operates or sponsors a team in a particular sport for members of one sex but operates or sponsors no such team for members of the other sex, and athletic opportunities for members of that sex have previously been limited, members of the excluded sex must be allowed to try-out for the team offered unless the sport involved is a contact sport. For the purposes of this part, contact sports include boxing, wrestling, rugby, ice hockey, football, basketball and other sports the purpose or major activity of which involves bodily contact.

(c) *Equal Opportunity.* A recipient which operates or sponsors interscholastic, intercollegiate, club or intramural athletics shall provide equal athletic opportunity for members of both sexes. In determining whether equal opportunities are available the Director will consider, among other factors:

> (1) Whether the selection of sports and levels of competition effectively accommodate the interests and abilities of members of both sexes;
> (2) The provision of equipment and supplies;
> (3) Scheduling of games and practice time;
> (4) Travel and per diem allowance;
> (5) Opportunity to receive coaching and academic tutoring;
> (6) Assignment and compensation for coaches and tutors;
> (7) Provision of locker rooms, practice and competitive facilities;
> (8) Provision of medical and training facilities and services;
> (9) Provision of housing and dining facilities and services;
> (10) Publicity. . . .

In 1978, several years after the promulgation of the regulations, the Office of Civil Rights published a proposed "Policy Interpretation," the purpose of which was to clarify the obligations of federal aid recipients under Title IX to provide equal opportunities in athletics programs. . . .

At issue in this appeal is the proper interpretation of the . . . so-called three-part test [developed to implement these regulations], which inquires as follows:

> (1) Whether intercollegiate level participation opportunities for male and female students are provided in numbers substantially proportionate to their respective enrollments; or
> (2) Where the members of one sex have been and are underrepresented among intercollegiate athletes, whether the institution can show a history and continuing practice of program expansion which is

demonstrably responsive to the developing interest and abilities of the members of that sex; or

(3) Where the members of one sex are underrepresented among intercollegiate athletes, and the institution cannot show a continuing practice of program expansion such as that cited above, whether it can be demonstrated that the interests and abilities of the members of that sex have been fully and effectively accommodated by the present program. . . .

The district court held that, "because Brown maintains a 13.01% disparity between female participation in intercollegiate athletics and female student enrollment, it cannot gain the protection of prong one." Nor did Brown satisfy prong two. While acknowledging that Brown "has an impressive history of program expansion," the district court found that Brown failed to demonstrate that it has "maintained a *continuing practice* of intercollegiate program expansion for women, the underrepresented sex." The court noted further that, because merely reducing program offerings to the overrepresented gender does not constitute program expansion for the underrepresented gender, the fact that Brown has eliminated or demoted several men's teams does not amount to a continuing practice of program expansion for women. As to prong three, the district court found that Brown had not "fully and effectively accommodated the interest and ability of the underrepresented sex 'to the extent necessary to provide equal opportunity in the selection of sports and levels of competition available to members of both sexes.'" . . .

The district court found that Brown predetermines the approximate number of varsity positions available to men and women, and, thus, that "the concept of any measure of unfilled but available athletic slots does not comport with reality." The district court concluded that intercollegiate athletics opportunities "means real opportunities, not illusory ones, and therefore should be measured by counting *actual participants*." . . .

IV

Brown contends that . . . the district court's interpretation and application of the test is irreconcilable with the statute, the regulation, and the agency's interpretation of the law, and effectively renders Title IX an "affirmative action statute" that mandates preferential treatment for women by imposing quotas in excess of women's relative interests and abilities in athletics. Brown asserts, in the alternative, that if the district court properly construed the test, then the test itself violates Title IX and the United States Constitution. . . .

Brown's talismanic incantation of "affirmative action" has no legal application to this case and is not helpful to Brown's cause. While "affirmative action" may have different connotations as a matter of politics, as a matter of law, its meaning is more circumscribed. True affirmative action cases have historically involved a voluntary undertaking to remedy discrimination (as in a program implemented by a governmental body, or by a private employer or institution), by means of specific group-based preferences or numerical goals, and a specific timetable for achieving those goals [citing, among other cases, Johnson v. Transportation Agency . . .].

Title IX is not an affirmative action statute; it is an anti-discrimination statute. . . . No aspect of the Title IX regime at issue in this case—inclusive of the statute, the relevant regulation, and the pertinent agency documents—mandates gender-based preferences or quotas, or specific timetables for implementing numerical goals.

Like other anti-discrimination statutory schemes, the Title IX regime *permits* affirmative action. In addition, Title IX, like other anti-discrimination schemes, permits an inference that a significant gender-based statistical disparity may indicate the existence of discrimination. . . .

From the mere fact that a remedy flowing from a judicial determination of discrimination is gender-conscious, it does not follow that the remedy constitutes "affirmative action." Nor does a "reverse discrimination" claim arise every time an anti-discrimination statute is enforced. . . .

Brown maintains that the district court's decision imposes upon universities the obligation to engage in preferential treatment for women by requiring quotas in excess of women's relative interests and abilities. With respect to prong three, Brown asserts that the district court's interpretation of the word "fully" "requires universities to favor women's teams and treat them better than men's [teams] . . . forces them to eliminate or cap men's teams . . . [and] forces universities to impose athletic quotas in excess of relative interests and abilities." . . .

Brown simply ignores the fact that it is required to accommodate fully the interests and abilities of the underrepresented gender, not because the three-part test mandates preferential treatment for women *ab initio*, but because Brown has been found (under prong one) to have allocated its athletics participation opportunities so as to create a significant gender-based disparity with respect to these opportunities, and has failed (under prong two) to show a history and continuing practice of expansion of opportunities for the underrepresented gender. . . .

To adopt [Brown's] relative interests approach would be . . . to . . . entrench and fix by law the significant gender-based disparity in athletics opportunities found by the district court to exist at Brown. . . . According to Brown's relative interests interpretation of the equal accommodation principle, the gender-based disparity in athletics participation opportunities at Brown is due to a lack of interest on the part of its female students, rather than to discrimination, and any attempt to remedy the disparity is, by definition, an unlawful quota. This approach is entirely contrary to "Congress's unmistakably clear mandate that educational institutions not use federal monies to perpetuate gender-based discrimination" . . . and makes it virtually impossible to effectuate Congress's intent to eliminate sex discrimination in intercollegiate athletics. . . .

Interest and ability rarely develop in a vacuum; they evolve as a function of opportunity and experience. The Policy Interpretation recognizes that women's lower rate of participation in athletics reflects women's historical lack of opportunities to participate in sports. . . .

[T]here exists the danger that, rather than providing a true measure of women's interest in sports, statistical evidence purporting to reflect women's interest instead provides only a measure of the very discrimination that is and has been the basis for women's lack of opportunity to participate in sports. Prong three requires some kind of evidence of interest in athletics, and the Title IX framework permits the use of statistical evidence in assessing the level of interest in sports. Nevertheless, to allow a numbers-based lack-of-interest defense to become the instrument of further discrimination against the underrepresented gender would pervert the remedial purpose of Title IX. We conclude that, even if it can be empirically demonstrated that, at a particular time, women have less interest in sports than do men, such evidence, standing alone, cannot justify providing fewer athletics opportunities for women than for men. Furthermore, such evidence is completely irrelevant where, as here, viable and successful women's varsity teams have been demoted or eliminated. . . .

Finally, the tremendous growth in women's participation in sports since Title IX was enacted disproves Brown's argument that women are less interested in sports for reasons unrelated to lack of opportunity. . . .

V . . .

Of course, a remedy that requires an institution to cut, add, or elevate the status of athletes or entire teams may impact the genders differently, but this will be so only if there is a gender-based disparity with respect to athletics opportunities to begin with, which is the only circumstance in which prong three comes into play. Here, however, it has not been shown that Brown's men students will be disadvantaged by the full and effective accommodation of the athletics interests and abilities of its women students. . . .

There can be no doubt that Title IX has changed the face of women's sports as well as our society's interest in and attitude toward women athletes and women's sports. . . . In addition, there is ample evidence that increased athletics participation opportunities for women and young girls, available as a result of Title IX enforcement, have had salutary effects in other areas of societal concern. . . .

One need look no further than the impressive performances of our country's women athletes in the 1996 Olympic Summer Games to see that Title IX has had a dramatic and positive impact on the capabilities of our women athletes, particularly in team sports. These Olympians represent the first full generation of women to grow up under the aegis of Title IX. . . . What stimulated this remarkable change in the quality of women's athletic competition was not a sudden, anomalous upsurge in women's interest in sports, but the enforcement of Title IX's mandate of gender equity in sports. . . .

Affirmed in part, reversed in part, and remanded for further proceedings. . . .

Biediger v. Quinnipiac University
691 F.3d 85 (2d Cir. 2012)

Reena RAGGI, Circuit Judge

Quinnipiac University appeals . . . from a permanent injunction ordered on July 22, 2010 . . . after a bench trial at which Quinnipiac was found to have violated Title IX of the Education Amendments of 1972 by failing to afford equal participation opportunities in varsity sports to female students. . . .

We affirm. . . .

[handwritten: Did not provide varsity sports to females]

I. Background

This lawsuit has its origins in Quinnipiac's March 2009 announcement that in the 2009–10 academic year, it would eliminate its varsity sports teams for women's volleyball, men's golf, and men's outdoor track and field, while simultaneously creating a new varsity sports team for women's competitive cheerleading. Plaintiffs . . . filed this action in April 2009, charging the university with violating Title IX by denying women equal varsity athletic participation opportunities, and seeking an injunction that, among other things, prevented Quinnipiac from eliminating its women's volleyball team. After a hearing, the district court preliminarily enjoined Quinnipiac from withdrawing support from its volleyball team, finding that Quinnipiac systematically and artificially increased women's teams' rosters and decreased men's teams' rosters to achieve the appearance of Title IX compliance. . . .

At trial, Quinnipiac maintained that it offered athletic participation opportunities to male and female undergraduates substantially proportionate to their respective enrollments. In support, it pointed to evidence showing that, of the 5,686 students enrolled in Quinnipiac's undergraduate programs in the 2009–10 academic year, 3,518 were female and 2,168 were male. Varsity rosters for the first day of team competitions in 2009–10 listed 440 varsity athletes, of whom 274 were female and 166 were male. Thus, Quinnipiac maintained that women represented 61.87% of the total student body and 62.27% of all varsity athletes, while men represented 38.13% of the student body and 37.73% of all varsity athletes.

Plaintiffs challenged Quinnipiac's count of its varsity athletes, arguing that (1) the university manipulated its team rosters to produce artificially undersized men's teams and artificially oversize women's teams; (2) counting the same women's membership on cross-country, indoor track, and outdoor track teams as three distinct athletic participation opportunities was unwarranted because Quinnipiac's indoor and outdoor track teams did not afford cross-country athletes genuine and distinct benefits; and (3) women who participated on the competitive cheerleading team should not be counted at all because the activity had not yet achieved the status of an intercollegiate varsity sport. . . .

II. Discussion . . .

Here, Quinnipiac elected to defend against plaintiffs' discrimination claim *only* by reference to the first safe harbor created by the three-part test, arguing that its athletics program provided "substantially proportionate" athletic participation opportunities to women. . . .

C. *Athletic Participation Opportunities for Women Runners: Discounting the Reported Numbers for Indoor and Outdoor Track*

During the 2009–10 academic year, the roster for Quinnipiac's women's cross-country team listed 18 athletes; the roster for its women's indoor track team listed 30 athletes; and the roster for its women's outdoor track team listed 30 athletes. Quinnipiac faults the district court for concluding that this represented 67 rather than 78 genuine athletic participation opportunities for women runners. We identify no error of law or fact in the district court's carefully reasoned resolution of this issue.

Before the district court, plaintiffs argued that Quinnipiac should not be allowed to count as 54 athletic participation opportunities the cross-country, indoor track, and outdoor track roster positions held by the same 18 women. As the district court recognized, the issue admitted no easy resolution. The 1996 Clarification plainly states that "an athlete who participates in more than one sport will be counted as a participant in each sport in which . . . she participates." 1996 Clarification at 3. But the trial evidence reflected circumstances not addressed in the 1996 Clarification: Quinnipiac's women cross-country runners were not afforded a choice as to whether to participate in more than one sport; they were required to do so. Specifically, their participation on the cross-country team was conditioned on their membership on the indoor and outdoor track teams. No other Quinnipiac athletes were required to join multiple sports teams. Notably, male cross-country runners were not required to join men's indoor and outdoor track teams. . . . Indeed, male cross-country runners were prohibited from representing Quinnipiac as individual entrants in indoor and outdoor track events. . . .

[T]he district court persuasively explained why a smaller number of cross-county runners, required to join Quinnipiac's track teams but participating in no competitions—or in one case, only one competition—could not be viewed as having been afforded multiple genuine athletic participation opportunities. . . . Specifically, five positions on the indoor track team and six

[handwritten margin note: No reg to join other V teams]

positions on the outdoor track team were held by cross-country runners who did not—and effectively could not—avail themselves of distinct participation opportunities on the track teams because they were injured or red-shirted. . . . Thus, the district court concluded that for injured and red-shirted cross-country runners, the athletic participation opportunities afforded by *mandated* membership on the indoor and outdoor track teams were "truly illusory."

What was not illusory, however, was Quinnipiac's ability to "pad[ ] its rosters" with female athletes who had "no hope of competing or otherwise participating meaningfully during the indoor and outdoor track seasons." As the district court aptly observed, it would be "unacceptable for Quinnipiac to pump up its women's track team rosters" by requiring every injured field hockey, soccer, and volleyball player to join these teams even though they "would never actually compete in the indoor and outdoor track seasons and, for that matter, would never want to enter a race." But, the district court found, "that is essentially what Quinnipiac is doing with its injured cross-country runners." Thus, the district court discounted Quinnipiac's claimed 30 athletic participation opportunities in indoor track by five, and its claimed 30 athletic participation opportunities in outdoor track by six. We conclude that this reduction in the total number of athletic participation opportunities for women runners in cross-country, indoor track, and outdoor track from Quinnipiac's claimed 78 to an actual 67 is fully supported by the record evidence and by the applicable law. . . .

Insofar as Quinnipiac questions the sufficiency of the trial evidence to establish a track participation requirement, the argument borders on the frivolous. When Carolyn Martin, who coached all Quinnipiac's running teams, was asked at her deposition about women cross-country runners also running track, she stated, "I require them to." . . .

D. Athletic Participation Opportunities for Women in Competitive Cheerleading: The Determination That the Activity Does Not Yet Qualify as a "Sport"

Competitive cheerleading, which Quinnipiac decided to create as a new women's varsity sport team for 2009–10, is a late twentieth-century outgrowth of traditional sideline cheerleading. Whereas sideline cheerleaders generally strive to entertain audiences or solicit crowd reaction at sport or school functions, a competitive cheerleading team seeks to pit its skills against other teams for the purpose of winning. . . .

The district court nevertheless concluded that the 30 roster positions that Quinnipiac assigned competitive cheerleading for 2009–10 could not be counted under Title IX because the activity did not yet afford the participation opportunities of a varsity "sport."

The district court observed that competitive cheerleading is not yet recognized as a "sport," or even an "emerging sport," by the NCAA, action that would have triggered a presumption in favor of counting its participants under Title IX. Nor has DOE recognized competitive cheerleading as a sport; to the contrary, in two letters in 2000, OCR indicated competitive cheerleading is presumptively not a sport, while leaving open the possibility for a different conclusion with respect to a particular cheerleading program. There is, however, no record evidence of any competitive cheerleading program being recognized by DOE as a sport.

Mindful of these circumstances, the district court proceeded carefully to review the structure, administration, team preparation, and competition of Quinnipiac's competitive cheerleading program to determine whether it nevertheless qualified as a sport whose athletic participation opportunities should be counted for purposes of Title IX. . . . The district court found that in terms of the team's operating budget, benefits, services, and coaching staff, competitive cheerleading was generally structured and administered by Quinnipiac's athletics department in a manner consistent with the school's other varsity teams. The district court noted two "minor" exceptions to this conclusion: Quinnipiac did not afford its competitive cheerleading team locker space; and because the NCAA did not recognize competitive cheerleading as a sport, the team did not receive NCAA catastrophic injury insurance and had to obtain it from a separate provider. With respect to factors relating to the team's preparation and competition, the district court found that the competitive cheerleading team's practice time, regimen, and venue were consistent with other varsity sports. . . . Finally, the purpose of the team—to compete athletically at the intercollegiate varsity level—was akin to that of other varsity sports.

At the same time, however, the district court identified a number of circumstances that sufficiently distinguished Quinnipiac's competitive cheerleading program from traditional varsity sports. . . . First, Quinnipiac did not—and, in 2009-10, could not—conduct any off-campus recruitment for its competitive cheerleading team. . . .

More important, no uniform set of rules applied to competitive cheerleading competition throughout the 2009-10 season. Indeed, in the ten competitions in which the Quinnipiac team participated during the regular season, it was judged according to five different scoring systems. Further, in these competitions, Quinnipiac did not face only varsity intercollegiate competitive cheerleading teams. Rather, it was challenged by "a motley assortment of competitors," including collegiate club opponents who did not receive varsity benefits, collegiate sideline cheerleading teams, and all-star opponents unaffiliated with a particular academic institution, some of whom may still have been high-school age. As the district court observed, "application of a uniform set of rules for competition and the restriction of competition to contests against other varsity opponents" are the "touchstones" of a varsity sports program. "Those features ensure that play is fair in each game, that teams' performances can be compared across a season, and that teams can be distinguished in terms of quality."

[Handwritten margin note: Cheerleading essentially the same as other sports, no lockers though]

The concerns raised by these irregularities in season competition were only aggravated by aspects of post-season play. Notably, competitive cheerleading offered no progressive playoff system leading to a championship game. Rather, it provided an open invitational, which neither excluded any team on the basis of its regular season performance nor ranked or seeded participating teams on that basis. . . .

Thus, [the district court] ruled that Quinnipiac's 30 roster positions for competitive cheerleading could not be counted for Title IX purposes because the activity did not yet afford women genuine participation opportunities in a varsity sport.

Accordingly, we conclude that the district court was correct not to count the 30 roster positions assigned to competitive cheerleading in determining the number of genuine varsity athletic participation opportunities that Quinnipiac afforded female students. [We agree.]

Cheerleading not a sport

E. Finding a Title IX Violation Based on a 3.62% Disparity

Having reduced Quinnipiac's claimed athletic participation opportunities for women by 41 — representing 30 competitive cheerleaders and 11 cross-country runners required to join the indoor and outdoor track teams but unable to compete on those teams because of their injuries or red-shirt status — the district court correctly found that the school had a total of 400 varsity athletic participation opportunities, of which 233, or 58.25%, were assigned to women. Because enrollment data established that 61.87% of Quinnipiac's undergraduate population were women, this indicated a 3.62% disparity in the athletic opportunities that Quinnipiac afforded women. The district court concluded that this disparity was sufficient to support a finding that Quinnipiac had failed to afford female students varsity athletic participation opportunities substantially proportionate to their enrollment. . . .

The district court itself recognized that "in strictly numerical terms," a 3.62% disparity presents "a borderline case of disproportionate athletic opportunities." But as the 1996 Clarification makes clear, substantial proportionality is not determined by any bright-line statistical test. . . . Instead, the Clarification instructs that substantial proportionality is properly determined on a "case-by-case basis" after a careful assessment of the school's "specific circumstances," including the causes of the disparity and the reasonableness of requiring the school to add additional athletic opportunities to eliminate the disparity.

Specifically, the district court pointed to record evidence showing that the 3.62% identified disparity was almost entirely attributable to Quinnipiac's own careful control of its athletic rosters. Although Quinnipiac claims that, but for a 0.27% increase in female enrollment in 2009–10 beyond its control, the disparity would have been only 3.35%, the difference is not one that undermines the district court's conclusion that Quinnipiac's voluntary actions largely caused the disparity. . . .

For TC

Accordingly, we reject Quinnipiac's challenge to the district court's finding that the school engaged in sex discrimination in violation of Title IX, and we affirm the order enjoining Quinnipiac from continuing such discrimination. . . .

Notes

1. Title IX and Women's Participation in Sports. At one time, strenuous physical activity was thought to be harmful to women's reproductive capacities and competition antithetical to their femininity. "Unsexed Amazons" on the playing fields were widely viewed as unattractive and some physicians worried that they would damage women's delicate nerves and physiques, or drain the "vital forces" necessary for reproduction.[182] The passage of Title IX reflected the more modern understanding that "girls who play sports have higher self-esteem, less risk of depression, a lower likelihood of engaging in high-risk behaviors, and perform better in school than girls who do not play sports."[183] Girls who participate in sports are also less likely to develop osteoporosis and breast cancer, less likely to have an unintended pregnancy, more likely to graduate from high school, and less likely to engage in an array of health-risk behaviors.[184] Although Title IX enforcement got off to a slow start, it is now widely regarded as having led to substantially increased opportunities for female athletes.[185] Under Title IX, participation in high school sports went from approximately 294,000 girls in 1971 to 3,173,000 in the 2010-2011 school year.[186] Participation in intercollegiate sports went from 32,000 before Title IX to over 196,000 in 2014.[187]

2. Title IX and Women's Interest in Sports. Since the ruling in *Cohen*, courts have uniformly upheld the three-part test against arguments from defendants that it amounts to reverse discrimination against men who, they argue, are more interested than women in playing sports.[188] Courts have ruled that men, as the overrepresented sex, are not protected by the three-part

182. Kathleen McCrone, Sport and the Physical Emancipation of English Women 1870-1914, at 6-7 (1988); Helen Lenskyi, Out of Bounds, Women, Sport, and Sexuality 38 (1986).

183. Deborah Brake, Revisiting Title IX's Legacy: Moving Beyond the Three-Part Test, 12 Am. U. J. Gender Soc. Pol'y & L. 453, 458 (2004).

184. Women's Sports Foundation, Title IX Facts Everyone Should Know (June 10, 2002), http://www.womenssportsfoundation.org/cgi-bin/iowa/issues/geena/record.html?record=862.

185. See Betsey Stevenson, Title IX and the Evolution of High School Sports, 25 Contemporary Economic Policy 486 (2007) (analyzing Title IX's impact statistically).

186. Nat'l Fed. of State High School Ass'ns, 2010-11 High School Athletics Participation Survey 52 (2011), www.nfhs.org.

187. See NCAA Sports Sponsorship and Participation Rates Report, 1981-82—2013-14, at 8, http://www.ncaapublications.com/productdownloads/PR1314.pdf.

188. See, e.g., Gonyo v. Drake Univ., 879 F. Supp. 1000 (S.D. Iowa 1995); Kelley v. Board of Trustees, 35 F.3d 265 (7th Cir. 1994); Miami Univ. Wrestling Club v. Miami Univ., 302 F.3d 608 (6th Cir. 2002).

test, and that the test's focus on expanding opportunities for the underrepresented sex is constitutional. The three-part test has also been applied to high school sports, and the OCR has repeatedly rebuffed requests by conservative groups to rescind its application in this context.[189] To the contrary, the OCR continues to actively enforce it against high schools.[190]

Despite courts' upholding of the three-part test, it remains controversial. President George W. Bush's administration made efforts to repeal or water-down the three-part test by making it difficult for women to show unmet interest in sports. In 2005, the OCR issued a policy clarification allowing schools to measure student interest via e-mail surveys, which triggered major criticisms from the NCAA, the Women's Sports Foundation, the National Women's Law Center, and the scholarly community.[191] One objection involves the survey methodology, which targets only current students and infers a lack of interest from a lack of response. Women students who have the interest and ability to play a particular varsity sport are unlikely to attend an institution that fails to offer it. Finally, and most fundamentally, it is charged that this strategy ignores one of the most fundamental lessons of Title IX and related social research; as Billie Jean King has succinctly put it, "interest reflects opportunities."[192]

The Bush administration guidance never gained widespread support and was short-lived; the Obama administration rescinded it in 2010.[193] Yet how else, apart from surveys, can institutions show that the interests and abilities of the underrepresented sex have been fully accommodated, as Title IX regulations require?

Some commentators continue to criticize the three-part test for failing to account for women's asserted lower athletic interest levels. Recently, some scholars have criticized the test from a cultural feminist perspective, arguing that the three-part test locks women into a model of sport that is designed for men's interests, and that women's athletic interests are more recreational and less competitive.[194] Do you agree? Are men inherently more interested (or well

---

189. See, e.g., Horner v. Kentucky High School Athletic Ass'n, 43 F.3d 265 (6th Cir. 1994).

190. Education Department Reaches Settlements of Title IX Athletics Complaints Against Four Districts, NSBA: Legal Clips (July 12, 2012), http://legalclips.nsba.org/?p=15271.

191. Office for Civil Rights, Additional Clarification of Intercollegiate Athletics Policy: Three Part Test – Part Three (2005).

192. Don Sabo & Christine H.B. Grant, Ctr. for Research on Physical Activity, Sport and Health, D'Youville College, Limitations of the Department of Education's Online Survey Method for Measuring Athletic Interest and Ability on U.S.A. Campuses (2005).

193. Office for Civil Rights, Intercollegiate Athletics Policy Clarification, The Three-Part Test, Part Three (2010). For a discussion of the relevant history, see Brake, Getting in the Game, supra note 174, at 219-21.

194. See, for example, B. Glenn George, Forfeit: Opportunity, Choice, and Discrimination Theory Under Title IX, 22 Yale J.L. & Feminism 1 (2010); Dionne L. Koller, Not Just One of the Boys: A Post-Feminist Critique of Title IX's Vision for Gender Equity in Sports, 43 Conn. L. Rev. 401 (2010).

served by) a hyper-competitive model of sport? How can we know whether gender differences in interest are authentic rather than socially constructed?

3. Affirmative Action or Remedy for Past Discrimination?   Is the three-part proportionality test adopted in *Cohen* an example of "affirmative action"? This depends, of course, on what one understands as a neutral fact or given, in relation to which some change might be understood as "affirmative" intervention.

Cohen rejects Brown's claim about the lack of greater women's interest in athletics based on factors controlled by Brown that historically seemed to have contributed to the problem. Scholars have identified numerous ways in which educational institutions have historically contributed to women's lack of interest. These include (1) the dominance of men in leadership positions in college athletics; (2) disparities in hiring, promotion, and pay between male and female coaches and resource inequalities in other expenditures for women's sports; (3) the linkage of sports with masculinity, which is evidenced in training methods built on norms of masculinity ("you throw like a girl"); (4) hostile or demeaning characterizations of female athletes; (5) lesbian-baiting; and (6) the objectification of women in sports (starting with the "quintessentially 'feminine' role" of cheerleaders who "[stand] at the periphery, offering unconditional support for the athletes who play the traditionally masculine role of competing in the primary athletic event").[195] One survey of Sports Illustrated coverage found that only 10 percent of the photographs were of women, and half of those were in provocative poses. Many female Olympic athletes appeared only in the swimsuit edition.[196]

Deborah Brake argues:

> [N]othing about sports as played in today's educational institutions is "natural"—not even what counts as a "sport." The popularity and revenue-producing potential of a sport is certainly not natural; it is carefully promoted and nurtured by the machinery of college (and professional) athletics. It is a product of countless social and institutional factors, including longstanding and continuing investments in facilities, personnel, programs, recruiting, marketing, and coaching. . . . These investments contribute to a certain image and status of a sport that greatly affect its marketability. The existence of average differences in male and female bodies in height and upper body strength does not "naturally" translate into inequality in markets and spectatorship.[197]

195. Deborah Brake, The Struggle for Sex Equality in Sport and the Theory Behind Title IX, 34 U. Mich. J.L. Reform 13, 74-122 (2001).

196. Janet S. Fink & Linda J. Kensicki, An Imperceptible Difference; Visual and Textual Constructions of Femininity in Sports Illustrated and Sports Illustrated for Women, 5 Mass Communication and Soc'y 317 (2002).

197. Brake, Revisiting Title IX's Legacy, supra note 183, at 481.

If Brake is right, what can Brown University do to "affirmatively" reverse the effects of its past practices? Should more sports be co-educational?[198] Or would shifting to a co-ed model of sports only further marginalize female athletes? Are there other ways of structuring sport that would make it more open to women?

4. Allocating Resources Under Title IX. In addition to requiring equal participation opportunities—the issue litigated in *Cohen*—Title IX also requires equal treatment of men's and women's teams. Some of the litigated cases address matters of unequal scheduling, access to fields, and equipment. For example, one case involved schools that scheduled girls' soccer in the spring, and boys' soccer in the fall, in order to stagger use of field space. As a result of the spring schedule, the girls' team was unable to compete in the New York Regional and State Championships, while the boys' team could compete. The appellate court found that this practice denied equality of athletic opportunity to the female team members, in violation of Title IX.[199]

The most frequent Title IX issue relates to the allocation of resources. Title IX regulations reviewed in *Cohen* make it clear that Title IX does not require that women's sports receive equal expenditures. The allocation of scholarships must match women's participation rates. With respect to athletic programs more generally, however, equality must be measured by consideration of a variety of open-ended factors relating to the availability of teams and levels of competition, equipment, supplies, scheduling, travel, tutoring, locker rooms, practice facilities, housing, publicity, and the like. Women account for 57 percent of college enrollments, but only 42 percent of athletes and 37 percent of program expenditures.[200]

A major problem, say many Title IX advocates, is the federal review policy. OCR does not audit or monitor the accuracy of data that schools report concerning gender equity, despite widespread evidence of error.[201] Nor does it routinely initiate Title IX compliance review proceedings on its own initiative. As a consequence, many experts worry that gender equity reports have become a "shell game," without strategies for holding the process accountable.[202] The "roster management" techniques used at Quinnipiac, at issue in

[handwritten margin note: No enforcement]

198. McDonagh & Pappano, supra note 171, at 252-55.

199. See McCormick v. Sch. Dist. of Mamaroneck, 370 F.3d 275 (2d Cir. 2004).

200. Vivian Acosta & Linda Carpenter, Women in Intercollegiate Sports: A Longitudinal, National Study—Thirty-Five Year Update: 1977-2012 (2012), http://acostacarpenter.org/AcostaCarpenter2012.pdf.

201. Paula Wasley, Education Dept. Ignores Rife Errors in Gender-Equity Data in College Sports Programs, USA Today Reports, Chron. of Higher Educ., Oct. 20, 2005.

202. Deborah L. Rhode & Christopher J. Walker, Gender Equity in College Athletics: Women Coaches as a Case Study, 4 Stan. J. C.R. & C.L. 1, 23 (2008) (quoting surveyed coach).

Biediger, are one example of this problem. The insufficiency of penalties is another widespread concern. Funding cut-offs are available in principle but not in practice. Nor does the OCR routinely pursue other options, such as referral of cases to the Department of Justice for further legal proceedings.[203] Surveyed college administrators have estimated that as many as 80 percent of schools may be out of compliance.[204]

5. Pregnant Student Athletes. Where do pregnant athletes fit in the male model of sport? This issue was thrust into the public eye in 2007 when ESPN's *Outside the Lines* ran a segment showcasing athletes who lost their athletic scholarships and dropped out of school when they became pregnant.[205] In response to criticism and controversy that followed, the OCR issued a "Dear Colleague" letter explaining the obligations under Title IX with respect to pregnant athletes.[206] The NCAA, which was taken to task in the ESPN program for not addressing pregnancy in its scholarship or eligibility rules, also took action. In 2008, it amended its scholarship rules to require members to treat pregnancy like other injuries or illnesses, which means that a school cannot withdraw a scholarship based on pregnancy alone.[207] It also issued a model policy on the treatment of pregnant and parenting students that it urges its members to adopt.[208] What would you expect a model policy to include? Should pregnant athletes have any restrictions or be entitled to any accommodations?

6. Title IX and Race. Girls and women of color have benefited from Title IX, but not as much as their white counterparts.[209] A report by the Women's Sports Foundation revealed that while the participation opportunities for women of color have increased dramatically since the passage of Title IX, they are still underrepresented when compared to enrollment—26 percent of the student body, but fewer than 18 percent of the athletes.[210] One reason for this is that the new sports that schools have added to come into compliance with the three-part test are often "country club" or suburban sports like soccer, lacrosse, golf, and tennis. Women of color are also clustered in certain sports, such as basketball. As Deborah Brake notes, nine

203. Women's Sports Foundation, Title IX Facts Everyone Should Know, supra note 184.

204. Jerome Solomon, Title IX, 30 Years Later: Sexes Still Unequal in Athletics, Houston Chron., June 23, 2002, at A1.

205. See Brake, Getting in the Game, supra note 174, at 170.

206. Office for Civil Rights, Dear Colleague Letter (June 25, 2007), http://www.ed.gov/about/offices/list/ocr/letters/colleague-20070625.html.

207. NCAA Division I and II Bylaw 15, §3.4.3; see also Bylaw 15, §3.2.2.

208. NCAA, Pregnant and Parenting Student-Athletes: Resources and Model Policies (2008), http://www.ncaa.org/documents/NCAAParentingHandbook.pdf.

209. See Deborah L. Brake & Verna L. Williams, The Heart of the Game: Putting Race and Educational Equity at the Center of Title IX, 7 Va. Sports & Ent. L.J. 199 (2008).

210. Women's Sports Foundation, Race and Sport (2015), https://www.womenssports foundation.org/en/home/advocate/title-ix-and-issues/title-ix-positions/race_and_sport.

out of ten black female athletes are on basketball or track and field teams.[211] Because Title IX has not spurred much growth in these traditional sports, women of color have not benefitted as much from the expansion in participation opportunities. Another problem is that girls of color are concentrated in nearly all-black schools in urban areas; with little offered to boys in those schools, "equality" does not bring many new additions for girls. In contrast, rich, suburban schools with well-funded athletic programs have had to add substantially to the girls' athletic programs to keep up with what is available to boys.[212] Are there any obvious solutions to the racial gap in obtaining the benefits of Title IX?

7. Redefining Sport. Is equality too limited a concept in college sports, if it means that women's intercollegiate sports will follow the road men's sports have taken? Some commentators recognized early on that Title IX reproduced in female sports the same pressure to produce high visibility and powerhouse teams that is endemic to male sports, rather than to increase participation in intramural and club programs and to promote the health and well-being of broad numbers of students. Before Title IX, the Association for Intercollegiate Athletics for Women (AIAW) pursued a less competitive model of sport than the NCAA. After passage of Title IX, which the NCAA had initially opposed, the Association successfully managed to swallow up the AIAW and take control over women's sports. This takeover, some have contended, imposed an overly commercial system on a program that had superior athlete-centered, educationally oriented values.[213] Do you agree? Would most female athletes? Could improving opportunities for women mean producing a more cooperative model of sport that better promotes physical and psychological health, teamwork, friendship, and recreation, rather than replicating the "male model"?

Putting Theory Into Practice

2-19. It is typical for co-ed intramural teams at colleges and universities to have requirements for participation by women in every game (for example, that at least two women be on the field, or in the batting line-up, at all times). What intramural rules exist at your school for, say, softball, or soccer? Do they

---

211. Brake, Getting in the Game, supra note 174, at 112-18.

212. See Regina Austin, Super Size Me and the Conundrum of Race/Ethnicity, Gender, and Class for the Contemporary Law-Genre Documentary Filmmaker, 40 Loyola L.A. L. Rev. 710 (2007); Katie Thomas, A City Team's Struggle Shows Disparity in Girls' Sports, N.Y. Times, June 14, 2009, at A1.

213. See, e.g., Mary A. Boutilier & Lucinda SanGiovanni, The Sporting Woman 173-76 (1983); Murray Sperber, College Sports Inc.: The Athletic Department vs. The University 322-32 (1990).

make sense from a gender quality perspective? What type of equality do they help to achieve? What is the cost?

2-20. A male student on a high school swim team was hazed by his teammates. The hazing including dragging him into a bathroom and shaving his head against his will; applying Icy Hot to him without consent to create a burning sensation; stealing his swim equipment; hitting him hard enough on the back to create a "five-star" handprint on his skin; and so on. He was not the only victim, but was the only one to seek help from the school. The coach told his mother that "it's best if we don't do anything about it at this point." The athletic director said "the boys don't look at [these actions] as hazing," but rather as "initiation." The superintendent said: "[h]ey lady, your kid's hair got cut." The hazing continued unabated. In a lawsuit, the boy alleged that the school officials "were willfully turning a blind eye to all of the awful things going on in the male swimming program because 'boys will be boys'," and that they did not permit similar types of hazing among female athletes.[214] Are the statements by the school officials sufficient to show the school's non-intervention was because of sex? If not, what other evidence would support or undermine his claim of sex discrimination?

2-21. In the United States, field hockey is typically a girls' sport. But when Keeling Pilaro moved to Long Island from Ireland, where he had been taught to play, he asked to play on the girls' team. As a sixth grader, he was invited to play for the local high school varsity field hockey team. He was a high scorer and earned "all-conference" honors. After two years, he was told that he was now "too skilled" to play for the girls' team. At 4 foot 8 inches tall and 82 pounds, he is no larger than the average female player on his team. The school administrators said they looked only at his skill level, which gives him an "unfair advantage," and decided that his presence was interfering with meaningful athletic opportunities for girls. Should he be allowed to play? Does it matter that he has been playing for two years already?[215]

2-22. Wesleyan University ordered its only two campus fraternities to admit women and to take steps to ensure they are "full members and well represented in the body and leadership of the organization." This announcement came at a time when other schools "were struggling with issues related to heavy drinking, dangerous behavior and sexual assault at fraternities and sororities."[216] What obstacles do you foresee in integrating women into a fraternity? Would you expect a co-ed fraternity to engage in less troubling

214. These facts are taken from J.H. v. School Town of Munster, __ F. Supp. 3d ___ (N.D. Ind. 2016).

215. Boy Wants to Play Girls' Field Hockey, timesunion.com (May 7, 2012), www.times union.com/default/article/Boy-wants-to-play-girls-field-hockey-3541070.php.

216. Marc Santora, Fraternity Sues Wesleyan University over Order to Admit Women, N.Y. Times, Feb. 19, 2015, at A24.

behaviors than an all-male one? In a lawsuit against the university challenging the order, who should prevail?

2-23. In *Biediger*, the district court refused to recognize cheerleading as a sport for Title IX purposes in part because the " 'application of a uniform set of rules for competition and the restriction of competition to contests against other varsity opponents' " are the 'touchstones' of a varsity sports program. Those features ensure that play is fair in each game, that teams' performances can be compared across a season, and that teams can be distinguished in terms of quality."[217] Are there other ways to determine whether an activity is a sport? Is this definition of sport gendered?

2-24. During his opening monologue at the 2016 Oscars, Comedian Chris Rock suggested that there was no reason for "actors" and "actresses" to compete in separate categories. Do you agree? Are the reasons for using sex segregation in sports or discouraging it for academics applicable?

D. SUBSTANTIVE EQUALITY IN THE FAMILY

1. The Right to Marry for Same-Sex Couples

The last two decades were witness to a flurry of legislation and litigation over whether gay and lesbian couples could marry. The earliest lawsuits claiming a right of same-sex couples to marry were filed in the 1970s. Same-sex couples in several states applied for marriage licenses and then sued after the clerks refused to issue them. Although the marriage codes at the time generally did not specify that only heterosexual couples could marry, courts construed them to exclude same-sex couples. In Jones v. Hallahan,[218] for example, an appellate court in Kentucky held that "marriage" in the state's statutes must be defined "according to common usage." It turned to Webster's dictionary and Black's Law dictionary to determine that marriage is the union between one man and one woman. It thus concluded that:

> It appears to us that appellants are prevented from marrying, not by the statutes of Kentucky or the refusal of the County Court Clerk of Jefferson County to issue them a license, but rather by their own incapability of entering into a marriage as that term is defined. . . .
>
> In substance, the relationship proposed by the appellants does not authorize the issuance of a marriage license because what they propose is not a marriage.[219]

217. Biediger v. Quinnipiac University, 691 F.3d 85, 104 (2d Cir. 2012) (citing district court opinion).
218. 501 S.W.2d 588 (Ky. Ct. App. 1973); see also Singer v. Hara, 11 Wash. App. 247 (1974).
219. *Hallahan*, 501 S.W.2d at 589-90.

The constitutional claims raised by the litigants in these early cases were dismissed out of hand. The U.S. Supreme Court granted certiorari in one cases, Baker v. Nelson, but ultimately dismissed the writ "for want of a substantial federal question."[220]

In the 1990s, a new round of lawsuits were filed alleging that state statutes that were silent on gender should be construed to permit same-sex couples to marry and that statutes that could not be so construed were unconstitutional under the equal protection and due process clauses of the respective state constitutions.[221] In Baehr v. Lewin, the Hawaii Supreme Court issued the first decision finding that a denial of the right to marriage to same-sex couples constituted sex discrimination.[222] Under its reasoning, the state constitution's equal protection clause required the government to show a compelling interest in denying marriage licenses to gay and lesbian couples. The court remanded the case to the trial court for resolution of that issue, but before that occurred, Hawaii voters approved an amendment to the state constitution providing that "[t]he legislature shall have the power to reserve marriage to opposite-sex couples." The legislature acted quickly to exercise that power and prohibit same-sex marriage.[223]

Although Hawaii did not legalize marriage for same-sex couples in the 1990s, the threat that it might fueled efforts at the state and federal level to ban the celebration and recognition of such marriages. Congress jumpstarted this movement with passage of the Defense of Marriage Act (DOMA) in 1996, which purported to give states the right to refuse recognition to same-sex marriages from other states and, more importantly, defined marriage as a union between a man and a woman for all federal-law purposes.[224] States followed suit with their own so-called mini-DOMAs; at the high point of anti-marriage-equality efforts, more than forty states had enacted statutes and/or constitutional amendments to ban the celebration and recognition of marriages by same-sex couples. Among other effects, these enactments prevented courts from applying the traditional rules of marriage recognition, which, as a matter of comity, tended to give effect to marriages as long as they were valid where celebrated.

Amid these growing obstacles, marriage equality proponents achieved their first state-level victory in Vermont in 1999. In Baker v. State, the Vermont Supreme Court held that the legislature had to allow same-sex couples to marry or to provide them with the same benefits.[225] The ruling in Vermont led to the

---

220. 191 N.W.2d 185 (Minn. 1971), appeal dismissed by Baker v. Nelson, 409 U.S. 810 (1972).

221. For a detailed description of these developments, see Joanna L. Grossman & Lawrence M. Friedman, Inside the Castle: Law and the Family in 20th Century America (2011).

222. 852 P.2d 44, 59-68 (Haw. 1993).

223. See Haw. Rev. Stat. §572-1 (2016) (amended to excluded same-sex marriage in 1997).

224. 28 U.S.C. §1738C (2012).

225. Baker v. State, 744 A.2d 864 (Vt. 1999).

legislative invention of the civil union. Then, in 2004, Massachusetts became the first state to legalize same-sex marriage. In Goodridge v. Department of Public Health, the Supreme Judicial Court ruled that the state constitutional guarantees of equal protection and due process were violated by prohibiting gays and lesbians equal access to marriage,[226] and, in a second ruling, that a civil union was not sufficient to cure the violation.[227] Gay and lesbian couples were thus permitted to marry on precisely the same terms as different-sex couples.

After *Goodridge*, there were a multitude of court decisions on the same issue, with mixed results.[228] The 2000s were a fraught political time, with significant developments for and against same-sex marriage across the country. Some states joined Massachusetts in legalizing same-sex marriage, while others fought it robustly. Meanwhile, tens of thousands of same-sex couples married, as marriage is not conditioned on residency. On the international front, many countries legalized same-sex marriage, including some, like Spain and Argentina, with strong Catholic populations. Same-sex couples also gained benefits in the private sector, even where the law did not require it. In 2007, about half of all Fortune 500 companies provided health benefits to domestic partners of their employees.[229]

The same-sex marriage revolution would eventually be resolved by the U.S. Supreme Court. Although the early cases were all filed in state court and under state constitutions—precisely to avoid review by the U.S. Supreme Court—some later challenges to state marriage bans and to DOMA were filed in federal court and raised federal constitutional claims. These cases queued up review by the Supreme Court.

≡ ***United States v. Windsor***
133 U.S. 2675 (2013)

Justice KENNEDY delivered the opinion of the Court. . . .

I

In 1996, as some States were beginning to consider the concept of same-sex marriage, and before any State had acted to permit it, Congress enacted

---

226. 798 N.E.2d 941 (Mass. 2003).

227. See Opinion of the Justices to the Senate, 802 N.E.2d 565 (2004).

228. Compare In re Marriage Cases, 43 Cal. 4th 757 (Cal. 2008) (striking down state ban on marriage by same-sex couples as a matter of state constitutional law) with Hernandez v. Robles, 855 N.E.2d 1 (N.Y. 2006) (upholding state ban against state constitutional challenge).

229. See The State of the Workplace for Gay, Lesbian, Bisexual and Transgender Americans 2006-2007 12 (2007), http://www.hrc.org/documents/State_of_the_Workplace.pdf; see also Catalyst, Lesbian, Gay, Bisexual, Transgender Workplace Issues (May 26, 2015), http://www.catalyst.org/knowledge/lesbian-gay-bisexual-transgender-workplace-issues.

the Defense of Marriage Act (DOMA). DOMA contains two operative sections: Section 2, which has not been challenged here, allows States to refuse to recognize same-sex marriages performed under the laws of other States. See 28 U.S.C. §1738C.

Section 3 is at issue here. It amends the Dictionary Act in Title 1, §7, of the United States Code to provide a federal definition of "marriage" and "spouse." Section 3 of DOMA provides as follows:

> In determining the meaning of any Act of Congress, or of any ruling, regulation, or interpretation of the various administrative bureaus and agencies of the United States, the word 'marriage' means only a legal union between one man and one woman as husband and wife, and the word 'spouse' refers only to a person of the opposite sex who is a husband or a wife. 1 U.S.C. §7.

The definitional provision does not by its terms forbid States from enacting laws permitting same-sex marriages or civil unions or providing state benefits to residents in that status. The enactment's comprehensive definition of marriage for purposes of all federal statutes and other regulations or directives covered by its terms, however, does control over 1,000 federal laws in which marital or spousal status is addressed as a matter of federal law. . . .

Edith Windsor and Thea Spyer met in New York City in 1963 and began a long-term relationship. Windsor and Spyer registered as domestic partners when New York City gave that right to same-sex couples in 1993. Concerned about Spyer's health, the couple made the 2007 trip to Canada for their marriage, but they continued to reside in New York City. The State of New York deems their Ontario marriage to be a valid one. . . .

Spyer died in February 2009, and left her entire estate to Windsor. Because DOMA denies federal recognition to same-sex spouses, Windsor did not qualify for the marital exemption from the federal estate tax, which excludes from taxation "any interest in property which passes or has passed from the decedent to his surviving spouse." . . . Windsor paid $363,053 in estate taxes and sought a refund. The Internal Revenue Service denied the refund, concluding that, under DOMA, Windsor was not a "surviving spouse." . . .

On the merits of the tax refund suit, the District Court ruled against the United States. . . . [T]he Court of Appeals for the Second Circuit affirmed. . . .

III

When at first Windsor and Spyer longed to marry, neither New York nor any other State granted them that right. After waiting some years, in 2007 they traveled to Ontario to be married there. It seems fair to conclude that, until recent years, many citizens had not even considered the possibility that two persons of the same sex might aspire to occupy the same status and dignity as that of a man and woman in lawful marriage. For marriage between a man and a woman no doubt had been thought of by most people as essential to the very definition of that term and to its role and function throughout the history of civilization. That belief, for many who long have held it, became even more urgent, more cherished when challenged. For others, however, came the beginnings of a new perspective, a new insight. Accordingly some States concluded that same-sex marriage ought to be given recognition and validity in the law for those same-sex couples who wish to define themselves by their commitment to each other. The limitation of lawful marriage to heterosexual couples, which for centuries had been deemed both necessary and fundamental, came to be seen in New York and certain other States as an unjust exclusion.

Slowly at first and then in rapid course, the laws of New York came to acknowledge the urgency of this issue for same-sex couples who wanted to affirm their commitment to one another before their children, their family, their friends, and their community. . . .

Against this background of lawful same-sex marriage in some States, the design, purpose, and effect of DOMA should be considered as the beginning point in deciding whether it is valid under the Constitution. By history and tradition the definition and regulation of marriage, as will be discussed in more detail, has been treated as being within the authority and realm of the separate States. Yet it is further established that Congress, in enacting discrete statutes, can make determinations that bear on marital rights and privileges. Just this Term the Court upheld the authority of the Congress to pre-empt state laws, allowing a former spouse to retain life insurance proceeds under a federal program that gave her priority, because of formal beneficiary designation rules, over the wife by a second marriage who survived the husband. . . .

Other precedents involving congressional statutes which affect marriages and family status further illustrate this point. . . .

Though these discrete examples establish the constitutionality of limited federal laws that regulate the meaning of marriage in order to further federal policy, DOMA has a far greater reach; for it enacts a directive applicable to over 1,000 federal statutes and the whole realm of federal regulations. And its operation is directed to a class of persons that the laws of New York, and of 11 other States, have sought to protect.

In order to assess the validity of that intervention it is necessary to discuss the extent of the state power and authority over marriage as a matter of history and tradition. State laws defining and regulating marriage, of course, must respect the constitutional rights of persons, see, *e.g.*, Loving v. Virginia, 388 U.S. 1 (1967); but, subject to those guarantees, "regulation of domestic relations" is "an area that has long been regarded as a virtually exclusive province of the States." . . .

The recognition of civil marriages is central to state domestic relations law applicable to its residents and citizens. . . . Consistent with this allocation of authority, the Federal Government, through our history, has deferred to state-law policy decisions with respect to domestic relations. . . . In order to respect this principle, the federal courts, as a general rule, do not adjudicate issues of marital status even when there might otherwise be a basis for federal jurisdiction. . . . Federal courts will not hear divorce and custody cases even if they arise in diversity because of "the virtually exclusive primacy . . . of the States in the regulation of domestic relations." . . .

Against this background DOMA rejects the long-established precept that the incidents, benefits, and obligations of marriage are uniform for all married couples within each State, though they may vary, subject to constitutional guarantees, from one State to the next. . . . DOMA, because of its reach and extent, departs from this history and tradition of reliance on state law to define marriage. . . .

The States' interest in defining and regulating the marital relation, subject to constitutional guarantees, stems from the understanding that marriage is more than a routine classification for purposes of certain statutory benefits. Private, consensual sexual intimacy between two adult persons of the same sex may not be punished by the State, and it can form "but one element in a personal bond that is more enduring." Lawrence v. Texas, 539 U.S. 558, 567 (2003). By its recognition of the validity of same-sex marriages performed in other jurisdictions and then by authorizing same-sex unions and same-sex marriages, New York sought to give further protection and dignity to that bond. . . .

IV

DOMA seeks to injure the very class New York seeks to protect. By doing so it violates basic due process and equal protection principles applicable to the Federal Government. . . . The Constitution's guarantee of equality "must at the very least mean that a bare congressional desire to harm a politically unpopular group cannot" justify disparate treatment of that group. Department of Agriculture v. Moreno, 413 U.S. 528, 534–535 (1973). In determining whether a law is motived by an improper animus or purpose, "'[d]iscriminations of an unusual character' " especially require careful consideration. [Romer v. Evans, 517 U.S. 620, 633.] DOMA cannot survive under these principles. The responsibility of the States for the regulation of domestic relations is an important indicator of the substantial societal impact the State's classifications have in the daily lives and customs of its people. DOMA's unusual deviation from the usual tradition of recognizing and accepting state definitions of marriage here operates to deprive same-sex couples of the benefits and responsibilities that come with the federal recognition of their marriages. This is strong evidence of a law having the purpose and effect of disapproval of that class. The avowed purpose and practical effect of the law here in question are to impose a disadvantage, a separate status, and so a stigma upon all who enter into same-sex marriages made lawful by the unquestioned authority of the States.

The history of DOMA's enactment and its own text demonstrate that interference with the equal dignity of same-sex marriages, a dignity conferred by the States in the exercise of their sovereign power, was more than an incidental effect of the federal statute. It was its essence. The House Report announced its conclusion that "it is both appropriate and necessary for Congress to do what it can to defend the institution of traditional heterosexual marriage . . . . H.R. 3396 is appropriately entitled the 'Defense of Marriage Act.' The effort to redefine 'marriage' to extend to homosexual couples is a truly radical proposal that would fundamentally alter the institution of marriage." . . . The House concluded that DOMA expresses "both moral disapproval of homosexuality, and a moral conviction that heterosexuality better comports with traditional (especially Judeo–Christian) morality." . . . The stated purpose of the law was to promote an "interest in protecting the traditional moral teachings reflected in heterosexual-only marriage laws." . . . Were there any doubt of this far-reaching purpose, the title of the Act confirms it: The Defense of Marriage. . . .

DOMA's principal effect is to identify a subset of state-sanctioned marriages and make them unequal. The principal purpose is to impose inequality, not for other reasons like governmental efficiency. Responsibilities, as well as rights, enhance the dignity and integrity of the person. And DOMA contrives to deprive some couples married under the laws of their State, but not other couples, of both rights and responsibilities. By creating two contradictory marriage regimes within the same State, DOMA forces same-sex couples to live as married for the purpose of state law but unmarried for the purpose of federal law, thus diminishing the stability and predictability of basic personal relations the State has found it proper to acknowledge and protect. By this dynamic DOMA undermines both the public and private significance of state-sanctioned same-sex marriages; for it tells those couples, and all the world, that their otherwise valid marriages are unworthy of federal recognition. This places same-sex couples in an unstable position of being in a second-tier marriage. The differentiation demeans the couple, whose moral and sexual choices the Constitution protects, see *Lawrence*, 539 U.S. 558, and whose relationship the State has sought to dignify. And it humiliates tens of thousands of children now being raised by same-sex couples. The law in question makes it even more difficult for the children to understand the integrity and closeness of their own family and its concord with other families in their community and in their daily lives. . . .

The power the Constitution grants it also restrains. And though Congress has great authority to design laws to fit its own conception of sound national policy, it cannot deny the liberty protected by the Due Process Clause of the Fifth Amendment.

What has been explained to this point should more than suffice to establish that the principal purpose and the necessary effect of this law are to demean those persons who are in a lawful same-sex marriage. This requires the Court to hold, as it now does, that DOMA is unconstitutional as a deprivation of the liberty of the person protected by the Fifth Amendment of the Constitution.

The liberty protected by the Fifth Amendment's Due Process Clause contains within it the prohibition against denying to any person the equal protection of the laws. While the Fifth Amendment itself withdraws from Government the power to degrade or demean in the way this law does, the equal protection guarantee of the Fourteenth Amendment makes that Fifth Amendment right all the more specific and all the better understood and preserved.

The class to which DOMA directs its restrictions and restraints are those persons who are joined in same-sex marriages made lawful by the State. DOMA singles out a class of persons deemed by a State entitled to recognition and protection to enhance their own liberty. It imposes a disability on the class by refusing to acknowledge a status the State finds to be dignified and proper. DOMA instructs all federal officials, and indeed all persons with whom same-sex couples interact, including their own children, that their marriage is less worthy than the marriages of others. The federal statute is invalid, for no legitimate purpose overcomes the purpose and effect to disparage and to injure those whom the State, by its marriage laws, sought to protect in personhood and dignity. By seeking to displace this protection and treating those persons as living in marriages less respected than others, the federal statute is in violation of the Fifth Amendment. This opinion and its holding are confined to those lawful marriages.

The judgment of the Court of Appeals for the Second Circuit is affirmed.

[The dissenting opinion by Chief Justice ROBERTS is omitted.]

Justice SCALIA, with whom Justice THOMAS joins, and with whom THE CHIEF JUSTICE joins as to Part I, dissenting. . . .

We have no power . . . to invalidate this democratically adopted legislation. . . .

The penultimate sentence of the majority's opinion is a naked declaration that "[t]his opinion and its holding are confined" to those couples "joined in same-sex marriages made lawful by the State." I have heard such "bald, unreasoned disclaimer[s]" before. *Lawrence*, 539 U.S., at 604. When the Court declared a constitutional right to homosexual sodomy, we were assured that the case had nothing, nothing at all to do with "whether the government must give formal recognition to any relationship that homosexual persons seek to enter." *Id.*, at 578. Now we are told that DOMA is invalid because it "demeans the couple, whose moral and sexual choices the Constitution protects," with an accompanying citation of *Lawrence*. It takes real cheek for today's majority to assure us, as it is going out the door, that a constitutional requirement to give formal recognition to same-sex marriage is not at issue here—when what has preceded that assurance is a lecture on how superior the

Condescending

majority's moral judgment in favor of same-sex marriage is to the Congress's hateful moral judgment against it. I promise you this: The only thing that will "confine" the Court's holding is its sense of what it can get away with.

. . . [T]he view that *this* Court will take of state prohibition of same-sex marriage is indicated beyond mistaking by today's opinion. As I have said, the real rationale of today's opinion, whatever disappearing trail of its legalistic argle-bargle one chooses to follow, is that DOMA is motivated by "'bare . . . desire to harm'" couples in same-sex marriages. *Supra,* at 18. How easy it is, indeed how inevitable, to reach the same conclusion with regard to state laws denying same-sex couples marital status. . . .

[T]hat Court which finds it so horrific that Congress irrationally and hatefully robbed same-sex couples of the "personhood and dignity" which state legislatures conferred upon them, will of a certitude be similarly appalled by state legislatures' irrational and hateful failure to acknowledge that "personhood and dignity" in the first place. As far as this Court is concerned, no one should be fooled; it is just a matter of listening and waiting for the other shoe.

By formally declaring anyone opposed to same-sex marriage an enemy of human decency, the majority arms well every challenger to a state law restricting marriage to its traditional definition. Henceforth those challengers will lead with this Court's declaration that there is "no legitimate purpose" served by such a law, and will claim that the traditional definition has "the purpose and effect to disparage and to injure" the "personhood and dignity" of same-sex couples. The majority's limiting assurance will be meaningless in the face of language like that, as the majority well knows. That is why the language is there. The result will be a judicial distortion of our society's debate over marriage—a debate that can seem in need of our clumsy "help" only to a member of this institution. . . .

[The dissenting opinion by Justice ALITO is omitted.]

Notes

1. *Windsor* Grounds. *Windsor* concerned the constitutionality of Section 3 of the Defense of Marriage Act (DOMA), which enacted a federal definition of marriage as one man and one woman, for purposes of federal benefits and entitlements. Section 2 of DOMA, which permits states to decline to recognize same-sex marriages from other states, remained in force. Nor did the *Windsor* decision reach the constitutionality of state bans on same-sex marriage.

What exactly is Justice Kennedy's reasoning in *Windsor*? Is it primarily a matter of federalism—i.e., states have the right to define marriage, to which the federal government should ordinarily defer? Obergefell v. Hodges, excerpted below, clarifies this question.

In previous state cases, the equal protection issue raised by challenges to state bans on same-sex marriage was whether discrimination based on sexual orientation is a form of discrimination "based on sex."[230] The argument was that a person banned from marrying someone of the same sex is being denied a privileged based on the sex of that person. The argument to the contrary was that there is no equal protection violation based on sex because men and women equally from marrying someone of the same sex. To the extent that, in *Windsor*, the equal protection issue was triggered by the plaintiff's sexual orientation, not whether she or her partner is male or female, the law has shifted ground significantly. How rigorous should judicial review of rules that disfavor persons based on their sexual orientation be? As much as sex-based rules and practices? Race-based rules and practices? This issue is examined in Chapter 1, Section B(2), Note 3.

2. Hollingsworth v. Perry. On the same day it issued the opinion in *Windsor*, the Supreme Court issued its ruling in Hollingsworth v. Perry,[231] a case in which it could have—but did not—rule on the question whether all state bans on same-sex marriage are invalid. That case involved the federal constitutionality of Prop 8, a voter referendum in California that banned the celebration and recognition of same-sex marriage. But the Supreme Court did not reach the question on the merits, ruling instead that the proponents of Prop 8, who stepped in to defend the law when state officials refused, did not have standing to appeal a district court ruling invalidating Prop 8. Dismissing the appeal, the Supreme Court ruling left in place the district court ruling—which meant that same-sex couples could then marry in California. But the Court left open the question whether other state bans were constitutional. It would reach that issue two years later.

Obergefell v. Hodges
135 S. Ct. 2584 (2015)

Justice KENNEDY delivered the opinion of the Court.

The Constitution promises liberty to all within its reach, a liberty that includes certain specific rights that allow persons, within a lawful realm, to define and express their identity. The petitioners in these cases seek to find that liberty by marrying someone of the same sex and having their marriages deemed lawful on the same terms and conditions as marriages between persons of the opposite sex.

---

230. See, e.g., Baehr v. Lewin, 852 P.2d 44 (Haw. 1993).
231. 133 S. Ct. 2652 (2013).

I

These cases come from Michigan, Kentucky, Ohio, and Tennessee, States that define marriage as a union between one man and one woman. The petitioners are 14 same-sex couples and two men whose same-sex partners are deceased. The respondents are state officials responsible for enforcing the laws in question. The petitioners claim the respondents violate the Fourteenth Amendment by denying them the right to marry or to have their marriages, lawfully performed in another State, given full recognition.

[Each suit was filed in the petitioners' favor at the district court level; the cases were consolidated and reversed by the Sixth Circuit.] This Court granted review, limited to two questions. The first . . . is whether the Fourteenth Amendment requires a State to license a marriage between two people of the same sex. The second . . . is whether the Fourteenth Amendment requires a State to recognize a same-sex marriage licensed and performed in a State which does grant that right.

II . . .

From their beginning to their most recent page, the annals of human history reveal the transcendent importance of marriage. The lifelong union of a man and a woman always has promised nobility and dignity to all persons, without regard to their station in life. Marriage is sacred to those who live by their religions and offers unique fulfillment to those who find meaning in the secular realm. Its dynamic allows two people to find a life that could not be found alone, for a marriage becomes greater than just the two persons. Rising from the most basic human needs, marriage is essential to our most profound hopes and aspirations. . . . [Marriage has been historically understood] as a union between two persons of the opposite sex.

That history is the beginning of these cases. The respondents say it should be the end as well. To them, it would demean a timeless institution if the concept and lawful status of marriage were extended to two persons of the same sex. Marriage, in their view, is by its nature a gender-differentiated union of man and woman. This view long has been held—and continues to be held—in good faith by reasonable and sincere people here and throughout the world.

The petitioners acknowledge this history but contend that these cases cannot end there. Were their intent to demean the revered idea and reality of marriage, the petitioners' claims would be of a different order. But that is neither their purpose nor their submission. To the contrary, it is the enduring importance of marriage that underlies the petitioners' contentions. This, they say, is their whole point. Far from seeking to devalue marriage, the petitioners seek it for themselves because of their respect—and need—for its privileges and responsibilities. And their immutable nature dictates that same-sex marriage is their only real path to this profound commitment.

Recounting the circumstances of three of these cases illustrates the urgency of the petitioners' cause from their perspective. Petitioner James Obergefell, a plaintiff in the Ohio case, met John Arthur over two decades ago. They fell in love and started a life together, establishing a lasting, committed relation. In 2011, however, Arthur was diagnosed with amyotrophic lateral sclerosis, or ALS. This debilitating disease is progressive, with no known cure. Two years ago, Obergefell and Arthur decided to commit to one another, resolving to marry before Arthur died. To fulfill their mutual promise, they traveled from Ohio to Maryland, where same-sex marriage was legal. It was difficult for Arthur to move, and so the couple were wed inside a medical transport plane as it remained on the tarmac in Baltimore. Three months later, Arthur died. Ohio law does not permit Obergefell to be listed as the surviving spouse on Arthur's death certificate. By statute, they must remain strangers even in death, a state-imposed separation Obergefell deems "hurtful for the rest of time." He brought suit to be shown as the surviving spouse on Arthur's death certificate.

April DeBoer and Jayne Rowse are co-plaintiffs in the case from Michigan. They celebrated a commitment ceremony to honor their permanent relation in 2007. They both work as nurses, DeBoer in a neonatal unit and Rowse in an emergency unit. In 2009, DeBoer and Rowse fostered and then adopted a baby boy. Later that same year, they welcomed another son into their family. The new baby, born prematurely and abandoned by his biological mother, required around-the-clock care. The next year, a baby girl with special needs joined their family. Michigan, however, permits only opposite-sex married couples or single individuals to adopt, so each child can have only one woman as his or her legal parent. If an emergency were to arise, schools and hospitals may treat the three children as if they had only one parent. And, were tragedy to befall either DeBoer or Rowse, the other would have no legal rights over the children she had not been permitted to adopt. This couple seeks relief from the continuing uncertainty their unmarried status creates in their lives. . . .

The cases now before the Court involve other petitioners as well, each with their own experiences. Their stories reveal that they seek not to denigrate marriage but rather to live their lives, or honor their spouses' memory, joined by its bond.

The ancient origins of marriage confirm its centrality, but it has not stood in isolation from developments in law and society. The history of marriage is one of both continuity and change. That institution—even as confined to opposite-sex relations—has evolved over time.

For example, marriage was once viewed as an arrangement by the couple's parents based on political, religious, and financial concerns; but by the time of the Nation's founding it was understood to be a voluntary contract between a man and a woman. See N. Cott, Public Vows: A History of Marriage and the Nation 9–17 (2000); S. Coontz, Marriage, A History 15–16 (2005). As the role and status of women changed, the institution further evolved. Under the centuries-old doctrine of coverture, a married man and woman were treated by the State as a single, male-dominated legal entity. See 1 W. Blackstone, Commentaries on the Laws of England 430 (1765). As women gained legal, political, and property rights, and as society began to understand that women have their own equal dignity, the law of coverture was abandoned. These and other developments in the institution of marriage over the past centuries were not mere superficial changes. Rather, they worked deep transformations in its structure, affecting aspects of marriage long viewed by many as essential.

History

These new insights have strengthened, not weakened, the institution of marriage. Indeed, changed understandings of marriage are characteristic of a Nation where new dimensions of freedom become apparent to new generations, often through perspectives that begin in pleas or protests and then are considered in the political sphere and the judicial process.

This dynamic can be seen in the Nation's experiences with the rights of gays and lesbians. Until the mid-20th century, same-sex intimacy long had been condemned as immoral by the state itself in most Western nations, a belief often embodied in the criminal law. For this reason, among others, many persons did not deem homosexuals to have dignity in their own distinct identity. A truthful declaration by same-sex couples of what was in their hearts had to remain unspoken. Even when a greater awareness of the humanity and integrity of homosexual persons came in the period after World War II, the argument that gays and lesbians had a just claim to dignity was in conflict with both law and widespread social conventions. Same-sex intimacy remained a crime in many States. Gays and lesbians were prohibited from most government employment, barred from military service, excluded under immigration laws, targeted by police, and burdened in their rights to associate.

For much of the 20th century, moreover, homosexuality was treated as an illness. . . . Only in more recent years have psychiatrists and others recognized that sexual orientation is both a normal expression of human sexuality and immutable.

In the late 20th century, following substantial cultural and political developments, same-sex couples began to lead more open and public lives and to establish families. This development was followed by a quite extensive discussion of the issue in both governmental and private sectors and by a shift in public attitudes toward greater tolerance. As a result, questions about the rights of gays and lesbians soon reached the courts, where the issue could be discussed in the formal discourse of the law.

This Court first gave detailed consideration to the legal status of homosexuals in Bowers v. Hardwick, 478 U.S. 186 (1986). There it upheld the constitutionality of a Georgia law deemed to criminalize certain homosexual acts. Ten years later, in Romer v. Evans, 517 U.S. 620 (1996), the Court invalidated an amendment to Colorado's Constitution that sought to foreclose any branch or political subdivision of the State from protecting persons against discrimination based on sexual orientation. Then, in 2003, the Court over-ruled *Bowers*, holding that laws making same-sex intimacy a crime "demea[n] the lives of homosexual persons." Lawrence v. Texas, 539 U.S. 558, 575 (2003). . . .

III

Under the Due Process Clause of the Fourteenth Amendment, no State shall "deprive any person of life, liberty, or property, without due process of law." The fundamental liberties protected by this Clause include most of the rights enumerated in the Bill of Rights. In addition these liberties extend to certain personal choices central to individual dignity and autonomy, including intimate choices that define personal identity and beliefs. . . .

Applying these established tenets, the Court has long held the right to marry is protected by the Constitution. In Loving v. Virginia, 388 U.S. 1, 12 (1967), which invalidated bans on interracial unions, a unanimous Court held marriage is "one of the vital personal rights essential to the orderly pursuit of happiness by free men." The Court reaffirmed that holding in Zablocki v. Redhail, 434 U.S. 374, 384 (1978), which held the right to marry was bur-dened by a law prohibiting fathers who were behind on child support from marrying. The Court again applied this principle in Turner v. Safley, 482 U.S. 78, 95, (1987), which held the right to marry was abridged by regulations limiting the privilege of prison inmates to marry. Over time and in other con-texts, the Court has reiterated that the right to marry is fundamental under the Due Process Clause.

It cannot be denied that this Court's cases describing the right to marry presumed a relationship involving opposite-sex partners. The Court, like many institutions, has made assumptions defined by the world and time of which it is a part. This was evident in Baker v. Nelson, 409 U.S. 810, a one-line sum-mary decision issued in 1972, holding the exclusion of same-sex couples from marriage did not present a substantial federal question.

Still, there are other, more instructive precedents. This Court's cases have expressed constitutional principles of broader reach. In defining the right to marry these cases have identified essential attributes of that right based in history, tradition, and other constitutional liberties inherent in this intimate bond. See, *e.g.*, *Lawrence*, 539 U.S., at 574. And in assessing whether the force and rationale of its cases apply to same-sex couples, the Court must respect the basic reasons why the right to marry has been long protected.

This analysis compels the conclusion that same-sex couples may exercise the right to marry. The four principles and traditions to be discussed demon-strate that the reasons marriage is fundamental under the Constitution apply with equal force to same-sex couples.

A first premise of the Court's relevant precedents is that the right to personal choice regarding marriage is inherent in the concept of individual autonomy. This abiding connection between marriage and liberty is why *Loving* invalidated interracial marriage bans under the Due Process Clause. Like choices concerning contraception, family relationships, procreation, and childrearing, all of which are protected by the Constitution, decisions concerning marriage are among the most intimate that an individual can make. Indeed, the Court has noted it would be contradictory "to recognize a right of privacy with respect to other matters of family life and not with respect to the decision to enter the relationship that is the foundation of the family in our society."

Choices about marriage shape an individual's destiny. As the Supreme Judicial Court of Massachusetts [in *Goodridge*] has explained, because "it fulfils yearnings for security, safe haven, and connection that express our common humanity, civil marriage is an esteemed institution, and the decision whether and whom to marry is among life's momentous acts of self-definition."

The nature of marriage is that, through its enduring bond, two persons together can find other freedoms, such as expression, intimacy, and spirituality. This is true for all persons, whatever their sexual orientation. See *Windsor*. There is dignity in the bond between two men or two women who seek to marry and in their autonomy to make such profound choices.

A second principle in this Court's jurisprudence is that the right to marry is fundamental because it supports a two-person union unlike any other in its importance to the committed individuals. This point was central to Griswold v. Connecticut, which held the Constitution protects the right of married couples to use contraception. Suggesting that marriage is a right "older than the Bill of Rights," *Griswold* described marriage this way:

> "Marriage is a coming together for better or for worse, hopefully enduring, and intimate to the degree of being sacred. It is an association that promotes a way of life, not causes; a harmony in living, not political faiths; a bilateral loyalty, not commercial or social projects. Yet it is an association for as noble a purpose as any involved in our prior decisions."

And in *Turner*, the Court again acknowledged the intimate association protected by this right, holding prisoners could not be denied the right to marry because their committed relationships satisfied the basic reasons why marriage is a fundamental right. The right to marry thus dignifies couples who "wish to define themselves by their commitment to each other." *Windsor*. Marriage responds to the universal fear that a lonely person might call out only to find no one there. It offers the hope of companionship and understanding and assurance that while both still live there will be someone to care for the other. . . . [W]hile *Lawrence* confirmed a dimension of freedom that allows individuals to engage in intimate association without criminal liability, it does not follow that freedom stops there. Outlaw to outcast may be a step forward, but it does not achieve the full promise of liberty.

A third basis for protecting the right to marry is that it safeguards children and families and thus draws meaning from related rights of childrearing, procreation, and education. The Court has recognized these connections by describing the varied rights as a unified whole: "[T]he right to 'marry, establish a home and bring up children' is a central part of the liberty protected by the Due Process Clause." *Zablocki*. Under the laws of the several States, some of marriage's protections for children and families are material. But marriage also confers more profound benefits. By giving recognition and legal structure to their parents' relationship, marriage allows children "to understand the integrity and closeness of their own family and its concord with other families in their community and in their daily lives." *Windsor*. Marriage also affords the permanency and stability important to children's best interests.

As all parties agree, many same-sex couples provide loving and nurturing homes to their children, whether biological or adopted. And hundreds of thousands of children are presently being raised by such couples. Most States have allowed gays and lesbians to adopt, either as individuals or as couples, and many adopted and foster children have same-sex parents. This provides powerful confirmation from the law itself that gays and lesbians can create loving, supportive families. . . .

Fourth and finally, this Court's cases and the Nation's traditions make clear that marriage is a keystone of our social order. Alexis de Tocqueville recognized this truth on his travels through the United States almost two centuries ago:

> "There is certainly no country in the world where the tie of marriage is so much respected as in America. . . . [W]hen the American retires from the turmoil of public life to the bosom of his family, he finds in it the image of order and of peace . . . . [H]e afterwards carries [that image] with him into public affairs." 1 Democracy in America 309 (H. Reeve transl., rev. ed. 1990).

In Maynard v. Hill, 125 U.S. 190 (1888), the Court echoed de Tocqueville, explaining that marriage is "the foundation of the family and of society, without which there would be neither civilization nor progress." Marriage, the *Maynard* Court said, has long been " 'a great public institution, giving character to our whole civil polity.' " This idea has been reiterated even as the institution has evolved in substantial ways over time, superseding rules related to parental consent, gender, and race once thought by many to be essential. Marriage remains a building block of our national community.

For that reason, just as a couple vows to support each other, so does society pledge to support the couple, offering symbolic recognition and material benefits to protect and nourish the union. Indeed, while the States are in general free to vary the benefits they confer on all married couples, they have throughout our history made marriage the basis for an expanding list of governmental rights, benefits, and responsibilities. These aspects of marital status include: taxation; inheritance and property rights; rules of intestate succession; spousal privilege in the law of evidence; hospital access; medical decision-making authority; adoption rights; the rights and benefits of survivors; birth and death certificates; professional ethics rules; campaign finance restrictions; workers' compensation benefits; health insurance; and child custody, support, and visitation rules. Valid marriage under state law is also a significant status for over a thousand provisions of federal law. See *Windsor*. The States have contributed to the fundamental character of the marriage right by placing that institution at the center of so many facets of the legal and social order. . . .

The limitation of marriage to opposite-sex couples may long have seemed natural and just, but its inconsistency with the central meaning of the fundamental right to marry is now manifest. With that knowledge must come the recognition that laws excluding same-sex couples from the marriage right impose stigma and injury of the kind prohibited by our basic charter. . . .

Objecting that this does not reflect an appropriate framing of the issue, the respondents refer to Washington v. Glucksberg, 521 U.S. 702 (1997), which called for a " 'careful description' " of fundamental rights. They assert the petitioners do not seek to exercise the right to marry but rather a new and nonexistent "right to same-sex marriage." *Glucksberg* did insist that liberty under the Due Process Clause must be defined in a most circumscribed manner, with central reference to specific historical practices. Yet while that approach may have been appropriate for the asserted right there involved (physician-assisted suicide), it is inconsistent with the approach this Court has used in discussing other fundamental rights, including marriage and intimacy. *Loving* did not ask about a "right to interracial marriage"; *Turner* did not ask about a "right of inmates to marry"; and *Zablocki* did not ask about a "right of fathers with unpaid child support duties to marry." Rather, each case inquired about the right to marry in its comprehensive sense, asking if there was a sufficient justification for excluding the relevant class from the right.

That principle applies here. If rights were defined by who exercised them in the past, then received practices could serve as their own continued justification and new groups could not invoke rights once denied. This Court has rejected that approach, both with respect to the right to marry and the rights of gays and lesbians. . . .

The right of same-sex couples to marry that is part of the liberty promised by the Fourteenth Amendment is derived, too, from that Amendment's guarantee of the equal protection of the laws. The Due Process Clause and the Equal Protection Clause are connected in a profound way, though they set forth independent principles. Rights implicit in liberty and rights secured by equal protection may rest on different precepts and are not always co-extensive, yet in some instances each may be instructive as to the meaning and reach of the other. In any particular case one Clause may be thought to capture the essence of the right in a more accurate and comprehensive way, even as the two Clauses may converge in the identification and definition of the right. This interrelation of the two principles furthers our understanding of what freedom is and must become.

The Court's cases touching upon the right to marry reflect this dynamic. In *Loving* the Court invalidated a prohibition on interracial marriage under both the Equal Protection Clause and the Due Process Clause. . . . The reasons why marriage is a fundamental right became more clear and compelling from a full awareness and understanding of the hurt that resulted from laws barring interracial unions. . . .

These considerations lead to the conclusion that the right to marry is a fundamental right inherent in the liberty of the person, and under the Due Process and Equal Protection Clauses of the Fourteenth Amendment couples of the same-sex may not be deprived of that right and that liberty. The Court now holds that same-sex couples may exercise the fundamental right to marry. No longer may this liberty be denied to them. Baker v. Nelson must be and now is overruled, and the State laws challenged by Petitioners in these cases are now held invalid to the extent they exclude same-sex couples from civil marriage on the same terms and conditions as opposite-sex couples.

[Part IV, in which Justice KENNEDY rejects the suggestion that the Court should defer to state democratic processes, is omitted.]

V

These cases also present the question whether the Constitution requires States to recognize same-sex marriages validly performed out of State. As made clear by the case of Obergefell and Arthur . . . the recognition bans inflict substantial and continuing harm on same-sex couples.

Being married in one State but having that valid marriage denied in another is one of "the most perplexing and distressing complication[s]" in the law of domestic relations. Williams v. North Carolina, 317 U.S. 287, 299 (1942). Leaving the current state of affairs in place would maintain and promote instability and uncertainty. For some couples, even an ordinary drive into a neighboring State to visit family or friends risks causing severe hardship in the event of a spouse's hospitalization while across state lines. In light of the fact that many States already allow same-sex marriage — and hundreds of thousands of these marriages already have occurred — the disruption caused by the recognition bans is significant and ever-growing. . . . The Court, in this decision, holds same-sex couples may exercise the fundamental right to marry in all States. It follows that the Court also must hold — and it now does hold — that there is no lawful basis for a State to refuse to recognize a lawful same-sex marriage performed in another State on the ground of its same-sex character. . . .

No union is more profound than marriage, for it embodies the highest ideals of love, fidelity, devotion, sacrifice, and family. In forming a marital union, two people become something greater than once they were. As some of the petitioners in these cases demonstrate, marriage embodies a love that may endure even past death. It would misunderstand these men and women to say they disrespect the idea of marriage. Their plea is that they do respect it, respect it so deeply that they seek to find its fulfillment for themselves. Their hope is not to be condemned to live in loneliness, excluded from one of civilization's oldest institutions. They ask for equal dignity in the eyes of the law. The Constitution grants them that right.

Justice SCALIA, with whom Justice THOMAS joins, dissenting. . . .

D-bag

The substance of today's decree is not of immense personal importance to me. The law can recognize as marriage whatever sexual attachments and living arrangements it wishes, and can accord them favorable civil consequences, from tax treatment to rights of inheritance. Those civil consequences—and the public approval that conferring the name of marriage evidences—can perhaps have adverse social effects, but no more adverse than the effects of many other controversial laws. So it is not of special importance to me what the law says about marriage. It is of overwhelming importance, however, who it is that rules me. Today's decree says that my Ruler, and the Ruler of 320 million Americans coast-to-coast, is a majority of the nine lawyers on the Supreme Court. The opinion in these cases is the furthest extension in fact—and the furthest extension one can even imagine—of the Court's claimed power to create "liberties" that the Constitution and its Amendments neglect to mention. This practice of constitutional revision by an unelected committee of nine, always accompanied (as it is today) by extravagant praise of liberty, robs the People of the most important liberty they asserted in the Declaration of Independence and won in the Revolution of 1776: the freedom to govern themselves.

State's rights

Until the courts put a stop to it, public debate over same-sex marriage displayed American democracy at its best. Individuals on both sides of the issue passionately, but respectfully, attempted to persuade their fellow citizens to accept their views. Americans considered the arguments and put the question to a vote. The electorates of 11 States, either directly or through their representatives, chose to expand the traditional definition of marriage. Many more decided not to. Win or lose, advocates for both sides continued pressing their cases, secure in the knowledge that an electoral loss can be negated by a later electoral win. That is exactly how our system of government is supposed to work. . . .

But the Court ends this debate, in an opinion lacking even a thin veneer of law. Buried beneath the mummeries and straining-to-be-memorable passages of the opinion is a candid and startling assertion: No matter *what* it was the People ratified, the Fourteenth Amendment protects those rights that the Judiciary, in its "reasoned judgment," thinks the Fourteenth Amendment ought to protect. . . .

This is a naked judicial claim to legislative—indeed, *super*-legislative—power; a claim fundamentally at odds with our system of government. Except as limited by a constitutional prohibition agreed to by the People, the States are free to adopt whatever laws they like, even those that offend the esteemed Justices' "reasoned judgment." A system of government that makes the People subordinate to a committee of nine unelected lawyers does not deserve to be called a democracy.

Judges are selected precisely for their skill as lawyers; whether they reflect the policy views of a particular constituency is not (or should not be) relevant. Not surprisingly then, the Federal Judiciary is hardly a cross-section of America. Take, for example, this Court, which consists of only nine men and women, all of them successful lawyers who studied at Harvard or Yale Law School. Four of the nine are natives of New York City. Eight of them grew up in east- and west-coast States. Only one hails from the vast expanse in-between. Not a single Southwesterner or even, to tell the truth, a genuine Westerner (California does not count). Not a single evangelical Christian (a group that comprises about one quarter of Americans), or even a Protestant of any denomination. The strikingly unrepresentative character of the body voting on today's social upheaval would be irrelevant if they were functioning as *judges*, answering the legal question whether the American people had ever ratified a constitutional provision that was understood to proscribe the traditional definition of marriage. But of course the Justices in today's majority are not voting on that basis; *they say they are not.* And to allow the policy question of same-sex marriage to be considered and resolved by a select, patrician, highly unrepresentative panel of nine is to violate a principle even more fundamental than no taxation without representation: no social transformation without representation. . . .

[The dissenting opinions by Justice ROBERTS and Justice THOMAS are omitted.]

Notes

1. The Internal Debate on Same-Sex Marriage.   The gay and lesbian community did not universally support the campaign for same-sex marriage. Early advocates argued that recognition of such marriages would ensure full legal benefits that were not otherwise available. In addition, it was thought, recognition of same-sex marriage would help to "normalize" the status of gays and lesbians, which could both stabilize those relationships and reduce the prejudice based on sexual orientation in society at large. But some worried that replicating the model of heterosexual unions would weaken the broader, extended relationships within lesbian communities; encourage possessive, patriarchal-style patterns of submission and dominance; and cultivate unacceptable distinctions between married and unmarried lesbians. This split was captured in a famous 1989 debate between Paula Ettelbrick, who was then the legal director of Lambda Legal Defense and Education Fund, and Tom Stoddard, her boss. While Stoddard argued for the aggressive pursuit of marriage equality, Ettelbrick argued as follows:

> [M]arriage will not liberate us as lesbians and gay men. In fact, it will constrain us, make us more invisible, force our assimilation into the mainstream, and undermine the goals of gay liberation. [A]ttaining the right to marry will not transform our society from one that makes narrow, but dramatic, distinctions between those who are married and those who are not married to one that respects and encourages choice of relationships and family diversity. Marriage runs contrary to two of the primary goals of the lesbian and gay movement: the affirmation of gay identity and culture; and the validation of many forms of relationships. . . .
>
> The moment we argue, as some among us insist on doing, that we should be treated as equals because we are really just like married couples and hold the same values to be true, we undermine the very purpose of our movement and begin the dangerous process of silencing our different voices. As a lesbian, I am fundamentally different from non-lesbian women. That's the point. . . .[232]

Despite Ettelbrick's argument, the fight for marriage equality became the centerpiece of the gay rights movement—culminating, successfully, in the *Obergefell* decision in 2015. But even now, some gay rights advocates continue to oppose marriage, or at least its centrality to the movement's agenda. Nancy Polikoff and others have argued that expanding the right to marry to same-sex couples simply ensures that marriage will continue to be the "only worthy form of family relationship," one that is "economically privileged above all others."[233] Newly endowed with the right to marry, same-sex couples will be forced to choose marriage, just as heterosexual couples have done, in order to obtain the benefits of state and societal support. Katherine Franke, also a long-standing skeptic of the push for marriage equality, draws on the history and experience of freed African-American slaves who gained the right to marry to write a cautionary tale. "What have we gotten ourselves into?" is the question she poses to the LGBT community in the wake of *Obergefell*. She fears the loss of alternative types of relationship recognition, which might allow all couples to customize their level and type of commitment, as well as the assimilation of

232. Paula L. Ettelbrick, Since When Is Marriage a Path to Liberation?, 2 Out/Look, Nat'l Gay & Lesbian Q. 9, 14 (Fall 1989); Thomas Stoddard, Why Gay People Should Seek the Right to Marry, Out/Look 8-12 (Autumn 1989). For a related view, see Katha Pollitt, Gay Marriage? Don't Say I Didn't Warn You, in Subject to Debate: Sense and Dissents on Women, Politics, and Culture 109 (Katha Pollitt ed., 2001).

233. Beyond Same-Sex Marriage: A New Strategic Vision for All Our Families and Relationships (July 26, 2006); Nancy Polikoff, Beyond (Straight and Gay) Marriage: Valuing All Families Under the Law (2008).

gay and lesbian couples into an institution that is perhaps inherently oppressive.[234] Do you agree with these arguments? Why or why not?

2. Backlash to Same-Sex Marriage. Backlash against *Obergefell* has been extensive. For discussion of resistance by some businesses to serving gay couples on religious grounds and the public accommodations laws that such refusals implicate, see Note 6 in Chapter 1, Section D. For discussion of efforts to strengthen federal law protecting the LGBT community from discrimination, see Note 6 in Chapter 1, Section C(2). For the issues raised by the clash between discrimination and religion more broadly, see Chapter 6, Section B. Specifically in the context of transgender rights, see Chapter 6, Section C.

Putting Theory Into Practice

2-25. Justice Alito asked, during oral argument in *Obergefell*, whether a ruling in favor of the petitioners would necessarily require states to issue licenses to groups of more than two consenting adults who wish to marry. Does it? Does polygamy threaten women's rights in the family?[235]

2. Marital Dissolution and Its Economic Consequences

a. The Traditional View

To the extent that women's role in the home has limited their opportunities in the world outside it, the traditional, heterosexual family has been a principal site of women's social and economic vulnerability. Under early Anglo-American common law, when a woman married, her identity merged with that of her husband. He assumed an obligation to support his wife and, in return, obtained total control of her property. Because wives lost their separate identity on marriage, they could not form contracts, keep their own earnings, acquire property, or bring their own legal actions.[236]

Gradually throughout the nineteenth century, legislation known generally as "married women's property acts" loosened these restrictions. However, well into the second half of the twentieth century, family law still disfavored women. Only eight states provided for joint ownership of "community property" acquired during the marriage. In the others, property acquired by husbands and wives typically was the property of the spouse who earned it—the husband in traditional households. As a result, women at divorce were often left with little or no property, even what they helped their husbands acquire.

---

234. See Katherine Franke, Wedlocked: The Perils of Marriage Equality (2015).
235. See Deborah Rhode, Adultery: Infidelity and the Law (2016).
236. See William Blackstone, 1 Commentaries on the Laws of England 430-32 (1765).

Orr → All receive alimony

At the same time, husbands typically owed their former wives continuing spousal support (often termed "maintenance" or "alimony"), unless the wife was determined to be at "fault" for the divorce.

Beginning in the late 1960s and 1970s, states began to pass no-fault divorce statutes and "equitable distribution" laws, designed to allow courts to divide property by taking into account a range of factors having to do with the child care as well as economic contributions of both spouses. As Chapter 1 indicated, the *Orr* case decided in 1979 that alimony had to be available on a gender-neutral basis to men as well as women. About the same time, often in the name of "equality," states moved to limit spousal support obligations to shorter periods in an effort to encourage women's economic independence and avoid reinforcing traditional stereotypes about women's role. Many states also moved to reduce the significance of fault in defining post-divorce obligations between the spouses.

With respect to parental rights, traditionally fathers had complete authority over their children, including the right to custody in the event of the parents' divorce. In the nineteenth century during what is sometimes referred to as the "cult of domesticity," states reversed that practice, creating legal presumptions giving mothers custody unless they were shown to be unfit (due to adultery, drunkenness, neglect and so forth). In the 1970s, explicit maternal presumptions were largely (although not entirely) eliminated in favor of the gender-neutral "best interests of the child" test.

Modern marriage and custody law reforms have been more controversial than one might expect because they have limited traditional protections for women without eliminating the economic vulnerability that women experience disproportionately at divorce. Most of the materials in this section explore the tension between formal and substantive equality principles: the desire to promote equal treatment and at the same time to ensure fairness for weaker parties, typically women, at divorce.

It bears emphasis that regulation of the family is primarily a matter of state, not federal, law. State statutes and court decisions vary widely on many questions, making it sometimes difficult to generalize about national trends. The cases and statutes in this section should be viewed as representative of their own time and jurisdiction, but not necessarily of the nation as a whole.

b. Modern Divorce

The divorce reforms that began in the 1970s had several objectives. One was the elimination of explicit gender distinctions, such as the rule invalidated in *Orr* that only wives could receive alimony and the presumptions favoring mothers in child custody cases. One of the questions explored in the next two sections is the extent to which this move to formal equality has promoted or undercut substantive equality between the sexes.

Not all aspects of the divorce reform movement explicitly concerned gender bias. One effort was to remove fault as a significant role in determining entitlement to divorce, custody, division of property, and spousal support. The requirement of fault often resulted in acrimony and false testimony, and was inconsistent with the modern notion of marriage as a complicated private relationship in which legal assignments of blame and innocence were often neither accurate nor constructive. It is not entirely clear whether the elimination of fault as a factor in divorce systematically favored, or disfavored, women. Although divorce is available now in every state on at least one ground that is not fault-based, fault continues to play a role in many divorces. Even in states that have only no-fault grounds for divorce, it is often hard to avoid fault considerations when judicial discretion is permitted in the distribution of property or the determination of spousal support.

Between forty and fifty percent of first marriages today end in divorce. Studies have consistently shown that women and children are, on average, worse off economically after divorce than men, although the extent of the disparity has declined over time and varies by study. Research based on the National Survey of Families and Households concluded that women who remain single after divorce now have, on average, a 14 percent drop in median per capita income, and remarried or cohabiting women a 3 percent decrease.[237] Women are also less dependent on others for economic support than in the past. Between 1980 and 2001, the percentage of divorced women who reported receiving spousal or child support declined from about one-third to one-fifth.[238]

Three factors affect economic well-being at divorce: property distribution; spousal support (or alimony or maintenance), and child support. Property distribution is a one-time distribution of the assets of the parties at divorce. Spousal support is an ongoing obligation of one spouse to the other after divorce. Child support is also a continuing obligation of one parent to the other, at least until the child reaches the age of majority.

It is relatively easy to make divorce laws in each of these areas formally equal; they simply have to apply the same rules to both sexes. Does equality require more than this? Should a substantive goal of divorce law be to ensure that women do not systematically leave marriage worse off than men? More broadly, what should be the priority of divorce law? Protecting the mutual expectations of the married couple when they got married? A clean break that encourages parties to get on with their lives? Equality? Justice? Women's

237. See Matthew McKeever & Nicholas H. Wolfinger, Reexamining the Economic Costs of Marital Disruption for Women, 82 Soc. Science Q. 202, 207 (Mar. 2001).
238. See Matthew McKeever & Nicholas H. Wolfinger, Shifting Fortunes in a Changing Economy, in Fragile Families and the Marriage Agenda 127, 149 (Lori Kowaleski-Jones & Nicholas H. Wolfinger eds., 2005).

autonomy? Self-sufficiency? Holding a guilty party accountable? What consequences follow from each of these possible goals?

Joan Williams, Do Wives Own Half? Winning for Wives After Wendt
32 Conn. L. Rev. 249, 253, 265-68 (1999)

[D]omesticity's peculiar organization of market work and family work first marginalizes mothers from market work, then limits their access to entitlements based on family work. The result is a system that is inconsistent with our commitment to gender equality, and leads to the widespread impoverishment of mothers and the children who depend on them. . . . [W]e need to deconstruct domesticity and develop in its place a new vision of morality in family life. . . .

The joint property theory begins from the principle that ideal workers who are parents are supported by a flow of family work from the primary caregiver of their children. If the ideal worker's performance depends on a flow of family work from his wife, then "his" wage is the product of two adults: his market work, and her family work. If an asset is produced by two family members, it makes no sense to award ownership to only one of them. We should abandon the "he who earns it, owns it" rule as an outdated expression of coverture, and give the wife half the accumulated family wealth based on her family work, without which that wealth would not have been created.

This is true whether or not the children are in child care. In the vast majority of families, the primary caregiver provides much of the child care even when the children are cared for by relatives, a nanny, or a day care center. Recent studies show that mothers spend three times as much time as fathers interacting with children. . . . Even when mothers' caregiving consists in part of finding child care and training and supervising child care workers, this, too, is work: managerial work. Studies show that women still do roughly 80% of the management work, even in families where men contribute substantially to the actual caretaking. We do not refuse to pay managers because their employees "really do all the work"; the same principle should apply to mothers.

The joint property theory has implications both for property division and for alimony. In the context of property division, it explains why wives should jointly own the family wealth, eliminating the unexplained jump in human capital theory between joint ownership and an enumeration of the specific contributions of the wife. It also provides the basis for arguing that the household of the custodial parent, often composed of three people, should have a greater share of family wealth than the household of the noncustodial parent, composed of only one. Certainly, in this context, a 50/50 split should be the floor, not the ceiling. In assessing how to split the family assets of a middle class family, the court should take into consideration how such families use their assets: to buy housing that offers a secure home environment and access to good schools, and to send children to college. Children should not lose these entitlements simply because their parents divorce and fathers prefer to found a new family rather than support the old one. In dividing family property, courts should begin from the principle that parents have the duty to share their wealth with their children. They should award more than 50% of family assets if that is necessary to ensure that the life chances of the family's children, to the extent possible, are unaffected by divorce.

In the context of very large estates consisting of more assets than are required to preserve the expectations of the family's children to decent housing and a good education, the joint property theory mandates a 50/50 split.

In most divorces, the key issue is not property division but human capital. This is true because no rule concerning property division makes much difference in most divorces: in our cash flow society, most families have accumulated few assets. Therefore, the key issue is income sharing: who owns the family wage after divorce. The joint property theory offers a new rationale for income sharing that begins from the observation that—after as well as before the divorce—the father can perform as an ideal worker only because the mother's family work allows him to do so. In an economy where ideal workers need to be supported by a flow of family work, a divorced father can continue to perform as an ideal worker only because his ex-wife continues to support his ability to be one by continuing as the primary caregiver of his children. Evidence of this is that divorced fathers with custody often cannot perform as ideal workers because they lack the flow of family work that supports fathers without custody. The joint property theory mandates not a 50/50 split but an equalization of the standard of living in the post-divorce two households.

Because the joint property theory mandates post-divorce sharing on the basis of its analysis of dependence in the modern family, it avoids the language of partnership and other commercial metaphors. . . .

The joint property theory also is quite different from the established theory that wives deserve half because of their contributions, particularly when lawyers focus on wives' direct contributions to husbands' businesses (as when a wife helps decorate the company offices). The joint property theory shifts the focus away from market work onto family work. The point is not that the wife helped the husband in business development, but that the husband could not have performed as an ideal worker without the marginalization of his wife.

If the joint property regime were put into effect, the next question is when it should end. I have proposed that joint property in wages should equalize the standard of living of the two post-divorce households for the period of the children's dependence, followed by a period of years designed to allow the wife to regain her ability to recover her earning potential (if she is young enough) or save for her future (if she is not). This additional period should be set at one additional year of income sharing for each two years of the marriage. . . . [T]his formula is designed to give the father an incentive to support his former wife's return to nonmarginalized market work: the more she earns, the less income he needs to provide her. The formula also gives the mother herself the incentive to develop a career. Because income sharing does not last for life, mothers who are young enough to do so will have to prepare themselves for a time when income sharing has ended.

Arneault v. Arneault
639 S.E.2d 720 (W. Va. 2006)

DAVIS, Chief Justice. . . .

[The parties divorced after a thirty-three year marriage that produced two now-adult children.] During the marriage, Mrs. Arneault stayed home with the children until 1990, when she returned to work on a part-time basis as a teacher. In 1995, Mrs. Arneault started her own business as a counselor providing college placement and career consulting services to high school students. While there is discord as to the effort Mrs. Arneault applied to her business, there is no dispute that Mrs. Arneault's business did not generate great income.

Mr. Arneault currently holds the same job position as he did at the time of the divorce. Mr. Arneault is Chairman, President, and Chief Executive Officer of MTR Gaming Group, Inc. (hereinafter "MTR"), which owns and controls Mountaineer Park, Inc., and operates video lottery terminals. Since 1995, Mr. Arneault has worked in Chester, West Virginia, away from the marital home. Prior to the divorce, he returned to Michigan on most weekends. There is no dispute that Mr. Arneault has been responsible for MTR's great success. In return for his achievements, Mr. Arneault has received a lucrative income from MTR, as well as MTR stock. . . .

[T]he family court determined that because Mr. Arneault had contributed significantly to the marital estate, a 50/50 split of the estate would be inequitable. Thus, the family court ordered that the parties' marital estate be divided 35/65, with Mr. Arneault receiving the larger share. . . . Mrs. Arneault now appeals to this Court. . . .

In a divorce proceeding, subject to some limitations, all property is considered marital property, which preference is reflected in our case law. . . .

With a few exceptions, all of the parties' property constituted marital property and should have been divided equally absent some compelling reason otherwise. Guidance is provided by . . . [West Virginia law], which provides as follows:

> In the absence of a valid agreement, the court shall presume that all marital property is to be divided equally between the parties, but may alter this distribution, without regard to any attribution of fault to either party which may be

alleged or proved in the course of the action, after a consideration of the following:

(1) The extent to which each party has contributed to the acquisition, preservation and maintenance, or increase in value of marital property by monetary contributions, including, but not limited to:

(A) Employment income and other earnings; and

(B) Funds which are separate property.

(2) The extent to which each party has contributed to the acquisition, preservation and maintenance or increase in value of marital property by nonmonetary contributions, including, but not limited to:

(A) Homemaker services;

(B) Child care services;

(C) Labor performed without compensation, or for less than adequate compensation, in a family business or other business entity in which one or both of the parties has an interest;

(D) Labor performed in the actual maintenance or improvement of tangible marital property; and

(E) Labor performed in the management or investment of assets which are marital property.

(3) The extent to which each party expended his or her efforts during the marriage in a manner which limited or decreased such party's income-earning ability or increased the income-earning ability of the other party, including, but not limited to:

(A) Direct or indirect contributions by either party to the education or training of the other party which has increased the income-earning ability of such other party; and

(B) Foregoing by either party of employment or other income-earning activity through an understanding of the parties or at the insistence of the other party.

(4) The extent to which each party, during the marriage, may have conducted himself or herself so as to dissipate or depreciate the value of the marital property of the parties: Provided, That except for a consideration of the economic consequences of conduct as provided for in this subdivision, fault or marital misconduct shall not be considered by the court in determining the proper distribution of marital property.

The [family court] judge explained the rationale for the unequal [65/35] distribution by finding that . . . Mr. Arneault's contributions to the marital estate overwhelmed the contributions made by Mrs. Arneault. Specifically, the family court reasoned as follows:

Having considered the factors enumerated in [the statute], this Court finds that the presumption of equal division has been rebutted. The petitioner's own overwhelming contribution make it completely inequitable to divide the marital estate equally. . . .

In that same order, the family court further explained that

> [t]he petitioner's intelligence and ability are unique to him and the development of these attributes can not [sic] be attributed equally to the petitioner and respondent, regardless of the environment which the respondent created in order to allow the petitioner to achieve the estate that has been amassed. He must be given some additional weight and credit in equitable distribution for existence of those attributes, intelligence, and abilities, which helped him achieve the marital estate currently in question. This Court looks at these personal attributes as substantial service contributions to the marital estate. There are many persons who have obtained an MBA and become a CPA during their marriage, but they have not accomplished nearly the achievements of the petitioner. These achievements go beyond the acquisition of degrees or experience, and must be given additional consideration in equitable distribution.

In essence, it appears that the family court judge believed Mr. Arneault's intelligence and ability led to his great financial success, and while Mrs. Arneault's homemaking and child-rearing duties were substantial, they did not compare to Mr. Arneault's contribution to the marital estate. . . .

Significantly, we disagree with the family court's undervaluement of the contributions made to the marital estate by Mrs. Arneault. In essence, the family court found that because Mrs. Arneault's contributions were not monetary in nature, they did not count as substantially as Mr. Arneault's contributions to the marital estate. This idea is contrary to West Virginia jurisprudence. We previously have held:

> Under equitable distribution, the contributions of time and effort to the married life of the couple—at home and in the workplace—are valued equally regardless of whether the parties' respective earnings have been equal. Equitable distribution contemplates that parties make their respective contributions to the married life of the parties in that expectation.

We likewise have stated that "general contributions, rather than economic contributions [a]re to be the basis for a distribution" of a marital estate. . . .

The facts of the present case highlight how important the contributions of both parties were to the marital estate. It was conceded that Mr. Arneault and Mrs. Arneault did not have any unusual fortune at the time of their marriage. Mrs. Arneault had recently received an undergraduate degree, and Mr. Arneault earned his undergraduate degree soon after they married. Mrs. Arneault then earned a masters degree, while Mr. Arneault went on to obtain his CPA license and a masters degree in business administration. The family court found that Mr. Arneault's innate abilities led to the financial wealth of the marital estate. However, the facts illustrate that the opposite is more probable. Mr. Arneault and Mrs. Arneault entered the marriage on fairly equal levels. Mr. Arneault earned a professional license and a graduate degree after the marriage commenced. It is very conceivable that this accumulation of knowledge, after the commencement of the marriage, led to the development of Mr. Arneault's innate abilities.

Even though Mrs. Arneault also had an advanced degree, she abandoned her own career in order to stay home with the couple's children. She also was responsible for the majority of the housework and the maintenance of the marital residence. Her responsibilities were manifestly increased by the fact that Mr. Arneault was completely absent from the marital home during the work week, leaving Mrs. Arneault with even greater responsibilities and household duties than is normally encountered in like circumstances. Rather than the conclusion made by the family court, the facts of this case show it is more likely that Mrs. Arneault's contributions to the marriage are precisely the reason that Mr. Arneault was able to succeed in his work.

While this Court has recognized that there are circumstances in which an unequal distribution of a marital estate is appropriate, this is not one of those cases. . . .

Thus, we conclude that the family court abused its discretion in fixing a 35/65 split of the marital estate. Mr. Arneault's intelligence and financial prowess is not sufficient justification for straying from the presumption of a 50/50 split. . . .

STARCHER, J., dissenting. . . .

This marriage was *not* a standard fifty/fifty marital partnership, where Mrs. Arneault was the homemaker/support mechanism and Mr. Arneault was the income earner outside the home. Although the couple lived together prior to Mr. Arneault's success (which has resulted in this dispute over the MTR Gaming stock), the Arneaults have lived and worked in separate states for more than a decade.

Since 1995, Mrs. Arneault lived in Michigan and Mr. Arneault spent the bulk of his time in West Virginia. He returned to Michigan a few days a week, being actively involved in various activities with his children, including coaching his son's teams in various sports, such as football, wrestling, basketball, and baseball, and performing household duties, while Mrs. Arneault engaged in her counseling business. Mrs. Arneault only visited West Virginia perhaps three times in ten years. The couple's children are now both emancipated adults and Mrs. Arneault, who received her masters' degree in 1971, works in her consulting business, which she has maintained on a full-time basis since 1995. There was no evidence that Mrs. Arneault's choices regarding work were compelled by Mr. Arneault or the couple's circumstances. Rather, since 1995, the couple pursued separate lives in separate states.

There is no evidence to support Mrs. Arneault's assertions that she provided substantial assistance in Mr. Arneault's success with MTR Gaming. For example, there is no evidence of record that Mrs. Arneault was a host for her husband's business functions. . . . Other than residing in the couple's

[handwritten margin note: Not even home most of the time]

Michigan home while Mr. Arneault toiled in West Virginia, Mrs. Arneault had nothing to do with MTR Gaming, even long after the children had gone to college. . . .

Essentially, Mrs. Arneault makes a "community property" argument, contending that because she was Mr. Arneault's long-time wife, she is automatically entitled to one-half of the stock of a corporation that Mr. Arneault built irrespective of their relative contributions to the corporation.

West Virginia, however, is *not* a "community property" state. Rather, West Virginia is an "equitable distribution" state in which its legislature has prescribed various factors to be considered in making, not an "equal" distribution of marital property, but an "equitable" distribution, based primarily upon the parties' relative contributions. . . .

Mrs. Arneault did almost nothing to refute the substantial evidence presented by Mr. Arneault which supported the thirty-five/sixty-five division of the stock. Consequently, there is a paucity of discussion in the majority opinion regarding her contributions to the marriage or the corporation. . . .

No details are provided about Mrs. Arneault's contributions to MTR Gaming because Mrs. Arneault made no contributions to MTR Gaming. . . .

Rather, Mrs. Arneault took the position that as Mr. Arneault's long-time wife, she was automatically entitled to one-half of everything, including the subject stock, and contrary to this Court's previous cases, she argues that the [statutory] factors apply only "in some extraordinary circumstance" or in "peculiar cases."

The statute, of course, does not require a finding that a case is "extraordinary" or "peculiar" before a court can find facts warranting an equitable distribution that is not equal. . . .

Mrs. Arneault likens a marriage to a law partnership whereby both parties are entitled to share in the good fortune of the other. Law partnerships, however, are governed by written partnership agreements that force whatever division of good or bad fortune the parties decide or other under governing statutory law.

The West Virginia Legislature, however, has not created a "marital partnership" in which each partner, whatever their relative contributions, is always entitled to share equally in the good fortune of the other. . . .

While married to Mr. Arneault, Mrs. Arneault reaped the benefits of his success and would be a multi-millionaire under the judgment of the Circuit Court of Hancock County. It is simply inequitable for her also to receive fifty percent of the stock in light of her negligible contribution to the success of the company, merely as the result of her status as his wife. MTR is not a "lottery ticket," the cost of which was purchased with marital funds and the equal division of which would be equitable. Rather, the overwhelming evidence was that Mr. Arneault was the heart and soul of MTR and it was his extraordinary personal efforts that built the company into what it is today. . . .

There are spouses, both husbands and wives, whose contributions to the success of their spouse's businesses are more or less, particularly considering their other contributions to the marriage, such as homemaker services, equal. For those spouses, they absolutely deserve a fifty percent distribution of the value of those businesses. . . . Had Mrs. Arneault, in reality, served the role of "corporate spouse" that she alleges, she might be entitled to half of the value of MTR stock.

In most cases, in the ordinary circumstances of divorce—which is that neither party can afford it—a relatively strict application of the presumption of equal distribution may be more appropriate. "Let both parties suffer equally" is not an unreasonable principle. But when the "super rich" start dividing things up, and even a person with the shorter end of the stick will be "rich" after a divorce, then it is less harmful to let the equities have their way. . . .

Michael v. Michael
791 S.W.2d 772 (Mo. Ct. App. 1990)

[handwritten margin note: Man appeal be depend on wife]

[handwritten margin note: Class?]

James A. PUDLOWSKI, Presiding Judge.

This is an appeal from a judgment and decree of dissolution which awarded respondent the majority of marital property and awarded appellant $500.00 in attorney's fees and no maintenance.

The evidence adduced at trial established that appellant and respondent were married in August 1972 and separated in April 1987. There were no children born of this marriage. Both appellant and respondent are well educated. Appellant holds a baccalaureate degree in political science and a master's degree in journalism. Respondent holds a baccalaureate degree in journalism and a master's degree in public administration.

In 1972, on the day following the parties' marriage, the couple moved to Little Rock, Arkansas where respondent was going to work for Southwestern Bell Corporation. While living in Little Rock, appellant was employed as a reporter for a local newspaper.

In June 1974, respondent received a promotion and was transferred back to St. Louis. In St. Louis, appellant worked for APC Skills Company and then for Maritz, Inc. In 1978, appellant was fired from Maritz, Inc. Upon appellant being fired, the couple agreed that appellant would not seek outside employment but instead would devote time to writing fiction. In that same year respondent received another transfer and the couple moved to Oklahoma City.

While living in Oklahoma, appellant continued to pursue a writing career, however, later abandoned this endeavor without ever having written a chapter in a book or a scene in a play. After giving up the attempt at writing, appellant worked briefly in a food store and spent 8-9 months working free-lance public relations. When appellant was not employed outside of the home, the couple agreed that appellant would be responsible for the general upkeep of the house and also for the preparation of the evening meal. Appellant spent several hours a day preparing the couple's dinner. Respondent claimed that appellant's other domestic chores were very lax. For two years while the couple was living in Oklahoma appellant drove respondent to and from work. However, for the rest of the mornings, appellant slept until 10 or 11:00 a.m.

In 1984 respondent was again transferred to St. Louis. After moving to St. Louis, appellant continued to cook the couple's dinner. He also periodically took the respondent to work but did not seek outside employment.

Throughout the marriage, the couple's lifestyle improved and they had a significant amount of disposable income. . . . At the time of trial, respondent had been working for Southwestern Bell for more than 15 years and was earning over $70,000 per year. Respondent's additional benefits from Southwestern Bell included vested pension benefits through the Southwestern Bell Corporation Management Pension Plan equal to $1,169.58 monthly payable at age sixty-five (65), as of March 1, 1988. Appellant's statement of income and expenses provides that he receives no income from employment, however he receives $75 per month in interest, and his share of the gross income on the previous year's Federal Income Tax Return was $1200.

It is with some interest that we note the gender roles of the parties in this marriage are reversed from the more traditional roles of husband and wife. In the present case the wife is the party who earned the lion's share of the income by working outside of the home during the marriage. The appellant is the party who remained at home throughout the majority of the marriage and did not work outside of the home for several years. However, certainly the sex of the parties should have no bearing on the division of marital property or on the allowance or prohibition of maintenance.

The trial court allocated $51,347 or 75.5% of the parties' marital property to respondent and $14,128 or 21.5% to appellant. The court granted appellant no maintenance but allowed appellant $500 for attorney's fees.

Appellant raises three points on his appeal. Appellant claims that the trial court abused its discretion by its distribution of the parties' marital property, abused its discretion by awarding appellant no maintenance, and abused its discretion by awarding appellant only $500 in attorney's fees. . . .

[Missouri law] directs the trial court to divide the marital property in a just manner, after considering all relevant factors including the five factors set out in the statute, as follows:

(1) The economic circumstances of each spouse at the time the division of property is to become effective, including the desirability of awarding the family home or the right to live therein for any reasonable periods to the spouse having custody of any children.

(2) The contribution of each spouse to the acquisition of the marital property, including the contribution of a spouse as a homemaker;

(3) The value of the non-marital property set apart to each spouse;

(4)   The conduct of the parties during the marriage; and
(5)   Custodial arrangements for minor children.

There are two guiding principles: "[F]irst property division should reflect the concept of marriage as a shared enterprise similar to a partnership; and, second property division should be utilized as a means of providing future support for an economically dependent spouse." . . .

When applying these guiding principles . . . to the present case we find that the trial court abused its discretion in its division of marital property. We first look at the economic circumstances of each spouse at the time the division of property is to become effective. Throughout the course of the marriage, appellant has become economically dependent on the respondent. At the time of the dissolution of marriage, appellant was unemployed, had not been employed in his chosen field of journalism for fifteen years, and had not been employed full-time since 1978. Conversely, [respondent] . . . was earning in excess of $70,000 per year. Additionally, respondent was the recipient of extensive employment benefits. . . .

With regard to the second statutory factor, the contribution of each spouse to the acquisition of marital property, including the contribution of a spouse as homemaker, the trial court found that the respondent, for the greater part of the marriage, had been the sole financial support of the parties and the funds used to acquire the marital property had been earned almost solely by her. Also, the court found that the appellant made no substantial contribution to the marriage as a homemaker because he showed a marked disinclination to undertake the normal domestic duties of a homemaker, engaging only in those duties, such as cooking the evening meal, which he found fulfilling, stimulating and interesting.

Although appellant did not work outside of the home for the majority of the years of the marriage, he did have outside employment for nearly one-third of the marriage. For two additional years appellant drove respondent to work and picked her up from work in the evening. While the appellant's performance of traditional domestic chores was often times lax, he did prepare dinner for himself and respondent throughout the duration of the marriage. We are not finding that appellant's contributions entitled him to an equal division of the marital property, however, we do hold that the trial court's division of property is against the weight of the evidence and therefore an abuse of discretion.

In his second point appellant claims that the trial court erred and abused its discretion in awarding no maintenance to appellant. . . .

We have said that maintenance is awarded when one spouse has detrimentally relied on the other spouse to provide the monetary support during the marriage. If the relying spouse's withdrawal from the marketplace so injures his/her marketable skills that he/she is unable to provide for his/her reasonable needs maintenance may be awarded. . . . "Rehabilitative maintenance" should be awarded for a term reasonably sufficient to receive job training. . . . Rehabilitative maintenance is appropriate where there is substantial evidence that the party seeking maintenance will or should become self-supporting. . . .

We have reviewed the record before us and we find that the trial court did err and abuse its discretion in finding that the appellant failed to show that his ten year absence from the journalism field has injured his ability to secure employment therein at this time and earn a sum sufficient to meet his reasonable needs and that appellant wholly failed to establish his entitlement to maintenance. . . .

At trial appellant testified that he intended to enroll for a semester at the University of Texas in a program on Latin American Studies in order to enable him to re-enter journalism as a reporter in Latin America. He indicated that he wrote to several of the major newspapers in Florida and received a response from the Miami Herald which indicated that the appellant's plans for further education would be attractive credentials for a newspaper like the Miami Herald. Appellant further testified that because his most recent articles are fifteen years old, he needs to develop some fresh stories that have been written in the recent past to show editors that he is still able to write and report.

Appellant's need to acquire fresh skills in order to re-enter the field of journalism is reasonable. . . . Appellant's plan to return to school in order to increase his marketability as a journalist would ensure that he become self-sufficient. Our disposition of the issues of marital property and maintenance is consistent with the generally accepted princip[le]s . . . that marriage is a shared enterprise and that maintenance should be utilized as a means of providing support for an economically dependent spouse until said spouse is self-reliant. . . .

This matter is remanded for further proceedings consistent with this opinion.

Judge WILLIAMS H. CRANDALL, Jr., dissenting. . . .

If we accept the concept of marriage as a shared enterprise similar to a partnership, husband had a negative impact on that partnership. Husband did not sacrifice his career for wife, rather he was a hindrance to her progress. On the issue of maintenance, husband has simply shown that he is unwilling, rather than unable, to support himself through appropriate employment.

For the foregoing reasons I would affirm the decree of dissolution.

Chen v. Warner
695 N.W.2d 758 (Wis. 2005)

Shirley S. ABRAHAMSON, C.J. . . . The circuit court granted Jane E. Chen's (the mother's) motion to amend the child support portion of a divorce judgment to require John J. Warner (the father) to pay $4,000 per month in child support. The circuit court rejected the father's argument that the mother's actions constituted "shirking" and declined to use the mother's earning capacity rather than her actual income in determining whether to award child support.

The court of appeals affirmed. . . . We affirm the decision of the court of appeals. . . .

The . . . issue is whether the circuit court erred in determining that the mother's decision to forgo employment outside the home and become an at-home full-time child care provider was reasonable under the circumstances. . . . [W]e conclude that the mother's decision was reasonable under the circumstances. . . .

I

The material facts are undisputed. The case at bar arises out of a post-divorce motion to modify child support. The mother and father, both physicians, were divorced in 1999 after an 18-year marriage. They have three children, born in 1991, 1993, and 1995.

The judgment of divorce incorporated the parties' agreement. It provided for joint custody and equal physical placement. The children spent alternating weeks with each parent. The judgment provided that neither party would pay child support to the other; each would be responsible for the children's daily expenses when they were in his or her care. Reasonable clothing expenses and other mutually agreed-upon expenses incurred on behalf of the children were equally divided. The father, however, was to pay $400 per child per month into a fund for the children's future education.

At the time of the divorce, both parties were employed full time at the Marshfield Clinic. The mother earned . . . $236,000 per year. The father earned . . . $256,452 per year. Both parents worked outside the home during the marriage.

After the divorce, the mother sought to reduce her employment to be more available for the children, who were of school age or nearing it. Both parents apparently agree that it is in the best interests of their children to have, if feasible, child care provided by a parent. The father testified at the child support modification hearing that, when possible, it was important to have a parent at home full time with the children rather than have someone else care for the children.

The mother voluntarily left her full-time position at the Marshfield Clinic in May 2000 when she was unable to reduce her schedule there to part time.

Leaving her position was not a rash decision. Prior to terminating her employment, the mother had consulted with a financial advisor and was advised that from her $1.1 million savings, she could expect an annual income of about $110,000. This sum was significant, but was less than the income she earned as a physician. The estimate of $110,000 was based on stock market returns over the past 50 years. The mother's estimated budget was $7,000 per month, or $84,000 per year. Because her expected income exceeded her budget, the mother did not seek child support from the father.

The stock market decline in 2001 took a toll on the mother's investment income. That year she earned only $32,000. In response to the income decline, the mother began to look for employment and began invading her assets in order to meet her and the children's expenses. The job search failed to yield any part-time opportunities within commuting distance of her home, although she could have obtained alternating-week work in distant communities. She did not want to live away from home during alternate weeks, so she declined to pursue those opportunities.

In 2002, the mother filed a motion to amend the divorce judgment to require the father to pay child support. She asserted a substantial change in circumstances to justify a child support award. Her income had diminished substantially; the father's income had increased.

Had the mother continued employment at the Marshfield Clinic, she would have been earning $415,000 per year. The father was earning $472,000 per year when the motion was filed in 2002, nearly twice what he earned at the time of the divorce. In addition, his employer contributed $73,000 per year to his retirement plan. The father had assets of $1,218,185, not including securities. He was eligible for nine weeks of paid vacation per year and two weeks of paid meeting time. He maintains three residences.

The father's monthly budget was $8,400, leaving him with discretionary income of $12,000 per month. The mother requested $4,000 per month in child support based on a monthly budget of $7,000.

The circuit court ordered the father to pay child support in the amount of $4,000, but excused him from his obligation to pay $1,200 per month into the children's education fund. Thus, the net effect of the circuit court's order is to require the father to pay an additional $2,800 per month for the children's support.

Not working outside the home full time has enabled the mother to spend significantly more time with the children. This increased time with the children also includes periods during the weeks when the father has placement of the children. She shepherds the children to medical appointments, attends their school activities, does volunteer work at the school, communicates more with their teachers, transports the children to their various extracurricular activities (tae kwon do, ballet, knitting, dancing, piano lessons), and monitors their participation in all their endeavors.

The record is also replete with evidence of the father's involvement in the children's lives.

By all accounts, the children were doing well and their needs were met before the mother left employment at the Marshfield Clinic, and they have continued to do well thereafter.

The father argued in the circuit court and on appeal that the mother's termination of employment in 2000 and her refusal to seek part-time work

[handwritten margin note: ♂ claim of refuse to work]

outside the Marshfield area were unreasonable and amounted to shirking her obligation to support their children.

II . . .

This is a child support modification case. The father asserts that in determining child support the circuit court should have used the mother's earning capacity, not her actual earnings. Obviously, in the present case there is a significant difference between the two numbers. A circuit court would consider a parent's earning capacity rather than the parent's actual earnings only if it has concluded that the parent has been "shirking," to use the awkward terminology of past cases. To conclude that a parent is shirking, a circuit court is not required to find that a former spouse deliberately reduced earnings to avoid support obligations or to gain some advantage over the other party. A circuit court need find only that a party's employment decision to reduce or forgo income is voluntary and unreasonable under the circumstances.

The parties, the circuit court, the court of appeals and this court agree that the mother's decision to reduce her income from employment outside the home was voluntary.

The focus of the parties' dispute is whether the mother's decision to forgo employment outside the home to become an at-home full-time child care provider was reasonable under the circumstances. . . .

The test of reasonableness under the circumstances is derived from the case law. . . . [T]he paying spouse should be afforded "a fair choice" of a means of livelihood as well as the ability to pursue what the spouse honestly feels are the best opportunities, even though the present financial return may be reduced from prior employment. The court further said that "[t]his rule is, of course, subject to reasonableness commensurate with [the spouse's] obligations to [the] children and [the former spouse]." The phrase "subject to reasonableness commensurate with a spouse's obligations to the children" has been repeated in numerous shirking cases, including unintentional shirking cases. The phrase "commensurate with a spouse's obligations to the children" does not explicitly refer to obligations of financial support; it includes other obligations, such as child care. . . .

The case law recognizes that the words "subject to reasonableness commensurate with a spouse's obligations to the children" mean that a court balances the needs of the parents and the needs of the child (both financial and otherwise, like child care) and the ability of both parents to pay child support.

Furthermore, Wis. Stat. §767.25(1m)(d) and (e) provide that a court may modify the amount of child support payments under the percentage standard if, after considering the listed economic factors, "[t]he desirability that the custodian remain in the home as a full-time parent," and "the value of custodial services performed by the custodian if the custodian remains at home," the court concludes that the percentage standard is unfair to the child or to any of the parties. Thus the legislature has explicitly recognized that in establishing financial child support obligations a circuit court considers the desirability and value of child care services performed by a custodian. . . .

With appropriate deference to the circuit court's ruling, we now determine the reasonableness of the mother's decision to forgo employment outside the home to become an at-home full-time child care provider.

While a family is intact, the parents' choice of employment, child care, and standard of living are left to the parties, as long as the children's basic needs are met. Upon divorce, however, courts are plunged into the divorced parents' personal lives to ensure that the interests of minor children are protected.

A divorced parent who voluntarily leaves gainful employment outside the home, for however good a reason, may be subject to judicial inquiry into that parent's responsibility to furnish child support. A divorced parent may voluntarily terminate employment but may not do so if the conduct inures to the detriment of child support. There is a limit to the unemployment or underemployment of a parent when the other parent "is presented the bill for the financial consequences."

When a divorced parent decides to forgo employment outside the home to render at-home full-time child care (but not for the purpose of avoiding a support obligation) . . . [a] court must weigh the right of a parent to make such a choice, while keeping in mind the public's interests that children be adequately cared for, that the financial needs of the children be met, and that the financial burdens of child care be apportioned fairly between the parents.

If it determines that a parent's decision to forgo employment outside the home to provide at-home full-time child care is unreasonable, a court can impose an obligation on that parent to support a child by imputing income to the parent based on that parent's earning capacity. . . .

We do not adopt a position favoring or disfavoring a parent's decision to forgo employment outside the home to become an at-home full-time or part-time child care provider. . . .

The factors to be considered in determining the reasonableness of a parent's decision to forgo employment outside the home, become an at-home full-time child care provider, and increase the support obligation of the other parent include, but are not limited to, the following: the number of children at home and their ages, maturity, health, and special needs; the availability of child care providers; the financial needs of the children; any detrimental effect on the child's support level if a parent is a full- or part-time at-home child care provider; the age and mental and physical condition of the parents; the educational background, training, skills, prior employment, and wage earning history of each parent; the earning potential of the parent who forgoes employment outside the home and that parent's efforts to find and retain employment; the status of the job market; the assets and income of each parent and the available resources if a parent is an at-home full- or part-time child care provider; the hardship and burden on the parent employed outside the home caused by the other parent's decision to forgo employment; and any other factors bearing on the needs of the children and each parent's ability to fund child support.

The gender of the parent forgoing employment outside the home to provide at-home full- or part-time child care is not a relevant factor.

The record in the present case supports the circuit court's determination that the mother's initial decision to terminate employment was reasonable. . . .

The question then becomes whether it was reasonable for the mother not to take full- or part-time employment as a physician when the income from her investments fell. It is this decision that precipitated the mother's child support motion and prompted the father's shirking allegation. . . .

The circuit court concluded, and we agree, that a parent's decision to provide at-home full-time child care may but does not, in and of itself, amount to shirking. As the circuit court explained, if the father is right that the mother's forgoing income from employment outside the home to become an at-home full-time child care provider is automatically unreasonable, then every arrangement in which one parent predominantly attends to the children while the other predominantly attends to an income-producing job is shirking. Furthermore, as the circuit court stated, under the father's theory it would no longer be appropriate to impute economic value to child care or homemaking services, as our statutes permit.

The father agreed at trial that if a family unit "can do it," that is, if it is feasible, it is preferable for the children to be with a parent rather than with someone else and that it is preferable to have a parent available as a full-time at-home child care provider rather than have one parent or both parents as part-time at-home child care providers. The father's briefs now seem to assert that the children might have greater opportunities had their mother continued to earn her substantial salary.

The circuit court properly considered the benefits to the children resulting from the mother's decision not to be employed outside the home. The father does not dispute the mother's accounting of her child-related activities, nor does he argue that the children do not benefit from her greater involvement in their lives. Rather, he argues that the benefits are not so great as to render reasonable her decision not to be employed outside the home in the face of her dwindling and inadequate investment returns. The father argues, and the mother does not dispute, that the children were doing well when both parents worked full time outside the home and that the children have no special needs or disabilities. Further, the father points out that the mother worked full time before the children were of school age and now stays home full time while they are in school. The usual practice, he contends, is for a parent to stay home while the children are very young and return to work when they start school.

The father makes good points, but we conclude, as did the circuit court, that the benefits to the children in the present case are a factor to be weighed in favor of the mother's decision not to be employed outside the home. This factor favoring the mother is not, however, determinative of the case.

This case presents the issue of whether it is fair to the father and to the children, in light of the mother's legal obligation to support the children, for a court not to impute to the mother her earning capacity, thereby increasing the father's child support obligations.

The father's key point is that the reasonableness of the mother's decision to be an at-home full-time child care provider should not be based solely on the fact that the father can afford to pay child support. We agree with the father. . . .

Certainly, if a working parent's income were low, that factor would weigh against a finding that the other parent's decision to forgo employment outside the home was reasonable. The converse should also be true.

In the present case the father's ability to make increased expenditures for the children is unusually high. As a result, the effect of increased support of $2,800 on the father's standard of living and financial picture is negligible. The father had monthly discretionary income of $12,000, over and above his monthly expenses and retirement savings. . . .

[T]he father argues that the children will suffer by the mother's decision to forgo paid employment outside the home. He argues that the court has terminated the father's obligation to contribute to the trust accounts for the children's post-high school education, thereby effectively forcing the children to subsidize their mother's early retirement and diminishing the children's funds for post-high school education. We disagree with the father. The mother's decision to forgo employment outside the home to become an at-home full-time child care provider was reasonable considering the present interests of the children and the other factors present in the case at bar. Further, nothing prevents the father from voluntarily continuing to pay $1,200 per month toward the children's education fund. . . .

[W]e conclude that the circuit court correctly concluded that the mother's decision to remain unemployed to be an at-home full-time child care provider was reasonable under the circumstances. . . .

We do not set forth a general rule that it is always reasonable for a parent to terminate employment to become an at-home full-time child care provider when the other parent has the ability to support the children. . . .

We affirm the court of appeals' decision affirming the circuit court's order that the father pay $4,000 per month to the mother as child support.

Notes

1. Property Distribution. As noted earlier, the traditional rule in most states (which have "common law property regimes") was that ownership of property at divorce followed title of that property, which in turn usually reflected who earned the money with which the property was purchased. The title rule caused substantial inequalities in cases where spouses acted as partners during the marriage, both contributing to the value of assets that were assigned at divorce to only one of them, usually the husband.[239] A minority of states have community property regimes, which have long considered the earnings of each spouse to be the property of both marriage partners. With respect to property division, most women traditionally were better off at divorce in community property states than they were in common law property states.

Equitable distribution reform swept the nation in the 1970s and 1980s in an effort to promote greater fairness in the division of property. Implicit in most equitable distribution statutes is the principle of a marital partnership, similar to the premise of community property law. This principle assumes an equitable division of responsibility during the marriage, and thus the need for an equitable division of the property at divorce. However, the statutes often try to accommodate competing principles as well. One such principle, contribution, invites consideration of how the assets were acquired, and thus tends to favor the spouse whose earnings or efforts produced the property; the effect of the contribution principle is sometimes offset by the "homemaker contribution" of the other spouse. Still another principle—need—emphasizes the spouses' comparative abilities to support themselves after the marriage, and thus favors the more financially dependent spouse.

The law in many jurisdictions recites a range of factors to consider in dividing property "equitably," including contribution, need, and the duration of the marriage. Other states, particularly ones with community property, call for equal division of assets between the parties. Which approach is more consistent with principles of gender equality? Which is the fairest? To what extent should property division reflect equal treatment and to what extent the needs of the lower-earning spouse? Should the answer be affected by the length of the marriage or the presence of children living at home? Was the *Arneault* case correctly decided? What about the *Michael* case? What results in these two cases best achieves gender equality? By what standard should that be judged?

2. Spousal Support. Traditional theories of spousal support called for compensation to a dependent wife for her divorcing husband's breach of marital vows and responsibilities. With the rise of no-fault divorce, a needs-based rationale supplanted the fault-based rationale. However, commentators have had difficulty constructing a viable theory for why one spouse should be the permanent insurer of the financial security of other, when modern marriage

---

239. See, e.g., Saff v. Saff, 402 N.Y.S.2d 690 (App. Div. 1978), appeal dismissed, 415 N.Y.S.2d 829 (N.Y. 1979). On the changes to the American family and family law over the course of the twentieth century, see Grossman & Friedman, supra note 223.

law generally allows either spouse to terminate the marriage. Need supplies a standard, but not an explanation for obligations that might define the contours of that standard.

The trend in the law has been (1) to disfavor spousal support, preferring to accomplish a "clean break" for the parties through property distribution alone, if possible; and (2) if spousal support is ordered, to favor short-term or "rehabilitative" awards designed to get a dependent spouse back on her (or his) feet so that a "clean break" can eventually be accomplished. When need comes into play, courts have applied relatively open-ended standards that produce widely varying results. About half of jurisdictions also consider fault in determining entitlement to support.

The American Law Institute proposes to treat spousal support as a return of non-economic investments in the marital partnership on behalf of the family, investments, that would otherwise be irrational or inefficient. The theory of this approach is that spousal support encourages (socially useful) investments in the marriage. The proposal provides for "compensatory spousal payments" to close the post-marriage gap between the parties' earning capacities attributable to lost opportunities by one spouse as a result of investments in the marriage. It uses length of marriage as a multiplier in the income-gap closing formula, thereby serving as a proxy for "lost opportunity." It further increases the amount when the dependent spouse assumed primary caretaking responsibilities for the couple's children during the marriage.[240] Does this approach reinforce marital role specialization? If so, is it good or bad for women?

3. Educational Degree: Property, Support, or Neither? One problem that falls between the cracks of marital property distribution and spousal support is how to treat an educational degree or professional license earned during the marriage with the economic support of the other spouse. When the parties divorce shortly after the degree has been obtained, there is often no property to distribute, and the supporting spouse may not be "dependent" in the usual sense (after all, she has been supporting the party who has earned the degree or license). Yet without recognition of the degree or license, one party to the marriage will benefit unfairly from "owning" an asset to which the other spouse made important contributions.

Courts reject the theory that a degree is property subject to division, on the theory that it has none of the transferability attributes of property and its value depends entirely on the future efforts of the degree-holder.[241] However,

---

240. American Law Institute, Principles of the Law of Family Dissolution, Chapter 4 (2002).

241. See In re Marriage of Graham, 574 P.2d 75, 77 (Colo. 1978). New York for some time treated educational degrees and other enhancements to one party's earning capacity acquired during the marriage as marital property subject to equitable division, O'Brien v. O'Brien, 489 N.E.2d 712 (N.Y. 1985), but a 2015 law has changed this approach. See N.Y. Dom. Rel.

a growing number of jurisdictions have applied theories of contract and equity, or other strained theories of spousal support, to arrive at awards that often combine features of maintenance and lump-sum property division.[242]

If an award is made for a spouse's contribution to the other spouse's degree, what about other human capital achieved through a partner's support? A working spouse typically enhances his or her income capacity through work experience. Should the spouse who has gained disproportionate earning capacity during the marriage be able to walk away with the benefits of that investment if the other spouse has sacrificed career opportunities in order to invest in the home and family?[243]

4. Child Support. Child support has also been a target of extensive reform. Close to one-third of American adults are either obligors or beneficiaries of such awards. Traditionally, courts used their discretion in setting amounts, which led to inconsistent and often inadequate payments and increased the number of families needing welfare. In an effort to address these problems, federal law conditions receipt of certain federal funds on the adoption by states of measures to improve the quantity, quality, and enforceability of child support. Among other things, states must have formula guidelines, which act as rebuttable presumptions of amounts owed, and they must implement automatic wage withholding of support payments in most cases. Federal law also provides for the interception of tax refunds, garnishment of federal wages, and locator services for delinquent parents. The Federal Child Support Recovery Act of 1992 makes it a federal crime to cross state lines to avoid payment of child support.

Aggressive state laws have been added to help improve child support collections. At least 15 states provide for the suspension, revocation, or denial of occupational or business licenses of individuals delinquent in their child support obligations. Fifteen states provide for the suspension or revocation of delinquents' drivers' licenses. Other statutes provide for the suspension of

---

§236 (2016) ("The court shall not consider as marital property subject to distribution the value of a spouse's enhanced earning capacity arising from a license, degree, celebrity goodwill, or career enhancement"); Lee Rosenberg, What a Difference a Year Makes: Changes to the Spousal Support Law and the End of *O'Brien*, 47 NYSBA Fam. L. Rev. 1 (Fall/Winter 2015).

242. See, e.g., Mace v. Mace, 818 So. 2d 1130 (Miss. 2002) (while husband's advanced degree is not marital property, wife has equitable interest in husband's medical practice); Meyer v. Meyer, 620 N.W.2d 382 (Wis. 2000) (appropriate for trial court to consider premarital contributions of one spouse to the medical education of the other in determining spousal maintenance).

243. For New York's effort to develop administrable standards to carry out its degree-as-property approach, see Sebastian Weiss, Note, Preventing Inequities in Divorce and Education: The Equitable Distribution of a Career Absent an Advanced Degree or License, 9 Cardozo Women's L.J. 133 (2002).

permanent license plates or motor vehicle registrations, hunting or fishing licenses, and even passports and marriage licenses.[244]

In choosing a formula for determining child support, most state guidelines either take a percentage of the obligor's income (percentage formula) or proportion liability based on the parents' relative incomes (income shares). Under both approaches, the level of support sought to be captured in a child support order is the marginal amount that a parent would be expected to spend on the child if the child still lived with the parent. Policymakers aim for this amount so that, theoretically at least, the obligor is paying only the child's expenses and not those of others in the household where the child primarily lives.[245]

The perceived fairness of child support awards under existing child support formulas depends on the goals one thinks should be achieved and, among other things, the relative earning powers of the two parents. When the parties' incomes are substantially different and the party with whom the child primarily lives is the lower-earning parent (as is typical), the standard of living enjoyed by the child in his or her primary residence is generally lower, sometimes far lower, than the standard of living enjoyed by the nonresidential parent. When the primary residential parent earns more, the child support order may require substantial sacrifice from the obligor parent in order to subsidize a household that is living quite comfortably. Remarriage of one or both parents further complicates the issue, since it introduces new obligations and/or resources. It is difficult for formulas to ensure results that are both consistent across cases and sensitive to such variations.[246]

Subsequent families pose especially difficult challenges. On the one hand, it seems fair to treat children of first families and second families alike, and thus make an adjustment in existing awards to reflect new family obligations. On the other hand, one might think that when parents undertake new family responsibilities, they do so as individuals with existing obligations to children whose needs remain the same. Sometimes the stepparent brings additional income, and the question arises whether that income should figure in the child support calculation as an asset of the obligor parent. None of these questions are answered consistently across states.[247]

244. See Carmen Solomon-Fears, Child Support Enforcement and Driver's License Suspension Policies, Congressional Research Service, Apr. 11, 2011, http://www.childsupport-guidelines.com/articles/art199906.html.

245. For a comparison of child support systems, see Douglas W. Allen & Margaret F. Brinig, Child Support Guidelines: The Good, the Bad, and the Ugly, 45 Fam. L.Q. 135 (2011).

246. For an overview, see Ira Mark Ellman & Tara O'Toole Ellman, The Theory of Child Support, 45 Harv. J. Legislation 107 (2008).

247. For some of the recent cases and a proposal for more determinate rules, see Yitshak Cohen, Issues Subject to Modification in Family Law: A New Model, 62 Drake L. Rev. 313 (2014).

Another issue is the effect of shared custody, when the obligor parent spends more parenting time with the child than the usual 20 percent arrangement. Typically states allow for a "shared custody child support adjustment" when the obligor's share of custody reaches a certain amount—say, 35 percent.[248] The adjustment reflects the extra costs that may be associated with custodial time, but not the fact that the primary custodian's fixed costs of raising the child are affected little, if at all. What do you think is the best way to handle this?

If a parent who is under a child support order loses a job and is unable to find another at the same wage, their ability to pay is affected, which may justify a modification of the child support award if the parent applies for it, although modification is not automatic and back awards, by federal law, are not retroactively modifiable.[249] But if the only job they can get pays much less than before, do they have to take it? Such cases tend to be decided on a case by case, much like *Chen*. *Chen* raises the question of when at-home parenting can substitute for earning at one's full capacity. Did the court in *Chen* reach the right conclusion on the facts? Do you think *Chen* would have come out the same way if the father, rather than the mother, chose to forego highly paid employment in favor of staying home with the couple's school-aged children?

The Obama Administration has focused greater attention on noncustodial parents who are overburdened by child support awards or arrearages and found ways to alleviate some of the burden.[250] Some argue that this has been done at the expense of custodial parents (mostly women) and children who will see less money awarded or paid. If you were an advocate for single mothers, would you support or oppose this policy shift? Are there ways in which mothers and children might benefit from a less strict approach to enforcement of child support orders against poor fathers?

At the other end of the spectrum are issues concerning high-income families, where a percentage formula may overstate the child's "needs." Consider an earner, for example, who earns $2 million annually, and who would ordinarily be expected to pay one-third of that in child support. Some states set

---

248. See Karen Syma Czapanskiy, The Shared Custody Child Support Adjustment: Not Worth the Candle, 49 Fam. L.Q. 409 (2015); Sanford L. Braver et al., Public Sentiments About the Parenting Time Adjustment in Child Support Awards, 49 Fam. L.Q. 433 (2015).

249. For the problem, see Julie Bosman, Fighting over Child Support After the Pink Slip Arrives, N.Y. Times, Mar. 29, 2009, at A1.

250. See White House, Promoting Responsible Fatherhood, June 2012, https://www.whitehouse.gov/sites/default/files/docs/fatherhood_report_6.13.12_final.pdf; see also Leslie Joan Harris, Questioning Child Support Enforcement Policy for Poor Families, 45 Fam. L.Q. 157, 159 (2011) (arguing that trying to collect child support from poor fathers should be curtailed, in favor of efforts to encourage absent father's efforts to provide for their children voluntarily).

caps on child support amounts; others leave it to the court's discretion.[251] Should there be a limit? If so, what factors should be considered in setting it?

Putting Theory Into Practice

2-26. Consider the following:

(a) George has been a highly paid executive for a Fortune-500 company. As a result of his earnings, at the time of his divorce from Kate, the couple has $50 million of assets. Kate never worked during the marriage but she managed the household and did the majority of childrearing for their one child, who is now 30 years old. Under what sex-neutral principle should the parties' assets be divided?

(b) In a case similar to (a), above, the husband complained of a judgment dividing the marital assets 50-50: "The biggest stress of the day for my wife was deciding what to tell the cook to make for dinner. There is a certain class of wealthy women who contribute nothing to the family wealth and then expect 50 percent on divorce. The court says she is entitled to continue the lifestyle you have provided. It's lunacy, absolute lunacy."[252] How would you respond to him?

(c) In a case similar to (a), above, the wife rejected a settlement offer of $10 million from her corporate-executive husband whose net worth was close to $100 million. She explained: "Marriage is a partnership, and I should be entitled to 50%. I gave thirty-one years of my life. I loved the defendant. I worked hard and I was very loyal." Although she admitted she could survive on $10 million, she asked "Why should he get $90 million? I entered this marriage as a partner. I don't know when he decided that it was not a partnership. [He] wanted to buy out my partnership, and I didn't want to be bought out. It's like a hostile takeover — he offered me a very small percentage, and I said that's not the price of a buyout."[253] Is her analogy persuasive?

2-27. Mary and Lewis both want to become lawyers and to open up a law practice together in their home town. They do not have enough funds to support themselves while both of them go to law school so they decide that Mary will support the couple as a data systems analyst while Lewis earns his law degree. Afterwards, Lewis will support them while Mary goes to law school.

251. See Lori W. Nelson, High-Income Child Support, 45 Fam. L.Q. 191 (2011).

252. Landon Thomas, Jr., Lawyer to Stars' Ex-Wives Has Never Been Busier, N.Y. Times, May 26, 2009, at B1 (quoting Brian Meyerson).

253. Judith H. Dobrzynski, A Corporate Wife Holds Out for a 50-50 Split of Assets, N.Y. Times, Jan. 24, 1997 (discussing divorce between Gary and Lorna Wendt); Wendt v. Wendt, 1998 Conn. Super. LEXIS 1023, at *55-56 (awarding wife $20 million in equitable distribution).

They follow the plan, except that on the day he gets his law degree, Lewis announces to Mary that he has fallen in love with someone else and he now wants a divorce. They have no assets. Lewis has taken a Wall Street position making $140,000 a year.

What financial rights should Mary have? What theory of equality supports that result? What if she no longer wants to go to law school, and instead hopes to be a full-time painter?

2-28. In an article entitled *Divorce Equality,* Allison Tait makes the following observation about marriages by same-sex couples:

> [A] number of studies have shown that, in terms of labor specialization, same-sex couples adopt a more egalitarian approach: "Much research on same-sex domesticity points to a strong egalitarian ideal for division of labour, a reluctance for one spouse to be dependent on the other, and an emphasis on negotiation." Instead of allocating household labor by gender (wife cooks dinner, husband takes out the trash), "most couples in same-sex relationships do not assign gender roles. The tasks are flexible, often interchangeable between the partners and are often divided by time, ability, and consideration." This egalitarian concept of domestic labor and marital bargaining correlates with the fact that "most gay men and lesbians are in dual-earner relationships, so neither partner is the exclusive breadwinner and each partner has some measure of economic independence."[254]

Do these studies suggest that the property and support law should be different for many same-sex couples than they are for different-sex couples?

2-29. An article in *Forbes* shares the stories of three women who were entitled to alimony upon divorce, but declined it. One woman, who had married at eighteen and stayed home to raise the daughter born soon thereafter before divorcing at 24, explained her decision to the reporter like this: "My marriage allowed me to stay home full-time with my daughter. . . . That was a luxury—not a job. I was compensated. I had a nice home, drove a nice car, had access to a bank account. Asking for alimony would be like asking for a pension for a job I no longer did. Why should he have to pay because he loved me enough to marry me? It just didn't seem fair."[255] If you were her lawyer, would you try to convince her to ask for alimony? If so, what arguments would you make?

2-30. In many states, spousal support payments terminate upon the remarriage of the payee spouse. Advocates, largely ex-husbands, have pushed

254. Allison Anna Tait, Divorce Equality, 90 Wash. L. Rev. 1246, 1268 (2015) (citations omitted).

255. Emma Johnson, "I Turned Down Alimony", 3 Women's Stories, Forbes, Nov. 13, 2014.

to make cohabitation a trigger for termination as well, and a 2014 law in New Jersey provides that "cohabitation" can potentially be established even if the payee and significant other maintain separate residences.[256] What is the rationale for such a rule? Is it fair to women?

2-31. The Supreme Court in Japan upheld a law requiring married couples to have the same surname.[257] The law is gender-neutral, in that a couple could choose either the husband's or the wife's surname, but more than 95 percent of couples pick the husband's surname. What arguments might you make about the relationship between this law and women's equality?

3. Child Custody

Although today's child custody standards focus on the best interests of the child, mothers continue to have custody of their children in the large majority of cases. About 82 percent of current custodial parents are mothers, a percentage largely unchanged over the two decades.[258] The prevailing best interests test encompasses a wide range of factors: the "quality of the emotional bonds between parent and child," "the ethical, emotional, and intellectual guidance the parent gives to the child throughout his formative years," the "moral fitness" and "ability" of the parents, and continuity of care. Such criteria have been criticized as overly subjective; they allow judges to act on their own instincts and biases (or those of the experts upon whom they rely), which results in uncertainty, inconsistency, recriminations among parents, and undesirable strategic behavior.[259]

Gender bias has been a particular problem. It can work both ways. Mothers sometimes benefit from traditional stereotypes and gender role expectations, but they also suffer if they fail to conform to idealized views of motherhood, or if fathers exceed the minimal expectations associated with fatherhood. In one case, for example, a father was awarded custody based on his "slightly more active engagement in their children's lives" even though the undisputed evidence showed that the father spent only 9 waking hours per week with the children, as compared with 20 hours by the working mother.[260]

---

256. See N.J. Stat. Ann. 2A:34-23(n) (West 2015).

257. See Jun Hongo, Japan's Top Court Rules Married Couples Must Have Same Surname, Wall St. J., Dec. 16, 2015.

258. See U.S. Census Bureau, Current Population Reports, Custodial Mothers and Fathers and Their Child Support 2 & Table 4 (Dec. 2011).

259. See Katharine T. Bartlett, Preference, Presumption, Predisposition, and Common Sense: From Traditional Custody Doctrines to the American Law Institute's Family Dissolution Project, 36 Fam. L.Q. 11 (2002).

260. See Hoover v. Hoover, 764 A.2d 1192, 1194 (Vt. 2000). According to the dissenting judge, time was credited to the father for activities such as helping with schoolwork in which the mother also engaged but for which she was not given credit.

Bias against lesbians, mothers with demanding jobs, and wives who have had extramarital affairs has also been apparent.

The difficulties of a standard focused on the best interests of the child have led many commentators to support a primary caretaker presumption. The main argument in favor of such a presumption is that it is a more determinate standard than the best interests test, and reduces the possibility of bias, stereotyping, uncertainty, and acrimonious litigation. It also is thought to encourage involvement in childrearing by rewarding parents who have assumed that responsibility. What should be the goal of custody law? To what extent should it reflect fairness to parents as well as the interests of their children? How important should gender neutrality be?

Patricia Ann S. v. James Daniel S.
435 S.E.2d 6 (W. Va. 1993)

Three children were born of the [parties'] marriage, [who are now ages 14, 11, and 7]. The [mother] was a kindergarten school teacher but left her employment upon the birth of their first child. The [father] is an architect. . . .

The primary issue in this case is the [mother]'s contention that she should be awarded custody of the parties' children. . . .

The parties agree that the guidelines for establishing custody are clearly set forth in Garska v. McCoy, [1981]. We defined primary caretaker . . . in *Garska*, as "that natural or adoptive parent who, until the initiation of divorce proceedings, has been primarily responsible for the caring and nurturing of the child." The law presumes that it is in the best interests of young children to be placed in the custody of the primary caretaker. . . .

It is the circuit court's responsibility to determine which parent is the primary caretaker. . . . In *Garska*, we listed the factors to be considered by the circuit court in making this determination. However, . . . we pointed out, "[i]f the trial court is unable to establish that one parent has clearly taken primary responsibility for the caring and nurturing duties of a child neither party shall have the benefit of the primary caretaker presumption."

It is clear from the evidence that the parties shared the primary caretaker duties as discussed in *Garska*. While the evidence presented established the fact that the [mother] was the homemaker and the [father] was the wage earner, this Court has recognized that the length of time a parent has alone with a child is not determinative of whether the primary caretaker presumption should attach. . . . The [mother] was at home for the children when they would return from school while the [father] would work throughout the day. However, the [father] was also a substantial participant in the child care duties once he came home from work.

With respect to the child care duties, the [mother] testified that she was a night person, meaning she would stay up late at night and sleep later in the morning. As a result, both parties testified that the [father] would be responsible for getting the boys ready for school and fixing their breakfast. Both parties further testified that the [mother] would primarily plan and prepare the evening meals on the weekdays, but on the weekends the [father] would often prepare the evening meals. The parties also testified that they shared the responsibility for getting the children ready for bed each night.

In terms of school and social activities for the children, the evidence is indicative of the fact that both parties were active in their children's social lives. . . . [The mother] participated in PTO (Parent Teacher Organization) meetings and school activities. [A teacher] also testified that the [father] was involved with the children's school activities; and, the [father] testified that he was instrumental in helping the children with their homework in the evenings.

Furthermore, each parent organized and participated in social activities with the children. [The mother] would organize birthday parties for the children, and she would often host pool parties for the children and their friends at the parties' home. On the other hand, the [father] would arrange and participate in camping, hiking, and biking trips as well as other sporting events with the children. . . .

Finally, the evidence suggests that the parties shared in the responsibility of disciplining the children. The [father] admitted that he used a belt to whip the boys, but he stated that he used his hand to whip Jennifer. The [mother], however, stated that she no longer uses the belt to whip the children. Rather, the [mother] testified that she had attended parenting classes, and as a result, she employed a new method of discipline such as taking away the children's privileges and grounding them for their wrongdoings. . . .

[W]e agree . . . that neither party is entitled to the status of primary caretaker because the child care duties were shared equally by the parties. Therefore, the issue of custody properly rests on the best interests of the child. . . .

With this in mind, we turn to the [mother's contention] that the circuit court erred in utilizing psychological expert witnesses prior to the circuit court's determination as to who was entitled to the status of primary caretaker. . . .

[The father] called psychologist, Mari Sullivan Walker, to testify before the family law master. Ms. Walker met with the [father] and the three children for approximately ninety minutes on September 22, 1990. Ms. Walker was of the opinion that the children perceive their father as the more nurturing person rather than their mother. Ms. Walker testified that all three children told her that the [mother] "beat" them. . . . Based upon the children's responses [to her question how they thought life would be with their father versus life with their mother,] Ms. Walker opined that the children have more faith in their father as opposed to their mother whom they were afraid of and with whom they were angry. . . .

Dr. Charles Yeargan, a child psychologist, . . . was initially hired by the [mother], but later the parties agreed to use him as a neutral expert to give his opinion regarding the welfare of the children. In October of 1990, Dr. Yeargan interviewed the entire S. family.

In response to questions asked by [father]'s counsel, Dr. Yeargan stated that he didn't ask the children where and with whom they wanted to live; however, based upon the children's comments, it was Dr. Yeargan's opinion that the children feel emotionally safer with the [father and that they would prefer to live with him].

Dr. Yeargan stated that the children perceive the [father] as emotional and supportive, and the [mother] is perceived as angry. Further, Dr. Yeargan testified that Jennifer told him that if her brothers live with the [father], then that is where she wants to live. Dr. Yeargan also opined that both parents have behavioral traits that they need to work out in order for them to be able to better cope with and relate to their children.

Ultimately, it was Dr. Yeargan's opinion that it was in the best interests of the two boys, Jason and Justin, that they live with the [father]. With respect to Jennifer, Dr. Yeargan admitted he did not have a lot to go on, but he recommended that Jennifer live with her mother because of "the interests of the two different parties," "the activity levels," "the socialization issues" and "the involvements."

Dr. Carl McGraw . . . interviewed all three children, the [father], and the [father]'s mother, because she had been helping care for the children. Dr. McGraw stressed the importance of keeping the children together in order to keep the family unit intact. Dr. McGraw noted that he had difficulty understanding Dr. Yeargan's reasoning for splitting the children between each parent. Dr. McGraw testified that the children told him they felt their mother was mean. Dr. McGraw stated he didn't ask the children who they wanted to live with, but he testified that they were adamant about wanting to live with their father. It was Dr. McGraw's opinion that the children would "have a better chance" if all three of them were to live with the [father], considering the rapport [he] has with [them]. . . .

The circuit court determined that the best interests of the children would be served by awarding custody to the [father]. There was an abundance of evidence presented in this case, which included the testimony of the parties, neighbors, teachers, family members, friends, and psychologists.

[In addition to the psychological testimony,] Jessica Halstead Sharp, a neighbor and friend of the parties, testified that she found the [father] to be loving and nurturing towards the children unlike the [mother] who, in Mrs. Sharp's opinion, had a problem dealing with the children. Mrs. Sharp also stated that, on more than one occasion, she overheard the [mother] calling the children vulgar names.

In addition, Nancy Jo S. and Reese and Ron Webb, Jr. testified that the children interact well with the [father]. However, they all felt the [mother] acted hostile with the children, and thus, the children did not respond well to her. All three witnesses further confirmed Mrs. Sharp's testimony that the [mother] called the children vulgar names, and they added, she used bad language around the children as well. . . .

Jason, the eldest son at fourteen years of age, is old enough to make a decision as to which parent he wants to live with, and the record clearly supports the circuit court's finding that Jason should live with his father. . . . Justin, on the other hand, is eleven years of age and not quite capable of making such a decision, but the evidence supports the circuit court's finding that he should live with his father. In addition, the [mother] admits that there is a lot of hostility between the boys and her, and because of this anger she might not be able to manage them. . . .

However, with respect to Jennifer, we do not believe that the record has been adequately developed. . . .

[W]e hold that the circuit court judge did not abuse his discretion by concluding that the best interests of the two boys would be served by awarding custody to the [father]. With respect to Jennifer, we remand the case to the circuit court for further development of the record in order to determine what is in her best interests. . . .

WORKMAN, CHIEF JUSTICE, dissenting.

The majority opinion marks a sharp departure from the primary caretaker rule which has been a viable and working concept in West Virginia for more than a decade. More disturbing, however, is the determination that it is in the best interests of children to place them in the custody of a parent who has abused both the wife and the children. In doing so, the majority implicitly places its stamp of approval on physical and emotional spousal abuse.

Deaths by domestic violence are increasing dramatically every year in West Virginia, and there is much discussion about the inefficacy of the judicial system in dealing with family violence. But until judicial officers on every level come to a better understanding of the phenomenon of family violence in its finer gradations, the response of the court system will continue to fall short. The majority demonstrates a tragic lack of understanding of the true nature of the dynamics that underlie family violence.

Erosion of Primary Caretaker Presumption

The primary caretaker rule as set forth in Garska v. McCoy . . . has been an important part of domestic relations law . . . for more than twelve years. . . .

> After stating the rationale for implementing the primary caretaker rule, this Court [in *Garska*] ruled that "in any custody dispute involving children of tender years it is incumbent upon the circuit court to determine as a threshold question which parent was the primary caretaker parent before the domestic strife giving rise to the proceeding began." . . .

In the instant case, it was clearly an abuse of discretion for the family law master and the circuit court to deny primary caretaker status to the mother. It is unfathomable that a woman who gives up her career (in this case, that of being a kindergarten teacher) to stay home to raise three children does not qualify as the primary caretaker, when as a full-time stay-at-home mother she breast-fed all three children; was so concerned about unnecessary additives and excess sugar that she processed her own baby food; was responsible for the majority of meal planning and preparation; was primarily responsible for laundering the family's clothing and housecleaning; was a Girl Scout troop leader; was a regular volunteer at her children's school and an active member of the parent-teacher organization; was responsible for scheduling and taking the children to their medical appointments; and was primarily responsible for managing the children's social activities. For some unarticulated reason, both the family law master and the circuit court appear to have been bowled over by the fact that the father helped in the evenings and weekends. Not unlike many modern fathers, the [father] did participate in some of the household and childrearing responsibilities. The mother and father jointly oversaw the bedtime routine of the children. Upon the birth of the third child, the father, by agreement of the parties, awoke the two oldest children and prepared their breakfasts, because the baby (Jennifer) was up a lot at night. As Jennifer grew older and began sleeping all night, the parties continued this routine. Although the mother stayed up late, during those evening hours she cleaned up from dinner, prepared lunches for the children to take to school the next day, and did other household duties. The [father] planned recreational activities such as camping and hiking trips, primarily for the boys. Given the father's admitted ten to twelve-hour work days combined with frequent business trips which took him away from home, it is difficult to conceive how he could ever qualify as having equal caretaking responsibility. . . . The majority in essence places a higher value on a father's time and contribution.

By upholding the circuit court's ruling, the majority begins an erosion of the primary caretaker rule, or at least sends a signal to domestic relations practitioners that it will be situationally ignored when expedient. . . . Sadly, . . . this case boils down to . . . one expert versus another [which the primary caretaker presumption was intended to avoid]. . . .

Majority Okays Spousal Abuse

This father not only takes a belt to the three children regularly, but he also has taken a belt to his wife. Phenomenally, the family law master did not permit the wife to testify in detail to the physical abuse she endured throughout the marriage, as he apparently concluded it had nothing to do with the children. In fact, spousal abuse has a tremendous impact on children.

> Children learn several lessons in witnessing the abuse of one of their parents. First, they learn that such behavior appears to be approved by their most important role models and that the violence toward a loved one is acceptable. Children also fail to grasp the full range of negative consequences for the violent behavior and observe, instead, the short term reinforcements, namely

compliance by the victim. Thus, they learn the use of coercive power and violence as a way to influence loved ones without being exposed to other more constructive alternatives.

In addition to the effect of the destructive modeling, children who grow up in violent homes experience damaging psychological effects. There is substantial documentation that the spouse abuser's violence causes a variety of psychological problems for children. Children raised in a home in which spouse abuse occurs experience the same fear as do battered children. . . .

Spouse abuse results not only in direct physical and psychological injuries to the children, but, of greatest long-term importance, it breeds a culture of violence in future generations. Up to 80 percent of men who abuse their wives witnessed or experienced abuse in their family of origin. Abused children are at great risk of becoming abusive parents. Thus, the ultimate question in assessing the relative fitness for custody of the abuser and victim is which parent is most likely to provide the children with a healthy, caring and *nonviolent* home. . . .

There is yet another aspect of spousal abuse that judges and many others find difficult to understand. These relationships are characterized not only by physical abuse, but also by repeated humiliation and other psychological abuse that "'reaches the level of a campaign to reduce the partner's sense of self-worth and to maintain control'"[;] and "a pattern on the part of the abusive partner to control the victim's daily actions. . . . " . . .

It is clear from Mr. S.'s testimony that he ran this family with an iron hand, a significant trait in abusive relationships being the total power and control of one party. The evidence reflects that for some period of time Mrs. S. was not allowed to have a cent, not even grocery money. She was permitted to write a grocery list, and if her husband was ever-so-gracious, he would include her requests. . . . Once she attempted to take $20 from his wallet and wound up in the emergency room after he wrestled with her over it. Mr. S. testified that he actually found the whole episode rather humorous, likening his wife clinging desperately to the $20 bill by hiding it in her mouth as resembling a lizard with lettuce sticking out of its mouth.

One of the complaints made about this mother is that she lacked the ability to manage the boys, ages twelve and ten at the time of the hearings, and surely the record is clear that it was difficult for her to manage these boys, especially Jason, the older of the two. In her petition for review, she pointed out that for several years, her husband had been "mentally, emotionally, and physically cruel" to her. Studies demonstrate that after ages five or six, children show strong indications of identifying with the aggressor and losing respect for the mother. . . .

In her personal petition for review to the circuit court, she [the mother] stated:

My two boys in particular identify with their father. Unfortunately, their father has downgraded me for years in front of them and continues to do so. I would become angry in response. The children have seen their father hit me with a belt. My oldest son Jason has bit me and kicked me so hard to have left bruises on me. Jason repeats to me in arguments what his father tells him happens in court. . . . My second son Justin is ten years old and is having difficulty adjusting. Since he has been with his father, his grades have gone from "A's" and "B's" to some "C's," "D's," and one "F." My six year old daughter, Jennifer is a 4.0 student in first grade. She is also in the gifted program. She has done fine under my care alone this past year.

The evidence reflects that Mr. S. modeled for these children the behavior of demeaning, discrediting, and otherwise disempowering the mother. For example, the father devised a point system to reward good behavior and punish bad behavior. When the mother attempted to participate in the system as a method of encouraging good behavior and managing the children, the children were told that "mommy's points don't count" and "mommy is crazy." The mother testified that the children's response was that "you're not the boss, daddy's the boss. . . ." Furthermore, the father would tally the points and take the children to the toy store for the payoff, which the mother had no financial resources to do. . . .

From Dr. Yeargan's report:

> Mr. S. reported that he can't see himself trying to tell the boys to be kinder and gentler to their mother for fear that he'll lose credibility with them. He said, "I'm not too interested in finding a way to help the enemy camp look good or better . . . until all three kids are together and this is resolved. My primary objective is to have the three kids."

Mrs. S. testified that she attended counselling, both in an effort to save the marriage and in an effort to get help in working with the children, and that she read a number of books on parenting and divorce. She admitted that she used bad language (as did the whole family) and that the husband's constant demeaning of her in front of the children made her angry. She acknowledged she had made mistakes and was working to correct them.

Mr. S., however, presents himself as the perfect father as demonstrated by his testimony that his rapport with the children was "exemplary," and "that it would be very difficult to improve upon." He described himself as "nurturing," "kind," "loving," "caring," "understanding," and "patient."

But a look at Dr. Yeargan's report presents a very different picture of this man:

> Some of the same parental behaviors that previously contributed to the children feeling torn between parents is continuing; those behaviors are (a) increasing the alienation between the children and their mother and (b) exacerbating the loneliness which the boys feel for their sister and vice versa. In this examiner's opinion the behaviors of Mr. [S.] . . . are of primary importance in the creation of more alienation and loneliness in the children. . . .

Mr. S. acknowledges that (although less frequently on five-year-old Jennifer), yes, he does use a belt on all three children, and according to unrefuted testimony he also has grabbed Jason by the shoulders and banged Jason's head against a tree. His own description of how he handles physical discipline shows best the kind of fear he uses to exert control over this family:

> Normally, the punishment is a smack on the behind with a belt. And I tell them what will happen if they transgress or exceed certain limitations; and, when they, on occasion — not recently, but on occasion — test an adult's authority, which all children are want (sic) to do, I have no choice but to follow through consistently with what I told them would happen. . . .
>
> On the occasions when I do smack their behinds with a belt, I will always make sure, after I have done it in a controlled and unemotional way — never in anger — that they understand what the punishment was for and why I had to do it, and I will always check their little bottoms to make sure that there is not sufficient force to seriously damage them, say bruising or whatever.

With all of these circumstances, one may wonder why the children were taken from the mother. A close reading of the record reveals that the most damaging things that can be said about Mrs. S. are that 1) she uses bad language; 2) she is very angry; 3) the children told the psychologists that they wanted to live with their father; and 4) one of the psychologists concluded that they "feel safer with their father."

Anger

What judges and indeed many therapists usually fail to understand is the behavior manifestations battered women frequently demonstrate. . . . Psychologists unfamiliar with all the circumstances and with the unique dynamics of family abuse may make these mistakes:

> 1. They fail to see that the victim's anger is appropriate and normal. . . .
> 2. They look to the victim's behavior and personality problems to explain the abuse. . . . Such blaming of the victim tends to reinforce the abuser's position that . . . the victim is crazy. 3. They seem to identify with the seemingly sociable, "appropriate" male as a man who has been pushed beyond his limits by an "angry woman." 4. They fail to see beneath the sincere, positive image of the abuser, but look instead for the "typical" abuser personality. . . . 7. Finally, they criticize [the woman] for focusing her anger on her husband. . . .

It does not appear that any of the psychologists had any information on the domestic abuse and none dealt with the physical abuse; only Dr. Yeargan seems to have had any information on the psychological abuse and domination. If family law masters and judges are to make decisions on the lives of troubled families, they must become sufficiently knowledgeable about physical and emotional domination to enable them to recognize that these factors are just as invidious, and probably more pervasive, than physical abuse alone. And we must begin to see anger on the part of the victim as healthy.

Children's Preference

These children learned from their father that their mother did not have even sufficient authority to purchase a package of Oreo cookies for them, that it was okay to demean, disobey, and verbally abuse her, and that physical violence awaited those who did not do as he said. The mother reacted with anger, and the father by word, deed, and dollar delivered the message that mommy's crazy and mommy's contemptible.

Jason was twelve years old at the time of the hearings before the family law master and thirteen by the time of the divorce. . . . Consequently, even though the mother was the primary caretaker, the circuit court cannot be said to have abused its discretion in giving weight to Jason's preference and placing him in the custody of his father. In all likelihood, and by all the evidence, this young man has already demonstrated a propensity to act out anger with violence, and we can only hope we do not see him in court in another generation.

Justin was ten years old and Jennifer six years old at the time their preferences were expressed. Although it could be argued that a ten-year-old's preference could be given some weight, Jennifer at six was too young to express a meaningful preference. Furthermore, a reading of the record makes it quite clear that Jennifer was spirited off to see psychologists by her father and instructed rather specifically on the way by her father and older brother regarding what to say. She related to her mother after-the-fact that she told lies and even Dr. Yeargan discerned that she had been coached.

Justin and Jennifer should have been placed in the custody of their mother. The majority wreaks further havoc on this family (especially Jennifer) by a remand for further evidence. It appears that anxiety and manipulation will again be the order of the day for this little girl, and life's most basic uncertainties will resume as the family is figuratively killed with due process. . . .

Notes

1. Primary Caretaker Presumption.   Although the primary caretaker presumption has been favored by many academics, only three states have ever enacted it.[261] Did the West Virginia state supreme court apply the presumption accurately in the *Patricia Ann S.* case?

---

261. See, e.g., Martha Albertson Fineman, The Illusion of Equality: The Rhetoric and Reality of Divorce Reform 180-85 (1991) (for all children); David L. Chambers, Rethinking the Substantive Rules for Custody Disputes in Divorce, 83 Mich. L. Rev. 477 (1985) (for children between six months and five years).

Substantive Equality in the Family

Some commentators have argued that the primary caretaker test is too heavily weighted in favor of the functions usually performed by women.[262] Is that a sufficient reason to abandon the test? What tasks are missing that ought to be on the list? Should wage-earning be a function that counts as "caretaking"? Even if a primary caretaker presumption does not reflect gender preferences, is it a problem that the rule perpetuates them? Even without the presumption, primary caretaking figures strongly in custody decisions.[263] Is that a problem?

West Virginia replaced its primary caretaker presumption in 2000 in favor of a past caretaking standard. See Note 3 below. Minnesota and Montana also tried the primary caretaker presumption, but neither retained it for long.

2. Joint Custody. All states allow some form of joint custody, and some provide a presumption or preference in its favor. Most commonly, however, despite statutory language encouraging participation in the child's life by both parents,[264] joint custody is one among a number of custody alternatives and not necessarily the favored one. In states with a preference for joint custody, some narrow it to circumstances in which the parents jointly agree,[265] or allow the presumption to be overcome by a showing that joint custody would not be in the child's best interests, or would be detrimental to the child.[266] Iowa requires the court to order joint custody on the request of either parent, unless clear and convincing evidence indicates that such an arrangement is unreasonable and not in the child's best interests, but joint custody in Iowa does not necessary mean joint physical care.[267] A few states disfavor joint custody awards.[268] A study of judges found that they developed a strong preference for joint custody between 1998 and 2011.[269] What might account for their changing attitudes?

Critics of joint custody argue that to the extent it reduces gender stereotypes, it does so by sacrificing the custodial rights of mothers who have acted as primary parents in favor of fathers who have not earned those rights. Another concern is "custody blackmail"—that laws favoring joint custody provide additional bargaining leverage to men at divorce, who use it to exact financial concessions from mothers who fear litigation over parental rights. A

262. Ronald K. Henry, Primary Caretaker: Is It a Ruse?, 17 Fam. Advoc. 53 (Summer 1994).

263. See, e.g., In re Custody of Kali, 792 N.E.2d 635 (Mass. 2003); In re McBrayer, 83 P.2d 936 (Or. Ct. App. 2004).

264. See, e.g., Colo. Rev. Stat. §14-10-124(1) (West 2016).

265. See, e.g., Cal. Fam. Code §3080 (West 2016).

266. See, e.g., D.C. Code Ann. §16-914(a)(2) (West 2016); Fla. Stat. Ann. §61.13(2)(c)(2) (West 2016).

267. Iowa Code Ann. §598.41(2) & (5) (West Supp. 2016).

268. Oregon, for example, prohibits an order unless both parents agree. Or. Rev. Stat. §107.169(3) (2016); see also Vt. Stat. Ann. tit. 15, §665(a) (2016) (when parents cannot agree, court must order primary or sole custody to one parent).

269. Julie E. Artis & Andrew V. Krebs, Family Law and Social Change: Judicial Views of Joint Custody, 1998-2011, 40 Law & Soc. Inquiry 723 (2015).

third criticism is that it gives spouses opportunities to harass their former partner and to prevent them from relocating. Similar critiques are leveled against "friendly parent" custody standards, which take into account the willingness and ability of a parent to cooperate in contact between the child and the other parent.[270] For example, Florida requires courts to examine "the demonstrated capacity and disposition of each parent to facilitate and encourage a close and continuing parent-child relationship, to honor the time-sharing schedule, and to be reasonable when changes are required."[271] Critics of such provisions argue that they enable vindictive individuals to harass and manipulate their former spouses and discourage well-intentioned parents—usually mothers—from opposing joint custody for fear that this opposition might be used to label them as a "non-friendly" parent and therefore an inappropriate candidate for primary custodian. Fathers' rights advocates, by contrast, argue that mothers sometimes falsely claim abuse in order to obtain custody, and that such allegations can be difficult to refute.

The effects of joint custody on child support are open to dispute. Supporters of joint custody note that it results in greater child support compliance than other arrangements. However, researchers note that is unclear whether joint custody encourages compliance or whether the kind of parents who seek joint custody are also the kind of parents who tend to take their child support obligations most seriously. Moreover, as discussed in Note 4 to Section 2, above, shared custody may reduce the amount of a child support order in a way that puts a greater strain on the lower-earning parent whose expenses on behalf of the child are not affected by the enhanced involvement of the other parent.

More generally, whether joint custody benefits children appears to depend upon the family circumstances. Children generally do well under shared arrangements when parents are able to value each other's contribution and have good psychological functioning, high self-esteem, and a low level of anger. By contrast, when parents have intense hostility, low self-esteem, and a tendency to blame or punish their former spouse, the children are likely to suffer.[272] There have been efforts in some states to push for a presumption of shared custody. Would you support such a proposal?

3. The "Approximation" or "Past Caretaking" Standard. The primary caretaking test was intended to give greater determinacy to the best interests test, which gave judges free rein to decide custody matters according

270. See Margaret K. Dore, The "Friendly Parent" Concept: A Flawed Factor for Child Custody, 6 Loy. J. Pub. Int. L. 41 (2004).

271. Fla. Stat. Ann. §61.13(3)(a) (West 2012).

272. On the relationship between high conflict and joint custody, see Janet Johnston, Building Multidisciplinary Professional Partnerships with the Court on Behalf of High-Conflict Divorcing Families and Their Children: Who Needs What Kind of Help?, 22 U. Ark. Little Rock L. Rev. 4543 (2000); Muriel Brotsky et al., Joint Custody Through Mediation: A Longitudinal Assessment of the Children, in Joint Custody and Shared Parenting 167 (1991).

to their own, subjective ideas about what is best for children. But the *Patricia Ann S.* case demonstrates that gender stereotypes can control a case, even in the face of a primary caretaker presumption.

If the best interests test is too subjective, the primary caretaker presumption too unfair to primary breadwinners, and the joint custody alternative too unrealistic for many couples, is there a preferable alternative?[273] Given the variety in circumstances in today's families and the importance of the actual custodial arrangements that parents make on their own, Elizabeth Scott suggests an alternative presumption, which she calls the "approximation standard." That standard calls for a custody arrangement that best approximates parenting patterns while the family was intact. Such an approach, she argues, promotes continuity and stability for children, encourages cooperative rather than adversarial behavior by parents, and provides incentives for both parents to invest in parenting before as well as after divorce.[274] This is also the approach taken by the American Law Institute, which calls it the "past caretaking standard."[275] Does this approach make gender bias less likely? Does it unfairly penalize fathers who are primary breadwinners? Douglas NeJaime argues that the marriage equality movement, because of its recognition of the needs of children being raised by same-sex couples, will help to promote a more intentional and functional view of parenthood.[276] Do you agree?

Another possibility is to give a custodial preference to the parent who is the same sex as the child. A few states have such a preference for children who are at or near adolescence; a few states expressly prohibit it.[277] Social science evidence on the benefits of such placements is mixed and may reflect gendered assumptions about what is healthy "sex role identification." Would

273. The Supreme Court of Wyoming reversed a trial court's finding that a husband's breadwinning was sufficient to allow him to share "primary caretaker" status with the child's mother. See Williams v. Williams, No. S-15-0148, 2016 WL 662020, at *6 (Wyo. Feb. 18, 2016); see also Laurie S. Kohn, Money Can't Buy You Love: Valuing Contributions by Non-Residential Fathers, 81 Brook. L. Rev. 53 (2015) (arguing that the legal system systematically sends the message that fathers' role is to provide financial support and denigrates the value of their caretaking efforts).

274. Elizabeth S. Scott, Pluralism, Parental Preference, and Child Custody, 80 Cal. L. Rev. 615 (1992).

275. American Law Institute, Principles of the Law of Family Dissolution §2.08 (2002).

276. Douglas NeJaime, Marriage Equality and the New Parenthood, 129 Harv. L. Rev. 1185 (2016); see also Joanna L. Grossman, Parentage Without Gender, 17 Cardozo J. Conflict Resolution 717 (2016).

277. Alabama appears to allow a same-sex parent preference, by statute. Other states, such as Arizona and Maine, explicitly prohibit it. See Ariz. Rev. Stat. Ann. §25-403.01(A) (West 2012); Me. Rev. Stat. Ann. tit. 19-A, §1653(4) (West 2012) ("court may not apply a preference for one parent over the other . . . because of a parent's gender or the child's age or gender"). In a few jurisdictions, including Illinois and North Dakota, courts have allowed a preference for a parent of the same sex during or right before adolescence on various role-modeling hypotheses. The majority rule, however, is that courts may not prefer a parent because he or she is the same sex as the child.

you expect that successful role modeling depends upon sharing a primary residence with the same-sex parent?

4. Lesbian Parents. Gay, lesbian, bisexual, or transgender parents may have custody issues even if they are the child's biological parent. Under the traditional view, homosexuality was sufficient to render a parent unfit to have custody of a child. While no court currently embraces such a categorical approach, a number of states permit the fact-finder to draw an inference that a parent's homosexual conduct is harmful to a child. In some cases, gay or lesbian parents have lost custody based upon kissing a same-sex partner in front of the children, admitting their homosexuality, or enrolling a child in a conservative school where it would cause embarrassment to the child to have a gay or lesbian parent.[278] In contrast, the emerging rule in a growing number of jurisdictions is that the sexual orientation of a parent may not be taken into account in a custody determination unless harm to the child is affirmatively demonstrated in a particular case.[279]

Generally, under the harm standard, real or imagined stigma from having a gay or lesbian parent is insufficient. The following analysis is increasingly typical:

> [O]ne of life's realities is that one of his parents is homosexual. In the absence of evidence that the homosexuality in some way harms the boy, limiting [his] relationship with that parent fails to permit him to confront his life situation, however unconventional it may be. . . . [The child's] best interest is served by exposing him to reality and not fostering in him shame or abhorrence for his mother's non-traditional commitment.[280]

Should state law prohibit consideration of a parent's sexual orientation in custody awards?[281]

Another set of issues arises with respect to a non-biological, lesbian co-parent who has acted as a parent with the consent of her partner, who is the biological mother and who seeks some custodial rights when the couple's relationship ends. Traditionally, courts denied visitation and custody rights to

---

278. See Suzanne A. Kim, The Neutered Parent, Yale J.L. & Feminism 1 (2012) (observing the tendency in custody law to prefer "sexually neutral" parenting, where parental sexuality is kept at a safe distance from children).

279. This is also the recommendation of the American Law Institute. See American Law Institute, Principles of the Law of Family Dissolution, §2.12(1)(d), (e) (2000). For a breakdown of the law among the states and a discussion of some of the cases, see Jovana Vujovic, Child Custody and Visitation, 5 Geo J. Gender & L. 477, 493 (2004).

280. Blew v. Verta, 617 A.2d 31, 36 (Pa. Super. Ct. 1992); see also Jacoby v. Jacoby, 763 So. 2d 410, 413 (Fla. Dist. Ct. App. 2000) (law cannot give effect to private biases, which in any event "flow not from the fact that the children were living with a homosexual mother, but from the fact that she is a homosexual").

281. See, e.g., D.C. Code Ann. §16-914(a)(1)(A) (2016).

lesbians who were de facto nonbiological parents, either because they lacked standing or because they failed to meet the substantive criteria for parenthood under the state's custody statute.[282] Starting in 1995, some states began developing a doctrine variously labeled de facto parentage, equitable parenthood, parenthood by estoppel, or in loco parentis (taking on all or some responsibilities of a parent), which allowed courts to award visitation rights to a lesbian co-parent who had raised the child on an equal basis with the biological parent, with that parent's approval.[283] A number of jurisdictions have changed, or are in the process of reviewing, decisions denying custodial status to a nonbiological co-parent.[284] In addition to the de facto parent rationale, a more recent theory is that when a co-parented child is conceived through artificial insemination in collaboration with her partner, she is a "parent" under a state's parentage act.[285] Under these theories, courts have also imposed support obligations on members of same-sex couples.[286] Courts in several states, however, have continued to reject de facto parentage, citing concerns about intruding on the biological mother's constitutionally protected parental rights and the lack of certainty about parental status that arises from a functional approach.[287]

Before the legalization of same-sex marriage nationwide, lesbian co-parents in some states were able to adopt the child they were co-parenting, notwithstanding the traditional prohibition against a child having more than one mother (or more than one father). Over a dozen states allowed "second-parent adoptions," a term developed as an equitable work-around for committed same-sex couples that could not avail themselves of stepparent adoptions because they were not permitted to marry.[288] When the California Supreme Court ruled in favor of same-sex second-parent adoptions in 2003, more than 20,000 had already been granted by family court judges.[289] But the national landscape on second-parent adoptions is still very mixed. The North Carolina Supreme Court, for example, ruled against second-parent adoption

---

282. See, e.g., Debra H. v. Janice R., 930 N.E.2d 184 (N.Y. 2010).

283. In re Custody of H.S.H.-K., 533 N.W.2d 419 (Wis. 1995); Rubano v. DiCenzo, 759 A.2d 959 (R.I. 2000).

284. See, e.g., Barone v. Chapman-Cleland, 129 A.D.3d 1578 (N.Y. App. Div. 2015), review granted sub nom. Brooke S.B. v. Elizabeth A. C.C., 26 N.Y.3d 901 (2015).

285. See, e.g., Chatterjee v. King, 280 P.3d 283 (N.M. 2012); Frazier v. Goudschaal, 295 P.3d 542 (Kan. 2013). For the argument, see Nancy D. Polikoff, From Third Parties to Parents: The Case of Lesbian Couples and Their Children, 77 L. & Contemp. Probs. 195, 209-19 (2014).

286. See, e.g., Elisa B. v. Superior Court, 117 P.3d 660, 663 (Cal. 2005).

287. See, e.g., Smith v. Gordon, 968 A.2d 1 (Del. 2009); White v. White, 293 S.W.3d 1 (Mo. Ct. App. 2009). A similar case in Maryland, Janice M. v. Margaret K., 948 A.2d 73 (Md. 2008), was recently overruled in Conover v. Conover, 2016 WL 3633062 (July 7, 2016).

288. Courtney G. Joslin, The Legal Parentage of Children Born to Same-Sex Couples, 39 Fam. L.Q. 683, 691 (2005).

289. Sharon S. v. Superior Court, 73 P.3d 554, 568 (Cal. 2003).

in 2010, invalidating not only a final adoption decree that had been previously granted in that particular case, but thousands more as well.[290] Utah bars adoptions by all unmarried couples, and Mississippi bars adoption by same-sex couples whether married or not.[291] Arkansas voters passed a referendum in 2008 to preclude adoption by any individual who was unmarried and "cohabiting with a sexual partner."[292] The state's supreme court struck down the referendum, however, as a violation of the state constitutional right to privacy. Only Florida had an outright prohibition on adoptions by gay or lesbian individuals, but the statute was held unconstitutional by an appellate court in 2010, and the state chose not to appeal.[293] The American Academy of Pediatrics has long supported same-sex co-parent adoption as beneficial to children.[294] Because state laws varied, questions arose about whether same-sex adoptions obtained in one state need to be recognized in another. The U.S. Supreme Court resolved this issue in V.I. v. E.I., in which it held even without the benefit of briefing on the merits that a final judgment of adoption in one state is entitled to full faith and credit in another.[295]

Obergefell has eliminated the need for second-parent adoptions because now that same-sex couples can marry, they presumably can use the step-parent adoption process that is available in every state. Mississippi had a separate law barring two people of the same sex from jointly adopting a child, but it was challenged in the wake of *Obergefell* and struck down by a federal court.[296] But should unmarried, same-sex couples still be permitted to use second-parent adoption? Also, now that same-sex couples have equal access to marriage, will courts be even less willing to recognize de facto parentage or second-parent adoption for unmarried same-sex couples, remedies that were designed to fill the gap left by discriminatory marriage laws? A Missouri appellate court recently observed that "the justification for rejecting an equitable parentage argument is stronger today" than in 2009 when it first rejected the doctrine.[297] Indeed, the court noted, "[w]e anticipate that in the wake of *Obergefell*, situations like this one, in which important issues involving children must be

290. Boseman v. Jarrell, 704 S.E.2d 494 (N.C. 2010).

291. Miss. Code Ann. §93-17-3(5) (2016); Utah Code Ann. §78B-6-117 (2016).

292. Ark. Code Ann. §9-8-204 (2010), invalidated by Dep't of Human Servs. v. Cole, 2011 Ark. 145 (2011).

293. In re Matter of Adoption of X.X.G. & N.R.G., 45 So. 3d 79, 81 (2010).

294. American Academy of Pediatrics, Co-Parent or Second Parent Adoption by Same-Sex Parents, 109 Pediatrics 339 (2002).

295. 136 S. Ct. 1017 (2016).

296. See Campaign for Southern Equality et al. v. Mississippi Dep't Human Servs., __ F. Supp. 3d (S.D. Miss. 2016) (invalidating Miss. Code Ann. §93-17-3(5) (2010)); Tamar Lewin, Mississippi Ban on Adoptions by Same-Sex Couples Is Challenged, N.Y. Times, Aug. 12, 2015, at A9. The Movement Advancement Project provides helpful tracking on these issues. Foster and Adoption Laws, MAP: Movement Advancement Project, http://www.lgbtmap.org/equality-maps/foster_and_adoption_laws (2015).

297. McGaw v. McGaw, 468 S.W.3d 435, 442 (Mo. Ct. App. 2015).

decided outside the established legal framework applicable to married couples, will occur less frequently."[298]

5. Relocation. Most families relocate after divorce. In 2014, approximately 18 percent of divorced or separated U.S. families reported having changed living quarters within the previous year. Of these, 62 percent relocated within the same county, 18 percent to a different county within the same state, and 18 percent to a different state or abroad.[299] One study of college students from divorced families found that in only 39 percent of cases did neither parent relocate after the divorce. It was equally likely that the child remained with the mother while the father relocated, and that the child relocated with the mother.[300] These moves often result in significant psychological disadvantages for children.[301]

The law in this area has been unstable, at best, but the clear trend has been toward increasing deference to the parent with whom the child has been primarily living. Typically, the kinds of reasons for relocation that courts view as acceptable are to take a significantly better job (or to allow a new spouse to take a significantly better job), to address significant health issues, to pursue educational opportunities not available in the original jurisdiction, to be close to other relatives, or to bring significant improvement in the family's quality of life.

Which of these reasons seem significant enough to deprive the non-custodial parent of frequent contact with the children? On the one hand, depriving a custodial parent of the right to move with his or her children is a high price to pay for custody. It often seems unfair to make the parent who has borne the primary responsibility for the children during the marriage incur relocation limitations that the other parent does not incur at divorce. On the other hand, the non-custodial parent will often face significant, sometimes almost insurmountable constraints, in maintaining a close relationship to a child who resides a long distance away. Yet preventing both parents from relocating may impose significant economic as well as personal disadvantages.

Because most children of divorced families are in the physical custody of their mothers, the relocation standard a court applies will have a gender impact. Should that impact be taken into account? If one objective of custody law is to encourage parenting by fathers, should the standard prefer protecting the custodial/visitation rights of fathers or the caretaking roles already assumed during the marriage?

298. Id. at 438.
299. See U.S. Census Bureau, Population Division, Current Population Survey, Geographic Mobility: 2014-2015 (Nov. 2015).
300. Sanford L. Braver et al., Relocation of Children After Divorce and Children's Best Interests: New Evidence and Legal Considerations, 17 J. Family Psych. 206, 212 (2003).
301. Id.

6. Fairness and Custody. To what extent should fairness be a factor in custody rules? In *Patricia Ann S.,* for example, assume that (1) the children are more comfortable with their father and want to live with him; (2) the reason for this is that the father has physically and emotionally abused the mother, eliminating her self-esteem and impairing her parental abilities; and (3) it is a reasonable prediction that the mother will not be able to regain the confidence and trust of her children. In these circumstances (which represent one reading of the case), should fairness to the mother be a factor in her favor?

7. Marriage, Cohabitation, and the American Paradox. In The Marriage-Go-Round, sociologist Andrew Cherlin notes that the United States is unlike any other country in the importance that it places both on marriage and on the ability to escape from marriage. Americans are more likely to marry and also to break up than couples in other nations. Cohabitation and its breakup are also more common in the United States.[302] Cohabiting couples are twice as likely to break up as married couples.[303] In short, the United States experiences exceptional social "turbulence—a coming and going of partners on a scale seen nowhere else."[304] This instability is not good for children. Cherlin, like other experts, concludes that families would be better off if parents were less quick to partner and repartner in marriage and cohabiting relationships. If that is true, does it have any implications for family law and policy?

Putting Theory Into Practice

2-32. Since the birth of her son, David, two years ago, Rhonda quit her job as an assistant office manager to care for her son at home, and relied on support by her husband Hugh, who is a high school teacher. They are divorcing. Since Hugh does not make enough money to support two households, Rhonda has agreed that she must return to full-time employment and that David will have to be placed in day care. Rhonda seeks primary custody of David based on her primary caretaking role during the marriage. Hugh argues that he should have primary custody because his mother has agreed to take care of David while he works, which he believes would be preferable to care by strangers. What rules should govern such a case? What further information should the court have to make its decision?

---

302. Andrew Cherlin, The Marriage-Go-Round: The State of Marriage and the Family in America Today 4, 18 (2009).
303. Lisa Selin Davis, Everything but the Ring, Time, May 25, 2009, at 58.
304. Cherlin, supra note 304, at 4.

What if Hugh is about to remarry and his new wife is prepared to provide full-time, in-home care for David along with her own young child? Is this a stronger or weaker case for Rhonda?

2-33. When Janet and Mark divorced after an eight-year marriage, Janet had no job skills or training. During the marriage, she stayed at home to care for her three children, the first of whom was born almost immediately upon her graduation from high school. At the divorce, Janet decided to give up primary custody of the children, then ages 3, 5, and 8, to Mark, who was planning to remarry, so that Janet would have two years to attend community college full-time. Still, Janet had custody of the children every weekend and during school vacations, talked to them every night on the telephone, and continued to take primary responsibility for such things as doctor appointments, clothing, haircuts, birthday presents, and the like. Janet missed seeing the children every day, but felt the arrangement was the only way she would be able to make herself economically independent. The children were cared for during the day, when they weren't in school, by their stepmother, who did not work outside the home.

The arrangement seemed to be working well, until one year into the arrangement, Mark announced that he had received a very large promotion and was moving to another state, 1500 miles away. He intends to take the children with him. Should Janet be able to stop him from moving with the children? Under what general rule?

2-34. The No Child Left Behind Act allows children in "failing" schools to transfer to a non-failing school in the same school district. Eight-year-old Charlie lives with Vivian, his mother, at one end of the school district, served by a very poor elementary school, to which Charlie can walk. His father, George, lives at the other end of the district near a school that the court determines is better educationally. George seeks a change of custody, so that Charlie can live with him and attend the better school. The parents live only 10 miles apart, but the commute by city bus is 45 minutes, George could not do the commute alone, and neither parent's work schedules would allow them to accompany George back and forth to school from Vivian's house.

Should George get custody of Charlie? Is changing custody from Vivian to George fair to Vivian? Should fairness matter?

2-35. At a custody trial between biological parents, the father offers evidence to show that a lesbian mother snuggles with her children and her female companion in bed, has the children march with her in a gay and lesbian rights parade, and has her children participate in a "commitment ceremony" with her companion. Her children also have an "astonishing grasp of anatomical terminology." Is this evidence proof of harm to the children? What are the arguments on each side?[305]

2-36. Thomas orally agreed with a lesbian couple to provide sperm that would inseminate one of them and to forgo all parental rights to any child born as a result. They also agreed that Thomas would be available to meet the child if she became curious about her origins. A child was born and when she was about five years old, the couple contacted Thomas so that she could meet him. For the next five or six years, Thomas visited with the child several times and developed a relationship with her, with the permission of the child's mothers. The parties eventually began to disagree, however, about the length and terms of the visits. Thomas files an action seeking court-ordered visitation. Should he succeed? Should advocates of the custodial rights of gay and lesbian parents favor Thomas' claim? If so, what access to the child should Thomas be allowed?

2-37. Two researchers have concluded, from a comparative longitudinal study, that while there is no significant difference in sexual attraction to someone of the same gender between those raised by lesbian single mothers and those raised by heterosexual single mothers, children raised in lesbian families are somewhat more likely to consider, and to have, homosexual involvement than are their peers raised by heterosexual mothers.[306] Should these findings play any role in custody decisions?

2-38. John seeks to have his 11-year-old son undergo "gay conversion" therapy so that he will live a happier life and because John's religion, in which the child was raised, believes that gays and lesbians will spend eternity in hell. His ex-wife, Louise, who is the child's mother, objects. How should this dispute be resolved? Should the dispute affect who gets custody of the child?[307]

2-39. It is estimated that one-fifth of children haven't seen their father in the last year.[308] If making divorced men more involved in parenting is an

305. See Hertzler v. Hertzler, 908 P.2d 946 (Wyo. 1995).

306. See Judith Stacey and Timothy J. Biblarz, (How) Does the Sexual Orientation of Parents Matter?, 66 Am. Soc. Rev. 159 (2001); Susan Golombok & Fiona Tasker, Do Parents Influence the Sexual Orientation of Their Children? Findings from a Longitudinal Study of Lesbian Families, 32 Dev. Psychol. 3, 7 (1996); Fiona Tasker & Susan Golombok, Growing Up in a Lesbian Family: Effects on Child Development 102-14 (1997).

307. Four states prohibit the practice. The laws are predicated on varying legislative findings, most notably harm to children and consumer fraud (on the theory that sexual orientation is innate and not subject to "conversion"). The American Psychological Association and American Academy of Pediatrics both condemn the practice. See Kim Bellware, Illinois Bans Gay Conversion Therapy for LGBT Youths, Huff. Post (Aug. 20, 2015), http://www.huffing tonpost.com/entry/illinois-bans-gay-conversion-therapy_us_55d668b4e4b020c386de2cc4.

308. Stephen Perrine, Keeping Divorced Dads at a Distance, N.Y. Times, June 16, 2006, at E13.

important goal, how can it be achieved? What would you think of a requirement that each parent exercise approximately 50 percent of physical custody
of his or her children? What are the advantages and disadvantages of such an
approach?[309]

4. Unmarried Parents

One area in which many sex-based distinctions persist involves the rights
of unmarried parents. The issue is increasingly important given the mete-
oric rise in nonmarital births. In 2010, more than 40 percent of all births
in the United States were to unmarried women, as many as 70 percent in
some racial groups.[310] At common law, the child of unmarried parents was
filius nullius—the child of no one. In the nineteenth century, states began to
recognize legal ties between unwed mothers and their children, but unwed
fathers were generally denied parental rights (though not always parental obligations) well into the twentieth century.[311] That system crumbled beginning
in the 1970s when the Supreme Court held, in a series of cases, that unwed
fathers could not be categorically stripped of legal parentage without violating the Fourteenth Amendments protections. These cases followed a series of
cases recognizing the equal protection rights of illegitimate children not to be
unfairly penalized by their parents' actions.[312]

In Stanley v. Illinois, the U.S. Supreme Court held that the state could
not make children of an unmarried father wards of the state when their mother
died based on a conclusive presumption that he was unfit.[313] Peter Stanley had
lived with his children and their mother for most of the 18 years before her
death. But because he was not married to the mother, he was not considered
a legal parent under the applicable statute. The Court invalidated the statute
on substantive and procedural due process grounds, holding that the children
could not be removed from their father unless he was first shown to be unfit. It
found the state's proffered justifications—to protect "the moral, emotional,
mental, and physical welfare of the minor and the best interests of the community" and to "strengthen the minor's family ties whenever possible"—to

---

309. See Ariel Ayanna, From Children's Interests to Parent Responsibility: Degendering
Parenthood Through Custodial Obligation, 19 UCLA Women's L.J. 1 (2012)

310. Brady E. Hamilton et al., Births: Preliminary Data for 2014, 64.6 Nat'l Vital Statistics Report 4 & 13 tbl. 6 (June 17, 2015).

311. See Mary Ann Mason, From Father's Property to Children's Rights: The History of
Child Custody in the United States 24 (1994).

312. See, e.g., Levy v. Louisiana, 391 U.S. 68 (1968). On the development of rights for
unwed fathers, see Joanna L. Grossman, The New Illegitimacy: Tying Parentage to Marital
Status for Lesbian Co-Parents, 20 J. Gender, Soc. Pol'y & L. 101, 122-32 (2012).

313. 405 U.S. 645 (1972).

be undermined by cutting off custodial, biological fathers solely based on marital status.[314]

Although *Stanley* put an end to the categorical denial of unwed father-hood, the Court considered in other cases the degree to which states could still differentiate between unmarried fathers and unmarried mothers. In Caban v. Mohammed (1979), the Supreme Court decided that a stepparent could not adopt a child without the biological father's consent if the father had developed an ongoing, meaningful relationship with the child.[315] If state law would not allow the termination of a mother's rights in similar circum-stances, the Court reasoned, it could not allow the termination of the rights of a father who had accepted his responsibilities as a parent. The Court rejected the state's justification that "a natural mother" usually has a "closer relation-ship with her child . . . than a father does."[316] Finally, in Lehr v. Robertson (1983), the Court considered an unwed father's rights to an infant before a substantial relationship has had time to develop.[317] The mother in that case married a man other than the biological father of her eight-month-old infant and petitioned for the stepfather to adopt the child when she was two. A court approved the adoption without notifying the biological father of the proceeding. New York maintained a "putative father registry" that allows men to notify the state of their intent to assert paternity over an actual or potential child. But the father had not registered, nor satisfied any other criteria such as listing on the birth certificate or living with the child that would entitle him to notice. The Court upheld the New York law, concluding that the father's biological tie to the child was not enough to justify full constitutional pro-tection of his parental rights. While a "developed parent-child relationship" deserves robust protection, an undeveloped one is only protected if the father has grasped every opportunity to develop one.[318]

Together, these rulings allow states to grant legal parentage automatically to unwed mothers, but to impose preconditions on legal parentage for unwed fathers. Most states have adopted a system similar to the one endorsed by the Uniform Parentage Act, in which a man is the legal father of a child if one of several criteria is met, including marriage to the mother, adjudication or acknowledgment of paternity, open and notorious acknowledgment of father-hood, or clear and convincing evidence of paternity.[319]

The federal government makes sex-based distinctions between unmar-ried mothers and unmarried fathers in circumstances that can produce harsh consequences. The Supreme Court has thrice upheld various provisions of immigration law that disallow citizen-fathers from passing citizenship to their

314. Id. at 652.
315. 441 U.S. 380 (1979).
316. Id. at 388.
317. 463 U.S. 248 (1983).
318. Id. at 250-62.
319. Unif. Parentage Act. §204, 9B U.L.A. 22-23 (Supp. 2011).

offspring born abroad in situations when a citizen-mother could have transmitted citizenship.[320] The Supreme Court in Nguyen v. Immigration and Naturalization Service (2001), for example, upheld a federal statute that sets forth different requirements for citizenship claimed through an American-born father than through the American-born mother.[321] Even though the child was abandoned by his Vietnamese mother, and raised exclusively by his American father in Texas, he was not eligible for citizenship because his father had not taken the right administrative steps within the allotted time to establish a legal parent-child relationship. Had his mother been the citizen, he would have inherited it automatically regardless of whether she actively participated in childrearing or took any affirmative steps to establish their relationship. But because his citizen-parent was his father, he was no longer eligible to apply for citizenship and was deported to Vietnam after conviction for a crime of moral turpitude. The Court upheld this gender differentiation against an equal protection challenge as justified by "a biological difference between the parents" because "the mother is always present at birth," but "the father need not be."[322]

Both lines of cases—considering the legality of state and federal distinctions between unwed mothers and fathers—are controversial. Some commentators argue that the rights of unmarried fathers and mothers should be identical; others claim that fathers and mothers are not similarly situated, and that the same rules should not apply. Justice Stevens has consistently followed the latter reasoning. Consider the following, from his dissent in Caban v. Mohammed:

> Men and women are different, and the difference is relevant to the question whether the mother may be given the exclusive right to consent to the adoption of a child born out of wedlock. Because most adoptions involve newborn infants or very young children, it is appropriate at the outset to focus on the significance of the difference in such cases.
>
> Both parents are equally responsible for the conception of the child out of wedlock. But from that point on through pregnancy and infancy, the differences between the male and the female have an important impact on the child's destiny. Only the mother carries the child; it is she who has the constitutional right to decide whether to bear it or not. In many cases, only the mother knows who sired the child, and it will often be within her power to withhold that fact, and even the fact of her pregnancy, from that person. If during pregnancy the

320. See Miller v. Albright, 523 U.S. 420 (1998); Nguyen v. INS, 533 U.S. 53 (2001); United States v. Flores-Villar, 131 S. Ct. 2312 (2010) (affirming without opinion, by a vote of 4-4, the appellate ruling, 536 F.3d 990 (9th Cir. 2008)).
321. 533 U.S. at 53. On how the citizenship-by-descent rules were used historically to deny citizenship to non-white children, see Kristin A. Collins, Illegitimate Borders: Jus Sanguinis Citizenship and the Legal Construction of Family, Race, and Nation, 123 Yale L.J. 2134 (2014).
322. *Nguyen*, 533 U.S. at 64.

mother should marry a different partner, the child will be legitimate when born, and the natural father may never even know that his "rights" have been affected. On the other hand, only if the natural mother agrees to marry the natural father during that period can the latter's actions have a positive impact on the status of the child; if he instead should marry a different partner during that time, the only effect on the child is negative, for the likelihood of legitimacy will be lessened.

These differences continue at birth and immediately thereafter. During that period, the mother and child are together; the mother's identity is known with certainty. The father, on the other hand, may or may not be present; his identity may be unknown to the world and may even be uncertain to the mother. These natural differences between unmarried fathers and mothers make it probable that the mother, and not the father or both parents, will have custody of the newborn infant.

In short, it is virtually inevitable that from conception through infancy the mother will constantly be faced with decisions about how best to care for the child, whereas it is much less certain that the father will be confronted with comparable problems. There no doubt are cases in which the relationship of the parties at birth makes it appropriate for the State to give the father a voice of some sort in the adoption decision. But as a matter of equal protection analysis, it is perfectly obvious that at the time and immediately after a child is born out of wedlock, differences between men and women justify some differential treatment of the mother and father in the adoption process.

Most particularly, these differences justify a rule that gives the mother of the newborn infant the exclusive right to consent to its adoption. Such a rule gives the mother, in whose sole charge the infant is often placed anyway, the maximum flexibility in deciding how best to care for the child. It also gives the loving father an incentive to marry the mother, and has no adverse impact on the disinterested father. Finally, it facilitates the interests of the adoptive parents, the child, and the public at large by streamlining the often traumatic adoption process and allowing the prompt, complete, and reliable integration of the child into a satisfactory new home at as young an age as is feasible. Put most simply, it permits the maximum participation of interested natural parents without so burdening the adoption process that its attractiveness to potential adoptive parents is destroyed.[323]

Consider also Justice Kennedy's plurality opinion in *Nguyen*:

To fail to acknowledge even our most basic biological differences—such as the fact that a mother must be present at birth but the father need not be—risks making the guarantee of equal protection superficial, and so disserving it. Mechanistic classification of all our differences as stereotypes would operate to obscure those misconceptions and prejudices that are real.[324]

---

323. Caban v. Mohammed, 441 U.S. 380, 404-08 (1979) (Stevens, J., dissenting).
324. 533 U.S. at 73.

Are Justices Stevens and Kennedy right? Granting the differences between mothers and fathers with respect to the birth process, should these differences have legal consequences? Does distinguishing between unmarried mothers and fathers promote, or undermine, gender equity?

Putting Theory Into Practice

2-40. Delaware law allows for the changing of a child's name, upon petition of a parent, if the change is in the child's best interests. A mother petitioned the court seeking to change the surname of her five-year-old daughter from her father's surname alone to a name that combined it with her mother's surname, without a hyphen. Denying the petition, the judge said the only benefit of the name change would be to "superficially execute [the mother's] desire to draw the child closer to her heritage," which was insufficient to make the change in the child's best interests?[325]

What arguments would you make on appeal for the mother?

2-41. Aala, a Muslim born of Syrian parents, had sex for the first time with John, after he had convinced her to try alcohol for the first time. She became pregnant, but did not tell John because she did not want him to interfere with her decision about the pregnancy. Aala placed the child for adoption without his knowledge for four reasons: (1) her parents are fundamentalist Muslims with strict views against pre-marital sex; (2) she is a college student and could not support a child; (3) she does not want her child raised by John because of his liberal cultural and political views; and (4) she believes that her child will be better off if raised in a two-parent family. During a statutory waiting period, John found out about the baby and petitioned to block the adoption. State law allows an unmarried mother to place a baby for adoption without the father's consent unless he has provided support during pregnancy or after birth.

Is this law constitutional? Is it wise? If the adoption is blocked, how should a court decide a custody dispute between Aala and John?

2-42. A newspaper article examining putative father registries concluded that "it's all smoke and mirrors. How can registries work if no one's heard of them? And it's just not reasonable to expect that men will register every time they have sex." It also reported that, in Florida in 2004, 47 men signed up for the state's registry, while there were 89,436 out-of-wedlock births.[326] Do those numbers signal an equality problem? Should states have the obligation to educate men of the steps necessary to protect parental rights?

325. In re Sophie LaVoie Boone, C.A. No. CPU 4-15-003549 (ct. Common Pleas New Castle Cty. Del., Dec. 21, 2015)

326. Tamar Lewin, Unwed Fathers Fight for Babies Placed for Adoption by Mothers, N.Y. Times, Mar. 19, 2006.

3

Nonsubordination

A nonsubordination perspective shifts the focus of attention from whether women and men are the same or different, to whether a rule or practice serves to subordinate women to men. This perspective, sometimes referred to as dominance theory, sees sex differences as part of a larger conceptual system designed to legitimate the power imbalance between men and women. Leading feminist legal theorist Catharine MacKinnon calls this theory feminism "unmodified," because it analyzes the situation of all women *as women* and abandons "gender-neutral absolutes, such as difference and sexuality and speech and the state" that, according to MacKinnon, are characteristic of liberal feminism.[1]

This chapter introduces nonsubordination theory by pairing John Stuart Mill's description of women's nineteenth-century "subjection" as a "solitary breach" in the fundamental laws of modern civilization with Catharine MacKinnon's characterization of women's legal subordination as the ability of those with power—men—to identify their own point of view, systematically, as universal "point-of-viewlessness." The remainder of the chapter explores nonsubordination theory's claim that the law defines sex and sexual difference in ways that naturalize women's relative powerlessness in this society, primarily through legal materials relating to sexual harassment, pornography, domestic violence, and heterosexuality.

It is no accident that most of the topics of this chapter relate to sexual behavior—particularly inside families, workplaces, and educational institutions. This is largely because the sexual realm is where dominance theory has

---

1. See Catharine A. MacKinnon, Feminism Unmodified: Discourses on Life and Law 16 (1987).

373

the most to offer. Traditional formal equality analysis has achieved significant improvements for women in employment, education, and other public benefits (although nonsubordination theorists tend to see these improvements as marginal exceptions—mostly on behalf of privileged women who fit the male profile). However, equality analysis is insufficient, MacKinnon argues, to address the central inequalities faced by women—sexual harassment, violence against women, poverty, and control of women's sexuality. To address these problems, MacKinnon contends that we must move beyond questions of sameness and difference to the construction of women's sexuality that underpins these more central inequalities. As you study the materials in this chapter, consider what nonsubordination theory contributes to the equality principles studied this far. Is it a supplement, a full replacement, or something else?

A. WOMEN'S RIGHTS AND POWER IN THE LIBERAL STATE

In the readings below, John Stuart Mill—the leading spokesman for nineteenth-century liberalism—finds the subordination of women an aberrational blind spot of liberalism. Catharine MacKinnon, on the other hand, finds the subordination of women a more or less inevitable consequence of liberalism's emphasis on the individual, its claim to objectivity, and its idealism. These two starting points frame much of the material in this chapter.

John Stuart Mill, The Subjection of Women
Three Essays by John Stuart Mill 427-28, 443-44, 449-50 (World's Classics ed. 1912) (1869)

[T]he principle which regulates the existing social relations between the two sexes—the legal subordination of one sex to the other—is wrong in itself, and now one of the chief hindrances to human improvement; . . . it ought to be replaced by a principle of perfect equality, admitting no power or privilege on the one side, nor disability on the other.

The . . . difficulty . . . is that which exists in all cases in which there is a mass of feeling to be contended against. So long as an opinion is strongly rooted in the feelings, it gains rather than loses in stability by having a preponderating weight of argument against it. For if it were accepted as a result of argument, the refutation of the argument might shake the solidity of the conviction; but when it rests solely on feeling, the worse it fares in argumentative contest, the more persuaded its adherents are that their feeling must have some deeper ground, which the arguments do not reach; and while the feeling remains, it is always throwing up fresh entrenchments of argument to repair any breach made in the old. And there are so many causes tending to make the feelings connected with this subject the most intense and most deeply-rooted of all those which gather round and protect old institutions and customs, that we need not wonder to find them as yet less undermined and loosened than any of the rest by the progress of the great modern spiritual and social transition; nor suppose that the barbarisms to which men cling longest must be less barbarisms than those which they earlier shake off.

All causes, social and natural, combine to make it unlikely that women should be collectively rebellious to the power of men. They are so far in a position different from all other subject classes, that their masters require something more from them than actual service. Men do not want solely the obedience of women, they want their sentiments. All men, except the most brutish, desire to have, in the woman most nearly connected with them, not a forced slave but a willing one; not a slave merely, but a favorite. They have therefore put everything in practice to enslave their minds. The masters of all slaves rely, for maintaining obedience, on fear; either fear of themselves, or religious fears. The masters of women wanted more than simple obedience, and they turned the whole force of education to effect their purpose. All women are brought up from the very earliest years in the belief that their ideal of character is the very opposite to that of men; not self-will, and government by self-control, but submission, and yielding to the control of others. All the moralities tell them that it is their nature, to live for others; to make complete abnegation of themselves, and to have no life but in their affections. And by their affections are meant the only ones they are allowed to have — those to the men with whom they are connected, or to the children who constitute an additional and indefeasible tie between them and a man. When we put together three things — first, the natural attraction between opposite sexes; secondly, the wife's entire dependence on the husband, every privilege or pleasure she has being either his gift, or depending entirely on his will; and lastly, that the principal object of human pursuit, consideration, and all objects of social ambition, can in general be sought or obtained by her only through him — it would be a miracle if the object of being attractive to men had not become the polar star of feminine education and formation of character. And, this great means of influence over the minds of women having been acquired, an instinct of selfishness made men avail themselves of it to the utmost as a means of holding women in subjection, by representing to them meekness, submissiveness, and resignation of all individual will into the hands of a man, as an essential part of sexual attractiveness. . . .

The social subordination of women thus stands out an isolated fact in modern social institutions; a solitary breach of what has become their fundamental law; a single relic of an old world of thought and practice exploded in everything else, but retained in the one thing of most universal interest. . . .

Catharine A. MacKinnon, Feminism Unmodified: Discourses on Life and Law
34-38, 40-41 (1987)

Under the sameness standard, women are measured according to our correspondence with man, our equality judged by our proximity to his measure. Under the difference standard, we are measured according to our lack of correspondence with him, our womanhood judged by our distance from his measure. Gender neutrality is thus simply the male standard, and the special protection rule is simply the female standard, but do not be deceived: masculinity, or maleness, is the referent for both. . . .

Feminists have this nasty habit of counting bodies and refusing not to notice their gender. As applied, the sameness standard has mostly gotten men the benefit of those few things women historically had—for all the good they did us. Almost every sex discrimination case that has been won at the Supreme Court level has been brought by a man. . . .

In reality, which this approach is not long on because it is liberal idealism talking to itself, virtually every quality that distinguishes men from women is already affirmatively compensated in this society. Men's physiology defines most sports, their needs define auto and health insurance coverage, their socially designed biographies define workplace expectations and successful career patterns, their perspectives and concerns define quality in scholarship, their experiences and obsessions define merit, their objectification of life defines art, their military service defines citizenship, their presence defines family, their inability to get along with each other—their wars and rulerships—defines history, their image defines god, and their genitals define sex. For each of their differences from women, what amounts to an affirmative action plan is in effect, otherwise known as the structure and values of American society. But whenever women are, by this standard, "different" from men and insist on not having it held against us, whenever a difference is used to keep us second class and we refuse to smile about it, equality law has a paradigm trauma and it's crisis time for the doctrine. . . .

The women that gender neutrality benefits, and there are some, show the suppositions of [the difference] approach in highest relief. They are mostly women who have been able to construct a biography that somewhat approximates the male norm, at least on paper. They are the qualified, the least of sex discrimination's victims. When they are denied a man's chance, it looks the most like sex bias. The more unequal society gets, the fewer such women are permitted to exist. Therefore, the more unequal society gets, the less likely the difference doctrine is to be able to do anything about it, because unequal power creates both the appearance and the reality of sex differences along the same lines as it creates its sex inequalities. . . .

There is an alternative approach, one that threads its way through existing law and expresses, I think, the reason equality law exists in the first place. . . . In this approach, an equality question is a question of the distribution of power. Gender is also a question of power, specifically of male supremacy and female subordination. The question of equality, from the standpoint of what it is going to take to get it, is at root a question of hierarchy, which—as power succeeds in constructing social perception and social reality—derivatively becomes a categorical distinction, a difference. Here, on the first day that matters, dominance was achieved, probably by force. By the second day, division along the same lines had to be relatively firmly in place. On the third day, if not sooner, differences were demarcated, together with social systems to exaggerate them in perception and in fact, because the systematically differential delivery of benefits and deprivations required making no mistake about who was who. Comparatively speaking, man has been resting ever since. Gender might not even code as difference, might not mean distinction epistemologically, were it not for its consequences for social power.

I call this the dominance approach. . . . The goal of this dissident approach is not to make legal categories trace and trap the way things are. It is not to make rules that fit reality. It is critical of reality. . . .

The dominance approach centers on the most sex-differential abuses of women as a gender, abuses that sex equality law in its difference garb could not confront. It is based on a reality about which little of a systematic nature was known before 1970. . . . This new information includes not only the extent and intractability of sex segregation into poverty, which has been known before, but the range of issues termed violence against women, which has not been. It combines women's material desperation, through being relegated to categories of jobs that pay nil, with the massive amount of rape and attempted rape . . . which is apparently endemic to the patriarchal family; the battery of women that is systematic in one quarter to one third of our homes; prostitution, women's fundamental economic condition, what we do when all else fails, and for many women in this country, all else fails often; and pornography, an industry that traffics in female flesh, making sex inequality into sex to the tune of eight billion dollars a year in profits largely to organized crime.

These experiences have been silenced out of the difference definition of sex equality largely because they happen almost exclusively to women. Understand: for this reason, they are considered not to raise sex equality issues. Because this treatment is done almost uniquely to women, it is implicitly treated as a difference, the sex difference, when in fact it is the socially situated subjection of women. The whole point of women's social relegation to inferiority as a gender is that for the most part these things aren't done to men. . . .

B. SEXUAL HARASSMENT

1. Sexual Harassment in the Workplace

The term "sexual harassment" did not come into use until the mid-1970s, and was not fully articulated as a form of discrimination based on sex until 1979, with the publication of Catharine MacKinnon's The Sexual Harassment of Working Women, excerpted below. This theory and the framework MacKinnon proposed was embraced by the EEOC in a set of guidelines issued in 1980, in which it interpreted Title VII to prohibit two types of harassment: (1) *quid pro quo* harassment, in which the harasser requires sexual contact or favors as a condition of employment or advancement, and (2) hostile environment harassment, based on unwelcome conduct of a sexual nature that "has the purpose or effect of unreasonably interfering with an individual's work performance or creating an intimidating, hostile, or offensive working environment."[2] Three major Supreme Court cases defining the contours of sexual harassment doctrine are excerpted below. The EEOC also proposed standards for determining when employers should be held liable for harassment by supervisors, co-workers, and third parties, a doctrinal question that spawned significant litigation and was eventually addressed by the Supreme Court.

Estimates of how many women have experienced sexual harassment range from 30 to 80 percent, depending upon who is asked and how sexual harassment is defined.[3] The prevalence of harassment did not change much from the earliest surveys, in the late 1970s, through 1994, when the federal government stopped collecting data on its own work force.[4] But a 2016 report from the EEOC Select Task Force on the Study of Harassment in the Workplace noted that 43 percent of all discrimination complaints filed by federal employees in 2015 alleged harassment, and almost a third of all charges of employment discrimination included a harassment allegation.[5] Still, the current prevalence thus remains a bit of an unknown. Sexual harassment

2. 29 C.F.R. §1604.11(a)(1)-(3) (1980); see also Joanna L. Grossman, Moving Forward, Looking Back: A Retrospective on Sexual Harassment Law, 95 B.U. L. Rev. 1029 (2015) (chronicling the development of sexual harassment law under Title VII).

3. See, e.g., Theresa M. Beiner, Gender Myths v. Working Realities: Using Social Science to Reformulate Sexual Harassment Law 1 (2004) (citing studies finding 40 percent to 80 percent); Joanna L. Grossman, The First Bite Is Free: Employer Liability for Sexual Harassment, 61 U. Pitt. L. Rev. 671, 673-74 (2000) (citing studies and case histories).

4. Joanna Grossman, The Culture of Compliance: The Final Triumph of Form Over Substance in Sexual Harassment Law, 26 Harv. Women's L.J. 3, 5-7 (2003) (citing surveys, studies, and cases showing little change in the prevalence of harassment over three decades).

5. U.S. Equal Employment Opportunity Comm'n, Select Task Force on the Study of Harassment in the Workplace 5, 8 (June 2016), https://www.eeoc.gov/eeoc/task_force/harassment/upload/report.pdf (concluding, based on a literature review, that between 25 and 85 percent of women "report having experienced sexual harassment in the workplace").

charges filed with the EEOC decreased between 1997 and 2011, but given how few victims complain, it is hard to draw a strong inference about prevalence from that measure.[6] Victims only report about 5 to 15 percent of instances of harassment, and less than 3 percent end up in litigation. Major barriers to reporting include guilt, shame, fears of retaliation or blacklisting, an unwillingness to jeopardize working relationships or to be known as a humorless whiner, concerns about loss of privacy, and doubts that an effective response to a complaint would be forthcoming. Women of color experience disproportionate rates of abuse: they account for 16 percent of the female labor force but 33 percent of women's sexual harassment claims. Women of color are ten times less likely to report harassing incidents internally than their white counterparts. Men account for about 17 percent of claims, up from approximately 9 percent of claims in 1992.[7] Other than large surveys, how else might we gauge whether the prevalence of harassment has gone down in response to greater enforcement efforts?

In what sense is sexual harassment a form of sex discrimination?

Catharine A. MacKinnon, The Sexual Harassment of Working Women
1, 9-10 (1979)

Intimate violation of women by men is sufficiently pervasive in American society as to be nearly invisible. Contained by internalized and structural forms of power, it has been nearly inaudible. Conjoined with men's control over women's material survival, as in the home or on the job, or over women's learning and educational advancement in school, it has become institutionalized. . . .

Sexual harassment, most broadly defined, refers to the unwanted imposition of sexual requirements in the context of a relationship of unequal power. Central to the concept is the use of power derived from one social sphere to

6. U.S. Equal Employment Opportunity Comm'n, Sexual Harassment Charges Combined: FY 1997-2011, http://www.eeoc.gov/eeoc/statistics/enforcement/sexual_harassment.cfm; see also U.S. Equal Employment Opportunity Comm'n, Charges Alleging Sexual Harassment, FY 2010-FY 2015, http://www.eeoc.gov/eeoc/statistics/enforcement/sexual_harassment_new.cfm.

7. U.S. Equal Employment Opportunity Comm'n, Sexual Harassment Charges: EEOC & FEPAs Combined: FY 1997-FY 2011, http://www.eeoc.gov/eeoc/statistics/enforcement/sexual_harassment.cfm; U.S. Equal Employment Opportunity Comm'n, Sexual Harassment Charges 2010-2015, http://www.eeoc.gov/eeoc/statistics/enforcement/sexual_harassment_new.cfm; Tresa Baldas, More Men Filing Workplace Lawsuits, Nat'l L.J., July 28, 2008, at A1; see also Tanya Kateri Hernandez, A Critical Race Feminism Empirical Research Project: Sexual Harassment and the Internal Complaints Black Box, 39 U.C. Davis L. Rev. 1235, 1255-60 (2006).

level benefits or impose deprivations in another. The major dynamic is best expressed as the reciprocal enforcement of two inequalities.

When one is sexual, the other material, the cumulative sanction is particularly potent. American society legitimizes male sexual dominance of women and employer's control of workers. . . .

[T]he sexual harassment of women can occur largely because women occupy inferior job positions and job roles; at the same time, sexual harassment works to keep women in such positions. Sexual harassment, then, uses and helps create women's structurally inferior status.

Kathryn Abrams, Gender Discrimination and the Transformation of Workplace Norms
42 Vand. L. Rev. 1183, 1207-09 (1989)

[S]exually oriented behavior in the workplace produces at least two responses among women that contribute to their subordination. . . . One response is a fear of sexual coercion. Sexually oriented behavior brings into the workplace echoes of a context in which men and women often are radically unequal. A woman struggling to establish credibility in a setting in which she may not be, or may not feel, welcome, can be swept off balance by a reminder that she can be raped, fondled, or subjected to repeated sexual demands. Her employment setting, already precarious, can be transformed instantly into an unwanted sexual encounter in which she is likely to feel even less control, a transformation that can cast shadows even when demands are not being made. The feelings of anxiety, fear, or vulnerability produced by the spectre of sexual coercion prevent women from feeling, or being viewed as, the equals of their male counterparts in the workplace.

But a woman need not be threatened with sexual coercion to feel, and to be perceived as, unequal in the workplace. Sexual inquiries, jokes, remarks, or innuendoes sometimes can raise the spectre of coercion, but they more predictably have the effect of reminding a woman that she is viewed as an object of sexual derision rather than as a credible co-worker. A woman who is continuously queried by male colleagues about her sexual preferences, referred to by co-workers as "the fucking flag girl," or depicted on the walls of men's restrooms in sexual poses is being told that she is not, first and foremost, a credible colleague and an equal. This message would be disturbing to any worker, even one who felt comfortable and secure in the workplace. For a woman worker, who may not have been socialized to feel comfortable in that role, and who may have faced numerous men who have difficulty viewing women as workers rather than wives or dates, this message can be devastating. Treatment that sexualizes women workers prevents them from feeling, and prevents others from perceiving them, as equal in the workplace.

L. Camille Hébert, *The Economic Implications of Sexual Harassment for Women*
3 Kan. J.L. & Pub. Pol'y 41, 47-50 (Spring 1994)

A common view is that sexual harassment . . . is motivated by sexual desire and that women are targets of sexual harassment because they are sexually attractive to their harasser. . . .

Existing patterns of sexual harassment in the workplace, however, are difficult to explain as caused by only sexual desire—even nonmutual, one-sided sexual desire.

One aspect of the pattern of sexual harassment in the workplace that suggests sexual harassment is motivated, or at least caused, by economic considerations is the profile of the women who are most often subjected to harassment. One characteristic common among women who report sexual harassment is economic vulnerability. . . .

[M]any women who report sexual harassment are very dependent on their jobs, which would make them economically vulnerable to sexual harassment. Women with low seniority and those in low-status and low-skill jobs are more frequently subjected to sexual harassment than women in higher status and higher skill jobs. . . .

[W]omen who are members of minority groups are more likely to be sexually harassed than nonminority women. . . .

. . . [S]imilarly, women moving into nontraditional jobs—jobs traditionally dominated by men—frequently are subjected to sexual harassment. There is no reason to believe that such women are more sexually attractive than other women.

Nor, however, are these women necessarily more economically vulnerable than other women. In fact, the converse is likely to be true. . . . This does not mean, however, that sexual harassment against these women is not the result of economic factors. In these situations, economic factors other than economic vulnerability appear to be at work, such as the desire of men to ensure continued economic dominance over women in the workplace by discouraging women from entering jobs in which they would compete with men.

Some commentators have argued that sexual harassment is motivated by factors other than power imbalances by pointing to the fact that sexual harassment most often occurs among co-workers rather than between a supervisor and a subordinate. Such a contention, however, fails to recognize that forms of economic power other than supervisory power exist in the workplace. Males may be able to exert economic power over female co-workers by withholding information and training necessary to job performance, particularly when women are moving into jobs that traditionally have been held by men. Men may also be able to assert economic power over female co-workers by threatening to sabotage work or job performance. Finally, men, because of their longer job tenure (and because of their maleness), may simply have more authority with supervisors than newer female employees and thereby be able to influence the supervisor's perception of the women's job performance.

Sexual harassment in the workplace may even be motivated by the frustration some men feel over the loss of economic power in the workplace. . . . Some men feel threatened, both socially and economically, by the advancement of women; some of these men react to these women with hostility.

It is not surprising that this hostility would manifest itself in abusive sexual activity directed toward women. Because of both biological and social factors, men often have, or believe themselves to have, power over women in their sexual relationships. Some men may resort to sexual harassment in the workplace to assert power in a sexual context, in which they believe they have an advantage over women, and to express frustration over their loss or lack of relative power over women in the workplace context. . . .

A final reason to doubt the sexual attractiveness theory of sexual harassment is that women surveyed in sexual harassment studies report that their harassers also harass others at work. This finding suggests that sexual harassment is more a pattern of abusive behavior than the result of "isolated instances of personal sexual attraction."

Kathryn Abrams, The New Jurisprudence of Sexual Harassment
83 Cornell L. Rev. 1169, 1206-08 (1998)

In some cases, sexual harassment has emerged as a means of preserving male control over the workplace, particularly where the entry of women into a particular work force appears to call that control into question. A prime example is sexual harassment directed at women who have entered predominantly male fields. Some types of harassment within this category are particularly flagrant, including physical or sexual aggression or persistent, targeted verbal abuse so severe as to serve unequivocal notice that women are not welcome. Women targeted in this way are often compelled to leave the workplace or transfer to a job with different co-workers or another supervisor. Even when they stay, it is clear that they remain at the sufferance of their male co-workers; they have no hope of getting sufficient purchase on the workplace to make it in any sense their own.

Other forms of harassment aimed at preserving male control are slightly subtler. Supervisors or co-workers may sexualize women employees by either propositioning them directly or treating them in a manner that highlights their sexuality, as opposed to other, work related characteristics. Supervisors may demand that women workers conform to dominant feminine stereotypes that operate outside the workplace by making repeated comments or suggestions regarding the employees' physical appearance, or through instructions to behave in a feminine manner. In some cases, it may be applied categorically to signal that women are not taken seriously: that they are considered sex objects or "pets" instead of competent workers. These latter forms of harassment may not be sufficient to compel all women to leave any particular workplace. Yet they make clear—to women and the men who work with them—that mere presence is not equal to influence or control. These forms of harassment suggest that whatever professional goals women pursue, they will continue to be viewed and judged by reference to more traditional female roles and whatever careers they enter, they still will occupy subordinate roles.

Pessimistic

Vicki Schultz, Reconceptualizing Sexual Harassment
107 Yale L.J. 1683, 1755, 1761, 1801 (1998)

Contrary to the assumption of the cultural-radical feminist tradition that inspired the development of harassment law, men's desire to exploit or dominate women sexually may not be the exclusive, or even the primary, motivation for harassing women at work. Instead, a drive to maintain the most highly rewarded forms of work as domains of masculine competence underlies many, if not most, forms of sex-based harassment on the job. . . . [B]y portraying women as less than equal at work, men can secure superior jobs, resources, and influence—all of which afford men leverage over women at home and everyplace else. . . . [The focus of legal inquiry should be whether the conduct at issue has] the purpose or effect of undermining women's "right to participate in the workplace on [an] equal footing."

Katherine M. Franke, What's Wrong with Sexual Harassment
49 Stan. L. Rev. 691, 693, 696 (1997)

According to the theory I develop . . . , the sexual harassment of a woman by a man is an instance of sexism precisely because the act embodies fundamental gender stereotypes: men as sexual conquerors and women as sexually conquered, men as masculine sexual subjects and women as feminine sexual objects. . . . Sexual harassment is a technology of sexism. It is a disciplinary practice that inscribes, enforces, and polices the identities of both harasser and victim according to a system of gender norms that envisions women as feminine, (hetero)sexual objects, and men as masculine, (hetero)sexual subjects. . . .

Re-inforce traditional roles

Similarly, sexual harassment operates as a means of policing traditional gender norms particularly in the same-sex context when men who fail to live up to a societal norm of masculinity are punished by their male co-workers through sexual means.

≡≡≡ ## *Meritor Savings Bank v. Vinson*
477 U.S. 57 (1986)

Justice REHNQUIST delivered the opinion of the court.

This case presents important questions concerning claims of workplace "sexual harassment" brought under Title VII of the Civil Rights Act of 1964. . . .

I

In 1974, respondent Mechelle Vinson met Sidney Taylor, a vice president of what is now petitioner Meritor Savings Bank (bank) and manager of one of its branch offices. . . . With Taylor as her supervisor, respondent started as a teller-trainee, and thereafter was promoted to teller, head teller, and assistant branch manager. She worked at the same branch for four years, and it is undisputed that her advancement there was based on merit alone. In September 1978, respondent notified Taylor that she was taking sick leave for an indefinite period. On November 1, 1978, the bank discharged her for excessive use of that leave.

Respondent brought this action against Taylor and the bank, claiming that during her four years at the bank she had "constantly been subjected to sexual harassment" by Taylor in violation of Title VII. She sought injunctive relief, compensatory and punitive damages against Taylor and the bank, and attorney's fees.

At the 11-day bench trial, the parties presented conflicting testimony about Taylor's behavior during respondent's employment. Respondent testified that during her probationary period as a teller-trainee, Taylor treated her in a fatherly way and made no sexual advances. Shortly thereafter, however, he invited her out to dinner and, during the course of the meal, suggested that they go to a motel to have sexual relations. At first she refused, but out of what she described as fear of losing her job she eventually agreed. According to respondent, Taylor thereafter made repeated demands upon her for sexual favors, usually at the branch, both during and after business hours; she estimated that over the next several years she had intercourse with him some 40 or 50 times. In addition, respondent testified that Taylor fondled her in front of other employees, followed her into the women's restroom when she went there alone, exposed himself to her, and even forcibly raped her on several occasions. These activities ceased after 1977, respondent stated, when she started going with a steady boyfriend. . . .

Taylor denied respondent's allegations of sexual activity, testifying that he never fondled her, never made suggestive remarks to her, never engaged in sexual intercourse with her, and never asked her to do so. He contended instead that respondent made her accusations in response to a business-related dispute. The bank also denied respondent's allegations and asserted that any sexual harassment by Taylor was unknown to the bank and engaged in without its consent or approval.

The District Court denied relief . . . [and the] Court of Appeals for the District of Columbia Circuit reversed. . . .

II . . .

Respondent argues . . . that unwelcome sexual advances that create an offensive or hostile working environment violate Title VII. Without question, when a supervisor sexually harasses a subordinate because of the subordinate's sex, that supervisor "discriminate[s]" on the basis of sex. Petitioner apparently does not challenge this proposition. It contends instead that in prohibiting discrimination with respect to "compensation, terms, conditions, or privileges" of employment, Congress was concerned with what petitioner describes as "tangible loss" of "an economic character," not "purely psychological aspects of the workplace environment." . . . In support of this claim petitioner observes that in both the legislative history of Title VII and this Court's Title VII decisions, the focus has been on tangible, economic barriers erected by discrimination.

We reject petitioner's view. First, the language of Title VII is not limited to "economic" or "tangible" discrimination. The phrase "terms, conditions, or privileges of employment" evinces a congressional intent " 'to strike at the entire spectrum of disparate treatment of men and women' " in employment. . . .

Second, in 1980 the EEOC issued Guidelines specifying that "sexual harassment," as there defined, is a form of sex discrimination prohibited by Title VII. . . . The EEOC Guidelines fully support the view that harassment leading to noneconomic injury can violate Title VII.

In defining "sexual harassment," the Guidelines first describe the kinds of workplace conduct that may be actionable under Title VII. These include "[u]nwelcome sexual advances, requests for sexual favors, and other verbal or physical conduct of a sexual nature." . . . Relevant to the charges at issue in this case, the Guidelines provide that such sexual misconduct constitutes prohibited "sexual harassment," whether or not it is directly linked to the grant or denial of an economic *quid pro quo*, where "such conduct has the purpose or effect of unreasonably interfering with an individual's work performance or creating an intimidating, hostile, or offensive working environment." . . .

In concluding that so-called "hostile environment" (i.e., non *quid pro quo*) harassment violates Title VII, the EEOC drew upon a substantial body of judicial decisions and EEOC precedent holding that Title VII affords employees the right to work in an environment free from discriminatory intimidation, ridicule, and insult. . . . Courts applied this principle to harassment based on race, religion, and national origin. Nothing in Title VII suggests that a hostile environment based on discriminatory sexual harassment should not be likewise prohibited. The Guidelines thus appropriately drew from, and were fully consistent with, the existing case law.

Since the Guidelines were issued, courts have uniformly held, and we agree, that a plaintiff may establish a violation of Title VII by proving that discrimination based on sex has created a hostile or abusive work environment. As the Court of Appeals for the Eleventh Circuit wrote in Henson v. Dundee, 682 F.2d 897, 902 (1982): "Sexual harassment which creates a hostile or offensive environment for members of one sex is every bit the arbitrary barrier to sexual equality at the workplace that racial harassment is to racial equality. Surely, a requirement that a man or woman run a gauntlet of sexual abuse in return for the privilege of being allowed to work and make a living can be as demeaning and disconcerting as the harshest of racial epithets." . . .

Of course, . . . not all workplace conduct that may be described as "harassment" affects a "term, condition, or privilege" of employment within the meaning of Title VII. . . . For sexual harassment to be actionable, it must be sufficiently severe or pervasive "to alter the conditions of [the victim's] employment and create an abusive working environment." Respondent's allegations in this case—which include not only pervasive harassment but also criminal conduct of the most serious nature—are plainly sufficient to state a claim for "hostile environment" sexual harassment. . . .

[T]he District court apparently believed that a claim for sexual harassment will not lie absent an economic effect on the complainant's employment. . . . Since it appears that the District Court made its findings without ever considering the "hostile environment" theory of sexual harassment, the Court of Appeals' decision to remand was correct.

[T]he District Court's conclusion that no actionable harassment occurred might have rested on its earlier "finding" that "[i]f [respondent] and Taylor did engage in an intimate or sexual relationship . . . , that relationship was a voluntary one." But the fact that sex-related conduct was "voluntary," in the sense that the complainant was not forced to participate against her will, is not a defense to a sexual harassment suit brought under Title VII. The gravamen of any sexual harassment claim is that the alleged sexual advances were "unwelcome." While the question whether particular conduct was indeed unwelcome presents difficult problems of proof and turns largely on credibility determinations committed to the trier of fact, the District Court in this case erroneously focused on the "voluntariness" of respondent's participation in the claimed sexual episodes. The correct inquiry is whether respondent by her conduct indicated that the alleged sexual advances were unwelcome, not whether her actual participation in sexual intercourse was voluntary.

Petitioner contends that even if this case must be remanded to the District Court, the Court of Appeals erred in one of the terms of its remand. Specifically, the Court of Appeals stated that testimony about respondent's "dress and personal fantasies", which the District Court apparently admitted into evidence, "had no place in this litigation." The apparent ground for this conclusion was that respondent's voluntariness vel non in submitting to Taylor's advances was immaterial to her sexual harassment claim. While "voluntariness" in the sense of consent is not a defense to such a claim, it does not follow that a complainant's sexually provocative speech or dress is irrelevant as a matter of law in determining whether he or she found particular sexual advances unwelcome. To the contrary, such evidence is obviously relevant. The EEOC Guidelines emphasize that the trier of fact must determine the existence of sexual harassment in light of "the record as a whole" and "the totality of circumstances, such as the nature of the sexual advances and the context in which the alleged incidents occurred." Respondent's claim that any marginal relevance of the evidence in question was outweighed by the potential for unfair prejudice is the sort of argument properly addressed to the District Court. In this case the District Court concluded that the evidence should be admitted, and the Court of Appeals' contrary conclusion was based upon the erroneous, categorical view that testimony about provocative dress and publicly expressed sexual fantasies "had no place in this litigation." While the District Court must carefully weigh the applicable considerations in deciding whether to admit evidence of this kind, there is no *per se* rule against its admissibility. . . .

IV. . . .

Accordingly, the judgment of the Court of Appeals reversing the judgment of the District Court is affirmed, and the case is remanded for further proceedings consistent with this opinion.

▤ ### *Harris v. Forklift Systems, Inc.*
510 U.S. 17 (1993)

Justice O'CONNOR delivered the opinion of the Court.

In this case we consider the definition of a discriminatorily "abusive work environment" (also known as a "hostile work environment") under Title VII. . . .

I

Teresa Harris worked as a manager at Forklift Systems, Inc., an equipment rental company, from April 1985 until October 1987. Charles Hardy was Forklift's president.

The Magistrate found that, throughout Harris' time at Forklift, Hardy often insulted her because of her gender and often made her the target of unwanted sexual innuendos. Hardy told Harris on several occasions, in the presence of other employees, "You're a woman, what do you know" and "We need a man as the rental manager"; at least once, he told her she was "a dumb ass woman." . . . Again in front of others, he suggested that the two of them "go to the Holiday Inn to negotiate [Harris'] raise." . . . Hardy occasionally asked Harris and other female employees to get coins from his front pants pocket. He threw objects on the ground in front of Harris and other women, and asked them to pick the objects up. . . . He made sexual innuendos about Harris' and other women's clothing.

In mid-August 1987, Harris complained to Hardy about his conduct. Hardy said he was surprised that Harris was offended, claimed he was only joking, and apologized. . . . He also promised he would stop, and based on this assurance Harris stayed on the job. But in early September, Hardy began anew: While Harris was arranging a deal with one of Forklift's customers, he asked her, again in front of other employees, "What did you do, promise the guy . . . some [sex] Saturday night?" . . . On October 1, Harris collected her paycheck and quit.

Harris then sued Forklift, claiming that Hardy's conduct had created an abusive work environment for her because of her gender. The United States District Court for the Middle District of Tennessee, adopting the report and recommendation of the Magistrate, found this to be "a close case," . . . but held that Hardy's conduct did not create an abusive environment. The court found that some of Hardy's comments "offended [Harris], and would offend the reasonable woman," . . . but that they were not "so severe as to be expected to seriously affect [Harris'] psychological well-being." A reasonable woman manager under like circumstances would have been offended by Hardy, but his conduct would not have risen to the level of interfering with that person's work performance. "Neither do I believe that [Harris] was subjectively so offended that she suffered injury. . . . Although Hardy may at times have genuinely offended [Harris], I do not believe that he created a working environment so poisoned as to be intimidating or abusive to [Harris]." . . . The United States Court of Appeals for the Sixth Circuit affirmed. . . .

II

Title VII . . . makes it "an unlawful employment practice for an employer . . . to discriminate against any individual with respect to his compensation, terms, conditions, or privileges of employment, because of such individual's race, color, religion, sex, or national origin." As we made clear in Meritor Savings Bank v. Vinson, this language "is not limited to 'economic' or 'tangible' discrimination. The phrase 'terms, conditions, or privileges of employment' evinces a congressional intent 'to strike at the entire spectrum of disparate treatment of men and women' in employment," which includes requiring people to work in a discriminatorily hostile or abusive environment. When the workplace is permeated with "discriminatory intimidation, ridicule, and insult," that is "sufficiently severe or pervasive to alter the condition of the victim's employment and create an abusive working environment," Title VII is violated.

This standard, which we reaffirm today, takes a middle path between making actionable any conduct that is merely offensive and requiring the conduct to cause a tangible psychological injury. As we pointed out in *Meritor*, "mere utterance of an . . . epithet which engenders offensive feelings in an employee," . . . does not sufficiently affect the conditions of employment to implicate Title VII. Conduct that is not severe or pervasive enough to create an objectively hostile or abusive work environment—an environment that a reasonable person would find hostile or abusive—is beyond Title VII's purview. Likewise, if the victim does not subjectively perceive the environment to be abusive, the conduct has not actually altered the conditions of the victim's employment, and there is no Title VII violation.

But Title VII comes into play before the harassing conduct leads to a nervous breakdown. A discriminatorily abusive work environment, even one that does not seriously affect employees' psychological well-being, can and often will detract from employees' job performance, discourage employees from remaining on the job, or keep them from advancing in their careers. Moreover, even without regard to these tangible effects, the very fact that the discriminatory conduct was so severe or pervasive that it created a work environment abusive to employees because of their race, gender, religion, or national origin offends Title VII's broad rule of workplace equality. The appalling conduct alleged in *Meritor*, and the reference in that case to environments "so heavily polluted with discrimination as to destroy completely the emotional and psychological stability of minority group workers," merely present some especially egregious examples of harassment. They do not mark the boundary of what is actionable.

We therefore believe the District Court erred in relying on whether the conduct "seriously affect[ed] plaintiff's psychological well-being" or led her to "suffe[r] injury." Such an inquiry may needlessly focus the factfinder's attention on concrete psychological harm, an element Title VII does not require. Certainly Title VII bars conduct that would seriously affect a reasonable person's psychological well-being, but the statute is not limited to such conduct. So long as the environment would reasonably be perceived, and is perceived, as hostile or abusive, *Meritor*, there is no need for it also to be psychologically injurious.

This is not, and by its nature cannot be, a mathematically precise test. We need not answer today all the potential questions it raises. . . . But we can say that whether an environment is "hostile" or "abusive" can be determined only by looking at all the circumstances. These may include the frequency of the discriminatory conduct; its severity; whether it is physically threatening or humiliating, or a mere offensive utterance; and whether it unreasonably interferes with an employee's work performance. The effect on the employee's psychological well-being is, of course, relevant to determining whether the plaintiff actually found the environment abusive. But while psychological harm, like any other relevant factor, may be taken into account, no single factor is required. . . .

We therefore reverse the judgment of the Court of Appeals, and remand the case for further proceedings consistent with this opinion.

Justice SCALIA, concurring. . . .

"Abusive" (or "hostile," which in this context I take to mean the same thing) does not seem to me a very clear standard—and I do not think clarity is at all increased by adding the adverb "objectively" or by appealing to a "reasonable person's" notion of what the vague word means. Today's opinion does list a number of factors that contribute to abusiveness, . . . but since it neither says how much of each is necessary (an impossible task) nor identifies any single factor as determinative, it thereby adds little certitude. As a practical matter, today's holding lets virtually unguided juries decide whether sex-related conduct engaged in (or permitted by) an employer is egregious enough to warrant an award of damages. One might say that what constitutes "negligence" (a traditional jury question) is not much more clear and certain than what constitutes "abusiveness." Perhaps so. But the class of plaintiffs seeking to recover for negligence is limited to those who have suffered harm, whereas under this statute "abusiveness" is to be the test of whether legal harm has been suffered, opening more expansive vistas of litigation.

Be that as it may, I know of no alternative to the course the Court today has taken. One of the factors mentioned in the Court's nonexhaustive list—whether the conduct unreasonably interferes with an employee's work performance—would, if it were made an absolute test, provide greater guidance to juries and employers. But I see no basis for such a limitation in the language of the statute. Accepting *Meritor*'s interpretation of the term "conditions of employment" as the law, the test is not whether work has been impaired, but whether working conditions have been discriminatorily altered. I know of no test more faithful to the inherently vague statutory language than the one the Court today adopts. For these reasons, I join the opinion of the Court.

Justice GINSBURG, concurring.

Today the Court reaffirms the holding of Meritor Savings Bank v. Vinson . . . : "[A] plaintiff may establish a violation of Title VII by proving that discrimination based on sex has created a hostile or abusive work environment." The critical issue, Title VII's text indicates, is whether members of one sex are exposed to disadvantageous terms or conditions of employment to which members of the other sex are not exposed. . . . As the Equal Employment Opportunity Commission emphasized . . . the adjudicator's inquiry should center, dominantly, on whether the discriminatory conduct has unreasonably interfered with the plaintiff's work performance. To show such interference, "the plaintiff need not prove that his or her tangible productivity has declined as a result of the harassment." . . . It suffices to prove that a reasonable person subjected to the discriminatory conduct would find, as the plaintiff did, that the harassment so altered working conditions as to "ma[k]e it more difficult to do the job." . . .

The Court's opinion, which I join, seems to me in harmony with the view expressed in this concurring statement.

Oncale v. Sundowner Offshore Servs., Inc.
523 U.S. 75 (1998)

Justice SCALIA delivered the opinion of the Court.

This case presents the question whether workplace harassment can violate Title VII's prohibition against "discrimination . . . because of . . . sex" when the harasser and the harassed employee are of the same sex.

I

The District Court having granted summary judgment for respondent, we must assume the facts to be as alleged by petitioner Joseph Oncale. The precise details are irrelevant to the legal point we must decide. . . . In late October 1991, Oncale was working for respondent Sundowner Offshore Services on a Chevron U.S.A., Inc., oil platform in the Gulf of Mexico. He was employed as a roust about on an eight-man crew which included respondents John Lyons, Danny Pippen, and Brandon Johnson. Lyons, the crane operator, and Pippen, the driller, had supervisory authority. On several occasions, Oncale was forcibly subjected to sex-related, humiliating actions against him by Lyons, Pippen and Johnson in the presence of the rest of the crew. Pippen and Lyons also physically assaulted Oncale in a sexual manner, and Lyons threatened him with rape.

Oncale's complaints to supervisory personnel produced no remedial action; in fact, the company's Safety Compliance Clerk, Valent Hohen, told Oncale that Lyons and Pippen "picked [on] him all the time too," and called him a name suggesting homosexuality. Oncale eventually quit—asking that his pink slip reflect that he "voluntarily left due to sexual harassment and verbal abuse." When asked at his deposition why he left Sundowner, Oncale stated, "I felt that if I didn't leave my job, that I would be raped or forced to have sex."

Oncale filed a complaint against Sundowner in the United States District Court for the Eastern District of Louisiana, alleging that he was discriminated against in his employment because of his sex. . . . [T]he district court held that "Mr. Oncale, a male, has no cause of action under Title VII for harassment by male co-workers." On appeal, a panel of the Fifth Circuit . . . affirmed. We granted certiorari.

II . . .

Title VII's prohibition of discrimination "because of . . . sex" protects men as well as women, and in the related context of racial discrimination in the workplace we have rejected any conclusive presumption that an employer will not discriminate against members of his own race. "Because of the many facets of human motivation, it would be unwise to presume as a matter of law that human beings of one definable group will not discriminate against other members of that group." Castaneda v. Partida, 430 U.S. 482 (1977). In Johnson v. Transportation Agency, Santa Clara Cty., 480 U.S. 616 (1987), a male employee claimed that his employer discriminated against him because of his sex when it preferred a female employee for promotion. Although we ultimately rejected the claim on other grounds, we did not consider it significant that the supervisor who made that decision was also a man. If our precedents leave any doubt on the question, we hold today that nothing in Title VII necessarily bars a claim of discrimination "because of . . . sex" merely because the plaintiff and the defendant (or the person charged with acting on behalf of the defendant) are of the same sex.

Courts have had little trouble with that principle in cases like *Johnson*, where an employee claims to have been passed over for a job or promotion. But when the issue arises in the context of a "hostile environment" sexual harassment claim, the state and federal courts have taken a bewildering variety of stances. Some, like the Fifth Circuit in this case, have held that same-sex sexual harassment claims are never cognizable under Title VII. Other decisions say that such claims are actionable only if the plaintiff can prove that the harasser is homosexual (and thus presumably motivated by sexual desire). Still others suggest that workplace harassment that is sexual in content is always actionable, regardless of the harasser's sex, sexual orientation, or motivations.

We see no justification in the statutory language or our precedents for a categorical rule excluding same-sex harassment claims from the coverage of Title VII. As some courts have observed, male-on-male sexual harassment in the workplace was assuredly not the principal evil Congress was concerned with when it enacted Title VII. But statutory prohibitions often go beyond the principal evil to cover reasonably comparable evils, and it is ultimately the provisions of our laws rather than the principal concerns of our legislators by which we are governed. Title VII prohibits "discrimination . . . because of . . . sex" in the "terms" or "conditions" of employment. Our holding that this includes sexual harassment must extend to sexual harassment of any kind that meets the statutory requirements.

Respondents and their *amici* contend that recognizing liability for same-sex harassment will transform Title VII into a general civility code for the American workplace. But that risk is no greater for same-sex than for opposite-sex harassment, and is adequately met by careful attention to the requirements of the statute. Title VII does not prohibit all verbal or physical harassment in the workplace; it is directed only at "*discrimination* . . . because of . . . sex." We have never held that workplace harassment, even harassment between men and women, is automatically discrimination because of sex merely because the words used have sexual content or connotations. "The critical issue, Title VII's text indicates, is whether members of one sex are exposed to disadvantageous terms or conditions of employment to which members of the other sex are not exposed." *Harris,* (Ginsburg, J., concurring).

Courts and juries have found the inference of discrimination easy to draw in most male-female sexual harassment situations, because the challenged conduct typically involves explicit or implicit proposals of sexual activity; it is reasonable to assume those proposals would not have been made to someone of the same sex. The same chain of inference would be available to a plaintiff alleging same-sex harassment, if there were credible evidence that the harasser was homosexual. But harassing conduct need not be motivated by sexual desire to support an inference of discrimination on the basis of sex. A trier of fact might reasonably find such discrimination, for example, if a female victim is harassed in such sex-specific and derogatory terms by another woman as to make it clear that the harasser is motivated by general hostility to the presence of women in the workplace. A same-sex harassment plaintiff may also, of course, offer direct comparative evidence about how the alleged harasser treated members of both sexes in a mixed-sex workplace. Whatever evidentiary route the plaintiff chooses to follow, he or she must always prove that the conduct at issue was not merely tinged with offensive sexual connotations, but actually constituted "*discrimination* . . . because of . . . sex."

And there is another requirement that prevents Title VII from expanding into a general civility code: As we emphasized in *Meritor* and *Harris,* the statute does not reach genuine but innocuous differences in the ways men and women routinely interact with members of the same sex and of the opposite sex. The prohibition of harassment on the basis of sex requires neither asexuality nor androgyny in the workplace; it forbids only behavior so objectively offensive as to alter the "conditions" of the victim's employment. "Conduct that is not severe or pervasive enough to create an objectively hostile or abusive work environment—an environment that a reasonable person would find hostile or abusive—is beyond Title VII's purview." *Harris,* citing *Meritor.* We have always regarded that requirement as crucial, and as sufficient to ensure that courts and juries do not mistake ordinary socializing in the workplace—such as male-on-male horseplay or intersexual flirtation—for discriminatory "conditions of employment."

We have emphasized, moreover, that the objective severity of harassment should be judged from the perspective of a reasonable person in the plaintiff's position, considering "all the circumstances." *Harris.* In same-sex (as in all) harassment cases, that inquiry requires careful consideration of the social context in which particular behavior occurs and is experienced by its target. A professional football player's working environment is not severely or pervasively abusive, for example, if the coach smacks him on the buttocks as he heads onto the field—even if the same behavior would reasonably be experienced as abusive by the coach's secretary (male or female) back at the office. The real social impact of workplace behavior often depends on a constellation of surrounding circumstances, expectations, and relationships which are not fully captured by a simple recitation of the words used or the physical acts performed. Common sense, and an appropriate sensitivity to social context, will enable courts and juries to distinguish between simple teasing or roughhousing among members of the same sex, and conduct which a reasonable person in the plaintiff's position would find severely hostile or abusive.

III

Because we conclude that sex discrimination consisting of same-sex sexual harassment is actionable under Title VII, the judgment of the Court of Appeals for the Fifth Circuit is reversed, and the case is remanded for further proceedings consistent with this opinion.

Justice THOMAS, concurring.

I concur because the Court stresses that in every sexual harassment case, the plaintiff must plead and ultimately prove Title VII's statutory requirement that there be discrimination "because of . . . sex."

≡ ### *Simonton v. Runyon*
225 F.3d 122 (2d Cir. 2000)

WALKER, Jr., Circuit Judge:

Plaintiff-appellant Dwayne Simonton sued the Postmaster General and the United States Postal Service . . . under Title VII of the Civil Rights Act of 1964 ("Title VII") for abuse and harassment he suffered by reason of his sexual orientation. The United States District Court for the Eastern District of New York . . . dismissed Simonton's complaint . . . for failure to state a claim, reasoning that Title VII does not prohibit discrimination based on sexual orientation. We agree. . . .

We must accept all facts alleged in the complaint as true. . . . The facts of this case are all too familiar in their general form. Simonton was employed as a postal worker in Farmingdale, New York for approximately twelve years. He repeatedly received satisfactory to excellent performance evaluations. He was, however, subjected to an abusive and hostile work environment by reason of his sexual orientation. The abuse he allegedly endured was so severe that he ultimately suffered a heart attack.

For the sake of decency and judicial propriety, we hesitate before reciting in detail the incidents of Simonton's abuse. Nevertheless, we think it is important both to acknowledge the appalling persecution Simonton allegedly endured and to identify the precise nature of the abuse so as to distinguish this case from future cases as they arise. We therefore relate some, but not all, of the alleged harassment that forms the basis for this suit.

Simonton's sexual orientation was known to his co-workers who repeatedly assaulted him with such comments as "go fuck yourself, fag," "suck my dick," and "so you like it up the ass?" Notes were placed on the wall in the employees' bathroom with Simonton's name and the name of celebrities who had died of AIDS. Pornographic photographs were taped to his work area, male dolls were placed in his vehicle, and copies of Playgirl magazine were sent to his home. Pictures of an erect penis were posted in his work place, as were posters stating that Simonton suffered from mental illness as a result of "bung hole disorder." There were repeated statements that Simonton was a "fucking faggot."

There can be no doubt that the conduct allegedly engaged in by Simonton's co-workers is morally reprehensible whenever and in whatever context it occurs, particularly in the modern workplace. Nevertheless, as the First Circuit recently explained in a similar context, "we are called upon here to construe a statute as glossed by the Supreme Court, not to make a moral judgment." Higgins v. New Balance Athletic Shoe, Inc. . . . The law is well-settled in this circuit and in all others to have reached the question that Simonton has no cause of action under Title VII because Title VII does not prohibit harassment or discrimination because of sexual orientation.

I

The Equal Employment Opportunity Act of 1972 extended Title VII's protections to certain federal employees, including U.S. postal service employees. Section 2000e-16(a) provides, in part, that all personnel actions affecting covered employees "shall be made free from any discrimination based on race, color, religion, sex, or national origin." Id. Simonton argues that discrimination based on "sex" includes discrimination based on sexual orientation. We disagree.

Admittedly, we have "little legislative history to guide us in interpreting the Act's prohibition against discrimination based on 'sex.'" Meritor Sav. Bank v. Vinson. But we are informed by Congress's rejection, on numerous occasions, of bills that would have extended Title VII's protection to people based on their sexual preferences. See, e.g., Employment Nondiscrimination Act of 1996, S. 2056, 104th Cong. (1996). . . . Although congressional inaction subsequent to the enactment of a statute is not always a helpful guide,

Congress's refusal to expand the reach of Title VII is strong evidence of congressional intent in the face of consistent judicial decisions refusing to interpret "sex" to include sexual orientation.

Moreover, we are not writing on a clean slate. In DeCintio v. Westchester County Med. Ctr., 807 F.2d 304 (2d Cir. 1986), we reversed a plaintiff's verdict in a Title VII suit alleging that a male employer had passed over several male applicants for a promotion in order to hire a woman with whom the employer had a romantic relationship. Interpreting the definition of "sex," we held that

> the other categories afforded protection under Title VII refer to a person's status as a member of a particular race, color, religion or nationality. "Sex," when read in this context, logically could only refer to membership in a class delineated by gender, rather than sexual activity regardless of gender. . . . The proscribed differentiation under Title VII, therefore, must be a distinction based on a person's sex, not on his or her sexual affiliations.

Id. at 306-307. Because the term "sex" in Title VII refers only to membership in a class delineated by gender, and not to sexual affiliation, Title VII does not proscribe discrimination because of sexual orientation.

Simonton argues that Oncale v. Sundowner Offshore Services, Inc. permits us to revisit our holding in *DeCintio*. We disagree that such an opportunity presents itself here. In *Oncale*, the Supreme Court rejected a *per se* rule that same-sex sexual harassment was non-cognizable under Title VII. . . . *Oncale* did not suggest, however, that male harassment of other males always violates Title VII. *Oncale* emphasized that every victim of such harassment must show that he was harassed *because he was male.*

Subsequent to the Supreme Court's decision in *Oncale*, the First Circuit has reaffirmed the inapplicability of Title VII to discrimination based on sexual orientation. *See Higgins,* 194 F.3d at 259 ("We regard it as settled law that, as drafted and authoritatively construed, Title VII does not proscribe harassment simply because of sexual orientation."). We likewise do not see how *Oncale* changes our well-settled precedent that "sex" refers to membership in a class delineated by gender. The critical issue, as stated in *Oncale*, "is whether members of one sex are exposed to disadvantageous terms or conditions of employment to which members of the other sex are not exposed." *Oncale,* 523 U.S. at 80. Simonton has alleged that he was discriminated against not because he was a man, but because of his sexual orientation. Such a claim remains non-cognizable under Title VII.

II

Simonton argues in the alternative that the harassment he suffered could be construed as discrimination based on sex rather than sexual orientation. . . . We disagree.

[T]here is no basis to infer from the complaint that the harassment Simonton suffered was because of his sex and not, as he urges throughout his complaint, because of his sexual orientation. In the context of male-female sexual harassment, involving more or less explicit sexual proposals, it is easy to infer discrimination because of sex since "it is reasonable to assume those proposals would not have been made to someone of the same sex." *Oncale,* 523 U.S. at 80. And, as the Supreme Court stated, "the same chain of inference would be available to a plaintiff alleging same-sex harassment, if there were credible evidence that the harasser was homosexual." Id. But since Simonton does not offer "direct comparative evidence about how the alleged harasser treated members of both sexes in [his] mixed-sex workplace" (id. at 80-81) and does not allege a basis for inferring gender-based animus, we are unable to infer that the alleged conduct would not have been directed at a woman. Accepting as true all the facts that Simonton has pled, the only inference we can draw is that he was harassed because of his sexual orientation. As we have explained, such harassment is not cognizable under Title VII.

Simonton also argues that discrimination because of sexual orientation is discrimination based on sex because it disproportionately affects men. We decline to adopt a reading of Title VII that would also "achieve by judicial 'construction' what Congress did not do and has consistently refused to do on many occasions," *DeSantis,* 608 F.2d at 330. Therefore, this argument is unavailing.

Simonton next relies on Price Waterhouse v. Hopkins, to argue that the abuse he suffered was discrimination based on sexual stereotypes, which may be cognizable as discrimination based on sex. We find this argument more persuasive but not sufficiently pled in this case.

The plaintiff in *Price Waterhouse* filed suit after having been denied partnership in an accounting firm, in part because she was "macho." . . . Justice Brennan, writing for the plurality, held that this was impermissible sex discrimination, and that "in the specific context of sex stereotyping, an employer who acts on the basis of a belief that a woman cannot be aggressive, or that she must not be, has acted on the basis of gender." . . .

The same theory of sexual stereotyping could apply here. Simonton argues that the harassment he endured was based on his failure to conform to gender norms, regardless of his sexual orientation. The Court in *Price Waterhouse* implied that a suit alleging harassment or disparate treatment based upon nonconformity with sexual stereotypes is cognizable under Title VII as discrimination because of sex. This would not bootstrap protection for sexual orientation into Title VII because not all gay men are stereotypically feminine, and not all heterosexual men are stereotypically masculine. But it would plainly afford relief for discrimination based upon sexual stereotypes.

We do not reach the merits of this issue, however, as Simonton has failed to plead sufficient facts for our consideration of the issue. . . .

For the reasons set forth above, the judgment of the district court is affirmed.

Nichols v. Azteca Restaurant Enterprises, Inc.
256 F.3d 864 (9th Cir. 2001)

Better argument of Simonton

GOULD, Circuit Judge

Antonio Sanchez brought this action against his former employer, Azteca Restaurant Enterprises, Inc., alleging, among other claims, sexual harassment and retaliation in violation of Title VII of the Civil Rights Act of 1964 ("Title VII") and its state law counterpart, the Washington Law Against Discrimination ("WLAD"). Sanchez claimed that he was verbally harassed by some male co-workers and a supervisor because he was effeminate and did not meet their views of a male stereotype. Sanchez further asserted that he was terminated in retaliation for opposing the harassment. Following a bench trial, the district court entered judgment in favor of Azteca on all claims. . . .

We agree with Sanchez that the behavior of his co-workers and supervisor violated Title VII and WLAD. We further agree that Azteca failed to take adequate steps to remedy the harassment. . . . We affirm the judgment of the district court with respect to Sanchez's retaliation claim.

I

Azteca operates a chain of restaurants in Washington and Oregon. It employed Sanchez from October 1991 to July 1995. Sanchez at first worked as a host in Azteca's Burien restaurant, and later worked as a food server at the Southcenter restaurant.

Throughout his tenure at Azteca, Sanchez was subjected to a relentless campaign of insults, name-calling, and vulgarities. Male co-workers and a supervisor repeatedly referred to Sanchez in Spanish and English as "she" and "her." Male co-workers mocked Sanchez for walking and carrying his serving tray "like a woman," and taunted him in Spanish and English as, among other things, a "faggot" and a "fucking female whore." The remarks were not stray or isolated. Rather, the abuse occurred at least once a week and often several times a day.

This conduct violated company policy. Since 1989, Azteca has expressly prohibited sexual harassment and retaliation and has directed its employees to bring complaints regarding such conduct directly to the attention of the corporate office. . . .

Upon receipt of a complaint, Azteca's policy is to conduct a thorough investigation, the results of which are reviewed by the company's EEO Board, which is then responsible for implementing an appropriate remedy.

In addition to this policy, Azteca has a bilingual (English and Spanish) training program about sexual harassment. This training, which all employees attend when hired, and annually thereafter, defines sexual harassment and instructs employees how to report complaints.

Sanchez attended Azteca's sexual harassment training and was familiar with the company's anti-harassment policy and reporting procedures. Yet he never complained to the corporate EEO officer or the area manager about the harassment he experienced, as required by the corporate policy. This is not to say, however, that Sanchez ignored the harassment. Indeed, the general manager of the Southcenter restaurant . . . testified that Sanchez complained about being called names, and an assistant manager testified that Sanchez made similar complaints to him. . . .

In response, Serna proposed the following solution: (1) Sanchez was to report any further harassment to the Southcenter general manager, who promised to address the issue; and (2) Serna was to follow up with "spot checks" over a two-week period to ensure that the harassment would stop. During the four or five spot checks that followed, Serna spoke with Sanchez only once and was told that conditions were improving. Serna replied that if the situation took a turn for the worse, Sanchez should tell the Southcenter general manager or call Serna directly. Sanchez made no further complaints.

On July 29, 1995, a couple of months after his meeting with Serna, Sanchez became involved in a heated argument with an assistant manager, and walked off the job. He was fired for leaving work in the middle of his shift. A month later, Sanchez filed a charge of discrimination with the EEOC. Thereafter, he initiated this lawsuit.

Following a bench trial, the district court concluded that Sanchez had not been subjected to a hostile environment. . . .

[Section II is omitted.]

III

Under Title VII, it is unlawful for an employer "to discriminate against any individual with respect to his compensation, terms, conditions, or privileges of employment, because of . . . sex." It is by now clear that sexual harassment in the form of a hostile work environment constitutes sex discrimination.

To prevail on his hostile environment claim, Sanchez was required to establish a "pattern of ongoing and persistent harassment severe enough to alter the conditions of employment." To satisfy this requirement, Sanchez needed to prove that his workplace was "both objectively and subjectively offensive, one that a reasonable person would find hostile or abusive, and one that the victim in fact did perceive to be so." In addition, Sanchez was required to prove that any harassment took place "because of sex." . . .

[Sections A and B, in which the court determined that Sanchez suffered both an objectively and subjectively hostile work environment, are omitted.]

C. Because of Sex

Sexual harassment is actionable under Title VII to the extent it occurs "because of" the plaintiff's sex. Sanchez asserts that the verbal abuse at issue was based upon the perception that he is effeminate and, therefore, occurred because of sex. In short, Sanchez contends that he was harassed because he failed to conform to a male stereotype.

Sanchez's theory derives from Price Waterhouse v. Hopkins . . . , in which the Supreme Court held that a woman who was denied partnership in an accounting firm because she did not match a sex stereotype had an actionable claim under Title VII. Hopkins, the plaintiff in *Price Waterhouse*, was described by various partners as "macho," in need of "a course in charm school," "a lady using foul language," and someone who had been "a tough-talking somewhat masculine hard-nosed manager." Hopkins was advised that she could improve her partnership chances if she would "walk more femininely, talk more femininely, dress more femininely, wear make-up, have her hair styled, and wear jewelry." Writing for the plurality, Justice Brennan held that "in the specific context of sex stereotyping, an employer who acts on the basis of a belief that a woman cannot be aggressive, or that she must not be, has acted on the basis of gender."

Sanchez contends that the holding in *Price Waterhouse* applies with equal force to a man who is discriminated against for acting too feminine. We agree. . . .

At its essence, the systematic abuse directed at Sanchez reflected a belief that Sanchez did not act as a man should act. Sanchez was attacked for walking and carrying his tray "like a woman"—i.e., for having feminine mannerisms. Sanchez was derided for not having sexual intercourse with a waitress who was his friend. Sanchez's male co-workers and one of his supervisors repeatedly reminded Sanchez that he did not conform to their gender-based stereotypes, referring to him as "she" and "her." And, the most vulgar name-calling directed at Sanchez was cast in female terms. We conclude that this verbal abuse was closely linked to gender.

Price Waterhouse sets a rule that bars discrimination on the basis of sex stereotypes. That rule squarely applies to preclude the harassment here.[7] The only potential difficulty arises out of a now faint shadow cast by our decision in DeSantis v. Pacific Telephone & Telegraph Co., Inc. *DeSantis* holds that discrimination based on a stereotype that a man "should have a virile rather than an effeminate appearance" does not fall within Title VII's purview. This holding, however, predates and conflicts with the Supreme Court's decision in *Price Waterhouse*. And, in this direct conflict, *DeSantis* must lose. To the extent it conflicts with *Price Waterhouse*, as we hold it does, *DeSantis* is no longer good law. Under *Price Waterhouse*, Sanchez must prevail.[7]

Following *Price Waterhouse*, we hold that the verbal abuse at issue occurred because of sex. Because we hold that Sanchez has established each element of his hostile environment claim, we further hold that the conduct of Sanchez's co-workers and supervisor constituted actionable harassment

---

7. We do not imply that all gender-based distinctions are actionable under Title VII. For example, our decision does not imply that there is any violation of Title VII occasioned by reasonable regulations that require male and female employees to conform to different dress and grooming standards.

under both Title VII and WLAD, and reverse the district court's contrary conclusion. . . .

Notes

1. Distinguishing Ordinary Social Exchange from Sexual Harassment. Courts have struggled with finding the line between "ordinary" social behavior between men and women and actionable sexual harassment, requiring that the conduct be sufficiently severe or pervasive, offensive (not only to the plaintiff, but to a reasonable person in the plaintiff's position), and unwelcome. Does the prohibition against sexual harassment leave room for ordinary sexual banter between men and women in the workplace? Under nonsubordination analysis, the ordinary is the problem—i.e., sex has been defined so that what has come to be accepted as everyday behavior, in fact, subordinates women. The ordinariness of sexual subordination makes it invisible, and thus all the more effective.

Those who have resisted recognizing sexual harassment as a wrong, on the other hand, see the law as a clumsy tool for restraining what is a "natural" attraction between the sexes. In one early case, in which defendant president of a company kissed the plaintiff, touched her breasts and buttocks, and put his hands up her dress, the court observed that "one of the traditional places where man meets woman is at the work place," and a "man should not have to gamble on civil liability on her 'yes' response."[8]

In another widely publicized case, the plaintiff introduced the following evidence of harassment: (1) her supervisor referred to her as a "pretty girl," as in "There's always a pretty girl giving me something to sign off on." (2) Once when she commented on how hot his office was, he raised his eyebrows and said, "Not until you stepped your foot in here." (3) Once when the announcement "may I have your attention, please" was broadcast over the public-address system, the supervisor stopped at her desk and said, "You know what that means, don't you? All pretty girls run around naked." (4) The supervisor once told her that his wife had told him "I had better clean up my act" and "better think of you as Ms. Anita Hill." (5) Once when she complained that his office was "smoky" from cigarette smoke, the supervisor replied, "Oh, really? Were we dancing, like in a nightclub?" (6) When she asked him whether he had gotten his wife a Valentine's Day card, he responded that he had not but he should because it was lonely in his hotel room, at which point he looked ostentatiously at his hand with a gesture suggesting masturbation. Judge Richard Posner analyzed this conduct as follows:

> He never touched the plaintiff. He did not invite her, explicitly or by implication, to have sex with him, or to go out on a date with him. He made no threats.

8. Jones v. Wesco Invs., Inc., 846 F.2d 1154, 1157 n.6 (8th Cir. 1988).

He did not expose himself, or show her dirty pictures. He never said anything to her that could not be repeated on prime time television. The comment about Anita Hill was the opposite of solicitation, the implication being that he would get into trouble if he didn't keep his distance. . . . Some of his repartee . . . has the sexual charge of an Abbott and Costello movie. The reference to masturbation completes the impression of a man whose sense of humor took final shape in adolescence. It is no doubt distasteful to a sensitive woman to have such a silly man one's boss, but only a woman of Victorian delicacy—a woman mysteriously aloof from contemporary American popular culture in all its sex-saturated vulgarity—would find [his] patter substantially more distressing than the heat and cigarette smoke of which the plaintiff does not complain.[9]

Does the sexual orientation of the "harasser" make a difference in what behaviors may be considered ordinary social exchange, and what constitutes harassment?

2. Same-Sex Harassment and Sex-Stereotyping. Since the Supreme Court's ruling in Oncale v. Sundowner Offshore Services,[10] it has been clear that male-on-male harassment can violate Title VII as long as the plaintiff can prove the harassment occurred because of sex. The Court in that case reasoned that a sexual harassment claim should not be precluded simply because the complainant and the harasser are of the same sex. In *Oncale,* the harassers appear to have thought that the complainant was gay, although he claimed he was straight. In contrast, *Nichols* involved an openly gay complainant, and the Ninth Circuit Court of Appeals, while citing *Oncale* at length, adopted a theory not discussed in *Oncale* and not yet adopted by the Supreme Court in a sexual harassment case—the theory of sex stereotyping. This theory posits that men often harass other men to enforce "the traditional heterosexual male gender role" by encouraging "stereotypical forms of 'masculine' behavior" and punishing or devaluing "feminine" conduct. Mary Anne Case provides this analysis:

> By examining the similarity of the taunts typically hurled at both women and gay or effeminate men in hostile environments, taunts that stress feminine sexual passivity . . . [it is apparent] that the sexual harassment inflicted on all three groups may have in common the desire of certain "active" masculine males to drive out of the workplace those they see as contaminating it with the taint of feminine passivity. Such harassment is, therefore, a form of gender discrimination against the feminine, one with serious effects on the job performance and security of its victims, who should have a legal remedy against it regardless of their sex.[11]

9. Baskerville v. Culligan Int'l Co., 50 F.3d 428, 431 (7th Cir. 1995).
10. 523 U.S. 75 (1998).
11. Mary Anne Case, Disaggregating Gender from Sex and Sexual Orientation: The Effeminate Man in the Law and Feminist Jurisprudence, 105 Yale L.J. 1, 7 (1995); see also Craig R. Waldo et al., Are Men Sexually Harassed? If So by Whom?, 22 Law & Hum. Behav. 59, 61 (1998).

One of the reasons for moving to the sex stereotyping theory was that many courts, before and after *Oncale*, have rejected sexual harassment claims by gays and lesbians, on the grounds that Congress intended the term "sex" to mean "biological male or female" and not one's sexuality or sexual orientation.[12] *Simonton* is still the majority approach; *Nichols* is in the minority. Which is more persuasive?

Given the reasoning cited above from the *Oncale* decision, do you see a risk, as commentators like Janet Halley have warned, that recognition of harassment based on sexual orientation may expose gays and lesbians to unwarranted claims of harassment by individuals who are threatened by any display of homosexual conduct in the workplace?[13]

3. Sexual Harassment as Discrimination "Because of Sex"? As discussed in *Oncale*, sexual harassment is a form of intentional discrimination under Title VII as long as it occurs *because of* sex. Given its foundation in equality analysis, under what circumstances should abusive or degrading behavior be considered actionable sexual harassment?

For example, what if a supervisor treats every worker in exactly the same way—abusively, and as a sexual object? Can this still be sex discrimination? Courts have not been consistent. Some have applied a comparative equality analysis and only recognized as discriminatory vulgar language, pictures, jokes, and other behaviors that affected plaintiffs in a particular way, or to a greater degree, because of their sex.[14] Other courts have concluded that a harasser cannot insulate him- or herself from a sexual harassment charge simply because his or her conduct is sufficiently egregious as to offend everyone.[15] For still other courts, the "because of sex" dimension is satisfied by the sexual nature of the offending behavior—in essence abandoning the equality paradigm in favor of a model that sees anything sexual as sex-based. To address the harms of sexual harassment, which approach makes most sense?

What if a supervisor's abusive conduct is not sexual or gendered in nature, but is targeted only at women? In EEOC v. National Education Ass'n,[16] the Ninth Circuit allowed plaintiffs to proceed with a hostile environment

12. See, e.g., DeSantis v. Pac. Telephone & Telegraph Co., 608 F.2d 327 (9th Cir. 1979); Bibby v. Phila. Coca-Cola Bottling Co., 260 F.3d 257 (3d Cir. 2001).

13. Janet Halley, Split Decisions: How and Why to Take a Break from Feminism 293-96 (2006).

14. See, e.g., Carpenter v. City of Torrington, 100 Fed. Appx. 858 (2d Cir. 2004) (conduct toward female employee not actionable because the harasser's conduct was "equally, if not more, sexually offensive to male employees").

15. McDonnell v. Cisneros, 84 F.3d 256, 260 (7th Cir. 1996) ("It would be exceedingly perverse if a male worker could buy his supervisors and his company immunity from Title VII liability by taking care to harass sexually an occasional male worker, although his preferred targets were female.").

16. 422 F.3d 840 (9th Cir. 2005).

harassment lawsuit on the basis of their supervisor's bullying. While his conduct did not include sexual advances or comments, he yelled at the plaintiffs with "little or no provocation," and his shouting rants were often accompanied by aggressive physical gestures like lunging, pumping fists, and grabbing plaintiffs while barking commands or complaints at them. The bulk of evidence in the record showed that he behaved this way only toward women. The court held that this comparative evidence could satisfy the "because of sex" requirement as elucidated in *Oncale.*

What if, in contrast, the conduct *is* very sexual in nature, but not targeted at anyone in particular or even women in general? In Lyle v. Warner Brothers Television Productions, a writer's assistant for the long-running sitcom *Friends* alleged she had been sexually harassed by being forced to be present and take notes during meetings where the comedy writers engaged in sexually explicit conversation, gestures (including pantomimed masturbation), and cartoon drawings.[17] The plaintiff complained especially about the writers' discussions of their own sexual preferences and experiences and their fantasies about the sex lives of the actresses on the show, as well as other topics like anal sex and naked cheerleaders. The defendant offered "creative necessity" as a defense, arguing that comedy writers needed to have "frank sexual discussions and tell colorful jokes and stories (and even make expressive gestures) as part of the creative process."[18] The California Supreme Court, interpreting a state law provision similar to Title VII, concluded that while there is no categorical defense to sexual harassment lawsuits for creative workplaces, the plaintiff could not prevail because she did not prove that the conduct was either targeted at her directly or created hostility for women in general. To be actionable, the court held, undirected conduct must be even more severe and pervasive than targeted conduct. It also held that workplace context is relevant to determining whether actionable harassment occurred.

What if the sexual conduct is consensual between a supervisor and employee, but unfair to other employees? So-called sexual favoritism complaints have not fared well under Title VII generally due to the "because of sex" requirement. If a male supervisor has an affair with a female subordinate, other employees, both male and female, may have a grievance if the supervisor treats his subordinate more favorably than he treats them, but those effects are not obviously because of sex. But what if it was clear to women that employees who slept with the boss would be treated more favorably? Does that create an implied *quid pro quo* for other female employees or create a hostile environment? The EEOC issued a policy guidance in 1990 stating the agency's position that while isolated incidents of sexual favoritism do not violate Title VII, widespread favoritism can create a hostile environment, as well as support

---

17. 132 P.3d 211 (Cal. 2006).
18. Lyle v. Warner, 117 Cal. App. 4th 1164, 1175 (2004).

an implicit *quid pro quo* claim.[19] The California Supreme Court, interpreting state anti-discrimination law, followed this guidance in a 2005 case, Miller v. Department of Corrections, which presents a textbook case of sexual favoritism.[20] There, the warden at a women's prison had sexual relationships with at least three female subordinates, often involving public displays of affection and emotional fights among the women over competing affairs. He admittedly treated these women more favorably than other employees, defending the decision to give one of them a promotion over more qualified applicants because he had no choice lest she "take him down" by revealing "every scar on his body." Plaintiffs claimed that female employees repeatedly questioned whether this was the type of workplace where they would have to "'F' my way to the top."[21] The court ruled that sexual favoritism is a valid claim when it is "sufficiently widespread" such that "the demeaning message is conveyed to female employees that they are viewed by management as 'sexual playthings' or that the way required for women to get ahead in the workplace is by engaging in sexual conduct with their supervisors or management." If you were an employer, what steps would you take to avoid liability for sexual favoritism? For further discussion of office romances, see Note 8.

Under MacKinnon's theory, can men ever be victims of sexual harassment? If sexual harassment is viewed primarily as a means of reinforcing gender subordination, what accounts for cases in which women harass male subordinates or co-workers? Although cases with male plaintiffs have been relatively rare, they have resulted in some of the largest verdicts, including the first $1 million damage award in a sexual harassment case.[22] Most of these cases involve *quid pro quo* harassment. Do these claims support the suspicion that sexual harassment charges are sometimes simply an act of revenge following a romantic attraction that ends badly? Or do they indicate that women, no less than men, are capable of abusing power in the workplace? Men have also received unusually high verdicts for the harm of being wrongly accused in sexual harassment cases. A jury awarded one executive $26 million (later overturned) after he was fired by the company based on repeated charges of sexual harassment, once on the basis of his description of a racy episode of *Seinfeld* to an offended female co-worker.[23]

4. The Standard for Determining Hostile Work Environment. *Harris* imposes both an objective and a subjective standard for determining a hostile

---

19. Policy Guidance on Employer Liability Under Title VII for Sexual Favoritism (Jan. 12, 1990), No. N-915-048, 2 EEOC Compliance Manual §615 (2016).

20. 115 P.3d 77 (Cal. 2005).

21. Id. at 82.

22. See Man Wins Sex-Harassment Suit Against a Woman, N.Y. Times, May 21, 1993, at A12.

23. Mackenzie v. Miller Brewing Co., 623 N.W.2d 739 (Wis. 2001).

work environment. The plaintiff must have been actually offended, and the offense taken must have been reasonable. A longstanding issue is whether "reasonable" should be interpreted in light of the plaintiff's sex—i.e., can conduct that would not be offensive to a male employee, if the tables were turned, be sufficiently offensive to the female plaintiff to be actionable as sexual harassment? Only the Ninth Circuit Court of Appeals has specifically applied a "reasonable woman" standard.[24] *Harris* and subsequent U.S. Supreme Court cases have firmly established the standard that the "objective severity of harassment should be judged from the perspective of a reasonable person in the plaintiff's position, considering 'all the circumstances.'"[25] In *Oncale*, Justice Scalia reaffirmed that the "objective severity of harassment should be judged from the perspective of a reasonable person in the plaintiff's position, considering 'all the circumstances.'" Is this broad enough to encompass a "reasonable woman" standard if the plaintiff is female? Must a jury take that perspective?

Should sexual harassment standards take into account research showing that women are more likely than men to perceive certain behaviors, such as unsolicited invitations for sex, as harassing?[26] Does a reasonable person standard ignore the perspectives of women, and legitimate behaviors that many female workers find offensive?[27] Or would women be harmed more than helped by the assumption that they are all alike, and easily offended?[28] Although this issue initially divided feminists, it has grown less important in light of (1) social science surveys suggesting that men and women do not significantly vary in their interpretations of conduct serious enough to trigger legal liability,[29] and (2) studies demonstrating that a change in the standard given to mock juries accounted for only about 2 percent of the variance in perceptions of hostile work environments.[30]

How should courts determine what acts are sufficiently pervasive and abusive to justify liability? Consider the proposal of Gillian K. Hadfield, who would

24. See Steiner v. Showboat Operating Co., 25 F.3d 1459, 1464 (9th Cir. 1994).

25. See Oncale v. Sundowner Offshore Servs., Inc., 523 U.S. 75, 81 (1998).

26. See Jeremy A. Blumenthal, The Reasonable Woman Standard: A Meta-Analytic Review of Gender Differences in Perceptions of Sexual Harassment, 22 Law & Hum. Behav. 33, 71 (1998); Richard L. Wiener et al., Perceptions of Sexual Harassment: The Effects of Gender, Legal Standard, and Ambivalent Sexism, 21 Law & Hum. Behav. 71 (1997).

27. Caroline A. Forrell & Donna M. Mathews, A Law of Her Own: The Reasonable Woman as a Measure of Man 35-58 (2000)

28. See Linda Kelly Hill, The Feminist Misspeak of Sexual Harassment, 57 Fla. L. Rev. 133, 172-80 (2005) (arguing that the "reasonable woman" standard raises concerns of "victimization, essentialism, and judicial neutrality").

29. Theresa Beiner, Gender Myths v. Working Realities: Using Social Science to Reformulate Sexual Harassment Law 57-59 (2004).

30. Barbara A. Gutek et al., The Utility of the Reasonable Woman Standard in Hostile Environment Sexual Harassment Cases: A Multimethod Multistudy Examination, 5 Psychol. Pub. Pol'y & L. Rev. 596, 623 (1999).

define sex-based harassment as "sex-based non-job-related workplace conduct that would lead a rational woman to alter her workplace behavior—such as by refusing overtime, projects, or travel that will put her in contact with a harasser, requesting a transfer, or quitting. . . ." In Hadfield's view, "[b]ecause Title VII targets sex discrimination . . . the issue is whether a workplace practice has systematically negative consequences for women vis-à-vis men. Even if significant numbers of women enjoy an atmosphere in which sexual jokes abound, if systematically more women than men find this costly, then the practice is discriminatory. . . ." This approach would also eliminate the need for individual plaintiffs to prove that the behavior was unwelcome (see Note 4, below), since "those behaviors that rational women would be willing to pay to avoid are by definition unwelcome." Such a standard, however, would place "the onus on men, employers, and organizations to become educated about what behavior on their subordinates' part would prompt employment changes by a rational female employee. The test rejects the notion that men are entitled to the protection of their misimpressions about how such behavior is interpreted by women."[31] Is Hadfield's approach consistent with equality analysis? Would it be desirable?

5. When Is Sexual Conduct "Unwelcome"? As discussed in *Meritor*, the plaintiff in a hostile environment sexual harassment case must prove that the conduct was "unwelcome." One function of this requirement is to prevent parties from using sexual harassment charges to punish each other when a consensual relationship fails. Critics have argued that, as in the case of proving rape, this requirement often seems to put on trial the plaintiff, whose sexually provocative speech or dress was thought by Justice Rehnquist in *Meritor* to be "obviously relevant." Evaluating it, according to Louise Fitzgerald and others, also reinforces double standards of morality that treat women's sexual expression more harshly than men's.[32] The Federal Rules of Evidence impose some limits on the evidence of dress or lifestyle that will be admissible: such evidence must be more probative than prejudicial.[33]

Evidence of the plaintiff's participation in workplace banter has been still more controversial. Court decisions concerning the relevance of such evidence are divided. In one case, the plaintiff admitted at trial that she cursed and used vulgar language while at work. Her co-workers also testified that she often made jokes about sex, including jokes about "screwing her boss," and

31. Gillian K. Hadfield, Rational Women: A Test for Sex-Based Harassment, 83 Cal. L. Rev. 1151, 1182, 1185-86 (1995).

32. Louise Fitzgerald, Who Says? Legal Psychological Construction of Women's Resistance to Sexual Harassment, in Directions in Sexual Harassment Law 94, 102 (Catharine A. MacKinnon & Reva B. Siegel eds., 2004).

33. See Theresa M. Beiner, Sexy Dressing Revisted: Does Target Dress Play a Part in Sex Harassment Cases?, 14 Duke J. Gender L. & Pol'y 125, 149 (2007).

that she participated in frequent discussions and bantering about sex. In light of this testimony, the trial judge concluded that "[a]ny harassment plaintiff received . . . was prompted by her own actions, including her tasteless joking. Considering plaintiff's contribution to and apparent enjoyment of the situation, it cannot be said that the defendants created 'an intimidating, hostile, or offensive working environment.' "[34] Other courts, however, have found that a plaintiff who has participated in some of the exchanges involving foul language and sexual innuendo does not lose all protection to be free from sexual harassment.[35]

What, besides consent to sexual advances, might explain an employee's participation in such conduct? Research suggests that such behavior might sometimes serve as a survival technique—a way to achieve acceptance or to defuse a potentially unpleasant situation.[36] A similar motive might explain situations in which a plaintiff discounts the significance of harassing behavior as "[not] that big of a deal" or maintains friendly relations with the harasser. Yet courts have sometimes considered such responses as proof that the conduct was not sufficiently abusive to establish liability.[37] Do such outcomes "ignore[] the reality of what women must do to make life bearable in an all-male workplace"?[38]

The most obvious way for an employee to signal that particular behavior is offensive and unwelcome is to complain about it. Courts have increasingly required such complaints, but questions remain about when an employee must register objections: After the first instance? When conditions have become intolerable? Somewhere in between? Note, again, the potential Catch-22 situation: if the woman complains too early, she is hypersensitive, humorless, and unreasonable; if she waits too long, she may have difficulty proving that the behavior was unwelcome.[39] Should it matter that surveys show filing a formal complaint to be the least likely response of a victim of workplace harassment?

---

34. Loftin-Boggs v. City of Meridian, 633 F. Supp. 1323, 1327 (S.D. Miss. 1986), aff'd, 824 F.2d 971 (5th Cir. 1987).

35. See, e.g., Carr v. Allison Gas Turbine Div., Gen. Motors Corp., 32 F.3d 1007, 1011 (7th Cir. 1994) (plaintiff's vulgar language and dirty jokes could not justify a barrage of derogatory language, pranks, and graffiti); Spencer v. Gen. Elec. Co., 697 F. Supp. 204 (E.D. Va. 1988), aff'd, 894 F.2d 651 (4th Cir. 1990), overruled on other grounds by Farrar v. Hobby, 506 U.S. 103 (1992) (joining in milder forms of sexual horseplay that occurred in the office did not waive plaintiff's protection against sexual harassment).

36. See Beth A. Quinn, The Paradox of Complaining: Law, Humor, and Harassment in the Everyday Work World, 25 Law & Soc. Inquiry 1151, 1179-81 (2000).

37. Highlander v. K.F.C. Nat'l Mgmt. Co., 805 F.2d 644 (6th Cir. 1986); Scott v. Sears, Roebuck & Co., 798 F.2d 210, 212-14 (7th Cir. 1986).

38. Wendy Pollack, Sexual Harassment: Women's Experience vs. Legal Definitions, 13 Harv. Women's L.J. 35, 72-73 (1990).

39. See Reed v. Shepard, 939 F.2d 484, 492 (7th Cir. 1991) (female police officer's receptiveness to co-workers' sexually suggestive jokes and activities because she wanted to be accepted by others on the police force was fatal to her sexual harassment claim).

6. Sexual Harassment as an Offense Against Dignity. A European Union Recommendation on the Protection of Dignity of Women and Men at Work defines the issue in terms of workplace dignity, rather than sex discrimination. Western European countries generally recognize harassment as an offense whether or not it is based on sex. "Bullying" is an actionable tort that includes everything from verbal harangues to social ostracism.[40] In the last several years, 13 states have considered legislation that would make unlawful behaviors that are threatening, intimidating, or humiliating. Some commentators have recommended remedies for harassment by extending current tort law concepts of intentional infliction of emotional distress. Such a remedy would allow victims to sue the persons responsible, rather than just the employer, and would encompass conduct that is not sexual or aimed at only certain groups.[41]

A 2014 national survey found that 27 percent of surveyed American workers reported bullying behavior, defined as verbal or psychological forms of aggressive (hostile) conduct that persists for at least six months. About 31 percent of the bullies were female, and in about 68 percent of those cases, the female bullies targeted other women.[42]

What conclusions do you draw from this research? Is the dignity approach preferable to the discrimination approach as a response to workplace harassment? Some critics worry that such legislation would encompass too much trivial behavior and impose undue legal costs. Others believe that it would prove largely meaningless since few victims could afford the costs of proceeding except in egregious cases. What is your view?

7. Employer Liability. An employee may experience sexual harassment in the workplace but still not be able to recover against the employer. Sexual harassment law involves two separate questions: (1) did actionable harassment occur; and (2) can the employer be held liable for it? Individual harassers cannot be held liable under Title VII, thus employer liability is crucial to providing a remedy to discrimination victims.[43]

40. See generally Susanne Baer, Dignity or Equality?: Responses to Workplace Harassment in European, German, and U.S. Law, in Directions in Sexual Harassment Law, supra note 32, at 582.

41. Wendy N. Davis, No Putting Up with Put Downs, ABA J., Feb. 2008, at 16; Martha Chamallas, Discrimination and Outrage: The Migration from Civil Rights to Tort Law, 48 Wm. & Mary L. Rev. 2115 (2007); L. Camille Hébert, Conceptualizing Sexual Harassment in the Workplace as a Dignitary Tort, 75 Ohio St. L.J. 1345 (2014).

42. Gary Namie, Workplace Bullying Inst., U.S. Workplace Bullying Survey (2014), http://workplacebullying.org/multi/pdf/WBI-2014-US-Survey.pdf.

43. See, e.g., Williams v. Banning, 72 F.3d 552, 555 (7th Cir. 1995); Grossman, The Culture of Compliance, supra note 4, at 9 n.25.

In *Meritor*, the Supreme Court declined to issue "a definitive rule" on employer liability, but the Court revisited the issue in 1998, when it established a new standard for employer liability for harassment by supervisors. In Faragher v. City of Boca Raton, a college student who worked as a city lifeguard alleged that her supervisors had created a "sexually hostile atmosphere" by repeatedly subjecting female lifeguards to " 'uninvited and offensive touching,' by making lewd remarks, and by speaking of women in offensive terms."[44] One lifeguard allegedly told her, "Date me or clean the toilets for a year." Although the city had a sexual harassment policy, it was not distributed to her supervisors, and they were unaware of its requirements.

The Supreme Court, speaking through Justice Souter, held:

> [W]e . . . agree with Faragher that in implementing Title VII it makes sense to hold an employer vicariously liable for some tortious conduct of a supervisor made possible by abuse of his supervisory authority. . . .
>
> In order to accommodate the principle of vicarious liability for harm caused by misuse of supervisory authority, as well as Title VII's equally basic policies of encouraging forethought by employers and saving action by objecting employees, we adopt the following holding. . . . An employer is subject to vicarious liability to a victimized employee for an actionable hostile environment created by a supervisor with immediate (or successively higher) authority over the employee. When no tangible employment action is taken, a defending employer may raise an affirmative defense to liability or damages, subject to proof by a preponderance of the evidence. The defense comprises two necessary elements: (a) that the employer exercised reasonable care to prevent and correct promptly any sexually harassing behavior, and (b) that the plaintiff employee unreasonably failed to take advantage of any preventive or corrective opportunities provided by the employer or to avoid harm otherwise. While proof that an employer had promulgated an antiharassment policy with complaint procedure is not necessary in every instance as a matter of law, the need for a stated policy suitable to the employment circumstances may appropriately be addressed in any case when litigating the first element of the defense. And while proof that an employee failed to fulfill the corresponding obligation of reasonable care to avoid harm is not limited to showing an unreasonable failure to use any complaint procedure provided by the employer, a demonstration of such failure will normally suffice to satisfy the employer's burden under the second element of the defense. No affirmative defense is available, however, when the supervisor's harassment culminates in a tangible employment action, such as discharge, demotion, or undesirable reassignment. . . .
>
> The City points to nothing that might justify a conclusion by the District Court on remand that the City had exercised reasonable care. Nor is there any reason to remand for consideration of Faragher's efforts to mitigate her own damages, since the award to her was solely nominal. . . .
>
> [Reversed and remanded for entry of judgment for Faragher.][45]

44. 524 U.S. 775 (1998).
45. 524 U.S. at 792, 802, 807-09.

In Burlington Industries v. Ellerth, the plaintiff was a salesperson who alleged that she was subjected to constant sexual harassment by her supervisor, a mid-level manager. The misconduct consisted of "repeated boorish and offensive remarks and gestures," including repeated warnings to "loosen up" in response to sexual comments and pressure to meet him at a hotel lounge under the threat that "you know, Kim, I could make your life very hard or very easy at Burlington."[46] The plaintiff never reported her supervisor's conduct to her employer, despite being aware that it had a policy against sexual harassment. The Court adopted the same legal standard for employer liability, but remanded Ellerth's case for application of it. The employer was likely to prevail given that she failed to take advantage of an available internal grievance procedure.

In two later cases, the Court further established that where an employee resigns as a result of conditions that have become intolerable (constructive discharge), the employer may avoid liability by showing that there was an effective remedial process that the employee unreasonably failed to use.[47] Punitive damages are available only if the employer has not made good-faith efforts to comply with Title VII.[48] A key determinant of liability is whether the harasser was a supervisor or co-worker; the Supreme Court adopted a narrow definition of "supervisor" in Vance v. Ball State University, pushing more cases to the side of the line where it is harder to holder employers accountable.[49]

Under the affirmative defense, employers who wish to avoid accountability must make prompt and thorough investigations and take remedial actions reasonably calculated to prevent further harassment and to protect the complainant. Thus, *Faragher* and *Ellerth* spurred many employers to adopt formal, written anti-harassment policies and procedures; some also adopted anti-harassment training programs. But there has been considerable litigation over what types of responses are required of employers and complainants under the affirmative defense. For example, what constitutes a reasonable remedial action? Case law suggests that employers may be able to avoid liability if they transfer complainants out of range of the harasser unless that involves a less desirable assignment.[50] As long as employers take some responsive measures, failure to stop the harassment is not necessarily fatal to the employer's proof of the affirmative defense.[51] As interpreted by lower courts,

---

46. 524 U.S. 742, 748-49 (1998).

47. Pennsylvania State Police v. Suders, 542 U.S. 129 (2004).

48. See Kolstad v. American Dental Ass'n, 527 U.S. 526, 545 (1999).

49 133 S. Ct. 2434 (2013).

50. Compare Robinson v. Sappington, 351 F.3d 317 (2003) (reassignment not a defense) with Sparks v. Reg'l Med. Ctr. Bd., 792 F. Supp. 735 (N.D. Ala. 1992) (reassignment a defense). See Smith v. Rock-Tenn Serv., 2016 WL 520073 (6th Cir. Feb. 10, 2016) (finding sufficient evidence of faulty investigation to deny summary judgment to employer and remand for trial).

51. See cases cited in Grossman, The First Bite Is Free, supra note 3, at 699.

the law does not require employers to be very proactive. A survey of some 200 post-*Faragher* and post-*Ellerth* cases found that as long as the employer had a viable anti-harassment policy and a grievance procedure that allows an employee to bypass a harassing supervisor, *Ellerth* and *Faragher* "did little to change employer incentives to reduce the incidence of sexual harassment by supervisors in the workplace."[52]

Another set of questions focuses on victim behavior. When is a victim's failure to complain unreasonable? Most women, including disproportionate numbers of women of color, fail to report harassment out of concerns for retaliation, blacklisting, loss of privacy, and doubts that effective responses will be forthcoming.[53] Although employers must demonstrate that a victim's failure to complain was unreasonable, judges have been skeptical of plaintiffs' reasons for delaying or failing to complain. A "generalized fear of retaliation" is insufficient. As one circuit court put it, "the bringing of a retaliation claim, rather than failing to report harassment, is the proper method for dealing with retaliation."[54] Courts have imposed strict standards on plaintiffs, ruling in one case that a new employee who complained on her eighth day at a new job that she had been harassed daily since the first day had waited too long.[55] Yet the majority of surveyed victims say that complaints make the situation worse.[56] Studies support this perception, finding that as many as 60 percent of employees who complain about harassment are subjected to retaliation.[57] How can the law take account of this reality while providing adequate incentives for employees to provide notice of harassing conditions?[58]

---

52. Anne Lawton, Operating in an Empirical Vacuum: The *Ellerth* and *Faragher* Affirmative Defense, 13 Colum. J. Gender & L. 197, 210 (2004); see also David Sherwyn et al., Don't Train Your Employees and Cancel Your "1-800" Harassment Hotline: An Empirical Examination and Correction of the Flaws in the Affirmative Defense to Sexual Harassment Charges, 69 Fordham L. Rev. 1265, 1304 (2001) (survey of 100 federal cases supports conclusion that in order to minimize liability, employers "should not engage in or should eliminate extensive preventive efforts such as expensive sexual harassment sensitivity training, or more particularly, harassment-reporting hotlines").

53. Vicki Schultz, The Sanitized Workplace, 112 Yale L.J. 2061, 2140 (2003); Hernandez, A Critical Race Feminism, supra note 7, at 1262-68.

54. Matvia v. Bald Head Island Mgmt., Inc., 259 F.3d 261, 270 (4th Cir. 2001).

55. Marsicano v. American Soc'y of Safety Engineers, No. 97-C7819, 1998 WL 603128 (N.D. Ill. Sept. 4, 1998).

56. Louise Fitzgerald et al., Why Didn't She Just Report Him? The Psychological and Legal Implications of Women's Responses to Sexual Harassment, 13 Harv. Women's L.J. 35, 100 (1995).

57. See id. at 122-23 (describing the results of a study of state employees finding that 62 percent of women who reported sexual harassment experienced retaliation, with the most assertive responses often triggering the harshest response); see also Deborah L. Brake & Joanna L. Grossman, 86 N.C. L. Rev. 859, 902-05 (2008) (summarizing retaliation data).

58. See Brake & Grossman, supra note 57, at 879-84 (analyzing the way in which prompt complaint doctrines interfere with the ability of discrimination victims to enforce substantive rights).

Some critics of the current law have charged that having an anti-harassment policy and a grievance process is not enough to change behaviors in the workplace. The law generally fails to require more proactive measures, such as training, and some management experts advise against strategies that would encourage reporting.[59] About 40 percent of surveyed businesses offer no training, and many programs that are in place have demonstrated no long-term positive effect on attitudes or behaviors.[60] Internal complaint mechanisms are often structured in ways that inadvertently discourage their use and diminish their ability to address underlying discrimination issues. For example, because employers cannot promise confidentiality during investigation of a complaint, many victims are unwilling to come forward.[61] Moreover, because internal grievance procedures tend to focus on individual problem-solving and preserving harmonious working relationships, experts have noted that they fail to address broader systemic conditions that perpetuate discrimination, such as gender segregation and stratification in the work force.[62]

8. Harassment Prevention Policies: Do They Go Too Far? While some believe that harassment policies do not effectively address discriminatory behaviors in the workplace, others argue that the current liability structure gives employers too great an incentive to regulate harmless behaviors, including "trivial" sexual conduct. According to Vicki Schultz:

> [T]he federal agency and the lower courts charged with interpreting Title VII define[d] harassment primarily in terms of sexual advances and other sexual conduct—an approach I call the sexual model. . . . [T]his sexual model is too narrow, because the focus on sexual conduct has obscured more fundamental problems of gender-based harassment and discrimination that are not primarily "sexual" in content or design. . . . [T]he sexual model is also too broad, because . . . [it is] leading *companies* to prohibit a broad range of relatively harmless sexual conduct, even when that conduct does not threaten gender equality on the job. . . . Many firms are banning or discouraging intimate relationships between their employees. Worst of all, companies are disciplining (and even firing) employees for these perceived sexual transgressions without bothering to examine whether they are linked to sex discrimination in purpose or effect.[63]

59. Sherwyn et al., supra note 52, at 1304. Lua Kamal Yuille, Liberating Sexual Harassment Law, 22 Mich. J. Gender & L. 345 (2015) (arguing that eradicating sexual harassment is beyond Title VII's scope, but that the statute has well served is educative function in the harassment context).

60. Train Right Solutions, EE Compliance Practices Benchmarking (2006); Deborah L. Rhode, Social Research and Social Change: Meeting the Challenge of Gender Inequality and Sexual Abuse, 30 Harv. J.L. & Gender 11, 14 (2007).

61. See Grossman, The Culture of Compliance, supra note 4, 26 Harv. Women's L.J. at 61-63; Schultz, supra note 53, at 2140.

62. See Grossman, The Culture of Compliance, supra note 4, at 42-47.

63. Schultz, supra note 53, at 2065.

Schultz worries, in addition, that both employers and employees use trivial examples of sexual conduct as a pretext for other concerns.[64] Other critics claim that liability concerns have encouraged employers to promulgate overly broad categorical prohibitions on sexual expression. In Robinson v. Jacksonville Shipyards, Inc., the plaintiff established a "hostile environment" in a workplace pervaded by pornographic pictures and repeated sexual and demeaning remarks and jokes.[65] The court found that the employer had condoned this conduct and issued an order enjoining such behaviors. The decree required the employer to prohibit the display, reading, or viewing of pictures, posters, calendars, graffiti, and other materials that were "sexually suggestive, sexually demeaning, or pornographic."[66]

Does such an order raise First Amendment issues? The court concluded it did not, because (1) the employer had "no intention to express itself through the sexually-oriented pictures" and had banned other speech as well (such as political campaign literature and buttons); (2) pictures and verbal harassment were "not protected speech [when] they act as discriminatory conduct in the form of a hostile work environment"; (3) "regulation of discriminatory speech in the workplace constitutes nothing more than time, place, and manner regulation of speech"; (4) "female workers were a captive audience in relation to the speech that comprised the hostile work environment"; (5) even if the speech is "treated as fully protected by the First Amendment," the governmental interest in "cleansing the workplace of impediments to the equality of women is . . . a compelling interest that permits [a regulation] . . . narrowly drawn to serve this interest"; and (6) even a governmental employer has the power to enforce workplace rules impinging on free speech rights, in order to maintain discipline and order in the workplace.[67]

Schultz maintains that such efforts to "sanitize the workplace" will "induce[] social stigma and enforce[] sexual conformity in a way that impoverishes life for everyone." In her view, what women need is a "sexually open" and "gender egalitarian" workplace.[68] She would reform sexual harassment law to eliminate its focus on sexual content; courts under her proposal would prohibit any harassment that occurs because of sex and impose lesser standards of liability on workplaces that were gender-integrated at all levels, because these have been shown to have a lower incidence of offensive conduct.

Eugene Volokh and Kingsley Browne, both strong critics of restrictions on workplace expression, argue that harassment laws should target only offensive conduct directed at a particular employee; they worry that broader vaguer prohibitions will encourage employers to avoid liability by unduly limiting

---

64. Id. at 2113-16, 2156.
65. 760 F. Supp. 1486 (M.D. Fla. 1991).
66. Id. at 1542 (Appendix).
67. Id. at 1534-36.
68. Schultz, supra note 53, at 2146, 2164.

workplace speech.[69] What is your view? Is the standard adopted by the court in Lyle v. Warner Bros. (*Friends*) a fair compromise?

Schultz, along with other commentators, is also critical of the growing tendency of employers to become "cupid cops." The limited research available suggests that somewhere between 20 to 40 percent of companies have policies or clear norms on workplace romances, and that the vast majority prohibits or discourages such relationships.[70] Critics of prohibitions on workplace romances worry that attempts to enforce them are often ineffective and intrusive, and likely to drive relationships underground. Enforcement is also likely to have gender-biased results; those in subordinate positions, typically women, are the ones typically subject to transfer or termination. Do categorical bans on workplace relationships ignore courtship realities? For a growing number of employees, the increasing length of workweeks means that they have less time to find potential partners outside of the workplace. In representative surveys, 40 to 50 percent of employees had dated someone at work, one-fifth had dated a subordinate, over a quarter ended up marrying a colleague, and three-quarters felt that they should be able to date anyone they wished.[71] Would it be reasonable for an employer to ask romantically involved employees to sign a "love contract" acknowledging the relationship and promising it will not interfere with work? Despite the prevalence of intraoffice dating, twice as many employers had policies regulating or prohibiting office romance in 2013 as did in 2005.[72]

9. Race and Sexual Harassment. Although research finds that women of color are especially vulnerable to sexual harassment, some courts seem unresponsive to the combined power of racial and sexual abuse. In one such case, the trial judge granted summary judgment against the plaintiff whose claims included an incident where a co-worker dropped his pants and ordered her to "suck my dick, you black bitch." Another co-worker told the woman that he wanted to hang her in a cornfield, and she also encountered a Ku Klux Klan card posted on a factory beam. The court concluded that the behavior was

---

69. See Eugene Volokh, What Speech Does "Hostile Work Environment" Restrict?, Sexual Harassment: Cases, Case Studies, and Commentary 180, 202 (Paul I. Weizer ed., 2002); Kingsley Browne, The Silenced Workplace: Employer Censorship Under Title VII, in Directions in Sexual Harassment Law, supra note 32, at 399.

70. Schultz, supra note 53, at 2129.

71. Office Romances Rarely Kept Secret, CNN.com (Feb. 12, 2008), http://www.cnn.com/2008/LIVING/worklife/02/13/office.romance/index.html?iref=mpstoryview (in Career Builder survey, 40 percent had dated a colleague, 29 percent had married one, and 27 percent had dated a superior).

72. Dana Wilkie, Society for Human Resource Management, Forbidden Love: Workplace-Romance Policies Now Stricter (Sept. 24, 2013), https://www.shrm.org/hrdisciplines/employeerelations/articles/pages/forbidden-love-workplace-romance-policies-stricter.aspx.

"deplorable, and even offensive, humiliating, and threatening," but insufficiently severe and pervasive to alter the terms of employment.[73]

Some commentators have suggested that standards of what is offensive may be affected by cultural expectations, including those based on race. Consider the highly publicized Senate confirmation hearing in which Clarence Thomas, nominated to serve on the U.S. Supreme Court, faced accusations of sexual harassment. Anita Hill, a former staff attorney under Thomas' supervision at the EEOC, claimed that she had been subject to repeated and unwelcome sexual comments and advances. In assessing Hill's claims, Harvard sociologist Orlando Patterson argued that "what constitutes proper and effective male-female relations varies across gender, class, ethnicity, and religion." To "most American feminists . . . an obscenity is always an obscenity . . . ; to everyone else . . . an obscene expression . . . has to be understood in context." With his "mainstream cultural guard down," Thomas may have engaged in conduct that might be offensive to some but not to others like Hill. To those of African-American southern working class backgrounds, such conversation might have seemed reflective of a "down home style of courting." Patterson also claimed that "[i]f women are to break through the glass ceiling, they must escape the trap of neo-Puritan feminism with its reactionary sacralization of women's bodies."[74]

What is your view? Should the racial or cultural background of the parties ever affect what constitutes harassment in the workplace?

Putting Theory Into Practice

3-1. Analyze each of the following situations to determine whether it establishes a case of "discrimination based on sex." What theories of sex discrimination help you make the determination?

(a) An employee uses obscene language and tells sexually explicit jokes, which are offensive to some co-workers, both male and female.

(b) A supervisor berates all of his subordinate staff, both men and women; he refers to male associates who are insufficiently combative as wimps and pussies, and he refers to assertive women as castrating bitches.

(c) A bisexual employee makes unwanted sexual advances to both male and female workers. After they refuse him twice, he stops, but his presence makes them uncomfortable.

---

73. EEOC v. Champion Int'l Corp., No. 93C20279, 1995 WL 488333, at *2 (N.D. Ill. Aug. 1, 1995).

74. Orlando Patterson, Race, Gender and Liberal Fallacies, N.Y. Times, Oct. 10, 1991, at A15; see also Waleska Suero, We Don't Think of It as "Sexual Harassment": The Intersection of Gender and Ethnicity on Latinas' Workplace Sexual Harassment Claims, 33 Chicano/a-Latino/a L. Rev. 129 (2015).

(d) An employee widely assumed to be gay invites a male co-worker to dance at the office Christmas party, stares at his anatomy in the restroom, and hangs around the co-worker's desk for no obvious work-related reason.

(e) At an all-female mortgage company office, female employees make lewd jokes, ask each other about their sexual experiences, discuss whose breasts are bigger, and change clothes in front of one another. One administrative assistant is offended and claims that it interferes with her work.

(f) In a correctional facility, a female officer discovers that night-shift workers have been using her desk at night for sexual liaisons.[75]

(g) A secretary who works in a physician's office announces that she is pregnant. The doctor's wife believes her husband was having an affair with the secretary and that the child might be his. After other measures to alleviate his wife's fears, the doctor fires his secretary to save his marriage. Does it matter whether they were actually having an affair?[76]

(h) Two first-year associates complain to their law firm managing partner that one of their colleagues, an attractive single woman, has consistently received better assignments than they have from the supervising partner in the litigation section. That partner is in the midst of a messy divorce and has made a point of including their colleague in evening strategy sessions and out-of-town depositions on a major case. The managing partner raises the issue with the supervisor, who responds that he is not having an affair with the associate, although he is seeing her "socially." He has channeled assignments to her because she is more available in the evening and for travel than her married colleagues. As long as the relationship is consensual, he views it as "none of the firm's business."

3-2. Of the things that a male boss might ask of a female employee, which is the most objectionable: (a) to kiss him, (b) to babysit his kids, or (c) to be responsible for serving coffee at staff meetings?[77] Does the law reflect your opinion?

3-3. Julie is a dedicated young scientist who received the following email from a senior scientist in the research institute for which they both work: "Forgive the truth bomb, but from the first day I talked to you, there hasn't been a single day or hour when you weren't on my mind. I find you incredibly attractive, adorably dorky, and worth promoting in all the ways I have done—some known to you, and some unknown. Being near you is wildly exhilarating and at the same time frustrating, as I am utterly unable to get a grip on myself. That's

75. Orton-Bell v. Indiana, 759 F.3d 768 (7th Cir. 2014).
76. Mittl v. N.Y. State Div. of Human Rights, 794 N.E.2d 660 (N.Y. 2003); see also Kahn v. Objective Solutions, Int'l, 86 F. Supp. 2d 377 (S.D.N.Y 2000).
77. These examples are taken from Laura Rosenbury, Work Wives, 36 Harv. J. Gender & L. 345 (2013).

just the way things are and you're gonna have to deal with me until one of us leaves."[78] Is this sexual harassment? What should Julie do?

3-4. A Minneapolis woman works as a cashier in a sex-toy shop. Day in, day out, she hears lewd conversations by co-workers. Does she have a hostile environment claim against her employer, for failing to stop, or shield her from, these conversations?[79]

3-5. A warehouse foreman in a workplace requiring heavy lifting stated repeatedly that he believes women are incapable of performing work in the warehouse and that he would never hire a woman. Although he was not found to have committed any discriminatory personnel action, he was demoted for violating the organization's nondiscrimination policy by expressing beliefs that reflected a discriminatory attitude. He challenges that disciplinary action. Should he be reinstated?[80]

3-6. How would you handle "street hassling"—crude behaviors such as wolf whistles, leers, catcalls, grabs, pinches, and sexual invitations? Some feminists have proposed liability for such conduct under tort doctrine or misdemeanor statutes.[81] What problems and benefits do you see from such efforts? An anti-harassment campaign was launched on Philadelphia transit, featuring ads such as "Nice a** is not a compliment," and "In a perfect world, what would your sister/daughter/girlfriend hear as she walks to the subway? Hey sexy? Can I have a smile? What, you gay? Good Morning!"[82] Are public awareness campaigns such as this one likely to change attitudes or behavior (or both)?

2. Sexual Harassment in Educational Institutions

a. School Legal Liability for Sexual Harassment

Title IX of the Education Amendments of 1972, discussed in Chapter 2, broadly prohibits sex discrimination by educational institutions that receive

---

78. A. Hope Jahren, She Wanted to Do Her Research. He Wanted to Talk "Feelings," N.Y. Times, Mar. 4, 2016, at SR4.

79. Gerald D. Skoning, 2000 Ten Wackiest Employment Lawsuits, Nat'l L.R. Apr. 2, 2001, at A21.

80. See Holland v. Dep't of the Air Force, 31 F.3d 1118 (Fed. Cir. 1994).

81. Olatokunbo Olukemi Laniya, Street Smut: Gender, Media, and the Legal Power Dynamics of Street Harassment, or "Hey Sexy" and Other Verbal Ejaculations, 14 Colum. J. Gender & L. 91 (2005); Cynthia Grant Bowman, Street Harassment and the Informal Ghettoization of Women, 106 Harv. L. Rev. 517 (1993).

82. Details of the SEPTA campaign can be found at http://www.stopstreetharassment.org/2013/-4/septaads.

any federal funding.[83] Although it is most closely associated with gender equity in athletics, Title IX has had substantial application in the sexual harassment context. The Supreme Court has interpreted Title IX to prohibit *quid pro quo* harassment and hostile environment harassment as forms of intentional sex discrimination and to permit lawsuits for money damages.[84] The standards of liability, however, are more favorable to educational institutions than to employers under Title VII. In Gebser v. Lago Vista Independent School District, parents of a female student sued the school district after police found that their eighth-grade daughter was having a sexual relationship with one of her teachers.[85] By a 5-4 vote, the Court held that schools are not liable for harassment of a student by an employee unless officials had actual notice of the specific misconduct and responded with "deliberate indifference." The school's failure in that case to have a nondiscrimination policy and internal grievance procedure, which are both required by Title IX's implementing regulations, was not sufficient to render it liable for the harassment. This sort of violation, however, can trigger enforcement and penalties by the Department of Education's Office for Civil Rights, the agency charged with implementing Title IX.

In explaining the result in *Gebser*, Justice O'Connor's majority opinion reasoned that any stricter standard would be at odds with the overall compliance scheme of Title IX, which requires federal enforcement agencies to provide notice of any violation of nondiscrimination requirements before initiating enforcement actions. The "central purpose" of this notice is to "avoid diverting education funding from beneficial uses where a recipient was unaware of discrimination in its programs and is willing to institute prompt corrective measures." Justice Stevens' dissenting opinion noted that the Court's opinion creates incentives to avoid the knowledge that should trigger corrective action. According to some commentators, the liability standard in *Gebser* may encourage the see-no-evil/hear-no-evil attitudes already in place in many school districts. "When ignorance is bliss, and a defense to legal judgments, why should schools establish effective complaint strategies?"[86] To some, this double standard for educational and employment settings seems perverse. "Students often have fewer options for avoiding an abusive situation than an adult employee, their capacities for resistance are less developed, and their values are more open to influence. Schools are powerful socializing institutions and their failure to address harassment perpetuates the attitudes that perpetuate problems."[87] What is your view?

---

83. 20 U.S.C. §1681 (2012).

84. See Franklin v. Gwinnett County Public Schools, 503 U.S. 60 (1992).

85. 524 U.S. 274 (1998).

86. Deborah L. Rhode, Sex in Schools: Who's Minding the Adults, in Directions in Sexual Harassment Law, supra note 32, at 290, 297.

87. Id.

Harassment by peers adds another layer. In co-educational environments, the abuse takes multiple forms.

Subtle oppression by boys, who act obviously bored, sighing, groaning and rolling their eyes, sends a powerful message when a girl contributes in class. . . . Boys verbally abuse girls in and outside the classroom. In addition to the constant attack on the intellectual and academic abilities of girls, boys degrade girls with language that is pejorative of women. . . . In addition to purposeful abuse, boys oppress girls by monopolizing physical space. . . . [T]eachers in England . . . found that while boys occupy the total area surrounding schools by playing football, girls observe from benches or wander in the periphery of the "boys' space."[88]

A 2011 survey of students in grades 7-12 found that harassment is "part of everyday life."[89] Girls are more likely to be harassed (56 percent), especially physically, but boys are not immune (40 percent). Boys describe being called gay as the worst type of harassment, while girls respond that unwelcome sexual comments, jokes, or gestures are the most troubling and online sexual rumors the second most troubling. The impact of harassment on students includes a variety of physical, emotional and educational consequences, including, most frequently, a desire not to go to school.

At the college level, 61 percent of male and 62 percent of female students report experiencing harassment, defined as unwanted and unwelcome sexual behavior that interferes with one's life. Conduct includes sexual comments, rumors, grabbing, and propositions. Men are more likely to be called homophobic names; women are more likely to be adversely affected.[90] Only 7 percent report such conduct to a faculty or school official, largely because they don't believe it is sufficiently serious. However, cases that are reported pose significant concerns: sexual harassment is now the largest source of liability claims against higher educational institutions.[91]

In Davis v. Monroe County Board of Education, a divided Supreme Court clarified the standards for schools' liability for peer harassment.[92] There, a fifth-grade female student alleged repeated acts of harassment by one of her male classmates, including verbal and physical assaults such as attempts to touch her genital area. Despite several complaints by the girl's mother to the teacher, principal, and, eventually, the school board, the school failed to take adequate remedial action. Even though the boy pled guilty to criminal sexual

---

88. Laurie LeClair, Note, Sexual Harassment Between Peers Under Title VII and Title IX: Why Girls Just Can't Wait to Be Working Women, 16 Vt. L. Rev. 303, 325-27 (1991).

89. See Am. Ass'n of Univ. Women, Crossing the Line: Sexual Harassment at School (2011).

90. Am. Ass'n of Univ. Women, Drawing the Line: Sexual Harassment on Campus (2005).

91. John L. Pulley, Risk Management Lawyer Says Boom in Sexual Harassment Lawsuits Should Make Colleges Handle Cases Carefully, Chron. of Higher Educ., Sept. 28, 2005.

92. 526 U.S. 629 (1999).

battery, the school took three months to even agree to change the girl's seat so she wouldn't have to sit next to him in every class. The majority in *Davis* held that a school district's "deliberate indifference to known acts of harassment" by students could give rise to liability, but only when the district "exercises substantial control over the harasser and the context in which the known harassment occurs" and the conduct is so "severe, pervasive, and objectively offensive that it can be said to deprive the victims of access to the educational opportunities or benefits provided by the school."[93] In assessing the adequacy of remedial responses, courts should not expect that administrators can entirely "purg[e] their schools of actionable peer harassment" and "should refrain from second-guessing [administrators'] disciplinary decisions."[94] The Court remanded the case, which ultimately settled for an undisclosed amount of damages.

Critics found *Davis* problematic on the same grounds as *Gebser*, in that it creates an incentive for educators to avoid knowledge that might subject them to legal accountability. Given the reluctance of students to complain to anyone, reporting requirements are said to create an unrealistic limitation on accountability where other, less senior school personnel have knowledge of a problem and fail to take reasonable remedial action. School officials have generally opposed stricter liability standards on the ground that they have limited control over abusive conduct, especially by student peers. While other employers can dismiss workers who persist in harassment, administrators believe that they have fewer options in the face of recalcitrant students or even faculty who have their own due process rights. Where facts are contested or ambiguous, officials feel "caught in the middle. . . . We weren't doing the harassing. We're the entity with the deep pockets."[95] How would you respond?

School officials also may be liable under another civil rights law, Section 1983, which creates liability for deprivations of constitutional rights. In Fitzgerald v. Barnstable School Committee, the Supreme Court held that parents could sue school officials for sex discrimination under that statute when they allegedly failed to respond to serious harassment of their daughter by another classmate.[96] The standard for school liability under this statute has yet to be determined in the harassment context.

Has the Supreme Court struck the right balance between avoiding undue liability and providing incentives for schools to prevent or remedy harassment? How proactive should schools be? Is there a danger of overreaction?

93. Id. at 633.
94. Id. at 648.
95. Guy W. Horsley, quoted in Robin Wilson, William and Mary Seeks to Shift Liability for Damages to Professor in Federal Sexual Harassment Case, Chron. of Higher Educ., June 9, 1995, at A20.
96. 128 S. Ct. 2903 (2009).

Simpson v. University of Colorado Boulder
500 F.3d 1170 (10th Cir. 2007)

HARTZ, Circuit Judge.

Lisa Simpson and Anne Gilmore (Plaintiffs) claim that they were sexually assaulted on the night of December 7, 2001, by football players and recruits of the University of Colorado at Boulder (CU). They brought this action against CU under Title IX. . . . The district court granted summary judgment for CU, and later denied motions to alter or amend the judgment and to reopen discovery. Plaintiffs appealed these rulings. . . .

I. BACKGROUND. . . .

A. Plaintiffs' Allegations

Plaintiffs were sexually assaulted in Ms. Simpson's apartment by CU football players and high-school students on a recruiting visit. The CU football team recruited talented high-school players each fall by bringing them to campus. Part of the sales effort was to show recruits "a good time." To this end, recruits were paired with female "Ambassadors," who showed them around campus, and player-hosts, who were responsible for the recruits' entertainment. At least some of the recruits who came to Ms. Simpson's apartment had been promised an opportunity to have sex. . . .

II. DISCUSSION

A. Governing Law. . . .

Both parties in the case before us have treated Plaintiffs' claims as claims of student-on-student harassment subject to the specific requirements of *Davis*. In our view, however, Plaintiffs' claims have critical elements that make the student-on-student-harassment framework an imperfect one for analysis of their claims. The alleged sexual assaults were not simply misconduct that happened to occur at CU among its students. Plaintiffs allege that the assaults arose out of an official school program, the recruitment of high-school athletes. Indeed, they allege that the assaults were the natural, perhaps inevitable, consequence of an officially sanctioned but unsupervised effort to show recruits a "good time". . . .

In *Gebser* the Supreme Court held that a student's claim for money damages based on sexual harassment by a teacher could arise under Title IX, but only if (1) "an official who at a minimum has authority to address the alleged discrimination and to institute corrective measures on the [funding] recipient's behalf has actual knowledge of discrimination in the recipient's programs and fails adequately to respond," and (2) the inadequate response "amount[s] to deliberate indifference to discrimination." . . .

The . . . the role and responsibility of CU—is the focus of this appeal. We do not believe, however, that the formulation of this component in *Gebser* and *Davis* translates perfectly to the context of this case. We find it significant that in those cases there was no element of encouragement of the misconduct by the school district. To be sure, in those cases the school district could anticipate that the very operation of a school would be accompanied by sexual harassment, but that is simply because, unfortunately, some flawed humans will engage in such misconduct when they are in the company of others. Here, however, the gist of the complaint is that CU sanctioned, supported, even funded, a program (showing recruits a "good time") that, without proper control, would encourage young men to engage in opprobrious acts. We do not think that the notice standards established for sexual-harassment claims in *Gebser* and *Davis* necessarily apply in this circumstance.

We conclude that a funding recipient can be said to have "intentionally acted in clear violation of Title IX," when the violation is caused by official policy, which may be a policy of deliberate indifference to providing adequate training or guidance that is obviously necessary for implementation of a specific program or policy of the recipient. . . .

B. Evidence at Summary Judgment. . . .

The CU football program is one of the premier programs in the country. . . . CU's success on the field has been partly the result of an effective recruiting program that attracts the attention of the country's elite high-school football prospects. . . .

Plaintiffs were assaulted during a recruiting visit in December 2001. CU won the Big 12 Conference championship on December 1. High-school recruits visited campus a few days later. According to one recruit who was present at the assaults, on the night of Thursday, December 6, some of his fellow recruits had sex with female students in a room at a local hotel. He had stayed in his own room, but the next day he was assured by players that he could expect similar treatment that night and every weekend if he came to CU.

CU football players talked to a female CU student, who was a tutor for the athletic department, about getting together with her and other female students on Friday, December 7. At least one of the players understood that the purpose was to provide recruits another chance to have sex. The tutor, along with Ms. Gilmore, Ms. Simpson and others, had planned to spend the evening at Ms. Simpson's apartment. The tutor asked Ms. Simpson if four football players could come over later, and Ms. Simpson agreed. Between 11:30 and 11:45 p.m. about 20 football players and recruits arrived. Although some apparently left shortly after arriving, others remained. One player who was leaving was told by the tutor that he should stay because "it was about to go down," which he understood to mean that the women would begin showing recruits a "good time."

Within an hour or so Ms. Simpson, who was intoxicated, went to her bedroom to sleep. She awoke later to find two naked men removing her clothes. The door was locked. She was then sexually assaulted, both orally and vaginally, by recruits and players surrounding her bed. In the same room at the same time, two players and a third man, who was either a player or a recruit, were sexually engaged with Ms. Gilmore, who was too intoxicated to consent. Ms. Simpson and Ms. Gilmore were not the only females allegedly assaulted that night; three other women were sexually harassed by players in the apartment and a fourth had nonconsensual sex with two players after leaving the apartment. Ms. Simpson later withdrew from CU, and Ms. Gilmore eventually left Colorado for a year.

The central question in this case is whether the risk of such an assault during recruiting visits was obvious. In our view, the evidence could support such a finding.

The association of sexual misconduct with college football programs had been a matter of widespread reporting and concern for many years. . . . Academic research in the early 1990s concluded that male student athletes were more prone to commit sexual assault than other male students. CU's 2001 handbook for football players contains the following paragraph:

> A recent three-year study conducted by the National Institute of Mental Health found that athletes participated in one-third of the 862 sexual attacks on college campuses. Another study conducted at Towson State University's Center for the Study and Prevention of Campus Violence found that athletes are 5.5 times more likely to commit date rape.

CU itself was a specific focus of concern. A 1989 Sports Illustrated article on unlawful conduct by CU football players reported a number of cases of sexual assault by the players. One passage stated that the head football coach at the time, Bill McCartney,

> sometimes doesn't seem to grasp the seriousness of the situation either. . . . [H]e told [a television reporter], "Rape by definition is a violent act; an act whereby there's real physical violence involved, and so I don't think that's what we're talking about here." Said Boulder district attorney Alex Hunter, "It's obvious to me that one more spot in that date-rape seminar should be reserved for the football coach."

. . . In 1990 two CU football players were charged with rape and sexual assault arising from separate incidents.

The CU recruiting program was implicated in such misconduct in 1997, when Rick Neuheisel was head coach. As the IIC Report detailed, on December 6 a group of high-school girls attended a party at an off-campus hotel hosted by a CU football player for two visiting recruits. One of the girls alleged that she had been sexually assaulted by recruits at the party. Although the victim was not a CU student protected by Title IX, that circumstance is irrelevant to evaluation of the risk to CU women.

In January 1998 CU Chancellor Richard Byyny learned that Boulder police were investigating the incident. He emailed Athletic Director Richard Tharp:

> I worry about the oversight we have of the recruits while they are in our charge. Allegedly the recruits were all drinking beer in their rooms. I realize we don't have control over immature potential students. However, we should clearly spell out our rules, responsibilities, and expectations.

After the incident came to the attention of Boulder County District Attorney Alex Hunter, he requested a meeting with CU officials. On February 18, 1998, Hunter and Assistant District Attorneys Peter Hofstrom and Mary Keenan met with Byyny, Tharp, and Chichester, who was working in CU's counsel's office. Byyny understood that the purpose of the meeting was to provide the DA's office with an opportunity to "ask [CU] to continue to try and help educate [its] students, make sure that [the] students and [the] coaches were well informed about University policies and expectations in order to work to prevent these . . . kinds of events from occurring."

At the meeting Keenan, who later became DA, said that she was concerned about women being made available to recruits for sex. She explained that a girl in the position of the high-school victim, who was drunk at the time, would have sex with football recruits, "whether consensual or nonconsensual." She asserted that the 1997 assault wasn't "isolated" and indicated a "*real* problem" from which people at CU were "turn[ing their] heads." According to Keenan, she recommended that CU adopt a policy of zero tolerance for alcohol and sex in the recruiting program, develop written policies and procedures for supervising recruits, and offer football players annual training by the DA on sexual assault. She told Tharp "that [he] need[ed] to take measures to prevent this because if it happens again, [the DA's office is] going to deal with it very seriously." CU was now, as she put it at the time, "on notice."

Hunter also emphasized the changes that he thought needed to be made in the CU football recruiting program. The most important was that the player-hosts needed to be instructed on what was and was not appropriate conduct. Furthermore, the head coach needed to be tougher with athletes, and the coaching staff needed to explain clearly what conduct was appropriate for player-hosts and others.

The parties dispute the vigor of CU's response after the meeting. CU claims that it made significant policy revisions, but Plaintiffs have questioned whether these revisions were actually aimed at remedying or correcting the problem. CU's primary response was not admitting the two recruits involved in the assault and suspending the player for a semester. In addition, in April

1998 Chancellor Byyny instructed Athletic Director Tharp to develop new policies on student-athlete behavior, including a zero-tolerance rule on activities threatening the health or safety of student-athletes and others. Tharp responded that new policies would be drafted, but he expressed concern that new policies—apparently including the zero-tolerance policy—would impose a higher standard upon student-athletes than other students. As Tharp acknowledged in his deposition, none of the eventual recruiting or policy changes—the most substantive of which was apparently a ban on alcohol or tobacco for recruits—addressed either sexual contact between recruits and females or the responsibilities of player-hosts (other than a general statement that student-athletes should comply with Colorado law). Furthermore, although CU adopted a revised sexual-harassment policy in 1998, it applied equally to everyone on campus. It included nothing specific to recruiting or athletics, and although Tharp had been involved in drafting the policy in 1995 and 1996, he admitted that he played no role in its development after December 1997, when the assault occurred. As for the recommendations by prosecutors Hunter and Keenan, "no changes . . . were apparent" to Chichester following the meeting.

New head coach Gary Barnett arrived at CU in 1999. Deposition testimony of three players suggests that player-hosts still received little or no direction on appropriate behavior or responsibilities. One player testified that he had been told that his responsibilities as a player-host were to "[s]how [the recruits] around," and that "[t]hey really don't go into detail [regarding] your responsibilit[ies]." Barnett, who had learned from Chichester about the 1997 assault and subsequent meeting with the DA, began distributing a football handbook that included one page (of 88) addressing "Date Rape and Social Policy." The page warned players "not [to] put [themselves] in a position to lose everything [they] ha[d] worked hard for by committing a sexually aggressive act." Id. It cautioned that "NO means NO; even if you think she means yes"; "[a] girl never owes you sex"; and "[n]ever initiate intercourse if the woman is intoxicated or passed out." Id. There is evidence that coaches or senior players reviewed at least some of the information in the handbook with players during training camp. The handbook does not, however, address the risk of sexual assault or harassment in the recruiting program, and does not provide guidance to player-hosts on appropriate behavior by themselves and recruits. . . .

More importantly, in late September 2001, about two months before Plaintiffs' assaults, a female student employed in the athletic department, Trainer A, was raped by a CU football player. Trainer A met with Barnett shortly after the rape. Barnett twice asked her if she planned to press charges, and she told him that she wasn't sure. He then told her that if she did, her "life would change," and that if the player had a different version of what happened, "he would support the player." She alleged that when she asked Barnett what he would do about the player, he responded that "he was the player's coach and not his father and that he would not punish him." Trainer A ultimately decided not to press charges because of her conversation with Barnett. Barnett testified that the player was ordered to do some extra running, but he could not recall the specifics. Also, the player wrote a letter of apology. . . .

CU contends that evidence of its conduct after the assaults on Plaintiffs is irrelevant. But the reaction by Barnett and other officials to Plaintiffs' allegations indicates an attitude that would be inconsistent with their having made any sincere effort in the past to instruct players not to engage in or promote sexual harassment or assault. After Ms. Simpson reported her assault to police, CU revoked spring-semester scholarships for four football players who were allegedly involved but did not deny eligibility to those players for the January 2002 Fiesta Bowl, where CU had a chance to win the national championship. Although CU did not admit that year two recruits who were implicated in the assaults, Coach Barnett acknowledges that after the assaults he continued to support admission for one of the recruits despite being told that evidence of his involvement in the assaults was "overwhelming." There is also evidence that the CU police officer who served as Coach Barnett's personal escort at football games obstructed the investigation into Plaintiffs' assaults by meeting with football players before the investigating officers could. . . .

Barnett and Tharp also continued to resist recruiting reforms. Barnett told Chichester that he thought that female students may have arranged for the events of December 7, effectively setting up the recruits. He claimed that at schools all over the country recruits were shown "a good time," met young women, and went to parties, and if such activities weren't allowed at CU, it would be a "competitive disadvantage" for the football team.

As for Tharp, in April 2002 Chancellor Byyny directed him to institute a number of recruiting changes, including requiring only "well-trained upperclassmen" to serve as recruiting hosts. Although Tharp made some changes, he resisted the order to limit hosts to upperclassmen. The record does not appear to indicate whether or when such a requirement was instituted, although CU eliminated the player-host program entirely by the 2004-2005 recruiting season.

In sum, the evidence before the district court would support findings that by the time of the assaults on Plaintiffs, (1) Coach Barnett, whose rank in the CU hierarchy was comparable to that of a police chief in a municipal government, had general knowledge of the serious risk of sexual harassment and assault during college-football recruiting efforts; (2) Barnett knew that such assaults had indeed occurred during CU recruiting visits; (3) Barnett nevertheless maintained an unsupervised player-host program to show high-school recruits "a good time"; and (4) Barnett knew, both because of incidents reported to him and because of his own unsupportive attitude, that there had been no change in atmosphere since 1997 (when the prior assault occurred) that would make such misconduct less likely in 2001. A jury could infer that "the need for more or different training [of player-hosts was] so obvious, and the inadequacy so likely to result in [Title IX violations], that [Coach Barnett could] reasonably be said to have been deliberately indifferent to the need." . . .

Summary judgment was therefore inappropriate. . . .

Videckis v. Pepperdine Univ.
2015 WL 8916764 (C.D. Cal. 2015)

D. PREGERSON, United States District Judge

. . . Plaintiffs in this case are Haley Videckis and Layana White. Videckis is a former member of Pepperdine's women's basketball team who transferred to Pepperdine from Arizona State University in July 2013. White is also a former member of Pepperdine's women's basketball team who transferred to Pepperdine from Arizona State University in January 2014. . . .

Plaintiffs' suit arises out of allegedly intrusive and discriminatory actions that Pepperdine and its employees committed against Plaintiffs on account of Plaintiffs' dating relationship. Plaintiffs allege that, in the spring of 2014, Coach Ryan and others on the staff of the women's basketball team came to the conclusion that Plaintiffs were lesbians and were in a lesbian relationship. Plaintiffs further allege that Coach Ryan and the coaching staff were concerned about the possibility of the relationship causing turmoil within the team. Plaintiffs allege that, due to their concerns, Coach Ryan and members of the coaching staff harassed and discriminated against Plaintiffs in an effort to force Plaintiffs to quit the team. . . .

Pepperdine [argues] that Title IX does not apply to claims based on sexual orientation discrimination. . . .

Title IX provides, in relevant part, that "[n]o person in the United States shall, on the basis of sex . . . be subjected to discrimination under any education program or activity receiving Federal financial assistance." 20 U.S.C. §1681(a). Congress enacted Title IX with the twin objectives of avoiding the use of federal resources to support discriminatory practices and providing individual citizens effective protection against those practices.

In interpreting Title IX, courts often look to interpretations of Title VII for reference. The Ninth Circuit has held that the legislative history of Title IX "strongly suggests that Congress meant for similar substantive standards to apply under Title IX as had been developed under Title VII." Emeldi v. Univ. of Oregon, 698 F.3d 715, 724 (9th Cir. 2012).

Title IX's prohibition of discrimination "on the basis of sex" encompasses both sex—in the biological sense—as well as gender. Schwenk v. Hartford, 204 F.3d 1187, 1202 (9th Cir. 2000). Furthermore, discrimination based on gender stereotypes constitutes discrimination on the basis of sex under Title VII. *Price Waterhouse; Nichols.* . . .

This Court . . . stated that "the line between discrimination based on gender stereotyping and discrimination based on sexual orientation is blurry, at best." After further briefing and argument, the Court concludes that the distinction is illusory and artificial, and that sexual orientation discrimination is not a category distinct from sex or gender discrimination. Thus, claims of discrimination based on sexual orientation are covered by Title VII and IX, but not as a category of independent claims separate from sex and gender stereotype. Rather, claims of sexual orientation discrimination are gender stereotype or sex discrimination claims.

Other courts have acknowledged the difficulty of distinguishing sexual orientation discrimination from discrimination based on sex or gender stereotypes. See, e.g., Prowel v. Wise Bus. Forms, Inc., 579 F.3d 285, 291 (3d Cir. 2009) (stating that "the line between sexual orientation discrimination and discrimination 'because of sex' can be difficult to draw"); Dawson v. Bumble & Bumble, 398 F.3d 211, 217 (2d Cir. 2005) (acknowledging that it would be difficult to determine if an actionable Title VII claim was stated when a plaintiff stated she was discriminated against based on her sex, her failure to conform to gender norms, and her sexual orientation, because "the borders [between these classes] are so imprecise" (alteration in original)); Centola v. Potter, 183 F. Supp. 2d 403, 408 (D. Mass. 2002) (acknowledging that "the line between discrimination because of sexual orientation and discrimination because of sex is hardly clear"). Simply put, the line between sex discrimination and sexual orientation discrimination is "difficult to draw" because that line does not exist, save as a lingering and faulty judicial construct.

Pepperdine cites to opinions from various federal courts that state categorically that sexual orientation discrimination is not covered under Title IX. However, the Ninth Circuit has held only that "an employee's sexual orientation is irrelevant for purposes of Title VII," and that "[i]t neither provides nor precludes a cause of action for sexual harassment." Rene v. MGM Grand Hotel, Inc., 305 F.3d 1061, 1063 (9th Cir. 2002) (en banc) (plurality opinion).[1] Furthermore, the cases upon which Pepperdine relies, for the most part, dismiss analogous sexual orientation-based claims in a cursory and conclusory fashion. The Court rejects the reasoning of these cases, which do not fully evaluate the nature of claims based on sexual orientation discrimination.

In sexual orientation discrimination cases, focusing on the actions or appearance of the alleged victim of discrimination rather than the bias of the alleged perpetrator asks the wrong question and compounds the harm. A plaintiff's "actual" sexual orientation is irrelevant to a Title IX or Title VII claim because it is the biased mind of the alleged discriminator that is the focus of the analysis. This is especially true given that sexuality cannot be defined on a homosexual or heterosexual basis; it exists on a continuum. It is not the victim of discrimination who should be forced to put his or her sexual orientation on trial. We do not demand of a victim of alleged religious discrimination, "Prove that you are a *real* Catholic, Mormon, or Jew." Just as it would be absurd to demand that a victim of alleged racial discrimination prove he is black, it is absurd to demand a victim of alleged sex discrimination based on sexual orientation prove she is a lesbian. The contrary view would turn a Title IX trial into a broad inquisition into the personal sexual history of the victim. Such an approach should be precluded as not only highly inflammatory and offensive, but also irrelevant for the purposes of the Title IX discrimination analysis.

Therefore, the Court finds that sexual orientation discrimination is a form of sex or gender discrimination, and that the "actual" orientation of the victim is irrelevant. It is impossible to categorically separate "sexual orientation discrimination" from discrimination on the basis of sex or from gender stereotypes; to do so would result in a false choice. Simply put, to allege discrimination on the basis of sexuality is to state a Title IX claim on the basis of sex or gender. . . .

Notes

1. Legal Issues under *Gebser* and *Davis*. Although the court in *Simpson* held that the recruiting program was tantamount to an official policy of harassment, most cases involving sexual harassment in schools do not contain such an allegation. They are litigated, instead, under *Gebser* and *Davis*. Four key issues arise in those cases. First, who in the school's chain of command must have "actual notice" of harassment? It depends on who has authority to respond to the problem. For harassment by students, some courts have said notice to a teacher is sufficient given that teachers have the authority to discipline students.[97] Notice to a principal or other administrator is almost certainly sufficient.[98] For harassment by students, the notice must reach higher in the chain. Knowledge by other teachers has been held insufficient, as has notice to department chairs and other mid-level administrators.[99] Second, what kind of notice must be provided? Some courts require that the official have actual knowledge of the harassment of the complaining victim, while others say that knowledge of previous victims or other incidents can be enough.[100] Third, did the school respond to actual knowledge of harassment with deliberate indifference? This standard is very hard for plaintiffs to meet unless school officials

---

97. See, e.g., Murrell v. School Dist. No. 1, 186 F.3d 1238 (10th Cir. 1999).

98. See, e.g., S.K. v. North Allegheny School Dist., 2016 WL 806483 (W.D. Pa. Mar. 2, 2016) (principal has power to take corrective action).

99. See, e.g., Miller v. Kentosh, 1998 U.S. Dist. LEXIS 9497 (E.D. Pa. June 29, 1998).

100. See, e.g., Doe v. Blackburn College, 2012 U.S. Dist. LEXIS 24797, at *23-25 (C.D. Ill. Feb. 27, 2012) (no liability because college had no notice of harassment of plaintiff or prior incidents creating a risk that plaintiff would be sexually assaulted that was "so great that they [were] almost certain to materialize if nothing [were] done").

did absolutely nothing.[101] Fourth, was the harassment so severe and pervasive that it effectively deprived the students of access to education? Courts have been relatively strict in applying this requirement, demanding tangible proof of harm such as lower grades, greater absenteeism, physical injury that prevents schooling or other educational difficulties.[102] Courts' interpretation of this prong is a rejection of the rule in the employment context under Harris v. Forklift Systems that harassment can be actionable regardless of whether it caused severe psychological injury or other tangible harm.[103] In addition to these issues raised by the unique standard for institutional liability under Title IX, plaintiffs must overcome the usual hurdles in harassment litigation such as proving that the conduct was unwelcome, because of sex, and sufficiently severe or pervasive.[104]

2. Administrative versus Judicial Enforcement.   *Gebser* and *Davis* set forth the standards for institutional liability for sexual harassment in schools when victims seek money damages in court. As noted at the beginning of this section, however, educational institutions covered by Title IX are independently subject to enforcement by the Office for Civil Rights. Through a series of policy guidances and "dear colleague" letters, OCR has made clear that it applies stricter standards than courts to determine compliance with

---

101. See, e.g., Sanches v. Carrollton-Farmers Branch Indep. Sch. Dist., 647 F.3d 156, 167-68 (5th Cir. 2011) ("neither negligence nor mere unreasonableness is enough" to qualify as deliberate indifference under Title IX); Doe v. Sch. Bd., 604 F.3d 1248, 1259-61 (11th Cir. 2010) (deliberate indifference is an "exacting standard" that does not require school's response to be reasonable or effective); Doe v. Crown Point Sch. Corp., 2015 WL 5038093 (N.D. Ind. Aug. 26, 2015) (holding that school cannot be held liable for teacher's sexual advances toward student because it acted swiftly to force the teacher's resignation after the fact); but see *S.K.*, 2016 WL 806483 (not all responses are sufficient, and appropriate response may have to evolve as situation progresses); BPS v. Colo. Sch. for the Deaf and Blind, 2015 WL 5444311 (D. Colo. Sept. 16, 2015) (failure to do much other than documenting incidents of one student's abuse of others in a dormitory could satisfy the deliberate indifference standard); Takla v. Regents of the Univ. of Cal., 2015 WL 6755190 (C.D. Cal. Nov. 2, 2015) (the fact that the harassment by a professor of a student did not recur does not prove the university's response was sufficient).

102. See, e.g., Gabrielle M. v. Park Forest-Chicago Heights, 315 F.3d 817, 822-23 (7th Cir. 2003) (no interference with education where kindergarten girl, although "diagnosed with some psychological problems," maintained "steady" grades and "her absenteeism from the school did not increase"); Burwell v. Pekin Community High School, 213 F. Supp. 2d 917 (C.D. Ill. 2002) (no interference with education because plaintiff received highest grades of school career during period of harassment).

103. See Harris v. Forklift Sys., Inc., 510 U.S. 17 (1993).

104. See, e.g., Morgan v. Town of Lexington, 2015 WL 5634463 (D. Mass. Sept. 30, 2015) (pulling down a boy's pants, at least once in front of a girl, was not "because of sex" for Title IX purposes); Hankey v. Town of Concord-Carlisle, 136 F. Supp. 3d 52 (D. Mass. 2015) (keying "cunt" into a female classmate's car was not harassment "because of sex").

Title IX.[105] In its 2001 Revised Sexual Harassment Guidance, OCR notes, for example, that it expects recipients to respond to harassment based on actual or constructive notice. It also expects a more robust response to harassment. If a school knows or should have known about a hostile environment and "fails to take prompt and effective corrective action," it has "violated Title IX even if the student has failed to use the school's existing grievance procedures or otherwise inform the school of the harassment."[106] OCR has broad authority to punish schools for noncompliance, up to and including the termination of federal funding. (The application of these standards to sexual violence on campus is taken up in Chapter 5, Section A(3).)

3. Sexual Orientation Discrimination Under Title IX. Most courts have ruled, as the court did in *Simonton* (see Section B of this chapter) that sexual orientation is not a form of sex discrimination under Title VII. The court in *Videckis*, however, bucked a longstanding trend, holding that sexual orientation discrimination is no different from any other claim of sex discrimination. What is the difference between those two opinions? How would you characterize the judges' disagreement? Some gay and lesbian plaintiffs have been successful where they have been able to prove that the discrimination was rooted in their non-conformity with gender stereotypes, a theory successfully deployed in *Nichols*. Does that make the holding in *Videckis* unnecessary? What type of claims might lose under *Nichols*, but win under *Videckis*?

b. Speech and Conduct Codes to Prevent Harassment

One approach to addressing sexual and racial harassment in educational institutions, especially at the college and university level, has been speech codes that prohibit "verbal conduct" or "expression" that interferes with a student's ability to benefit from the educational environment. Some proposals relate specifically to the Internet and email systems. These codes have drawn fierce criticism from free speech advocates, who consider them a form of censorship and urge that the appropriate remedy for hurtful speech is not less, but more, speech. By contrast, advocates of regulation argue that in a sexist, racist society, "free speech" is available only to those with the power to use it, and that anti-harassment codes are critical to protect the dignity and integrity of individuals who cannot effectively "fight back" with counterspeech. In the university setting, racist and sexist speech is said to prevent some students

---

105. See Office for Civil Rights, Dep't of Educ., Revised Sexual Harassment Guidance: Harassment of Students By School Employees, Other Students, or Third Parties 19, at iv (Jan. 2001), http://www2.ed.gov/about/offices/list/ocr/docs/shguide.pdf.

106. Id. at 13-14.

from participating fully in the university community and from developing their psychological and intellectual potential.[107]

The tension between schools' interests in both preventing harassment and protecting expression has provoked increasing disputes, but no Supreme Court decision. Harassment codes at some public institutions have been struck down by lower courts on First Amendment grounds. For example, a federal appellate court struck down as vague and overbroad a policy defining harassment as "verbal, written or physical conduct which offends, denigrates or belittles an individual . . . [including] unsolicited derogatory remarks, jokes, demeaning comments or behaviors, slurs, mimicking, name calling, graffiti, innuendo, gestures, physical conduct, stalking, [and] threatening [or] bullying [conduct]."[108] When such codes have been enforced against professors for conduct in the classroom, courts have been similarly protective of First Amendment concerns. For example, one federal trial court held that a university could not impose sanctions under a policy prohibiting "verbal or physical conduct of a sexual nature" against a writing professor who made frequent references to sex (such as comments about belly dancing and vibrators), often as analogies to the writing process.[109] The First Amendment does not, however, prevent schools from maintaining anti-harassment policies. Explicitly sexual or lewd statements, for example, are not protected speech within an educational environment.[110] Schools may also be able to justify their policies under strict scrutiny, even as a content-based restriction on speech, because of the compelling interest in preventing discrimination. They can also defend policies and their enforcement under the standard in Tinker v. Des Moines Indep. Sch. Dist. if the speech might "substantially interfere with the work of the school or impinge upon the rights of other students."[111]

The law has developed in Canada in a direction more supportive of speech codes. There, the Supreme Court of Canada upheld a statute penalizing the communication of statements that willfully promote hatred against

---

107. Compare Nadine Strossen, Defending Pornography: Free Speech, Sex, and the Fight for Women's Rights (1995) with Mari J. Matsuda et al., Words That Wound: Critical Race Theory, Assaultive Speech, and the First Amendment (1993).

108. Saxe v. State Coll. Area School Dist., 240 F.3d 200 (3d Cir. 2001); see also UWM Post, Inc. v. Bd. of Regents of Univ. of Wisconsin, 774 F. Supp. 1163 (E.D. Wis. 1991) (striking down a Wisconsin code that prohibited conduct that "create[s] an intimidating, hostile, or demeaning environment for education").

109. Silva v. Univ. of New Hampshire, 888 F. Supp. 293 (D.N.H. 1994).

110. See Bethel Sch. Dist. v. Fraser, 478 U.S. 675 (1986) (upholding school's right to discipline student for making sexually explicit speech at school function).

111. 393 U.S. 503, 509 (1969); see also West v. Derby Unified Sch. Dist., 206 F.3d 1358 (10th Cir. 2000) (applying *Tinker* to uphold punishment of student under racial harassment policy for drawing a confederate flag); Zamecnik v. Indian Prairie Sch. Dist., 636 F.3d 874 (7th Cir. 2011) (student wearing t-shirt saying "be happy, not gay" was protected by the First Amendment because no risk of substantial disruption under *Tinker*).

any identifiable racial, religious, or ethnic group, as applied to a high school teacher who expressed anti-Semitic views, including the belief that the Holocaust was a myth.[112]

How should academic institutions deal with offensive speech? Are strategies other than prohibitions preferable, such as student protests, negative course evaluations, and open forums?

c. Faculty-Student Dating

Faculty-student dating has been another subject of campus concern. The limited available data suggest that such relationships are not uncommon. The conventional assumption is that broad prohibitions are unnecessary, unenforceable, or unduly paternalistic. Common views include:

> "Being sexually propositioned . . . is a normal and healthy part of life. (The real psychological and emotional tragedy probably befalls those who are not). . . . It is hardly self evident that the 'power imbalance' in such [relationships] favors the teacher. . . . If matters turn out badly, his career is finished."[113]
>
> "You can't legislate love."[114]
>
> A prohibition on faculty-student sexual relations "portrays students as timid and in need of protection." "It's like saying I can't make choices about who I want to date."[115]
>
> "It would take cult-like reprogramming to stop professors and students from dating. 'From everything we know sociologically, anthropologically, and biologically, males tend to be attracted to nubile potential mates, and women tend to be attracted to older men who . . . are successful and represent symbols of power.'"[116]

Feminist literary critic Jane Gallop acknowledges that women are at a "disadvantage" in a faculty-student relationship, but believes that "denying women the right to consent further infantilizes us."[117] Law professor Sherry Young similarly maintains:

112. See Regina v. Keegstra, [1990] 3 S.C.R. 697.

113. Edward Greer, What's Wrong with Faculty-Student Sex? Response I, 47 J. Legal Educ. 437, 438 (1997).

114. Dan Blatt, quoted in University of Virginia Considers Wide Ban on Intimate Teacher-Student Ties, N.Y. Times, Apr. 14, 1993, at A22.

115. Sara Rimer, Love on Campus: Trying to Set Rules for the Emotions, N.Y. Times, Oct. 1, 2003, at A21 (quoting Berkeley student newspaper editorial and Berkeley student journalist Virginia Griffey).

116. Tanya Shevitz, Dating Rule Was Defined at Cal, S.F. Chron., Dec. 3, 2001, at A25 (quoting Barry Dan, Professor of Sociology).

117. Jane Gallop, Feminism and Harassment Policy, Academe, Sept.-Oct. 1994, at 16, 22; see also Jane Gallop, Feminist Accused of Sexual Harassment 41-43 (1997).

Feminists should not be in the business of reducing the range of choice available to women, no matter how much they may question the wisdom of some of the choices that are made. . . . Feminists should not promote an image of women as helpless victims incapable of functioning under conditions of inequality of power. . . . The most pernicious idea to emerge from the debate on consensual relationship policies is the notion that feminists should be in the business of questioning the capacity of women, limiting the choices available to women, or urging institutions to disregard the testimony of women about their lives, their aspirations, and their emotional commitments.[118]

Compare Robin West's analysis:

Smart male students view themselves as all sorts of things, including young intellectuals. A good male student will often attach himself to a brilliant professor, and will aspire to *be like* him. . . . Unlike the male student, [the good female student] is more likely to be attracted to the brilliant professor, and aspire not to be like him, but to give herself *to* him. . . . For the female student, the intellectual self must fight the giving self, both in external and internal reality. The women who lose this battle have lost far more than the women who lost the A to which they were entitled, and so has the world. . . .

"Falling-in-love" with high school teachers, college professors, or research assistants really does destroy the productivity, the careers, the earning potential, and eventually the self-respect of many gifted women. Smart women drop out of high school, college and graduate school (and pretty women are at the highest risk) to date, marry, to help, and to serve those they perceive as intellectual giants. Eventually they learn boredom, the weariness of inactivity, and the self-contempt of nonproductivity.[119]

Other feminists agree. In part, their concerns are based on students' own accounts of sexual overtures by faculty. In one representative study, almost three-quarters of those who rejected a professor's advances considered them coercive and about half of those who had sexual relationships believed that some degree of coercion was involved.[120] Moreover, "faculty whose self-image and self-interest are at stake may underestimate the pressures that students experience. Regardless of the teacher's own intentions, students may believe that their acceptance or rejection of sexual overtures will have academic consequences. Given the power disparities involved, even relationships that appear consensual at the outset may become less so over time."[121] Except in egregious

---

118. Sherry Young, Getting to Yes: The Case Against Banning Consensual Relationships in Higher Education, 4 Am. U. J. Gender & L. 269, 298, 302 (1996).

119. Robin L. West, The Difference in Women's Hedonic Lives: A Phenomenological Critique of Feminist Legal Theory, 3 Wis. Women's L.J. 81, 109-11 (1987).

120. See surveys discussed in Caroline Forrell, What's Wrong with Faculty-Student Sex? The Law School Context, 47 J. Legal Educ. 47 (1997).

121. Rhode, Sex in Schools, supra note 86, at 296.

cases, however, few students have been willing to file complaints, and few institutions have been willing to impose serious sanctions. Even where the rules are clear, the evidence often is not. Moreover, most campus enforcement structures address only those faculty-student sexual relationships that meet conventional definitions of sexual harassment. Yet the harms to both individuals and institutions can be significant even in the absence of an explicit *quid pro quo* or a pervasive hostile environment. In relationships where the professor has any advisory or supervisory authority over the student, both the fact and the appearance of academic integrity are at risk.[122]

A growing number of institutions attempt to discourage faculty-student relationships. A few, such as William and Mary, ban all "amorous relations between faculty and undergraduates," or between graduate students and their supervisors.[123] Other schools counsel against such relationships and place a heavy burden on the faculty member to establish consent if a student complains. Some institutions prohibit faculty-student relationships where the professor has direct academic responsibility for the student. If a relationship arises, the faculty member must make other arrangements for supervision of the student's work. What kind of policy would you recommend for your own school?

Putting Theory Into Practice

3-7. For each of the following problems, consider (1) whether the conduct constitutes sexual harassment; (2) whether it would be appropriate for a university to prohibit the conduct through rules and regulations; and (3) if the conduct is undesirable, what strategies short of prohibition might be appropriate.

(a) A male college student repeatedly pursues a female student for a date. He calls her frequently on the phone, and approaches her in person when he sees her on campus. She continues to refuse and finally demands that he leave her alone and stop calling. He does so, but then a month later asks again in the hopes she has changed her mind. He has never touched her.

(b) One fraternity on campus has an annual "red light district" party. All female students who attend are required to dress as prostitutes. At the

---

122. Forrell, supra note 120; see also Carol Sanger, Consensual Sex and the Limits of the Law, in Directions in Sexual Harassment Law, supra note 32, at 86-87; Neal Hutchens, The Legal Effect of College and University Policies Prohibiting Romantic Relationships Between Students and Professors, 32 J.L. & Educ. 411 (2003); Paul M. Secunda, Getting to the Nexus of the Matter: A Sliding Scale Approach to Faculty-Student Consensual Relationship Policies in Higher Education, 55 Syracuse L. Rev. 55 (2004).

123. See www.wm.edu/about/administration/provost/documents/consensual_relations .pdf (rev. Apr. 2008).

party, the male students simulate "pick-ups" of the prostitutes. Invariably, some "mock" solicitations develop during that evening into actual seductions. Another fraternity invites a stripper to perform on campus the routine she offers at a local club.

(c) A university professor finds himself attracted to one of his students, who he feels is also attracted to him. Aware of the problems that can arise with faculty-student dating, he attempts to put his feelings of attraction aside. After picking up more and more "signals" that the student would welcome some initiative on his part, however, he finally asks her out for coffee. Her acceptance leads to more invitations to accompany him to campus events.

(d) Students post anatomically explicit and derogatory remarks on a male-only computer bulletin board. Other students circulate a poster with a nude caricature of a woman candidate for office of a student organization and send to an email list of 20 friends a parody titled "Top 75 Reasons Why Women [Bitches] Should Not Have Freedom of Speech."[124]

(e) Male students claim that an openly gay male professor has come on to them sexually by leering at them after class and by including favorable references to same-sex relationships in his lectures on ancient Greece. One student claims that the professor brushed his buttocks when leaving class in a crowded corridor.

3-8. Administrators at a middle school sent a notice to parents announcing that female students would no longer be allowed to wear shorts, leggings, or yoga pants because those types of clothing might be "too distracting" for their male peers. A petition with more than 500 student signatures urged the school to abandon the policy because it is not the obligation of the girls to accommodate the boys' inability to concentrate. A poster put up throughout the school asked: "Are my pants lowering your test scores?" Parents wrote a letter complaining that "this kind of message lands itself squarely on a continuum that blames girls and women for assault by men. It also sends the message to boys that their behaviors are excusable, understandable given what the girls are wearing. We really hope that you will consider the impact of these policies and how they contribute to rape culture."[125] Do you agree with the students and parents who objected to the policy? Why or why not?

3-9. Yik Yak is a popular social media app that does not include any user profiles. It sorts messages only by geographic location (1.5-mile radius) and is entirely anonymous. The app's developers say they intended it to make social

---

124. Thomas J. De Loughry, Cornell Top 75 Reasons, Chron. of Higher Educ., Dec. 1, 1995.

125. Tara Culp-Ressler, Middle School Girls Protest Sexist Dress Code: "Are My Pants Lowering Your Test Scores?", thinkprogress.com (Mar. 25, 2014), http://thinkprogress.org/health/2014/03/25/3418482/middle-school-dress-code-protest.

media more democratic, by allowing people to share their views widely even if they did not have a lot of followers or friends. A junior at the University of Mary Washington, who was a vocal leader in the campus group called "Feminists United" and had been outspoken about an incident involving the rugby team and its efforts to incite violence against women, was murdered. Prior to her murder, there were 700 sexist "yaks," including many that called for violence against this particular student and other members of her group in retaliation for calling for suspension of the rugby team. A former rugby player was eventually arrested for her murder. The surviving members of Feminists United filed a Title IX suit alleging that the university failed to protect them against discrimination and gender-based violence.[126] Did the university have sufficient notice to trigger its obligation to respond? What response would be appropriate given the technological features of this particular app? Advocacy groups have petitioned OCR to provide guidance to schools on their obligations with respect to this and other forms of online harassment.[127] What institutional responses should be recommended?

3-10. One of the subjects of a Human Sexuality course offered at Northwestern University is the use of sex toys for sexual stimulation. During one class, the professor displayed a variety of sex toys and described how they work. After class, he invited students to stick around for a demonstration, at which a naked woman was brought to orgasm using one of the toys. In the face of a firestorm of criticism, the university's president said he was "troubled and disappointed" by the incident, and that an investigation into the matter was underway. "I feel it represented extremely poor judgment on the part of our faculty member," the president's statement said. "I simply do not believe this was appropriate, necessary or in keeping with Northwestern University's academic mission."

"Sticks and stones may break your bones, but watching naked people on stage doing pleasurable things will never hurt you," the professor told his class in response to the controversy. The student newspaper quoted him as saying, "Do I have any regrets? It is mostly too early to say. I certainly have no regrets concerning students, who have demonstrated that they are open-minded grown-ups rather than fragile children. . . . To the extent that this event provokes a discussion of my reasoning, above, I welcome it. I expect

---

126. Justin Jouvenal & T. Rees Shapiro, Feminists at Mary Washington Say They Were Threatened on Yik Yak, Wash. Post, May 6, 2015.

127. Peter Schmidt, Women's Groups Urge Colleges and Government to Rein in Yik Yak, Chron. Higher Ed., Oct. 21, 2015; see also Yeasin v. Univ. of Kansas, 360 P.3d 423 (Kan. Ct. App. 2015) (holding that the university did not have the authority to punish student for online harassment because its policy only applied to conduct on campus or at university-sponsored events).

many people to disagree with me. Thoughtful discussion of controversial topics is a cornerstone of learning."[128]

Does this controversy implicate any equality concerns? Nonsubordination concerns?

C. DOMESTIC VIOLENCE

1. Domestic Violence: Legal Strategies for Protecting Victims

According to William Blackstone, the husband at English common law was legally entitled to use some physical force to provide his wife with "moderate correction."[129] So too, under early American common law, a husband, as master of his household, could subject his wife to "chastisement" short of permanent physical injury.[130] By the end of the Civil War, partly through efforts by early feminists, the American legal system had repudiated the doctrine of chastisement. However, during the Reconstruction Era, a new body of common law emerged under which judges concluded that "the legal system should not interfere in cases of wife beating, in order to protect the privacy of the marriage relationship and to promote domestic harmony."[131]

By the end of the nineteenth century, wife beating was viewed as a crime, but increasingly characterized as solely the practice of "lawless or unruly men of the 'dangerous classes,'" particularly African-American men and men from low-status immigrant ethnic groups such as Germans and Irish Americans. Domestic violence among the economically and racially privileged classes disappeared from public view.[132] By the 1920s, the victims of wife beating and child abuse had been transferred from "protection societies," which sought to provide women and children a safe haven from abusive men, to "child welfare agencies," which attempted to regulate domestic life more broadly. In the process, women were increasingly seen as part of the problem and "domestic trouble cases" often became an occasion to help wives "master the habits of cleanliness, nutrition, and child care."[133] The goal of the new family court

---

128. Professor John Michael Bailey Issues Statement on After-Class Event Controversy (Mar. 1, 2011), http://dailynorthwestern.com/2011/03/01/campus/campusarchived/prof-john-michael-bailey-issues-statement-on-after-class-event-controversy.

129. William Blackstone, 1 Commentaries on the Laws of England 432-33 (1765).

130. Reva B. Siegel, "The Rule of Love": Wife Beating as Prerogative and Privacy, 105 Yale L.J. 2117, 2118 (1996).

131. Id. at 2120.

132. Id. at 2137-39.

133. Evan Stark, Re-Presenting Woman Battering: From Battered Woman Syndrome to Coercive Control, 58 Alb. L. Rev. 973, 992-93 (1995). For further historical accounts of violence against women in Anglo-American social life and efforts to control it, see Linda Gordon,

system was to keep the family intact; accordingly, judges encouraged battered women to accept responsibility for their role in provoking the violence and discouraged them from filing criminal charges. Those views, and the perception of domestic violence as a private matter, lasted well into the 1970s.

Beginning in the 1960s, the women's movement sought to make "private" violence a public issue. Feminists created shelters to protect the health and safety of battered women and children. Activists also undertook public education campaigns to call attention to male violence and state inaction. So, too, advocates began using legal strategies to reform how law enforcement officials responded to cases of intimate abuse.

As the legal landscape has changed, so has the language used to describe it. Battered women's advocates initially introduced the term "domestic violence" to replace more colloquial terms such as "wife beating." More recently, the terms "intimate violence" and "intimate partner violence" serve to encompass the abuse of elders, children, domestic partners, men, and siblings. Descriptions of such violence also are evolving. The popular meaning of "battering" is physical assault, but many researchers now argue that the quest for control, and not physical violence per se, best describes an abusive relationship, and can involve threats, isolation, and control over necessities. Indeed, some evidence suggests that psychological abuse can be at least or more harmful to victims as physical assaults.[134]

It is estimated that a quarter to a third of women and 14 percent of men in the United States have experienced physical or sexual violence by an intimate partner or acquaintance at some point in their lifetime. About 14 percent of men are estimated to have experienced such violence.[135] Approximately 15 percent of women have experienced stalking from which they felt very fearful, or believed that they or someone close to them would be harmed as a result.[136]

Heroes of Their Own Lives: The Politics and History of Family Violence (1988); Elizabeth Pleck, Domestic Tyranny: The Making of Social Policy Against Family Violence from Colonial Times to the Present (1987).

134. Margaret E. Johnson, Balancing Liberty, Dignity, and Safety: The Impact of Domestic Violence Lethality Screening, 32 Cardozo L. Rev. 519, 526 (2010); Jennifer Langhinrichsen-Rohling, Top 10 Greatest "Hits": Important Findings and Future Directions for Intimate Partner Violence Research, 20 J. of Interpersonal Violence 108, 113 (2005).

135. Nat'l Domestic Hotline, Statistics (2016), http://www.thehotline.org/resources/statistics (quarter); Ctrs. for Disease Control and Prevention, National Data on Intimate Partner Violence, Sexual Violence, and Stalking (2014), http://www.cdc.gov/violenceprevention/pdf/nisvs-fact-sheet-2014.pdf (quarter); Nat'l Coalition Against Domestic Violence, National Statistics (2016), http:www.ncadv.org/learn/statistics (third).

136. Mathew J. Feiding et al., Ctrs. for Disease Control and Prevention, Prevalence and Characteristics of Sexual Violence, Stalking, and Intimate Partner Violence Victimization (2014).

About 75 percent of stalking victims are female.[137] Almost two-thirds of homeless women (63 percent) have experienced intimate partner violence.[138]

Most systematic studies conclude that women are significantly more likely to be victims of intimate violence than men. One Department of Justice report found that about four out of five victims of intimate partner violence were female.[139] Other research suggests that women are at least as physically aggressive as men, but less likely to inflict serious injury.[140] According to the Centers for Disease Control and Prevention, domestic violence is a leading cause of death for women ages 15 to 44, and the leading cause of death of pregnant women. Over 90 percent of female homicide victims are killed by men with whom they have had a relationship.[141] African-American women and Native American women are at the highest risk of intimate partner homicide.[142]

Women are most likely to be injured in an intimate relationship in the course of trying to end it. One study found that married women who lived apart from their husbands were nearly four times more likely to report that their husbands had raped, physically assaulted, and/or stalked them than women who lived with their husbands (20 percent and 5.4 percent, respectively).[143]

Women of color are disproportionately likely to experience intimate partner violence. African American women have a rate of domestic violence 35 percent higher than that of white women, yet are less likely to use social

137. Bureau of Justice Statistics, Stalking Victims in the United States (2012), http://www.bjs.gov/content/pub/pdf/svus_rev.pdf.

138. Nat'l Network to End Domestic Violence, Housing (2016), http://nnedv.org/policy/issues/housing.html.

139. Bureau of Justice Statistics, Intimate Partner Violence, 1993-2010 (rev. 2015), http://www.bjs.gov/content/pub/pdf/ipv9310.pdf. For further data, see Violence Policy Ctr., When Men Murder Women (2014), http://www.vpc.org/studies/wmmw2014.pdf.

140. For data on female violence and male victims, see The Surprising Truth About Women and Violence, Time, June 25, 2014; see also Jamie R. Abrams, The Feminist Case for Acknowledging Women's Acts of Violence, 27 Yale J.L. & Feminism 287 (2016).

141. Prediction of Homicide of and by Battered Women in Assessing Dangerousness: Violence by Batterers and Child Abusers 85, 86, (Jacqueline C. Cambell ed., 2d ed., 2007); see also Bureau of Justice Statistics, Female Victims of Violence (2009), http://www.bjs.gov/content/pub/pdf/fvv.pdf.

142. Minority Women and Intimate Partner Violence, Minority Nurse (2015), http://minoritynurse.com/minority-women-and-intimate-partner-violence; Elizabeth M. Schneider, Domestic Violence Law Reform in the Twenty-First Century: Looking Back and Looking Forward, 42 Fam. L.Q. 353, 361 (2008).

143. Patricia Tjaden & Nancy Thoennes, Full Report of the Prevalence, Incidence, and Consequences of Violence Against Women, findings from the National Violence Against Women Survey, Nov. 2000, http://www.ncjrs.org; see also Molly Dragiewicz & Yvonne Lindgren, The Gendered Nature of Domestic Violence: Statistical Data for Lawyers Considering Equal Protection Analysis, 17 Am. U. J. Gender Soc. Pol'y & L. 229 (2009) (reviewing studies); Walter S. DeKeseredy, Sexual Assault During and After Separation/Divorce: An Exploratory Study (U.S. Dep't of Justice 2007) (49 percent of survivors abused in the course of attempting to leave relationship).

services, medical services, and battered women's programs.[144] Between 40 to 60 percent of Asian American and Pacific Islander women reported physical and or sexual violence by intimate partners during their lifetime.[145] Native American women experience higher rates of intimate partner violence than other women of color.[146] Even after controlling for income, being a member of a minority group is a risk factor for domestic abuse.[147]

Being a member of a highly observant religious community also makes individuals particularly vulnerable.[148] Unresponsive clergy, pressure to preserve the family unit, and an absence of targeted support services pose ongoing challenges.[149]

Research on the incidence of domestic violence across class consistently finds a link between poverty and abuse. Low-income women have rates of intimate partner violence that are two to ten times higher than those among other women.[150] Residents of rural communities also face disproportionate dangers both because of the inaccessibility of shelters and support services, and the persistence of "old boy networks" that trivialize abuse.[151] Poor women are particularly vulnerable to violence because their lack of financial resources and employment skills traps them in abusive relationships. By the same token, violence impairs individuals' ability to find and retain work, which perpetuates economic dependence. Research finds that between one- and two-thirds of women who were welfare recipients have been victims of domestic violence.[152]

144. Minority Women and Intimate Partner Violence, supra note 142.

145. Id.

146. Id.

147. Deborah M. Capaldi et al., A Systematic Review of Risk Factors for Intimate Partner Violence, 3 Partner Abuse 231 (Apr. 2012).

148. Michal Gilad, In God's Shadow: Unveiling the Hidden World of Victims of Domestic Violence in Observant Religious Communities, 11 Rutgers J.L. & Pub. Pol'y 471 (2014).

149. Id. at 538, 541-42.

150. For twice the rate, see Erika Harrell et al., Bureau of Justice Statistics, Household Poverty and Nonfatal Violent Victimization, 2008-2012 (Nov. 2014). For higher rates, see research discussed in Hannah Brenner, Transcending the Criminal Law's One Size Fits All Response to Domestic Violence, 19 Wm. & Mary Women & L. 301, 313 (2012-2013); Anna Kastner, The Other War at Home: Chronic Nuisance Laws and the Revictimization of Survivors of Domestic Violence, 103 Calif. L. Rev. 1047, 1054 (2015). For other research, see Am. Psychological Ass'n, Violence and Socioeconomic Status Fact Sheet, http://www.apa.org/pi/ses/resources/publications/factsheet-violence.aspx.

151. Sara R. Benson, Failure to Arrest: A Pilot Study of Police Response to Domestic Violence in Rural Illinois, 17 Am. J. Gender Soc. Pol'y & L. 685, 697-99 (2009).

152. Angelo M. Moe & Myrtle Bell, Abject Economics: The Effects of Battering and Violence on Women's Work and Employability, 10 Violence Against Women 29, 35-36 (2004) (citing surveys finding that between one- and two-thirds of women on welfare experience violence); Rachel Gallagher, Welfare Reform's Inadequate Implementation of the Family Violence Option: Exploring the Dual Oppression of Poor Domestic Violence Victims, 19 Am. U. J. Gender, Soc. Pol'y & L. 987 (2011).

Research on lesbian, bisexual, and gay individuals finds a high incidence of domestic violence, and one that until recently has been largely overlooked. According to a study co-sponsored by the National Institute of Justice and the Centers for Disease Control and Prevention, the lifetime prevalence of rape, physical violence, or stalking by an intimate partner was 61 percent for bisexual women, 44 percent for lesbians, and 35 percent for heterosexual women. Among men, it was 37 percent for bisexuals, 29 percent for heterosexuals, and 26 percent for gays.[153] A fear of encountering homophobia or "making the community look bad" keeps many survivors from seeking help.[154] Research by the National Coalition of Anti-Violence Programs found that only 17 percent of LGBT survivors reported abuse to the police and only 4 percent reported seeking shelters.[155] Biases based on sexual orientation remain all too common within the domestic violence community.[156]

Teens and elderly Americans are also targets for abuse. The Centers for Disease Control and Prevention reports that about 10 percent of high school students reported physical victimization and 10 percent reported sexual victimization from a dating partner in the preceding year.[157] Accurate estimates of elder abuse are unavailable, but some research finds that 8 to 10 percent of adults experienced abuse in the prior year.[158]

Since 1994, the rate of nonfatal domestic violence has declined 63 percent.[159] The decline is commonly attributed to: (1) the increased provision of legal services for victims of intimate partner abuse, (2) improvements in some women's economic status, and (3) the overall drop in violent crime, which reflects demographic trends, most notably the aging of the population.[160] Domestic violence programs enable many women to leave relationships before they feel that they need to use deadly force in self-protection. However, the National Network to End Domestic Violence finds no decrease

153. Ctrs. for Disease Control and Prevention, An Overview of 2010 Findings on Victimization by Sexual Orientation (2013).

154. Maya Shwayder, Same Sex Domestic Violence Epidemic is Silent, The Atlantic, Nov. 5, 2013 (quoting Jesse Newman of Violence Recovery Program in Boston).

155. Id.

156. Deborah M. Weissman, Rethinking a New Domestic Violence Pedagogy, 5 U. Miami Race & Soc. Just. L. Rev. 635, 653 (2015).

157. Ctrs. for Disease Control and Prevention, Teen Dating Violence (2016), http://www.cdc.gov/violenceprevention/intimatepartnerviolence/teen_dating_violence.html.

158. Nat'l Ctr. on Elder Abuse, Fact Sheet (2016), http://www.ncea.aoa.gov/library/data/.

159. Are Domestic Violence Rates Dropping?, Domestic Shelters (Apr. 20, 2015), https://www.domesticshelters.org/domestic-violence-articles-information/are-domestic-violence-rates-dropping; Stacy Teicher Khadaroo, In US, a Decline in Domestic Violence, Christian Science Monitor, Aug. 26, 2014, http://www.csmonitor.com/World/Progress-Watch/2014/0826/In-US-a-decline-in-domestic-violence.

160. Amy Farmer & Jill Tiefenthaler, Explaining the Recent Decline in Domestic Violence, 21 Contemp. Econ. Pol'y 158 (Apr. 2003).

in the need for services; 88 percent of their programs are experiencing an increase in requests for assistance at the same time that 80 percent of states are reporting a drop in funding.[161]

Karla Fischer, Neil Vidmar & René Ellis,
The Culture of Battering and the Role of
Mediation in Domestic Violence Cases
46 SMU L. Rev. 2117, 2120-21, 2126-29,
2137-38 (1993)

The culture of battering refers to the relationship context of an abusive relationship. The first of the three elements of the culture of battering is the abuse, which includes at least one of the following types: physical, emotional, sexual, familial, and property. Professionals have increasingly recognized non-physical forms of abuse as harmful to domestic violence victims. The second element is the systematic pattern of domination and control that the batterer exerts over his victim. This pattern may be initiated by the batterer's gradual imposition of a series of rules that his victim must follow or be punished for violating. Over time, victims may censor their own behavior in anticipation of yet-unexpressed rules. The abuser's rein on the members of the household is enhanced by the use of emotional abuse and financial and social isolation, all of which help keep the victim in fear of impending abuse. Victims may engage in episodes of rebellion or resistance to the rules, which are nearly always met with more serious violence. Even separating from the abuser, an act of rebellion by itself, does not secure the end of the abuse; rather, it frequently escalates it. The third element, hiding, denying, and minimizing the abuse, refers to typical coping strategies that battered women use to reduce the psychological impact of the abuse. Each of these elements to some degree must be present in order for a culture of battering to be established. . . .

Battered women have frequently reported that abusers are extremely controlling of the everyday activities of the family. This domination can be all encompassing: as one of the batterers from Angela Browne's study was fond of stating, "[y]ou're going to dance to my music . . . be the kind of wife I want you to be." Charlotte Fedders' account of the escalating rules imposed by her husband [who was a prominent lawyer and high-level government official] over the course of their seventeen year, extremely violent marriage is particularly illuminating about the range of control that abusers can exert. Her husband insisted that no one (including guests and their toddler children) wear shoes in the house, that the furniture be in the same indentations in the carpet, that the vacuum marks in the carpet be parallel, and that any

Abusers like control

---

161. Are Domestic Violence Rates Dropping?, supra note 159.

sand spilled from the children's sandbox during their play be removed from the surrounding grass. Charlotte was not allowed to write checks from their joint checking account. Any real or perceived infraction of these rules could result in her husband beating her, or at the very least, the expression of his irritation that was frequently a harbinger to a beating.

Typically, battered women talk to the men about the abuse, partly as an attempt to concretize the rules that are connected to the absence of abuse. In turn, many abusers promise to stop the abuse. One abuser in Browne's study formalized such discussions into a written document, where he set forth a list of conditions that his victim was to agree to in exchange for cessation of his violence. These conditions were: (1) the children were to keep their rooms clean without being told; (2) the children could not argue with each other; (3) he was to have absolute freedom to come and go as he wished, and could have a girlfriend if he wanted one; (4) she would perform oral sex on him anytime he requested; and (5) she would have anal sex with him. He enforced this document shortly after she "agreed" to it and continued to sexually assault her until his death. This abuser simply made explicit the rules in the relationship and made it obvious that abuse was the punishment for violating the rules.

In many abusive relationships, however, the rules do not need to be verbally expressed to create a family atmosphere controlled by the batterer. Charlotte Fedders' story is a prototype of a battered woman who becomes very good at reading nonverbal messages from her abuser. She writes of how she restricted the play of her four young boys in order to avoid her husband's increasingly subtle signs of displeasure:

> Eventually . . . we just stopped using the living room and the family room because little things out of place would make him angry. . . . If [the boys'] rooms were a mess, he'd complain to me, so I was reluctant to let them play there. So they pretty much played in the basement. . . . I'd let them play only in the backyard, not the front, because John was so proud and particular about it. He wanted it perfectly green, and orderly. . . . He didn't like my putting a swing set up for the kids in the backyard, so it had to go all the way in the back, where no one would see it. . . .

What fuels this . . . process is the responsibility the victim feels, both as a woman socialized into believing that making relationships work is her job, and the responsibility added by the abuser, who blames her for the "failure" of the relationship, as evidenced by the occurrence of abuse. . . .

Our argument that abuse occurs within a relationship context of control and domination is an explicit rejection of the popular belief that abuse is simply a logical extension of a heated argument or disagreement. . . . Battered women's narratives of the context of abuse suggest quite the opposite of conflict. Women are typically beaten in a variety of situations that could hardly be classified as conflict: while sleeping, while using the toilet, and while in another room that the batterer suddenly entered to begin his beating. The usual scenario women describe is that at one moment all is calm and in the next, there is a major, seemingly untriggered explosion:

> I remember walking in, got undressed, and put my robe on, and I was going to get a glass of milk. At one moment we were laying together and kissing and everything seemed fine. And, it was like a second later, he was saying that I stayed out too late, and asked who was there and stuff, and then just . . . everything blew up. I know he threw me off the bed. And he told me he was going to beat me to death. And, then he said, "I'm going to set the trailer on fire with you and your daughter in it." And then he goes, "well, first, bitch, you are going to get me a glass of ice water."

In addition to the information about context, batterers' behavior during abusive incidents does not support an image that these men are out of control with anger. Women have reported deliberate, calculating behavior, ranging from searching for and destroying a treasured object of hers to striking her in areas of her body that do not show bruises (e.g. her scalp) or in areas where she would be embarrassed to show others her bruises.

Anger and conflict may be frequently confused with violence because both can be a proxy for abuse. The abuser may in fact be angry when he beats his victim or a conflict over what she has served for dinner may have developed before the incident of violence. But this simple coexistence in time does not mean that the anger or conflict has caused the violence. Lurking underneath the surface anger or conflict is the batterer's need to express his power over his victim. Even if the anger is controlled and all sources of conflict are removed from the relationship, violence still occurs. After all, batterers are usually involved in other social relationships, at work or elsewhere, where they become angry or have conflicts with others that they do not abuse. Their ability to cope with anger in some situations but not at home suggests that conflict and anger are not at the root of domestic violence. Perhaps the best evidence, however, that abuse is not about anger or conflict is that violence continues to occur, frequently escalating, after women leave their abusers.

≡≡≡ *Martha R. Mahoney, Legal Images of*
≡≡≡ *Battered Women: Redefining the*
≡≡≡ *Issue of Separation*
≡≡≡ 90 Mich. L. Rev. 1, 5-7 (1991)

The question "why didn't she leave?" shapes both social and legal inquiry on battering; much of the legal reliance on academic expertise on battered women has developed in order to address this question. At the moment of separation or attempted separation—for many women, the first encounter with the authority of law—the batterer's quest for control often becomes most acutely violent and potentially lethal. Ironically, although the proliferation of shelters and the elaboration of statutory structures facilitating the grant of protective orders vividly demonstrate both socially and legally the dangers attendant on separation, a woman's "failure" to permanently separate from a violent relationship is still widely held to be mysterious and in need of explanation, an indicator of her pathology rather than her batterer's. We have had neither cultural names nor legal doctrines specifically tailored to the particular assault on a woman's body and volition that seeks to block her from leaving, retaliate for her departure, or forcibly end the separation. I propose that we name this attack "separation assault."

Separation assault is the common though invisible thread that unites the equal protection suits on enforcement of temporary restraining orders, the cases with dead women that appear in many doctrinal categories, and the cases with dead men — the self-defense cases. As with other assaults on women that were not cognizable until the feminist movement named and explained them, separation assault must be identified before women can recognize our own experience and before we can develop legal rules to deal with this particular sort of violence. Naming one particular aspect of the violence then illuminates the rest: for example, the very concept of "acquaintance rape" moves consciousness away from the stereotype of rape (assault by a stranger) and toward a focus on the woman's volition (violation of her will, "consent"). Similarly, by emphasizing the urgent control moves that seek to prevent the woman from ending the relationship, the concept of separation assault raises questions that inevitably focus additional attention on the ongoing struggle for power and control in the relationship.

Stevenson v. Stevenson
714 A.2d 986 (N.J. Super. Ct. Ch. Div. 1998)

Cook, J.S.C. . . .

In what appears as a matter of first impression in New Jersey, this case presents the question whether a final restraining order issued under the Prevention of Domestic Violence Act . . . must be dissolved in all cases where the plaintiff so requests. For the reasons expressed below, this court determines that dissolution of a final restraining order at the request of plaintiff is not mandatory. Rather, dissolution in such cases is at the court's discretion, and should depend upon a showing of good cause, with an independent finding by the court based upon the facts presented in each case. . . .

On November 6, 1997, the parties appeared before this court for a hearing on plaintiff's complaint charging defendant with numerous violations of the Prevention of Domestic Violence Act (the Act). The testimony of plaintiff, the photographic exhibits offered by her counsel, and the graphic appearance at the hearing of the residual effects of the severe physical injuries she suffered, established by a clear preponderance of the evidence that defendant was guilty of attempted criminal homicide, aggravated assault, terroristic threats, criminal restraint and burglary, all in violation of the Act. These violations arose from a brutal, sadistic and prolonged attack by defendant on his wife during the late evening and early morning hours of October 29-30, 1997.

Plaintiff, who appeared at the hearing with two black and severely swollen eyes, testified that on the late evening of October 29, 1997, defendant came into the marital bedroom, went into a total rage, punched plaintiff with both fists, held her down with his knees, kicked her in the back and ribs, and continued beating her there for approximately 25 minutes. Defendant then dragged her by her hair down the stairs and out of the house, and shoved her into his van, saying that they were going to go to a friend's house. Plaintiff was bleeding from her ears, nose and mouth. She got out of the van, ran to a neighbor's house and banged on the door. Defendant chased her, screaming he would kill her, and that he should have killed her before. She was "petrified." He caught up to her outside the neighbor's house, and choked her with both hands around her throat. He then dragged her down the street and pushed her back into the van. She escaped again and ran to another neighbor's house. At that point, defendant's vicious attack on his wife had been going on for 45 minutes. She went inside the neighbor's house and asked her neighbor to call the police, while she went into a powder room, closed the door, and tried to hide from defendant. Defendant went into the neighbor's house and proceeded to rip the powder room door off its hinges. The door landed on plaintiff. He dragged her out of the house, and back towards their house. Plaintiff grabbed onto trees along the way, trying to resist. He was furious because she had asked her neighbor to call the police. Finally, he let go of her, got into the van and left. She was badly injured and very scared. A neighbor came with a blanket and rendered first aid. She was rushed by ambulance to the Emergency Room . . . [and] medevac'd by helicopter to the Cooper Hospital Trauma Center. She had a fractured skull, a concussion, four broken ribs, and a punctured lung (pneumothorax), in addition to the injuries noted above. She remained hospitalized at Cooper for several days, and was still under medical care at the time of the hearing on November 6, 1997.

At the hearing, the court had the opportunity not only to hear the testimony of plaintiff, but to observe her injuries and review the photographic exhibits submitted by her counsel as well. . . . The photographic exhibits submitted by plaintiff's counsel depicted her injuries, as well as the powder room door that defendant ripped off its hinges in the neighbor's home where plaintiff sought refuge. The photos, including those of plaintiff's facial and head injuries, and the hole in her chest where a tube was inserted to re-inflate her punctured lung, depicted a severally beaten and battered woman.

Plaintiff testified she was in fear of defendant. She related a prior history of domestic violence on his part, including previous assaults. She was afraid he would take their ten year-old son and leave the area, noting that he would do anything and everything to get physical custody and keep their son away from her. She added that their ten year-old son was in the house throughout the forty-five minute period that the beating of his mother took place.

Defendant, who was represented by counsel at the hearing, did not testify. No evidence was presented to controvert plaintiff's testimony, or the domestic violence charges she made against him. . . .

Because of (1) the barbaric conduct of the defendant during the nightmarish incident of October 29-30, 1997; (2) the evidence of his drunkenness that night and in the past; (3) his prior history of domestic violence; and (4) plaintiff's clearly expressed fear that defendant would take her son away if not restrained, a final restraining order was entered. The order prohibited any further acts of domestic violence, and barred him from having any contact or communication with the plaintiff and from harassing or stalking her. The order also required defendant to undergo substance abuse and psychological evaluations, and restricted him to supervised visitation only. He was also ordered to pay plaintiff's attorneys' fees of $2,400 by December 12, 1997; child and spousal support; all household expenses; and other expenses enumerated in the order.

At the hearing on plaintiff's request that the court dissolve the final restraining order, several violations of the order came to light. For example, it appeared that the defendant has engaged in *unsupervised visitation* with the child, including trips out-of-state. He has continually attempted to contact plaintiff. He has not abided by the psychotherapy recommendations of the Steininger Center, nor with the substance abuse recommendations of Segaloff. Both of those reports are discussed below. He has not paid any of the attorney's fees he was ordered to pay. In short, the defendant has flouted and violated the final restraining order. . . .

At the hearing on March 13, 1998, plaintiff asked the court to dissolve the final restraining order. She claimed she had reconsidered her relationship with the defendant and wanted him to be involved with their son's life. She requested that the restraints be dissolved, but only on the condition that he commit no future violence.

The final restraining order permitted *supervised visitation only*, pending a risk assessment and further order of the court. Risk assessment evaluations, substance abuse evaluations, and psychological evaluations of defendant were received by the court. At the request of and by agreement of both parties, through their counsel, copies of those evaluation reports were provided to the parties and their counsel. Plaintiff testified she had read the reports. . . .

Those reports include (1) a psychological evaluation of defendant by Dr. Stuart Kurlansik, Chief Psychologist, The Steininger Center; and (2) a drug and alcohol abuse evaluation of defendant by Patricia Thurman, a substance abuse counsellor. . . .

Dr. Karlansik reported inter alia that:

When asked to describe the events which resulted in his referral to this office, Mr. Stevenson reported that "I assaulted my wife. I beat her up very badly." . . .

He reported prior fights with his wife, but "nothing to this degree." He claimed that *every time they fought, he was drunk*. He stated that she never had to go to the hospital in previous fights. He stated that the previous fights involved punching, although not to the face. He stated that he bruised her in prior fights, but then claimed that she bruises easily. He reported that he had been in fights with other people during the period of his marriage as well. He stated that he boxes and plays hockey, and fought during the course of a game. He stated that he has had a few fights outside of the sport events, however. He then said there had been a handful, the most recent occurring [a year ago] at a roller rink [when] the other coach had been a poor sport, and "we ended up in a physical confrontation." . . . Another time, four years ago, he stated that he was a spectator at an ice hockey [game] in which his son was playing. He stated that a parent of one of his teams' children became involved in a fight with three of the opposing team's parents, and he "intervened." *He reported having a fight five years ago in a bar, and stated that he was intoxicated at the time.* He stated that he had played a game of pool for twenty dollars and the other person lost the game, and did not want to pay, "so I hit him." . . .

He denied any arrests as a result of fighting as an adult. As a juvenile, he stated that he was incarcerated at Glen Mills for a total of three years, and stated that "we could go on for hours" regarding juvenile incidents. He stated that he was at Glen Mills twice—once at age thirteen for assault, and the second time at age fourteen for robbery.

His current marriage has been his only marriage. He married on December 28, 1986. The most recent separation occurred October 29, 1997. He reported one other separation, two years ago. He stated that "things just weren't working well." This separation lasted about three months.

He reported that he has a *short temper*, although "not now." He claimed that the experience which brought him here has changed his life and a short temper is "not gonna be a trait for me anymore." . . .

An objective measure of personality functioning, the Million Clinical Multiaxial Inventory—III, was administered. . . . [T]he interpretive report stated that "on the basis of the test data (assuming denial is not present), it may be reasonable to assume that the patient is exhibiting psychological dysfunction of mild to moderate severity." An Axis I (an "acute" disorder) diagnosis of Generalized Anxiety Disorder is suggested, while Axis II (enduring features of an individual's personality, and therefore more "chronic") diagnosis of: "*Antisocial Personality Traits*," "*Passive-Aggressive Personality Traits*," "*Avoidant Personality Traits*," and "*Sadistic Personality Features*" are suggested. The NCS report hypothesizes . . . that he may manifest (among other things) a lack of empathy, intolerance, and display "impulsive and quixotic emotionality." It goes on to state that *individuals with his profile can "be easily provoked into sudden and unpredictable reactions," which "may be punctuated periodically by angry outbursts."*

Recommendations:

It is strongly urged that Mr. Stevenson participate in psychotherapy, to help him learn to control his anger (and to find more appropriate ways of expressing it), *as well as to reduce his anxiety.* Psychotherapy might also address what appears to be an issue with *excessive use of alcohol at times.*

In her substance abuse evaluation of defendant, Ms. Thurman, a substance abuse counsellor . . . reported that: . . .

Robert, a 34 year-old white male, was interviewed on November 29, 1997, at 8:30 a.m. Eye contact was fair, affect closed, guarded and *very accusatory toward his estranged wife, Melody.*

When asked about his use of drugs and alcoholic beverages, Mr. Stevenson states he's never used drugs of any kind and attempts to portray himself as a modest drinker, however, says the day he was charged "*I had a little too much to drink*". . . . But, Robert was quick to defend his actions by blaming the problem on "I caught my wife trying to buy drugs on the phone" and sees no relationship between his drinking and his current family problems. . . .

Concluding, based upon the limited information available to us, we strongly suspect Mr. Stevenson is drinking more than he reports and we feel he would greatly benefit from outpatient counseling to enable him to cease drinking and evaluate his family problems in a drug free state. The fact the client admits he was under the influence at the time of the altercation with his wife prompts us to question the severity of his drinking and its relationship to his family problems. . . . If Mr. Stevenson is not already in treatment for substance abuse, *we would then recommend he be mandated to complete at least 3 months in substance abuse treatment.* . . .

At a risk assessment conference with a Family Court staff therapist, plaintiff expressed concern over defendant's "*need for control,*" and again said she feared he would flee with their son, perhaps to Arizona. . . . She also said that on more than one occasion, defendant has threatened that he "will do anything and everything he has to" in order to gain custody of his son. Plaintiff requested that supervised visitation continue.

There remain several criminal charges pending against defendant as a result of his sadistic attack on his wife, including criminal attempt–murder; aggravated assault; burglary; criminal mischief; threatened violence; and criminal restraint. He is reportedly free on $75,000 cash bail, and is awaiting further proceedings in the criminal case.

When considering a plaintiff's request to dissolve the Final Restraining Order, a court must not forget that it is the public policy of the State of New Jersey, expressed by the Legislature in the Act, *that victims of domestic violence must be assured the maximum protection from abuse the law can provide; that the official response to domestic violence, including that of the courts, shall communicate the attitude that domestic violent behavior will not be excused or tolerated; and that it is the responsibility of the courts to protect victims of domestic violence* by ordering those remedies and sanctions that are *available to assure the safety of the victims* and the public. . . .

In addition, the Legislature has mandated that a final restraining order cannot be dissolved [or modified], *unless good cause is shown.* . . . Even where good cause is shown, the language of the statute, [the Act] expressly makes dissolution *discretionary*, not mandatory (". . . final order *may* be dissolved").

Plaintiff's dissolution request, made despite the latest brutal beating she suffered at the hands of a drunken husband who has a past history of wife-beating and an alcohol abuse problem, is consistent with phase three of "the battered woman's syndrome." That phase of the battering cycle is character-ized by a period of loving behavior by the batterer, during which pleas for forgiveness and protestations of devotion are often mixed with promises to seek counselling, stop drinking and refrain from further violence. A period of relative calm may last as long as several months, but in a battering rela-tionship the affection and contrition of the batterer will eventually fade, and phases one and two, the "tension-building" phase and the "acute battering incident" phase, will start anew. . . . Plaintiff has gone through the batter-ing cycle with defendant at least twice. Through this dissolution request she seeks to remain in the situation. She thus meets the definition of a "battered woman." . . . The New Jersey Legislature recognized the plight of battered women when it enacted the Act and provided battered women with the rem-edy of *permanent* restraining orders against wife-beaters and other batterers of women.

Obviously, if there were no basis at all for plaintiff to fear further vio-lence—as most certainly there is, given the nature and extent of this attack and defendant's past history of violence, including domestic violence against plaintiff; then there would be no need to condition dissolution on the absence of further violence. But there is that inherent fear, a fear that this court and any reasonable person viewing this situation would certainly share.

[Because fear is vital to the continuance of power and control in a domes-tic violence relationship, and this fear can impact the victim's ability to act in the best interests of her child, it is important to consider the victim's fear of the defendant.] When considering the question of fear of defendant, . . . the test should not be the victim's subjective fear. Rather, the test is one of objec-tive fear, i.e., that fear which a reasonable victim similarly situated would have under the circumstances. . . .

When considering a victim's application to dissolve, and whether there is good cause to do so, a court must determine whether objective fear can be said to continue to exist, and also whether there is a real danger of domestic violence recurring, in the event the restraining order is dissolved. . . . Whether or not this plaintiff would agree, it is clear that *from the standpoint of objec-tive fear*, that a reasonable victim of such a brutal beating by a husband, who has assaulted her in the past and has a history of other violent behavior, and is the subject of experts' findings of uncontrolled anger and excessive use of

Reasonable fear of husband

alcohol, would have a reasonable fear that future violence by her husband would occur, were the restraining order dissolved.

Even in cases of reconciliation, the court must still make *an independent finding* that continued protection is unnecessary before vacating a restraining order. . . . In this case, given the uncontroverted evidence of defendant's brutality against his wife, his history of violence both within and without the domestic arena, his alcohol abuse and uncontrolled assaultive behavior when under the influence, and the reports before the court, including those of The Steininger Center and Segaloff, a reasonable, objective and independent determination of the facts leads to the inescapable conclusion that a real threat of recurrence of domestic violence by defendant upon his battered wife will exist, if the Final Restraining Order is dissolved. This court will not be an accomplice to further violence by this defendant, by wholly dissolving at this point the restraints that have been entered against him. Accordingly, and for lack of good cause shown, plaintiff's application to dissolve the Final Restraining Order is denied.

Keep Protection order

The court does find cause to modify the Final Restraining Order with respect to certain matters concerning the child of the parties, as follows. The final restraining order shall remain in full force and effect, except that contact or communication between plaintiff and defendant relating to supervised visitation, and to the safety, health, education, welfare, status or activities of the minor child of the parties, shall be permitted. There shall be no further modification of the final restraining order, without application to and with the express approval of the court.

Defendant shall promptly undergo psychotherapy as recommended in the report of Dr. Kurlansik of The Steininger Center. He shall also promptly undergo at least three months of substance abuse treatment. . . . Upon completion of psychotherapy and substance abuse treatment, the court will consider unsupervised visitation.

Jeannie Suk, Criminal Law Comes Home
116 Yale L.J. 2, 8, 10, 16, 18-19, 45, 48-50, 69-70 (2006)

Beginning with the court-ordered prohibition of the alleged abuser's presence in the home, this Article ultimately points to a criminal law practice that I call "state-imposed de facto divorce," wherein prosecutors use the routine enforcement of misdemeanor DV to seek to end (in all but name) intimate domestic relationships. I show an emerging shift in emphasis from punishment of violence between spouses and intimate partners to criminalization of individuals' decisions to live like spouses or intimate partners. Even when a formal marriage may remain, the practical and substantive continuation of the intimate relationship becomes criminal. And perhaps unsurprisingly, this phenomenon is thoroughly class-contingent because it largely affects poor urban minorities and immigrants. . . .

[The article] examines a protection order practice in criminal courts in Manhattan that exemplifies criminal law control of the home. I argue that the routine issuance of criminal protection orders pursuant to a defendant's arrest and prosecution for DV—and the protection order's subsequent role in plea bargaining, conviction, and sentencing—is a form of state-imposed de facto divorce that subjects the practical and substantive continuation of the relationship to criminal sanction. In this system, the government (rather than one of the parties) initiates and dictates the end of the intimate relationship as a solution to DV. . . .

Today, protection orders are primarily enforced through criminal misdemeanor charges. Almost every state has made the violation of a DV protection order a crime. Violations of orders are generally misdemeanors, but in some states they are felonies. Laws in almost every state authorize warrantless arrests and apply mandatory arrest rules to protection order violations. . . .

Prosecutions for protection order violations can be a way of "short-circuiting proof problems for the prosecution," and thus a more efficient and effective means of convicting and punishing domestic abusers. A violation of a protection order is far easier to prove than the target crime of DV. The testimony of the victim is generally less important. No physical injury need be shown. The existence of the protection order and the defendant's presence in the home, to which the arresting officer can usually bear witness, are sufficient to establish violation of the protection order. With a "no-contact" order, all that may need to be shown is that the defendant made a phone call to the protected party. Thus, one function of protection orders can be to relax or circumvent the burden of proof for DV. . . .

The enforcement protocol consists of the following practices. Police officers must make an arrest if there is reasonable cause to believe that a DV crime, including violation of a protection order, has been committed. Officers therefore sometimes make DV arrests without inquiry into the victims' wishes. Once a DV arrest is made, the D.A.'s Office has a no-drop prosecution policy, according to which the decision to charge and prosecute does not hinge on the victim's willingness to cooperate. Prosecutors continue to pursue cases in the face of the victim's opposition and routinely inform victims that the choice to prosecute belongs to the state. . . .

At the arraignment of any defendant charged with a DV crime, the D.A.'s Office's mandatory practice involves asking the criminal court to issue a temporary order of protection (TOP) as a condition of bail or pretrial release. The order of protection, issued on a standard form for a "family offense," normally prohibits any contact whatsoever with the victim, including phone, e-mail, voice-mail, or third-party contact. Contact with children is also banned. The order excludes the defendant from the victim's home, even if it is the defendant's home. It also bans the defendant from the victim's school, business, and place of employment. Ascertaining whether the victim wants the order is not part of the mandatory protocol. The prosecutor generally requests a full stay-away order even if the victim does not want it.

The criminal court routinely issues the order of protection at arraignment, the defendant's first court appearance. The brief, formulaic, and compressed nature of arraignments in criminal court, which run around the clock to ensure that all defendants are arraigned within twenty-four hours of arrest, means that courts often issue orders with little detailed consideration of the particular facts. DV orders are generally requested and issued as a matter of course.

When the protection order goes into effect, the defendant cannot go home or have any contact with the victim (usually his wife) and his children. If the defendant does go home or contact the protected parties, he could be arrested, prosecuted, and punished for a fresh crime. This is so even if the victim initiates contact or invites the defendant to come home. Police officers then make routine unannounced visits to homes with a history of domestic violence. If a defendant subject to a protection order is present there, he is arrested. . . .

Already in effect on a temporary basis since the defendant's arraignment, the protection order is deployed as follows: the prosecutor offers the defendant a plea bargain consisting of little or no jail time (or time served) and a reduction of the charge, or even an adjournment in contemplation of dismissal, in exchange for the defendant's acceptance of a final order of protection prohibiting his presence at home and contact with the victim. This is an attractive offer. It presents the opportunity to dispose of the criminal case immediately with little or no jail time, and in some cases, no criminal conviction or record. The offer is particularly attractive for a defendant who has remained in jail since arraignment pending disposition of his case; if he agrees he will be released.

Depending on the terms of the plea bargain, the court issues the final protection order as part of the defendant's sentence pursuant to a guilty plea, or as a condition of an adjournment in contemplation of dismissal. In light of the evidentiary difficulties of obtaining a DV conviction at trial, especially when victims are uncooperative, many defendants do not take pleas, in anticipation of eventual acquittal or dismissal. But many do.[232]

About a third of all DV misdemeanor defendants plead guilty and roughly 15 percent more take adjournments in contemplation of dismissal. . . . Only about a third of convicted DV defendants get jail sentences; most get conditional discharges, which may include requirements such as batterer intervention programs. . . .

In the world of misdemeanor DV, then, prosecutors routinely use arraignment, bail, and plea bargaining to obtain defendants' agreements to protection orders forcing long-term separation—de facto divorce—from their spouses. As a product of the plea bargain, de facto divorce goes into effect without the benefit of traditional criminal process or proof of the crime. The arrest may have come at the behest of neighbors rather than the victim herself. Or the victim may have called the police to seek specific intervention in that moment.

But as a result of the initial arrest and through the operation of mandatory arrest and no-drop prosecution policies, the relationship can be, for practical purposes, dissolved by the force of the criminal law. Recall that this is a world in which the violence of DV has been defined down, and in which a mandatory protocol designed to deal with dangerous batterers applies in every case. De facto divorce is thus by and large imposed in misdemeanor cases, which by definition do not involve serious physical injury, and often involve little or no physical injury.

Finally, state-imposed de facto divorce is so class-contingent that it could be called poor man's divorce. The initial DV arrest that sets the wheels in motion is much more likely to occur if people live in close quarters in buildings with thin walls, and neighbors can easily hear a disturbance and call the police. . . .

State-imposed de facto divorce may well be appropriate for truly violent and dangerous abusive relationships; in these cases, the state may more readily conclude that victims' autonomy and consent are already worn so thin that paternalism will best enhance them. But the extraordinary legal innovation wherein de facto divorce becomes a standard prosecutorial tool needs close interrogation before it becomes a uniform, mechanical solution for the large number of cases now coming into the criminal system under the rubric of DV that do not involve serious physical injury. . . .[162]

Notes

1. Assessments of Danger. The *Stevenson* decision raises the question of how much evidence of past violence is necessary to override a victim's own preferences. Because past predictions of future violence by courts and clinicians have often proven inaccurate, experts have developed a Danger Assessment tool and a related Lethality Assessment program that use multiple factors to evaluate the likelihood of further abuse. In addition to the abusers' histories of violence, these frameworks look at threats and strategies of control. On average, these tools have proven more accurate than clinicians' judgments, but not more accurate than women's own predictions.[163] Should that fact influence courts in cases like *Stevenson*?

2. The Violence Against Women Act. The Violence Against Women Act of 1994 (VAWA) responded to domestic violence on multiple fronts. For example, it tightened sanctions by requiring courts to sentence first-time

---

162. For an expanded version of these views, see Jeannie Suk, At Home in the Law: How the Domestic Violence Revolution is Transforming Privacy (2009).

163. Margaret E. Johnson, Balancing Liberty, Dignity, and Safety: The Impact of Domestic Violence Lethality Screening, 32 Cardozo L. Rev. 519, 531 (2010).

offenders to prison or probation, rather than to general deferred or diverted prosecution programs, and to condition probation on participation in an approved nonprofit rehabilitation program. Assault with intent to rape, sexual abuse, and an attempt or solicitation to commit these offenses qualify as "serious violence felonies" under the federal "three strikes and you're out" sentencing structure. The Safe Homes for Women Act, created under VAWA, provides law enforcement personnel with the authority to enforce civil protection orders from other states, and provides databases and technical assistance to courts handling domestic violence. VAWA also expanded the State Justice Institute's authority and mission to study and eliminate gender bias in all criminal justice and court systems. On issues related to women of color, VAWA provided for the improvement of delivery services to racial, cultural, ethnic, and language minorities. It also expanded the remedies available to battered immigrant women, which were further broadened in the 2005 VAWA reauthorization legislation. Finally, VAWA created new substantive law, making it a federal crime to cross state lines for the purpose of, or in the course of, "harassing, intimidating, or injuring a spouse or intimate partner."[164] In 2013, the reauthorization of VAWA concentrated on improving prevention and response services among communities that have traditionally been underserved: Native Americans, LGBT individuals, and immigrant women.[165] For example, VAWA 2013 included provisions that ensure access to services and programs to all victims of domestic violence, regardless of their sexual orientation or gender identity, and allowed states to use federal funding to improve responses to domestic violence among the LGBT community.[166]

Spurred by federal assistance, states have also expanded services for victims of domestic violence. However, in most jurisdictions, the need substantially exceeds the programs available. Every year, the National Network to End Domestic Violence conducts a one day count of individuals seeking services from U.S. domestic violence shelter programs. In the most recent available survey, over 10,000 requests for services were unmet, including over 4300 requests for emergency shelter.[167] Male victims are particularly underserved.[168]

---

164. VAWA was passed as part of the Violent Crime Control and Law Enforcement Act of 1994, Pub. L. No. 103-322, 108 Stat. 1796 (codified as amended in scattered sections of 8 U.S.C., 16 U.S.C., 18 U.S.C., 28 U.S.C., and 42 U.S.C.).

165. Violence Against Women Reauthorization Act of 2013, Pub. L. No. 113-114, 127 Stat. 54, codified as amended in scattered sections of 8, 18, 20, 22, 25, 28, 42, 47, and 48 U.S.C. (2013).

166. 42 U.S.C. §13925 (2012); 42 U.S.C. §3796(g) (2012).

167. Nat'l Network to End Domestic Violence, Domestic Violence Counts 2014, http://nnedv.org/projects/census/4481-domestic-violence-counts-census-2014-report.html.

168. Korey Lewis, The Road to Inequality Is Paved with Good Intentions; The Effect of Language in Domestic Violence Statutes on Male Victims, 83 UMKC L. Rev. 789, 795-96 (2015).

3. Mandatory Arrest, No-Drop Prosecution and Restraining Orders, and Mandatory Reporting Policies. Mandatory or pro-arrest policies require police officers to arrest a suspect if there is probable cause to believe that an assault or battery has occurred, or that a domestic restraining order has been violated, without regard to the victim's consent or objection. These policies began to appear in the wake of a landmark Minneapolis study showing that arrest lowered recidivism rates in domestic violence cases. This study, along with several high-profile lawsuits against unresponsive police departments, helped launch policies now in force in about half of the states.[169] These policies have dramatically increased arrest rates. In one National Institute of Justice study, 37 percent of domestic violence incidents resulted in arrest, and 43 percent resulted in conviction.[170] Other changes have complemented and strengthened these policies, such as creation of offender databases, mandatory documentation of domestic violence incidents, and the development of specialized domestic violence police teams, prosecution units, and courts.[171]

Another initiative has been mandatory or no-drop prosecution policies, which require prosecutors to pursue domestic violence cases regardless of victims' wishes. These policies take two forms. The "hard approach" requires the victim to cooperate or face penalties; the "soft" approach does not penalize the victim for refusing to participate.[172] The limited evidence available suggests that the vast majority of victims are reluctant to testify against an abuser due to fear of retaliation, financial dependence, emotional attachment, or family and community pressure.[173] An estimated 60 to 80 percent of victims either recant their testimony or refuse to testify.[174] Under these circumstances, prosecutors may use strategies similar to those used in murder cases where victims are unavailable: introducing spontaneous statements made by the victim at the time of arrest, police officers' testimony, and videos or photographs taken at the time of the injury in lieu of victims' testimony. However, while evidence given by the victim in an effort to obtain help are admissible,

---

169. Atinuke O. Awoyomi, The State-Created Danger in Domestic Violence Cases: Do We Have a Solution in *Okin v. Village of Cornwall-on Hudson Police Department?*, 20 Colum. J. Gender & L. 1, 9 (2010).

170. David Hirschel, Nat'l Institute of Justice, Domestic Violence Cases: What Research Shows About Arrest and Dual Arrest Rates (2008).

171. See Schneider, Domestic Violence Law Reform in the Twenty-First Century, supra note 142, at 355; Emily J. Sack, Battered Women and the State: The Struggle for the Future of Domestic Violence Policy, 2004 Wis. L. Rev. 1657, 1671.

172. Leigh Goodmark, A Troubled Marriage: Domestic Violence and the Legal System 112 (2012); Caitlin Valiulis, Domestic Violence, 15 Geo. J. Gender & L. 123, 142 (2014).

173. Goodmark, A Troubled Marriage, supra note at 172; Keith Guzik, The Forces of Conviction: The Power and Practice of Mandatory Prosecution upon Misdemeanor Domestic Battery Suspects, 32 Law & Soc. Inquiry 41, 48 (2007).

174. Kimberly Bailey, Lost in Translation: Domestic Violence, "The Personal Is Political," and the Criminal Justice System, 100 J. Crim. L. & Criminology 1255, 1257 (2010).

evidence collected by the police as part of their investigation (known as "testimonial evidence") is not admissible against a criminal defendant unless the witness who made the statements at issue is unavailable and the defendant had a prior opportunity for cross-examination. Except in cases involving serious documented injuries, juries tend to be reluctant to convict if victims are uncooperative.[175] But prosecutors in many of these cases are able to obtain plea agreements at least to misdemeanors by charging defendants with more serious offenses, or by threatening to prosecute violations of restraining orders. The *Stevenson* case illustrates the further instance of not allowing women themselves to end restraining orders.

Medical screening for violence and mandatory reporting laws are another form of intervention. Over four-fifths of the states require reporting by healthcare providers if the patient has an injury that appears to have resulted from a deadly weapon.[176] In some states, service providers at Family Justice Centers, which coordinate the provision of services to domestic violence victims by a number of different agencies and community services, have a duty to report.[177] Advocates of these laws see them as a way to take domestic violence seriously and to ensure early law enforcement intervention when women's lives and health are at risk, and note that women are more likely to visit doctors than call the police. In an effort to encourage screening that too often falls through the cracks, the recently enacted Patient Protection and Affordable Care Act provides that covered insurance plans cover domestic violence screening and counseling free of copays by the insured individual.[178]

Proponents of these mandatory policies argue that they are the best way to force law enforcement officials and various service providers to take domestic violence seriously. By taking the decision to proceed away from victims, they contend, a mandatory approach can deter future abuse, reduce the exposure of victims to pressure and retaliation from the abuser, and enable them to receive much needed services. Under nonsubordination theory, aren't mandatory policies necessary?

These policies, however, have been subject to considerable criticism. Evidence concerning their effectiveness is mixed.[179] On the one hand, some studies indicate that some police officers remain unresponsive even under

---

175. Guzik, supra note 173, at 49.

176. Linda K. Bledsoe et al., Understanding the Impact of Intimate Partner Violence Mandatory Reporting Law, 10 Violence Against Women 536, 544 (2004).

177. See Jane K. Stoever, Mirandizing Family Justice, Harv. J.L. & Gender 189 (2016).

178. Patient Protection and Affordable Care Act, Pub. L. No. 111-148, 124 Stat. 119. For discussion of the inadequacy of screening and new Affordable Care Act Provisions, see Karen Oehme, Ember Urbach, & Nat Stern, Unheard Voices of Domestic Violence Victims: A Call to Remedy Physician Neglect, 15 Geo. J. Gender & L. 613, 615-22 (2014).

179. For an overview, see Goodmark, A Troubled Marriage, supra note 172, at 128-29; Laurie S. Kohn, The Justice System and Domestic Violence: Engaging the Case but Divorcing the Victim, 32 N.Y.U. Rev. L. & Soc. Change 191, 237-38 (2008).

mandatory policies because they retain discretion to determine the existence of probable cause to believe that domestic violence has occurred.[180] On the other hand, many studies find little deterrent impact, increased risk of retaliation, and decreased likelihood that victims will contact police or service providers.[181] Some research finds that mandatory arrest policies increase the frequency of arrests, but not successful prosecutions or victim safety.[182] One recent study found an increased death rate among domestic violence survivors whose partners were arrested and jailed.[183] Research also indicates that arrest and prosecution work best with those who have the most to lose from criminal sanctions, and that the risks of violence escalate among those who have the least to lose: those who are unemployed, poorly educated, and unmarried, and who already have a criminal record.[184]

Critics also charge that interventions over which victims have no control compound victims' trauma and erode their senses of efficacy, autonomy, and self-esteem—all aspects of their lives that are already weakened by the violence itself.[185] Mandatory arrest laws also increase the likelihood of dual arrests, in which victims who fight back are also charged, although rates of dual arrest are still relatively low.[186] In some jurisdictions, victims have even been jailed for refusing to testify after filing an abuse complaint. Critics also stress the likelihood that arrest and prosecution will remain more frequent in African-American and Latino communities, which are already disproportionately targeted by law enforcement officials.[187]

Similar problems arise when courts refuse victims' requests to dissolve restraining orders or to issue protection orders that permit non-abusive ongoing contact. Practices vary; in some jurisdictions, courts defer to victims' preferences, in others they make independent inquiries concerning coercion and

---

180. Bailey, supra note 174, at 1273: Benson, supra note 151, at 698-70.

181. For an overview, see Kohn, supra note 179, at 237-38; Sally F. Goldfarb, Reconceiving Civil Protection Orders for Domestic Violence: Can Law Help End the Abuse Without Ending the Relationship?, 29 Cardozo L. Rev. 1511, 1537 (2008).

182. Leigh Goodmark, Autonomy Feminism: An Anti-Essentialist Critique of Mandatory Interventions in Domestic Violence Cases, 37 Fla. St. U. L. Rev. 1, 35 (2009).

183. Lawrence W. Sherman & Heather M. Harris, Increased Death Rates of Domestic Violence Victims from Arrests Vs. Warning Suspects in the Milwaukee Domestic Violence Experiment, J. Experimental Criminology 1 (2015).

184. See Guzik, supra note 173, at, 44; Deborah Epstein et al., Transforming Aggressive Prosecution Policies: Prioritizing Victims' Long-Term Safety in the Prosecution of Domestic Violence Cases, 12 Am. U. J. Gender Soc. Pol'y & L. 465, 476-77 (2003).

185. Goodmark, A Troubled Marriage, supra note 172, at 118-24.

186. Emerson Beishline, An Examination of the Effects of Institutional Racism and Systematic Prejudice on Intimate Partner Violence in Minority Communities, 4 Wm. Mitchell L. Raza J. 2, 22-23 (2013); David Hirschel et al., Domestic Violence and Mandatory Arrest Laws: To What Extent Do They Influence Police Arrest Decisions, J. Crim. L. & Criminology 255 (2007) (finding that only 1 percent of incidents resulted in dual arrest).

187. Beishline, supra note 186, at 23-24.

risks, and in some instances they deny requests as a matter of policy. However, pressure is hard to assess, and when in doubt many judges err on the side of keeping protections in place; no one wants to be the one who dissolved an order for a woman "found face down in the morning."[188] Yet refusing to defer to women's own risk assessments may discourage them from filing requests for restraining orders in the first instance, and deny them bargaining leverage that may help end the abuse.[189]

As to medical interventions, critics worry that women whose history of abuse makes them aware of reporting requirements may be deterred from seeking treatment. Alternatively, their abusive partners may prevent victims from seeking assistance. Some research suggests that most women fear that mandatory reporting would increase their risk of abuse.[190] The American Medical Association opposes mandatory reporting out of concerns for patients' safety, confidentiality, and autonomy.

Given these problems, some feminists conclude that strategies providing women with material resources such as housing, food, clothing, or money should take priority over policies that seek greater accountability by batterers.[191] They also propose that law enforcement agencies should make victims' long-term safety the preeminent concern and provide more outreach to victims to ensure that protective orders are effective. Advocates of this approach often support presumptive arrest policies, in which officers will arrest unless the victim expressly opposes arrest and the officer determines that the victim is safe.[192] A "survivor-centered" strategy also calls for flexible policies that permit dropping charges where victims are at high risk for retaliation and abusers are unlikely to get lengthy sentences or where an alternative like completion of a substance abuse and counseling program might assist the parties more than prosecution. The limited available evidence suggests that focusing on

188. Tamara L. Kuennen, Analyzing the Impact of Coercion on Domestic Violence Victims; How Much Is Too Much?, 22 Berkeley J. Gender, L. & Just. 2, 25 (2007).

189. Goldfarb, supra note 181, at 1501-05, 1523 (citing evidence that only a small minority of women subject to physical assault obtain protective orders, and that many women want protection without ending the relationship). In Williams v. State (Alaska Ct. App. 2006), an appellate court in Alaska held that a mandatory law prohibiting someone accused of domestic violence of returning to the residence was unconstitutional as applied to defendants on pre-trial release. 51 P.3d 460 (2006). In that case, the defendant had petitioned for permission to return home for Christmas, and his wife supported his petition with evidence that they had taken vacations together, that separate residences was a financial burden, and that "she did not feel her husband was a threat." Id. at 462-63.

190. Thomas L. Hafemeister, If All You Have Is a Hammer: Society's Ineffective Response to Intimate Partner Violence, 60 Cath. U. L. Rev. 919, 962 (2011).

191. Schneider, Domestic Violence Law Reform in the Twenty-First Century, supra note 142, at 358; Donna Coker, Shifting Power for Battered Women: Law, Material Resources, and Poor Women of Color, 33 U.C. Davis L. Rev. 1009 (2000).

192. Hafemeister, supra note 190, at 982.

women's needs increases their willingness to cooperate with prosecutors and reduces their exposure to repeated abuse.[193]

Can women be counted on to make the right decisions to protect themselves when subject to the pressures that domestic violence exerts upon them? If you were a domestic violence judge, what evidence would be most relevant to your decision about whether to honor a woman's decision to dissolve a restraining order? Should victims have the option of requesting protection orders that do not prohibit all contact with the requesting party?[194] If Suk is right that domestic violence protection orders amount to de facto divorce, what follows?

Some judges have imposed fines or jail sentences for a battered woman's contempt of a civil protection order. For example, Kentucky Judge Megan Lake Thornton fined an impoverished woman $100 for reconciling with her husband a few days after she had obtained a protective order. Thornton explained, "I find that offensive. It drives me nuts when people just decide to do whatever they want." Like a vocal minority of family court judges, she has made it clear that no-contact orders apply equally to abusers and targets of abuse. "People are ordered to follow them and I don't care which side you are on."[195] Domestic violence advocates view this kind of formalistic egalitarian approach as unrealistic, unjust, and "a barrier that stops abused women from seeking protection of the court."[196] They believe that victims should be able to request orders that do not bar all contact. When parties have children, financial difficulties, or continuing love for their abusers, "[i]t's pretty hard to say, 'Never speak again.'"[197]

A minority of states make protective orders available for nonviolent forms of domestic abuse, and some commentators believe that all states should do so.[198] One recent bill proposes to recognize abusive contact through emails and phone calls, and the malicious destruction of property, as forms of domestic violence.[199] Research suggests that women find psychological abuse more

193. Epstein, supra note 184, at 486-98.

194. Goldfarb, supra note 181.

195. Francis X. Clines, Judge's Domestic Violence Ruling Creates an Outcry in Kentucky, N.Y. Times, Jan. 8, 2002, at A14 (quoting Thornton). For other examples, see Debora L. Threedy, Legal Archeology and Feminist Legal Theory: A Case Study of Gender and Domestic Violence, 29 Women's Rts. L. Rep. 171, 189 (2008).

196. Clines, supra note 195, at A14 (quoting Carol Jordan, director of the Kentucky Governor's Office of Child Abuse and Domestic Violence).

197. Id. at A14 (quoting Sherry Currens, Executive Director of the Kentucky Domestic Violence Ass'n). For arguments supporting orders that do not ban all contact, see Goldfarb, supra note 181.

198. Margaret E. Johnson, Redefining Harm, Reimagining Remedies, and Reclaiming Domestic Violence Law, 42 U.C. Davis L. Rev. 1107, 1133-37 (2009).

199. Bill Sponsor Seeks to Close Loophole in Domestic Violence Law, Mar. 9, 2016, http://www.wbaltv.com/politics/bill-sponsor-seeks-to-close-loophole-in-domestic-violence-law/38424912.

painful than physical abuse, and psychological abuse often leads to physical abuse.[200] Restricting women's freedom or access to money, sabotaging their attempts to find or keep a job, and isolating them from friends and families are part of patterns of domination that experts believe should be subject to restraining orders. Should a victim be able to choose to end protective orders when the abuse is not physical?

Federal law prohibits individuals convicted of domestic violence misdemeanors involving force or attempted use of physical force from owning a firearm.[201] That statute was enacted to close a loophole that had allowed access to guns by abusers who had not been convicted of a felony. In United States v. Castleman, the Supreme Court held that a crime satisfying the common law definition of battery satisfied the force requirement of the federal statute.[202] In Voisine v. United States, the Court concluded that a misdemeanor crime with the mens rea of recklessness qualified as a misdemeanor crime of domestic violence under the statute.[203] The Court did not review claims that the statute was unconstitutional.

4. Civil Damage Claims.   Another legal resource for survivors of intimate violence is the civil damages suit. VAWA had created a federal civil rights remedy for "crimes of violence motivated by gender," but the Supreme Court in United States v. Morrison determined that such a right of action was up to the states to create, and was beyond Congress' constitutional authority.[204] However, a few states and localities have adopted gender-motivated violence laws that cover domestic assaults.[205] State tort law also generally provides remedies for assault, and 48 jurisdictions have abolished barriers to spouses suing each other.[206] Such claims are, however, infrequent, partly because defendants lack deep pockets and insurance policies do not cover intentional torts.[207]

Beginning in the 1980s, some leading decisions also allowed actions under Section 1983 of the Federal Civil Rights Act against municipalities whose police were grossly negligent in responding to domestic violence complaints. However, in 2005, the Supreme Court limited such remedies. In Castle Rock v. Gonzales, the Court held that a jurisdiction's mandatory arrest policy does

200. Johnson, supra note 198, at 1113, 1121.

201. 18 U.S.C. §922 (g)(9).

202. United States v. Castleman, 134 S. Ct. 1405 (2014).

203. 2016 WL 3461559.

204. United States v. Morrison, 529 U.S. 598 (2000). The case arose from a sexual assault by two college football players. One of them, after raping the victim, told her that "You better not have any fucking diseases." He later announced in the dormitory's dining room that "I like to get girls drunk and fuck the shit out of them."

205. Camille Carey, Domestic Violence Torts: Righting a Civil Wrong, 62 Kan. L. Rev. 695, 712 (2014).

206. Valiulis, supra note 172, at 145.

207. Carey, supra note 205, at 728-29.

not create the necessary "special relationship" with the state or an entitlement under the due process clause that would justify liability under Section 1983. There, Jessica Gonzales repeatedly requested that local police arrest her ex-husband for violation of a civil restraining order after he abducted their three daughters who were playing in the family's front yard.[208] According to the facts in the complaint, which the Court accepted for purposes of the decision, the respondent contacted the police six times between 7:30 p.m. and 1:00 a.m. the next morning. She even went to the police station to file an incident report and begged the officers to look for her husband, who had a history of instability and violence. The officer who took the report made "no reasonable effort to enforce the [restraining order] or locate the three children. Instead he went to dinner." Shortly after 3:00 a.m., the husband arrived at the police station and opened fire. Officers shot back, killing him in the exchange, and then discovered the dead bodies of his daughters in his pick-up truck.

Colorado has a mandatory arrest law for violations of restraining orders. It provides that:

> (a) Whenever a protection order is issued, the protected person shall be provided with a copy of such order. A peace officer shall use every reasonable means to enforce a protection order.
> (b) A peace officer shall arrest, or, if an arrest would be impractical under the circumstances, seek a warrant for the arrest of a restrained person when the peace officer has information amounting to probable cause that [the order has been violated].

Speaking for the majority, Justice Scalia reasoned that these statutory provisions have not "truly made enforcement of restraining orders mandatory. A well-established tradition of police discretion has coexisted with apparently mandatory arrest statutes." Moreover, even if Gonzales had been entitled to enforcement, the majority concluded that such an entitlement would not constitute a property interest protected by the Due Process Clause and enforceable under Section 1983. Justice Souter, joined by Justice Breyer, concurred in the judgment but wrote separately to emphasize the concern that finding a property right to enforcement would in effect "federalize every mandatory state-law direction to executive officers whose performance on the job can be vitally significant to individuals affected." Justice Stevens, joined by Justice Ginsburg, dissented. As he read the statute, in light of its legislative history, "the police were required to provide enforcement. They lacked the discretion to do nothing."[209]

---

208. 545 U.S. 748 (2005).
209. Id. at 760; id. at 772 (Souter, J., concurring in the judgment); id. at 784-85 (Stevens, J., dissenting).

Following that decision, the mother brought a suit before the Inter-American Commission on Human Rights, affiliated with the Organization of American States. In essence, she claimed that the United States violated her rights under the American Declaration of the Rights and Duties of Man, denying her right to be free from gender-based violence and discrimination. State Department lawyers countered that the Declaration imposes no duty to prevent crimes inflicted by private individuals and that the state acted reasonably on the information it had available. In rejecting that argument, the Commission found that the State failed to act with "due diligence" to protect the Gonzales children and their mother from domestic violence, which violated "the State's obligation not to discriminate and to provide for equal protection before the law under the American Declaration." The Commission also found that the state failed to undertake reasonable measures to protect the lives of the children, in violation of their right to life under the Declaration. Under the Commission's analysis, the "state apparatus was not duly organized, coordinated, and ready to protect these victims from domestic violence by adequately and effectively implementing the restraining order at issue . . . [which] constituted a form of discrimination in violation of Article II of the American Declaration."[210] Based on those conclusions, the Commission made recommendations to the United States including that:

- it undertake a "serious, impartial and exhaustive investigation" into the deaths of the Gonzales children and the failures to enforce Jessica Lenahan Gonzales's protection order, and hold those responsible accountable;
- it offer full reparations to Jessica Lenahan;
- it adopt multifaceted legislation at the federal and state levels, or reform existing legislation to protect women and children from imminent violence and to ensure effective implementation mechanisms.[211]

How would you evaluate the Commission's ruling? If the United States were to follow its recommendations, what initiatives would be likely?

Lower federal courts have also been willing to hold states liable under civil rights law where law enforcement officials increase the danger to domestic violence victims. Circuits are split on the evidence required to make such a showing. Some have required more than inaction, such as failure to arrest.[212] The Second Circuit, however, in Okin v. Village of Cornwall-on-Hudson Police Department, has held that "repeated sustained inaction by government officials, in the face of potential acts of violence, might . . . [give rise] to the

210. Jessica Lenahan (Gonzales) et al. v. United States, Report No. 80/11, Case 12.626, paragraphs 5 & 60 (Merits, July 21, 2011).

211. Id., para. 201.

212. See cases discussed in Awoyomi, supra note 169, at 13-20.

level of an affirmative condoning of private violence," and if the indifference is so egregious as to "shock the conscience" the victim can recover damages under Section 1983.[213] In *Okin*, police officers' failure to arrest a batterer, and discussion of football with him, could be taken as condoning future violence. If more circuits adopt such an approach, it could strengthen enforcement policies.

5. Stalking and Domestic Violence in the Workplace. According to Bureau of Justice reports, about 3.4 million individuals, three-quarters of them women, report being subject to stalking, defined as conduct causing reasonable persons to fear for their safety.[214] Estimates also suggest that anywhere between 75 to 95 percent of those who are subject to domestic violence experience related problems at work.[215] Problems include assaults, stalking, harassing or threatening phone calls, destruction of work products, and lateness or absenteeism due to physical injuries, legal proceedings, and disruption of childcare and transportation arrangements. Domestic violence in the United States is estimated to cost companies 8 million days in paid labor and 4.9 billion dollars in medical costs, lost productivity, and lost earnings.[216] Employers sometimes respond by penalizing or terminating employees who are victims, which compounds their problems and reinforces economic dependence on abusers. Workplaces that do not provide adequate security force many women to leave their jobs out of safety concerns.

All states now have anti-stalking laws, and almost all have criminal statutes that make violating a protection order a criminal offense. Many domestic violence victims report losing a job after the violence, and a growing number have recourse under federal or state law. The EEOC notes that although federal law does not explicitly protect domestic violence victims from employment discrimination, they may be entitled to protection under federal anti-discrimination law.[217] For example, an employer that terminates

213. 577 F. 3d 415, 428, 431 (2d Cir. 2009).

214. Elizabeth Olson, Though Many Are Stalked, Few Report It, Study Finds, N.Y. Times, Feb. 5, 2009, at A1.

215. See Workplaces Respond, The Facts on the Workplace and Domestic Violence, http://www.workplacesrespond.org/learn/the-facts/the-facts-on-the-workplace-and-domestic-violence; Marie Tessier, More States Give Abuse Victims Right to Time Off (Jan. 18, 2005), http://womensenews.org/2005/01/more-states-give-abuse-victims-right-time.

216. Stephen R. Arnott & Margaret C. Hobday, It's a Human Right: Using International Human Rights Principles to Assist Employees Experiencing Domestic Violence, 18 Emp. Rts. & Emp. Pol'y J. 1, 9 (2014); Angela M. Moe & Myrtle Bell, Abject Economics: The Effects of Battering and Violence on Women's Work and Employability, 10 Violence Against Women 29, 34 (2004); McKinsey Global Institute, The Power of Parity: Advancing Women's Equality in the United States (Apr. 2016), http://www.mckinsey.com/globalthemes.

217. EEOC, The Application of Title VII and the ADA to Applicants or Employees Who Experience Domestic or Dating Violence, Sexual Assault, or Stalking (2012), http://www.eeoc.gov/eeoc/publications/upload/qa_domestic_violence.pdf.

an employee subject to domestic violence out of fear of the potential "drama battered women bring to the workplace" may be liable for discrimination on the basis of sex.[218] Rather than firing a domestic violence victim, employers should consider alternatives such as increasing workplace security or obtaining a temporary restraining order. An increasing number of states expressly prohibit employment discrimination against domestic violence survivors or have common law remedies for wrongful termination or for negligence in response to foreseeable violence.[219] Not all courts have been sympathetic, however.[220] In Carroll v. Shoney's, for example, the court denied relief to the estate of a murdered woman, which sued her restaurant employer for negligence.[221] The woman was a counter worker on the evening shift who had been beaten by her husband. She informed her assistant manager about the abuse and asked him to call the police if her husband came to the restaurant. When the husband arrived and made threats, the police escorted him from the premises, but released him after the restaurant did not press charges. The following day, management rejected the woman's requests to be excused from work and promised to call the police if the man showed up. He did, and shot her in the head before law enforcement officials could be alerted. The majority of the Alabama Supreme Court held that the restaurant was not liable because the murder was not foreseeable. The dissent, by contrast, claimed that the standard under prior cases was not "that the particular consequences should have been anticipated, but rather that some general harm or consequence could have been anticipated."[222] Such harm was "expectable" as the dissent viewed the facts, and the defendant had amplified the risks by placing the woman at the front counter.

Strategies to increase workplace protections are proceeding on several fronts. The Corporate Alliance to End Partner Violence brings together companies across the country to collaborate on ways to increase awareness among employers and to support policy initiatives.[223] These initiatives include laws that ban discrimination based on domestic violence and provide unpaid leave for employees to deal with violence-related concerns. About half of the states have enacted laws explicitly granting unemployment benefits in some circumstances, such as where loss of employment reflects individuals' reasonable actions to protect themselves or their families from domestic violence.

---

218. Id.

219. Legal Momentum, State Law Guide: Employment Rights for Victims of Domestic or Sexual Violence (2013). For an example, see Danny v. Laidlaw Transit Servs., Inc. 193 P.3d 128 (Wash. 2008) (finding public policy of prohibiting an employer from discharging an employee because of domestic violence issues).

220. See Sabric v. Lockheed Martin, 2012 WL 1952197 (M.D. Pa. May 30, 2012).

221. 775 So. 2d 753 (Ala. 2000).

222. Id.

223. See Our Purpose, Corporate Alliance to End Partner Violence, http://www.caepv. org/about/purpose.php.

Congress has also considered federal legislation such as the Security and Financial Empowerment Act, which would prohibit discrimination based on domestic violence, guarantee eligible employees time off to address domestic violence issues, and ensure unemployment compensation for those who lose employment due to domestic violence.[224] A number of commentators have urged that state and local governments require employers to offer reasonable accommodations to employees subject to domestic violence that would enable them to maintain their employment.[225] A few states and localities have enacted such requirements, which include measures such as modifying work schedules or transferring the employee to another location.[226]

What strategies do you believe are most essential to deal with workplace violence? What stands in the way? How would you respond to the employers' legitimate concerns? Would it be appropriate, for example, to require individuals who are under a restraining order to wear global positioning satellite devices that track their location and alert police when they enter a prohibited zone?[227] A growing number of states have legislation authorizing courts to require electronic monitoring under certain conditions.[228] A number of studies suggest that such monitoring has reduced offenders' likelihood of reoffending.[229]

6. Domestic Violence and Housing Discrimination. A related issue involves housing discrimination based on domestic violence. The Violence Against Women Act and the Federal Fair Housing Act both offer protection to victims of domestic violence living in federally subsidized housing.[230] The U.S. Department of Housing and Urban Development has pursued a growing number of enforcement actions involving such issues. In one typical case, the Department settled complaints against two New Hampshire landlords who refused to rent or renew a lease because of police visits responding to domestic violence incidents.[231] Women's rights advocates have also success-

---

224. Security and Financial Empowerment Act of 2015, HR 3841 and S 2208 (114th Congress, 2015).

225. Arnott & Hobday, supra note 216, at 6, 15, 31-34; see also Joan Zorza, New Study on Domestic Violence in the Workplace, 3 Fam. & Intimate Partner Violence Q. 217 (2011).

226. Arnott & Hobday, supra note 216, at 15.

227. Jennifer Hahn, Tracking the Abusers, Ms., Summer 2008, at 18 (noting that such devices are widely used to track parolees and sex offenders but only seven states permit it for domestic violence cases).

228. Brenner, supra note 150, at 341.

229. Suraji R. Wagage, When the Consequences Are Life and Death: Pretrial Detention for Domestic Violence Offenders, 7 Drexel L. Rev. 195, 210 (2014).

230. U.S. Dep't of Housing and Urban Development, Assessing Claims of Housing Discrimination Against Victims of Domestic Violence Under the Fair Housing Act and the Violence Against Women Act (2011).

231. Mary C. Curtis, HUD Settles Case Alleging Housing Discrimination Against Domestic Violence Victim, Wash. Post., July 22, 2014.

fully challenged local nuisance laws that penalize victims for seeking police protection. In one recent case, the ACLU settled a case involving an ordinance under which three calls to the police in four months could result in revocation of a landlord's rental license and fines that could be avoided if the landlord evicted the tenant initiating the calls.[232]

7. Domestic Violence and Child Custody. Children can give partners additional ways to exercise domination and abuse. Male batterers are more likely than non-abusive men to seek custody of their children.[233] A mother is all the more reluctant to leave her batterer if by doing so she jeopardizes the safety and economic support of her children and, as the Mahoney excerpt explains, the period after separation from the batterer—when a custody action is most likely to be filed[234]—is the one of the most dangerous times for abused women and their children.[235] Moreover, victims' psychological profiles or reluctance to cooperate with an abuser may work against their efforts to secure permanent custody of the children, and they may even be blamed for failing to protect children from abuse.[236] Visitation rights and joint custody arrangements may also give batterers the ability to continue their abuse.

In principle, at least, family law has recognized such problems. At least 22 states have some form of a rebuttable presumption against awarding custody to a parent who has engaged in domestic violence, and many other states direct the court to take such violence into account in making custody and visitation decisions.[237] However, critics claim that judges and experts who make custody evaluations often fail to accord sufficient weight to evidence of domestic violence, and discount incidents as "occasional," provoked, uncorroborated, or

---

232. Sandra Park, Victory! Town Will No Longer Treat Domestic Violence Victims as Nuisances, ACLU Blog (Sept. 8, 2014), http://www.aclu.org/blog/victory-town-will-no-longer-treat-domestic-violence-victims-as-nuisances.

233. Allen M. Bailey, Prioritizing Child Safety as the Prime Best-Interest Factor, 47 Fam. L.Q. 35, 38 (2013) (citing sources).

234. Id. at 37.

235. In addition to the Mahoney article, see Peter G. Jaffe et al., Custody Disputes Involving Allegations of Domestic Violence: Toward a Differentiated Approach to Parenting Plans, 46 Fam. Ct. Rev. 500, 501-02 (2008); Daniel G. Saunders & Angela Browne, Intimate Partner Homicide, Case Studies in Family Violence 415, 420-21 (Robert Ammerman & Michel Hersen, 2nd ed. 2000).

236. Lynn F. Beller, When in Doubt, Take Them Out: Removal of Children from Victims of Domestic Violence Ten Years After Nicholson v. Williams, 22 Duke J. Gender L. & Pol'y 205 (2015); see Nicholson v. Scoppetta, 820 N.E.2d 840 (N.Y. 2004) (holding that a policy of removing children from their mother's custody was not justified where the only allegation of neglect was that the child witnessed the mother's abuse; the reasonableness of the mother's action must be considered in light of all the circumstances).

237. For the last reliable inventory, along with a description of statutory refinements, see Leslie Joan Harris, Failure to Protect from Exposure to Domestic Violence in Private Custody Contests, 44 Fam. L.Q. 169, 173-77 (2010).

unlikely to recur.[238] The existence of "friendly parent" provisions, discussed in Chapter 2, can further complicate the matter by penalizing a battered mother who "alienates" the child from the abuser.

Another difficult issue in battering relationships is allocating culpability when the children themselves are abused. If children are present when police arrive at the home of a domestic violence incident, in some jurisdictions "the officers, as mandated reporters of child maltreatment, will routinely report not only the perpetrator, but also the victim to the child protection agency"; the government may then "charge a victim with 'failure to protect' her children by permitting domestic violence to occur while they are living in the home."[239] Such practices can deter women from reporting violence.

The tragic case of Andrea Yates raises issues of whether fathers are subject to the same standard as mothers concerning child protection. Yates, who had a history of serious mental health difficulties and suicidal tendencies, drowned her five children in a bathtub. Shortly before the killings, her husband recognized that she was no longer taking medication, and was exhibiting signs of serious dysfunction. He contacted a mental health facility to request her admission and asked his mother to stay at the family home to minimize his wife's time alone with the children. He did not, however, take other measures to prevent abuse. After the killings, prosecutors concluded that there was insufficient evidence to press charges against the husband. Shelby Moore disagrees, and argues that the case reflects the double standards underpinning the abuse and neglect system, which faults abused mothers for failure to intervene when they have fewer and more dangerous options than fathers.[240] As Moore and other scholars note, men also are not held liable for neglecting children whom they abandon to the care of the mother. Should the law require less of mothers or more of both parents? Or should it require more of the state in terms of services such as adequate shelters, legal advocacy, family therapy, social services referrals, and housing assistance?[241]

Finally, how should the law respond when a battered woman flees with the children — or when an abuser does? Various federal statutes seek to protect

---

238. Id.; Schneider, Domestic Violence Law Reform in the Twenty-First Century, supra note 142, at 360 (describing inadequate consideration of violence in custody cases); Leigh Goodmark, When Is a Battered Woman Not a Battered Woman? When She Fights Back, 20 Yale J.L. and Feminism 75, 116 (2008) (describing judicial belief that women fabricate claims to gain custody leverage); Joan S. Meier, Domestic Violence, Child Custody, and Child Protection: Understanding Judicial Resistance and Imagining the Solutions, 11 Am. U. J. Gender Soc. Pol'y & L. 657, 673-64 & n.50 (2003) (citing cases).

239. Harris, Failure to Protect, supra note 237, at 178-83; Sack, supra note 171, at 1684.

240. Shelby A.D. Moore, Understanding the Connection Between Domestic Violence, Crime, and Poverty: How Welfare Reform May Keep Battered Women from Leaving Abusive Relationships, 12 Tex. J. Women & L. 451, 484 (2003).

241. Beller, supra note 236, at 238.

victims of abduction and promote coordination among states.[242] When abductors flee the United States altogether, the Hague Child Abduction Convention mandates the return of children to their place of "habitual residence" for a custody determination unless that would pose a "grave risk of harm."[243] Judicial remedies known as "undertakings" can return families to the country of origin to arrange custody. Whether courts have interpreted the Convention in ways responsive to domestic violence that prompts abduction remains open to dispute. Some commentators charge that courts do not consider violence directed only against mothers when assessing harm. If their children are subject to return, these mothers may accompany them and become vulnerable to further abuse.[244]

Putting Theory Into Practice

3-11. Immigrant women face special difficulties in escaping abusive relationships due to lack of language ability, cultural backgrounds that tolerate violence, unfamiliarity with the U.S. legal system and local social services, and dependence on husbands for financial support and for eligibility for resident status. Some of these women come to the United States as "mail-order brides." What special measures would you recommend for protecting these women?[245] Should they have a special right to legal assistance and adequate court services, including interpreters and appropriate social services, even if these are not available to other individuals who need them?

3-12. Rendez-Vous is a small, upscale eating establishment that caters to the Manhattan theater crowd. One of its best waitresses is being stalked by an ex-boyfriend who has come to the restaurant several times to harass her and has occasionally prevented her from arriving on time. After one loud abusive incident in which the owner had to call the police, he fires the waitress. "I don't need this," he tells her. "Business is bad enough as it is." Would it be fair to the employer to hold him liable for firing her? The boyfriend also has stalked her apartment complex, and his violent actions have alarmed other tenants. Should the landlord be able to evict her if she does not get a no-contact protective order? If not, what remedies should be available to him?

242. The Uniform Child Custody Jurisdiction and Enforcement Act (UCCJEA) generally favors the "home state" of the child and custodial parent. Other relevant statutes are the Parental Kidnapping Prevention Act (PKPA), and the full faith and credit requirements of the Violence Against Women Act (VAWA).
243. Hague Convention of October 25, 1980 on the Civil Aspects of Child Abduction, Article 13(b).
244. Merle H. Weiner, Using Article 20, 38 Fam. L.Q. 583 (2004).
245. See discussion in Chapter 5.

3-13. Pamela Hird obtained a protective order against the defendant based on domestic violence. She subsequently allowed him to live in her basement and have occasional meals with her because she felt sorry for him when he was intoxicated and had no place to go, and because she worried that she might be in trouble for not calling the police immediately when he showed up. Should her consent be relevant in a prosecution of the defendant for violating the protective order?[246]

2. Domestic Violence and Substantive Criminal Law

Under longstanding Anglo-American law, killing in the "sudden heat of passion" is not murder, but rather the lesser crime of voluntary manslaughter; the theory is that "adequate provocation" by the victim may cause a reasonable man to lose his reason.[247] Catching one's spouse in the act of adultery traditionally has been described as the quintessential example of adequate provocation. Sexual taunting, as in People v. Berry, excerpted below, provides a classic example. Until the 1960s, juries in some states also recognized an "unwritten law" of "honor defense" that allowed for acquittal of a defendant who killed his wife or his wife's lover out of sexual jealousy.

Under the Model Penal Code (MPC), a homicide that would otherwise be murder may be reduced to manslaughter if defendants can show that they acted under the influence of "extreme mental or emotional disturbance for which there is reasonable explanation or excuse." Whether there is such an explanation or excuse is to be judged from the point of view of "a person in the actor's situation under the circumstances as he believes them to be." The intention of the MPC drafters was to focus on the defendant's disturbed state of mind, rather than on the existence of justifying circumstances. *Berry* reflects this approach.

Another criminal law doctrine that applies in some domestic violence cases is the law of self-defense. This doctrine exonerates a killing when reasonably necessary to save oneself from imminent death or great bodily harm. This is the law at issue in State v. Norman, excerpted below. Both *Berry* and *Norman* involve a lapse of time between the victim's provocation of the defendant and defendant's violent acts. How does that lapse of time factor in? How should it?

246. State v. Branson, 167 P.3d 370 (Kan. Ct. App. 2007).
247. See Joshua Dressler, Understanding Criminal Law §31.07[A], [B], at 527-28 (3d ed. 2001).

People v. Berry
556 P.2d 777 (Cal. 1976)

SULLIVAN, Justice.

Defendant Albert Joseph Berry was charged by indictment with one count of murder and one count of assault by means of force likely to produce great bodily injury. . . . The assault was allegedly committed on July 23, 1974, and the murder on July 26, 1974. In each count, the alleged victim was defendant's wife, Rachel Pessah Berry. A jury found defendant guilty as charged and determined that the murder was of the first degree. Defendant was sentenced to state prison for the term prescribed by law. He appeals from the judgment of conviction.

Defendant contends that there is sufficient evidence in the record to show that he committed the homicide while in a state of uncontrollable rage caused by provocation and flowing from a condition of diminished capacity and therefore that it was error for the trial court to fail to instruct the injury on voluntary manslaughter as indeed he had requested. . . .

Manslaughter bc rage

Defendant, a cook, 46 years old, and Rachel Pessah, a 20-year-old girl from Israel, were married on May 27, 1974. . . .

After their marriage, Rachel lived with defendant for only three days and then left for Israel. Immediately upon her return to San Francisco she told defendant about her relationship with and love for Yako. This brought about further argument and a brawl that evening in which defendant choked Rachel and she responded by scratching him deeply many times. Nonetheless they continued to live together. Rachel kept taunting defendant with Yako and demanding a divorce. She claimed she thought she might be pregnant by Yako. She showed defendant pictures of herself with Yako. Nevertheless, during a return trip from Santa Rosa, Rachel demanded immediate sexual intercourse with defendant in the car, which was achieved; however upon reaching their apartment, she again stated that she loved Yako and that she would not have intercourse with defendant in the future.

On the evening of July 22d defendant and Rachel went to a movie where they engaged in heavy petting. When they returned home and got into bed, Rachel announced that she had intended to make love with defendant, "But I am saving myself for this man Yako, so I don't think I will." Defendant got out of bed and prepared to leave the apartment, whereupon Rachel screamed and yelled at him. Defendant choked her into unconsciousness.

Two hours later defendant called a taxi for his wife to take her to the hospital. He put his clothes in the Greyhound bus station and went to the home of his friend Mrs. Berk for the night. The next day he went to Reno and returned the day after. Rachel informed him by telephone that there was a warrant for his arrest as a result of her report to the police about the choking incident. On July 25th defendant returned to the apartment to talk to

Rachel, but she was out. He slept there overnight. Rachel returned around 11 a.m. the next day. Upon seeing defendant there, she said, "I suppose you have come here to kill me." Defendant responded, "yes," changed his response to "no," and then again to "yes," and finally stated "I have really come to talk to you." Rachel began screaming. Defendant grabbed her by the shoulder and tried to stop her screaming. She continued. They struggled and finally defendant strangled her with a telephone cord.

Dr. Martin Blinder, a physician and psychiatrist, called by the defense, testified that Rachel was a depressed, suicidally inclined girl and that this suicidal impulse led her to involve herself ever more deeply in a dangerous situation with defendant. She did this by sexually arousing him and taunting him into jealous rages in an unconscious desire to provoke him into killing her and thus consummating her desire for suicide. Throughout the period commencing with her return from Israel until her death, that is from July 13 to July 26, Rachel continually provoked defendant with sexual taunts and incitements, alternating acceptance and rejection of him. This conduct was accompanied by repeated references to her involvement with another man; it led defendant to choke her on two occasions, until finally she achieved her unconscious desire and was strangled. Dr. Blinder testified that as a result of this cumulative series of provocations, defendant at the time he fatally strangled Rachel, was in a state of uncontrollable rage, completely under the sway of passion.

We first take up defendant's claim that on the basis of the foregoing evidence he was entitled to an instruction on voluntary manslaughter as defined by statute which is "the unlawful killing of a human being, without malice . . . upon a sudden quarrel or heat of passion." [In an earlier case the court approved the following quotation of the law:] "[T]he fundamental of the inquiry is whether or not the defendant's reason was, at the time of his act, so disturbed or obscured by some passion—not necessarily fear and never, of course, the passion for revenge—to such an extent as would render ordinary men of average disposition liable to act rashly or without due deliberation and reflection, and from this passion rather than judgment."

We further held . . . that there is no specific type of provocation required . . . and that verbal provocation may be sufficient. [In a previous case] in the course of explaining the phrase "heat of passion" used in the statute defining manslaughter we pointed out that "passion" need not mean "rage" or "anger" but may be any "[v]iolent, intense, high-wrought or enthusiastic emotion" and concluded there "that defendant was aroused to a heat of 'passion' by a series of events over a considerable period of time. . . ." Accordingly we there declared that evidence of admissions of infidelity by the defendant's paramour, taunts directed to him and other conduct, "supports a finding that defendant killed in wild desperation induced by [the woman's] long continued provocatory conduct." We find this reasoning persuasive in the case now before us. Defendant's testimony chronicles a two-week period of provocatory conduct by his wife Rachel that could arouse a passion of jealousy, pain

Man provoked

Woman asking for it

and sexual rage in an ordinary man of average disposition such as to cause him to act rashly from this passion. It is significant that both defendant and Dr. Blinder testified that the former was in the heat of passion under an uncontrollable rage when he killed Rachel.

The Attorney General contends that the killing could not have been done in the heat of passion because there was a cooling period, defendant having waited in the apartment for 20 hours. However, the long course of provocatory conduct, which had resulted in intermittent outbreaks of rage under specific provocation in the past, reached its final culmination in the apartment when Rachel began screaming. . . .

. . . There was no clear direction to the jury to consider the evidence of Rachel's course of provocatory conduct so as to determine whether defendant, as an ordinary man of average disposition, having been exposed to such conduct, was provoked into committing the homicide under a heat of passion. [The failure to give the jury proper instructions on this question was prejudicial error and requires us to reverse the conviction of murder of the first degree.]

Donna K. Coker, Heat of Passion and Wife Killing: Men Who Batter/Men Who Kill

2 S. Cal. Rev. L. & Women's Stud. 71, 93-94, 118-20, 128 (1992)

[H]omicide law divides sane individuals who intentionally kill into two major categories: those who premeditate murder and those who act in the heat of passion. Social stereotypes of wife-killing that characterize the killer as a previously non-violent man who "snapped" under pressure, roughly parallel the understandings which underlie heat-of-passion doctrine. However, this social stereotype is grossly inaccurate when applied to men who are identified as "batterers" and when applied to the general category of husband-wife killings. Violence perpetrated by abusive men is purposeful, not spontaneous; the majority of men who kill their wives have a documented history of violent assaults. Furthermore, one would expect to find empirical evidence of wife-killers who fit the stereotype of the heat-of-passion killer in those reports of forensic psychiatrists whose job it is to aid defense counsel, yet these reports seem to confirm that men who kill and men who batter have remarkably similar personality traits and similar motivations. . . .

In essence, Berry's defense was that he was the sort of man who abused women — but the twist was [Dr.] Blinder's psychiatric explanation that Berry's violence was a result of his choosing women who enraged him and provoked him to violence. The fact that Berry had a prior conviction for assaulting his ex-wife with a butcher knife, that in past relationships with other women he had destroyed their property, forcing former girlfriends to "put him out of the

Dr. blame women not Berry

house, locking the door," indicated to Blinder the personality of the women with whom Berry involved himself, more than it demonstrated Berry's dangerous and abusive nature. Blinder testified that these women "offer[ed] him the promise of comfort but ultimately deliver[ed] emotional pain." Yet Blinder's testimony provides a classic portrait of an abuser. Berry was most dangerous when women threatened to leave him. Berry was "emotionally dependent" on wives and girlfriends; he threatened physical violence in order to control women; he destroyed women's property; and he had a history of violent relationships with wives and lovers. The Supreme Court's opinion read Dr. Blinder's testimony to focus narrowly on the effect of Rachel's "provocative" behavior on Berry's mental state. Dr. Blinder's testimony, however, refers to a cumulative rage resulting from the provocation of all the women in Berry's entire life:

Q: . . . How would you characterize [Berry's] state of mind . . . [at the time of the homicide]?

A: . . . I would say that he was in a state of uncontrollable rage which was a product of having to contend with what seems to me an incredibly provacative [sic] situation, an incredibly provacative [sic] young woman, and that this immediate situation was superimposed upon Mr. Berry having encountered the situation time and time again. So that we have a cumulative effect dating back to the way his mother dealt with him. . . .

Q: . . . [Y]ou say that the situation involving Rachel Berry and Albert Berry . . . was the product of . . . cumulative . . . provocations. Now, specifically, what would you base your opinion as to provocations on? . . .

A: . . . We have two factors here. . . . The past history, that is, the history of this man well in advance of his meeting the deceased. And then the history of his relationship with her. And I think the two go together. . . . After 15 years [of marriage to his second wife] and five children, his wife leaves him for . . . another man. . . . They continued to live together, during which time his wife taunted him about her boyfriend. . . .

One night while they were having sex, his wife [called him by the name of her boyfriend]. Despondent and enraged at the same time, he went into the kitchen, obtained a knife, and stabbed his wife in the abdomen. And she was not serious [sic]. He only got to spend a year in jail for that. . . .

So we have this pattern of enormous dependency on these women and then rupture of the relationship with tremendous rage, almost uncontrollable. I think in one instance he put his foot through the stereo . . . he had purchased for one of these girls [sic]. . . .

So we see a succession of women, beginning with his mother, who offer the promise of comfort but ultimately deliver indifference and emotional pain. . . .

The irony of this defense . . . [is that] Berry's past abuse of other women was used to strengthen his claim of Rachel's provocative nature: Berry had a pattern of involvement with emotionally abusive women; his violence was in response to their "abuse"—never the other way around. . . .

The California Supreme Court opinion repeatedly echoes the tenor of Blinder's words—using terms such as "the result" or "culmination"—terms that diffuse responsibility and make Berry's violence seem inevitable and uncontrollable. . . .

Though Blinder's testimony focused on Rachel's "provocative" sexual behavior, the truth is that Berry didn't kill Rachel until it appeared that she might make good on her threat to leave him. . . . [*Berry's*] perspective . . . suggests that a woman's "abandonment" of a husband is provocative—and that a woman's preference of another lover is provocation of the worst sort.

≡≡≡ ### *State v. Norman*
≡≡≡ **378 S.E.2d 8 (N.C. 1989)**

MITCHELL, Justice.

. . . At trial, the State presented the testimony of Deputy Sheriff R.H. Epley of the Rutherford County Sheriff's Department, who was called to the Norman residence on the night of 12 June 1985. Inside the home, Epley found the defendant's husband, John Thomas Norman, lying on a bed in a rear bedroom with his face toward the wall and his back toward the middle of the room. He was dead. . . . A later autopsy revealed three gunshot wounds to the head, two of which caused fatal brain injury. The autopsy also revealed a .12 percent blood alcohol level in the victim's body.

Later that night, the defendant related an account of the events leading to the killing. . . . The defendant told Epley that her husband had been beating her all day and had made her lie down on the floor while he slept on the bed. After her husband fell asleep, the defendant carried her grandchild to the defendant's mother's house. The defendant took a pistol from her mother's purse and walked the short distance back to her home. She pointed the pistol at the back of her sleeping husband's head, but it jammed the first time she tried to shoot him. She fixed the gun and then shot her husband in the back of the head as he lay sleeping. After one shot, she felt her husband's chest and determined that he was still breathing and making sounds. She then shot him twice more in the back of the head. The defendant told Epley that she killed her husband because "she took all she was going to take from him so she shot him." *Pre-meditated*

The defendant presented evidence tending to show a long history of physical and mental abuse by her husband due to his alcoholism. At the time of the killing, the thirty-nine-year-old defendant and her husband had been married almost twenty-five years and had several children. The defendant testified that her husband had started drinking and abusing her about five years after they were married. His physical abuse of her consisted of frequent assaults that included slapping, punching and kicking her, striking her with various objects, and throwing glasses, beer bottles and other objects at her.

The defendant described other specific incidents of abuse, such as her husband putting her cigarettes out on her, throwing hot coffee on her, breaking glass against her face and crushing food on her face. Although the defendant did not present evidence of ever having received medical treatment for any physical injuries inflicted by her husband, she displayed several scars about her face which she attributed to her husband's assaults.

The defendant's evidence also tended to show other indignities inflicted upon her by her husband. Her evidence tended to show that her husband did not work and forced her to make money by prostitution, and that he made humor of that fact to family and friends. He would beat her if she resisted going out to prostitute herself or if he was unsatisfied with the amounts of money she made. He routinely called the defendant "dog," "bitch" and "whore," and on a few occasions made her eat pet food out of the pets' bowls and bark like a dog. He often made her sleep on the floor. At times, he deprived her of food and refused to let her get food for the family. During those years of abuse, the defendant's husband threatened numerous times to kill her and to maim her in various ways.

The defendant said her husband's abuse occurred only when he was intoxicated, but that he would not give up drinking. She said she and her husband "got along very well when he was sober," and that he was "a good guy" when he was not drunk. She had accompanied her husband to the local mental health center for sporadic counseling sessions for his problem, but he continued to drink.

In the early morning hours on the day before his death, the defendant's husband, who was intoxicated, went to a rest area off I-85 near Kings Mountain where the defendant was engaging in prostitution and assaulted her. While driving home, he was stopped by a patrolman and jailed on a charge of driving while impaired. After the defendant's mother got him out of jail at the defendant's request later that morning, he resumed his drinking and abuse of the defendant.

The defendant's evidence also tended to show that her husband seemed angrier than ever after he was released from jail and that his abuse of the defendant was more frequent. That evening, sheriff's deputies were called to the Norman residence, and the defendant complained that her husband had been beating her all day and she could not take it anymore. The defendant was advised to file a complaint, but she said she was afraid her husband would kill her if she had him arrested. The deputies told her they needed a warrant before they could arrest her husband, and they left the scene.

The deputies were called back less than an hour later after the defendant had taken a bottle of pills. The defendant's husband cursed her and called her names as she was attended by paramedics, and he told them to let her die. A sheriff's deputy finally chased him back into his house as the defendant was put into an ambulance. The defendant's stomach was pumped at the local hospital, and she was sent home with her mother.

While in the hospital, the defendant was visited by a therapist with whom she discussed filing charges against her husband and having him committed for treatment. Before the therapist left, the defendant agreed to go to the mental health center the next day to discuss those possibilities. The therapist testified at trial that the defendant seemed depressed in the hospital, and that she expressed considerable anger toward her husband. He testified that the defendant threatened a number of times that night to kill her husband and that she said she should kill him "because of the things he had done to her."

The next day, the day she shot her husband, the defendant went to the mental health center to talk about charges and possible commitment, and she confronted her husband with that possibility. She testified that she told her husband later that day: "J.T., straighten up. Quit drinking. I'm going to have you committed to help you." She said her husband then told her he would "see them coming" and would cut her throat before they got to him.

The defendant also went to the social services office that day to seek welfare benefits, but her husband followed her there, interrupted her interview and made her go home with him. He continued his abuse of her, threatening to kill and to maim her, slapping her, kicking her, and throwing objects at her. At one point, he took her cigarette and put it out on her, causing a small burn on her upper torso. He would not let her eat or bring food into the house for their children.

That evening, the defendant and her husband went into their bedroom to lie down, and he called her a "dog" and made her lie on the floor when he lay down on the bed. Their daughter brought in her baby to leave with the defendant, and the defendant's husband agreed to let her baby-sit. After the defendant's husband fell asleep, the baby started crying and the defendant took it to her mother's house so it would not wake up her husband. She returned shortly with the pistol and killed her husband.

The defendant testified at trial that she was too afraid of her husband to press charges against him or to leave him. She said that she had temporarily left their home on several previous occasions, but he had always found her, brought her home and beaten her. Asked why she killed her husband, the defendant replied: "Because I was scared of him and I knowed when he woke up, it was going to be the same thing, and I was scared when he took me to the truck stop that night it was going to be worse then he had ever been. I just couldn't take it no more. There ain't no way, even if it means going to prison. It's better than living in that. That's worse hell than anything."

The defendant and other witnesses testified that for years her husband had frequently threatened to kill her and to maim her. When asked if she believed those threats, the defendant replied: "Yes. I believed him; he would, he would kill me if he got a chance. If he thought he wouldn't a had to went to jail, he would a done it." . . .

Two expert witnesses in forensic psychology and psychiatry who examined the defendant after the shooting, Dr. William Tyson and Dr. Robert

Rollins, testified that the defendant fit the profile of battered wife syndrome. This condition, they testified, is characterized by such abuse and degradation that the battered wife comes to believe she is unable to help herself and cannot expect help from anyone else. She believes that she cannot escape the complete control of her husband and that he is invulnerable to law enforcement and other sources of help.

Dr. Tyson, a psychologist, was asked his opinion as to whether, on 12 June 1985, "it appeared reasonably necessary for Judy Norman to shoot J.T. Norman?" He replied: "I believe that . . . Mrs. Norman believed herself to be doomed . . . to a life of the worst kind of torture and abuse, degradation that she had experienced over the years in a progressive way; that it would only get worse, and that death was inevitable. . . . " Dr. Tyson later added: "I think Judy Norman felt that she had no choice, both in the protection of herself and her family, but to engage, exhibit deadly force against Mr. Norman, and that in so doing, she was sacrificing herself, both for herself and for her family."

Dr. Rollins, who was the defendant's attending physician at Dorothea Dix Hospital when she was sent there for evaluation, testified that in his opinion the defendant was a typical abused spouse and that "[s]he saw herself as powerless to deal with the situation, that there was no alternative, no way she could escape it." Dr. Rollins was asked his opinion as to whether "on June 12th, 1985, it appeared reasonably necessary that Judy Norman would take the life of J.T. Norman?" Dr. Rollins replied that in his opinion, "that course of action did appear necessary to Mrs. Norman."

Based on the evidence that the defendant exhibited battered wife syndrome, that she believed she could not escape her husband nor expect help from others, that her husband had threatened her, and that her husband's abuse of her had worsened in the two days preceding his death, the Court of Appeals concluded that a jury reasonably could have found that her killing of her husband was justified as an act of perfect self-defense. The Court of Appeals reasoned that the nature of battered wife syndrome is such that a jury could not be precluded from finding the defendant killed her husband lawfully in perfect self-defense, even though he was asleep when she killed him. We disagree.

The right to kill in self-defense is based on the necessity, real or reasonably apparent, of killing an unlawful aggressor to save oneself from *imminent* death or great bodily harm at his hands. . . . Our law has recognized that self-preservation under such circumstances springs from a primal impulse and is an inherent right of natural law. . . .

The killing of another human being is the most extreme recourse to our inherent right of self-preservation and can be justified in law only by the utmost real or apparent necessity brought about by the decedent. For that reason, our law of self-defense has required that a defendant claiming that a homicide was justified and, as a result, inherently lawful by reason of perfect self-defense must establish that she reasonably believed at the time of the killing she otherwise would have immediately suffered death or great bodily harm. Only if defendants are required to show that they killed due to a reasonable belief that death or great bodily harm was imminent can the justification for homicide remain clearly and firmly rooted in necessity. The imminence requirement ensures that deadly force will be used only where it is necessary as a last resort in the exercise of the inherent right of self-preservation. . . .

The term "imminent," as used to describe such perceived threats of death or great bodily harm as will justify a homicide by reason of perfect self-defense, has been defined as "immediate danger, such as must be instantly met, such as cannot be guarded against by calling for the assistance of others or the protection of the law." . . .

The evidence in this case did not tend to show that the defendant reasonably believed that she was confronted by a threat of imminent death or great bodily harm. The evidence tended to show that no harm was "imminent" or about to happen to the defendant when she shot her husband. The uncontroverted evidence was that her husband had been asleep for some time when she walked to her mother's house, returned with the pistol, fixed the pistol after it jammed and then shot her husband three times in the back of the head. The defendant was not faced with an instantaneous choice between killing her husband or being killed or seriously injured. Instead, *all* of the evidence tended to show that the defendant had ample time and opportunity to resort to other means of preventing further abuse by her husband. . . .

Dr. Tyson . . . testified that the defendant "believed herself to be doomed . . . to a life of the worst kind of torture and abuse, degradation that she had experienced over the years in a progressive way; that it would only get worse, and that death was inevitable." Such evidence of the defendant's speculative beliefs concerning her remote and indefinite future, while indicating she had felt generally threatened, did not tend to show that she killed in the belief—reasonable or otherwise—that her husband presented a threat of imminent death or great bodily harm. . . .

The reasoning of our Court of Appeals in this case . . . proposes justifying the taking of human life not upon the reasonable belief it is necessary to prevent death or great bodily harm—which the imminence requirement ensures—but upon purely subjective speculation that the decedent probably would present a threat to life at a future time and that the defendant would not be able to avoid the predicted threat. . . .

. . . The relaxed requirements for perfect self-defense proposed by our Court of Appeals would tend to categorically legalize the opportune killing of abusive husbands by their wives solely on the basis of the wives' testimony concerning their subjective speculation as to the probability of future felonious assaults by their husbands. Homicidal self-help would then become a lawful solution, and perhaps the easiest and most effective solution, to this problem. . . . It has even been suggested that the relaxed requirements of self-defense found in what is often called the "battered woman's defense" could be extended in *principle to any type of case* in which a defendant testified that he or she subjectively believed that killing was necessary and proportionate to any perceived threat. . . .

In conclusion, we decline to expand our law of self-defense beyond the limits of immediacy and necessity which have heretofore provided an appropriately narrow but firm basis upon which homicide may be justified. . . .

Reversed.

MARTIN, Justice, dissenting.

At the outset it is to be noted that the peril of fabricated evidence is not unique to the trials of battered wives who kill. The possibility of invented evidence arises in all cases in which a party is seeking the benefit of self-defense. Moreover, in this case there were a number of witnesses other than defendant who testified as to the actual presence of circumstances supporting a claim of self-defense. This record contains no reasonable basis to attack the credibility of evidence for the defendant. . . .

Evidence presented by defendant described a twenty-year history of beatings and other dehumanizing and degrading treatment by her husband. In his expert testimony a clinical psychologist concluded that defendant fit "and exceed[ed]" the profile of an abused or battered spouse, analogizing this treatment to the dehumanization process suffered by prisoners of war under the Nazis during the Second World War and the brainwashing techniques of the Korean War. The psychologist described the defendant as a woman incarcerated by abuse, by fear, and by her conviction that her husband was invincible and inescapable:

> Mrs. Norman didn't leave because she believed, fully believed that escape was totally impossible. There was no place to go. He, she had left before; he had come and gotten her. She had gone to the Department of Social Services. He had come and gotten her. The law, she believed the law could not protect her; no one could protect her, and I must admit, looking over the records, that there was nothing done that would contradict that belief.

. . . For the battered wife, if there is no escape, if there is no window of relief or momentary sense of safety, then the next attack, which could be the fatal one, is imminent. In the context of the doctrine of self-defense, "imminent" is a term the meaning of which must be grasped from the defendant's point of view. Properly stated, the second prong of the question is not whether the threat was in fact *imminent*, but whether defendant's belief in the impending nature of the threat, given the circumstances as she saw them, was reasonable in the mind of a person of ordinary firmness.

Defendant's intense fear, based on her belief that her husband intended not only to maim or deface her, as he had in the past, but to kill her, was evident in the testimony of witnesses who recounted events of the last three days of the decedent's life. This testimony could have led a juror to conclude that defendant reasonably perceived a threat to her life as "imminent," even while her husband slept. . . .

From this evidence of the exacerbated nature of the last three days of twenty years of provocation, a juror could conclude that defendant believed that her husband's threats to her life were viable, that serious bodily harm was imminent, and that it was necessary to kill her husband to escape that harm. And from this evidence a juror could find defendant's belief in the necessity to kill her husband not merely reasonable but compelling. . . .

Notes

1. "Heat of Passion" Manslaughter and the Reasonable "Man." Victoria Nourse's landmark study compiled heat of passion cases from across several jurisdictions. She found that a woman's attempt to leave the relationship, or the man's belief in her infidelity, was the most common "provocation" when men killed women and then sought reduction of their crime to manslaughter. In Model Penal Code jurisdictions, she found that there were three times as many infidelity cases involving separation as cases involving infidelity in a continuing relationship. Nourse asked: "If intimate homicide frequently involves separated couples why does our canonical legal image still revolve around sexual infidelity?"[248] In another study of separation assaults, jealousy was a major factor; male partners frequently warned women whom they later killed, "If I can't have you, nobody can."[249] Doctrines such as "heat of passion," along with similar cultural attitudes, have traditionally resulted in lesser sentences for wife killers.

Gender biases may also affect expert testimony that influences judicial and jury decisions. Is it relevant that Dr. Binder, who testified in the *Berry* case, had a troubled marital history? Two of his wives committed suicide; one assaulted him before taking her own life, perhaps fueled by jealousy.[250]

2. Heat of Passion and Sex Equality. For three centuries, English courts reserved the heat of passion defense to men, and early American law followed suit. Before the 1960s, many states retained laws that allowed a husband to kill his wife's lover, but made no concession for the wife who killed her husband or her husband's lover. Although the current heat of passion

248. Victoria Nourse, Passion's Progress: Modern Law Reform and the Provocation Defense, 106 Yale L.J. 1331, 1345 (1997).
249. Ruth E. Fleury et al., When Ending the Relationship Does Not End the Violence, 6 Violence Against Women 1363, 1365 (2000).
250. Mike Weiss, Mayhem Shadowed Therapist's Life: Expert on Relationships Examines Why Many of His Ended Badly, S.F. Chron., May 22, 2001, at A1.

doctrine is gender neutral in form, women rarely assert the defense, perhaps because women are socialized to respond less aggressively than men to most provocation, including infidelity.[251]

Are juries likely to react the same way to women and men who invoke the heat of passion defense? No statistical evidence is available, but some experts cite representative examples to suggest gender bias. A case in point is that of Houston dentist Clara Harris, who killed her husband after he failed to keep his promise to end his extramarital affair with his office's receptionist. Harris confronted her husband and his mistress at a hotel, and the two women became involved in a violent fight. Hotel employees separated them, and Harris, still enraged, got in her car and ran over her husband twice in the parking lot. She was convicted of murder, despite her testimony that she was "in a fog" at the time, and that it was a "blackout," period, a "crazy time." Eyewitnesses reported that after she had hit her husband, she jumped from the car, asked him repeatedly whether he was "okay" and screamed, "I am sorry." The jury convicted her of murder, and of using a deadly weapon, which enhanced the offense. During the sentencing phase, the jury also found that she had acted in the heat of passion, but imposed the maximum sentence of 20 years.[252] During the trial, both sides capitalized on gender stereotypes. The prosecution painted Harris as a wife who ignored her husband's needs and who was a selfish spendthrift. The defense painted the mistress as an unscrupulous and promiscuous woman with a history of "abnormal relationships," including an alleged lesbian affair.[253]

Compare the result in *Harris* with Maryland v. Peacock.[254] There, the defendant shot and killed his wife when he discovered her having sex with another man. He pleaded guilty to manslaughter and was sentenced for three years, with immediate eligibility for work release and possible home detention. In justifying the sentence, the judge explained that "to be betrayed in your personal life when you are out working to support the spouse" was "almost unmanageable." "I seriously wonder how many married men . . . would have the strength to walk away, but without inflicting some corporal punishment. . . . I shudder to think what I would do. . . ."[255]

---

251. See Christine R. Harris, A Review of Sex Differences in Sexual Jealousy, Including Self-Report Data, Psychosociological Responses, Interpersonal Violence, and Morbid Jealousy, 2 Personality & Soc. Psychol. Rev. 102 (2003).

252. Nick Madigan, Wife Testifies She Was "In a Fog" Just Before Her Car Struck Husband, N.Y. Times, Feb. 8, 2003, at A11; Ron Nissamov, Parham Shares Views on *Harris*, Hous. Chron., Feb. 16, 2003, at 33.

253. Lucas Wall, Common Link in Uncommon Lives: Clara Harris: Mother of Twins Kept to Herself, Hous. Chron., Aug. 4, 2002, at 37; Ruth Rendon, "I Could Kill Him," Harris Told Teen: Defense Says Words Taken Out of Context, Hous. Chron., Jan. 17, 2003, at 36.

254. No. 94-CR-0943 (Balt. Cty. Ct., Oct. 17, 1994).

255. Quoted in Catharine A. MacKinnon, Sex Equality 730-31 (2d ed. 2007).

What message do sentences like those in *Harris* and *Peacock* send? What sentences would you impose? Should "hot-blooded" separation murders and assaults be seen as deserving of less culpability? Or would you favor the approach of Minnesota, which authorizes a finding of first-degree murder based on repeated abuse?[256]

If equality is a goal in these cases, is it best achieved by restricting the heat of passion doctrine or by enlarging it to mitigate women's killings, such as those described below? Should the provocation defense be modified to consider the justifiability of the defendant's response?[257]

3. The Battered Person Syndrome. Every year, a small percentage of women kill their abuser and typically invoke a defense based on the battered person syndrome, originally formulated as the battered woman's syndrome (BWS).[258] All states, either by statute or case law, admit evidence of the battered person defense.[259] It is a subcategory of post-traumatic stress disorder involving "thoughts, feelings, and actions that logically follow a frightening experience that one expects could be repeated." The syndrome is associated with three major symptom clusters, each of which can be accompanied by neurochemical and other physical changes. These clusters are (1) cognitive disturbances, including repetitive memories that cause battered women to re-experience previous abusive incidents and that increase their perception of danger; (2) high arousal symptoms that cause battered women to be nervous and hyper-vigilant to cues of potential danger; and (3) avoidance symptoms, including depression, denial, minimization, and repression, often leading to isolation as the batterer exerts his power and control.[260] Researchers offer two psychological theories to help juries understand the syndrome: learned helplessness and the cycle theory of violence. The theory of learned helplessness was first developed by experimental psychologist Marvin Seligman to explain the fact that dogs and other animals subjected to electric shocks that they are powerless to control will soon stop trying to escape or to avert the

256. See Minn. Stat. Ann §609.185(6) (West 2016) (defining murder in the first degree as, among other things, causing "death of a human being while committing domestic abuse, when the perpetrator has engaged in a past pattern of domestic abuse upon the victim or upon another family or household member and the death occurs under circumstances manifesting an extreme indifference to human life").

257. Carolyn B. Ramsey, Provoking Change: Comparative Insights on Feminist Homicide Law Reform, J. Crim. L. & Criminology 33 (Winter 2010).

258. Kirstin Cole, Barbara Sheehan On What Happened the Day of the Shooting, PIX11.com, Oct. 28, 2011 (estimating 500 women); See Kelly Weisberg, Domestic Violence: Legal and Social Reality 302 (2012) (citing surveys finding that only .05 percent of intimate partner–related crimes involve battered women who kill their spouses).

259. Weisberg, supra note 258, at 304.

260. Lenore E.A. Walker, Battered Women Syndrome and Self-Defense, 6 Notre Dame J.L. Ethics & Pub. Pol'y 321, 327-28 (1992).

shocks. In the context of battered women, Lenore E.A. Walker pioneered the theory of learned helplessness to explain a cycle that traps women in abusive relationships. That cycle includes a tension-building phase, an acute battering incident, and a period of loving-contrition or absence of tension. The pattern leads the battered woman to believe that she is unable to help herself, that others cannot help her, and that the batterer might in fact reform.

In this state of learned helplessness, what causes a victim of abuse to turn on the batterer? Many abused individuals do not, but others at some point experience a "turning point." The turning point may come when there is a marked increase in the severity of the abuse, when the abuse becomes visible to others who question the victim's denial or rationalizations, or when the "loving-contrition" phase becomes increasingly short or disappears altogether. At that point, victims move from the state of learned helplessness to a state of the "victimized self," and conclude that they must either assert themselves or be killed. For some victims, this means finally being able to leave their batterers; others stay and a few kill.

4. The Battered Person in Self-Defense Law: Substantive and Procedural Proposals. The most common criticism of the law of self-defense in the battered person context is that it reflects patterns of male aggression: a "fair fight" between physical equals meeting in a single, discrete confrontation. Critics say this approach fails to take into account the realities of battered persons. Its "objective" standard of reasonableness ignores the special circumstances facing individuals in abusive relationships, and fails to consider the risk that verbal threats may convey in light of the history of battering. Requirements of "imminence" and proportionate force also discount women's lesser strength, which may make delay and deadly force seem necessary. Do these criticisms seem justified in the context of *Norman*? If so, do they support some critics' call for a "reasonable woman" or a "reasonable battered woman" standard? Assuming that expert testimony on the battered person syndrome should have gone to the jury in *Norman*, should the defendant's circumstances constitute a justification, exonerating her from guilt, or merely an excuse or mitigating factor affecting the degree of crime or the sentence?

A more recent case in France has raises the question of how to handle severely abused victims who kill their abusers. Jacqueline Sauvage married her husband when they were teenagers. She sustained 47 years of physical and psychological abuse. She had once tried to kill herself but the doctor who treated her never asked the reason. Her husband also physically and sexually abused their three daughters. One of her daughters complained to the police about the sexual abuse, but instead of taking the charges seriously, the police called the father, causing the daughter to recant. One night, the husband woke Ms. Sauvage from a nap with a blow to the face demanding that she make him dinner. Instead, she retrieved a hunting rifle from the closet, went to the terrace where he was sitting drinking whiskey, and shot him three times in the back. She was found guilty of murder and given a 10-year prison sentence. President Francois Hollande commuted part of her sentence in 2016.[261]

5. Concerns About the Battered Person Syndrome. Uneasiness about use of the battered person syndrome reflects various concerns. The *Norman* court's objection was that such evidence could be too easily manipulated, and might encourage opportunistic premeditated killings. Other critics similarly warn that the defense could permit "vigilante justice" and give battered persons a "license to kill."[262] How would you respond?

In response to such concerns, one scholar collected data from numerous studies comparing battered women who killed their husbands to those who did not. He concluded that women who kill their husbands suffer from far more frequent, more severe, and more prolonged abuse than other battered women; they have less ability to support themselves and thus to escape from their situations; they are more likely to have children who are also being abused by the batterer; and they are more likely to live in an environment where a gun is present and where the batterer abuses alcohol or other drugs.[263] Other research indicates that some groups of women are more likely than others to respond with force. African-American women are disproportionately likely to resort to physical violence in part because they have less access to services than more affluent white women; they feel pressure not to shame or force imprisonment of a "black brother"; and they do not "really trust" law enforcement officials to help them.[264] Lesbians also have disproportionately high rates of violent responses because they too lack confidence that police and courts would be responsive, and because they experience bias based on sexual orientation from police, judges, and service providers.[265] A reluctance to come out publicly as a lesbian or to expose violence in the lesbian community, along with greater comfort and capacity in fighting back, also help to

261. Lilia Blaise, He Abused Her for Years. She Shot Him. France Asks: Is It Self-Defense?, N.Y. Times, Mar. 11, 2016, at A8.

262. Donald A. Downs & James Fisher, Battered Woman's Syndrome: Tool of Justice or False Hope in Self-Defense Cases, in Current Controversies on Family Violence 241, 252 (Donileen R. Loseke et al. eds. 2005). For discussion of such claims, see Sue Osthoff & Holly Maguigan, Explaining Without Pathologizing: Testimony on Battering and Its Effects, in Current Controversies on Family Violence, supra, at 225, 233.

263. See Charles Patrick Ewing, Battered Women Who Kill: Psychological Self-Defense as Legal Justification 23-40 (1987).

264. Goodmark, When Is a Battered Woman Not a Battered Woman?, supra note 238, at 96-98.

265. Id. at 102.

explain the use of force rather than other strategies of resistance.[266] What are the reform implications of these conclusions?

David L. Faigman and Amy J. Wright assert that "[t]he battered woman syndrome illustrates all that is wrong with the law's use of science."[267] They and other critics note that Lenore Walker's research, based on a small group of racially homogenous women, failed to establish either the duration of the cycle of violence or that all subjects experienced all three stages. The relevance of research on dogs to battered women is also problematic, particularly given that the dogs exhibited total passivity, while battered women generally resist in some form, including instances in which they assault or kill their batterers.[268]

Moreover, when invoked in court, the battered person syndrome implies an excuse through mitigation based on the victim's passivity, while self-defense generally requires justification based on the reasonableness of the defendant's behavior. Women who do not match the battered person profile may be assumed (by themselves as well as others) as failing to meet standards for self-defense. The risk appears particularly great for African-American and lesbian women; their resistance, viewed through the lens of racial and homophobic stereotypes, is inconsistent with the image of helpless victim.[269] A final concern is that the syndrome will reinforce the view of woman as passive, dysfunctional, powerless, and victimized, a view from which so many negative consequences flow, especially in child custody contexts.

How could these harms be mitigated? To what extent would more accurate testimony about battered persons help in cases like *Norman*? Would it be enough to show that a "reasonable" person, in the face of past experiences of abuse and no certain options for escaping it, might respond with deadly force? Could a defendant reasonably claim that "a sleeping abuser is merely seconds away from being an awakened abuser" who poses an imminent threat?[270]

---

266. Id.; Janice L. Ristock, No More Secrets: Violence in Lesbian Relationships, 99 (2002); Adele M. Morrison, Queering Domestic Violence to Straighten out Criminal Law: What Might Happen When Queer Theory and Practice Meet Criminal Law's "Conventional" Responses to Domestic Violence, 13 S. Cal. L. & Women's Stud. 8, 147 (2003); Sheila M. Seelau & Eric P. Seelau, Gender-Role Stereotypes and Perceptions of Heterosexual, Gay, and Lesbian Domestic Violence, 20 J. Fam. Violence 363, 363 (2005).

267. David L. Faigman & Amy J. Wright, The Battered Woman's Syndrome in the Age of Science, 39 Ariz. L. Rev. 67, 68 (1997).

268. For critiques, see Marian Angel, The Myth of Battered Woman Syndrome, 24 Temple P. & Civ. Rts. L. Rev. 301 (2015).

269. Goodmark, When Is a Battered Woman Not a Battered Woman?, supra note 238, at 120-22; Alafair S. Burke, Rational Actors, Self-Defense, and Duress: Making Sense, Not Syndromes, Out of the Battered Woman, 81 N.C. L. Rev. 212, 230-47 (2002); Adele M. Morrison, Changing the Domestic Violence (Dis)course: Moving Away from White Victim to Multi-Cultural Survivor, 39 U.C. Davis L. Rev. 1061 (2006).

270. Joan Krause, Distorted Reflections of Women Who Kill: A Response to Professor Dressler, 4 Ohio St. J. Crim. L. 555, 563 (2007); Burke, supra note 269, at 266.

6. Post-Conviction Strategies for Battered Persons Who Kill. After Judy Norman had served four years of her six-year sentence, the state governor commuted her sentence to time served. He gave no reasons.[271] What would you have done as governor, or as a member of her jury?

Systematic efforts for clemency on behalf of convicted women in over 20 other states have sometimes yielded similar results. Estimates suggest that about 125 women convicted of killing an abuser have been freed since 1978. However, the trend toward clemency has slowed. Almost all the petitions were granted during the 1980s and early 1990s. In some states, no requests have ever been successful, even in cases where defendants were convicted before expert testimony on battered women was available at trial.[272]

Men's rights groups generally oppose efforts to mitigate penalties for battered women. According to Warren Farrell, feminists argue " 'there's never an excuse for violence against women.' Now they [are] saying 'but there's always an excuse for violence against men.' "[273] How would you respond? What criteria would you advise governors to apply in considering clemency requests by battered persons convicted of killing their abusers?

7. Domestic Violence and the Public/Private Dichotomy. Regulating domestic violence has been traditionally viewed as private, and therefore, at best, a state rather than a federal matter. It was on this basis that the Supreme Court invalidated the federal civil rights remedy for sex-based violence enacted under VAWA (see Note 5 in Section C(1), above).[274]

Critics have long rejected the traditional dichotomy between public and private, on the ground that it leaves women unprotected where they are most vulnerable. Victims experience abuse, and the conditions that perpetuate it—lack of income, family and cultural expectations—on a very personal level. Yet the social expectations surrounding battering and the resources that are available to battered persons reflect broader social and political forces.[275]

What follows from this critique of the public/private distinction? Is the exercise of public power represented in the *Stevenson* case, or reflected in mandatory no-drop prosecution policies, any better? Are there contexts in which greater public control over private violence compounds the power imbalances it seeks to address? Are there realms that the law should not reach? Consider

271. Elizabeth Leland, Abused Wife's Sentence Commuted, Charlotte Observer, July 8, 1989, at B1.

272. See Burke, supra note 269.

273. Deborah L. Rhode, Speaking of Sex: The Denial of Gender Equality 115 (1997) (quoting Farrell).

274. See United States v. Morrison, 529 U.S. 598 (2000).

275. Catharine A. MacKinnon, Disputing Male Sovereignty: On *United States v. Morrison*, 114 Harv. L. Rev. 135, 170 (2002).

this issue in light of the following discussion of pornography, reproductive rights, and same-sex relationships.

8. Domestic Violence as a Basis for Asylum.   Whether domestic violence should be treated as a human rights violation has arisen in several contexts including asylum. In the United States, the right to asylum is governed by the international definition of a "refugee." The United Nations Convention Relating to the Status of Refugees defines a refugee in part as any person who "owing to a well-founded fear of being persecuted for reasons of race, religion, national origin, membership in a particular social group or political opinion, is outside the country of his nationality and is unable or, owing to such fear, is unwilling to avail himself of the protection of that country." Victims of domestic violence have generally based their claims for asylum on the "membership in a particular social group."[276]

For two decades, courts and immigration authorities struggled with such claims. In 2014, in the Matter of A-R-C-G, the Board of Immigration Appeals held in a published opinion that an applicant can qualify for asylum based on domestic violence.[277] The principal respondent in the case was a Guatemalan mother of three whose husband raped and beat her repeatedly. When calls to the police and attempts to escape proved unavailing, she entered the United States and filed for asylum soon after. The hearing judge found her testimony about abuse credible, but that she had failed to show that persecution or membership in a social group rather than arbitrary criminal acts had caused her abuse. On appeal, a unanimous Board held that the respondent belonged to a social group—married women in Guatemala who are unable to leave their relationship—that could form the basis of an asylum claim.[278] Because the Department of Homeland Security had conceded that her membership in this group was at least one central reason for her persecution, the Board remanded the case to the immigration judge for further findings, including whether the Guatemalan government was able to control the respondent's husband and whether she could relocate within Guatemala and avoid persecution.[279] Other international law sources also provide support for treating domestic violence as a human rights issue. The Declaration on the Elimination of Violence Against Women and the UNHCR Guidelines on the Protection of Refugee Women recognize domestic violence as a form of gender discrimination, and thus a human rights violation. The UN Convention Against Torture is another possible foundation for asylum claims when women flee domestic violence. The

276. See Andrea Binder, Gender and the "Membership in a Particular Social Group" Category of the 1951 Refugee Convention, 10 Colum. J. Gender & L. 167 (2001).
277. 26 I. & N. Dec. 388 (B.I.A. 2014). For discussion see, Recent Adjudication, Asylum Law, 128 Harv. L. Rev. 2090 (2015).
278. A-R-C-G, 26 I & N. Cec. At 388-89.
279. Id. at 395.

United Nations Special Rapporteur on Violence Against Women has "recommended that bodies that report on human rights abuses and violence against women and treaty bodies consider treating domestic violence as an internationally proscribed form of torture."[280] Should all women fleeing domestic violence in their home countries be entitled to claim asylum in the United States? If not, what limiting principles should be applicable?[281]

9. Prevention and Treatment. Although most domestic violence initiatives have focused on assisting victims and punishing perpetrators, many experts believe that more attention needs to center on prevention and rehabilitation. Since the late 1970s, at least 2000 batterer treatment programs have been developed in prisons or as alternatives to incarceration.[282] Such programs aim to change attitudes and improve anger management skills. Yet despite the prevalence of such initiatives, there is surprisingly little data on their long-term effectiveness, and much of the research available is conflicting or hampered by small and non-random samples.[283] As one expert put it, "the field of batterer intervention is still in its infancy."[284] Particularly given the significant backlash against domestic violence programs among men's rights groups, there is an urgent need for better data on what can promote changes in male attitudes and behaviors.[285] There is also a need for more educational and employment services for abusers, which some experts believe may do more than batterer intervention programs in preventing further violence.[286]

Reliable information is also lacking on the effectiveness of other violence prevention and remedial initiatives. For example, some police agencies participate in programs designed to increase outreach to specific populations and to reduce teen violence. Little is known about the impact of these efforts.[287] What we do know underscores the need for effective interventions. As noted earlier, a significant number of high school students report being physically

280. Amanda Blanck, Domestic Violence as a Basis for Asylum Status: A Human Rights Based Approach, 22 Women's Rts. L. Rep. 47, 72 (2001).

281. See Spencer Kyle, Safety Over Semantics: The Case for Statutory Protection for Domestic Violence Asylum Applicants, 16 The Scholar 505, 535 (2014) (noting that Canada's experience with permitting asylum for domestic violence survivors had resulted in only 2 percent of refugee claims being gender based, and concluding that few survivors are willing and able to flee their country and navigate the asylum process).

282. D. Kelly Weisberg, Domestic Violence: Legal and Social Reality 803 (2012).

283. Deborah L. Rhode, Social Research and Social Change: Meeting the Challenge of Gender Inequality and Sexual Abuse, 30 Harv. J.L. & Gender 21 (2007) (reviewing studies).

284. Suzanne Batchelor, Programs for Batterers Changing Their Focus, Women's eNews (Jan. 1, 2006), http://womensenews.org/2006/01/programs-batterers-changing-their-focus (quoting Shelly Jackson).

285. Molly Dragiewicz, Equality with a Vengeance: Men's Rights Groups, Battered Women, and Antifeminist Backlash (2011).

286. Goodmark, A Troubled Marriage, supra note 172, at 191.

287. Rana Sampson, U.S. Dep't of Justice, Domestic Violence 20 (2007).

hurt by a partner and these youths are more likely to do poorly in school and to suffer from mental health and substance abuse problems.[288] Perpetrators of teen violence may also carry those patterns into future relationships. Among adult victims of rape, stalking, or violence by an intimate partner, almost a quarter of women first experienced some form of partner violence when they were adolescents.[289] The Centers for Disease Control and Prevention has recently launched pilot projects in high-risk urban communities aimed at promoting healthy teen dating relationships.[290] We need more such projects, along with comprehensive evaluations that can identify interventions that work. Schools in other nations have done a better job of integrating materials aimed at reducing violence, and similar efforts should be institutionalized and evaluated in this country.[291]

10. Integrated Courts and Services. Reliable information is also lacking on the effectiveness of integrated domestic violence courts that combine civil and criminal functions and attempt to deal with all the concerns regarding abusers and victims.[292] However, the evidence available suggests that offenders who feel that they were treated unfairly by the criminal justice system are more likely to offend again, which suggests the need to consider another model.[293] Providing courts that ensure due process safeguards for defendants who feel coerced into treatment programs, and cross disciplinary services for victims, can improve the law enforcement response to domestic violence. So too, holistic family justice centers that address all of victims' needs for legal and social services can assist abused parties escape the conditions that perpetuate abuse.[294]

Putting Theory Into Practice

3-14. Child welfare authorities removed Sharon's three children from her home based on findings that her husband had subjected them to repeated abuse, such as cursing and beating them. A mental health evaluation of Sharon showed that she did not always put the needs of the children first, that her

288. Id.
289. Ctrs. for Disease Control and Prevention, National Intimate Partner and Sexual Violence Survey: 2010 Summary Report (2011), http://www.cdc.gov/violencePrevention/pdf/nisvs_report2010-a.pdf.
290. Ctrs. for Disease Control and Prevention, Dating Matters, http://www.cdc.gov/violenceprevention/datingmatters.
291. Deborah L. Rhode, What Women Want: An Agenda for the Women's Movement 119 (2014).
292. See Elizabeth L. MacDowell, When Courts Collide: Integrated Domestic Violence Courts and Court Pluralism, 20 Tex. J. Women & L. 95, 98 (2011).
293. Id. at 125.
294. Susie Boss, Under One Roof, Stan. Soc. Innovation Rev. 21 (Spring 2011).

parenting skills were weak, and that she was a battered wife who had a history of relationships with batterers. Her social profile and personality type suggested that she was particularly vulnerable to abuse. The child welfare authorities now seek to terminate Sharon's parental rights to her children on the theory that even if she leaves her current husband, she is likely to enter into another relationship that will be dangerous to the children.

Under your state's abuse and neglect law, parental rights can be terminated on a showing that a parent has failed to prevent another person from abusing a child and that it is reasonably likely that the child will be abused if returned to the parent.

As Sharon's lawyers, what arguments would you make against termination of her parental rights? Should she win?

3-15. Debra and Terrance are cocaine addicts, arrested for the commission of several armed robberies. Debra admits the crimes, but claims a defense of duress, which is unlawful threat or coercion creating an immediate threat of injury that causes someone to act as he or she would not otherwise act. Debra argues that she participated in the robberies out of fear that Terrance would kill her if she did not. In support of her defense, Debra seeks to present expert testimony indicating that she suffers from battered person's syndrome; she has a history of physical and emotional abuse that escalated every time she tried to leave Terrance.

Evidence of battered person's syndrome has been admitted in the jurisdiction in cases in which victims of domestic violence have killed their batterers and claim self-defense. Duress in the criminal law ordinarily does not exonerate a defendant but it can reduce the severity of the crime or the sentence. Should the defense of duress be available in Debra's circumstances? In any felony case?[295]

3-16. In People v. Beltran, the defendant killed a woman with whom he had previously cohabited and who was involved with another man. He testified that he acted in the heat of passion after the woman stated that she "could get better than [him]" and that "I knew you were going to walk away someday. That's why I killed your bastard. I got an abortion."[296] If the jury had believed him, would that be a sufficient basis for finding that the defendant was guilty only of manslaughter? The test under California law is whether the defendant's reason was "at the time of his act, so disturbed or obscured by some passion to such an extent as would render ordinary men of average dis-

---

295. Dixon v. United States, 548 U.S. 1 (2006) (holding that in a case where the defendant claimed that her boyfriend threatened to kill her if she did not buy guns for him in violation of federal law, the accused has the burden of production and persuasion on the issue of duress).

296. People v. Beltran, 301 P.3d 1120, 1124 (Cal. 2013).

position liable to act rashly or with due deliberation and refection, and from this passion rather than from judgment."[297]

3-17. What would you do if you had been Laura Beth Lamb, an attorney who fraudulently took the bar exam in her husband's place, after he physically abused her and threatened to kill both her and her unborn child if she did not take the exam? She pled guilty to felony impersonation, and received probation on condition of paying a fine and completing 200 hours of community service. The California Bar then recommended disbarment. Is disbarment appropriate?[298]

3-18. A highly publicized case of battering involved Barbara Sheehan, who shot and killed her husband after 17 years of physical and emotional abuse. He was a retired New York police officer and, according to testimony at trial by Sheehan and her children, his abuse included throwing boiling pasta sauce in her face and punching her in the face on the evening before the killing. Sheehan told the jury that on the day of the shooting, she took a loaded revolver that belonged to her husband and attempted to sneak out of the house following an argument in which he threatened to kill her if she continued to refuse to accompany him on a Florida vacation. As she passed by the bathroom where her husband was shaving, he tried to stop her by taking a semiautomatic pistol and aiming it at her head. She then shot him, and he reportedly fell to the floor and screamed that he was going to kill her. As he reached for his pistol, she then shot him ten more times.[299] Prosecutors attempted to characterize Sheehan as a pathological liar who murdered her husband because she despised him after years of a dysfunctional marriage and then cloaked herself in a false story of chronic abuse. They also claimed that her fatal shot occurred after her husband presented no real threat, and that Sheehan had not sought help from the police or from family members living close by.

Jurors had the option of convicting her for anything ranging from second degree murder (with a possible sentence of 25 years) to unlawful possession of a firearm (with a possible sentence of three-and-a-half to five years), or acquitting her on all charges. If you were on the jury, how would you vote? How would you respond to other jurors with a different view?

---

297. Id. at 1120. The Court rejected the prosecution's argument that the provocation must be of a kind that would cause an ordinary person of average disposition to kill.

298. See In re Lamb, 776 P.2d 765 (Cal. 1989).

299. Cole, supra note 258; see also Dan Bilefsky, Queens Woman Testifies She Killed Her Husband in Self Defense, N.Y. Times, Sept. 19, 2011; see also Dan Bilefsky, Wife Who Fired 11 Shots is Acquitted of Murder, N.Y. Times, Oct. 6, 2011, at A1; Dan Bilefsky, Cleared of Murder, Sheehan Reports to Jail on Gun Conviction, N.Y. Times, Oct. 12, 2011, at A26.

D. PORNOGRAPHY

Sex sells. That has always been true, but increased technological innovations have created increased opportunities for private consumption of pornography. Video sales and rentals, pay-per-view movies on cable and websites, phone sex, and Internet websites are estimated to generate close to $13 billion annually in the United States.[300] Americans spend more on pornography than on all other movies, performing arts, and professional football, basketball, and baseball combined.[301] Nielsen ratings indicated that about a quarter of all Internet users in the United States, some 60 million users, visited a pornography website. Two-thirds of these viewers were male.[302]

Since the early 1980s, some feminists have joined with religious conservatives and other activists to combat pornography on several fronts. While the conservative case against pornography focuses on the corruption of morals and erosion of "family values," the feminist rationale emphasizes the role of pornography in subordinating women through objectifying and degrading images, and eroticization of abuse.

The traditional legal approach to pornography is encompassed within obscenity doctrine. The leading case, Miller v. California, permits the government to ban material if, under contemporary community standards, the work as a whole appeals to the "prurient interest," depicts sex in a "patently offensive" way, and lacks serious literary, artistic, political, or scientific value.[303] Feminists charge that this standard cannot be effective in challenging pornographic materials because it incorporates the very community standards that have made subordination sexually appealing. Moreover, it asks judges to admit to an uncomfortable psychological state of finding material both sexually arousing *and* patently offensive.[304]

What legal theories best apply to pornography? Is pornography a form of discrimination based on sex?

300. Pornography Statistics, Annual Report 2015, http://www.covenanteyes.com/pornstats.
301. Frank Rich, Naked Capitalists, N.Y. Times Mag., May 20, 2001, at 51.
302. Natasha Vargas-Cooper, Hard Core, Atlantic (Jan./Feb. 2011), http://www.the-atlantic.com/magazine/archive/2011/01/hard-core/308327.
303. 413 U.S. 15 (1973).
304. Rhode, Speaking of Sex, supra note 273, at 130-35.

1. The Feminist Critique of Pornography

Catharine A. MacKinnon, Feminism Unmodified: Discourses on Life and Law
171-72 (1987)

Pornography sexualizes rape, battery, sexual harassment, prostitution, and child sexual abuse; it thereby celebrates, promotes, authorizes and legitimizes them. More generally, it eroticizes the dominance and submission that is the dynamic common to them all. It makes hierarchy sexy and calls that "the truth about sex" or just a mirror of reality. Through this process pornography constructs what a woman is as what men want from sex. . . .

The content of pornography is one thing. There, women substantively desire dispossession and cruelty. We desperately want to be bound, battered, tortured, humiliated, and killed. . . . What pornography does goes beyond its content: it eroticizes hierarchy, it sexualizes inequality. It makes dominance and submission into sex. Inequality is its central dynamic; the illusion of freedom coming together with the reality of force is central to its working. . . .

From this perspective, pornography is neither harmless fantasy nor a corrupt and confused misrepresentation of an otherwise natural and healthy sexual situation. It institutionalizes the sexuality of male supremacy, fusing the eroticization of dominance and submission with the social construction of male and female. To the extent that gender is sexual, pornography is part of constituting the meaning of that sexuality.

Catharine A. MacKinnon, Pornography as Defamation and Discrimination
71 B.U. L. Rev. 793, 796-97, 801-02 (1991)

Pornography has a central role in actualizing . . . [a] system of subordination in the contemporary West, beginning with the conditions of its production. Women in pornography are bound, battered, tortured, harassed, raped, and sometimes killed; or in the glossy men's entertainment magazines, "merely" humiliated, molested, objectified, and used. In all pornography, women are prostituted. . . . It is done because someone who has more power than they do, someone who matters, someone with rights, a full human being and a full citizen, gets pleasure from seeing it, or doing it, or seeing it as a form of doing it. In order to produce what the consumer wants to see, it must first be done to someone, usually a woman, a woman with few real choices. . . .

The evidence shows that the use of pornography makes it impossible for men to tell when sex is forced, that women are human, and that rape is rape. Pornography makes men hostile and aggressive toward women, and it makes women silent. While these effects are not invariant or always imme-diate, and do not affect all men to the same degree, there is no reason to think they are not acted upon and every reason and overwhelming evidence to think that they are — if not right then, then sometime, if not violently, then through some other kind of discrimination. . . . When men use pornography, they experience in their bodies, not just their minds, that one-sided sex — sex between a person (them) and a thing (it) — is sex, that sexual use is sex, sex-ual abuse is sex, sexual domination is sex. This is the sexuality that they then demand, practice, purchase, and live out in their everyday social relations with others. Pornography works by making sexism sexy.

2. The Judicial, First Amendment Response

American Booksellers Association, Inc. v. Hudnut
771 F.2d 323 (7th Cir. 1985), aff'd mem.,
475 U.S. 1001, reh'g denied, 475 U.S. 1132 (1986)

EASTERBROOK, Circuit Judge.

Indianapolis enacted an ordinance defining "pornography" as a practice that discriminates against women. "Pornography" is to be redressed through the administrative and judicial methods used for other discrimination. The City's definition of "pornography" is considerably different from "obscenity," which the Supreme Court has held is not protected by the First Amendment.

To be "obscene" under Miller v. California, . . . "a publication must, taken as a whole, appeal to the prurient interest, must contain patently offen-sive depictions or descriptions of specified sexual conduct, and on the whole have no serious literary, artistic, political, or scientific value." . . . Offensiveness must be assessed under the standards of the community. Both offensiveness and an appeal to something other than "normal, healthy sexual desires" are essential elements of "obscenity."

"Pornography" under the ordinance is "the graphic sexually explicit sub-ordination of women, whether in pictures or in words, that also includes one or more of the following: (1) Women are presented as sexual objects who enjoy pain or humiliation; or (2) Women are presented as sexual objects who experience sexual pleasure in being raped; or (3) Women are presented as sexual objects tied up or cut up or mutilated or bruised or physically hurt, or as dismembered or truncated or fragmented or severed into body parts; or (4) Women are presented as being penetrated by objects or animals; or (5) Women are presented in scenarios of degradation, injury, abasement, torture, shown as filthy or inferior, bleeding, bruised, or hurt in a context that makes these conditions sexual; or (6) Women are presented as sexual objects for domination, conquest, violation, exploitation, possession, or use, or through postures or positions of servility or submission or display." . . . The statute provides that the "use of men, children, or transsexuals in the place of women in paragraphs (1) through (6) above shall also constitute pornography under this section." . . . The Indianapolis ordinance does not refer to the prurient interest, to offensiveness, or to the standards of the community. It demands attention to particular depictions, not to the work judged as a whole. It is irrelevant under the ordinance whether the work has literary, artistic, political, or scientific value. The City and many amici point to these omissions as virtues. They maintain that pornography influences attitudes, and the statute is a way to alter the socialization of men and women rather than to vindicate community standards of offensiveness. And as one of the principal drafters of the ordinance has asserted, "if a woman is subjected, why should it matter that the work has other value?" . . .

The plaintiffs are a congeries of distributors and readers of books, magazines, and films. . . . Civil rights groups and feminists have entered this case as amici on both sides. Those supporting the ordinance say that it will play an important role in reducing the tendency of men to view women as sexual objects, a tendency that leads to both unacceptable attitudes and discrimination in the workplace and violence away from it. Those opposing the ordinance point out that much radical feminist literature is explicit and depicts women in ways forbidden by the ordinance and that the ordinance would reopen old battles. It is unclear how Indianapolis would treat works from James Joyce's Ulysses to Homer's Iliad; both depict women as submissive objects for conquest and domination. . . .

"If there is any fixed star in our constitutional constellation, it is that no official, high or petty, can prescribe what shall be orthodox in politics, nationalism, religion, or other matters of opinion or force citizens to confess by word or act their faith therein." . . . Under the First Amendment the government must leave to the people the evaluation of ideas. Bald or subtle, an idea is as powerful as the audience allows it to be. A belief may be pernicious—the beliefs of Nazis led to the death of millions, those of the Klan to the repression of millions. A pernicious belief may prevail. Totalitarian governments today rule much of the planet, practicing suppression of billions and spreading dogma that may enslave others. One of the things that separates our society from theirs is our absolute right to propagate opinions that the government finds wrong or even hateful. . . .

Under the ordinance graphic sexually explicit speech is "pornography" or not depending on the perspective the author adopts. Speech that "subordinates" women and also, for example, presents women as enjoying pain, humiliation, or rape, or even simply presents women in "positions of servility or submission or display" is forbidden, no matter how great the literary or political value of the work taken as a whole. Speech that portrays women in positions of equality is lawful, no matter how graphic the sexual content. This is thought control. It establishes an "approved" view of women, of how they may react to sexual encounters, of how the sexes may relate to each other. Those who espouse the approved view may use sexual images; those who do not, may not.

Indianapolis justifies the ordinance on the ground that pornography affects thoughts. Men who see women depicted as subordinate are more likely to treat them so. Pornography is an aspect of dominance. It does not persuade people so much as change them. It works by socializing, by establishing the expected and the permissible. In this view pornography is not an idea; pornography is the injury.

There is much to this perspective. Beliefs are also facts. . . . Depictions of subordination tend to perpetuate subordination. The subordinate status of women in turn leads to affront and lower pay at work, insult and injury at home, battery and rape on the streets. In the language of the legislature, "[p]ornography is central in creating and maintaining sex as a basis of discrimination. Pornography is a systematic practice of exploitation and subordination based on sex which differentially harms women. The bigotry and contempt it produces, with the acts of aggression it fosters, harm women's opportunities for equality and rights [of all kinds]."

Yet this simply demonstrates the power of pornography as speech. All of these unhappy effects depend on mental intermediation. Pornography affects how people see the world, their fellows, and social relations. If pornography is what pornography does, so is other speech. Hitler's orations affected how some Germans saw Jews. . . . Racial bigotry, anti-semitism, violence on television, reporters' biases—these and many more influence the culture and shape our socialization. None is directly answerable by more speech, unless that speech too finds its place in the popular culture. Yet all is protected as speech, however insidious. Any other answer leaves the government in control of all of the institutions of culture, the great censor and director of which thoughts are good for us. . . .

Much of Indianapolis's argument rests on the belief that when speech is "unanswerable," and the metaphor that there is a "marketplace of ideas" does not apply, the First Amendment does not apply either. The metaphor is honored; Milton's Areopagitica and John Stewart [sic] Mill's On Liberty defend freedom of speech on the ground that the truth will prevail, and many of the most important cases under the First Amendment recite this position. The Framers undoubtedly believed it. As a general matter it is true. But the Constitution does not make the dominance of truth a necessary condition of freedom of speech. To say that it does would be to confuse an outcome of free speech with a necessary condition for the application of the amendment.

A power to limit speech on the ground that truth has not yet prevailed and is not likely to prevail implies the power to declare truth. At some point the government must be able to say (as Indianapolis has said): "We know what the truth is, yet a free exchange of speech has not driven out falsity, so that we must now prohibit falsity." If the government may declare the truth, why wait for the failure of speech? Under the First Amendment, however, there is no such thing as a false idea, . . . so the government may not restrict speech on the ground that in a free exchange truth is not yet dominant. . . .

We come, finally, to the argument that pornography is "low value" speech, that it is enough like obscenity that Indianapolis may prohibit it. Some cases hold that speech far removed from politics and other subjects at the core of the Framers' concerns may be subjected to special regulation. . . . These cases do not sustain statutes that select among viewpoints, however. In [one case], the FCC sought to keep vile language off the air during certain times. The Court held that it may; but the Court would not have sustained a regulation prohibiting scatological descriptions of Republicans but not scatological descriptions of Democrats, or any other form of selection among viewpoints.

At all events, "pornography" is not low value speech within the meaning of these cases. Indianapolis seeks to prohibit certain speech because it believes this speech influences social relations and politics on a grand scale, that it controls attitudes at home and in the legislature. This precludes a characterization of the speech as low value. True, pornography and obscenity have sex in common. But Indianapolis left out of its definition any reference to literary, artistic, political, or scientific value. The ordinance applies to graphic sexually explicit subordination in works great and small. The Court sometimes balances the value of speech against the costs of its restriction, but it does this by category of speech and not by the content of particular works. . . . Indianapolis has created an approved point of view and so loses the support of these cases.

Any rationale we could imagine in support of this ordinance could not be limited to sex discrimination. Free speech has been on balance an ally of those seeking change. Governments that want stasis start by restricting speech. Culture is a powerful force of continuity; Indianapolis paints pornography as part of the culture of power. Change in any complex system ultimately depends on the ability of outsiders to challenge accepted views and the reigning institutions. Without a strong guarantee of freedom of speech, there is no effective right to challenge what is.

. . . The offense of coercion to engage in a pornographic performance . . . has elements that might be constitutional. Without question a state may prohibit fraud, trickery, or the use of force to induce people to perform—in pornographic films or in any other films. Such a statute may be written without regard to the viewpoint depicted in the work. New York v. Ferber . . . suggests that when a state has a strong interest in forbidding the conduct that makes up a film (in *Ferber* sexual acts involving minors), it may restrict or forbid dissemination of the film in order to reinforce the prohibition of the conduct. A state may apply such a rule to non-sexual coercion (although it need not). . . .

But the Indianapolis ordinance, unlike our hypothetical statute, is not neutral with respect to viewpoint. . . .

The ban on distribution of works containing coerced performances is limited to pornography; coercion is irrelevant if the work is not "pornography," and we have held the definition of "pornography" to be defective root and branch. A legislature might replace "pornography" in [the ordinance] with "any film containing explicit sex" or some similar expression, but even the broadest severability clause does not permit a federal court to rewrite as opposed to excise. Rewriting is work for the legislature of Indianapolis. . . .

No amount of struggle with particular words and phrases in this ordinance can leave anything in effect. The district court came to the same conclusion. Its judgment is therefore Affirmed.

Cannot outlaw porn.
First Amend.

Notes

1. Pornography and the First Amendment. Some commentators have argued that regulation of pornography is consistent with the First Amendment, in that pornography is like other forms of speech that can be regulated because of their low value (such as advertising) or their social harm (such as libel, fraud, and sexual harassment). They also claim that pornography ordinances are no less vague than existing obscenity law. MacKinnon further claims that

> while the First Amendment supports pornography on the belief that consensus and progress are facilitated by allowing all views, however divergent and unorthodox, it fails to notice that pornography . . . is not at all divergent or unorthodox. It is the ruling ideology. Feminism, the dissenting view, is suppressed by pornography.[305]

Is she right? How effectively does *Hudnut* respond to these claims?

Legislation somewhat similar to the Indianapolis ordinance has been upheld by the Canadian Supreme Court. In Regina v. Butler, the Court sustained a statute that criminalizes "any publication a dominant characteristic of which is the undue exploitation of sex, or of sex and any one or more of the following subjects, namely crime, horror, cruelty and violence." The Court interpreted the statute to prohibit any "materials that subordinate, degrade or dehumanize women."[306] In determining that the restriction of speech expression was justified, the Court concluded:

> [T]his kind of expression lies far from the core of the guarantee of freedom of expression. It appeals only to the most base aspect of individual fulfillment and it is primarily economically motivated. The objective of the legislation on the

---

305. Catharine A. MacKinnon, Toward a Feminist Theory of the State 205 (1989).
306. 89 D.L.R.4th 449 (S.C.C. 1992).

other hand is of fundamental importance in a free and democratic society. . . . It thus seeks to enhance respect for all members of society and non-violence and equality in their relations with each other.[307]

Is this a desirable approach? Is your view affected by the fact that the first targets of the legislation included a gay and lesbian bookstore, a lesbian magazine, and two books by anti-pornography activist Andrea Dworkin?[308]

Another alternative is the approach of some sexually progressive societies that ban portrayals of "extreme abuse," such as rape, bestiality, and pedophilia.[309] Would such an approach be constitutional in this country? Desirable?

One additional area of controversy involving the First Amendment involves the use of zoning regulations to curtail adverse community effects associated with adult entertainment businesses. In City of Los Angeles v. Alameda Books, Inc., the Court sustained such a regulation as a justifiable response to increases in prostitution, robbery, assault, and theft in areas where adult entertainment establishments are centered.[310] Free-speech advocates have criticized such uses of zoning on grounds that the evidence for increased crime is weak, and that their effect is to stigmatize erotic materials and limit the rights of individuals to construct their own sexualities.[311] If you were a city leader, how would you balance these competing concerns? Has the rise in Internet access to pornography made such zoning less necessary?

2. Evaluating the Harm of Pornography. Evidence concerning the harms of pornography remains conflicting and contested. In 2004, the Subcommittee on Science, Technology, and Space of the Senate Committee on Commerce held a hearing on The Science Behind Pornography Addiction.[312] The hearing included evidence that prolonged exposure to pornography promotes sexual callousness, increases proclivity to rape, promotes adverse perceptions of women, and erodes trust and honesty in intimate relationships. Other experts at the hearing and in subsequent reports claimed that frequent viewing of pornography leads to unrealistic expectations concerning female appearance and behavior, greater acceptance of sexual aggression and

307. Id. at 487-88.

308. Nadine Strossen, A Feminist Critique of "the" Feminist Critique of Pornography, 79 Va. L. Rev. 1099, 1145-46 (1993).

309. Int'l Ctr. for Missing and Exploited Children, Child Pornography: Model Legislation and Global Review (6th ed. 2010).

310. 535 U.S. 425 (2002).

311. See Stephanie Lasker, Comment, Sex and the City: Zoning Pornography Peddlers and Live Nude Shows, 49 UCLA L. Rev. 1139, 1158-59, 1181-84 (2002).

312. The Science Behind Pornography Addiction, Hearing on S. 2056, 108th Cong. (2004).

harassment, and difficulties in forming sexually satisfying relationships.[313] Part of the reason is that the best selling pornography emphasizes physical aggression by men apparently enjoyed by women.[314] In a Kaiser Family Foundation study, about half of the 15- to 24-year-olds surveyed believed that adolescents who see pornography on the Internet are more likely to have sex before they are ready and that such material promotes bad attitudes toward women.[315] The review of research by the Children's Commissioner in Great Britain found a link between exposure to pornography among children and adolescents with unrealistic attitudes about sex, less progressive gender roles, and greater likelihood of engagement in sexually risky behaviors.[316] A study of battered women also found that pornography use by the batterer was correlated with an increased likelihood of sexual as well as physical abuse.[317]

By contrast, other experts maintain that the vast majority of pornography viewers are occasional, recreational users, not addicts, and that such use can be beneficial in sparking desire, enhancing satisfaction, and constructively channeling sexual fantasies. Many researchers also believe that the causal relationships between pornography and sexual violence have not been established.[318] An equally contested issue is what kinds of explicit sexual imagery are the most damaging. The premise of an Indianapolis-style ordinance is that violent pornography is more harmful and therefore more appropriate for regulation than nonviolent pornography. By contrast, some feminists contend that the most adverse effects on women's self-image come from nonviolent mainstream images that appear acceptable and normal.[319] In a sense, this point is fully consistent with one principle of dominance theory, which is that legal rules proscribing only the most severe forms of certain behaviors thereby legitimize the remainder. Would tighter controls on violent pornography further eroticize violence against women? Is the answer to regulate more, or less?

---

313. Id.; Report of the American Psychological Association Task Force on the Sexualization of Girls 29, 31, 34 (2006); Belinda Luscombe, Porn and the Threat to Virility, Time, Apr. 11, 2016, 42-46; studies cited in Alison Baxter, How Pornography Harms Children: The Advocates' Role, 33 Child. L. Practice 113 (2014); Lihi Yona, Politicizing Health, Medicalizing Porn: Rethinking Modern Pornography, 16 Marq. Elder's Advisor 113, 149 (2014).

314. Ana Bridges et al., Aggression and Sexual Behavior in Best-Selling Pornography Videos: A Content Analysis Update, 16 Violence Against Women 1065 (2010).

315. Pamela Paul, The Porn Factor, Time, Jan. 19, 2004, at 99.

316. Miranda A.H. Horvath et al., Basically . . . Porn Is Everywhere: A Rapid Evidence Assessment on the Effects that Access and Exposure to Pornography Has on Children and Young People (2013).

317. Janet Hinson Shope, When Words Are Not Enough: The Search for the Effect of Pornography on Abused Women, 10 Violence Against Women 56, 67-68 (2004).

318. For discussion of studies, see Horvath et al., supra note 317; David Segal, Does Porn Hurt Children?, N.Y. Times, Mar. 28, 2014.

319. Carlin Meyer, Sex, Sin, and Women's Liberation: Against Porn Suppression, 72 Tex. L. Rev. 1097 (1994).

Many scholars argue for less regulation, both because they do not believe that violent pornography causes the harms that opponents cite, and because, even if it did, trying to prevent it through law would be counterproductive. On the latter point, David Cole agrees:

> Sexual expression . . . inevitably confounds society's attempts to regulate it. It subverts every taboo by making it a fetish. The forbidden is simultaneously eroticized. As a result, attempts to regulate sexual expression are doomed to failure; by creating taboos to transgress, regulation only adds to sexual expression's appeal.[320]

Feminists opposing the *Hudnut* regulation argued that pornography regulation reinforces damaging stereotypes—stereotypes that men are "attack dogs" or "irresponsible beasts"; that only women are demeaned or degraded by pornography; that women are incapable of consent to sex; or that good women do not seek and enjoy sex.[321] Are they right?

Others have focused on the negative effects on men themselves. Sociologist Michael Kimmel argues that "porn gives guys a world in which no one has to take no for an answer." It serves a "refuge from the harsh reality of a more gender equitable world. . . . It's about anger at the loss of privilege." Escape into this world, Kimmel argues, fosters attitudes "that won't serve [men] in the long term. . . . They're missing out on developing the skills, sexual and otherwise, that might help them to sustain relationships with women in the real world," relationships that demand "at least a modicum of dignity, respect, and care."[322] Is he right?

3. Pornography and Sex-Positive Feminism. Sex-positive or pro-sex feminism is a movement that began in the early 1980s that emphasizes the importance of sexual freedom as part of women's overall freedom. Some activists became involved in the movement in response to anti-pornography feminist efforts. Wendy McElroy, a prominent defender of the sex-positive position, opens her book, XXX A Woman's Right to Pornography, with the claim, "Pornography benefits women, both personally and politically."[323] In her view, "every woman has the right to define what is degrading and liberating for herself." Pornography can be liberating by (1) giving a "panoramic

---

320. David Cole, Playing by Pornography's Rules: The Regulation of Sexual Expression, 143 U. Pa. L. Rev. 111, 116 (1994).

321. See Nan D. Hunter & Sylvia A. Law, Brief Amici Curiae of Feminist Anti-Censorship Taskforce et al., in American Booksellers Association v. Hudnut, 21 U. Mich. J.L. Reform 69, 125-31 (Fall 1987-Winter 1988).

322. Michael Kimmel, Guyland 173, 177, 188 (2008).

323. Wendy McElroy, XXX: A Woman's Right to Pornography (1997). For a more recent account, see Wendy McElroy, A Feminist Overview of Pornography Ending in a Defense Thereof, http://www.wendymcelroy.com/freeinqu.htm.

view of the world's sexual possibilities;" (2) allowing women to avoid shame and "enjoy scenes and situations that would be anathema in real life;" and (3) providing a sexual outlet for those who have no sexual partner.[324] Some sex-positive feminists create what they term "feminist porn," which stresses women's agency and pleasure even as it sometimes depicts sado-masochistic acts that anti-porn activists find subordinating.[325] Candida Royalle, a prominent creator of feminist porn, argues that it can "help people become comfortable with a particular fantasy they or their partner may have. Pornography can reboot a couple's sex life. It can give ideas or help you get in touch with what turns you on."[326]

A former porn star makes a similar point:

> I'm just very happy with what I've done. On a social level, I think these movies are helping people's lives. A lot of our crowd, our audience, is made up of guys who maybe aren't the best-looking dudes in town. Maybe they're dorks or disabled or something like that, and there's no chance they're ever going to get laid. And I think the adult business definitely gives those guys an outlet. Otherwise, they'll explode.
>
> And lately, a lot of couples are benefiting from our films as well. . . . There are so many people who are so unhappy sexually. But now, because of the way sex has become so important in the media and so open, and people are finally talking about stuff and showing stuff sexually, people are realizing how unhappy they are and doing something about it. For the guys to bring these movies home to their spouses or girlfriends, sometimes it can really stimulate their relationship. Sometimes it works, sometimes it doesn't. But at least if a guy is unhappy with the way his wife is performing, he can watch porno and jerk off maybe, rather than have an affair. Everyone can disagree, but I think it's definitely at least an outlet for guys.[327]

Some feminists have objected to the labels "sex positive" and "sex negative." Meghan Murphy argues that those who are called sex negative are critical of pornography because they "want to work towards a real, liberated, *feminist* understanding of sex and sexuality, rather than one that sexualizes inequality, domination, and subordination. To me, that sounds far more 'sex positive' (from a feminist perspective, anyway), than blind support for

324. McElroy, A Feminist Overview, supra note 323.

325. Rebecca Santiago, Feminist Porn 101: Your Guide to Empowering Sexytimes (2013), http://www.bustle.com/articles/10042-feminist-porn-101-your-guide-to-empowering-sexytimes.

326. Candida Royalle, Pornography Can Be Good for Consumers, N.Y. Times, Nov. 11, 2012.

327. Brad Armstrong, Porn Star, in Gig: Americans Talk About Their Jobs at the Turn of the Millennium 359, 364 (John Bowe et al. eds., 2000).

anything sex-related. . . ."[328] Other feminists argue that "it's saddening to see us fighting each other; women who have been called prudes for asserting their sexual choices attacking women who have been called whores for asserting their sexual choices . . . and vice versa."[329]

Where do you situate yourself in this debate? Is it productive? Is it unavoidable?

4. Pornography and Individual Agency. At the heart of the debate over pornography regulation is the extent to which people are capable of defining their own sexuality. Those favoring regulation of pornography assume that its proliferation prevents women from being independent agents; women's choices appear constrained by the ways in which sex has been defined in *men's* interests. Those opposing regulation assume that women have the capacity to think and act for themselves, and to know what they want. Many young "third wave" feminists and gays and lesbians have taken this approach and stressed the subversive and self-expressive aspects of pornography.[330] What is your view?

Is there some "natural" set of sexual drives and desires that pornography, advertising, and other social forces distort? Or is sexuality always socially constructed? If the latter, how could society promote the most healthy understandings of sex and sexuality?

5. Pornography, the Internet, and Children. The increasingly accessible Internet has expanded opportunities for the creation and distribution of sexually explicit images. Research shows that adolescents' exposure to online pornography has led to more unrealistic sexual beliefs, and consumption of violent pornography is correlated with increased sexually aggressive behavior. In the absence of education, exposure to high-risk practices is correlated with high-risk behavior.[331] Online pornography poses special challenges for regulation. The first problem is detection. The sheer size of cyberspace makes it difficult to police. A second problem is accountability. Even if illegal content

---

328. Meghan Murphy, The Divide Isn't Between "Sex Negative" and "Sex Positive" Feminists—It's Between Liberal and Radical Feminism, Feminist (Apr. 11, 2014), http://www.feministcurrent.com/2014/04/11/the-divide-isnt-between-sex-negative-and-sex-positive-feminist-its-between-liberal-and-radical-feminism.

329. Kitty Stryker, The 80s Called And They Want Their Sex Wars Back, The Frisky (Apr. 10, 2014), http://www.thefrisky.com/2014-04-10/the-soapbox-the-80s-called-and-they-want-their-sex-wars-back.

330. Vargas-Cooper, supra note 303; Bridget J. Crawford, Toward a Third-Wave Feminist Legal Theory: Young Women, Pornography and the Praxis of Pleasure, 14 Mich. J. Gender & Law 99, 139-52 (2007); Jeffrey G. Sherman, Love Speech: The Social Utility of Pornography, 47 Stan. L. Rev. 661 (1995).

331. Eric W. Owens et al., The Impact of Internet Pornography on Adolescents: A Review of the Research, 19 Sexual Addiction & Compulsivity 99, 116 (2012).

is discovered online, the responsible party may be impossible to track. Both of these difficulties are exacerbated by encryption technology, which allows parties to disguise their identities. A third problem is jurisdiction: How can courts exercise authority over out-of-state providers? Other difficulties arise in determining which "community standards" govern online materials that can be downloaded anywhere. The Internet's decentralized structure also resists regulation by permitting users to reroute access around "blocks." In addition, users can post messages anonymously through the use of remailers, making it difficult to suspend privileges or identify senders.

The vast majority of nations prohibit the sale of pornography to children but such prohibitions are difficult to enforce. The same technologies that make it easy for individuals to disguise their identity make it equally easy to disguise their age. Courts have struggled with how to reconcile child protection with First Amendment interests, and have struck down early congressional regulations as overly broad restrictions on speech.[332] For example, the Child Pornography Prevention Act (CPPA) prohibited the production, transportation, receipt, or distribution of visual depictions that involve the use of a minor (any person under the age of 18) engaged in sexually explicit conduct, where the producer or distributor knows or has reason to know, that the depiction was or will be transported in interstate commerce or was created using a camera (or the like) that had traveled in interstate commerce. When the statute came before the Supreme Court for oral argument, Justice Scalia questioned whether there would in fact be "radical tragic consequences" for First Amendment jurisprudence if audiences could not see "minors copulating." When Justice Stevens smilingly interjected a reference to Romeo and Juliet, Justice Scalia responded, "You've seen a different version of that play than I have."[333] In Ashcroft v. Free Speech Coalition, the Court held that the statute proscribed material that was neither obscene nor child pornography, and violated the First Amendment.[334] In so ruling, the Court rejected the government's argument that such works could be banned because they contributed to child abuse when pedophiles used them to stimulate an appetite for sexual contact or to lure children into criminal acts. In the Court's view, child pornography had not been demonstrated to be "intrinsically related" to child abuse and the link between abuse and virtual child pornography was only "contingent and indirect."[335]

However, the Supreme Court upheld the Children's Internet Protection Act (CIPA) that requires publicly funded elementary schools, secondary

332. Reno v. ACLU, 521 U.S. 844 (1997); Ashcroft v. ACLU, 542 U.S. 656 (2004); ACLU v. Gonzales, 478 F. Supp. 2d 775 (E.D. Pa. 2007).

333. Tony Mauro, Virtual Reality Check, Am. Lawyer 70 (Dec. 2001) (quoting Justice Scalia).

334. 535 U.S. 234 (2002).

335. Id. at 250.

schools, and libraries that provide Internet access to (1) block or filter adults' access to visual depictions of obscenity or child pornography and (2) block or filter children's access to obscenity, child pornography, or other material that is "harmful to minors." In upholding CIPA, the Court's decision left open the possibility of later challenge if, as applied, software erroneously blocked constitutionally protected material and librarians were not willing, or able, to unblock it.[336]

Other important legislation includes the PROTECT Act, passed in 2003, which attempts to curb the spread of child pornography on the Internet by making it a crime to offer or solicit sexually explicit images of children. The PROTECT Act applies even if the material at issue consists solely of computer-generated images or digitally altered photographs of adults, as well as to fraudulent offers of child pornography in which the material does not exist at all.[337]

Two issues that recently have divided federal courts involve punishment for possession of child pornography. Many courts have used their discretion to revise sentences downward for individuals convicted of possession or distribution of child pornography on the ground that penalties are too high for a victimless offense and that offenders are themselves victims of mental health disorders.[338] In some instances, punishments for the possession of child pornography have exceeded those for actual child abuse.[339] By contrast, other courts have viewed such offenses more seriously and have required even those convicted only of possessing pornography to pay restitution to victims in amounts ranging from $3000 to $150,000.[340] The Violence Against Women Act authorizes restitution to victims who are harmed as a result of commission of a crime involving sexual exploitation of children.[341] Lower courts divided over this remedy in pornography possession cases, because the number of potential victims and offenders is "staggering," the amount of losses directly attributable to a single owner is difficult to calculate, and inconsistent verdicts are likely.[342] In Paroline v. United States, the Supreme Court held that where it

---

336. 539 U.S. 194 (2003).

337. See United States v. Williams, 553 U.S. 285 (2008).

338. United States v. Irey, 612 F.3d 1160 (11th Cir. 2010) (en banc) (reversing a district court's sentence of 17 years for having sex with children and distributing the images and imposing a 30-year sentence); Melissa Hamilton, Sentencing Adjudication: Lessons from Child Pornography Policy Nullification, 30 Ga. St. U. L. Rev. 375, 378 (2014) (citing study finding that more than half of child pornography sentences were below the recommended range).

339. Carissa Byrne Hessick, The Limits of Child Pornography, 89 Ind. L.J. 1437, 1439 (2014).

340. Dina McLeod, Section 2259 Restitution Claims and Child Pornography Possession, 109 Mich. L. Rev. 1327 (2011).

341. 18 U.S.C. §2259 (2012).

342. McLeod, supra note 341, at 1342 (noting that each year there are about 200 victims of child pornography and 3000 prosecutions for possession, and that some offenders collect thousands of images).

was impossible to trace a particular amount of the plaintiff's losses to an individual defendant's possession, the court should order restitution in an amount "that comport[s] with the defendant's relative role in the causal process that underlay the victim's general losses."[343] Relevant factors should include the number of images the defendant possessed of the victim and whether the defendant reproduced or distributed them. The difficulties in enforcing restitution have prompted a variety of congressional reform proposals.[344]

How serious is the crime of possession of pornography? Is a life sentence appropriate for a 26-year-old man convicted of 454 counts of possessing child pornography?[345] Should pretrial diversion for offenders be available?[346] If restitution is appropriate, how should damages be measured? Should a lawyer convicted of possession be disbarred if the material he owned was legally made in the country in which he purchased it?[347]

6. Sexting.   An issue that is gaining increased attention is sexting—sending nude or seminude pictures over cell phones. Studies find that between 20 to 30 percent of teens have reported sending or receiving such pictures and almost half of boys in co-ed high schools had seen a nude picture of a female classmate.[348] Adolescents have faced exploitation, harassment, bullying, blackmail, and psychological trauma as a result of nonconsensual distribution of such images, and a number have committed suicide.[349]

Students have been expelled or suspended or denied the right to participate in school activities in response to such offenses.[350] Prosecutors in several states also have filed or threatened child pornography charges against stu-

343. 134 S. Ct. 1710, 1727 (2014).

344. Alanna D. Francois, *Paroline v. United States*: Mandatory Restitution: An Empty Gesture, Leaving Victims of Child Pornography Holding the Bag, 42 S. U. L. Rev. 293, 324-25 (2015).

345. Jacob Carpenter, East Naples Man's Life Sentence for Child Porn Too Harsh, Attorney Says, Naplesnews.com (Nov. 3, 2011).

346. Sarah J. Long, The Case for Extending Pretrial Diversion to Include Possession of Child Pornography 9 U. Mass. L. Rev. 306 (2014).

347. In re Boudreau, 815 So. 2d 76 (La. 2002) (the models were of legal age in Norway).

348. See surveys reviewed in Whitney Strachan, A New Statutory Regime Designed to Address the Harms of Minors Sexting While Giving a More Appropriate Punishment: A Marrying of New Revenge Porn Statutes with Traditional Child Pornography Laws, 24 S. Cal. L. Rev L. & Soc. Just. 267, 275 (2015); Raychelle Cassada Lohmann, Teen Sexting—The Real Issue, Psychol. Today, Apr. 7, 2013; Jane Bailey & Mouna Hanna, The Gendered Dimensions of Sexting: Assessing the Applicability of Canada's Child Pornography Provision, 23 Canadian J. Women & L., 405, 409-10 (2011).

349. Bailey & Hanna, supra note 348, at 407, 411-21; April Gile Thomas & Elizabeth Cauffman, Youth Sexting as Child Pornography? Developmental Science Supports Less Harsh Sanctions for Juvenile Sexters, 17 New Crim. L. Rev. 631, 639-40 (2014).

350. Bailey & Hanna, supra note 348, at 413-14.

dents involved in sending or forwarding such photos.[351] Sanctions for such offenses could include long prison terms and 10 to 20 years registration as a sex offender. In one case, the parents of two 15-year-old girls who circulated provocative photos of themselves wearing bras sued the district attorney. He had threatened prosecution of the girls if they did not attend a ten-hour class dealing with pornography and sexual violence. The American Civil Liberties Union lawyer representing the families denounced the "nuclear-weapon-type charge like child pornography against kids who have no criminal intent and are merely doing stupid things."[352] Opponents of prosecution point out that even if students aren't convicted, searchable records exist of charges that my affect college and job applications.[353] Prosecutors, by contrast, defend the charges as a way to "protect these kids from themselves" and from acting in ways that can "follow them for the rest of their lives."[354] Particularly where students have ignored school warnings not to engage in the practice, local district attorneys have viewed criminal charges, with the possibility of a suspended sentence, as a useful deterrent. Courts, however, have imposed limits on the sanctions that can be imposed. In Miller v. Mitchell, the Third Circuit Court of Appeals granted a preliminary injunction against requiring a student to attend an educational class on sexting on the grounds that it infringed her parent's autonomy and her own right of free expression.[355]

Sexting has evolved against a growing cultural backdrop of sexualization of adolescents.[356] Girls often use sexting as a form of "relationship currency;" it also serves to initiate or sustain intimacy, as well as to entertain friends and humiliate enemies.[357] Girls are more likely to send sexualized photos than boys, feel more pressure to do so, and suffer more adverse consequences. A common perception is that girls who sext are sluts, while boys are studs.

How would you respond to "sexting," as a parent, principal, or prosecutor? Are there legitimate issues of sexual self-expression and agency at issue? Should you punish those who send sexts as part of a relationship, or only those

---

351. Erik Eckholm, Prosecutors Weigh Teenage Sexting: Folly or Felony?, N.Y. Times, Nov. 14, 2015, at A13.

352. Sean D. Hamill, Students Sue Prosecutors in Cellphone Photos Case, N.Y. Times, Mar. 26, 2009, at A18 (quoting Witold J. Walczak).

353. Eckholm, supra note 351, at A17.

354. Comments of Michal McAlexander, Chief Deputy, Prosecutor's Office, Allen County, PA, in Racy Teen Messaging Could Be Illegal, Talk of the Nation, NPR, Feb. 18, 2009.

355. 598 F.3d 139 (3d Cir. 2010). The class would have required the student to write an essay about what was wrong with what she did.

356. M. Gigi Durham, The Lolita Effect: The Media Sexualization of Young Girls and What We Can Do About It (2008).

357. Andrea Lenhart, Teens and Sexting (2009); Alex Morris, They Know What Boys Want, N.Y. Mag., Jan. 30, 2011; Jim Hoffman, Girl's Nude Photo and Altered Life, N.Y. Times, Mar. 27, 2011, at A1.

who forward them or pressure others to engage in the practice?[358] About 20 states have adopted laws to address juvenile sexting, with penalties such as misdemeanor charges that may be expunged, and required community service or counseling.[359] Is this good policy?

7. Nonconsensual Pornography: Revenge Porn. A practice that has attracted increasing concern is nonconsensual pornography—the distribution of sexually explicit images without the subject's consent. A subset involves revenge porn, in which a former intimate partner is responsible for the distribution. The distributor may have obtained the image with subject's consent, captured it without the subject's knowledge, or hacked it from the subject's computer. Often the distributor includes the subject's name, location and links to the subject's social media accounts, which facilitates stalking, harassment, and reputational injuries. Some research suggests that 80 percent of victims of nonconsensual pornography are female.[360] A number of online sites cater to such postings, and one, at its height, claimed over 350,000 views a day.[361]

Victims of revenge porn have a number of remedies. If they took the photo themselves, they are owners under copyright law and can demand that sites remove them or face infringement claims. Victims can also sue posters for intentional infliction of emotional distress and invasion of privacy (or disclosure of private facts). Such suits, however, are expensive and difficult to win, and defendants are often judgment proof. Thirty-four states have statutes prohibiting nonconsensual pornography, and federal legislation has also been proposed.[362] Google now honors requests to remove which fall under their criteria for revenge porn and provides a quick online form for making such requests.[363] First Amendment advocates express concern about the breadth of such legislation and believe that current remedies are adequate.[364] How would you respond to revenge porn?

---

358. See id. at 439-41 (arguing against compounding the adverse consequences for girls who naively trust an intimate partner not to share sexualized representations).

359. Eckholm, supra note 351, at A13.

360. Emily Poole, Fighting Back Against Non-Consensual Pornography, 49 U.S.F. L. Rev. 181, 192 (2015).

361. Austin McCullough, Criminalization of Revenge Porn: Protecting Victims with a Realistic Legal Avenue, Am. Crim. L. Rev. Oct. 31, 2015.

362. Id.; Lydia Wheeler, Lawmaker Eyes Revenge Porn Crackdown, The Hill, July 15, 2015; Aubrey Burris, Hell Hath No Fury Like a Woman Porned: Revenge Porn and the Need for a Federal Nonconsensual Pornography Statute, 66 Fla. L. Rev. 2325 (2014); Cyber Civil Rights Initiative, http://www.cybercivilrights.org/revenge-porn-laws.

363. Jessica Guynn, Google to Remove "Revenge Porn" from Search Results, USA Today, June 19, 2015.

364. See Sarah Jeong, Revenge Porn Is Bad: Criminalizing It Is Worse, Wired (Oct. 26, 2013).

Putting Theory Into Practice

3-19. You are a university lawyer who is contacted by the campus women students' organization that is offended by the practices of several fraternities, which show porn films and invite strippers to perform on campus at all-male parties. The students believe that these practices encourage date rape. They also protest the fraternity's practice of circulating provocative photos that members receive from their girlfriends. The fraternity officers believe that their members are entitled to exercise their First Amendment rights. How would you respond? What strategies would you propose?

3-20. You are a state legislator who has been contacted in connection with a campaign to criminalize posting a private nude photo online without obtaining the individual's consent. Should you propose legislation making such actions a misdemeanor or felony? Should you require specific intent to harm? Your state is also considering an increase of criminal penalties for possession of child pornography from a misdemeanor to a felony. Advocates of reform argue that such penalties are necessary to discourage demand. Opponents respond that felony convictions are inappropriate for first-time offenders who simply view images of sexual conduct by minors and that there is little or no link between those who view child pornography and those who sexually abuse children.[365] What is your advice?

3-21. You are the Dean of Humanities at a university that offers a student-devised course on "Male Sexuality." The course includes a field trip to a gay strip club, class discussion of photographs of the students' genitals, and a requirement that each student produce a sexually explicit work. Adverse publicity has led to demands that the university cease offering the course. How should this be handled?[366]

3-22. Danish schools have piloted curricula that use pornography to discuss gender equality, safe sex, and the meaning of consent. Educators note that the overwhelming majority of adolescents have encountered pornographic images and "[i]t's important [that] young people learn to be critical consumers."[367] Would you support such educational initiatives for high schools or colleges?

---

365. Hanna Roos, Trading the Sexual Child: Child Pornography and the Commodification of Children in Society, 23 Tex. J. Women & L. 131, 141 (2014).

366. See Cathy Young, Skin Flicks 101: What Porn Studies Profs Don't Get About Sex, 35 Reason 20 (May 2003).

367. Porn (1): A User's Manual, The Economist, Sept. 24, 2015 (quoting Christian Graugaard).

4
Difference

Formal equality assumes a basic sameness between men and women, and the obligation of law to respect that sameness. Substantive equality assumes some meaningful differences, and seeks to eliminate the disadvantages of those differences through various legal strategies. Nonsubordination theory treats sameness and difference both as artificial constructs, designed to keep women in their place.

Difference theory (also referred to as cultural feminism, relational feminism, or the ethic of care) offers still another perspective on gender and the law. Like substantive equality, difference theory underscores important differences between women and men. Unlike substantive equality, however, difference theory sees at least some of these differences not as problems to be overcome but rather as potentially valuable resources that might provide a better model for legal and social institutions than do "male" characteristics and values. Within this theory, women tend to be associated with the values of relationship, protection of the vulnerable, and context-based reasoning, while men are identified with autonomy, individualism, and risk-taking. This chapter investigates the nature of these claimed differences and their implications for law.

Feminist theorists often view difference theory with suspicion because of the risk that attributing certain traditional virtues to women will reinforce the stereotypes upon which ideologies of subordination rest. At the same time, it is generally assumed that the increasing presence of women in law schools, legal practice, elected office, juries, and the judiciary will affect how law is created, taught, practiced, and applied. This chapter explores the tension between the embrace of gender differences as a means of improving legal institutions and the rejection of gender stereotypes.

A. THE ETHIC OF CARE AND ITS LEGAL IMPLICATIONS

This section sets forth the basic case for difference theory: that women have distinctive traits and values that should be affirmatively valued in the public realm as well as the realm of private relationships and family.

Some feminist scholars who helped develop difference theory in law were influenced by Carol Gilligan's 1982 publication, In a Different Voice: Psychological Theory and Women's Development. This work challenged a widely accepted model of moral development articulated by psychologist Lawrence Kohlberg, a model that charted a progression in moral thinking through increasingly abstract levels of reasoning. Gilligan argued that this model missed the more contextualized, relationship-sensitive style of reasoning more typical of girls. In one of her most well-known studies, Gilligan compared how boys and girls responded to "Heinz's dilemma," in which Heinz's wife is dying of cancer and requires a drug that Heinz cannot afford to purchase from the local pharmacist. The children are asked whether Heinz should steal the drug. Summarizing Gilligan's findings, Carrie Menkel-Meadow explains:

> Jake, an eleven-year-old boy, sees the problem as one of "balancing rights," like a judge who must make a decision or a mathematician who must solve an algebraic equation. Life is worth more than property, therefore Heinz should steal the drug. For Amy, an eleven-year-old girl, the problem is different. Like a "bad" law student who "fights the hypo" she wants to know more facts. Have Heinz and the druggist explored other possibilities, like a loan or credit transaction? Why couldn't Heinz and the druggist simply sit down and talk it out so that the druggist would come to see the importance of Heinz's wife's life? In Gilligan's terms, Jake explores the Heinz dilemma with the "logic of justice" while Amy uses the "ethic of care." Amy scores lower on the Kohlberg scale because she sees the problem rooted in the persons involved rather than in the larger universal issues posed by the dilemma.[1]

It is important to note that Gilligan did not reject abstract reasoning; rather, she believed that the more contextualized form of reasoning (at which girls were more likely to excel) was no less valuable or advanced a way of thinking. In appropriating Gilligan's research, however, some of the feminist legal scholars have tended to be highly critical of "masculine" values and forms of reasoning, and to be strong advocates for "feminine" alternatives.

---

1. Carrie Menkel-Meadow, Portia in a Different Voice: Speculations on a Women's Lawyering Process, 1 Berkeley Women's L.J. 39, 46 (1985). For an overview of the "connection thesis" literature, see Patricia W. Hatamyar & Kevin M. Simmons, Are Women More Ethical Lawyers? An Empirical Study, 31 Fla. St. L. Rev. 785, 839-41 (2004).

Leslie Bender, A Lawyer's Primer on Feminist Theory and Tort

38 J. Legal Educ. 3, 31-36 (1988)

Negligence law could begin with Gilligan's articulation of the feminine voice's ethic of care—a premise that no one should be hurt. We could convert the present standard of "care of a reasonable person under the same or similar circumstances" to a standard of "conscious care and concern of a responsible neighbor or social acquaintance for another under the same or similar circumstances." . . .

The recognition that we are all interdependent and connected and that we are by nature social beings who must interact with one another should lead us to judge conduct as tortious when it does not evidence responsible care or concern for another's safety, welfare, or health. Tort law should begin with a premise of responsibility rather than rights, of interconnectedness rather than separation, and a priority of safety rather than profit or efficiency. The masculine voice of rights, autonomy, and abstraction has led to a standard that protects efficiency and profit; the feminine voice can design a tort system that encourages behavior that is caring about others' safety and responsive to others' needs or hurts, and that attends to human contexts and consequences. . . .

One of the most difficult areas in which questions of duty and the standard of care arise is the "no duty to rescue" case. The problem is traditionally illustrated by the drowning-stranger hypothetical and the infamous case of Yania v. Bigan [in which one businessman jumped into a trench partially filled with water and drowned, although his business competitor was also in the trench and could have saved him if he had tried].

Each year that I teach torts I watch again as a majority of my students initially find this legal "no duty" rule reprehensible. After the rationale is explained and the students become immersed in the "reasoned" analysis, and after they take a distanced, objective posture informed by liberalism's concerns for autonomy and liberty, many come to accept the legal rule that intuitively had seemed so wrong to them. They are taught to reject their emotions, instincts, and ethics, and to view accidents and tragedies abstractly, removed from their social and particularized contexts, and to apply instead rationally-derived universal principles and a vision of human nature as atomistic, self-interested, and as free from constraint as possible. They are also taught that there are legally relevant distinctions between acts and omissions.

How would this drowning-stranger hypothetical look from a new legal perspective informed by a feminist ethic based upon notions of caring, responsibility, interconnectedness, and cooperation? If we put abstract reasoning and autonomy aside momentarily, we can see what else matters. In defining duty, what matters is that someone, a human being, a part of us, is drowning and will die without some affirmative action. That seems more urgent, more imperative, more important than any possible infringement of individual autonomy by the imposition of an affirmative duty. If we think about the stranger as a human being for a moment, we may realize that much more is involved than balancing one person's interest in having his life saved and another's interest in not having affirmative duties imposed upon him in the absence of a special relationship, although even then the balance seems to me to weigh in favor of imposing a duty or standard of care that requires action. The drowning stranger is not the only person affected by the lack of care. He is not detached from everyone else. He no doubt has people who care about him—parents, spouse, children, friends, colleagues; groups he participates in—religious, social, athletic, artistic, political, educational, work-related; he may even have people who depend upon him for emotional or financial support. He is interconnected with others. If the stranger drowns, many will be harmed. It is not an isolated event with one person's interests balanced against another's. When our legal system trains us to understand the drowning-stranger story as a limited event between two people, both of whom have interests at least equally worth protecting, and when the social ramifications we credit most are the impositions on personal liberty of action, we take a human situation and translate it into a cold, dehumanized algebraic equation. We forget that we are talking about human death or grave physical harms and their reverberating consequences when we equate the consequences with such things as one person's momentary freedom not to act. People are decontextualized for the analysis, yet no one really lives an acontextual life. . . .

If instead we impose a duty of acting responsibly with the same self-conscious care for the safety of others that we would give our neighbors or people we know, we require the actor to consider the human consequences of her failure to rescue. . . .

The duty to act with care for another's safety, which under appropriate circumstances would include an affirmative duty to act to protect or prevent harm to another, would be shaped by the particular context. One's ability to aid and one's proximity to the need would be relevant considerations. Whether one met that duty would not be determined by how a reasonable person would have acted under the circumstances but by whether one acted out of a conscious care and concern for the safety, health, and well-being of the victim in the way one would act out of care for a neighbor or friend. . . . This seemingly minor change would transform the core of negligence law to a human, responsive system.

≡≡≡ ### Richard A. Posner, *Conservative Feminism*
≡≡ 1989 U. Chi. Legal F. 191, 214

[Most] people are what they are; most neighbors are not caring, and most accident victims are not neighbors. Human nature will not be altered by holding injurers liable for having failed to take the care that a caring neighbor would have taken. The only effect of adopting Bender's proposal would be to shift negligence liability in the direction of strict liability. Her "caring neighbor" is an unnecessary step in the analysis. Bender might as well argue directly for strict liability on the ground that it is the more altruistic regime than negligence.

Is it? Strict liability is sometimes defended on the ground that it provides more compensation to more accident victims. This is a partial analysis. Strict liability can also result in higher prices, and the burden may be borne by consumers. The net distributive impact is unclear. If these complications are ignored, maybe a feminine outlook on law could be expected to stress compensation—obviously Bender associates altruism with women. On the other hand, strict liability is more rule-like, less standard-like, less contextualist, less sensitive to the particulars of the individual accident, than negligence is; in that respect it is the more masculine standard.

≡≡≡≡≡ *Kingsley R. Browne, Sex and Temperament in Modern Society: A Darwinian View of the Glass Ceiling and the Gender Gap*
37 Ariz. L. Rev. 971, 984, 1016, 1065-66, 1071, 1081-82 (1995)

It is my central thesis that much of what we call the glass ceiling and gender gap is the product of basic biological sex differences in personality and temperament. These differences have resulted from differential reproductive strategies that have been adopted by the two sexes during human history and are every bit as much a product of natural selection as our bipedal locomotion and opposable thumbs. Although these temperamental traits evolved in our hunting-and-gathering ancestral environment, they remain with us today whether or not they remain adaptive. . . .

Evolutionary theory predicts that men will tend to exhibit greater status-seeking, competitiveness, and risk-taking than women, and that women will exhibit more nurturance and affiliative behavior. These predictions are borne out in every known human society. With respect to all of these traits, the differences are statistical, in the sense that they are generalizations that do not hold true for all individuals. However, even relatively small between-group differences can have a dramatic effect on the sex ratio at the extremes. Moreover, since the glass ceiling and the gender gap in compensation are themselves both group-based phenomena, it seems appropriate to seek an explanation for them in terms of group-based traits. . . .

It is a common observation—sometimes a complaint—that in order for women to attain the highest levels of success in the working world they must "be like men." Prominent among the qualities of successful female executives are the "male" traits of aggressiveness, ambition and drive, strong career orientation ("a passion for success"), and risk-taking. Women are consistently perceived to have a lesser level of these traits than men. Even apart from commitment to children, women as a class differ in important temperamental ways from men. Combined with women's greater commitment to families these temperamental differences have a powerful effect. . . .

If a substantial contributor to the "glass ceiling" is the fact that women tend not to display, to the same degree that men do, the temperamental traits and accompanying behaviors that result in achieving the highest levels, then in order for women to achieve parity, something must change: either the job requirements or women themselves. Many students of the glass ceiling have advocated both changes: employers should stop rewarding driven and ambitious people, and girls should be socialized to manifest the same drive and ambition as males. For a whole host of reasons, both of these suggestions are unlikely to bear fruit.

It seems unlikely in the extreme that employers will cease rewarding employees who exhibit a high degree of commitment to the employer. All else being equal—and in the absence of some prohibition—an employer will generally prefer a worker who puts in more hours to one who puts in fewer; it will prefer a worker who will travel or relocate to one who will not; and it will prefer a worker whose career is not interrupted by lengthy absences from the labor market to one whose is. Those employees are simply more valuable. Moreover, it is a fact of life in modern America that men work more hours, are more willing to travel and relocate, and are less likely to leave the labor force for extended periods. . . .

[T]he simplistic observation that men and women have different average earnings tells one very little, but the fact that earnings are easier to quantify and compare than other important job attributes has led to an undue focus on wage disparities. To the extent that compensation differences are due to the kinds of differences described above, it is not clear why there should be societal intervention. The studies described above suggest that if women make the same kinds of human-capital investments and occupational choices as men, their compensation will be much more similar to men's than it is now. If they choose to work fewer hours, seek less job-related training, and select jobs that have advantages that for them outweigh the lower pay, it is difficult to see why there is any need for correction. Preventing employers from giving higher pay to employees who work more hours, have greater job-related training, or occupy riskier jobs seems foolish.

Notes

1. Explaining Women's Differences. Is it meaningful to speak in terms of "women's" values or characteristics? If certain characteristics are sex-related, where did these differences come from? Philosopher Sara Ruddick locates gender differences in the social practice of mothering, in which boys develop their identities by separating from their differently gendered mothers, which reinforces for boys the values of separation and individualism, while girls develop by identifying with their mothers, to whom they remain connected, which reinforces for girls the values of relationship and communal identity.[2] How does this view compare with Robin West's?

Do women value care and connection because of their biological role in sex and reproduction, or because they have been placed in a social and political hierarchy that values, and thus sustains, these values? Consider the following:

> It truly would be extremely odd, as [Gilligan] argued, if it turned out that the vastly greater amount of child raising and homekeeping, the world over and throughout history, in which women engage—a fact apparently conceded by all—has *no impact whatsoever* on the moral orientations of the two sexes. Similarly it really would be extremely odd if it turned out that our shared experience as infants and children under the protection and tutelage and love of *women*—our shared experiences derived from the fact that we are all *to woman* born—also has *no* differentiating effect or impact on the way the two sexes view relational ethics. It would be odd if it turned out that the experiences of pregnancy and childbirth, shared by the majority of all women everywhere, have no effect, and lend to women's perspectives no unifying and distinguishing threads. The null hypothesis, if we are questioning sameness or difference, might more defensibly be identified as the claim of difference, rather than the claim of sameness, in the face of these quite different early experiences of the world.[3]

2. Mainstreaming the Ethic of Care in the Law. As both a critique of existing "male" law and a substantive reform agenda, difference theory or the "ethic of care" has been applied to virtually every area of law. For example, over 25 years ago Kathleen Lahey and Sarah Salter challenged the "patriarchal nature of the dominations upon which corporate culture depends" and urged legal reforms in corporate law that reflect "the ethics of care, responsibility, connection and sharing" and are organized around the "values of contextuality, continuity, and holistic participation."[4] Joan MacLeod Heminway argues

---

2. Sara Ruddick, Maternal Thinking: Toward a Politics of Peace (1989).

3. Robin West, Caring for Justice 18-19 (1997).

4. Kathleen A. Lahey & Sarah W. Salter, Corporate Law in Legal Theory and Legal Scholarship: From Classicism to Feminism, 23 Osgoode Hall L.J. 543, 555-56. 570 (1985); see also Kellye Y. Testy, Capitalism and Freedom—For Whom?: Feminist Legal Theory and Progressive Corporate Law, 67 Law & Contemp. Probs. 87, 99 (2004) (urging a union of progressive corporate law and feminist legal theory, which articulates "a normative vision of the relationship between life and law, one that prescribes a moral vision for social ordering, based upon the principles of equality and human flourishing"); Theresa A. Gabaldon, Assumptions About Relationships Reflected in the Federal Securities Laws, 17 Wis. Women's L.J. 215

that because women and men use different factors and processes in deciding whom to trust, greater gender diversity on corporate boards will enhance "trust diversity" and hence the independence of corporate boards.[5] Marjorie Kornhauser has defended progressive income tax rules from a "female voice" perspective that emphasized interdependence and altruism.[6] Aviva Orenstein has proposed a new "apology exception" to evidentiary rules relating to admissions by party-opponents based on feminist relational values.[7] Judith Resnik has criticized the relegation of mundane, fact-specific cases, such as prisoner petitions and Social Security cases, to Article I judges or state courts, as well as the treatment of "the complex and messy activity of interacting with litigants, witnesses, and lawyers" as "mere housekeeping." She urges "[r]etrieving—without romanticizing—the importance of 'humble' activities" that may be "repetitive and non-engaging," but nonetheless necessary to maintain the daily maintenance of a judicial system.[8]

For a while, proposals along these lines largely vanished. The notes that follow describe some possible reasons. The remainder of the chapter then explores the contemporary relevance of the difference approach.

3. The Feminist Critique of Difference Theory and an Ethic of Care. The primary criticism of difference theory is that the values that it seeks to redeem and celebrate are the same as those that have been used to justify women's subordination to men. Catharine MacKinnon argues, for example, that the theory "mak[es] it seem as though [women's] attributes, with their consequences, really are somehow ours, rather than what male supremacy has attributed to us for its own use. For women to affirm difference, when

---

(2002) (examining the role of relationships in the context of federal securities laws); Barbara Ann White, Feminist Foundations for the Law of Business: One Law and Economics Scholar's Survey and (Re)View, 10 UCLA Women's L.J. 39 (1999) (urging feminist methods of recognizing the excluded voice and the feminist ethic of care in business law).

5. See Joan MacLeod Heminway, Sex, Trust, and Corporate Boards, 18 Hastings Women's L.J. 173 (2007).

6. Marjorie Kornhauser, The Rhetoric of the Anti-Progressive Income Tax Movement: A Typical Male Reaction, 86 Mich. L. Rev. 464 (1987).

7. Aviva Orenstein, Apology Excepted: Incorporating a Feminist Analysis into Evidence Policy Where You Would Least Expect It, 28 Sw. U. L. Rev. 113 (1999); see also Kit Kinports, Evidence Engendered, 1991 U. Ill. L. Rev. 413 (criticizing evidence law for characteristics such as abstractness, formality, hierarchy, and adversarialness, which tend both to institutionalize female disadvantage in concrete cases and to reinforce values that are not congenial to many women; Rosemary C. Hunter, Gender in Evidence: Masculine Norms vs. Feminist Reforms, 19 Harv. Women's L.J. 127, 129 (1996) (criticizing rules of evidence for, among other things, privileging "fact over value, reason over emotion, presence over absence, physical over psychological, perception over intuition").

8. See Judith Resnik, Housekeeping: The Nature and Allocation of Work in Federal Trial Courts, 24 Ga. L. Rev. 909, 945, 960-61 (1990).

difference means dominance, as it does with gender, means to affirm the qualities and characteristics of powerlessness."[9] Does she have a point?

Linda McClain, after reviewing the dangers of difference theory, concludes that the voice of care is important but is better attributed to liberal humanist values than specifically "female" values. Liberalism has plenty of room for these values, she argues. Rather than forcing a "stark pick between mothering and contract, or care and justice, or connection and separation," feminists should engage in dialogue about how their insights about interdependency, connection, and responsibility can be incorporated within the liberal legal system. "[P]rinciples of justice, equality, and autonomy can coexist with and inform care and responsibility, just as care and connection, for both liberals and feminists, aid in the pursuit of justice."[10] Joan Tronto echoes this theme, arguing that "we need to stop talking about 'women's morality' and start talking instead about a care ethic that includes the values traditionally associated with women."[11]

Is this gender-neutral approach appealing? Consider Leslie Bender's objection:

> [S]ome who have been attracted by the advantages of an ethic of care have argued that it has non-gender-based sources and could be adopted as a "humanist" approach to law, that is, one that promotes the value of caring apart from any language of gender relations. Frankly, while I am sympathetic to feminists who make this argument, I believe it is politically, theoretically, and factually unsound to move women from center stage in this proposed reconstruction of legal and ethical discourse based on an ethic of care. Interpersonal caregiving is something that women have specialized in for years. We have special knowledge and insights to offer. After many, many years of being submerged, we have finally come above the surface and caught our long-awaited breath. The air tastes good. A change to "humanism," I fear, will ultimately press us under water again. While we clearly must be very cautious about perpetuating disempowering or disadvantaging stereotypes, the move from "women" to "human" seems to dupe us into an even worse co-optation of being reabsorbed, resilenced, and resubmerged into a newly invisible system of male dominance. Consequently, I reject critiques of a gender-based ethic of care that locate the ethic of care in a humanist approach.[12]

What is your view? What is gained, or lost, by a gender-neutral strategy?

9. Catharine A. MacKinnon, Feminism Unmodified: Discourses on Life and Law 38-39 (1987).

10. Linda C. McClain, "Atomistic Man" Revisited: Liberalism, Connection, and Feminist Jurisprudence, 65 S. Cal. L. Rev. 1171, 1196-1202, 1263 (1992).

11. Joan C. Tronto, Moral Boundaries: A Political Argument for an Ethic of Care 3 (1993).

12. Leslie Bender, From Gender Difference to Feminist Solidarity: Using Carol Gilligan and an Ethic of Care in Law, 15 Vt. L. Rev. 1, 40 (1990).

4. The Normative Claims of the Evolutionary Thesis. The extent to which differences between men and women, including characteristics ordinarily viewed as social, are rooted in biology has produced an extensive scientific literature—too extensive to permit a representative sampling. Without the opportunity to fully explore the research, the question for this chapter will have to be not *whether* the premises of evolutionary biology (also called "developmental biology" and "sociobiology") are true, but rather *what follows* if they are true.

To Richard Epstein, different personality types and social roles are a matter of efficiency—nature's efficiency. Efforts to change the instincts that have emerged as adaptive behaviors are simply inefficient.

[C]onsider the question of differences in spatial perception. Here, the traditional account of its origins is quite persuasive. So long as there is any division of labor between the two sexes, it must be decided who will stay with the newborn child and who will venture forth to explore, to fight, and to hunt. This is true because there are clear losses to the family unit if both parents have identical tasks. In economic terms, the potential gains from specialization and trade are too large to be ignored, especially under conditions of extreme scarcity. The mere fact that the mother carries with her a supply of milk makes it clear that she is the better candidate for staying with the child, consequently leaving the male of the species to engage in a broad class of explorative activities. The nurturing instincts usually attributable to women are a set of attitudinal adaptations that reduce the cost of doing activities that help promote the survival of both her and her offspring. Although modern women operate in settings far different from those of their ancient mothers, the initial tendency still remains: If nurturing brings greater pleasure or requires lower cost for women than for men, then we should expect to see women devote a greater percentage of their resources to it than men. This specialization will endure in the aggregate and should be accepted for what it is: a healthy adaptation that works for the benefit of all concerned, and not as a sign of inferiority or disrespect.

There are offsetting adjustments in the male, for the devotion of greater mental resources to spatial arrangements at the cost of other advantages carries with it a strong reproductive payoff. The ability to give this characteristic selectively to one sex to the exclusion of the other also carries with it a strong reproductive advantage in that it is possible to leave superior endowments in all offspring. The alternative strategy, which gives the same cognitive skills and basic attitudes to all offspring, will leave both males and females at a relative disadvantage for their biologically specialized tasks, especially since there is no gain from reversing the sex roles in parenting. The other gains from specialization are still too great to be overcome. This explanation involves the interaction of social function with biological fitness. Is there any purely social explanation that can account for these differences?[13]

---

13. Richard A. Epstein, Gender Is for Nouns, 41 DePaul L. Rev. 981, 989-90 (1992).

Kathryn Abrams challenges the factual premises of Epstein's sociobiological analysis, as well as the implications:

> Breast milk is not, nor has it in memory been, the only alternative for nourishing infants. . . . To enshrine this difference as central, at a time when we have the technological capacity to generate adequate substitutes is a bit like describing the structure of contemporary society as arising from the human inability to master air travel. . . . [Moreover,] it is not clear . . . why the initial division of labor arising from breastfeeding would necessarily reinforce [his explorative and spatial perception advantages]. Why should the male adventurer have more opportunity to develop these capacities than the female, who is constantly balancing and shifting her infants, or cannily judging the distance between her children and danger?[14]

Kingsley Browne, while he states that there are no "necessary" implications in finding a biological basis for women's difference, makes it clear that once the "glass ceiling" or the gender gap in women's earnings is explained as a product of natural selection processes, there is no longer sex discrimination for which a legal remedy is necessary. Elsewhere he states that efforts to prohibit sexual harassment are doomed, insofar as they go "against the grain" of human psychology.[15]

George Gilder takes still another tack. According to Gilder, women who abandon traditional, biology-created gender roles do so at the expense of both children who need their care and also men, whose sexual energies and aggressions will be directed either toward the long-term goal of providing for their families or toward various dangerous, anti-social pursuits.

> A man without a woman has a deep inner sense of dispensability, perhaps evolved during the millennia of service in the front lines of tribal defense. He is sexually optional. Several dominant males could impregnate all the women and perpetuate the tribe. It is this sense of dispensability that makes young men good fighters, good crusaders, good martyrs. But it also weakens the male ability to care deeply and long and stunts young men's sense of the preciousness of human beings. Because the woman has always been directly responsible for infants and almost always exclusively responsible, she is dubious about the dying and killing that have surrounded male activities.

14. Kathryn Abrams, Social Construction, Roving Biologism, and Reasonable Women: A Response to Professor Epstein, 41 DePaul L. Rev. 1021, 1024-25 (1992).

15. See Kingsley R. Browne, An Evolutionary Perspective of Sexual Harassment: Seeking Roots in Biology Rather Than Ideology, 8 J. Contemp. Legal Issues 5 (1997); see also Kingsley R. Browne, Women at War: An Evolutionary Perspective, 49 Buff. L. Rev. 51, 56 (2001) (using evolutionary psychology and the literature of sex-linked cognitive and behavioral differences to challenge the assumption that "all it will take to integrate women into combat roles is educating men out of their ideology of masculinism").

Once the man marries he can change. He has to change, for his wife will not long have him if he remains in spirit a single man. He must settle his life, and commit it to the needs of raising a family. He must exchange the moral and spiritual rhythms of the hunt for a higher, more extended mode of sexual life. He must submit, ethically and sexually, to the values of maternal morality and futurity.[16]

How do you respond?

5. Evolutionary Biology: The Critique. In response to the claims of scholars like Epstein and Browne, some feminists have observed that even if sex-based differences exist, they do not account for the full range of occupational segregation and wage differentials that exist. Deborah Weiss argues, for example, that "heritable" (i.e., genetic) differences interact with various forms of discrimination, including unconscious discrimination, irrational discrimination, and structural discrimination, in ways that are impossible to untangle. Because the effects of sex-based differences are indeterminate, anti-discrimination policies remain fully necessary, even if the goal of evenly distributing women throughout all labor markets is unjustified.[17]

More broadly, legal scholar Amy Wax argues that even if the sexually dimorphic scramble to keep one's genes alive produce gender differences, society still has a choice about what behaviors to promote. Despite human biological urges, society develops moral codes to discourage drunk driving, teen pregnancy, and sexual violence, and it likewise may undertake policies to encourage a "greater impulse for 'nurturing' or a diminished attraction to competition in the male population."[18] The significance of sociobiological findings, according to Wax, is that when desired behavior goes "against nature," it must be furthered by building a sense of moral duty and social obligation, rather than by trying to transform feelings or attitudes. Sociobiology does not mean, however, that biological differences must be embraced.

[M]an does indeed have tendencies, some stronger, more pervasive, and more "hard wired" than others. To say that, however, is not to say that the tendencies cannot be curbed or overcome by the forces of culture or morality.[19]

16. George F. Gilder, Men and Marriage 15-16 (1986). Other scholarship based on the evolutionary perspective includes Owen D. Jones & Timothy H. Goldsmith, Law and Behavioral Biology, 105 Colum. L. Rev. 405 (2005).

17. See Deborah Weiss, The Annoyingly Indeterminate Effects of Sex Differences, 19 Tex. J. Women & Law 99 (2010).

18. Amy L. Wax, Against Nature—On Robert Wright's "The Moral Animal," 63 U. Chi. L. Rev. 307, 355-56 (1996).

19. Id. at 329-30.

to work interferes with individual freedom and choice. The presence of these discourses has moved me to articulate a feminist vision of the significance of paid work to the good life, to equality, and to women. I agree that it is vitally important to create society-wide mechanisms for allocating the costs of household labor and for allowing people to realize their preferences. But, unless we pay attention to the institutional contexts through which housework is valued and individual choice realized, stubborn patterns of gender inequality will continue to reassert themselves—including the gender-based distribution of work that is at the root of women's disadvantage. In the search for social justice, separatism simply won't suffice. . . .

In my view, a robust conception of equality can be best achieved through paid work, rather than despite it. Work is a site of deep self-formation that offers rich opportunities for human flourishing (or devastation). To a large extent, it is through our work—how it is defined, distributed, characterized, and controlled—that we develop into the "men" and "women" we see ourselves and others see us as being. . . .

Paid work has the potential to become the universal platform for equal citizenship it has been imagined to be, but only if we ensure meaningful participation in the workforce by attending to the specific needs of various social groups and individuals. . . . This means that, in the future, we will have to supplement employment discrimination law with measures like job-creation programs, wage subsidies, universal child care and health care programs, enhanced employee representation, and a reduced workweek for everyone. . . .

It is vitally important to acknowledge the hidden labor that is performed in households, and to create society-wide mechanisms for allocating its costs rather than continuing to impose them on individual family members (too often, women). One method of doing so is already being implemented on a massive scale: collectivizing housework by converting it into employment. A great deal of work once performed in private households has been handed over to day-care providers, cleaning services, home health aides, landscapers, and the like. Feminists could think creatively about how to capitalize on this trend by supporting efforts to upgrade the pay, promotional prospects, and working conditions associated with work once performed by at-home spouses. Compared to marriage and intimate relationships, labor markets and workplaces are spaces in which it is easier for workers to mobilize to obtain public accountability and protection. By transforming at least some forms of household work into paid employment, we could more easily protect those who do the work from discrimination, unfair labor practices, wage and hour violations, adverse working conditions, health and safety threats, and other problems on the job. We could also make it easier for those who perform household labor to engage in collective action to improve their situation. . . .

Converting household work into paid employment not only provides jobs for many people who need them, it also frees those who provide unpaid family labor to pursue more fully for pay the work that suits them best. Countless middle- and working-class families buy time or convenience by purchasing such things as child care, cleaning services, dinners from McDonald's, lawn mowing, haircuts, car repair, and other services that should count as commercialized forms of household labor. There may, of course, be some forms of household labor that cannot or should not be commodified. There may also be some services that average- or low-income people cannot afford. But, there is no reason why a commercialization strategy must be limited to pure market forces. Some services could be subsidized for those who cannot afford them, or even made available for free to everyone (like public schooling, a now universal service that was once provided exclusively within the family setting).

Despite the fact that converting household labor into paid work collectivizes it and renders it more visible and publicly accountable, feminists in the movement to value housework tend to shun this approach. Instead, these feminists are proposing schemes to compensate women for performing household labor in private homes. . . . [Some] feminists promote state-based "welfare" strategies in which the government pays caregiver stipends that are not tied to paid employment, but are instead intended to permit women to choose full-time or near full-time homemaking and child care. . . .

Wittingly or unwittingly, advocates of these family-based approaches replicate some of the same conservative assumptions that have been used traditionally to justify women's disadvantage. Indeed, feminists in this movement tend to rely on the human capital literature to assert that it is women's disproportionate responsibility for housework and child care that accounts for our lower wages and our inferior position in the workforce. Unfortunately, many of these feminists seem unaware of (or uninformed about) the body of sociological work that casts doubt on the validity of human capital theory. Within the social sciences, the debate is between conventional economists—who pin women's plight on our family roles—and feminist sociologists (and sociologically-inclined economists)—who have produced evidence that discriminatory workplace dynamics are a more fundamental cause. The sociological literature points toward a more contextual approach that rejects static family-based conceptions of women's difference; it shows instead that socially-constructed features of the workworld help create the very gender differences (manifested in work aspirations, employment patterns, and familial divisions of labor) that human capital theory attributes to women themselves. Such an approach creates greater possibilities for change. If the sources of women's disadvantage lie not in sociobiological forces that commit women more heavily to child care and housework but instead in the political economy of paid work, we can challenge the sex bias in allegedly gender-neutral forces in labor markets and work places. We can create more empowering gender arrangements by demanding work and working conditions that will give women more economic security, more political clout, more household bargaining power, and perhaps even more personal strength with which to pursue our dreams.

[Additional portions of this article are set forth in Chapter 5.]

Dorothy Roberts, Spiritual and Menial Housework

9 Yale J.L. & Feminism 51, 55-59 (1997)

The "cult of domesticity" legitimized the confinement of women to the private sphere by defining women as suited for motherhood (and unsuited for public life) because of their moral or spiritual nature. Thus, the very idealization of women's spirituality bolstered the opposition between maternal nurturing in the home and masculine work in the cutthroat marketplace.

Household labor, however, is not all spiritual. It involves nasty, tedious physical tasks—standing over a hot stove, cleaning toilets, scrubbing stains off of floors and out of shirts, changing diapers and bedpans. The notion of a purely spiritual domesticity could only be maintained by cleansing housework of its menial parts. The ideological separation of home from market, then, dictated the separation of spiritual and menial housework. Housework's undesirable tasks had to be separated physically and ideologically from the moral aspects of family life.

This dichotomy has two important consequences. First, women may delegate housework's menial tasks to others while retaining their more valuable spiritual duties. Second, this fragmentation fosters a hierarchy among women because the menial aspects of housework are typically delegated by more privileged women to less privileged ones. At the same time, the availability of a class of menial workers, sustained by race and class subordination, makes this division of women's housework possible. Although women's participation in the market is now widely accepted, the assignment of household work to women and the distinction between spiritual and menial housework both persist. In the hit movie *The First Wives' Club*, the character played by Diane Keaton complains to her friends about the work she did for her ex-husband: "I washed his shorts, I ironed them, and I starched them." "You did?" her friends respond in amazement. "Well, I supervised," Keaton clarifies. This scene conveys the spiritual housewife's relationship to menial housework: she supervises the labor of less privileged women.

An early example of the distinction between spiritual and menial housework is embodied in the relationship between Mammy and her mistress. The image of Mammy was that of a rotund, handkerchiefed house servant who humbly nursed her master's children. Mammy was both the perfect mother and the perfect slave; whites saw her as a "passive nurturer, a mother figure who gave all without expectation of return, who not only acknowledged her inferiority to whites but who loved them." It is important to recognize, however, that Mammy did not reflect any virtue in Black motherhood. The ideology of Mammy placed no value in Black women as the mothers of their own children. Rather, whites claimed Mammy's total devotion to the master's children, without regard to the fate of Mammy's own offspring. Moreover,

Mammy, while caring for the master's children, remained under the constant supervision of her white mistress. She had no real authority over either the white children she raised or the Black children she bore. Mammy's domestic labor is the perfect illustration of menial housework; her mistress, on the other hand, performed the spiritual work in the house.

Today, the spiritual/menial split enables many professional women to go to work without disturbing the sexual division of housework or relinquishing their role as spiritual housekeepers. . . .

The modern household worker's job is defined in a way that prevents its interference with the female employer's spiritual prerogatives. Even if a child spends the entire day with her nanny while her mother is at work, the hour of "quality time" mother and child share at bedtime is considered most important. Of course, the mother expects the nanny to develop a warm and caring relationship with the child. She wants the nanny to treat the child as a special person, and not as a chore. But the mother nevertheless desires her own relationship with her child to be superior to—closer, healthier, and more influential than—the relationship the child has with the nanny. . . .

These incompatible motives parallel another dilemma that mothers face in delegating child care to a less privileged employee. In another study of private child care arrangements, Julia Wrigley discovered that parents were torn between their desire to hire a high-status substitute mother and their preference for a manageable subordinate. "They would like caregivers who share their child-rearing values and who operate independently," Wrigley explains, "but they also want inexpensive, reliable, controllable employees." Parents often resolve this dilemma by relying on their spiritual supervision of the low-status employees' menial work. For example, one employer commented that "sometimes it was better to accept 'dumb' employees who are under the parents' control rather than deal with cocky ones." In both studies, employers resolved their contradictory desires by distinguishing between their own spiritual and the employees' menial housework.

Thus, the mother's spiritual moments with her child are far more valuable than the long hours the nanny spends caring for the child. Moreover, the working mother might not be able to devote quality time to her child at all if she came home to face the chores that the nanny took care of during the day. Some working mothers also hire another woman, who has even lower status, to clean the house and run errands. By delegating work to a nanny and/or maid, affluent women can fulfill their spiritual calling as mother despite their career in the market.

What is wrong with distinguishing between the roles played by the mother and by the woman she hires to care for her children? Would we not expect to find a difference between a child's relationship with her parents and with the paid household help? My point is not that we should eradicate all distinctions among people who perform housework, but to demonstrate how the distinction made between spiritual and menial housework fosters both a gendered and racialized devaluation of this type of labor. By separating spiritual from menial housework, both the mother and the nanny continue to be undercompensated for their work in the home despite working women's supposed liberation from domestic confinement.

Notes

1. Substantive Equality vs. Difference Theory as a Basis for Legal Reform. Both substantive equality and difference theory support greater public responsibility for children and family leave policies, as well as more flexible work policies. The difference is that while substantive equality models justify supportive measures as necessary to eliminate the disadvantages women experience, and thus to equalize the sexes' legal and economic status (see Chapter 2, Section B), difference theory justifies such measures as part of a better, more nurturing world for everyone. Which approach seems more compelling? Which is more politically viable? Is there an advantage to characterizing these measures as a positive, societal ideal, rather than as an accommodation to women's "difference"?

Why does Anne-Marie Slaughter resist "balance" as the ideal? Susan Dominus writes that the term "balance" suggests some zero-sum game in which one achieves a "state of grace" between "work" at one end of the fulcrum and "life" on the other. An alternative is the term "work-life fit," which "capture[s] the way workers try to piece the disparate parts of their lives together."[24]

Martha Fineman's emphasis on "derivative dependency" leads her to focus on restructuring society's institutions to better accommodate caretaking functions.[25] Vicki Schultz's emphasis on the importance of women's work as a path to equal citizenship leads her toward reforming workplace institutions, in particular. Joan Williams has been a leader in advocating numerous concrete policies for changing the workplace, including flexible, reduced hours and leave policies that do not penalize those who take advantage of them.[26]

24. Susan Dominus, Rethinking the Work-Life Equation, N.Y. Times Mag., Feb. 25, 2016, at MM46.

25. In addition to the principal reading, see Martha Albertson Fineman, Cracking the Foundational Myths: Independence, Autonomy, and Self-Sufficiency, 8 Am. U.J. Gender Soc. Pol'y & L. 13, 18 (2000) ("[C]aretaking work creates a collective or societal debt. . . . In order to move . . . to a more just resolution for the dilemma of caretaking and dependency, . . . [t]he active state must . . . structure accommodation of the needs of caretaking into society's institutions.").

26. See Joan Williams, Reshaping the Work-Family Debate (2010); see also Sylvia Ann Hewlett & Carolyn Buck Luce, Off-Ramps and On-Ramps: Keeping Talented Women on the Road to Success, Harv. Bus. Rev. (Mar. 2005).

Do workers have a legal right to work-life balance (or "fit")? One district court, in dismissing a class-action complaint brought by mothers against Bloomberg News alleging that the company had reduced the pay of pregnant women and mothers, reduced their responsibilities, excluded them from management meetings, and subjected them to stereotypes about female caregivers, stated that the law "does not mandate 'work-life balance.' . . . In a company . . . which explicitly makes all-out dedication its expectation, making a decision that preferences family over work comes with consequences."[27] The court concludes that the plaintiffs could not show a pattern and practice of treating pregnant women and mothers differently from other workers. Does this reasoning show the need for a theory that is not tied to the concept of equality?

Research is ongoing that shows that, in some industries at least, workplace reform can help workers achieve a better work-life fit without compromising work productivity. A pilot program at Best Buy, for example, granted a group of randomly-assigned workers almost total control of their schedules, measuring productivity by results rather than on the number of hours worked. In addition, "[m]anagers were trained to be supportive of their employee's personal issues and were formally encouraged to open up about their own priorities outside work—an ill parent, or a child wanting her mom to watch her soccer games. Managers were given iPods that buzzed twice a day to remind them to think about the various ways they could support their employees as they managed their jobs and home lives."[28] The workers in this experimental group met their goals as reliably as those in the control group and were much happier. They slept better, experienced less stress, and were healthier. Even their children did better. Three years later, employees in the experimental group reported less interest in leaving the organization than those in the control group.[29] What do you take from this study?

2. Women's Disproportionate Caretaking Burdens. Sociologist Arlie Hochschild coined the term "second shift" to describe the social norm by which women who work for wages are also expected to take care of the house and the children.[30] The phenomenon has abated somewhat; when hours worked are combined with hours spent on housework and child care, the load in dual income households in 2011 was roughly equal between women and

---

27. EEOC v. Bloomberg L.P., 778 F. Supp. 2d 458, 485-86 (S.D.N.Y. 2011).
28. Dominus, supra note 24.
29. Id.
30. Arlie Russell Hochschild, The Second Shift: Working Parents and the Revolution at Home (1989).

men.[31] Still, working mothers spend about twice as much time with their children as working fathers do (13.5 hours per week compared to 18).[32]

Drawing on sociological theory, Naomi Cahn suggests that wives take responsibility for a disproportionate share of housework and child care as a way of "performing gender": Since women are expected to mother and to take care of the house, doing so gives wives both social approval and interpersonal power.[33] By contrast, men may suffer social stigma when they are full-time "househusbands."

Will these attitudes and patterns change among millennials? Maybe, but the data so far is not especially encouraging. One recent survey indicates that while millennial men aspire to be equal parents to their children, there is considerable gap between those aspirations and the child-care responsibilities that they actually assume when they have children.[34] What might be effective in changing not just behavior, but attitudes? The "Lego hipster dad" toy, just released, which pushes a small Lego stroller?[35]

The "chore gap" is not confined to married American couples. Melinda Gates focused on the unpaid labor chore gap in her 2016 philanthropy letter, noting that "[u]nless things change, girls today will spend hundreds of thousands more hours than boys doing unpaid work simply because society assumes it's their responsibility. . . . It ends up robbing them of their potential."[36] She cited data from the Organisation for Economic Co-operation and Development showing that women do more unpaid labor than men in virtually every country, even Finland.[37]

---

31. See Pew Research Center, Modern Parenthood: Roles of Moms and Dads Converge as They Balance Work and Family 4, 6 (Mar. 14, 2013), http://www.pewsocialtrends.org/2013/03/14/modern-parenthood-roles-of-moms-and-dads-converge-as-they-balance-work-and-family.

32. Id. at 6; see also Bureau of Labor Statistics, American Time Use Survey Summary (June 24, 2015), http://www.bls.gov/news.release/atus.nr0.htm (working women living in households with children under the age of 18 spend an average of one hour per day providing physical care, compared to 23 minutes for men).

33. Naomi Cahn, Gendered Identities: Women and Household Work, 44 Vill. L. Rev. 525, 532 (1999); Naomi Cahn, The Power of Caretaking, 12 Yale J.L. & Feminism 177 (2000).

34. Claire Cain Miller, Millennial Men Aren't the Dads They Thought They'd Be, N.Y. Times, July 30, 2015, at A1 (reporting that only 35 percent of employed millennial men believe in the traditional allocation of child-care roles, but most of those who believe in equal roles do not assume these roles when they become parents; of the 24 percent of millennial men who thought they would shoulder most of the child-care responsibilities, only 8 percent did so).

35. Elissa Strauss, Lego Launches Stay-at-Home Dad Figurine, Slate (Feb. 22, 2016), http://www.slate.com/blogs/xx_factor/2016/02/22/lego_launches_stay_at_home_dad_figurine.html.

36. Olga Khazan, The Scourge of the Female Chore Burden, The Atlantic (Feb. 23, 2016), http://www.theatlantic.com/business/archive/2016/02/the-scourge-of-the-female-time-crunch/470379.

37. Id.

3. Women "Opting Out." One of the explanations for why, despite an upward trend in women's labor force participation, they continue to bear a disproportionate share of housework and child-care work is that women disproportionately drop out of the work force. Although women make up approximately half of the graduates of graduate programs in law, medicine, and business, their representation in these fields is much lower.[38] The opt-out explanation gained popularity with an influential 2003 New York Times article by Lisa Belkin, who told the stories of professional women who found that they could not both raise families and pursue demanding professions.[39] This narrative was fed by research documenting a high "opt-out" rate among women, especially professional women. For example, a study by the Center for Work-Life Policy of some 3000 high-achieving American women and men (defined as those with graduate or professional degrees or high honors under-graduate degrees) showed that nearly four in ten women reported leaving the work force voluntarily at some point over their careers. The same proportion reported sometimes choosing a job with lesser compensation and fewer responsibilities than they were qualified to assume in order to accommodate family responsibilities. By contrast, only one in ten men left the work force primarily for family-related reasons.[40] Recent books have continued to highlight the difficulties women have in both raising a family and holding down a demanding job.[41]

More recent research has painted a more complex, sometimes conflicting story about women opting out of the work force when they have children.[42] One study concludes that, while the upward trend in women's labor force participation has appeared to have leveled out or even reversed course, the opting out has been disproportionately concentrated among women with degrees from elite institutions.[43] The author of the study notes that women who attend elite institutions and then drop out of the work force have not only taken up the space of someone else who might have used their degree to stay in the work force, but also have more time to invest in their children, increasing the likelihood that their children, too, will attend elite schools.[44] Is this a problem?

38. See Lisa Belkin, The Opt-Out Revolution, N.Y. Times Mag., Oct. 26, 2003 (reporting that women were only 16 percent of law firm partners and only 16 percent of corporate officers).

39. Id.

40. See Hewlett & Luce, supra note 26, at 43-45.

41. See, e.g., Anne-Marie Slaughter, Unfinished Business: Women Men Work Family (2015)

42. For citations to some of the studies, see Joni Hersch, How Opting Out Among Women with Elite Education Contributes to Social Inequality, 3 Ind. J. L & Soc. Equality 192, 192-94 (2015).

43. Id. at 195-98.

44. Id. at 195.

Would Kingsley Browne (see reading in the previous section) find women's opting-out problematic? How about Martha Fineman? Vicki Schultz? Linda Hirshman writes that when women opt out, they are "cutting their ambitions off at the knees." In her view, those who put family first have "fewer opportunities for full human flourishing" in public life. Assigning this role to women "is unjust. Women assigning it themselves is equally unjust."[45] Leslie Bennetts argues that it has become "inescapably clear that choosing economic dependency as a lifestyle is the classic feminine mistake."[46] Do you agree?

4. Child Care. Early in the second wave of feminism, a common assumption was that the state would step in to provide quality child care for families.

> When Betty Friedan wrote [The Feminine Mystique (1963)], she assumed that very soon there would be a national system of subsidized child care centers that would be as free, accessible, and high in quality as public libraries. She actually believed this. Not only did she believe this, it was not an implausible vision. After all, that is what has happened in Belgium. That's what happened in France. . . . Ninety-five percent of nursery school age children in those countries are in government-subsidized child care.[47]

Friedan's vision came nowhere close to realization. Instead, as Joan Williams notes:

> In 1971, when Congress passed a Comprehensive Child Development Act, President Nixon vetoed it under pressure from an intense lobbying campaign that decried the proposal as "a radical piece of social legislation" designed to deliver children to "communal approaches to child-rearing over and against the family-centered approach." A 1975 proposal was also defeated, decried as an effort to "[s]ovietize the family." As a result, the U.S. offers less governmental support for child care than does any other industrialized nation.[48]

Current law provides federal funds for various child-care assistance programs for disadvantaged children. The federal Child and Dependent Care Tax Credit allows a credit for a percentage of money certain taxpayers spend on

---

45. Linda Hirshman, Get to Work 23, 24-25 (2006). For the popularized version of this theme, see Sheryl Sandberg, Lean In: Women, Work, and the Will to Lead (2013).

46. Leslie Bennetts, The Feminine Mistake: Are We Giving Up Too Much? xxiii-xxiv (2007).

47. Symposium, Unbending Gender: Why Family and Work Conflict and What to Do About It, 49 Am. U. L. Rev. 901, 904 (2000) (remarks by Joan Williams).

48. Joan Williams, Toward a Reconstructive Feminism: Reconstructing the Relationship of Market Work and Family Work, 19 N. Ill. U. L. Rev. 89, 150-51 (1998). On the feminist campaign for universal child care, see Deborah Dinner, The Universal Childcare Debate: Rights Mobilization, Social Policy, and the Dynamics of Feminist Activism, 1966-74, 28 Law & Hist. Rev. 577 (2010).

child care.[49] The Personal Responsibility and Work Opportunity Reconciliation Act of 1996 offsets some of the losses to poor families under "welfare reform" through a $4 billion increase in child-care funding. This Act is discussed more broadly in Chapter 5, Section C. As a general matter, however, funding for federal programs has failed to keep up with inflation. Moreover, states vary widely in their use of federal funds and their own resources to support child-care assistance programs. As a result, children in some states are better off than before, while others are worse off.[50]

Employer-subsidized child care is another option for some families. Employers can establish a Dependent Care Assistance Plan through which their employees can put a certain percentage of their earnings up to $5000 into tax-free savings accounts.[51] Employers may also choose to provide on-site or off-site day care, or subsidize their employees' day-care costs as a part of their compensation packages. Indeed, demand is sufficiently high that businesses have sprung up specifically to address the day-care needs of the employees of their corporate clients.[52] Workers in white-collar occupations are more than twice as likely to have employer subsidies for child care as blue-collar or service workers. Employers with 100 workers or more are five times more likely to provide child-care subsidies, and more than four times more likely to have on-site and off-site child-care facilities.[53]

Most Western countries have gone considerably further than the United States in assisting families with children. Sweden, for example, not only provides paid caretaking leave, but also a basic child allowance for all families, increased allowances for families with three or more children, and additional subsidies to replace support that a non-custodial parent is unable or unwilling to pay. There are additional income supports for post-childbirth leave and for care of children with disabilities, as well as an extensive publicly financed child-care system. Single parents receive preferential treatment for housing and child care. The tax system encourages the entry of women into the work force by taxing the second earner separately, rather than at the marginal rate of the primary wage earner. France, like Sweden, has a family allowance system, one that is particularly generous to large families. France also has a nearly

---

49. 26 U.S.C. §21 (2012).

50. For a National Women's Law Center comprehensive study of child-care assistance policies, including eligibility requirements, funding trends, waiting lists, and differences among the state programs through which federal funds are distributed, see Karen Schulman & Helen Blank, Pivot Point: State Child Care Assistance Policies (2013), http://nwlc.org/wp-content/uploads/2015/08/final_nwlc_2013statechildcareassistancereport.pdf.

51. 26 U.S.C. §129 (2012). For a summary of the detailed rules, see https://www.law.cornell.edu/uscode/text/26/129.

52. See, e.g., Care.com Launches Care@Work App Offering 24/7 on-Demand Access to Family Care Benefits, https://www.law.cornell.edu/uscode/text/26/129.

53. U.S. Bureau of Labor Statistics, National Compensation Survey: Employee Benefits in Private Industry in the United States (Mar. 2005) at 26, tbl. 22.

universally available child-care and preschool education system, regardless of whether the parent or parents are in the paid work force. Are these countries to be emulated, or is the United States simply based on different principles, more appropriate to its history and values?[54]

Even the most generous policies abroad do not necessarily translate into gender equality. For example, Swedish women take most of the 16 months in parental leave to which they are entitled; fathers use only about one-fourth of that amount.[55] Paid leave programs may also do more to reveal than to reduce the gap between high- and low-wage workers. California's Paid Family Leave program (which provides 55 percent wage replacement with a capped ceiling on weekly benefits) was designed to close the socioeconomic gap in access to and use of paid family leave; yet California workers who are eligible for family leave but do not take one are disproportionately nonwhite, older, foreign-born, and less educated. Over 60 percent of respondents who could have taken a leave but didn't earn less than $35,000 annually. The main reason appears to be fear of retaliation at work for taking family leave.[56]

Moreover, income supplements for families with dependents, greater tax subsidies for child-care expenses, and mandatory paid leave tend to leave existing employment and family patterns relatively intact, with government assistance to lessen their burdens. Does an ethic of care demand more? What kinds of measures would satisfy Anne-Marie Slaughter's call for truly valuing care? The proposals that go beyond economic measures tend to emphasize a revamping of the workplace itself to make it more flexible and amendable to parents. Joan Williams has been a principal proponent of such approaches.[57] Clare Huntington looks beyond these measures to changes in family law that might strengthen family relationships, and even to changes in zoning laws that would better facilitate family life.[58] To what extent do you think the government should support families?

5. Is Caretaking a Public Good? From an equality perspective, the debate over caretaking is about the disadvantages women experience when the family is organized to give them primary responsibility for their "private" decision to have children while the "ideal worker" in the workplace is assumed

---

54. Compare Thomas B. Edsall, Why Can't America Be Sweden?, N.Y. Times (May 29, 2013), with Livin' Bernie Sanders's Danish Dream, N.Y. Times, Feb. 12, 2016.

55. Gender Equality in Sweden, https://sweden.se/society/gender-equality-in-sweden. See also Bryce Covert, Women Won't Have Equality Until Dads Stay Home, The Nation (Apr. 20, 2016).

56. See Catherine Albiston & Lindsey Trimble O'Connor, Just Leave, 39 Harv. J.L. & Gender 1, 1, 25, 29, 32 (2016).

57. Among her many books and articles on the subject, see Williams, Unbending Gender, supra note 47.

58. See Clare Huntington, Failure to Flourish: How Law Undermines Family Relationships (2014).

to be available full time, and unburdened by significant family responsibilities. But theorists such as Martha Fineman stress that caretaking is not just a private consumption decision; it is a public good, upon which society depends, and for which society bears some responsibility.[59]

A number of feminist theorists take issue with the premise that caretaking is a public good. Katherine Franke's primary concern is the further privileging of reproduction, along with its various cultural associations and a sexual division of labor that oppresses women.

> Reproduction has been so taken for granted that only women who are not parents are regarded as having made a choice—a choice that is constructed as nontraditional, nonconventional, and for some, non-natural.[60]

Franke also raises fairness issues about the public support for an activity over which the public retains so little control.

> The politics of public value, public subsidy, but private accountability with respect to raising children is revealed to be quite paradoxical under close examination. . . . [For example, a] large number of home schoolers are fundamentalist christian families who . . . "are no longer fighting against the mainstream—they're 'dropping out' and creating their own private America." Many families . . . are heeding the call of Paul Weyrich, a founder of the Christian Right, to "drop out of this culture, and find places . . . where we can live godly, righteous, and sober lives." Not coincidentally, these families, and many others like them, are also making the loudest demands for public subsidies or vouchers that will finance home-schooling as well as private, parochial school tuition for families that seek to remove their children from the public school system. It must be worth at least thinking about the carte blanche we give the privatized family to refuse to teach "our" future citizens public norms of tolerance, equality, and humanity—or worse. . . .
>
> What also strikes me as worthy of examination is the degree to which parenting is described as productive society activity while, in many regards, parenting has become as much or more about consumption than production. Sylvia Anne Hewlett, the founder of the National Parenting Association, mused in a recent op-ed piece . . . about how the public fails to recognize the financial sacrifices that mothers make to raise children. What with "therapy, summer camp, computer equipment and so on," kids are just darn expensive, she argued. The "and so on" explicitly entails Pokemon accessories, My Little Pony dolls, Barbies, fancy sneakers, and other expensive articles of consumption that are aggressively marketed to children these days. While I don't think that children of any economic class should be deprived of the toys and other items that bring

---

59. For another robust political theory calling for a "supportive state," see Maxine Eichner, The Supportive State: Families, Government, and America's Political Ideals (2010).

60. Katherine Franke, Theorizing Yes: An Essay on Feminism, Law, and Desire, 101 Colum. L. Rev. 181, 186-87 (2001).

joy into their lives, I am concerned about the bourgeois framing of an issue that gives the larger public the tab for the marketing-induced "needs" of children. And all in the name of "society-preserving work." That children want things, or their parents wish to provide them to their children, is an insufficient justification for shifting the costs of those needs to the public.[61]

Another critic, Mary Anne Case, focuses on the unfairness of shifting the burden of caretaking to those who choose not to have children.

> The difficulty I have experienced goes beyond privileging certain kinds of family over others, and more broadly extends to a privileging of family matters over an employee's other life concerns.
>
> [I]f the premise of some parents' advocates really is one of strong equality of result (i.e., that parents should, in effect, be held harmless in time and money from their decision to have children; that their decision to have children should be made as close as possible to costless), then we really are talking, if not quite about a zero-sum game, then at least about a massive redistribution from non-parents to parents, one which, on grounds, *inter alia*, of inequity to people like myself, I would strongly oppose.[62]

Aren't efforts to create family-friendly workplaces and provide subsidies for workers with children in fact a form of discrimination based on marital and parental status? If so, is this discrimination illegal?[63] Is it sound public policy?

Even if caretaking is a public good, is there a reason why it should be singled out for priority over other public goods such as health care or the environment? Is there such a thing as too much caretaking?[64]

How far should caretaking obligations extend? In his influential 2009 book, The Life You Can Save, Princeton philosopher Peter Singer argues that if relatively well-off individuals can save the lives of starving children in other nations with little harm to themselves, they have a moral obligation to do so. Do you think that feminists like Fineman and Bender would agree? Is there a logical stopping point to an ethic of care?

6. Dependent Care and the Market in Domestic Workers. As Martha Fineman observes, the primary approach to child and elder care in

61. Id. at 191-92.

62. Mary Anne Case, How High the Apple Pie? A Few Troubling Questions About Where, Why, and How the Burden of Care for Children Should Be Shifted, 76 Chi.-Kent L. Rev. 1753, 1767, 1771 (2001). For a rich historical analysis of how feminism came to "abandon" the interests of single women, see Rachel F. Moran, How Second-Wave Feminism Forgot the Single Woman, 33 Hofstra L. Rev. 223 (2004).

63. For the argument that it should be, see Trina Jones, Single and Childfree! Reassessing Parental and Marital Status Discrimination, 46 Ariz. St. L.J. 1253 (2014).

64. See Judith Warner, Perfect Madness: Motherhood in the Age of Anxiety 220 (2005) (on the "helicopter parent" phenomenon).

the United States has been to treat it as a "private" issue to be negotiated by individual women. Government involvement has largely been limited to providing mothers with resources to track down "deadbeat dads." Women who must work but cannot afford high-quality in-home assistance or day care look to their own relatives, to babysitters, or to low-cost, frequently unlicensed family day-care centers that feature frequent turnover and poorly trained workers. Those workers are 95 percent female and poorly paid.[65] And, as Dorothy Roberts argues, the convergence of gender roles, racial norms, and market forces has meant that a disproportionate part of that undervalued labor force is non-white. A sizable proportion of domestic workers are immigrants who typically do not have the protections of traditional labor and employment laws. By one count, 46 percent of domestic help were born abroad.[66]

Domestic work also lacks effective legal protections. It is explicitly excluded from coverage under the National Labor Relations Act (which guarantees the right to organize and engage in collective bargaining). It is also outside the protection of the Occupational Safety and Health Act, Title VII, and most state workers' compensation acts. Domestic workers typically have only limited eligibility for unemployment benefits. Collective action is difficult for domestic workers because they are isolated from one another, and enforcement of applicable laws and regulations is a serious problem, particularly when workers are undocumented. Many of these workers lack entitlement to overtime or health benefits, unemployment or disability benefits, or social security when they retire.

How might a true "ethic of care" restructure the market for caretaking? What mix of organizing strategies, government subsidies, tax incentives, and statutory protections would be most helpful?

Putting Theory Into Practice

4-5. How much responsibility should private employers have to support employees with families? Paid leave? Flex-time and part-time options? Child-care assistance? Benefit plans with choices that include family-related assistance? Does it depend on the employer's labor market position? What

---

65. Full-time child-care workers in private households earned, on average, $442 per week. U.S. Bureau of Labor Statistics, Highlights of Women's Earnings in 2014, Rep. 1058, at 17 (Nov. 2015). Caretakers for the elderly are also disproportionately women of color and experience low wages and often unsafe and exploitative working conditions. See Peggie R. Smith, Aging and Caring in the Home: Regulating Paid Domesticity in the 21st Century, 92 Iowa L. Rev. 1835, 1848 (2007).

66. Shirley Lin, "And Ain't I A Woman?": Feminism, Immigrant Caregivers, and New Frontiers for Equality, 39 Harv. J.L. & Gender 67, 76 (2016).

problems do you foresee in obtaining such initiatives? Are any of them unfair to workers who do not have families?

4-6. What are the implications of difference theory for laws relating to women's reproductive rights? Would the state be entitled or compelled, for example, to take greater control over the mother's risk-taking behavior during pregnancy, to express a stronger "ethic of care"?

4-7. A program at the University of Michigan, funded in part by the National Science Foundation to address the acute shortage of female scientists, provides small grants to allow female scientists to hire

> . . . an extra set of hands in the lab or a substitute teacher in the classroom so they can spend more time at home without watching their careers stall. . . . Michigan has even paid for weekend day care so that female scientists have quiet time to write grants and journal articles. . . .
>
> [At Harvard, under a similar program,] the vast majority of the grants have gone to women with children. But [one male doctor] has turned his $25,000 fellowship over to the hospital to hire doctors to cover a portion of his work week in the emergency room so that he can attend a new clinical-research training program at Harvard . . . and spend more time with his 2-year-old daughter. . . . [The doctor] says he initially felt guilty about taking a fellowship designed for women. "I'm sensitive to the idea that women have it harder than men in making their academic and family careers work, and I didn't want to be competing for an award with women who deserve it," he says. But his wife, who is pregnant with their second child, is a lawyer with the Office of the Massachusetts General. "Her career is just as demanding and high-powered as mine," says [the doctor,] so he felt he qualified for the grant.[67]

Are government grants to assist scientists manage the tough laboratory hours required of first-rate scientists a good policy? If so, does the acute underrepresentation of female scientists justify giving priority to women?

4-8. How do you plan to cope with the challenges involved in fitting together your personal and professional commitments? Do you expect to work full time throughout your career? Do you plan to have children? If so, who will take care of them? What accommodations do you think are fair to expect from your employer? From your co-workers?

---

67. Robin Wilson, Family Science, Chron. Higher Educ., July 22, 2005, at A6, A7-A-8.

C. WOMEN IN THE JUSTICE SYSTEM

Women participate in the justice system in every respect—as parties, judges, lawyers, and witnesses. Would you expect women to bring different values than men to the system, or are the generalizations discussed in this section the product of stereotyping? Are lawyers, judges, and jurors likely to bring gender biases to the courtroom, or to be subject to such biases in the workplace? If so, how should the legal system respond?

1. Women as Lawyers

a. *Women in Legal Education*

The first woman entered an American law school (Washington University in St. Louis) in 1869. Admission to the other elite law schools did not come until much later. Many schools did not enroll women until the late 1920s and 30s, and Harvard remained all-male until 1950. Not until 1972 did all accredited law schools eliminate explicit sex-based restrictions. Until the 1960s, women constituted about 3 percent of enrollment in law schools, less than 3 percent of the profession, and less than 1 percent of law professors.

The reasons for exclusion involved concerns not only about the proper role of women but also about the distraction and discomfort of men. Administrators at Harvard worried about unchaperoned interchange in the library; at Hastings about the rustling of female skirts in the classroom; and at Columbia, about the "cranks and freaks" who would adversely affect the school's culture and competitive edge.[68] Other law school and law firm leaders put the problem of prejudice in pragmatic terms. Given discrimination by clients and colleagues, and pressures from family that would keep women from establishing successful careers, it made little sense to waste a position on them. The fact of bias thus became a sufficient reason for perpetuating it. In the absence of any accountability for restrictive policies, many decisionmakers saw no reason even to give an explanation. When a woman barred from applying to Columbia Law School in 1922 asked Dean Harlan Stone (later Chief Justice of the United States Supreme Court) why the school didn't allow women, his response was "[w]e don't because we don't."[69]

Discrimination against racial, ethnic, and religious minorities was also pervasive. Throughout the nineteenth and early twentieth centuries, many

---

68. For Harvard, see Deborah L. Rhode, Perspectives on Professional Women, 40 Stan. L. Rev. 1163, 1171 (1988); for Hastings, see Barbara Babcock, Woman Lawyer: The Trials of Clara Foltz 7-8 (2011); for Columbia, see Jerold Auerbach, Unequal Justice: Lawyers and Social Change in America 295 (1976).

69. Cynthia Fuchs Epstein, Women in Law 51 (1981) (quoting Stone).

employers, law schools, and bar associations excluded Jews, Eastern European immigrants, and applicants of color.[70] Not until the mid-1960s were all members of the Association of American Law Schools able to report that they did not officially discriminate on the basis of race or ethnicity. Once admitted to the bar, minority lawyers faced continued resistance from potential employers and clients. Barriers to women of color were especially great because the few institutions that did not discriminate on the basis of race often did so on the basis of sex. Charlotte Ray, one of the first black women to graduate from law school (Howard, 1873), gained admittance by using her initials rather than her first name on application papers. After an unsuccessful struggle to obtain legal work, she returned to her earlier career of teaching in public schools. Between 1875 and 1925, no more than 25 black women were reported to be practicing law in the entire nation. By 1940, the number had only doubled.[71]

Until women began entering law schools in substantial numbers during the 1970s, a common practice was to ignore their classroom presence as much as possible except for special issues or ceremonial occasions. For example, some professors observed Ladies' Days, on which they called only on women students for selected cases or hypothetical problems involving "women's concerns." Rape and needlework were favored topics. Dean Erwin Griswold of Harvard was notorious for inviting all the women students to dinner and asking them individually to explain why they were taking the place of a man.[72] Schools had no organizations for women law students, although associations were often available for wives of law students; activities included teas, bake sales, fashion shows, and speaker series with topics such as the importance of the well-informed wife (a woman "educated but not equal").[73] During this era, formal complaint channels for matters like sexual harassment were nonexistent. When harassment happened, it had neither a label nor a remedy. Women spoke of having a "problem" with a professor, and the problem was always theirs, never his.

Discrimination in the placement process was less the exception than the rule:

> Many interviewers candidly acknowledged that their firms "did not and would not hire a woman." Some partners offered a secretarial position, provided that the woman law graduate could pass a typing test; Supreme Court Justice Sandra Day O'Connor had that experience. Others were simply apologetic. As one put

70. Auerbach, supra note 68.

71. Geraldine Segal, Blacks in the Law 1, 4, 215, 240 (1983).

72. Celebration 45: The Alumnae of Harvard Law Return to Cambridge, Harvard News Bulletin (Spring 1999), http://today.law.harvard.edu/bulletin/issue/spring-1999/# (quoting Judith Hope).

73. Barbara Aronstein Black, Something to Remember, Something to Celebrate: Women at Columbia Law School, 102 Colum. L. Rev. 1451, 1454 (2002); Ruth Bader Ginsburg, Women at the Bar: A Generation of Change, 2 Puget Sound L. Rev. 1, 6 (1978).

it to an early Stanford law student: "You are highly qualified for the position, but what do you plan to do about being a woman?" A Harvard woman applicant was told that "[u]nfortunately we hired a woman lawyer several months ago and I'm sure you can understand how we would feel about having two at the same time." Placement directors who learned of such incidents generally just passed the information along to women applicants to save them the time and frustration of fruitless interviews. It apparently did not occur to law school administrators that they might actually do something to discourage such discrimination by denying interview facilities to employers who engaged in it.[74]

Sol Linowitz, a prominent Washington practitioner, summarized men's response to these patterns:

> There were only two women in my class at Cornell Law School, and to tell the truth we felt somewhat uncomfortable when they were around. It never occurred to us to wonder whether *they* felt uncomfortable.
>
> Nobody in those days thought of bigoted exclusion from the higher levels of legal practice as an ethical problem. For those who were excluded, it would have been pretentious; for others, with few exceptions, it was the way of the world—unfair, perhaps, but manageable. After all, you couldn't ask lawyers to be partners with people with whom they did not feel "comfortable."[75]

During the late 1960s and 1970s, the climate for both white women and women of color improved substantially. The women's rights and civil rights movements encouraged more women, including racial and ethnic minorities, to apply to law schools and to challenge discriminatory practices. During the Vietnam War, a reduction in the pool of qualified male law school applicants also helped to boost women's admission. By the mid-1980s, over a third of new entrants to law school were women. The growth of affirmative action and financial aid programs also increased the representation of women of color. Similar progress occurred in most European and Anglo-American countries. Since the turn of the twenty-first century, women typically have accounted for a quarter to a third of the legal profession and close to half of new entrants to the profession.[76]

Since the time women began to enter law schools in significant numbers, some have argued that legal education systematically disadvantages women. Studies in the 1980s and 1990s often found that female students received lower grades than their male classmates, given predictions based on test scores and college performance, and that they also participated less in class, held

---

74. Deborah L. Rhode, Midcourse Corrections: Women in Legal Education, 53 J. Legal Educ. 475, 479 (2003); see also Judith Richards Hope, Pinstripes and Pearls 155-62 (2004).

75. Sol M. Linowitz with Martin Mayer, The Betrayed Profession 6 (1994).

76. See Ulrike Schultz, Introduction: Women in the World's Legal Profession: Overview and Synthesis, in Women in the World's Legal Profession xxv, xxxvii (Ulrike Schultz & Gisela Shaw eds., 2003).

fewer leadership positions, and received less mentoring.[77] Subsequent studies have shown more mixed results. Women have achieved equal representation in law review leadership and judicial clerkships, although some studies have shown a persistent gap in the most prestigious judicial clerkships and in authorship of student notes.[78] At many institutions, male students still talk more in class and receive higher grades.[79] Women law students also have had higher rates of dissatisfaction, disengagement, and self-doubt than men.[80]

Are women themselves responsible for the gender disparities that persist? In commenting on the lower class participation rates of women at Harvard

77. The findings were especially pronounced for lesbian and gay students and students of color. Some basic studies include: Linda F. Wightman, Law School Admission Council Research Report Series, Women in Legal Education: A Comparison of the Law School Performance and Law School Experience of Women and Men 25 (1996); Lani Guinier, Michael Fine & Jane Balin, Becoming Gentlemen 41 (1997); Elizabeth Mertz et al., What Difference Does Difference Make: The Challenge for Legal Education, 48 J. Legal Educ. 1 (1998); Janice L. Austin et al., Results from a Survey: Gay, Lesbian, and Bisexual Students' Attitudes About Law School, 48 J. Legal Educ. 157 (1998).

78. Women constitute 54 percent of women in leadership positions on law reviews, and 49 percent of editors-in-chief; they account for 51 percent of judicial clerkships. ABA Commission on Women in the Profession, The Unfinished Agenda (2001); see also Ms. JD, Women on Law Review: A Gender Diversity Report (2012). For women's underrepresentation in prestigious clerkships, see Dahlia Lithwick, Who Feeds the Supreme Court?, Slate (Sept. 14, 2015) (one-third of Supreme Court clerks are female); Felice Batlan et al., Not Our Mother's Law School? A Third Wave Feminist Study of Women's Experiences in Law School, 39 U. Balt. L. Forum 124, 129-30, 140 (2009); see also D.H. Kaye & Joseph L. Gastwirth, Where Have All the Women Gone? The Gender Gap in Supreme Court Clerkships, 49 Jurimetrics 411 (2009). For women's underrepresentation among note writers, see Jennifer Mullins & Nancy Leong, The Persistent Gender Disparity in Student Note Publications, 23 Yale J. Law & Feminism 385 (2011).

79. Alice Shih, Yale Law Women, Yale Law School Faculty and Students Speak Up About Gender, Ten Years Later (2012), https://issuu.com/yalelawwomen/docs/ylw_speak_up_study (finding that men were responsible for 57 percent of class participation, a rate higher than in 2002, and a perception that women may be penalized socially for participating more than average); Lauren Graber, Are We There Yet? Progress Toward Gender-Neutral Legal Education, 33 B.C. J.L. & Soc. Just. 45, 68, 75 (2013) (Boston College female law students reported significantly less class participation than their male classmates, and men were nearly three times as likely as women to assert that they had never felt a loss of confidence in the classroom); Batlan et al., supra note 78, at 129-31, 140 (reviewing studies finding lower grades and participation rates for women); The Study on Women's Experiences at Harvard Law School (2004), discussed in "Women's Experience" Raises Concerns, Harv. L. S. Record, Feb. 26, 2004, at 1 (noting that male students were 50 percent more likely to speak voluntarily at least once during a class meeting than female students, and that female students constituted a significantly smaller proportion of "frequent talkers").

80. Batlan et al., supra note 78, at 131; Elizabeth Mertz, Inside the Law School Classroom: Toward a New Legal Realist Pedagogy, 60 Vand. L. Rev. 483, 509 (2007); Adam Neufield, Costs of an Outdated Pedagogy? Study on Gender at Harvard Law School, 13 J. Gender, Social Pol'y & L. 511, 516-17, 530-39 (2005); Claire G. Schwab, A Shifting Gender Divide: The Impact of Gender on Education at Columbia Law School in the New Millennium, 36 Colum. J.L. & Soc. Probs. 229, 325 (2003).

Law School, an editorial in the student newspaper faulted women for "consciously choosing to let their male peers do most of the talking" and asserted that female students had a "duty" to speak up.[81] Another commentator, in response to feminists' arguments that the aggressive, competitive atmosphere of law school classrooms silences women, claimed that such assertions revive nineteenth-century stereotypes about women's inability to engage in the "hot strifes of the bar."[82] How would you respond?

Women law professors have made substantial progress. The Association of American Law Schools stopped collecting data on faculty diversity in 2009, but in a 12-year survey prior to that point, law schools hired women at higher rates than men for all but one of those years; their cumulative success rate was 14 percent compared with 11 percent for men. Women of color were also more successful than other applicants over the same period; their cumulative success rate is 17 percent compared with 12 percent for non-minority applicants.[83] However, women still remained substantially underrepresented in positions of greatest status, influence, and job security. Although women constituted about two-fifths of tenure track faculty, they accounted for only about 30 percent of tenured professors and 21 percent of deans. Women of color constituted 10 percent of tenure-track faculty, but only 6 percent of tenured professors and 3 percent of deans.[84] Subsequent research based on 2010-2011 data show that 36 percent of tenure and tenure-track faculty and 23 percent of deans at AALS-member schools are female.[85]

In explaining these disparities, some research suggests that unconscious discrimination, unequal family commitments, and different career priorities are all at work.[86] Women appear less willing to relocate in pursuit of the most prestigious jobs and clerkships, and less focused on obtaining deanships or publishing articles in the most elite academic journals. "If women want different career paths than men," one researcher concludes, "then we shouldn't measure their advancement along traditional lines."[87] In commenting on

---

81. The Study on Women's Experiences, supra note 79, at 1.

82. John O. McGinnis, At Law School, Unstrict Scrutiny, Wall St. J., July 27, 2005, at D10 (discussing Dan Subotnik, Toxic Diversity (2005)).

83. For a review of studies, see Dan Subotnik, Do Law Schools Mistreat Women Faculty? Or, Who's Afraid of Virginia Woolf?, 44 Akron L. Rev. 867, 872-73 (2011).

84. For statistics on deans and associate deans, see the ABA's A Current Glance at Women in the Law 2014, http://www.americanbar.org/dam/aba/marketing/women/ current_glance_statistics_july2014.authcheckdam.pdf. For statistics on tenured and tenure-track professors, see Am. Bar Ass'n, Law School Faculty and Staff by Ethnicity and Gender (2013), http://www.americanbar.org/groups/legal_education/resources/statistics.html.

85. Robert Steinbuch, Finding Female Faculty: Empirically Assessing the Current State of Women in the Legal Academy, 36 Women's Rts. L. Rep. 375, 411-12 (2015).

86. Deborah Jones Merritt, Are Women Stuck on the Academic Ladder? An Empirical Perspective, 10 UCLA Women's L.J. 241 (2000); Ann McGinley, Reproducing Gender on Law School Faculties, 2009 BYU L. Rev. 99.

87. Merritt, supra note 86, at 247.

women's overrepresentation in less prestigious fields, Dan Subotnik notes, "[i]t is said that if there is no problem there is no solution . . . . Do we want deans to ram courses down faculty throats to right gender imbalances?"[88]

What constitutes equal opportunity in the law school context? Should we assume that women's different priorities are always freely chosen or that they are the primary explanation for different levels of advancement? Consider Deborah Rhode's account of largely unconscious forms of gender bias:

[Women professors are] subject to the same double standards and double binds that women encounter in other professional settings. Their competence is subject to heightened scrutiny and they risk criticism for being too assertive or not assertive enough. Multiple studies document unconscious bias in scholarly evaluations; for example, the same resumes or publications are rated higher when they are assumed to belong to men rather than women. Given the subjectivity of academic hiring and promotion standards, such biases are extremely difficult to identify or remedy. The same is true of biases in student course evaluations. Comments like "she's too liberated for me" are still depressingly common. Even more frequent are the assessments that reflect such biases but are not candid in expressing them.

Women also assume a disproportionate share of academic "housekeeping" work that interferes with the time available for scholarly research, which is, of course, what matters most in law school reward structures. Substantial gender disparities are reported in time spent on advising students and student organizations, attending law school events, and serving on committees. At most institutions, the small number of women of color further increases their burdens. And the devaluation of such service in the academic pecking order reinforces gender inequalities.

Women's disproportionate family responsibilities also carry a cost when pitted against substantial research, teaching, and committee obligations. Although academics' work schedules generally permit more flexibility than those in other professional contexts, performance pressures and time demands can be even more unbounded. The problem is exacerbated by the overlap between women's biological and tenure clocks. About two-thirds of surveyed women law professors cite work/family conflicts as a significant problem.

Women's unequal domestic and academic service burdens also reduce the time available for the informal networking and mentoring that are often critical for career advancement. The relatively small number of senior women, particularly women of color, in many institutions and substantive specialties also leads to professional isolation and marginalization. There are still too many "good old boys" and too few "good old girls" to create level playing fields in most academic settings. . . .

The devaluation of teaching and scholarship that focuses on gender, race, ethnicity, and sexual orientation also discourages junior faculty from pursuing such interests and disadvantages those who persist. In short, too many women, particularly women who are "different" along other dimensions, still feel

---

88. Subotnik, supra note 83, at 875.

uncomfortable in the educational environment; too few have advanced to positions where they can significantly affect it.[89]

Considerable evidence suggests that all of these problems are greater for women of color, who lack the presumption of competence accorded to other academics, and who are subject to less respect, more hostile evaluations, and more exclusion from informal networks.[90] Gay and lesbian academics often encounter similar problems.[91] If these are the barriers that impede equity, do law schools have an obligation to respond? How?

b. Women in Legal Practice

By the turn of the twentieth century, various political, legal, and social forces had coalesced to secure women's rights to admission to the bar in about half the states, and by 1920, formal barriers were largely removed. But informal obstacles remained substantial. One District of Columbia judge captured widespread attitudes: "Bring on as many women lawyers as you choose, I do not believe they will be a success."[92]

Since the 1960s, the representation of women in the American legal profession has increased from about 3 to 34 percent, and since the turn of the

89. Rhode, Midcourse Corrections, supra note 74, at 482-83, 487 (2003); see also Martha Chamallas, The Shadow of Professor Kingsfield; Contemporary Dilemmas Facing Women Law Professors, 11 Wm. & Mary J. Women & L. 195, 200-02 (2005) (discussing unconscious biases and the accumulation of small disadvantages); Marjorie E. Kornhauser, Rooms of Their Own: An Empirical Study of Occupational Segregation by Gender Among Law Professors, 73 UMKC L. Rev. 293 (2004) (finding that four-fifths of law school courses have a gender identity, in that they are taught largely by members of one sex or the other, and that the courses disproportionately taught by women, such as family law, juvenile law, poverty, and legal research and writing, have less prestige than those disproportionately taught by men, such as constitutional law, corporations, federal tax, and law and economics); Marjorie E. Kornhauser, Why a Duck? Are Feminist Legal Journals an Endangered Species, and If So, Are They Worth Saving?, 12 Hastings Women's L.J. 478 (2003) (documenting the bias against publishing feminist articles by leading law journals).

90. See Presumed Incompetent: The Intersections of Race and Class for Women in Academia (Gabriella Gutierrez y Muhs et al. eds., 2012); Carmen G. Gonzalez, Women of Color in Legal Education: Challenging the Presumption of Incompetence, 61 Fed. La. 48 (2014); Meera E. Deo, The Ugly Truth About Legal Academia, Brooklyn L. Rev. 943 (2015); Robert S. Chang & Adrienne Davis, Making Up Is Hard to Do: Race/Gender/Sexual Orientation in the Law School Classroom, 33 Harv. J.L. & Gender 1 (2010).

91. Chang & Davis, supra note 90; Vanessa Lynn Ewing et al., Student Prejudice Against Gay Male and Lesbian Lecturers, 143 J. Soc. Psych. 569 (2003); Michael R. Siebecker, To Be or Not to Be? . . . Out in the Legal Academy, 22 Law & Ineq. 143 (2004).

92. Belva Lockwood, My Efforts to Become a Lawyer, in Women and the American Economy: A Documentary History 1675-1929, at 297-301 (W. Elliot Brownlee & Mary M. Brownlee eds., 1976).

twenty-first century, women have constituted almost half of entering law students. Yet female practitioners remain underrepresented at the top and over-represented at the bottom in terms of status, power, and financial reward. Women account for only 17 percent of equity law firm partners, and 21 percent of Fortune 500 company general counsels.[93] Women are also underrepresented in leadership positions such as firm chairs and members of management and compensation committees. Only 12 of the nation's hundred largest firms have a woman as a chair or managing partner.[94]

The gap widens for women of color, who account for less than 3 percent of law firm partners and 5 percent of general counsel.[95] Eighty-five percent of minority female attorneys will leave large firms within seven years of starting.[96] Minority representation in the bar lags behind that in most other professions, as well as in the labor force generally. According to the most recent available data, minorities constituted about 25 percent of the civilian labor force, 25 percent of physicians, 23 percent of computer scientists, 20 percent of accountants, and 18 percent of academics, compared to 10 percent of lawyers. Women account for a higher percentage of minority lawyers than of white lawyers (44 percent compared to 30 percent).[97]

A substantial gender pay gap also persists. Overall, female attorneys earned 83 percent of what male attorneys earned.[98] In private practice, the gap for women equity partners is 20 percent.[99] Gaps persist even for female partners who are equally productive as their male colleagues in generating revenue for their firms.[100] None of the law firms responding to the National Association of Women Lawyers' 2015 survey had a woman as its highest

93. ABA Commission on Women in the Profession, A Current Glance at Women in the Law 2014 (2014); ABA Women of the Section of Litigation, Nov. 6, 2014.

94. Id.; Jake Simpson, Only 12 BigLaw Firms Have Women Running the Show, Law 360, Apr. 21, 2015.

95. For law firms, see Liane Jackson, Invisible Then Gone, ABA J., Mar., 2016, at 37. For general counsel, see Minority Corporate Counsel Association, Sustaining Pathways to Diversity: A Comprehensive Examination of Diversity Demographics, Initiatives, and Policies in Corporate Legal Departments (2011).

96. Jackson, supra note 95, at 37.

97. Elizabeth Chambliss, Miles to Go: Progress of Minorities in the Legal Profession (Commission on Racial and Ethnic Diversity in the Legal Profession 2005).

98. Bureau of Labor Statistics Reports, Women in the Labor Force: A Databook 66 (Table 18) (Dec. 2015), http://www.bls.gov/opub/reports/cps/women-in-the-labor-force-a-databook-2015.pdf.

99. Nat'l Ass'n of Women Lawyers, Report of the Ninth Annual National Survey on Retention and Promotion of Women in Law Firms (2015); see also Dau-Schmidt et al., Men and Women of the Bar: An Empirical Study of the Impact of Gender on Legal Careers, 16 Mich. J. of Gender & L. 49 (2009) (finding that 15 years after law school, women on average earn approximately $100,000 less than men; women who have done childcare show the most negative impact on income, although they enjoy higher career satisfaction).

100. Id.; see also Theresa M. Beiner, Some Thoughts on the State of Women Lawyers and Why Title VII Has Not Worked for Them, 44 Ind. L. Rev. 685, 688 (2011).

earner.[101] Female equity partners worked longer hours than their male colleagues for less reward.[102]

One main challenge in achieving gender equity in the legal profession involves retention and promotion. The problem is not simply that women have not been in the pipeline long enough to achieve substantial representation at the highest levels. In studies comparing women's and men's likelihood of making partner, "the rate for men ranges from two to five times greater than for women. Even women who never take time out of the labor force and who work long hours have a lower chance of partnership than similarly situated men."[103] The disparities are most pronounced at the highest levels. Underrepresentation is greatest for women of color. Minority women account for just 2.5 percent of law firm partners and minority men account for twice as many partners as minority women.[104] Eighty-five percent of women of color leave within seven years of starting with a firm.[105]

Men and women are now similarly distributed in most legal settings, although women are disproportionately underrepresented in business (which accounts for 12.3 percent of female lawyers and 14.6 percent of male lawyers) and overrepresented in public interest positions (which account for 7.8 percent of female lawyers and 4.2 percent of male lawyers). In private practice, the ratio of female to male lawyers is 51 percent to 55.4 percent. In government, men and women are evenly represented (both around 13 percent).[106]

American Bar Association Commission on Women in the Profession, Fair Measure: Toward Effective Attorney Evaluations
17-23 (2d ed. 2008)

B. Specific Types of Gender Bias . . .

(i) The maternal wall: how stereotypes link motherhood and part-time work with lack of competence and commitment . . .

Negative competence assumptions. A 2004 study found that adding the words "has a two-year-old child" to a woman's resume led evaluators to rate a woman as less capable and skillful and to decrease their interest in

---

101. Nat'l Ass'n of Women Lawyers, supra note 99.
102. Id.
103. Rhode, The Trouble with Lawyers 61 (2015).
104. Liane Jackson, Minority Women Are Disappearing from Big Law—and Here's Why, ABA Journal, Mar. 1, 2016; Jessica Faye Carter, Leave None Behind, Nat'l L.J., Dec. 8, 2008, at 23.
105. Jackson, supra note 104.
106. Catalyst, Women in Law in the U.S. at 5 (July 2012).

training and promoting her. Mothers were held to higher performance and time commitment standards than nonmothers, although fathers were held to lower performance and time commitment standards than nonfathers. A 2007 study found that mothers were 79% less likely to be hired, 100% less likely to be promoted, offered an average of $11,000 less in salary, and held to higher punctuality and performance standards. Mothers were seen as less suitable for hire, promotion, and management training, and deserving of lower salaries. It is often noted that "when men need time off to handle family matters, people think it reflects well on them. When women need time off to handle family matters, it is seen as a lack of commitment or a weakness." Women's absence (but not men's) often is attributed to lack of commitment. This is an example of *attribution bias*: note how the stereotype that women, but not men, lack commitment drives different interpretations of men's and women's behavior.

The pregnancy plummet.   Job evaluations of managers "plummeted," according to one study, when they became pregnant. Pregnant women, the study found, tend to be viewed as "overly emotional, often irrational . . . and less committed to their jobs. They were not seen as valued or dependable employees." . . .

The good mother v. the norm of work devotion.   While "the good father" and "the good mother" share many attributes, one important difference emerges: the good mother (but not the good father) is "always available to her children." The implicit stereotype of "the good mother" is a married mother who "will do anything for [her] children (e.g., children come first, always on call, wants the best for her kids)." This ideal clashes with the ideal of a lawyer who is always available for clients. The notion that a lawyer with a "good work ethic" is always on call reflects "the norm of work devotion," which requires that professionals "manifest singular 'devotion to work,' unencumbered with family responsibilities." When "[t]ime becomes a proxy for dedication and excellence," lawyers who need to place limits on their availability for work tend to be judged as lacking in both commitment and competence. . . .

"Killing moms with kindness."   Benevolent prescriptive stereotyping, in a kinder and gentler tone of voice, enforces employers' sense of how mothers should behave. An example: A husband and wife worked for the same law firm. After they had a baby, the mother was sent home promptly at 5:30, on the assumption that she had a baby to care for. The father was kept later than ever, on the assumption that he had a family to support. Note how the employer, in effect, is pressuring the family into traditional gender roles. For a lawyer, such well-intended actions could lead to exclusion from challenging assignments or beneficial client contacts, and ultimately to denial of partnership. This is stereotyping, despite the good intentions: the better approach is simply to ask each parent what he or she wants.

"Role incongruity." Role incongruity sends the message that one cannot be a good mother and hold a certain job. For example, in one Fourth Circuit case, a supervisor told a lawyer that she needed to decide if she wanted to be "a successful mommy or a successful lawyer." In a Massachusetts case, an investigation revealed that a managing partner said that a woman with children was not a suitable candidate for a full-time position because her priorities lay "elsewhere."

Giving the benefit of the doubt to others, but not mothers. "The rule appears to be, when judgments are uncertain, give an in-group member the benefit of the doubt." Merit reviews have been found to be particularly vulnerable to stereotyping of this kind, called *leniency bias.* An example from an in-house lawyer who is a mother: "[B]efore I went part-time, people sort of gave me the benefit of the doubt. They assumed that I was giving them as fast a turnaround as was humanly possible. After I went part-time, this stopped, and they assumed that I wasn't doing things fast enough because of my part-time schedule." The vast majority of attorneys working flexible work schedules are women, and they do so for childcare reasons. The combination of being a woman and working a flexible schedule makes motherhood salient, which may well trigger leniency bias.

Mothers are assumed to be uncommitted. As noted above, part-time work can trigger maternal wall bias by making gender salient. The mother quoted in the previous section continued, "[B]efore I went part-time, when people called and found I was not at my desk, they assumed that I was elsewhere at a business meeting. But after I went part-time, the tendency was to assume that I was not there because of my part-time schedule—even if I was out at a meeting." This again is *attribution bias*: note how the lawyer's absence was attributed to a work reason while she was full time, but to a family reason once her part-time status triggered the schema of the "good mother" who is always available to her children. . . .

Double jeopardy. Studies that inquire whether women of color encounter different kinds of maternal wall stereotypes are few and far between. One found that African-American mothers are even less likely to be promoted than white mothers. Another reported that white women are sometimes offered flexible work arrangements that are not offered to women of color.

(ii) Double standards: why women have to work harder to prove competence . . .
The common saying "women must try twice as hard to achieve half as much" is documented by more than a quarter century of social science.

Women are judged as less competent than men in traditionally masculine domains such as the law.

Studies document that women need to provide more evidence of job-related skills (relative to white men) before evaluators feel confident of their competence and that this has an effect on performance evaluations. Not only do women have to work harder to establish competence; they also can make fewer mistakes than men before they are judged incompetent.

The following are basic patterns of descriptive stereotyping that can make it harder for women to establish competence, driven by unspoken stereotypes that associate competence with men.

He's skilled, she's lucky. Men's successful performance of masculine tasks tends to be attributed to stable personality traits (he has the right stuff) while women's successes tend to be attributed to transitory situational factors (she lucked out or drew a receptive judge).

He's busy, she has trouble with deadlines. Conversely, men's failures tend to be attributed to situational factors (he's busy working on other matters), while women's tend to be attributed to stable personality traits (she has trouble with deadlines).

Are men given larger rewards for the same accomplishments? When men's successes are attributed to personality traits while women's are attributed to transitory factors, men will be seen as deserving of larger rewards than women for the same accomplishment. . . .

Do women need to prove their competence over and over again? Stereotypes are resistant to disconfirming information. Thus women may have to prove their competence over and over while men do not, because men's good performance is consistent with their assumed competence, whereas women's good performance is inconsistent with the stereotype of them as less competent at masculine tasks and in predominantly male work environments. . . .

Are women's mistakes remembered long after men's are forgotten? Similarly, stereotype-consistent information is recalled better than stereotype-inconsistent information, so that women's mistakes (confirming their lack of competence) are remembered long after men's are forgotten.

Are men judged on their potential and women strictly on their achievements? The tendency to judge men on their potential but women strictly on their achievements again reflects the automatic assumption (until proven otherwise) that men are competent. . . .

Presto change-o. In one study, subjects preferred an educated candidate over an experienced one when the male candidate had outstanding educational credentials. But this "education advantage" disappeared when the female candidate was better educated. Then many respondents stressed experience over education—and still favored the male over the female. In the evaluation context, criteria may be given different weight depending on the gender of the person being evaluated.

Double jeopardy. A 2006 study found that women lawyers of color reported being perceived less favorably than their counterparts in almost every one of the 14 categories covered in a survey. . . . Extensive literature documents the negative competence assumptions triggered by race for African-Americans. One study found that a favorable letter of recommendation for a black candidate was interpreted by third parties as indicating a less objectively good performance than a similar recommendation for a white candidate because of competence assumptions. Another study found that white women were seen as significantly more competent and more intelligent than black women. A third found that, when subjects were given identical resumes—one with a white-sounding name and the other with an African-American sounding name—African-Americans had to have eight years more experience than whites in order to receive the same number of callbacks. . . .

The evidence on Asian-American women is both scarcer and more mixed. On the one hand, Asians are seen as "too competent, too ambitious, too hardworking," which might be expected to mitigate the stereotypes of women (and racial minorities) as less competent. On the other hand, one stereotype of Asian-American women is that they are deferential and passive, a characterization that might be expected to trigger negative competence assumptions.

(iii) Double-binds and "deference-challenged" women: when the job requires a "go-getter" but assertive women are disliked . . .

Whereas descriptive stereotyping impacts assessments of competence, "deference-challenged" women often encounter prescriptive stereotyping that faults them for their failure to conform to feminine norms of selflessness and sensitivity to the comfort of others. (These are the interpersonal skills that are felt to be lacking.) . . .

Moreover, many behaviors considered inappropriate for women are precisely those deemed necessary in order to be seen as competent in a traditionally male job, thereby creating a double bind. If women behave in traditionally feminine ways, their competence is undervalued, whereas if they behave in traditionally masculine ways, their interpersonal skills are derogated and their mental health questioned. "Because advancement in organizations depends not only on competence but also on social acceptance and approval," negative reactions to women who seek to achieve in "areas that traditionally are off-limits to them can be lethal when they strive to get ahead."

What a witch. Some women are unpleasant; others lack inter-personal skills. That said, studies show that behavior that would be accepted in men often is considered unacceptable in women. When a woman in a traditionally masculine job is called a "witch" or "too ambitious" in situations where a man would be characterized as "hard-driving," "having a temper," or "not suffering fools lightly," the unspoken prescription that women should be "helpful, warm, understanding, and kind" is at work. Decades of studies document that behavior that is praised and applauded in men often is regarded as unattractive in women, and that women who do not display feminine characteristics often are judged less psychologically healthy and evaluated less favorably than those who do. Women who violate the mandates of femininity are often viewed as "aggressive, selfish, greedy and cold." In some workplaces, women are seen either as "likable, dependent . . . traditional women" who are nice but not competent or as "dominant, competent, nontraditional women" (e.g., career women, feminists) who are competent, but are disliked for violating unspoken norms that women should be inclusive and nurturing. This pattern is called *ambivalent sexism.*

He's incisive; she's abrasive. Ambivalent sexism also lies behind the finding that the "same critical remark was found to be abrasive coming from a woman, but incisive and direct coming from a man."

She's a shameless self-promoter; he knows his own worth. Hiding one's light under a bushel is not a promising strategy for success. Not surprisingly, self-promotion enhances performance ratings and thus impacts evaluations. Yet self-promotion in women is often viewed with distaste. One study found, in the context of a masculine job, that women who "spoke in a direct, self-confident manner, highlighted past accomplishments," and attributed successes to skill rather than luck were viewed less positively than women who were more modest about skills and accomplishments and 209 included disclaimers ("I'm no expert") and hedges ("Don't you think?"). Another found that women had "to show that they were not seeking status at the expense of other group members." Self-promotion in women flouts the norm that "women cooperate, men compete," and that women are selfless and supportive of others.

Notes

1. Women Lawyers: Seeking a Different Professional Life? Should it be of concern that women do not occupy the same status as men in private practice, and that they are grossly underrepresented in large firms? Consider Carrie Menkel-Meadow's observation:

Achievement of high-status and lucrative positions in large law firms represents the liberal feminist achievement of the American Dream. But is it a dream or a nightmare? Monetary and prestige measures of success, drawn from conventional male-constructed sociology, all too often are taken as the measure of women's progress in the profession, even where there is some evidence women themselves look to other measures, like doing socially useful work or having meaningful relationships at work with clients and co-workers. Both cultural and more radical feminist critiques remind us that becoming surrogate males is not the feminist-humanist transformative vision. Committing many hours to routinized tasks, within a highly stratified hierarchy, on cases and transactions with debatable social utility, while leaving one's children in the care of low-income women is hardly the feminist vision of a more humane world. . . . Women want to be in the workforce but may want to reconstruct what it means to be a productive worker.[107]

Does this suggest a different "women's" vision of a professional life? Discrimination? Or both? Some evidence suggests that women and men have somewhat different motivations for choosing law as a career. Men are more interested in high incomes, women in serving others.[108] Studies of career change reflect similar gender differences. For example, in one in-depth Colorado bar study, virtually all men moved up in status over the course of the 12 years surveyed. That was true of only about half of women. Male lawyers' primary explanation for leaving their last job was new opportunities in law (46 percent); the second most common reason was unhappiness with compensation (23 percent). Women were slightly more likely to cite dissatisfaction with compensation (26 percent), and far less likely to cite new opportunities in law (27 percent). Women also gave reasons that almost no men report: lifestyle concerns (10 percent), unhappiness with legal practice (6 percent), and opportunities outside of law (4 percent).[109]

Satisfaction rates also reveal a substantial gender gap. Although female lawyers report about the same overall career satisfaction as their male colleagues, women also experience greater dissatisfaction with most dimensions of practice: salary, level of responsibility, recognition for work, content of work, chances for advancement, and control over their work lives. In an ABA survey of large firm lawyers, white men graded their career satisfaction A; white women and minority men graded theirs B, and minority women

107. Carrie Menkel-Meadow, Exploring a Research Agenda of the Feminization of the Legal Profession: Theories of Gender and Social Change, 14 L. & Soc. Inquiry 289, 307-08 (1989).

108. Lauren A. Graber, Are We There Yet? Progress Toward Gender-Neutral Legal Education, 33 B.C. J.L. & Soc. Just. 45, 62 (2013).

109. Nancy Reichman & Joyce S. Sterling, Gender Penalties Revisited 14-15, 25 (Colo. Bar Ass'n 2004).

hovered between B minus and C plus.[110] Women of color are the least satisfied of all lawyers with almost all aspects of their workplaces.[111]

In attempting to account for this "paradox of success," theorists suggest two explanations. One involves values. Women may ascribe less significance to aspects of their work environment on which they are disadvantaged, such as compensation and promotion, than to other factors such as intellectual challenge, which evokes greater satisfaction among female than male attorneys. A second theory is that women have a lower sense of entitlement, in part because their reference group is other women or because they "have made peace with second best."[112]

What implications do you draw from these differences? Is Kingsley Browne right that there is no glass ceiling, only different career paths? Or is Deborah Rhode right that "female lawyers' dissatisfaction with certain aspects of practice, which is reflected in disproportionate rates of attrition, should be cause for concern in a profession committed to diversity and equity"?[113] Do women want something different from a career in law than men do?

2. Structural Bias and Unconscious Bias.   More significant than conscious bias against women in legal practice are structural barriers and unconscious attitudes and assumptions. Two central problems are the excessive hours in many practice settings, and the inadequacy of part-time options, parental leave, and flexible schedule arrangements. Although the vast majority of legal employers provide paid maternity leave, the duration is often insufficient and only about 10 to 15 percent of surveyed employers provide the same opportunities for men. Additionally, while over 90 percent of law firms report offering part-time policies, only about 6 percent of lawyers actually use them.[114] Women who take advantage of part-time policies often report "schedule creep" and second-class status in work assignments and advancement possibilities; their reduced hours aren't respected, and they fall off the partnership track. Few law firms have followed the lead of major corporations

110. Nancy Levit & Douglas O. Linder, The Happy Lawyer: Making a Good Life in the Law 14 (2010).

111. For client development opportunities and work assignments, see ABA Commission on Women in the Profession, Visible Invisibility: Women of Color in Law Firms, 19, 21 (2006). For satisfaction, see Theresa M. Beiner, Not All Lawyers Are Equal: Difficulties That Plague Women and Women of Color, 58 Syracuse L. Rev. 317, 329 (2008); Ronit Dinovitzer et al., After the JD: First Results of a National Study of Legal Careers 3, 58, 64-65 (2004).

112. Rhode, The Trouble with Lawyers, supra note 103, at 62.

113. Id.

114. Nat'l Ass'n for Law Placement, Most Lawyers Working Part Time Are Women—Overall Number of Lawyers Working Part-time Remains Small, Dec. 17, 2009, http://www.nalp.org/parttimesched2009; see also Deborah L. Rhode & Lucy Buford Ricca, Diversity in the Legal Profession: Perspectives from Managing Partners and General Counsel, 83 Fordham L. Rev. 2484, 2499-2501 (2015).

and accounting firms in providing help to employees in securing affordable, quality child care and elder care, particularly for emergencies, weekends, and evenings. Such failures carry significant costs in recruitment, retention, absenteeism, and job-related stress.[115]

Another commonly cited obstacle involves the exclusion of women, particularly women of color, from challenging work assignments and informal networks of support, mentoring, and business development. ABA research found that

- Fifty-five percent of white women and 43 percent of women of color in law firms, compared with 3 percent of white men and 24 percent of men of color, reported limited access to client development opportunities.
- Thirty-nine percent of white women and 44 percent of women of color in law firms, compared with 2 percent of white men and 25 percent of men of color, reported being passed over for desirable assignments.[116]

More mixed findings emerged from a study by the Minority Corporate Counsel Association. There, the vast majority of minority lawyers and female associates in large firms believed that their firm's leadership of their firm was committed to diversity (81 percent and 79 percent, respectively). Still higher numbers of whites (90 percent) and male partners (94 percent) had similar assessments. Only 13 to 14 percent of minority partners and female associates reported experiencing discrimination. Yet many also reported substantially less satisfaction than their white male counterparts concerning assignments, mentoring, and business development.[117] As one woman of color noted, "There are subtle forms of 'discrimination' that are difficult to truly pinpoint or detail. . . . [H]ow is one to know whether missed opportunities are a result of a racial or gender bias . . . ? However, it is very apparent that being of the same race, ethnicity or gender as a powerful partner" can be an advantage when it makes the partner "fee[l] comfortable with the associate."[118] Some minority female lawyers also reported feeling like "tokens" when they were included on teams just to make the firm's "numbers" look good for corporate clients.[119]

By contrast, some white male lawyers objected to efforts at "'diversity' and 'inclusion' [as] pernicious forms of racial . . . discrimination." In their

---

115. For recommendations and examples of model workplace policies, see Cynthia Calvert et al., Project for Attorney Retention, Reduced Hours, Full Success: Part-Time Partners in U.S. Law Firms (2009).

116. See ABA Commission on Women in the Profession, Visible Invisibility, supra note 111, at 19, 21.

117. MCCA, Sustaining Pathways to Diversity, supra note 95, at 13, 23-30.

118. Id. at 20.

119. Id. at 14.

view, "reverse discrimination" fostered a "victim mentality and an expectation that success does not need to be earned."[120] How would you respond?

Strategies for addressing these obstacles fall into two categories. One is to assist women, particularly women of color, to compete on a playing field that is not yet equal. These strategies include formal mentoring programs and women's initiatives that provide opportunities for support, guidance, and business development. Many bar associations and women's organizations are also active in providing research, educational materials, training, and programs. So, for example, a study by Catalyst, an organization for advancing professional women, catalogs "unwritten rules" that are critical in career development. The most important rules cited by survey participants were to

- network and build relationships within and outside the organization (71 percent);
- find ways to become visible (51 percent);
- communicate effectively and ask for frequent feedback (43 percent);
- perform well and produce results (35 percent);
- find a mentor, coach, or sponsor (32 percent);
- work long hours (29 percent); and
- develop a good career plan (20 percent).[121]

A second set of strategies aims at reforming institutional structures to create fairer evaluation, assignment, and reward systems, as well as more effective work/family policies. A report by the National Association of Women Lawyers identified the following strategies for breaking down gender barriers:

- Ensure a broadened selection of leaders by diversifying the nominating process; publicizing explicit selection criteria; and holding partners accountable for achieving diversity;
- Correct for hidden biases by tracking retention, increasing the objectivity of evaluation processes, and ensuring diverse representation in high-profile teams and leadership positions;
- Promote meaningful mentoring through strategies such as training and reward systems;
- Promote workplace flexibility by offering customized schedules to all lawyers, employing a balanced-life coordinator; and monitoring the usage and impact of reduced hour schedules on retention and promotion.[122]

---

120. Id. at 25.

121. Laura Sabattini, Unwritten Rules: What You Don't Know Can Hurt Your Career 5 (Catalyst 2008).

122. Nat'l Ass'n of Women Lawyers, Actions for Advancing Women into Law Firm Leadership (2008).

The Minority Corporate Counsel Association's report echoes many of these recommendations and also proposes that law firms implement "360-degree feedback loops" to provide bottom-up evaluations and gather information from all lawyers concerning their experiences and opportunities.[123]

Other commentators have recommended that legal employers centralize responsibility for diversity initiatives, obtain buy-in from leaders, engage in meaningful self-assessment, and ensure accountability for developing and monitoring those initiatives.[124] Further proposals are that bar associations support "no glass ceiling" campaigns in which participating law firms adopt goals and timetables for women in leadership; that clients direct business only to firms with demonstrable commitments to diversity; and that students pressure employers to improve their diversity and family-friendly policies.[125] How would you evaluate these strategies? What others would you add? What stands in their way?

3. Women in the Legal Profession: A Different Voice? Matthew Hale Carpenter, in unsuccessfully defending the right of Myra Bradwell to become a member of the Illinois Bar, argued that while some cases may require the "rough qualities possessed by men, . . . [t]here are many causes in which the silver voice of a woman would accomplish more than the severity and sternness of man could achieve."[126] Whether or not you agree with this statement, do you think women bring special qualities to legal practice?

Many commentators have argued that women lawyers practice in a "different voice," more sensitive to values of care, compassion, and cooperation than prevailing legal norms.[127] Such differences are assumed to account for sex-linked differences in choice of specialties, such as women's disproportionate representation among family lawyers, family court judges, and teachers of family law. Yet social science research does not confirm the sharp gender-linked variations in male and female lawyering that many practitioners and commentators assume.[128]

---

123. MCCA, Sustaining Pathways, supra note 95, at 38-39.

124. Rhode, The Trouble with Lawyers, supra note at 103; Beiner, supra note 111, at 697.

125. Judith S. Kaye & Ann C. Reddy, The Progress of Women Lawyers at Big Firms: Steadied or Simply Studied?, 76 Fordham L. Rev. 1941, 1969-70 (2008).

126. Bradwell v. Illinois, 83 U.S. 130, 137 (1872).

127. See, e.g., Susan P. Sturm, From Gladiators to Problem-Solvers: Connecting Conversations About Women, the Academy, and the Legal Profession, 4 Duke J. Gender L. & Pol'y 119 (1997).

128. William Felstiner et al., The Effect of Lawyers' Gender on Client Perceptions of Lawyers, in Women in the World's Legal Profession, supra note 76, at 23, 26 (finding that both sexes are seen as friendly, polite, organized, confident, and trustworthy); Lynn Mather, Gender in Context: Women in Family Law, in Women in the World's Legal Professions, supra note 76, at 39-40 (both male and female lawyers prefer amicable settlements).

One context in which gender differences have been extensively researched involves negotiating behavior. Over the past two decades, a large body of theoretical and empirical research has attempted to determine whether men and women have different negotiating styles and effectiveness. One finding is that gender appears to be mediated by other aspects of the negotiating context that vary across research settings. These other aspects include the relative social status, perceived power, and attitudes toward conflict of the participants.[129] It also matters whether negotiators are the same sex, whether they have negotiating experience or ongoing relationships, and whether they are acting for themselves or as representatives for someone else. However, a recent meta-analysis of studies suggests that overall, men achieve better outcomes.[130] Common findings are that women are less likely than men to initiate negotiations and ask for what they need, that women set lower goals, and that they feel less confident than men even when there are no objective differences in outcome.[131] In the context of compensation, where research consistently finds gender differences, women tend to have lower expectations than men, feel less entitled to higher salaries, and place less value on pay than on other aspects of their jobs. The result is that women demand and accept less in negotiations, and are less confident and satisfied with their negotiation performance.[132] One reason for the gender disparity is that stereotypes make assertive behavior more costly for women than men: women who act assertively are deemed less likable and are less likely to be hired and viewed as good colleagues than men.[133]

How should women respond to these findings? Some researchers advise women to be "relentlessly pleasant" and to stress benefits for others, including

---

129. For the importance of status, see Emily T. Amanatullah & Catherine H. Tinsely, Ask and Ye Shall Receive? How Gender and Status Moderate Negotiation Success, 6 Negot. & Conflict Mgmt. Res. 253 (2013).

130. Jens Mazei et al., A Meta-Analysis on Gender Differences in Negotiation Outcomes and Their Moderators, 141 Psychol. Bull. 85 (2015). For factors that moderate this finding, see Jessica A. Kennedy & Laura J. Kray, A Pawn in Someone Else's Game? The Cognitive, Motivational, and Paradigmatic Barriers to Women's Excelling in Negotiation, 35 Res. Org. Behav. 3, 6 (2015).

131. For reviews of multiple studies, see Deborah M. Kolb, Negotiating in the Shadow of Organizations: Gender Negotiation, and Change, 28 Ohio St. J. Dispute Res. 241, 243 (2013). When there is no explicit statement that wages are negotiable, men are likely to negotiate for a higher wage and women more likely to signal their willingness to work for a lower wage. Andrew Leibbrandt & John A. List, Do Women Avoid Salary Negotiations? Evidence from a Large-Scale Natural Field Experiment, 61 Mgmt. Sci. 2016 (2015).

132. Kolb, supra note 131, at 243-44; Kennedy & Kray, supra note 130, at 7.

133. Emily T. Amanatullah & Catherine H. Tinsely, Punishing Female Negotiators for Asserting Too Much . . . Or Not Enough: Exploring Advocacy as a Moderator of Backlash Against Assertive Female Negotiators, 120 Org. Behav. & Hum. Decision Processes 110 (2013); Kennedy & Kray, supra note 130, at 6.

employers and family members.[134] Commentators also recommend that organizations devise compensation systems that rely more on objective performance criteria and peer review and less on individual ability to self-promote.[135] What other strategies seem useful?

On a more positive note, some research finds that women are more likely than men to disparage ethically questionable tactics, and are less likely to lower their ethical standards when doing so would benefit their economic outcomes.[136] This fact is often obscured by evaluating negotiating performance only with respect to economic outcomes. If, as research suggests, women excel at cooperative behavior and ethical standards, might their influence help reorient practice in socially valuable directions?

More broadly, are the non-adversarial methods and problem-solving techniques that are associated (rightly or wrongly) with women simply better lawyering?

Do you think it more likely that the profession will change women or that women will change the profession?

Putting Theory Into Practice

4-9. The ABA Commission on Women in the Profession has recommended that law schools establish committees to identify and address gender-related concerns.[137] If you were on such a committee, what strategies might you recommend for your law school?

4-10. Have there been any gender patterns in class participation in the course for which you have been reading this book? Analyze these dynamics. How does one get recognition in your class? What factors seem to affect who gets called on, who asks questions, and who stays after class to ask questions? Is this class typical? How would you assess the climate for women in your law school? What about women of color?

To the extent that female students participate less in class and feel more alienated from the educational process, what strategies should law professors consider to address these disparities? How would you evaluate these strategies in terms of the different perspectives examined in this course?

---

134. See Kennedy & Kray, supra note 130, at 21; Hannah Riley Bowles & Linda Babcock, How Can Women Escape the Compensation Negotiation Dilemma? Relational Accounts Are One Answer, 37 Psych. Women Q. 80 (2013).

135. Amanatullah & Tinsely, supra note 133, at 119-20.

136. See research reviewed in Kennedy & Kray, supra note 130, at 16.

137. ABA Commission, Don't Just Hear It Through the Grapevine: Studying Gender Questions at Your Law School (1998).

4-11. Lelia Robinson, the first woman lawyer in Massachusetts, counseled her female colleagues: "Do not take sex into the practice. Don't be 'lady lawyers.' Simply be lawyers and recognize no distinction between yourselves and the other members of the bar."[138] Is that still good advice? Why or why not? What strategies would be most effective in building coalitions for change within the legal profession?

4-12. In 1879, Clara Shortridge Foltz, the first woman lawyer in the Pacific, brought suit to force Hastings College of Law to admit women. In court, her opposing counsel argued that women "would be 'dangerous to justice, inasmuch as an impartial jury would be impossible were a lovely woman to plead the case of the criminal.'" She would "have an advantage of which the Bar might well complain." Indeed, the lawyer cautioned that impartiality was imperiled in this very case before a judge "whose well-known gallantry may succumb to such grace and beauty." Is there any present-day validity to this concern?[139]

4-13. Have you observed or experienced any of the workplace biases described above? What was done, or should have been done, to address them?

4-14. A firm's billboard states "Divorce: Men Only," and its website states that the firm believes in "fighting for men's rights."[140] Would it be legal for the firm to accept only male clients? Ethical?[141] If not, is marketing itself that way also illegal?

4-15. The Austin Manifesto on Women in Law, adopted at a 2009 Women's Power Summit on Law and Leadership, maintained that "[a] critical mass of women lawyers is a significant element in providing a work environment that is hospitable and nurturing to women lawyers."[142] Yet the preceding year, a study by the American Bar Association found that a majority of women lawyers under 40 preferred male supervisors, who received higher marks than women for constructive criticism and keeping confidences. In explaining the survey results, consultants noted that women expect more nurturing from

---

138. Letter from Lelia J. Robinson [Sawtelle] to the Equity Club (Apr. 9, 1887), reprinted in Women Lawyers and the Origins of Professional Identity in America: The Letters of the Equity Club, 1887 to 1890, 66 (Virginia G. Drachman ed., 1993).

139. Barbara Babcock, Woman Lawyer: The Trials of Clara Foltz 50 (2011).

140. Michele N. Struffolino, For Men Only: A Gap in the Rules Makes Sex Discrimination in the Client Selection Process Ethical, 23 Am U. J. Gender, Soc. Pol'y & L. 487 (2015).

141. Stropnicky v. Nathanson, 2003 WL 22480688 (Mass. Super. Sept. 16, 2003) (affirming a ruling by the Massachusetts Commission Against Discrimination finding a woman lawyer liable for refusing to represent men in domestic relations matters).

142. Austin Manifesto on Women in Law, https://law.utexas.edu/cwil/the-austin-manifesto.

other women than from men and so are more readily disappointed when it is not forthcoming. Competition among women for credit and power is also particularly likely to be divisive.[143] Has that been your experience? How should legal employers and women's initiatives respond to these findings?

2. Judging

The proportion of judges who are women has increased dramatically over the last two decades. Women now make up 35 percent of the federal bench and 40 percent of the state court bench.[144] Women of color still remain substantially underrepresented.[145]

Empirical studies of gender differences in judicial voting behaviors have reached varying results. Some have found that women judges were more sympathetic to divorced wives and gay rights plaintiffs; others have found no significant differences or more male support for women's rights issues.[146] One study of state supreme court justices found that female justices after 1991 (but not before) were more likely to rule for the criminal defendants.[147] Yet another study reports that increasing the number of female judges in a district is associated with lower gender disparities in sentencing for serious crimes, possibly because female offenders benefit from the paternalistic biases of male judges.[148]

Since the 1990s, the majority of studies have found some relationship between a judge's gender and voting behavior in gender-related cases.[149] For example, women of color are more likely to cast liberal votes in sex discrimination

143. Vivia Chen, The End of Sisterhood, Amer. Lawyer, May 1, 2009.

144. Jay Newton-Small, More Women in the Judiciary Means Justice for All, Nat'l L.J., Jan. 11, 2016.

145. Nat'l Women's L. Ctr., Women in the Federal Judiciary: Still A Long Way to Go (2016), http://nwlc.org/resources/women-federal-judicary-still-long-way-go (noting that only 82 women of color serve as active federal judges).

146. Deborah L. Rhode & Barbara Kellerman, Women and Leadership: The State of Play, in Women and Leadership: The State of Play and Strategies for Change 51-52, n.104 (Barbara Kellerman & Deborah L. Rhode eds., 2008); Theresa M. Beiner, Female Judging, 36 U. Tol. L. Rev. 821, 821-29 (2005); Fred O. Smith, Jr., Gendered Justice: Do Male and Female Judges Rule Differently on Questions of Gay Rights? 57 Stan. L. Rev. 2087, 2089-91 (2005).

147. See Madhavi McCall & Michael A. McCall, How Far Does the Gender Gap Extend? Decision Making on State Supreme Courts in Fourth Amendment Cases, 1980-2000, 44 Soc. Sci. J. 67 (2007); Madhavi McCall, Structuring Gender's Impact: Judicial Voting Across Criminal Justice Cases, 36 Am. Pol. Res. 264 (2007).

148. See Max Schanzenbach, Racial and Sex Disparities in Prison Sentences: The Effect of District-Level Judicial Demographics, 24 J. Legal Stud. 57 (2005).

149. Susan Haire & Laura P. Moyer, Diversity Matters: Judicial Policy Making in the U.S. Courts of Appeals 53-54 (2015); Rosalind Dixon, Female Justices, Feminism, and the Politics of Judicial Appointment: A Re-Examination, 21 Yale J.L. & Feminism 297, 312 (2010).

matters.[150] One study concluded that (1) having a female judge increased the probability of a finding for the plaintiff by 86 percent (from 22 percent to 41 percent) in sexual harassment cases and by 65 percent (from 17 percent to 28 percent) in sex discrimination cases; and (2) having a female on a panel of judges more than doubled the probability that a male judge, regardless of his ideology, ruled for the plaintiff in sexual harassment cases (increasing the probability from 16 percent to 35 percent) and nearly tripled the probability in sex discrimination cases (increasing it from 11 percent to 30 percent).[151]

The author of the study explores four possible explanations for these results: (1) female judges influence male judges through simple deliberation; (2) male judges defer to female judges in sex discrimination cases; (3) male judges make implicit strategic bargains with female judges for their votes in future cases; and (4) female judges cause male judges to moderate their anti-plaintiff preferences.[152] Which explanation(s), if any, seem plausible to you? A survey of federal and state appellate decisions found that female judges were significantly more likely than male judges to rule in favor of gay and lesbian rights.[153]

Could the statistics about the difference women judges make in how cases are decided be turned against women? In Blank v. Sullivan & Cromwell, Judge Constance Baker Motley denied a motion seeking her recusal in a gender discrimination case on grounds that her sex and prior experience as a civil rights attorney would bias her in favor of the plaintiff.[154] In rejecting that motion, the court ruled that if the "background or sex or race of each judge were, by definition, sufficient grounds for removal, no judge on this court could hear this case, or many others."[155] Does the motion make any more sense than one to recuse a male judge in such a case?

Consider a 2003 case in which an attorney requested recusal of a female judge in a case involving allegations that the defendant had groped a female nurse and used vulgar language. The attorney could not see how a female

150. Haire & Moyer, supra note 149, at 78.
151. Jennifer L. Peresie, Female Judges Matter: Gender and Collegial Decisionmaking in the Federal Appellate Courts, 114 Yale L.J. 1759, 1776, 1778 (2005); see also Christina L. Boyd et al., Untangling the Causal Effects of Sex on Judging, 54 Am. J. Pol. Sci. 389 (2010) (probability of judge deciding in favor of plaintiff in a discrimination case decreases about 10 percent when the judge is male, and increases when a woman serves on a panel with men). For a collection of analysis of many of the studies of the impact of gender on case outcomes and the influence of female judges on their colleagues, see Fiona Kay & Elizabeth Gorman, Women in the Legal Profession, 4 Ann. Rev. L. Soc. Sci. 299, 321-23 (2008) and Haire & Moyer, supra note 149, at 98.
152. Peresie, supra note 151, at 1781-86.
153. Smith, supra note 146, at 2097.
154. 418 F. Supp. 1 (S.D.N.Y. 1975).
155. Id. at 4.

judge "would be fair because of the nature of the allegations."[156] Can you? Would a male judge necessarily be more "fair"? To what extent do we want judges to build on their experience of group membership in deciding cases? Is it coherent to claim both that women have a "different voice" and that they bring no bias to their own decisionmaking?

What is the best guarantee of a lack of bias in the courts—judges who are detached and objective, or those who are empathetic and understanding of other perspectives? In 2009, when a vacancy on the Court opened, President Obama announced his views on the qualities of the Justice that he would appoint:

> I will seek somebody with a sharp and independent mind and a record of excellence and integrity. I will seek someone who understands that justice isn't about some abstract legal theory or footnote in a casebook. It is also about how our laws affect the daily realities of people's lives—whether they can make a living and care for their families; whether they feel safe in their homes and welcome in their own nation.
>
> I view that quality of empathy, of understanding and identifying with people's hopes and struggles as an essential ingredient for arriving at just decisions and outcomes.[157]

Commentators from the right were quick to condemn the President's statement. On Fox Forum, S.E. Cupp noted:

> The word empathy, according to its Greek derivation, means "physical affection, passion, and partiality." I thought Aristotle said the law is reason free from passion? And, if justice is blind, I'm fairly certain she's also impartial. But more importantly, who is on the receiving end of [empathy] by Obama's definition?[158]

Karl Rove echoed similar themes in criticizing "empathy" as too "amorphous a basis on which to pick a justice. Should the 'empathy standard' apply to the unborn? How about gun owners? . . . What Mr. Obama wants in a nominee isn't really 'empathy' and 'understanding.' He wants a liberal . . . ."[159] Thomas Sowell claimed that the "very idea of the rule of law becomes meaningless

---

156. Lynn Hecht Schafran, Not from Central Casting: The Amazing Rise of Women in the American Judiciary, 36 U. Tol. L. Rev. 953, 959 (2005).

157. President Barack Obama, Remarks by the President on Justice David Souter (May 1, 2009), http://www.whitehouse.gov/the_press_office/Remarks-By-The-President-On-Justice-David-Souter.

158. S.E. Cupp, Obama's Wacky Supreme Court Vision, Fox Forum, at FoxNews.com (May 2009), http://foxforum.blogs.foxnews.com/2009/05/05/cupp_supreme_court.

159. Karl Rove, Op. Ed., Republicans and Obama's Court Nominees, Wall St. J., May 7, 2009.

when it is replaced by the empathies of judges."[160] Senator Orrin Hatch of Utah weighed in that empathy is a "code word for an *activist* judge."[161] John Kyl of Arizona, a member of the Senate Judiciary Committee, pledged to block any nominee who "takes into account human suffering and employs empathy from the bench."[162] By contrast, two-thirds of surveyed Americans assigned empathy the highest degree of importance in selecting a Supreme Court Justice, and those most knowledgeable about the Court were particularly likely to value empathy. The most commonly desired characteristic, endorsed by three-quarters of Americans, was that Justices "uphold the values of those who wrote the Constitution long ago." Are those positions always consistent, particularly on women's rights issues?[163]

What is the alternative to "empathy"? Is detachment possible? Desirable? Are empathy and objectivity compatible? Drawing on research concerning regulation of emotions, Terry Maroney argues that it is unrealistic and counterproductive to expect judges to put feelings aside in their decisionmaking. Rather, she proposes a model of engagement in which judges anticipate and respond thoughtfully to emotions and integrate lessons from those emotions into their future decisionmaking processes.[164] Susan Bandes similarly argues that empathy is both inevitable and essential to good judging; it enables judges to understand conflicting claims, but it does not dictate how they should be resolved. Thus, in her view, "it is misleading to discuss whether judges should exercise empathy . . . the questions are for whom they exercise it, how accurately they exercise it, how aware they are of their own limitations and blind spots, and what they do to correct for those blind spots."[165]

In the context of non-judicial conflict resolution, Susan Sturm and Howard Gadlin question the assumption that " 'detached neutrality' is the only or even the best way to achieve impartiality and reduce the expression of bias." They offer as an alternative the ideal of "multi-partiality," which they define as the ability to "critically analyz[e] a conflict from multiple vantage

160. Thomas Sowell, "Empathy" vs. Law, Nat'l Rev. Online (May 5, 2009).

161. William Safire, On Language, N.Y. Times Mag., May 17, 2009, at 26.

162. Douglas O. Linder & Nancy Levit, The Good Lawyer: Seeking Quality in the Practice of Law 29 (2014) (quoting Kyl).

163. James L. Gibson, Expecting Justice and Hoping for Empathy, Pacific Standard (2010), http://www.psmag.com/politics-and-law/expecting-justice-and-hoping-for-empathy-17677 (defining empathy as being able to understand how the law hurts or helps people).

164. Terry A Maroney, Emotional Regulation and Judicial Behavior, 99 Calif. L. Rev. 1485 (2011).

165. Susan A. Bandes, Empathetic Judging and the Rule of Law, Cardozo L. Rev. De Novo 133, 135-36 (2009).

points—as a way to check the inevitable biases in decision making that have to be continually surfaced and corrected."[166]

Are any of these models preferable for judicial decisionmaking?

Another issue is bias against female attorneys in the courtroom. Beginning in 1982, courts began establishing gender bias task forces to respond to such conduct by all participants in the justice system. Some jurisdictions also established separate commissions on racial and ethnic bias or gave one commission responsibility to consider all diversity-related issues. By the turn of the twenty-first century, some 65 state and federal courts had issued reports on bias in the justice system. The ABA Commission on Women in the Profession summarizes the problems exemplified by these studies and the reforms necessary to address them:

> Between two-thirds and three-quarters of women report experiencing bias, while only a quarter to a third of men report observing it and far fewer report experiencing it. Women are also more likely than men to believe that bias is a significant problem and that female attorneys are treated less favorably than male attorneys by judges and opposing counsel. Two-thirds of African American lawyers, but less than a fifth of white lawyers, report witnessing racial bias in the justice system in the last three years. About forty percent of surveyed lawyers report witnessing or experiencing sexual orientation bias in professional settings, even in jurisdictions that have ordinances prohibiting it. Between about a quarter to a half of lawyers with disabilities also experience various forms of bias in the legal system. . . .
>
> Demeaning conduct takes a variety of forms. To be sure, gender bias rules and educational programs have reduced the most egregious problems. Female lawyers no longer routinely cope with labels such as "pretty girl," "little lady," "lawyerette," "baby doll," "sweetie" and "attorney generalette." . . . However, some of these problems persist, particularly those involving disrespectful forms of address. Female lawyers, administrative personnel, and witnesses are still addressed by their first names, while male counterparts are not. . . .
>
> Women also report recurring instances of being ignored, interrupted, or mistaken for nonprofessional support staff. And support staff, for their part, often experience similarly demeaning comments and have been expected to perform menial personal services, such as making coffee or running non-work related errands. . . .
>
> When men observe such incidents, they often seem like isolated, idiosyncratic, or inadvertent slights. A common reaction is that women should just "grow up and stop whining." Such reactions both silence and stigmatize complainants. Many women are unwilling to jeopardize a client's case or their own career prospects by antagonizing decision makers or earning a reputation as "humorless," "oversensitive," or a "troublemaker." . . .

166. Susan Sturm & Howard Gadlin, Conflict Resolution and Systemic Change, 3 J. Dispute Resol. 1, 4 (2007).

A common finding of gender bias studies is that the credibility of female lawyers, litigants, and witnesses is often discounted. Examples range from the occasional overt comment, such as "Shut up. Let's hear what the men have to say," to the much more common and subtle patterns of devaluation, such as openly ignoring or trivializing claims.

In some instances, judicial attitudes are tied to perceptions about the substantive rights or injuries at issue. Claims involving violence, acquaintance rape, sexual harassment, and employment discrimination face special skepticism. In New Jersey's recent follow-up survey of gender bias, about 60 to 70 percent of women (compared with about a quarter of men) reported that victims of domestic violence and sex harassment had less credibility than other victims.[167]

Examples on the record are relatively rare. In one New York divorce case concerning the validity of a premarital agreement, the judge commented that the wife had no background in business or material wealth and "[h]ad nothing going for her except for her physical attractiveness," and that the husband "had come out of a very unpleasant, very unhappy marriage," had gotten a divorce "which cost him a million dollars," "was reluctant to get married again," and "did not look like John Wayne." Under those circumstances, the court reasoned, "I cannot accept the fact that, as she said, he was the one that proposed marriage to her. That would be the last thing that would be on his mind. And why, in heaven's name, do you buy the cow when you get the milk free, as we used to say." The court thus concluded that "the impetus for marriage must [have come] from her side, because there's nothing [the husband] is going to get out of it."[168] Are these statements evidence of gender bias? Another New York judge stated that domestic violence cases were a "waste of the court's time" and that most women asked to get "smacked around."[169] Is this gender bias? If you were a lawyer encountering demeaning comments, how would you respond?

The ABA Model Code of Judicial Conduct 3B(6) provides:

> A judge shall perform judicial duties without bias or prejudice . . . and shall not permit staff, court officials and others subject to the judge's direction and control to do so. . . .
>
> A judge shall require lawyers in proceedings before the judge to refrain from manifesting, by words or conduct, bias or prejudice . . . against parties, witnesses, counsel or others. This Section does not preclude legitimate advocacy when race, sex, religion national origin, disability, age, sexual orientation, or socioeconomic status, or other similar factors, are issues in the proceeding. . . .

---

167. ABA Commission, supra note 78, at 20-21 (2001). For a comprehensive bibliography, see Nat'l Ctr. for State Courts, Racial and Ethnic Bias in the Courts: Bibliography, prepared for the National Consortium of Task Forces and Commissions on Racial and Ethnic Bias in the Courts (2002).

168. In re Marriage of Iverson, 15 Cal. Rptr. 2d 70 (Ct. App. 1992).

169. Joan Dempsey Klein, Remarks, 36 U. Tol. L. Rev. 918 (2005).

A Comment to Rule 8.4 of the Model Rules of Professional Conduct speaks to the lawyer's obligations:

> A lawyer who, in the course of representing a client, knowingly manifests by words or conduct, bias or prejudice based upon race, sex, religion, national origin, disability, age, sexual orientation or socioeconomic status violates [this rule] when such actions are prejudicial to the administration of justice. Legitimate advocacy respecting the foregoing factors does not violate [this rule].

> What sanctions are appropriate for sexist litigation practices? In 2016, in a wrongful death action, Claypole v. County of Monterey, a federal magistrate found that Peter Bertling, counsel for the defendant, engaged in various forms of discovery abuse.[170] At a contentious deposition, when plaintiff's counsel asked Bertling not to interrupt her, Bertling responded, "[D]on't raise your voice at me. It's not becoming of [sic] a woman. . . ." In a brief declaration filed in response to the motion for sanctions, Bertling wrote, "In retrospect, the proper term for me to have used in this context would have been 'attorney.' I apologize to Ms. Rifkin if I offended her by referring to her as a 'woman' instead of as an 'attorney.'" However, Bertling claimed that his remarks were made "in the context of Ms. Rifkin literally yelling at my client and creating a hostile environment during the deposition."[171] The magistrate characterized this response as "only a halfhearted politician's apology," and noted that Bertling had failed to apologize at a hearing on the matter. Accordingly, the magistrate found that Bertling had acted in "bad faith." In the magistrate's view, "A sexist remark is not just a professional discourtesy . . . . The bigger issue is that comments like Bertling's reflect and reinforce the male-dominated attitude of our profession."[172] Because the magistrate had already awarded fees and costs for Bertling's other discovery abuse, the magistrate added the additional sanction that Bertling donate $250 to the Women Lawyers Association of Los Angeles Foundation. Was that an appropriate sanction? What if a female magistrate had imposed it?

Putting Theory Into Practice

4-16. In France, 80 percent of new judges are female. As in other civil law countries, the judiciary is a separate career track. To become a member of the bench, individuals apply for positions at a special college either directly from law school or from positions in the bar. Applicants are selected based on performance on an exam. In recent years, about three-quarters of the applicants have been women and they do slightly better on the exam than men; women's pass rate has been 11 percent compared to 8 percent for men. Part of the explanation for the disparities in applications is that judges average

---

170. Claypole v. Monterey, No. 14-cv-02730_BLF, 2016 WL 145557 (N.D. Cal., Jan. 12, 2016).
171. Id.
172. Id.

three times less income than lawyers, and occupy a relatively low status in the profession.

The current concern is that men, who are 80 percent of defendants in the courts, might lose confidence in a system dominated by women judges. According to the French Justice Minister, quotas might be necessary if the current trends continue. Women judges have been highly critical of the suggestion. As the vice president of the Magistrates Union noted, "No one ever talked about quotas when the judiciary was dominated by men."[173]

Should quotas be imposed or should qualified men be given preference in the selection process?

4-17. A Ugandan woman with the first name Jane came before a Massachusetts immigration judge seeking asylum. Her claim was based on incidents of torture and rape in her homeland. Before denying her request, the judge quipped, "Jane, Come here. Me Tarzan."[174]

In a hearing in Orange County, California, the judge opened the proceedings by asking the female lawyer of record for her business card to substantiate the fact that she was an attorney. The court then inquired of the woman, who was wearing maternity clothes, "Are you ready to have your baby? Is it momentarily?" He then added, "Well, your appearance, Ms. Roberson, leaves a lot to be desired, as far as your clothing is concerned."[175]

If you had been the lawyer in either of these cases, how would you have responded? If you had a filed a formal complaint, should either of the judges have been subject to sanctions?

4-18. Ginnah Muhammad, a conservative Muslim, wore a full veil that left only her eyes exposed when she appeared in a Michigan small claims court to resolve a dispute over a rental car. The judge asked her to remove her veil before testifying. As he explained:

> One of the things I need to do as I am listening to testimony is I need to see your face and I need to see what's going on and unless you take that off, I can't see your face and I can't tell whether you're telling me the truth and I can't see certain things about your demeanor and temperament that I need to see in a court of law.

Muhammad responded: "I'm a practicing Muslim. . . . I wish to respect my religion and so I will not take off my clothes."

173. Adam Sage, Women on Top in Race to Sit on the Bench, London Times, June 3, 2003, at 3 (quoting Veronique Imbert).

174. Gail Diane Cox, And as Cheetah . . . , Nat'l L.J., Aug. 11, 2003, at 3.

175. Anthony P. Capozzi, Gender Bias Is Alive and Well, Cal. Bar J., June 2004, at 9.

In an effort to clarify his concern, the judge explained that he wasn't asking her to take off her clothes but just to "take off the part that's covering your face [while] . . . you testify, and then you can put the veil back on."

"Well, your honor with all due respect," Muhammad responded, "this is part of my clothes."

The court then noted that the issue had come up before in his courtroom, and that practicing Muslims had told him that veiling was not a "religious thing. . . . It's a custom thing."

Mohammad responded, "Well, that's not correct."

The court dismissed her complaint.[176] Should his dismissal be reversed? Should the judge be subject to a reprimand? Would your answer be affected by research showing that the ability to recognize deception through demeanor is rare, even among trained professionals?[177] For further consideration of veiling, see Chapter 6, Section B, Note 2.

4-19. The chief justice of the Delaware Supreme Court used his state email account to send to thirty-eight male colleagues a video depicting a professional-looking young woman in a bar competing with a glamorous blonde for the attention of a man by simulating oral sex with a wine bottle. One critic observed: "[The woman] in the video could be a clerk in the court, a stenographer, a secretary. She's a woman in professional garb. It's a classic theme in porn. She's being ignored by men. She's unworthy of attention except to give men [oral sex]." The justice, who said he has daughters who are professionals and a wife who is a businesswoman, said he felt the video showed "assertive" women in their "own right."[178]

Does this violate the state judicial rules of conduct, which requires judges to "avoid impropriety and the appearance of impropriety"? Does it suggest he cannot be fair to women in his court? Should he be subject to sanctions?

3. Juries

The jury system reflects a tension between the right to be judged by one's peers, and the right to an impartial tribunal. The peremptory strike is both a potential aid to achieving these goals, and an instrument of bias. On balance, should litigants to able to take account of their experiences and instincts about

---

176. The transcript is quoted in Stephen Lubet, Lawyer's Poker 150-53 (2006), and http://volokh.com/posts/1166121763.shtml.

177. When one set of tests was given to judges, police officers, trial lawyers, psychotherapists, and CIA agents, no group was able to do better than 50 percent in weeding out deceit, the same success rate that would come through random guessing. Id. at 151-52.

178. See Maureen Milford, Supreme Court Chief Justice Sent Racy Video to Colleagues, News J., Apr. 30, 2009. A complaint was dismissed in a confidential order.

gender in using their peremptory strikes? Or is this an example of the kind of gender bias that should be eliminated, if possible, from the justice system?

J.E.B. v. Alabama ex rel. T.B.
511 U.S. 127 (1994)

Justice BLACKMUN delivered the opinion of the Court, in which STEVENS, O'CONNOR, SOUTER, and GINSBURG, JJ., joined.

I

On behalf of [the mother of a minor child], respondent State of Alabama filed a complaint for paternity and child support against petitioner J.E.B. in the District Court of Jackson County, Alabama. . . . The trial court assembled a panel of 36 potential jurors, 12 males and 24 females. After the court excused three jurors for cause, only 10 of the remaining 33 jurors were male. The State then used 9 of its 10 peremptory strikes to remove male jurors; petitioner used all but one of his strikes to remove female jurors. As a result, all the selected jurors were female.

Before the jury was empaneled, petitioner objected to the State's peremptory challenges on the ground that they were exercised against male jurors solely on the basis of gender, in violation of the Equal Protection Clause. . . . Petitioner argued that the logic and reasoning of Batson v. Kentucky, which prohibits peremptory strikes solely on the basis of race, similarly forbids intentional discrimination on the basis of gender. The court rejected petitioner's claim and empaneled the all-female jury. The jury found petitioner to be the father of the child and the court entered an order directing him to pay child support. . . .

. . . Today we reaffirm what, by now, should be axiomatic: Intentional discrimination on the basis of gender by state actors violates the Equal Protection Clause, particularly where, as here, the discrimination serves to ratify and perpetuate invidious, archaic, and overbroad stereotypes about the relative abilities of men and women.

II

Discrimination on the basis of gender in the exercise of peremptory challenges is a relatively recent phenomenon. Gender-based peremptory strikes were hardly practicable for most of our country's existence, since, until the 19th century, women were completely excluded from jury service. So well-entrenched was this exclusion of women that in 1880 this Court, while finding that the exclusion of African-American men from juries violated the Fourteenth Amendment, expressed no doubt that a State "may confine the selection [of jurors] to males." Strauder v. West Virginia [1880].

Many States continued to exclude women from jury service well into the present century, despite the fact that women attained suffrage upon ratification of the Nineteenth Amendment in 1920. States that did permit women to serve on juries often erected other barriers, such as registration requirements and automatic exemptions, designed to deter women from exercising their right to jury service. . . .

. . . In this country, supporters of the exclusion of women from juries tended to couch their objections in terms of the ostensible need to protect women from the ugliness and depravity of trials. Women were thought to be too fragile and virginal to withstand the polluted courtroom atmosphere. . . .

This Court in Ballard v. United States [1946], first questioned the fundamental fairness of denying women the right to serve on juries. Relying on its supervisory powers over the federal courts, it held that women may not be excluded from the venire in federal trials in States where women were eligible for jury service under local law. In response to the argument that women have no superior or unique perspective, such that defendants are denied a fair trial by virtue of their exclusion from jury panels, the Court explained:

> It is said . . . that an all male panel drawn from the various groups within a community will be as truly representative as if women were included. The thought is that the factors which tend to influence the action of women are the same as those which influence the action of men — personality, background, economic status — and not sex. Yet it is not enough to say that women when sitting as jurors neither act nor tend to act as a class. Men likewise do not act like a class. . . . The truth is that the two sexes are not fungible; a community made up exclusively of one is different from a community composed of both; the subtle interplay of influence one on the other is among the imponderables. To insulate the courtroom from either may not in a given case make an iota of difference. Yet a flavor, a distinct quality is lost if either sex is excluded. . . .

Fifteen years later, however, the Court still was unwilling to translate its appreciation for the value of women's contribution to civic life into an enforceable right to equal treatment under state laws governing jury service. In Hoyt v. Florida [1961], the Court found it reasonable, "despite the enlightened emancipation of women," to exempt women from mandatory jury service by statute, allowing women to serve on juries only if they volunteered to serve. The Court justified the differential exemption policy on the ground that women, unlike men, occupied a unique position "as the center of home and family life." . . .

In 1975, the Court finally repudiated the reasoning of *Hoyt* and . . . struck down, under the Sixth Amendment, an affirmative registration statute nearly identical to the one . . . [upheld in 1961 in Hoyt v. Florida]. We explained: "Restricting jury service to only special groups or excluding identifiable segments playing major roles in the community cannot be squared with the constitutional concept of jury trial." The diverse and representative character of the jury must be maintained " 'partly as assurance of a diffused impartiality and partly because sharing in the administration of justice is a phase of civic responsibility.' " [Taylor v. Louisiana (1975).]

III

Taylor relied on Sixth Amendment principles, but the opinion's approach is consistent with the heightened equal protection scrutiny afforded gender-based classifications. . . .

While the prejudicial attitudes toward women in this country have not been identical to those held toward racial minorities, the similarities between the experiences of racial minorities and women, in some contexts, "overpower those differences." . . .

Certainly, with respect to jury service, African-Americans and women share a history of total exclusion, a history which came to an end for women many years after the embarrassing chapter in our history came to an end for African-Americans. . . . Under our equal protection jurisprudence, gender-based classifications require "an exceedingly persuasive justification" in order to survive constitutional scrutiny. . . .

Far from proffering an exceptionally persuasive justification for its gender-based peremptory challenges, respondent maintains that its decision to strike virtually all the males from the jury in this case "may reasonably have been based upon the perception, supported by history, that men otherwise totally qualified to serve upon a jury might be more sympathetic and receptive to the arguments of a man alleged in a paternity action to be the father of an out-of-wedlock child, while women equally qualified to serve upon a jury might be more sympathetic and receptive to the arguments of the complaining witness who bore the child." . . .

We shall not accept as a defense to gender-based peremptory challenges "the very stereotype the law condemns." . . . Respondent's rationale, not unlike those regularly expressed for gender-based strikes, is reminiscent of the arguments advanced to justify the total exclusion of women from juries. Respondent offers virtually no support for the conclusion that gender alone is an accurate predictor of juror's attitudes; yet it urges this Court to condone the same stereotypes that justified the wholesale exclusion of women from juries and the ballot box. Respondent seems to assume that gross generalizations that would be deemed impermissible if made on the basis of race are somehow permissible when made on the basis of gender.

Discrimination in jury selection, whether based on race or on gender, causes harm to the litigants, the community, and the individual jurors who are wrongfully excluded from participation in the judicial process. The litigants are harmed by the risk that the prejudice which motivated the discriminatory selection of the jury will infect the entire proceedings. . . . The community is harmed by the State's participation in the perpetuation of invidious group stereotypes and the inevitable loss of confidence in our judicial system that state-sanctioned discrimination in the courtroom engenders.

When state actors exercise peremptory challenges in reliance on gender stereotypes, they ratify and reinforce prejudicial views of the relative abilities of men and women. Because these stereotypes have wreaked injustice in so many other spheres of our country's public life, active discrimination by litigants on the basis of gender during jury selection "invites cynicism respecting the jury's neutrality and its obligation to adhere to the law." . . . The potential for cynicism is particularly acute in cases where gender-related issues are prominent, such as cases involving rape, sexual harassment, or paternity. . . .

In recent cases we have emphasized that individual jurors themselves have a right to nondiscriminatory jury selection procedures. . . . Contrary to respondent's suggestion, this right extends to both men and women. . . . All persons, when granted the opportunity to serve on a jury, have the right not to be excluded summarily because of discriminatory and stereotypical presumptions that reflect and reinforce patterns of historical discrimination. Striking individual jurors on the assumption that they hold particular views simply because of their gender is "practically a brand upon them, affixed by law, an assertion of their inferiority." Strauder v. West Virginia [1880]. It denigrates the dignity of the excluded juror, and, for a woman, reinvokes a history of exclusion from political participation. The message it sends to all those in the courtroom, and all those who may later learn of the discriminatory act, is that certain individuals, for no reason other than gender, are presumed unqualified by state actors to decide important questions upon which reasonable persons could disagree.

IV

Our conclusion that litigants may not strike potential jurors solely on the basis of gender does not imply the elimination of all peremptory challenges. . . . Parties still may remove jurors whom they feel might be less acceptable than others on the panel; gender simply may not serve as a proxy for bias. Parties may also exercise their peremptory challenges to remove from the venire any group or class of individuals normally subject to "rational basis" review. . . . Even strikes based on characteristics that are disproportionately associated with one gender could be appropriate, absent a showing of pretext.

If conducted properly, voir dire can inform litigants about potential jurors, making reliance upon stereotypical and pejorative notions about a particular gender or race both unnecessary and unwise. Voir dire provides a means of discovering actual or implied bias and a firmer basis upon which the parties may exercise their peremptory challenges intelligently. . . .

V

Equal opportunity to participate in the fair administration of justice is fundamental to our democratic system. It not only furthers the goals of the jury system. It reaffirms the promise of equality under the law — that all citizens, regardless of race, ethnicity, or gender, have the chance to take part directly in our democracy. . . .

Justice O'CONNOR, concurring.

I agree with the Court that the Equal Protection Clause prohibits the government from excluding a person from jury service on account of that person's gender. . . . But today's important blow against gender discrimination is not costless. I write separately to discuss some of these costs, and to express my belief that today's holding should be limited to the government's use of gender-based peremptory strikes.

The principal value of the peremptory is that it helps produce fair and impartial juries. Moreover, "[t]he essential nature of the peremptory challenge is that it is one exercised without a reason stated, without inquiry and without being subject to the court's control." . . . Indeed, often a reason for it cannot be stated, for a trial lawyer's judgments about a juror's sympathies are sometimes based on experienced hunches and educated guesses, derived from a juror's responses at voir dire or a juror's "bare looks and gestures." That a trial lawyer's instinctive assessment of a juror's predisposition cannot meet the high standards of a challenge for cause does not mean that the lawyer's instinct is erroneous. . . . Our belief that experienced lawyers will often correctly intuit which jurors are likely to be the least sympathetic, and our understanding that the lawyer will often be unable to explain the intuition, are the very reason we cherish the peremptory challenge. But, as we add, layer by layer, additional constitutional restraints on the use of the peremptory, we force lawyers to articulate what we know is often inarticulable.

In so doing we . . . increase the possibility that biased jurors will be allowed onto the jury, because sometimes a lawyer will be unable to provide an acceptable gender-neutral explanation even though the lawyer is in fact correct that the juror is unsympathetic. Similarly, in jurisdictions where lawyers exercise their strikes in open court, lawyers may be deterred from using their peremptories, out of the fear that if they are unable to justify the strike the court will seat a juror who knows that the striking party thought him unfit. Because I believe the peremptory remains an important litigator's tool and a fundamental part of the process of selecting impartial juries, our increasing limitation of it gives me pause.

Nor is the value of the peremptory challenge to the litigant diminished when the peremptory is exercised in a gender-based manner. We know that like race, gender matters. A plethora of studies make clear that in rape cases, for example, female jurors are somewhat more likely to vote to convict than male jurors. . . . Moreover, though there have been no similarly definitive studies regarding, for example, sexual harassment, child custody, or spousal or child abuse, one need not be a sexist to share the intuition that in certain cases a person's gender and resulting life experience will be relevant to his or her view of the case. "Jurors are not expected to come into the jury box and leave behind all that their human experience has taught them." . . . Individuals are not expected to ignore as jurors what they know as men—or women.

Today's decision severely limits a litigant's ability to act on this intuition, for the import of our holding is that any correlation between a juror's gender and attitudes is irrelevant as a matter of constitutional law. But to say that gender makes no difference as a matter of law is not to say that gender makes no difference as a matter of fact. . . . Today's decision is a statement that, in an effort to eliminate the potential discriminatory use of the peremptory, . . . gender is now governed by the special rule of relevance formerly reserved for race. Though we gain much from this statement, we cannot ignore what we lose. In extending *Batson* to gender we have added an additional burden to the state and federal trial process, taken a step closer to eliminating the peremptory challenge, and diminished the ability of litigants to act on sometimes accurate gender-based assumptions about juror attitudes.

These concerns reinforce my conviction that today's decision should be limited to a prohibition on the government's use of gender-based peremptory challenges. The Equal Protection Clause prohibits only discrimination by state actors. . . .

Accordingly, I adhere to my position that the Equal Protection Clause does not limit the exercise of peremptory challenges by private civil litigants and criminal defendants. . . . This case itself presents no state action dilemma, for here the State of Alabama itself filed the paternity suit on behalf of petitioner. But what of the next case? Will we, in the name of fighting gender discrimination, hold that the battered wife—on trial for wounding her abusive husband—is a state actor? Will we preclude her from using her peremptory challenges to ensure that the jury of her peers contains as many women members as possible? I assume we will, but I hope we will not.

Justice KENNEDY, concurring in the judgment.

I am in full agreement with the Court.

The importance of individual rights to our analysis prompts a further observation concerning what I conceive to be the intended effect of today's decision. We do not prohibit racial and gender bias in jury selection only to encourage it in jury deliberations. Once seated, a juror should not give free rein to some racial or gender bias of his or her own. The jury system is a kind of compact by which power is transferred from the judge to jury, the jury in turn deciding the case in accord with the instructions defining the relevant issues for consideration. The wise limitation on the authority of courts to inquire into the reasons underlying a jury's verdict does not mean that a jury ought to disregard the court's instructions. A juror who allows racial or gender bias to influence assessment of the case breaches the compact and renounces his or her oath.

In this regard, it is important to recognize that a juror sits not as a representative of a racial or sexual group but as an individual citizen. Nothing would be more pernicious to the jury system than for society to presume that persons of different backgrounds go to the jury room to voice prejudice. . . . The jury pool must be representative of the community, but that is a structural mechanism for preventing bias, not enfranchising it. . . . Thus, the Constitution guarantees a right only to an impartial jury, not to a jury composed of members of a particular race or gender. . . .

Justice SCALIA, with whom THE CHIEF JUSTICE and Justice THOMAS join, dissenting.

Today's opinion is an inspiring demonstration of how thoroughly up-to-date and right-thinking we Justices are in matters pertaining to the sexes (or as the Court would have it, the genders), and how sternly we disapprove the male chauvinist attitudes of our predecessors. . . . The parties do not contest that discrimination on the basis of sex[1] is subject to what our cases call "heightened scrutiny" . . . .

The core of the Court's reasoning is that peremptory challenges on the basis of any group characteristic subject to heightened scrutiny are inconsistent with the guarantee of the Equal Protection Clause. That conclusion can be reached only by focusing unrealistically upon individual exercises of the peremptory challenge, and ignoring the totality of the practice. Since all groups are subject to the peremptory challenge (and will be made the object of it, depending upon the nature of the particular case) it is hard to see how any group is denied equal protection. . . . That explains why peremptory challenges coexisted with the Equal Protection Clause for 120 years. This case is a perfect example of how the system as a whole is even-handed. While the only claim before the Court is petitioner's complaint that the prosecutor struck male jurors, for every man struck by the government petitioner's own lawyer struck a woman. To say that men were singled out for discriminatory treatment in this process is preposterous. The situation would be different if both sides systematically struck individuals of one group, so that the strikes evinced group-based animus and served as a proxy for segregated venire

---

1. Throughout this opinion, I shall refer to the issue as sex discrimination rather than (as the Court does) gender discrimination. The word "gender" has acquired the new and useful connotation of cultural or attitudinal characteristics (as opposed to physical characteristics) distinctive to the sexes. That is to say, gender is to sex as feminine is to female and masculine to male. The present case does not involve peremptory strikes exercised on the basis of femininity or masculinity (as far as it appears, effeminate men did not survive the prosecution's peremptories). The case involves, therefore, sex discrimination plain and simple.

lists. . . . The pattern here, however, displays not a systemic sex-based animus but each side's desire to get a jury favorably disposed to its case. That is why the Court's characterization of respondent's argument as "reminiscent of the arguments advanced to justify the total exclusion of women from juries" is patently false. Women were categorically excluded from juries because of doubt that they were competent; women are stricken from juries by peremptory challenge because of doubt that they are well disposed to the striking party's case. . . . There is discrimination and dishonor in the former, and not in the latter—which explains the 106-year interlude between our holding that exclusion from juries on the basis of race was unconstitutional, Strauder v. West Virginia, and our holding that peremptory challenges on the basis of race were unconstitutional, Batson v. Kentucky.

Although the Court's legal reasoning in this case is largely obscured by anti-male-chauvinist oratory, to the extent such reasoning is discernible it invalidates much more than sex-based strikes. . . . [The Court's analysis] places all peremptory strikes based on any group characteristic at risk, since they can all be denominated "stereotypes." Perhaps, however (though I do not see why it should be so), only the stereotyping of groups entitled to heightened or strict scrutiny constitutes "the very stereotype the law condemns"—so that other stereotyping (e.g., wide-eyed blondes and football players are dumb) remains OK. Or perhaps when the Court refers to "impermissible stereotypes," it means the adjective to be limiting rather than descriptive—so that we can expect to learn from the Court's peremptory/stereotyping jurisprudence in the future which stereotypes the Constitution frowns upon and which it does not. . . .

[M]ake no mistake about it: there really is no substitute for the peremptory. Voir dire (though it can be expected to expand as a consequence of today's decision) cannot fill the gap. The biases that go along with group characteristics tend to be biases that the juror himself does not perceive, so that it is no use asking about them. It is fruitless to inquire of a male juror whether he harbors any subliminal prejudice in favor of unwed fathers. . . .

In order, it seems to me, not to eliminate any real denial of equal protection, but simply to pay conspicuous obeisance to the equality of the sexes, the Court imperils a practice that has been considered an essential part of fair jury trial since the dawn of the common law. The Constitution of the United States neither requires nor permits this vandalizing of our people's traditions.

For these reasons, I dissent.

NOTE ON EQUALITY AND IMPARTIALITY IN THE JURY CONTEXT

As Justice O'Connor notes, there are some cases in which gender does make a difference. Does pretending otherwise improve the accuracy of the jury system? What exactly does impartiality mean in the context of the constitutional right to a jury of one's peers? Is it that a potential juror should have no views on any relevant subject? Or that jury perspectives in some sense should be drawn from a cross section of the community, and "not arbitrarily skewed for or against any particular group or characteristic"? Should the goal be proportional representation on juries?

Although *J.E.B.* has met with considerable support in theory, it has proven more problematic in practice. Part of the difficulty, Charles Ogletree notes, is that while gender may be an imperfect proxy for relevant attitudes, it is not an entirely irrational one. The stereotypes that influence lawyers in jury selection may also be ones that "affect the behavior of men and women in the jury box."[179] Moreover, inventive lawyers can always summon nondiscriminatory reasons for a challenge, and most trial courts are reluctant to reject them as pretextual unless they are patently implausible or clearly incorporate impermissible stereotypes. Appellate courts are similarly reluctant to reverse lower court rulings, which often turn on factual determinations of credibility. Lawyers who feel ethically obligated to gain sympathetic hearings for their clients may be equally reluctant to acknowledge—even to themselves—the role that impermissible stereotypes play in their juror selections. Experienced litigators and jury consultants believe that concerns such as race, sex, ethnicity, and religion routinely figure in juror selection.[180]

Given these evidentiary hurdles, it is perhaps unsurprising that claims of gender discrimination in peremptory challenges are relatively rare. A survey of cases in the first five years under *J.E.B* found only 127 reported complaints and 23 reversals in all state and federal systems. Clearly the ruling has not been as burdensome as critics predicted. But neither has it been as effective as supporters hoped. Surveyed cases include numerous examples of peremptories that have been sustained despite the stereotypes underlying them. Women have been struck for being "timid," "not assertive," "weak," "vacillating," overweight, and single mothers.[181] One particularly striking case, Talley v. State,[182] involved a battered woman on trial for murder of her husband. The state used all 13 of its strikes against women, and the court upheld the exclusions. Among the reasons that the prosecutor offered were that a female prospective juror had "heard of the battered woman syndrome," "agree[d] with feminists ideals and goals," or had read romance novels, "indicating that she

---

179. Charles Ogletree, Just Say No! A Proposal to Eliminate Racially Discriminatory Uses of Peremptory Challenges, 31 Am. Crim. L. Rev. 1099, 1104 (1994).

180. See Leonard Post, A Loaded Box of Stereotypes, Nat'l L.J., Apr. 25, 2005, at A1, A18.

181. Susan Hightower, Sex and the Peremptory Strike: An Empirical Analysis of *J.E.B. v. Alabama*'s First Five Years, 52 Stan. L. Rev. 895, 924-26 (2000).

182. 687 So. 2d 1261 (Ala. Crim. App. 1996).

did not look at life as it is."[183] In a 2016 case, Foster v. Chatman, the Supreme Court reversed a 30-year-old murder conviction because the prosecutors relied on illegal race-based peremptory challenges.[184] With respect to one juror, the Court found the prosecutors' "neutral" explanations to be pretextual because they had "willingly accepted white jurors with the same traits" that rendered the black juror "unattractive." Is this comparative analysis likely to make it easier to challenge gender-based peremptories? Which traits and qualities are most likely to motivate the exclusion of female jurors today?

Putting Theory Into Practice

4-20. In the trial of O.J. Simpson for murder of his battered white wife, jury consultants for both sides found that black women were the group most likely to vote for acquittal; they were least likely to credit inculpating domestic violence evidence, or to respond favorably to Marcia Clark, a white woman who was the lead prosecutor.[185] If you had been one of the defense lawyers in the *Simpson* case, would you have tried to use your peremptory strikes to increase the representation by black women on the jury?

4-21. How should courts deal with strikes based on an individual's sexual orientation?[186] Should lawyers be entitled to ask jurors questions about their living arrangements and about conduct that might suggest a lesbian or gay identity?

4-22. The defendant was on trial for violating a restraining order that protected his battered wife. The prosecutor used her three peremptory challenges to strike the first three jurors on the panel who had indicated prior involvement with a protective order. The defendant was convicted and appealed, claiming gender bias in jury selection. The prosecutor admitted that she assumed that men involved in such a dispute would likely have been defendants rather than complainants. Does the defendant have grounds for appeal?[187]

4-23. A prosecutor uses his three peremptory challenges to exclude three overweight African-American women from the jury. In explaining his decision

183. Id. at 1267.
184. Foster v. Chatman, 136 S. Ct. 1737 (2016).
185. Albert W. Alschuler, How to Win the Trial of the Century: The Ethics of Lord Brougham and the O.J. Simpson Defense Team, 29 McGeorge L. Rev. 311, 312 (1998).
186. SmithKline Beecham Corp. v. Abbott Labs., 740 F.3d 471, 484 (9th Cir. 2014) (striking down the use of peremptory challenges based on sexual orientation).
187. See State v. Jensen, 76 P.3d 188 (Utah Ct. App. 2003); Debora L. Threedy, Legal Archeology and Feminist Legal Theory: A Case Study of Gender and Domestic Violence, 29 Women's Rts. L. Rep. 171 (2008).

to the court, he cites their dress and hairstyles, as well as their youth. Two women had braided hair, which he had always regarded "as somewhat radical." One was "grossly overweight and . . . [wearing] a little tiny skirt that doesn't fit her . . . a skirt that's hiked halfway up her thighs when she stands, and then when she sits, you can see everything that God gave the woman." Her appearance made him "uncomfortable" trusting her with a case of "this seriousness."[188] Are these constitutionally permissible reasons for exclusion?

In comments to a reporter outside of court, the prosecutor acknowledged, "Young, obese, black women are really dangerous to me. . . . I've never liked young obese black women and I think they sense that."[189] If he had made that statement in court, should that have affected the legitimacy of his peremptory challenges?

4-24. Should the prosecution and defense in criminal cases be treated the same with respect to peremptory challenges? Can a case be made for holding prosecutors to higher standards?[190]

4. Criminal Sentencing

Traditionally, judges considered the individual circumstances of defendants when determining punishment. Women generally received more lenient sentences than men who committed similar crimes partly because they had more family and community ties and less extensive criminal records, and because male judges were often motivated by chivalry or paternalism.[191] Other sentencing disparities reflected racial and gender bias, and idiosyncratic views of judges.

During the 1980s, in a general effort to promote more consistency and proportionality in punishment, Congress passed the Sentencing Reform Act, which attempted to prescribe uniform sentences for similar conduct. The Federal Sentencing Commission established the Federal Sentencing Guidelines in order to shift the focus of punishment away from the characteristics of the defendant to the characteristics of the crime. The Guidelines

188. People v. Galbert, 1995 WL 108696 (Cal. App. Jan. 30, 1995), discussed in Sondra Solovay, Tipping the Scales of Justice: Fighting Weight-Based Discrimination 94-95 (2000).

189. Galbert v. Merkle, 1997 U.S. Dist. LEXIS 2081, at *3 (N.D. Cal. Feb. 24, 1997); Tanya Schevitz, Appeals Court Backs Banning of Fat Jurors, S.F. Examiner, Feb. 8, 1995, at A1, A12 (quoting William Tingle).

190. Anna Roberts, Asymmetry as Fairness: Reversing a Peremptory Trend, 92 Wash. U. L. Rev. 1503 (2015).

191. See Nancy Gertner, Women Offenders and the Sentencing Guidelines, 14 Yale J.L. & Feminism 291, 292 (2002); Amy Farrell, Geoff Ward & Danielle Rousseau, Intersections of Gender and Race in Federal Sentencing: Examining Court Contexts and the Effects of Representative Court Authorities, 14 J. Gender, Race, & Just. 85, 89-90 (2010).

prohibited consideration of traditional "individualizing" factors, except in "extraordinary" situations, and specified that family ties and responsibilities were not ordinarily relevant. Supreme Court decisions have determined that Federal Sentencing Guidelines cannot be mandatory, although they remain as advisory. States, which handle the vast majority of criminal cases, have their own guidelines.

Despite these guidelines, most research reveals significant gender, racial, and ethnic differences. Women are generally treated more leniently than men, controlling for the severity of the offense and their prior criminal record, and white defendants are treated more leniently than non-whites. Gender disparities appear partly attributable to assumptions that women are less dangerous, more remorseful, more open to reform, more likely to be victims themselves, and more likely to have family responsibilities and community ties.[192] However, women who commit particularly egregious crimes tend to receive even harsher sentences than men, probably in part because they deviate so far from accepted notions of femininity.[193]

The Federal Guidelines permit a downward adjustment for family circumstances only in truly exceptional circumstances. Being a single parent is not generally viewed as an exceptional circumstance. A primary concern is that greater discretion for family circumstances would reward women for their status as mothers or, alternatively, penalize women who do not have children. It would say in effect, "you have violated the criminal law, but we'll overlook that so you can do what you are supposed to do—care for your children."[194] The same goes for pregnant women. One court noted that "pregnancy of convicted female felons is neither atypical nor unusual," and that giving a downward departure for pregnancy would send "an obvious message to all female defendants that pregnancy is 'a way out.'"[195]

Despite the Guidelines, research indicates that judges in practice tend to give mothers with children and pregnant women lighter sentences.[196] Is that

---

192. Farrell, Ward, & Rousseau, supra note 191, at 91-92; Ryan Elias Newby, Evil Women and Innocent Victims: The Effect of Gender on California Sentences for Domestic Homicide, 22 Hastings Women's L.J. 113, 117-19 (2011). For commentators' justifications, see Carissa Byrne Hessick, Race and Gender as Explicit Sentencing Factors, 14 J. Gender, Race, & Just. 127, 139-40 (2010).

193. Newby, supra note 192, at 119-20, 155, 156.

194. Ilene H. Nagel & Barry L. Johnson, Gender Issues and the Criminal Law: The Role of Gender in a Structured Sentencing System: Equal Treatment, Policy Choices, and the Sentencing of Female Offenders Under the United States Sentencing Guidelines, 85 J. Crim. L. & Criminology 181, 208 (1994).

195. United States v. Pozzy, 902 F.2d 133, 138-39 (1st Cir. 1990).

196. See, e.g., United States v. Mateo, 299 F. Supp. 2d 201, 212-13 (S.D.N.Y. 2004) (giving a lighter sentence to a mother who did not have a spouse to care for her newborn child); see also Sean B. Berberian, Protecting Children: Explaining Disparities in the Female Offender's Pretrial Process, and Policy Issues Surrounding Lenient Treatment of Mothers, 10

fair? Or does it constitute sex discrimination? Some commentators argue that it does not.

> The purpose of just punishment emphasizes consistency in sentencing. If the "same" sentence has an inconsistent impact on two different defendants, then considering the two sentences as equivalent is unjust. An incarcerative sentence may have a distinctly different impact on a parent than it has on a non-parent. For example, in many states incarceration constitutes a ground for termination of parental rights. A two year prison sentence does not equal two years in prison accompanied by permanent loss of child custody. . . . [197]

What is your view?

Some countries have not tried so hard to be sex-neutral. In 1994, President Nelson Mandela of the Republic of South Africa signed a Presidential Act providing an early release from prison for certain categories of prisoners, including "all mothers in prison on 10 May 1994, with minor children under the age of twelve (12) years." Fathers were not included. President Mandela explained that he was motivated predominantly by a concern for children who had been deprived of the nurturing and care that their mothers would ordinarily have provided.[198]

A father with a child under the age of twelve who was not entitled to early release under the order challenged his exclusion under the anti-discrimination provisions of the interim South African Constitution. Is there any question about how this case would be decided in the United States? A majority of the South African Constitutional Court rejected the challenge on the grounds that the early release order was not "unfair discrimination." One justice dissented, and another determined that although the Act constituted "unfair discrimination," it was justified.[199]

In the United States, one of the factors "not ordinarily relevant" to determining whether to depart from the federal Sentencing Guidelines is a defendant's mental or emotional condition, but prior abuse has been considered by some courts if the defendant can establish a nexus between the abuse and the offense. In 1994, only two weeks after receiving custody of her two young sons, Susan Smith loaded them into her car, drove to a nearby lake,

---

Hastings Women's L.J. 369 (1999) (finding that women with children were significantly more likely to receive pretrial release and lower bail/bond amounts).

197. Eleanor Bush, Considering the Defendant's Children at Sentencing, 2 Fed. Sent'g Rep. 194, 194 (1990); see also Myrna Raeder, Gender and Sentencing: Single Moms, Battered Women, and Other Sex-Based Anomalies in the Gender-Free World of the Federal Sentencing Guidelines, 20 Pepp. L. Rev. 905, 961 (1993) (blindly imposing equal treatment on parents at sentencing when the rest of society does not "makes a mockery of so-called gender neutrality in sentencing").

198. President of the Republic of South Africa v. Hugo, 1997 (4) SA 1 (CC).

199. Id.

pointed the car toward the lake, released the hand brake and jumped out. She told the police that she and her children had been abducted by an African-American carjacker. After a fruitless nine-day search for the offender, Smith confessed to the murders. Her capital murder trial was short, and during the penalty phase, her attorneys argued for leniency based on a history of depression brought on in large part by sexual abuse she suffered as a child. The jury sentenced her to life imprisonment, sparing her the death penalty.[200] Does this seem appropriate?

In a more recent, well-publicized case, Andrea Yates, who suffered from severe postpartum depression, drowned her five children, ages six months to seven years, in the family bathtub. She was convicted for the murders of three of the children. A jury deliberated for 40 minutes before sentencing her to life in prison instead of the death penalty. Her conviction was subsequently reversed. On retrial, she was found not guilty by reason of insanity and sentenced to an indefinite civil commitment.

What facts would you need before deciding on guilt and sentencing in the Yates case? One commentator explains:

> The "baby blues," or "blues," occurs in fifty to seventy percent of women in the first six to eight weeks after birth; symptoms include crying, general depression, and fatigue. The "blues" does not impair a mother's judgment and is probably not a disorder or disease. Postpartum depression occurs in ten to twenty percent of women and may persist for one year. It is categorized as a type of reaction depression and involves feelings of hopelessness, inadequacy, anxiety, and moodiness. Although studies are few, the level of support that the mother receives from the father and family is more determinative of the depression than are demographic and biological factors. Postpartum psychosis occurs in one to two of every one thousand births and can lead to suicide or infanticide. It involves a major deviation from the normal processes of thinking, behavior, and emotion. Emotional reactions may be inappropriate to the circumstances, and actions may not be related to facts. For example, a mother may say that she sees the room upside down, express concern that a small pimple on her child's face is a misplaced testis, or fear that the hospital staff is part of a conspiracy to kill the baby. Anxiety can lead to panic attacks; a mother often has obsessive thoughts about harming the baby by putting it in the oven, drowning it, cutting off its body parts, or dropping it from an elevated surface. Hospitalization is necessary for the protection of both the mother and the child.[201]

Is compassion appropriate in the Andrea Yates case? Does it matter that postpartum depression is a female-specific defense? One study of 24 cases in

200. See Chris Burritt & Jack Warner, The *Susan Smith* Trial, Atlanta Const., July 22, 1995, at C8; Jurors in *Susan Smith* Trial Say They Don't Have Any Regrets, Atlanta Const., Aug. 28, 1995, at C6.

201. Michele Connell, The Postpartum Psychosis Defense and Feminism: More or Less Justice for Women?, 63 Case W. Res. L. Rev. 143, 146-47 (2002).

which postpartum psychosis was offered as a defense found that 8 women were acquitted and 4 were given probation, while 10 were sentenced to between 3 and 20 years, and 2 received life sentences.[202] Are those disparities defensible?

Prior abuse was not presented as a factor in the Yates case but, as noted above, it was an important part of Susan Smith's sentencing hearing. In federal courts, past victimization has been found as a basis for downward departure from the Sentencing Guidelines as well. In one case, the court found that a history of abuse so severe that the defendant was "virtually a mind puppet" was extraordinary and that a downward departure was not forbidden by the Guidelines.[203]

Should sentencing be affected by a woman's involvement in a controlling relationship? The issue arises in the context of drug conspiracies. A significant number of the female defendants involved in those conspiracies—sometimes called "women of circumstance"—are "wives, mothers, sisters, daughters, girlfriends, and nieces, who become involved in crime because of fear, financial dependence or romantic attachment arising from relationships with male drug traffickers."[204] Many are "desperate, unsuspecting or coerced women who often have no prior criminal history and serve as the sole caretakers of young children," charged with conspiracy and subject to harsh sentencing laws.[205] Women may also suffer disproportionate sentences, either because they refuse to snitch, out of loyalty or fear, or because they do not know enough valuable information to obtain a reduced sentence as a cooperating witness. A "safety valve" in the federal Violent Crime Control and Drug Enforcement Act of 1994 provides relief to nonviolent, low-level drug offenders who cooperate with the authorities, but this will not help women too fearful to cooperate or too uninformed to provide valuable evidence. Nor does it assist women facing state charges.[206]

Kemba Smith was a student at Hampton University with no prior criminal record. She became involved with a man eight years older, who was the ringleader of a cocaine enterprise. By the time Smith realized that her boyfriend was a drug dealer, he was abusing her, and she feared retaliation (he eventually killed his best friend for informing on him). Smith never handled any of the drugs, but she received a 24-year prison sentence for conspiracy to distribute cocaine. President Clinton pardoned her after six years of incarceration and a mass media campaign.[207] What sentence would have been appropriate?

---

202. Id. at 147-48.

203. United States v. Roe, 976 F.2d 1216, 1218 (9th Cir. 1992).

204. Shimica Gaskins, Note, "Women of Circumstance"—The Effects of Mandatory Minimum Sentencing on Women Minimally Involved in Drug Crimes, 41 Am. Crim. L. Rev. 1533, 1534 (2004).

205. Id. at 1536.

206. Id. at 1547.

207. See id. at 1535.

Putting Theory Into Practice

4-25. Most states remove infants from imprisoned mothers almost immediately after birth, and these women do not have the opportunity to nurse or bond with their newborns. Children of imprisoned parents are five to six times as likely as their peers to end up behind bars, and 10 percent land in foster care.[208] In 2002, Jodie received a four-year sentence for a fourth offense of operating a motor vehicle while intoxicated and fleeing an officer. She placed her 2-year-old son with her mother, but in 2004, her mother was no longer able to take care of the child. At that point, the state moved to permanently terminate Jodie's rights to her son so that he could be adopted into a stable family. What should the controlling law be?[209]

4-26. A young woman, referred to at the time as "Miss America Bandit," was convicted of a string of bank robberies. At sentencing, the judge ordered a downward departure based on the defendant's domination by her boyfriend, even though there were no indications of physical abuse. The judge's comments during the sentencing hearing included: "men have exercised traditional control over the activities of women, and I'm not going to ignore that, no matter how much flak I get from women's lib"; and "I think it's a fact of life that men can exercise a Svengali influence over women"; and "women are a soft touch, particularly if sex is involved."[210] Is this judge taking the social reality of the defendant into consideration, or is he instead reasoning from his own gender stereotypes?

4-27. In 2016, Brock Turner, a Stanford University athlete, was convicted of sexually assaulting an unconscious intoxicated woman. On the recommendation of the probation office, the judge sentenced him to only six months in jail, which could be reduced to three months for good behavior. Turner was caught by two graduate students who witnessed the attack behind a fraternity house dumpster. Jurors rejected Turner's claim that he believed the woman consented. They convicted him of intent to rape an incapacitated person, along with two related crimes, which altogether carried a maximum punishment of fourteen years and a minimum of two years in prison.[211] The

---

208. For an overview of problems, see Susan F. Sharp & M. Elaine Eriksen, Imprisoned Mothers and Their Children, in Women in Prison: Gender and Social Control (Barbara H. Zaitzow & Jim Thomas eds., 2003).

209. Kenosha Cnty. Dep't of Human Servs. v. Jodie W., 716 N.W.2d 845 (Wis. 2006) (reversing the permanent termination of Jodie's parental rights).

210. The case is United States v. Mast, No. CR-88-0720-AAH-1 (C.D. Cal. 1989), rev'd on other grounds, 925 F.2d 1472 (9th Cir. 1991). See John Griffith, Woman Faces Counts in Bank Case, Oregonian, Feb. 4, 1992, at C8; Kim Murphy, "Soft Touch" Bandit Gets a Break from Judge on Term, L.A. Times, May 13, 1989.

211. Liam Stack, Light Sentence for Brock Turner in Stanford Rape Case Draws Outrage, N.Y. Times, June 6, 2016, at A15; Thomas Fuller, Court Papers Give Insight into Stanford Sex Assault, N.Y. Times, June 12, 2016, at A8.

judge, himself a former Stanford athlete, said that his decision to impose a lesser sentence reflected the defendant's lack of a prior criminal record or likely danger to others, his intoxication at the time of the incident, 39 character letters from friends and family that indicated "a period of, essentially, good behavior," the "severe impact" of a prison sentence, and the adverse collateral consequences that the defendant had already suffered from the felony conviction and the publicity accompanying it.[212]

The case attracted a firestorm of protest, exacerbated by a letter from Turner's father, who asserted that the verdict was a "steep price to pay for 20 minutes of action."[213] Critics also pointed out that the defendant had refused to accept full responsibility for his action.[214] Although he expressed regret for the incident, he blamed the campus drinking culture and "sexual promiscuity," and even claimed the victim seemed to enjoy the experience.[215] Over a million people signed a petition to remove the judge from the bench.[216] Should he be removed? How should judges weigh various factors in determining the appropriate punishment for sexual assault?

212. Sam Levin, Stanford Sexual Assault: Read the Full Text of the Judge's Controversial Decision, The Guardian, June 14, 2016.

213. Max Hamilton, Stanford Sex Offenders Friends and Relatives Wrote to Persuade Judge to Keep Him Out of Prison," LA Times.com, June 7, 2016.

214. Fuller, supra note 211.

215. Emily Bazelon, Why the Stanford Rape Conviction Actually Represents Progress, N.Y. Times Mag., June 9, 2016; see also, Abby Jackson, 39 Separate Letters; Eliana Dockterman, On Campuses, "Party Culture" No Longer Excuses Rape, Time, June 27, 2016, at 21.

216. Eliott C. McLaughlin, One Million Sign Petition to Oust Judge in Brock Turner Case: Will It Matter?, N.Y. Times Mag., June 10, 2016.

5 *Autonomy*

For women's rights advocates, equality is a critical value, but so, too, is autonomy. This chapter shifts the emphasis from women having what men have, to women being able to stand on their own, make their own decisions, and pursue their own notion of a life well lived.

The concept of autonomy is woven deeply into Anglo-American liberal legal premises. The law governing contracts, torts, and crimes typically assumes that the individual is capable of formulating a specific "intent" to act, of exercising free "choice" or "consent," and of behaving as a "reasonable" person. Women's rights advocates make similar assumptions when they argue that women should have freedom to control their own lives and make their own reproductive choices.

Contemporary social theory has challenged the Enlightenment view of the self as autonomous and capable of acting independently of external influence. Today, the individual is more often understood as constituted through multiple sources of identity and as subject to social, institutional, and ideological forces that construct and constrain individuals' desires, choices, and perceptions of reality. This more complex view reveals limitations in the traditional view of autonomy and underscores the need for pragmatic strategies for overcoming these limitations. From this vantage point, freedom is a relative concept rather than an absolute one, but the assumption remains that, in most matters, more is better than less.

Another complexity arises from different views concerning what constitutes autonomy. Typically, autonomy is thought to reside in the individual person, and means the right to be free from interference by others. The contemporary women's rights movement, however, has often considered relationships as the foundation of autonomy rights and has argued for concepts of autonomy that encompass the freedom to flourish in a positive sense, not just freedom free from the interference of others. This chapter explores these themes in contexts in which autonomy, choice, and consent are most deeply implicated—rape, prostitution, pregnancy, abortion, and welfare.

A. SEX AND CONSENT

1. "Statutory" Rape: The (Ir)relevance of Consent

One of the most difficult and contested issues in the law of rape is that of consent. The chapter begins with the law of statutory rape, which presumes the lack of consent to sex by victims below a certain age.

Michael M. v. Superior Court of Sonoma County
450 U.S. 464 (1981)

Justice REHNQUIST announced the judgment of the Court and delivered an opinion, in which THE CHIEF JUSTICE, JUSTICE STEWART, and JUSTICE POWELL joined.

The question presented in this case is whether California's "statutory rape" law . . . violates the Equal Protection Clause of the Fourteenth Amendment. §261.5 defines unlawful sexual intercourse as "an act of sexual intercourse accomplished with a female not the wife of the perpetrator, where the female is under the age of 18 years." The statute thus makes men alone criminally liable for the act of sexual intercourse.

In July 1978, a complaint was filed in the Municipal Court of Sonoma County, Cal., alleging that petitioner, then a 17-year-old male, had had unlawful sexual intercourse with a female under the age of 18, in violation of §261.5. The evidence, adduced at a preliminary hearing showed that at approximately midnight on June 3, 1978, petitioner and two friends approached Sharon, a 16-year-old female, and her sister as they waited at a bus stop. Petitioner and Sharon, who had already been drinking, moved away from the others and began to kiss. After being struck in the face for rebuffing petitioner's initial advances, Sharon submitted to sexual intercourse with petitioner. Prior to trial, petitioner sought to set aside the information on both state and federal constitutional grounds, asserting that §261.5 unlawfully discriminated on the basis of gender. The trial court and the California Court of Appeal denied petitioner's request for relief and petitioner sought review in the Supreme Court of California. . . .

The justification for the statute offered by the State, and accepted by the Supreme Court of California, is that the legislature sought to prevent illegitimate teenage pregnancies. That finding, of course, is entitled to great deference. . . .

We are satisfied not only that the prevention of illegitimate pregnancy is at least one of the "purposes" of the statute, but also that the State has a strong interest in preventing such pregnancy. At the risk of stating the obvious, teenage pregnancies, which have increased dramatically over the last two decades, have significant social, medical, and economic consequences for both the mother and her child, and the State. Of particular concern to the State is that approximately half of all teenage pregnancies end in abortion. And of those children who are born, their illegitimacy makes them likely candidates to become wards of the State.

We need not be medical doctors to discern that young men and young women are not similarly situated with respect to the problems and the risks of sexual intercourse. Only women may become pregnant, and they suffer disproportionately the profound physical, emotional, and psychological consequences of sexual activity. The statute at issue here protects women from sexual intercourse at an age when those consequences are particularly severe.

The question thus boils down to whether a State may attack the problem of sexual intercourse and teenage pregnancy directly by prohibiting a male from having sexual intercourse with a minor female. We hold that such a statute is sufficiently related to the State's objectives to pass constitutional muster.

Because virtually all of the significant harmful and inescapably identifiable consequences of teenage pregnancy fall on the young female, a legislature acts well within its authority when it elects to punish only the participant who, by nature, suffers few of the consequences of his conduct. It is hardly unreasonable for a legislature acting to protect minor females to exclude them from punishment. Moreover, the risk of pregnancy itself constitutes a substantial deterrence to young females. No similar natural sanctions deter males. A criminal sanction imposed solely on males thus serves to roughly "equalize" the deterrents on the sexes.

We are unable to accept petitioner's contention that the statute is impermissibly under-inclusive and must, in order to pass judicial scrutiny, be *broadened* so as to hold the female as criminally liable as the male. It is argued that this statute is not *necessary* to deter teenage pregnancy because a gender-neutral statute, where both male and female would be subject to prosecution, would serve that goal equally well. The relevant inquiry, however, is not whether the statute is drawn as precisely as it might have been, but whether the line chosen by the California Legislature is within constitutional limitations.

In any event, we cannot say that a gender-neutral statute would be as effective as the statute California has chosen to enact. The State persuasively contends that a gender-neutral statute would frustrate its interest in effective enforcement. Its view is that a female is surely less likely to report violations of the statute if she herself would be subject to criminal prosecution. In an area already fraught with prosecutorial difficulties, we decline to hold that the Equal Protection Clause requires a legislature to enact a statute so broad that it may well be incapable of enforcement. . . .

There remains only petitioner's contention that the statute is unconstitutional as it is applied to him because he, like Sharon, was under 18 at the time of sexual intercourse. Petitioner argues that the statute is flawed because it presumes that as between two persons under 18, the male is the culpable aggressor. We find petitioner's contentions unpersuasive. Contrary to his assertions, the statute does not rest on the assumption that males are generally the aggressors. It is instead an attempt by a legislature to prevent illegitimate teenage pregnancy by providing an additional deterrent for men. The age of the man is irrelevant since young men are as capable as older men of inflicting the harm sought to be prevented.

In upholding the California statute we also recognize that this is not a case where a statute is being challenged on the grounds that it "invidiously discriminates" against females. To the contrary, the statute places a burden on males which is not shared by females. But we find nothing to suggest that men, because of past discrimination or peculiar disadvantages, are in need of the special solicitude of the courts. Nor is this a case where the gender classification is made "solely for . . . administrative convenience," . . . or rests on "the baggage of sexual stereotypes." . . . As we have held, the statute instead reasonably reflects the fact that the consequences of sexual intercourse and pregnancy fall more heavily on the female than on the male.

Accordingly, the judgment of the California Supreme Court is Affirmed.

Justice BLACKMUN, concurring in the judgment.

I think . . . that it is only fair, with respect to this particular petitioner, to point out that his partner, Sharon, appears not to have been an unwilling participant in at least the initial stages of the intimacies that took place the night of June 3, 1978.* Petitioner's and Sharon's nonacquaintance with each other before the incident; their drinking; their withdrawal from the others of the group; their foreplay, in which she willingly participated and seems to

---

*Sharon at the preliminary hearing testified as follows: "Q. [by the Deputy District Attorney]. On June the 4th, at approximately midnight—midnight of June the 3rd, were you in Rohnert Park?" A. [by Sharon]. Yes. "Q. Is that in Sonoma County?" A. Yes. "Q. Did anything unusual happen to you that night in Rohnert Park?" A. Yes. "Q. Would you briefly describe what happened that night? Did you see the defendant that night in Rohnert Park?" A. Yes. "Q. Where did you first meet him?" A. At a bus stop. "Q. Was anyone with you?" A. My sister. "Q. Was anyone with the defendant?" A. Yes. "Q. How many people were with the defendant?" A. Two. "Q. Now, after you met the defendant, what happened?" A. We walked down to the railroad tracks. "Q. What happened at the railroad tracks?" A. We were drinking

have encouraged; and the closeness of their ages (a difference of only one year and 18 days) are factors that should make this case an unattractive one to prosecute at all, and especially to prosecute as a felony, rather than as a misdemeanor chargeable under §261.5. But the State has chosen to prosecute in that manner, and the facts, I reluctantly conclude, may fit the crime.

Justice BRENNAN, with whom Justices WHITE and MARSHALL join, dissenting. . . .

[E]ven assuming that prevention of teenage pregnancy is an important governmental objective and that it is in fact an objective of §261.5 . . . ,

---

at the railroad tracks and we walked over to this bush and he started kissing me and stuff, and I was kissing him back, too, at first. Then, I was telling him to stop—"Q. Yes." A.—and I was telling him to slow down and stop. He said, "Okay, okay." But then he just kept doing it. He just kept doing it and then my sister and two other guys came over to where we were and my sister said—told me to get up and come home. And then I didn't—"Q. Yes." A.—and then my sister and—"Q. All right." A.—David, one of the boys that were there, started walking home and we stayed there and then later—"Q. All right." A.—Bruce left Michael, you know. "The Court: Michael being the defendant?" The Witness: Yeah. We was lying there and we were kissing each other, and then he asked me if I wanted to walk him over to the park; so we walked over to the park and we sat down on a bench and then he started kissing me again and we were laying on the bench. And he told me to take my pants off. I said, "No," and I was trying to get up and he hit me back down on the bench and then I just said to myself, "Forget it," and I let him do what he wanted to do and he took my pants off and he was telling me to put my legs around him and stuff—

"Q. Did you have sexual intercourse with the defendant?" A. Yeah. "Q. He did put his penis into your vagina?" A. Yes. "Q. You said that he hit you?" A. Yeah. "Q. How did he hit you?" A. He slugged me in the face. "Q. With what did he slug you?" A. His fist. "Q. Where abouts in the face?" A. On my chin. "Q. As a result of that, did you have any bruises or any kind of an injury?" A. Yeah. "Q. What happened?" A. I had bruises. "The Court: Did he hit you one time or did he hit you more than once?" The Witness: He hit me about two or three times.

"Q. Now, during the course of that evening, did the defendant ask you your age?" A. Yeah. "Q. And what did you tell him?" A. Sixteen. "Q. Did you tell him you were sixteen?" A. Yes. "Q. Now, you said you had been drinking, is that correct?" A. Yes. "Q. Would you describe your condition as a result of the drinking?" A. I was a little drunk.

CROSS-EXAMINATION "Q. Did you go off with Mr. M. away from the others?" A. Yeah. "Q. Why did you do that?" A. I don't know. I guess I wanted to. "Q. Did you have any need to go to the bathroom when you were there." A. Yes. "Q. And what did you do?" A. Me and my sister walked down the railroad tracks to some bushes and went to the bathroom. "Q. Now, you and Mr. M., as I understand it, went off into the bushes, is that correct?" A. Yes. "Q. Okay. And what did you do when you and Mr. M. were there in the bushes?" A. We were kissing and hugging. "Q. Were you sitting up?" A. We were laying down. "Q. You were lying down. This was in the bushes?" A. Yes. "Q. How far away from the rest of them were you?" A. They were just bushes right next to the railroad tracks. We just walked off into the bushes; not very far.

"Q. So your sister and the other two boys came over to where you were, you and Michael were, is that right?" A. Yeah. "Q. What did they say to you, if you remember?" A. My sister didn't say anything. She said, "Come on, Sharon, let's go home." "Q. She asked you to go

California still has the burden of proving that there are fewer teenage pregnancies under its gender-based statutory rape law than there would be if the law were gender neutral. To meet this burden, the State must show that because its statutory rape law punishes only males, and not females, it more effectively deters minor females from having sexual intercourse.[5]

The plurality assumes that a gender-neutral statute would be less effective than §261.5 in deterring sexual activity because a gender-neutral statute would create significant enforcement problems. . . . However, a State's bare assertion that its gender-based statutory classification substantially furthers an important governmental interest is not enough to meet its burden of proof under Craig v. Boren . . . .

The State has not produced such evidence in this case. Moreover, there are at least two serious flaws in the State's assertion that law enforcement problems created by a gender-neutral statutory rape law would make such a statute less effective than a gender-based statute in deterring sexual activity.

---

home with her?" A. (Affirmative nod.) "Q. Did you go home with her?" A. No. "Q. You wanted to stay with Mr. M.?" A. I don't know. "Q. Was this before or after he hit you?" A. Before.

"Q. What happened in the five minutes that Bruce stayed there with you and Michael?" A. I don't remember. "Q. You don't remember at all?" A. (Negative head shake.) "Q. Did you have occasion at that time to kiss Bruce?" A. Yeah. "Q. You did? You were kissing Bruce at that time?" A. (Affirmative nod.) "Q. Was Bruce kissing you?" A. Yes. "Q. And were you standing up at this time?" A. No, we were sitting down.

"Q. Okay. So at this point in time you had left Mr. M. and you were hugging and kissing with Bruce, is that right?" A. Yeah. "Q. And you were sitting up." A. Yes. "Q. Was your sister still there then?" A. No. Yeah, she was at first. "Q. What was she doing?" A. She was standing up with Michael and David. "Q. Yes. Was she doing anything with Michael and David?" A. No, I don't think so. "Q. Whose idea was it for you and Bruce to kiss? Did you initiate that?" A. Yes. "Q. What happened after Bruce left?" A. Michael asked me if I wanted to go walk to the park. "Q. And what did you say?" A. I said, "Yes." "Q. And then what happened?" A. We walked to the park.

"Q. How long did it take you to get to the park?" A. About ten or fifteen minutes. "Q. And did you walk there?" A. Yes. "Q. Did Mr. M. ever mention his name?" A. Yes. . . .

5. Petitioner has not questioned the State's constitutional power to achieve its asserted objective by criminalizing consensual sexual activity. However, I note that our cases would not foreclose such a privacy challenge. The State is attempting to reduce the incidence of teenage pregnancy by imposing criminal sanctions on those who engage in consensual sexual activity with minor females. We have stressed, however, that "[i]f the right of privacy means anything, it is the right of the individual, married or single, to be free from unwarranted governmental intrusion into matters so fundamentally affecting a person as the decision whether to bear or beget a child." Eisenstadt v. Baird, [1972]. Minors, too, enjoy a right of privacy in connection with decisions affecting procreation. Carey v. Population Services International, [1977]. Thus, despite the suggestion of the plurality to the contrary . . . , it is not settled that a State may rely on a pregnancy-prevention justification to make consensual sexual intercourse among minors a criminal act.

First, the experience of other jurisdictions, and California itself, belies the plurality's conclusion that a gender-neutral statutory rape law "may well be incapable of enforcement." There are now at least 37 States that have enacted gender-neutral statutory rape laws. Although most of these laws protect young persons (of either sex) from the sexual exploitation of older individuals, the laws of Arizona, Florida, and Illinois permit prosecution of both minor females and minor males for engaging in mutual sexual conduct. California has introduced no evidence that those States have been handicapped by the enforcement problems the plurality finds so persuasive.[7] Surely, if those States could provide such evidence, we might expect that California would have introduced it.

In addition, the California Legislature in recent years has revised other sections of the Penal Code to make them gender-neutral. For example [other California criminal law statutes], prohibiting sodomy and oral copulation with a "person who is under 18 years of age," could cause two minor homosexuals to be subjected to criminal sanctions for engaging in mutually consensual conduct. Again, the State has introduced no evidence to explain why a gender-neutral statutory rape law would be any more difficult to enforce than those statutes.

The second flaw in the State's assertion is that even assuming that a gender-neutral statute would be more difficult to enforce, the State has still not shown that those enforcement problems would make such a statute less effective than a gender-based statute in deterring minor females from engaging in sexual intercourse. Common sense, however, suggests that a gender-neutral statutory rape law is potentially a greater deterrent of sexual activity than a gender-based law, for the simple reason that a gender-neutral law subjects both men and women to criminal sanctions and thus arguably has a deterrent effect on twice as many potential violators. Even if fewer persons were prosecuted under the gender-neutral law, as the State suggests, it would still be true that twice as many persons would be subject to arrest. The State's failure to prove that a gender-neutral law would be a less effective deterrent than a gender-based law, like the State's failure to prove that a gender-neutral law would be difficult to enforce, should have led this Court to invalidate §261.5.

III

Until very recently, no California court or commentator had suggested that the purpose of California's statutory rape law was to protect young

---

7. There is a logical reason for this. In contrast to laws governing forcible rape, statutory rape laws apply to consensual sexual activity. Force is not an element of the crime. Since a woman who consents to an act of sexual intercourse is unlikely to report her partner to the police—whether or not she is subject to criminal sanctions—enforcement would not be undermined if the statute were to be made gender neutral. . . .

women from the risk of pregnancy. Indeed, the historical development of §261.5 demonstrates that the law was initially enacted on the premise that young women, in contrast to young men, were to be deemed legally incapable of consenting to an act of sexual intercourse.[9] Because their chastity was considered particularly precious, those young women were felt to be uniquely in need of the State's protection.[10] In contrast, young men were assumed to be capable of making such decisions for themselves; the law therefore did not offer them any special protection.

It is perhaps because the gender classification in California's statutory rape law was initially designed to further these outmoded sexual stereotypes, rather than to reduce the incidence of teenage pregnancies, that the State has been unable to demonstrate a substantial relationship between the classification and its newly asserted goal. . . .

I would hold that §261.5 violates the Equal Protection Clause of the Fourteenth Amendment, and I would reverse the judgment of the California Supreme Court.

Justice STEVENS, dissenting.

Local custom and belief—rather than statutory laws of venerable but doubtful ancestry—will determine the volume of sexual activity among unmarried teenagers. The empirical evidence cited by the plurality demonstrates the futility of the notion that a statutory prohibition will significantly affect the volume of that activity or provide a meaningful solution to the problems created by it. Nevertheless, as a matter of constitutional power, unlike my Brother Brennan . . . , I would have no doubt about the validity of a state law prohibiting all unmarried teenagers from engaging in sexual intercourse. The societal interests in reducing the incidence of venereal disease and teenage pregnancy are sufficient, in my judgment, to justify a prohibition of conduct that increases the risk of those harms.

9. California's statutory rape law had its origins in the Statutes of Westminster enacted during the reign of Edward I at the close of the 13th century. . . . The age of consent at that time was 12 years, reduced to 10 years in 1576. . . . This statute was part of the common law brought to the United States. Thus, when the first California penal statute was enacted, it contained a provision . . . that proscribed sexual intercourse with females under the age of 10. In 1889, the California statute was amended to make the age of consent 14. . . . In 1897, the age was advanced to 16. . . . In 1913 it was fixed at 18, where it now remains. . . .

Because females generally have not reached puberty by the age of 10, it is inconceivable that a statute designed to prevent pregnancy would be directed at acts of sexual intercourse with females under that age. . . .

10. Past decisions of the California courts confirm that the law was designed to protect the State's young females from their own uninformed decision making. . . . It was only in deciding *Michael M.* that the California Supreme Court decided for the first time in the 130-year history of the statute, that pregnancy prevention had become one of the purposes of the statute.

My conclusion that a nondiscriminatory prohibition would be constitutional does not help me answer the question whether a prohibition applicable to only half of the joint participants in the risk-creating conduct is also valid. It cannot be true that the validity of a total ban is an adequate justification for a selective prohibition; otherwise, the constitutional objection to discriminatory rules would be meaningless. The question in this case is whether the difference between males and females justifies this statutory discrimination based entirely on sex. . . .

In my judgment, the fact that a class of persons is especially vulnerable to a risk that a statute is designed to avoid is a reason for making the statute applicable to that class. The argument that a special need for protection provides a rational explanation for an exemption is one I simply do not comprehend. . . .

If pregnancy or some other special harm is suffered by one of the two participants in the prohibited act, that special harm no doubt would constitute a legitimate mitigating factor in deciding what, if any, punishment might be appropriate in a given case. But from the standpoint of fashioning a general preventive rule—or, indeed, in determining appropriate punishment when neither party in fact has suffered any special harm—I regard a total exemption for the members of the more endangered class as utterly irrational.

In my opinion, the only acceptable justification for a general rule requiring disparate treatment of the two participants in a joint act must be a legislative judgment that one is more guilty than the other. The risk-creating conduct that this statute is designed to prevent requires the participation of two persons—one male and one female. In many situations it is probably true that one is the aggressor and the other is either an unwilling, or at least a less willing, participant in the joint act. If a statute authorized punishment of only one participant and required the prosecutor to prove that that participant had been the aggressor, I assume that the discrimination would be valid. Although the question is less clear, I also assume, for the purpose of deciding this case, that it would be permissible to punish only the male participant, if one element of the offense were proof that he had been the aggressor, or at least in some respects the more responsible participant in the joint act. The statute at issue in this case, however, requires no such proof. The question raised by this statute is whether the State, consistently with the Federal Constitution, may always punish the male and never the female when they are equally responsible or when the female is the more responsible of the two.

It would seem to me that an impartial lawmaker could give only one answer to that question. The fact that the California Legislature has decided to apply its prohibition only to the male may reflect a legislative judgment that in the typical case the male is actually the more guilty party. Any such judgment must, in turn, assume that the decision to engage in the risk-creating conduct is always—or at least typically—a male decision. . . . But the possibility that such a habitual attitude may reflect nothing more than an irrational prejudice makes it an insufficient justification for discriminatory treatment that is otherwise blatantly unfair. For, as I read this statute, it requires that one, and only one, of two equally guilty wrongdoers be stigmatized by a criminal conviction. . . .

[I do not] find at all persuasive the suggestion that this discrimination is adequately justified by the desire to encourage females to inform against their male partners. Even if the concept of a wholesale informant's exemption were an acceptable enforcement device, what is the justification for defining the exempt class entirely by reference to sex rather than by reference to a more neutral criterion such as relative innocence? Indeed, if the exempt class is to be composed entirely of members of one sex, what is there to support the view that the statutory purpose will be better served by granting the informing license to females rather than to males? If a discarded male partner informs on a promiscuous female, a timely threat of prosecution might well prevent the precise harm the statute is intended to minimize.

Finally, even if my logic is faulty and there actually is some speculative basis for treating equally guilty males and females differently, I still believe that any such speculative justification would be outweighed by the paramount interest in evenhanded enforcement of the law. A rule that authorizes punishment of only one of two equally guilty wrongdoers violates the essence of the constitutional requirement that the sovereign must govern impartially.

I respectfully dissent.

Notes

1. Consent and Statutory Rape. Technically, consent is not an element of statutory rape. Yet the extent to which Sharon participated willingly seems important to the Justices. Note that Justice Rehnquist and Justice Blackmun reach the same conclusion in the case, but apparently based on different views about Sharon's level of consent. From Justice Rehnquist, all we know is that Sharon was "struck in the face" for "rebuffing" Michael's advances and that then she "submitted" to sexual intercourse. Under Justice Blackmun's detailed reading of the facts, Sharon's participation in the incident was "not unwilling." Which rationale for statutory rape laws does each narrative support? In what sense, if any, did Sharon lack capacity? Was she taken advantage of because of her age? If Sharon was "willing," what does this say about the majority's justification for the sex-based statute—that the fear of pregnancy is an effective deterrent?

What does it mean for a teenage girl to "consent" to sex? Michelle Oberman explains:

> [E]ven assuming that girls do experience sexual pleasure and desire, these are only two of a multiplicity of factors which induce their consent to sex.

The stories girls tell about the "consensual" sex in which they engage reflect a poignant subtext of hope and pain. Girls express longing for emotional attachment, romance, and respect. At the same time, they suffer enormous insecurity and diminished self-image. These two factors are clearly interrelated—the worse girls feel about themselves, the more they look to males for ratification of the women that they are becoming. The importance of being attractive to males takes on a central role in many girls' lives. . . . Girls want boyfriends, relationships, or somebody who will hold them and tell them that they are wanted.

Girls negotiate access to the fulfillment of these emotional needs by way of sex. A girl who wants males to find her attractive, who wants acceptance and popularity, might reasonably consent to sex with a popular boy, to multiple popular boys, or with any partner who can persuade her that she is attractive and desirable. Males recognize, and occasionally exploit, girls' insecurity. . . . Modern statutory rape law . . . classifies intercourse as either consensual sex or rape. However, from the girl's vantage point, her consent may have been so fraught with ambivalence that it was meaningless. . . .

If girls' autonomy is to be taken seriously, the law must evaluate the sexual decisions they make, and formulate a legal response which enhances the likelihood that those decisions are autonomous ones.[1]

If Oberman is right, what would such a legal response look like? Are the considerations for boys concerning unwanted sex any different than they are for girls?

Consider Wendy Williams' comment about statutory rape laws:

At this point, we need to think as deeply as we can about what we want the future of women and men to be. Do we want equality of the sexes—or do we want justice for two kinds of human beings who are fundamentally different?[2]

2. Statutory Rape Laws. At one time, the legal age of sexual consent was 10 or younger. The nineteenth-century reformers who succeeded in persuading states to increase the statutory age were motivated both by a desire to protect young women from sexual exploitation, and to control their sexuality.[3]

The legal consent age now ranges from 12 to 18, the most common being 16. The statutory rape laws of all states except Idaho are now sex-neutral. The move to neutrality appears to have had less to do with a recognition of female sexual autonomy than with a recognition of male vulnerability to sexual exploitation. Recent well-publicized cases involving the solicitation

1. Michelle Oberman, Turning Girls into Women: Re-Evaluating Modern Statutory Rape Law, 85 J. Crim. L. & Criminology 15, 70 (1994).

2. Wendy W. Williams, The Equality Crisis: Some Reflections on Culture, Courts, and Feminism, 7 Women's Rights L. Rep. 175, 200 (1982).

3. See J. Shoshanna Ehrlich, You Can Steal Her Virginity But Not Her Doll: The Nineteenth Century Campaign to Raise the Legal Age of Sexual Consent, 15 Cardozo J.L. & Gender 229, 231 (2009).

of sex from underage boys by priests, teachers, and coaches have dramatically altered social attitudes. (See Note 4, below.)

Many state statutes now focus on the number of years that separate the parties, either ignoring relationships between adolescents of similar ages, or making these interactions less serious. In California, for example, any person who engages in sexual intercourse with a minor who is not more than three years older or three years younger than the perpetrator is guilty of a misdemeanor, whereas any person over the age of 21 years who engages in sexual intercourse with a minor under 16 years of age may be guilty of either a misdemeanor or a felony.[4] Laws that treat sexual acts between teenagers more leniently, or ignore them altogether, are sometimes called "Romeo and Juliet laws." The American Law Institute is considering proposed changes in the Model Penal Code that would include an offense titled sexual penetration of minor, a felony of the third degree. It would impose liability on a person who engages in intercourse and "knows or recklessly disregards the risk that the other person is a minor who . . . is not the spouse of the actor and is less than 16 years old and the actor is more than four years older than such minor." Another proposed offense would make an actor guilty of rape of a child if the child "is less than twelve years old and the actor is more than two years older than the child."[5] If you were drafting such provisions, are these the formulations that you would propose?

3. Gender Neutrality and Differential Treatment of Male and Female Offenders.   Most countries with legal traditions similar to the United States, such as Great Britain, Canada, and Australia, have adopted gender-neutral statutory rape laws.[6] However, many prosecutors, judges, and juries, as well as society generally, tend to view the crime differently when the victims are male, particularly when the offenders are female. In justifying gender-specific language in the Model Penal Code, its commentators claim that the "potential consequences of coerced intimacy [for males] do not seem so grave. For one thing there is no prospect of unwanted pregnancy. And however devalued virginity has become for the modern woman, it would be difficult to believe that its loss constitutes comparable injury to the male."[7] Is this right? Should the sex of the victim affect the penalties?

Double standards regarding statutory rape remain common. A widespread attitude is that underage men welcome the encounter; otherwise they would not be physically capable of engaging in the sexual act. However,

4. Cal. Penal Code §261.5 (West 2016).
5. Am. Law Inst., Model Penal Code, §213.2, Tentative Draft No. 5 (Sept. 8, 2015).
6. Philip N.S. Rumney, In Defense of Gender Neutrality Within Rape, 6 Seattle J. Soc. Just. 481, 486 (2007).
7. Susan Estrich, Rape, 95 Yale L.J. 1087, 1150 (1986) (quoting Model Penal Code §213.1 comment at 338 (1980)).

research indicates that male sexual responses are stimulated not only by desire, but sometimes fear and anger.[8] Boys may often be reluctant to acknowledge sexual abuse by women because the culture conditions them to view such encounters as "getting lucky."[9] Many male adolescents fear that resistance will make them look like a "sissy" or a "fag," and that complaints will result in disbelief or ridicule. However, even victims who repress their sense of injury may suffer psychological harm.[10]

The culture's persistent double standards concerning sexual victimization help explain the harsher sentences that male sex offenders normally receive.[11] However, in some cases female offenders are beginning to receive harsh treatment if it appears that they exploited an underage male. One of the most well-known cases was a Seattle grade school teacher, Mary Kay Letourneau, who at age 35 had sex with her 13-year-old student, for which she received a 7.5-year prison sentence. All but six months of the sentence was suspended conditional upon her entering a sex-offender treatment program and refraining from contact with the boy. Shortly thereafter, her sentence was reinstated after she was found in his company. She had one child with the boy prior to sentencing and conceived another during her brief release. The couple married once the boy became of age, and reunited after she served her prison sentence.[12] Other cases include female teachers in Tennessee and Florida. Lisa Lynette Clark of Georgia was impregnated by her son's 15-year-old friend, whom she married a day before she was arrested. Another woman was sentenced to 30 years in 2005 for having sex with teenagers, to whom she provided drugs and alcohol.[13] Are these cases any different from the more traditional statutory rape of girls by men?

Female sexual offenders have varying profiles. Some are teachers who fall in love with young students and pursue them in the hope that they will return their affection. Others were victims of child sexual abuse or experienced other intergenerational abuse.[14] Should such different background circumstances matter?

8. Kay L. Levine, No Penis, No Problem, 33 Fordham Urban L.J. 357, 363-64 (2006).
9. Alicia Graham, Simply Sexual: The Discrepancy in Treatment Between Male and Female Sex Offenders, 7 Whittier J. Child. & Fam. Advoc. 145, 160 (2007).
10. Levine, supra note 8, at 404.
11. Graham, supra note 9, at 153.
12. Jennifer Joseph et al., Mary Kay Letourneau Fualaau, Vili Fualaau Detail Their Path from Teacher-Student Sex Scandal to Raising Teenagers, ABC News (Apr. 10, 2015), http://abcnews.go.com/US/mary-kay-letourneau-fualaau-vili-fualaau-detail-path/story?id=30160737.
13. Kate Zernike, The Siren Song of Sex with Boys, N.Y. Times, Dec. 11, 2005, at SR3.
14. Levine, supra note 8, at 395.

Putting Theory Into Practice

5-1. A law in State X defines statutory rape as sexual intercourse with a child under the age of 16. Colleen, age 20, gives birth to a baby fathered by 16-year-old Shane, who at the time of conception was 15. Colleen was, for several years, Shane's babysitter, and Shane never complained to his parents about the sexual liaison with Colleen. Colleen is charged with statutory rape, but pleads to the lesser crime of contributing to a child's misconduct. After the child's birth, Colleen applies for public assistance, whereupon the Department of Social Services petitions the court to order Shane to contribute to the child's financial support. The Parentage Act of State X, which mandates that parents provide support for their children, makes no exception for minors and courts have held that society has a legitimate interest in holding parents rather than the state responsible for support.[15] Does this make sense? Should Shane be liable for child support?

5-2. A former New York sportscaster who buys sex from a 14-year-old victim is initially charged with statutory rape and then allowed to plead guilty to endangering the welfare of a child.[16] Should prosecutors use statutory rape laws to curb demand for child prostitution, which otherwise exposes customers to only misdemeanor liability?

5-3. Two 16-year-olds voluntarily have sex. Should either of them be charged with statutory rape? Both of them?[17]

5-4. A number of states allow underage pregnant teenagers to consent to marriage but not to sex. Should men arrested for statutory rape be allowed to marry their pregnant partners in lieu of jail time?[18]

5-5. In a celebrated case involving students at St. Paul's prep school, an 18-year-old senior competed with other male students over who could "score"

15. Alia Beard, Rau, Arizona Statutory Rape Victim Forced to Pay Child Support, Arizona Republic, Sept. 2, 2014 (man who fathered a child at 14 forced to pay child support when he reached early twenties). For other cases, see Michael R. Hudzik & Anthony E. Chiola, Statutory Rape and the Duty to Pay Child Support (When One Crime Is Not Enough), 27 D.C.B.A. Brief 26 (2015).

16. Laura Italiano, Former Sportscaster Marvell Scott Pleads Guilty in Child Prostitute Case, N.Y. Post, Aug. 16, 2011. See Amanda Shapiro, Buyer Beware: Why Johns Should Be Charged with Statutory Rape for Buying Sex from a Child, 23 J.L. & Pol'y 449 (2014).

17. Louise McCarthy, 16-year-old Faces Statutory Rape Charge for Having Consensual Sex with Girl the Same Age as Him, Yahoo! News (Mar. 5, 2016), https://uk.news.yahoo.com/16-old-faces-statutory-rape-charge-having-consensual-142846600.html.

18. See Rumney, supra note 6, at 486; see also Claire Bushey, Age of Consent Muddles Law on Marriage v. Rape, Alternet, June 10, 2007, http://www.alternet.org/story/53628/age_of_consent_muddles_law_on_marriage_vs._rape (reporting on new law eliminating pregnancy as a basis for underage marriage and requiring judicial permission to marry).

with the most girls. Just before his 2014 graduation, Owen Labrie invited a 15-year-old girl to join him for a "senior salute," which could involve anything from kissing to sexual intercourse. The girl claimed that she had said no three times to intercourse, but acknowledged on cross examination that she lifted up her arms so that Labrie could take her shirt off, and raised her hips so he could pull off her shorts. She also explained that "I wanted to not cause a conflict" and "I felt like I was frozen." Labrie denied that sexual penetration took place, but acknowledged that he was wearing a condom. He claimed that "I thought she was having a great time."[19] The jury acquitted Labrie of aggravated felonious assault, which required a showing of nonconsent. It convicted him of three charges of misdemeanor sexual assault (based on the fact that the victim was under 16) and one misdemeanor count of endangering the welfare of a minor. He was sentenced to one year in jail, followed by five years of probation, and required to register for life as a sex offender.[20] Was this an appropriate result? How would the case have come out under the proposed Model Penal Code formulation? How should the school respond?

2. Defining and Explaining Rape: Distinguishing Consent and Nonconsent

According to governmental and crime center research, about 16 to 18 percent of American women and 5 to 14 percent of American men have experienced an attempted or completed rape.[21] Rates for African American women are slightly higher (22 percent) and for Hispanic women are slightly lower (14 percent) than for white women (18 percent). About 12 percent of victims are 10 years old or younger; 30 percent are 11 to 17, and 37 percent are 18 to 24.[22] Gay, bisexual, and transgender individuals are particularly vulnerable.[23]

---

19. Emily Bazelon, The St. Paul's Rape Case Shows Why Sexual-Assault Laws Must Change, N.Y. Times Mag., Aug. 26, 2015.

20. Jeannie Suk, St. Paul's School and a New Definition of Rape, New Yorker, Nov. 3, 2015.

21. Rates for men are particularly hard to calculate. See Hanna Rosin, When Men are Raped, Slate (Apr. 29, 2014), http://www.slate.com/articles/double_x/doublex/2014/04/male_rape_in_america_a_new_study_reveals_that_men_are_sexually_assaulted.html; see also Bennett Capers, Real Rape Too, 99 Cal. L. Rev. 1259 (2011) (discussing male rape); see discussion in Section 4, infra.

22. Nat'l Center for Injury Prevention and Control, CDC, National Intimate Partner and Sexual Violence Survey (2010); surveys cited in Testimony of Susan B. Carbon, Director, Office on Violence Against Women, Rape in the United States, Testimony before the Subcommittee on Crime and Drugs, Committee on the Judiciary, United States Senate (Sept. 14, 2010), https://www.justice.gov/sites/default/files/testimonies/witnesses/attachments/09/14/10/09-14-10-carbon-rape-in-the-usa.pdf.

23. See surveys reviewed in The White House Council on Women and Girls, Rape and Sexual Assault: A Renewed Call to Action 10-11 (2014) (hereinafter "White House Council").

In some research, 98 percent of female and 93 percent of male rape survivors report that their assailants were male.[24] Estimates of the frequency of prison rape vary. According to Department of Justice statistics between 4 and 10 percent of prison inmates report being sexually victimized in the preceding 12 months or since admission to the facility.[25] Survivors of rape suffer a wide range of related injuries including sexually transmitted infections, depression, anxiety, and post-traumatic stress disorder.[26]

Explanations for rape fall along three main dimensions: individual, socio-biological, and cultural. At the individual level,

> many rapists are attracted to power; they want the feeling of domination, adventure, and status that comes from coercing sex. Other men are motivated by anger; rape serves to punish or avenge some wrong by a particular woman, women in general, or another perceived adversary. Most rapists blame their victims, and some stress situational influences such as peer pressure or drug and alcohol abuse. Exposure to family violence during childhood increases the probability that men will become sexually violent as adults.[27]

The sociobiological explanation is that, at an evolutionary level, men having intercourse with a large number of fertile females has "favorable reproductive consequences." For men who have difficulty attracting willing partners, coercive sex is "adaptive" and likely to be favored by natural selection.[28] Critics of this account note that they do not explain the substantial variation in rape rates across time and culture, or the frequency of sexual assaults involving non-vaginal intercourse or female victims too young or too old to bear children.

Cultural explanations stress the eroticization of male aggression in popular films, television, fiction, pornography, and video games. Such frameworks also underscore the role of male-dominated institutions such as the military, fraternities, and athletic teams in fostering attitudes that legitimate male sexual aggression.

A major issue is what constitutes the line between coercive and consensual sex. What makes this line so difficult? Have you ever had an experience in which you had difficulty seeing the difference?

24. Nat'l Center for Injury Prevention and Control, supra note 22. Other research finds higher rates of female perpetrators. See Rosin, supra note 21.

25. Dep't of Justice, Nearly 10 Percent of Former State Prisoners Reported Being Sexually Victimized During Confinement (May 17, 2012), http://www.ojp.usdoj.gov/newsroom/pressreleases/2012/ojppr051712.pdf; U.S. Dep't of Justice, Bureau of Justice Statistics, Allen Beck et al., Sexual Victimization in Prisons and Jails Reported by Inmates, 2011-12 (2013).

26. See research reviewed in White House Council, supra note 23, at 12-13.

27. Deborah L. Rhode, What Women Want: An Agenda for the Women's Movement 120 (2014).

28. See Owen D. Jones & Timothy H. Goldsmith, Law and Behavioral Biology, 105 Colum. L. Rev. 405 (2005).

Susan Estrich, Rape
95 Yale L.J. 1087, 1102-05 (1986)

My view is that . . . a "negligent rapist" should be punished, albeit—as in murder—less severely than the man who acts with purpose or knowledge, or even knowledge of the risk. First, he is sufficiently blame-worthy for it to be just to punish him. Second, the injury he inflicts is sufficiently grave to deserve the law's prohibition.

The traditional argument against negligence liability is that punishment should be limited to cases of choice, because to punish a man for his stupidity is unjust and, in deterrence terms, ineffective. Under this view, a man should only be held responsible for what he does knowingly or purposely or at least while aware of the risks involved. . . .

If inaccuracy or indifference to consent is [the best that a man can do] because he lacks the capacity to act reasonably, then it might well be unjust and ineffective to punish him for it. But such men will be rare . . . at least as long as voluntary drunkenness is not equated with inherent lack of capacity. More common is the case of the man who could have done better but didn't; could have paid attention, but didn't; heard her say no, or saw her tears, but decided to ignore them. Neither justice nor deterrence argues against punishing this man.

In holding a man to such a standard of reasonableness, the law signifies that it considers a woman's consent to sex to be significant enough to merit a man's reasoned attention. In effect, the law imposes a duty on men to open their eyes and use their heads before engaging in sex—not to read a woman's mind, but to give her credit for knowing her own mind when she speaks it. The man who has the inherent capacity to act reasonably, but fails to do so, has made the blameworthy choice to violate this duty. While the injury caused by purposeful conduct may be greater than that caused by negligent acts, being negligently sexually penetrated without one's consent remains a grave harm, and being treated like an object whose words or actions are not even worthy of consideration adds insult to injury. This dehumanization exacerbates the denial of dignity and autonomy which is so much a part of the injury of rape, and it is equally present in both the purposeful and negligent rape.

By holding out the prospect of punishment for negligence, the law provides an additional motive for men to "take care before acting, to use their faculties and draw on their experience in gauging the potentialities of contemplated conduct." We may not yet have reached the point where men are required to ask verbally. But if silence does not negate consent, at least the word "no" should, and those who ignore such an explicit sign of non-consent should be subject to criminal liability.

State v. Alberts
722 N.W.2d 402 (Iowa 2006)

STREIT, Justice.

Is skinny-dipping a form of sexual behavior? Michael John Alberts allegedly sexually assaulted R.M., his nephew's twenty-two-year-old girlfriend. Alberts was convicted of third-degree sexual abuse following a jury trial in Johnson County, Iowa. . . . Because we find the district court erred by failing to determine whether R.M. made a prior false allegation of sexual misconduct relating to a skinny-dipping incident, we reverse the district court judgment on this error and remand for further proceedings.

On the night of October 19, 2003, R.M. attended a bachelorette party at a Cedar Rapids bar named Borrowed Bucks. Alberts was also at the bar, and the two struck up a conversation. Alberts and R.M. knew each other through R.M.'s boyfriend, Jesse Goeller. Alberts is Jesse's forty-two-year-old uncle. R.M. attended a half dozen or so family gatherings with Jesse where Alberts was present.

Additionally, a few weeks prior to the bachelorette party, Jesse, R.M., and a friend of R.M. ran into Alberts at Borrowed Bucks. There, the four of them danced as a group and at times Alberts and R.M. danced together in a provocative manner. When the bar closed, R.M. and Jesse sat with Alberts in the cab of Alberts' semi-truck. R.M.'s friend waited in the car. R.M. and Alberts smoked marijuana. Before leaving, R.M. unhooked her bra under her shirt and hung it on Alberts' rearview mirror. R.M. left the cab and Jesse followed a couple minutes later after Alberts handed Jesse R.M.'s bra.

During the bachelorette party, R.M. drank several beers and a shot of tequila. At closing time, R.M. went with Alberts to his family's lake house instead of remaining with the bachelorette group. When they arrived at the lake house, R.M. ate some food, headed for the bathroom, and vomited. She then told Alberts she felt "like crap" and needed to "sleep this off." Alberts followed R.M. into one of the bedrooms and sat next to her on the bed. With Alberts still in the room, R.M. took off her skirt and climbed into bed.

Sometime later, R.M. woke to find Alberts sucking her breasts. According to R.M., she did not respond to his actions. Alberts then performed oral sex on her and had intercourse with her. R.M. claims she pretended to be asleep during the entire episode. Alberts thereafter left to sleep in another bedroom.

The next morning, Alberts drove R.M. to her home. R.M. showered as soon as she got there. Jesse, the boyfriend, who had been visiting friends in Ames, returned home early in the afternoon. After speaking with R.M. about the previous night's events, Jesse took R.M. to the hospital.

At the hospital, R.M. told the nurse she needed to report a rape. A sexual assault examination ensued. The nurse found semen inside her vagina, but did not observe any evidence of trauma or injury. Police officers spoke with R.M.

at the hospital and told her she had the option to press charges, which she did three days later. . . .

Because Alberts had elicited statements from witnesses during depositions regarding R.M.'s flirtatious nature, her past sexual comments, and prior allegation of being trapped by a man during a skinny-dipping incident, the State filed a motion in limine asking the court to determine whether such evidence was admissible. The State contended such testimony was either inadmissible under the Iowa rape-shield law or irrelevant to the case at hand.

In the unreported pretrial hearing, the State pointed to several incidents involving R.M. it considered inadmissible and irrelevant. One specific instance was a Fourth of July party where Jesse's brother Josh discovered R.M. skinny-dipping with Chris Slach. In his deposition, Josh described how he saw R.M. with her arms around Slach in the Cedar River. Josh said he "busted them" because R.M. was supposed to be dating his brother. According to Josh, R.M. came out of the water crying. She told Josh "[t]hank God you saw me. I didn't know what to do out there. . . . I couldn't get away from him. I didn't know what to do." R.M. later explained that nothing sexual had happened between the two. Slach was also prepared to testify it was R.M.'s idea to go skinny-dipping and there was no sexual contact between the two.

Alberts argued the rape-shield law was not applicable to this situation because there was no sexual contact and therefore no "past sexual behavior." Alternatively, he argued that if this was sexual activity or sexual behavior, then it was admissible under the false-claim exception to the rape-shield law.

The district court sustained most of the State's motion *in limine* and specifically excluded any evidence pertaining to the skinny-dipping incident. The court also excluded any testimony which described R.M.'s character as flirtatious or promiscuous. However, the court allowed the jury to hear evidence that R.M. had engaged in "dirty dancing" with Alberts a few weeks before the alleged sexual abuse, smoked marijuana with him in the cab of his semi-truck, and removed her bra and hung it on his rear-view mirror. . . .

Alberts claimed the district court erred when it ruled he could not present evidence about the skinny-dipping incident or question R.M. about the incident during cross-examination. . . .

Rule 5.412 prohibits introduction of reputation or opinion evidence of a complainant's "past sexual behavior" and substantially limits admissibility of evidence of specific instances of a complainant's past sexual behavior. Rule 5.412(d) defines "past sexual behavior" as "sexual behavior other than the sexual behavior with respect to which sexual abuse is alleged." We recently clarified this definition:

> "past sexual behavior" means a volitional or non-volitional physical act that the victim has performed for the purpose of the sexual stimulation or gratification of either the victim or another person or an act that is sexual intercourse, deviate

sexual intercourse or sexual contact, or an attempt to engage in such an act, between the victim and another person. . . .

In his brief to the district court, Alberts argued the skinny-dipping incident was not "past sexual behavior" and "not a claim of prior sexual activity because no actual sexual contact occurred." In support of this argument, Alberts offered the deposition testimony of both skinny-dippers.

When questioned at her deposition about the incident, R.M. denied any sexual activity occurred:

> We were skinny dipping in the river together, and he got close to me and asked me if he could kiss me, and I said, "No, I have a boyfriend."

Slach corroborated R.M.'s testimony that she declined his request for a kiss. Both parties expressly denied any sexual activity occurred. . . .

At the outset, we concede the difficulty in determining what sexual behavior is for purposes of our rape-shield law. [In a prior case, the court held that nude posing was not sexual conduct per se but in some circumstances could be determined to be so.]

Just like nudity alone is not sexual, skinny-dipping in and of itself is not sexual behavior. But in this case, the skinny-dipping incident should be deemed sexual behavior based on the circumstances described. Slach testified he was at a Fourth of July party drawing a beer from the keg when R.M. approached him and asked him if he would like to go swimming. It was approximately midnight and the two of them had never previously spoken. At his deposition, Slach said:

> I didn't see any reason to decline her. I wasn't seeing anybody at the time, and I just assumed from the way that she come up to me that she was somewhat interested, and it didn't appear to be at the time that she was attached to anybody either.

According to Slach, R.M. took her clothes off first and encouraged him to do the same. He recalls both of them being completely naked. While they were in the river, R.M. put her arms around Slach's shoulders, which prompted him to ask for permission to kiss her. Slach stated "it kind of seemed to me like she was coming on to me." After R.M. declined the kiss, the two of them continued to have their arms around each other for another five minutes until Josh interrupted them, causing them to get out of the water.

Based on these facts, the skinny-dipping was likely a precursor to sexual activity. This is evidenced by Slach asking for a kiss. To say it was not sexual behavior would be to say a circumstance where the complaining witness was thwarted in her attempt to meet someone for an amorous rendezvous was not sexual behavior. Such a result would be contrary to the purpose of the rape-shield law, which is to protect the victim's privacy, encourage the reporting and prosecution of sex offenses, and prevent the parties from delving into distractive, irrelevant matters. . . . Thus, this particular episode of skinny-dipping is covered by the rape-shield law unless R.M. made a related false allegation of sexual misconduct. . . .

[T]he court failed to take the additional step of determining whether R.M. made a false claim of sexual misconduct relating to the incident, which would make the rape-shield law not applicable. . . .

In her deposition, R.M. stated Slach never "forced himself" on her while they were skinny-dipping. However, at the time of the incident, R.M. allegedly came out of the water crying. According to Josh, the person who discovered R.M. and Slach skinny-dipping, R.M. said: "Thank God you saw me. I didn't know what to do out there. . . . I couldn't get away from him. I didn't know what to do." R.M.'s statements to Josh, if she did say them, are relevant for two reasons. First, they reflect on her credibility as a witness. Second, the alleged statements may reveal a motive to lie. If a fact finder were to conclude she made untruthful statements to preserve her boyfriend's perception of her virtue when she was discovered skinny-dipping with another man, the fact finder might reasonably conclude she's also untruthful with respect to her allegations that Alberts raped her for the same reason.

Even if the evidence was relevant, it may still "be excluded if its probative value is substantially outweighed by danger of unfair prejudice, confusion of the issues, or misleading the jury, or by considerations of undue delay, waste of time, or needless presentation of cumulative evidence." . . .

Under Rule 5.403, the primary focus is not upon the witness, but the interests of the defendant and the right of the defendant to present a defense. . . . Based on the record before us, we do not find any of the aforementioned dangers potentially outweighed the probative value of this evidence. This evidence would not have been confusing to the jury, nor would it have been cumulative or a waste of time. Moreover, the evidence would not have been misleading to the jury because R.M. would have had ample opportunity to deny or explain her allegedly untruthful statements. Finally, while it may have been embarrassing for R.M. to testify about going skinny-dipping, this is not the kind of unfair prejudice that will outweigh the probative value of clearly relevant evidence. This is especially true when the countervailing right of a defendant to present a defense to a criminal charge is at stake. . . .

We find the trial court abused its discretion by excluding evidence of the skinny-dipping incident without first giving Alberts the opportunity to prove . . . that R.M. made a prior false claim of sexual misconduct involving the man with whom she went skinny-dipping. For the sake of judicial economy, we remand for a hearing to determine whether R.M. made these statements and if so, whether they are false. If the trial court finds Alberts meets the threshold showing set forth in this opinion, then a new trial shall be granted. If Alberts fails to make such a showing, then his conviction stands. This matter is remanded to the trial court for proceedings consistent with this opinion.

Notes

1. Rape Law Reform. Rape law reform in this country has come in three waves: (1) the Model Penal Code (MPC) revision of the 1950s, (2) legislation enacted in the 1970s through the 1990s responding to the critique of rape laws by women's advocates; and (3) recent legal and educational initiatives to address rape, particularly among acquaintances and particularly vulnerable populations such as prisoners and members of the military. The MPC, which stimulated statutory reform in many states, abolished a common provision requiring the victim to offer the "utmost" or "reasonable" resistance. This reform refocused the crime from the consent of the woman to the conduct of the defendant. To increase the likelihood of convictions and to reduce the scope for idiosyncratic or biased judgments, the MPC also divided rape into three categories. First-degree felony rape was reserved for life-threatening conduct where the parties were strangers or where the defendant inflicted serious bodily harm. Life-threatening rape between acquaintances was a second-degree felony. Less serious abuses were grouped under a new third-degree felony of "gross sexual imposition." The choice continues to raise subtle questions about naming the crime. Does the decision to call such conduct something other than "rape" matter?

The next wave of law reform brought new legislation, such as rape shield statutes, which sought to protect victims, encourage reporting, and exclude prejudicial evidence. By the close of the 1990s, all states had such provisions. In addition, in 1994, Congress enacted Federal Rules of Evidence 413 and 415, which make evidence of the defendant's prior instances of sexual violence admissible in federal cases, even if relevant only to the defendant's disposition or propensity to engage in such conduct. The rules have been controversial and states have divided on whether to follow them. Advocates see them as necessary to convict repeat offenders. A case in point involved a Baltimore man cleared in four trials based on similar allegations that he broke into a home and sexually assaulted a woman. The defendant claimed that all of the encounters were consensual and trial judges excluded evidence of the prior incidents.[29] Critics of the federal approach have objected that evidence of prior crimes is unduly prejudicial and that defendants have been subject to intrusive pretrial proceedings in cases where evidence of the claimed assault is dubious.

Other reforms spurred by women's rights advocates included reformulation of statutory provisions with gender-neutral language, elimination or relaxation of the marital rape exemption, alterations in the substantive requirements of force and non-consent, and modification of federal definitions of

---

29. Ian Duncan, Rape Acquittals Spur Calls for Law Change, Balt. Sun, Oct. 29, 2013.

rape that collected crime statistics only on rapes that involved "the carnal knowledge of a female forcibly and against her will."[30]

A third wave of reform, reflected in a number of initiatives including a new revision of the Model Penal Code, concerns further modifications to the consent requirement. See Note 3, below. Current reform efforts have also focused on prosecutions of sexual assault in educational institutions (see Section 3, below) and in the military (see Section 4, below).

2. Marital Rape. Early common law assumed that a married woman gave her irrevocable consent to intercourse with her husband. This assumption followed from the law's treatment of married women as their husbands' property. When this rationale became outdated, other justifications emerged for the marital exemption from rape law. According to the Model Penal Code, courts should not intrude on the "privacy" of the family relationship; forced sex by a husband is not as harmful as other sexual assaults; and spousal rape would be too easy to charge, too hard to disprove, and too readily available for blackmail. In many countries in Africa and the Middle East, attitudes toward marital rape still mirror those that sustained traditional exemption in Anglo-American law and 123 countries do not recognize the crime.[31]

By 1993, all jurisdictions in the United States had abolished the marital rape exemption by statute or judicial decision, although some continued to treat spouses who rape differently than other rapists.[32] For example, a few states require spouses to show force or threat of force, not just coercion. Other states only permit prosecution when the parties have a written separation agreement or are in the process of a divorce.[33]

Is there a convincing justification for treating marital rape with greater leniency than other sexual assault? The traditional arguments for the exemption are that criminalizing nonconsensual marital sex undermines marital intimacy and provides a way for a "vindictive wife" to use fabricated claims to

30. The definition updated in 2012 eliminates the word "forcible" and defines rape as "the penetration . . . of the vagina or anus with any body part or object, or oral penetration by a sex organ of another person without the consent of the victim." U.S. Dep't of Justice, Attorney General Holder Announces Revisions to the Uniform Crime Reports Definition of Rape (Jan. 6, 2012), http://www.fbi.gov/news/pressrel/press-releases/attorney-general-eric-holder-announces-revisions-to-the-uniform-crime-reports-definition-of-rape.

31. Megan Lutz-Priefert, A Call for a More Permanent International Definition of Rape, 6 Creighton Int'l & Comp. L.J. 85 (2015); Michelle J. Anderson, Marital Immunity, Intimate Relationships, and Improper Inferences: A New Law on Sexual Offenses by Intimates, 54 Hastings L.J. 1465, 1468-73, 1557-74 (2003).

32. Samantha Allen, Marital Rape Is Semi-Legal in 8 States, The Daily Beast (June 9, 2015), http://www.thedailybeast.com/articles/2015/06/09/marital-rape-is-semi-legal-in-8-states.html; Anderson, supra note 31, at 1470-71, 1537-74.

33. See, e.g., Ohio Rev. Code Ann. 2907.01(L). For discussion, see Patricia J. Falk, Husbands Who Drug and Rape Their Wives: The Injustice of the Marital Exemption in Ohio's Sexual Offenses, 36 Women's Rts. L. Rep. 265 (2015).

gain leverage in a divorce case.[34] No research, however, finds that wives are prone to make false charges.[35] What the evidence does show is that the greatest adverse psychological effects on women who have been raped are those resulting from sexual assaults by a husband or a relative. In one study, 52 percent of women raped by a husband and 52 percent of women raped by a relative reported long-term effects on their lives. For women raped by a stranger, the figure was 39 percent; for women raped by an acquaintance, 25 percent; and for women raped by a friend, date, or lover, 22 percent.[36] Based on such evidence, a few courts have specifically rejected the rationale that marital rape is less traumatic than stranger rape. Does it follow that the law should treat marital rape exactly the same as other forms of sexual assault?

3. Consent. Nowhere in the law are issues of consent as divisive as in the context of rape. Perspectives range from the traditional assumption that consent can be inferred from "evidence of public displays of general interest in sexual activity"[37] to Catharine MacKinnon's claim that consent is merely a label that the law places on the kind of sex acceptable under conditions of gender inequality.[38] Note that the traditional view presupposes the greatest amount of female self-control, MacKinnon's the least. Which understanding is likely to lead to rules that promote women's sexual autonomy?

Much of the contemporary debate on rape law has centered on how to define consent and how much importance to attach to its presence. Most states require a showing of force; non-consent without force is a misdemeanor.[39] In some states, including New York, the question is whether a reasonable person would believe that sex was consensual, considering all the surrounding circumstances.

Stephen Schulhofer and Joan McGregor argue that the focus of criminal prohibitions should be protecting women's autonomy—her physical integrity and her capacity to choose, unconstrained by impermissible pressures. To that end, Schulhofer proposes a crime of nonviolent sexual misconduct for invading women's bodily integrity in the face of ambivalence, objection, or silence. "No" would mean "no," whether or not a defendant used physical force. Such a statute would encompass economic pressure or other coercive

34. Jill Elaine Hasday, Contest and Consent: A Legal History of Marital Rape, 88 Cal. L. Rev. 1373, 1486-89 (2000).

35. Id. at 1489.

36. Diana E. H. Russell, Rape in Marriage 192-93 (rev. ed. 1990).

37. See State v. Colbath, 540 A.2d 1212 (N.H. 1988) (opinion by now-retired Justice Souter).

38. Catharine A. MacKinnon, Toward a Feminist Theory of the State 172-74 (1989).

39. Deborah Tuerkheimer, Rape On and Off Campus, 65 Emory L.J. 1, 15 (2015); Courtney Fraser, From "Ladies First" to "Asking for It": Benevolent Sexism in the Maintenance of Rape Culture, 103 Cal. L. Rev. 141, 177 (2015).

behavior to obtain sex.[40] McGregor believes that the law should require affirmative consent.[41]

In 2016, the American Law Institute specifically rejected a proposed affirmative consent standard for the Model Penal Code, instead defining consent to mean "a person's behavior, including words and conduct—both action and inaction—that communicates the person's willingness to engage in a specific act of sexual penetration or sexual contact." The consent definition makes clear both that the absence of explicit, affirmative consent does not prove lack of consent, and that consent may be express or inferred—i.e., that "neither verbal nor physical resistance is required to establish the absence of consent" and that a person's behavior "must be assessed in the context of all the circumstances to determine whether the person has consented."[42] How does this definition compare to Susan Estrich's proposal that the law should focus on the reasonableness of the defendant's intent and should assume that a reasonable man understands "no" to mean "no"?[43] How would either of these proposals address circumstances in which a woman has had too much to drink to give meaningful consent,[44] or is traumatized into passivity?

Still under consideration by the American Law Institute is a proposal that makes a person guilty of rape, a felony of the second degree, if he or she knowingly or recklessly uses physical force or threat of force to cause another person to engage in sexual intercourse or the other person is sleeping, unconscious, unable to express refusal because of a mental disability, or lacks substantial capacity to appraise or control his or her conduct because of drugs or alcohol administered by the actor. An actor is guilty of sexual penetration without consent, a misdemeanor, if he or she engages in act of sexual penetration and knows or recklessly disregards a risk that the other person has expressed by words or conduct his or her refusal to consent.[45]

Jed Rubenfeld rejects sexual autonomy as the core value protected by rape law. He notes that sex achieved by deception, although it violates autonomy, is not considered rape under American criminal law.[46] Rubenfeld argues that rape is best conceptualized not as a violation of autonomy but of

---

40. Stephen Schulhofer, Unwanted Sex: The Culture of Intimidation and the Failure of Law (2000).

41. Joan McGregor, Is It Rape?: On Acquaintance Rape and Taking Women's Consent Seriously 190-93 (2005).

42. Am. Law Inst., Model Penal Code: Sexual Assault and Related Offenses, Tentative Draft No. 2, §213.0(3), (Apr. 15, 2016).

43. See Susan Caringella, Addressing Rape Reform in Law and Practice (2009) (arguing that a society that can scarcely accept "no means no" is unlikely to adapt to "only yes means yes").

44. For further consideration of alcohol use in the context of acquaintance rape, see Section 3, infra.

45. Sexual Assault and Related Offenses, Tentative Draft No. 2, supra note 42, at §§2.13(1) and (2).

46. Jed Rubenfeld, The Riddle of Rape-by-Deception and the Myth of Sexual Autonomy, 122 Yale L.J. 1372 (2013).

self-possession, analogous to slavery and torture. It follows, under his analysis, that lack of consent should not be sufficient to prove rape, but that force should also be shown. How would you respond? [47]

Consider the celebrated prosecution of WikiLeaks Founder Julian Assange. According to a confidential Swedish police report, one woman claimed that Assange prevented her from reaching for a condom while they were having sex. A second woman claimed that after having protected sex with Assange, she woke to find him having sex with her without a condom. When the two women discovered that they had both had unprotected sex, they decided to insist that Assange get tested for sexually transmitted diseases. They went to a police station for advice, and gave statements that led prosecutors to charge Assange with third-degree rape. The women have been vilified on the Internet and face regular death threats. A former equal opportunities ombudsman who is representing them explained that it was common for men who force sex on women without a condom to be subject to prosecution: "It's a violation of sexual integrity and it can be seen as rape."[48] Would it be seen that way by American prosecutors? Should it?

4. Rape Shield Laws and Defendant's Rights. All states have rape shield laws. Half of these laws generally prohibit admission of evidence of prior sexual conduct subject to one or more legislated exceptions, such as where the evidence would show prior sexual conduct between the complainant and the accused; an alternative source of semen, pregnancy, or injury; bias or motive to fabricate; a pattern of prior sexual conduct like prostitution; a mistaken belief by the accused in the complainant's consent; and prior false accusations of sexual assault by the complainant. A minority of states allow judicial discretion, or have a catchall provision allowing evidence where necessary to protect the defendant's constitutional rights. A few states determine the admissibility of a woman's sexual history based on the purpose for which the evidence is offered. For example, sexual history offered to prove the complainant's consent to sexual intercourse may be prohibited, but sexual history offered to attack credibility is admissible. The converse is the case in other jurisdictions.[49]

47. For detailed critiques, see Corey Rayburn Yung, Rape Law Fundamentals, 27 Yale J.L. & Feminism 1 (2015); Kiel Brennan-Marquez, A Quite Principled Conceit, 80 U. Chi. L. Rev. 81 (2013), and the symposium in 123 Yale L.J. Online (2013).

48. John Burns & Ravi Somaiya, Confidential Swedish Police Report Details Allegations Against WikiLeaks Founder, N.Y. Times, Dec. 18, 2010.

49. Nat'l District Attorneys Ass'n, Rape Shield Statutes (2011), http://www.ncdaa.org/pdf/NCPCA%20Rap; Michelle J. Anderson, From Chastity Requirement to Sexuality License: Sexual Consent and a New Rape Shield Law, 70 Geo. Wash. L. Rev. 51 (2002).

The complexities of applying shield statutes is well illustrated by a federal appellate ruling in Gagne v. Booker.[50] There a state court excluded evidence that the complainant had previously engaged in three-way consensual intercourse with one of the defendants whom she was dating at the time. A federal court of appeals on a habeas petition found that the decision violated the defendants of a meaningful opportunity to present a defense. A fractured en banc court reversed the panel, with eight separate opinions. The primary issue dividing the judges was whether the conduct of the woman in consenting to a threesome with a man she was dating was almost "identical" to the threesome sex she had with that same man whom she was no longer dating and another party. What is your view? Is consent to group sex on one occasion probative about likely consent on another?

Rape shield statutes have drawn criticism from all sides. Civil libertarians and criminal defense counsel often claim that the protections compromise defendants' rights to a fair trial. As stated by one defense counsel:

> Now a public-policy decision designed to correct vestiges of Victorian-era morality has stacked the deck against every citizen accused of a sex crime. . . .
>
> Our justice system depends on the belief that a randomly drawn jury, culled only for prejudice and partiality, can detect truth and falsity. But if a jury is given a skewed presentation of the facts, or if important facts are withheld from a jury, we cannot expect it to do justice.
>
> Most rape cases that turn on whether a sex act was consensual . . . [will] ultimately come down to a "he said/she said" contest between the accused and the accuser. But how can a jury accurately judge the credibility of the two parties if the accused has been presented in the worst possible light while the accuser is enshrouded in a cloak of purity?[51]

By contrast, many women's advocates claim that the exemptions compromise complainants' rights to privacy and deter other victims from reporting the crime. The problem is particularly acute for prostitutes, who are frequently vulnerable to sexual assault.[52] Shield laws do not prevent police and prosecutors from considering sexual history, nor do they prevent nongovernmental actors and the media from publicizing such behavior.[53] Some commentators have also argued that the message implicitly communicated by shield laws is that jurors should assume that the complainant is a "good

---

50. Gagne v. Booker, 606 F.3d 278 (6th Cir. 2010), rev'd en banc, 680 F.3d 493 (6th Cir. 2012).

51. Barry Tarlow, Criminal Justice: Rape Suspects' Uphill Road, L.A. Times, Aug. 17, 2003, at M3.

52. Michele Alexander, "Girls Gone Wild" and Rape Law: Revising the Contractual Concept of Consent and Ensuring an Unbiased Application of "Reasonable Doubt" When the Victim Is Nontraditional, 17 Am. U.J. Gender Soc. Pol'y & L. 41 (2009).

53. Aya Gruber, Rape, Feminism, and the War on Crime, 84 Wash. L. Rev. 581, 646-47 (2009).

girl" untarnished by too much or the wrong kind or sexual behavior. On this view, feminists have "reinscribed the very chastity requirement they hoped to abolish."[54] How would you respond?

In one Oregon case involving admission of social media evidence, a grand jury declined to authorize a prosecution for sexual assault after seeing the teen victim's MySpace page where she talked about drinking and "getting some," and posted provocative pictures of herself. Such a self-portrait was inconsistent with her claim to the police that she would never willingly have had sex.[55] In a California sexual assault case, the appellate court ruled that it was reversible error to exclude social media evidence to impeach a rape survivor's testimony that she was a virgin.[56] Some commentators have criticized such decisions as inconsistent with the intent of shield laws, while others have maintained that social media postings are inherently public and should be admissible.[57] What is your view?

A similar debate has surfaced over defendant's rights. One issue involves the admission of prior sexual misconduct. Prior bad acts are ordinarily not admissible in a criminal trial, because they are thought to be overly prejudicial.[58] The justifications for allowing evidence of prior sexual conduct in rape cases are that sexual offenders are more likely to re-offend than other criminals, false accusations of rape are rare, and sexual offenses are particularly hard to prove. Allowing prior acts may also encourage other victims to come forward.[59] However, as a Report by the Judicial Conference noted, "the overwhelming majority of judges, lawyers, law professors and legal organizations" have opposed the admission of prior sexual misconduct.[60] As experts have noted, recidivism rates are not disproportionately high for sex offenses except those involving deviant interests (e.g., pedophilia) and those reflecting other antisocial tendencies.[61] Although the frequency of false charges is difficult to measure, it is noteworthy that one-third of convicted defendants who have

---

54. I. Bennett Capers, Real Women, Real Rape, 60 UCLA L. Rev. 826, 874 (2013).

55. Beth C. Boggs & Misty L. Edwards, Does What Happens on Facebook Stay on Facebook? Discovery, Admissibility, Ethics, and Social Media, 98 Ill. Bar J. 366, 367 (2010).

56. People v. Flynn, No. F062483, 2013 WL 6047625 (Cal. Ct. App. Nov. 15, 2013).

57. See Kim Loewen, Rejecting the Purity Myth: Reforming Rape Shield Laws in the Age of Social Media, 22 UCLA Women's L.J. 151, 160 (2015).

58. Federal Rules of Evidence §§413-415.

59. Tamara Lave & Aviva A. Orenstein, Empirical Fallacies of Evidence Law: A Critical Look at the Admission of Prior Sex Crimes, 81 U. Cin. L. Rev. 795, 806-07 (2013).

60. Report of the Judicial Conference of the United States on the Admission of Character Evidence in Certain Sexual Assault Cases (1995).

61. Lave & Orenstein, supra note 59, at 817; see also Charles H. Rose, III, Should the Tail Wag the Dog?: The Potential Effects of Recidivisim Data on Character Evidence Rules, 36 N.M. L. Rev. 341, 344 (2006); R. Karl Hanson & Kelly Morton-Bourgon, Predictors of Sexual Recidivism: An Updated Meta-Analysis (2004), http://www.static99.org/pdfdocs/hansonandmortonbourgon2004.pdf.

been exonerated by DNA evidence were individuals convicted of rape.[62] So too, some commentators claim that the effects of laws requiring registration of sex offenders and limitations on where they can live and work are excessive and ineffective forms of punishment.[63] How would you respond?

Another potential difficulty, particularly in cases involving substantial publicity, is that the complainant may be identified in the media. In a celebrated case involving basketball player Kobe Bryant, the complainant was so vilified that she refused to testify and the prosecutor dropped the case.[64] In a New York Times op-ed, Dahlia Lithwick offered this assessment of the Bryant prosecution:

> Enacted with the best of intentions, rape shield statutes don't work, particularly in high-profile cases. . . . There is a class of cases that are simply beyond the ability of the legal system to resolve, both because some truths are ultimately unknowable, and because it isn't "justice" when everyone emerges from a trial so damaged that it hardly matters who won.[65]

Do you agree? Are there offsetting benefits to victims from media coverage if it encourages others to come forward? Some fifty women have accused famed comedian Bill Cosby of sexually molesting them, and details of his exploitation have become widely available.[66]

5. Rape and Scientific Evidence. Following a sexual assault, women victims often agree to an exam that yields a "rape kit"—a collection of hair, semen, and skin cell samples. The DNA extracted from these kits can be checked against databases of DNA from violent criminals and a match can lead to successful prosecutions. Because the average rapist commits between 8 and 16 sexual assaults before being caught, and serial offenders account for the vast majority of rapes, kit evidence can be a crucial law enforcement tool. However, it is estimated that hundreds of thousands of kits remain untested

62. Samuel R. Gross et al., Exonerations in the United States 1989 through 2003, 95 J. Crim. L. & Criminology 523, 529 (2005).

63. Roger Lancaster, Sex Offenders: The Last Pariahs, N.Y. Times, Aug. 21, 2011, at SR6.

64. She then filed a civil suit, which ultimately settled. Kirk Johnson, As Accuser Balks, Prosecutors Drop Bryant Rape Case, N.Y. Times, Sept. 2, 2004; Bill Saporito, Kobe Rebounds, Time, Sept. 13, 2004, at 72.

65. Dahlia Lithwick, The Shield That Failed, N.Y. Times, Aug. 8, 2004, at SR11.

66. Justin Wm. Moyer, The Prosecutor Undone by a 'Secret Agreement' with Bill Cosby, Wash. Post, Feb. 4, 2015; Graham Bowley & Sydney Ember, Bill Cosby, in Deposition, Said Drugs and Fame Helped Him Seduce Women, N.Y. Times, July 19, 2015. Cosby has been charged with sexual assault in one of these cases. See Sydney Ember & Graham Bowley, Cosby Is Charged with Sex Assault in Criminal Case, N.Y. Times, Dec. 31, 2001, at A1.

due to lack of resources.[67] Public outcry has begun making addressing that backlog a priority and federal and local governments, as well as nonprofit groups, have allocated additional funding to the effort.[68] Some women's rights advocates argue that processing most of these kits should not be a high priority because the vast majority of cases involve acquaintances where the defense focuses on consent, so DNA would be irrelevant.[69] Other advocates suggest limiting the use of kits to cases of stranger rape as a way of minimizing backlog and trauma to the victim.[70] How should women's rights groups respond?

6. The Rape Crisis Counselor Privilege. A related issue is whether and to what extent a rape complainant should have the right to shield disclosures made to rape crisis counselors. About forty states and the District of Columbia have enacted privilege statutes that protect such information, but the statutes vary in whether the privilege is absolute or whether a judge may decide in camera whether the probative value of the evidence to the defendant outweighs the victim's interests in confidentiality.[71]

The justifications for the privilege are self-evident. Victims of sexual assault are likely to obtain higher quality counseling if confidentiality can be assured, and without that assurance the injuries of a sexual assault may be compounded by public disclosure of intimate details from therapeutic sessions. Rape crisis centers are often the primary source of assistance for victims, and failure to protect confidential disclosures to counselors at these centers whether or not they are licensed physicians would compromise treatment and reporting, particularly consequential for individuals who cannot afford to pay for assistance from psychiatrists who can assert the privilege.[72]

The justifications for allowing defendants access to therapeutic records are equally apparent. In some rape cases, the boundaries of consent and coercion are blurred at best, and subtle, even unintended, encouragement by rape counselors to define an interaction as rape may affect how a complainant later recalls the event.[73] Other relevant details in therapeutic records may include

67. The extent of the problem is unknown because many cities have failed to compile statistics or have destroyed untested kits. Erik Eckholm, No Longer Ignored, Evidence Solves Rape Cases Years Later, N.Y. Times, Aug. 2, 2014.

68. Id.; Anita Little, Passing the Test, Ms. at 11 (Spring 2015).

69. Wendy Murphy, Most Rape Cases Are About Consent, Not DNA, Women's eNews, Feb. 9, 2011.

70. Taylor Gamble, Thinking Outside the Box: Limiting the Collection of Rape Kit Evidence in Acquaintance Rape Trials, 20 Cardozo J.L. & Gender 743, 760-62 (2014).

71. Barry G. Stratford, *State v. Worthen*: Demonstrating Utah's Need for an Expanded, Absolute Victim-Counselor Testimonial Privilege, 2013 Utah L. Rev. On Law 124, 128 (2013).

72. Jennifer Bruno, Pitfalls for the Unwary: How Sexual Assault Counselor-Victim Privileges May Fall Short of Their Intended Protections, 2002 U. Ill. L. Rev. 1373.

73. See Rachel Capoccia, Piercing the Veil of Tears: The Admission of Rape Crisis Counselors' Records in Acquaintance Rape Trials, 68 S. Cal. L.J. 1335, 1342 (1995).

the complainant's prior involvement with the accused and a history of mental health problems.

Given the enormous costs to the defendant of an unjust conviction, is some relinquishment of the complainant's privacy interests reasonable? How would you strike the balance?

7. Cultural Attitudes, "Rape Myths," and Law Enforcement Responses. Of all major felonies, rape is the "least reported, least indicted, and least likely to end in a conviction."[74] One study finds that of 100 rapes committed, an estimated 5 to 20 are reported to police, .4 to 5.4 are prosecuted, .2 to 5.2 percent result in conviction, and .2 to 2.8 percent result in incarceration.[75] Major factors affecting the likelihood of conviction include the degree of acquaintance between the victim and accused; the appearance and reputation of the victim; the capacity of the victim to recall key details; the availability of physical evidence; and the presence and degree of intoxication.[76] Low conviction rates are partly attributed to "myths" about rape shared by judges, juries, and law enforcement personnel: (1) only certain women (i.e., those with "bad" reputations) are raped; (2) only certain men (i.e., psychopaths) rape; (3) women invite or deserve rape by their appearance and behavior; and (4) women fantasize or fabricate rape, motivated by desire, revenge, blackmail, jealousy, guilt, or embarrassment.

Consider the following examples:

- Missouri Congressman Todd Akin, opposing an exception for rape in an anti-abortion statute, argues that pregnancy from rape is rare because "if it's a legitimate rape, the female body has ways to try to shut the whole thing down."[77]
- Women who accused celebrated athletes like Kobe Bryant and Mike Tyson received death threats and harassment for being "gold diggers" who needlessly destroy revered role models for conduct that they invite by going to athletes' hotel rooms alone.[78]

74. Deborah L. Rhode, Rape on Campus and in the Military: An Agenda for Reform, UCLA Women's L.J. (forthcoming 2016).

75. Kimberly A. Lonsway & Joanne Archambault, The "Justice Gap" for Sexual Assault Cases: Future Directions for Research and Reform, 18 Violence Against Women 145, 157 (2012).

76. Francis X. Shen, How We Still Fail Rape Victims: Reflecting on Responsibility and Legal Reform, 22 Colum. J. Gender & L. 1, 14-27 (2011); Henry F. Fradell & Kagan Brown, The Effects of Using Social Scientific Rape Typologies on Juror Decisions to Convict, 31 Law & Psych. Rev. 1, 1-16 (2007).

77. John Eligon & Michael Schwirtz, Senate Candidate Provokes Ire with "Legitimate Rape" Comment, N.Y. Times, Aug. 19, 2012, at A13.

78. See Saporito, supra note 64.

- A juror who voted to acquit William Kennedy Smith of the rape of a woman he picked up in a bar explained that "he's too charming and too good-looking to have to resort to violence for a night out."[79]
- A Montana judge sentenced a teacher to 30 days for a rape of a 14-year-old student and commented that the victim was "older than her chronological age."[80]
- During a fraternity pledge initiation ritual, Yale students chanted "No means yes, yes means anal" outside the university's women's center.[81]
- Camille Paglia argues that a "girl who lets herself get dead drunk at a fraternity party is a fool. A girl who goes upstairs alone with a brother at a fraternity party is an idiot. Feminists call this 'blaming the victim.' I call it common sense."[82]
- A Toronto police officer told a group of college women that if they wanted to avoid sexual assault, they should avoid dressing like "sluts." In response, young women have marched in "slutwalks" in more than 70 cities around the world, dressed in bras, halter tops, and garter belts.[83]

Why do you suppose rape norms have taken so long to change? Katharine Baker suggests three factors: (1) the criminal burden of proof makes it often too difficult, as a realistic matter, to prove lack of consent; (2) constructions of the rapist as "profoundly deviant and distinctly criminal" do not correspond to the characteristics of many men accused of rape; and (3) rape reform efforts often assume that women lack agency, a view that women themselves resist. Baker suggests that civil approaches to rape, and in particular the federal Department of Education's efforts to use Title IX to curb sexual assault on college campuses, may be more effective in reducing nonconsensual sex and in dislodging current sex norms than further efforts to tighten the criminal law would be.[84] What advantages might come from a civil rather than a criminal approach to rape? Disadvantages? For further discussion of sexual assault on college campuses, see the next section on Acquaintance Rape and Campus Rape.

8. Rape Trauma Syndrome. In the course of improving clinical treatment for rape victims, researchers have developed a profile known as the "rape

79. Lynn Hecht Schafran, The Importance of Voir Dire in Rape Trials, Trial 26 (Aug. 1992).

80. Zusha Elinson, Montana Rape Cases Draw Scrutiny, Wall St. J., Mar. 5, 2014, at A4.

81. Jake New, The "Yes Means Yes" World, Inside Higher ED, Oct. 17, 2014.

82. Camille Paglia, Sex, Art, and American Culture 51 (1992).

83. Rebecca Traister, Ladies, We Have a Problem, N.Y. Times Mag., July 24, 2011, at 9.

84. Katharine K. Baker, Why Rape Should Not (Always) Be a Crime, 100 Minn. L. Rev. 221, 223-24 (2015).

trauma syndrome." The syndrome is characterized by two phases: Phase I, the "acute phase," is a period of disorganization in which the victim is either emotionally out of control—crying, sobbing, restless, or tense—or extraordinarily controlled—calm, composed, or subdued. Headaches, fatigue, and gastrointestinal or sleep disturbances are common during this period. Phase II, the "long-term reorganization process," is a period of nightmares, phobic reactions, sexual fears, and changes in routine.[85]

Some courts have approved use of expert testimony about rape trauma syndrome to help prove that a forcible assault, rather than consensual sex, occurred. However, disputes about the scientific basis for the theory have encouraged limitation of its use to rehabilitating the victim's credibility rather than proving the prosecution's case-in-chief. In both contexts, expert testimony regarding rape trauma syndrome may be effective in dispelling rape myths regarding victim's behavior after the rape. In one New York case, the court noted:

> [T]he reaction of a rape victim in the hours following her attack is not something within the common understanding of the average lay juror. Indeed, the defense would clearly want the jury to infer that because the victim was not upset following the attack, she must not have been raped. This inference runs contrary to the studies cited earlier, which suggest that half of all women who have been forcibly raped are controlled and subdued following the attack. . . . Thus, we conclude that evidence of this type is relevant to dispel misconceptions that jurors might possess regarding the ordinary responses of rape victims in the first hours after their attack.[86]

Some feminists have been concerned that rape trauma evidence focuses too much on the behavior of the victim rather than the accused, and that it might be misused to show that an alleged victim's behavior was atypical, and thus inconsistent with claims of rape. The Indiana Supreme Court, for example, held that it was an abuse of discretion to exclude expert testimony that the victim's conduct in returning to the bar where the rape allegedly had taken place was inconsistent with that of a person who had been forcibly raped.[87] Is it fair for women's rights advocates to support admission of rape trauma evidence only when it helps female complainants, not when it exculpates male defendants?

---

85. See Ann Wolbert Burgess & Lynda Lytle Holmstrom, Rape Trauma Syndrome, in Forcible Rape: The Crime, the Victim, and the Offender 315 (Duncan Chappell et al. eds., 1977).

86. People v. Taylor, 552 N.E.2d 131, 138 (N.Y. 1990).

87. Henson v. State, 535 N.E.2d 1189 (Ind. 1989).

9. Racial Bias. At one time, rape of a non-white woman was not a crime.[88] By contrast, the rape of a white woman by a black man was long considered the most horrific sexual offense and provided the most common justification for lynching. At various times, the law required that blacks convicted of raping white women be castrated.[89]

Although most rapes, like most other crimes, are intraracial rather than interracial, rapes in which black men are the perpetrators and white women the victims continue to receive the greatest attention and the most serious sanctions.

In one survey of cases involving no weapons, prosecutors were over four times as likely to file charges if the victim was white.[90] In explaining their decisions, prosecutors often claim that jurors are less willing to convict in cases involving poor and minority victims.[91] How might these prejudices be addressed?

A controversial case involving racial dynamics involved a young African-American exotic dancer who claimed that she was raped by several white members of the Duke University lacrosse team that had asked her to perform as a stripper. A medical exam showed evidence of forcible sex. There was evidence that the dancer had been subject to racial epithets. Several of the university's athletic teams had a history of alcohol-related offenses, and town-gown relations were complicated by class and racial tensions. The immediate media and community reaction was to assume that rape had occurred at the party, a reaction fueled by the white prosecutor who was facing a difficult election campaign. Bringing charges gained him the support from the black community necessary for victory. The university administration, in the wake of considerable adverse media coverage, fired the coach and prevented the team from competition for the remainder of the season.

It soon became apparent, however, that there were considerable inconsistencies in the victim's account and other critical weaknesses in the case. Although the victim picked out players she said were her attackers from pictures of those present at the party, the photo spread did not conform to accepted practice because it included no other pictures that might have produced a false identification. One of the players whom the woman identified had photographic and telephone records that placed him elsewhere. DNA tests on the woman's underwear showed traces of sperm and other material

---

88. See George v. State, 37 Miss. 316 (1859).

89. See A. Leon Higginbotham, Jr., & Anne F. Jacobs, The "Law Only as an Enemy": The Legitimization of Racial Powerlessness Through the Colonial Laws of Virginia, 70 N.C. L. Rev. 969, 1055-60 (1992).

90. Cassia Spohn & David Holleran, Prosecuting Sexual Assault: A Comparison of Charging Decisions in Sexual Assault Cases Involving Strangers, Acquaintances, and Intimate Partners, 18 Just. Q. 651, 680 (2001).

91. Jeffrey J. Pokorak, Rape as a Badge of Slavery: The Legal History of, and Remedies for, Prosecutorial Race of Victim Charging Disparities, 7 Nev. L.J. 1, 39 (2006).

that failed to match any of the lacrosse players. The prosecutor maintained that despite these weaknesses, he had enough evidence to put the matter to a jury. However, he also failed to disclose exculpatory DNA evidence to the defense and falsely claimed to the court that he was unaware of any such evidence. That conduct subsequently resulted in his disbarment. The rape charges were dropped and the players sued the city and the university alleging various breaches of duty. The lacrosse case generated several books and months of media coverage, much of which emphasized the gullibility of the public toward accusations of rape.[92] Does the case prove that rape "myths" are sometimes true? That race can work both ways? That race and rape are still a volatile combination?

10. Male Rape.   For centuries, the problem of male rape went largely unrecognized and some countries still do not recognize it as a crime.[93] In the United States, the frequency with which men are victimized by rape has traditionally been hard to assess, in part because until 2012 it was excluded from the federal definitions of rapes that needed to be nationally reported and because many surveys have excluded inmates of prison and jails where male rape is prevalent. As noted earlier, estimates of the percentage of men who have been raped typically have ranged between 5 and 14 percent, a lower percentage than among women, but one recent survey by the Centers for Disease Control found that men and women had had a similar prevalence of nonconsensual sex in the previous 12 months.[94] Men subject to sexual abuse are at increased risk for physical and psychological problems, as well as substance abuse, and many feel that their masculinity has been called into question. Humiliation and self-blame, together with an absence of resources for men at rape crisis centers, discourage reporting of the offense. In military and prison contexts, men also worry about retaliation. According to Department of Justice anonymous surveys, between 69 and 82 percent of prison inmates who experienced sexual abuse reported it to corrections officials.[95] A Department of Defense anonymous survey of men in the armed

92. The prosecutor argued that despite the inconsistencies, he had an "obligation" to put the victim's positive identification to the jury. Bennett L. Gershman & Joel Cohen, No Gatekeeper of Justice, Nat'l L.J., Feb. 19, 2007, at A22 (quoting Michael Nifong). For critical accounts, see Race to Injustice: Lessons Learned from the Duke Lacrosse Rape Case (Michael L. Siegel ed., 2009); Stuart Taylor & K.C. Johnson, Until Proven Innocent: Political Correctness and the Shameful Injustices of the Duke Lacrosse Rape Case (2007).

93. Megan Lutz-Priefert, A Call for a More Permanent International Definition of Rape, 6 Creighton Int'l & Comp. L.J. 85, 86 (2015).

94. For discussion of these findings see Lara Stemple & Ilan H. Meyer, The Sexual Victimization of Men in America: New Data Challenge Old Assumptions, 104 Am. J. Pub. Health 19 (2014).

95. U.S. Dep't of Justice, Prison Rape Elimination Act Regulatory Impact Assessment 17-18 (2013), http://ojp.gov/programs/pdfs/prea_ria.pdf.

forces who had experienced but had not reported sexual crimes found that the predominant reasons were not wanting anyone to know (about a half), not believing that anything would be done (about a third), and fearing reprisals (close to a third).[96]

Putting Theory Into Practice

5-6. At Richard's trial for rape, witnesses testified that they saw him in the bar that evening with the complainant, Candice, who was sitting on his lap and "making out with Richard and a few others." Richard testified that he had felt Candice's breasts and bottom while at the bar and that she had been rubbing his crotch. When she finally left the bar with him, witnesses said that she was "hanging all over" him like she had been hanging all over others earlier in the evening. Richard and Candice went from the bar to his trailer where they engaged in sex. Before they left Richard's trailer, the woman with whom Richard lived came home unexpectedly and saw them together. She became enraged and dragged Candice out of the trailer by the hair. Candice returned immediately to town, at which point she went to the police and charged Richard with rape.[97]

Should evidence of Candice's activity with other men on the evening of the events in question be admissible in Richard's rape trial? How about the fact that Candice was wearing skimpy clothing? That she was making out with Richard, including rubbing his crotch?

5-7. Some defendants have sought to prevent terms such as "rape," "attack," and "victim" from being used in court on the grounds that they express legal conclusions. Should they succeed?

In one such case, which resulted in a hung jury, the complainant refused to testify on retrial if she could not use the terms "attack" or "rape," on the grounds that it made her less credible and denied her right to testify to the "truth of what happened."[98] What is your view?

5-8. A single mother of three young children who can't make ends meet has unwanted sex with her landlord in order to persuade him not to evict her.[99] Should he be guilty of a crime? What additional facts would be relevant to your analysis?

---

96. Jesse Ellison, The Military's Secret Shame, Newsweek, Apr. 11, 2011, at 42.

97. See State v. Colbath, 540 A.2d 1212 (N.H. 1988).

98. Vesna Jaksic, Playing with the Power of Words, Nat'l L.J., July 23, 2007, at A1, A26 (describing Nebraska v. Safi, No. CR 05-87 (Dist. Ct. Lancaster Co. Neb. 2007)).

99. For a discussion of this and other hypotheticals, see Stephen Schulhofer, Taking Sexual Autonomy Seriously, 11 Law & Phil. 35 (1992).

5-9. J.L. drives home from a party with two men she has just met. She testifies that they told her to give them oral sex and that she could leave the car "as soon as we're done." One of them says, "I don't want to rape you," and she responded that he could go ahead as long he "stops when I tell him to." When he inserted his penis into her vagina, "it hurt" and she told him to stop. He did so only after he continued for "about five seconds," apparently long enough for him to reach orgasm. Can he be prosecuted for rape? Should he be?[100]

3. Acquaintance Rape and Campus Rape

According to U.S. government statistics, about seven in ten rapes or sexual assaults against women are by a relative, a friend, or an acquaintance. About one in five college women, and a higher percentage of other women between 18 and 24, experience sexual assault.[101] Only about 12 to 20 percent of campus rapes are reported to the police or campus authorities.[102] Major reasons for non-reporting include self-blame, lack of proof, fear of retribution, fear of disbelief by legal and medical authorities, desire for privacy, and lack of faith in the likely response.[103] Survivors suffer high rates of PTSD, depression, and drug or alcohol abuse, which are linked to higher school dropout rates and impaired work performance.[104] Acquaintance rape is often no less psychologically harmful than other assaults because it calls into question a complainant's behavior, judgment, and sense of trust in ways that acts of strangers do not.[105] Yet law enforcement officials have traditionally been reluctant to pursue such cases because they often present difficult problems of proof or because complainants appear partly responsible. In one survey of sexual assaults investigated by police at six campuses, only 7 percent resulted in

---

100. State v. Baby, 946 A.2d 463, 467 (Md. 2008).

101. White House Council, supra note at 23; United States Centers for Disease Control and Prevention, Sexual Violence Facts at a Glance (2012); Callie Marie Rennison, Privilege, Among Rape Victims, N.Y. Times, Dec. 23, 2014. For an overview of some of the problems with these frequency estimates see Dana Goldstein, The Dueling Data on Campus Rape, The Marshall Project (2014), https://www.themarshallproject.org/2014/12/11/the-dueling-data-on-campus-rape#.mrUwbukpL.

102. White House Council, supra note at 23 (12 to 13 percent); Sofi Sinozich & Lynn Langton, U.S. Dep't of Justice, Bureau of Justice Statistics, Rape and Sexual Assault Victimization Among College-Age Females, 1995-2013 (2014) (20 percent).

103. See research discussed in Nancy Chi Cantalupo, Title IX's Civil Rights Approach and the Criminal Justice System in The Crisis of Campus Sexual Violence: Critical Perspectives on Prevention and Response 129-30 (Sara Carrigan Wooten & Roland W. Mitchell eds., 2016); Rhode, Rape on Campus, supra note 74.

104. White House Council, supra note 23, at 14.

105. Rhode, Rape on Campus, supra note 74.

arrest and 4 percent in conviction.[106] The problem is particularly pronounced when male athletes are involved. In one college town, the failure to prosecute campus rape cases was so egregious that the Department of Justice launched an investigation and negotiated an agreement providing for independent oversight of law enforcement decisionmaking.[107] The major issue concerning acquaintance rape is, again, how to distinguish coercive from consensual sex. The difficulties are compounded by the use of drugs and alcohol and a social context in which ambiguous and inconsistent understandings coexist. How much responsibility do women have for making their non-consent clear? When, if ever, is "blaming the victim" appropriate? When male and female perspectives differ, who should bear the risk of misunderstood signals? How can such misunderstandings be minimized?

During the second wave of rape reform, women's rights advocates focused attention on changing laws and practices to recognize that "no means no." At the time, this was not uncontroversial. Some commentators invoked studies indicating that women sometimes protested when they wanted sex to avoid looking promiscuous. Commentators such as John Leo argued that "the mating game does not proceed by words alone." In Leo's view, the "demonization" of men that is common in feminists' writing on date rape is profoundly unjust. If women cannot be clear about their preferences, men should not pay the price.[108] Other commentators worried that broadening definitions of rape would give women unreasonable control to define, after the fact, what is or is not acceptable, consensual sex.[109] These objections intensified during the third wave of rape reform, when activists sought to institutionalize requirements of affirmative consent and address deficiencies in the way that state statutes dealt with campus assaults.[110]

An estimated 1400 colleges and universities now use some type of affirmative consent definition in their sexual assault policies, according to the National Center for Higher Education Risk Management, and two states,

106. Nancy Chi Cantalupo, Burying Our Heads in the Sand: Lack of Knowledge, Knowledge Avoidance, and the Persistent Problem of Campus Peer Sexual Violence, 43 Loy. U. Chi. L.J. 205, 239 (2011).

107. Jon Krakauer, Missoula: Rape and the Justice System in a College Town 340 (2015). For a celebrated case involving a star Florida football player, see Walt Bogdanich, A Star Player Accused, and a Flawed Rape Investigation, N.Y. Times, Apr. 16, 2014.

108. John Leo, Two Steps Ahead of the Thought Police 247 (1994).

109. See Neil Gilbert, The Phantom Epidemic of Sexual Assault, 103 Pub. Int. 54 (Spring 1991).

110. For the inadequacy of state statutes particularly regarding consent and intoxication, see David Dematteo et al., Sexual Assault on College campuses: A 50 State Survey of Criminal Sexual Assault Statutes and Their Relevance to Campus Sexual Assault, 21 Psychol. Pub. Pol'y & L. 227 (2015).

New York and California, require state-funded schools to adopt such policies.[111] The California statute defines "affirmative consent" as "affirmative, conscious and voluntary agreement to engage in sexual activity. . . . Lack of protest or resistance does not mean consent, nor does silence mean consent. Affirmative consent must be ongoing throughout a sexual activity and can be revoked at any time." The statute further specifies that it "shall not be a valid excuse that the accused believed that the complainant affirmatively consented to the sexual activity if the accused knew or reasonably should have known that the complainant was unable to consent to the sexual activity [because] . . . the complainant was asleep or unconscious [or] . . . was incapacitated due to the influence of drugs, alcohol or medication, so that the complainant could not understand the fact, nature or extent of the sexual activity."[112] A few campuses have gone further and required that the consent be "enthusiastic."[113]

Opponents of such initiatives have claimed that they are an example of "creeping Big-Sisterism," that they are unfair to men who do not get clear signals of what women want, and that they will risk making everyone "hypersensitive, even delusional, about victimizations."[114] According to Jed Rubenfeld, "[p]eople can and frequently do have fully voluntary sex without communicating unambiguously." Under "yes means yes" policies, "that can be deemed rape if one party later feels aggrieved."[115] These kinds of considerations raise potential due process problems, and a few campus policies based on such standards have been struck down on due process grounds.[116]

In a majority of campus rape cases, the complainant has been drinking or taking drugs and many alleged offenders have suffered from impaired judgment related to substance abuse.[117] Some commentators argue that alcohol is "often used to create a gray area, a realm of plausible deniability where no one

111. See Sandy Keenan, Affirmative Consent: Are Students Really Asking?, N.Y. Times, July 28, 2015; Cal. Ed. Code, §67386 (2015); N.Y. CLS Education §6441 (2015).

112. Cal. Ed. Code §67386 (2015).

113. Jeannie Suk, St. Paul's School and a New Definition of Rape, New Yorker, Nov. 3, 2015.

114. Cathy Young, California's Absurd Intervention Over Dorm Room Sex, Reason (June 22, 2014), http://reason.com/archives/2014/06/22/Californias-absurd-intervention-over-dor/print; George Will, Colleges Become the Victims of Progressivism, Wash. Post, June 6, 2014.

115. Jed Rubenfeld, Opinion, Mishandling Rape, N.Y. Times, Nov. 15, 2014.

116. See, e.g., Mock v. University of Tennessee at Chattanooga (Chancery Ct. Davidson Cty. Tenn. Twentieth Judicial Dist. No. 14-1687-II, Aug. 4, 2015) at http://chronicle.com/items/biz/pdf/memorandum-mock.pdf (finding that the affirmative consent standard improperly shifts the burden of proof to defendant).

117. Rhode, Rape on Campus, supra note 74. Some research finds that as many as 72 to 82 percent of students who experienced unwanted sexual intercourse were intoxicated at the time. Aaron White & Ralph Hingson, The Burden of Alcohol Use: Excessive Alcohol Consumption and Related Consequences Among College Students, 35 Alcohol Research: Current Reviews 201, 212 (2013). For a particularly egregious example, see Problem 4-27 at the end of Chapter 4.

supposedly has to take responsibility for what he (or she) wanted to do."[118] Should alcohol abuse be a mitigating factor for the perpetrator (he wasn't fully in control of his actions) and/or an aggravating factor for the complainant (she shouldn't have put herself in that position)? Do defendants need to know that victims' intoxication make them incapable of consent? Or is it enough for the prosecution just to prove such intoxication?[119]

Andrew Taslitz argues that a primary explanation for acquaintance rape is self-deception:

> The common thread in all the relevant types of self-deception is that semiconscious or unconscious processes, motivated by serving an overriding self-interest, suppress from the conscious mind certain thoughts and feelings that might work against that interest, thereby permitting us to act contrary to our sincerely professed conscious principles.[120]

> Drawing on social science research, Taslitz explores cognitive biases and semiconscious or unconscious self-deception ranging from willful ignorance, systematic ignoring, emotional detachment, and rationalization (semiconscious), which reinforce self-interest.

> Self-deception can be overcome by sustained efforts. . . . A "reasonableness" standard that is defined by jurors as a duty of reasonable inquiry to determine an intended sexual partner's desires is an effective way to combat male self-deception. . . . Because self-deception in this area is morally worse than the simple ignorance involved in ordinary criminal negligence, self-deceptive negligence . . . merits more severe punishment than is generally accorded to crimes of negligence.[121]

If Taslitz's diagnosis is correct, is criminal punishment the right prescription? Is "education" or peer pressure likely to be effective?[122]

What prevention programs make the most sense? Some commentators have stressed the need to empower women and girls to "stand up for what they do or don't want" in sexual relationships.[123] One Canadian program cut the risk of rape by nearly half through training female students on assessing risk among male acquaintances, resisting coercion, and focusing on their own desires and values.[124] Some feminists object that this approach deflects

118. Caroline Knapp, Drinking: A Love Story (1996).
119. State v. Jones, 804 N.W.2d 409 (S.D. 2011) (requiring knowledge).
120. Andrew E. Taslitz, Willfully Blinded: On Date Rape and Self-Deception, 28 Harv. J.L. & Gender 381, 394 (2005).
121. Id. at 434, 446.
122. For analysis of other cognitive biases that may incline individuals, particularly women with hierarchical world views, to be highly judgmental of complainants' conduct in acquaintance rape cases, see Dan M. Kahan, Culture, Cognition and Consent: Who Perceives What, and Why, in Acquaintance Rape Cases, 158 U. Penn. L. Rev. 728 (2010).
123. Suk, supra note 113.
124. Emily Bazelon, The Return of the Sex Wars, N.Y. Times Mag., Sept. 10, 2015.

attention from changing the male behaviors that are primarily responsible for assault. They would like to see more emphasis on bystander intervention training and peer education among all-male groups such as athletic teams and fraternities.[125] What is your view? Has your campus done an adequate job of rape prevention? What can be done in elementary and secondary schools to address attitudes that lead to sexual abuse?[126]

Title IX of the Education Amendments of 1972 requires schools that receive federal financial assistance to take necessary steps to prevent sexual assaults and to respond promptly and effectively when an assault is reported.[127] The Clery Act requires schools that participate in federal financial aid programs to report annual statistics on crime, including sexual assault and rape, on or near their campuses, and to develop prevention policies.[128] The Department of Education's Federal Student Aid Office is responsible for enforcing the Clery Act, and conducts on-site reviews to ensure compliance. Violations of the Act can result in fines and orders to comply. The Campus Sexual Violence Elimination Act amends the Clery Act to require procedural protections for those reporting an assault, to establish standards for disciplinary procedures governing assault, and to require prevention and awareness programming for students and employees.[129] The Department of Education's Office for Civil Rights is charged with enforcing Title IX. It may initiate an investigation either proactively or in response to a formal complaint. If OCR finds a Title IX violation, it can in theory withdraw federal funds. In practice, that penalty has never been invoked.[130] Rather, schools that are found to be in violation enter into agreements requiring them to take specified actions to remedy the problem.

A case against Eastern Michigan University shows the interplay of these requirements. OCR initiated enforcement proceedings based on the university's issuance of a misleading statement about a student who was sexually assaulted and murdered in her dorm room by a fellow student that there was "no evidence of foul play." During the investigation, however, OCR discovered several sexual assault and harassment complaints that had been inadequately investigated or resolved. The university entered a voluntary resolution in which it agreed to take a number of proactive measures to educate students and staff about the problem of sexual assault, to widely disseminate information about the policies and procedures for dealing with it, and to develop

125. See sources cited in Rhode, Rape on Campus supra note 74; White House Council, supra note 23, at 27.

126. Serena Patel, Gender Respect Education: A Proposal to Combat Commercial Sexual Exploitation, 23 J. Gender, Soc. Pol'y & L. 393, 406-10 (2015).

127. 20 U.S.C. §1681 et seq. (2012).

128. 20 U.S.C. §1092 (2012).

129. 20 U.S.C. §1092(f) (2012).

130. Mary Beth Marklein, Colleges Put on Notice over Rape, USA Today, July 31, 2014, at 3A.

procedures to assist victims.[131] The university was also fined under the Clery Act for failing to disclose the sexual assault and murder. In 2011, OCR issued a "Dear Colleague" letter (DCL) to remind institutions covered by Title IX of their obligations in dealing with complaints of sexual violence. OCR shared data from a National Institute of Justice report finding that "1 in 5 women are victims of completed or attempted sexual assault while in college," and, during the 2007-08 school year, there were 800 reported incidents of rape and attempted rape and 3,800 reports of other sexual batteries at public high schools.[132] The letter emphasizes the deleterious effects on education experienced by victims of sexual violence and the need for prompt and effective investigations of complaints. It provides step-by-step guidance for schools that receive complaints, emphasizing, for example, that schools can neither await the outcome of criminal investigations before initiating their own investigations, nor impose a heightened "clear and convincing" evidentiary standard.[133]

Beginning with the 2011 letter, OCR has significantly increased its involvement in campus sexual violence cases. By 2016, the Department of Education (DOE) had 194 sexual violence cases under investigation at 159 postsecondary institutions.[134] In many cases, OCR has been effective in pressuring institutions to improve their sexual assault procedures. However, the DOE process has been plagued by lack of resources and realistic penalties. In one Chronicle of Higher Education survey of complaints brought between 2003 and 2013, only 10 percent ended with an agreement on reform.[135]

Some commentators have also worried that the pressure to respond to activists' concerns has led institutions to shortchange the rights of the accused. In some institutions, including Harvard, the Title IX enforcement office acts as investigator, prosecutor, judge, and jury, and also handles appeals, which raises obvious due process issues that faculty have aired.[136] Many institutions do not provide lawyers to students who cannot afford them. According to the founder of Families Advocating for Campus Equality, "[i]n their rush to

131. Resolution, OCR Docket #15-09-6002, http://www2.ed.gov/about/offices/list/ocr/docs/investigations/15096002-a.pdf.

132. Office for Civil Rights, Dep't of Educ., Dear Colleague Letter, Apr. 4, 2011, http://www.whitehouse.gov/sites/default/files/dear_colleague_sexual_violence.pdf.

133. On litigation in the wake of *Gebser* and *Davis*, see Nancy Chi Cantalupo, Burying Our Heads in the Sand: Lack of Knowledge, Knowledge Avoidance, and the Persistent Problem of Campus Peer Sexual Violence, 43 Loy. U. Chi. L.J. 205 (2011).

134. Federal Campus Rape Investigations Near 200, and Finally Get More Funding, Huff. Post (Jan. 5, 2016).

135. Jonah Newman & Libby Sander, A Promise Unfulfilled, Chron. of Higher Educ., Apr. 30, 2014.

136. Judith Shulevitz, Accused College Rapists Have Rights Too, New Republic, Oct. 11, 2014; Rethink Harvard's Sexual Harassment Policy, Boston Globe, Oct. 14, 2014.

judgment, colleges are now substituting one class of victims for another."[137] In a rapidly growing number of cases, accused students have sued their institutions for abridging their rights.[138] In responding to such concerns, *Guardian* columnist Jessica Valenti writes, "on the one side, there are the 20 percent of college women who can expect to be victimized by rapists and would-be rapists; on the other side is a bunch of adult men (and a few women) worrying themselves to death that a few college-aged men might have to find a new college to attend."[139] Does that trivialize the harm of being labeled a rapist and forced to apply to another school with that record? How fair and adequate are your school's sexual assault procedures?

In 2016, a former female Harvard student sued the university for failing to protect her by forcing her to live in the same dorm as an alleged attacker. According to the lawsuit, a male student with whom she had a sexual relationship grew abusive and she reported his conduct to university counselors, officers, and the police several times. A university investigation found that he was not responsible for any rape, assault, abuse, harassment, or retaliation and the university declined to ask him to move from the dormitory where they both lived. She did, however, claim that he continued to harass her and obtained a judicial restraining order shortly before her graduation. The university then moved him to another building.[140] How should universities respond to safety concerns while investigations are pending? If she legitimately felt threatened by the student's presence, would it have been fair to him to require that his housing be changed? How would you assess the costs and benefits of lawsuits against universities as a way of securing greater accountability? In 2014 and again in 2015, a group of senators introduced the Campus Accountability and Safety Act, which sought to expand and codify some of what the Department of Education was already encouraging or requiring colleges and universities to do under Title IX. Among other things, the bill would require institutions to conduct and publish results of anonymous surveys of students regarding their experience with sexual misconduct and to provide confidential advisors for victims. It would also create financial penalties for noncompliance.[141] Why do you suppose that legislation has not passed? What other reform strategies would you suggest? In 2011, a widely reported scandal emerged involving alleged sexual abuse of young boys by a coach affiliated with Penn State University's football program. Jerry Sandusky was indicted for multiple counts

137. Robin Wilson, Presumed Guilty, Chron. of Higher Educ., Sept. 1, 2014 (quoting Judith E. Grossman).

138. Id. Ariel Kaminer, A New Factor in Campus Sexual Assault Cases, N.Y. Times, Nov. 19, 2014.

139. Zoë Heller, Rape on the Campus, N.Y. Rev. Books, Feb. 5, 2015 (quoting Valenti).

140. Christine Hauser, Former Student Sues Harvard over Handling of Sexual Crimes Complaints, N.Y. Times, Feb. 19, 2016.

141. The Campus Accountability and Safety Act, S. 590, 114th Cong. (2015-2016).

of sexual assault of boys that he had worked with through a charity. According to the grand jury's presentment, many of the alleged assaults, which included forced oral sex and anal rape, occurred in the locker room and showers of the football building. On at least one occasion, a low-ranking member of the coaching staff saw Sandusky anally raping a pre-adolescent boy. He reported the incident to the head coach, Joe Paterno, the "winningest" coach in college football history. Paterno passed along some version of the report to upper level university officials, but the incident was never reported to the police and no action was taken against Sandusky, although he was told not to bring children to university facilities and his keys to the locker room were assertedly taken away. When the scandal became public in 2011, Paterno and the university president were fired for their failure to respond appropriately to what they had been told about Sandusky. But witnesses differed on how specific the information was that reached them. In an interview with the Washington Post, Paterno said the eyewitness was reluctant to "get specific" about the nature of the abuse and suggested that it might have been "inappropriate . . . fondling." And, Paterno stated, "To be frank with you, I don't know that it would have done any good [to hear more details], because I never heard of, of rape and a man."[142]

Putting Theory Into Practice

5-10. In a 2014 case at Yale, a young woman drinking with friends exchanged text messages with a former sexual partner in which she told him that she was getting drunk and stated "don't let me try to seduce you. . . . Sex is awesome . . . and I might try to get it from you. But I shouldn't. I don't think." The two engaged in sex and she later charged him with assault, claiming she was too intoxicated to do anything other than "capitulate." An adjudicative panel found that while "alcohol may have reduced [her] inhibitions,"

142. Sally Jenkins, Joe Paterno's First Interview Since the Penn State-Sandusky Scandal, Wash. Post, Jan. 14, 2014. "I Just Did What I Thought Was Best," (quoting Paterno). Paterno died shortly after the scandal broke; Sandusky was convicted by a jury of multiple counts of child sexual assault; and Louis Freeh, hired by Penn State to conduct an independent investigation into the scandal, issued a scathing indictment of the university for failing to act on its prior knowledge of Sandusky's conduct. For Freeh's report see Freeh Sporkin & Sullivan, LLP, Report of the Special Investigative Counsel Regarding the Actions of the Pennsylvania State University Related to the Child Sexual Abuse Committed by Gerald A. Sandusky (July 12, 2012), http://www.scribd.com/doc/99901850/Freeh-Report-of-the-Actions-of-Penn-State-University; see also Richard Goldstein, Joe Paterno, Longtime Penn State Coach, Dies at 85, N.Y. Times, Jan. 22, 2012; Joe Drape, Sandusky Guilty of Sexual Abuse of 10 Young Boys, June 22, 2012, at A1.

her actions "taken as a whole, do not indicate that she lacked the ability to make or act on considered decisions."[143] Would you agree?

5-11. A fraternity at Old Dominion University greeted parents and freshman on move-in day with giant banners hanging off the front of their house. The signs said things like: "Rowdy and fun, hope your baby girl is ready for a good time"; "Freshman daughter drop-off"; and "Go ahead and drop off Mom too." Fraternities at other colleges have engaged in similar behavior with signs saying "daughter day care" and "21 to drink/18ish to stay the night." Should the universities take action to stop this conduct?[144] On what theory? Should universities themselves have any liability if they take no action?[145]

5-12. In a 2015 case against the University of California San Diego, a student accused of sexual assault claimed that the campus procedures violated his due process rights. Among other things, he objected to procedures giving the chair of the disciplinary panel discretion about whether to ask key witnesses questions that he had submitted. Only 9 of the accused student's 32 questions were put to the complainant. The chair also failed to allow follow up questions that the accused claimed were essential to his defense. For example, the complainant declined to answer a question about her relationship with the student after the alleged incident on the ground that the relationship was irrelevant, and the chair permitted this non-responsive answer. The student also objected that he was unable at the hearing to question the examiner who prepared an investigative report or any of the witnesses interviewed by the examiner. Finally, the student objected that hearing panel gave improper weight to his exercise of the Fifth Amendment Privilege Against Self-Incrimination. The panel's finding stated that although the student denied sexual penetration, "he abstained from providing additional information regarding the incident . . . and the panel would have liked to hear more information from him."[146] How should the court rule on the accused student's claims?

5-13. In a widely publicized case involving Columbia University, a male student who was found not responsible for sexual misconduct sued the university for sex discrimination. He claimed that the administration had allowed

---

143. Robin Wilson, Colleges Wrestle with How to Define Rape, Chron. of Higher Educ., Jan. 16, 2015.

144. Jake New, A Common Sign, insidehighered.com (Aug. 28, 2015), https://www.insidehighered.com/news/2015/08/28/sexist-banners-old-dominion-point-practice-many-campuses.

145. See Lisa Belkin, After Class, Skimpy Equality, N.Y. Times, Aug. 26, 2011, at ST1; Elizabeth Armstrong et al., Sexual Assault on Campus: A Multilevel Integrative Approach to Party Rape, 53 Soc. Probs. 483 (2006).

146. Doe v. Regents of the University of San Diego, Cal Super. Court, Case No. 37-2015-00010549-CU-WM-CTL (Mar. 25, 2015).

a campaign to harass him and that it would never have let a male student target a female student in the same way that he had been targeted. Among other things, the university had allowed the complaining witness to carry a mattress everywhere she went while on campus, including the graduation ceremony, and had given her academic credit and logistical support for her "Mattress Performance (Carry That Weight)," which doubled as her senior thesis project. The university art gallery also displayed an exhibit that featured prints of a couple having sex that included an obscenity and an inked-over New York Times article about the accused student.[147] How would you evaluate the university's conduct?

5-14. According to a female Swarthmore student, a male friend with whom she had been sexually involved fell asleep on her bed. Because the two had decided, she thought mutually, just to be friends, she climbed in next to him. When he began taking off her clothes, she "basically said, 'No, I don't want to have sex with you.' And then he said, 'Okay, that's fine,' and stopped. . . . And then he started again a few minutes later, taking off my panties, taking off his boxers. I just kind of laid there and didn't do anything—I had already said no. I was just tired and wanted to go to bed. I let him finish. I pulled my panties back on and went to sleep." She told a drug and alcohol counselor about the incident, who responded that the student was "such a good guy" that she must be mistaken. Three months later she complained to a dean. The students both graduated, and she never learned the outcome of any investigation.[148] If the facts were as she stated them, what if any sanctions would have been appropriate for the male student?

4. Rape, War, and the Military: Violence Against Women as a Human Rights Issue.

Women have long been targets of mass rape during wartime.[149] Accounts of brutalization are common in the literature of ancient Greece and Rome. The Old Testament similarly chronicles the invasion of Canaan by Hebrew tribes, whose spoils of war included "sheep, cattle, asses, and thirty-two thousand girls who had had no intercourse with a man."

---

147. Emily Bazelon, Have We Learned Anything from the Columbia Rape Case?, N.Y. Times, May 29, 2015. The student's lawsuit against Columbia was dismissed. See Max Kutner, Lawsuit Against Columbia over "Mattress Protest" Dismissed, Newsweek.com (Mar. 12, 2016), http://www.newsweek.com/paul-nungesser-columbia-mattress-lawsuit-dismissed-436273.

148. Simon Van Zuylen-Wood, Rape Happens Here, Philadelphia Mag., Apr. 24, 2014.

149. For an overview, see Sexual Violence in Conflict Zones: From the Ancient World to the Era of Human Rights (Elizabeth D. Heineman ed., 2011).

As Susan Brownmiller notes, the degradation of women has traditionally served to enhance the degradation of men:

> Rape by a conqueror is compelling evidence of the conquered status of masculine impotence. . . . Rape by a conquering soldier destroys all remaining illusions of power and property for men of the defeated side. The body of a raped woman becomes a ceremonial battlefield . . . a message passed between men. . . .[150]

Early prohibitions on such abuse were largely unenforced. In the United States, initial prohibitions on rape in wartime appeared in the 1863 military code for the Union Army, which codified early humanitarian law protecting non-combatants. At the international level, Article 46 of the Hague Convention of 1907 outlawed rape during occupations, and the Geneva Convention of 1929, which governed treatment of prisoners of war, guaranteed female prisoners all the regard "due their sex."

These prohibitions did little to deter massive rapes during World War II. The most notorious cases involved Japanese soldiers' "comfort facilities" or brothels, staffed by "comfort women." Most of these women were disfavored minorities, such as Koreans and Filipinos who were abducted or otherwise coerced into sexual slavery. An estimated 200,000 women were involved, often listed in official military documents as "military supplies"; almost three-quarters died from their treatment. Most of those who survived the camps were murdered or abandoned in dangerous areas at the close of the war.[151] Although the International Military Tribunal of the Far East gathered evidence on these abuses, its charter did not include sexual offenses and its proceedings (the Tokyo Trials) largely ignored them except when they were coupled with other offenses.[152] In Germany, rape was subsumed under crimes against humanity but was not included in a single indictment. The Allies who ran the Nuremberg Tribunal also ignored atrocities committed by their own soldiers, including an estimated rape of some 100,000 to 800,000 women in the Soviet capture of Berlin.

After World War II, international law began to include explicit prohibitions on rape during wartime. Article 27 of the 1949 Geneva Conventions, and subsequent Protocols of 1977 protect women against rape, enforced prostitution, or any form of indecent assault. More recently, the 1998 Rome Statute, which defines the jurisdiction of the International Criminal Court (ICC), defines "rape, sexual slavery, enforced prostitution, forced pregnancy, enforced sterilization, or any other form of sexual violence of comparable

---

150. Susan Brownmiller, Against Our Will: Men, Women and Rape 35 (1976).

151. Shellie K. Park, Broken Silence: Redressing the Mass Rape and Sexual Enslavement of Asian Women by the Japanese Government in an Appropriate Forum, 3 Asian-Pac. L. & Pol'y J. 2, 28 (2002).

152. Kelly D. Askin, A Decade of the Development of Gender Crimes in International Courts and Tribunals: 1993 to 2003, 11 (No. 3) Hum. Rts. Brief 16, 16 (2004).

gravity" as crimes against humanity, war crimes, and potentially part of genocide. Although the United States is not currently a signatory to the Rome Statute, U.S. courts have provided civil relief to victims of wartime rape under the Alien Tort Claims Act. In 1995, for example, the Second Circuit Court of Appeals held that Radovan Karadzic, leader of the Bosnian-Serb territory, could be held accountable for rape as an act of genocide and other war crimes committed during the Yugoslav conflict. A jury subsequently awarded the plaintiffs $745 million in compensatory and punitive damages.[153]

The international community first began to prosecute rape as a human rights violation largely in response to the atrocities committed in Rwanda and Yugoslavia in the early 1990s. Estimates of the number of rapes that occurred during the Yugoslavian conflict range from 20,000 to 50,000. What made these rapes distinctive was their role in ethnic cleansing. For example, Muslim and Croatian women were raped in order to make women tainted and therefore unmarriageable within their cultures, as well as to produce Serbian babies. Many women were murdered after rape, or held in camps where they were raped repeatedly, often until they died.[154] In Rwanda, an estimated 250,000 to 535,000 Tutsi women were raped, and some 200,000 murdered. Most of those who survived are now HIV-positive.[155]

What also distinguishes these mass rapes is the response of the international community, prompted by women's rights advocates. Their efforts have been critical in chronicling the abuses, drawing attention to the cultural context that legitimated them, and establishing rape as a crime against humanity within the jurisdiction of the International Criminal Tribunal for the former Yugoslavia (ICTY) and the International Criminal Tribunal for Rwanda (ICTR). For the first time, an international tribunal recognized rape as a tool of genocide and a crime against humanity and indicted a former head of government, Slobodan Milosevic, for mass rapes constituting such a crime.[156] Women's groups have also pressured the Japanese government to contribute to the Asian Women's Fund, which has also raised $4 million in non-governmental funds to compensate former comfort women. Some of these women have refused to accept such reparations on the grounds that this approach allows Japan to continue to avoid issuing a formal apology.[157]

153. Kadic v. Karadzic, 70 F.3d 232 (2d Cir. 1995).

154. Lynda E. Boose, Crossing the River Drina: Bosnian Rape Camps, Turkish Impalement, and Serb Cultural Memory, 28 Signs 71, 73-74 (Autumn 2002).

155. Jennifer M. Hentz, The Impact of HIV on the Rape Crisis in the African Great Lakes Region, 12 (No. 2) Hum. Rts. Brief 12, 13 (2005).

156. See Adrienne Kalosieh, Consent to Genocide?: The ICTY's Improper Use of the Consent Paradigm to Prosecute Genocidal Rape in FOCA, 24 Women's Rts. L. Rep. 121, 129 (2003).

157. Afreen R. Ahmed, The Shame of *Hwang v. Japan*: How the International Community Has Failed Asia's "Comfort Women," 14 Tex. J. Women & L. 121, 147 (2004).

Other efforts on the international front have centered on clarifying the law, supporting survivors, and preventing gender violence from occurring in future conflicts. One initiative involved implementation of command responsibility, which is now codified in the Rome Statute, establishing that military and non-military leaders can be held responsible for crimes under the ICC's jurisdiction. Another initiative involved the establishment of an unofficial Women's International War Crimes Tribunal, which heard testimony and passed judgment on high-ranking Japanese military and political leaders for their role in authorizing sexual slavery. Although the judgment carried no binding force, it has served an important role in clarifying international law and gaining compensation for comfort women.

Despite these efforts, rape remains common in armed conflict. According to organizations such as Amnesty International, more women have been raped in the Democratic Republic of the Congo (DRC) than in any other conflict. Some estimates have put the number at about 2 million, with 1 woman raped per minute.[158] Armed bands of soldiers have developed a "signature" form of rape: Local defense forces (known as Mai Mai) use branches or bayonets, and Rwandans gang rape their victims. An estimated 30 percent of women raped during the conflict are HIV-positive as a consequence.[159] In war-torn Liberia, 92 percent of surveyed women had experienced sexual violence.[160] Convictions for these crimes are rare. The International Rescue Committee rape centers in Sierra Leone have treated more than 9000 survivors since 2003 and fewer than half of 1 percent of those rapes have resulted in criminal convictions.[161] In many other conflicts, rape victims also die from attempted abortions and lack of health care during childbirth. Those who survive are often subject to permanent injuries or infertility, social ostracism, and desertion by their husbands. In Libya, where female chastity is highly valued, Moammar Gadhafi's troops raped women on a massive scale, and some survivors were subject to honor killings for bringing shame on their families.[162] More resources are urgently needed for organizations such as HEAL Africa, which attempts to help victims with medical assistance and social services, including basic education and job

158. Jeffrey Gettleman, Congo Study Sets Estimates for Rapes Much Higher, N.Y. Times, May 12, 2011, at A4; see also the study on which Gettleman's article is based: Amber Peterman et al., Estimates and Determinants of Sexual Violence Against Women in the Democratic Republic of Congo, 101 Am. J. of Pub. Health 1060 (June 2011).

159. Hentz, supra note 155, at 13.

160. United Nations, Office of the High Commissioner of Human Rights, Rape: Weapon of War (2016), http://www.ohchr.org/en/newsevents/pages/rapeweaponwar.aspx.

161. Nicholas D. Kristof, In This Rape Center, the Patient Was 3, N.Y. Times, Oct. 8, 2011, at SR11.

162. Hilmi M. Zawati, Hidden Deaths of Libyan Rape Survivors, Nat'l L. J., Jan 9, 2012.

skills. Commentators have also called for more progressive definitions of consent and stronger rape shield protections.[163]

United Nations peacekeeping forces have not only been often ineffective in preventing sexual abuse, they have also contributed to the problem. Over 100,000 peacekeepers serve in some of the world's most volatile areas, and UN reports have documented chronic problems of sexual assaults and exploitation, particularly sex coerced by offers of food, money, or employment.[164] Part of the problem is that the peacekeepers are often inadequately trained and those guilty of abuse fall under the legal jurisdictions of their home countries, which are reluctant to prosecute.[165] The UN Secretary General has called the abuse "a cancer in our system," urged the General Assembly to consider an international convention on crimes committed in peacekeeping operations, and called on member states to obtain DNA samples of those alleged to have committed exploitation and abuse.[166] Human Rights Watch has called for additional measures, including monitoring the status of prosecutions, publicly demanding accountability by those responsible for abuse, and providing more support for survivors.[167]

Rape is also a significant problem in the United States armed services. The best available studies indicate that 1 percent of men and 4.9 percent of women serving in the military experienced a sexual assault in the last year. Overall, 2 percent of men and 15 percent of women have experienced a sexual assault since joining the military.[168] Only 21 percent of women and 7 percent of men filed an official report of the assault, and of those who did so, 52 percent experienced professional or social retaliation.[169] Men were more likely than women to have been assaulted repeatedly and were more likely to describe the incident as designed to humiliate or abuse them.[170]

---

163. For example, the requirement of proof that the accused knew that sex achieved through force was not consensual seems unnecessary in the context of armed conflict. Phillip Weiner, The Evolving Jurisprudence of the Crime of Rape in International Criminal Law, 54 B.C. L. Rev. 1207, 1235 (2013).

164. United Nations Report of the Secretary General, Special Measures for Protection from Sexual Exploitation and Sexual Abuse (Feb. 15, 2016); Marie Deschamps, Hassan B. Jallow, & Yasmin Sooka, Taking Action on Sexual Exploitation and Abuse by Peacekeepers, Report of an Independent Review on Sexual Exploitation and Abuse by International Peacekeeping Forces in the Central African Republic (Dec. 17, 2015).

165. Kevin Sieff, The Growing U.N. Scandal over Sex Abuse and Peacekeeper Babies, Washington Post, Feb. 27, 2016.

166. Id. (quoting Ban Ki-moon); United Nations Report of the Secretary General, supra note 164 .

167. UN: Stop Sexual Abuse by Peacekeepers, Human Rights Watch (Mar. 4, 2016), http://reliefweb.int/report/central-african-republican/un-stop-sexual-abuse-peacekeepers.

168. Rand Corporation, Sexual Assault and Sexual Harassment in the U.S. Military xviii, xx (2015), http://www.rand.org/pubs/research_reports/RR870z2.html.

169. Id. at xx.

170. Id. at xix.

In commenting on the problem, President Obama in 2013 told reporters, "The bottom line is, I have no tolerance for this. If we find out somebody's engaging in this stuff, they've got to be held accountable, prosecuted, stripped of their positions, court-martialed, fired, dishonorably discharged—period."[171] Obama said he had instructed Defense Secretary Chuck Hagel "to step up our game exponentially."[172]

Yet despite efforts to do just that, progress remains uneven. A study by Human Rights Watch chronicled the failures. As it noted, just 5 percent of sexual assault cases investigated with a reportable outcome in 2014 led to a sex offense conviction. Servicemembers who reported an assault were 12 times more likely to suffer retaliation for doing so than to see their offender convicted for a sex offense.[173] The fear of retaliation is particularly great in military contexts because victims cannot simply quit or transfer. An army nurse told the co-chair of a new Congressional caucus on military sexual assault, "I'm more afraid of my own soldiers than of the enemy."[174]

The problem is compounded by a structure that gives commanding officers the power to determine whether to institute charges and what sanctions to impose. According to statistics provided to Congress, commanders reduced as many as a third of sexual abuse punishments.[175] Less than one-third of perpetrators in substantiated charges receive legal or administrative sanctions.[176] In two recent cases, Air Force Generals set aside jury convictions for sexual assault, in one instance reasoning that the defendant could not be guilty because he was a "doting father and husband."[177]

Some commentators believe that the most promising response to these persistent problems is to create an independent prosecutor to handle sex abuse cases in the military. Other countries that have taken sexual assault cases out of the chain of command have witnessed substantial improvement.[178] Yet proposals to remove responsibility from commanders has been opposed by the military and blocked in Congress.[179]

---

171. Craig Whitlock, Obama Delivers Blunt Message on Sexual Assaults in Military, Wash. Post, May 7, 2013.

172. Id.

173. Human Rights Watch, Embattled: Retaliation Against Sexual Assault Survivors in the US Military (2015).

174. Sabrina Ruben Erdely, The Rape of Petty Officer Blumer, Rolling Stone, Feb. 14, 2013, at 59.

175. Tom Vanden Brook & Gregg Zoroya, Why the Military Hasn't Stopped Sexual Abuse, U.S.A. Today, May 16, 2013, at 1A.

176. Carl Andrew Castro et al., Sexual Assault in the Military, 17 Current Psychiatry Reps. 54 (2015).

177. Id. at 1A.

178. Pending Legislation Regarding Sexual Assaults in the Military: Hearings Before the Senate Committee on Armed Services, 113th Cong. 320, at 91 (2014).

179. Leo Shane III, Miltary Sexual Assault Reform Plan Fails Again, Military Times, June 18, 2015.

What do you think accounts for the pervasiveness of rape in military and wartime settings?[180] How might it be more effectively addressed?

5. Prostitution: Consent Under Conditions of Constraint

Prostitution has been a common practice across time and culture, but in the United States, it remained relatively invisible until the antebellum period. With industrialization, urbanization, and Western migration, markets for sex increased and provoked significant challenge. The first major initiatives, variously characterized as "moral reform" and "social purity" campaigns, began in the 1830s and resurfaced in the late nineteenth and early twentieth centuries. At the outset, the leaders were mainly male clergy and philanthropists, but women's organizations soon joined the crusade. Their goals were to reform prostitutes and to discourage men from employing or recruiting them. These efforts led to expanded criminal prohibitions and enforcement strategies.

The criminalization of prostitution has been justified on multiple grounds: promoting morality, protecting public health, avoiding public nuisance, and preventing sexual exploitation and abuse. Class, race, and ethnic prejudice also underpinned many of the early "anti-vice" campaigns. Moral reformers were particularly concerned by the vision of husbands of white women consorting with lower-class immigrants and women of color.

Today, the legal status of prostitution varies widely around the world. Most countries either prohibit or regulate the sale of sex, but the scope of permissible behavior, the severity of penalties, and the practices of enforcement agencies differ considerably.

In the United States, every state but Nevada prohibits buying or selling sexual intercourse for money or offering to do so. Every state but Nevada also makes it a crime to knowingly encourage or compel a person to sell sex for money (pandering) or to receive "something of value" knowing that it was earned through an act of prostitution (pimping).[181] Most jurisdictions classify first-time offenses as misdemeanors, but typically punish repeat behavior as a felony. About half of all states have a "patron clause," which subjects customers to the same penalty as prostitutes. Other jurisdictions classify purchase of

---

180. Valerie A. Stander & Cynthia J. Thomsen, Sexual Harassment and Assault in the U.S. Military: A Review of Policy and Research Trends, 181 Military Medicine 20, 22 (2016) (discussing factors such as military lifestyle, demographics, and culture).

181. Sylvia Law, Commercial Sex: Beyond Decriminalization, 73 S. Cal. L. Rev. 523, 530 (2000); Melissa Farley, Prostitution and Trafficking in Nevada: Making the Connections (2007).

sex as a less serious offense.[182] New York is the only state that has higher penalties for the customer than the prostitute.[183]

Nevada permits prostitution in counties with populations under 200,000 persons, subject to highly restrictive licensing conditions. Prostitutes must be registered and fingerprinted by the police and must work in brothels where they typically have no control over their hours or customers.[184] County police have broad discretion to regulate the conditions under which commercial sex is permissible. For example, prostitutes generally may not have their children live in the same community in which they work, drive a car in city limits, or appear on the streets after 5 p.m. In the areas surrounding brothels, this system has effectively reduced street solicitation and incidental crime, and has largely eliminated the risks of sexually transmitted diseases. However, it has failed to curtail illegal prostitution elsewhere in the state. About a thousand women work in 33 licensed brothels and account for only a small percentage of prostitutes estimated to be working in Nevada.[185] The stigma and lack of control make licensed brothel work an unattractive option for most prostitutes.[186]

Although anti-prostitution statutes in this country are generally sex-neutral in form, they are sex-biased in practice. Law enforcement officials prosecute mainly prostitutes, not customers or pimps, who are overwhelmingly male. According to some studies, less than 1 percent of prostitution-related arrests are for pimping.[187] Female prostitutes are also prosecuted at far higher rates than males, and women of color are disproportionately targeted.[188] Current policies are expensive and largely ineffective deterrents. Thousands are spent prosecuting woman offenders, who typically return almost immediately to the streets. In one study, almost two-thirds of incarcerated prostitutes reported at least five arrests, and their jail time increased the intensity and

182. See Joann Miller, Prostitution in Contemporary American Society, in Sexual Coercion: A Sourcebook on Its Nature, Causes and Prevention 45 (Elizabeth Grauerholz & Mary Koralewski eds., 1991).

183. U.S. Federal and State Prostitution Laws, ProCon.org (2010), http://prostitution.procon.org/view.resource.php?resourceID=000119#2.

184. Law, supra note 181, at 543, 552-54.

185. Id. at 560. See Danielle Augustson & Alyssa George, Prostitution and Sex Work, 16 Geo. J. Gender & L. 229, 245 (2015).

186. Brynn N.H. Jacobson, Addressing the Tension Between the Dual Identities of the American Prostitute: Criminal and Victim; How Problem-Solving Courts Can Help, 37 Seattle U. L. Rev. 1023, 1043 (2014).

187. John Elrod, Filling the Gap: Refining Sex Trafficking Legislation to Address the Problem of Pimping, 68 Vand. L. Rev. 961, 979 (2015).

188. Augustson & George, supra note 185, at 255, 258; Cheryl Nelson-Butler, A Critical Race Feminist Perspective on Prostitution & Sex Trafficking in America, 27 Yale J.L. & Feminism 95, 132 (2015).

duration of involvement in streetwalking.[189] A Texas study found that it cost over four times as much to incarcerate prostitutes as to fund their participation in rehabilitative programs.[190] Although some evidence suggests that most streetwalkers would like to quit, a variety of forces make exit difficult: lack of education and employment skills, the stigma of an arrest record, substance abuse and mental health problems, and control by pimps.[191]

The criminal approach also increases women's vulnerability to physical abuse and economic coercion. Studies of streetwalkers typically find that about two-thirds to four-fifths are subject to physical assault and to extremely high rates of rape, murder, and post-traumatic stress disorders.[192] Women are reluctant to report abuses that could lead to prostitution charges, and police systematically fail to pursue complaints by sex workers. Arrest records heighten women's difficulties in moving to alternative work and often force them to rely on pimps and middlemen to screen customers or provide money for bail and fines.

Those who work in high-end escort services typically incur fewer risks either of arrest or physical abuse, and often make substantial sums. Details of such services emerged in 2007, with the arrest of the "D.C. Madame" and, in 2008, with the forced resignation of New York governor Eliot Spitzer, who patronized the Emperor's Club, an escort service charging between $1000 and $5000 an hour.[193]

Accurate figures on the total amount of prostitution in the United States are unavailable. However, most studies indicate that about 10 to 20 percent of American men acknowledge having purchased sex at some point in their lives.[194] The rise in Internet-facilitated prostitution has compounded

189. Maureen A. Norton-Hawk, The Counterproductivity of Incarcerating Female Street Prostitutes, 22 Deviant Behav. 403, 405 (2001).

190. Kim Wilks, Texas Criminal Justice Coalition, Effective Approaches for Reducing Prostitution in Texas: Proactive and Cost-Efficient Strategies to Help People Leave the Streets (2013).

191. C. Aaron McNeece & Elizabeth Mayfield Arnold, Program Closure: The Impact on Participants in a Program for Female Prostitutes, 12 Res. Soc. Work Prac. 159, 168 (2002) (reporting that 90 percent of interviewees expressed desire to leave. For other research, see Michael Shively et al., A National Overview of Prostitution and Sex Trafficking Demand Reduction Efforts, Final Report to the Department of Justice 14 (2012); Catharine MacKinnon, Trafficking, Prostitution, and Inequality, 46 Harv. Civ. Rights-Civ. Lib. L. Rev. 271, 290 (2011).

192. See MacKinnon, Trafficking, supra note 191, at 282; Catharine A. MacKinnon, Sex Equality 1233-40 (2d ed. 2007); Melissa Farley, Prostitution, Trafficking, and Cultural Amnesia: What We Must Not Know in Order to Keep the Business of Sexual Exploitation Running Smoothly, 18 Yale J.L. & Feminism 109, 113-16 (2006).

193. Eric Lipton, Woman in Escort Case Plans to Name Names in Defense, N.Y. Times, Apr. 29, 2007, at A20; Stefano Eposito et al., "I Offer an Authentic Experience": Prostitute Says Going Rate Here Is Only $700 to $800 an Hour, Chicago Sun-Times, Mar. 16, 2008.

194. Shively et al., supra note 191, at 7.

challenges in measuring and sanctioning offenses because it enables customers to more readily access commercial sex and evade arrests through temporary brothels and tips about sting operations.[195] Some evidence suggests that Internet-based prostitution is also less risky for sex workers and enables more of them to avoid reliance on pimps.[196]

Most European countries have repealed prohibitions on engaging in prostitution but have retained laws against soliciting, pimping, pandering, running a disorderly house, or transporting a woman across national boundaries for purposes of prostitution. Other restrictions range from fairly laissez-faire approaches in countries like Denmark and the Netherlands, to tightly controlled zoning systems for licensed brothels in many German cities. Sweden criminalizes the purchase but not the sale of sex, and New Zealand has fully decriminalized prostitution.[197] Even where commercial sex is legal and taxable, workers often lack basic rights and benefits, such as pensions, health insurance, and unemployment assistance. The same is true in Nevada, where prostitutes are classified as independent contractors rather than employees.[198]

In other countries, particularly those in Asia, South America, and the Mideast, prostitution remains a criminal offense. The prohibitions in some tradition-oriented societies are quite severe. In other nations, a de facto licensing system has evolved despite formal prohibitions. Through de facto or de jure licensing structures, a growing number of Asian and European countries are also developing sex tourism industries.

Dorchen Leidholdt, Prostitution: A Violation of Women's Human Rights
1 Cardozo Women's L.J. 133, 135-38 (1993)

Prostitution is not about women making money. It is about other people—usually men—making money off women's bodies. Pimps, brothel owners, club owners, hotel chains, travel agencies, pornographers, organized crime syndicates, and governments are the real economic beneficiaries of the sex trade in women. . . .

Prostitution is not about individuals. It is an institution of male dominance, and it is also a global industry in which the prostituting of women is

195. Id. at 18-19.

196. Scott R. Peppet, Prostitution 3.0?, 98 Iowa L. Rev. 1989 (2013).

197. MacKinnnon recounts the legislative history of the law and considers it "sex equality in inspiration and effect." Mackinnon, Trafficking, supra note 191, at 301. For discussion of comparative approaches, see Emily Bazelon, Oppression or Profession?, N.Y. Times Mag., May 8, 2016 at 35-43, 55-57.

198. Law, supra note 181, at 543, 552-54.

constantly being packaged in new ways, using new forms of technology, tapping new markets: sex-tourism, mail-order bride selling, sex entertainment, sex immigration, dial-a-porn, computer pornography.

Just as prostitution isn't about individuals, it isn't about choice. Instead, prostitution is about the absence of meaningful choices; about having alternative routes to survival cut off or being in a situation where you don't have options to begin with. . . . [T]he majority of women in prostitution in the country—most studies estimate 60 to 70 percent—have histories of sexual abuse in childhood. . . . Add to this the reality that the population targeted by pimps and traffickers is teenagers. It becomes clear that the majority of prostitutes are socialized into "sex work" in childhood and adolescence when consent is meaningless and choice an illusion.

Then there are the related factors of poverty, lack of education, and homelessness. . . .

Choice vanishes when, in order to endure the prostitution, women become addicted to alcohol or drugs, or become prostitutes to support their addiction. In the Portland, Oregon, study, 85 percent of the women were drug or alcohol abusers.

Nor is choice present when a woman is so traumatized by having stranger after stranger use her body as a seminal spittoon that she accepts prostitution as her destiny.

Just as prostitution is not about choice, it's not about work. Or if it is, it is work in the same way that slavery or bonded labor is work—work that violates human dignity and every other human right. What other kind of work has as job training years of being sexually abused in childhood? What other job has as its working conditions: rape . . . beatings . . . and premature death and murder?

Notes

1. Alternative Regulatory Structures.   The alternatives to the existing criminal approach to prostitution are

- full decriminalization, i.e., removal of penalties from all consensual sexual activities and related commercial practices;
- partial decriminalization, i.e., removal of penalties from the sale of sexual services but not from other related activities such as purchasing, pimping, pandering, soliciting, or advertising; and
- regulation, i.e., removal of penalties from activities that meet state-imposed requirements, such as zoning restrictions, licensing regulations, and health exams.

Most women's rights advocates and sex workers agree on two points: Criminal penalties for workers are not appropriate, and more strategies are necessary to ensure their safety. From this perspective, many feminists point out that the best way for society to minimize the harms associated with prostitution is to maximize women's other employment choices, increase their access to social services, and reduce the safety risks and social stigma associated with consensual commercial sex.

Most women's rights advocates and sex workers are also united in opposing regulation as an alternative to decriminalization. Workers generally object to the highly restrictive conditions imposed by licensing structures and to the large share of profits taken by brothel owners (typically 50 percent). Counties in Nevada exclude women with criminal records or sexually transmitted diseases, brothels limit women's mobility and choices, and licensing structures permanently stigmatize women as sex workers. It is for this reason that only a small percentage of Nevada's prostitutes operate out of licensed establishments, despite the relatively safe working conditions and substantial incomes available. Although conditions can be better in worker-owned collectives, these are relatively rare in sex work.

Windsor, Canada offers a less stigmatized model. There, the city sought to create a safe "adult entertainment destination" while respecting escorts' "right to self determination in their work." Sex work is licensed, advertised, and "normalized;" and workers are given information about health, safety, social services, and financial planning.[199] Experience in other countries is more mixed. In Australia, legalization resulted in higher levels of illegal and child prostitution, organized crime, and trafficking.[200] In the Netherlands, brothels are legal, as is street prostitution in certain zones, and sex workers have access to pensions, social security benefits and state-organized health care. However, illegal prostitution and trafficking remain problems, and many workers are unwilling to take advantage of benefits that would stigmatize them as prostitutes.[201]

To what extent would legalization of prostitution represent state collaboration in the exploitation and commodification of female sexuality? Some research suggests that countries that have legalized prostitution have a larger reported incidence of trafficking.[202] Does that suggest that decriminalization is an unacceptable risk?

---

199. Eleanor Maticka-Tyndale et al., Making a Place for Escort Work: A Case Study, 42 J. Sex. Res. 1, 2, 7-8 (2005).

200. Mary Sullivan, What Happens When Prostitution Becomes Work? An Update on Legalization of Prostitution in Australia 23 (2005), http://www.turnofftheredlight.ie/wp-content/uploads/2011/02/What-happens-when-prostitution-becomes-work.pdf.

201. Jacobson, supra note 186, at 1039; Janet Halley et al., From the International to the Local in Feminist Legal Responses to Rape, Prostitution/Sex Work, and Sex Trafficking: Four Studies in Contemporary Governance Feminism, 29 Harv. J.L. & Gender 335, 398 (2006); MacKinnon, Trafficking, supra note 191, at 304-06.

202. Seo-Young Cho et al., Does Legalized Prostitution Increase Human Trafficking?, 41 World Dev. 67 (2012).

The public generally opposes decriminalization. Surveys over the last decade find that about 60 to 80 percent of voters are against legalized prostitution for consenting adults, with women less supportive than men.[203] Ballot initiatives to decriminalize sex work have been unsuccessful. A 2008 initiative to legalize prostitution in San Francisco was defeated by a 58 to 42 percent margin, and a 2004 Berkeley, California, proposal to make prostitution the city's lowest law enforcement priority (along with marijuana possession) lost by a two-to-one margin. Voters and city leaders have often opposed such measures because they would insulate pimps, not just prostitutes, from prosecution and increase risks of public nuisance.[204] More politically acceptable are diversion programs pioneered by a number of problem-solving courts, such as Hartford, Connecticut's Community Court and New York City's Midtown Community Court. These programs allow defendants who plead guilty to prostitution to avoid incarceration if they participate in individualized treatment plans. Such plans include social services designed to address underlying problems, such as substance abuse or lack of education and employment skills. As an added incentive for participation, commentators urge that successful completion of the program should expunge prostitution-related crimes.[205] These initiatives have substantially reduced recidivism rates, as have some similar efforts targeted at rehabilitating juvenile offenders.[206] Why do you think more communities have not adopted such approaches?

A final strategy, proposed by Andrea Dworkin in the 1980s, and supported by some contemporary women's rights advocates, is to decriminalize selling of sex by prostitutes but prohibit purchase of sex by customers, pimps, and traffickers. As noted earlier, Sweden has such a law, and the approach has also spread to Iceland, South Korea, and Norway. Swedish law provides fines or prison of up to one year for those convicted and also provides social assistance such as shelters, education, and job training to women seeking to leave sex work.[207] It is credited with reducing the frequency of street prostitu-

203. Quinnipiac University Poll (2008), http://www.quinnipiac.edu/polling.xml; Social Science Research Center (1995), http://prostitution.procon.org/view.resource. php?resourceID=000121#G (81 percent of adults, and 74 percent of males oppose legalization; 62 percent of New Yorkers, 54 percent of men, and 68 percent of women oppose legalization).

204. See Johnny California, Measure K in California Defeated — Prostitution Laws Still Enforced (Nov. 6, 2008), http://johnnycalifornia.com/?p=1145; Jess McKinley, San Francisco's Prostitutes Support a Proposition, N.Y. Times, Oct. 31, 2008, at A10; Rebecca W. Turek, Prostitutes' Rights Measure Defeated in Berkeley, (Nov. 3, 2004), http://journalism. berkeley.edu/projects/election2004/archives/berkeley; Chip Johnson, A Look Back at the Year's News Stories, S.F. Chron., Dec. 31, 2004, at B1.

205. Jacobson, supra note 186, at 1051.

206. Christina Hoag, New Laws Treat Teen Prostitutes as Abuse Victims, AP and ABC News, Apr. 18, 2009; Bernice Yeung, Throw Away Girls, Cal. Lawyer, Nov. 2003, at 59.

207. Roger Mathews, Prostitution, Politics, and Policy, 113 (2008); Sweden Unveils Tougher Penalties for Buying Sex, The Local: Sweden's News in English (Jan. 27, 2011), http://www.thelocal.se/20110127/31680.

tion and trafficking and enjoys the support of about four-fifths of the public.[208] Although arrests are infrequent, the law has reduced the acceptability of purchasing sex.[209] However, sex workers oppose this approach on the ground that it makes their lives less safe by forcing them underground to protect patrons. When prostitution is invisible, workers are more vulnerable to violence and are less able to insist on condoms and to seek health and safety services.[210] No empirical evidence is available to quantify such risks.[211] After evaluating the options available, the European Parliament in 2014 endorsed the Nordic approach and called on Member states to repeal repressive legislation against prostitutes, expand their access to social services, and pursue efforts at demand reduction.[212]

What is your view? Does the Swedish partial decriminalization approach seem preferable or politically plausible for the United States? Is it fair that women like Deborah Jeane Palfrey, known as the D.C. Madame, faced a 55-year prison term for arranging sexual liaisons for powerful men, while her male customers faced no prosecution and some retained influential government positions?[213]

Could technology be harnessed to make sex work safer? Scott Peppet has advocated changing laws to permit the growth of intermediaries that would enable verification of whether customers and workers were free of sexually transmitted disease or had a criminal record, and whether workers had characteristics that suggested trafficking.[214] What would be the advantages and disadvantages of such an approach?

What constitute effective enforcement strategies? According to recent research, strategies that focus on demand reduction are more effective than those directed at suppliers.[215] Some municipalities have attempted to crack

---

208. Farley, supra note 192, at 138; Gunilla S. Ekberg, The Swedish Law That Prohibits the Purchase of Sexual Services, 10 Violence Against Women 1187, 1189-93 (2004); Sheila Jeffreys, The Industrial Vagina: The Global Sex Trade 203 (2009). Street prostitution has reportedly declined by 50 percent since the law's passage. Sweden's Law a Success: Report, The Local: Sweden's News in English (July 3, 2010), http://www.thelocal.se/20100703/27580. For a comprehensive review of the mixed evidence on Sweden's law, see Katie Beran, Revisiting the Prostitution Debate: Uniting Liberal and Radical Feminism in Pursuit of Policy Reform, 30 J. Law & Ineq, 19, 49-53, 55 (2012).

209. Beran, supra note 208, at 51, 53.

210. Aziza Ahmed, Feminism, Power, and Sex Work in the Context of HIV/AIDs Consequences for Women's Health, 34 Harv. J.L. & Gender 225, 255 (2011); see also Jacobson, supra note 186, at 1041; Bazelon, supra note 197, at 40.

211. Michelle Madden Dempsey, Decriminalizing Victims of Sex Trafficking, 52 Am. Crim. L. Rev. 207, 228 (2015).

212. Resolution of 26 February 2014 on Sexual Exploitation and Prostitution and Its Impact on Gender Equality (2014), discussed in Dempsey, supra note 211, at 227.

213. Mark Benjamin, Fall Girls, Ms., Summer 2008, at 37.

214. Peppet, supra note 196, at 2037-43.

215. Shively et al., supra note 191, at 4.

down on customers by launching sting operations targeted at buyers rather than sellers; publishing the names and photos of those convicted); impounding vehicles or taking away the driving licenses of those convicted of solicitation from their cars; posting on the Internet videos of men soliciting prostitutes; and requiring attendance at "John schools", which educate participants on the harms and risks of prostitution.[216] Would you recommend any of these strategies? In surveys in England, Scotland, and the United States, men agreed that being placed on a sex offender registry would be the most effective deterrent to their purchase of sex. Other effective deterrents would be prison time and public exposure.[217]

Which of these approaches seem most desirable? How could they be achieved?

2. Prostitution and the Autonomy of Workers.   At issue in debates over prostitution are fundamental issues about the meaning of consent and the nature of sexual expression. Among the most divisive issues are whether most individuals who engage in commercial sex have made truly free choices to do so, and whether commercial sex is work like any other.

What complicates the debate is the diversity of stories among prostitutes and the inadequate or conflicting data concerning their experiences. As one worker put it, "[s]ome [women] feel they are victims. Some *are* victims. And then there are others who say that they made that choice and celebrate that choice."[218] Some prostitutes claim that the first time they felt powerful was the first time they turned a trick.[219] According to one worker:

> [B]eing able to earn [a substantial income] is a blessing. . . . I have no regret for my experiences. Prostitution brought me social life, money, sex and entertainment. . . . I was alone in college, on welfare with a son. He wanted football clothes. He got them.[220]

Another woman agreed:

> I've always considered my place in sex work really privileged because I've always worked indoors and I've always been really in control of my work. I really love what I do. It's an amazing income and it's putting me through college. . . . [But

---

216. For evaluation of these strategies, see Shively et al., supra note 191, at 24-83.

217. Melissa Farley et al., Men Who Buy Sex: Who They Buy and What They Know 26 (2009).

218. Sex Trade Workers and Feminists: Myths and Illusions, in Good Girls/Bad Girls: Feminists and Sex Trade Workers Face to Face 202 (Laurie Bell ed., 1987).

219. Gail McPherson, The Whore Stigma: Female Disorder and Male Unworthiness, 37 Soc. Text 39, 54 (1993).

220. Anonymous, Prostitution: A Narrative by a Former "Call Girl," 1 Mich. J. Gender & L. 105 (1993).

as a woman of color] I've been busted over and over again more so than the peers that I work with, who are mainly educated and white.[221]

One prostitute who had previously worked in a male-dominated occupation servicing telephone lines recalled that "I came home exhausted every day plus I was harassed by guys on the job. Working as a prostitute in a massage parlor is far less draining and I still get that kick of being an assertive woman."[222] The prominent Hollywood Madame, Heidi Fleiss, "wouldn't recommend prostitution as a career because it doesn't have great long-term prospects." But in the short term, the money can help someone finish school, start a business, or do something else "positive with her life."[223]

One Stanford law school graduate, Cristina Schultz Warthen, appears to have pursued such a strategy by working as an escort during her legal education. Her Internet site featured topless photos and listed rates ranging from $1250 for two hours to $3000 for six hours. According to one posting on the site, "I have paid off 100 percent of my student loans and I have tried to send a positive message to SF escorts re: assumptions about the nature and social status of women in the business."[224] In another posting, Warthen states, "During my education, I was continually taught to question paradigms and assumptions. I never understood, however, why this questioning had to stop when it bumped up against accepted social and sexual norms. I never understood why you had to be a down-to-earth educated chaste career-girl or a sexual, sensual adventuress or temptress."[225] She eventually pled guilty to tax evasion and agreed to pay $243,000 and serve a year of home detention and three years of probation.[226] Was this an appropriate result? If Warthen eventually applies to the bar, could she ever satisfy the standard requiring applicants to demonstrate "good moral character"?

221. Hannah Alsgaard, Introduction: Symposium, Uncovered: The Policing of Sex Work, 26 Berkeley J. Gender L. & Justice, 198, 200 (2011) (quoting Luette Chavez).

222. McPherson, supra note 219, at 57.

223. Heidi Fleiss, as told to Nadya Labi, In Defense of Prostitution, Legal Affairs (Sept./ Oct. 2003), http://www.legalaffairs.org/issues/September-October-2003/feature_fleiss_ sepoct03.msp. For other positive accounts, see Nelson-Butler, supra note 188, at 116.

224. Dan Reed, Stanford Law Grad, U.S. Clash over Cache of Cash, San Jose Mercury News, Oct. 6, 2004, at B1.

225. John Roemer, Degree of Flexibility: Stanford Law Grad Turned Escort Says Her Legal Training Taught Her to Question Assumptions, S.F. Daily J., Oct. 25, 2004, at A1; Howard Mintz, Stanford Law School Grad Pleads Guilty to Running Escort Service, San Jose Mercury News (Jan. 26, 2009), http://www.mercurynews.com/breakingnews/ ci_11558089?source=rss.

226. Mintz, supra note 225; She Works Hard for the Money, Playboy, Feb. 1, 2005, at 49.

Research on male prostitutes reflects a similar diversity of experience. Although some are young, impoverished, addicted, and abused, others appear to freely choose their work and appear to suffer few ill effects.[227]

Even for well-compensated sex workers, however, many feminists, such as Dorchen Leidholdt in the reading above, question whether prostitution represents the kind of free, informed, individual choice that is worthy of respect. Many prostitutes enter sex work as minors before capacities for autonomous decision-making are well developed. So too, Catharine MacKinnon notes, "[i]f prostitution is a free choice, why are the women with the fewest choices the ones most often found doing it?"[228] In her view, "[u]nderstood as a practice of sexual exploitation, prostitution cannot be made safe."[229] According to some sociologists, when prostitutes give favorable accounts of their experience, they are engaging in "neutralizing techniques":

> Sociologists use the term to describe the way in which socially despised and marginalized groups survive their marginal condition. Such techniques may be employed because the only alternative available may be the painful one of self-contempt. The idea that prostitution is freely chosen is such a technique.[230]

By contrast, defenders of sex work are offended by the dismissal of their own perceptions as false consciousness. As members of one Canadian organization of sex workers put it:

> When you are a prostitute that says, "Well, I don't agree with the way you're interpreting my life, I don't feel oppressed or I don't feel exploited in the way that you're saying," they say things like "she's too blinded to her own oppression to see her experience for what it really is, and it really is the patriarchy." They find it necessary to interpret prostitutes' experience of their lives and then feed it back to the prostitutes to tell them what's really happening, whereas they wouldn't dare be so condescending or patronizing with any other group of women.[231]

In a world of true equality, would commercial sex be inherently exploitative? Are the degrading aspects of current prostitution largely attributable to its social and legal status rather than to its intrinsic nature? Consider these views:

227. Thayne D. Stoddard, Male Prostitution and Equal Protection: An Enforcement Dilemma, 21 Duke J. Gender L. & Pol'y 227, 233-35 (2013).

228. Catharine MacKinnon, Prostitution and Civil Rights, 1 Mich. J. Gender & L. 13, 27-28 (1996).

229. MacKinnon, Trafficking, supra note 191, at 299.

230. Sheila Jeffreys, The Idea of Prostitution 137 (1997).

231. Realistic Feminists: An Interview with Valerie Scott, Peggy Miller, and Ryan Hotchkiss of the Canadian Organization for the Rights of Prostitutes, in Good Girls/Bad Girls, at 204, 213 (Laurie Bell ed., 1987). For similar views among sex workers, see Bazelon, supra note 197, at 35-43.

Anonymous sex has validity in its own right. Since when is sex only acceptable and valid and good sex if it's linked to love or linked to someone that they have invested in, in terms of a relationship? There are a lot of people who feel unwilling or reluctant or unable to express a lot of pockets of their sexuality and their sexual needs unless it is with someone they don't have to look at afterwards. There's an excitement that goes with a new person, a novelty. Needing novelty is perfectly acceptable around other needs that we have. . . . Humanity benefits from giving legitimacy to all kinds of needs as long as they're consensual. . . . [Prostitutes'] ideal situation is like anybody else's—that we have control over our work environment. . . .[232]

Legal and illegal sex businesses are places where men can commit sexual . . . exploitation without fear and where they are socialized to inflict those same acts on other women in their lives. When prostitution is tolerated or legalized by the state, sexual, predation is normalized. . . .[233]

We need to reflect on whether romantic love is really the only valid foundation for sexual interaction; to question the view that "legitimate" sexual intimacy must be tied to spiritual connection. All too many of us seem to have swallowed wholesale this ideology: we abhor . . . "impersonal" sex; we yearn for intimate "pillow talk"; we disdain the prostitute for engaging in sex without "real connection." (Which of us hasn't engaged in sex without connection? It wasn't prostitutes who told their daughters to "close your eyes and think . . . [of the Empire]"). . . . Must we all learn to see the subjects of our sexual desire as whole, equal, non-partial, and unsegmented? Even were it desirable, *can* we eliminate inequality in the realm of the intimate? Can we do so before we eliminate pervasive economic and social inequality? And if not, what do we do in the meantime?[234]

Does women's purchase of sex from men stand on the same footing as men's purchase from women? The limited available evidence suggests that women tend to "shy away from straightforward cash for sex transactions," and prefer at least the illusion of affection and romance.[235] Does a romantic façade make the transaction any less exploitative? Are men's purchases of sex from men different from women's purchases of sex from men? Is it the nature of the act, the working conditions, or the social context that should be most critical in shaping our cultural norms and legal policies?

3. Trafficking. After drugs, trafficking is the largest criminal enterprise globally with annual profits in America estimated at over $9 billion.[236] Most

---

232. Id. at 206, 209.

233. Farley, Prostitution, Trafficking and Cultural Amnesia, supra note 192, at 142.

234. Carlin Meyer, Decriminalizing Prostitution: Liberation or Dehumanization?, 1 Cardozo Women's L.J. 105, 117 (1993).

235. Mireya Navarro, The West Gets Wilder, N.Y. Times, Jan. 8, 2006, at S2 (quoting Amalia Cazebas).

236. Nancy Hubasek & Kaela Herrera, Combatting Domestic Sex Trafficking: A Time for a New Approach, 24 Tex. J. Women, Gender & L. 167, 170 (2015); Steven Seidenberg, Of

trafficking involves sexual exploitation, and although there are no solid estimates of the number of persons who are victims of sex trafficking, there is no doubt that most offenders are male and most victims are female.[237] Some estimates suggest that 95 to 98 percent of sex trafficking victims are women and girls.[238] The United States is a major destination country for traffickers, largely from Southeast Asia, Eastern Europe, Latin America, and the independent states of the former Soviet Union, including Russia. In 2012, President Obama called sex trafficking a "debasement of our common humanity" that ought to concern every person, community, business, and nation.[239] Trafficking encompasses a range of crimes, including sex tourism, debt bondage, involuntary servitude, forced prostitution, child marriage, and rape. The 2000 United Nations Convention Against Transnational Organized Crime; Protocol to Prevent, Suppress, and Punish Trafficking in Persons, Especially Women and Children includes as trafficking "the recruitment, transportation, transfer, harboring or receipt of persons, by means of the threat or use of force or other forms of coercion, of abduction, of fraud, of deception, of the abuse of power or of a position of vulnerability or of the giving or receiving of payments or benefits to achieve the consent of a person having control over another person, for the purposes of exploitation." Exploitation includes "the prostitution of others or other forms of sexual exploitation, forced labor or services, slavery, or practices similar to slavery, servitude, or the removal of organs." The United States has adopted a similar, although somewhat narrower, definition in the Victims of Trafficking and Violence Protection Act of 2000. It prohibits:

> (A) sex trafficking in which a commercial sex is induced by force, fraud, or coercion, or in which the person induced to perform such an act has not attained 18 years of age; or
> (B) the recruitment, harboring, transportation, provision, or obtaining a person for labor or services, through the use of force, fraud, or coercion for the purpose of subjection to involuntary servitude, peonage, debt bondage, or slavery.

A significant part of the current trafficking industry involves deception, kidnapping, or outright purchase of women and girls for work in the sex

Human Bondage, ABA J. Apr., 2013, 54; see also U.S. Dep't of Health & Human Services, About Human Trafficking (2012).

237. United Nations Office on Drugs and Crime, Global Report on Trafficking in Persons 16, 23, 33-34 (2014) (hereinafter United Nations, Global Report). Figures compiled by the United Nations indicate that that about 53 percent of victims are subjected to sexual exploitation and forced labor accounted for 40 percent. Id. at 33.

238. Id. at 73; U.S. Dep't of State, Trafficking in Persons Report 45 (2012).

239. Barack Obama, Remarks by the President at the Clinton Global Initiative (Sept. 25, 2012), https://www.whitehouse.gov/the-press-office/2012/09/25/remarks-president-clinton-global-initiative.

trade. Some women or their families are duped by advertisements or agents promising jobs such as waitresses, au pairs, sales clerks, actresses, and exotic dancers. Other women voluntarily accompany a new husband or a boyfriend to another country where they are sold into bondage. Women and children are also drugged or kidnapped and smuggled across state lines. Many are then sold into child marriages or to brothels and kept against their will by a variety of methods. Typically, they are taken to a city or foreign country where they lack marketable skills and familiarity with the language and legal culture. Their passports and other forms of identification are confiscated and they are threatened with assault, murder, or prosecution by local authorities if they try to escape. Some are told that if they do manage to leave, their family members will suffer retaliation. Female refugees displaced by war or disasters may also land in "survival sex."[240] Once women have entered the sex trade, the social stigma that they encounter further restricts their employment and marriage options; many face ostracism if they return to their original communities.[241] Children who are abused or orphaned as a result of HIV and armed conflict may also end up in brothels.[242]

Some women are promised freedom after they have earned enough to repay their travel, purchase price, room and board, and interest on these debts. Often, however, such promises are not kept or the costs remain prohibitive. Women who refuse to work may be raped, physically assaulted, denied food, or forcibly restrained from leaving houses of prostitution.[243] Many prostitutes have 10- to 18-hour shifts in squalid conditions with no choice of customers and little birth control or health care. The rising rate of sexually transmitted disease, coupled with longstanding beliefs about the value of intercourse with virgins, has heightened demand for ever-younger partners of both sexes, and purchase of preteens and adolescents has become increasingly common. A representative account appears in a State Department Trafficking Report:

> Neary grew up in rural Cambodia. Her parents died when she was a child, and, in an effort to give her a better life, her sister married her off when she was 17. Three months later they went to visit a fishing village. Her husband rented a room in what Neary thought was a guest house. But when she woke the next morning, her husband was gone. The owner of the house told her she had been sold by her husband for $300 and that she was actually in a brothel.
>
> For five years, Neary was raped by five to seven men every day. In addition to brutal physical abuse, Neary was infected with HIV and contracted AIDS.

---

240. Gaiutra Bahadur, Survival Sex, Ms., Summer 2008, 28-29.
241. See U.S. Dep't of State, Trafficking in Persons Report, supra note 238.
242. Julia O'Connell Davidson, Children in the Global Sex Trade (2005).
243. Id. at 8-9 (reporting rates of rape between 60 and 75 percent, and rates of physical assault between 70 and 95 percent).

The brothel threw her out when she became sick, and she eventually found her way to a local shelter. She died of HIV/AIDS at the age of 23.[244]

Nicholas Kristof's *New York Times* profile of Long Pross, a Thai thirteen-year-old sold into slavery, is still more horrific. She was painfully stitched up to look like a virgin four times, and subjected to electric shocks and beatings if she protested. When recovering from a painful second abortion, she pled for rest and enraged the brothel owner, who gouged out her eye. It was only the resulting infection and disfigurement that finally enabled her escape.[245]

Trafficking also supports the rapidly increasing sex tourism industry. A growing number of companies offer "sex tours" to countries such as Thailand and the Philippines, where purchasers have ready access to bars and brothels.[246] A California travel agency ad read: "Sex Tours to Thailand, Real Girls, Real Sex, Real Cheap. These women are the most sexually available in the world. Did you know you can actually buy a virgin girl for as little as $200? You could fuck a different girl for the rest of your life." The agency offers a prize to the man who has sex with the most girls on the tour. "Travel and the Single Male" offers its customers a "sexual Disneyland" capable of fulfilling their most exotic fantasies.[247]

Such prostitution reflects racist as well as sexist dynamics. Male tourists can convince themselves that women and children from other races and nationalities are hyper-sexed exotic "others" who willingly cater to sexual fantasies and benefit economically from doing so. Children are particularly attractive because they are easily exploited and relatively cheap. In rationalizing his sexual transactions with 14- and 15-year-old girls in Mexico and Colombia, one retired school teacher noted: "If they don't have sex with me, they may not have enough food. If someone has a problem with me doing this, let UNICEF feed them. I've never paid more than $20 to these young women, and that allows them to eat for a week."[248] Similar rationalizations, along with the other revenue and corruption generated by sex tourism, encourage officials in many impoverished countries to tolerate child prostitution.[249]

The U.S. State Department, as well as many experts in the field, has advocated a four-pronged approach to human trafficking: prevention, punishment, protection, and partnership. Prevention approaches focus on challenging the

---

244. Id. at 6.

245. Nicholas Kristof, If This Isn't Slavery, What Is?, N.Y. Times, Jan. 4, 2009, at SR8. For a more recent, but similar account, see Nicholas Kristof, Meet a 21st-Century Slave, N.Y. Times, Oct. 25, 2015.

246. Luchina Fisher, Judge to Rule on Ground-Breaking Sex Tourism Case (Sept. 22, 2003), www.womensenews.org.

247. Davidson, supra note 242, at 130.

248. Fed. Bureau of Investigation, 76 FBI Law Enforcement Bulletin 1, 16-21 (2007).

249. Kathy Steinman, Sex Tourism and the Child: Latin America's and the United States' Failure to Prosecute Sex Tourists, 13 Hastings Women's L.J. 53, 65 (2002).

cultural devaluation of women, expanding their education and employment opportunities, providing services for victims, reducing poverty in the countries that supply the global trade, and distributing better information to vulnerable groups about the strategies of traffickers and the legal remedies available. Partnerships among governments and non-governmental organizations are crucial in that effort.[250] State anti-trafficking legislation has dramatically increased and in 2015, Congress passed the Justice for Victims of Trafficking Act, which increased support for trafficking prosecution, expanded services and restitution for victims, and enhanced penalties for offenders.[251]

Some experts have criticized these approaches as well intentioned in principle but ineffective in practice. Inadequate resources have been available for prevention and protective strategies and customers have been subject to minimal sanctions.[252] Moreover, only a minority of states have "safe harbor" laws that immunize child victims for prostitution-related offenses, vacate convictions of adult victims, and provide specialized services to assist individuals in exiting prostitution.[253]

The inadequacy of resources, training, and penalties is partly responsible for making the global sex trade an expanding vehicle for international crime. In many foreign countries, enforcement of anti-trafficking laws remains grossly inadequate due to lack of funding, corruption of police and immigration officials, and governmental ambivalence about curtailing profitable sex tourism activities.[254]

The Trafficking Victims Protection Act (TVPA) of 2000, reauthorized in 2003, 2008, and 2013, attempts to respond to these problems by increasing the maximum penalties for trafficking to 20 years, providing a civil damages remedy for victims, increasing assistance to international law enforcement efforts, and giving the President discretionary power to impose sanctions on nations that fail to meet minimum standards for enforcement of anti-trafficking prohibitions. In addition, the TVPA establishes an annual Trafficking in Persons (TIP) Report, published by the State Department, that separates

250. U.S. Dep't of State, Trafficking in Persons Report, supra note 238, at 9.

251. The federal act is Public Law 114-22, 129 Stat. 227. In a one-year period between October 2014 and October 2015, 236 trafficking bills were enacted. Rebecca Beitsch, More States Separate Prostitution, Sex Trafficking, PEW Charitable Trusts Research and Analysis (Oct. 21, 2015), http://www.pewtrusts.org/en/research-and-analysis/blogs/stateline/2015/10/21/more-states-separate-prostitution-sex-trafficking.

252. Heather C. Gregorio, More than "Johns", Less than Traffickers: In Search of Just and Proportional Sanctions for Buyers of Sex with Trafficking Victims, 90 N.Y.U. L. Rev. 626 (2015).

253. Dempsey, supra note at 211; Nicholas R. Larche, Victimized by the State: How Legislative Inaction Has Led to the Revictimization and Stigmatization of Victims of Sex Trafficking, 38 Seton Hall Legis. J. 281, 295 (2014).

254. For the low number of trafficking convictions, see United Nations Office on Drugs and Crime, Global Report, supra note 237, at 13, 52.

countries into Tier 1 countries, which meet the minimum standards set by the U.S. government for eliminating trafficking; Tier 2 countries, which do not comply with the minimum standards but are making "significant efforts to bring themselves into compliance"; and Tier 3 countries, which do not comply with the minimum standards and are not making "significant efforts to bring themselves into compliance." The United States will not provide "nonhumanitarian, nontrade-related foreign assistance" to Tier 3 countries and will also direct the International Monetary Fund to vote against "any loan or other utilization of the funds of the respective institution to that country." However, in the first five years under the Act, only three countries were subject to sanctions, despite widespread evidence of noncompliance.[255]

To combat child sexual tourism, Congress in 2003 passed the Prosecutorial Remedies and Other Tools to End the Exploitation of Children Today (PROTECT) Act and the Trafficking Victims Reauthorization Act, which increase penalties to a maximum of 30 years of imprisonment for engaging in child sexual trafficking. However, enforcement has been minimal, which has led some commentators to advocate more reliance on other strategies, such as civil suits against sex tourists, consumer protests, and adoption of voluntary codes of conduct by hotels and travel agencies.[256] The 2000 Trafficking Act also addresses the third area in which increased efforts are necessary: protection of victims. Traditionally, the targets of trafficking have been subject to immediate deportation, which deters reporting and cooperation with enforcement efforts. Under the Act, some 5000 "T" visas as well as social services are available each year for women who are assisting investigators and who would "suffer extreme hardship" if deported. However, that remedy remains underutilized because many victims are unable to provide usable information to law enforcement or fear that they or their families will be subject to retaliation if they cooperate.[257]

At the international level, the United Nations Protocol to Prevent, Suppress, and Punish Trafficking in Persons, Especially Women and Children (supplementing the United Nations Convention Against Transnational Organized Crime) directs signatory nations to consider implementing measures to assist victims, such as medical, psychological, and counseling services, and employment, education, and training opportunities. To that end, the United States has pledged financial assistance to groups that work against

255. Susan W. Tiefenbrun, Updating the Domestic and International Impact of the U.S. Victims of Trafficking Protection Act of 2000: Does Law Deter Crime?, 38 Case W. Res. J. Int'l L. 249, 286 (2006).

256. David Lee Mundy, Using Transnational Tort to Combat Sex Trafficking and Sex Tourism, 9 Regent J. Int'l L. 247 (2013); Vincent Bevins, Brazil Targets Sex Tourism Before the World Cup, L.A. Times, Apr. 26, 2014.

257. Lise Olsen, Sex Trafficking Victims Live in Visa Limbo, Houston Chron., Nov. 24, 2008; Jayrashri Srikantiah, Perfect Victims and Real Survivors: The Iconic Victim in Domestic Human Trafficking Law, 87 B.U. L. Rev. 157, 178-80 (2007).

trafficking and provide assistance to its victims. However, there has been controversy over policies targeting funds only to domestic and international groups that oppose prostitution.

One dispute involved the "anti-prostitution pledge," a requirement that organizations receiving funding for HIV/AIDS prevention must have a policy opposing prostitution.[258] Advocates of the pledge, including a coalition of feminists and religious organizations, stressed the harms to women from prostitution and trafficking. Critics charged that it would prevent grants to HIV initiatives involving sex workers, whose support is critical to reducing incidence of the disease.[259] In 2013, the Supreme Court held that the requirement violated the First Amendment as applied to American organizations by requiring them to "pledge allegiance to the Government's policy of eradicating prostitution."[260]

4. Juvenile Prostitution. Another recent dispute involves whether to treat juvenile prostitutes as victims or offenders. International estimates suggest that as many as 10 million children are involved in the sex trade, and that approximately 1 million enter each year.[261] In the United States, as noted earlier, most women enter prostitution as juveniles. Yet in some states, the prevailing laws are internally inconsistent. Minors are treated as incapable of consenting to sex under statutory rape law, but as capable of being prosecuted for commercial sex under prostitution law. State criminal prohibitions on juvenile prostitution are also inconsistent with federal anti-trafficking laws treating minors as victims, and giving them a safe harbor from incarceration.[262] To deal with these inconsistencies, growing number of states have passed their own safe harbor legislation protecting child prostitutes from prosecution, but as noted earlier, most jurisdictions still lack such protections.

5. International Matchmaking. Another practice with the potential for sexual abuse involves "mail-order brides." International matchmaking involves two primary forms. One is pen pal clubs. These organizations offer information to and about men and women for free. The second type of organization is the mail-order bride agency, which generally recruits and screens

258. The pledge was added as an amendment to the United States Leadership Against HIV/AIDs, Tuberculosis, and Malaria Act of 2003, 22 U.S.C.A. §7601, 1117 Stat. 711, at 733-34 (West 2012).

259. Ahmed, supra note 210, at 242-45.

260. Agency for Int'l Dev v. Alliance for Open Soc'y Int'l, 133 S.Ct. 2321 (2013). The funding ban still applies to foreign organizations. See Bazelon, supra note 197, at 40.

261. Int'l Human Rights Law Inst., DePaul University College of Law, Demand Dynamics: The Forces of Demand in Global Sex Trafficking 92 (Morrison Torrey & Sara Dubin eds., 2004).

262. Britta S. Loftus, Coordinating U.S. Law on Immigration and Human Trafficking: Lifting the Lamp to Victims, 43 Colum. Hum. Rts. L. Rev. 143. 186, 210 (2011).

potential candidates from economically disadvantaged communities through newspaper and magazine advertisements. Most recruits come from Asia, Latin America, Eastern Europe, and the former Soviet Union. These agencies market catalogs to men that include women's names, pictures, and biographical data including physical measurements and personal interests. The World Association of Introduction Agencies recognizes some 2700 agencies worldwide, and an estimated 14,000 women enter the United States annually after meeting men on mail-order bride websites.[263] Close to 2 million websites provide information on mail-order brides, and attempt to make finding a wife "as easy as ordering pizza."[264] This industry represents a modern variation on an earlier tradition of picture brides, a system in which individual families arranged marriages between their daughters and men of the same racial or ethnic groups abroad using only pictures and recommendations. That practice was encouraged by restrictive immigration laws, such as U.S. anti-Asian exclusion acts, which largely limited legal immigration status to male laborers and prevented them from traveling back and forth to their native lands to arrange their own marriages. Once a man selected a picture bride, the marriage would be legalized in Asia, and the wife would be eligible to immigrate to the United States. The practice died out in the mid-twentieth century as a result of the repeal of the exclusion acts and the growth of the Asian population in the United States. However, a superficially similar practice resurfaced in the 1970s, partly due to the Vietnam War and the experience of American soldiers with Asian prostitutes. Former military personnel are prominent founders of modern bridal agencies and constitute a large percentage of their customers.[265]

Mail-order bride catalogs are highly profitable in and of themselves, as they feature attractive women and provide a fantasy for American men who have been "unlucky in love." The women are typically portrayed as exotic, dutiful, and accommodating. A website listing for Brides 4U describes Asian brides as "attractive physically, very feminine, petite and slender, . . . gentle and polite, . . . charming and attentive to their partner, . . . and respecting [of] traditions." Latin brides are described as having "exotic beauty, refreshingly sunny disposition[s] . . . and traditional upbringings where old fashioned values and family virtues remain a vital way of life." Cherry Blossoms portrays

---

263. Victoria I. Kusel, Gender Disparity, Domestic Abuse, and the Mail-Order Bride Industry, 7 Albany Gov't L. Rev. 166, 167 (2014).

264. Olga Grosh, Foreign Wives, Domestic Violence: U.S. Law Stigmatizes and Fails to Protect "Mail-Order Brides," 22 Hastings Women's L.J. 81, 88 (2011) (quoting website); Jane Kim, Trafficked: Domestic Violence, Exploitation in Marriage, and the Foreign-Bride Industry, 51 Va. J. Int'l L. 443, 468 (2011).

265. Donna R. Lee, Mail Fantasy: Global Sexual Exploitation in the Mail-Order Bride Industry and Proposed Legal Solutions, 5 Asian L.J. 139, 160 (1998).

Filipinos who are "subservient and docile."[266] The website of Chance for Love maintains: "The Russian woman has not been exposed to the world of rampant feminism that asserts its rights in America. She is the weaker gender and knows it."[267]

The catalogs target men from industrialized countries such as the United States, Australia, and Canada who consider American women too independent, selfish, and career-oriented. Broker services reinforce and accommodate this view. One website, Goodwife.com, features images of scantily clad homemakers in sexually provocative poses while cooking and cleaning. The site explains:

> We, as men, are more and more wanting to step back from the types of women we meet now. With many women taking on the "me first" feminist agenda and the man having to take a back seat to her desire for power and control, many men are turned off by this and look back to having a more traditional woman as our partner.[268]

For a fee, men buy the addresses of the women they select from the catalogs. Some agencies also offer video presentations, and services such as private investigators and clinical psychologists. Customers then mail letters to potential brides or join a group tour that allows members to interview potential applicants. Typically the man travels to the home country of the potential bride, often through arrangements made by the agency. If, after meeting, the couple agrees to marry, the wedding occurs in the woman's home country or the husband-to-be applies for a fiancée visa, which allows the prospective bride to travel to the man's country. U.S. immigration law requires the couple to marry within 90 days. Once they are married, the bride obtains resident status on a two-year conditional basis. Ninety days before the expiration of the two-year period, the couple must jointly petition for unrestricted permanent residency status for the wife. The burden of proof is on the couple to establish that the marriage is viable and was not fraudulently arranged to evade immigration restrictions.

Expectations are frequently disappointed. Although the practice appeals to men seeking submissive wives, the women who participate are sufficiently independent and resourceful to leave their country and often do not fit the stereotype of the docile helpmate. So, too, many women's knowledge of American society comes from romanticized media portrayals, encouraging the belief that American husbands treat their wives better than husbands in their

---

266. Beverly Encarguez Perez, Woman Warrior Meets Mail-Order Bride: Finding an Asian American Voice in the Women's Movement, 18 Berkeley Women's L.J. 211, 221 (2003).
267. David Crary, Protecting Mail-Order Brides, Ariz. Rep., July 6, 2003, at A2.
268. Kim, supra note 264, 470-71 (2011) (quoting GoodWife.com).

home countries.[269] When asked why they are seeking an American to marry, women generally say that they believe that Americans make good husbands while men from their own country do not.[270] However, the men seeking foreign brides frequently have negative attitudes toward women. Many have experienced a bitter divorce or break-up, and a substantial number become physically, sexually, and emotionally abusive toward new wives who do not fulfill their fantasies.[271] For some women, a risk of such abuse may seem the necessary price of immigration.[272]

The extent of domestic violence in mail-order marriages is impossible to estimate with any accuracy, since police records do not reveal this information and women have well-documented reasons not to report abuse. They frequently fear further retaliation against themselves or their children and loss of economic support. These concerns are common in any violent relationship but are especially prominent among mail-order wives for multiple reasons. These women typically have no family or support network on which they can rely and lack the language and employment skills for financial independence. Few have funds to seek legal assistance or to return to their native country. Many fear deportation and the cultural stigma of divorce. Those who come from nations with a tradition of gender subordination may also see some abuse as a standard feature of marital relationships. Some research finds that foreign women who marry American men are between three and six times more likely to be victims of domestic abuse than American women.[273]

In response to these problems, the U.S. Immigration and Nationality Act, the Violence Against Women Act, and the Battered Immigrant Women Protection Act provide for a waiver of the joint petition requirement for permanent residency in certain circumstances, including spousal abuse.[274] The International Marriage Broker Regulation Act [IMBA] became part of the 2005 Violence Against Women Reauthorization Act.[275] It provides prospective brides with information about the immigration process, domestic violence

269. Perez, supra note 266, at 221.

270. Robert J. Scholes, with Anchalee Phataralaoha, The "Mail-Order Bride" Industry and Its Impact on U.S. Immigration, Report to Congress (2006).

271. For examples of violence and sexual exploitation, see Kim, supra note 264, at 471.

272. Scholes, supra note 270, at 5.

273. Kusel, supra note 263, at 173. But see Marcia Anne Yablon-Zug, Mail Order Feminism, 21 Wm. & Mary J. Women & L. 153, 166-67 (2014) (questioning statistics finding higher levels of abuse).

274. Immigration and Nationality Act, June 27, 1952, ch. 477, 66 Stat. 163 (8 U.S.C. §1101 et seq.); Violence Against Women Act of 2000, Pub. L. 106-386, div. B, Oct. 28, 2000, 114 Stat. 1491; Battered Immigrant Women Protection Act of 2000, Pub. L. 106-386, div. B, title V, Oct. 28, 2000, 114 Stat. 1518.

275. International Marriage Broker Regulation Act of 2005, Pub. L. 109-162, title VIII, subtitle D (Sec. 831 et seq.), Jan. 5, 2006, 119 Stat. 3066; Violence Against Women Reauthorization Act of 2005, Pub. L. 109-162, Sec. 3, titles I to IX, Jan. 5, 2006, 119 Stat. 2964-3077.

resources, and their prospective husbands' prior marital and criminal records. The Act also limits the number of fiancée visas that an American can seek within a particular time period in order to prevent serial abuse. Claims that the statute represents unconstitutional discrimination against men seeking brides abroad have been rejected on the ground that higher risks of violence justify such background checks.[276] The 2013 reauthorization of the Violence Against Women Act strengthened regulations of the international marriage brokering industry. It clarified who is responsible for investigating and prosecuting IMBA violations, prohibited marketing brides who are under 18 years of age, strengthened background checks for U.S. citizens using brokers, and increased penalties for brokers who violate the law.[277] Some countries of origin have also attempted to restrict abuses. The Philippines, for example, makes it illegal to broker mail-order marriages.[278]

However, enforcement of IMBA has been plagued with difficulties and commentators have called for increased civil liability suits against marriage brokers.[279] In the first successful matchmaker lawsuit, Nataliya Fox obtained a $430,000 award against Encounters International for failing to screen customers for violence, misstating deportation risks, and omitting required disclosures about the legal rights of domestic-violence victims. She suffered severe physical abuse from her husband, who had a prior history of battering. He eventually divorced Nataliya, paid her $110,000 in a settlement, and obtained a new mail-order bride.[280]

Putting Theory Into Practice

5-15. In 2015, The Erotic Service Providers Legal, Education and Research Project filed suit in federal district court challenging California's anti-prostitution law on the ground that it deprives individuals of the fundamental right to engage in consensual private sexual activity.[281] Plaintiffs were three sex workers and a disabled man who wished to purchase sexual services.

---

276. See, e.g., European Connections & Tours, Inc. v. Gonzales, 480 F. Supp. 2d 1355 (N.D. Ga. 2007).

277. 8 U.S.C. §1375 (2012).

278. Republic Act No. 6955 (1990 Phil. & Republic Act No. 9208 (2003)).

279. Kusel, supra note 263, at 182-85. For problems in IMBA enforcement, See U.S. Government Accountability Office, Immigration Benefits: Improvements Needed to Fully Implement the International Marriage Broker Regulation Act 24 (2014).

280. Fox v. Encounters International, No. 05-1139, 05-1404, 2006 WL 952317 (4th Cir. Apr. 16, 2006); D. Murali, Mail-Order Brides Beware, Bus. Line, 2004 WLNR 24197612 (Dec. 6).

281. Erotic Service Providers Legal Education & Research Project v. Gascon, No. 15-1007 (N.D. Cal. filed Mar. 4, 2015).

What arguments would you make in support of plaintiffs? What arguments would you make in opposition?

5-16. The Shady Lady Ranch brothel, two-and-a-half hours northwest of Las Vegas, offers male prostitutes to female customers.[282] In what respect, if any, does this business reflect progress for women? In what respect is it bad for women?

5-17. In 2015, a controversy erupted over Amnesty International's resolution supporting full decriminalization of consensual sex work and calling on governments to ensure that sex workers enjoy full legal protection from exploitation, trafficking, and violence.[283] An editorial in the *Lancet* medical journal supported the resolution partly on the ground that its research estimated that decriminalization of sex work would result in the reduction of 33 to 46 percent of HIV infections in the next decade.[284] Equality Now and The Coalition Against Trafficking in Women opposed the Amnesty International measure on the ground that prostitution and trafficking were inextricably linked and that decriminalization of the purchase of sex would support exploitation. If you were voting on the proposal, what would you decide?

B. PREGNANCY AND AUTONOMY

1. Control of Conception and Other Aspects of Women's Health

Woman's role in reproduction has always been a factor in limiting her life choices and opportunities. Thus, contraception, pregnancy, abortion, and

---

282. Hollywood Madame Heidi Fleiss Abandons Plan for Stud Farm, Fox News, Feb. 10, 2009. For her former plans, see Navarro, supra note 235, at S1.

283. Global Movement Votes to Adopt Policy to Protect Human Rights of Sex Workers, Amnesty International (Aug. 11, 2015), https://www.amnesty.org/en/latest/news/2015/08/global-movement-votes-to-adopt-policy-to-protect-human-rights-of-sex-workers.

284. Keeping Sex Workers Safe, 386 The Lancet 504 (2015). See HIV and Sex Workers, The Lancet (July 23, 2014), http://www.thelancet.com/series/hiv-and-sex-workers. For a defense of Amnesty International's policy and the extensive consultation and research that led to its adoption, see Catherine Murphy, Sex Worker's Rights Are Human Rights, https://www.amnesty.org/en/latest/news/2015/08/sex-workers-rights-are-human-rights. In the wake of the controversy, former President Jimmy Carter wrote an op-ed opposing decriminalization on the grounds that normalizing the act of buying sex conveys to men that "women and girls are commodities to be bought and sold." Jimmy Carter, To Curb Prostitution, Punish Those Who Buy Sex Rather Than Those Who Sell It, Wash. Post, May 31, 2016. For discussion of the controversy over the Amnesty International resolution, see Bazelon, supra note 197, at 38.

other reproductive issues have been central to controversial debates about women's autonomy.

Women's reproductive choices were not broadly regulated in the United States until the nineteenth century. The momentum for legal control of women's options came largely from moral reformers and physicians who, in response to the increased demand by women for contraception and abortion, wanted to assert technical, ethical, and social superiority over their competitors, particularly midwives. In 1873, Congress passed the Comstock Law, which prohibited dissemination of information about abortion and contraception. While the early efforts to overturn this regulation asserted women's right to control their own bodies, feminist pioneers such as Margaret Sanger also used eugenic arguments in favor of birth control. Reflecting this mix of motivations, throughout the early twentieth-century fertility control emerged as a right for the privileged and a duty for the poor. By the middle of the twentieth century, more liberal sexual mores, opportunities for women in paid employment, economic pressure within families to control fertility, and the availability of oral contraception helped liberalize public attitudes and practices, but many state laws banning contraception remained on the books.[285]

Griswold v. Connecticut
381 U.S. 479 (1965)

Mr. Justice DOUGLAS delivered the opinion of the Court.

[Appellants, Planned Parenthood personnel who prescribed contraceptives for "married persons," were charged as accessories to the violation of the Connecticut statute prohibiting the use of contraceptives. The Court first held that they had standing to assert their patients' privacy rights.]

[W]e are met with a wide range of questions that implicate the Due Process Clause of the Fourteenth Amendment. . . . We do not sit as a super-legislature to determine the wisdom, need, and propriety of laws that touch economic problems, business affairs, or social conditions. This law, however, operates directly on an intimate relation of husband and wife and their physician's role in one aspect of that relation.

The association of people is not mentioned in the Constitution nor in the Bill of Rights. The right to educate a child in a school of the parents' choice—whether public or private or parochial—is also not mentioned. Nor is the right to study any particular subject or any foreign language. Yet the First Amendment has been construed to include certain of those rights. . . . In

---

285. Deborah L. Rhode, Justice and Gender 202-07 (1989). For a comprehensive history of the regulation of contraception, see Linda Gordon, Woman's Body, Woman's Right: Birth Control in America (rev. ed. 1990).

other words, the First Amendment has a penumbra where privacy is protected from governmental intrusion. . . .

The foregoing cases suggest that specific guarantees in the Bill of Rights have penumbras, formed by emanations from those guarantees that help give them life and substance. Various guarantees create zones of privacy. The right of association contained in the penumbra of the First Amendment is one, as we have seen. The Third Amendment in its prohibitions against the quartering of soldiers "in any house" in time of peace without the consent of the owner is another facet of that privacy. The Fourth Amendment explicitly affirms the "right of the people to be secure in their persons, houses, papers, and effects, against unreasonable searches and seizures." The Fifth Amendment in its Self-Incrimination Clause enables the citizen to create a zone of privacy which government may not force him to surrender to his detriment. The Ninth Amendment provides: "The enumeration in the constitution, of certain rights, shall not be construed to deny or disparage others retained by the people." . . . We have had many controversies over these penumbral rights of "privacy and repose." These cases bear witness that the right of privacy which presses for recognition here is a legitimate one.

The present case, then, concerns a relationship lying within the zone of privacy which, in forbidding the use of contraceptives rather than regulating their manufacture or sale, seeks to achieve its goals by . . . having a maximum destructive impact upon that relationship. Such a law cannot stand in light of the familiar principle, so often applied by the Court, that a "governmental purpose to control or prevent activities constitutionally subject to state regulation may not be achieved by means which sweep unnecessarily broadly and thereby invade the area of protected freedoms." NAACP v. Alabama [ex rel. Flowers, 377 U.S. 288, 1964]. Would we allow the police to search the sacred precincts of marital bedrooms for telltale signs of the use of contraceptives? The very idea is repulsive to the notions of privacy surrounding the marriage relationship.

We deal with a right of privacy older than the Bill of Rights—older than our political parties, older than our school system. Marriage is a coming together for better or worse, hopefully enduring, and intimate to the degree of being sacred. It is an association that promotes a way of life, not causes; a harmony in living, not political faiths; a bilateral loyalty, not commercial or social projects. Yet it is an association for as noble a purpose as any involved in our prior decisions.

Reversed.

Mr. Justice GOLDBERG, whom THE CHIEF JUSTICE and Mr. Justice BRENNAN join, concurring. . . .

[I]t should be said of the Court's holding today that it in no way interferes with a State's proper regulation of sexual promiscuity or misconduct. As my Brother Harlan so well stated in his dissenting opinion in Poe v. Ullman [1961]:

Adultery, homosexuality and the like are sexual intimacies which the State forbids . . . but the intimacy of husband and wife is necessarily an essential and accepted feature of the institution of marriage, an institution which the State not only must allow, but which always and in every age it has fostered and protected. It is one thing when the State exerts its power either to forbid extra-marital sexuality . . . or to say who may marry, but it is quite another when, having acknowledged a marriage and the intimacies inherent in it, it undertakes to regulate by means of the criminal law the details of that intimacy.

In sum, I believe that the right of privacy in the marital relation is fundamental and basic—a personal right "retained by the people" within the meaning of the Ninth Amendment.

Burwell v. Hobby Lobby Stores, Inc.
134 S. Ct. 2751 (2014)

Justice ALITO delivered the opinion of the Court.

We must decide in these cases whether the Religious Freedom Restoration Act of 1993 (RFRA) permits the United States Department of Health and Human Services (HHS) to demand that three closely held corporations provide health-insurance coverage for methods of contraception that violate the sincerely held religious beliefs of the companies' owners. We hold that the regulations that impose this obligation violate RFRA, which prohibits the Federal Government from taking any action that substantially burdens the exercise of religion unless that action constitutes the least restrictive means of serving a compelling government interest. . . .

I

A

Congress enacted RFRA in 1993 in order to provide very broad protection for religious liberty. RFRA's enactment came three years after this Court's decision in *Employment Div., Dept. of Human Resources of Ore. v. Smith,* which largely repudiated the method of analyzing free-exercise claims that had been used in cases like *Sherbert v. Verner,* and *Wisconsin v. Yoder.* In determining whether challenged government actions violated the Free Exercise Clause of the First Amendment, those decisions used a balancing test that took into account whether the challenged action imposed a substantial burden on the practice of religion, and if it did, whether it was needed to serve a compelling government interest. . . .

In *Smith,* however, the Court rejected "the balancing test set forth in *Sherbert.*" *Smith* concerned two members of the Native American Church who were fired for ingesting peyote for sacramental purposes. When they sought unemployment benefits, the State of Oregon rejected their claims on the ground that consumption of peyote was a crime, but the Oregon Supreme Court, applying the *Sherbert* test, held that the denial of benefits violated the Free Exercise Clause.

This Court then reversed, observing that use of the *Sherbert* test whenever a person objected on religious grounds to the enforcement of a generally applicable law "would open the prospect of constitutionally required religious exemptions from civic obligations of almost every conceivable kind." The Court therefore held that, under the First Amendment, "neutral, generally applicable laws may be applied to religious practices even when not supported by a compelling governmental interest." *City of Boerne v. Flores.*

Congress responded to *Smith* by enacting RFRA. "[L]aws [that are] 'neutral' toward religion," Congress found, "may burden religious exercise as surely as laws intended to interfere with religious exercise." In order to ensure broad protection for religious liberty, RFRA provides that "Government shall not substantially burden a person's exercise of religion even if the burden results from a rule of general applicability." If the Government substantially burdens a person's exercise of religion, under the Act that person is entitled to an exemption from the rule unless the Government "demonstrates that application of the burden to the person—(1) is in furtherance of a compelling governmental interest; and (2) is the least restrictive means of furthering that compelling governmental interest."

As enacted in 1993, RFRA applied to both the Federal Government and the States, but the constitutional authority invoked for regulating federal and state agencies differed. As applied to a federal agency, RFRA is based on the enumerated power that supports the particular agency's work, but in attempting to regulate the States and their subdivisions, Congress relied on its power under Section 5 of the Fourteenth Amendment to enforce the First Amendment. In *City of Boerne*, however, we held that Congress had overstepped its Section 5 authority because "[t]he stringent test RFRA demands" "far exceed[ed] any pattern or practice of unconstitutional conduct under the Free Exercise Clause as interpreted in *Smith.*"

Following our decision in *City of Boerne*, Congress passed the Religious Land Use and Institutionalized Persons Act of 2000 (RLUIPA). That statute, enacted under Congress's Commerce and Spending Clause powers, imposes the same general test as RFRA but on a more limited category of governmental actions. And, what is most relevant for present purposes, RLUIPA amended RFRA's definition of the "exercise of religion." Before RLUIPA, RFRA's definition made reference to the First Amendment. In RLUIPA, in an obvious effort to effect a complete separation from First Amendment case law, Congress deleted the reference to the First Amendment and defined the "exercise of religion" to include "any exercise of religion, whether or not compelled by, or central to, a system of religious belief." And Congress mandated that this concept "be construed in favor of a broad protection of religious exercise, to the maximum extent permitted by the terms of this chapter and the Constitution."

B

At issue in these cases are HHS regulations promulgated under the Patient Protection and Affordable Care Act of 2010 (ACA). ACA generally requires employers with 50 or more full-time employees to offer "a group health plan or group health insurance coverage" that provides "minimum essential coverage." Any covered employer that does not provide such coverage must pay a substantial price. Specifically, if a covered employer provides group health insurance but its plan fails to comply with ACA's group-health-plan requirements, the employer may be required to pay $100 per day for each affected "individual." And if the employer decides to stop providing health insurance altogether and at least one full-time employee enrolls in a health plan and qualifies for a subsidy on one of the government-run ACA exchanges, the employer must pay $2,000 per year for each of its full-time employees.

Unless an exception applies, ACA requires an employer's group health plan or group-health-insurance coverage to furnish "preventive care and screenings" for women without "any cost sharing requirements." Congress itself, however, did not specify what types of preventive care must be covered. Instead, Congress authorized the Health Resources and Services Administration (HRSA), a component of HHS, to make that important and sensitive decision. The HRSA in turn consulted the Institute of Medicine, a nonprofit group of volunteer advisers, in determining which preventive services to require.

In August 2011 . . . the HRSA promulgated the Women's Preventive Services Guidelines. The Guidelines provide that nonexempt employers are generally required to provide "coverage, without cost sharing" for "[a]ll Food and Drug Administration [(FDA)] approved contraceptive methods, sterilization procedures, and patient education and counseling." Although many of the required, FDA-approved methods of contraception work by preventing the fertilization of an egg, four of those methods (those specifically at issue in these cases) may have the effect of preventing an already fertilized egg from developing any further by inhibiting its attachment to the uterus.

HHS also authorized the HRSA to establish exemptions from the contraceptive mandate for "religious employers." That category encompasses "churches, their integrated auxiliaries, and conventions or associations of churches," as well as "the exclusively religious activities of any religious order." See *ibid.* In its Guidelines, HRSA exempted these organizations from the requirement to cover contraceptive services.

In addition, HHS has effectively exempted certain religious nonprofit organizations, described under HHS regulations as "eligible organizations," from the contraceptive mandate. An "eligible organization" means a nonprofit organization that "holds itself out as a religious organization" and "opposes providing coverage for some or all of any contraceptive services required to be covered . . . on account of religious objections." To qualify for this accommodation, an employer must certify that it is such an organization. . . .

In addition to these exemptions for religious organizations, ACA exempts a great many employers from most of its coverage requirements. Employers providing "grandfathered health plans" — those that existed prior to March 23, 2010, and that have not made specified changes after that date — need not comply with many of the Act's requirements, including the contraceptive mandate. And employers with fewer than 50 employees are not required to provide health insurance at all. . . .

II

A

Norman and Elizabeth Hahn and their three sons are devout members of the Mennonite Church, a Christian denomination. The Mennonite Church opposes abortion and believes that "[t]he fetus in its earliest stages . . . shares humanity with those who conceived it."

Fifty years ago, Norman Hahn started a wood-working business in his garage, and since then, this company, Conestoga Wood Specialties, has grown and now has 950 employees. Conestoga is organized under Pennsylvania law as a for-profit corporation. The Hahns exercise sole ownership of the closely held business; they control its board of directors and hold all of its voting shares. One of the Hahn sons serves as the president and CEO.

The Hahns believe that they are required to run their business "in accordance with their religious beliefs and moral principles."

As explained in Conestoga's board-adopted "Statement on the Sanctity of Human Life," the Hahns believe that "human life begins at conception." It is therefore "against [their] moral conviction to be involved in the termination of human life" after conception, which they believe is a "sin against God to which they are held accountable." The Hahns have accordingly excluded from the group-health-insurance plan they offer to their employees certain contraceptive methods that they consider to be abortifacients.

The Hahns and Conestoga sued HHS and other federal officials and agencies under RFRA and the Free Exercise Clause of the First Amendment, seeking to enjoin application of ACA's contraceptive mandate insofar as it requires them to provide health-insurance coverage for four FDA-approved contraceptives that may operate after the fertilization of an egg. These include two forms of emergency contraception commonly called "morning after" pills and two types of intrauterine devices. . . .

B

David and Barbara Green and their three children are Christians who own and operate two family businesses. Forty-five years ago, David Green started an arts-and-crafts store that has grown into a nationwide chain called Hobby Lobby. There are now 500 Hobby Lobby stores, and the company has more than 13,000 employees. Hobby Lobby is organized as a for-profit corporation under Oklahoma law.

One of David's sons started an affiliated business, Mardel, which operates 35 Christian bookstores and employs close to 400 people. Mardel is also organized as a for-profit corporation under Oklahoma law.

Though these two businesses have expanded over the years, they remain closely held, and David, Barbara, and their children retain exclusive control of both companies. David serves as the CEO of Hobby Lobby, and his three children serve as the president, vice president, and vice CEO. . . .

[T]he Greens believe that life begins at conception and that it would violate their religion to facilitate access to contraceptive drugs or devices that operate after that point. They specifically object to the same four contraceptive methods as the Hahns and, like the Hahns, they have no objection to the other 16 FDA-approved methods of birth control. . . .

III

A

RFRA prohibits the "Government [from] substantially burden[ing] *a person's* exercise of religion even if the burden results from a rule of general applicability" unless the Government "demonstrates that application of the burden to *the person*—(1) is in furtherance of a compelling governmental interest; and (2) is the least restrictive means of furthering that compelling governmental interest." The first question that we must address is whether this provision applies to regulations that govern the activities of for-profit corporations like Hobby Lobby, Conestoga, and Mardel.

HHS contends that neither these companies nor their owners can even be heard under RFRA. According to HHS, the companies cannot sue because they seek to make a profit for their owners, and the owners cannot be heard because the regulations, at least as a formal matter, apply only to the companies and not to the owners as individuals. HHS's argument would have dramatic consequences. . . .

[B] RFRA applies to "a person's" exercise of religion, and RFRA itself does not define the term "person." We therefore look to the Dictionary Act, which we must consult "[i]n determining the meaning of any Act of Congress, unless the context indicates otherwise."

Under the Dictionary Act, "the wor[d] 'person' . . . include[s] corporations, companies, associations, firms, partnerships, societies, and joint stock companies, as well as individuals." . . .

We see nothing in RFRA that suggests a congressional intent to depart from the Dictionary Act definition, and HHS makes little effort to argue otherwise. We have entertained RFRA and free-exercise claims brought by nonprofit corporations, and HHS concedes that a nonprofit corporation can be a "person" within the meaning of RFRA. . . .

2

The principal argument advanced by HHS and the principal dissent regarding RFRA protection for Hobby Lobby, Conestoga, and Mardel focuses not on the statutory term "person," but on the phrase "exercise of religion." According to HHS and the dissent, these corporations are not protected by RFRA because they cannot exercise religion. Neither HHS nor the dissent, however, provides any persuasive explanation for this conclusion.

Is it because of the corporate form? The corporate form alone cannot provide the explanation because, as we have pointed out, HHS concedes that nonprofit corporations can be protected by RFRA. The dissent suggests that nonprofit corporations are special because furthering their religious "autonomy . . . often furthers individual religious freedom as well." But this principle applies equally to for-profit corporations: Furthering their religious freedom also "furthers individual religious freedom." In these cases, for example, allowing Hobby Lobby, Conestoga, and Mardel to assert RFRA claims protects the religious liberty of the Greens and the Hahns.

If the corporate form is not enough, what about the profit-making objective? In *Braunfeld*, we entertained the free-exercise claims of individuals who were attempting to make a profit as retail merchants, and the Court never even hinted that this objective precluded their claims. . . . Business practices that are compelled or limited by the tenets of a religious doctrine fall comfortably within that definition. Thus, a law that "operates so as to make the practice of . . . religious beliefs more expensive" in the context of business activities imposes a burden on the exercise of religion.

If, as *Braunfeld* recognized, a sole proprietorship that seeks to make a profit may assert a free-exercise claim, why can't Hobby Lobby, Conestoga, and Mardel do the same?

Some lower court judges have suggested that RFRA does not protect for-profit corporations because the purpose of such corporations is simply to make money. This argument flies in the face of modern corporate law. . . . While it is certainly true that a central objective of for-profit corporations is to make money, modern corporate law does not require for-profit corporations to pursue profit at the expense of everything else, and many do not do so. For-profit corporations, with ownership approval, support a wide variety of charitable causes, and it is not at all uncommon for such corporations to further humanitarian and other altruistic objectives. . . .

HHS would draw a sharp line between nonprofit corporations (which, HHS concedes, are protected by RFRA) and for-profit corporations (which HHS would leave unprotected), but the actual picture is less clear-cut. Not all corporations that decline to organize as nonprofits do so in order to maximize profit. For example, organizations with religious and charitable aims might organize as for-profit corporations because of the potential advantages of that corporate form, such as the freedom to participate in lobbying for legislation or campaigning for political candidates who promote their religious or charitable goals. . . .

In any event, the objectives that may properly be pursued by the companies in these cases are governed by the laws of the States in which they were incorporated—Pennsylvania and Oklahoma—and the laws of those States permit for-profit corporations to pursue "any lawful purpose" or "act," including the pursuit of profit in conformity with the owners' religious principles.

3

HHS and the principal dissent make one additional argument in an effort to show that a for-profit corporation cannot engage in the "exercise of religion" within the meaning of RFRA: HHS argues that RFRA did no more than codify this Court's pre-*Smith* Free Exercise Clause precedents, and because none of those cases squarely held that a for-profit corporation has free-exercise rights, RFRA does not confer such protection. This argument has many flaws.

First, nothing in the text of RFRA as originally enacted suggested that the statutory phrase "exercise of religion under the First Amendment" was meant to be tied to this Court's pre-*Smith* interpretation of that Amendment. . . .

Second, if the original text of RFRA was not clear enough on this point—and we think it was—the amendment of RFRA through RLUIPA surely dispels any doubt. That amendment deleted the prior reference to the First Amendment. . . .

Finally, the results would be absurd if RFRA merely restored this Court's pre-*Smith* decisions in ossified form and did not allow a plaintiff to raise a RFRA claim unless that plaintiff fell within a category of plaintiffs one of whom had brought a free-exercise claim that this Court entertained in the years before *Smith*. . . .

Presumably in recognition of the weakness of this argument, both HHS and the principal dissent fall back on the broader contention that the Nation lacks a tradition of exempting for-profit corporations from generally applicable laws. . . .

4

Finally, HHS contends that Congress could not have wanted RFRA to apply to for-profit corporations because it is difficult as a practical matter to ascertain the sincere "beliefs" of a corporation. . . .

These cases, however, do not involve publicly traded corporations, and it seems unlikely that the sort of corporate giants to which HHS refers will often assert RFRA claims. HHS has not pointed to any example of a publicly traded corporation asserting RFRA rights, and numerous practical restraints would likely prevent that from occurring. . . . The companies in the cases before us are closely held corporations, each owned and controlled by members of a single family, and no one has disputed the sincerity of their religious beliefs.[28] . . .

For all these reasons, we hold that a federal regulation's restriction on the activities of a for-profit closely held corporation must comply with RFRA.

IV

Because RFRA applies in these cases, we must next ask whether the HHS contraceptive mandate "substantially burden[s]" the exercise of religion. We have little trouble concluding that it does.

A

As we have noted, the Hahns and Greens have a sincere religious belief that life begins at conception. They therefore object on religious grounds to providing health insurance that covers methods of birth control that . . . may result in the destruction of an embryo. By requiring the Hahns and Greens and their companies to arrange for such coverage, the HHS mandate demands that they engage in conduct that seriously violates their religious beliefs.

If the Hahns and Greens and their companies do not yield to this demand, the economic consequences will be severe. If the companies continue to offer group health plans that do not cover the contraceptives at issue, they will be taxed $100 per day for each affected individual. For Hobby Lobby, the bill could amount to $1.3 million per day or about $475 million per year. . . .

B

Although these totals are high, *amici* supporting HHS have suggested that the $2,000 per-employee penalty is actually less than the average cost of providing health insurance. . . .

[I]t is far from clear that the net cost to the companies of providing insurance is more than the cost of dropping their insurance plans and paying the ACA penalty. Health insurance is a benefit that employees value. If the companies simply eliminated that benefit and forced employees to purchase their own insurance on the exchanges, without offering additional compensation, it is predictable that the companies would face a competitive disadvantage in retaining and attracting skilled workers. . . .

In sum, we refuse to sustain the challenged regulations on the ground—never maintained by the Government—that dropping insurance coverage eliminates the substantial burden that the HHS mandate imposes.

---

28. To qualify for RFRA's protection, an asserted belief must be "sincere"; a corporation's pretextual assertion of a religious belief in order to obtain an exemption for financial reasons would fail.

We doubt that the Congress that enacted RFRA—or, for that matter, ACA—would have believed it a tolerable result to put family-run businesses to the choice of violating their sincerely held religious beliefs or making all of their employees lose their existing healthcare plans.

C

In taking the position that the HHS mandate does not impose a substantial burden on the exercise of religion, HHS's main argument (echoed by the principal dissent) is basically that the connection between what the objecting parties must do (provide health-insurance coverage for four methods of contraception that may operate after the fertilization of an egg) and the end that they find to be morally wrong (destruction of an embryo) is simply too attenuated. HHS and the dissent note that providing the coverage would not itself result in the destruction of an embryo; that would occur only if an employee chose to take advantage of the coverage and to use one of the four methods at issue.

This argument dodges the question that RFRA presents (whether the HHS mandate imposes a substantial burden on the ability of the objecting parties to conduct business in accordance with *their religious beliefs*) and instead addresses a very different question that the federal courts have no business addressing (whether the religious belief asserted in a RFRA case is reasonable). The Hahns and Greens believe that providing the coverage demanded by the HHS regulations is connected to the destruction of an embryo in a way that is sufficient to make it immoral for them to provide the coverage. This belief implicates a difficult and important question of religion and moral philosophy, namely, the circumstances under which it is wrong for a person to perform an act that is innocent in itself but that has the effect of enabling or facilitating the commission of an immoral act by another. Arrogating the authority to provide a binding national answer to this religious and philosophical question, HHS and the principal dissent in effect tell the plaintiffs that their beliefs are flawed. For good reason, we have repeatedly refused to take such a step. . . .

[T]he Hahns and Greens and their companies sincerely believe that providing the insurance coverage demanded by the HHS regulations lies on the forbidden side of the line, and it is not for us to say that their religious beliefs are mistaken or insubstantial. Instead, our "narrow function . . . in this context is to determine" whether the line drawn reflects "an honest conviction," and there is no dispute that it does. . . .

V

Since the HHS contraceptive mandate imposes a substantial burden on the exercise of religion, we must move on and decide whether HHS has shown that the mandate both "(1) is in furtherance of a compelling governmental interest; and (2) is the least restrictive means of furthering that compelling governmental interest."

A

HHS asserts that the contraceptive mandate serves a variety of important interests, but many of these are couched in very broad terms, such as promoting "public health" and "gender equality." RFRA, however, contemplates a "more focused" inquiry: It "requires the Government to demonstrate that the compelling interest test is satisfied through application of the challenged law 'to the person'—the particular claimant whose sincere exercise of religion is being substantially burdened." *O Centro.* This requires us to "loo[k] beyond broadly formulated interests" and to "scrutiniz[e] the asserted harm of granting specific exemptions to particular religious claimants"—in other words, to look to the marginal interest in enforcing the contraceptive mandate in these cases.

In addition to asserting these very broadly framed interests, HHS maintains that the mandate serves a compelling interest in ensuring that all women have access to all FDA-approved contraceptives without cost sharing. Under our cases, women (and men) have a constitutional right to obtain contraceptives, and HHS tells us that "[s]tudies have demonstrated that even moderate copayments for preventive services can deter patients from receiving those services." . . .

We find it unnecessary to adjudicate this issue. We will assume that the interest in guaranteeing cost-free access to the four challenged contraceptive methods is compelling within the meaning of RFRA, and we will proceed to consider the final prong of the RFRA test, *i.e.,* whether HHS has shown that the contraceptive mandate is "the least restrictive means of furthering that compelling governmental interest."

B

The least-restrictive-means standard is exceptionally demanding, and it is not satisfied here. HHS has not shown that it lacks other means of achieving its desired goal without imposing a substantial burden on the exercise of religion by the objecting parties in these cases. See §§2000bb-1(a), (b) (requiring the Government to "demonstrat[e] that application of [a substantial] burden to *the person* . . . is the least restrictive means of furthering [a] compelling governmental interest" (emphasis added)).

The most straightforward way of doing this would be for the Government to assume the cost of providing the four contraceptives at issue to any women who are unable to obtain them under their health-insurance policies due to their employers' religious objections. This would certainly be less restrictive of the plaintiffs' religious liberty, and HHS has not shown, that this is not a viable alternative. . . . It seems likely, however, that the cost of providing the forms of contraceptives at issue in these cases (if not all FDA-approved contraceptives) would be minor when compared with the overall cost of ACA. . . .

In the end, however, we need not rely on the option of a new, government-funded program in order to conclude that the HHS regulations fail the least-restrictive-means test. HHS itself has demonstrated that it has at its disposal an approach that is less restrictive than requiring employers to fund contraceptive methods that violate their religious beliefs. As we explained above, HHS has already established an accommodation for nonprofit organizations with religious objections. Under that accommodation, the organization can self-certify that it opposes providing coverage for particular contraceptive services. If the organization makes such a certification, the organization's insurance issuer or third-party administrator must "[e]xpressly exclude contraceptive coverage from the group health insurance coverage provided in connection with the group health plan" and "[p]rovide separate payments for any contraceptive services required to be covered" without imposing "any cost-sharing requirements . . . on the eligible organization, the group health plan, or plan participants or beneficiaries."[38]

We do not decide today whether an approach of this type complies with RFRA for purposes of all religious claims. At a minimum, however, it does not impinge on the plaintiffs' religious belief that providing insurance coverage for the contraceptives at issue here violates their religion, and it serves HHS's stated interests equally well.

The principal dissent identifies no reason why this accommodation would fail to protect the asserted needs of women as effectively as the contraceptive mandate, and there is none. . . .

C

HHS and the principal dissent argue that a ruling in favor of the objecting parties in these cases will lead to a flood of religious objections regarding a wide variety of medical procedures and drugs, such as vaccinations and blood transfusions, but HHS has made no effort to substantiate this prediction. HHS points to no evidence that insurance plans in existence prior to the enactment of ACA excluded coverage for such items. Nor has HHS provided evidence that any significant number of employers sought exemption, on religious grounds, from any of ACA's coverage requirements other than the contraceptive mandate. . . .

In any event, our decision in these cases is concerned solely with the contraceptive mandate. Our decision should not be understood to hold that an insurance-coverage mandate must necessarily fall if it conflicts with an employer's religious beliefs. Other coverage requirements, such as immunizations, may be supported by different interests (for example, the need to combat the spread of infectious diseases) and may involve different arguments about the least restrictive means of providing them. . . .

The contraceptive mandate, as applied to closely held corporations, violates RFRA. Our decision on that statutory question makes it unnecessary to reach the First Amendment claim raised by Conestoga and the Hahns. . . .

It is so ordered.

Justice GINSBURG, with whom Justice SOTOMAYOR joins, and with whom Justice BREYER and Justice KAGAN join as to all but Part III-C-1, dissenting.

I

"The ability of women to participate equally in the economic and social life of the Nation has been facilitated by their ability to control their reproductive lives." Planned Parenthood of Southeastern Pa. v. Casey. Congress acted on that understanding when, as part of a nationwide insurance program intended to be comprehensive, it called for coverage of preventive care responsive to women's needs. Carrying out Congress' direction, the Department of Health and Human Services (HHS), in consultation with public health experts, promulgated regulations requiring group health plans to cover all forms of contraception approved by the Food and Drug Administration (FDA). The genesis of this coverage should enlighten the Court's resolution of these cases.

A

The Affordable Care Act (ACA), in its initial form, specified three categories of preventive care that health plans must cover at no added cost to the plan participant or beneficiary. Particular services were to be recommended by the U.S. Preventive Services Task Force, an independent panel of experts. The scheme had a large gap, however; it left out preventive services that "many women's health advocates and medical professionals believe are critically important." 155 Cong. Rec. 28841 (2009) (statement of Sen. Boxer). To correct this oversight, Senator Barbara Mikulski introduced the Women's Health Amendment, which added to the ACA's minimum coverage requirements a new category of preventive services specific to women's health.

Women paid significantly more than men for preventive care, the amendment's proponents noted; in fact, cost barriers operated to block many women from obtaining needed care at all. And increased access to contraceptive services, the sponsors comprehended, would yield important public health gains.

As altered by the Women's Health Amendment's passage, the ACA requires new insurance plans to include coverage without cost sharing of "such additional preventive care and screenings . . . as provided for in comprehensive guidelines supported by the Health Resources and Services Administration [(HRSA)]," a unit of HHS. Thus charged, the HRSA developed recommendations in consultation with the Institute of Medicine (IOM). The IOM convened a group of independent experts, including "specialists in disease prevention [and] women's health"; those experts prepared a report evaluating the efficacy of a number of preventive services. Consistent with the findings of "[n]umerous health professional associations" and other organizations, the IOM experts determined that preventive coverage should include the "full range" of FDA-approved contraceptive methods.

In making that recommendation, the IOM's report expressed concerns similar to those voiced by congressional proponents of the Women's Health Amendment. The report noted the disproportionate burden women carried for comprehensive health services and the adverse health consequences of excluding contraception from preventive care available to employees without cost sharing.

In line with the IOM's suggestions, the HRSA adopted guidelines recommending coverage of "[a]ll [FDA-]approved contraceptive methods, sterilization procedures, and patient education and counseling for all women with reproductive capacity." Thereafter, HHS, the Department of Labor, and the Department of Treasury promulgated regulations requiring group health plans to include coverage of the contraceptive services recommended in the HRSA guidelines . . . This opinion refers to these regulations as the contraceptive coverage requirement.

B

While the Women's Health Amendment succeeded, a countermove proved unavailing. The Senate voted down the so-called "conscience amendment," which would have enabled any employer or insurance provider to deny coverage based on its asserted "religious beliefs or moral convictions." That amendment, Senator Mikulski observed, would have "pu[t] the personal opinion of employers and insurers over the practice of medicine." Congress left health care decisions—including the choice among contraceptive methods—in the hands of women, with the aid of their health care providers. . . .

III . . .

B

[T]he Court sees RFRA as a bold initiative departing from, rather than restoring, pre-*Smith* jurisprudence. To support its conception of RFRA as a measure detached from this Court's decisions, one that sets a new course, the Court points first to [RLUIPA], which altered RFRA's definition of the term "exercise of religion." . . . That definitional change, according to the Court, reflects "an obvious effort to effect a complete separation from First Amendment case law."

The Court's reading is not plausible. RLUIPA's alteration clarifies that courts should not question the centrality of a particular religious exercise. But the amendment in no way suggests that Congress meant to expand the class of entities qualified to mount religious accommodation claims, nor does it relieve courts of the obligation to inquire whether a government action substantially burdens a religious exercise.

Next, the Court highlights RFRA's requirement that the government, if its action substantially burdens a person's religious observance, must demonstrate that it chose the least restrictive means for furthering a compelling interest. "[B]y imposing a least-restrictive-means test," the Court suggests, RFRA "went beyond what was required by our pre-*Smith* decisions." But as RFRA's statements of purpose and legislative history make clear, Congress intended only to restore, not to scrap or alter, the balancing test as this Court had applied it pre-*Smith*.

The Congress that passed RFRA correctly read this Court's pre-*Smith* case law as including within the "compelling interest test" a "least restrictive means" requirement. And the view that the pre-*Smith* test included a "least restrictive means" requirement had been aired in testimony before the Senate Judiciary Committee by experts on religious freedom. . . .

C

With RFRA's restorative purpose in mind, I turn to the Act's application to the instant lawsuits. That task, in view of the positions taken by the Court, requires consideration of several questions, each potentially dispositive of Hobby Lobby's and Conestoga's claims: Do for-profit corporations rank among "person[s]" who "exercise . . . religion"? Assuming that they do, does the contraceptive coverage requirement "substantially burden" their religious exercise? If so, is the requirement "in furtherance of a compelling government interest"? And last, does the requirement represent the least restrictive means for furthering that interest?

Misguided by its errant premise that RFRA moved beyond the pre-*Smith* case law, the Court falters at each step of its analysis.

1

RFRA's compelling interest test, as noted, see *supra*, at 2790, applies to government actions that "substantially burden *a person's exercise of religion*." This reference, the Court submits, incorporates the definition of "person" found in the Dictionary Act. . . . The Dictionary Act's definition, however, controls only where "context" does not "indicat[e] otherwise." Here, context does so indicate. RFRA speaks of "a person's *exercise of religion*." Whether a corporation qualifies as a "person" capable of exercising religion is an inquiry one cannot answer without reference to the "full body" of pre-*Smith* "free-exercise caselaw." *Gilardi*. There is in that case law no support for the notion that free exercise rights pertain to for-profit corporations.

Until this litigation, no decision of this Court recognized a for-profit corporation's qualification for a religious exemption from a generally applicable law, whether under the Free Exercise Clause or RFRA. The absence of such precedent is just what one would expect, for the exercise of religion is characteristic of natural persons, not artificial legal entities. As Chief Justice Marshall observed nearly two centuries ago, a corporation is "an artificial being, invisible, intangible, and existing only in contemplation of law." *Trustees of Dartmouth College v. Woodward,* 4 Wheat. 518 (1819). Corporations, Justice Stevens more recently reminded, "have no consciences, no beliefs, no feelings, no thoughts, no desires." *Citizens United v. Federal Election Comm'n* (opinion concurring in part and dissenting in part).

The First Amendment's free exercise protections, the Court has indeed recognized, shelter churches and other nonprofit religion-based organizations. "For many individuals, religious activity derives meaning in large measure from participation in a larger religious community," and "furtherance of the autonomy of religious organizations often furthers individual religious freedom as well." *Corporation of Presiding Bishop of Church of Jesus Christ of Latter-day Saints v. Amos* (Brennan, J., concurring in judgment). The Court's "special solicitude to the rights of religious organizations," *Hosanna-Tabor Evangelical Lutheran Church and School v. EEOC,* however, is just that. No such solicitude is traditional for commercial organizations. Indeed, until today, religious exemptions had never been extended to any entity operating in "the commercial, profit-making world." *Amos.*

The reason why is hardly obscure. Religious organizations exist to foster the interests of persons subscribing to the same religious faith. Not so of for-profit corporations. Workers who sustain the operations of those corporations commonly are not drawn from one religious community. Indeed, by law, no religion-based criterion can restrict the work force of for-profit corporations. The distinction between a community made up of believers in the same religion and one embracing persons of diverse beliefs, clear as it is, constantly escapes the Court's attention. . . .

The Court's determination that RFRA extends to for-profit corporations is bound to have untoward effects. Although the Court attempts to cabin its language to closely held corporations, its logic extends to corporations of any size, public or private. Little doubt that RFRA claims will proliferate, for the Court's expansive notion of corporate personhood—combined with its other errors in construing RFRA—invites for-profit entities to seek religion-based exemptions from regulations they deem offensive to their faith.

2

Even if Hobby Lobby and Conestoga were deemed RFRA "person[s]," to gain an exemption, they must demonstrate that the contraceptive coverage requirement "substantially burden[s] [their] exercise of religion." Congress no doubt meant the modifier "substantially" to carry weight. In the original draft of RFRA, the word "burden" appeared unmodified. . . .

The Court barely pauses to inquire whether any burden imposed by the contraceptive coverage requirement is substantial. . . . I agree with the Court that the Green and Hahn families' religious convictions regarding contraception are sincerely held. But those beliefs, however deeply held, do not suffice to sustain a RFRA claim. RFRA, properly understood, distinguishes between "factual allegations that [plaintiffs'] beliefs are sincere and of a religious nature," which a court must accept as true, and the "legal conclusion . . . that [plaintiffs'] religious exercise is substantially burdened," an inquiry the court must undertake. . . .

Undertaking the inquiry that the Court forgoes, I would conclude that the connection between the families' religious objections and the contraceptive coverage requirement is too attenuated to rank as substantial. The requirement carries no command that Hobby Lobby or Conestoga purchase or provide the contraceptives they find objectionable. Instead, it calls on the companies covered by the requirement to direct money into undifferentiated funds that finance a wide variety of benefits under comprehensive health plans. . . .

Importantly, the decisions whether to claim benefits under the plans are made not by Hobby Lobby or Conestoga, but by the covered employees and dependents, in consultation with their health care providers. . . . Any decision to use contraceptives made by a woman covered under Hobby Lobby's or Conestoga's plan will not be propelled by the Government, it will be the woman's autonomous choice, informed by the physician she consults.

3

Even if one were to conclude that Hobby Lobby and Conestoga meet the substantial burden requirement, the Government has shown that the contraceptive coverage for which the ACA provides furthers compelling interests in public health and women's well being. Those interests are concrete, specific, and demonstrated by a wealth of empirical evidence. To recapitulate, the mandated contraception coverage enables women to avoid the health problems unintended pregnancies may visit on them and their children. The coverage helps safeguard the health of women for whom pregnancy may be hazardous, even life threatening. And the mandate secures benefits wholly unrelated to pregnancy, preventing certain cancers, menstrual disorders, and pelvic pain.

That Hobby Lobby and Conestoga resist coverage for only 4 of the 20 FDA-approved contraceptives does not lessen these compelling interests. Notably, the corporations exclude intrauterine devices (IUDs), devices significantly more effective, and significantly more expensive than other contraceptive methods. Moreover, the Court's reasoning appears to permit commercial enterprises like Hobby Lobby and Conestoga to exclude from their group health plans all forms of contraceptives. . . .

Perhaps the gravity of the interests at stake has led the Court to assume, for purposes of its RFRA analysis, that the compelling interest criterion is met in these cases. It bears note in this regard that the cost of an IUD is nearly equivalent to a month's full-time pay for workers earning the minimum wage; that almost one-third of women would change their contraceptive method if costs were not a factor; and that only one-fourth of women who request an IUD actually have one inserted after finding out how expensive it would be.

Stepping back from its assumption that compelling interests support the contraceptive coverage requirement, the Court notes that small employers and grandfathered plans are not subject to the requirement. If there is a compelling interest in contraceptive coverage, the Court suggests, Congress would not have created these exclusions. . . .

The Court ultimately acknowledges a critical point: RFRA's application "*must* take adequate account of the burdens a requested accommodation may impose on nonbeneficiaries." No tradition, and no prior decision under RFRA, allows a religion-based exemption when the accommodation would be harmful to others — here, the very persons the contraceptive coverage requirement was designed to protect.

4

After assuming the existence of compelling government interests, the Court holds that the contraceptive coverage requirement fails to satisfy RFRA's least restrictive means test. But the Government has shown that there is no less restrictive, equally effective means that would both (1) satisfy the challengers' religious objections to providing insurance coverage for certain contraceptives (which they believe cause abortions); and (2) carry out the objective of the ACA's contraceptive coverage requirement, to ensure that women employees receive, at no cost to them, the preventive care needed to safeguard their health and well being. A "least restrictive means" cannot require employees to relinquish benefits accorded them by federal law in order to ensure that their commercial employers can adhere unreservedly to their religious tenets.

Then let the government pay (rather than the employees who do not share their employer's faith), the Court suggests. "The most straightforward [alternative]," the Court asserts, "would be for the Government to assume the cost of providing . . . contraceptives . . . to any women who are unable to obtain them under their health-insurance policies due to their employers' religious objections." The ACA, however, requires coverage of preventive services through the existing employer-based system of health insurance "so that [employees] face minimal logistical and administrative obstacles." 78 Fed. Reg. 39888. Impeding women's receipt of benefits "by requiring them to take steps to learn about, and to sign up for, a new [government funded and administered] health benefit" was scarcely what Congress contemplated. . . .

And where is the stopping point to the "let the government pay" alternative? Suppose an employer's sincerely held religious belief is offended by health coverage of vaccines, or paying the minimum wage, or according women equal pay for substantially similar work? Does it rank as a less restrictive alternative to require the government to provide the money or benefit to which the employer has a religion-based objection? . . .

In sum, in view of what Congress sought to accomplish, *i.e.*, comprehensive preventive care for women furnished through employer-based health plans, none of the proffered alternatives would satisfactorily serve the compelling interests to which Congress responded. . . .

IV

Among the pathmarking pre-*Smith* decisions RFRA preserved is *United States v. Lee.* Lee, a sole proprietor engaged in farming and carpentry, was a member of the Old Order Amish. He sincerely believed that withholding Social Security taxes from his employees or paying the employer's share of such taxes would violate the Amish faith. This Court held that, although the obligations imposed by the Social Security system conflicted with Lee's religious beliefs, the burden was not unconstitutional. The Government urges that *Lee* should control the challenges brought by Hobby Lobby and Conestoga. In contrast, today's Court dismisses *Lee* as a tax case. Indeed, it was a tax case and the Court in *Lee* homed in on "[t]he difficulty in attempting to accommodate religious beliefs in the area of taxation."

But the *Lee* Court made two key points one cannot confine to tax cases. "When followers of a particular sect enter into commercial activity as a matter of choice," the Court observed, "the limits they accept on their own conduct as a matter of conscience and faith are not to be superimposed on statutory schemes which are binding on others in that activity." The statutory scheme of employer-based comprehensive health coverage involved in these cases is surely binding on others engaged in the same trade or business as the corporate challengers here, Hobby Lobby and Conestoga. Further, the Court recognized in *Lee* that allowing a religion-based exemption to a commercial employer would "operat[e] to impose the employer's religious faith on the employees." No doubt the Greens and Hahns and all who share their beliefs may decline to acquire for themselves the contraceptives in question. But that choice may not be imposed on employees who hold other beliefs. Working for Hobby Lobby or Conestoga, in other words, should not deprive employees of the preventive care available to workers at the shop next door, at least in the absence of directions from the Legislature or Administration to do so. . . .

Would the exemption the Court holds RFRA demands for employers with religiously grounded objections to the use of certain contraceptives extend to employers with religiously grounded objections to blood transfusions (Jehovah's Witnesses); antidepressants (Scientologists); medications derived from pigs, including anesthesia, intravenous fluids, and pills coated with gelatin (certain Muslims, Jews, and Hindus); and vaccinations (Christian Scientists, among others)?

The Court, however, sees nothing to worry about. Today's cases, the Court concludes, are "concerned solely with the contraceptive mandate. . . ." But the Court has assumed, for RFRA purposes, that the interest in women's health and well being is compelling and has come up with no means adequate to serve that interest, the one motivating Congress to adopt the Women's Health Amendment.

There is an overriding interest, I believe, in keeping the courts "out of the business of evaluating the relative merits of differing religious claims," *Lee* (Stevens, J., concurring in judgment), or the sincerity with which an asserted religious belief is held. Indeed, approving some religious claims while deeming others unworthy of accommodation could be "perceived as favoring one religion over another," the very "risk the Establishment Clause was designed to preclude." The Court, I fear, has ventured into a minefield, by its immoderate reading of RFRA. I would confine religious exemptions under that Act to organizations formed "for a religious purpose," "engage[d] primarily in carrying out that religious purpose," and not "engaged . . . substantially in the exchange of goods or services for money beyond nominal amounts."

* * *

For the reasons stated, I would reverse the judgment of the Court of Appeals for the Tenth Circuit and affirm the judgment of the Court of Appeals for the Third Circuit.

Notes

1. The Constitutional Right to Contraception. The right in *Griswold* was based squarely on the special status of marriage in this society. In Eisenstadt v. Baird, the Court extended *Griswold* to prevent Massachusetts from barring distribution of contraceptives to unmarried persons. In so ruling, the Court reasoned that "the goals of deterring premarital sex and regulating the distribution of potentially harmful articles cannot reasonably be regarded as legislative aims of [the contraception law]" since it would be irrational to make an unwanted child the "punishment for fornication." In the Court's view: "If the right of privacy means anything, it is the right of the individual, married or single, to be free from unwarranted governmental intrusion into matters so fundamentally affecting a person as the decision whether to bear or beget a child."[286]

---

286. 405 U.S. 438, 453 (1972).

How far should this right extend? Should it apply to minors? How about a constitutional right to have sex? Although, in Carey v. Population Serv. Int'l, the Court invalidated a New York law that, among other things, restricted the sale of contraceptives to minors younger than sixteen, it sidestepped the question whether minors have a constitutional right of access to contraception.[287] Similarly, in striking down a Texas statute prohibiting same-sex sodomy in Lawrence v. Texas, the Supreme Court cited *Eisenstadt* and *Carey* for the proposition that the liberty interest protected sexual decisions by unmarried persons, but stopped short of declaring a fundamental right to all sexual activity between consenting adults.[288]

Popular acceptance of *Griswold* has been deep and wide, despite the fact that many scholars at one time questioned its grounding as a matter of constitutional law.[289] Support has been so strong, in fact, that one nominee to a seat on the U.S. Supreme Court, Robert Bork, was defeated in 1987 largely because of his opposition to the ruling.[290] Nevertheless, the 2012 campaign for the Republican nomination for President, reflecting a growing conservatism about issues dealing with women's control of their reproductive lives, exposed considerable backlash on the issue of payment for contraceptives. Proposed federal legislation that would have permitted any employer to omit coverage for contraceptives from its employee health insurance plans based on any moral or religious objection was narrowly defeated by a vote of 51 to 48 in a Democratic-controlled Senate.[291] Even the most moderate of the four men then seeking the Republican nomination, Mitt Romney, said he supported the legislation.[292] When a female Georgetown law student was denied the opportunity to testify about the proposed legislation, she told the press that she would have talked about the women who have been affected by Georgetown's failure to include contraception in its student health plan.[293] In response to her statements, Rush Limbaugh called her a "slut" and a "prostitute" on his national radio show, repeatedly telling listeners that the student has "so much sex she can't afford it" and that she seeks someone to pay her for having

287. 431 U.S. 678 (1977).

288. 539 U.S. 558 (2003).

289. See, e.g., Robert P. George & David L. Tubbs, The Bad Decision That Started It All, National Review, July 18, 2005, at 39-40.

290. See Mark Gitenstein, Matters of Principle: An Insider's Account of American's Rejection of Robert Bork's Nomination to the Supreme Court (1992). For Bork's view of *Griswold*, see Robert H. Bork, Neutral Principles and Some First Amendment Problems, 47 Ind. L.J. 1, 7-12 (1971) (arguing that *Griswold* was an unprincipled decision).

291. 158 Cong. Rec. S. 1162 (Mar. 1, 2012); Robert Pear, Senate Rejects Step Targeting Coverage of Contraception, N.Y. Times, Mar. 1, 2012.

292. See Romney Clarifies His Position on Blunt Amendment, The Miami Herald, Feb. 29, 2012.

293. See Sarah Kiff, Meet Sandra Fluke: The Woman You Didn't Hear at Congress' Contraceptives Hearing, Wash. Post, Feb. 16, 2012.

sex.[294] Outrage over those statements caused over one hundred advertisers to pull ads from his program. Public opinion polling at the time of the controversy indicated that eight in ten Democrats supported requiring employers to include coverage for contraceptives in their employer-based health insurance plans, but that only four in ten Republicans did.[295]

2. Contraception and Women's Autonomy. It seems obvious that female contraception allows women to maintain greater control over their reproductive lives. But Catharine MacKinnon points out some disadvantages:

> So long as women do not control access to our sexuality, abortion facilitates women's heterosexual availability. In other words, under conditions of gender inequality, sexual liberation in this sense does not free women; it frees male sexual aggression. The availability of abortion removes the one remaining legitimized reason that women have had for refusing sex besides the headache.[296]

What do you think? Historian Linda Gordon underlines the class and gender ideologies of birth control, explaining how men, particularly those of lower socioeconomic status, tend to associate masculinity with sexual images of virility—an identity that is undercut by the use of contraception "because it introduces calculation and negotiation with women into sexual relations." Among the prosperous, masculinity is associated to a greater extent with earning power, responsibility, children's high achievement, and other goals that tend to be served by contraceptive use. Race and ethnicity are further complicating factors. At various times and circumstances, racial and ethnic pride might stimulate fertility, or it might stimulate greater use of contraception. Race and ethnicity also affect the availability of competing opportunities to motherhood and thus the motivation to reproduce.[297]

Male condom use has increased dramatically. Almost 10 percent of women of reproductive age rely on their partners' use of condoms, 15.5 percent of women rely on female sterilization, 16 percent use birth control pills, 5.1 percent rely on male sterilization, and 11.4 percent use injectable contraceptives, vaginal rings, or IUDs.[298] The remaining 52 percent rely on various

---

294. See Matt Negrin, Sandra Fluke Says Rush Limbaugh's Apology Doesn't Change Anything, OTUS News (Mar. 5, 2012), http://abcnews.go.com/Politics/OTUS/rush-limbaugh-apologizes-calling-sandra-fluke-slut/story?id=15841687#.T1fasPUyF8E.

295. Erik Eckholm, Poll Finds Divisions over Requiring Coverage, N.Y. Times, Mar. 1, 2012, at A15.

296. Catharine MacKinnon, Feminism Unmodified: Discourses on Life and Law 99 (1987).

297. Gordon, supra note 285, at 480-481, xix-xxi.

298. See Guttmacher Inst., Contraceptive Use in the United States (Oct. 2015); Kimberly Daniels et al., U.S. Dep't Health & Human Servs., Current Contraceptive Status Among Women Aged 15-44: United States, 2011-2013 (Dec. 2014).

levels of abstinence or do not use any form of contraception. Significantly, of course, female contraceptive alternatives do not protect against AIDS and other sexually transmitted diseases.

3. Emergency Contraception and Conscience Laws. The "morning after pill" is a form of emergency contraception that is most effective when taken 12 to 24 hours after intercourse and can be effective up to 72 hours afterwards. Emergency contraception works by several methods: suppressing ovulation, preventing fertilization, disrupting transport of a fertilized egg, or preventing its implantation in the uterus. Of the 3 million unintended pregnancies that occur in the United States each year, estimates suggest that access to emergency contraception could prevent 1.5 million pregnancies, of which half now end in abortion.[299]

In 1999, the FDA approved the "morning-after pill" by prescription as a form of emergency birth control, but resisted the decision to make it available on an over-the-counter basis. An enormous controversy ensued. Unfettered over-the-counter access was finally approved for women 18 and older in August of 2006, and, by 2013, for women of all ages.[300]

As the morning-after pill was working its way through the regulatory process, a related controversy was playing out in pharmacies and religious hospitals. Forty-five states and the federal government have "conscience laws" that enable institutions and individuals to refuse abortion, contraception, or sterilization services that are "contrary to [their] religious beliefs or moral principles."[301] The 2005 Weldon Amendment also prohibits federal funding for any federal, state, or local agency that discriminates against any "health care entity" that does not provide or offer referrals or insurance coverage for abortions. Accordingly, Catholic hospitals follow the National Conference of Bishops Ethical and Religious Directives for Catholic Health Care Services, which prohibit all forms of contraceptive services and counseling, medical and surgical abortions, sterilizations, and even emergency contraception to victims of rape.[302] Some hospitals prohibit affiliated doctors from performing similar medical procedures elsewhere. The impact of these restrictions has increased

299. Deana Pisoni, Ninth Annual Review of Gender and Sexuality Law: Health Law Chapter: Access to Contraceptives, 9 Geo. J. Gender & L. 1125, 1131 (2008).

300. See Gardiner Harris, F.D.A. Easing Access to "Morning After" Pill, N.Y. Times, Apr. 22, 2009, at A14; Michael D. Shear & Pam Belluck, U.S. Drops Bid to Limit Sales of Morning-After Pill, June 10, 2013, at A1.

301. See, e.g., 42 U.S.C. §300a-7(c)(B) (2011); Guttmacher Inst., Refusing to Provide Health Services, Feb. 1, 2016.

302. See U.S. Conference of Catholic Bishops, http://www.usccb.org/issues-and-action/human-life-and-dignity/health-care/upload/Ethical-Religious-Directives-Catholic-Health-Care-Services-fifth-edition-2009.pdf (Nov. 2009); see also Sandhya Somashekhar, A Pregnant Woman Wanted Her Tubes Tied. Her Catholic Hospital Said No., Wash. Post., Sept.

with the trend of religiously-affiliated health care facilities merging with non-sectarian institutions.

Efforts have failed to enact federal legislation that would require hospitals to provide access to a full range of reproductive services. A number of states, however, require all hospitals to provide either information about emergency contraception, a referral for the morning-after pill, or on-site emergency contraception treatment, which means that "conscience clauses" apply only to procedures such as abortion, sterilization, and artificial insemination, and not to emergency contraception. California's Women's Contraception Equity Act requires Catholic institutions, including hospitals, to provide their employees with contraceptive coverage if they provide prescription drug coverage.[303]

In recent years, controversies have centered on the right of pharmacists to refuse to fill prescriptions for the "morning after" pill. Pharmacists who believe that life begins at conception consider emergency contraception to be similar to abortion because it may prevent implantation of an embryo. (This is similar to the argument of the defendants in *Hobby Lobby*, who argued that four of the contraceptives covered by the HHS mandate are "abortifacients.") The FDA classifies the morning-after pill as a contraceptive, and supporters deny that it is like abortion because it does not destroy an embryo. In small communities, pharmacists' refusals to fill prescriptions or make referrals have undermined access to this medication. Six states have laws permitting pharmacists' refusals on ethical or religious grounds, and many more have considered adopting such laws.[304] Seven states have laws requiring pharmacists to fill prescriptions, others require timely referrals or are considering such legislation, and a few have pharmacy boards that have affirmed such obligations.[305] Since 1998, the American Pharmacists Association has had a policy supporting members' right to "refuse to dispense medication" while encouraging pharmacies to provide alternative arrangements for ensuring that prescriptions are filled. In one representative poll, 80 percent of Americans believed that pharmacists should not be able to refuse to dispense birth control.[306]

Both sides in the debate claim the moral high ground. Pharmacists argue that customer's "convenience should not trump another person's moral conscience." Neither, they contend, should pharmacists be forced to say "I don't kill people myself but let me tell you about the guy down the street

---

13, 2015 (describing 2015 Michigan case in which Catholic hospital refused a tubal ligation to a woman with a brain tumor).

303. For an overview, see Guttmacher Inst., Rights vs. Responsibilities: Professional Standards and Provider Refusals (2005).

304. Guttmacher Inst., Refusing to Provide Health Services (2016).

305. Nat'l Women's Law Ctr., Pharmacy Refusals; State Laws, Regulations, and Policies (Apr. 2012), http://www.nwlc.org/resource/pharmacy-refusals-state-laws-regulations-and-policies.

306. CBS News, Religion at the Drugstore (Nov. 23, 2004), http://www.cbsnews.com/stories/2004/11/23/opinion/polls/main657413.shtml.

who does."[307] Women's rights advocates like Ellen Goodman respond that "the pharmacist's license does not include the right to dispense morality."[308] Should state law or pharmacy boards dictate policy in this area? Or should we let the market decide?

4. The Fight for Contraceptive Equity Insurance and Women's Health. Does it violate Title VII for an employer to omit coverage for prescription contraceptives, which are only used by women, from an otherwise comprehensive insurance plan? This issue was litigated in several cases in the early 2000s, when relatively few employers voluntarily provided coverage for prescription contraceptives and the Affordable Care Act (discussed at length in *Hobby Lobby*) had not yet been enacted. Plaintiffs in these cases urged that access to contraception is an issue of sex equality.[309] These cases raised the question whether the Pregnancy Discrimination Act, covered in Chapter 2, applies to the entire reproductive process—including efforts to control it. In Erickson v. Bartell Drug Co., the court sided with the plaintiffs: "Title VII does not require employers to offer any particular type or category of benefit. However, when an employer decides to offer a prescription plan covering everything except a few specifically excluded drugs and devices, it has a legal obligation to make sure that the resulting plan does not discriminate based on sex-based characteristics and that it provides equally comprehensive coverage for both sexes."[310] Is *Erickson* correctly decided? What exactly is the nature of the discrimination? Does it matter whether the insurance plan covers drugs used only by men, such as Viagra?

Federal district courts split on whether such exclusions constitute unlawful discrimination under Title VII, as amended by the PDA.[311] Only one federal appellate court has considered this issue. The Eighth Circuit, in Standridge v. Union Pacific Railroad Company, held that it was neither pregnancy nor sex discrimination for the employer to exclude coverage for all forms of contraception, including sterilization. The court concluded that contraception is not a "related medical condition" under the terms of the PDA, even though the Supreme Court held in *Johnson Controls*, discussed in Chapter 2, that "poten-

307. Sheila G. Liaugminas, Pharmacists Battling Lawsuits over Conscience Issues, Nat'l Cath. Reg., Feb. 13-19, 2005, at 1; Editorial, Prescription Politics Hard to Swallow, Balt. Sun, Apr. 22, 2005, at 13A.

308. Ellen Goodman, Pharmacists and Morality, Boston Globe, Apr. 14, 2005, at A14.

309. Cornelia T.L. Pillard articulates an equality-based theory for contraceptive access in Our Other Reproductive Choices: Equality in Sex Education, Contraceptive Access, and Work-Family Policy, 56 Emory L.J. 941, 963-77 (2007).

310. 141 F. Supp. 2d 1266 (W.D. Wash. 2001).

311. Compare Stocking v. AT&T Corp., 436 F. Supp. 2d 1014 (W.D. Mo. 2006) (PDA requires coverage) and EEOC v. UPS, 141 F. Supp. 2d 1216 (D. Minn. 2001) (exclusion constitutes sex discrimination under Title VII) with Cummins v. Illinois, 2005 U.S. Dist. LEXIS 42634 (S.D. Ill.) (PDA does not require coverage).

tial pregnancy" is covered by that same language.[312] The *Standridge* court found "unpersuasive" a decision from the EEOC that interpreted the PDA to require coverage of prescription contraceptives for women if they cover "other prescription drugs and devices, or other types of services, that are used to prevent the occurrences of other medical conditions."[313] It also concluded that the employer's plan was gender-neutral because it excluded coverage for male contraception (condoms) and sterilization.

The impact of these rulings both in favor of and against contraceptive equity has lessened over the last decade, as the number of employers providing insurance with contraceptive benefits has dramatically increased. By 2010, nine in ten employer-provided insurance plans covered prescription contraceptives, compared with only three in ten a decade earlier.[314] This change came about primarily through state adoption of contraceptive coverage mandates. Beginning with Maryland in 1998, twenty-eight states adopted some type of mandated benefit law for prescription contraceptives.[315] Since 1998, health plans participating in the Federal Employees Health Benefit Program have been required to provide prescription contraceptive coverage if other prescription drugs are covered.[316]

Efforts to pass a federal contraceptive equity bill were unsuccessful until the Affordable Care Act was signed into law in 2010 and the HHS regulations at issue in Burwell v. Hobby Lobby Stores were enacted. Even after the U.S. Supreme Court upheld these regulations from a RFRA challenge in *Hobby Lobby* on the basis of the religious exemption provided in the regulations, RFRA challenges continued. In Zubik v. Burwell, a number of non-church employers, including a Roman Catholic-supported home for low-income elderly and several religiously-based colleges, claimed that the requirement that they submit notice of the exemption to their insurer itself impermissibly requires their involvement in the provision of contraception, in violation of their religious liberty.[317] In the latest round of activity, the U.S. Supreme Court, after oral argument and supplemental briefing requested by the Court in which the federal government represented that it was "feasible" to provide contraception coverage to women without the notice to which the challengers

312. 479 F.3d 936, 942 (8th Cir. 2007).

313. Id. at 943 (citing EEOC Commission Decision on Coverage of Contraception (Dec. 14, 2000)), http://www.eeoc.gov/policy/docs/decision-contraception.html.

314. Guttmacher Inst., Contraceptive Use in the United States (Oct. 2015), http://www.guttmacher.org/pubs/fb_contr_use.html.

315. Guttmacher Inst., Insurance Coverage of Contraceptives (Feb. 1, 2016), http://www.guttmacher.org/statecenter/spibs/spib_ICC.pdf (analyzing state contraceptive coverage mandates).

316. See Pub. L. 108-7, 117 Stat. 474 (2003).

317. Briefs available at http://www.scotusblog.com/case-files/cases/zubik-v-burwell.

objected, remanded the case back to the various circuit courts involved in the case to settle the matter.[318]

5. Religion and Women's Equality. *Hobby Lobby* involves a longstanding, and perhaps increasing, tension between religion and equality. It raises a similar issue to those involved in the public accommodations cases discussed in Chapter 1, Section D (religious objections to providing goods and services for gay weddings) and in the discussion in Chapter 6 of other conflicts between religion and women's interests in equality. Are you satisfied with the way the majority weighed religious freedom against advancement of women's health and the economic consequences of lessening their ability to control reproduction? Or was Justice Ginsburg's account more persuasive? Is there a limit to the protection for religious freedom when the Court defers not only to the business owners' statements about their religious beliefs but also to their beliefs about whether particular methods qualify as "abortifacients"? Priscilla Smith argues that the plaintiffs' beliefs about when pregnancy occurs (upon fertilization of an egg) and whether contraceptive devices can prevent implantation of an embryo in the uterine wall are contrary to scientific consensus and reminiscent of the arguments made in defense of Comstock laws.[319] Is there room under the *Hobby Lobby* decision for a debate about the scientific truth underlying the claimed "belief"?

Consider Elizabeth Sepper's perspective on *Hobby Lobby*:

> The Supreme Court could have treated *Hobby Lobby* as implicating women's status in society. As feminists have long recognized, without control over their reproductive health, women can pursue their professional and educational ambitions only with great difficulty. Empirical studies confirm that access to contraception contributes to higher educational attainment and more financially desirable jobs for women, in turn reducing the gender pay gap. Women themselves experience the use of contraception as enabling them "to take better care of themselves or their families, support themselves financially, complete their education, or get or keep a job."
>
> The fact that only women bear children and (due to the limits of today's technology) use prescription contraceptives is biological, but the imposition of financial burdens on reproductive control is social. By allowing employers to exclude contraceptives from insurance plans, society, not biology, has subjected women to inequality. With the women's preventive services mandate, Congress responded to this inequality.

318. Zubik v. Burwell, 578 U.S. __ (2016).

319. Priscilla J. Smith, Contraceptive Comstockery: Reasoning from Immorality to Illness in the Twenty-First Century, 47 Conn. L. Rev. 971 (2015).

The courts instead treated gender equality as extraneous to the federal contraceptive mandate.[320]

Do you agree with her critique?

6. Access to Treatment for Infertility. Women have also challenged their employers' response to infertility as a form of sex discrimination. The CDC estimates that as many as 7 million women suffer some degree of infertility.[321] With advances in reproductive technology, women have many more options for treating infertility. Twelve percent of women of childbearing age have sought medical help for infertility or prevention of miscarriage.[322] Because most treatments for infertility are expensive, prohibitively so for many women, insurance coverage is an important issue. By and large, however, plaintiffs have not succeeded in litigation challenging insurance exclusions under Title VII and the PDA. In Krauel v. Iowa Methodist Medical Center, the Eighth Circuit Court of Appeals held that infertility is not a "related medical condition" under the PDA because both men and women can suffer from it. It is thus unlike the "potential pregnancy" recognized in Johnson Controls, which is unique to women.[323] The Second Circuit in Saks v. Franklin Covey Co. rejected a similar claim, ruling that it was neither pregnancy nor sex discrimination for an employer to deny insurance coverage for surgical impregnation procedures (such as artificial insemination and in vitro fertilization) performed only on women.[324] The court noted that including "infertility within the PDA's protection as a 'related medical condition[ ]' would result in the anomaly of defining a class that simultaneously includes equal numbers of both sexes and yet is somehow vulnerable to sex discrimination."[325] To fall under the PDA, the court concluded, the condition "must be unique to women." The Seventh Circuit, however, held in Hall v. Nalco that an employer could not fire a woman because she requested time off to undergo in vitro fertilization without violating the PDA. If her allegations were true, the plaintiff "was terminated not for the gender-neutral condition of infertility, but rather for the gender-specific quality of childbearing capacity."[326] Employees "terminated for taking time off to undergo IVF—just like those terminated for taking time off to give birth or receive other pregnancy-related care—will

---

320. Elizabeth Sepper, Gendering Corporate Conscience, 38 Harv. J.L. & Gender 193, 208-09 (2015).
321. Anjani Chandra et al., Nat'l Health Stat. Rep., Infertility Service Use in the United States: Data from the National Survey of Family Growth, 1982-2010, at 1 (Jan. 2014).
322. Id.
323. 95 F.3d 674, 679-80 (8th Cir. 1996).
324. 316 F.3d 337, 346-49 (2d Cir. 2003).
325. Id. at 346.
326. 534 F.3d 644, 649 (7th Cir. 2008).

always be women."[327] Can *Saks* and *Hall* be reconciled? Which one has the better reading of *Johnson Controls*?

7. Gender Bias in Health Care. Health concerns about female contraception are part of a broader set of issues related to gender bias in health care. Some of these complaints concern the failure to provide adequate warnings and instructions for contraceptives, and to provide research and treatment for women with conditions such as heart disease, renal disease, and lung cancer, for which men receive better health care.[328]

One representative study found that emergency rooms incorrectly sent home a disproportionate number of women and blacks despite warning signs of heart attacks.[329] Other problems concern the overuse of certain invasive procedures or restrictive instructions. Such biases may be related to the fact that, for decades, women were disproportionately excluded from medical research and drug test trials.[330] To rectify such exclusions the NIH Revitalization Act of 1993 required the National Institutes of Health of the Department of Health and Human Services to ensure that women and minorities were among the subjects of clinical research.

Concerns about the lack of attention to women's health have been fueled by the discovery of numerous drugs and other products that, as in the case of some contraceptives, have turned out to be medically unsafe for women. Examples have included the Dalkon Shield contraceptive; DES, a synthetic estrogen hormone prescribed for miscarriages, later linked to cancer and birth defects; and Bendectin, an anti-nausea medication also found to cause birth defects. Concerns have also been raised about silicone breast implants. In the 1990s, the makers of the implants spent more than 6 billion dollars settling about 370,000 claims for arthritic and autoimmune disorders claimed to have resulted from the rupture and leakage of silicone from the implants. During this time, the FDA withdrew approval of the implants except for "urgent need" patients who had had mastectomies, at which point saline implants dominated the market. Subsequently, in 2006, a new type of silicone implant was approved, with the requirement of ten years of follow-up study.[331] In 2010, half of the almost 300,000 breast augmentation procedures performed

327. Id. at 648-49.

328. See Mary Crossley, Infected Judgment: Legal Responses to Physician Bias, 48 Vill. L. Rev. 195, 225, 227-29 (2003) (citing studies); Sandra C. Gan et al., Treatment of Acute Myocardial Infarction Among Men and Women, 343 New Eng. J. Med. 8 (July 2000).

329. See, e.g., Maya Dusenbery, Is Medicine's Gender Bias Killing Young Women?, Pacific Standard, Mar. 23, 2015.

330. Crossley, supra note 328, at 224 (citing studies).

331. See FDA Approves Silicone Gel-Filled Breast Implants After In-Depth Evaluation, (Nov. 17, 2006), http://www.fda.gov/NewsEvents/Newsroom/PressAnnouncements/2006/ucm108790.htm. On the history of breast implants, see Florence Williams, Breasts: A Natural and Unnatural History (2012).

in the United States made use of silicone implants.[332] Based on five years of post-approval studies, the FDA determined that silicone implants "have a reasonable assurance of safety and effectiveness when used as labeled" and "despite frequent local complications and adverse outcomes, the benefits and risks . . . are sufficiently well understood for women to make informed decisions about their use."[333]

One women's health care controversy centers on whether states should require or promote vaccination of school-age girls with Gardasil, a vaccine designed to protect against four strands of the human papilloma virus (HPV). HPV is the most common sexually transmitted disease with which 20 million people are currently infected.[334] It is responsible for almost all cervical cancers, as well as a significant percentage of cancers of the vulva, vagina, penis, anus, mouth, and throat, and 90 percent of genital warts. There are about 12,000 new cervical cancer cases every year and about 4,000 deaths from the disease. Black and Hispanic women have disproportionately high rates of cervical cancer and face worse outcomes.[335] In 2006, the FDA approved Gardasil for females ages nine to twenty-six.[336] Conservative groups like the Family Research Council have opposed the vaccine because female adolescents could see it as "license to engage in premarital sex."[337] Such opposition has helped block proposed legislation in about half of the states to require vaccination, as well as efforts to require its coverage in insurance policies.[338] New evidence shows that the rate of HPV infection in girls has decreased by 64 percent since

---

332. See FDA Update on the Safety of Silicone Gel-Filled Breast Implants at 3 (June 2011), http://www.fda.gov/downloads/MedicalDevices/ProductsandMedicalProcedures/ImplantsandProsthetics/BreastImplants/UCM260090.pdf.

333. Id. at 34.

334. See Ctrs. for Disease Control and Prevention (CDC), HPV Vaccine Information for Clinicians—Fact Sheet (July 8, 2012), http://www.cdc.gov/std/HPV/STDFact-HPV-vaccine-hcp.htm.

335. See Ctrs. for Disease Control & Prevention, Cervical Cancer Rates by Race & Ethnicity (Aug. 20, 2015), http://www.cdc.gov/Features/dsCervicalCancer.

336. See Letter from Norman W. Baylor, Dep't of Health & Human Serv., to Patrick Brill-Edwards, M.D., Worldwide Regulatory Affairs (June 8, 2006), http://www.fda.gov/BiologicsBloodVaccines/Vaccines/ApprovedProducts/ucm111283.htm.

337. Nancy Gibbs, Defusing the War over the "Promiscuity" Vaccine, Time, June 21, 2006 (quoting Bridget Maher).

338. Women in Government, the State of Cervical Cancer Prevention in America 7-8 (2008) (noting that only one state requires vaccination and five require coverage). Arguing for broader access to Gardasil, see Micah Globerson, Gardasil a Year Later: Cervical Cancer as a Model of Inequality of Access to Health Services, 15 Cardozo J. Law & Gender 247 (2009); see also Henry J. Kaiser Family Foundation, The HPV Vaccine: Access and Use in the U.S. (Sept. 3, 2015), http://kff.org/womens-health-policy/fact-sheet/the-hpv-vaccine-access-and-use-in.

the introduction of the vaccine.[339] Is that a sufficient counter to the moral opposition?

In 2009, the FDA approved Gardasil for use in boys nine through twenty-six years of age.[340] In 2011, an advisory committee of the FDA recommended that all boys of the requisite ages receive the vaccine. In support of the recommendation, the committee stated: "HPV vaccination of males offers an opportunity to decrease the burden of HPV related disease in both males and females. In addition to providing direct benefit to boys by preventing future genital warts or anal cancer there is also the potential that vaccinating boys will reduce the spread of HPV from males to females and reduce some of the HPV-related burden that women suffer from."[341] As a legislator, would you support a mandate for both boys and girls to receive the vaccine? If so, how would you respond to conservative critics who object to mandatory use of a vaccine to prevent sexually transmitted disease?

8. Sterilization. As Note 2 indicates, sterilization is currently the second-most widely used birth control technique. Almost 16 percent of women rely on female sterilization for contraception, and 6 percent of women rely on the sterilization of their male partners.

Sterilization has an unbecoming history, due to its compulsory application to poor, minority, and mentally disabled women. In a 1927 case permitting such sterilization, Justice Oliver Wendell Holmes infamously declared: "Three generations of imbeciles is enough."[342] The view of the Supreme Court toward compulsory sterilization ultimately changed,[343] but some states continue to authorize sterilization for certain offenses such as child sexual abuse.[344]

Sterilization for poor and minority women as a condition of receiving welfare has led to federal and state regulations designed to prevent such coercion. However, as forced sterilization laws tightened, it became more difficult for parents and guardians to obtain the procedure for developmentally disabled women whose best interests—including their autonomy—might benefit from sterilization. Attention then shifted to how sterilization standards

---

339. Jan Hoffman, HPV Sharply Reduced in Teenage Girls Following Vaccine, Study Says, N.Y. Times, Feb. 22, 2016, at A14.

340. See Letter from Wellington Son, M.D., Dep't of Health & Human Serv., to Patrick Brill-Edwards, Merck & Co., Inc. (Oct. 16, 2009), http://www.fda.gov/BiologicsBloodVaccines/Vaccines/ApprovedProducts/ucm186991.htm.

341. CDC, Online Newsroom Press Briefing Transcript (Oct. 25, 2011), www.cdc.gov/media/releases/2011/t1025_hpv_12yroldvaccine.html.

342. Buck v. Bell, 274 U.S. 200, 207 (1927).

343. See Skinner v. Oklahoma, 316 U.S. 535 (1942).

344. See, e.g., Cal. Penal Code §645 (West 2016) (authorizing hormone suppression treatment for parolees convicted of certain sexual offenses); Wash. Rev. Code §9.92.100 (West 2016) (authorizing sterilization for persons convicted of sex with female under age ten).

should both protect women, but also enable them to live richer, sexually active lives. Some jurisdictions such as Connecticut attempt to accommodate these competing concerns by allowing courts to authorize sterilization if presented with clear and convincing evidence that it is in the best interests of the individual or that the individual would choose it for herself if able.[345] Is this a good balance?

Putting Theory Into Practice

5-18. The Women's Health and Cancer Rights Act of 1998 was passed to require that insurance plans that include coverage for mastectomy also cover reconstruction of the removed breast, and also the other breast in order to produce a symmetrical appearance. Is this entitlement best viewed as a gender equality issue? An autonomy issue? Does it serve to reinforce the concept of women as sexual objects? Or does it expand their life choices in a positive way?

5-19. You have been appointed the guardian ad litem for Beth, an 18-year-old woman who has the mental function of an 8-year-old. Beth is able to work in a sheltered workshop setting and to take care of her own basic, physical needs, but she is not able to cook, drive, read, balance a checkbook, or follow complicated instructions. She would like to move from her parents' home to a supervised group-home setting with people her own age. Her parents are agreeable to the move, as long as she has a tubal ligation first so that, if she becomes sexually active, she cannot become pregnant. Because she is incompetent, state law requires a judicial order authorizing the procedure. Your role is to make a recommendation to the court about whether the procedure is in Beth's best interests.

What will you recommend to the court? What additional evidence, if any, would you need to gather to support your recommendation?

5-20. A 2005 Executive Order in Illinois provided that "[u]pon receipt of a valid, lawful prescription for a contraceptive, a pharmacy must dispense the contraceptive, or a suitable alternative permitted by the prescriber, to the patient . . . without delay, consistent with the normal time frame for filling any other prescription."[346] Pursuant to this order, Walgreens requires its pharmacists to sign statements promising to fill contraceptive prescriptions. It suspended four pharmacists who refused to do so based on their religious beliefs.

---

345. Conn. Gen. Stat. §45a-699(b) (2016).
346. 68 Ill. Admin. Code §1330.91(j) (2005). The order was the subject of a state and federal lawsuit, see Menges v. Blagojevich, 451 F. Supp. 2d 992 (C.D. Ill. 2006) and Morr-Fitz, Inc. v. Blagojevich, 901 N.E.2d 373 (Ill. 2008), and subsequently repealed. 33 Ill. Reg. 12992 (2009).

Should pharmacists who morally oppose contraception (especially the morning-after pill, which they consider a form of abortion) be protected from adverse employment action for acting on their consciences? Should states enact laws protecting them from such consequences? Is there a compromise position?[347]

5-21. In *Hobby Lobby*, the majority made clear that only a sincere religious belief could be the basis for an exemption from the contraceptive coverage mandate. Would it be appropriate in litigation to ask business owners who are seeking the exemption whether they have ever personally used contraception? Why or why not?

2. Abortion

Access to abortion has been the most contested site for women's claims to reproductive autonomy. As noted in the prior section, the legal regulation of abortion began in earnest in the nineteenth century. Physicians advocated the criminalization of abortion using arguments that related not only to protecting potential life, but also to ensuring women's performance of marital and maternal obligations, preserving the ethnic character of the nation, and maintaining the social order.[348] By the 1960s, about 1 million abortions were being performed annually, most of them illegally. Because of their illegality, many abortions were performed under unsafe conditions by unskilled practitioners. Between 1000 and 10,000 individuals, who were disproportionately poor and minority women, died each year from botched abortions. These human costs were a catalyst of reform activity.[349]

While attitudes about abortion were changing in the 1960s and about one-third of states liberalized their statutes, at the time of the Roe v. Wade decision in 1973, half the states still prohibited termination of pregnancy except where necessary to preserve maternal life.[350]

347. For the "market" argument, see Robert K. Vischer, Conscience in Contest: Pharmacist Rights and the Eroding Moral Marketplace, 17 Stan. L. & Pol'y Rev. 83, 119 (2006) (if "moral pluralism is going to mean anything in our society it has to mean something at Walgreen's").

348. Reva Siegel, Reasoning from the Body: A Historical Perspective on Abortion Regulation and Questions of Equal Protection, 44 Stan. L. Rev. 261, 279 (1992).

349. Deborah L. Rhode, Justice and Gender 207 (1989) (citing sources).

350. Id. at 208.

≣ *Roe v. Wade*
≣ **410 U.S. 113 (1973)**

Justice BLACKMUN delivered the opinion of the Court. . . .

[Texas law makes] it a crime to "procure an abortion," as therein defined, or to attempt one, except with respect to "an abortion procured or attempted by medical advice for the purpose of saving the life of the mother." Similar statutes are in existence in a majority of the States. . . .

Three reasons have been advanced to explain historically the enactment of criminal abortion laws in the 19th century and to justify their continued existence.

It has been argued occasionally that these laws were the product of a Victorian social concern to discourage illicit sexual conduct. Texas, however, does not advance this justification in the present case. . . .

A second reason is concerned with abortion as a medical procedure. When most criminal abortion laws were first enacted, the procedure was a hazardous one for the woman. . . . Modern medical techniques have altered this situation. . . .

The third reason is the State's interest—some phrase it in terms of duty—in protecting prenatal life. Some of the argument for this justification rests on the theory that a new human life is present from the moment of conception. The State's interest and general obligation to protect life then extends, it is argued, to prenatal life. . . .

The Constitution does not explicitly mention any right of privacy. In a line of decisions, however going back perhaps as far as [1891], the Court has recognized that a right of personal privacy, or a guarantee of certain areas or zones of privacy, does exist under the Constitution. In varying contexts, the Court or individual Justices have, indeed, found at least the roots of that right in the First Amendment . . . ; in the Fourth and Fifth Amendments . . . ; in the penumbras of the Bill of Rights . . . ; or in the concept of liberty guaranteed by the first section of the Fourteenth Amendment. . . . These decisions make it clear that only personal rights that can be deemed "fundamental" or "implicit in the concept of ordered liberty," . . . are included in this guarantee of personal privacy. They also make it clear that the right has some extension to activities relating to marriage, Loving v. Virginia [1967]; procreation, Skinner v. Oklahoma [1942]; contraception, Eisenstadt v. Baird [1972]; family relationships, Prince v. Massachusetts [1944]; and child rearing and education, Pierce v. Society of Sisters [1925], Meyer v. Nebraska [1923].

This right of privacy, whether it be founded in the Fourteenth Amendment's concept of personal liberty and restrictions upon state action, as we feel it is, or, as the District Court determined, in the Ninth Amendment's reservation of rights to the people, is broad enough to encompass a woman's decision whether or not to terminate her pregnancy. The detriment that the State would impose upon the pregnant woman by denying this choice altogether is apparent. Specific and direct harm medically diagnosable even in early pregnancy may be involved. Maternity, or additional offspring, may force upon the woman a distressful life and future. Psychological harm may be imminent. Mental and physical health may be taxed by child care. There is also the distress, for all concerned, associated with the unwanted child, and there is the problem of bringing a child into a family already unable, psychologically and otherwise, to care for it. In other cases, as in this one, the additional difficulties and continuing stigma of unwed motherhood may be involved. All these are factors the woman and her responsible physician necessarily will consider in consultation. . . .

We, therefore, conclude that the right of personal privacy includes the abortion decision, but that this right is not unqualified and must be considered against important state interests in regulation . . .

The appellee and certain *amici* argue that the fetus is a "person" within the language and meaning of the Fourteenth Amendment. In support of this, they outline at length and in detail the well-known facts of fetal development. If this suggestion of personhood is established, the appellant's case, of course, collapses, for the fetus' right to life would then be guaranteed specifically by the Amendment. . . .

The Constitution does not define "person" in so many words. Section 1 of the Fourteenth Amendment contains three references to "person." . . . None indicates, with any assurance, that it has any possible pre-natal application.

All this, together with our observation . . . that throughout the major portion of the 19th century prevailing legal abortion practices were far freer than they are today, persuades us that the word "person," as used in the Fourteenth Amendment, does not include the unborn. . . .

. . . We need not resolve the difficult question of when life begins. When those trained in the respective disciplines of medicine, philosophy, and theology are unable to arrive at any consensus, the judiciary, in the development of man's knowledge, is not in a position to speculate as to the answer. . . .

[W]e do not agree that, by adopting one theory of life, Texas may override the rights of the pregnant woman that are at stake. [The State does, however,] does have an important and legitimate interest in preserving and protecting the health of the pregnant woman, whether she be a resident of the State or a nonresident who seeks medical consultation and treatment there, and [it] has still *another* important and legitimate interest in protecting the potentiality of human life. These interests are separate and distinct. Each grows in substantiality as the woman approaches term and, at a point during pregnancy, each becomes "compelling."

With respect to the State's important and legitimate interest in the health of the mother, the "compelling" point, in the light of present medical knowledge, is at approximately the end of the first trimester. This is so because of the now-established medical fact . . . that until the end of the first trimester mortality in abortion may be less than mortality in normal childbirth. It follows that, from and after this point, a State may regulate the abortion procedure to the extent that the regulation reasonably relates to the preservation and protection of maternal health. Examples of permissible state regulation in this area are requirements as to the qualifications of the person who is to perform the abortion[,] . . . the facility in which the procedure is to be performed, and the like.

This means, on the other hand, that, for the period of pregnancy prior to this "compelling" point, the attending physician, in consultation with his patient, is free to determine, without regulation by the State, that, in his medical judgment, the patient's pregnancy should be terminated. If that decision is reached, the judgment may be effectuated by an abortion free of interference by the State.

With respect to the State's important and legitimate interest in potential life, the "compelling" point is at viability. This is so because the fetus then presumably has the capability of meaningful life outside the mother's womb. State regulation protective of fetal life after viability thus has both logical and biological justifications. If the State is interested in protecting fetal life after viability, it may go so far as to proscribe abortion during that period, except when it is necessary to preserve the life or health of the mother.

Measured against these standards, [Texas law], in restricting legal abortions to those "procured or attempted by medical advice for the purpose of saving the life of the mother," sweeps too broadly. The statute makes no distinction between abortions performed early in pregnancy and those performed later, and it limits to a single reason, "saving" the mother's life, the legal justification for the procedure. The statute, therefore, cannot survive the constitutional attack made upon it here. . . .

Planned Parenthood of Southeastern Pennsylvania v. Casey
505 U.S. 833 (1992)

Justice O'CONNOR, Justice KENNEDY, and Justice SOUTER announced the judgment of the Court and delivered the opinion of the Court [with Justice BLACKMUN and Justice STEVENS joining in certain parts of the opinion].

I

Liberty finds no refuge in a jurisprudence of doubt. Yet 19 years after our holding that the Constitution protects a woman's right to terminate her pregnancy in its early stages, Roe v. Wade [1973], that definition of liberty is still questioned. Joining the respondents as amicus curiae, the United States, as it has done in five other cases in the last decade, again asks us to overrule *Roe.* . . .

II . . .

[T]he reservations any of us may have in reaffirming the central holding of *Roe* are outweighed by the explication of individual liberty we have given combined with the force of *stare decisis*. . . .

. . . [F]or two decades of economic and social developments, people have organized intimate relationships and made choices that define their views of themselves and their places in society, in reliance on the availability of abortion in the event that contraception should fail. The ability of women to participate equally in the economic and social life of the Nation has been facilitated by their ability to control their reproductive lives. The Constitution serves human values, and while the effect of reliance on *Roe* cannot be exactly measured, neither can the certain cost of overruling *Roe* for people who have ordered their thinking and living around that case be dismissed. . . .

IV . . .

The trimester framework no doubt was erected to ensure that the woman's right to choose not become so subordinate to the State's interest in promoting fetal life that her choice exists in theory but not in fact. We do not agree, however, that the trimester approach is necessary to accomplish this objective. A framework of this rigidity was unnecessary and in its later interpretation sometimes contradicted the State's permissible exercise of its powers.

Though the woman has a right to choose to terminate or continue her pregnancy before viability, it does not at all follow that the State is prohibited from taking steps to ensure that this choice is thoughtful and informed. Even in the earliest stages of pregnancy, the State may enact rules and regulations designed to encourage her to know that there are philosophic and social arguments of great weight that can be brought to bear in favor of continuing the pregnancy to full term and that there are procedures and institutions to allow adoption of unwanted children as well as a certain degree of state assistance if the mother chooses to raise the child herself. "[T]he Constitution does not forbid a State or city, pursuant to democratic processes, from expressing a preference for 'normal childbirth.'" . . . It follows that States are free to enact laws to provide a reasonable framework for a woman to make a decision that has such profound and lasting meaning. This, too, we find consistent with *Roe*'s central premises, and indeed the inevitable consequence of our holding that the State has an interest in protecting the life of the unborn. . . .

Numerous forms of state regulation might have the incidental effect of increasing the cost or decreasing the availability of medical care, whether for abortion or any other medical procedure. The fact that a law which serves a valid purpose, one not designed to strike at the right itself, has the incidental effect of making it more difficult or more expensive to procure an abortion cannot be enough to invalidate it. Only where state regulation imposes an undue burden on a woman's ability to make this decision does the power of the State reach into the heart of the liberty protected by the Due Process Clause. . . .

A finding of an undue burden is a shorthand for the conclusion that a state regulation has the purpose or effect of placing a substantial obstacle in the path of a woman seeking an abortion of a nonviable fetus. A statute with this purpose is invalid because the means chosen by the State to further the interest in potential life must be calculated to inform the woman's free choice, not hinder it. . . .

Some guiding principles should emerge. What is at stake is the woman's right to make the ultimate decision, not a right to be insulated from all others in doing so. Regulations which do no more than create a structural mechanism by which the State, or the parent or guardian of a minor, may express profound respect for the life of the unborn are permitted, if they are not a substantial obstacle to the woman's exercise of the right to choose. . . . Unless it has that effect on her right of choice, a state measure designed to persuade her to choose childbirth over abortion will be upheld if reasonably related to that goal. Regulations designed to foster the health of a woman seeking an abortion are valid if they do not constitute an undue burden. . . .

These principles control our assessment of the Pennsylvania [Abortion Control Act of 1982], and we now turn to the issue of the validity of its challenged provisions.

V . . .

Except in a medical emergency, the statute requires that at least 24 hours before performing an abortion a physician inform the woman of the nature of the procedure, the health risks of the abortion and of childbirth, and the "probable gestational age of the unborn child." The physician or a qualified nonphysician must inform the woman of the availability of printed materials published by the State describing the fetus and providing information about medical assistance for childbirth, information about child support from the father, and a list of agencies which provide adoption and other services as alternatives to abortion. An abortion may not be performed unless the woman certifies in writing that she has been informed of the availability of these printed materials and has been provided them if she chooses to view them. . . .

To the extent [two prior Supreme Court cases] find a constitutional violation when the government requires, as it does here, the giving of truthful, nonmisleading information about the nature of the procedure, the attendant health risks and those of childbirth, and the "probable gestational age" of the fetus, those cases go too far, are inconsistent with *Roe*'s acknowledgment of an important interest in potential life, and are overruled. . . . It cannot be questioned that psychological well-being is a facet of health. Nor can it be doubted that most women considering an abortion would deem the impact on the fetus relevant, if not dispositive, to the decision. In attempting to ensure that a woman apprehend the full consequences of her decision, the State furthers the legitimate purpose of reducing the risk that a woman may elect an abortion, only to discover later, with devastating psychological consequences, that her decision was not fully informed. If the information the State requires to be made available to the woman is truthful and not misleading, the requirement may be permissible.

We also see no reason why the State may not require doctors to inform a woman seeking an abortion of the availability of materials relating to the consequences to the fetus, even when those consequences have no direct relation to her health. An example illustrates the point. We would think it constitutional for the State to require that in order for there to be informed consent to a kidney transplant operation the recipient must be supplied with information about risks to the donor as well as risks to himself or herself. . . .

The idea that important decisions will be more informed and deliberate if they follow some period of reflection does not strike us as unreasonable, particularly where the statute directs that important information become part of the background of the decision. The statute, as construed by the Court of Appeals, permits avoidance of the waiting period in the event of a medical emergency and the record evidence shows that in the vast majority of cases, a 24-hour delay does not create any appreciable health risk. In theory, at least, the waiting period is a reasonable measure to implement the State's interest in protecting the life of the unborn, a measure that does not amount to an undue burden.

Whether the mandatory 24-hour waiting period is nonetheless invalid because in practice it is a substantial obstacle to a woman's choice to terminate her pregnancy is a closer question. The findings of fact by the District Court indicate that because of the distances many women must travel to reach an abortion provider, the practical effect will often be a delay of much more than a day because the waiting period requires that a woman seeking an abortion make at least two visits to the doctor. The District Court also found that in many instances this will increase the exposure of women seeking abortions to "the harassment and hostility of anti-abortion protestors demonstrating outside a clinic." . . . As a result, the District Court found that for those women who have the fewest financial resources, those who must travel long distances, and those who have difficulty explaining their whereabouts to husbands, employers, or others, the 24-hour waiting period will be "particularly burdensome."

These findings are troubling in some respects, but they do not demonstrate that the waiting period constitutes an undue burden. We do not doubt that, as the District Court held, the waiting period has the effect of "increasing the cost and risk of delay of abortions," but the District Court did not conclude that the increased costs and potential delays amount to substantial obstacles. . . .

[One provision] of Pennsylvania's abortion law provides, except in cases of medical emergency, that no physician shall perform an abortion on a married woman without receiving a signed statement from the woman that she has notified her spouse that she is about to undergo an abortion. The woman has the option of providing an alternative signed statement certifying that her husband is not the man who impregnated her; that her husband could not be located; that the pregnancy is the result of spousal sexual assault which she has reported; or that the woman believes that notifying her husband will cause him or someone else to inflict bodily injury upon her. A physician who performs an abortion on a married woman without receiving the appropriate signed statement will have his or her license revoked, and is liable to the husband for damages.

[The District Court found that the reasons some women do not consult their husbands about the decision to obtain an abortion include domestic violence, sexual abuse, rape, and sexual mutilation.] . . .

[T]he District Court's findings reinforce what common sense would suggest. In well-functioning marriages, spouses discuss important intimate decisions such as whether to bear a child. But there are millions of women in this country who are the victims of regular physical and psychological abuse at the hands of their husbands. Should these women become pregnant, they may have very good reasons for not wishing to inform their husbands of their decision to obtain an abortion. Many may have justifiable fears of physical abuse, but may be no less fearful of the consequences of reporting prior abuse to the Commonwealth of Pennsylvania. Many may have a reasonable fear that notifying their husbands will provoke further instances of child abuse; these women are not exempt from [the] notification requirement. Many may fear devastating forms of psychological abuse from their husbands, including verbal harassment, threats of future violence, the destruction of possessions, physical confinement to the home, the withdrawal of financial support, or the disclosure of the abortion to family and friends. These methods of psychological abuse may act as even more of a deterrent to notification than the possibility of physical violence, but women who are the victims of the abuse are not exempt from [the] notification requirement. And many women who are pregnant as a result of sexual assaults by their husbands will be unable to avail themselves of the exception for spousal sexual assault, because the exception requires that the woman have notified law enforcement authorities within 90 days of the assault, and her husband will be notified of her report once an investigation begins. If anything in this field is certain, it is that victims of spousal sexual assault are extremely reluctant to report the abuse to the government; hence, a great many spousal rape victims will not be exempt from the notification requirement. . . .

The spousal notification requirement is thus likely to prevent a significant number of women from obtaining an abortion. It does not merely make abortions a little more difficult or expensive to obtain; for many women, it will impose a substantial obstacle. We must not blind ourselves to the fact that the significant number of women who fear for their safety and the safety of their children are likely to be deterred from procuring an abortion as surely as if the Commonwealth had outlawed abortion in all cases. . . .

This conclusion is in no way inconsistent with our decisions upholding parental notification or consent requirements. . . . Those enactments, and our judgment that they are constitutional, are based on the quite reasonable assumption that minors will benefit from consultation with their parents and that children will often not realize that their parents have their best interests at heart. We cannot adopt a parallel assumption about adult women.

We recognize that a husband has a "deep and proper concern and interest . . . in his wife's pregnancy and in the growth and development of the fetus she is carrying." . . . With regard to the children he has fathered and raised, the Court has recognized his "cognizable and substantial" interest in their custody. . . . If this case concerned a State's ability to require the mother to notify the father before taking some action with respect to a living child raised by both, therefore, it would be reasonable to conclude as a general matter that the father's interest in the welfare of the child and the mother's interest are equal.

Before birth, however, the issue takes on a very different cast. It is an inescapable biological fact that state regulation with respect to the child a woman is carrying will have a far greater impact on the mother's liberty than on the father's. The effect of state regulation on a woman's protected liberty is doubly deserving of scrutiny in such a case, as the State has touched not only upon the private sphere of the family but upon the very bodily integrity of the pregnant woman. . . . The Court has held that "when the wife and the husband disagree on this decision, the view of only one of the two marriage partners can prevail. Inasmuch as it is the woman who physically bears the child and who is the more directly and immediately affected by the pregnancy, as between the two, the balance weighs in her favor." . . .

Women do not lose their constitutionally protected liberty when they marry. The Constitution protects all individuals, male or female, married or unmarried, from the abuse of governmental power, even where that power is employed for the supposed benefit of a member of the individual's family. These considerations confirm our conclusion that [the spousal notification provision] is invalid.

[The Court also upheld a provision requiring consent to an abortion, except in a medical emergency, for an unemancipated minor under 18, unless the court determines that she is mature and capable of giving informed consent, or that an abortion would be in her best interests.]

Justice BLACKMUN, concurring in part, concurring in the judgment in part, and dissenting in part. . . .

State restrictions on abortion violate a woman's right of privacy. . . .

A State's restrictions on a woman's right to terminate her pregnancy also implicate constitutional guarantees of gender equality. State restrictions on abortion compel women to continue pregnancies they otherwise might terminate. By restricting the right to terminate pregnancies, the State conscripts women's bodies into its service, forcing women to continue their pregnancies, suffer the pains of childbirth, and in most instances, provide years of maternal care. The State does not compensate women for their services; instead, it assumes that they owe this duty as a matter of course. This assumption—that women can simply be forced to accept the "natural" status and incidents of motherhood—appears to rest upon a conception of women's role that has triggered the protection of the Equal Protection Clause. See, e.g., Mississippi Univ. for Women v. Hogan [1982]; Craig v. Boren [1976]. The joint opinion recognizes that these assumptions about women's place in society "are no longer consistent with our understanding of the family, the individual, or the Constitution." . . .

Justice SCALIA, with whom THE CHIEF JUSTICE, Justice WHITE, and Justice THOMAS join, concurring in the judgment in part and dissenting in part. . . .

The States may, if they wish, permit abortion-on-demand, but the Constitution does not require them to do so. The permissibility of abortion, and the limitations upon it, are to be resolved like most important questions in our democracy: by citizens trying to persuade one another and then voting. . . .

That is, quite simply, the issue in this case: not whether the power of a woman to abort her unborn child is a "liberty" in the absolute sense; or even whether it is a liberty of great importance to many women. Of course it is both. The issue is whether it is a liberty protected by the Constitution of the United States. I am sure it is not. I reach that conclusion not because of anything so exalted as my views concerning the "concept of existence, of meaning, of the universe, and of the mystery of human life." . . . Rather, I reach it for the same reason I reach the conclusion that bigamy is not constitutionally protected—because of two simple facts: (1) the Constitution says absolutely nothing about it, and (2) the longstanding traditions of American society have permitted it to be legally proscribed. . . .

In truth, I am as distressed as the Court is . . . about the "political pressure" directed to the Court: the marches, the mail, the protests aimed at inducing us to change our opinions. How upsetting it is, that so many of our citizens (good people, not lawless ones, on both sides of this abortion issue, and on various sides of other issues as well) think that we Justices should properly take into account their views, as though we were engaged not in ascertaining an objective law but in determining some kind of social consensus. The Court would profit, I think, from giving less attention to the fact of this distressing phenomenon, and more attention to the *cause* of it. That cause permeates today's opinion: a new mode of constitutional adjudication that relies not upon text and traditional practice to determine the law, but upon what the Court calls "reasoned judgment," . . . which turns out to be nothing but philosophical predilection and moral intuition. . . .

As long as this Court thought (and the people thought) that we Justices were doing essentially lawyers' work up here — reading text and discerning our society's traditional understanding of that text — the public pretty much left us alone. Texts and traditions are facts to study, not convictions to demonstrate about. But if in reality our process of constitutional adjudication consists primarily of making *value judgments* . . . then a free and intelligent people's attitude towards us can be expected to be (*ought* to be) quite different. The people know that their value judgments are quite as good as those taught in any law school — maybe better. If, indeed, the "liberties" protected by the Constitution are, as the Court says, undefined and unbounded, than the people *should* demonstrate, to protest that we do not implement their values instead of *ours*. . . .

We should get out of this area, where we have no right to be, and where we do neither ourselves nor the country any good by remaining.

Reva Siegel, Reasoning from the Body: A Historical Perspective on Abortion Regulation and Questions of Equal Protection
44 Stan. L. Rev. 261, 267, 361-63, 370 (1992)

Social forces play a powerful part in shaping the process of reproduction. Social forces define the circumstances under which a woman conceives a child, including how voluntary her participation in intercourse may be. Social forces determine whether a woman has access to methods of preventing and terminating a pregnancy, and whether it is acceptable for her to use them. Social forces determine the quality of health care available to a woman during pregnancy, and they determine whether a pregnant woman will be able to support herself throughout the term of gestation, or instead will be forced to depend on others for support. Social relations determine who cares for a child once it is born, and what resources, rewards, and penalties attend the work of gestating and nurturing human life. . . .

[T]oday, as in the nineteenth century, legislators enacting restrictions on abortion may act from judgments about the sexual and maternal conduct of the women they are regulating, and not merely from a concern about the welfare of the unborn. Legislators may condemn abortion because they assume that any pregnant woman who does not wish to be pregnant has committed some sexual indiscretion properly punishable by compelling pregnancy itself. Popular support for excusing women who are victims of rape or incest from the proscriptions of criminal abortion laws demonstrates that attitudes about abortion do indeed rest on normative judgments about women's sexual conduct. Opinion polls like Louisiana's suggest that the public assumes a woman can be coerced into continuing a pregnancy because the pregnancy is her sexual "fault."

Along distinct, but related lines, legislators may view abortion as repellant because it betrays a lack of maternal solicitude in women, or otherwise violates expectations of appropriately nurturing female conduct. If legislators assume that women are "child-rearers," they will take for granted the work women give to motherhood and ignore what it takes from them, and so will view women's efforts to avoid some two decades of life-consuming work as an act of casual expedience or unseemly egoism. Thus, they will condemn women for seeking abortion "on demand," or as a mere "convenience," judging women to be unnaturally egocentric because they do not give their lives over to the work of bearing and nurturing children—that is, because they fail to act like mothers, like normal women should. . . .

Even if state actors have adopted restrictions on abortion out of a genuine and single-minded concern for the welfare of the unborn, archaic or stereotypical assumptions about women may nonetheless deeply bias their deliberations, making fetal life-saving by compelled pregnancy seem reasonable where otherwise it would not. A legislature's attitudes about women may cause it to underestimate or disregard the burdens it would impose on them by compelling pregnancy. A latent assumption that motherhood is women's "normal" condition can easily render state actors oblivious to the life-consuming consequences of forcing women to perform its work—just as a latent assumption that motherhood is women's "deserved" condition will cause indifference to the burdens the legislation will inflict. In short, a legislature may not decide that it is reasonable to save unborn life by compelling pregnancy, "but for" the archaic or stereotypic assumptions about women it holds. If restrictions on abortion are adopted in these circumstances, they offend constitutional guarantees of equal protection. . . .

[S]tate action restricting abortion injures women. . . . First, restrictions on abortion do not merely force women to bear children; powerful gender norms in this society ensure that almost all women who are forced to bear children will raise them as well, a result that legislatures adopting restrictions on abortion both desire and expect. Second, the work legislatures would force women to perform defines women's social status along predictable, gender-delineated lines. Women who perform the socially essential labor of bearing and rearing children face diverse forms of stigmatization and injury, none of which is ordained by the physiology of gestation, and all of which is the doing of the society that would force women to bear children. Third, when states adopt restrictions on abortion, they compel women to become mothers, while in no respect altering the conditions that make the institution of motherhood a principal cause of women's subordinate social status. When the gender-based impositions of abortion-restrictive regulation are considered in light of the forms of gender bias that may animate it, it is clear abortion-restrictive regulation is and remains caste legislation which subordinates women in ways that offend constitutional guarantees of equal protection. . . .

Robin West, The Supreme Court 1989 Term, Foreword: Taking Freedom Seriously
104 Harv. L. Rev. 43, 82-85 (1990)

From a postdemocratic liberal perspective, support for reproductive freedom—like all freedom—should rest on the demonstrated capacity of pregnant women to decide whether to carry a fetus to term or to abort responsibly. Correlatively, support for expanded reproductive freedom should rest on the claim that only by accepting the responsibility to make these judgments do women manifest their freedom to pursue their authentically chosen and desired life goals. . . . [W]hat a rights-focused liberalism obscures is that the meaningful distinction between murder and abortion is not in the nominal and question-begging difference between a "fetus" and a "baby," but rather in the moral quality of the underlying decision that liberal legalism insulates from scrutiny. Unlike the homicidal decision to take another's life, the decision to abort is more often than not a morally responsible decision. The abortion decision typically rests not on a desire to destroy fetal life but on a responsible and moral desire to ensure that a new life will be borne only if it will be nurtured and loved. . . .

[While there are risks to basing reproductive freedom on responsibility, a] failure to rest reproductive freedom on a theory of responsibilities may ensure the complete erosion of the right. . . . The Court's manifest ambivalence over the constitutional status of the right to privacy that undergirds reproductive freedom has compromised the persuasiveness of the appeal to rights and constitutional authority that has to date characterized the pro-choice movement. Pro-choice groups consequently must turn their attention away from courts and to the legislatures and the public who will increasingly be responsible for either protecting or obliterating this individual liberty. As the audience of the "pro-choice/pro-life" debate shifts away from courts and to legislatures, it may be prudent—whether or not philosophically wise—to focus attention on reproductive responsibility as well as on reproductive rights. If the premise of the rights-based argument—a Court willing to guard the individual liberty protected by the right against even well-intended state infringement—ceases to exist, the argument must change. Liberals and feminists must develop alternative, public-regarding arguments supporting those rights and the liberty they protect that transcend the circular and increasingly false insistence that they simply exist.

Minimally, a responsibility-based argument for reproductive freedom that would justify rather than supplant the rights-based claim of Roe v. Wade would more accurately correspond to the experience of women. Women need the freedom to make reproductive decisions not merely to vindicate a right to be left alone but often to strengthen their ties to others: to plan responsibly and have a family for which they can provide, to pursue professional or work commitments made to the outside world, or to continue supporting their families or communities. At other times the decision to abort is necessitated not by a murderous urge to end life, but by the harsh reality of a financially irresponsible partner, a society indifferent to the care of children, and a workplace incapable of accommodating or supporting the needs of working parents. At many other times the need to abort follows directly from a violent sexual assault. When made for any of these reasons, the decision to abort is not one made in an egoistic private vacuum. Whatever the reason, the decision to abort is almost invariably made within a web of interlocking, competing, and often irreconcilable responsibilities and commitments.

By focusing on the moral quality of reproductive decisions rather than insulating them from understanding, liberals could redirect societal attention toward this web of shared responsibilities and societal failures. We might then begin to recognize that we have a collective responsibility to address the variable causes that result in unwanted pregnancies, from the pervasive acceptance of sexual violence in our culture to our collective refusal to provide meaningful material assistance for the nurturing of children and families. Whatever the fate of *Roe*, widespread understanding of the moral nature of the abortion decision, the profound sense of responsibility that often accompanies it, and the societal failure to assume responsibility for the causes and effects of unwanted pregnancy, childbirth, and motherhood would strengthen, not weaken, the case for abortion rights and the freedoms those rights ought to protect. Without a Court willing to protect those rights in the face of societal opposition, however, that understanding may be necessary to the liberty's very existence.

 ### *Gonzales v. Carhart*
550 U.S. 124 (2007)

Justice KENNEDY delivered the opinion of the Court.

These cases require us to consider the validity of the Partial-Birth Abortion Ban Act of 2003 (Act), a federal statute regulating abortion procedures. [The Act is more specific and precise than the Act addressed in Stenberg v. Carhart (2000), which the Court found to be unconstitutional.] . . .

The operative provisions of the Act provide in relevant part:

(a) Any physician who, in or affecting interstate or foreign commerce, knowingly performs a partial-birth abortion and thereby kills a human fetus shall be fined under this title or imprisoned not more than 2 years, or both. This subsection does not apply to a partial-birth abortion that is necessary to save the life of a mother whose life is endangered by a physical disorder, physical illness, or physical injury, including a life-endangering physical condition caused by or arising from the pregnancy itself. This subsection takes effect 1 day after the enactment.

(b) As used in this section —

(1) the term "partial-birth abortion" means an abortion in which the person performing the abortion —

(A) deliberately and intentionally vaginally delivers a living fetus until, in the case of a head-first presentation, the entire fetal head is outside the body of the mother, or, in the case of breech presentation, any part of the fetal trunk past the navel is outside the body of the mother, for the purpose of performing an overt act that the person knows will kill the partially delivered living fetus; and

(B) performs the overt act, other than completion of delivery, that kills the partially delivered living fetus. . . .

[The District Courts in these two cases each found the Act to be unconstitutional, one because it lacked an exception where necessary for the health of the mother and because it covered not merely intact D&E but also certain other D&Es, and the other because it imposed an undue burden on a woman's ability to choose a second-trimester abortion, was unconstitutionally vague, and lacked a health exception. The decisions were upheld on appeal.] . . .

The Act proscribes a method of abortion in which a fetus is killed just inches before completion of the birth process. Congress stated as follows: "Implicitly approving such a brutal and inhumane procedure by choosing not to prohibit it will further coarsen society to the humanity of not only newborns, but all vulnerable and innocent human life, making it increasingly difficult to protect such life." . . .

The Act's ban on abortions that involve partial delivery of a living fetus furthers the Government's objectives. No one would dispute that, for many, D&E is a procedure itself laden with the power to devalue human life. . . .

Respect for human life finds an ultimate expression in the bond of love the mother has for her child. The Act recognizes this reality as well. Whether to have an abortion requires a difficult and painful moral decision. . . . While we find no reliable data to measure the phenomenon, it seems unexceptionable to conclude some women come to regret their choice to abort the infant life they once created and sustained. . . . Severe depression and loss of esteem can follow. . . .

In a decision so fraught with emotional consequence some doctors may prefer not to disclose precise details of the means that will be used, confining themselves to the required statement of risks the procedure entails. From one standpoint this ought not to be surprising. Any number of patients facing imminent surgical procedures would prefer not to hear all details, lest the usual anxiety preceding invasive medical procedures become the more intense. This is likely the case with the abortion procedures here in issue. . . .

It is, however, precisely this lack of information concerning the way in which the fetus will be killed that is of legitimate concern to the State. . . . The State has an interest in ensuring so grave a choice is well informed. It is self-evident that a mother who comes to regret her choice to abort must struggle with grief more anguished and sorrow more profound when she learns, only after the event, what she once did not know: that she allowed a doctor to pierce the skull and vacuum the fast-developing brain of her unborn child, a child assuming the human form.

It is a reasonable inference that a necessary effect of the regulation and the knowledge it conveys will be to encourage some women to carry the infant to full term, thus reducing the absolute number of late-term abortions. The medical profession, furthermore, may find different and less shocking methods to abort the fetus in the second trimester, thereby accommodating legislative demand. The State's interest in respect for life is advanced by the dialogue that better informs the political and legal systems, the medical profession, expectant mothers, and society as a whole of the consequences that follow from a decision to elect a late-term abortion.

It is objected that the standard D&E is in some respects as brutal, if not more, than the intact D&E, so that the legislation accomplishes little. What we have already said, however, shows ample justification for the regulation. Partial-birth abortion, as defined by the Act, differs from a standard D&E because the former occurs when the fetus is partially outside the mother to the point of one of the Act's anatomical landmarks. It was reasonable for Congress to think that partial-birth abortion, more than standard D&E, "undermines the public's perception of the appropriate role of a physician during the delivery process, and perverts a process during which life is brought into the world." . . .

The Act's furtherance of legitimate government interests bears upon, but does not resolve, the next question: whether the Act has the effect of imposing an unconstitutional burden on the abortion right because it does not allow use of the barred procedure where " 'necessary, in appropriate medical judgment, for [the] preservation of the . . . health of the mother.' " . . . The prohibition in the Act would be unconstitutional, under precedents we here assume to be controlling, if it "subject[ed] [women] to significant health risks." . . . The evidence presented in the trial courts and before Congress demonstrates both sides have medical support for their position.

Respondents presented evidence that intact D&E may be the safest method of abortion. . . . Respondents, in addition, proffered evidence that intact D&E was safer for women with certain medical conditions or women with fetuses that had certain anomalies. . . .

The Court has given state and federal legislatures wide discretion to pass legislation in areas where there is medical and scientific uncertainty. . . . Considerations of marginal safety, including the balance of risks, are within the legislative competence when the regulation is rational and in pursuit of legitimate ends. When standard medical options are available, mere convenience does not suffice to displace them; and if some procedures have different risks than others, it does not follow that the State is altogether barred from imposing reasonable regulations. The Act is not invalid on its face where there is uncertainty over whether the barred procedure is ever necessary to preserve a woman's health, given the availability of other abortion procedures that are considered to be safe alternatives. . . .

[T]he judgments of the Courts of Appeals are reversed.

Justice GINSBURG, with whom Justice STEVENS, Justice SOUTER, and Justice BREYER join, dissenting. . . .

Seven years ago, in *Stenberg* v. *Carhart*, . . . the Court invalidated a Nebraska statute criminalizing the performance of a medical procedure that, in the political arena, has been dubbed "partial-birth abortion." With fidelity to the *Roe-Casey* line of precedent, the Court held the Nebraska statute unconstitutional in part because it lacked the requisite protection for the preservation of a woman's health.

Today's decision is alarming. It refuses to take *Casey* and *Stenberg* seriously. It tolerates, indeed applauds, federal intervention to ban nationwide a procedure found necessary and proper in certain cases by the American College of Obstetricians and Gynecologists (ACOG). It blurs the line, firmly drawn in *Casey,* between previability and postviability abortions. And, for the first time since *Roe*, the Court blesses a prohibition with no exception safeguarding a woman's health. . . .

I

As *Casey* comprehended, at stake in cases challenging abortion restrictions is a woman's "control over her [own] destiny." . . . "There was a time, not so long ago," when women were "regarded as the center of home and family life, with attendant special responsibilities that precluded full and independent legal status under the Constitution." . . . Those views, this Court made clear in *Casey*, "are no longer consistent with our understanding of the family, the individual, or the Constitution." . . . Women, it is now acknowledged, have the talent, capacity, and right "to participate equally in the economic and social life of the Nation." Their ability to realize their full potential, the Court recognized, is intimately connected to "their ability to control their reproductive lives." . . . Thus, legal challenges to undue restrictions on abortion procedures do not seek to vindicate some generalized notion of privacy;

rather, they center on a woman's autonomy to determine her life's course, and thus to enjoy equal citizenship stature. . . .

In keeping with this comprehension of the right to reproductive choice, the Court has consistently required that laws regulating abortion, at any stage of pregnancy and in all cases, safeguard a woman's health. . . .

In *Stenberg*, we expressly held that a statute banning intact D&E was unconstitutional in part because it lacked a health exception. . . . We noted that there existed a "division of medical opinion" about the relative safety of intact D&E, . . . but we made clear that as long as "substantial medical authority supports the proposition that banning a particular abortion procedure could endanger women's health," a health exception is required. . . .

In 2003, a few years after our ruling in *Stenberg*, Congress passed the Partial-Birth Abortion Ban Act—without an exception for women's health. . . . The congressional findings on which the Partial-Birth Abortion Ban Act rests do not withstand inspection, as the lower courts have determined and this Court is obliged to concede. . . .

Many of the Act's recitations are incorrect. . . . For example, Congress determined that no medical schools provide instruction on intact D&E. . . . But in fact, numerous leading medical schools teach the procedure. . . .

More important, Congress claimed there was a medical consensus that the banned procedure is never necessary. . . . But the evidence "very clearly demonstrate[d] the opposite." . . .

Similarly, Congress found that "[t]here is no credible medical evidence that partial-birth abortions are safe or are safer than other abortion procedures." . . . But the congressional record includes letters from numerous individual physicians stating that pregnant women's health would be jeopardized under the Act, as well as statements from nine professional associations, including ACOG, the American Public Health Association, and the California Medical Association, attesting that intact D&E carries meaningful safety advantages over other methods. . . . No comparable medical groups supported the ban. In fact, "all of the government's own witnesses disagreed with many of the specific congressional findings."

In contrast to Congress, the District Courts made findings after full trials at which all parties had the opportunity to present their best evidence. The courts had the benefit of "much more extensive medical and scientific evidence . . . concerning the safety and necessity of intact D&Es." . . .

During the District Court trials, "numerous" "extraordinarily accomplished" and "very experienced" medical experts explained that, in certain circumstances and for certain women, intact D&E is safer than alternative procedures and necessary to protect women's health. . . .

According to the expert testimony plaintiffs introduced, the safety advantages of intact D&E are marked for women with certain medical conditions, for example, uterine scarring, bleeding disorders, heart disease, or compromised immune systems. . . . Further, plaintiffs' experts testified that intact D&E is significantly safer for women with certain pregnancy-related conditions, such as placenta previa and accreta, and for women carrying fetuses with certain abnormalities, such as severe hydrocephalus. . . .

Intact D&E, plaintiffs' experts explained, provides safety benefits over D&E by dismemberment for several reasons: *First,* intact D&E minimizes the number of times a physician must insert instruments through the cervix and into the uterus, and thereby reduces the risk of trauma to, and perforation of, the cervix and uterus—the most serious complication associated with nonintact D&E. . . . *Second,* removing the fetus intact, instead of dismembering it *in utero,* decreases the likelihood that fetal tissue will be retained in the uterus, a condition that can cause infection, hemorrhage, and infertility. . . . *Third,* intact D&E diminishes the chances of exposing the patient's tissues to sharp bony fragments sometimes resulting from dismemberment of the fetus. . . . *Fourth,* intact D&E takes less operating time than D&E by dismemberment, and thus may reduce bleeding, the risk of infection, and complications relating to anesthesia. . . .

Today's opinion supplies no reason to reject [the District Courts'] findings. Nevertheless, despite the District Courts' appraisal of the weight of the evidence, and in undisguised conflict with *Stenberg,* the Court asserts that the Partial-Birth Abortion Ban Act can survive "when . . . medical uncertainty persists." . . . This assertion is bewildering. Not only does it defy the Court's longstanding precedent affirming the necessity of a health exception, with no carve-out for circumstances of medical uncertainty, . . . it gives short shrift to the records before us, carefully canvassed by the District Courts. . . .

The law saves not a single fetus from destruction, for it targets only a *method* of performing abortion. . . . And surely the statute was not designed to protect the lives or health of pregnant women. . . . In short, the Court upholds a law that, while doing nothing to "preserv[e] . . . fetal life," . . . bars a woman from choosing intact D&E although her doctor "reasonably believes [that procedure] will best protect [her]." . . .

As another reason for upholding the ban, the Court emphasizes that the Act does not proscribe the nonintact D&E procedure. . . . But why not, one might ask. Nonintact D&E could equally be characterized as "brutal," . . . involving as it does "tear[ing] [a fetus] apart" and "ripp[ing] off" its limbs. . . . "[T]he notion that either of these two equally gruesome procedures . . . is more akin to infanticide than the other, or that the State furthers any legitimate interest by banning one but not the other, is simply irrational." . . .

Delivery of an intact, albeit nonviable, fetus warrants special condemnation, the Court maintains, because a fetus that is not dismembered resembles an infant. . . . But so, too, does a fetus delivered intact after it is terminated by injection a day or two before the surgical evacuation, . . . a fetus delivered through medical induction or cesarean. . . . Yet, the availability of those procedures—along with D&E by dismemberment—the Court says, saves the ban on intact D&E from a declaration of unconstitutionality. . . . Never mind that the procedures deemed acceptable might put a woman's health at greater risk. . . .

Ultimately, the Court admits that "moral concerns" are at work, concerns that could yield prohibitions on any abortion. . . . Notably, the concerns expressed are untethered to any ground genuinely serving the Government's interest in preserving life. By allowing such concerns to carry the day and case, overriding fundamental rights, the Court dishonors our precedent. . . .

Revealing in this regard, the Court invokes an antiabortion shibboleth for which it concededly has no reliable evidence: Women who have abortions come to regret their choices, and consequently suffer from "[s]evere depression and loss of esteem." . . . Because of women's fragile emotional state and because of the "bond of love the mother has for her child," the Court worries, doctors may withhold information about the nature of the intact D&E procedure. . . . The solution the Court approves, then, is *not* to require doctors to inform women, accurately and adequately, of the different procedures and their attendant risks. . . . Instead, the Court deprives women of the right to make an autonomous choice, even at the expense of their safety.

This way of thinking reflects ancient notions about women's place in the family and under the Constitution—ideas that have long since been discredited. . . .

One wonders how long a line that saves no fetus from destruction will hold in face of the Court's "moral concerns." . . . The Court's hostility to the right *Roe* and *Casey* secured is not concealed. Throughout, the opinion refers to obstetrician-gynecologists and surgeons who perform abortions not by the titles of their medical specialties, but by the pejorative label "abortion doctor." . . . A fetus is described as an "unborn child," and as a "baby;" . . . second-trimester, previability abortions are referred to as "late-term," . . . and the reasoned medical judgments of highly trained doctors are dismissed as "preferences" motivated by "mere convenience". . . . Instead of the heightened scrutiny we have previously applied, the Court determines that a "rational" ground is enough to uphold the Act. . . . And, most troubling, *Casey*'s principles, confirming the continuing vitality of "the essential holding of *Roe*," are merely "assume[d]" for the moment, . . . rather than "retained" or "reaffirmed". . . .

. . . In candor, the Act, and the Court's defense of it, cannot be understood as anything other than an effort to chip away at a right declared again and again by this Court—and with increasing comprehension of its centrality to women's lives. . . .

Jeannie Suk, The Trajectory of Trauma: Bodies and Minds of Abortion Discourse
110 Colum. L. Rev. 1193-1201 (2010)

The idea of women traumatized by abortion has recently acquired a constitutional foothold. . . . Justice Kennedy, writing for the Court, said it was "unexceptionable to conclude" that some women who have abortions later feel "regret" resulting in "severe depression and loss of esteem." Then he noted that some who undergo the late-term procedure at issue may be unaware of its details (piercing and vacuuming the skull of the fetus before removing its intact body) at the time. Finally, he thought it was "self-evident that a mother who comes to regret her choice to abort must suffer grief more anguished and sorrow more profound when she learns, only after the event, what she once did not know. . . ."

Justice Ginsburg's dissent . . . called the Court's reference to abortion regret "an antiabortion shibboleth" that assumes "women's fragile emotional state." Though she acknowledged that "for most women, abortion is a painfully difficult decision," she pointedly suggested that the weight of scientific authority resisted "post-abortion syndrome"—purportedly a kind of post-traumatic stress disorder. The court's reasoning, she said, "reflects ancient notions about women's place in the family and under the Constitution—ideas that have long since been discredited."

The strong rejoinder to Justice Kennedy's salvo presents this battle of ideas as having a clear, rightful winner: On one side are modern constitutional ideals of right-thinking people heeding scientific evidence; on the other side are retrograde stereotypes supported by ideologically tainted junk science. The supposition is that defenders of abortion rights value the autonomy of women, while those undermining the right reveal latent sexism in depicting women as regretful beings who must be protected from themselves. There is perhaps an understandable desire, in an ideological war, to discredit a line of reasoning that threatens to gain ground. Critics of the notion of women suffering after abortion thus emphasize the connection between today's concern for such emotional pain and age-old sexism. . . .

I argue, however, that rather that representing such a departure, . . . [the Kennedy reasoning] continues a legal discourse of trauma around women's bodies and sexuality. This intellectual context, which has been all but ignored, gives important meaning to the present discourse of women's psychological pain in our legal system. . . .

Variations now abound in legal contexts in which we routinely see claims of psychological disorder arising from traumatic experiences. Battered Woman Syndrome and Rape Trauma Syndrome, for example, have gained acceptance as traumatic disorders considered relevant for some legal purposes. Trauma resulting from violation of the body has been a focus in feminist legal reform, particularly in domestic violence, rape, sex abuse, and sexual harassment. The concern for abortion trauma is a recognizable outgrowth of legal thinking of psychological trauma as a core of women's experience. . . .

Abortion trauma is a notion with which those committed to abortion rights are deeply uncomfortable. To some, the idea that women might suffer from psychological harm that can trace to their abortions may be more alarming than the argument that abortion is murder. If the idea is indeed threatening, it is not merely because it revists old sexism that we all know to be outmoded. Rather it is because it resonates so profoundly with now common legal sensibilities of more recent vintage: feminist visions of women with bodies violated and minds traumatized.

Khiara M. Bridges, When Pregnancy Is an Injury: Rape, Law, and Culture
65 Stan. L. Rev. 457, 457-58 (2013)

In several jurisdictions in the United States, a rapist who causes his victim to become pregnant commits an aggravated sexual assault. Having committed an aggravated crime, he will be subjected to a longer prison sentence relative to his counterpart whose victim does not become pregnant consequent to the rape. . . . That is, *the victim's pregnancy is treated the same as a broken bone, a concussion, or a gunshot wound.* . . . These laws . . . function to construct pregnant as an injury. . . .

In decades past, advocates for the abortion right made their case in the language of injury: unwanted pregnancies were injuries to the women forced to bear them. Abortion figured as a healing modality, serving to heal a woman of her injury. This advocacy never quite made it into abortion jurisprudence. As a consequence, perhaps, the construction of unwanted pregnancy as an injury disappeared from the language of abortion rights activism. However, recent developments in antiabortion argumentation counsel its retrieval. There has been a shift in antiabortion argumentation away from a focus on the fetus and toward a focus on the woman. In this shift, abortion is wrong, not because it harms the fetus, but rather because it harms the pregnant woman. The Court in Gonzales v. Carhart (Carhart II) accepted this position, upholding a law that restricted access to abortion because it seemed "unexceptionable" to conclude that "some women come to regret their choice to abort the infant life they once created and sustained. Severe depression and loss of esteem can follow." Because the Court accepted as true that abortion harms women, it is reasonable to expect that opponents of abortion rights will continue to advocate in this register. In light of this, the incredible significance of constructing unwanted pregnancy as an injury is revealed: unwanted pregnancies *also*, literally, harm women. If true, then women bearing unwanted pregnancies are faced with two injuries—the pregnancy itself and the abortion that would end it. Antiabortion activists, and the Court, would need to articulate a basis for compelling women to remain injured (that is, pregnant) in order to protect them from a harm (that is, abortion). Moreover, if unwanted pregnancy is an injury, then perhaps abortion does not harm women but rather *heals* them. Which is to say, recent developments in antiabortion argumentation counsel the retrieval of the claim that unwanted pregnancies are injuries to women; the sexual assault laws . . . are a means to legitimize this claim.

Whole Woman's Health v. Hellerstedt
579 U.S. __ (2016)

Justice BREYER delivered the opinion of the Court.

. . . We must here decide whether two provisions of Texas' House Bill 2 violate the Federal Constitution as interpreted in *Casey*[: the "admitting-privileges" requirement and "surgical center" requirement.] . . . We conclude that neither of these provisions offers medical benefits sufficient to justify the burdens upon access that each imposes. Each places a substantial obstacle in the path of women seeking a previability abortion, each constitutes an undue burden on abortion access, *Casey,* and each violates the [Fourteenth Amendment of the] Federal Constitution.

I

In July 2013, the Texas Legislature enacted House Bill 2 (H.B. 2 or Act). . . .

On April 6, . . . petitioners, a group of abortion providers . . . filed the present lawsuit. They sought an injunction preventing enforcement of the admitting-privileges provision as applied to physicians at two abortion facilities [in McAllen and El Paso]. . . . They also sought an injunction prohibiting enforcement of the surgical-center provision anywhere in Texas. They claimed that the admitting-privileges provision and the surgical-center provision violated the Constitution's Fourteenth Amendment, as interpreted in *Casey*.

[The District Court granted the injunction and the Court of Appeals reversed on the merits.]

[The Court's discussion of issues relating to the effect of a prior, unsuccessful facial attack against the Act, before the Act went into effect, is omitted.]

III

Undue Burden—Legal Standard

We begin with the standard, as described in *Casey*. We recognize that the "State has a legitimate interest in seeing to it that abortion, like any other medical procedure, is performed under circumstances that insure maximum safety for the patient." But, we added, "a statute which, while furthering [a] valid state interest, has the effect of placing a substantial obstacle in the path of a woman's choice cannot be considered a permissible means of serving its legitimate ends." Moreover, "[u]nnecessary health regulations that have the purpose or effect of presenting a substantial obstacle to a woman seeking an abortion impose an undue burden on the right."

The Court of Appeals wrote that a state law is "constitutional if: (1) it does not have the purpose or effect of placing a substantial obstacle in the path of a woman seeking an abortion of a nonviable fetus; and (2) it is reasonably related to (or designed to further) a legitimate state interest." The Court of Appeals went on to hold that "the district court erred by substituting its own judgment for that of the legislature" when it conducted its "undue burden inquiry," in part because "medical uncertainty underlying a statute is for resolution by legislatures, not the courts."

The Court of Appeals' articulation of the relevant standard is incorrect. The first part of the Court of Appeals' test may be read to imply that a district court should not consider the existence or nonexistence of medical benefits when considering whether a regulation of abortion constitutes an undue burden. The rule announced in *Casey*, however, requires that courts consider the burdens a law imposes on abortion access together with the benefits those laws confer. And the second part of the test is wrong to equate the judicial review applicable to the regulation of a constitutionally protected personal liberty with the less strict review applicable where, for example, economic legislation is at issue. The Court of Appeals' approach simply does not match the standard that this Court laid out in *Casey*, which asks courts to consider whether any burden imposed on abortion access is "undue."

The statement that legislatures, and not courts, must resolve questions of medical uncertainty is also inconsistent with this Court's case law. Instead, the Court, when determining the constitutionality of laws regulating abortion procedures, has placed considerable weight upon evidence and argument presented in judicial proceedings. . . .

[The District Court] considered the evidence in the record—including expert evidence, presented in stipulations, depositions, and testimony. It then weighed the asserted benefits against the burdens. We hold that, in so doing, the District Court applied the correct legal standard.

IV

Undue Burden—Admitting–Privileges Requirement

Turning to the lower courts' evaluation of the evidence, we first consider the admitting-privileges requirement. Before the enactment of H.B. 2, doctors who provided abortions were required to "have admitting privileges *or* have a working arrangement with a physician(s) who has admitting privileges at a local hospital in order to ensure the necessary back up for medical complications." The new law changed this requirement by requiring that a "physician performing or inducing an abortion . . . must, on the date the abortion is performed or induced, have active admitting privileges at a hospital that . . . is located not further than 30 miles from the location at which the abortion is performed or induced." The District Court held that the legislative change imposed an "undue burden" on a woman's right to have an abortion. We conclude that there is adequate legal and factual support for the District Court's conclusion.

The purpose of the admitting-privileges requirement is to help ensure that women have easy access to a hospital should complications arise during an abortion procedure. But the District Court found that it brought about no such health-related benefit. The court found that "[t]he great weight of evidence demonstrates that, before the act's passage, abortion in Texas was extremely safe with particularly low rates of serious complications and virtually no deaths occurring on account of the procedure." Thus, there was no significant health-related problem that the new law helped to cure.

The evidence upon which the court based this conclusion included, among other things:

- A collection of at least five peer-reviewed studies on abortion complications in the first trimester, showing that the highest rate of major complications—including those complications requiring hospital admission—was less than one-quarter of 1%.
- Figures in three peer-reviewed studies showing that the highest complication rate found for the much rarer second trimester abortion was less than one-half of 1% (0.45% or about 1 out of about 200).
- Expert testimony to the effect that complications rarely require hospital admission, much less immediate transfer to a hospital from an outpatient clinic.
- Expert testimony stating that "it is extremely unlikely that a patient will experience a serious complication at the clinic that requires emergent hospitalization" and "in the rare case in which [one does], the quality of care that the patient receives is not affected by whether the abortion provider has admitting privileges at the hospital."
- Expert testimony stating that in respect to surgical abortion patients who do suffer complications requiring hospitalization, most of these complications occur in the days after the abortion, not on the spot.
- Expert testimony stating that a delay before the onset of complications is also expected for medical abortions, as "abortifacient drugs take time to exert their effects, and thus the abortion itself almost always occurs after the patient has left the abortion facility."
- Some experts added that, if a patient needs a hospital in the day or week following her abortion, she will likely seek medical attention at the hospital nearest her home.

We have found nothing in Texas' record evidence that shows that, compared to prior law (which required a "working arrangement" with a doctor with admitting privileges), the new law advanced Texas' legitimate interest in protecting women's health.

We add that, when directly asked at oral argument whether Texas knew of a single instance in which the new requirement would have helped even one woman obtain better treatment, Texas admitted that there was no evidence in the record of such a case. . . .

At the same time, the record evidence indicates that the admitting-privileges requirement places a "substantial obstacle in the path of a woman's choice [citing *Casey*]." The District Court found, as of the time the admitting-privileges requirement began to be enforced, the number of facilities providing abortions dropped in half, from about 40 to about 20. Eight abortion clinics closed in the months leading up to the requirement's effective date. Eleven more closed on the day the admitting-privileges requirement took effect.

Other evidence helps to explain why the new requiement led to the closure of clinics. We read that other evidence in light of a brief filed in this Court by the Society of Hospital Medicine. That brief describes the undisputed general fact that "hospitals often condition admitting privileges on reaching a certain number of admissions per year." Returning to the District Court record, we note that, in direct testimony, the president of Nova Health Systems, implicitly relying on this general fact, pointed out that it would be difficult for doctors regularly performing abortions at the El Paso clinic to obtain admitting privileges at nearby hospitals because "[d]uring the past 10 years, over 17,000 abortion procedures were performed at the El Paso clinic [and n]ot a single one of those patients had to be transferred to a hospital for emergency treatment, much less admitted to the hospital." In a word, doctors would be unable to maintain admitting privileges or obtain those privileges for the future, because the fact that abortions are so safe meant that providers were unlikely to have any patients to admit.

Other *amicus* briefs filed here set forth without dispute other common prerequisites to obtaining admitting privileges that have nothing to do with ability to perform medical procedures.

In our view, the record contains sufficient evidence that the admitting-privileges requirement led to the closure of half of Texas' clinics, or thereabouts. Those closures meant fewer doctors, longer waiting times, and increased crowding. Record evidence also supports the finding that after the admitting-privileges provision went into effect, the "number of women of reproductive age living in a county . . . more than 150 miles from a provider increased from approximately 86,000 to 400,000 . . . and the number of women living in a county more than 200 miles from a provider from approximately 10,000 to 290,000." We recognize that increased driving distances do not always constitute an "undue burden." But here, those increases are but one additional burden, which, when taken together with others that the closings brought about, and when viewed in light of the virtual absence of any health benefit, lead us to conclude that the record adequately supports the District Court's "undue burden" conclusion.

The dissent's only argument why these clinic closures, as well as the ones discussed in Part V, may not have imposed an undue burden is this: Although "H. B. 2 caused the closure of *some* clinics," other clinics may have closed for other reasons (so we should not "actually count" the burdens resulting from those closures against H.B. 2). But petitioners satisfied their burden to present evidence of causation by presenting direct testimony as well as plausible inferences to be drawn from the timing of the clinic closures. The District Court credited that evidence and concluded from it that H.B. 2 in fact led to the clinic closures. The dissent's speculation that perhaps other evidence, not presented at trial or credited by the District Court, might have shown that some clinics closed for unrelated reasons does not provide sufficient ground to disturb the District Court's factual finding on that issue.

In the same breath, the dissent suggests that one benefit of H.B. 2's requirements would be that they might "force unsafe facilities to shut down." To support that assertion, the dissent points to the Kermit Gosnell scandal. Gosnell, a physician in Pennsylvania, was convicted of first-degree murder and manslaughter. He "staffed his facility with unlicensed and indifferent workers, and then let them practice medicine unsupervised" and had "[d]irty facilities; unsanitary instruments; an absence of functioning monitoring and resuscitation equipment; the use of cheap, but dangerous, drugs; illegal procedures; and inadequate emergency access for when things inevitably went wrong." Gosnell's behavior was terribly wrong. But there is no reason to believe that an extra layer of regulation would have affected that behavior. Determined wrongdoers, already ignoring existing statutes and safety measures, are unlikely to be convinced to adopt safe practices by a new overlay of regulations. Regardless, Gosnell's deplorable crimes could escape detection only because his facility went uninspected for more than 15 years. Pre-existing Texas law already contained numerous detailed regulations covering abortion facilities, including a requirement that facilities be inspected at least annually. The record contains nothing to suggest that H. B. 2 would be more effective than pre-existing Texas law at deterring wrongdoers like Gosnell from criminal behavior.

V

Undue Burden—Surgical–Center Requirement

The second challenged provision of Texas' new law sets forth the surgical-center requirement. Prior to enactment of the new requirement, Texas law required abortion facilities to meet a host of health and safety requirements. Under those pre-existing laws, facilities were subject to annual reporting and recordkeeping requirements; a quality assurance program; personnel policies and staffing requirements; physical and environmental requirements; infection control standards; disclosure requirements; patient-rights standards; and medical- and clinical-services standards, including anesthesia standards. These requirements are policed by random and announced inspections, at least annually as well as administrative penalties, injunctions, civil penalties, and criminal penalties for certain violations.

H.B. 2 added the requirement that an "abortion facility" meet the "minimum standards . . . for ambulatory surgical centers" under Texas law. The surgical-center regulations include, among other things, detailed specifications relating to the size of the nursing staff, building dimensions, and other building requirements. . . .

There is considerable evidence in the record supporting the District Court's findings indicating that the statutory provision requiring all abortion facilities to meet all surgical-center standards does not benefit patients and is not necessary. The District Court found that "risks are not appreciably lowered for patients who undergo abortions at ambulatory surgical centers as compared to nonsurgical-center facilities." The court added that women "will not obtain better care or experience more frequent positive outcomes at an ambulatory surgical center as compared to a previously licensed facility." And these findings are well supported.

The record makes clear that the surgical-center requirement provides no benefit when complications arise in the context of an abortion produced through medication. That is because, in such a case, complications would almost always arise only after the patient has left the facility. The record also contains evidence indicating that abortions taking place in an abortion facility are safe—indeed, safer than numerous procedures that take place outside hospitals and to which Texas does not apply its surgical-center requirements. The total number of deaths in Texas from abortions was five in the period from 2001 to 2012, or about one every two years (that is to say, one out of about 120,000 to 144,000 abortions). Nationwide, childbirth is 14 times more likely than abortion to result in death, but Texas law allows a midwife to oversee childbirth in the patient's own home. Colonoscopy, a procedure that typically takes place outside a hospital (or surgical center) setting, has a mortality rate 10 times higher than an abortion. [The mortality rate for liposuction, another outpatient procedure, is 28 times higher than the mortality rate for abortion.] Medical treatment after an incomplete miscarriage often involves a procedure identical to that involved in a nonmedical abortion, but it often takes place outside a hospital or surgical center. And Texas partly or wholly grandfathers (or waives in whole or in part the surgical-center requirement for) about two-thirds of the facilities to which the surgical-center standards apply. But it neither grandfathers nor provides waivers for any of the facilities that perform abortions. These facts indicate that the surgical-center provision imposes "a requirement that simply is not based on differences" between abortion and other surgical procedures "that are reasonably related to" preserving women's health, the asserted "purpos[e] of the Act in which it is found."

Moreover, many surgical-center requirements are inappropriate as applied to surgical abortions. Requiring scrub facilities; maintaining a one-way traffic pattern through the facility; having ceiling, wall, and floor finishes; separating soiled utility and sterilization rooms; and regulating air pressure, filtration, and humidity control can help reduce infection where doctors conduct procedures that penetrate the skin. But abortions typically involve either the administration of medicines or procedures performed through the natural opening of the birth canal, which is itself not sterile. Nor do provisions designed to safeguard heavily sedated patients (unable to help themselves) during fire emergencies, provide any help to abortion patients, as abortion facilities do not use general anesthesia or deep sedation. Further, since the few instances in which serious complications do arise following an abortion almost always require hospitalization, not treatment at a surgical center, surgical-center standards will not help in those instances either. . . .

At the same time, the record provides adequate evidentiary support for the District Court's conclusion that the surgical-center requirement places a substantial obstacle in the path of women seeking an abortion. The parties stipulated that the requirement would further reduce the number of abortion facilities available to seven or eight facilities, located in Houston, Austin, San Antonio, and Dallas/Fort Worth. In the District Court's view, the proposition that these "seven or eight providers could meet the demand of the entire State [by the 60,000 to 72,000 Texas women seeking abortions annually] stretches credulity. [Although the Court of Appeals held that the District Court's finding was "clearly erroneous,"] we take this statement as a finding that these few facilities could not "meet" that "demand." . . .

More fundamentally, in the face of no threat to women's health, Texas seeks to force women to travel long distances to get abortions in crammed-to-capacity superfacilities. Patients seeking these services are less likely to get the kind of individualized attention, serious conversation, and emotional support that doctors at less taxed facilities may have offered. Healthcare facilities and medical professionals are not fungible commodities. Surgical centers attempting to accommodate sudden, vastly increased demand, may find that quality of care declines. Another commonsense inference that the District Court made is that these effects would be harmful to, not supportive of, women's health.

Finally, the District Court found that the costs that a currently licensed abortion facility would have to incur to meet the surgical-center requirements were considerable, ranging from $1 million per facility (for facilities with adequate space) to $3 million per facility (where additional land must be purchased). This evidence supports the conclusion that more surgical centers will not soon fill the gap when licensed facilities are forced to close.

We agree with the District Court that the surgical-center requirement, like the admitting-privileges requirement, provides few, if any, health benefits for women, poses a substantial obstacle to women seeking abortions, and constitutes an "undue burden" on their constitutional right to do so. . . .

For these reasons the judgment of the Court of Appeals is reversed, and the case is remanded for further proceedings consistent with this opinion.

Justice GINSBURG concurring. . . .

When a State severely limits access to safe and legal procedures, women in desperate circumstances may resort to unlicensed rogue practitioners, *faute de mieux*, at great risk to their health and safety. So long as this Court adheres to Roe v. Wade and Planned Parenthood of Southeastern Pa. v. Casey, Targeted Regulation of Abortion Providers laws like H.B. 2 that "do little or nothing for health, but rather strew impediments to abortion," cannot survive judicial inspection.

Justice THOMAS, dissenting. . . .

I remain fundamentally opposed to the Court's abortion jurisprudence. Even taking *Casey* as the baseline, however, the majority radically rewrites the undue-burden test in three ways. First, today's decision requires courts to "consider the burdens a law imposes on abortion access together with the benefits those laws confer." Second, today's opinion tells the courts that, when the law's justifications are medically uncertain, they need not defer to the legislature, and must instead assess medical justifications for abortion restrictions by scrutinizing the record themselves. Finally, even if a law imposes no "substantial obstacle" to women's access to abortions, the law now must have more than a "reasonabl[e] relat[ion] to . . . a legitimate state interest." These precepts are nowhere to be found in *Casey* or its successors, and transform the undue-burden test to something much more akin to strict scrutiny. . . .

I respectfully dissent.

[The dissenting opinion of Justice Alito, with whom the Chief Justice and Justice Thomas join, focuses on issues of *res judicata*, preclusion, standing, and severability, and is omitted here.]

Notes

1. Grounding the Abortion Right. Few, if any, Supreme Court cases have received as much criticism as Roe v. Wade. Critics have pointed to the lack of a constitutional basis for the right[351] as well as the failure of *Roe*'s trimester system to fully acknowledge the state's interest in protecting

---

351. A classic critique by a scholar who supported abortion as a matter of policy but thought it had no constitutional basis is John Hart Ely, The Wages of Crying Wolf, 82 Yale L.J. 920 (1973).

unborn life.[352] Some scholars support the right to privacy foundation of *Roe* but believe, as exemplified in the excerpt by Reva Siegel, that an equality framework would better capture the important social dimensions of women's reproductive choice. Equality arguments figured in Justice Blackmun's concurring opinion in *Casey,* but they have not been accepted by the Court. Is Siegel's analysis a sound application of equality analysis? Or is nonsubordination theory more apt?

Is it necessary to choose between the privacy and equality-based rationales? One scholar reasons that both analyses are necessary—equality analysis to understand that the right to make reproductive decisions is fundamentally a problem of unequal power, and privacy analysis to ensure that the end goal remains autonomous decisionmaking.[353] Is this right? As a practical matter, does it matter whether the right to have an abortion is based on privacy or equality?

West's responsibility-based theory offers no additional constitutional hook, but some believe that the rhetoric is more appealing than choice, and more likely to persuade politicians and the public. Marjorie M. Shultz worries that the "uncritical embrace of extreme autonomy rhetoric and *exclusively* woman-regarding positions . . . undermine[s] our persuasiveness, [renders] us vulnerable on grounds of principle, and [damages] our aspirations for a humane and responsible world." Shultz also raises concerns that, on principle, an unrestricted autonomy-based right would affect other legal principles in an undesirable way, such as undercutting the responsibility of doctors and employers to take reasonable measures to protect the safety of a fetus.[354] Linguist and political analyst George Lakoff argues that proponents of women's rights should avoid terms like "choice," which are too consumer-oriented, and even "abortion," which sounds negative. They should instead focus on personal freedom from government interference and the lack of support for contraception and sex education.[355] William Saletan goes further: "What we need is an explicit pro-choice war on the abortion rate." Activists should concede that

---

352. See, e.g., Patrick Lee & Robert P. George, The Wrong of Abortion, in Abortion, in Contemporary Debates in Applied Ethics 13 (Andrew Cohen & Christopher Heath Wellman eds., 2005).

353. See Stephen J. Schnably, Beyond Griswold: Foucauldian and Republican Approaches to Privacy, 23 Conn. L. Rev. 861, 932-34 (1991). For a similar argument that emphasizes the importance of viewing women's reproductive rights from the point of view of women's experiences, not as analogs to or derivations from men's experiences, see Jennifer S. Hendricks, Body and Soul: Equality, Pregnancy, and the Unitary Right to Abortion, 45 Harv. C.R.-C.L. L. Rev. 329 (2010).

354. Vicki Schultz, Abortion and the Maternal-Fetal Conflict: Broadening Our Concerns, 1 S. Cal. Rev. L. & Women's Stud. 79, 81 (1992).

355. George Lakoff, The Foreign Language of Choice, Alternet, reviewed in Katha Pollitt, If the Frame Fits, The Nation, July 11, 2005.

abortion is wrong but focus on reducing its necessity while avoiding dragging the criminal law into "personal tragedies."[356]

On the other hand, commentators like Linda McClain have cautioned against responsibility-based theories for the abortion right, whether strategic or principled, on the ground that such theories will trigger too much second-guessing of women's decisions without adequate societal or governmental commitment to family support and reproductive health. It will also leave women vulnerable to charges of irresponsibility. Even the most compelling cases of constraint will still be found by some abortion opponents to be instances of mere "convenience."[357]

Khiara Bridges states that an "injury" rationale is necessary to counteract the jurisprudential move made in *Carhart* toward justifying restrictions on abortion based on maternal welfare. In some sense, the rationale evokes an earlier defense of abortion by moral philosopher Judith Jarvis Thomson based on the right of a person to control their own body when that right comes into conflict with the interests—even the right to live—of another person:

> You wake up in the morning and find yourself back to back in bed with an unconscious violinist. A famous unconscious violinist. He has been found to have a fatal kidney ailment, and the Society of Music Lovers has canvassed all the available medical records and found that you alone have the right blood type to help. They have therefore kidnapped you, and last night the violinist's circulatory system was plugged into yours, so that your kidneys can be used to extract poisons from his blood as well as your own. The director of the hospital now tells you, "Look, we're sorry the Society of Music Lovers did this to you—we would never have permitted it if we had known. But still, they did it, and the violinist is now plugged into you. To unplug you would be to kill him. But never mind, it's only for nine months. By then he will have recovered from his ailment, and can safely be unplugged from you."[358]

Is this analogy persuasive? Does Bridges' theory of injury strengthen woman's right to choose an abortion? Or does it subject that right to a balancing test that women cannot hope to win?

Coming full circle, Katha Pollitt argues that "the only way feminists will regain ground in the abortion wars is to let go of language framing abortion as an icky but necessary evil, and instead push for a more positive view of

---

356. William Saletan, Three Decades After *Roe*, An Abortion War We Can All Support, N.Y. Times, Jan. 22, 2006, at E17.

357. Linda C. McClain, The Poverty of Privacy?, 3 Colum. J. Gender & L. 119, 173 (1992); see also Pamela S. Karlan & Daniel R. Ortiz, In a Diffident Voice: Relational Feminism, Abortion Rights, and the Feminist Legal Agenda, 87 Nw. U. L. Rev. 858 (1993) (expressing concern over relational feminism in the abortion context).

358. Judith Jarvis Thomson, A Defense of Abortion, 1 Phil. & Pub. Affairs 47, 48-49 (1971).

abortion as a 'good thing for society,' precisely because it allows women 'to commit to education and work and dreams without having at the back of the mind . . . that maybe it's all provisional because at any moment an accidental pregnancy could derail them for life.' "[359]

Who is right? Which theory for grounding the abortion right is the strongest? Is it strong enough?

Should facts about why women have abortions make a difference? In explaining their decisions to have an abortion, three-fourths of surveyed women say they cannot afford a child; three-fourths say that having a baby would interfere with work, school, or the ability to care for dependents; and half say they do not want to be a single parent or are having problems with their husband or partner.[360] Should these reasons be sufficient? An amicus brief submitted to the U.S. Supreme Court in Whole Woman's Health v. Cole, a case discussed in Note 4, below, presents the stories of 113 lawyers who claimed that without having had an abortion, their ability to pursue a professional career would have been substantially compromised, or completely thwarted.[361] Are these stories relevant to the debate? If so, how about the brief on behalf of 3348 women who claim to have been injured, physically or psychologically, by an abortion procedure?[362]

2. Stare Decisis, Reliance, and Autonomy.   Part of *Casey's* rationale for preserving *Roe* is that women have come to rely upon the right to choose abortion. In what sense is this true? One possibility is that they are accustomed to relying on abortion as a backup if they fail to use other forms of contraception or those methods fail. Can this be what the three Justices of the lead opinion in *Casey* had in mind? An alternative view is that women have come to see themselves as having some control and autonomy in personal decision-making, which *Roe* has come to symbolize, and it is this autonomy that enables them to plan their lives in long-range terms. Is *this* what the

---

359. Katha Pollitt, Pro: Reclaiming Abortion Rights (2014).

360. Lawrence B. Finer et al., Reasons U.S. Women Have Abortions: Quantitative and Qualitative Perspectives, 37 Perspectives on Sexual and Reproductive Health 110, 113 (2005). Sixty-nine percent of women who get an abortion are at or below the poverty level. See Rickie Solinger, Reproductive Politics: What Everyone Needs to Know 75 (2013).

361. Brief of Janice MacAvoy et al., Whole Woman's Health v. Cole, filed Jan. 4, 2016, http://www.reproductiverights.org/sites/crr.civicactions.net/files/documents/Janice%20 Macavoy%20Paul%20Weiss.pdf. For another brief on behalf of actress Amy Brenneman and other women who tell their reasons for obtaining an abortion, see Brief for Kate Banfield et al. as Amici Curiae Supporting Petitioners, Whole Woman's Health v. Cole, filed on Dec. 30, 2015, http://www.scotusblog.com/wp-content/uploads/2016/01/Kate-Banfield-Kramer-Levin.pdf.

362. See Brief of 3,384 Women Injured by Abortion & the Justice Found. Supporting Respondents, Whole Woman's Health v. Cole (Dec. 10, 2015), http://www.scotusblog.com/wp-content/uploads/2016/02/15-274_amicus_resp_3348Women.authcheckdam.pdf.

plurality of Justices had in mind? If so, this reasoning is specifically rejected by Justice Rehnquist in his *Casey* dissent, which is joined by four other Justices:

> The joint opinion . . . turns to what can only be described as an unconventional—and unconvincing—notion of reliance, a view based on the surmise that the availability of abortion since *Roe* has led to "two decades of economic and social developments that would be undercut if the error of *Roe* were recognized." . . . The joint opinion's assertion of this fact is undeveloped and totally conclusory. In fact, one cannot be sure to what economic and social developments the opinion is referring. Surely it is dubious to suggest that women have reached their "places in society" in reliance upon *Roe*, rather than as a result of their determination to obtain higher education and compete with men in the job market, and of society's increasing recognition of their ability to fill positions that were previously thought to be reserved only for men.[363]

What different assumptions about individual autonomy and choice do the authors of the dissent and the plurality opinion make?

Abortion is fairly widely accepted, at least in some circumstances. In a 2012 Quinnipiac University poll, 64 percent of respondents said that they agree with Roe v. Wade, and only 14 percent say that abortion should be illegal in all cases—numbers that have remained relatively constant since 2005.[364] Polling evidence also shows that many people consider themselves both pro-choice and pro-life.[365] The reality is that most Americans believe that the decision to have an abortion should be a personal choice between a woman and her doctor, but at the same time disapprove of abortion because of, say, the sex of the fetus, or when the woman should have been able to control the circumstances leading to the pregnancy.[366] What are the implications of these surveys? To what extent should public opinion control the abortion issue?

3. "Informed Consent" Requirements. State legislatures continue to pass abortion regulations, and pro-choice advocates continue to oppose them.[367] Many of these regulations are packaged as "informed consent"

---

363. Planned Parenthood v. Casey, 505 U.S. at 956, 957(1992) (Rehnquist, C.J., dissenting).

364. This poll and others with comparable findings can be found at Abortion & Birth Control, Polling Report (Dec. 2-6, 2015), http://www.pollingreport.com/abortion.htm.

365. For a graphic presentation of the evidence, see Public Religion Research Inst., Pro-Choice/Pro/Life; Overlapping Identities (Jan. 25, 2013), http://publicreligion.org/research/graphic-of-the-week/pro-choicepro-life-overlapping-identities/#.VtB2okZH4Yc.

366. See Karlyn Bowman & Jennifer Marsico, Opinions About Abortion Haven't Changed Since *Roe v. Wade*, Atlantic (Jan. 22, 2014), http://www.theatlantic.com/politics/archive/2014/01/opinions-about-abortion-havent-changed-since-em-roe-v-wade-em/283226.

367. A frequently updated website on abortion regulation state by state is Guttmacher Inst., Abortion (Mar. 10, 2016), http://www.guttmacher.org/sections/abortion.php.

requirements. As of February 2016, 38 states require that women receive counseling before they can obtain an abortion. Thirty of these states detail the information a woman must be given. Twenty-seven of these states also require women to wait a specified amount of time—most often 24 hours, but sometimes up to 72 hours—between counseling and the procedure. Twenty-eight states specify what information a woman must be given—usually information about the gestational age of the fetus, the extent of fetal development, and the ability of a fetus to feel pain. In addition, some states require information about the medical and psychological risks of abortion. Some states require information that overstates the risks of abortion to future fertility or that is medically inaccurate, such as that a medication abortion can be stopped after the woman takes the first dose of pills, or that there is a link between abortion and an increased risk of breast cancer.[368] Proposed federal legislation—the Stop Deceptive Advertising for Women's Services Act—would require the Federal Trade Commission to enforce truth in advertising standards for organizations claiming to offer reproductive services; it has been introduced most years since 2006, so far without being enacted into law.[369]

Twenty-five states regulate the provision of ultrasound by abortion providers, with 10 of these states mandating an ultrasound for each woman seeking an abortion and the opportunity for the woman to view the image.[370] Does this image provide useful information for the pregnant woman? Or is it unduly coercive? Taking it one step further, Texas enacted a law requiring vaginal ultrasound in order to pick up a fetal heartbeat sound earlier than with a standard abdominal ultrasound procedure. Some advocates argued that this was state-imposed rape.[371] In Virginia, after strong public protest, a similar law was withdrawn.[372]

Two studies have examined the effects of mandatory delay laws in Mississippi. One study found that the total rate of abortions for Mississippi residents decreased by approximately 16 percent after "informed consent" laws required counseling 24 hours in advance of the procedure, but that the proportion of Mississippi residents traveling to other states to obtain abortions

---

368. For a state-by-state breakdown of laws relating to mandatory counseling and waiting periods, see Guttmacher Inst., Counseling and Waiting Periods for Abortion (Feb. 2, 2016), http://www.guttmacher.org/statecenter/spibs/spib_MWPA.pdf.

369. See To Direct the Federal Trade Commission to Prescribe Rules Prohibiting Deceptive Advertising of Abortion Services, H.R. 2030, 113th Cong. (May 16, 2013), https://www.govtrack.us/congress/bills/113/hr2030.

370. Guttmacher Inst., Requirements for Ultrasound (Feb. 1, 2016), http://www.guttmacher.org/statecenter/spibs/spib_RFU.pdf.

371. See, e.g., Nicholas D. Kristof, When States Abuse Women, N.Y. Times, Mar. 3, 2012, at SR11.

372. See Jessica Grose, Virginia Gov. Bob McDonnell Backs Off the Invasive Ultrasound Law (Feb. 22, 2012), http://www.slate.com/blogs/xx_factor/2012/02/22/virginia_gov_bob_mcdonnell_changes_his_mind_about_ultrasound_law.html.

increased 37 percent and that the proportion of second-trimester abortions among all Mississippi women obtaining abortions increased 40 percent. A second study found that the rate of second-trimester abortions in Mississippi after enactment of the law increased by 53 percent among women whose closest health care provider is in-state, but only 8 percent among women living close to an out-of-state provider.[373] To what extent do these studies put mandatory wait laws into question?

As the Mississippi studies show, mandatory counseling and delay requirements are especially disadvantageous to low-income women.

> A forty-eight hour waiting period . . . may not be an "undue burden" for affluent professional women, and a hospitalization requirement may only serve to make her abortion more expensive. But for an 18-year-old girl in the rural South, unmarried, pregnant, hoping to finish school and build a decent life, who has little or no access to transportation, a hospitalization requirement can mean an abortion that will cost nearly one-thousand dollars and involve a trip of hundreds of miles; a waiting period can mean two long trips and an overnight stay in a strange and distant city.[374]

Women of limited means living in rural areas are particularly affected by abortion restrictions, given the difficulties of transportation and the lack of confidentiality in small communities.[375]

Do counseling requirements amount to compelled disclosures of a government viewpoint, contrary to the First Amendment?[376]

4. Targeted Regulation of Abortion Providers ("TRAP"). The laws at issue in *Whole Woman's Health* represent an approach to limiting abortion through tighter restrictions on abortion providers—an approach sometimes referred to as TRAP, for "targeted regulation of abortion providers." Much of this regulation is founded on an assumption that abortion is an exceptional procedure and thus warrants controls beyond those applied to other medical procedures that may be similar in terms of medical risk. Abortion exceptionalism is apparent with respect to informed consent requirements, examined in Note 3 above, which are more rigorous and substantively detailed than in

---

373. See Theodore Joyce et al., The Impact of Mississippi's Mandatory Delay Law on Abortions and Births, 278 JAMA 653, 655 (1997); Ted Joyce & Robert Kaestner, The Impact of Mississippi's Mandatory Delay Law on the Timing of Abortion, 32 Family Planning Perspectives 4 (2000).

374. Walter Dellinger & Gene B. Sperling, Abortion and the Supreme Court: The Retreat from *Roe v. Wade*, 138 U. Pa. L. Rev. 83, 102 (1989).

375. Lisa R. Pruitt, Toward a Feminist Theory of the Rural, 2 Utah L. Rev. 421, 470-73 (2007).

376. See Caroline Mala Corbin, Compelled Disclosures, 65 Ala. L. Rev. 1277 (2014) (arguing yes).

other medical contexts.[377] What is Justice Breyer's response to the implied assumption that abortion is exceptional?

Texas attempted to defend the admitting-privileges regulations and surgical-center requirements at issue in *Whole Woman's Health* on the basis of its interest in enhancing safety for women—a defense the Court rejected based upon factual findings by the District Court. Is the Court's approach consistent with its opinion in Gonzales v. Carhart? Justice Breyer distinguishes *Carhart* both on the ground that the Court in that case stated that legislative findings, while entitled to deference, were not dispositive, and on the ground that the statute at issue in *Whole Woman's Health* did not set forth legislative findings. Are these distinctions satisfactory, or does *Whole Woman's Health*, in fact, bring significantly greater judicial skepticism to bear on the factual underpinnings used to justify TRAP laws? Isn't Justice Thomas correct in his dissenting opinion that, in requiring courts to consider both the law's burdens and benefits, to determine the facts for themselves, and to closely examine the relationship between the law and a legitimate state purpose, *Whole Woman's Health* represents a significant change in abortion law and a substantially higher burden on abortion regulation than *Casey* imposes?

In the litigation in *Whole Woman's Health*, the state's solicitor general stated that the law was not only to enhance women's health but also "to advance the State's interest in promoting and protecting fetal life."[378] How would you respond to this rationale? How did the Court respond?

The impact of *Whole Woman's Health* on other TRAP laws is as yet unclear.[379] Some states have already dropped their defense of laws with regulations similar to the ones struck down in the case,[380] but other cases are likely to continue.

Tied in with the trend toward tighter restrictions on abortion providers is the decreasing number of physicians prepared to perform them. Only 45 percent of residency training programs in obstetrics and gynecology provide some exposure to abortion and only 32 percent offer at least one abortion-related lecture during the clinical years. Only 14 percent of doctors currently

377. For this and other examples of abortion exceptionalism, see Caroline Mala Corbin, Abortion Distortions, 71 Wash. & Lee L. Rev. 1175, 1176 (2014); Linda Greenhouse & Reva Siegel, When "Protecting Health" Obstructs Choice, 125 Yale L.J. 428 (2016).

378. See Linda Greenhouse, The Fact About Abortion Rights, N.Y. Times, Sunday Review at 1, 4 (Feb. 28, 2016).

379. For a graphic presentation showing the spread of similar state laws and the effects of an affirmance in the case, see Ford Fessenden, How the Supreme Court Case Could Change Women's Access to Abortion, N.Y. Times, Mar. 2, 2016.

380. See Emily Crockett, Texas-like Abortion Laws are Already Starting to Fall After the Supreme Court's Ruling, Vox Identities (June 28, 2016) http://www.vox.com/2016/6/28/12050784/abortion-laws-struck-down-mississippi-wisconsin (reporting that the Court declined to hear cases with similar laws in Mississippi and Wisconsin, and that Alabama's attorney announced that he was dropping legal appeals to a similar Alabama law).

practicing as obstetrician/gynecologists provide abortions.[381] Since 1982, the number of abortion providers has fallen by one-third, and over 85 percent of U.S. counties have none.[382] Besides the increasingly restrictive abortion laws, another factor is the violence and abuse directed at abortion providers, described in Note 8, below.

5. Restrictions on Late-Term Abortions. Eighty-eight percent of abortions occur before the end of the first trimester. Women who obtain "late-term" abortions—i.e., after the first trimester—are disproportionately young and victims of physical abuse or rape. Many women do not realize earlier that they are pregnant or that the fetus has serious abnormalities, or they have difficulty making arrangements.[383]

The "partial-birth" abortion regulation at issue in *Carhart* is part of a larger body of regulation aimed to restricting abortions after the first trimester. Forty-three states prohibit at least some abortions after a certain point in pregnancy—often fetal viability (20 states) or a particular gestational age, such as 20 weeks (12 states). The circumstances in which later-term abortions are permitted vary by state. In 25 states, late-term abortion is permitted to preserve the life or health of the woman.[384] Some states require the involvement of a second physician for late-term abortions, including 13 states that require that a second physician attend the procedure to treat a fetus if it is born alive, and 9 states that require that a second physician certify that the abortion is medically necessary.[385]

6. Abortion "Regret." Criticism of the gender paternalism reflected in the *Carhart* decision was extensive. Reva Siegel documents the growing use of claims about post-abortion syndrome (or PAS) as an anti-abortion strategy that would attract broad support for the fetal rights argument. She quotes David Reardon, an anti-abortion activist:

> While committed pro-lifers may be more comfortable with traditional "defend the baby" arguments, we must recognize that many in our society are too

381. See Am. College of Obstetricians and Gynecologists, Abortion Training and Education (Nov. 2014), http://www.acog.org/Resources-And-Publications/Committee-Opinions/Committee-on-Health-Care-for-Underserved-Women/Abortion-Training-and-Education.

382. See Sarah Kliff, Has Violence Deterred Doctors From Performing Abortions?, Wash. Post, Mar. 6, 2012; Rene Almeling et al., Abortion Training in U.S. Obstetrics & Gynecology Residency Programs 1998, 32 Family Planning Perspectives 268-71, 320 (2000).

383. See Rachel K. Jones & Lawrence B. Finer, Who Has Second-Trimester Abortions in the United States? (2011), at http://www.guttmacher.org/pubs/journals/j.contraception.2011.10.012.pdf.

384. See Guttmacher Inst., State Policies on Later Abortions (Feb. 1, 2016), http://www.guttmacher.org/statecenter/spibs/spib_PLTA.pdf.

385. Id.

morally immature to understand this argument. They must be led to it. And the best way to lead them to it is by first helping them to see that abortion does not help women, but only makes their lives worse.[386]

"Abortion regret" arguments, in the name of women's welfare, arguably exploit, and magnify, the stigma associated with having an abortion. [387] These arguments, coupled with other advocacy positions that appeal to women such as expansion of the Pregnancy Discrimination Act and more support for families, also to help de-stigmatize the pro-life position on abortion.[388]

Is it true, as Justice Ginsburg states, that abortion-regret arguments are based on paternalistic stereotypes and anti-woman rhetoric? Is it enough that no reputable studies support the causal link between abortion and women's depression or suicidal tendencies?[389] Or is Jeannie Suk right that post-abortion syndrome fits the pattern of explanations of women's victimization used by legal reformers to secure more protection for women in other areas, such as sexual violence and harassment? Or does Khiara Bridges have it right that if women's regret is relevant to the analysis, so is the "injury" of pregnancy? Could all these analyses be correct?

What research, if any, would affect your views on whether, and to what extent, abortion harms women? In 2009, one set of researchers concluded that, compared to women who had never had an abortion, women who had had an abortion were at increased risk of several anxiety, mood, and substance abuse disorders.[390] Subsequent research using the same data but controlling for prior mental health difficulties and experience of violence found no such anxiety and mood disorders, although it did find an association with substance abuse, which the researchers attributed to the likelihood they had been unable to control for other relevant risk factors.[391] On what facts does Justice Kennedy rely?

---

386. Reva B. Siegel, Dignity and the Politics of Protection: Abortion Restrictions Under *Casey/Carhart*, 117 Yale L.J. 1695, 1718-19 (2008) (quoting David Reardon, Politically Correct vs. Politically Smart: Why Politicians Should be Both Pro-Woman and Pro-Life, 2 Post-Abortion Rev. 3 (Fall 1994)).

387. On abortion stigma, see Anuradha Kumar et al., Conceptualising Abortion Stigma, 11 Culture, Health & Sexuality 625 (2009).

388. See Tali R. Leinwald, Strange Bedfellows: The Destigmatization of Anti-Abortion Reform, 30 Colum. J. Gender & L. 429 (2016).

389. Corbin, Abortion Distortions, supra note 377, at 1175, 1179-81.

390. See Priscilla K. Coleman et al., Induced Abortion and Anxiety, Mood, and Substance Abuse Disorders: Isolating the Effects of Abortion in the National Comorbidity Survey, 43 J. Psychiatric Research 770 (2009).

391. See Julia R. Steinberg & Lawrence B. Finer, Examining the Association of Abortion History and Current Mental Health: A Reanalysis of the National Comorbidity Survey Using a Common-Risk-Factors Model, 72 Social Sci. & Medicine 72 (2011).

7. A State or Federal Matter?   The Partial Birth Abortion Ban Act at issue in *Carhart* is unusual in that, unlike virtually all other abortion restrictions, it was enacted by Congress at the federal level, rather than by a state legislature. Is this significant? Should there be a national abortion policy, or is this a matter best left up to the states, subject to review under the U.S. Constitution?

What should be the right balance between judicial and legislative power in regulating reproductive decisions? Justice Ginsburg has criticized the majority decision in *Roe* for going too far when the "legislatures all over the United States were moving on this question. The law was in a state of flux," and the Court "bit off more than it could chew." It would have been enough to invalidate the extremely restrictive Texas statute and leave the rest to legislative developments. In her view, that would have avoided the backlash against "unelected judges" making such fundamental decisions.[392]

Some scholars disagree that this approach would have been preferable. They rely on evidence indicating that a majority of the public in the 1970s supported giving women the right to choose but some legislatures were moving in the direction of less not greater recognition of that right.[393] How do you think control over reproductive decisions should be allocated among courts, legislatures, and women?

In the context of weakening support for the right to abortion in the federal courts, a number of state courts have interpreted their own state constitutions to provide more protection than the U.S. Constitution.[394] Sixteen state constitutions now provide greater protection for a woman's right to obtain an abortion than does the federal constitution.[395]

8. Anti-Abortion Activism.   Anti-abortion advocates have long sought to dissuade women from obtaining an abortion through clinic pickets and protest activities. After the Supreme Court found civil rights statutes inapplicable to protect clinic access, Congress passed the Freedom of Access to

392. Adam Liptak, Gay Vows, Repeated from State to State, N.Y. Times, Apr. 12, 2009, at SR1 (quoting Justice Ginsburg).

393. Samantha Luks & Michael Salamone, Abortion, in Public Opinion and Constitutional Controversy 81 (Nathaniel Persily et al. eds., 2008); see also Linda Greenhouse & Reva B. Siegel, Before (and After) Roe v. Wade: New Questions About Backlash, 120 Yale L.J. 100 (2011) (arguing that the polarization of debates about abortion was due not to Roe v. Wade but instead to a party realignment caused when Republicans campaigning for Richard Nixon in 1972 took an anti-abortion stance in order to draw Catholics and social conservatives away from the Democratic Party).

394. See, e.g., Planned Parenthood of Middle Tenn. v. Sundquist, 38 S.W.3d 1 (Tenn. 2000) (mandatory waiting period requirement failed to meet strict scrutiny required under privacy protections of Tennessee constitution).

395. For a map of the states, see State Constitutional Protection, NARAL Pro-Choice America (Mar. 10, 2016), http://www.prochoiceamerica.org/what-is-choice/maps-and-charts/map.jsp?mapID=24.

Clinic Entrances Act (FACE).[396] FACE allows for civil remedies and/or criminal penalties against anyone who "by force or threat of force or by physical obstruction, intentionally injures, intimidates or interferes with or attempts to injure, . . . or intimidate such person from, obtaining or providing reproductive health services." Violators are subject to one year in prison or up to $10,000 in fines, or both, for the first violation, and up to three years in prison and up to $25,000 in fines for the second. If bodily injury or death results, other penalties are possible. The Act also authorizes a private right of action in favor of physicians, clinic staff, and patients who are injured by conduct proscribed by the Act. Critics of FACE have argued that it violates the First Amendment, the Eighth Amendment, the Tenth Amendment, and the Religious Freedom Restoration Act, but the Act has survived numerous constitutional attacks at the federal appellate level.

State laws also provide some protection for health care providers and for women seeking abortions. These include general trespass laws and actions for tortious interference with business, false imprisonment, and intentional infliction of emotional distress. Thirteen states and the District of Columbia prohibit certain specified actions. For example, some state laws provide specific protections such as "bubble zones" around clinics, within which protesters may not approach clinic workers and clients, or prohibit excessive noise outside a clinic, possess or have access to a weapon during a demonstration at a medical facility, threaten or intimidate staff, or block the entrance to a clinic.[397] Some of these restrictions have been upheld, while others have been struck down.[398]

---

396. See, e.g., Bray v. Alexandria Women's Health Clinic, 506 U.S. 263 (1993) (holding that Section 1985 of the Civil Rights Statutes did not provide a federal cause of action to stop demonstrations at abortion clinics based on a violation of the civil rights of women). For FACE, see 18 U.S.C. §248(a)(1) (2012).

397. See Guttmacher Inst., Protecting Access to Clinics (Feb. 1, 2016), http://www.guttmacher.org/statecenter/spibs/spib_PAC.pdf.

398. See, e.g., Madsen v. Women's Health Center, 512 U.S. 753 (1994) (upholding injunctive restraints on demonstrating within 36 feet of clinic, making loud noises within earshot of the clinic, and making loud noises within 300 feet of an employee's residence, but striking down prohibitions against displaying images, approaching patients within 300 feet of the clinic, and peacefully picketing within 300 feet of an employee's residence); Schenck v. Pro-Choice Network of Western New York, 519 U.S. 357 (1997) (upholding injunction for 15-foot buffer zone within 215 feet of clinic entrances and driveways and within 15 feet of vehicles and patients entering or leaving the clinic, but striking down as overbroad injunction for floating 15-foot buffer zones within 15 feet of cars and people); Hill v. Colorado, 530 U.S. 703 (2000) (upholding Colorado law requiring protesters to stay eight feet from anyone entering or leaving an abortion clinic as long as clinic visitor is within 100 feet of the entrance); McCullen v. Coakley, 134 S. Ct. 2518 (2014) (holding that Massachusetts law that created 35-feet fixed buffer zones around abortion clinics violated First Amendment); see also Scheidler v. NOW, 547 U.S. 9 (2006) (holding that federal extortion and racketeering laws (the Hobbs Act) cannot be used to ban abortion demonstrations).

Targeted harassment of clinic doctors and staff has substantially increased since 2010. A 2014 survey of 242 providers conducted by the Feminist Majority Foundation found that nearly 70 percent of abortion providers said they had experienced frequent harassment, and that there had been a 25 percent increase in threats and targeted intimidation tactics between 2010 and 2014. This includes extensive use of "Wanted" and "Killers Among Us" posters and pamphlets that give doctors' and nurses' personal information.[399] Anti-abortion activists sometimes target doctors' homes (Operation Housecall) and use media ads and websites. In one campaign, radio ads proclaimed: "Some doctors deliver babies. Some doctors kill babies."[400] In another instance, the American Coalition of Life Activists portrayed a medical provider and its affiliated doctors on a website, in posters with the physicians' names and addresses labeled "GUILTY," "Deadly Dozen GUILTY," and "Nuremberg Files." This campaign followed in the wake of the murder of other doctors who had been identified in a series of posters labeled "WANTED" and "UNWANTED."[401] In an action against the website developers under both FACE and the Racketeer Influenced and Corrupt Organizations Act (RICO), plaintiffs won an injunction shutting down the website and a verdict of $4.8 million (reduced from $108 million at the trial level).[402]

Since 1993, at least 11 people have been killed in attacks on abortion clinics in the United States. In November 2015, three people were killed when a gunman opened fire with an assault-style rifle at a facility in Colorado Springs, mumbling "no more baby parts" in an interview after his arrest.[403] Another murder involved a Wichita doctor, George Tiller, in his church sanctuary. An Operation Rescue "Tiller Watch" web page had featured vitriolic postings, and pro-life leaders had denounced Tiller as "a baby killer" and "mass murderer."[404] The doctor who attempted to take Dr. Tiller's place has faced harassment and a number of threats, including a letter from an antiabortion

399. Alanna Vagianos, Threats and Targeted Intimidation Against Abortion Clinic Staff Have Significantly Increased Since 2010, Huffpost Women (Feb. 10, 2015), http://www.huffingtonpost.com/2015/02/09/threats-against-abortion-clinics-increased-2015_n_6581536.html.

400. Eyal Press, My Father's Abortion War, N.Y. Times Mag., Jan. 22, 2006, at 59.

401. For extended accounts of anti-abortion activism, see David S. Cohen & Krysten Connon, Living in the Crosshairs: The Untold Stories of Anti-Abortion Terrorism (2015).

402. See Planned Parenthood v. American Coalition of Life Activists, 422 F.3d 949 (9th Cir. 2005).

403. Liam Stack, A Brief History of Deadly Attacks on Abortion Providers, N.Y. Times, Nov. 29, 2015.

404. The Tiller Watch page was taken down after his murder. See George Tiller Killed: Abortion Doctor Shot at Church, Huff. Post (July 1, 2009), http://www.huffingtonpost.com/2009/05/31/george-tiller-killed-abor_n_209504.html.

activist who befriended the killer of Dr. Tiller, warning the doctor to check under her car for explosives before turning the key.[405]

9. Spousal Notice and Consent Provisions. Is *Casey* right to find spousal consent provisions unconstitutional? At a time when many feminists are urging measures to encourage fathers to be more engaged in childrearing, does it make sense to deny them the right to participate in the abortion decision? In a widely circulated New York Times op-ed piece, Dalton Conley argues that "if we want to make fathers relevant, they need rights too. If a father is willing to legally commit to raising a child with no help from the mother, he should be able to obtain an injunction against the abortion of the fetus he helped create."[406] Similarly, Glenn Sacks objects to the "anti-male double standards" that require men to be responsible for child support if the woman carries an unplanned pregnancy to term, but gives them "no say" in that decision or the decision to terminate the pregnancy.[407]

How would you respond? Why do you suppose that paternal consent arguments are no longer a principal strategy of anti-abortion forces?

10. Parental Consent and Notification Requirements. *Casey* upheld provisions requiring minors to have parental consent before obtaining an abortion, as long as the state made available a bypass procedure permitting exemptions from the consent requirement. Under that procedure, a judge must allow an abortion for a minor who has demonstrated that she is mature and capable of giving informed consent, or has shown that the abortion would be in her best interests. This holding was consistent with the Court's prior and subsequent decisions upholding both parental consent and parental notification requirements, despite evidence that they resulted in delays causing health risks, financial costs, trauma, and unwanted births.[408]

Thirty-eight states now require parental involvement in a minor's decision to have an abortion. Of these, 12 require only parental notification (one of which requires notification of both parents), 21 require only parental consent (three of these requiring consent of both parents), and five require both notification and consent. Most states make an exception for a medical emergency, and 16 states make an exception in cases of abuse, assault, incest, or neglect. All but 1 of the 38 states provide an alternative judicial bypass

---

405. Jenny Deam, Doctor Struggles to Fill Role of Slain Kansas Abortion Provider, L.A. Times, Mar. 5, 2012.

406. Dalton Conley, A Man's Right to Choose, N.Y. Times, Dec. 1, 2005, at A35.

407. Glenn Sacks, Alito and the Rights of Men, L.A. Times, Nov. 1, 2005, at B11.

408. The most recent U.S. Supreme Court decision on the subject is Ayotte v. Planned Parenthood of Northern New England, 546 U.S. 320 (2006) (striking down parental notification law because it did not make an exception for a medical emergency). For a continuously updated state-by-state survey of parental consent laws, see Guttmacher Inst., State Policies in Brief (Mar. 1, 2016), http://www.guttmacher.org/statecenter/spibs/spib_PIMA.pdf.

procedure; 15 of these states require judges to use the clear and convincing evidence standard in determining that the minor is mature and that the abortion is in her best interests.[409] Courts in a few states have struck down parental consent or parental notification statutes under their own state constitutional provisions, although anti-abortion advocates in one of these states, California, have sought repeatedly to overrule one such decision through a referendum to amend the state constitution.[410] At the federal level, legislation is introduced from time to time, most recently in 2011, that would require all minors who travel outside their home state for an abortion to obtain parental consent and wait 24 hours.[411]

At one time, it seemed that most minors who pursued a bypass procedure obtained judicial permission to obtain an abortion.[412] However, a study involving interviews of professionals from every state with a bypass provision found numerous difficulties faced by minors in pursuing bypass petitions, including the inability of minors to obtain helpful and reliable information, pay the costs, and find a judge who will hear the petition. Minors who are in state custody face additional problems, including confusion within the system about who is authorized to provide consent. Once a petition is before the court, abuse of judicial discretion is also a problem. Some judges grill the minors on their sex lives, or deliver stern lectures on the need for parental consultation.[413] Is this appropriate? If not, what could be done to prevent the practice? Should the law assume that parents act in their children's best interests? Should the law assume that parents do not act in their children's best interests?

11. Federal Policy Relating to Minors and Abortion. The federal government in recent decades has provided various funding programs to support pregnancy prevention for teenagers. For much of this period, the funds have been available only for programs premised on abstinence as the sole prevention strategy. Thus, qualifying programs have been required to teach that

---

409. Guttmacher Inst., Parental Involvement Law in Minors' Abortions, and New Governance (Feb. 1, 2016), http://www.guttmacher.org/statecenter/spibs/spib_PIMA.pdf.

410. See A Resolution to Propose to the People of the State of California an Amendment to the Constitution of the State, Assembly Constitutional Amendment No. 5, 2013-14 Reg. Sess. (Cal. 2014), http://leginfo.legislature.ca.gov/faces/billNavClient.xhtml?bill_id=201320140ACA5 (2014 version of the bill to amend state constitution).

411. See Editorial, Yet Another Curb on Abortion, N.Y. Times, Mar. 13, 2012, at A24; Federal Parental Notification Law Introduced (Mar 18, 2011), http://www.feminist.org/news/newsbyte/uswirestory.asp?id=13015.

412. A 10-year study in Massachusetts cited by a state appellate judge in 1997 showed that all bypass petitions but 13 were granted, and of these 13, all but one were reversed on appeal; in the one remaining case, the parents eventually gave consent. See American Academy of Pediatrics v. Lungren, 940 P.3d 797, 836 n.12 (Cal. 1997) (Kennard, J., dissenting).

413. See Rachel Rebouche, Parental Involvement Law and New Governance, 34 Harv. J. Law & Gender 175, 188-196 (2011).

abstaining from sex "is the only certain way to avoid out-of wedlock pregnancy, sexually transmitted diseases, and other associated health problems," that a "mutually faithful monogamous relationship in context of marriage is the expected standard of human sexual activity," and that "sexual activity outside of marriage is likely to have harmful physical and psychological effects."[414] Much of the funding for these programs expired in 2009 and 2010 but then was renewed as part of the Affordable Care Act signed into law by President Obama in 2010.[415] President Obama's 2017 budget, however, eliminates the $10-million-a-year grant for abstinence-only education run by the Department of Health and Human Services, while increasing funds for other programs aimed at pregnancy prevention for teenagers.[416]

The political popularity of abstinence-only programs has not been matched by any demonstration of effectiveness. The vast majority of abstinence-only curricula include errors and distortions, and none have been found to delay sexual activity. A large-scale analysis from researchers from the University of Georgia showed that states that prescribe abstinence-only sex education programs in public schools have significantly higher teenage pregnancy and birth rates than states with more comprehensive sex education programs.[417] One study showed that students who take virginity pledges — a common feature of abstinence-only programs — delayed sexual activity slightly, but when they did have sex, they used condoms less frequently and were less likely to be tested for STIs. Students who take part in abstinence-only programs are also more likely to believe, incorrectly, that condoms do not protect against STIs.[418] According to data from the Centers for Disease Control and Prevention, one in four teenage girls has a sexually-transmitted infection (STI), and African-American girls are at more than twice the risk of white girls.[419]

Critics of abstinence-only programs generally do not object to approaches that encourage teens to resist unwanted sex, but believe that teens should also have accurate information about sexual activity and birth control. Some critics also argue that abstinence-only initiatives violate minors' constitutional rights concerning health and procreation decisions, and that some federally-funded

---

414. 42 U.S.C. §710(b)(2) (2012). For a history of the federal programs, see No More Money: Abstinence-Only-Until-Marriage Funding (Nov. 2010), http://www.nomoremoney.org/index.cfm?pageid=947.

415. 42 U.S.C. §710(b)(2) (2012).

416. Michael Stone, Obama Removes All Funding for "Abstinence-Only" Sex Education, Progressive Secular Humanist (Feb. 16, 2016), http://www.patheos.com/blogs/progressivesecularhumanist/2016/02/obama-removes-all-funding-for-abstinence-only-sex-education.

417. See Kathrin F. Stanger-Hall & David W. Hall, Abstinence-Only Education and Teen Pregnancy Rates: Why We Need Comprehensive Sex Education in the U.S., 6(10) PLoS One 1371 (2011), http://journals.plos.org/plosone/article?id=10.1371/journal.pone.0024658.

418. Julie F. Kay, What's Not Being Said About Sex and Who It's Hurting (Mar. 27, 2008), https://www.americanprogress.org/issues/education/news/2008/03/27/4082/whats-not-being-said-about-sex-and-who-its-hurting.

419. Id.

programs include religious material in violation of the First Amendment establishment clause, which requires separation between church and state. One federal court struck down a Louisiana program on that ground.[420]

12. Funding the Abortion Right. Underfunding of family planning programs disproportionately restricts poor women's reproductive choices and increases the number of abortions. Nearly half of pregnancies are unintended, and 40 percent of these end in abortion (down from 47 percent in 2001). Black women are twice as likely to have unintended pregnancies as non-Hispanic white women, and poor women are five times as likely as women at the highest income level.[421] Two-thirds of the 1.5 million unplanned births in 2010 were paid for by public insurance programs, primarily Medicaid, as compared to 38 percent of planned births.

Federal funding legislation, known as the "Hyde Amendment," limits federal reimbursement for abortions to very narrow exceptions, such as when necessary to save the life of the mother or to end pregnancies resulting from rape or incest. The restriction applies to funding provided through the Department of Health and Human Services and primarily affects Medicaid. The Supreme Court has sustained such legislation on the ground that it does not impose an unconstitutional condition on women's exercise of their fundamental right to an abortion but simply leaves them in the same place they would be absent any federal funding program.[422] Although 32 states and the District of Columbia provide their own funds for indigent women, only 4 states voluntarily provide funds for all or most medically necessary abortions, with 13 additional states providing funds pursuant to court order.[423] In response to the requirements of the Patient Protection and Affordable Care Act for the establishment of state-level health care exchanges to assist individuals and small businesses purchase a private health insurance plan, 25 states have enacted significant restrictions on abortion coverage, and 10 states restrict insurance coverage of abortion in all private insurance plans written in the state.[424]

13. Personhood Amendments and Other Efforts to Ban Abortion. At one time it seemed possible, as the majority in *Roe* maintained, that legal issues about abortion could be decided without having to resolve the "difficult

---

420. ACLU of Louisiana v. Foster, No. Civ.A. 02-1440, 2002 WL 1733651 (E.D. La. July 24, 2002).

421. See Guttmacher Inst., Unintended Pregnancy in the United States (July 2015), http://www.guttmacher.org/pubs/FB-Unintended-Pregnancy-US.html.

422. Harris v. McRae, 448 U.S. 297 (1980).

423. Guttmacher Inst., State Funding of Abortion Under Medicaid (Feb. 1, 2016), http://www.guttmacher.org/statecenter/spibs/spib_SFAM.pdf.

424. Guttmacher Inst., Restricting Insurance Coverage of Abortion (Feb. 1, 2016), http://www.guttmacher.org/statecenter/spibs/spib_SFAM.pdf.

question of when life begins." One of the strategies pursued in recent years by anti-abortion advocates, however, is proposed legislation or constitutional amendments providing that life begins at conception. At least 20 states have considered measures declaring that personhood begins at conception. Measures have been defeated in Mississippi,[425] Colorado, and North Dakota.[426] In 2012, the Oklahoma Supreme Court struck down a bill that declared that life begins at conception and would have afforded all unborn children "at every stage of development all the rights, privileges, and immunities available to other persons, citizens, and residents of this state."[427]

If a "Personhood Amendment" becomes law, what would be its effect? It would certainly ban abortion (its declared primary purpose) and probably eliminate any potential exceptions in the case of rape or incest. Would any miscarriage necessitate a state murder investigation? How would it affect frozen embryos? Would a pregnant woman be able to declare her fetus as a dependent for tax purposes? Would she be entitled to welfare benefits immediately upon becoming pregnant?

In a satirical effort to draw attention to the gender implications of the efforts to expand the definition of personhood, Oklahoma state representative Constance Johnson introduced a bill to amend the "Personhood" bill introduced in the Oklahoma legislature to say: ". . . provided, however, any action in which a man ejaculates or otherwise deposits semen anywhere but in a woman's vagina, shall be interpreted and construed as an action against an unborn child."[428] Is this just silly, or does it identify a real problem in this kind of legislation?

425. The measure was a constitutional amendment that would define "persons" to include "every human being from the moment of fertilization, cloning, or the functional equivalent thereof." See Miss. Initiative 26 (2011), discussed in Christopher R. Green, A Textual Analysis of the Possible Impact of Measure 26 on the Mississippi Bill of Rights, 81 Miss. L.J. Supra 39 (2011). This bill and numerous initiatives from other states is described at the Personhood USA website, Personhood (Mar. 10, 2016), http://www.personhoodusa.com.

426. See Tara Culp-Ressler, Even in Deep Red States, Voters Reject Radical "Personhood" Measures, ThinkProgress (Nov. 5, 2014), http://thinkprogress.org/health/2014/11/05/3589112/voters-reject-personhood.

427. In re Initiative Petition No. 395 State Question No. 761, 286 P.3d 637 (Okla. 2012), cert. denied, Personhood Okla. v. Barber, 133 S. Ct. 528 (2012). See Warren Richey, Supreme Court Turns Away Case on Oklahoma "Personhood" Amendment, The Christian Science Monitor, Oct. 29, 2012, http://www.csmonitor.com/USA/Justice/2012/1029/Supreme-Court-turns-away-case-on-Oklahoma-personhood-amendment. In acknowledgment of the potential unconstitutionality of such amendments, Virginia's proposed legislation is "subject . . . to the laws and constitutions of Virginia and the United States." See Va. H.B. 1 Unborn children; construing the word "person" under Virginia law to include (introduced Nov. 2011), http://leg1.state.va.us/cgi-bin/legp504.exe?121+sum+HB1.

428. See Constance Johnson, About My "Spilled Semen" Amendment to Oklahoma's Personhood Bill, The Guardian, Feb. 9, 2012, http://www.guardian.co.uk/commentisfree/cifamerica/2012/feb/09/spilled-semen-amendment-oklahoma-personhood-bill; see also Harvey L. Riser & Paula K. Garrett, Life Begins at Ejaculation: Legislating Sperm as the Po-

Recent bills in a few states have been more direct, prohibiting the performance of an abortion at any stage of the pregnancy. An Oklahoma bill that recently passed the legislature would have made it a felony for a doctor to perform an abortion except to save the life of the mother or to remove the fetus after a miscarriage.[429] The bill was vetoed by Governor Mary Fallin.[430]

14. The Impact of Increasing Abortion Restrictions. Many states have positioned themselves in the event that the Supreme Court overturns Roe v. Wade. As of February 2016, 19 states had either pre-*Roe* laws or post-*Roe* laws that would immediately ban abortion if *Roe* were overturned.[431] If the Supreme Court were to eliminate the constitutional right of a woman to choose to have an abortion, the result would be a patchwork of regulations, with some states completely denying abortion rights except to protect maternal life, and others providing stringent regulations. After *Whole Woman's Health*, does this seem likely?

More restrictive abortion laws do not necessarily mean fewer abortions. Data show that in states where abortions are hardest to get because of the inaccessibility of services, there are more live births, but not as many as pregnancy rates would predict; one economist finds reason to suspect that some of the pregnancies are terminated through self-induced abortions. One indication of this is that Google searches for advice on self-abortion are higher in states where clinic abortions are harder to obtain. The state with the most Google searches for self-induced abortion is Mississippi, which now has only one clinic that performs abortions. A recent survey shows an especially high number of attempted self-induced abortions in Texas, where 4.1 percent of women were sure, or suspected, that their best friend had tried a self-induced abortion.[432]

More generally, abortion rates are lower in countries where it is legal; for example, in Western Europe, where abortions are broadly available, the

---

tential to Create Life and the Effects on Contracts for Artificial Insemination, 21 Am. U. J. Gender & Soc. Pol'y 39 (2012).

429. Erik Eckholm, Oklahoma Passes Bill That Would Subject Abortion Doctors to Felony Charges, N.Y. Times, May 19, 2016, at A10.

430. Emily Crockett, Oklahoma's Governor Just Vetoed the Bill that Would Have Made Abortion a Felony, Vox (May 22, 2016), at http://www.vox.com/2016/4/26/11510874/oklahoma-abortion-outlaw-felony-doctors (mentioning efforts in other states). Oklahoma had earlier attempted to ban use of the drug misoprostol to induce abortions. After the Oklahoma State Supreme Court found the law to be unconstitutional, the U.S. Supreme Court agreed to hear the case, but then sent it back to the Oklahoma court to certify whether the statute banned the use of misoprostol even when used under a protocol approved by the Food and Drug Administration. See Cline v. Okla. Coalition for Reprod. Justice, 133 S. Ct. 2887 (2013). The state case is Okla. Coalition v. Cline, 292 P.3d 27 (Okla. 2012).

431. Guttmacher Inst., Abortion Policy in the Absence of Roe (Feb. 1, 2016), http://www.guttmacher.org/statecenter/spibs/spib_APAR.pdf.

432. See Seth Stephens-Davidowitz, The Return of the D.I.Y. Abortion, N.Y. Times, Mar. 5, 2016, at SR2.

abortion rate is 12 per 1,000 women. Countries with highly restrictive abortion laws tend to have higher abortion rates; in Latin America, for example, the rate is 32 per 1,000 women. Abortions are also safer where they are legal because of the methods used, the sanitary conditions, and the later gestational age at which women seek illegal abortions. In South Africa, the annual number of abortion-related deaths fell by 91 percent after the liberalization of the abortion law. Worldwide, although abortion rates declined significantly between 1995 and 2003, they have now leveled off at 28 per 1,000 women between ages 15 and 44.[433]

Putting Theory Into Practice

5-22. Research shows consistently that, even in the United States, most families prefer boys to girls, especially as first or only children.[434] A number of states now make it illegal to intentionally perform an abortion when that abortion is sought solely on account of the sex of the unborn child.[435] Are these laws constitutional? Are they enforceable, or wise? What about laws to prohibit sex selection in in-vitro fertilization?

5-23. When diagnosed before birth, genetic abnormalities prompt couples to have an abortion 90 percent of the time. A number of states, including North Dakota, now ban the abortion of fetuses with severe genetic abnormalities, like Down Syndrome.[436] How should the courts rule on the constitutionality of this law?

5-24. There are more than 4000 centers, sometimes called Crisis Pregnancy Centers, which purport to offer comprehensive services to women with unwanted pregnancies. Typically these centers advertise by offering free pregnancy tests and counseling. They then attempt to dissuade women from obtaining an abortion, often with false claims relating to abortion to sterility,

433. See Guttmacher Inst., Facts on Induced Abortion Worldwide (Nov. 2015), http://www.guttmacher.org/pubs/fb_IAW.html.

434. See Frank Newport, Americans Prefer Boys to Girls, Just as They Did in 1941 (June 23, 2011), http://www.gallup.com/poll/148187/americans-prefer-boys-girls-1941.aspx (in 2011 polling, 40 percent of respondents would prefer a boy if they are only going to have one child, while 28 percent would prefer a girl, as compared to 38 to 24 percent in 1941). The evidence for male favoritism is stronger in China and India. See Therese Hesketh, The Consequences of Son Preference and Sex-Selective Abortion in China and Other Asian Countries, 183 Canadian Medical Association J. 1374 (Sept. 6, 2011); Jeff Jacoby, Choosing to Eliminate Unwanted Daughters, Boston Globe, Apr. 6, 2008.

435. See, e.g., N.D. Cent. Code §14-02.1-04.1 (2016); N.C. Gen. Stat. §90-21.121 (2015).

436. N.D. Cent. Code 14-02.1-04.1 (2016).

breast cancer, and other harms. These centers, which do not provide abortions, are not regulated or licensed. Should they be required to post notices that they do not provide or make referral for abortion services? Should they be required to tell women where they can obtain those services?[437]

5-25. A bill in Kansas would, if passed, make it illegal for any state employee to perform an abortion, and would thereby, among other things, preclude abortion training to medical students or medical residents in the University of Kansas Medical Center.[438] Is this bill constitutional? Should it be?

5-26. A Michigan father defended against a paternity suit in which he was ordered to pay $500 per month in child support, on the grounds that the law on which it was based constitutes sex discrimination. The father, represented by the National Center for Men, argued that he had been deprived of the right to avoid parenthood. He claimed that the mother had falsely assured him that she was unable to get pregnant due to a medical condition, and that she was using birth control just in case. The state also denied him any right to determine whether the pregnancy would be carried to term.[439] Should his defense be accepted?

5-27. A 1997 Louisiana law provides that "[a]ny person who performs an abortion is liable to the mother of the unborn child for any damage occasioned or precipitated by the abortion." A signed consent may reduce damages, but not eliminate them.[440] A group of abortion providers and their patients brought suit. What should be the outcome?[441] Are tort remedies a

---

437. For different views, compare http://www.prochoiceamerica.org/what-is-choice/abortion/abortion-crisis-pregnancy-centers.html, with http://www.aul.org/2012/12/americans-united-for-life-leaders-head-to-richmond-virginia-for-free-speech-case-arguments-in-the-4th-circuit-court-of-appeals. In Greater Baltimore Center for Pregnancy Concerns v. Mayor and City Council of Baltimore, 721 F.3d 264 (4th Cir. 2013) (en banc) (vacating injunction against city ordinance to post disclaimer that center does not provide or make referrals for abortions or certain birth-control services, largely on procedural grounds) and Centro Tepeyac v. Montgomery Cnty., 722 F.3d 184 (4th Cir. 2013) (en banc) (on First Amendment challenge, upholding injunction against city ordinance requiring clinic to post statement encouraging women "who are or may be pregnant to consult with a licensed health care provider" against First Amendment challenge and affirming district court's failure to enjoin disclosure that "the Center does not have a licensed medical professional on staff").

438. See Doctor Training at Issue in Kansas Abortion Bill, Kansas City Star, Mar. 8, 2012, http://www.kansascity.com/2012/03/08/3478488/doctor-training-at-issue-in-kansas.html.

439. Dubay v. Wells, 506 F.3d 422 (6th Cir. 2007).

440. La. Rev. Stat. Ann. §9:2800.12 (2016).

441. Okpalobi v. Foster, 244 F.3d 405 (5th Cir. 2001) (en banc) (dismissed on standing grounds); Women's Health Clinic v. State, 825 So.2d 1210 (La. Ct. App. 2002) (same).

logical extension of the regret analysis in *Carhart*, or do they violate the U.S. Constitution?[442]

5-28. Two weeks before her sentencing hearing on a forgery conviction, Yuriko wrote to the judge telling him that she was pregnant and wished to have an abortion. The judge offered her a deal: If she agreed to bring the fetus to term, he would give her probation instead of a prison sentence.[443] Should this kind of plea bargain be permissible?

5-29. Some abortion protesters photograph and videotape women entering abortion clinics; the photographs are later posted on the Internet, in some cases along with age, height, and location. Protestors hope that the increased publicity will deter women from seeking abortions and claim that the postings are protected under the First Amendment. Should these postings be allowed? If not, what remedies should be available to women whose photographs are published?

3. Pregnancy and Contractual Autonomy

This section addresses what legal rules should govern women who are willing to bear children for someone else, as a surrogate, or through other arrangements arising from non-traditional methods of reproduction. In this area, the law has been unable to keep up with either medical technology or evolving social practice. This new frontier presents crucial challenges for women's autonomy and public policy.

In re Baby M
537 A.2d 1227 (N.J. 1988)

WILENTZ, C.J.

In this matter the Court is asked to determine the validity of a contract that purports to provide a new way of bringing children into a family. For a fee of $10,000, a woman agrees to be artificially inseminated with the semen of another woman's husband; she is to conceive a child, carry it to term, and after its birth surrender it to the natural father and his wife. The intent of the

---

442. See Maya Manian, Privatizing Bans on Abortion: Eviscerating Constitutional Rights Through Tort Remedies, 80 Temple L. Rev. 123 (2007).

443. The facts were taken from Cleveland Bar Association v. Clearly, 754 N.E.2d 235 (Ohio 2001), described and critiqued in April L. Cherry, The Detention, Confinement, and Incarceration of Pregnant Women for the Benefit of Fetal Health, 16 Colum. J. Gender & L. 147 (2007).

contract is that the child's natural mother will thereafter be forever separated from her child. The wife is to adopt the child, and she and the natural father are to be regarded as its parents for all purposes. The contract providing for this is called a "surrogacy contract," the natural mother inappropriately called the "surrogate mother."

We invalidate the surrogacy contract because it conflicts with the law and public policy of this State. While we recognize the depth of the yearning of infertile couples to have their own children, we find the payment of money to a "surrogate" mother illegal, perhaps criminal, and potentially degrading to women. Although in this case we grant custody to the natural father, the evidence having clearly proved such custody to be in the best interests of the infant, we void both the termination of the surrogate mother's parental rights and the adoption of the child by the wife/stepparent. We thus restore the "surrogate" as the mother of the child. We remand the issue of the natural mother's visitation rights to the trial court. . . .

We find no offense to our present laws where a woman voluntarily and without payment agrees to act as a "surrogate" mother, provided that she is not subject to a binding agreement to surrender her child. . . .

I. FACTS

In February 1985, William Stern and Mary Beth Whitehead entered into a surrogacy contract. It recited that Stern's wife, Elizabeth, was infertile, that they wanted a child, and that Mrs. Whitehead was willing to provide that child as the mother with Mr. Stern as the father.

The contract provided that through artificial insemination using Mr. Stern's sperm, Mrs. Whitehead would become pregnant, carry the child to term, bear it, deliver it to the Sterns, and thereafter do whatever was necessary to terminate her maternal rights so that Mrs. Stern could thereafter adopt the child. Mrs. Whitehead's husband, Richard, was also a party to the contract; Mrs. Stern was not. Mr. Whitehead promised to do all acts necessary to rebut the presumption of paternity under the Parentage Act. Although Mrs. Stern was not a party to the surrogacy agreement, the contract gave her sole custody of the child in the event of Mr. Stern's death. . . .

Mr. Stern, on his part, agreed to attempt the artificial insemination and to pay Mrs. Whitehead $10,000 after the child's birth, on its delivery to him. In a separate contract, Mr. Stern agreed to pay $7,500 to the Infertility Center of New York ("ICNY"). The Center's advertising campaigns solicit surrogate mothers and encourage infertile couples to consider surrogacy. ICNY arranged for the surrogacy contract by bringing the parties together, explaining the process to them, furnishing the contractual form, and providing legal counsel.

The history of the parties' involvement in this arrangement suggests their good faith. William and Elizabeth Stern were married in July 1974, having met at the University of Michigan, where both were Ph.D. candidates. Due to financial considerations and Mrs. Stern's pursuit of a medical degree and residency, they decided to defer starting a family until 1981. Before then, however, Mrs. Stern learned that she might have multiple sclerosis and that the disease in some cases renders pregnancy a serious health risk. Her anxiety appears to have exceeded the actual risk, which current medical authorities assess as minimal. Nonetheless that anxiety was evidently quite real, Mrs. Stern fearing that pregnancy might precipitate blindness, paraplegia, or other forms of debilitation. Based on the perceived risk, the Sterns decided to forego having their own children. The decision had special significance for Mr. Stern. Most of his family had been destroyed in the Holocaust. As the family's only survivor, he very much wanted to continue his bloodline.

Initially the Sterns considered adoption but were discouraged by the substantial delay apparently involved and by the potential problem they saw arising from their age and their differing religious backgrounds. They were most eager for some other means to start a family.

The paths of Mrs. Whitehead and the Sterns to surrogacy were similar. Both responded to advertising by ICNY. . . . Mrs. Whitehead's response apparently resulted from her sympathy with family members and others who could have no children (she stated that she wanted to give another couple the "gift of life"); she also wanted the $10,000 to help her family.

Both parties, undoubtedly because of their own self-interest, were less sensitive to the implications of the transaction than they might otherwise have been. Mrs. Whitehead, for instance, appears not to have been concerned about whether the Sterns would make good parents for her child; the Sterns, on their part, while conscious of the obvious possibility that surrendering the child might cause grief to Mrs. Whitehead, overcame their qualms because of their desire for a child. At any rate, both the Sterns and Mrs. Whitehead were committed to the arrangement; both thought it right and constructive.

. . . On February 6, 1985, Mr. Stern and Mr. and Mrs. Whitehead executed the surrogate parenting agreement. After several artificial inseminations over a period of months, Mrs. Whitehead became pregnant. The pregnancy was uneventful and on March 27, 1986, Baby M was born. . . .

Mrs. Whitehead realized, almost from the moment of birth, that she could not part with this child. She had felt a bond with it even during pregnancy. . . . She apparently broke into tears and indicated that she did not know if she could give up the child. . . .

Nonetheless, Mrs. Whitehead was, for the moment, true to her word. Despite powerful inclinations to the contrary, she turned her child over to the Sterns on March 30 at the Whiteheads' home.

The Sterns were thrilled with their new child. They had planned extensively for its arrival, far beyond the practical furnishing of a room for her. It was a time of joyful celebration—not just for them but for their friends as well. The Sterns looked forward to raising their daughter, whom they named Melissa. . . .

Later in the evening of March 30, Mrs. Whitehead became deeply disturbed, disconsolate, stricken with unbearable sadness. She had to have her child. She could not eat, sleep, or concentrate on anything other than her need for her baby. The next day she went to the Sterns' home and told them how much she was suffering.

The depth of Mrs. Whitehead's despair surprised and frightened the Sterns. She told them that she could not live without her baby, that she must have her, even if only for one week, that thereafter she would surrender her child. The Sterns, concerned that Mrs. Whitehead might indeed commit suicide, not wanting under any circumstances to risk that, and in any event believing that Mrs. Whitehead would keep her word, turned the child over to her. . . .

The struggle over Baby M began when it became apparent that Mrs. Whitehead could not return the child to Mr. Stern. Due to Mrs. Whitehead's refusal to relinquish the baby, Mr. Stern filed a complaint seeking enforcement of the surrogacy contract. . . .

The Whiteheads immediately fled to Florida with Baby M. They stayed initially with Mrs. Whitehead's parents, where one of Mrs. Whitehead's children had been living. For the next three months, the Whiteheads and Melissa lived at roughly twenty different hotels, motels, and homes in order to avoid apprehension. From time to time Mrs. Whitehead would call Mr. Stern to discuss the matter; the conversations, recorded by Mr. Stern on advice of counsel, show an escalating dispute about rights, morality, and power, accompanied by threats of Mrs. Whitehead to kill herself, to kill the child, and falsely to accuse Mr. Stern of sexually molesting Mrs. Whitehead's other daughter.

Eventually the Sterns discovered where the Whiteheads were staying, commenced supplementary proceedings in Florida, and obtained an order requiring the Whiteheads to turn over the child. Police in Florida enforced the order, forcibly removing the child from her grandparents' home. She was soon thereafter brought to New Jersey and turned over to the Sterns. . . .

The trial took thirty-two days over a period of more than two months. . . . [The trial court] held that the surrogacy contract was valid; ordered that Mrs. Whitehead's parental rights be terminated and that sole custody of the child be granted to Mr. Stern; and, after hearing brief testimony from Mrs. Stern, immediately entered an order allowing the adoption of Melissa by Mrs. Stern, all in accordance with the surrogacy contract. . . .

II. INVALIDITY AND UNENFORCEABILITY OF SURROGACY CONTRACT.

. . . A. Conflict with Statutory Provisions

The surrogacy contract conflicts with: (1) laws prohibiting the use of money in connection with adoptions; (2) laws requiring proof of parental unfitness or abandonment before termination of parental rights is ordered or an adoption is granted; and (3) laws that make surrender of custody and consent to adoption revocable in private placement adoptions.

(1) Our law prohibits paying or accepting money in connection with any placement of a child for adoption. Violation is a high misdemeanor. Excepted are fees of an approved agency (which must be a non-profit entity) and certain expenses in connection with childbirth.

Considerable care was taken in this case to structure the surrogacy arrangement so as not to violate this prohibition. . . . Nevertheless, it seems clear that the money was paid and accepted in connection with an adoption. . . .

Mr. Stern knew he was paying for the adoption of a child; Mrs. Whitehead knew she was accepting money so that a child might be adopted; the Infertility Center knew that it was being paid for assisting in the adoption of a child. The actions of all three worked to frustrate the goals of the statute. . . .

. . . The evils inherent in baby-bartering are loathsome for a myriad of reasons. The child is sold without regard for whether the purchasers will be suitable parents. The natural mother does not receive the benefit of counseling and guidance to assist her in making a decision that may affect her for a lifetime. In fact, the monetary incentive to sell her child may, depending on her financial circumstances, make her decision less voluntary. Furthermore, the adoptive parents may not be fully informed of the natural parents' medical history. . . .

(2) The termination of Mrs. Whitehead's parental rights, called for by the surrogacy contract and actually ordered by the court, fails to comply with the stringent requirements of New Jersey law. . . .

In order to terminate parental rights under the private placement adoption statute, there must be a finding of "intentional abandonment or a very substantial neglect of parental duties without a reasonable expectation of a reversal of that conduct in the future." . . .

In this case a termination of parental rights was obtained not by proving the statutory prerequisites but by claiming the benefit of contractual provisions. . . . [A] contractual agreement to abandon one's parental rights, or not to contest a termination action, will not be enforced in our courts. . . .

(3) The provision in the surrogacy contract stating that Mary Beth Whitehead agrees to "surrender custody . . . and terminate all parental rights" contains no clause giving her a right to rescind. It is intended to be an irrevocable consent to surrender the child for adoption—in other words, an irrevocable commitment by Mrs. Whitehead to turn Baby M over to the Sterns and thereafter to allow termination of her parental rights. . . .

. . . Such a provision, however, making irrevocable the natural mother's consent to surrender custody of her child in a private placement adoption, clearly conflicts with New Jersey law. . . .

The[] strict prerequisites to irrevocability constitute a recognition of the most serious consequences that flow from such consents: termination of parental rights, the permanent separation of parent from child, and the ultimate adoption of the child. Because of those consequences, the Legislature severely limited the circumstances under which such consent would be irrevocable. The legislative goal is furthered by regulations requiring approved agencies, prior to accepting irrevocable consents, to provide advice and counseling to women, making it more likely that they fully understand and appreciate the consequences of their acts. . . .

The provision in the surrogacy contract whereby the mother irrevocably agrees to surrender custody of her child and to terminate her parental rights conflicts with the settled interpretation of New Jersey statutory law. . . .

B. Public Policy Considerations

The surrogacy contract's invalidity . . . is further underlined when its goals and means are measured against New Jersey's public policy. The contract's basic premise, that the natural parents can decide in advance of birth which one is to have custody of the child, bears no relationship to the settled law that the child's best interests shall determine custody. . . .

The surrogacy contract guarantees permanent separation of the child from one of its natural parents. Our policy, however, has long been that to the extent possible, children should remain with and be brought up by both of their natural parents. . . . This is not simply some theoretical ideal that in practice has no meaning. The impact of failure to follow that policy is nowhere better shown than in the results of this surrogacy contract. A child, instead of starting off its life with as much peace and security as possible, finds itself immediately in a tug-of-war between contending mother and father.

The surrogacy contract violates the policy of this State that the rights of natural parents are equal concerning their child, the father's right no greater than the mother's. . . . The whole purpose and effect of the surrogacy contract was to give the father the exclusive right to the child by destroying the rights of the mother.

The policies expressed in our comprehensive laws governing consent to the surrender of a child stand in stark contrast to the surrogacy contract and what it implies. Here there is no counseling, independent or otherwise, of the natural mother, no evaluation, no warning. . . .

Under the contract, the natural mother is irrevocably committed before she knows the strength of her bond with her child. She never makes a totally voluntary, informed decision, for quite clearly any decision prior to the baby's birth is, in the most important sense, uninformed, and any decision after that, compelled by a pre-existing contractual commitment, the threat of a lawsuit, and the inducement of a $ 10,000 payment, is less than totally voluntary. . . .

Although the interest of the natural father and adoptive mother is certainly the predominant interest, realistically the *only* interest served, even they are left with less than what public policy requires. They know little about the natural mother, her genetic makeup, and her psychological and medical history. Moreover, not even a superficial attempt is made to determine their awareness of their responsibilities as parents.

Worst of all, however, is the contract's total disregard of the best interests of the child. There is not the slightest suggestion that any inquiry will be made at any time to determine the fitness of the Sterns as custodial parents, of Mrs. Stern as an adoptive parent, their superiority to Mrs. Whitehead, or the effect on the child of not living with her natural mother.

This is the sale of a child, or, at the very least, the sale of a mother's right to her child, the only mitigating factor being that one of the purchasers is the father. Almost every evil that prompted the prohibition on the payment of money in connection with adoptions exists here. . . .

The main difference [between adoption and surrogacy], that the unwanted pregnancy is unintended while the situation of the surrogate mother is voluntary and intended, is really not significant. Initially, it produces stronger reactions of sympathy for the mother whose pregnancy was unwanted than for the surrogate mother, who "went into this with her eyes wide open." On reflection, however, it appears that the essential evil is the same, taking advantage of a woman's circumstances (the unwanted pregnancy or the need for money) in order to take away her child, the difference being one of degree.

In the scheme contemplated by the surrogacy contract in this case, a middle man, propelled by profit, promotes the sale. Whatever idealism may have motivated any of the participants, the profit motive predominates, permeates, and ultimately governs the transaction. The demand for children is great and the supply small. The availability of contraception, abortion, and the greater willingness of single mothers to bring up their children has led to a shortage of babies offered for adoption. . . .

Intimated, but disputed, is the assertion that surrogacy will be used for the benefit of the rich at the expense of the poor. In response it is noted that the Sterns are not rich and the Whiteheads not poor. Nevertheless, it is clear to us that it is unlikely that surrogate mothers will be as proportionately numerous among those women in the top 20 percent income bracket as among those in the bottom twenty percent. Put differently, we doubt that infertile couples in the low-income bracket will find upper income surrogates. . . .

The long-term effects of surrogacy contracts are not known, but feared—the impact on the child who learns her life was bought, that she is the offspring of someone who gave birth to her only to obtain money; the impact on the natural mother as the full weight of her isolation is felt along with the full reality of the sale of her body and her child; the impact on the natural father and adoptive mother once they realize the consequences of their conduct. . . .

The surrogacy contract is based on, principles that are directly contrary to the objectives of our laws. It guarantees the separation of a child from its mother; it looks to adoption regardless of suitability; it totally ignores the child; it takes the child from the mother regardless of her wishes and her maternal fitness; and it does all of this, it accomplishes all of its goals, through the use of money.

Beyond that is the potential degradation of some women that may result from this arrangement. In many cases, of course, surrogacy may bring satisfaction, not only to the infertile couple, but to the surrogate mother herself. The fact, however, that many women may not perceive surrogacy negatively but rather see it as an opportunity does not diminish its potential for devastation to other women. . . .

IV. CONSTITUTIONAL ISSUES

Both parties argue that the Constitutions—state and federal—mandate approval of their basic claims. . . . The right asserted by the Sterns is the right of procreation; that asserted by Mary Beth Whitehead is the right to the companionship of her child. We find that the right of procreation does not extend as far as claimed by the Sterns. As for the right asserted by Mrs. Whitehead, since we uphold it on other grounds . . . , we need not decide that constitutional issue. . . .

V. CUSTODY

. . . Our reading of the record persuades us that the trial court's decision awarding custody to the Sterns (technically to Mr. Stern) should be affirmed. . . .

Our custody conclusion is based on strongly persuasive testimony contrasting both the family life of the Whiteheads and the Sterns and the personalities and characters of the individuals. The stability of the Whitehead family life was doubtful at the time of trial. Their finances were in serious trouble. . . . Mr. Whitehead's employment, though relatively steady, was always at risk because of his alcoholism, a condition that he seems not to have been able to confront effectively. Mrs. Whitehead had not worked for quite some time, her last two employments having been part-time. . . . Certain of the experts noted that Mrs. Whitehead perceived herself as omnipotent and omniscient concerning her children. She knew what they were thinking, what they wanted, and she spoke for them. As to Melissa, Mrs. Whitehead expressed the view that she alone knew what that child's cries and sounds meant. Her inconsistent stories about various things engendered grave doubts about her ability to explain honestly and sensitively to Baby M—and at the right time—the nature of her origin. . . . In short, while love and affection there would be, Baby M's life with the Whiteheads promised to be too closely controlled by Mrs. Whitehead. The prospects for wholesome, independent psychological growth and development would be at serious risk.

The Sterns have no other children, but all indications are that their household and their personalities promise a much more likely foundation for Melissa to grow and thrive. There *is* a track record of sorts—during the one-and-a-half years of custody Baby M has done very well, and the relationship between both Mr. and Mrs. Stern and the baby has become very strong. The household is stable, and likely to remain so. Their finances are more than adequate, their circle of friends supportive, and their marriage happy. Most important, they are loving, giving, nurturing, and open-minded people. They have demonstrated the wish and ability to nurture and protect Melissa, yet at the same time to encourage her independence. . . . All in all, Melissa's future appears solid, happy, and promising with them. . . .

VI. VISITATION

The trial court's decision to terminate Mrs. Whitehead's parental rights precluded it from making any determination on visitation. . . . We therefore remand the visitation issue to the trial court for an abbreviated hearing. . . .

We also note the following for the trial court's consideration: First, this is not a divorce case where visitation is almost invariably granted to the non-custodial spouse. . . . Mrs. Whitehead spent the first four months of this child's life as her mother and has regularly visited the child since then. Second, she is not only the natural mother, but also the legal mother, and is not to be penalized one iota because of the surrogacy contract. Mrs. Whitehead, as the mother (indeed, as a mother who nurtured her child for its first four months—unquestionably a relevant consideration), is entitled to have her own interest in visitation considered. . . .

CONCLUSION

This case affords some insight into a new reproductive arrangement: the artificial insemination of a surrogate mother. . . .

We have found that our present laws do not permit the surrogacy contract used in this case.

. . . [T]he Legislature remains free to deal with this most sensitive issue as it sees fit, subject only to constitutional constraints.

If the Legislature decides to address surrogacy, consideration of this case will highlight many of its potential harms. . . . Legislative consideration of surrogacy may also provide the opportunity to begin to focus on the overall implications of the new reproductive biotechnology—*in vitro* fertilization, preservation of sperm and eggs, embryo implantation and the like. The problem is how to enjoy the benefits of the technology—especially for infertile couples—while minimizing the risk of abuse. The problem can be addressed only when society decides what its values and objectives are in this troubling, yet promising, area. . . .

Notes

1. Decisional Autonomy. One justification for the court's ruling in *Baby M* was a concern that women may irrevocably consent to relinquishing a child without fully understanding and appreciating the consequences of their acts. When providing guidance to the lower court on visitation for Mrs. Whitehead, the court offered this view:

> It seems to us that given her predicament, Mrs. Whitehead was rather harshly judged—both by the trial court and by some of the experts. She was guilty of a breach of contract, and indeed, she did break a very important promise, but we think it is expecting something well beyond normal human capabilities to suggest that this mother should have parted with her newly born infant without a struggle. Other than survival, what stronger force is there?

Is this accurate, condescending, or both? What assumptions about women's ability to make decisions, particularly those involving reproduction, underlie the court's view? Do similar ones underlie the U.S. Supreme Court's ruling in Gonzales v. Carhart, excerpted in the prior section, that Congress can constitutionally prohibit a particular method of abortion in part to save "a mother who comes to regret her choice to abort" from "grief more anguished and sorrow more profound" when she learns later how the abortion was performed?[444] Are empirical studies, which tend to show that most surrogates are happy with the experience and would do it again, relevant to the legal questions about surrogacy?

2. Gestational Surrogacy. In *Baby M*, Mary Beth Whitehead was the child's biological mother because of her genetic contribution to the child. The agreement entailed what is now referred to as "traditional surrogacy." Because she was the mother, after the New Jersey Supreme Court determined that her rights could not be terminated on the basis of a contract signed before the birth of the child, the custody of the child was adjudicated between her and the child's biological father under the customary test applied in custody disputes between biological parents—i.e., the best interests of the child.

When the genetic and gestational functions are separated, the issue becomes more complicated. With "gestational surrogacy," the surrogate provides the womb, but not the egg. With sperm and egg provided either by the intended parents or donors, conception is achieved through *in vitro* fertilization. Today, almost all surrogacy arrangements are done this way. In Johnson v. Calvert, the gestational mother asserted parental rights against the intended parents, who were also both the genetic parents of the child.[445] The California

---

444. 550 U.S. 124, 159-60 (2007).
445. 19 Cal. Rptr. 2d 494 (Cal. 1993).

Supreme Court interpreted the state's version of the Uniform Parentage Act to permit a finding of parenthood on either genetic or gestational grounds, concluding that "when the two means do not coincide in one woman, she who intended to procreate the child—that is, she who intended to bring about the birth of a child that she intended to raise as her own—is the natural mother under California law."[446] As for the concern expressed by *Baby M* court about when a pre-birth contract could be truly voluntary, the court responded:

> The argument that a woman cannot knowingly and intelligently agree to gestate and deliver a baby for intending parents carries overtones of the reasoning that for centuries prevented woman from attaining equal economic rights and professional status under the law. To resurrect this view is both to foreclose a personal and economic choice on the part of the surrogate mother, and to deny intending parents what may be their only means of procreating a child of their own genes.[447]

In a subsequent California case involving another surrogate who was not the genetic mother, it was the intended father who changed his mind; he no longer wished to be either married or a father. In this case, as well, the court held that the party's original intent should be controlling and that the father would remain responsible for child support.[448]

Some commentators have criticized approaches that give gestational carriers fewer rights to change their minds than those surrogates who are also genetic mothers. The concern is that this both devalues the care invested during gestation and also encourages more couples to undergo egg extraction, a prolonged and difficult process that results in more high-risk pregnancies, so that the surrogate will only have a gestational and not genetic relationship to the infant.[449] If these are valid concerns, what follows? Could the act of gestation create strong emotional ties for which surrogacy law needs to account? A pregnant surrogate in California filed suit to invalidate an agreement she had made to bear triplets for a single man in Georgia. In her complaint, she refers to herself as a mother "as a matter of biologic fact" and cites studies on the physiologic and emotional aspects of pregnancy.[450] Should any of this be relevant to a legal dispute over the enforceability of the contract?

Matters can become even more complicated when neither claimant is the genetic mother. In one egg donor case, a Pennsylvania court voided a surrogacy contract and declared that the legal mother of triplets was the gestational

---

446. Id. at 500.

447. Id. at 503.

448. In re Marriage of Buzzanca, 61 Cal. Rptr. 2d 280 (Ct. App. 1998).

449. Jennifer Hendricks, Essentially a Mother, 13 William & Mary J. Women & L. 429, 477 (2007).

450. M.C. v. C.M., No. __, Ca. Super. Ct. (Jan. 4, 2016).

surrogate, not the contracting couple. The court determined that the egg donor was comparable to a sperm donor.[451] Celebrity talk-show host Sherri Shepard attempted to avoid her responsibilities for a child carried by a surrogate because Sherri and her husband parted ways during the pregnancy. The child was not related genetically to Sherri or to the surrogate; an egg donor was used instead. Her ex-husband, the biological father, is raising the child as a single father and sought child support from Shepard. Sherri sought to invalidate the agreement as against public policy. A Pennsylvania trial court held that the surrogacy agreement was enforceable, tying Sherri to a child who was brought into this world because of her actions but whom she has never met and to whom she is not genetically related.[452] Does her ex ante intent make her more of a mother than the gestational carrier?

Several cases involving lesbian parents and non-traditional reproductive procedures have recognized the parental status of both women.[453] Issues involving lesbian parents are explored more fully in Chapter 2, Section D.

3. The Use and Regulation of Surrogacy. The *Baby M* ruling thrust the surrogacy issue into the public eye. In the year after the ruling, legislatures all over the country considered bills to permit, prohibit, or regulate surrogacy. Most did not become law, but several states, including New York, have since banned surrogacy.[454] But the demand for surrogacy has increased dramatically. Worldwide it is estimated that approximately 7 million children have been born through some means of assisted reproductive technology.[455] Surrogacy is one option for infertile couples, although the cost is often prohibitive. Gay male couples also sometimes turn to surrogacy in order to have a child with a genetic tie to one partner. Exact numbers on surrogacy are hard to get, but the American Society for Reproductive Medicine estimates that the number of surrogate births doubled in seven years, from 738 in 2004 to 1593 in 2011.[456]

---

451. J.F. v. D.B., 66 Pa. D. & C. 4th 1 (Pa. Ct. Comm. Pl. 2004).

452. In re Baby S., 128 A.3d 296 (Pa. 2015).

453. See, e.g., K.M. v. E.G., 117 P.3d 673 (Cal. 2005) (recognizing rights of former lesbian partner who supplied ova; court declined to treat partner like semen donor); Carvin v. Britain, 122 P.3d 161 (Wash. 2005) (lesbian partner standing to seeking custody rights after mother conceived child through artificial insemination).

454. N.Y. Dom. Rel. §123 (2016). Other states that ban paid surrogacy include Arizona, Indiana, Louisiana, Michigan, Nebraska, North Dakota, and Utah. On *Baby M*'s influence, see Elizabeth S. Scott, Surrogacy and the Politics of Commodification, 72 L. Contemp. Prob. 109 (2009). On the role of brokers, see Carol Sanger, Developing Markets in Baby-Making: In the Matter of Baby M, 29 Harv. J.L. & Gender (2007).

455. Emily Galpern, Assisted Reproductive Technologies: Overview and Perspective Using a Reproductive Justice Framework (Dec. 2007), http://geneticsandsociety.org/downloads/ART.pdf.

456. Suzanne Rico, Surrogacy: Joyful, Frightening, Always Risky, The Atlantic, Apr. 2013; Sara Rimer, No Stork Involved, but Mom and Dad Had Help, N.Y. Times, July 12, 2009, at A1.

The vast majority of surrogacy contracts are honored by both parties whether or not they are legally enforceable, but the law develops through the cases in which there are conflicts between the intended parents and the surrogate. In the absence of controlling statutory authority, state courts rulings have produced mixed results. The rulings reflect two primary approaches: (1) an intent-based approach, which seeks to fulfill the intentions of the parties (*Calvert*); or (2) the genetic contribution test, which looks to the genetic tie between parent and child.[457] The Wisconsin Supreme Court has held that surrogacy agreements are enforceable under conventional contract law as long as enforcement is not contrary to the child's best interests.[458] Is that a good compromise, or does it defeat the very purpose of a pre-conception surrogacy agreement?

A number of models for regulating surrogacy have been proposed. The Uniform Status of Children of Assisted Conception Act,[459] adopted by the National Conference of Commissioners on Uniform State Law in 1988, gave jurisdictions a choice about whether to allow surrogacy arrangements. Alternative A spelled out the terms under which surrogacy arrangements were permissible. Alternative B provided that surrogacy agreements are void and unenforceable. Only two states enacted this law, choosing different alternatives. This Act was withdrawn and superseded in 2002 by the amended Uniform Parentage Act (UPA). Section 8 of the UPA, which provides for enforceable agreements using either traditional or gestational surrogacy, is "bracketed," which means it is designed so that legislatures that object to surrogacy can omit it without undermining the other provisions of the Act.

Section 8 of the UPA imposes some restrictions on valid gestational agreements. For example, a married gestational mother's husband must be a party to the agreement, and the gestational agreement cannot "limit the right of the gestational mother's right to make decisions to safeguard her health or that of the embryos or fetus." The provision also mandates pre-conception validation of the gestational agreement by a court, which must find that either the mother or the intended parents have resided in the state for at least ninety days, that the consideration paid is reasonable, that the parties have entered into the agreement voluntarily and with full knowledge of its contents, and that adequate provision has been made for all health-care expenses associated with conception, pregnancy, and childbirth. A non-validated agreement cannot be enforced in court, and may result in unintended assignments of legal parentage and child support obligations.

In the last several years, a handful of state legislatures have adopted laws that permit, but regulate, surrogacy. These laws tend to be more restrictive

---

457. On competing approaches, see Browne C. Lewis, Three Lies and a Truth: Adjudicating Maternity in Surrogacy Disputes, 49 U. Louisville L. Rev. 371 (2011).

458. In re the Paternity of F.T.R., 833 N.W.2d 634 (Wis. 2013).

459. 9 B.U.L.A. 102-17.

than the UPA provision. The Illinois Gestational Surrogacy Act, enacted in 2004, only allows for gestational surrogacy. The act requires that a gestational surrogate be at least twenty-one years old, have given birth already at least once, receive mental and physical health evaluations, and receive independent legal advice. The surrogate must be allowed to choose her own doctor, but the intended parents can insist on behavioral changes that protect fetal health such as giving up smoking and undergoing prenatal testing. The intended parents must prove infertility or a documented medical reason for resorting to surrogacy. At least one of them must provide a gamete used to conceive any resulting child.[460] The New Jersey legislature has passed a similar bill to allow gestational surrogacy under certain conditions, but Governor Chris Christie vetoed it.[461] California, which has allowed surrogacy by judicial decision since 1993, adopted a surrogacy-enabling statute in 2015.[462] This statute does not impose as many restrictions on surrogacy as the Illinois statute, focusing instead on the formality of the agreement and disclosures about the payment of medical expenses. Is one approach preferable? Which concerns about surrogacy does Illinois' more restrictive law try to answer? Does it do so effectively?

The legal landscape for surrogacy thus remains quite checkered. A handful of jurisdictions treat surrogacy agreements as void and unenforceable.[463] Another group of states allow surrogacy under some but not all circumstances.[464] Some states, such as Virginia, require that the surrogate mother be married and already have a child.[465] Other jurisdictions require prior court approval of the arrangement.[466] Some statutes require proof of the intended mother's infertility or other medical need.[467] The most common restrictions are prohibitions or limits on what can be paid. At least four states require the intended parents to be married.[468] Before the Obergefell v. Hodges ruling, discussed in Chapter 2, Section D, the marriage requirement meant that gay

460. 750 Ill. Comp. Stat. Ann. §47/1 et seq. (2016); see also Fla. Stat. §745.15 (2016); N.H. Rev. Stat. §§168-B:1 (2016); Nev. Rev. Stat. §126.045 (2016); Va. Code Ann. §20-159 (2016).

461. See New Jersey Gestational Carrier Agreement Act, N.J. S.B. 1599 (introduced Feb. 13, 2012).

462. Cal. Fam. Code §7962 (2016).

463. See, e.g., Ind. Stat. §31-21-1-1 (2016) (prohibiting surrogacy in all circumstances); Mich. Comp. Laws Ann. §722.851-861 (2016) (same).

464. See, e.g., La. Rev. Stat. Ann. §9:2713 (2016) (prohibiting traditional and compensated surrogacy, but permitting altruistic gestational surrogacy).

465. Va. Code Ann. §20-158 (2016).

466. Utah Code Ann. §78b-15-801-809 (2016).

467. See, e.g., N.H. Rev. Stat. Ann. §168-B:17 (2016) (paid surrogacy permitted if intended mother has demonstrated medical need).

468. Fla. Stat. Ann. §742.11-16 (2016); Tenn. Code Ann. §36-1-102 (2016); Tex. Fam. Code Ann. §160.754 (2016); Utah Code Ann. §§78b-15-801-809 (2016); Va. Code Ann. §20-158; see also Tiffany L. Palmer, The Winding Road to the Two-Dad Family: Issues Arising in Interstate Surrogacy for Gay Couples, 8 Rutgers J.L. & Pub. Pol'y 895, 905 (2011);

couples could not avail themselves of surrogacy as a path to parenthood. Now, however, surrogacy is available to any couple that chooses to marry. Is the elimination of marriage's gender requirement likely to have repercussions for parentage law generally or surrogacy in particular? Does the use of surrogacy by gay male couples raise the same concerns about exploitation of women that some see with hiring one woman to carry a baby for another?

Due to the wide variation in state law on surrogacy, there is considerable uncertainty among parties when they are from different jurisdictions. A case in point involved a man from Ohio and his fiancée from Texas, who entered into a surrogacy contract with a Pennsylvania woman through an Indiana-based agency. After the biological mother gave birth to triplets, a Pennsylvania court voided the contract and gave custody to the mother. An Ohio court contradicted that decision and identified the Texas woman as the legal mother. When the triplets were two years old, a Pennsylvania appellate court overturned the trial court decision and ordered the children to be placed with their biological father.[469] Could any of the underlying state policies be as important as stability in the life of the affected children? In another case, the surrogate fled to Michigan, where surrogacy agreements are unenforceable, to avoid turning over a child with significant birth defects to the intended parents, who indicated they would place the child for adoption.[470] Do these stories justify federal intervention or a unified approach to surrogacy?

The world community reflects similar divisions in legal approaches, with all pre-conception arrangements prohibited in most Middle Eastern countries, China, Denmark, Norway, Switzerland, Costa Rica, and Germany, and only unpaid surrogacy allowed in Korea and Australia. In Great Britain, surrogacy agreements are unenforceable, and it is illegal to advertise for or broker surrogacy arrangements.[471] Surrogacy has increasingly become a feature of "reproductive tourism," in which couples from countries like the United States and England hire surrogate carriers in places like India, where it can be done more cheaply and without legal regulation.[472] Surrogacy in the United States can

---

Elizabeth Meltzer, Eighth Annual Review of Gender and Sexuality Law: Health Care Law Chapter: Assisted Reproductive Technologies, 8 Geo. J. Gender & L. 807, 821-24 (2007).

469. Theresa Glennon, Inaction Causes Harm, Nat'l L.J. July 24, 2006, at 31.

470. Elizabeth Cohen, Surrogate Offered $10,000 to Abort Baby, CNN.com, Mar. 6, 2013; see also Tamar Lewin, Surrogates and Couples Face a Maze of Laws, State by State, N.Y. Times, Sept. 17, 2014.

471. See Jill Elaine Hasday, Intimacy and Economic Exchange, 119 Harv. L. Rev. 491 (2005); Margaret Foster Riley, with Richard A. Merrill, Regulating Reproductive Genetics: A Review of American Bioethics Commissions and Comparison to the British Human Fertilization and Embryology Authority, 6 Colum. Sci. & Tech. L. Rev. 1, 4 (2005).

472. See Debora Spar, Reproductive Tourism and the Regulatory Map, 352 New Eng. J. Med. 531-33 (2005); Debora Spar, The Baby Business: How Money, Science, and Politics Drive the Commerce of Conception (2006); Nilanjana S. Roy, Protecting the Rights of Surrogate Mothers in India, N.Y. Times, Oct. 4, 2011.

cost between $40,000 and $100,000, of which about $25,000 is paid to the surrogate. Surrogacy in India costs between $5,000 and $12,000, with the surrogate receiving only $3,000-$6,000 for her services. Despite the higher price in the United States, it has become one of the leading destinations for surrogacy because of the perception that the law supports enforcement of paid surrogacy contracts, at least in particular states.[473] The Indian government has stated it plans to ban surrogacy for non-Indian couples, but so far it remains unregulated.[474] International surrogacy arrangements, however, have led to conflicts about parentage, citizenship, and other matters when the surrogate and the intended parents come from countries with conflicting laws.[475] The lack of personal contact between intended parents and surrogates may also open the door to greater fraud.[476] Does international surrogacy also heighten concerns about the potential exploitation of women (see Note 5)? Is it a coincidence that India has one-third of the world's poorest people and has become a "surrogacy hub"?

4. Feminist Responses to Surrogacy. Feminist scholars have divided over the issue of surrogacy in general and its implications for autonomy in particular. When the trial court in *Baby M* ordered the surrogacy agreement enforced (a ruling later overturned), Betty Friedan saw "frightening implications for women" and a "terrifying denial of what should be basic rights for women."[477] The principal feminist defense of surrogate contracts credits the surrogate's expression of intent that her role will be limited to gestation and legitimates the contracting father's intent to play an equal parental role. According to Marjorie Shultz:

> Rules that would determine legal parenthood on the basis of individual intentions about procreation and parenting—at least in the context of reproductive technology—would recognize, encourage and reinforce men's choices to nurture children. By adopting a sex-neutral criterion such as intention, the law would partially offset the biological disadvantages men experience in accessing child-nurturing opportunities. The result would parallel recent legal efforts to

473. See Tamar Lewin, Coming to U.S. for Baby, and Womb to Carry It: Foreign Couples Heading to America for Surrogate Pregnancies, N.Y. Times, July 5, 2014, at A1.

474. India to Ban Foreign Surrogate Services, BBC News (Oct. 28, 2015), http://www.bbc.com/news/world-asia-india-34655084.

475. See Hague Conference on Private International Law, A Study of Legal Parentage and the Issues Arising from International Surrogacy Arrangements (Mar. 2014), http://www.hcch.net/upload/wop/gap2014pd03c_en.pdf.

476. See, e.g., Alan Zarembo, Scam Targeted Surrogates as Well as Couples, L.A. Times, Aug. 13, 2011 (describing a criminal enterprise for which surrogates were impregnated for intended parents who did not actually exist, then used as bait for desperate couples willing to pay above-market prices for an already-pregnant surrogate).

477. James Barron, Views on Surrogacy Harden After *Baby M* Ruling, N.Y. Times, Apr. 2, 1987, at A1.

offset the burdens that childbearing imposes on women who seek equal access to market employment.[478]

Of what significance to the debate over surrogacy arrangements are the economic pressures that might lead a surrogate to enter into an arrangement? Toward which legal approach does recognition of these pressures lead? Margaret Radin is concerned about the "commodification of personhood" that surrogacy represents.[479] By contrast, Judge Richard Posner takes an economics efficiency approach in arguing that the financial constraints that push a woman toward becoming a surrogate are no different and no more objectionable than the considerations that motivate all kinds of decisionmaking throughout the economy.[480] This is essentially the framework applied by one court:

> Although common sense suggests that women of lesser means serve as surrogate mothers more often than do wealthy women, there has been no proof that surrogacy contracts exploit poor women to any greater degree than economic necessity in general exploits them by inducing them to accept lower-paid or otherwise undesirable employment.[481]

Who is right? Can women give meaningful consent to act as surrogates without any future parental rights, or are these arrangements unacceptably exploitative? Consider the words of one woman, who served as a surrogate for a gay male couple, in an essay entitled "Mutual Exploitation":

> The obvious assumption is the possibility of exploitation by the intended parents towards the surrogate. However, the reverse is just as easily possible and likely much more prevalent than people realize. In fact, the process may work best when there is mutual exploitation, to a degree. . . . [T]he experience was absolutely ideal. I had amazing people doting on me constantly, and I had the enjoyable pregnancy I had previously missed. It was a spiritual experience to be able to help create a life for two people who so desired a child, and I got to play the nurturing role. . . . On top of all this, I was compensated, and after it all, my life went back to being my life. So I can say, with absolute certainty, that any construed exploitation done 'against' me was equally matched.[482]

---

478. Marjorie Maguire Shultz, Reproductive Technology and Intent-Based Parenthood: An Opportunity for Gender Neutrality, 1990 Wis. L. Rev. 297, 302-03.

479. Margaret Jane Radin, Market Inalienability, 100 Harv. L. Rev. 1849, 1885 (1987).

480. Richard Posner, The Ethics and Economics of Enforcing Contracts of Surrogate Motherhood, 5 J. Contemp. Health L. & Pol'y 21, 26 (1989) (just as only wealthy people can afford butlers and expensive cars, so only wealthy people will be able to afford surrogate mothers).

481. Johnson v. Calvert, 19 Cal. Rptr. 494, 503 (Cal. 1993).

482. Beth Jones, Mutual Exploitation: A Response, in Pregnant Man? A Conversation, 22 Yale J.L. & Feminism 207, 257 (2010).

Critics of surrogate contracts like Nancy Ehrenreich have emphasized how surrogacy arrangements support ideological messages about having a child "of one's own" that have reinforced male dominance and women's sense of obligation to bear children:

> Given the discourse surrounding this issue, which treats infertility as a human tragedy of immense proportions and child rearing as an inviolable right, enforcing such contracts would seem to suggest that it is absolutely essential for women to become mothers by whatever means possible.[483]

Do you agree? Is there another way to read women's desire for surrogacy arrangements? What about men's desire? Is the intended father acting out of a male chauvinist vanity in "wanting a child that is 'his,' or is he expressing a male commitment to nurturing a child?"[484]

Is there a race component to surrogacy arrangements? Consider Anita Allen's concern:

> Minority women increasingly will be sought to serve as "mother machines" for embryos of middle and upper-class clients. It's a new, virulent form of racial and class discrimination. Within a decade, thousands of poor and minority women will be used as a "breeder class" for those who can afford $30,000 to $40,000 to avoid the inconvenience and danger of pregnancy.[485]

April Cherry and Dorothy Roberts also worry that such reproductive technologies reinforce racial hierarchy, particularly in light of current estimates of the cost of the procedure, ranging from $30,000 to $70,000.[486] How should policymakers respond?

Lori B. Andrews, who has vigorously defended surrogacy contracts, is concerned about the implications of assuming that women cannot make responsible reproductive decisions. If gestation gives rise to "special rights" for surrogates to change their minds, could it not also justify "special responsibilities," such as a woman's responsibility to have a Caesarean section if doctors believe it would be beneficial to the child? Andrews concludes:

> Some feminists have criticized surrogacy as turning participating women, albeit with their consent, into reproductive vessels. I see the danger of the anti-surrogacy arguments as potentially turning *all* women into reproductive vessels,

---

483. Nancy Ehrenreich, Surrogacy as Resistance? The Misplaced Focus on Choice in the Surrogacy and Abortion Funding Contexts, 41 DePaul L. Rev. 1369, 1376 (1992).

484. Shultz, supra note 478, at 353.

485. Anita L. Allen, The Black Surrogate Mother, 8 Harv. Blackletter J. 17, 30 (1991).

486. April L. Cherry, Nurturing the Service of White Culture: Racial Subordination, Gestational Surrogacy, and the Ideology of Motherhood, 10 Tex. J. Women & L. 83 (2001); Dorothy E. Roberts, Race and the New Reproduction, 47 Hastings L.J. 935 (1996). For costs, see Alex Kuczynski, Her Body, My Baby, N.Y. Times Mag., Nov. 30, 2008, at 45.

without their consent, by providing government oversight for women's decisions and creating a disparate legal category for gestation.[487]

What is your view? What regulations do you believe should govern surrogacy arrangements?

5. Reproductive Rights in the Surrogacy Context. A recurring conflict in surrogacy cases—at least those that make national news—is whether a provision in the contract allowing the intended parents to make the decision whether to terminate a pregnancy can be enforced. It is common for surrogacy contracts to provide that the gestational surrogate must terminate the pregnancy (or reduce the number of fetuses being carried) upon request of the intended parents. While a few statutes specifically prohibit this type of clause, most states have no rules regarding the scope or content or surrogacy agreements.[488] Can this provision be enforced? Consider the implications of either specific performance—a court order that a woman must have an abortion—or damages for breach of contract. Would either be appropriate and/or constitutional in this context? Deborah Forman writes:

> Although contracts often contain abortion and selective reduction provisions such as these, practitioners routinely describe these as unenforceable, even while advocating their inclusion in the contract. A closer look reveals a somewhat more nuanced perspective: consensus that specific performance of such provisions would never occur but disagreement about whether a surrogate could be liable in damages for breach of contract. Scholars have been a bit more willing to challenge conventional wisdom on the specific performance point, but they by and large echo the practitioner perspective—that provisions relating to abortion are either unenforceable altogether or at best subject to a suit for damages.[489]

If the conventional wisdom is correct, why do lawyers continue to include termination clauses in surrogacy contracts? What purpose do they serve? As a lawyer, what would you say to a client about such a clause? Does a statute prohibiting this type of clause answer any of the concerns about surrogacy described in the preceding materials?

6. Frozen "Pre-embryos": Balancing Wanted and Unwanted Parenthood. As many as a million embryos lie in frozen storage, with

---

487. Lori Andrews, Surrogate Motherhood: The Challenge for Feminists, 16 Law, Med. & Health Care 72, 78 (1988).

488. See, e.g., Utah Code Ann. §78B-15-808(2) & (3) (2016) ("A gestational agreement may not limit the right of the gestational mother to make decisions to safeguard her health or that of the embryo or fetus.").

489. Deborah L. Forman, Abortion Clauses in Surrogacy Contracts: Insights from a Case Study, 49 Fam. L.Q. 29, 34-35 (2015).

little clear law on how to resolve disputes that arise about their use.[490] In one Tennessee case, Davis v. Davis, a couple had planned on using frozen embryos to start a family, but divorced before a pregnancy had been achieved. At divorce, the wife sought custody of the embryos for possible future implantation and the husband sought authority to prevent implantation. The trial court declared that the embryos were "human beings" and awarded custody to the wife on the grounds that such action was the most likely to protect their best interests. The Tennessee Court of Appeals reversed, concluding that the parties shared an equal interest in the embryos, that the husband had a constitutionally protected right not to beget a child where no pregnancy had yet taken place, and that there was no compelling state interest to justify implantation against the will of either party.

On appeal to the state supreme court, the wife changed her position, deciding that rather than use the embryos to become pregnant herself, she wanted to donate them to a childless couple. The court rejected the approaches of both the trial court and the court of appeals, holding that "preembryos are not, strictly speaking, either 'persons' or 'property,' but occupy an interim category that entitles them to special respect because of their potential for human life." The court stated that, if possible, a contest over pre-embryos should be resolved according to prior agreement. Where no such agreement exists, each party's constitutional privacy interests require that their individual positions, burdens, and interests be weighed against those of the other party, with the court's choosing the disposition that avoids the most harm. In *Davis*, the court balanced the interests as follows:

> Beginning with the burden imposed on Junior Davis, we note that the consequences are obvious. Any disposition which results in the gestation of the preembryos would impose unwanted parenthood on him, with all of its possible financial and psychological consequences. The impact that this unwanted parenthood would have on Junior Davis can only be understood by considering his particular circumstances, as revealed in the record.
>
> Junior Davis testified that he was the fifth youngest of six children. When he was five years old, his parents divorced, his mother had a nervous breakdown, and he and three of his brothers went to live at a home for boys run by the Lutheran Church. Another brother was taken in by an aunt, and his sister stayed with her mother. From that day forward, he had monthly visits with his mother but saw his father only three more times before he died in 1976. Junior Davis testified that, as a boy, he had severe problems caused by separation from his parents. He said that it was especially hard to leave his mother after each monthly visit. He clearly feels that he has suffered because of his lack of

490. See Tamar Lewin, Industry's Growth Leads to Leftover Embryos, and Painful Choices, N.Y. Times, June 17, 2015, at A1.

opportunity to establish a relationship with his parents and particularly because of the absence of his father.

In light of his boyhood experiences, Junior Davis is vehemently opposed to fathering a child that would not live with both parents. Regardless of whether he or Mary Sue had custody, he feels that the child's bond with the non-custodial parent would not be satisfactory. He testified very clearly that his concern was for the psychological obstacles a child in such a situation would face, as well as the burdens it would impose on him. Likewise, he is opposed to donation because the recipient couple might divorce, leaving the child (which he definitely would consider his own) in a single-parent setting.

Balanced against Junior Davis's interest in avoiding parenthood is Mary Sue Davis's interest in donating the preembryos to another couple for implantation. Refusal to permit donation of the preembryos would impose on her the burden of knowing that the lengthy IVF procedures she underwent were futile, and that the preembryos to which she contributed genetic material would never become children. While this is not an insubstantial emotional burden, we can only conclude that Mary Sue Davis's interest in donation is not as significant as the interest Junior Davis has in avoiding parenthood. If she were allowed to donate these preembryos, he would face a lifetime of either wondering about his parental status or knowing about his parental status but having no control over it. He testified quite clearly that if the preembryos were brought to term he would fight for custody of his child or children. Donation, if a child came of it, would rob him twice—his procreational autonomy would be defeated and his relationship with his offspring would be prohibited.

The case would be closer if Mary Sue Davis were seeking to use the preembryos herself, but only if she could not achieve parenthood by any other reasonable means. We recognize the trauma that Mary Sue has already experienced and the additional discomfort to which she would be subjected if she opts to attempt IVF again. Still, she would have a reasonable opportunity, through IVF, to try once again to achieve parenthood in all its aspects—genetic, gestation, bearing, and rearing.

Further, we note that if Mary Sue Davis were unable to undergo another round of IVF, or opted not to try, she could still achieve the child-rearing aspects of parenthood through adoption. The fact that she and Junior Davis pursued adoption indicates that, at least at one time, she was willing to forego genetic parenthood and would have been satisfied by the child-rearing aspects of parenthood alone.[491]

Is this analysis consistent with the principle of equality? Is it an application of the "ethic of care"? Pragmatism? Stereotyped thinking? Resistance to stereotypes?

Mary Sue Davis was unable to conceive children through the usual means because, after six painful tubal pregnancies, both of her fallopian tubes were inoperative. Each of the six IVF attempts involved a month of subcutaneous

---

491. Davis v. Davis, 842 S.W.2d 588, 597 (Tenn. 1992).

injections and five anesthetizations for the aspiration procedure. Should this painful series of treatments have been considered in the balancing of interests?

Is it clear to you why Junior Davis' strong feelings — about not fathering children he could not raise himself in a nuclear family — weighed more heavily than Mary Sue Davis' wish to succeed in her efforts to produce one or more children for herself or for others? The court stated that "[o]rdinarily, the party wishing to avoid procreation should prevail, assuming that the other party has a reasonable possibility of achieving parenthood by means other than use of the preembryos in question."[492] The court seemed to suggest that further IVF procedures or adoption would offer reasonable possibilities for Mary Sue Davis to achieve parenthood.

While the law is still emerging in this area, the trend in this context has favored the right not to procreate over the right to procreate, as the court did in *Davis*. But when the frozen embryo represents a party's last chance to conceive a biological child, courts have split on the right approach. A judge in California upheld a consent form a couple signed shortly after they married, which provided that any embryos stored at the fertility clinic would be destroyed if the couple divorced. The couple, Mimi Lee and Stephen Findley, created and stored the embryos because Lee had just been diagnosed with breast cancer and worried about the effects of treatment on her fertility. The couple eventually divorced, and Lee sought to use the embryos to become pregnant. At age 46, she argued in court that these embryos represented her last chance to have a child with a genetic tie to her. Findley objected to the possibility of involuntary parenthood. A judge in San Francisco sided with Findley and ordered that the embryos be thawed and discarded, concluding that he "should be free from court compelled fatherhood and the attendant uncertainties it would bring."[493] Would the judge have reached the same conclusion if the parties had not agreed in advance to the destruction of the embryos? That was the situation in a recent Pennsylvania case. In Reber v. Reiss, the court applied the same balancing test used in *Davis*, supra, because the parties had not entered into an agreement prior to creating the pre-embryos about their disposition in the event of divorce or disagreement. The court concluded that the wife's interest in biological parenthood outweighed the husband's interest in non-parenthood, particularly because the pre-embryos in dispute were her "only opportunity to achieve biological parenthood and her best chance to achieve parenthood at all."[494] In Szafranski v.

---

492. Id. at 604; see also J.B. v. M.B., 783 A.2d 707, 717 (N.J. 2001) (refusing to allow husband to have pre-embryos for use by a surrogate over his soon-to-be ex-wife's objection because he was fertile and had other opportunities to procreate).

493. See Findley v. Lee, No. FDI-13-780539 (Cal. Super. Ct. Nov. 18, 2015); Maura Dolan, Divorced Couple's Frozen Embryos Must be 'Thawed and Discarded,' Judge Rules, L.A. Times, Nov. 18, 2015.

494. 42 A.3d 1131, 1142 (Pa. Super. Ct. 2012).

Dunston, an Illinois appellate court also ruled that a woman could make use of cryopreserved pre-embryos, over the objection of her former partner, in part because they had orally agreed that she could use them regardless of whether the relationship lasted and in part because the pre-embryos represented her "last and only opportunity to have a biological child with her own eggs," and thus her interests outweighed his.[495]

How should courts balance a person's last chance at parenthood versus another person's strong desire to avoid it? Does it matter whether the party seeking to use the embryos is male or female? Some commentators have criticized rulings that deny a party a last chance at parenthood, arguing that there is no convincing evidence of psychological harm from involuntary genetic parenthood, and that whatever interest individuals have in avoiding genetic parenthood should be waivable in advance.[496] Is a person's interest in biological parenthood strong enough that it should outweigh an agreement to the contrary? Several courts have held that a pre-procedure agreement to destroy embryos in the event of one party's death or divorce is enforceable and consistent with public policy.[497] The highest court in Massachusetts wrote in dictum that it would refuse to enforce an agreement giving one party the power to make use of pre-embryos if doing so "would compel one donor to become a parent against his or her will."[498] Thus, even in the face of a contrary agreement, this court seems inclined to favor the right to avoid procreation over the right to procreate. Do you agree with that approach?

A few states have enacted statutes addressing the status or use of cryopreserved preembryos. For example, Florida requires couples and IVF programs to agree in advance about the disposition of preembryos in the event of a divorce or the death of a spouse.[499] Louisiana requires the treatment of pre-embryos as "juridical persons" and prohibits the destruction of preembryos or their use for research purposes.[500] How would you resolve the competing concerns? Is there a "feminist" answer?

---

495. 34 N.E.3d 1132 (Ill. App. 2015).

496. Glenn Cohen, The Constitution and the Rights Not to Procreate, 60 Stan. L. Rev. 1135 (2008). For other commentary, see Jessica Berg, Owning Persons: The Application of Property Theory to Embryos and Fetuses, 40 Wake Forest L. Rev. 159, 161 (2005).

497. Kass v. Kass, 696 N.E.2d 174 (N.Y. 1998); Roman v. Roman, 193 S.W.3d 40 (Tex. App. 2006); In re Marriage of Dahl & Angle, 194 P.3d 834 (Or. Ct. App. 2008).

498. A.Z. v. B.Z., 725 N.E.2d 1051 (Mass. 2000).

499. Fla. Stat. Ann. §742.17 (West 2016).

500. La. Rev. Stat. §9:121 et seq. (West 2016).

Putting Theory Into Practice

5-30. Facebook and Apple now offer to pay for female employees to freeze their eggs.[501] Is this good for working women? Or is it just a way to influence women to subordinate their reproductive choices to someone else (i.e., their employers)?

5-31. In March 2013, a surrogate who had contracted to act as a gestational surrogate carrier for an infertile couple learned from ultrasound tests that the fetus she was carrying suffered from multiple birth defects, including a cleft palate, a brain cyst, and serious heart abnormalities, that would require multiple surgeries upon birth and leave the child with only a 25 percent chance of having a "normal life." The intended parents already had three special-needs children and wanted to spare another child from suffering. The contract required an abortion under such circumstances. The woman states that she has always been against abortion, and refuses to terminate the pregnancy.[502] Who should prevail?

5-32. Mari Smith underwent two rounds of egg stimulation and created and preserved 12 embryos for use by a surrogate. She had no medical need for assisted reproduction, but did not want to be out of work for any lengthy period of time for fear of losing her clientele. Moreover, after watching a friend give birth, she exclaimed: "I don't want to go through that if I don't have to."[503] A week later she wired money to a broker to start searching for a surrogate. Does a case like this affect your views on surrogacy? Why or why not?

5-33. Patricia Williams has argued that "to try to criminalize surrogacy is a bit like trying to criminalize contraception or abortion, in that it comes too close to criminalizing sexuality, libido, intimacy . . ."[504] Is that an apt comparison? Why or why not?

5-34. Every year since 2002, Congress has authorized the spending of between 1 and 2 million dollars to promote the donation of frozen embryos

---

501. Sarah Buhr, Facebook and Apple Offer to Pay for Female Employees to Freeze Their Eggs (Oct. 14, 2014), http://techcrunch.com/2014/10/14/facebook-and-apple-offer-to-pay-for-female-employees-to-freeze-their-eggs.

502. The problem is described in Forman, supra note 489. See also Brittney Kern, "You Are Obligated to Terminate This Pregnancy Immediately": The Contractual Obligations of a Surrogate to Abort Her Pregnancy, 36 Women's Rts. L. Rep. 344 (2015).

503. Sarah Elizabeth Richards, Birth Rights: Inside the Social Surrogacy Debate, Elle (Apr. 17, 2014).

504. Patricia J. Williams, Womb Wars: Fetal Factories, Virgin Vessels and Our Misguided Surrogacy Debate, The Nation, Feb. 24, 2014.

to recipients who intend to use the embryos to bear and raise a child. Is this a good policy?

5-35. Dr. Eleanora Porcu, who helped to develop the technology for freezing of eggs (or oocyte cryopreservation), saw the possibility of freezing unfertilized eggs as a way of sidestepping the Roman Catholic Church's ban on freezing embryos, which the Church deems immoral. However, she is opposed to giving healthy women the opportunity to freeze their eggs so that they can postpone childbearing for their own convenience. This practice is harmful to feminism, she says, because "[i]t means that we're accepting a mentality of efficiency in which pregnancy and motherhood are marginalized." "We've demonstrated that we are able to do everything like men. . . . Now we have to do the second revolution, which is not to become dependent on a technology that involves surgical intervention. We have to be free to be pregnant when we are fertile and young."[505] Do you agree?

5-36. Would enactment of a "personhood amendment," discussed in the previous section, have an effect on surrogacy? On the regulation of cryopreserved preembryos or embryos?

4. The Pregnant Woman and Fetus as Adversaries

A different kind of control of pregnant women concerns their prosecution and confinement for abusing drugs or engaging in other behaviors detrimental to the fetus.

≡≡≡ *Ferguson v. City of Charleston*
532 U.S. 67 (2001)

Justice STEVENS delivered the opinion of the Court.

In this case, we must decide whether a state hospital's performance of a diagnostic test to obtain evidence of a patient's criminal conduct for law enforcement purposes is an unreasonable search if the patient has not consented to the procedure. More narrowly, the question is whether the interest in using the threat of criminal sanctions to deter pregnant women from using cocaine can justify a departure from the general rule that an official nonconsensual search is unconstitutional if not authorized by a valid warrant.

---

505. Rachel Lehmann-Haupt, Why I Froze My Eggs, Newsweek, May 11 & 18, 2009, at 50-51.

I

In the fall of 1988, staff members at the public hospital operated in the city of Charleston by the Medical University of South Carolina (MUSC) became concerned about an apparent increase in the use of cocaine by patients who were receiving prenatal treatment. In response to this perceived increase, as of April 1989, MUSC began to order drug screens to be performed on urine samples from maternity patients who were suspected of using cocaine. If a patient tested positive, she was then referred by MUSC staff to the county substance abuse commission for counseling and treatment. However, despite the referrals, the incidence of cocaine use among the patients at MUSC did not appear to change.

Some four months later, Nurse Shirley Brown, the case manager for the MUSC obstetrics department, heard a news broadcast reporting that the police in Greenville, South Carolina, were arresting pregnant users of cocaine on the theory that such use harmed the fetus and was therefore child abuse. Nurse Brown discussed the story with MUSC's general counsel, Joseph C. Good, Jr., who then contacted Charleston Solicitor Charles Condon in order to offer MUSC's cooperation in prosecuting mothers whose children tested positive for drugs at birth.

After receiving Good's letter, Solicitor Condon took the first steps in developing the policy at issue in this case. He organized the initial meetings, decided who would participate, and issued the invitations, in which he described his plan to prosecute women who tested positive for cocaine while pregnant. The task force that Condon formed included representatives of MUSC, the police, the County Substance Abuse Commission and the Department of Social Services. Their deliberations led to MUSC's adoption of a 12-page document entitled "POLICY M-7," dealing with the subject of "Management of Drug Abuse During Pregnancy."

The first three pages of Policy M-7 set forth the procedure to be followed by the hospital staff to "identify/assist pregnant patients suspected of drug abuse." The first section, entitled the "Identification of Drug Abusers," provided that a patient should be tested for cocaine through a urine drug screen if she met one or more of nine criteria. It also stated that a chain of custody should be followed when obtaining and testing urine samples, presumably to make sure that the results could be used in subsequent criminal proceedings. The policy also provided for education and referral to a substance abuse clinic for patients who tested positive. Most important, it added the threat of law enforcement intervention that "provided the necessary 'leverage' to make the policy effective." That threat was, as respondents candidly acknowledge, essential to the program's success in getting women into treatment and keeping them there.

The threat of law enforcement involvement was set forth in two protocols, the first dealing with the identification of drug use during pregnancy, and the second with identification of drug use after labor. Under the latter protocol, the police were to be notified without delay and the patient promptly arrested. Under the former, after the initial positive drug test, the police were to be notified (and the patient arrested) . . . [unless she consented] to substance abuse treatment.

The last six pages of the policy contained forms for the patients to sign, as well as procedures for the police to follow when a patient was arrested. The policy also prescribed in detail the precise offenses with which a woman could be charged, depending on the stage of her pregnancy. If the pregnancy was 27 weeks or less, the patient was to be charged with simple possession. If it was 28 weeks or more, she was to be charged with possession and distribution to a person under the age of 18—in this case, the fetus. If she delivered "while testing positive for illegal drugs," she was also to be charged with unlawful neglect of a child. Under the policy, the police were instructed to interrogate the arrestee in order "to ascertain the identity of the subject who provided illegal drugs to the suspect." Other than the provisions describing the substance abuse treatment to be offered to women who tested positive, the policy made no mention of any change in the prenatal care of such patients, nor did it prescribe any special treatment for the newborns.

II

Petitioners are 10 women who received obstetrical care at MUSC and who were arrested after testing positive for cocaine. . . .

Petitioners' complaint challenged the validity of the policy under various theories, including the claim that warrantless and nonconsensual drug tests conducted for criminal investigatory purposes were unconstitutional searches. Respondents advanced two principal defenses to the constitutional claim: (1) that, as a matter of fact, petitioners had consented to the searches; and (2) that, as a matter of law, the searches were reasonable, even absent consent, because they were justified by special non-law-enforcement purposes. The District Court rejected the second defense because the searches in question "were not done by the medical university for independent purposes. [Instead,] the police came in and there was an agreement reached that the positive screens would be shared with the police." [The Fourth Circuit Court of Appeals reversed on the grounds that the searches were reasonable under the "special needs" exception.]

We granted certiorari . . . to review the appellate court's holding on the "special needs" issue.

III

Because MUSC is a state hospital, the members of its staff are government actors, subject to the strictures of the Fourth Amendment. . . . Moreover, the urine tests conducted by those staff members were indisputably searches within the meaning of the Fourth Amendment. . . . Neither the District Court nor the Court of Appeals concluded that any of the nine criteria used to identify the women to be searched provided either probable cause to believe that they were using cocaine, or even the basis for a reasonable suspicion of such use. Rather, the District Court and the Court of Appeals viewed the case as one involving MUSC's right to conduct searches without warrants or probable cause. . . . The reasonable expectation of privacy enjoyed by the typical patient undergoing diagnostic tests in a hospital is that the results of those tests will not be shared with nonmedical personnel without her consent. . . . In none of our prior cases was there any intrusion upon that kind of expectation.

The critical difference between those [previous] four drug-testing cases and this one, however, lies in the nature of the "special need" asserted as justification for the warrantless searches. In each of those earlier cases, the "special need" that was advanced as a justification for the absence of a warrant or individualized suspicion was one divorced from the State's general interest in law enforcement. . . . In this case, however, the central and indispensable feature of the policy from its inception was the use of law enforcement to coerce the patients into substance abuse treatment. This fact distinguishes this case from circumstances in which physicians or psychologists, in the course of ordinary medical procedures aimed at helping the patient herself, come across information that under rules of law or ethics is subject to reporting requirements, which no one has challenged here. . . .

Respondents argue in essence that their ultimate purpose—namely, protecting the health of both mother and child—is a beneficent one. . . . While the ultimate goal of the program may well have been to get the women in question into substance abuse treatment and off of drugs, the immediate objective of the searches was to generate evidence for law enforcement purposes in order to reach that goal. The threat of law enforcement may ultimately have been intended as a means to an end, but the direct and primary purpose of MUSC's policy was to ensure the use of those means. In our opinion, this distinction is critical. Because law enforcement involvement always serves some broader social purpose or objective, under respondents' view, virtually any nonconsensual suspicionless search could be immunized under the special needs doctrine by defining the search solely in terms of its ultimate, rather than immediate, purpose. Such an approach is inconsistent with the Fourth Amendment. Given the primary purpose of the Charleston program, which was to use the threat of arrest and prosecution in order to force women into treatment, and given the extensive involvement of law enforcement officials at every stage of the policy, this case simply does not fit within the closely guarded category of "special needs."

Accordingly, the judgment of the Court of Appeals is reversed, and the case is remanded for further proceedings consistent with this opinion.

Dissenting opinion by Justice SCALIA, with whom THE CHIEF JUSTICE and Justice THOMAS join as to Part II.

There is always an unappealing aspect to the use of doctors and nurses, ministers of mercy, to obtain incriminating evidence against the supposed objects of their ministration—although here, it is correctly pointed out, the doctors and nurses were ministering not just to the mothers but also to the children whom their cooperation with the police was meant to protect. But whatever may be the correct social judgment concerning the desirability of what occurred here, that is not the issue in the present case. The Constitution does not resolve all difficult social questions, but leaves the vast majority of them to resolution by debate and the democratic process—which would produce a decision by the citizens of Charleston, through their elected representatives, to forbid or permit the police action at issue here. The question before us is a narrower one: whether, whatever the desirability of this police conduct, it violates the Fourth Amendment's prohibition of unreasonable searches and seizures. In my view, it plainly does not.

I . . .

Until today, we have never held—or even suggested—that material which a person voluntarily entrusts to someone else cannot be given by that person to the police, and used for whatever evidence it may contain. Without so much as discussing the point, the Court today opens a hole in our Fourth Amendment jurisprudence, the size and shape of which is entirely indeterminate. . . .

II . . .

The conclusion of the Court that the special-needs doctrine is inapplicable rests upon its contention that respondents "undertook to obtain [drug] evidence from their patients" not for any medical purpose, but "for the specific purpose of incriminating those patients." In other words, the purported medical rationale was merely a pretext; there was no special need. . . . This contention contradicts the District Court's finding of fact that the goal of the testing policy "was not to arrest patients but to facilitate their treatment and protect both the mother and unborn child." . . . This finding is binding upon us unless clearly erroneous. . . .

The cocaine tests started in April 1989, neither at police suggestion nor with police involvement. Expectant mothers who tested positive were referred by hospital staff for substance-abuse treatment—an obvious health benefit to both mother and child. . . . And, since "infants whose mothers abuse cocaine during pregnancy are born with a wide variety of physical and neurological abnormalities," . . . which require medical attention, . . . the tests were of additional medical benefit in predicting needed postnatal treatment for the child. Thus, in their origin—before the police were in any way involved—the tests had an immediate, not merely an "ultimate" . . . purpose of improving maternal and infant health. . . .

[I]t is not the function of this Court—at least not in Fourth Amendment cases—to weigh petitioners' privacy interest against the State's interest in meeting the crisis of "crack babies" that developed in the late 1980's. I cannot refrain from observing, however, that the outcome of a wise weighing of those interests is by no means clear. The initial goal of the doctors and nurses who conducted cocaine-testing in this case was to refer pregnant drug addicts to treatment centers, and to prepare for necessary treatment of their possibly affected children. When the doctors and nurses agreed to the program providing test results to the police, they did so because (in addition to the fact that child abuse was required by law to be reported) they wanted to use the sanction of arrest as a strong incentive for their addicted patients to undertake drug-addiction treatment. And the police themselves used it for that benign purpose, as is shown by the fact that only 30 of 253 women testing positive for cocaine were ever arrested, and only 2 of those prosecuted. . . . It would not be unreasonable to conclude that today's judgment, authorizing the assessment of damages against the county solicitor and individual doctors and nurses who participated in the program, proves once again that no good deed goes unpunished.

Notes

1. Drug Testing of Welfare Recipients.   The 1996 welfare reform act, discussed in Section C, below, included a provision making clear that states would not be prohibited by federal law from sanctioning welfare applicants who tested positive for controlled substances.[506] As of 2015, 13 states required drug testing or screening for all public assistance applicants and another 18 were considering such requirements.[507] States vary in the sanctions that they impose for drug use. In some states, such as Tennessee, applicants can receive benefits while in treatment. And in Tennessee, even if parents don't enroll in treatment, the state can designate a "protective payee" so that their children can still get benefits.[508] No state legislation, however, gives priority for drug treatment to welfare applicants nor allocates additional funding for treatment

---

506. 21 U.S.C. §862 (b) (1996).

507. Nat'l Conference of State Legislatures, Drug Testing for Welfare Recipients and Public Assistance (July 27, 2015), http://www.ncsl.org/research/human-services/drug-testing-and-public-assistance.aspx.

508. Arthur Delaney, States Continue Welfare Drug Tests Despite Underwhelming Results, Huff. Post (Oct. 8, 2015).

programs.[509] States also vary in terms of the privacy protection they provide for test results. In one survey, only one jurisdiction barred the use of results in other investigations and proceedings; most states allowed records to be shared with other state agencies and only two mandated disclosure to child protection agencies.[510]

In 2014, the Eleventh Circuit Court of Appeals enjoined Florida's system of mandatory drug tests for all TANF applicants. According to the Governor, the measure was a valid means of saving revenue and ensuring that benefits accomplish their intended purpose. "Welfare is for the benefit of children, and the money should go to the benefit of children," he stated. "This makes all the sense in the world."[511] However, the court found that the state had made no showing of a special need for mandatory suspicionless testing sufficient to suspend normal Fourth Amendment search and seizure protections. Nor was consent to the tests by beneficiaries freely and voluntarily given. Relevant to the court's analysis was a study finding a lower rate of drug use among TANF applicants than in the Florida population generally.[512]

National studies similarly find that the rate of drug use among TANF recipients is generally below 1 percent, compared with 9 percent among the general public.[513] After the Eleventh Circuit decision, states that maintained testing programs generally tested only those who have been identified by a preliminary questionnaire as raising reasonable suspicion of drug use.

Is the denial of welfare benefits for not agreeing to a drug test, or passing it, permissible after *Ferguson*? Even if it does not violate the Fourth Amendment, is it unlawfully discriminatory? What if there are not adequate drug treatment facilities? Would you support Tennessee's approach? Should welfare authorities be allowed to share results with child protective services?[514]

2. Criminal Prosecutions of Drug-Abusing Pregnant Women. According to the Department of Health and Human Services, about 5.4 percent of pregnant women in 2013 used illicit drugs.[515] Drug abuse by

509. Wendy A. Bach, The Hyperregulatory State: Women, Race, Poverty, and Support, 25 Yale J.L. & Feminism 317, 360-61 (2014).

510. Id. at 363-68.

511. Michael C. Bender, Drug Test Law Faces Challenge, St. Petersburg Times, Sept. 8, 2011, at A1 (quoting Rick Scott).

512. Lebrun v. Secretary, Florida Dep't of Children and Families, 772 F.3d 1352 (11th Cir. 2014).

513. Bryce Covert & Josh Israel, What 7 States Discovered After Spending More Than $1 Million Drug Testing Welfare Recipients, Think Progress (Feb. 26, 2015), http://think progress.org/economy/2015/02/26/3624447/tanf-drug-testing-welfare-recipients.

514. See Bach, supra note 509, for arguments that welfare recipients should not be punished for submitting to drug tests.

515. DHHS, Results from the 2013 National Survey on Drug Use and Health: Summary of National Findings 26 (2014).

a pregnant woman, especially crack cocaine, enhances certain serious risks to the unborn child, including growth retardation, smaller head circumference, impaired motor development, greater difficulty with tasks that require visual attention and focus, and higher incidences of depression, anxiety, attention-deficit disorders, and delinquent and aggressive behaviors. Boys appear to be more vulnerable than girls to behavior problems. However, the long-term damage does not appear to be as serious as was once thought. A study based on 4,419 cocaine-exposed children showed that I.Q. scores averaged only about four points lower than those of unexposed children, and that children outgrow some of the effects in terms of brain and body size.[516] New research suggests that *in utero* exposure to methamphetamine is a growing problem and may pose similar or ever greater dangers than cocaine.[517]

In response to growing concern about the risks of fetal damage from drug use, prosecutors in a significant majority of states have charged drug-addicted pregnant women under various criminal statutes prohibiting delivery of a controlled substance to a minor, child abuse or endangerment, and homicide.[518] Many charges have been rejected, at least on appeal, on the grounds that the statutes under which charges were brought were not intended to apply to unborn children as victims. The Kentucky Supreme Court, for example, reversed a criminal conviction of a woman whose baby tested positive for cocaine at birth. In construing the child endangerment law to exclude a pregnant woman's conduct, the court relied in part on the state's Maternal Health Act of 1992, in which the legislature stated that "punitive actions taken against pregnant alcohol or substance abusers would create additional problems, including discouraging these individuals from seeking the essential prenatal care and substance abuse treatment necessary to deliver a healthy newborn."[519] Substance abuse by pregnant women, according to the Kentucky legislature, should be treated "solely as a public health issue."[520] To the same end, the South Carolina Supreme Court in 2008 overturned the conviction of a defendant for homicide by child abuse, on grounds of ineffective counsel. Although the defendant's fetus was stillborn and tested positive for cocaine, the court concluded that the state relied upon "outdated" research about the consequences of cocaine use on the fetus, and that defendant's counsel had failed to call experts who would have testified about "recent studies showing that cocaine is no more harmful to a fetus than nicotine use, poor nutrition,

---

516. Susan Okie, The Epidemic That Wasn't, N.Y. Times, Jan. 27, 2009, at D1.

517. Linda L. LaGasse et al., Prenatal Methamphetamine Exposure and Childhood Behavior Problems at 3 and 5 Years of Age, 129 Pediatrics 680 (2012).

518. See Lynn M. Paltrow & Jeanne Flavin, Arrests and Forced Medical Interventions on Pregnant Women in the United States, 38 J. Health Politics, Pol'y & L. 299, 309 (2013); Deborah L. Rhode, What Women Want: An Agenda for the Women's Movement 92 (2014).

519. Cochran v. Commonwealth, 315 S.W.3d 325, 329 (Ky. 2010).

520. Maternal Health Act of 1992, 1992 Ky. Acts, ch. 442 (H.B. 192) (preamble).

lack of prenatal care, or other conditions commonly associated with the urban poor."[521] Courts in South Carolina and Alabama, however, have upheld convictions for drug use during pregnancy.[522] In 2014, Tennessee became the first state to expressly criminalize drug use by a pregnant woman.[523]

There is little doubt that statutes specifically targeted at drug abuse by pregnant women would be constitutional and enforceable, and legislatures in a number of states have begun to pass such laws. One example that has become a model for other states is a Utah law enacted in 2010 that makes it criminal homicide for a woman to engage in conduct that intentionally or knowingly causes a miscarriage.[524] Is this a reasonable statute?[525] A 2006 Alabama law prohibits a "responsible person" from "exposing a child to an environment in which he or she . . . knowingly, recklessly or intentionally causes of permits a child to be exposed to, to ingest or inhale, or to have contact with a controlled substance, chemical substance or drug paraphernalia." The law was intended to protect children from the dangers of methamphetamine labs, but prosecutors have expanded the law's definition of "child" to mean "fetus" and interpreted the term "environment" to also mean the "womb." According to the New York Times, there have been approximately sixty chemical-endangerment prosecutions of new mothers since the law was passed. The minimum sentence under the law is ten years.[526] Is this a reasonable approach?

In one Indiana case, a despondent pregnant woman who was 33-weeks pregnant swallowed rat poison in an effort to end her life after her boyfriend abandoned her. Although the woman lived, the baby, who was delivered by emergency C-section, did not. She was convicted of murder, and the conviction was upheld by the Indiana Court of Appeals.[527] Is a murder prosecution reasonable under these circumstances?[528]

---

521. McKnight v. State, 661 S.E.2d 354 (S.C. 2008). *McKnight* appeared to mark a shift from an earlier decision in South Carolina, Whitner v. State, 492 S.E.2d 777 (S.C. 1997), which rejected an ineffective counsel claim and upheld a criminal child neglect conviction under the child endangerment law, based on the conclusion that a viable fetus is a "child" and that proof of cocaine metabolites in the infant at birth proved endangerment by the mother in the last trimester.

522. *Whitner*, 492 S.E.2d at 777; see also Ex Parte Ankrom, 152 So. 3d 397 (Ala. 2013).

523. Tenn. Code Ann. §39-13-107 (2016).

524. See 2010 Ut. HB 462.

525. See Lynn M. Paltrow & Farah Diaz-Tello, Caution: Pregnancy May Be Hazardous to Your Liberty, Huff. Post (Mar. 2, 2010) (arguing "no," and citing a number of other state law examples).

526. See Ada Calhoun, The Criminalization of Bad Mothers, N.Y. Times Mag., Apr. 25, 2012, at 30.

527. See Bei Bei Shuai v. State, 966 N.E.2d 619 (Ind. Ct. App. 2012). For a news video account of the case, see Attorney Rips Prosecutor in Infant Rat Poison Death, ABC (Mar. 16, 2011), http://www.theindychannel.com/news/27215238/detail.html.

528. For the argument that such prosecutions "fly in the face of medical and public health recommendations regarding the most effective and appropriate ways to respond to suicide at-

In the 2-1 decision, the dissenting judge suggested that holding the woman's actions covered by Indiana's feticide statute could result in the criminalization of pregnant women who smoke, drink, or take over-the-counter cold remedies and sleep aids. The majority responded that the statute requires the intention to terminate a pregnancy.[529] Is this a satisfactory limiting principle? According to the Department of Health and Human Services, 10.8 percent of pregnant women use alcohol during pregnancy, and 16.3 percent use tobacco—two to three times, respectively, the number of pregnant women who abuse illegal drugs.[530]

An upstate New York woman was charged with child endangerment after she delivered a baby whose blood alcohol was 0.18 percent; the charges were later dismissed on the grounds that the state's child-endangerment statute was not intended to apply to the unborn.[531] If the state amended the statute to include such conduct, what penalties would be appropriate? What about pregnant women who drive too fast, fail to use seat belts, or work extended hours against the advice of their doctors? Jennifer Jorgensen was pregnant and not wearing a seatbelt when she was in a car accident in 2008. At the hospital, she consented to an emergency cesarean section at 34-weeks of gestation because the fetus was showing signs of distress. The baby died six days later from injuries caused by the accident. She was charged with manslaughter for the baby's death, as well as for the death of two people in the car she hit. She was alleged to have been speeding and under the influence of a prescription drug and alcohol. A jury found her not guilty on all counts except for manslaughter in connection with the death of her child. On appeal, however, the state's highest court held that the criminal law was not intended "to hold pregnant women criminally responsible for conduct with respect to themselves and their unborn fetuses unless such conduct is done intentionally."[532] What might have led the jury to convict Jorgensen for manslaughter of her child, but not of the two strangers killed in the same accident?

The effects of substance abuse can interact with other risk factors and cultural biases. For example, research shows that among women who drink at the same rate, children born to low-income women have a 70.9 percent rate of fetal alcohol syndrome, compared to a 4.5 percent rate for those of upper-income women. Better nutrition is the difference. A Northwestern University study suggests that outcomes in pregnancies complicated by cocaine abuse

tempts and drug-dependency disorders," see Lynn Paltrow, Is Locking Up Pregnant Women the New Cure for State Financial Woes and Mental Health Problems?, RH Reality Check (Mar. 30, 2011), http://www.rhrealitycheck.org/blog/2011/03/30/locking-pregnant-women-cure-state-financial-woes-mental-health-problems.

529. Id.

530. See DHHS, supra note 515, at 29, 43.

531. Jordan Carleo, Evangelist, Charge Dropped in Drunken Baby Case, Albany Times Union, Apr. 9, 2004, at B1.

532. People v. Jorgensen, 41 N.E.3d 778, 780 (N.Y. 2015).

may be improved by comprehensive prenatal care.[533] Race and class also affect how service providers respond to high-risk factors. One study found that despite similar rates of substance abuse, black women are ten times more likely than white women to be reported to government authorities.[534]

Should a pregnant woman who is in an abusive relationship and does not leave her batterer be prosecuted under a child abuse statute? Her abuser is subject to additional penalties. Federal legislation criminalizes harm caused to a "child in utero" during the course of other specified offenses. So, for example, a man who assaults his pregnant partner can also be guilty of a separate crime under federal law if he causes injury to the fetus.

Some courts have ordered female offenders with a history of substance abuse to avoid becoming pregnant, as a term of probation. Such a probationary condition has generally been overturned because it is not reasonably related to the crime committed (which often has nothing to do with childrearing) or to the goal of rehabilitation. However, some trial courts have ordered women who have been convicted of child abuse not to become pregnant as a condition of probation. Many of these cases, too, have been overturned on appeal.[535]

Does it matter whether courts and legislatures are acting on inaccurate scientific information when imposing restrictions and penalties on pregnant women who use drugs or alcohol? In 2013, science and medical experts wrote a letter to media outlets and policy makers urging them to take an evidence-based approach to writing about and reacting to the problem of pregnant women who use prescription opiates.[536] For example, the letter observes that the babies born to these women are frequently described as "addicted" to drugs, when that term is accurately used only with respect to "compulsive behavior that continues in spite of adverse consequences" and can never accurately be used to describe a child in utero or in infancy. Whose responsibility is it to educate lawmakers?

3. Civil Alternatives to Criminal Prosecution. What about a form of "civil commitment" (not requiring a criminal conviction) for women who are in grave danger of drug abuse during a pregnancy? In 1998, South Dakota became the first state to require pregnant women who abuse alcohol or drugs

---

533. Dorothy E. Roberts, Race and the New Reproduction, 47 Hastings L.J. 935, 953-54 (1996).

534. Id. at 947-48.

535. See, e.g., Trammell v. State, 751 N.E.2d 283 (Ind. Ct. App. 2001) (no-pregnancy condition excessively infringes on defendant's privacy rights and serves no rehabilitative purpose).

536. Press Statement, Experts Urge Media to End Inaccurate Reporting on Prescription Opiate Use by Pregnant Women (Mar. 13, 2013), http://advocatesforpregnantwomen.org/issues/pregnancy_and_drug_use_the_facts/experts_urge_media_to_end_inaccurate_reporting_on_prescription_opiate_use_by_pregnant_women.php.

to be taken into custody and to undergo mandatory rehabilitation. Wisconsin and Minnesota soon followed, and several other states have considered adopting a similar approach.[537] Would you support such legislation? Does it present different concerns than treatment required as a condition of probation?

The Canadian Supreme Court considered this issue. In Winnipeg Child and Family Services v. G.D.F., a trial court granted an order to confine a pregnant woman who was addicted to glue sniffing, which can damage the fetal nervous system. Two of the woman's previous children were born permanently disabled and were wards of the state. The Canadian Supreme Court held that the court lacked authority to order confinement to protect the unborn under its parens patriae jurisdiction, which sometimes allows courts to step into the shoes of the parent to safeguard the best interests of a child. In so holding, the court expressed concerns not only about the restriction of women's rights, but also the possibility that confinement would "drive the problem underground" by deterring women from seeking prenatal care. Two dissenting Justices would have permitted intervention to prevent "abusive activity that will cause serious and irreparable harm to the [fetus]," where the remedy was the "least intrusive option" and the process was procedurally fair. In the dissent's view, "when a woman chooses to carry a fetus to term, she must accept some responsibility for its well-being and the state has an interest in trying to ensure the child's health."[538] What is your view? Should it matter whether the woman chose not to take advantage of voluntary treatment programs?

State child abuse and neglect statutes provide another response to the problem. These civil statutes are available only if a court concludes that they were intended to apply to prenatal conduct. Civil child abuse laws in more than a dozen states apply to substance abuse during pregnancy.[539] In a 2013 case, New Jersey Dep't of Children & Families, Div. of Youth & Family Servs. v. A.L, 59 A.3d 576 (N.J. 2013), the New Jersey Supreme Court held that a court cannot make a finding of abuse or neglect based on an expectant mother's drug use during pregnancy unless there is evidence of actual or imminent harm when the baby is born, and a positive drug test at birth is insufficient evidence of such harm. With respect to an entry on the baby's medical record, which noted "the presence of the following cocaine metabolite(s) . . . Benzoylecgonine = 88 ng/g" in the baby's meconium, the court wrote:

---

537. See Guttmacher Inst., State Policies in Brief: Substance Abuse During Pregnancy (2016), http://www.guttmacher.org/statecenter/spibs/spib_SADP.pdf (noting that 18 states treat substance abuse during pregnancy as a form of child abuse, while 3 deem it sufficient grounds for civil commitment).

538. 3 S.C.R. 925 (1997).

539. See, e.g., Fla. Stat. Ann. §415.503(9)(g)(1) (West 2016); 705 Ill. Comp. Stat. Ann. §405/2-18(2)(c) & (d) (2016); Nev. Rev. Stat. Ann. §432B.330(1)(b) (2016).

Neither the hospital records nor any other document explains what benzoylec-gonine is or discloses the meaning of the level reported in this case. On its own, the one entry does not tell us whether the mother is an addict or used an illegal substance on a single occasion. The notation does not reveal the severity or extent of the mother's substance abuse or . . . the degree of future harm posed to the child . . . Judges at the trial and appellate level cannot fill in missing information on their own or take judicial notice of harm. Instead, the fact-sensitive nature of abuse and neglect cases turns on particularized evidence.

Would the individualized, evidence-based inquiry called for by this court be possible under many of the laws and proposed laws discussed in this section? Does a more generalized approach offer sufficient benefits to offset the possible harm of overreaching?

In Florida, Samantha Burton was hospitalized without her consent after she was admitted to hospital in her seventh month of pregnancy on a false alarm of premature labor. Her doctor argued that she was risking a miscarriage if she didn't quit smoking immediately and stay on bed rest in the hospital, and a judge agreed.[540] Should a second opinion have been required, at least?

If drug abuse during pregnancy constitutes child neglect, what governmental responses are most appropriate? Removal of the child from the parent and in some cases termination of parental rights are the most likely options, but is that a good option for the child?

Every leading medical organization, including the American Medical Association and the American College of Obstetricians and Gynecologists, has concluded that the best response to substance abuse during pregnancy is education and treatment rather than punishment.[541] As they note, the primary effect of punitive policies is to force substance abuse underground and deter women from seeking drug treatment and prenatal care. Although most states have provided some resources for such approaches, many programs come nowhere close to meeting the need.[542] Several of the pregnant addicts facing well-publicized prosecutions for criminal child abuse had sought treatment, but found either that waiting lists were long or that the programs available would not accept

540. See Bill Kaczor, Florida Woman Fights Ruling that Kept Her in Hospital (Jan. 26, 2010), http://apnews.myway.com/article/20100126/D9DFDKO0.html.

541. Rhode, What Women Want, supra note 518, at 91; see also Linda C. Fentiman, The New "Fetal Protection": The Wrong Answer to the Crisis of Inadequate Health Care for Women and Children, 84 Denv. U. L. Rev. 537, 594-97 (2006) (proposing a more aggressive battle against poverty, universal health care, expanded and targeted substance abuse programs for pregnant women, improved environmental and workplace health laws, and a no-fault program to compensate children who suffer prenatal harm).

542. David C. Brody & Heidee McMillin, Combating Fetal Substance Abuse and Governmental Foolhardiness Through Collaborative Linkages, Therapeutic Jurisprudence, and Common Sense: Helping Women Help Themselves, 12 Hastings Women's L.J. 243, 268 (2001).

pregnant women. In New York City, 87 percent of drug treatment programs reject pregnant Medicaid patients addicted to crack cocaine, and yet these are the women most likely to be targeted for prosecution.[543]

In partial response to this problem, Congress passed the Alcohol, Drug Abuse, and Mental Health Administration Reorganization Act.[544] This legislation expands block grants provided to states for drug treatment programs, including money targeted at addressing the particular needs of pregnant, drug-addicted women. A number of states have enacted legislation to prohibit drug treatment facilities from discriminating against pregnant women.[545]

Putting Theory Into Practice

5-37. A nonprofit organization founded as Children Requiring a Caring Kommunity (C.R.A.C.K.), later renamed Project Prevention, was established to provide "effective prevention measures to reduce the tragedy of numerous drug-affected pregnancies." The Project offers $300 to drug-abusing females who promise to be sterilized or to receive long-term birth control. As of February 2016, 5543 addicts or alcoholics had taken advantage of the offer. Of those whose race is noted, 32 percent are black or Hispanic.[546] Is Project Prevention a good approach? Is its approach any more, or less, defensible than court-mandated probation conditions?

5-38. To be eligible for Medicaid-subsidized prenatal care in New York, a pregnant woman is compelled by law to be interviewed by a battery of professionals, including nurses, health educators, financial officers, HIV counselors, and social workers. The questions include personal details about any past and current romantic relationships, experience with domestic violence, use of alcohol and drugs, mental illness, eating habits, earning capacity, and the earning capacity of any boyfriends.[547] Is this appropriate? Are poor, pregnant

---

543. Rachel Roth, Making Women Pay: The Hidden Costs of Fetal Rights 140 (2000).

544. Pub. L. No. 102-321, 106 Stat. 323 (codified as amended in scattered sections of 42 U.S.C.A. §§201-300 (West Supp. 2012)).

545. See Jean Reith Schroedel & Pamela Fiber, Punitive Versus Public Health Oriented Responses to Drug Use by Pregnant Women, 1 Yale J. Health Pol'y L. & Ethics 217 (2001).

546. See http://www.projectprevention.org/statistics/; see also Lynn Paltrow, Why Caring Communities Must Oppose C.R.A.C.K./Project Prevention: How C.R.A.C.K. Promotes Dangerous Propaganda and Undermines the Health and Well Being of Children and Families, 5 J.L. Soc'y 11, 13-15 (2003) (challenging negative racial and gender stereotypes that the program promotes).

547. For details about the New York State Prenatal Assistance Program, see Khiara M. Bridges, Privacy Rights and Public Families, 34 Harv. J. Law & Gender 113 (2011). For discussion of the larger issue of what conditions the state may place on public assistance, see Dorothy Roberts, The Only Good Poor Woman: Unconstitutional Conditions and Welfare, 72 Denv. U.L. Rev. 931 (1995).

women entitled to any privacy with respect to their personal relationships and habits, or is this divulging information a reasonable quid pro quo for public assistance?

5-39. Wisconsin state Senator Glenn Grothman has proposed SB507, which provides for statewide education and public awareness campaigns about child abuse and neglect. The bill specifies that "[i]n promoting these campaigns and materials, the [Child Abuse and Neglect Prevention Board] shall emphasize nonmarital parenthood as a contributing factor to child abuse and neglect."[548] How would you respond to this proposed legislation?

5-40. A 28-year-old woman from Salt Lake City failed to follow medical advice to have a Caesarean section. As a result, one of her twins was stillborn, although he could have been saved if the mother had undergone the procedure. She was arrested for first-degree criminal homicide and child endangerment. What defenses could be raised on her behalf? Should her conduct be criminalized? The woman later pled guilty to two counts of child endangerment and the homicide charge was dropped.[549] Is this an appropriate outcome? Should the failure of a mother to consent to a medically recommended Caesarean section be an appropriate factor to consider in a subsequent abuse and neglect action on behalf of the child, even if the vaginal birth was successful?[550]

5-41. The increased use of in vitro fertilization (IVF) procedures over the years has led to an increasing number of multiple births, which in turn has increased the number of low-birth-weight babies. The increased risk results from the limitations of the uterus, resulting in a greater likelihood of preterm labor, and medical care that is ten times as great in the first year than for an average-weight newborn. A legislator has proposed a bill that would (1) make it a crime for a doctor to transfer any more than three embryos to a woman's womb in a single IVF procedure, and, (2) in the event of multiple conceptions through IVF, it would authorize government funds to pay for the "selective reduction" of one or more fetuses. The proposed legislation was prompted by public outcry after an unmarried woman, who already had six children ages

548. Glenn Grothman, Wisconsin Senator, Proposes Law That Declares Single Parenthood Child Abuse, Huff. Post, Mar. 2, 2012.

549. See Monica K. Miller, Refusal to Undergo a Cesarean Section: A Woman's Right or a Criminal Act?, 15 Health Matrix 383 (2005).

550. See N.J. Div. of Youth & Family Servs. v. V.M., 974 A.2d 448 (N.J. Super. Ct. App. Div. 2009) (yes), discussed critically in Jessica L. Waters, In Whose Best Interest? New Jersey Division of Youth and Family Services v. V.M. and B.G. and the New Wave of Court-Controlled Pregnancies, 34 Harv. J. Law & Gender 81 (2011).

seven and under, became pregnant with octuplets through an IVF procedure supervised by a doctor.[551] Would you support this legislation? Why or why not?

5-42. An Indiana woman, Purvi Patel, induced an abortion with pills she ordered from Hong Kong (the same pills were available in the United States with a prescription). Bleeding and in pain, she went to an emergency room. She told the doctors that she miscarried and that the baby was stillborn. When asked what she had done with the fetal remains, she said she didn't know what to do and thus had left them in a dumpster. Police recovered the body, and she was eventually charged with child felony neglect and feticide. At trial, experts for the prosecution and defense disagreed both about how far along she was in the pregnancy (23-24 weeks vs. 25-30 weeks) and whether the baby was born alive. She was convicted on both counts and sentenced to twenty years in prison.[552] Should women who self-induce abortions be subject to criminal penalties?

5-43. Should welfare benefits be subject to a clean drug test? See Section C below.

5-44. There are nearly 50,000 new HIV infections a year, over 20 percent of them under the age of 24. An antiretroviral medication, Truvada, originally approved to treat HIV has been found to *prevent* HIV infection.[553] What strategies, if any, would you favor to obtain wider use of this drug? Should information about it be provided in sex education classes? Should it be available to teenagers without the consent of their parents? Should it be *required* for children in high-risk families?

C. ECONOMIC AUTONOMY AND WOMEN'S POVERTY

One of the most significant constraints on women's autonomy is not primarily legal, but economic. The final section of this chapter explores the welfare system and its impact on poverty among women and their children.

Welfare began in the United States as part of state "mother's pensions" programs for destitute families. Use of the term "pension" implied that the payment was a substitute for money that might otherwise be received in paid

---

551. For some provocative views, see Kate Zernike, And Baby Makes How Many?, N.Y. Times, Feb. 9, 2009, at ST1; Lisa Belkin, How Many Children Is Too Many? N.Y. Times, Feb. 9, 2009.

552. Emily Bazelon, *Purvi Patel* Could Be Just the Beginning, N.Y. Times Mag. (Apr. 1, 2015).

553. For results of her appeal, see Patel v. State, 2016 WL 3959344 (July 22, 2016). See Jason Potter Burda, PREP and Our Youth: Implications in Law and Policy, 30 Colum. J. Gender & L. 295, 296 (2016).

employment. Implicit in these early programs was the understanding that childrearing was work and that a mother's devotion to the care of her children was important.[554] The initial purpose was to relieve impoverishment caused by mothers having been widowed or abandoned by their husband—i.e., "worthy" mothers. From the very beginning, blacks, immigrants, and unwed mothers were systematically excluded, either by the failure to establish programs in locations where these populations were concentrated or through discriminatory eligibility requirements, including residency and moral character requirements. In 1931, the first national survey of mother's pensions, broken down by race, found that only 3 percent of recipients were black.[555]

With the civil rights movement of the 1960s came successful legal challenges to welfare criteria that excluded racial and ethnic minorities. As a result, an increasing proportion of welfare recipients were never married, non-Caucasian, and adolescent. As this demographic transformation occurred, so too did the image of women on welfare, who were often viewed as lazy, promiscuous, and socially irresponsible. Accordingly, attention began to focus less on child welfare and more on mothers' sexual and reproductive practices.

In 1996, national welfare policy shifted significantly. Rather than a potentially long-term public entitlement of support for poor, single-parent families, it became a time-limited benefit that assumed that every able-bodied parent should work to support his or her own children.

≡≡≡ *Judith Koons, Motherhood, Marriage and Morality:*
≡≡≡ *The Pro-Marriage Moral Discourse of American*
≡≡≡ *Welfare Policy*
≡≡≡ **19 Wis. Women's L.J. 1, 1-3, 6-8, 10-14, 20-24, 41-42 (2004)**

During a campaign speech in 1991, Bill Clinton vowed to "put an end to welfare as we know it." Five years later, with the adoption of the Personal Responsibility and Work Opportunity Reconciliation Act (PRWORA), that promise was given effect. . . .

Aid to Families with Dependent Children (AFDC), which had been construed to provide welfare assistance as a matter of statutory entitlement,

554. See Jill Duerr Berrick, From Mother's Duty to Personal Responsibility: The Evolution of AFDC, 7 Hastings Women's L.J. 257, 258-59 (1996); Bridgette Baldwin, Stratification of the Welfare Poor: Intersections of Gender, Race & "Worthiness" in Poverty Discourse and Policy, 6 Modern American 4, 4-5 (2010).

555. See Linda Gordon, Pitied but Not Entitled: Single Mothers and the History of Welfare 48 (1994). General sources on women and welfare include Mimi Abramovitz, Regulating the Lives of Women: Social Welfare Policy from Colonial Times to the Present (1988); Jill Quadagno, The Color of Welfare: How Racism Undermined the War on Poverty (1994); Dorothy E. Roberts, Welfare and the Problem of Black Citizenship, 105 Yale L.J. 1563 (1996).

was replaced by TANF, a fixed block grant program. . . . Given flexibility to design work-oriented, transitional assistance programs, states were permitted to use TANF funds for cash assistance, childcare, education, training, and transportation. . . .

For the central work requirement, the federal government required a welfare-reliant mother to engage in an approved work activity within two years of receiving her first welfare check or face sanctioning. The work activity requirement was slated to increase . . . to thirty hours per week in 2000. Optional individual responsibility plans were designed to move welfare recipients into the work force as quickly as possible. . . .

Traditional "family values" were asserted in the PRWORA in five inter-related ways. First, the PRWORA explicitly expressed a purpose of promoting two-parent families. Construing the purpose as one of promoting marriage, a number of states adopted pro-marriage programs for welfare recipients. A growing Marriage Movement endorsed these and other pro-marriage and "responsible fatherhood" initiatives.

Second, the purpose of the PRWORA explicitly discouraged out-of-wedlock pregnancies. States were required to track out-of-wedlock pregnancy rates and to take steps to reduce illegitimate births. Bonuses for "Illegitimacy Reduction" were established for states that achieved the highest decreases of out-of-wedlock births without increases in abortions. . . .

Third, the PRWORA regulated non-marital sexuality by allowing states to impose "family caps" on recipient households. Under "family cap" legislation, a family could not receive additional benefits due to the birth of a child who was conceived during a period in which the family was eligible for TANF. . . .

Fourth, the PRWORA opened the door for states to promote family planning and to encourage welfare-reliant mothers to relinquish their children for adoption. In fifteen states, family planning information and counseling initiatives were integrated into the TANF program. Three states devised programs to encourage mothers who receive welfare to give up children for adoption. In addition to offering services such as "positive information" about adoption, two states provided cash incentives for relinquishing newborns.

Fifth, the PRWORA demonstrated that welfare is a site of sexual regulation by mandating paternity identification as well as child support enforcement cooperation.

≡≡≡ ### *Ann Cammett, Deadbeat Dads & Welfare*
Queens: How Metaphor Shapes Poverty Law
34 B.C. J.L. & Soc. Jus. 233, 233-38, 265 (2014)

In 2011, presidential candidate Newt Gingrich kicked off his campaign for the Republican Party's nomination to thunderous applause by deriding Barack

Obama as "the most successful food stamp president in American history." The symbolism of linking the nation's first African American president with food stamps, a social welfare program that often is associated with poor Blacks, was not lost on his Georgia audience or on the electorate as a whole. By cynically stoking racial resentment about entitlements, Gingrich deployed a well-worn and effective trope to galvanize supporters while minimizing the effects of an acute economic crisis among the poor and middle classes across all racial and ethnic groups. As poverty scholar Mark R. Rank notes, "few[] topics in American society have more myths and stereotypes surrounding them than poverty, misconceptions that distort both our politics and our domestic policymaking." The "food stamp president" metaphor is only the latest rhetorical device laden with strong racial undercurrents that serves to trigger the politics of resentment, rather than empathy, during a time of economic insecurity for many Americans.

Since the high-water mark of the anti-poverty programs of President Lyndon B. Johnson's Great Society in the 1960s and 1970s, conservative theorists and policymakers have launched attacks on the existence of the economic safety net as a whole. They have been most vehemently opposed to Aid to Families with Dependent Children ("AFDC"), commonly known as welfare. Politicians proffered their concerns about the cost of public assistance programs to taxpayers as a rationale for scaling back the social welfare state, but the rhetoric quickly devolved into racial stigmatization of welfare recipients. According to political scientist Martin Gilens, exhaustive studies examining Americans' attitudes on race and their views on welfare spending have demonstrated that "perceptions of blacks continue to play the dominant role in shaping the public's attitudes toward welfare." Therefore, although the majority of public assistance recipients are White, welfare's association with Blacks in the public imagination continues to drive policy around poverty issues as a whole. The rhetorical discourse about self-sufficiency, personal responsibility, and deservedness has laid the groundwork for the transformation or, more accurately, the evisceration of the social safety net. By 1996, the enactment of the Personal Responsibility and Work Opportunity Reconciliation Act ("PRWORA")—also known as welfare reform—effectively eliminated the federal AFDC program, replacing it with far less robust, more discretionary, and steadily shrinking state block grant programs that no longer keep families out of dire poverty. This is where we stand today. . . .

[Traditionally], the social construction of poor Black single mothers deemed them the agents of their own misfortune due to their unmarried status—assumed to indicate loose morals, hypersexuality, and presumed laziness—framed as reliance on public assistance rather than work. For example, stigmatizing metaphors such as the "Welfare Queen" were built on longstanding race and gender stereotypes and widely held beliefs. . . .

[M]any scholars have explored the history and construction of welfare reform and the use of the Welfare Queen as "race code" for undeserving beneficiaries of welfare. Far less has been written about another simultaneous but related phenomenon: its intersection with aggressive child support enforcement. This change in policy was designed to transfer the burden of financial support from the government to non-resident fathers. If the Welfare Queen is a public identity, her corollary is the "Deadbeat Dad." The political backlash over expanded access to assistance for Black mothers evolved in tandem with the identification of Deadbeat Dads as the engines of child poverty, even when fathers were poor themselves. This concept of a "broken" family, another ubiquitous metaphor, headed by a poor single mother in need of rehabilitation, and an "absent" father is another powerful cultural narrative informing the social construction of poor Black families. . . .

The use of tropes like the Welfare Queen and the Deadbeat Dad have shifted the focus of policy debates surrounding poverty programs from helping those in difficult economic situations to punishing those perceived to be at the heart of economic problems. Instead of focusing on negative racial metaphors, the discourse surrounding welfare programs should re-focus on the intended beneficiaries of the social safety net, the deserving children living in poverty.

Martha Albertson Fineman, Cracking the Foundational Myths: Independence, Autonomy, and Self-Sufficiency
8 Am. U. J. Gender Soc. Pol'y & L. 13, 22-23, 25-26 (2000)

In popular and political discourse, the idea of "subsidy" is viewed as an equally negative companion to dependence, the opposite of the ideal of self-sufficiency. But a subsidy is nothing more than the process of allocating collective resources to some persons or endeavors rather than other persons or endeavors because a social judgment is made that they are in some way "entitled" or the subsidy is justified. . . .

Typically, subsidy is thought of as the provision of monetary or economic assistance. But subsidy can also be delivered through the organization of social structures and norms that create and enforce expectations. Taking this observation into account, along with the earlier discussion of inevitable and derivative dependency, it seems obvious that we must conclude that subsidy is also universal. We all exist in context, in social and cultural institutions, such as families, which facilitate, support and subsidize us and our endeavors.

. . . We all live subsidized lives. Sometimes the benefits we receive are public and financial, such as in governmental direct transfer programs to certain individuals like farmers or sugar growers. Public subsidies can also be indirect, such as the benefits given in tax policy. Private economic subsidy systems work in the forms of foundations, religions and charities. But a subsidy can also be non-monetary, such as the subsidy provided by the uncompensated labor of others in caring for us and our dependency needs.

It seems clear that all of us receive one or the other or both types of subsidy throughout our lives. The interesting question in our subsidy shaped society, therefore, has to be why only some subsidies are differentiated and stigmatized while others are hidden. In substantial part, subsidies are hidden when they are not called subsidy (or welfare, or the dole), but termed "investments," "incentives," or "earned" when they are supplied by government, and called "gifts," "charity," or the product of familial "love" when they are contributions of caretaking labor. . . .

As a result of such discussion, the very terms of independence and self-sufficiency might well be redefined or re-imagined in the public mind. Independence is not the same as being unattached. Independence from subsidy and support is not attainable, nor is it desirable—we want and need the contexts that sustain us. A different understanding of independence is needed and attainable. Independence is gained when an individual has the basic resources that enable her or him to act consistent with the tasks and expectations imposed by the society. This form of independence should be every citizen's birthright, but independence in this sense can only be achieved when individual choices are relatively unconstrained by inequalities, particularly those inequalities that arise from poverty. Independence, as well as justice, requires that those who are assigned a vital societal function are also provided with the wherewithal to do those tasks. This is a state or collective responsibility and may not be relegated to potentially exploitative private institutions.

≡ *Vicki Schultz, Life's Work*
100 Colum. L. Rev. 1881, 1914-15, 1928-35 (2000)

[T]raditional welfare strategies can be detrimental to women. . . . Joint property approaches [whereby individual men pay their partners for taking care of the house and children] rely on individual breadwinners to fund household labor, while welfare strategies rely on the state. State funding is advantageous for women, because it frees them from serving individual men and sheds class bias by funding household work at a uniform level regardless of the earnings of the family members who support it. Nonetheless, by paying women to stay home with their children rather than providing real support for parents (especially single parents) to work at paid jobs, welfare strategies still encourage women to invest in homemaking and caregiving to the exclusion of their job skills—which may harm women and their families in the long run. . . .

I realize that work alone is no panacea. It is the platform on which equal citizenship should be built, not the entire edifice. Still, the importance of work to the future cannot be overemphasized; abandoning work as a political and cultural ideal would be a serious mistake. People need more than money or property: We need life projects. We need goals and activities to which we can commit our hearts, minds, and bodies. We need to struggle with our capacities and our limits, in sustained ways in stable settings. We need to work alongside others in pursuit of common goals. We need to feel that we are contributing to something larger than ourselves and our own families. Most of us even need something that requires regular rhythms and structure, and provides a mechanism for deferring gratification. We need to feel that we are earning our keep—that we have a source of wherewithal that is our own. We also need public recognition for our labors. It is difficult to imagine any single activity that can fulfill all these purposes for the vast majority of people other than working. We have seen what happens to people when they don't have work to give life structure and meaning, and it is not exemplary. There is a reason why democratic societies have organized themselves as employment societies. Paid work is the only institution that can be sufficiently widely distributed to provide a stable foundation for a democratic order. It is also one of the few arenas—perhaps the only one—in which diverse groups of people can come together and develop respect for each other through shared experience. Can we think of a society anywhere in the world we would want to emulate in which most people do not work for a living? . . .

We can also view the transition from welfare to work as part of this trend. I realize that the impetus for welfare-to-work programs has come from the political right, who may not have the best interests of poor people at heart. But it would be a mistake to attribute all of the new emphasis on work to conservatives alone. Some of the demand has come from members of the working poor who do not receive welfare, and who do not have the luxury of keeping a parent at home to take care of their own children. . . .

Poor single parents have long expressed a desire for work that will allow them to support their children; they know that a decent job is the only path that provides real hope for their empowerment in the long run. Most people who receive welfare payments have been working for pay all along, as they must in order to ensure the survival of their families. But, partly because so many of them are women and racial minorities, single parents have not been perceived as "authentic" workers who have the capacity to contribute to productive endeavors beyond raising their own children. Women who draw on welfare are overrepresented among classic contingent workers, who fare worse on a variety of dimensions than people in more permanent employment. . . .

Even if many welfare-to-work programs have been adopted for the wrong reasons, their existence does provide a political opening to turn things around. Not only is paid work important to people's ability to get ahead and their sense of community and self-esteem; it is also a more easily politicized setting than the privatized home. By creating social systems that allow poor (and other) parents to combine caregiving with stable employment, we enable them to move into the workforce—a space in which they can more easily engage in collective action to improve their situation. . . .

[handwritten margin note: Assuming everyone who works loves their job]

Free edu.?

Viewed from this perspective, the best welfare-to-work programs push in the direction of a more expansive set of social programs that guarantee and support a right to work for everyone. If work is to provide the foundation for citizenship (as welfare-to-work programs imply), then everyone must have access to a suitable job, as well as the training and education needed to do the job. There is no reason to find or create jobs exclusively for people who have drawn on welfare, when so many others are struggling to find jobs, often under fiercely competitive conditions. The goal should be to ensure that everyone—mothers on welfare, fathers struggling to pay child support, poor women and men without children, people with disabilities, middle-class homemakers or divorcees, people in temporary jobs who want steady employment, older people, youth who are trying to finance continuing education, and, yes, even well educated displaced workers—has work.

Notes

1. Poverty, Gender, and Race.   Poverty is strongly correlated with gender, race, ethnicity, and marital status. Official Census Bureau figures put the poverty rate at 14.9 percent, while a new supplemental formula, which takes account of non-cash benefits and essential expenditures, put the rate at 15.3 percent.[556] The figure is highest among households headed by a single mother (28.7 percent) and lowest among two-parent households (9.4 percent). Women are 32 percent more likely to be poor than men, and single mothers are 1000 percent more likely to be poor than single fathers. [557] The poverty rate for U.S. single mothers is almost twice the average rate in other high-income countries.[558] Poverty is greater among racial and ethnic minorities. For non-Hispanic whites, the poverty rate was 10.7 percent; for Blacks, it was 23.4 percent; for Hispanics, it was 25.4 percent; and for Asians, it was 16.8 percent.[559] Poverty is associated with a host of problems, including food insecurity, homelessness, poor education, and chronic illness. As Chapter 3 noted, poverty also traps women in violent relationships.

2. International Comparisons.   Poverty experts have ranked the United States in comparison with other peer countries terms of its relative poverty rates. Peer countries are largely countries within the Organisation

556. U.S. Census Bureau, The Research Supplemental Poverty Measure: 2014 5 (2015), https://www.census.gov/content/dam/Census/library/publications/2015/demo/p60-254.pdf; see also Teresa Tritch, Reading Between the Poverty Lines, N.Y. Times, Nov. 19, 2011, at SR2.

557. Timothy Casey, Women's Poverty in the United States, 2013 (Legal Momentum, 2013).

558. Id.

559. U.S. Census Bureau, The Research Supplemental Poverty Measure, supra note 556.

for Economic Co-operation and Development (OECD) with roughly similar GDP per hour worked as the United States. Relative poverty rates measure the share of the population living below half the median household income. By this criterion, the United States has the highest relative poverty rate among OCED peers.[560] The United States also most has one of the lowest rates of social expenditure on the poor. It spends a smaller percentage of its economy on cash transfer programs to help the needy than 26 other developed countries.[561]

3. Low-Wage Work as a Cause of Poverty. In a widely circulated report by the Center for American Progress, The Shriver Report: A Woman's Nation Pushes Back from the Brink, a number of contributors underscored the need to "stop blaming poverty on the poor."[562] Barbara Ehrenreich, the author of a widely acclaimed account of trying to get by on low-paying entry level jobs, puts it this way:

> Poverty is not a character failing or a lack of motivation. Poverty is a shortage of money. For most women in poverty, in both good times and bad, the shortage of money arises largely from inadequate wages. When I worked on my book *Nickel and Dimed: On (Not) Getting by in America*, I took jobs as a waitress, nursing-home aide, hotel housekeeper, Wal-Mart associate, and a maid with a house-cleaning service. I did not choose these jobs because they were low-paying. I chose them because these are the entry-level jobs most readily available to women. What I discovered is that in many ways, these jobs are a trap: They pay so little that you cannot accumulate even a couple of hundred dollars to help you make the transition to a better-paying job. They often give you no control over your work schedule, making it impossible to arrange for child care or take a second job. . . . To be poor—especially with children to support and care for—is a perpetual high wire act. . . .
>
> Instead of treating low-wage mothers as the struggling heroines they are, our political culture still tends to view them as miscreants and contributors to the "cycle of poverty." . . . Sadly, this has become the means by which the wealthiest country in the world manages to remain complacent in the face of alarmingly high levels of poverty: by continuing to blame poverty not on the economy or inadequate social supports, but on the poor themselves.

---

560. Elise Gould & Hilary Wething, Economic Policy Inst., U.S. Poverty Rates Higher, Safety Net Weaker Than in Peer Countries (July 24, 2012).

561. Jordan Weissmann, How Poor Are America's Poor, Really?, Slate (Jan. 5, 2015), http://www.slate.com/blogs/moneybox/2015/01/05/america-s_poor.

562. Barbara Ehrenreich, Time to Wake Up: Stop Blaming Poverty on the Poor, in The Shriver Report: A Woman's Nation Pushes Back from the Brink 40 (Olivia Morgan & Karen Skelton eds., 2014).

It's time to revive the notion of a collective national responsibility to the poorest among us, who are disproportionately women and especially women of color.[563]

So too, Peter Edelman, the Director of the Georgetown Center on Poverty, Inequality and Public Policy, who has served in the federal government working on poverty-related issues, writes:

[T]he fundamental problem with regard to poverty and economic insecurity today is the flood of extremely low-wage work that keeps families stuck on the lower rungs. . . .

A quarter of [the jobs in America] pay less than the federal poverty level for a family of four. . . . While money has poured into the upper reaches of our economy, wages in the lower half are basically stagnant, having increased by a mere 7 percent over the past 40 years—just one-fifth of a percent per year. The people who hold these low-wage jobs are disproportionately women especially women with children. . . .

[O]ur most glaring public policy error is what we have done to the safety net for the most vulnerable women and children in our nation. And [o]ur most glaring omission is our failure to address the proliferation of poorly-paid jobs that leave working families struggling.[564]

Do you agree with these diagnoses? If so, how should public policy respond? How effective is the current welfare system in addressing these issues?

4. Challenges to the Welfare System. During the 1980s and 1990s, American conservatives launched a sustained challenge to the traditional welfare system on the grounds that it entrenched, rather than reduced, poverty. In their view, the poor make rational choices based on the existing incentive structures. Welfare discourages work and rewards out-of-wedlock childrearing. Critics like Charles Murray not only called for ending the entitlement-based welfare system, but also supported shaming those dependent upon welfare and praising self-sufficiency. Without a distinction between the deserving and the undeserving poor, Murray argued that indigent parents would have no reason to take responsibility for providing for themselves and their families.[565]

Individual agency figures strongly in this line of analysis. Those critical of public welfare tend to assume that the poor could work if only they chose to, and that they choose instead to take government benefits. Others describe an economic structure in which the opportunities for self-sufficiency are steadily

563. Id. at 42-43.
564. The Shriver Report, supra note 562, at 272-73; see also Peter Edelman, So Rich, So Poor: Why It's So Hard to End Poverty in America (2012).
565. Charles Murray, Losing Ground: American Social Policy 1950-1980, at 154-62, 178-81 (1984).

worsening for the "have-nots." According to some observers, one silver lining of this reform is that recipients are no longer demonized as shirkers; they are now part of the working poor and their poverty cannot be simply be attributed to their own shiftlessness.[566] In your view, is this correct? Was the reform worth the price?

5. The Impact of Welfare Reform. The Koons reading describes the major overhaul of the U.S. welfare system that occurred with the passage of the Personal Responsibility and Work Opportunity Reconciliation Act of 1996. The impact of welfare reform has been mixed. In the first decade following welfare reform, the number of welfare recipients declined, and paid employment and earnings among low-income single mothers increased. It is, however, difficult to tell how much of that improvement was due to general gains in the economy during the first five years following welfare reform.[567]

The economic downturn that began in 2008 increased the economic vulnerability of the poor while posing new challenges for the welfare system. Because the federal block grant system provided no additional funding to meet increased need and many state and local governments confronted declining revenue, they were unable to address soaring unemployment and economic hardship. The central premise of welfare reform that all able-bodied parents should work was impossible to accommodate in the declining job market. The hardships reached across the economic spectrum as a growing number of formerly middle-class parents were unable to meet basic subsistence needs although they often have too many assets to qualify for aid.[568] Even after the economy rebounded, it proved unable to deliver the types of jobs that poor people can fill, and many of the jobs available did not provide a living wage.[569]

A related problem is that benefits don't reach many eligible individuals and are set so low that they do not bring a family's income even to half the poverty line in any state.[570] In 2013, about 4 million Americans were receiving TANF, compared with 14 million who were receiving AFDC in 1993.[571] Only a quarter of poor people with children received cash benefits.[572] Because

566. Marissa Chappell, The War on Welfare: Family, Poverty, and Policies in Modern America 247 (2010).

567. Robert Pear & Erik Eckholm, A Decade After Welfare Overhaul, a Fundamental Shift in Policy and Perception, N.Y. Times, Aug. 21, 2006, at 12.

568. Amy Goldstein, Welfare Rolls See First Climb in Years, Wash. Post, Dec. 17, 2008, at A1; Molly Hennessy-Fiske, Middle-Class Jobless Run into a Welfare Wall, L.A. Times, Mar. 26, 2009, at A1.

569. Marianne Page, Are Jobs the Solution to Poverty?, Pathways (Summer 2014).

570. Kathryn J. Edin & H. Luke Shaefer, $2.00 a Day: Living on Almost Nothing in America 169-70 (2015).

571. Thomas Gabe, Congressional Research Service Welfare, Work and Poverty Status of Female-Headed Families with Children: 1987-2013 (2014).

572. Edin & Shaefer, supra note 570, at 7.

states can use TANF block grants for many purposes other than cash assistance to the needy, they have an incentive to discourage applicants and critics claim that the system has become "welfare for the states rather than families in need."[573]

However, the poverty rate among female-headed households has also fallen, from 55 percent in 1991 to 46 percent in 2013.[574] Part of the reason is that more single mothers are working and their income is substantially increased by other forms of aid, particularly the Supplemental Nutritional Assistance Program (SNAP, formerly food stamps) and the Earned Income Tax Credit.[575] Still, because TANF benefits do not guarantee meeting subsistence needs, half of TANF recipients have income below the poverty line.[576] Only one in six eligible families receives child-care subsidies.[577] The human costs are substantial. Many families report insufficient food, housing, utilities, and health care, and the inadequacy of assistance keeps some women trapped in violent relationships.[578] As Chapter 3 indicated, between one- and two-thirds of women on welfare have been subject to violence, and although all states have exercised a Family Violence Option, which allows them to waive TANF benefit requirements for victims, the waiver is infrequently exercised.[579] Studies of what happens to poor families after they leave welfare show that most remain poor.[580] One reason is that many states do not consider college attendance as meeting work requirements; the number of recipients enrolled in college has dropped since reform.[581] Difficulties in understanding and complying with welfare requirements pose other problems. Because welfare subsidies are so inadequate, many recipients rely on unreported income, which,

[handwritten margin note: Ineligible if criminal conviction]

---

573. Id. at 169.

574. Gabe, supra note 571.

575. Id. at 45; Hilary W. Hoynes, A Revolution in Poverty Policy, Pathways (Summer, 2014) (noting that the EITC "has become the cornerstone of U.S. anti-poverty policy" and is the largest cash transfer program for low-income families with children); Michele Estrin Gilman, The Return of the Welfare Queen, 22 J. Gender, Social Pol'y & L. 247 (2014) (noting that TANF serves 1.8 million families and the ETIC serves 26 million families).

576. Gilman, supra note 575, at 268.

577. Id. at 278.

578. Legal Momentum, Welfare Reform at Age 15: A Vanishing Safety Net for Women and Children 7 (Apr. 1, 2011) http://www.legalmomentum.org/resources/welfare-reform-age-15-vanishing-safety-net-women-and-children.

579. Rachel Gallagher, Welfare Reform's Inadequate Implementation of the Family Violence Option: Exploring the Dual Oppression of Poor Domestic Violence Victims, 19 Am. U. J. Gender, Soc. Pol'y & L. 987 (2011).

580. Chappell, supra note 566, at 245.

581. Noah Zatz, What Welfare Requires From Work, 54 UCLA L. Rev. 373, 415 (2006) (citing state definitions); Juliette Terzieff, Welfare Clock Should Stop for College Moms (Apr. 20, 2006), http://womensenews.org/2006/04/study-welfare-clock-should-stop-college-moms (noting that only 10 percent of single mothers hold a degree and number has dropped since reform).

if detected, can subject them to substantial penalties, including extended or permanent bans from further assistance.[582] For those on the bottom rung of the income scale, an estimated 10 to 20 percent of recipients, the situation has worsened since reform. These "disconnected" parents have problems of substance abuse, mental health or learning disabilities, domestic violence, inadequate education, and criminal records, which make getting a living wage impossible.[583] Children of parents who are working also may suffer due to the lack of supervision and additional responsibilities in caring for younger siblings. Poorer school performance is the consequence.[584]

Kathryn Edin and Luke Shaefer offer case histories of the hardships among the poorest of the poor, those living on $2.00 in cash income, who account for a fifth of families living below the poverty line. Modonna Harris, one such woman, lost her cashier's job and was unable to find other work. She and her 15-year-old daughter lived in a homeless shelter, and received meals from the shelter and other non-profits during the week. They struggled with food shortages on weekends. Chicago had so many people on the wait list for housing assistance that it was accepting no new applicants. She had not applied for TANF because she didn't know anyone getting benefits and she had assumed that government officials "just weren't giving it anymore." When prompted to apply, she showed up at the government office only a half hour before it opened and already there were too many applicants for staff to schedule her an appointment.[585] Yet despite such hardships, cash-strapped states and a deficit-conscious Congress have shown little support for enhancing the safety net of the poor, who have little leverage in the political process.[586] How would you suggest addressing these obstacles?

6. Welfare Reform and the Promotion of Marriage. An important objective of PRWORA is the reduction of out-of-wedlock pregnancies and childbirths. Proponents of marriage-based programs point to studies that have shown that children who grow up with both of their biological parents are more successful across a broad range of outcomes than children who grow up

582. Kaaryn S. Gustafson, Public Assistance and the Criminalization of Poverty 67-69, 141, 143, 160 (2011).

583. Richard Wolf, How Welfare Reform Changed America: 10 Years Later, Success Stories Common but Many Families Still Struggle to Get By, USA Today, July 18, 2006, at A1; Pear & Eckholm, supra note 567, Erik Eckholm, A Welfare Law Milestone Finds Many Left Behind, N.Y. Times, Aug. 22, 2006, at 13; Rebecca M. Blank, Improving the Safety Net for Single Mothers Who Face Serious Barriers to Work, 17 The Future of Children 183, 184 (Fall 2007).

584. Pamela Morris et al., Soc'y for Research in Child Dev., Effects of Welfare Reform and Employment Policies on Young Children (2005).

585. Edin & Shaefer, supra note 570, at 6-9, 33.

586. Jake Blumgart, Happy Birthday, Welfare Reform, American Prospect, Aug. 19, 2011.

with only one parent, including higher educational attainment, better behavioral outcomes, and mental health. However, it is not clear to what extent these positive outcomes are due to pre-existing characteristics of the parents who choose to marry (and not to divorce) rather than to marriage itself.[587]

Since 2002, the federal government has funded A Healthy Marriage Initiative, designed to promote stable marriages and responsible fatherhood. Activities include marriage education programs, public service announcements, and courses in relationship skills for adults and adolescents.[588] The vast majority of states have changed their rules to eliminate pre-1996 welfare eligibility barriers to two-parent families. Bonuses of as much as $25 million are also available to states that meet targets in reducing out-of-wedlock births and abortions.[589] According to conservatives such as Marco Rubio, marriage is "the greatest tool" for lifting people out of poverty.[590]

Critics of the "healthy marriage" approach to welfare reform charge that, even if marriage is a legitimate government goal, marriage alone is not sufficient to lift couples out of poverty and that promotion programs are ineffective in promoting it. Researchers have generally found no consistent correlation between state expenditures on marriage programs and marriage or divorce rates.[591] One review of a federal program, Building Strong Families, which gave counseling and support to unwed couples with children, revealed no positive impact on whether the couples got married or remained involved, or whether fathers supported their children.[592] Critics also argue that the marriage promotion approach reflects an unduly narrow definition of healthy families, and that the money would be better spent on programs that are critically underfunded, such as child care. Marriage promotion is particularly problematic for black and Latino families, given the ways in which incarceration and joblessness have narrowed the pool of eligible men, and the extended family patterns that are common in these racial groups.[593] Research

---

587. Kimberly A. Yuracko, The Meaning of Marriage: Does Marriage Make People Good or Do Good People Marry?, 42 San Diego L. Rev. 889 (2005); Jennifer M. Randles, Marriage Promotion Policy and Family Inequality, 6 Sociology Compass 671, 673 (2012).

588. See Julia M. Fisher, Marriage Promotion Policies and the Working Poor: A Match Made in Heaven?, 25 B.C. Third World L.J. 475, 485 n.71 (2005).

589. Marnie Eisenstadt, Birth Figures Deliver Bonus: State Receives $25 Million in Federal Money as Out-of-Wedlock Births Decline, The Post-Standard (Syracuse, New York), Oct. 14, 2004, at A8.

590. Bryce Covert, Nearly a Billion Dollars Spent on Marriage Promotion Programs Have Achieved Next to Nothing, Think Progress (Feb. 11, 2014), http://thinkprogress.org/economyu/2014/02/11/3275811/marriage-romotion-programs-have-achieved-next-to-nothing (quoting Rubio).

591. Id.

592. Id; see also Randles, supra note 587, at 674.

593. Angela Onwuachi-Willig, The Return of the Ring: Welfare Reform's Marriage Cure as the Revival of Post-Bellum Control, 93 Cal. L. Rev. 1647, 1690 (2005); Randles, supra note 587, at 676.

on low-income women finds that many see marriage as a luxury but children as a necessity, a chief source of identity and meaning.[594] The Center for Law and Social Policy proposes "Marriage Plus" as an alternative, which would include not only marriage counseling and relationship training, but pregnancy prevention, mental health support, greater child-care services, reform of the child support system, and employment training and placement.[595]

Other critics, such as Anna Marie Smith, have challenged the priority given to heterosexual marriages over other household arrangements. In her view, a just society would ensure that every person is "equally valued and respected," and would recognize that caretakers irrespective of marital status have a "special claim to public support," given their contributions to the nurture of dependents and the "good of the community." These individuals should have an entitlement to support equivalent to a living wage, and should enjoy the "same right to determine their intimate lives that privileged citizens take for granted."[596]

Do you agree? Is marriage promotion a legitimate governmental objective? Is it a better use of federal funds than child-care subsidies? What data might you need to answer that question?

7. Welfare and Autonomy. To what extent should autonomy be a goal for the welfare system? Can the views of Fineman, Smith, and Schultz be reconciled? Is it possible that the emphasis on women's autonomy actually has undermined their well-being? Consider this further analysis by Fineman:

> Rejection of the idea that there is some collective responsibility for dependency is not surprising in a society such as ours. American political ideology offers an iconic construct of the autonomous individual and trusts the abstraction of an efficiency-seeking market as an ordering mechanism. We have an historic and highly romanticized affair with the ideals of the private and the individual, as contrasted with the public and the collective, as the appropriate units of focus in determining social good. . . .
>
> The theory of dependency I set forth develops a claim of "right" or entitlement to support and accommodation from the state and its institutions on the part of caretakers—those who care for dependents. Their labor should be treated as equally productive even if unwaged, and should be measured by its societal value, not by economic or market indicators. The fact that dependency work has been un- or under-valued in the market is an argument *for* governmental inter-

594. Randles, supra note 587, at 677 (citing studies).

595. For the Marriage Plus proposal, see Theodora Ooms et al., Center for Law and Social Policy, Beyond Marriage Licenses: Efforts in States to Strengthen Marriage and Two-Parent Families, Apr. 2004, http://www.clasp.org/publications/beyond_marr.pdf.

596. Anna Marie Smith, Welfare Reform and Sexual Regulation 228, 230, 248 (2007).

vention and restructuring to mandate adjustment and market accommodation, as well as more direct reparations.[597]

8. Income Inequality. According to the Congressional Research Service, "the U.S. income distribution appears to be among the most unequal of all major industrialized countries and the United States appears to be among the nations experiencing the greatest increases in measures of income dispersion."[598] In 2011, the Occupy Wall Street Movement drew national attention to the growing inequality in American society. Spin-off groups such as Women Occupying Wall Street (WOW), Occupy Patriarchy, and Women Occupy underscored the way that women, because they are overrepresented among the poor, have borne the brunt of this inequality.[599] In 2016, Democratic Presidential Candidate Bernie Sanders drew national attention to the issue of wealth inequality. As he repeatedly claimed, "America now has more wealth and income inequality than any major developed country on earth. . . . [T]here is something profoundly wrong when the top one tenth of one percent owns almost as much wealth as the bottom 90 percent."[600] How do you respond? Are such inequalities the natural and inevitable product of a market system, in which people differ in how hard they work, how talented they are, and how much risk they assume?[601] Or a now-built-in barrier to equal opportunity and political participation?[602]

Income affects many factors that affect equal opportunity, such as education, nutrition, health, housing, and physical safety. As a consequence, the accident of birth is highly predictive of life chances. Upward mobility is less common in the United States than in most other industrial nations. A child born

597. Martha Albertson Fineman, The Autonomy Myth: A Theory of Dependency xiii-xv (2004).

598. Linda Levine, The U.S. Income Distribution and Mobility: Trends and International Comparisons, Cong. Research Serv. (2012).

599. Sarah Seltzer, We Are the Many, Not the Few, Ms., Winter 2012, at 34.

600. On the Issues: Income and Wealth Inequality (2016), https://berniesanders.com/issues/income-and-wealth-inequality (citing sources).

601. See Igor Bobic, Rand Paul: Of Course Income Inequality Is Linked to How Hard You Work, Huffpost Politics, Aug. 11, 2015.

602. Frank Newport, Americans Continue to Say U.S. Wealth Distribution is Unfair, Gallup (May 4, 2015), http://www.gallup.com/poll/182987/americans-continue-say-wealth-distribution-unfair.aspx (almost two-thirds of the public believes that the current wealth distribution is unfair); Ron Haskins et al., Getting Ahead or Losing Ground: Economic Mobility in America, The Brookings Inst. 19 (Feb. 2008), http://www.brookings.edu/research/reports/2008/02/economic-mobility-sawhill.

in the bottom one-fifth of the socioeconomic spectrum in the United States has only about a 17 percent chance of making it into the upper two-fifths.[603]

A second reason for concern about growing inequalities in wealth is that they translate into inequalities in political power. Money buys access and influence, and the result is to entrench existing entitlements. Much of the gap in life prospects is due to laws, institutions, and tax policies that reflect the interests of the rich, rather than the vast majority of Americans. Almost two-thirds of the public believes that the current wealth distribution is unfair.[604] What is your view?

If you believe that current income inequalities are unjust, what responses would you propose? Legal historian Deborah Dinner argues that one reason for the growing income gap is that the concept of equality in U.S. employment law has been interpreted as if it were justified by economic efficiency concerns, i.e., eliminating inaccurate stereotypes rather than by the needs of working class women and men. The anti-stereotyping principle, she argues, has reinforced and legitimated the premises of market libertarianism, thereby sidetracking advocates and lawmakers from structural reforms of the workplace that would raise working class wages, accommodate the needs of pregnant women and parents with children, and otherwise treat workers with greater fairness. According to Dinner, the challenge to a more robust and positive version of equality has not been maternalist ideologies, which have often been present in feminist advocacy (these ideologies are explored in Chapter 4 of this book), but market libertarianism values which treat reproduction as a private activity, not one of public responsibility, and fail to admit how market structures themselves foreclose opportunities to individuals on a class basis.[605] If Dinner is right, are feminists partially to blame? Is is possible that the anti-stereotyping principle not only doesn't go far enough to address class-based injustice, but by assuming stereotypes are the problem helps to reinforce that injustice?

How much would that agenda do to address women in poverty? What other strategies would you suggest?

603. Julia B. Isaacs et al., The Brookings Inst., Getting Ahead or Losing Ground: Economic Mobility in America (Feb. 2008), at 19, http://www.pewstates.org/uploadedFiles/PCS_Assets/2008/PEW_EMP_GETTING_AHEAD_FULL(2).pdf; Rana Foroohar, Whatever Happened to Upward Mobility, Time, Nov. 14, 2011, at 28.

604. Bryan Montopoli, Poll: 43 Percent Agree with Views of "Occupy Wall Street," CBS News (Oct. 25, 2011), http://www.cbsnews.com/8301-503544_162-20125515-503544/poll-43-percent-agree-with-views-of-occupy-wallstreet/?tag=cbsnewsMainColumnArea.

605. See Deborah Dinner, Beyond "Best Practices": Employment Discrimination Law in the Neoliberal Era, 92 Ind. L.J. ___ (forthcoming 2017); Deborah Dinner, The Costs of Reproduction: History and the Legal Construction of Sex Equality, 46 Harv. C.R.-C.L. L. Rev. 415 (2011).

Putting Theory Into Practice

5-45. Your state legislature is considering a measure to give low-income individuals and couples who periodically attend parenting classes an annual tax deduction (or cash benefits if they do not pay taxes). Would you support the proposal? Should schools be required to offer marriage relationship skills and fatherhood classes? How about giving poor couples an annual cash "bonus" for staying married?

5-46. You are chairing a coalition of women's rights organizations that is advising Congress on changes to the welfare program. What reforms would you propose?[606]

5-47. You are a single mother with two children under five. You have a minimum wage job at a local grocery store. It does not provide health benefits. Prepare a budget based on living expenses in your locality. Could you manage without welfare assistance? If not, what benefits would be most critical? With welfare assistance, could you meet basic subsistence needs?

---

606. For suggestions, see Edin & Shaefer, supra note 572, at 160-70.

6

Identity

This final chapter examines four sets of issues relating to identity and gender. The first involves the interrelationship of a person's multiple identities, especially race and gender. Does race interact with gender in ways that make discrimination more difficult to recognize than when only one or the other characteristic is at issue? Does it amplify the experience of inequality, or transform it? To what extent do claims on behalf of women generally marginalize the experiences of some women?

A second issue expands the intersectionality debate to include issues of culture and religion. When are other values more important than gender equality? Can anyone speak for women when women's perceptions of their own interests vary across religion and culture? More specifically, when Western feminists criticize cultural practices of other nations or religions that contribute to sexual inequality, are they being arrogant, or even "imperialist"?

A third issue concerns the evolving definition of male and female. Is the difference natural, biological, psychological, or social—or some combination? This section explores this question in the context of transgender identity. Transgender individuals challenge the law's assumption that an individual's identity as man or woman is fixed. What is the consequence of shattering this assumption? Should a transgender female be able to marry a male? A female? Is discrimination against transgender persons "because of sex"?

Finally, the chapter addresses masculinities. Most of this book is focused on the interests of women, but gender also constrains opportunities for men. How does the concept of masculinity shape men's privilege and how does it constrain men's choices? What attention does it warrant from women?

Readings in the other chapters of this book tend to take for granted various identity assumptions—what a woman is, what sex is, and what it means that a law or practice is (or is not) in women's interests. The identity issues raised in this chapter challenge some of these assumptions. In an important sense, much of the material in this chapter could be viewed as a form of self-critique. Does that critique go too far? Far enough?

A. GENDER AND RACE

The term "women" is used freely throughout the book. Yet differences among women may complicate the use of this term. This section focuses on the intersection of race and gender. Some discrimination results from the combination of race and gender; this discrimination may be invisible if the intersections of race and gender are ignored. Moreover, advocacy on behalf of women that ignores their race is a form of "essentialism" that marginalizes the interests of some women on behalf of other women. What are the consequences of generalizations about women that ignore their race?

Devon W. Carbado & Mitu Gulati, The Fifth Black Woman
11 J. Contemp. Legal Issues 701, 710-15, 717-20 (2001)

Consider the following hypothetical. Mary, a black woman, works in an elite corporate firm. There are eighty attorneys at the firm, twenty of whom are partners. Only two of the partners are black, and both are men. The firm has three female partners, and all three are white. There are no Asian American, Native American, or Latina/o partners. The firm is slightly more diverse at the associate rank. There are fifteen female associates: three, including Mary, are black, two are Asian American, and one is Latina. The remaining female associates are white. Of the forty-five male associates, two are black, two are Latino, three are Asian American, and the rest are white.

Mary is a seventh-year associate at the firm. She, along with five other associates, is up for partnership this year. Her annual reviews have been consistently strong. The partners for whom she has worked praise her intellectual creativity, her ability to perform well under pressure, her strong work ethic, her client-serving skills, and her commitment to the firm. She has not brought in many new clients, but, as one of the senior partners puts it, "that is not unusual for a person on the cusp of partnership."

For the past three years, the Chair of the Associate's Committee, the committee charged with making partnership recommendations to the entire partnership, has indicated to Mary that she is "on track." Being "on track" was important to Mary because, were she not on track, she would have seriously explored the option of moving either to another firm with better partnership prospects for her or in-house to an investment bank that provided greater job security. It was generally understood, however, and the Chair made sure to make it clear that "being on track is not a guarantee that you will ultimately make partner." . . .

The Associate Committee recommends that the firm promote all six. However, the partners vote only four into the partnership: one black man, one Asian American male, one white man, and one white woman. They deny partnership to Mary and a white male associate. The partnership's decision to depart from the Associate Committee's recommendation is not unusual. . . . [I]t accepts the committee's positive recommendation only half of the time.

Subsequently, Mary brings a disparate treatment discrimination suit under Title VII. She advances three separate theories: race discrimination, sex discrimination, and race and sex discrimination. She does not, however, have any direct evidence of animus against her on the part of the employer. In other words, Mary can point to no explicit statements such as "We don't like you because you are a woman," or "We think that you are incompetent; all blacks are." The evidence is all circumstantial: Mary was highly qualified, but was rejected for a position that was arguably open.

The court, ruling in favor of the firm's summary judgment motion, rejects all three of Mary's claims. With respect to the race discrimination claim, the court reasons that it is not supported by evidence of intentional or animus-based discrimination. According to the court, there is no evidence that the firm dislikes (or has a taste for discrimination against) blacks. In fact, argues the court, the evidence points in the other direction. The very year the firm denied partnership to Mary, it extended partnership to another African-American. Further, within the past five years, the firm had promoted two other African-Americans to the partnership. The court notes that both of these partners participated in the deliberations as to whether Mary would be granted partnership, and neither has suggested that the firm's decision to deny Mary partnership was discriminatorily motivated. The court concludes that the simple act of denying one black person a promotion is, especially when other blacks have been promoted, insufficient to establish discrimination.

The court disposes of Mary's gender discrimination claim in a similar way. That is, it concludes that the fact that the firm has in the past promoted women to the partnership, that the partners who voted to deny partnership to Mary extended partnership to another woman, and that women participated in the firm's deliberations as to whether Mary would be promoted, and none of these women have claimed that Mary was treated unfairly because she is a woman, suggests that the firm did not engage in sex-based discrimination against Mary.

The court concludes its dismissal of Mary's compound discrimination claim (the allegation of discrimination based on her race and sex) with an argument about cognizability. . . . According to the court, there is no indication in the legislative history of Title VII that the statute intended "to create a

Court rationale: give one
group higher ground

Ironic to think discr.
affects everyone the
same then cause
discrimination

new classification of 'black women' who would have greater standing than, for example, a black male." According to the court, "the prospect of the creation of new classes of protected minorities, governed only by mathematical principles of permutation and combination, clearly raises the prospect of opening the hackneyed Pandora's box."

The foregoing hypothetical articulates the classic intersectionality problem wherein black women fall through an anti-discrimination gap constituted by black male and white female experiences. The problem can be framed in terms of essentialism. Consider first the court's response to Mary's race discrimination claim. In determining whether Mary experienced race discrimination, the court assumes that there is an essential black experience that is unmodified by gender. The court's adjudication of Mary's race discrimination claim conveys the idea that racism is necessarily total. It is a particular kind of animus that reaches across gender, and affects men and women in the same way. It is about race—a hostility against all black people. . . .

Consider now the court's adjudication of Mary's sex discrimination. Here, too, the court's analysis reflects essentialism. The essentialism in this context conveys the idea that women's experiences are unmodified by race. The court assumes that if a firm engages in sex discrimination, such discrimination will negatively affect all women—and in the same way. . . .

Finally, consider the court's rejection of Mary's compound discrimination claim. Here, the court doctrinally erases black women's status identity as black women. Its conclusion that this identity status is not cognizable means that, for purposes of Title VII, black women exist only to the extent that their experiences comport with the experiences of black men or white women. Under the court's view, and in the absence of explicit race/gender animus, black women's discriminatory experiences as black women are beyond the remedial reach of Title VII. . . .

To appreciate the identity performance problem, assume again that Mary is an African American female in a predominantly white elite corporate law firm. As before, Mary is up for partnership and her evaluations have been consistently strong. Stipulate now that four other black women are up for partnership, as are two white women and two white men. The Associate's Committee recommends that the firm extends partnership to all nine associates. The members of the partnership, however, decide to depart from this recommendation. They grant partnership to four of the black women. The fifth black woman, Mary, does not make partner. Of the four white associates, the firm extends partnership to one of the men and one of the women.

The partnership's decision creates a buzz around the firm. The firm had never before granted partnership to so many non-white attorneys. Moreover, in the firm's fifty year history, it had only ever promoted two black people to partnership. Both of these partners are men, and the firm promoted both of them in the mid-1980s, a period during which the firm, along with many others, had enjoyed a high level of prosperity.

Prior to 1980, the firm had never hired a black female associate. Furthermore, most of those who were hired after that date left within two to three years of their arrival. Given the history of black women at the firm—low hiring rate, high attrition rate, low promotion rate—associates at the firm dubbed this year the "year of the black woman."

Mary, however, does not agree. Subsequent to the partnership decision, she files a Title VII discrimination suit, alleging (1) race and sex compound discrimination, i.e., discrimination against her on account of her being a black woman, and (2) discrimination based on identity performance. The firm moves for summary judgment on two theories. First, it argues that Mary may not ground her discrimination claim on her race and sex. According to the firm, Mary may separately assert a race discrimination claim and/or a sex discrimination claim; however, she may not, under Title VII, advance a discrimination claim combining race and sex. Second, the firm contends that whatever identity Mary invokes to ground her claim, there is simply no evidence of intentional discrimination.

With respect to the first issue, the court agrees with Mary that a discrimination claim combining race and sex is, under Title VII, legally cognizable. The court has read, and understood, and it agrees with the literature on intersectionality. Under the court's view, black women should be permitted to ground their discrimination claims on their specific status identity as black women. According to the court, failing to do so would be to ignore the complex ways in which race and gender interact to create social disadvantage: a result that would be inconsistent with the goals of Title VII.

With respect to the second issue, the court agrees with the firm. The court reasons that recognizing Mary's status identity does not prove that the firm discriminated against her because of that identity. It explains that the firm promoted four associates with Mary's precise status identity—that is, four black women. Why, the court rhetorically asks, would a racist/sexist firm extend partnership to these women? The court suggests that when there is clear evidence of non-discrimination against the identity group within which the plaintiff is situated, that produces an inference that the plaintiff was not the victim of discrimination.

The court rejects the plaintiff's arguments that Title VII itself and the Supreme Court's interpretation of Title VII focuses on protecting individuals, not groups, from discrimination. . . .

The problem with the court's approach is that it fails to consider whether Mary was the victim of an intra-racial (or intra-gender) distinction based not simply on her identity status as a black woman but on her performance of that identity. In effect, the court's approach essentializes the identity status "black female." More specifically, the court assumes that Mary and the other four black women are similarly situated with respect to their vulnerability to discrimination. However, this might not be the case. The social meaning of being a black woman is not monolithic and static but contextual and dynamic.

Need to take bg into acct can't say
black woman & everyone understand

An important way in which it is shaped is by performance. In other words, how black women present their identity can (and often does) affect whether and how they are discriminated against.

Consider, for example, the extent to which the following performance issues might help to explain why Mary was not promoted, but the other black women were.

Dress. While Mary wears her hair in dreadlocks, the other black women relax their hair. On Casual Fridays, Mary sometimes wears West African influenced attire. The other black women typically wear khaki trousers or blue jeans with white cotton blouses.

Institutional Identity. Mary was the driving force behind two controversial committees: the committee for the Recruitment and Retention of Women and Minorities and the committee on Staff/Attorney Relations. She has been critical of the firm's hiring and work allocation practices. Finally, she has repeatedly raised concerns about the number of hours the firm allocates to pro bono work. None of the other four black women have ever participated on identity-related or employee relations-related committees. Nor have any of them commented on either the racial/gender demographics of the firm or the number of hours the firm allocates for pro bono work.

Social Identity. Mary rarely attends the firm's happy hours. Typically, the other four black women do. Unlike Mary, the four black women each have hosted at least one firm event at their home. All four play tennis, and two of them play golf. Mary plays neither. Finally, while all four black women are members of the country club to which many of the partners belong, Mary is not.

Educational Affiliations. Two of the other four black women graduated from Harvard Law School, one graduated from Yale, and the other graduated from Stanford. Mary attended a large local state law school at the bottom of the second tier of schools.

Marital Status. All four of the other black women are married. Two are married to white men and each of them is married to a professional. Mary is a single mother.

Residence. Each of the other four black women lives in predominantly white neighborhoods. Mary lives in the inner city, which is predominantly black.

Professional Affiliation. Mary is an active member of the local black bar association, the Legal Society Against Taxation, and the Women's Legal Caucus. None of the four black women belongs to any of these organizations. One of them is on the advisory board of the Federalist Society. One of the four black women is a Catholic, two are Episcopalian, and the other does not attend church. Mary is a member of the Nation of Islam. . . .

Intersectionality does not capture this form of preferential treatment. While intersectionality recognizes that institutions make intra-group distinctions, that understanding is situated in an anti-discrimination context that is buttressed by a status conception of identity.

Reword to make termination justified

Assuming the foregoing performance issues obtain in Mary's case, do they reflect impermissible discrimination? The answer is not obviously yes. Perhaps the partners simply do not like Mary. Based on the description of how Mary performs her identity, could one not reasonably conclude the following: She does not attend happy hours, she creates trouble, she is not a team player, she does not dress or act professionally. Redescribing Mary's performance in this way makes the employer's decision to deny her partnership appear non-discriminatory (and even legitimate). After all, working and succeeding in an organization is not only about doing work. It is also about getting along with people and getting them to like you. An argument can be made that Mary simply did not do much work in the direction of getting the people who mattered to like her. The other four black women did; and they got promoted. On its face some—perhaps—will see this as fair. Those who do the extra work of making people like them should get promoted. Given our claim that this line of reasoning is flawed, the question is: What exactly is the relationship between identity performance and workplace discrimination? . . .

Broadly speaking, there are two ways to make the point that intra-group distinctions based on identity performance implicate workplace discrimination. The first is to focus on the preferred group members. In our hypothetical, they are the four black women. The second way is to focus on the disfavored group members. Mary, the fifth black woman, falls into this category. . . .

In a prior article, *Working Identity* [85 Cornell L. Rev. 1259 (2000)], we argued that an employee's awareness that identity-based assumptions about her are at odds with the institutional norms and criteria of a firm creates an incentive for that employee to work her identity. There are a number of ways an employee might do this. The employee might laugh in response to, or engage in racist humor (signaling collegiality). She might socialize with her colleagues after work (signaling that she can fit in; is one of the boys). She might avoid contact with other employees with negative workplace standing (signaling that she is not really "one of them"). The list goes on. The point is that whatever particular strategy the employee deploys, her aim will likely be to comfort her supervisors/colleagues about her negative workplace standing. Specifically, the employee will attempt to signal that she can fit in, that she is not going to make her supervisors/colleagues uncomfortable about her identity—or theirs—and, at bottom, that the negative stereotypes that exist about her status identity are inapplicable to her. *Working Identity* refers to these strategies collectively as "comfort strategies." These strategies are constituted by identity performances.

Stipulate that the four black women in the hypothetical performed comfort strategies. The claim that the performance of such strategies constitutes discrimination is based on the idea that people with negative workplace standing (e.g., people of color) have a greater incentive to perform comfort strategies than people with positive workplace standing. This means that identity performances burden some employees (e.g., blacks) more than others (e.g., whites).

Without more, this racial distribution of identity performances is problematic. The problem is compounded by the fact that identity performances constitute work, a kind of "shadow work." This work is simultaneously expected and unacknowledged. Plus, it is work that is often risky. Finally, this work can be at odds with the employee's sense of her identity. That is, the employee may perceive that she has to disassociate from or disidentify with her identity in order to fit in. To the extent the employee's continued existence and success in the workplace is contingent upon her behaving in ways that operate as a denial of self, there is a continual harm to that employee's dignity.

Recall that the claim is that the firm's discrimination against Mary derives from an intra-group distinction based on Mary's dress, institutional identity, marital status, professional and educational affiliations, and residence. The question becomes, why is this discrimination impermissible? The short answer is that the distinction creates an intra-racial and an inter-racial problem. The problem is that the firm draws a line between black people who do (or whom the firm perceives as performing) identity work to fit in at the firm and black people who do not perform (or whom the firm perceives as not performing) such work. The interracial problem is that white people are not subject to this subcategorization.

Angela P. Harris, Race and Essentialism in Feminist Legal Theory
42 Stan. L. Rev. 581, 588-89, 595 (1990)

[T]he story [feminists] tell about "women," despite its claim to universality, seems to black women to be peculiar to women who are white, straight, and socioeconomically privileged—a phenomenon Adrienne Rich terms "white solipsism." . . .

The notion that there is a monolithic "women's experience" that can be described independent of other facts of experience like race, class, and sexual orientation is one I refer to . . . as "gender essentialism." A corollary to gender essentialism is "racial essentialism"—the belief that there is a monolithic "Black Experience," or "Chicano Experience." The source of gender and racial essentialism (and all other essentialisms, for the list of categories could be infinitely multiplied is the . . . voice that claims to speak for all. The result of essentialism is to reduce the lives of people who experience multiple forms of oppression to addition problems: "racism + sexism = straight black women's experience," or "racism + sexism + homophobia = black lesbian experience." Thus, in an essentialist world, black women's experience will always be forcibly fragmented before being subjected to analysis, as those who are "only interested in race" and those who are "only interested in gender" take their separate slices of our lives. . . .

[T]he "nuance theory" approach to the problem of essentialism . . . [is to offer generalization] about "all women" while qualifying statements, often in footnotes, supplement the general account with the subtle nuances of experience that "different" women add to the mix. Nuance theory thus assumes the commonality of all women—differences are a matter of "context" or "magnitude"; that is, nuance.

The problem with nuance theory is that by defining black women as "different," white women quietly become the norm, or pure, essential woman.

Catharine A. MacKinnon, Women's Lives, Men's Laws
87-88, 90 (2005)

Discerning commonalities in experience is not the same as searching for an "essence." The socially constructed "woman" has no "essence." If women "as women" are social and concrete, they must encompass all of women's experiences of social hierarchy, because race, class, and sexual orientation (for instance) contribute to making women's concrete situation and status as women be what it is. A genuinely feminist method is thus open to real women in the social world and builds its category, "women," from them. . . .

[F]eminism does not take the view that gender is all there is. It takes the view that gender is almost never not there. Feminism claims not that all women are affected the same by male power or are similarly situated under it. It claims that no woman is unaffected by it. Feminism does not see all women as the same; it criticizes this view. It claims that all women are seen and treated as women in some way under male supremacy. This is not to say that feminism is always practiced, even by feminists. This is not to say that feminism does not need to be more race-conscious; it does. Neither is it to say that some work, claiming to be feminist, has not been racist; it has. It is to say that some of the feminist analysis that has been dismissively tagged with what has become the academic epithet of "essentialism," as exemplary of the "straight, white, and economically privileged," is not. . . .

The "essentialism" charge has become a sneer, a tool of woman-bashing, with consequences that far outrun its merits. The widespread acceptance of the claim seems due more to its choice of target than its accuracy in hitting it. Male power is ecstatic; its defenders love the accusation that feminism is "essentialist," even though they don't really know what this means. They do know that it has divided women, which sure takes a lot of heat off. The charge brings the moral authority of opposition to racism to the support of male dominance. "Essentialist" name-calling has become a weapon of choice against those who oppose pornography, prostitution, clitoridectomy, dowry burning, and other misogynist cultural practices, practices that target women as women across cultures, although often in culturally specific forms. Avoiding "essentialism" has become a politically and intellectual respectable pretext for dismissing and ignoring gender and the realities of sexual politics. . . .

Anti-"essentialism," as practiced, thus corrodes group identification and solidarity and leaves us with one-at-a-time personhood; liberal individualism. What a coincidence. With the inability to assert a group reality—an ability that only the subordinated need—comes the shift away from realities of power in the world and toward the search for "identity," excuse me, "identities." It changes the subject, as it were, or tries to. But who wins? Can a postmodern humanism be far behind? "Identity" in its currently psychologically shrunk sense is not women's problem. Reality is: a reality of group oppression that exists whether we identify with our group or not.

Notes

1. Racial Tensions in the First Wave of Feminism.   Nineteenth-century suffragettes exploited both the civil rights principles underlying abolition and the racism that persisted after the Civil War. Elizabeth Cady Stanton, for example, claimed both affinity with Negro slaves and superiority over them, reminding white political leaders of the obvious injustice that black men could vote while white women could not: "[Y]ou place the [N]egro, so unjustly degraded by you, in a superior position to your own wives and mothers," she complained.[1] Later suffragettes used even more explicitly racist arguments asserting the desirability of diluting the Negro vote as a rationale for supporting women's suffrage. For example, one Southern suffragist at a 1903 convention of the National American Women Suffrage Association claimed that "[t]he enfranchisement of women would insure immediate and durable white supremacy, honestly attained."[2]

Does any of this sound familiar today? Recall the concern expressed by Dorothy Roberts about privileged women's exploitative delegation of menial tasks to low-income women of color.[3] Does white women's equality continue to depend upon the inequality of minority women? Do majority women feel entitled, at least unconsciously, to status and income at least as high as

---

1. Elizabeth Cady Stanton, Address to the Legislature of the State of New York (Feb. 14, 1854). This address is excerpted in Chapter 1, Section A of this book.

2. Sara M. Evans, Born for Liberty: A History of Women in America 155 (1989). For discussion of how feminist advocates used the race analogy in complex ways, often in collaboration with African American women, to help secure women's rights, and also disaggregated race from sex when it became a liability, see Serena Mayeri, Reasoning From Race: Feminism, Law, and the Civil Rights Revolution (2011). See also bell hooks, Ain't I a Woman: Black Women and Feminism 127-39 (1981) (describing historical tensions over race within the women's movement).

3. Dorothy Roberts, Spiritual and Menial Housework, 9 Yale J.L. & Feminism 51 (1997), excerpted in Chapter 4, Section B of this book.

minority women? What, if anything does the Black Lives Matter movement suggest about the relationship of racism to sexism? Has racism been shown to be the more intractable problem? Does it matter which is worse? For further consideration of the relationship, see Section D, Note 3 in this Chapter, and Problem 6-19.

2. The Intersectionality Critique.   A case that helped to stimulate the intersectionality critique involved a challenge by a black woman to an airline grooming policy prohibiting employees from wearing a braided hairstyle. The court held that because the policy applied to all employees—women and men, black and white—it was not discrimination on the basis of either race or gender. In rejecting claims that the style was crucial to black women, the judge pointed out that the plaintiff did not begin to wear the hairstyle until just after a white actress, Bo Derek, popularized corn rows in the movie "10," rather than several years earlier when Cicely Tyson wore the hairstyle at the Academy Awards.[4]

Critics attacked the case for ignoring "intersectionality"—or the interrelationships between race and gender. According to Paulette Caldwell:

> Wherever they exist in the world, black women braid their hair. They have done so in the United States for more than four centuries. African in origin, the practice of braiding is as American—black American—as sweet potato pie. A braided hairstyle was first worn in a nationally-televised media event in the United States—and in that sense "popularized"—by a black actress, Cicely Tyson, nearly a decade before the movie "10." More importantly Cicely Tyson's choice to popularize (i.e., to "go public" with) braids, like her choice of acting roles, was a political act made on her own behalf and on behalf of all black women.
>
> The very use of the term "popularized" to describe Bo Derek's wearing of braids—in the sense of rendering suitable to the majority—specifically subordinates and makes invisible all of the black women who for centuries have worn braids in places where they and their hair were not overt threats to the American aesthetic.[5]

How compelling is this critique?

To what extent do the theoretical perspectives examined in this book assume, as Angela Harris charges, that the "women" who would be aided by the perspective are white, middle-class, able-bodied individuals? Harris' claim is that with respect to some experiences, like rape, being black is not simply additive, but that it transforms the experience.

---

4. Rogers v. American Airlines, 527 F. Supp. 229 (S.D.N.Y. 1981)

5. Paulette M. Caldwell, A Hair Piece: Perspectives on the Intersection of Race and Gender, 1991 Duke L.J. 365, 379.

[T]he paradigm experience of rape for black women has historically involved the white employer in the kitchen or bedroom as much as the strange black man in the bushes. During slavery, the sexual abuse of black women by white men was commonplace. Even after emancipation, the majority of working black women were domestic servants for white families, a job which made them uniquely vulnerable to sexual harassment and rape.

Moreover, as a legal matter, the experience of rape did not even exist for black women. During slavery, the rape of a black woman by any men, white or black, was simply not a crime. Even after the Civil War, rape laws were seldom used to protect black women against either white or black men, since black women were considered promiscuous by nature. In contrast to the partial or at least formal protection white women had against sexual brutalization, black women frequently had no legal protection whatsoever. "Rape," in this sense, was something that only happened to white women; what happened to black women was simply life.

Finally, for black people, male and female, "rape" signified the terrorism of black men by white men, aided and abetted, passively (by silence) or actively (by "crying rape"), by white women. . . . [S]ocial activist Ida B. Wells . . . saw that both the law of rape and Southern miscegenation laws were part of a patriarchal system through which white men maintained their control over the bodies of all black people: "[W]hite men used their ownership of the body of the white female as a terrain on which to lynch the black male." Moreover, Wells argued, white women, protected by the patriarchal idealization of white womanhood, were able to remain silent, unhappily or not, as black men were murdered by mobs. . . .

[T]he experience of rape for black women includes not only a vulnerability to rape and a lack of legal protection radically different from that experienced by white women, but also a unique ambivalence. Black women have simultaneously acknowledged their own victimization and the victimization of black men by a system that has consistently ignored violence against women while perpetrating it against men.[6]

Can you think of other examples where race transforms the experience of sexual subordination, rather than merely intensifying it?

A study examining a sample of judicial opinions in federal courts from 1965 through 1999 concluded, among other things, that plaintiffs who make intersectional claims in discrimination cases are only half as likely to win their cases as plaintiffs who allege a single basis of discrimination.[7] The explanation that emerged from the intersectionality critique is that courts make the mistake of looking at race and sex separately, thus missing the cumulative or

---

6. Angela P. Harris, Race and Essentialism in Feminist Legal Theory, 42 Stan. L. Rev. 581, 601 (1990).

7. See Rachel Kahn Best et al., Multiple Disadvantages: An Empirical Test of Intersectionality Theory in EEO Litigation, 45 Law & Soc'y Rev. 991 (2011).

transformative effects of race and gender.[8] A more recent doctrinal articulation of the problem is that by insisting that discrimination be established by comparison to someone else who does not have the characteristics of the plaintiff, courts systematically exclude plaintiffs who have been discriminated against based on more than one factor.[9]

3. The Critiques of the Intersectionality Critique. Richard Ford responds to Paulette Caldwell's argument excerpted above in Note 2:

> Suppose some black women employed by American Airlines wished to wear cornrows and advance the political message they ostensibly embody, while others thought cornrows damaged the interests of black women in particular and reflected badly on the race as a whole (given the cultural politics of black America in the mid-to-late 1970s, there almost certainly were such black women employed by American Airlines and even more certainly there were such black women among its customers). Suppose further that the management of American Airlines, either formally or informally, sought out and considered the opinions of its employees as well as of its customers and made its grooming policies based at least in part on such information. Now Rogers's claim is no longer plausibly described as a claim on behalf of black women. Instead it is a claim on behalf of some black women over the possible objections of other black women.
>
> Rogers and her supporters might object: "What business is it of other black women whether we wear braids—no one will be forced to wear them." But this individualistic account of the stakes of the case flatly contradicts the proffered rationale for conceiving of the hairstyle as a legal right: cornrows are the "cultural essence," not of one black *woman*. If this claim is to be taken seriously then cornrows cannot be the cultural essence of only those black women who choose to wear them—they must be the cultural essence of *all* black women. And in this case *all* black women have a stake in the rights claim and the message about them that it will necessarily send—not only those who support the political and cultural statement conveyed by cornrows but also those who oppose that statement.
>
> We'd need a fairly detailed account of the cultural and political stakes of cornrows to have a real sense of the political dimensions of this legal conflict. Does the wearing of cornrows track social class (are most cornrow wearers working class "authentics" or bourgeois trendies?) or ideological splits (nationalist v. integrationist?) within the black community? Do cornrows reflect a sophisticated racial politics in which the essentialist message is subordinate, ambiguous or even ironic or is a crude essentialism a central or indispensable part of the politics of cornrows? Is the symbolism of cornrows widely shared and well understood at least within some subset of American society or is it ambiguous?[10]

---

8. The classic exposition of this theory is Kimberlé Crenshaw, Demarginalizing the Intersection of Race and Sex: A Black Feminist Critique of Antidiscrimination Doctrine, Feminist Theory and Antiracist Politics, 1989 U. Chi. Legal F. 139.

9. See Suzanne B. Goldberg, Discrimination by Comparison, 120 Yale L.J. 718 (2011).

10. Richard T. Ford, Racial Culture: A Critique 24-25 (2005).

Is Ford right? How would you have decided the *Rogers* case? What evidence would have been relevant to your decision?

Does Angela Harris herself "essentialize" black women?

Do many gender critiques essentialize men? This topic will be explored in Section D, below.

Is MacKinnon right that an over-obsession with essentialism "corrodes group identification and solidarity" and thus the political basis for changing women's reality of subordination? Is there a middle ground that recognizes the need for both the critical edge that MacKinnon's dominance theory provides and caution about claims made on behalf of all women?[11]

4. The Problem of Categorization.   Gender interacts with other characteristics as well as race. One study of harassment charges brought under the Americans with Disabilities Act, for example, found that disabled individuals who are female, who are members of a racial minority, older, or who work for a small or a very large company are at higher risk of experiencing disability harassment than others.[12]

Is there a danger in applying the intersectionality critique to all categories that distinguish us? To what extent are the problems of intersectionality and essentialism an inevitable result of the inadequacy of *all* categories?

Linda Krieger outlines how difficult the problem is, even from the standpoint of a single category:

> Every person, and perhaps even every object that we encounter in the world, is unique, but to treat each as such would be disastrous. Were we to perceive each object *sui generis*, we would rapidly be inundated by an unmanageable complexity that would quickly overwhelm our cognitive processing and storage capabilities. Similarly, if our species were "programmed" to refrain from drawing inferences or taking action until we had complete, situation-specific data about each person or object we encountered, we would have died out long ago. To function at all, we must design strategies for simplifying the perceptual environment and acting on less-than-perfect information. A major way we accomplish both goals is by creating categories. . . .
>
> What happens when we group objects into categories? First, we tend to perceive members of the same category as being more similar to each other, and

---

11. Examples of the broad range of efforts to promote solidarity while recognizing difference and different forms of resistance include Janet Halley, Split Decisions: How and Why to Take a Break From Feminism (2006) (arguing for a form of feminism that neither denies harm nor assumes guilt); Katharine T. Bartlett, Feminist Legal Methods, 103 Harv. L. Rev. 829, 880-85 (1990) (describing the "positional" stance that both commits to specific truths and values and acknowledges the importance of contingency and perspective); Kathryn Abrams, Feminist Lawyering and Legal Method, 16 Law & Soc. Inquiry 373 (1991) (describing concrete methodological innovations that avoid both absolute and relativistic assumptions).

12. See Linda R. Shaw et al., Intersectionality and Disability Harassment: The Interactive Effects of Disability, Race, Age, and Gender, 55 (2) Rehab. Bulletin 82, 88 (2012).

members of different categories as more dissimilar to each other, than when all the objects are viewed in aggregate. The same results adhere when the "objects" we categorize are other human beings. . . .

Second, although some debate exists on this issue, it appears that we create a mental prototype, often visual, of the "typical" category member. To determine whether an item is a member of a particular category, we match the object perceived with the category prototype and determine the "distance" between the two. We experience an object first as a member of its "basic" category—the category most accessible at the moment. Only with additional mental processing do we identify it as a member of its superordinate or subordinate categories. . . .

But the price of this cognitive economy is that categorical structures . . . bias what we see, how we interpret it, how we encode and store it in memory, and what we remember about it later. In intergroup relations, these biases, mediated through perception, inference, and judgment, can result in discrimination, whether we intend it or not, whether we know it or not.[13]

As the Carbado and Gulati excerpt suggests, categorization based on multiple categories leads not only to discriminatory decision-making by employers of the sort Krieger describes but also to pressure on individuals to emphasize, or suppress, key aspects of their identity. Kenji Yoshino notes that members of subordinate groups have to choose when to assert their identity and when to "cover" their differences to fit within the dominant culture.[14] This choice constrains "intersectionals" in ways that others are not constrained.[15] Does this dynamic help to explain the conduct of some of the female lawyers in the Carbado and Gulati excerpt? Does everyone perform their gender and their race in some way, or is this only an issue for racial minorities and women? Is there a legal fix to the pressures to conform to (subordinating) expectations?

Putting Theory Into Practice

6-1. Reconsider Problem 2-8 involving the pregnant teenage girl, fired from her job at the community center because of concern that she would be a poor role model for the teenagers served by the community center programs. What, if anything, does the intersectionality critique add to your analysis of her case?

6-2. As a gift to her mother, Seandria purchased the Miracle Morning package from an Elizabeth Arden Red Door Salon and Spa in suburban Washington D.C., which included a facial, massage, manicure, and lunch. While

---

13. Linda Hamilton Krieger, The Content of Our Categories, 47 Stan. L. Rev. 1161, 1188-90 (1995).

14. Kenji Yoshino, Covering, 11 Yale L.J. 769, 772 (2002).

15. See Gowri Ramachandran, Intersectionality as "Catch-22": Why Identity Performance Demands Are Neither Harmless Nor Reasonable, 69 Alb. L. Rev. 299 (2005).

her mother, who is African American, was at the salon, she asked that the salon also color and style her hair. The receptionist refused, telling her that the salon "did not do black people's hair."[16] Is this unlawful discrimination?

B. GENDER, CULTURE, AND RELIGION

Is it appropriate to impose the theories developed in this book upon non-Western cultures or religious communities that do not have the same commitment to women's equality? The conflict between women's interests and religion within the United States has been explored in other sections of this book, including Chapter 1, Section C(2) (ministerial exception to Title VII), Chapter 1, Section B (public accommodations laws that conflict with antidiscrimination laws), and Chapter 3, Section D (sexual orientation discrimination). This section addresses issues concerning women who adhere to non-Western cultural practices. Are Western feminists who advocate for reform of societies whose cultures and religions "oppress" women arrogant, or even "imperialist"?

Genital mutilation for immigration

Bah v. Mukasey
529 F.3d 99 (2d Cir. 2008)

STRAUB, Circuit Judge:

Petitioners, three women from Guinea who underwent female genital mutilation in the past, petition for review of decisions of the Board of Immigration Appeals ("BIA") affirming, inter alia, the denial of their claims for withholding of removal and Convention Against Torture ("CAT") relief based on female genital mutilation. . . .

Female genital mutilation "is the collective name given to a series of surgical operations, involving the removal of some or all of the external genitalia, performed on girls and women primarily in Africa and Asia." . . . According to the World Health Organization, female genital mutilation can be classified into four different categories:

Type I Excision of the prepuce with or without excision of part or all of the clitoris.

---

16. See Denny v. Elizabeth Arden Salons, 456 F.3d 427 (4th Cir. 2006). The court ruled against the plaintiff on the Title II claim on the grounds that a beauty salon is not a place of public accommodation, but it remanded the case for trial on whether the salon had violated Section 1981's prohibition on race discrimination in the making of contracts. For a critique of the case, see Radiance A. Walters, *Denny v. Elizabeth Arden Salons, Inc.*: Condoning Race Discrimination in Resembling Places of Public Accommodation Under Title II, 8 U. Md. L.J. Race, Religion, Gender & Class 407 (2008).

Type II Excision of the prepuce and clitoris together with partial or total excision of the labia minora.

Type III Excision of part or all of the external genitalia and stitching/narrowing of the vaginal opening (infibulation).

Type IV Unclassified: Includes pricking, piercing or incision of clitoris and/or labia; stretching of clitoris and/or labia; cauterization by burning of clitoris and surrounding tissues; . . . scraping . . . of the vaginal orifice or cutting . . . of the vagina; Introduction of corrosive substances into the vagina to cause bleeding or herbs into the vagina with the aim of tightening or narrowing the vagina; any other procedure which falls under the definition of FGM. . . .

The U.S. Department of State has largely adopted this classification. . . .

Genital mutilation "is often performed under unsanitary conditions with highly rudimentary instruments." . . .

The procedure is carried out with special knives, scissors, scalpels, pieces of glass or razor blades [in] poor light and septic conditions. The procedures are usually carried out by an elderly woman of the village who has been specially designated for this task, or by traditional birth attendants. . . . Anaesthetics and antiseptics are not generally used. Assistants and/or family members hold down the girl to prevent her struggling. . . . Paste mixtures made of herbs, local porridge, ashes, or other mixtures are rubbed on to the wound to stop bleeding. . . .

Genital mutilation can have devastating, permanent effects on its victims, including immediate and long-term physical problems such as infection, difficulty during urination and menstruation, incontinence, and sexual dysfunction; complications during child birth such as fetal and maternal death, birth defects, and internal damage to the mother; and severe psychological problems. . . .

In light of the long-lasting and severe consequences of genital mutilation, paired with the reasons for its infliction, the practice has been largely condemned by the international community. See, e.g., World Health Organization, Eliminating Female Genital Mutilation: An Interagency Statement OHCHR, UNAIDS, UNDP, UNECA, UNESCO, UNFPA, UNHCR, UNICEF, UNIFEM, WHO (2008), http://www.who.int/reproductive-health/publications/fgm/fgm_statement_2008.pdf; Committee on the Elimination of All Forms of Discrimination Against Women, Female Circumcision General Recommendation No. 14, U.N. GAOR, 45th Sess., Supp. No. 38 & Corr. 1, at 80, P 438, U.N. Doc. A/45/38 (1990); Declaration on the Elimination of Violence against Women, G.A. Res. 104, U.N. GAOR, 48th Sess., Art. 2(a), U.N. Doc. A/48/629 (1993). It has also been criticized and condemned by many activist groups within the countries where it is practiced. See, e.g., Inter-African Committee on Traditional Practices Homepage, http://www.iac-ciaf.com. Moreover, in recognition of the harmful effects of genital mutilation, the United States Congress has criminalized female genital mutilation of minors in the United States. See 18 U.S.C. §116(a) (2012).

Petitioner Salimatou Bah, . . . a native and citizen of Guinea, entered the United States without valid travel documents in June 2003, and in January 2005 was placed in removal proceedings by service of a Notice to Appear ("NTA"). She applied for asylum, withholding of removal, and relief under the CAT, alleging, inter alia, that as a young girl she "suffered" the "barbarous act" of female genital mutilation, and the event "still has dire consequences on [her] adult life."

In a statement accompanying her application, Salimatou explained that she belongs to the Fulani ethnic group, which strongly supports the practice of genital mutilation as "the best way to prevent the Fulani girls from having pre-marital sex," and "to force the Fulani girls to keep their virginity until the marriage." She claimed that at the age of eleven, her mother and aunt took her to a "small area fenced with wood and stuffed with coconut leaves." She was taken into a tent where five "old ladies" with knives and other tools undressed her and had her lie on the ground. Salimatou, "scared and shaking," tried to escape, but the women restrained her. She was then held down by two of the women while two others opened her legs so that a fifth could make a "deep cut of [her] 'private part'" without "any anesthetic or sanitary precaution." Salimatou screamed throughout the mutilation, and experienced "pain all over [her] body." She began "bleeding heavily" and feeling dizzy to the point where she was unable to stand on her own. After she was given "traditional medicines," she convalesced for weeks during which time she was "treated traditionally with dried leaves and some other local potions." Salimatou further stated that she later had "problems with [her] menstrual period," as well as complications during the deliveries of her children. She also stated that she "can barely feel any pleasure" during sexual intercourse with her husband. She sought asylum in order to "live free from that barbarous act still in practice" in Guinea. . . .

Pursuant to 8 U.S.C. §1231(b)(3)(A), an alien may not be removed to a country if "the alien's life or freedom would be threatened in that country because of the alien's race, religion, nationality, membership in a particular social group, or political opinion." . . .

Here, the records below provide ample evidence that Guinean and/or Fulani women are routinely subjected to various forms of persecution and harm beyond genital mutilation. For example, the 2004 State Department Country Report on Human Rights Practices for Guinea states that "[d]omestic violence against women [is] common," and that "police rarely intervene[] in domestic disputes." . . . Moreover, the report states that women in Guinea are commonly subject, without recourse, to crimes such as rape and sex trafficking. . . . Under the regulations, once the petitioners established past persecution on account of a protected ground in the form of female genital mutilation, it should have been presumed that their lives or freedom would be threatened in the future.

L. Amede Obiora, Bridges and Barricades: Rethinking Polemics and Intransigence in the Campaign Against Female Circumcision

47 Case W. Res. L. Rev. 275, 288-90, 295-99, 316-17, 329 (1997)

Cultural phenomenon

Genital scarification and reconstruction are time-honored and worldwide practices. As extant cultural traditions, the practices are particularly prevalent in Africa where they are reported to occur in about twenty-six countries; the exact number of women affected is unknown, but it is estimated between 80 and 110 million. Within the African context, the age at which it is performed varies between localities and it is possible to distinguish at least four major forms of incidence. The ritualized marking of female genitalia begins with the mildest forms of the procedures, where the clitoris is barely nicked or pricked to shed a few drops of blood. This procedure is innocuous and has a strictly symbolic connotation.

The next range of surgeries extend to the removal of the clitoral prepuce, hood, or outer skin. This is the form that ritual Muslims refer to as sunna, and medical data indicates that it poses minimal health risks if scientifically performed and monitored. Sunna is most comparable to male circumcision and there is some suggestion that it may serve the purpose of hygiene and cleanliness. A more radical form of female genital surgeries is known as excision or clitoridectomy. In this procedure, the clitoral glans and some of the nympha or labia minora, the narrow lip-like enclosures of the genital anatomy, are severed. The most extreme form of the surgeries is called infibulation, and it has been identified as the form that presents the most significant risks and hazards. This procedure entails scraping the labia majora, the two rounded folds of tissue that contour the external boundaries of the vulva, and stitching the remaining raw edges together in a manner that ensures that only a tiny opening will be left after the surgery heals. . . .

Desc.

Describing a vital aspect of African cultural identity as "mutilation" has proven offensive, if not psychically mutilating, to critical African constituencies like the Premier Group des Femmes d'Afrique who prefer to employ the term "female circumcision." . . .

Female circumcision is embedded in an intricate web of habits, attitudes, and values, along with having both functional and symbolic connotations. In Africa, the practice is validated and undergirded by a wide spectrum of principles, in addition to temporal and spiritual beliefs. Recurring themes such as sexuality and fertility express preeminent indigenous values like solidarity among women, public recognition of lifecycle change, and procreation for social continuity. Some of these themes are not peculiar to cultures that practice circumcision. Adherence to rites of passage, for example, is an abiding phenomenon in the West.

[Obiora surveys a number of different symbolic meanings for female circumcision in different tribes, including circumcision as a test of courage; as a symbolic linking with tribal history; as a means of making the body symbolically fertile; as a sacrifice to a fertility deity; as a rite of purification; as a means of sex differentiation; as an aesthetic practice; as a symbol of individual identity; as a kind of cosmetic surgery akin to ear piercing; as a contraceptive device; as a means of inaugurating a girl into sexual womanhood; and finally as a way to discourage premarital sex. Obiora argues that it is this last function of female circumcision that Western critics have focused on to the exclusion of its other meanings and functions. She notes that female circumcision in the nineteenth-century West was primarily practiced for the control of female sexuality, and she suggests that Western observers therefore read their own cultural history onto the practice of female circumcision. Obiora also argues that Western academics tend to treat African people as lacking in agency, compelled by their "cultures" to behave in certain ways.] . . .

Through the years in Africa, outside interventionists, whether colonialist or missionary (and now feminist), continue to presume that it is their duty as the "advanced" to elevate and enlighten the "backward." It is characteristic of these interventionists to pay scant attention to crucial issues including the wishes and opinions of the supposed beneficiaries of their benevolence, the overall implications of intervention, and the possibility of more "benign" intervention. Not surprisingly, their campaigns, often couched in terms of virtual monopoly on good judgment, are perceived as unduly ethnocentric and presumptuous. Such campaigns conform to patterns and habits that have historically provoked righteous indignation and engendered cultural resistance to Western "missionary" exploits. Moreover, they tend to pre-judge and alienate the only forces—women, the "victims" and perpetrators—capable of facilitating or subverting meaningful change.

Madhavi Sunder, Piercing the Veil
112 Yale L.J. 1399, 1402-03, 1405 (2003)

Current scholarship posits an inherent conflict between women's rights and culture. But . . . religion qua religion is less the problem than is our traditional legal construction of this category. Premised on a centuries-old, Enlightenment compromise that justified reason in the public sphere by allowing deference to religious despotism in the private, human rights law continues to define religion in the twenty-first century as a sovereign, extralegal jurisdiction in which inequality is not only accepted, but expected. Law views religion as natural, irrational, incontestable, and imposed—in contrast to the public sphere, the only viable space for freedom and reason. Simply put, religion is the "other" of international law.

Today, fundamentalists are taking advantage of this legal tradition. Yet, contrary to law's centuries-old conception, religious communities are internally contested, heterogeneous, and constantly evolving over time through internal debate and interaction with outsiders. And this has never been so true as in the twenty-first century. Individuals in the modern world increasingly demand change within their religious communities in order to bring their faith in line with democratic norms and practices. Call this the New Enlightenment: Today, individuals seek reason, equality, and liberty not just in the public sphere, but also in the private spheres of religion, culture, and family. Current law, however, elides these claims for modernization. Failing to recognize cultural and religious communities as contested and subject to change, legal norms such as the "freedom of religion," the "right to culture," and the guarantee of "self-determination" defer to the claims of patriarchal, religious elites, buttressing their power over the claims of modernizers. Paradoxically, law's failure to question or revisit its old Enlightenment views is obstructing the emergence of the New Enlightenment. In short, human rights law, not religion, is the problem. . . .

So long as law continues to hold a fundamentalist view of religion and culture, it will transfer more power to fundamentalists and traditionalists at the expense of human rights.

Notes

1. Female Genital "Surgeries." The World Health Organization estimates that over 200 million women alive today in 30 countries in Africa, the Middle East, and Asia have had some form of female genital surgeries (FGS), or as the WHO calls it, female genital mutilation (FGM). The practice is carried out mostly on young girls between infancy and age 15 and, as the Obiora reading details, involves a range of different practices from pricking to removing or cauterizing parts of the genital area.[17]

In 1996, the United States became the second country in the world to ban female genital surgeries.[18] U.S. Directors of international financial institutions are required to oppose non-humanitarian loans to countries where FGM is commonly practiced if local governments have not undertaken educational measures to combat the practice.[19] Federal legislation also makes it illegal to "knowingly circumcise[], excise[] or infibulate[] the whole or any part of the labia majora or labia minora or clitoris of another person who has not attained the age of 18 years." The maximum sentence is five years. The statute

---

17. World Health Organization, Female Genital Mutilation Fact Sheet, updated February 2016, http://www.who.int/mediacentre/factsheets/fs241/en/.
18. Federal Prohibition of Female Genital Mutilation Act, 18 U.S.C. §116 (2012).
19. 22 U.S.C. §262k-2 (2012).

explicitly rejects the possibility of a cultural defense: "No account shall be taken of the effect on the person on whom the operation is to be performed of any belief on the part of that person, or any other person, that the operation is required as a matter of custom or ritual."[20] Is this the right policy?

As Bah v. Mukasey makes evident, FGM is considered to be a form of persecution on the basis of group membership (i.e., women) that may support an asylum petition. Is this an example of Western ethnocentrism, as Obiora suggests, or does it exemplify a basic "universal obligation to protect human functioning and its dignity"?[21]

In addressing the role of criminal and human rights law in combating practices that subordinate women, Helen Stacy notes that legal prohibitions are most likely to be successful when they work in tandem with broader social movements. So, for example, laws against footbinding in China were not effective until anti-footbinding societies enlisted parents to take an oath that they would not bind their daughters' feet or allow their sons to marry a woman who had been subjected to the practice. By analogy, Stacy argues that courts that want to take some effective action against FGM could direct governments to establish programs that promulgate alternative, safe, coming of age rituals.[22] Does this strike you as a desirable approach? What other alternatives might be feasible?

2. Multiculturalism and the Veil.   Islamic veiling is not just a religious practice, but also "a highly contested political symbol within Muslim societies and the global political arena."[23] Some traditions call for covering of the entire body (the burqa) and others for only headscarves (hijab).

The European Court of Human Rights has upheld bans on headscarves including a French ban enacted in 2010, making it illegal for anyone to cover their face in a public place.[24] The challenger, a French citizen of Pakistani

---

20. 18 U.S.C. §116 (2012).

21. Martha Nussbaum, Sex & Social Justice 29-30 (1999) (referring generally to international human rights). For general discussion of feminism and religious-based cultural practices that, from a Western viewpoint, violate women's basic human rights, see Patricia A. Broussard, Female Genital Mutilation: Exploring Strategies For Ending Ritualized Torture: Shaming, Blaming, and Utilizing the Convention Against Torture, 15 Duke J. Gender L. & Pol'y 19 (2008); International Law: Modern Feminist Approaches (Doris Buss & Ambreena Manji eds., 2005); Ayelet Shachar, Religion, State, and the Problem of Gender: New Modes of Citizenship and Governance in Diverse Societies, 50 McGill L.J. 49 (2005); Sally Engle Merry, Constructing a Global Law: Violence Against Women and the Human Rights System, 28 Law & Soc. Inquiry 941 (2003).

22. Helen M. Stacy, Human Rights for the 21st Century: Sovereignty, Civil Society, Culture 110, 177 (2009).

23. Valorie K. Vojdik, Politics of the Headscarf in Turkey: Masculinities, Feminism, and the Construction of Collective Identities, 33 Harv. J. Law & Gender 661, 661 (2010).

24. See France's Burqa Ban Upheld by Human Rights Court, The Guardian, July 1, 2014, http://www.theguardian.com/world/2014/jul/01/france-burqa-ban-upheld-human-rights-court.

origin, claimed that the ban was "inhumane and degrading, against the right of respect for family and private life, freedom of thought, conscience and religion, freedom of speech and discriminatory."[25] The French government claimed that the law was not aimed at the veil or the burqa, but at any head covering, including hoods and helmets when not worn on a motor vehicle. The ban was defended on the grounds that it served the purpose of social integration and "the right to interact with someone by looking them in the face and about not disappearing under a piece of clothing." The Court held that a certain idea of "living together" was a "legitimate aim" of France.[26] The Court had previously upheld bans on headscarves in educational establishments, public buildings, and for purposes of security checks.[27] Other countries, like the United States and Great Britain, believe that bans violate women's right to religious freedom.[28]

There are many reasons for wearing the veil. Some women engage in the practice as a form of identification with and loyalty to conservative, male-controlled Muslim communities. Others may wear it as a form of resistance, but what they are resisting itself may vary widely. One writer explains that, "[c]ontrary to what outsiders generally suppose, the typical Muslim woman in a Muslim city doesn't wear the veil because her grandmother did so, but because her grandmother did *not*."[29] Some Muslim women—who tend to be "young, urban, and typically the daughters of migrants from rural areas—deliberately embrace[] the choice to cover, challenging . . . both the secular construction of the headscarf as a means of Islamic male oppression [and] the Islamic masculinist construction of the veil as a protector of women's modesty and place in . . . the domestic sphere."[30] Some Muslim women also embrace the veil as a protection from sexual assault and harassment, as well as a challenge to Western imperialism and objectification of women's bodies. "Why is a veil more oppressive than a miniskirt?" asks one woman.[31] Is it?

Several cases under U.S. discrimination law have raised questions about Muslim women wearing the veil. Title VII requires employers to accommodate the religious practices of their employees, as long as it does not constitute an "undue hardship." A 1990 Title VII case upheld the right of a school board to refuse to allow a teacher to wear a hijab on the grounds that accommodating

25. Id.

26. Id.

27. See, e.g., Sahin v. Turk., App. 44774/98, Eur. Ct. H.R. (Nov. 10, 2005).

28. Vojdik, supra note 23, at 662 (citing examples and sources); see also Pnina Werbner, Veiled Interventions in Pure Space: Honour, Shame and Embodied Struggles among Muslims in Britain and France, 24(2) Theory, Culture & Society 161 (2007) (comparing British and French approaches).

29. Quoted in Werbner, supra note 28, at 173.

30. Vojdik, supra note 23, at 664-65.

31. Estelle Freedman, No Turning Back 223-24 (2002); see Joan Scott, The Politics of the Veil (2007).

the teacher's religious practice would be an undue hardship on the school.[32] What hardship do you think the school faced? Did it act reasonably? In a more recent case that has not yet been decided, a Muslim woman was discharged as a restaurant hostess by Disney Corporation after she began wearing a hijab and would not accept being accommodated by being moved to the back of the restaurant, or by wearing a large hat to mitigate the conspicuous nature of the head covering.[33] Are the cases distinguishable? Should Alamo Rent-A-Car be able to prohibit its Muslim employees from wearing a head covering during the holy month of Ramadan unless they are willing to move to the back office, away from customers?[34] How broad an expansion of Title VII should there be to accommodate persons practicing the Muslim faith?[35]

3. The "Cultural Defense" in Criminal Law. Another context in which the culture clash occurs is the controversial "cultural defense." This criminal law defense would permit evidence describing accepted practices in an immigrant defendant's native country in order to bolster a claim of justification or excuse. Advocates of the defense claim that it is consistent with principles of religious liberty, equal protection, and cultural pluralism.[36] Opponents argue that it reinforces stereotypes, legitimates gender subordination, invites anti-immigrant backlash, and promotes inconsistent treatment. "If you want to live here, live by our rules" is a common reaction.[37]

Two landmark examples are a New York case, People v. Chen, and a California case, People v. Wu.[38] In *Chen*, the defendant was a 54-year-old Chinese immigrant who killed his wife by smashing her skull with a claw

32. U.S. v. Bd. of Educ. for Sch. Dist. of Phila., 911 F.2d 882 (3d Cir. 1990).

33. This case is described in Nida Alvi, Dressed to Oppress? An Analysis of the Legal Treatment of the First Amendment and Its Effect of Muslim Women Who Wear Hijabs, 21 Cardozo J.L. & Gender 785, 796-98 (2015); see also E.E.O.C. v. Abercrombie & Fitch Stores, Inc., 731 F.3d 1106, 1106 (10th Cir. 2013) (throwing out case brought against Abercrombie & Fitch by female applicant who wore a hijab for customer floor representative, because woman had not made clear when she applied that she wore a hijab for religious reasons).

34. See EEOC v. Alamo Rent-A-Car, 432 F. Supp. 2d 1006 (D. Ariz. 2006) (employee should have been granted an exception because the possibility that other employees might request deviations was hypothetical and did not constitute undue hardship).

35. See Sahar F. Aziz, Coercive Assimilationism, The Perils of Muslim Women's Identity Performance in the Workplace, Mich. J. Race & L. 1 (2014) (arguing for a broad expansion to alleviate the many stereotypes and identity performance challenges and contradictions faced by Muslim women).

36. Alison Dundes Renteln, The Use and Abuse of the Cultural Defense, in Multicultural Jurisprudence: Comparative Perspectives on the Cultural Defense 62 (Marie Claire Foblets & Alison Dundes Renteln eds., 2009).

37. Steven E. Briggs, Letter to the Editor, Cal. Bar J., Apr. 2009, at 9. For backlash, see Arthur R. Silen, Letter to the Editor, id.

38. People v. Chen, No. 87-7774 (N.Y. Sup. Ct. Dec. 2, 1988); People v. Wu, 286 Cal. Rptr. 868 (Ct. App. 1991). Both of these cases are explored in Leti Volpp, (Mis)Identifying Culture: Asian Women and the "Cultural Defense," 17 Harv. Women's L.J. 57 (1994).

hammer. Chen argued that he lacked the intent to kill but rather had acted under "extreme emotional disturbance" in part because of his Chinese cultural values. Chen had become suspicious that his wife was having an affair and attacked her after she admitted that she was seeing another man. Chen's attorney introduced an anthropologist who testified that, "[i]n general terms, I think that one could expect a Chinese to react in a much more volatile, violent way to those circumstances than someone from our own society. I think there's no doubt about it." According to this expert, social control is more strict and unchanging in China than in the West. A Chinese man whose wife had committed adultery would be dishonored, and both parties would have difficulty remarrying. In the United States, the anthropologist also claimed, a Chinese man whose wife had committed adultery would be considered a "pariah" among Chinese women, and would have no chance of finding a white woman. On cross-examination, the expert contrasted Chinese people with "the average American," whom he described as a white professional male, and argued that Chinese immigrants assimilated into American society "very slowly, if ever." Impressed by this testimony, the trial judge found Chen guilty of manslaughter rather than murder and sentenced him to five years probation instead of time in prison.

In *Wu*, the defendant, Helen, who grew up in China, became romantically involved with a man, Gary Wu, who emigrated to the United States and married another woman. Many years later, however, he contacted Helen and told her he was unhappily married and that if Helen emigrated to the United States he would marry her and she could bear a child for him. Helen did emigrate to the United States, but Gary did not offer to marry her, even after the two of them had a child, a son named Sidney. Gary did divorce his wife, but did not tell Helen.

Helen, who was unable to speak English or drive a car, was unhappy in the United States, and eventually told Gary she would return to Macau. She did so without Sidney, but for the next eight years repeatedly asked Gary to visit her with Sidney. Gary continually asked for money, at one point proposing marriage after Helen showed him a certificate of deposit for a million Hong Kong dollars. Finally Helen and Gary were married in Las Vegas, but when pressed Gary would not say whether he had married her for her money. Shortly thereafter, Helen saw Gary beating their son, and Sidney told her the house they were staying in belonged to another woman, Gary's girlfriend. At that point, Helen told Sidney she wanted to die and asked if he would go too. He clung to her neck and cried. Helen cut the cord off a window blind and strangled her son. She then attempted to kill herself by slashing her wrist with a kitchen knife, but she was revived at the local emergency room.

At the murder trial, the judge refused to instruct the jurors that they could choose to consider Helen's cultural background in determining the presence or absence of malice, and Wu was convicted of murder. On appeal, the California Court of Appeals reversed, holding that evidence of her cultural background was relevant to the issues of premeditation and deliberation and could potentially reduce the murder charge to one of voluntary manslaughter. The experts in this case were not anthropologists but "transcultural psychologists," who explained that Helen's behavior represented love and maternal altruism: ". . . in her own culture, in her own mind, there are no other options but to, for her at the time, but to kill herself and take the son along with her so that they could sort of step over to the next world where she could devote herself, all of herself to the caring of the son, caring of Sidney. . . . Her purpose . . . in many ways . . . is a benevolent one."

There are hundreds of cases in which individuals have attempted to invoke a cultural defense. They involve a wide variety of cultural claims in a wide variety of contexts, including homicide, rape, drugs, custody, child abuse, animal cruelty, custody, employment discrimination suits, and the treatment of the dead.[39] A disproportionate number of these cases involve Asian immigrants. In such proceedings, Daina Chiu argues that the debate over the "cultural defense" is in large part a debate over three different ways of "managing Asian difference" in American society. The first is the "exclusion" approach: it argues for a cultural defense as "special treatment" to protect immigrants and to preserve American identity as white. Chiu argues that this approach is particularly harmful to Asian women because it legitimates their traditional subordinate role in Asian culture. A second framework, the "assimilation" approach, rejects the defense and demands conformity to dominant norms. A third, intermediate position, which admits cultural evidence to show state of mind or mitigate punishment, reflects what Chiu calls "guilty liberalism." Chiu argues that this position enables "white society . . . to reinforce its prejudices through the other culture while purporting to act in tolerance of difference. In particular, this approach allows white society to reconstruct the subordination of women through the medium of another culture." Chiu argues that the *Chen* case is an example of guilty liberalism. The judge in that case, she argues, reduced Chen's culpability not because he was acting under "different" cultural values, but because he held the "same" cultural values as Americans: "The subordination of women and the privileging of the male sex-right are common to both cultures."[40] Cynthia Lee similarly argues that the defense is most likely to succeed when it is "culturally convergent" with patriarchal norms in our own society.[41] If these commentators are correct, what does it suggest about when cultural evidence should be admissible?

39. See generally Alison Dundes Renteln, The Cultural Defense (2004).

40. Daina C. Chiu, The Cultural Defense: Beyond Exclusion, Assimilation, and Guilty Liberalism, 82 Cal. L. Rev. 1053, 1057, 1114 (1994).

41. Cynthia Lee, Cultural Convergence: Interest Convergence Theory Meets the Cultural Defense, 49 Ariz. L. Rev. 911, 918 (2007). For an argument that narratives of cultural difference function to reinforce xenophobia, see Leti Volpp, Framing Cultural Difference: Immigrant Women and Discourses of Tradition, 22 Differences: A J. of Feminist Cultural Studs. 90 (2011).

B. Gender, Culture, and Religion ═══ **833**

4. Feminist Multiculturalism. Cyra Akila Choudhury compares the complex struggles of women in non-Western cultures to the struggles of non-white feminists within the West. She observes that both "postcolonial and critical race feminists have resisted attacks based on culture by white feminists" while also having "to articulate the fight for change against dominant cultural norms within their communities."[42] She suggests further that the best strategy among feminists in these struggles is "a politics of solidarity—one in which feminists come together to engage in unflinching critique from positions of equality rather than civilizational superiority."[43] Is this the answer—both resisting communities and finding alliances within them? What do you think this means in practice?

Putting Theory Into Practice

6-3. In 1996, a group of Somali immigrants living in Seattle sought to persuade a hospital to perform largely symbolic circumcisions on their daughters, a procedure that involved simply pricking the clitoral hood and that was less intrusive than male circumcision. The parents presented this as an alternative to sending their daughters to Africa for a more extreme procedure. The hospital initially agreed but changed course when it was inundated with complaints.[44] What would you have done? Should such a procedure be banned given that circumcision is now performed on a majority of male newborns?[45]

6-4. A Hmong immigrant attempted to defend against a charge of child sexual assault in Wisconsin on the grounds that he was married to the child, who was 14 years old at the time, according to Hmong custom.[46] How would you evaluate the defense?

6-5. An elite university set aside six hours a week in one of its gyms solely for use by its female Muslim students. In the absence of such a policy, these women would be unable to exercise in appropriate attire. Critics viewed it as

42. Cyra Akila Choudhury, Beyond Culture: Human Rights Universalisms Versus Religious and Cultural Relativism in the Activism for Gender Justice, 30 Berkeley J. Gender L. & Justice 226, 230 (2015).
43. Id. at 230-31.
44. See Doriane Lambelet Coleman, The Seattle Compromise: Multicultural Sensitivity and Americanization, 47 Duke L.J. 717 (1998).
45. Child Trends Databank, Infant Male Circumcision, http://www.childtrends.org/?indicators=infant-male-circumcision (58 percent in 2010, down from 63 percent in 2001).
46. See State v. Mong Lor, 768 N.W.2d. 730 (Wis. Ct. App. 2009) (holding because Wisconsin does not recognize a "cultural marriage defense," the defendant did not have grounds to charge that his lawyer was ineffective in not raising the defense).

a concession to sexist cultural norms that included Shari'a and honor killings and invoked visions of women in veils and chadors on treadmills.[47] If you were an administrator at the university, how would you respond?

6-6. A police department regulation prohibits altering its prescribed police uniform in any manner, including to incorporate religious attire. A woman police officer would like to start wearing a hijab. Should the police department be required to accommodate her?[48]

6-7. A female U.S. Air Force fighter pilot challenges the constitutionality of regulations requiring female military personnel to be accompanied by a male companion and to wear a full-length dark abaya on trips off base in Saudi Arabia. The pilot claims that these regulations violate her equal rights.[49] Is she right?

6-8. In a number of different immigrant groups in the United States, parents are expected to arrange for their daughters' marriages. A survey of agencies throughout the world that had encountered forced marriage cases reported multiple forms of fraud, force, or coercion to make girls (some as young as 13) enter or stay in a forced marriage. Tactics included emotional blackmail, isolation, social ostracism, economic threats, and threats of physical violence and loss of immigration status.[50] Over half of cases involved Muslim families.[51] Should forced marriages be banned in the United States or regulated in some manner, or should they be tolerated in the name of religious liberty?

The United Kingdom estimated that 5000 to 8000 forced marriages were reported across the country in 2009.[52] In response, the country established a "Forced Marriage Unit" and national helpline, passed a law creating a special "forced marriage protective order" in family court, made changes to the visa sponsorship process, and conducted overseas "rescue" operations

47. Katha Pollitt, Sweatin' to the Koran?, The Nation, Apr. 28, 2008, at 14.

48. See Alvi, supra note 33, at 799-800 (no).

49. In response to Congressional legislation in 2002 outlawing the practice of making female soldiers wear Muslim religious garb, the Department of Defense agreed to change the regulations from requiring women to wear the abaya to "strongly advise." But some say that, in the military, encouragement is "tantamount to a demand." Caroline May, Don't Forget Your Hijab, Soldier! American Servicewomen Encouraged to Wear Headscarves in Afghanistan, in The Daily Caller (Mar. 31, 2011), http://dailycaller.com/2011/03/31/dont-forget-your-hijab-soldier-american-servicewomen-encouraged-to-wear-headscarves-in-afghanistan.

50. See Tahirih Justice Center, Forced Marriages in Immigrant Communities in the United States: 2011 National Survey Results, Sept. 2011, at 8, http://www.tahirih.org/site/wp-content/uploads/2011/09/REPORT-Tahirih-Survey-on-Forced-Marriage-in-Immigrant-Communities-in-the-United-States-September-2011.pdf/.

51. Id. at 11.

52. Id. at 7.

as well as extensive community education, outreach, and training. Is this the right approach? Can you think of other measures that might be part of a regulatory solution?

6-9. Obama Abou Salama is a professor of botany at Cairo University and a member of the Muslim Brotherhood. Mr. Salama runs premarital counseling classes. "A woman," he teaches, "takes pleasure in being a follower and finds ease in obeying a husband who loves her." Female members of his classes agree readily. One female supporter of the Muslim Brotherhood's family values agenda explains, "Let's face it, if your work took you away from your fundamental duties at home and if your success came at the cost of your family life and stability of your children, then you are the one who stands to lose."[53] Do Western feminists have a positive role to play in influencing such attitudes in Egypt? Or is this a matter for the Egyptian women themselves?

6-10. Mary Anne Case writes:

> At a time when so many different religious fundamentalisms are coming to the foreground and demanding legal recognition, I want to vindicate something I have come to call feminist fundamentalism, by which I mean an uncompromising commitment to the equality of the sexes as intense and at least as worthy of respect as, for example, a religiously or culturally based commitment to female subordination or fixed sex roles.[54]

Evaluate this statement. What do you think Case means? What would change, if anything, if United States public policy fully reflected the values of feminist fundamentalism?

C. WHAT IS A WOMAN? THE SPECIAL CASES OF TRANSGENDER AND INTERSEX

Throughout this book, male and female are assumed (for the most part) to be clear, easily ascertainable categories. This section examines the challenge that transgender individuals and people with an intersex condition make to this assumption and to the law generally.

The San Francisco Human Rights Commission defines "transgender" as "an umbrella term that includes male and female cross-dressers, transvestites, female and male impersonators, pre-operative and post-operative transsexuals,

---

53. Mona El-Naggar, Family Life According to the Brotherhood, N.Y. Times, Sept. 7, 2012, at A1.

54. Mary Anne Case, Feminist Fundamentalism as an Individual and Constitutional Commitment, 19 Am. U. J. Gender, Soc. Pol'y & L. 549, 550 (2011).

and transsexuals who choose not to have genital reconstruction, and all persons whose perceived gender and anatomic sex may conflict with the gender expression, such as masculine-appearing women and feminine-appearing men. All other terms—cross-dresser, transvestite, transsexual—are subsets of the umbrella term transgender." The term "intersex" is used to describe "anyone with a congenital condition whose sex chromosomes, gonads, or internal or external sexual anatomy do not fit clearly into the binary male/female norm."[55]

Transgender individuals and people with an intersex condition challenge the law's assumptions that a person is either male or female and that a sex designation at birth is permanent. Current cases tend to involve changing identity documents, employment rights, or access to sex-segregated facilities (everything from bathrooms to prisons).

In re Petition for Change of Birth Certificate
22 N.E.3d 707 (Ind. Ct. App. 2014)

Allowed

FRIEDLANDER, Judge.

Appellant is a transgender male who identifies as a man, lives as a man, and has undergone extensive medical treatment for gender transition, including gender reassignment surgery. Appellant filed a petition to change his legal gender so that he could correct the gender markers on his birth certificate. The trial court denied the petition based upon a perceived lack of authority to grant such a request. In this uncontested appeal, Appellant contends that the trial court erred by refusing to grant the petition.

We reverse and remand.

In 1988, Appellant was born in Indiana as a genotypical female. Since 2008, Appellant has received ongoing psychotherapy to address longstanding gender dysphoria (formerly known as gender identity disorder). As Appellant's desire and readiness to pursue gender reassignment became clear, Appellant began living as a male in January 2011 and shortly thereafter started testosterone treatment, which he has since continued. Appellant legally changed his name in 2012, and he completed sex reassignment surgery the following year. According to his surgeon, Appellant's true gender, based upon psychological and medical testing, is male. Appellant has changed his name and gender mark on his driver's license, as well as with the Social Security Administration. His birth certificate is the only significant life document that remains to be changed.

On March 26, 2013, Appellant filed a petition for change of gender in Tippecanoe Circuit Court. The petition sought an order changing Appellant's legal gender from female to male "for the purposes of meeting

Typical precursor ↗

---

55. Julie A. Greenberg, Health Care Issues Affecting People with an Intersex Condition or DSD: Sex or Disability Discrimination?, 45 Loy. L.A. L. Rev. 849, 853 (2012).

the requirements of the Indiana State Department of Health for changing the gender designation on birth records." Appellant stated in the petition that he had successfully transitioned to a male role in society, in accordance with accepted medical standards of care for gender dysphoria, and that he desired to change his gender designation so that his birth record "may be more congruent with his appearance and social role."

Appellant appeared pro se at the uncontested hearing on the petition on February 12, 2014. He presented evidence from his surgeon, therapist, and endocrinologist detailing his gender transition. He also provided the court with a letter from the Indiana State Department of Health (the ISDH) setting out its official process for changing the gender marker on birth records. In the letter, the ISDH Birth Record Amendment Supervisor stated in relevant part:

> The [ISDH] Registrar's manual states that we need a court order to change the gender on a birth record for a person who has gone through Gender Reassignment Surgery. The court order needs to tell us the person's name, date and place of birth and needs to tell us to change the original gender of the person on the person's birth certificate. The [ISDH] Vital Records office will accept any court ordered gender change from any valid court in the United States.

The court took the matter under advisement after specifically finding that the petition had been made in good faith and not for a fraudulent or unlawful purpose.

On February 14, 2014, the trial court issued an order denying the petition. The court concluded that it did not have authority to grant such a request, noting that the Indiana General Assembly had not yet spoken on the issue. On appeal, Appellant contends that the trial court had authority pursuant to [the Code], as well as the court's inherent equitable authority.

[The Code] provides in relevant part: "The state department may make additions to or corrections in a certificate of birth on receipt of adequate documentary evidence". Like name changes, the ISDH defers to the courts by requiring a court order to establish adequate documentary evidence for an amendment of gender on a birth certificate. Courts in our state have entered such orders. Further, the Indiana Bureau of Motor Vehicles expressly recognizes "certified amended birth certificate[s] showing a change in . . . gender" as proof of identity to obtain, renew, or amend an Indiana driver's license or identification card.

Though never addressed by this court, the amendment of a birth certificate with respect to gender is not novel. The vast majority of states, including Indiana, have allowed it in practice for some time. *See In re Heilig* (2003) (recognizing that, at the time, twenty-two states had enacted statutes expressly enabling such amendments and twenty states had statutes dealing generally with amendments to birth certificates; only Tennessee statutorily forbade an amendment as to gender). *See also* Dean Spade, Documenting Gender, 59 Hastings L.J. 731, 768 (2008) (forty-seven states allow gender reclassification on birth certificates (Idaho, Ohio, and Tennessee do not);[2] twenty-eight of these states "specifically authorize gender reclassification by statute or administrative ruling, while the other nineteen have no written rule stating that they allow sex designation change, but in practice do provide sex designation change upon application").[3]

I.C. §16-37-2-10 provides general authority for the amendment of birth certificates, without any express limitation (in the statute or elsewhere) regarding gender amendments. In light of this statute, as well as the inherent equity power of a court of general jurisdiction, we conclude that the trial court had authority to grant the petition at hand.

We recognize the trial court's concern over what evidence is required in support of such a petition. In its order, the court queried in part:

> Can the court grant such a request merely because someone holds themselves out as a member of the other gender? If so, how long must they hold themselves out as a member of the other gender? Is gender reassignment surgery required? Is hormone therapy required? Is a medical opinion required?

The legislature is free to craft specific requirements. Without such guidance, however, it is our view that the ultimate focus should be on whether the petition is made in good faith and not for a fraudulent or unlawful purpose.[4]

There can be no question in this case that Appellant made an adequate showing in support of his petition. He presented ample medical evidence

---

2. Tennessee is the only state that statutorily bans such amendments. See Tenn. Code Ann. §68-3-203(d) (West, Westlaw current through end of the 2014 2nd Regular Session) ("[t]he sex of an individual shall not be changed on the original certificate of birth as a result of sex change surgery"). Ohio's denial is based on a ruling from a probate court interpreting Ohio's statute as "strictly a 'correction' type statute," which permits correction only "if in fact the original entry was in error." In re Ladrach, 32 Ohio Misc. 2d 6, 8, 513 N.E.2d 828 (Ohio Prob. Ct. 1987). See also Ohio Rev. Code Ann. §3705.15 (providing for correction where registration of birth "has not been properly and accurately recorded"). The basis of Idaho's denial is unclear but commentators appear to agree that gender amendments are not permitted by Idaho's Office of Vital Statistics.

3. The Model State Vital Statistics Act and Regulations issued by the U.S. Department of Health and Human Services has, since the 1977 revision, provided in §21 for the amendment of a birth certificate upon the receipt of a certified copy of an order indicating the individual's sex has been changed by surgical procedure.

4. The Social Security Administration (the SSA) no longer requires documentation of sex reassignment surgery for individuals seeking to change their gender designation in their Social Security records. Individuals can submit, among other things, an amended birth certificate with the new sex, a court order directing legal recognition of the change of sex, or a physician's verified statement that "the individual has had appropriate clinical treatment for gender transition". Soc. Sec. Admin., Program Operations Manual Sys., RM 10212.200 Changing Numident Data for Reasons Other than Name Change (2013), https://secure.ssa. gov/poms. nsf/lnx/0110212200.

regarding his gender transition, which culminated in sex reassignment surgery. Moreover, Appellant's genuine desire to have all identifying documents conform to his current physical and social identity is apparent.

The trial court erred in denying the petition. On remand, the trial court is directed to grant Appellant's petition and issue an order directing the ISDH to amend his birth certificate to reflect his male gender.

Reversed and remanded.

VAIDIK, C.J., and MAY, J., concur.

Schroer v. Billington
577 F. Supp. 2d 293 (D.D.C. 2008)

ROBERTSON, J.:

Diane Schroer is a male-to-female transsexual. Although born male, Schroer has a female gender identity—an internal, psychological sense of herself as a woman. In August 2004, before she changed her legal name or began presenting as a woman, Schroer applied for the position of Specialist in Terrorism and International Crime with the Congressional Research Service (CRS) at the Library of Congress. The terrorism specialist provides expert policy analysis to congressional committees, members of Congress and their staffs. The position requires a security clearance.

Schroer was well qualified for the job. She is a graduate of both the National War College and the Army Command and General Staff College, and she holds masters degrees in history and international relations. During Schroer's twenty-five years of service in the U.S. Armed Forces, she held important command and staff positions in the Armored Calvary, Airborne, Special Forces and Special Operations Units, and in combat operations in Haiti and Rwanda. Before her retirement from the military in January 2004, Schroer was a Colonel assigned to the U.S. Special Operations Command, serving as the director of a 120-person classified organization that tracked and targeted high-threat international terrorist organizations. In this position, Colonel Schroer analyzed sensitive intelligence reports, planned a range of classified and conventional operations, and regularly briefed senior military and government officials, including the Vice President, the Secretary of Defense, and the Chairman of the Joint Chiefs of Staff. At the time of her military retirement, Schroer held a Top Secret, Sensitive Compartmented Information security clearance, and had done so on a continuous basis since 1987. After her retirement, Schroer joined a private consulting firm, Benchmark International, where, when she applied for the CRS position, she was working as a program manager on an infrastructure security project for the National Guard.

When Schroer applied for the terrorism specialist position, she had been diagnosed with gender identity disorder and was working with a licensed clinical social worker . . . to develop a medically appropriate plan for transitioning from male to female. The transitioning process was guided by a set of treatment protocols formulated by the leading organization for the study and treatment of gender identity disorders, the Harry Benjamin International Gender Dysphoria Association. Because she had not yet begun presenting herself as a woman on a full-time basis, however, she applied for the position as "David J. Schroer," her legal name at the time. In October 2004, two months after submitting her application, Schroer was invited to interview with three members of the CRS staff, [including Charlotte Preece, who] was the selecting official for the position. Schroer attended the interview dressed in traditionally masculine attire—a sport coat and slacks with a shirt and tie.

Schroer received the highest interview score of all eighteen candidates. In early December, Preece called Schroer, told her that she was on the shortlist of applicants still in the running, and asked for several writing samples and an updated list of references. After receiving these updated materials, the members of the selection committee unanimously recommended that Schroer be offered the job. In mid-December, Preece called Schroer, offered her the job, and asked, before she processed the administrative paper work, whether Schroer would accept it. Schroer replied that she was very interested but needed to know whether she would be paid a salary comparable to the one she was currently receiving in the private sector. The next day, after Preece confirmed that the Library would be able to offer comparable pay, Schroer accepted the offer, and Preece began to fill out the paperwork necessary to finalize the hire.

Before Preece had completed and submitted these documents, Schroer asked her to lunch on December 20, 2004. Schroer's intention was to tell Preece about her transsexuality. She was about to begin the phase of her gender transition during which she would be dressing in traditionally feminine clothing and presenting as a woman on a full-time basis. She believed that starting work at CRS as a woman would be less disruptive than if she started as a man and later began presenting as a woman.

When Schroer went to the Library for this lunch date, she was dressed in traditionally masculine attire. Before leaving to walk to a nearby restaurant, Preece introduced her to other staff members as the new hire who would soon be coming aboard. Preece also gave Schroer a short tour of the office, explaining where her new colleagues' offices were and describing Schroer's job responsibilities. As they were sitting down to lunch, Preece stated that they were excited to have Schroer join CRS because she was "significantly better than the other candidates." Schroer asked why that was so, and Preece explained that her skills, her operational experience, her ability creatively to answer questions, and her contacts in the military and in defense industries made her application superior.

About a half hour into their lunch, Schroer told Preece that she needed to discuss a "personal matter." She began by asking Preece if she knew what "transgender" meant. Preece responded that she did, and Schroer went on to explain that she was transgender, that she would be transitioning from male to female, and that she would be starting work as "Diane." Preece's first reaction was to ask, "Why in the world would you want to do that?" Schroer explained that she did not see being transgender as a choice and that it was something she had lived with her entire life. Preece then asked her a series of questions, starting with whether she needed to change Schroer's name on the hiring documentation. Schroer responded that she did not because her legal name, at that point, was still David. Schroer went on to explain the Harry Benjamin Standards of Care and her own medical process for transitioning. She told Preece that she planned to have facial feminization surgery in early January and assured her that recovery from this surgery was quick and would pose no problem for a mid-January start date. In the context of explaining the Benjamin Standards of Care, Schroer explained that she would be living full-time as a woman for at least a year before having sex reassignment surgery. Such surgery, Schroer explained, could normally be accomplished during a two-week vacation period and would not interfere with the requirements of the job.

. . . Because Schroer expected that there might be some concern about her appearance when presenting as a woman, she showed Preece three photographs of herself, wearing traditionally feminine professional attire. Although Preece did not say it to Schroer, her reaction on seeing these photos was that Schroer looked like "a man dressed in women's clothing." . . .

Although Schroer initially thought that her conversation with Preece had gone well, she thought it "ominous" that Preece ended it by stating "Well, you've given me a lot to think about. I'll be in touch."

[After speaking with other Library of Congress personnel, Preece rescinded the job offer.] . . .

ANALYSIS

I.

None of the five assertedly legitimate reasons that the Library has given for refusing to hire Schroer withstands scrutiny. [These concerns included (1) Schroer's ability to maintain her contacts within the military because she is transgender; (2) Schroer's credibility when testifying before Congress; (3) Schroer's trustworthiness because she had not been up front about her transition from the beginning of the interview process; (4) Schroer's transition might distract her from her job; and (5) Schroer's ability to maintain her security clearance. All of these concerns were pretextual.]

II.

Schroer contends that the Library's decision not to hire her is sex discrimination banned by Title VII, advancing two legal theories. The first is unlawful discrimination based on her failure to conform with sex stereotypes. The second is that discrimination on the basis of gender identity is literally discrimination "because of . . . sex."

A. *Sex Stereotyping*

Plaintiff's sex stereotyping theory is grounded in the Supreme Court's decision in Price Waterhouse v. Hopkins. In that case, a female senior manager was denied partnership in a large accounting firm in part because she was perceived to be too "macho" for a woman. Her employer advised that she would improve her chances at partnership if she would "take 'a course at charm school'" and would "'walk more femininely, talk more femininely, dress more femininely, wear make-up, have her hair styled, and wear jewelry.'" In ruling for the plaintiff, the Court held that Title VII reaches claims of discrimination based on "sex stereotyping." . . .

[D]iscrimination against a plaintiff who is transsexual—and therefore fails to act and/or identify with his or her gender—is no different from the discrimination directed against Ann Hopkins in *Price Waterhouse*, who, in sex-stereotypical terms, did not act like a woman. Sex stereotyping based on a person's gender nonconforming behavior is impermissible discrimination, irrespective of the cause of that behavior.

What makes Schroer's sex stereotyping theory difficult is that, when the plaintiff is transsexual, direct evidence of discrimination based on sex stereotypes may look a great deal like discrimination based on transsexuality itself, a characteristic that, in and of itself, nearly all federal courts have said is unprotected by Title VII. . . .

Ultimately, I do not think that it matters for purposes of Title VII liability whether the Library withdrew its offer of employment because it perceived Schroer to be an insufficiently masculine man, an insufficiently feminine woman, or an inherently gender-nonconforming transsexual. . . .

B. *Discrimination Because of Sex*

Schroer's second legal theory is that, because gender identity is a component of sex, discrimination on the basis of gender identity is sex discrimination. In support of this contention, Schroer adduced the testimony of Dr. Walter Bockting, a tenured associate professor at the University of Minnesota Medical School who specializes in gender identity disorders. Dr. Bockting testified that it has long been accepted in the relevant scientific community that there are nine factors that constitute a person's sex. One of these factors is gender identity, which Dr. Bockting defined as one's personal sense of being male or female.[1]

---

1. The other eight factors . . . are chromosomal sex, hypothalamic sex, fetal hormonal sex, pubertal hormonal sex, sex of assignment and rearing, internal morphological sex, external morphological sex, and gonads.

The Library adduced the testimony of Dr. Chester Schmidt, a professor of psychiatry at the Johns Hopkins University School of Medicine and also an expert in gender identity disorders. Dr. Schmidt disagreed with Dr. Bockting's view of the prevailing scientific consensus and testified that he and his colleagues regard gender identity as a component of "sexuality" rather than "sex." According to Dr. Schmidt, "sex" is made up of a number of facets, each of which has a determined biologic etiology. Dr. Schmidt does not believe that gender identity has a single, fixed etiology.

Resolving the dispute between Dr. Schmidt and Dr. Bockting as to the proper scientific definition of sex . . . is not within this Court's competence. More importantly (because courts render opinions about scientific controversies with some regularity), deciding whether Dr. Bokting or Dr. Schmidt is right turns out to be unnecessary.

The evidence establishes that the Library was enthusiastic about hiring David Schroer—until she disclosed her transsexuality. The Library revoked the offer when it learned that a man named David intended to become, legally, culturally, and physically, a woman named Diane. This was discrimination "because of . . . sex." . . .

Imagine that an employee is fired because she converts from Christianity to Judaism. Imagine too that her employer testifies that he harbors no bias toward either Christians or Jews but only "converts." That would be a clear case of discrimination "because of religion." No court would take seriously the notion that "converts" are not covered by the statute. Discrimination "because of religion" easily encompasses discrimination because of a change of religion. But in cases where the plaintiff has changed her sex, and faces discrimination because of the decision to stop presenting as a man and to start appearing as a woman, courts have traditionally carved such persons out of the statute by concluding that "transsexuality" is unprotected by Title VII. In other words, courts have allowed their focus on the label "transsexual" to blind them to the statutory language itself. . . .

For Diane Schroer to prevail on the facts of her case, however, it is not necessary to draw sweeping conclusions about the reach of Title VII. Even if the decisions that define the word "sex" in Title VII as referring only to anatomical or chromosomal sex are still good law—after that approach "has been eviscerated by *Price Waterhouse*,"—the Library's refusal to hire Schroer after being advised that she planned to change her anatomical sex by undergoing sex reassignment surgery was literally discrimination "because of . . . sex." . . .

In refusing to hire Diane Schroer because her appearance and background did not comport with the decisionmaker's sex stereotypes about how men and women should act and appear, and in response to Schroer's decision to transition, legally, culturally, and physically, from male to female, the Library of Congress violated Title VII's prohibition on sex discrimination.

Elvia R. Arriola, Law and the Gendered Politics of Identity: Who Owns the Label "Lesbian"?

8 Hastings Women's L.J. 1, 1-3, 5-6, 8-9 (1997)

Several years ago, I was a member of a predominantly lesbian women's support group. The group offered a "womanspace" for individuals who wanted to share their experiences, strength, and hope as survivors of rape and sexual abuse. On a weekly basis, anywhere from fifteen to thirty women of all racial, ethnic and social backgrounds, who knew each other only by first name, rented a meeting room from a community church and shared stories of sexual victimization and abuse, with the singular goal of healing themselves through mutual support. . . . In the company of other survivors, the women felt safe enough, sometimes for the first time in their adult lives, to weep or get angry; for in this safe space they trusted that their companions would not mock, negate, or minimize their feelings. Of course, the critical sense of safety was ensured by the practice of someone standing guard at the door to make sure no man accidentally walked into the rented rooms. If that happened, all talk would suspend until the man was gone. This ground rule grew out of the plainly obvious fact that this was a meeting for women healing from sexual abuse by the men in their lives; only an all-women atmosphere could guarantee an emotionally safe environment.

Imagine, then, the turmoil created in this "womanspace" when one day a tall, quiet woman who had shown up regularly at meetings for several weeks suddenly came out to the group as a transsexual female. Not only that, she was a transsexual female who identified as a lesbian. Suddenly "Micki," who had simply appeared as an unusually tall, rather quiet and professionally dressed woman, looked very different to the group's members. Some of the women were too involved with their own issues to take in immediately what had just happened. In the following weeks, however, a few women, both lesbian and not, reacted strongly, sharing that they felt threatened by Micki's continued presence. Micki's feminine appearance bore witness to the wonders of modern medicine, but to some she was nothing but a fake. Her revelation explained at last the slightly masculine build around the shoulders and neck: this supposed woman was a man, or at least had been born male. Further, although she had given up her male identity, Micki's self confident demeanor betrayed residual hints of her socialization as a privileged white male.

Her chosen identity as a lesbian posed another gender and sexuality enigma. Having castrated "his" penis while leaving "his" sexual orientation unscathed, to what label was s/he entitled? The choice of a lesbian identity to express her (his) new identity as a "woman-loving-woman" communicated an unfamiliar sex and gender ambiguity. For some, the ambiguity only generated feelings of hostility and feelings of mockery for this once-man's appropriation of a label—lesbian—which they felt belonged only to "real women."

In the conflict and confusion that surfaced for several weeks after her coming out, Micki encountered both support and prejudice from fellow members of the incest survivors' group. A few sought out Micki's friendship, trying to assure her that she was welcome. Others kept their distance and in private conversations voiced their distrust and interest in removing Micki from the group. They felt abandoned by their group, angry and enraged that not everyone agreed that Micki should leave. Too many individuals supported Micki to force a formal demand that she leave and not come back. The resistors expressed a sense of betrayal by the group's unwillingness to oust Micki, whose perceived crime was in once having had a penis and now being viewed as neither truly female, nor woman, nor lesbian. She was at best a not-man. Eventually, the conflict led to a split, as Micki's resistors formed their own group, with membership limited to women who had been born into a female body. Micki herself eventually left the group. She ultimately formed her own support group, focusing on gender identity and abuse issues. . . .

By leaving to form another support group, Micki opened the door for healing from incest and sexual abuse to other transsexual females. Yet, the women who separated from the original group never had to examine the source of their fears. No one thought to ask whether some of their reactions to Micki, based upon preconceived ideas about the meaning of sex, gender or sexuality, might have stemmed from the same hetero-patriarchal value system which accounted for their own sexual victimization. Certainly no one felt the need to understand or address the unique form of gender oppression that leads an individual to such a drastic measure as sex reassignment surgery (SRS). The fact that Micki's recovery involved stories of how s/he had been shamed and traumatized from the time of his (her) childhood for engaging in gender-nonconforming behavior did not interest her opponents. Yet I wonder how the group never questioned the inclusion of "butchy" lesbians, some of whom dressed in very masculine attire, and who described similar childhood examples of abusive treatment for their own gender-nonconforming behavior. I have asked and answered my own question: it is all gender-based oppression. . . .

I have often wondered what would have happened in that group if Micki had not left. In the few weeks she was there, did it make any difference for someone like Micki, who had been raised as a boy and had become a man, to hear the depth of anger experienced by women who had survived male rape or incest and who now felt desperate at being unable to escape even a hint of residual male energy in a transgender female? Was it unreasonable for the women-from-birth to see Micki as a burden, rather than as someone who might help their healing by vouching as a once-man for the reality of abusive male power, and affirming to them, "yes, this is what men do and you were unjustly violated"? Could either side have seen the source of their fears and their unjust experiences as rooted in societal attitudes based on male power and privilege which continue to induce heightened levels of female sexual victimization, or which so oppress some boys/men that their only escape is to castrate the physical signs of the male gender identity they were assigned at birth?

Notes

1. Who Is a Woman? Was "Micki" a woman? Was Diane Schroer? Was the unnamed appellant in the Indiana case a man? What factors should determine the answer to those questions? Many of the judicial opinions on gender determination involved marriage because the validity of a marriage, until very recently, turned on the participation of one man and one woman. In that context, many courts set forth strict definitions of gender that made it difficult or impossible to change one's gender legally. In Kantaras v. Kantaras, for example, an appellate court in Florida concluded that the marriage between a postoperative transgender male and a female was invalid because both were legally female—the term "female" refers "to immutable traits determined at birth."[56] A Texas court, in a similar marriage case, observed with respect to any person's sex that "[e]very schoolchild, even of tender years, is confident he or she can tell the difference, especially if the person is wearing no clothes."[57] But is it that simple? The Supreme Court's ruling in *Obergefell v. Hodges*, in invalidating all remaining state bans on marriages by same-sex couples, moots the gender question in the context of marriage.[58] Might we expect courts to take less stringent views of one's ability to change gender now that it cannot affect marriage, custody, or parentage? In a first, an Oregon judge granted Jamie Shupe's petition to change her legal sex "from female to non-binary."[59] Is this a good solution?

The rights of transgender individuals have become increasingly complicated as jurisdictions resolve the issue of whether, when, and how one's legal sex can be changed in different ways. As the Indiana case discusses, there are variations in state laws as to whether gender can be changed on a birth certificate and, if so, what evidence is required to justify such a change.[60] Similar variations can be found in standards for changing other identity documents such as driver's licenses and passports. In 2011, the State Department announced a new policy regarding gender designations on passports, which

56. 884 So. 2d 155 (Fla. Dist. Ct. App. 2004).

57. Littleton v. Prange, 9 S.W.3d 223, 223 (Tex. App. 1999); see also In re Estate of Gardiner, 22 P.3d 1086 (Kan. 2001) (invalidating marriage between man and transsexual woman on grounds that legal sex cannot be changed for purposes of marriage law).

58. 135 S. Ct. 2584 (2015).

59. In the Matter of the Sex Change of Jamie Shupe, Case No. 16CV13991 (Or. Cir. Ct. June 10, 2016).

60. For exhaustive coverage of these variations and their possible meaning, see Dean Spade, Documenting Gender, 59 Hastings L.J. 731 (2008).

provides that a transgender person can obtain a passport reflecting a new gender with a physician's certification that the gender transition is either in process (entitling the applicant to a limited-duration passport) or complete.[61] But a person seeking a change on a passport may end up with other identity documents that do not reflect the same sex because the standards for changing the designation are higher or lower, or change is not permitted at all. In addition to the bureaucratic headache this might impose, do the possible variations among documents invite discrimination against transgender individuals who might otherwise want and be able to conceal that their gender had changed since birth?[62] Does the lack of uniformity in legal rules regarding gender designations suggest that there is no consensus about who is female and who is male? In the academic setting, should professors and administrators ask students which pronouns they prefer?[63]

2. "Intersex" Children. Consider the situation of those who possess biological features that are neither completely "male" nor "female." Estimates vary as to the percentage of the world's population with an intersex condition in part because definitions of the condition also vary widely. With a broad definition, including anyone born with sex chromosomes, gonads, or internal or external sexual anatomy that does not neatly correspond with "male" or "female," the estimated intersex rate is 1 to 2 percent of the population.[64] A narrower definition focusing only on those with severe atypicalities, perhaps severe enough to warrant discussion with sex differentiation specialists and consideration of surgical alteration, produces estimates closer to 1 in 4,500 births.[65]

The issue of surgery to "correct" intersexed conditions in infants so that they are more clearly male, or female, is controversial. Reassignment surgery on infants with such a condition has been a standard protocol since the late

61. U.S. Dep't of State, Gender Transition Applicants, https://travel.state.gov/content/passports/en/passports/information/gender.html.

62. See, e.g., Elliot S. Rozenberg, The NCAA's Transgender Student-Athlete Policy: How Attempting to Be More Inclusive Has Led to Gender and Gender-Identity Discrimination, 22 Sports L.J. 193 (2015) (arguing that NCAA rules regarding documentation of gender-eligibility force transgender athletes to reveal their status).

63. See Jessica Bennett, She? Ze? They? What's in a Gender Pronoun, N.Y. Times, Jan. 30, 2016, at ST2.

64. See Melanie Blackless et al., How Sexually Dimorphic Are We? Review and Synthesis, 12 Am. J. Hum. Biology 151, 161 (2000); see also Julie A. Greenberg, Defining Male and Female: Intersexuality and the Collision Between Law and Biology, 41 Ariz. L. Rev. 265, 267 (1999).

65. See Peter A. Lee et al., Consensus Statement on Management of Intersex Disorders, 118 Pediatrics 488 (2006); Julie A. Greenberg, Intersexuality and the Law: Why Sex Matters 1-2 (2012) (discussing difficulties of measuring rates given different definitions of "intersex"). Prevalence and other issues relating to intersex conditions are tracked by the Intersex Society of North America, http://www.isna.org.

1950s and early 1960s. Clinicians have assured parents over the years that the surgical potential for normal-looking genitalia should dictate the child's gender and that any innate gender propensity of the child can be changed by careful upbringing. They have also counseled parents that children who do not have the surgery as infants become confused and distressed by their sexual ambiguity, are often teased and rejected by other children, and are not as successful in adapting to one sex or the other if they undergo surgery later on. For more than a decade, intersex advocacy groups have strongly opposed infant surgery, preferring to have parents raise their intersex children as social males or females, and then let the children decide for themselves at puberty whether they would like to change their social sex, with or without surgical assistance.[66] The delay prevents some "mistakes" from being made, although, as a practical matter, lack of financial resources, support networks, and safe educational environments often prevent exercise of free choice by the affected children.[67]

Feminists have found the intersex issue a difficult one. Nancy Ehrenreich explores the arguments on both sides, and concludes that intersex surgery is like female genital cutting and other genital surgeries in that both are cultural practices with the potential to reinforce misogynist gender norms.[68]

Why do we think that intersex individuals need to become identified either as male or female? Can you imagine a world in which one didn't need to be one or the other? In the state of Oaxaca in southern Mexico, the local Zapotec people have made room for a third category, which they call "muxes"—men who consider themselves women and live in a socially sanctioned netherworld between the two genders. Some dress as women and take hormones to change their bodies; others favor male clothes.[69] Do even the Muxe seem overly committed to a two-gender world? A similar model is represented in the Navajo recognition of the category "nadle" (or "nadleehe")—intersex individuals

66. E.J. Graff, The M/F Boxes, The Nation, Dec. 17, 2001, at 20, 21. For a survey of views on the question of how to respond to "ambiguous genitals," with some rich narratives, see Elizabeth Weil, What If It's (Sort of) a Boy and (Sort of) a Girl?, N.Y. Times Mag., Sept. 24, 2006; Hanna Rosin, A Boy's Life, The Atlantic Online, Nov. 8, 2008. The lead advocacy group today is Advocates for Informed Choice; information about this group is available at aiclegal. org. On the emerging intersex movement and legal issues affecting people with an intersex condition, see Greenberg, Intersexuality and the Law, supra note 65.

67. See Amanda Kennedy, Because We Say So: The Unfortunate Denial of Rights to Transgender Minors Regarding Transition, 19 Hastings Women's L.J. 281 (2008).

68. Nancy Ehrenreich (with Mark Barr), Intersex Surgery, Female Genital Cutting, and the Selective Condemnation of "Cultural Practices," 40 Harv. C.R.-C.L. L. Rev. 71 (2005). For both medical and legal issues of gender assignment, see Greenberg, Intersectionality and the Law, supra note 65; Legal Aspects of Gender Assignment, 13 Endocrinologist 277 (2003); Anne Tamar-Mattis, Exceptions to the Rule: Curing the Law's Failure to Protect Intersex Infants, 21 Berkeley J. Gender L. & Just. 59 (2006).

69. See Marc Lacey, A Lifestyle Distinct: The Muxe of Mexico, N.Y. Times (Dec. 6, 2008), at wk 4.

who are considered to be good luck to their families, greatly respected for being able to do the work of both men and women, and often the custodians of wealth.[70]

Australia now provides three gender options for passport applicants—male, female, and X. The "X" marker is available to those with medical certification that "the person has had, or is receiving appropriate clinical treatment for gender transition to a new gender, or that they are intersex and do not identify with the sex assigned to them at birth."[71] What would be the consequences of challenging the two-gender world for children without ambiguous genitalia? Two families made headlines for refusing to reveal the gender of their babies—a Swedish baby named Pop and a Canadian baby named Storm—and declaring their intent to raise them gender-free.[72]

3. Transgender and Discrimination "Because of Sex." Transgender individuals face intense employment discrimination and, until recently, they have had no legal protection.[73] Just as courts generally have held that discrimination based on sexual orientation is not discrimination based on sex, they have frequently excluded transgender individuals, as well, from the protection of Title VII.[74] However, a growing number of courts have, as in *Schroer*, applied the sex stereotyping theory recognized in Price Waterhouse v. Hopkins (discussed in Chapter 1, Section C and Chapter 3, Section B, above) to discrimination against transgender employees. As one federal appellate court

70. See Alison Shaw, Is It a Boy, or a Girl? The Challenges of Genital Ambiguity, in Changing Sex and Bending Gender 20, 25-26 (Alison Shaw & Shirley Ardener eds., 2005); see also Jessica Knouse, Intersexuality and the Social Construction of Anatomical Sex, 12 Cardozo J L. & Gender 135, 150 (2005).

71. The new policy is described at https://www.passports.gov.au/web/sexgenderappli cants.aspx.

72. See Swedish Parents Keep 2-Year-Old's Gender Secret, The Local (Jun. 9, 2009), http://www.thelocal.se/20232/20090623. After five years, Pop's parents revealed that he is a boy. David Wilkes, Boy or Girl? The Parents Who Refused to Say for FIVE Years Finally Reveal Sex of Their "Gender-Neutral" Child, The Daily Mail (Jan. 20, 2012), http://www.dailymail. co.uk/news/article-2089474/Beck-Laxton-Kieran-Cooper-reveal-sex-gender-neutral-child-Sasha.html (It's a boy.).

73. Shanelle Matthews, Transgender Rights Run into Bathroom Politics, Women's eNews, Apr. 28, 2008; San Francisco Human Rights Commission, Economic Empowerment for the Lesbian, Gay, Bisexual, and Transgender Communities 10 (2000) (estimating unemployment rate of 70 percent); Shannon Minter & Christopher Daley, A Legal Needs Assessment of San Francisco's Transgender Communities (2003), http://www.ftmi.org/images/0TransFinal. pdf. See generally Transgender Rights (Paisley Currah et al. eds., 2006).

74. See, e.g., Etsitty v. Utah Transit Authority, 502 F.3d 1215, 1224 (10th Cir. 2007) (Title VII does not cover discrimination against transsexuals); Dobre v. National R.R. Passenger Corp., 850 F. Supp. 284 (E.D. Pa. 1993) (requiring male-to-female transition transsexual to use male washroom and dress in traditionally male attire is not discrimination "against a female because she is female"); James v. Rank Mart Hardware Inc., 881 F. Supp. 478 (D. Kan. 1995) (discrimination against male transvestite is permissible as long as female transsexuals are treated no better).

put it in a case involving a transitioning fire department employee, "Sex stereotyping based on a person's gender non-conforming behavior is impermissible discrimination, irrespective of the cause of that behavior."[75] In 2012, the EEOC took this approach as well. In Macy v. Holder, the Commissioners concluded that discrimination against a transgender person "because that person is transgender is, by definition, discrimination 'based on . . . sex,' and such discrimination therefore violates Title VII."[76] The Eleventh Circuit applied the same reasoning to an equal protection challenge brought by a transgender public employee whose supervisor thought it was "unnatural" and "unsettling" for a biological male to appear at work dressed as a woman.[77] In 2014, President Obama issued an Executive Order banning discrimination by federal contractors on the basis of gender identity.[78]

One argument that persuaded the court in *Schroer* and the EEOC in *Macy* is that transgender discrimination is not based on sex, per se, but on an individual's decision to *change* sex. Paisley Currah and Shannon Minter analyze the distinction:

> [A]lthough it is difficult to see how an employer's decision to terminate an employee for undergoing sex-reassignment could plausibly be deemed anything other than a form of sex-based discrimination, courts have adopted the Orwellian notion that there is a meaningful legal distinction between discrimination because of sex and discrimination because of a change of sex. [I]n Underwood v. Archer Management Services, Inc. [D.D.C. 1994], [for example,] the plaintiff alleged that she had been terminated from her job because, as a transsexual woman, she retained some masculine traits. The court held that insofar as "she was discriminated against because . . . she transformed herself into

---

75. Smith v. Salem, 378 F.3d 566, 575 (6th Cir. 2004) (sexual harassment against transgender individual is discrimination because of sex and also sex stereotyping in violation of *Price Waterhouse*); see also Rosa v. Park W. Bank & Trust Co., 214 F.3d 213 (1st Cir. 2000); Lie v. Sky Publishing Corp., 15 Mass. L. Rptr. 412 (Super. Ct. 2002); Schwenk v. Hartford, 204 F.3d 1187 (9th Cir. 2000). On protection of transgender workers through sex discrimination laws, see David B. Cruz, Acknowledging the Gender in Anti-Transgender Discrimination, 32 Law & Inequality 257 (2014); L. Camille Hebert, Transforming Transsexual and Transgender Rights, 15 Wm. & Mary J. of Women & L. 535 (2009).

76. EEOC Appeal No. 0120120821 (Apr. 20, 2012), http://www.washingtonblade.com/content/files/2012/04/90910497-EEOC-Ruling.pdf. The significance of this ruling is discussed in Joanna L. Grossman, The EEOC Rules That Transgender Discrimination is Sex Discrimination, Justia's Verdict, May 1, 2012, http://verdict.justia.com/2012/05/01/the-eeoc-rules-that-transgender-discrimination-is-sex-discrimination. For a list of cases under Title VII on behalf of transgender individuals with EEOC involvement, see EEOC, Fact Sheet: Recent EEOC Litigation Regarding Title VII and LGBT-Related Discrimination, last updated Mar. 1, 2016, https://www1.eeoc.gov/eeoc/litigation/selected/lgbt_facts.cfm?renderforprint=1.

77. Glenn v. Brumby, 663 F.3d 1312 (11th Cir. 2011).

78. See Executive Order 13762 (July 21, 2014), https://www.whitehouse.gov/the-press-office/2014/07/21/executive-order-further-amendments-executive-order-11478-equal-employment.

a woman" rather than "because she is a woman," she had failed to state a viable sex discrimination claim.

The incoherence of this purportedly meaningful distinction (between sex and change of sex) is apparent the moment one imagines a court applying a similar distinction in a case involving discrimination on any other ground. It is unlikely, for example, that an employer who terminated an employee for changing her religious affiliation or nationality would be absolved of liability on the ground that he did not object to the employee's new religion or national origin, but only to the change of religion or national origin. Yet, the only difference between these situations and that of a transsexual person is that while changing one's religion or nationality is generally considered to be a legitimate personal choice, "the very idea that one sex can change into another" is likely to engender "ridicule and horror."[79]

The proposed federal Employment Non-Discrimination Act (ENDA), discussed at length in Chapter 1, Section C, above, was plagued with controversy among advocates over whether it should protect against both sexual orientation and gender identity discrimination; the theory on excluding gender identity was that passage was more likely if it did not cover transgender employees. The 2007 version that passed in the House did not include gender identity protection. Openly gay Massachusetts Congressman Barney Frank introduced the Act, and argued that it will pave the way for subsequent more inclusive protections.[80] Critics claim that it will be harder to get protection for transgender individuals as a separate measure than as part of a broader statute. Why do you think that greater bias exists against transgender persons than against gays or lesbians?

Twenty states prohibit gender identity discrimination in employment, housing, and/or public accommodations.[81] In addition, more than one hundred cities and counties have passed laws prohibiting gender identity discrimination. An early test case was a 2008 ballot initiative in Montgomery County, Maryland, to overturn an action adding gender identity to the County's antidiscrimination code. Among the key concerns of the citizens' group was that "any man thinking that he has a particularly strong interest in women and

---

79. Paisley Currah & Shannon Minter, Unprincipled Exclusions: The Struggle to Achieve Judicial and Legislative Equality for Transgender People, 7 Wm. & Mary J. Women & L. 37, 40-41 (2000).

80. See ENDA to Be Separated into Two Bills: Sexual Orientation and Gender Identity, http://www.advocate.com/news_detail_ektid49439.asp (Sept. 29, 2007-Oct. 1, 2007). Current versions of ENDA in both the House and the Senate include gender identity. See S. 811, A Bill to Prohibit Employment Discrimination on the Basis of Sexual Orientation or Gender Identity, 112th Cong., 1st Sess. (2011); H.R. 1397, A Bill to Prohibit Employment Discrimination on the Basis of Sexual Orientation or Gender Identity, 112th Cong., 1st Sess. (2011).

81. A current map of relevant state laws is available at http://www.aclu.org/maps/non-discrimination-laws-state-state-information-map.

children who are not related to him can put on makeup and a dress and wander into the women's restroom." The group cited an example of women in a gym locker room frightened by a masculine individual in makeup and a ruffled skirt.[82] Are these valid concerns?

Most recently, these concerns were the impetus for a 2016 North Carolina law mandating public agencies and public schools to designate and limit multiple-occupancy bathrooms and changing facilities to members of a single sex, based on their biological sex. The law, known as HB2, was passed and signed by Governor Pat McCrory in 12 hours without the opportunity for legislative or public debate in response to the "emergency" of the city of Charlotte passing an ordinance permitting transgender individuals to use the bathroom of their chosen gender identity.

The terms of HB2 went well beyond the bathroom issue. HB2 created new limits on the state policy prohibiting sex discrimination by providing that the policy applied only to *biological* sex, thus precluding protection from discrimination based on sexual orientation or gender identity; it preempted local and county anti-discrimination ordinances and prohibited any further passage of such laws at the local level; and it eliminated a private right of action under the state anti-discrimination policy, leaving enforcement in the hands of a state administrative agency. The law led to boycotts by some businesses, entertainers, the National Basketball Association and the governments of other states, and to still unresolved lawsuits and countersuits involving advocacy groups, state officials, and the U.S. Department of Justice.[83]

HB2 is likely unconstitutional under Romer v. Evans,[84] since the "emergency" appears to have been a pretext from the enactment of comprehensive provisions designed to cut out the LGBT community from anti-discrimination protections—provisions enacted in a context that can only be explained by animus against that community. In insisting that individuals be treated according to their biological sex rather than the gender with which they identify, the bathrooms provisions of HB 2, which apply to facilities used by employees of

---

82. Matthews, supra note 73 (quoting Michelle Turner). The Maryland Court of Appeals later held that the referendum had been improperly certified because many of the signatures were invalid. See Doe v. Montgomery County Bd. of Elections, 962 A.2d 342 (Md. 2009); see also P. Solomon Banda & Nicholas Riccardi, Coy Mathis Case: Colorado Civil Rights Division Rules in Favor of Transgender 6-Year-Old in Bathroom Dispute, Huff. Post (June 24, 2013), http://www.huffingtonpost.com/2013/06/24/coy-mathis_n_3488306.html.

83. See Alan Blinder et al., Countersuits over North Carolina's Bias Law, N.Y. Times, May 9, 2016; Joanna L. Grossman, A Room with a View: Federal Appeals Courts Says School District Cannot Bar Transgender Boy from Using the Bathroom Aligned with His Gender Identity, Justia's Verdict, 2016, at https://verdict.justia.com/2016/05/03/a-room-with-a-view.

84. 517 U.S. 620 (1996).

public agencies and educational institutions, also violate the EEOC's interpretation of Title VII,[85] as well the interpretation of Title IX promulgated by the Department of Education Office of Civil Rights,[86] to which the Fourth Circuit of Appeals has held deference is due.[87] Other states, including Texas, are following North Carolina's lead by queuing up new "bathroom laws" designed to fire up opponents of LGBT rights,[88] and 13 states have joined a suit against the federal government objecting to the Obama administration's interpretations of Title VII and Title IX.[89] Much of this could be avoided, of course, with stronger anti-discrimination laws at the federal level. See Note 6 in Chapter 1, Section C(2).

European courts generally have held that gender reassignment surgery does not alter an individual's sex for purposes of family law but that discrimination against transgender individuals is discrimination based on sex for purposes of human rights law. Canadian courts have taken the same position regarding discrimination.[90] England's Gender Recognition Act of 2004 goes further, allowing a transgender person to change legal sex and gain all the rights of the new sex, including those that relate to marriage and parentage.[91]

4. Transgender and Intersex Athletes. As awareness of transgender and intersex issues grows, so have controversies in athletics, where sex-segregation is the norm for most sports, at most levels. Title IX's application to sex-segregation in sports is discussed in Chapter 2. A controversy erupted at the World Track Championships in 2009 over a South African runner, Caster Semenya, whose gender was scrutinized after she won the 800 meters by 2.45 seconds.[92] Semenya was not stripped of her medal, but was ordered to

85. See supra notes 75-77; but see also cases cited in note 74.

86. OCR, Case No. 05-14-1055 (Nov. 2, 2015). More recently, see Julie Hirschfeld Davis & Matt Apuzzo, U.S. Directs Public Schools to Allow Transgender Access to Restrooms, N.Y. Times, May 12, 2016.

87. See G.G. v. Gloucester County School Board, Appeal No. 15-2056 (4th Cir. Apr. 19, 2016), at http://apps.washingtonpost.com/g/documents/local/court-opinion-4th-circuit-sides-with-transgender-high-school-student-suing-school-board-for-access-to-boys-bathroom/1960/ (Education Department's interpretation that Title IX requires transgender individuals to be allowed access to school bathrooms according to their gender identity is owed deference.).

88. See Patrick Svitek, Bathroom Law Battle Begins to Take Hold in Texas, The Texas Tribune, Apr. 27, 2016, at https://www.texastribune.org/2016/04/27/bathroom-law-battle-begins-take-hold-texas/.

89. David Montgomery & Alan Blinder, States Sue Obama Administration over Transgender Bathroom Policy, N.Y. Times, May 25, 2016.

90. See Laura Grenfell, Embracing Law's Categories: Anti-Discrimination Laws and Transgenderism, 15 Yale J.L. Feminism 51, 70-71, 78-81 (2003).

91. Gender Recognition Act, 2004, c. 7 (Eng.).

92. See Christopher Clarey, Gender Test After a Gold-Medal Finish, N.Y. Times, Aug. 19, 2009, at B13.

undergo gender testing by the governing international body, which revealed that she is intersex. She has internal testicles, no ovaries, and no uterus. After a forced 11-month layoff, she was cleared to continue competing as a woman and later qualified for South Africa's 2012 Olympic team. In the London Olympics, she carried the flag for her country and won a silver medal in the 800 meters.[93] In 2015, the International Association of Athletics Federations was forced to abandon its then-existing policy of policing gender in international sports through various gender verification strategies, including requirements that testosterone levels for female athletes be within certain limits, after a three-judge Court of Arbitration determined in a case involving Indian athlete Dutee Chand that the policy was not justified by current scientific research. The panel wrote:

> While the evidence indicates that higher levels of naturally occurring testosterone may increase athletic performance, the Panel is not satisfied that the degree of that advantage is more significant than the advantage derived from the numerous other variables which the parties acknowledge also affect female athletic performance: for example, nutrition, access to specialist training facilities and coaching and other genetic and biological variations.[94]

In 2016, the International Olympic Committee relaxed the rules for transgender athletes; now, female-to-male athletes can compete without restriction, and male-to-female athletes must undergo only hormone therapy (as opposed to surgery) to compete as women.[95]

In 2011, the NCAA adopted a new policy on transgender athletes, which allows student-athletes to participate in sex-segregated sports in accordance with their gender identity as long as certain medical criteria are met. A trans male who has been treated with testosterone can compete only on men's teams. A trans female can continue to compete on men's teams, or can compete on women's teams following one calendar year of documented testosterone-suppression treatment.[96] These rules only apply to post-season

93. Peroshni Govender, South African Caster Semenya Cleared to Return, reuters.com, July 6, 2010, http://uk.reuters.com/article/2010/07/06/uk-athletics-semenya-idUK-TRE6652M520100706; Jeré Longman, Farah Wins 5,000 to Give Home Team Another Title, N.Y. Times, Aug. 11, 2012, at SP3. On the issues raised by Semenya's case, see Erin Buzuvis, Caster Semenya and the Myth of a Level Playing Field, 6 Modern Am. 36 (2010).

94. Chand v. Athletics Federation of India, CAS 2014/A/3759, at 154.

95. Transgender Athletes Can Now Compete in Olympics Without Surgery, N.Y. Times, Jan. 25, 2016.

96. See NCAA Inclusion of Transgender Student-Athletes (2011), https://www.ncaa.org/sites/default/files/Transgender_Handbook_2011_Final.pdf. On these issues, see Erin E. Buzuvis, Transgender Student-Athletes and Sex-Segregated Sport: Developing Policies of Inclusion for Intercollegiate and Interscholastic Athletics, 21 Seton Hall J. Sports & Ent. L. 1 (2011); Christina Cauterucci, Harvard's Evolved Response to a Trans Male Swimmer Is a Joy to Watch, Slate (Apr. 12, 2016), http://www.slate.com/blogs/outward/2016/04/12/harvard_s_evolved_response_to_a_trans_male_swimmer_is_a_joy_to_watch.html.

play; individual schools have discretion in handling athlete placement during the regular season. The International Olympic Committee also adopted new rules on transgender athletes, permitting them to compete as the opposite sex after having undergone sex reassignment surgery, legally changing their sex, and completing two years of hormone therapy. What is the right approach to determining the sex of an athlete? Who should decide? Do these controversial cases suggest a problem with the overall system that segregates athletes by sex?

5. "Sex" and "Gender." Legal issues raised by transgender individuals re-invoke a whole line of questions about the distinction between "sex" and "gender." Feminist theorist Linda Nicholson argues that feminists have used the word "gender" in two distinct ways. On the one hand, gender was developed and is still often used as a contrasting term to sex, to depict that which is socially constructed as opposed to that which is biologically given. On this usage, gender is typically thought to refer to personality traits and behavior in distinction from the body. Here, gender and sex are thought to be distinct. On the other hand, gender has increasingly become used to refer to any social construction having to do with the male/female distinction, including those constructions that separate "female" bodies from "male" bodies. This latter usage emerged when many came to realize that society not only shapes personality and behavior, it also shapes the ways in which the body appears. But if the body is itself always seen through social interpretation, then sex is not something that is separate from gender but is, rather, that which is subsumable under it.[97]

Which conception of gender is more appropriate for feminism? Nicholson argues for the second. In her view, treating gender as something distinct from sex assumes that there is uniform sexual difference that is constant across cultures; this belief she calls "biological foundationalism." Nicholson argues that such a framework is inappropriate for feminists because it assumes without proof that all cultures experience sexual and bodily difference in the same way. Similarly, Katherine Franke argues that it is gender that determines sex, and not the other way around. In Franke's view, "sexual equality jurisprudence has uncritically accepted the validity of biological sexual differences. By accepting these biological differences, equality jurisprudence reifies as foundational fact that which is really an effect of normative gender ideology."[98] For example, physical differences that are assumed to have biological bases in fact are influenced by gendered cultural norms. It follows for Franke, and most other feminists, that discrimination against transgender people should be understood

---

97. Linda Nicholson, Interpreting Gender, 20 Signs: J. of Women in Culture and Soc'y 79 (1994).

98. See Katherine M. Franke, The Central Mistake of Sex Discrimination Law: The Disaggregation of Sex from Gender, 144 U. Pa. L. Rev. 1, 2 (1995).

as a form of sex discrimination. Nicholson's and Franke's arguments seem to suggest that the distinction between "sex" and "gender" is not a useful one.

In contrast to Franke's focus on the primacy of social gender, Mary Anne Case argues that unless sex and gender are "disaggregated," forms of sex discrimination that turn on gender-role expectations rather than physical attributes will not be readily recognized. Case argues that *Price Waterhouse, VMI,* and the numerous cases in which effeminate men have been penalized for breaching gender norms are cases of gender, not sex, discrimination.[99] Does it matter who is right for purposes of protecting transgender individuals? What else is at stake?

Judges as well as academic feminists disagree about the proper relationship between the concepts of "sex" and "gender." Some members of the Supreme Court use the terms "sex" and "gender" interchangeably. The issue became a matter of discussion between the Justices in J.E.B. v. Alabama (excerpted in Chapter 4, Section C(3)). The opinion for the Court written by Justice Blackmun, the separate concurring opinions by Justice O'Connor and Justice Kennedy, and the dissenting opinion by Justice Rehnquist all addressed whether use of peremptory strikes to exclude potential jurors because they are men or because they are women is "gender" discrimination. Justice Scalia explained why the term "sex discrimination" is more appropriate to the case:

> [G]ender is to sex as feminine is to female and masculine to male. The present case does not involve peremptory strikes exercised on the basis of femininity or masculinity (as far as it appears, effeminate men did not survive the prosecution's peremptories). The case involves, therefore, sex discrimination plain and simple.[100]

Justice Ginsburg had made the move from sex to gender by 1975, when she decided that the word "sex" was too disturbing in that it "may conjure up improper images" of what occurs in theaters showing pornography.[101] Similar issues have arisen in international human rights and refugee law.[102]

How should law use the terms "sex" and "gender"?

99. Mary Anne Case, Disaggregating Gender from Sex and Sexual Orientation: The Effeminate Man in the Law and Feminist Jurisprudence, 105 Yale L.J. 1 (1995).

100. 511 U.S. 127, 157 n.1 (1994) (Scalia, J., dissenting).

101. See Ruth Bader Ginsburg, Gender in the Supreme Court: The 1973 and 1974 Terms, 1975 Sup. Ct. Rev. 1 at n.1.

102. See Valerie Oosterveld, The Definition of "Gender" in the Rome Statute of the International Criminal Court: A Step Forward or Back for International Criminal Justice? 18 Harv. Hum. Rts. J. 55, 66-71 (2005).

Putting Theory Into Practice

6-11. Women's colleges have struggled in recent years with the decision whether to admit transgender students. Mills College was the first to adopt a trans-inclusive admissions policy, but many others have followed suit.[103] Bryn Mawr, for example, welcomes applications from individuals "who have identified and continue to identify as women (including cisgender and trans women), intersex individuals who do not identify as male, individuals assigned female at birth who have not taken medical or legal steps to identify as male, and individuals assigned female at birth who do not identify within the gender binary."[104] Mount Holyoke excludes only an applicant who was both born male and identifies as a man.[105] Is there a difference between these two policies? If you were on a gender-inclusion task force at a women's college, what admissions policy would you suggest?

6-12. Frank is fired from his job as a police officer after he reveals to his supervisor that he will be undergoing the transition from male to female under the close supervision of his doctor and psychiatric counselor. Frank sues under Title VII, and the police department defends the lawsuit on the grounds that a transgender person will not have the "street credibility" necessary to maintain order in the tough community in which he works. Even if the approach in *Schroer* is followed and discrimination against transgender persons is viewed as discrimination because of sex, should the police department be required to retain Frank in this case? Or does the BFOQ exception apply here?

6-13. A rape counseling organization employs only female volunteers and rejects a transgender person who had transitioned from being male to female. Although subject to a law prohibiting discrimination based on sexual identity, the organization claims that it has a compelling interest in having women who are sexually assaulted helped by those who have "suffered oppression from birth."[106] Should the organization be allowed to reject the transgender applicant?

---

103. Paul G. Lannon, Transgender Student Admissions: The Challenge of Defining Gender in a Gender Fluid World, 59 Boston Bar J. 5 (Spring 2015).

104. Bryn Mawr College, Transgender Applicants, https://www.brynmawr.edu/admissions/transgender-applicants.

105. Mount Holyoke, Admission of Transgender Students, https://www.mtholyoke.edu/policies/admission-transgender-students.

106. Nixon v. Vancouver Rape Relief Society, 2002 C.L.L.C 230-009, 42 C.H.R.R. D/20.

6-14. A transgender biologically male middle-school student seeks to wear female clothing. How would you advise the school board?[107]

6-15. A state legislature passes a bill providing that students in public schools can only use bathrooms or locker rooms designated for their chromosomal or birth sex. Transgender students can request an accommodation, but the accommodation cannot include allowing them to use a bathroom or locker room designated for use by students of the other sex. Schools may provide a unisex bathroom, a single-occupancy bathroom, or allow controlled use of a faculty bathroom. What harms might this rule impose? Do the permissible accommodations adequately respond to them? What if the law applied to restrooms in all public places as well? Would your analysis be different?

6-16. Mikki, a woman with an intersex condition, was sentenced to fourteen months in prison for writing bad checks. Where should she be housed? Is the prison within its rights to place her in solitary confinement rather than with the female population?

D. MASCULINITIES

The emphasis of this book is on women, but there is little doubt that understandings of masculinity are important because of their impact not only on women's interests, but on men's interests as well. By the late 1970s, the study of masculinities because a topic in its own right. As two theorists have put it, "[m]asculinities theorists would agree with feminists that men as a group have power over women as a group, but they tend to complicate the situation . . . by examin[ing] the effects of the social construction of men."[108]

What are the connections between constructions of masculinity and femininity? Do the theories explored in the other chapters of the book understate the distinctive burdens faced by men in a gendered society? As women have made advances in the name of equality, is it possible to think, for some purposes at least, of men now being the subordinated sex? The section helps to explore these questions, along with issues related to intersectionality of masculinity and race.

---

107. See Doe v. Yunits, 15 Mass. L. Rptr. 278 (Mass. Super. Ct. 2001). This and related cases discussed in Transgender Law and Policy Institute, Litigation: Case Law—Youth, at http://www.transgenderlaw.org/cases/index.htm#youth.

108. Ann C. McGinley & Frank Rudy Cooper, Introduction: Masculinities, Multidimensionality, and Law: Why They Need One Another, in Masculinities and the Law: A Multidimensional Approach 1, 3 (Frank Rudy Cooper & Ann C. McGinley eds., 2012).

Nancy E. Dowd, *Asking the Man Question:* *Masculinities Analysis and Feminist Theory*

33 Harv. J. Law & Gender 415, 416-19 (2010)

Masculinities work can be used to understand more clearly how male privilege and dominance are constructed. It can make us see harms suffered by boys and men that we have largely ignored. It may also reinforce and strengthen the commitment to anti-essentialism in feminist theory. Exposing the complexities and multiplicity of masculinities leads toward understanding intersection and multiple forms of discrimination more clearly. . . .

Masculinities analysis may also remind us to be attentive to different patterns of inequality and to our interpretation of those patterns. Where one sex is sole or dominant, dominance should be something that triggers scrutiny. This should matter both when the dominant sex benefits (as in occupying high paid jobs) or is harmed (as in occupying more prison cells). We should question not only why one sex fills or dominates the pattern, but also the gendered meaning of both who is present and who is absent. Oddly, when one sex is dominant, sometimes gender issues are rendered invisible. Examples of this are male predominance in the juvenile and adult criminal justice systems, and women's predominance in the welfare system. Invisibility is fostered by gender-neutral language that covers the predominance of gender patterns, but also by the acceptance of the pattern as usual, normal, and taken for granted.

On the other hand, where both sexes are present, one or both may claim bias. We tend to frame competing claims of bias as requiring prioritization or hierarchy rather than seeing how they interconnect. We tend to argue over who has the more important issues to address or the most pressing "crisis." Resisting this "either/or" approach of a hierarchy of inequalities is critical. For example, in education there are inequality issues for both girls and boys, women and men. Rather than exclusively focusing on the issues of one sex to the exclusion of the other, as if only one can claim our focus or deserve our attention, we should see and insist on addressing both. Inequalities often interlock. A battle of the sexes, moreover, may only divert attention from more serious issues of race and class. Examining subordination in isolation undermines our understanding and our attack upon the interacting dynamic, even if gender-specific problem solving is needed. . . .

Raising issues about men when so many issues about women remain generates resistance and distrust. . . . Masculinities analysis needs to continually challenge itself to challenge the hegemony of men and male power. The project of imagining positive, affirming, egalitarian masculinities is ongoing, but it is absolute essential. . . .

These are what I have identified as core propositions [of masculinities scholarship]:

1. Men are not universal or undifferentiated.
2. Men pay a price for privilege.
3. Intersections of manhood, particularly with race, class, and sexual orientation, are critical to the interplay of privilege and disadvantage, to hierarchies among men, and factors that may entirely trump male gender privilege.
4. Masculinity is a social construction and not a biological given.
5. Hegemonic masculinity recognizes that one masculinity norm dominates multiple masculinities.
6. The patriarchal dividend is the benefit that all men have from the dominance of men in the overall gender order.
7. The two most common pieces defining masculinity are, at all costs, to not be like a woman and not be gay.
8. Masculinity is as much about relation to other men as it is about relation to women.
9. Men, although powerful, feel powerless.
10. Masculinities study exposes how structures and cultures are gendered male.
11. The spaces and places that men and women daily inhabit and work within are remarkably different.
12. The role of men in achieving feminist goals is uncertain and unclear.
13. The asymmetry of masculinities scholarship and feminist theory reflects the differences in the general position of men and women.

The implications of these teachings . . . are that feminists should "ask the man question."

Frank Rudy Cooper, "Who's the Man?": Masculinities Studies, Terry Stops, and Police Training

18 Colum. J. Gender & Law 671, 671-72, 674-76, 741 (2009)

We men have some strange rituals. One occurs on the basketball court. A player will make a move around a defender and score a basket. Then he'll shout, "Who's the man?" He wants his opponent to say, "*You* are the man." This episode is a paradigmatic description of how masculinities work. Men often act with the goal of impressing other men. We gain our masculine esteem and relative masculine stature from other men's acknowledgements of our masculinity. Sociologist Michael Kimmel puts it best: "[w]e are under the constant careful scrutiny of other men. Other men watch us, rank us, grant our acceptance into the realm of manhood. Manhood is demonstrated for other men's approval. . . .

How does masculinity affect policing? This is an important question, given that policemen have nearly unique powers to make others acknowledge them as "the man" while ostensibly merely performing their duties.

The short answer is that officers may get "macho" with civilians. Specifically, they may enact a command presence in situations where it only serves to boost the officer's masculine esteem. To enact command presence is to take charge of a situation. It involves projecting an aura of confidence and decisiveness. It is justified by the need to control dangerous suspects. A situation that does not justify enacting command presence is what I call a "masculinity contest." A masculinity contest is a face-off between men where one party is able to bolster his masculine esteem by dominating the other. A prototypical masculinity contest is a bar fight. Men will glare at each other and ratchet up their challenges until one party backs down or is subdued. Male police offers may sometimes be tempted to turn encounters with male civilians into masculinity contests.

The insight that policemen may sometimes enact command presence is order to stage masculinity contests and boost their masculine esteem is important because it helps explain patterns of law enforcement. . . . [S]cholars have long noted that officers sometimes use their Terry v. Ohio stop-and-frisk powers to racially profile. The usual explanation for that practice is racial animus. However, concentrating solely on race as an explanation for police behaviors ignores the fact that the overwhelming majority of police officers are men and the overwhelming majority of those they stop are men. As David Sklansky says, "One train may hide another." I contend that the desire to boost one's masculine esteem is a train traveling behind, and obscured by, the desire to boost one's racial esteem in some officers' decision to disproportionately stop and frisk men belonging to racial minorities. . . .

If policemen are using *Terry* stops and frisks to play the game of "who's the man?" rather than just to gather evidence of crime, then we need to change the gender dynamics of policing. I propose that we do so by changing the cultures of police forces. This can be achieved by establishing extensive training programs designed to root out the attitudes and rituals that perpetuate a macho police culture. . . .

Aside from the question of whether policemen should bully civilians, we might ask whether such actions can ever actually sate the desire to prove one's masculinity. According to Kimmel, they cannot:

> [T]he bully is the *least* secure about his manhood, and so he is constantly trying to prove it. But he proves it by choosing opponents he is absolutely certain he can defeat; thus the standard taunt to a bully is to "pick one someone your own size." He can't, though, and after defeating a smaller and weaker opponent, which he was sure would prove his manhood, he is left with the empty gnawing feeling that he has not proved it after all, and he must find another opponent, again one smaller and weaker, than he can again defeat to prove it to himself. . . . When does it end? Never.

So bullying is a counter-productive activity for the bully himself. . . .

The bully's conundrum demonstrates that no one really benefits from the current structure of masculinity. Ultimately, hegemonic masculinity is the source of the problem of police harassment of men.

≡≡≡ *Darren Rosenblum, Unsex Mothering:*
≡≡≡ *Toward a New Culture of Parenting*
35 Harv. J. Law & Gender 57, 58 (2012)

I was, until recently, a pregnant man. . . . My husband and I began the process of having a child several years ago when we hired a surrogacy agency that works primarily with gay male couples. After a complex process, we are now raising our daughter.

As a parent, I confront a far more sexed area of life than I have ever encountered before. Everyone congratulates my partner and me on being "fathers," even though within our home we share responsibilities and flip roles, including a mothering role, with some fluidity. The outside world, it seems, needs to box us into the "daddy" category as much as it invests women with the power of motherhood.

Some time ago, I was in a taxi with my daughter. . . . She fussed a bit and the driver said, "Where's the mother? Only the mother knows how to do this." Avoiding a complex explanation that I view myself as both mother and father, I said she has two dads. He still seemed perplexed that a man could know how to care for a child. I left the taxi and wiped a saliva-soaked Cheerio from my daughter's chin, feeling less of a parent because I was perceived as only a father, and not the primary parent—a mother. It is a feeling constantly reinforced for gay male parents I know who report that when in public, at markets, stores, and restaurants—they get asked by women: "Is it mommy's day off?" It is challenging to come up with a responsible response.

Notes

1. Defining Masculinity. Contemporary views about masculinity tend to divide into two broad normative categories: (1) the celebration of traditional masculine values, and (2) the desire to eliminate strict gender roles, for men as well as for women. Prominent advocates for traditional masculine values often appeal to biological understandings of masculinity. Harvard Professor Harvey Mansfield, for example, argues that men are by nature dominant, aggressive, self-confident risk takers. At its best, manliness encourages men to defend higher ends, and this role is threatened by "feminist nihilism." Although in the public sphere, the sexes should have equal rights, in the

Evolutionary argument

private sphere, Mansfield advocates respect for differences and wants society to stop trying to "feminize boys." "Men should be expected, not merely free to be manly."[109] Poet Robert Bly, an active proponent of the "men's movement," urged men in the 1990s to "retreat from the world of women to temporary male sanctuaries in order to recapture some 'deep' or 'wild' masculinity that has become dormant in today's modern technological society in which women actively participate."[110]

Other commentators, while not necessarily supporting the movement to celebrate traditional male values, seek to put men's anxiety about their manhood in a sympathetic light. Susan Faludi, for example, argues that hypermasculine behavior is often a response to men's feeling of being "downsized," economically and emotionally, both by the rise in women's rights and the erosion of traditional male jobs.[111] Christina Hoff Sommers takes it a step further, specifically blaming feminists for men's sense of disempowerment and disadvantage.[112] The theme of men and boys falling behind has been augmented by more recent claims that women have overtaken men in work, education, and in love and marriage.[113]

On the other side of the spectrum is a growing acceptance of more positive, androgynous visions of masculinity. Many of these visions would enlist men in the same struggles against male violence, homophobia, and gender inequality in which feminists have engaged.[114] This effort builds on a long tradition that has included historic leaders such as John Stuart Mill, Frederick Douglass, and W.E.B. Dubois.[115] Others, like Darren Rosenblum in the excerpted reading above, emphasize the ways in which men, as well as women, suffer from gender stereotypes.

Within this spectrum are a number of different versions of masculinity. In some fields, as the excerpted reading by Frank Rudy Cooper exemplifies, masculinity is defined principally in terms of strength and toughness. One study has documented how working conditions in the construction industry

109. Harvey C. Mansfield, Manliness 244 (2006).

110. Michael S. Kimmel, Issues for Men in the 1990s, 46 U. Miami L. R. 671, 672, (1992), citing Robert Bly, Iron John: A Book About Men 6, 222-37, 244-49 (1990).

111. Susan Faludi, Stiffed: The Betrayal of the American Man (2000).

112. Christina Hoff Sommers, The War Against Boys: How Misguided Feminism Is Harming Our Young (2000).

113. See, e.g., Hanna Rosin, The End of Men (2012). For a law review symposium responding to Rosin's book, see Symposium: Evaluating Claims About the "End of Men": Legal and Other Perspectives, 93 B.U. L. Rev. 663 (2013).

114. For examples, see Handbook of Studies on Men & Masculinities (Michael S. Kimmel et al. eds., 2005); The Black Male Handbook (Kevin Powell ed., 2007); Michael Kimmel, Guyland (2008); R.W. Connell, The Men and the Boys (2000); R.W. Connell, Masculinities (1995); Michael Kimmel, Manhood in America: A Cultural History (1996).

115. Shira Tarrent, Men and Feminism 28-39 (2009); Against the Tide: Pro-Feminist Men in the United States 1776-1990, A Documentary History (Michael S. Kimmel & Thomas E. Mosmiller eds., 1991).

help produce hyper-masculinized behaviors of "manning up," risk-taking, aggressiveness, and denigrating women, especially among undocumented immigrants.[116] Along similar lines, an analysis of Ricci v. DeStefano, a U.S. Supreme Court case finding that a city's failure to certify the result of promotional exams for firefighters that had a pronounced disparate impact against blacks and Hispanics was unconstitutional, argues that the case was

> about white masculinity and heterosexuality and breadwinner status. It was about heroism: the noble job of firefighters who risk their lives to save others. It was about self-respect and a sense of fairness. It was about ethnic heritage — Italian and Irish and even Puerto Rican. It was about the American dream and the ability of all who work hard and act responsibly to accomplish their goals.[117]

Responding to the congratulations of the white plaintiffs by some U.S. Senators, McGinley writes:

> The explicit message was that the nearly all-white plaintiffs were "real men" and "real firefighters" who worked hard and cared for their families. The implicit message was that female firefighters of all races were not qualified to do the job and that African American and Hispanic firefighters who complained about the disparate impact were lazy and could not measure up.[118]

Is this version of masculinity anti-feminist?

In other fields, masculinity is defined quite differently. A large national survey by the Center for Work-Life Policy on the female "brain drain" in science, engineering, and technology documents the macho cultures that prevail in these fields.[119] Sociologist Marianne Cooper, who has analyzed the Silicon Valley culture, explains that men in this culture express their masculinity by working lots of hours. As one man explains: "Guys constantly try to out-macho each other, but in engineering it's really perverted because out-machoing someone means being more of a nerd than the other person. . . .

---

116. See Letitia M. Saucedo & Maria Christina Morales, Masculinities Narratives and Latino Immigrant Workers: A Case Study of the Law Vegas Residential Construction Trades, 33 Harv. J. Law & Gender 625 (2010). For a description of the "gender divide" on law faculties, whereby women not only teach a disproportionate percentage of female-identified courses (and men a disproportionate percentage of male-identified courses), but also experience differential expectations from colleagues and students and often bear the brunt of their colleagues' bullying behavior, see Ann C. McGinley, Reproducing Gender on Law School Faculties, 2009 B.Y.U. L. Rev. 99.

117. Ann C. McGinley, *Ricci v. DeStefano*: A Masculinities Theory Analysis, 33 Harv. J. Law & Gender 581, 584 (2010). For the case itself, see Ricci v. DeStefano, 557 U.S. 557 (2009).

118. Id. More generally, see Ann C. McGinley, Through a Different Lens: Multidimensional Masculinities and Employment Discrimination Law (2013).

119. Sylvia Ann Hewlett, The Athena Factor: Reversing the Brain Drain in Science, Engineering, and Technology, Harv. Bus. Rev. Research Rep. (May 2008).

It's not like being a brave firefighter and going up one more flight than your friend. There's a lot of see how many hours I can work. . . . He's a real man, he works ninety-hour weeks; he's a slacker, he works fifty hours a week."[120] Cooper summarizes: "The successful enactment of this masculinity involves displaying one's exhaustion, physically and verbally, in order to convey the depth of one's commitment, stamina, and virility."[121] Do you recognize this pattern in your own experience in the legal profession? If so, do you associate it with masculinity?

Another area of investigation has been the military. Consider the following:

> What is the role of law, in the context of the military, in reinforcing stereotypes about men as courageous? Theoretically, female soldiers can be punished for cowardice, but, so far, none have, as though martial courage were only expected of men. On the other hand, two of the most publicized military cases in recent memory involve the first woman B-52 bomber pilot, Kelly Flinn, and Lt. Colonel Karen Tew, both court marshaled [sic], not for lacking the male virtue of courage, but for having sexual relations with male soldiers. The two female officers were thus punished for being absent the virtue that is chiefly ascribed to women — chastity.[122]

How do these various visions of masculinity fit together? Some commentators say that many men, including those in blue-collar occupations, are caught in the "daddy double-bind"; they are expected to be both breadwinners and involved fathers in settings that provide inadequate support for that dual role.[123] Do you agree? How does this double-bind compare with burdens women face in being both parents and workers? See Chapter 4, Section B, Note 1.

Are issues different for gay male parents?[124] Recent data from the Families and Work Institute suggest that gay couples tend to divide household chores more evenly than straight couples.[125]

A survey in the 1990s asked women and men what they were most afraid of. "Women responded that they were most afraid of being raped and

---

120. Marianne Cooper, Being the "Go-To Guy": Fatherhood, Masculinity, and the Organization of Work in Silicon Valley, 23 Qualitative Sociology 379, 382 (2000).

121. Id. at 383.

122. John M. Kang, The Burdens of Manliness, 33 Harv. J. Law & Gender 477, 495 (2010).

123. Kari Palazzari, The Daddy Double-Bind: How the Family and Medical Leave Act Perpetuates Sex Inequality Across All Class Levels, 16 Colum. J. Gender & L. 429 (2008).

124. For an extended conversation between a dozen professors about gay male parenthood, see Darren Rosenblum et al., Pregnant Man?: A Conversation, 22 Yale J. Law & Feminism 207 (2010).

125. Emily Peck, 2 Things Gay Couples Can Teach Straight Couples About Marriage, Huffpost Queer Voices (Feb. 2, 2016), http://www.huffingtonpost.com/2015/06/04/gay-couples-dividing-household-work_n_7513624.html/.

murdered. Men responded that they were most afraid of being laughed at."[126] Do you suppose this is still true? Does the asserted difference have potential legal and policy implications? For example, would the training Frank Cooper suggests be appropriate only for men, or for policewomen as well?

2. The Intersection of Gender, Race, Class, and Sexual Orientation. The various versions of masculinity described in Note 1, above, suggest that generalizations about masculinity might fail to capture (and instead "essentialize") the experience of all men. As three scholars have put it, while men's collective privilege "puts men as a group above women as a group, and infuses structures, culture, and policy with masculinities because men have historically held positions of power. At the same time, gender for men and boys does not operate uniformly, and is particularly affected by intersections with race, class, and sexual orientation."[127]

Some of the discussion about masculinity has focused the extent to which men have fallen behind women in some important measures, like education and employment. An entire issue of the Boston University Law Review is focused on a book claiming that women are in the ascendancy, while men are on the wane.[128] Some responders answer that not only are generalizations about women overtaking men inaccurate but that, to the extent they are true, they have more to do with class than with gender. By this account, the increasing gap between rich and poor has meant a decline in the position of working-class men, but not necessarily a benefit to women. June Carbone and Naomi Cahn, who have made this point, do not deny that women have made gains in access to education and employment. They argue, rather, that as society becomes more unequal, a greater percentage of men experience imprisonment, chronic unemployment, substance abuse, and mental instability, while women are left raising their families on their own, often unable to find stable partners or to escape from low-paying jobs.[129] By this analysis, elite men are the winners in today's economy, not women.[130]

In addition to class, as is explored elsewhere in Section A of this chapter, race is also an important variable. As many scholars have pointed out, black men have vastly disproportionate rates of unemployment, police stops, incarceration, and substance abuse, and lower rates of college attendance and

126. Michael S. Kimmel, Masculinity as Homophobia: Fear, Same, and Silence in the Construction of Gender Identity, in Theorizing Masculinities 119, 133 (Harry Brod & Michael Kaufman eds., 1994).

127. Nancy E. Dowd et al., Feminist Legal Theory Meets Masculinities Theory, in Masculinities and the Law, supra note 108, at 25.

128. Rosin, supra note 113.

129. June Carbone & Naomi Cahn, The End of Men or the Rebirth of Class, 93 B.U. L. Rev. 871, 872-75 (2013).

130. Id. at 876-78.

marriage.[131] How do these differences affect the meanings of masculinity? Do these meanings affect the racist attitudes that may have helped create them?

What about sexual orientation? To what extent do the meanings of masculinity suggested in this section assume a heterosexual ideal?

3. Masculinity and the Black Lives Matter Movement. One of President Obama's signature initiatives, My Brother's Keeper,[132] seeks to remove barriers to education and employment for black men. A non-profit spinoff, My Brother's Keeper Alliance, has raised more than $80 million from major corporations for specialized programs for young black and Latino men.[133] Is the focus on men appropriate?

In his groundbreaking work about black disembodiment, Ta-Nehisi Coates addresses the experience of black males in the form of a letter to his son:

> Disembodiment is a kind of terrorism . . . [t]he dragon that compelled the boys I knew, way back, into extravagant theater of ownership. . . . The demon that pushed the middle-class black survivors into aggressive passivity, our conversation restrained in public quarters, our best manners on display, our hands never out of pockets, our whole manner ordered as if to say, "I make no sudden moves." . . . The serpent of school years, demanding I be twice as good, though I was but a boy.[134]

Does the "Black Lives Matter" movement have a gender? The #WhyWeCan'tWait movement, led by women of color and various activist groups, including the NAACP Legal Defense and Educational Fund, the National Women's Law Center, and the African American Policy Forum, advocates the inclusion of women in initiatives now focused on black boys and men. Representing this voice, Kimberlé Crenshaw argues that the My Brother's Keeper and Black Lives Matter movements create a false impression that black girls do not need the same kind of emphasis. "The gender-exclusive focus on

131. See, e.g., Ta-Nehisi Coates, Between the World and Me (2015); Frank Rudy Cooper, We Are Always Already Imprisoned: Hyper-Incarceration and Black Male Identity Performance, 93 B.U. L. Rev. 1185 (2013); Ralph Richard Banks, Are African Americans Us?, 93 B.U. L. Rev. 681 (2013); Olatunde C.A. Johnson, Disparity Rules, 107 Colum. L. Rev. 374 (2007). See also Khiara M. Bridges, TANF and the End (Maybe?) of Poor Men, 93 B.U. L. Rev. 1141, 1143 (2013) ("if we are witnessing the end of men . . . then we are witnessing the end of non-white men, not the end of men generally"); Nancy E. Dowd, What Men?: The Essentialism Error of the "End of Men," 93 B.U. L. Rev. 1205, 1208 (2013) ("Male hierarchy is raced, classed, and gendered on the basis of sexual orientation.").

132. See https://www.whitehouse.gov/my-brothers-keeper. For the initiative, Empowering Men of Color, see http://www.emocdc.org/.

133. See President Obama Announces Launch of My Brother's Keeper Alliance, Ebony, May 6, 2015, http://www.ebony.com/news-views/president-obama-announces-launch-of-my-brothers-keeper-alliance-503#axzz3ZZMmW7A9.

134. Coates, supra 131, at 114.

boys (of color) as ground zero . . . continues to undermine the well-being of our entire community."[135] What do you think? Do the problems of black boys and men warrant a distinct, separate set of initiatives?

Putting Theory Into Practice

6-17. Mark, who is divorced from his ex-wife, Margaret, is charged with child sexual abuse, based on evidence that he (1) allowed his two-year-old daughter to sleep alone with him in bed; (2) let her walk into the bathroom while he was naked in the shower; and (3) in changing her diapers, often applied diaper cream to her vagina.[136] Part of Mark's defense is that Margaret also engaged in these behaviors, and yet she is not charged with child abuse. Can behavior that is not child sexual abuse if engaged in by mothers constitute child sexual abuse by fathers?

6-18. According to one scholar, "sport has been a site where masculinity is learned, performed, and reproduced."[137] In what sense is this true? In what sense is it a problem to be fixed?

6-19. Reconsider the issue examined in Chapter 2, Section C of whether separate schools or classes should be allowed for boys. Could separate schools do a better job of addressing damaging stereotypes about men? Would all-male, all-black schools better address the disproportionate rates of black men incarceration, unemployment, drug use, and family instability?

6-20. Do you assume that when women become terrorists, it is because they are under the influence of the men in their lives? The evidence shows that women have long been voluntarily involved in terrorism,[138] and that women terrorists, for strategic reasons, are actually more successful and more deadly

---

135. See Melinda D. Anderson, Black Girls Should Matter, Too, Atlantic, May 11, 2015, http://www.theatlantic.com/education/archive/2015/05/black-girls-should-matter-too/392879/.

136. Cases involving these kinds of behaviors are discussed in Camille Gear Rich, Innocence Interrupted: Reconstructing Fatherhood in the Shadow of Child Molestation Law, 101 Calif. L. Rev. 609 (2013). Rich argues that the gendered interpretation of child molestation laws helps to reinforce gendered parenting norms. Id.

137. Deborah L. Brake, Sport and Masculinity: The Promise and Limits of Title IX, in Masculinities and the Law, supra note 108, at 207.

138. Jayne Huckerby, When Women Become Terrorists, N.Y. Times, Jan. 21, 2015, at A27 (arguing that despite stereotypes about women's domesticity and passivity, and the belief that women terrorists must be under men's influence and tricked into joining the Islamic State, women have long been involved in terrorism and the failure of the West to recognize this fact impedes counterterrorism efforts).

than male terrorists on a per-episode basis.[139] Being a parent is no guarantee to the contrary; one of the 2015 San Bernardino terrorists was the mother of a six-month-old infant.[140] Why do you suppose debates over asylum and immigration continue to assume that women and their children are the victims of terrorism, rather than potential perpetrators?[141]

139. Fionnuala Ní Aoláin, Situating Women in Counterterrorism Discourses: Undulating Masculinities and Luminal Femininities, 93 B.U. L. Rev. 1085, 1092 (2013) (women terrorists have an average of 8.4 victims per attack, as compared to 5.3 for men, and more often succeed in carrying out suicide attacks).

140. This fact seemed to make the incident seem especially "twisted." See San Bernardino: The Most Twisted Terrorist Plot Yet, The Daily Beast (Dec. 4, 2015), http://www.thedaily beast.com/articles/2015/12/04/san-bernardino-the-most-twisted-terrorist-plot-yet.html.

141. See, e.g., UNHCR Appeals for Urgent Action to Address Deteriorating Humanitarian Situation in Calais, Sept. 26, 2014, http://www.unhcr.org/542563199.html (describing UN refugee agency expressing special concern about women and children asylum seekers from Syria and other Middle East and North African countries).

Table of Cases

Principal cases are indicated by italics.

Index

Native American women, domestic violence and, 441, 442, 457

Navajo people, 848

Navarro, Mireya, 655n235, 666n282

Navy, women in, 42

NCAA. *See* National Collegiate Athletics Association (NCAA)

Nebraska, surrogacy in, 761n454

Negrin, Matt, 689n294

Neil, Martha, 159n268

NeJaime, Douglas, 359, 359n276

Nelson, Lori W., 345n251

Nelson-Butler, Cheryl, 645n188, 653n223

Netherlands
   affirmative action, 188
   prostitution, 647, 649

Neufield, Adam, 547n80

Nevada
   BFOQ for correctional officers, 141
   prostitution laws, 644, 645, 649

New, Jake, 624n81, 637n144

Newby, Ryan Elias, 586nn192–193

New Jersey
   cohabitation, 347
   family leave, 224
   parental leave, 224
   surrogacy, 750–758, 763

Newman, Jesse, 443n154

Newman, Jonah, 634n135

New Mexico, public accommodations, 160

Newport, Frank, 748n434, 804n602

Newton-Small, Jay, 566n144

New York
   acquaintance rape and campus rape, 631
   appearance standards, 117
   equal pay law, 66
   pay equity, 66
   pregnant women, alcohol or drug abuse by, 783, 787
   Prenatal Assistance Program, 787n547
   professional degree as not marital property, 341n241–342n241
   prostitution laws, 645, 650
   putative father registry, 368
   rape and consent, 616, 631
   surrogacy, 761, 761n454

New Zealand, prostitution in, 647

Nicholson, Linda, 855, 855n97, 856

Nifong, Michael, 627n92

NIH Revitalization Act of 1993, 696

Nineteenth Amendment, 11–12

Nissamov, Ron, 484n252

Nixon, Richard, 180, 739n393

No Child Left Behind Act of 2001, 270, 365

Nonsubordination, 373–512
   domestic violence, 439–494. *See also* Domestic violence

pornography and, 496–497

sexual harassment, 378–418. *See also* Sexual harassment

sexual orientation discrimination, 428–430, 432. *See also* Sexual orientation

women's rights, 373–377

Norman, Judy, 489

North Carolina
   bathroom law, 265, 852, 853
   gay parent adoption, 361–362
   sexual orientation and gender identity discrimination, 95

North Dakota
   abortion, 748
   child custody, same-sex parent preference, 359n277
   personhood amendments, 746
   surrogacy, 761n454

Northwestern University, 783

Norton-Hawk, Maureen A., 646n189

Norway
   affirmative action, 188
   family leave policy, 239
   pre-conception arrangements, prohibition against, 764
   prostitution, 650

Nourse, Victoria, 483, 483n248

Nursing mothers. *See* Breastfeeding

Nussbaum, Emily, 121n196

Nussbaum, Martha, 828n21

Obama, Barack
   abortion, 744
   Affordable Care Act, 744
   appearance of attorney general, 123, 123n203
   child support awards or arrearages, 344, 344n250
   "Don't ask, don't tell" policy, 44
   gender identity, executive order on, 850
   judging, 568, 568n157
   My Brother's Keeper, 867
   pay equity, 65
   school athletics, 293
   sex trafficking, 656
   sexual assaults in military, 643
   Title VII and Title IX, 853

Oberman, Michelle, 602–603, 603n1

Obiora, L. Amede, 825–826, 828

Obscenity doctrine, 495. *See also* Pornography

Occupational Safety and Health Act of 1970 (OSHA), 542

Occupy Patriarchy, 804

Occupy Wall Street Movement, 804

O'Connor, Lindsey Trimble, 224n78, 539n56

O'Connor, Sandra Day, 51, 181, 251, 582, 856

OCR. *See* Office for Civil Rights